P9-DWI-722

Developing Minds

A Resource Book for Teaching Thinking

DISCARD
LCCC LIBRARY

3rd Edition

Edited by Arthur L. Costa

 ® Association for Supervision and Curriculum Development
Alexandria, Virginia USA

Association for Supervision and Curriculum Development
1703 N. Beauregard St. • Alexandria, VA 22311-1714 USA
Telephone: 1-800-933-2723 or 703-578-9600 • Fax: 703-575-5400
Web site: http://www.ascd.org • E-mail: member@ascd.org

Copyright © 2001 by the Association for Supervision and Curriculum Development (ASCD). All rights reserved. No part of this publication may be reproduced or transmitted in any form or by any means, electronic or mechanical, including photocopy, recording, or any information storage and retrieval system, without permission from ASCD. Readers who wish to duplicate material copyrighted by ASCD may do so for a small fee by contacting the Copyright Clearance Center (CCC), 222 Rosewood Dr., Danvers, MA 01923, USA (telephone: 978-750-8400; fax: 978-750-4470). ASCD has authorized the CCC to collect such fees on its behalf. Requests to reprint rather than photocopy should be directed to ASCD's permissions office at 703-578-9600.

Because ASCD does not hold copyright to the following chapters, they may not be reproduced in any form without the consent of the authors, their publishers, or the agents listed in the copyright notice on the first page of each chapter:

1, 4, 7, 11, 13, 16, 17, 21, Section IV Introduction, 26, 28, 29, 31, 39, 40, 41, 45, 46, 50, 52, 62, 63, 66, 67, 70, 74, 80, 83, 84

ASCD publications present a variety of viewpoints. The views expressed or implied in this book should not be interpreted as official positions of the Association.

Printed in the United States of America.

ASCD Product No. 101063   s6/2001

ASCD member price: $32.95   nonmember price: $39.95

Library of Congress Cataloging-in-Publication Data

Developing minds: a resource book for teaching thinking/edited by Arthur L. Costa.—3rd ed.
     p. cm.
Includes bibliographical references and index.
     ISBN 0871203790 (alk. paper)
  1. Thought and thinking—Study and teaching.   2. Cognition in children. Costa, Arthur L.
     LB1590.3 .D 48 2001
     370.15/2 21

                                                       2001006466

07 06 05 04 03 02 01   10 9 8 7 6 5 4 3 2 1

With deep respect, admiration, and love, this book is dedicated to Ron Brandt, long-time executive editor of Educational Leadership *and other publications for the Association for Supervision and Curriculum Development. Over many years he has provided inspiration and encouragement to untold numbers of educators; he has made clearer the vision of thoughtful education and has opened pathways of communication among schools in all corners of the earth. Because of his devotion to learning, the world is becoming a more thoughtful place.*

—ARTHUR L. COSTA

Let us put our minds together and see what life we can make for our children.

—Sitting Bull, 1877

Developing Minds

A Resource Book for Teaching Thinking

3RD EDITION

ACKNOWLEDGMENTS ix

PREFACE TO THE 3RD EDITION *Arthur L. Costa* x

FOREWORD *Ron Brandt* xii

INTRODUCTION: THE VISION *Arthur L. Costa* xv

SECTION I. THE NEED TO TEACH THINKING

INTRODUCTION *Arthur L. Costa* 2

1. MAKING AMERICA SMARTER: THE REAL GOAL OF SCHOOL REFORM *Lauren B. Resnick* 3

2. THINKING SKILLS FOR THE INFORMATION AGE *LeRoy Hay* 7

3. THINKING IN CONTEXT: TEACHING FOR
OPEN-MINDEDNESS AND CRITICAL UNDERSTANDING *Sheldon Berman* 11

4. FIVE HUMAN PASSIONS: THE ORIGINS OF EFFECTIVE THINKING
Arthur L. Costa and Robert J. Garmston 18

5. LEARNING AND THINKING IN THE WORKPLACE *John Edwards* 23

6. STANDARDS-BASED THINKING AND REASONING SKILLS
Robert J. Marzano and Jane E. Pollock 29

7. TEACHING THINKING SKILLS—DEFINING THE PROBLEM *Barry K. Beyer* 35

SECTION II. THINKING: BUILDING COMMON UNDERSTANDINGS

INTRODUCTION *Arthur L. Costa* 42

8. GOALS FOR A CRITICAL THINKING CURRICULUM AND ITS ASSESSMENT *Robert H. Ennis* 44

9. THINKING SKILLS: MEANINGS AND MODELS REVISITED *Barbara Z. Presseisen* 47

10. WHAT IS PROBLEM SOLVING? *Jack Lochhead and Aletta Zietsman* 54

11. THINKING ABOUT DECISIONS *Robert J. Swartz* 58

12. CREATIVE THINKING: AN ESSENTIAL LIFE SKILL *Gerard J. Puccio and Mary C. Murdock* 67

13. ADDED VALUE: A DISPOSITIONAL PERSPECTIVE ON THINKING *Shari Tishman* 72

14. ACTIVELY OPEN-MINDED THINKING *Jonathan Baron* 76

15. HABITS OF MIND *Arthur L. Costa* 80

16. WHAT PHILOSOPHY OFFERS TO THE TEACHING OF THINKING *Barry K. Beyer* 87

SECTION III.   CREATING THOUGHT-FULL ENVIRONMENTS

INTRODUCTION *Arthur L. Costa* 94

17. CAPITALIZING ON THE INVISIBLE DIMENSION OF ORGANIZATIONAL LEARNING
Geoffrey Caine and Renate Nummela Caine 96

18. THOUGHTFUL PARENTING *Dee Dickinson* 101

19. DESIGNING THE INVITATIONAL ENVIRONMENT *John Barell* 106

20. PREPARING TEACHERS OF THINKING *David S. Martin and Nicholas M. Michelli* 111

21. FROM STAFF DEVELOPMENT TO PROFESSIONAL DEVELOPMENT: SUPPORTING
THOUGHTFUL ADULTS FOR THINKING SCHOOLS *Laura Lipton and Bruce Wellman* 118

22. FOR ADMINISTRATORS: KEEPING THE FOCUS *David S. Martin* 123

23. BUILDING A THOUGHTFUL HIGH SCHOOL *William C. Martin* 126

24. MANAGING FOR REFLECTION: A SUPERINTENDENT'S DILEMMA *Sherry P. King* 131

25. MEDIATIVE ENVIRONMENTS *Arthur L. Costa* 135

SECTION IV.   OUR CHANGING PERSPECTIVES ON THINKING

INTRODUCTION *Robin Fogarty* 142

26. OUR CHANGING PERSPECTIVE OF INTELLIGENCE:
MASTER ARCHITECTS OF THE INTELLECT *Robin Fogarty* 144

27. BECOMING A CONSTRUCTIVIST TEACHER
Jacqueline Grennon Brooks and Martin G. Brooks 150

28. THE SOCIAL SIDE OF THINKING *David Perkins* 158

29. IN THE GRIPS OF EMOTION *Robert J. Swartz* 164

30. ON TEACHING BRAINS TO THINK: A CONVERSATION WITH ROBERT SYLWESTER
Ron Brandt 170

31. THE BIOLOGICAL BASIS FOR THINKING *Lawrence F. Lowery* 175

32. A NEW TAXONOMY OF EDUCATIONAL OBJECTIVES *Robert J. Marzano* 181

SECTION V.   HUMAN VARIABILITY AND THINKING

INTRODUCTION *Sandra Parks* 190

33. A SURVEY OF THINKING AND LEARNING STYLES *Armando Lozano* 192

34. THINKING STYLES *Robert J. Sternberg* 197

35. TEACHING FOR, WITH, AND ABOUT MULTIPLE INTELLIGENCES *David G. Lazear* 202

36. THINKING AND THE SPECIAL-NEEDS LEARNER *David S. Martin* 211

37. CULTURAL INFLUENCES ON CRITICAL THINKING AND PROBLEM SOLVING
Douglas F. Brenner and Sandra Parks 216

38. REVERSING UNDERACHIEVEMENT IN URBAN STUDENTS: PEDAGOGY OF CONFIDENCE
Yvette Jackson 222

39. THINKING IN A CULTURE OF POVERTY *Ruby K. Payne* 229

40. THE BIOLOGICAL BASIS FOR LEARNING *Lawrence F. Lowery* 234

SECTION VI.   THINKING ACROSS THE CURRICULUM

INTRODUCTION *Arthur L. Costa* 246

41. DEVELOPING A SCOPE AND SEQUENCE FOR THINKING SKILLS INSTRUCTION *Barry K. Beyer* 248

42. Teacher as "Thought-Full" Designer *Bena Kallick and Marian Leibowitz* 253

43. Big Rocks and Powerful Kingdoms: Problem-Based Learning
    in Science and Social Studies *John Barell, Cheryl Hopper, and Ann White* 256

44. Resetting the Table: A Balanced Diet of Thought-Filled Integration
    Burton Cohen and Peter Hilts 262

45. Infusing Critical and Creative Thinking into Content Instruction
    Robert J. Swartz 266

46. What Research Says About Teaching Thinking Skills *Barry K. Beyer* 275

Section VII. Thinking in School Subjects

Introduction *John Barell* 284

47. Mathematics: The Thinking Arena for Problem Solving *Marcy Cook* 286

48. Improving Thinking Abilities Through Reading Instruction *Cathy Collins Block* 292

49. What Is Write for Thinking?
    Arthur Whimbey, Jack Lochhead, Myra J. Linden, and Carol Welsh 298

50. Teaching Thinking in Science *Robert J. Swartz and Stephen David Fischer* 303

51. The Role of the Arts in Cognition and Curriculum *Elliot W. Eisner* 310

52. Infusing Thinking in History and the Social Sciences *Barry K. Beyer* 317

53. A View from the Foxhole: Elevating Foreign Language Classrooms
    Virginia Pauline Rojas 326

54. Music and Skillful Thinking *Ruth M. Loring* 332

55. Developing a Lifetime of Literacy *Rebecca Reagan* 337

56. Developing Thinking Skills in Physical Education
    Daniel M. Landers, William Maxwell, Jessica Butler, and Lex Fagen 343

Section VIII. Techniques for Teaching Thinking

Introduction *Arthur L. Costa* 352

57. Teaching For, Of, and About Thinking *Arthur L. Costa* 354

58. Teacher Behaviors That Enable Student Thinking *Arthur L. Costa* 359

59. Teaching for Transfer *David Perkins and Gavriel Salomon* 370

60. Teaching the Language of Thinking *Arthur L. Costa and Robert J. Marzano* 379

61. Cueing Thinking in the Classroom: The Promise of Theory-Embedded Tools
    Jay McTighe and Frank T. Lyman Jr. 384

62. Practical Strategies for Direct Instruction in Thinking Skills *Barry K. Beyer* 393

63. Visual Tools for Mapping Minds *David Hyerle* 401

64. Mediating the Metacognitive *Arthur L. Costa* 408

65. Making Sense of Thinking *Jack Lochhead* 413

66. Putting It All Together to Improve Student Thinking *Barry K. Beyer* 417

Section IX. Strategies for Teaching Thinking

Introduction *Jack Lochhead* 426

67. Dialogical and Dialectical Thinking *Richard W. Paul* 427

68. CONCEPT DEVELOPMENT   *Sydelle Seiger-Ehrenberg* .... .437

69. TEACHING FOR CREATIVE LEARNING AND PROBLEM SOLVING
Donald J. Treffinger and Scott G. Isaksen .... .442

70. THINKING FOR UNDERSTANDING   *David Perkins* .... .446

71. TEACHING PROBLEM SOLVING AS A WAY OF LIFE   *Robert J. Sternberg* .... .451

72. COOPERATION AND CONFLICT: EFFECTS ON COGNITION AND METACOGNITION
David W. Johnson and Roger T. Johnson .... .455

73. THE ART AND CRAFT OF "GENTLY SOCRATIC" INQUIRY   *Thomas E. Jackson* .... .459

74. TEACHING COGNITIVE STRATEGIES FOR READING, WRITING, AND PROBLEM SOLVING
Michael Pressley and Karen R. Harris .... .466

SECTION X.   TEACHING THINKING THROUGH TECHNOLOGY

INTRODUCTION   *Bena Kallick* .... .472

75. TECHNOLOGY AND THINKING: THE EVOLVING RELATIONSHIP   *James M. Wilson III* .... .474

76. THINKING IN THE INFORMATION AGE   *Gary R. Morrison and Deborah L. Lowther* .... .479

77. LEARNING IN A DIGITAL WORLD   *John Richards* .... .484

78. INTEGRATING RESEARCH, THINKING, AND TECHNOLOGY
Joanne Marien, Elaine Vislocky, and Linda Chapman .... .489

SECTION XI.   ASSESSING GROWTH IN THINKING ABILITIES

INTRODUCTION   *Bena Kallick* .... .496

79. TO THINK OR NOT TO THINK: THINKING AS MEASURED
ON STATE AND NATIONAL ASSESSMENTS   *Elliott Asp* .... .497

80. STATE EXAMS FLUNK TEST OF QUALITY THINKING   *Monty Neill* .... .511

81. BUILDING A SYSTEM FOR ASSESSING THINKING   *Arthur L. Costa and Bena Kallick* .... .517

82. HOW TEACHERS CAN ASSESS THE THINKING SKILLS THEY ARE TEACHING   *Robert Stone* .... .525

83. PERFORMANCES TO ASSESS STANDARDS AND INTELLECTUAL GROWTH   *Kay Burke* .... .528

84. A FORMAT FOR ASSESSING THINKING SKILLS   *Barry K. Beyer* .... .533

85. ASSESSING THINKING SKILLS   *Alec Fisher* .... .541

APPENDIXES AND RESOURCES

INTRODUCTION   *Arthur L. Costa* .... .547

GLOSSARY OF THINKING TERMS   *Barry K. Beyer, Arthur L. Costa, and Barbara Z. Presseisen* .... .548

APPENDIX A: SELF-REFLECTION ON OUR OWN MODELS OF TEACHING   *John Barell* .... .551

APPENDIX B: CLASSROOM OBSERVATION CHECKLIST   *Lee Winocur Field* .... .552

APPENDIX C: HOW THOUGHTFUL IS YOUR SCHOOL?   *Arthur L. Costa* .... .555

APPENDIX D: CHECKLIST FOR THINKING SKILLS PROGRAMS   *Barry K. Beyer* .... .556

RECOMMENDED RESOURCES .... .558

ABOUT THE AUTHORS .... .564

INDEX TO AUTHORS .... .579

INDEX .... .580

Acknowledgments

This book is largely the brainchild of Ron Brandt, formerly executive editor of *Educational Leadership* and other ASCD publications. It was through his encouragement and guidance over many years that the previous two editions as well as this third revision have flourished.

Many minds have been engaged in preparing this third edition of *Developing Minds*. On November 21, 1998, a group met at the ASCD headquarters to generate a new format, to identify which chapters from previous editions should be retained, and to suggest contents and authors for the third edition. The product of their thinking is now in your hands. They made helpful suggestions, volunteered their time and talents, and persisted throughout the entire development of this project.

For their guidance, encouragement, and giving of their talents, I wish to express deep appreciation to:

John Barell, Montclair State College, New Jersey
Barry Beyer, George Mason University, Fairfax, Virginia
Ron Brandt, Alexandria, Virginia
Bena Kallick, Westport, Connecticut
Jack Lochhead, Amherst University, Massachusetts
David S. Martin, Gallaudet College, Washington, D.C.
Robert J. Marzano, Mid-continent Research for Education and Learning, Aurora, Colorado
Robert Swartz, National Center for Teaching Thinking, Boston, Massachusetts

Still others were invited to review the previous version of *Developing Minds*—the revised edition—and to make recommendations for this new round of revisions. Their thoughtful analysis and suggestions were extremely helpful in preparing this 3rd edition. They are:

Jay McTighe, Sandra Parks, Robin Fogarty, and
Arnold Ostfield.

Special appreciation is also expressed to Michael Barrett and his students of the Teaching Thinking Course in Shelby, Michigan, for their review of the previous edition of *Developing Minds* and their helpful suggestions for this revision.

I wish to express appreciation to the many contributors to this publication. They are a veritable "who's who" of outstanding contemporary cognitive educators. They have produced what I believe to be the most extensive, helpful, and scholarly publication on this topic to date. They've been patient with my prodding, determined with my deadlines, and agreeable to my editorial exclusions.

I wish to give special recognition to Bena Kallick, John Barell, Robin Fogarty, Sandra Parks, and Jack Lochhead, who volunteered to take on the additional responsibility for editing particular sections of this book.

Members of the ASCD Publications team who supported and guided this project through its arduous journey to completion included:

Nancy Modrak
Julie Houtz
John O'Neil
Terrey Hatcher Quindlen
Gary Bloom
Georgia McDonald
Tracey Smith

I wish to acknowledge and express appreciation to my assistant, Kim Welborn, who provided not only the technical assistance but also the sorely needed organizational capacities for so vast a project as this.

Finally, I wish to thank my wife, Nancy, who at times mistakenly may have thought my computer was more important than she.

Preface to the 3rd Edition

The world is endless, the universe inexhaustible, and the human brain will never be threatened with unemployment.
—*Genrich Altshuller, author of* The Innovation Algorithm

As I compose this preface on my laptop plugged into the power source of my seat while flying across the Pacific Ocean on a 767, I reflect on my learning journey since the first edition of *Developing Minds* in 1984. I reminisce about my first and feeble computerized attempts on my then-new Apple IIe that taught me the invaluable lesson to save as I worked. It was a time for a renaissance, a rebirth of thinking in the curriculum—not that we ever left it. In the great cycle of educational innovations, we hadn't had a healthy look at thinking since the post-Sputnik era. (I am chronologically gifted enough to have experienced four back-to-basics movements in my professional lifetime.) There were new and intriguing programs for teaching thinking that schools and districts were beginning to explore and adopt: Talents Unlimited, Structure of the Intellect, Instrumental Enrichment, Philosophy for Children, CoRT, and Odyssey. It was a time when we debated the use of open books while students were taking tests.

The first edition was an attempt to develop a broader awareness of the need for thinking to permeate the educational enterprise. In many ways the effort was successful. Today we can see school, district, state, and national standards reflecting the application of complex thought processes in each subject area, and our assessment practices are being refined to better assess students' more thoughtful performance.

The previous, revised edition of *Developing Minds* was composed on my Apple IIe with a screen so small that it would tax my eyes today. (In 1988 all faculty at California State University were given computers in the university's efforts to help professors become more computer literate.) At that time ASCD made a commitment to devote programs and resources to thinking skills for a five-year period. The revised edition of

Developing Minds as well as the Tactics for Thinking and Dimensions of Learning programs were born of that effort. At that time an avalanche of additional new thinking skills programs tempted educators: Higher Order Thinking Skills (HOTS), Impact, Creative Problem Solving, and Thinking to Learn. Confusion centered on whether to infuse thinking into content, to adopt a separate program, or both. We debated if students should be allowed to use calculators while taking their tests.

Since that time, many of the thinking skills programs have been winnowed. Teaching students to think has become accepted practice. Thoughtfulness in the workplace has become the standard, and industries realize the intellectual capital of their employees commands the investment of the major portion of their resources. Intellectual engagement and growth are internalized into most educational environments and endeavors. Educational practices that expect less are demeaning, detestable, and indefensible. Today we are debating whether students should be allowed to bring to their tests their cell phones and their Palm Pilots with access to www.askjeeves.com.

ASCD is a professional organization dedicated to making the world a better place for future generations. Realizing that our children are our most precious resource and that through them we will achieve a better tomorrow, I believe it is the most significant organization concerned with all youth. Children are our legacy, and we know that the degree of civilization of any nation is equivalent to the degree of civilization of its youth.

This third and expanded edition of *Developing Minds* is a compilation of research, practical applications, theory, and international perspectives from a wide range of authors, including those from Australia, England, and Mexico. About 10 percent of the chapters are retained from previous editions because of their classic and timeless quality. The remainder provide fresh new insights, accumulated research, and illumination of contemporary issues. This book is intended to be a resource for those educational decision makers who influence curriculum and instruction. This new edition is rededicated to the development of a new focus of the pervasive intellect—thoughtful people in all walks of life: government, the military, education, health care, and the corporate world—people who know how to live in a rational, humane, peaceful, and compassionate relationship with each other and with the environment.

This book is intended for educators who believe that education is one of the most powerful mechanisms for developing intellectual prowess; that meaningful interaction with adults, peers, and the environment is essential in mediating the learner's intellectual development; that learning is a continual transformation of inner perceptions, knowledge, and experiences; and that all human beings have the potential to continually develop their intellectual powers throughout their lives. It is intended to help educational leaders—teachers, administrators, curriculum workers, staff developers, and teacher educators—infuse curriculum, instruction, and school organization with practices that more fully develop the intellectual potentials of all the organizations' inhabitants.

Because the research in brain growth, development, and functioning is amplifying our understanding of the neurosciences, because of advancement in our classification of the genetic structure of human beings, because of our better understanding of how humans learn, and because of the rapid changes overtaking our world community, this edition is *not* intended to be comprehensive. Rather, it is intended to serve as a practical resource to help initiate change, to validate the enhancement of the intellect as a legitimate goal of education, to invite critical assessment of emerging school practices for their contributions to children's intellectual growth, and to foster the expansion of thinking throughout the curriculum, the school, the community, and ultimately the world.

This resource book provides an organized space for those educators who are involved with curriculum decision making. Grounded in reliable research, scholarly theory, and practical experience, the information contained herein is intended to provoke dialogue, stimulate discussion, and serve as a foundation for more responsible curriculum and instructional decision making.

On the day of its publication, *Developing Minds* will be obsolescent—there will have been new programs developed, additional research generated, and new articles and books written and published. These additions should be welcomed in a continuing journey toward better understanding of human learning and intellectual development.

While this book is copyrighted, you are invited to duplicate those portions you find suitable for distribution to community groups, school staffs, and boards of education. We merely ask that you identify the source on all duplicated materials, give credit to the authors, and not use these materials for resale. Our goal is to improve educational practices, and this book should provide a valuable resource toward that end.

Developing Minds is not a recipe book nor does it provide simple answers or immediate solutions to educational dilemmas. As a curriculum for thinking, this revised edition is intentionally unfinished. Its design is symbolic of the field of educational inquiry today—controversial, tentative, incomplete, and fascinating. Several chapters intentionally present alternative approaches, multiple definitions, and differing points of view. Instructional leaders, working with other educators and interested community members, will strive for improvement by continuing to stimulate dialogue, gathering additional resources and data, clarifying meaning, synthesizing definitions, conducting action research, and searching for better ways of learning to think through educational problems. Out of this confusion comes enlightenment. Thus the process of developing curriculum, improving instructional strategies, and assessing and reporting on students' growth in cognitive abilities, habits, and skills is in itself a form of inquiry and should be an intellectually stimulating experience.

Arthur L. Costa, Ed. D.
Kalaheo, Hawaii

Foreword

Ron Brandt

Who can say when and how it began? Long before our own day, educators sought to teach their students to think. Philosopher John Dewey first published his analysis titled *How We Think* in 1910, and a substantial movement devoted to critical thinking flourished in the 1960s. For me, though, the current thinking skills movement began in 1981, when I edited an issue of ASCD's *Educational Leadership* magazine called "Teaching Thinking Skills." Something was in the wind. I wasn't entirely sure what, but it was very exciting.

Cognitive psychology had displaced behaviorism, with its limited approach to mental activity. Mathematics and science educators were stressing problem solving. Critical thinking was making a comeback, especially on college campuses. Several instructional programs had been developed to improve students' thinking, which some equated with intelligence. A major factor helping to consolidate these efforts was a project that had been launched in Venezuela in 1978, led by national minister Luis Machado, to make all that country's citizens more intelligent (Perkins, 1995). Project Intelligence, as it was called, not only was using existing programs, such as Edward de Bono's CoRT thinking program, but also had commissioned the creation of a second generation curriculum, later to be published in the United States as Odyssey.

In the early 1980s most experts claimed (and some still do) that intelligence is unalterable. People are born with a certain level of intellectual ability, the IQ tests seemed to show, and you can't do much about it. At that time researchers such as Howard Gardner and Robert Sternberg were just beginning to explore expanded definitions of intellectual ability, and though true believers were convinced, the evidence was pretty skimpy that—using the title of a book published in 1976—*Intelligence Can Be Taught* (Whimbey, A., & Whimbey, L. S.).

One of the authors in that early issue of *Educational Leadership* was Arthur Costa, then a professor at California State University, Sacramento, and a member of ASCD's Executive Council. In his article, Art neatly dodged the question of whether schools could change measured intelligence. Instead, he focused on intelligent behavior, which surely they could influence. Art Costa continued to play key roles in the development of ASCD's program. In the summer of 1983, he and I organized an institute on thinking skills, introducing participants to programs such as Reuven Feuerstein's Instrumental Enrichment. The following year we held an invitational conference at the Wingspread center in Racine, Wisconsin, to plan a more comprehensive set of activities. The conference produced several recommendations, including a suggestion that ASCD publish a "resource book." I wasn't sure what such a book would be, but I invited Art to serve as editor, and he generously agreed. The result was the first edition of *Developing Minds*, which at the time was the largest book ASCD had published and which also has become one of the most successful and influential.

Basic Issues

The thinking skills movement examined in this volume has been bedeviled by at least three questions. The first is "What skills are you talking about?" The next, quite naturally, is "Can such skills be taught?" When that question is answered by citing examples of apparent success, usually achieved under relatively controlled conditions, the third question becomes "Should (can) thinking be taught not as a separate curriculum but in regular classes in conjunction with teaching subject matter?"

Before briefly discussing these questions, I will address the many possible meanings of "teaching thinking." Arthur Costa and I sometimes divide the field into three categories: teaching for thinking, teaching about thinking, and teaching of thinking. Even these categories mean different things to different people.

Here is what I mean by them. Teaching of thinking is what program developers like Matthew Lipman, creator of the Philosophy for Children program, have learned to do, using teaching methods and special materials not usually found in the typical school curriculum. In such programs, thinking becomes a subject like reading and writing, with specific skills you can learn to do and can improve upon. Thinking is not quite like reading, of course, because everyone can think to some extent without any training. But it is similar in that with guided practice—for example, in detecting errors in reasoning—we can become better at it. (I formulated those last two sentences by asking myself, "How is thinking similar to and different from reading?" I then rearranged my answer several times to avoid ambiguity and to make my statement as clear as possible.)

Teaching about thinking is the least clear of the three types, and I have heard differing explanations of its meaning. I understand it to mean encouraging students to think about their thinking—to become conscious of their own thought processes and improve their ability to control them to some degree. The idea was being promoted in the 1980s by psychologists and reading specialists, who used the term metacognition.

The third category, teaching for thinking, encompasses all the practices teachers have used for generations to induce their students to think. It includes assigning difficult reading material and problems to solve, asking open questions, giving essay tests, and so on. Most people assume the value of such practices and do not require scientific proof that they work. How best to teach for thinking remains an appropriate subject for research, but the evidence question applies more to the other two categories of teaching thinking, which are the object of my three questions.

WHAT SKILLS?

Nearly 20 years after that 1981 issue of *Educational Leadership*, the question of whether thinking skills can be taught is still somewhat open to debate. The first step toward answering the question is to define what is meant by "thinking." Benjamin Bloom (1956) and his colleagues provided a useful start a half century ago with their well-known taxonomy. The hierarchical structure of the taxonomy later enabled Bloom (1981) and others to refer to skills such as synthesis and analysis as "higher level."

But each of the published programs that attracted educators' attention in the 1980s had its own conceptual scheme and its own list of skills. To help clarify what schools might need to include in a comprehensive program, I recruited a group of interested educators. They reviewed available literature and prepared *Dimensions of Thinking* (Marzano et al., 1988), an analysis of the particular aspects of thinking (such as critical thinking, metacognition, classifying, and decision mak-

ing) emphasized by various authorities. The clusters we chose for that publication were subsequently transformed by Bob Marzano, Deborah Pickering, and their associates into a practical model for teachers known as Dimensions of Learning (Marzano, 1992; Marzano & Pickering, 1997).

But that framework (skills such as abstracting are for extending and refining, processes such as problem solving are for meaningful use) is just one more way of selecting and arraying the various skills. There continues to be no single compendium—other than the now somewhat outmoded Bloom taxonomy—widely accepted by the various proponents of thinking. (When I described the Dimensions framework to de Bono, he observed wryly, "There are many great cuisines in the world—French, Italian, German, Chinese—and you seem to want to make a great stew out of all of them.")

CAN THINKING SKILLS BE TAUGHT?

The only way to deal with the second question, then, is to ask whether program developers have succeeded in teaching the particular skills they set out to teach. Scholars who have reviewed the evidence are generally positive but cautious. David Perkins (1995), for example, asks "Can people learn more intelligence?" and answers "Yes, in a number of ways." But he quickly points to a number of problems, including the "modest impact" of published programs. An honest advocate, Perkins looks forward to the possibility that "newer ways of enhancing intelligence, fundamentally more powerful, will emerge from current work" (p. 210).

CAN THINKING BE TAUGHT IN REGULAR CLASSES?

The third basic question builds on the second. If, as David Perkins reports, we have evidence of "modest" success in teaching the skills of thinking by trained teachers using specially designed curriculums, can other teachers be expected to incorporate the teaching of such skills into regular subject-matter classes? Although many advocates support the idea, the evidence for this position is much skimpier. Nearly all would agree that it can happen only with continuing emphasis, which includes strong leadership, training, and logistical support.

Even so, some of the most respected authorities on learning and cognition, such as Lauren Resnick of the Learning Research and Development Center at the University of Pittsburgh, advise against special courses in thinking. In her influential booklet, *Education and Learning to Think*, prepared for the National Research Council, Resnick (1987) stressed the need to develop higher-order thinking but advised that it be done through capable teaching of complex subject matter. "Isolated instruction in thinking skills, no matter how elegant the training provided, is unlikely to produce broadly used thinking ability," she wrote. "Higher order skills must suffuse the school program from kindergarten on and in every subject matter" (p. 48).

Since she wrote those words, Resnick has been an influential figure, serving as a member of several advisory bodies and as codirector of the New Standards Project, which helped shape the current standards and assessment movement. With standards and matching state assessments now dominating American education, the view that thinking is best taught through challenging content seems—for the time being, at least—to be firmly in place. Many state standards specifically call for students to "analyze," "compare," and "explain." The less well informed may assume that good thinking will be an automatic byproduct of teaching traditional content. To the contrary, Resnick and other cognitive scientists recognize how much must be done to achieve the goal of "embedding instruction in thinking skills within the academic disciplines" (p. 48). If students are to meet higher standards—especially if assessments are valid—they must be capable thinkers.

Regardless of how it is done, now more than ever, educators confront the challenge of developing minds.

REFERENCES

Bloom, B. S., Englehart, M. D., Furst, E. J., Hill, W. H., & Krathwohl, D. R. (Eds.). (1956). *Taxonomy of educational objectives: The classification of educational goals. Handbook I: Cognitive domain.* New York: David McKay.

Bloom, B. S. (1981). *All our children learning.* New York: McGraw-Hill.

Dewey, J. (1910). *How we think.* Boston: D. C. Heath.

Marzano, R. J. (1992). *A different kind of classroom: Teaching with Dimensions of Learning.* Alexandria, VA: Association for Supervision and Curriculum Development.

Marzano, R. J., Brandt, R. S., Hughes, C. S., Jones, B. F., Presseisen, B. Z., Rankin, S. C., & Suhor, C. (1988). *Dimensions of thinking: A framework for curriculum and instruction.* Alexandria, VA: Association for Supervision and Curriculum Development.

Marzano, R. J., & Pickering, D. J. (1997). *Dimensions of Learning Trainer's Manual* (2nd ed.). Alexandria, VA: Association for Supervision and Curriculum Development; and Aurora, CO: Mid-continent Regional Educational Laboratory.

Perkins, D. N. (1995). *Outsmarting IQ: The emerging science of learnable intelligence.* New York: Free Press.

Resnick, L. B. (1987). *Education and learning to think.* Washington, DC: National Academy Press.

Whimbey, A., & Whimbey, L. S. (1976). *Intelligence can be taught.* New York: Bantam Books.

Introduction: The Vision

Arthur L. Costa

We are riding the crest of what may well be the greatest opportunity for educational reform in history—a growing dissatisfaction with the current quality of education; a realization of educational reform as a political platform; a concern about nations' global economic dependence upon an educated and highly skilled work force; and a heightened awareness that we are preparing students for a future filled with uncertainties.

As we enter an era in which knowledge doubles in less than five years—the projection is that by the year 2020 it will double every 73 days—it is no longer feasible to anticipate an individual's future information requirements. We now have more information than the collective minds in science can understand.

Our world has shifted away from an industrial model of society to a learning society, from Newtonian to quantum sciences, and from a linear to a complex and chaotic world view. These changes require education to develop individuals with the knowledge, problem-solving skills, cognitive processes, intellectual dispositions, and habits of mind necessary to engage in lifelong learning.

Students entering the new millennium must come fully equipped with skills that enable them to think for themselves and be self-initiating, self-modifying, and self-directing. They must acquire the capacity to learn and change consciously, continuously, and quickly. They will require skills that cannot be gained learning content alone. They must possess process capabilities beyond just fixing problems. Rather, they must anticipate what might happen and search continuously for more creative solutions. Our society further recognizes a growing need for informed, skilled, and compassionate citizens who value truth, openness, creativity, interdependence, balance, and love as well as the search for personal and spiritual freedom in all areas of one's life. This demands that the school's curriculum must be open and flexible enough to accommodate these new perspectives.

Curriculum is the most critical component of school reform. It is the central focus around which all other variables are constructed—assessment, teacher evaluation, textbook and media selection, professional development, student achievement, collegial discussions, and parent-teacher communications. As such, curriculum, instruction, learning, and assessment are the pulse of the school. They drive everything else. They are the currency through which we exchange thoughts and ideas. They are the passions that bind our organization together.

We are at a time in education when professional educators are being pressured for immediate, measurable results on standardized performances (Colvin & Helfand, 2000). This assumes that if teachers taught academic subjects and students were evaluated on how well they learned the minute subskills in those content areas, they would "somehow become the kind of people we want them to become" (Seiger-Ehrenberg, 1991, p. 6).

While politicians' and legislators' desires to improve education are commendable, such misguided efforts as increasing reliance on test scores and requiring high-stakes accountability are the antithesis of our desire to make learning and instruction more reflective, more complex, and more relevant to society's and students' diverse needs and interests now and in the future.

THE MULTIPLE PURPOSES OF THIS BOOK

The major purpose of this book, therefore, is to rejuvenate our focus on thinking throughout the curriculum. Having read, organized, and reflected on all the contributions to this book, five pervasive themes or patterns seem to emerge. Not only might these five themes provide lenses through which the contents of this volume may be examined, they may also constitute some unfinished tasks, suggesting an agenda for action in moving toward a more "thought-full" curriculum for a more thought-filled world. The purpose of this endeavor may be reinterpreted in light of these five themes. They are disclosed at several levels of complexity. The first, focusing on students' capacities to think, is an obvious, immediate goal. The others—thinking to learn, thinking together, thinking about our own thoughtfulness, and thinking big—are more subtle and complex and require longer-range attention.

LEARNING TO THINK

One obvious purpose of this book is to reinvigorate our attention on students' capacities to think. All of us think. Indeed, we come to this earth with the capacity, ability, and inclination to think. Nobody has to "teach us how to think," just like no one teaches us how to move or walk. We do it innately when we are ready. Thinking, therefore, may be taken for granted.

However, it takes much time and coaching for human movement to be performed with precision, style, and grace. It takes years of practice, concentration, reflection, and coaching to become a skilled gymnast or ice skater. Improvement is demonstrated by the increasing mastery of complex and intricate maneuvers performed repeatedly on command with sustained, seemingly effortless agility. The distinction between awkwardness and grace is obvious even to the most undisciplined observer.

Like strenuous movement, effective, skillful thinking is also hard work. Similarly, with proper instruction human thought processes can become more broadly applied, more spontaneously generated, more precisely focused, more intricately complex, more metaphorically abstract, and more insightfully divergent. Such refinement also requires practice, concentration, reflection, and coaching. Unlike athletics, however, thinking is most often idiosyncratic and covert. Awkwardness and agility, therefore, are not as easily distinguished in thinking as they are in athletics. Definitions of thought processes, strategies for their development, and assessment of the stamina required for their increased mastery are therefore illusive.

The positive effects become increasingly apparent when schools and communities forge a common vision and focus efforts and resources on developing the attributes of the ideal thinking person. These could be characteristics of the "critical thinker"; dispositions of intelligent human beings; qualities of the thought-full person; or performances of efficient, effective, and reasoned problem solvers. The name is not as important as the shared meaning and vision these terms convey.

This book provides many useful definitions of thinking and related terminology as well as an understanding of the significance of developing thoughtfulness as a prerequisite of lifelong learning. But a grander intent of such definitions is to forge a common vision among all members of the educational community—individual teachers from all levels of instruction and teams of administrators, librarians, staff developers, teacher educators, school board members, and parents—of what characterizes effective and creative thinkers and problem solvers.

THINKING TO LEARN

Meaning making is not a spectator sport. It is an engagement of the mind that transforms the mind. Knowledge is a constructive process rather than a finding. The brain's capacity and desire to make or elicit patterns of meaning is one of the keys of brain-based learning. We never really understand something until we can create a model or metaphor derived from our unique personal world. The reality we perceive, feel, see, and hear is influenced by the constructive processes of the brain as well as by the cues that impinge upon it. It is not the content stored in memory but the activity of constructing it that gets stored. Humans don't *get* ideas; they *make* ideas.

Furthermore, meaning making is not just an individual operation. The individual interacts with others to construct shared knowledge. There is a cycle of internalization of what is socially constructed as shared meaning, which is then externalized to affect the learner's social participation. Constructivist learning, therefore, is viewed as a reciprocal process in which the individual influences the group and the group influences the individual (Vygotsky, 1978).

Naturally, many suggestions for instructional strategies and techniques are presented herein. Yet, a larger purpose is to shift our perceptions of teaching from educational outcomes that are primarily an individual's collection of subskills to include successful participation in socially organized activities and the development of students' identities as conscious, flexible, effective, and interdependent meaning makers. We must let go of having learners acquire our meanings and have faith in the processes of individuals' construction of their own and shared meanings through individual activity and social interaction. This thought makes some people uneasy, because the individual and the group may not construct the meaning we want them to. Such an approach represents a real challenge to the basic educational framework with which most school leaders are comfortable.

While many practical suggestions are provided for teaching thinking directly as well as infusing thought into all areas of the curriculum, the greater purpose is to enhance instructional decision making to employ content, not as an end of instruction, but rather as a vehicle for activating and engaging the mind. Content is selected merely as a vehicle for experiencing the joy ride of learning.

Thinking Together

I never saw an instance of one or two disputants convincing the other by argument.

—*Thomas Jefferson*

A great problem facing education is caused by the fragmentation of thinking and acting—a way of thinking that divides and fails to see the interconnections and coherence of divergent views. Fixated on his own certainties, each stakeholder perceives the solution to educational reform from his individual perspective. Invested in present ways of working, many educators, parents, legislators, and board members believe that if we can just do what we are presently doing better—give more money to education, purchase more computers, hire more teachers, extend the school year, mandate high-stakes testing, reduce class size, "toughen" teacher certification standards, hold schools more accountable—everything will improve. People become convinced that their own perspectives on the problem are essentially right and that others have it wrong. But thinking in this way prevents us from gaining a wider perspective—one that would enable all of us to determine what we are missing. This egocentric view hinders serious reflection and honest inquiry.

Therefore, while there are numerous suggestions for cooperative and social discourse, another purpose of this book is to stimulate dialogue as a means of building an "ecology of thought" (Isaacs, 1999)—a living network of memory and awareness that becomes a complex web linking community members together. This is a difficult task, as it means temporarily suspending what we individually think—relaxing our grip on our certainties, entertaining others' points of view, and acting with a willingness to abide by and support the group's decisions arrived at through deep and respectful listening and dialogue. Out of this collective atmosphere in which we think and work together unfolds a fresh group intelligence that promotes action toward common goals.

This implies encountering the unknown: the psychologically unknown risks of a new venture, the physically unknown demands on time and energy, and the intellectually unknown requirement for different views and definitions. Thinking together demands a shift away from our own traditional and obsolescent thinking. Achieving such an ecology of thought will require patience, stamina, and courage. The benefits, however, are resplendent.

Thinking About Our Own Thoughtfulness

In this volume, there are many descriptions of the benefits of and suggestions for inviting students to think about their thinking: metacognition. Indeed, human beings, to the best of our knowledge, are the only form of life with the capacity to stand off and examine their own thoughts while they engage in them. Although the human brain is able to generate reflective consciousness, however, not everyone seems to use it equally (Csikszentmihalyi, 1990). Thus a broader intent of this publication is heightened consciousness for all of us, not only students.

Thinking involves the whole of us—our emotions, our ways of feeling in the body, our ideas, our beliefs, our qualities of character, and our visions of being. Learning to think begins with recognizing how we are thinking now. Generally we are not all that conscious of how we are thinking. We can begin to think by listening first to ourselves and to our own reactions—by learning to watch how our thoughts encapsulate us. Much of what we think happens simply by virtue of our agreement that it should, not because of any close examination of our bounded assumptions, limited history, and existing mental models.

This volume presents research on human effectiveness, descriptions of remarkable performers, and analyses of the characteristics of efficacious people. These descriptions should serve as mental disciplines not only for our students, but for each of us as well. When confronted with problematic situations, we all must learn to habitually monitor our reactions by asking ourselves, "What is the most intelligent thing I can do right now?"

Further self-probing questions include the following:

• How can I learn from this? What are my resources? How can I draw on my past successes with problems like this? What do I already know about the problem? What resources do I have available or need to generate?

• How can I approach this problem flexibly? How might I look at the situation in another way? How can I look at this problem from a fresh perspective? Am I remaining open to new possibilities and further learning?

• How can I illuminate this problem to make it clearer, more precise? Do I need to check out my data sources? How might I break this problem down into its component parts and develop a strategy for understanding and accomplishing each step?

• What do I know or not know? What questions do I need to ask? What strategies are in my mind now? What am I aware of in terms of my own beliefs, values, and goals related to this problem? What feelings or emotions am I aware of that might be blocking or enhancing my progress?

• How is this problem affecting others? How can we solve it together? What can I learn from others that would help me become a better problem solver?

Taking a reflective stance in the midst of active problem solving is often difficult.

The goal of education, therefore, should be to support others and ourselves in liberating, developing, and habituating greater self-thought and reflection. Thinking about our own thoughtfulness becomes the force directing us toward becoming increasingly authentic, congruent, and ethical. It is the primary vehicle in the lifelong journey toward integration.

THINKING BIG

To be found in this extensive volume are many prescriptions for teaching and assessing thinking skills, creativity, problem solving, decision making, and information processing. As professional educators, however, we have a larger, more spiritual agenda to which this book is dedicated.

When the first astronauts went into space and looked back on earth, they realized that there were no lines on the planet. The scars of national boundaries were gone. Dividing lines disappear when you get enough perspective. And yet, divisions still exist among people, children, nations, institutions, religions, and political ideologies.

Another mission of this book, therefore, is to build a more thoughtful world as an interdependent learning community, where all people are continually searching for ways to trust each other, to learn together, and to grow toward greater intelligence. By caring for and learning from one another and sharing the riches and resources in one part of the globe, we can help the less fortunate others achieve their fullest intellectual potential and together build

• A world community that strives to generate more thoughtful approaches to solving problems in peaceful ways rather than resorting to violence and terrorism to resolve differences.

• A world community that values human diversity of other cultures, races, religions, language systems, time perspectives, and political and economic views in an effort to bring harmony and stability.

• A world of greater consciousness of our human effects on each other and on the earth's limited resources in an effort to live more respectfully, graciously, and harmoniously in our delicate environment.

• A world of better communication with other peoples, regardless of what language they speak, to employ clear and respectful dialogue rather than weapons to resolve misunderstandings.

The larger mission of this book, therefore is to support a vision of a world filled with classrooms, schools, and communities that are more thoughtful places. We must learn to unite and not divide. As Alan Kay (1990) stated, "The best way to predict the future is to invent it."

If we want a future that is much more thoughtful, vastly more cooperative, greatly more compassionate, and a lot more loving, then we have to invent it. The future is in our schools and classrooms today.

REFERENCES

Colvin, R. L., & Helfand, D. (2000, July 1). Millions for schools tied to Stanford 9 test scores. *Los Angeles Times*, pp. A20–21.

Csikszentmihalyi, M. (1990). *Flow: The psychology of optimal experience.* New York: Harper & Row Publisher.

Isaacs, W. (1999). *Dialogue and the art of thinking together: A pioneering approach to communicating in business and in life.* New York: Currency.

Kay, Alan (1990, March). *The best way to predict the future is to invent it.* Keynote presentation delivered at the 45th Annual Conference of the Association for Supervision and Curriculum Development, San Antonio, TX.

Seiger-Ehrenberg, S. (1991). Educational outcomes for a K-12 curriculum. In A. Costa (Ed.), *Developing Minds: A Resource Book for Teaching Thinking* (Rev. ed., Vol. 1, pp. 6–9). Alexandria, VA: Association for Supervision and Curriculum Development.

Vygotsky, L. S. (1978). *Mind in society: The development of higher psychological processes.* Cambridge, MA: Harvard University Press.

I

The Need to Teach Thinking

The object of education is to prepare the young to educate themselves throughout their lives.

—ROBERT MAYNARD HUTCHINS

Introduction

ARTHUR L. COSTA

The three major purposes of public education have remained consistent over many decades. Although different authors may use different terminology, the purposes are

- To help individuals develop to their fullest potential—physically, emotionally, philosophically, aesthetically, and intellectually.
- To prepare students for economic self-sufficiency and the world of work, teaching them how to obtain and produce desired goods and services and efficiently manage personal resources.
- To instill responsibility for participating in society—maintaining an environment conducive to human survival and functioning effectively for the well-being of the community.

Although these goals may be perennial, their interpretation and manifestations change constantly depending on the changing needs of society and the resources available. During the Industrial Revolution of the 18th and 19th centuries, for example, students prepared for the world of work by developing the capacity to perform repetitive tasks and use physical stamina to be productive. In the knowledge revolution of the 21st century, the emphasis is on using ingenuity, creativity, and intellectual prowess. In addition, the concept of social responsi-bility has changed, as our view of society has broadened to encompass the global community rather than just our immediate community or nation.

This section substantiates the need for teaching students to think. It is structured around the three basic objectives of education, exploring the intellectual demands of the future from the perspective of the individual, society, and the world of work.

The section opens with Lauren Resnick's provocative chapter prompting us to reconsider some obsolescent interpretations of the purposes of education. Futurist LeRoy Hay next examines the intellectual needs of the future and suggests that a changing world will demand changes in our instructional and curriculum practices. Sheldon Berman considers the need for thinking in social contexts, while Arthur Costa and Robert Garmston suggest that the capacity for critical and creative thinking arises from innate passions within each human being. John Edwards explores the need for thinking in the workplace. Robert Marzano and Jane Pollock examine the degree to which national standards in different subject areas incorporate the teaching of complex thought processes. Finally, Barry Beyer outlines some of the challenges ahead if schools are to fulfill their obligation to prepare students for successful lives in which problem solving, continual learning, and creativity are paramount.

1

Making America Smarter: The Real Goal of School Reform

LAUREN B. RESNICK

Standards, tests, and accountability programs are today's favored policy tools for raising overall academic achievement. Testing policies are also meant to increase equity, to give poor and minority students a fairer chance by making expectations clear and providing instruction geared to them. In practice, though, it is proving hard to meet the twin goals of equity and higher achievement. This is because our schools are trapped in a set of beliefs about the nature of ability and aptitude that make it hard to evoke effective academic effort from students and educators.

What we learn is a function of both our aptitudes for particular kinds of learning and the effort we put forth. Americans mostly assume that aptitude largely determines what people can learn in school, although they allow that hard work can compensate for lower doses of innate intelligence. Our schools are largely organized around this belief. IQ tests or their surrogates are used to determine who has access to enriched programs. As a result, some students never get the chance to study a high-demand, high-expectation curriculum (Resnick, 1995).

Traditional achievement tests are normed to compare students against one another rather than against a standard of excellence. This approach makes it difficult to see the results of learning and thereby discourages effort. (If one is going to stay at about the same relative percentile rank no matter how much one has learned, what is the point of trying hard?) Similarly, college entrance depends heavily on aptitude-like tests that have little to do with the curriculum studied. Like IQ tests, they are designed to spread the student population out on a statistical scale rather than to define what any particular individual has learned.

These commonplace features of the American educational landscape are institutionalized expressions of a persistent belief in the importance of inherited aptitude. The system they are part of is self-sustaining. Assumptions about aptitude are continually reinforced by the results of practices based on those assumptions. Students who are held to low expectations do not try to break through that barrier, because they accept the judgment that inborn aptitude matters most and that they have not inherited enough of that capacity. Not surprisingly, their performance remains low. Children who have not been taught a demanding, challenging, thinking curriculum do poorly on tests of reasoning or problem solving, confirming many people's original suspicions that they lack the talent for high-level thinking.

Two converging lines of research—one from cognitive science, one from social psychology—now give us reason to believe that we don't have to continue in this way. We don't need to pit excellence against equity. We can harness effort to create ability and build a smarter America (Resnick & Hall, 1998).

INTELLIGENCE-IN-PRACTICE: HABITS OF MIND

For more than 30 years, psychologists and other students of the human mind have been experimenting with ways of teaching the cognitive skills associated with intelligence. These include techniques as varied as generating analogies, making logical deductions, creating and using memory aids, and monitoring one's own state of knowledge (*metacognition*). Early experiments on teaching specific, isolated components of intelligence yielded a common pattern of results: Most of the training was successful in producing immediate gains in performance, but people typically ceased using the cognitive techniques they had been taught as soon as the specific conditions of training were removed. In other words, they became *capable* of performing whatever skill was taught, but they acquired no

Adapted with permission. The original article, "Making America Smarter" by L. B. Resnick, first appeared in *Education Week*, June 16, 1999, Volume 8, Issue Number 40, pp. 38–40.

general *habit* of using it or capacity to judge for themselves when it was useful.

As a result of these findings, cognitive researchers began to shift their attention to educational strategies that immerse students in demanding, long-term intellectual environments. Positive results are now coming in. In experimental programs and in practical school reforms, we are seeing that students who, over an extended period of time, are treated *as if* they are intelligent, actually become so. If they are taught demanding content and are expected to explain and find connections as well as memorize and repeat, they learn more and learn more quickly. They think of themselves as learners. They are able to bounce back in the face of short-term failures.

This experience is giving rise to a new conceptualization of intelligence-in-practice: Intelligence is the habit of persistently trying to understand things and make them function better. Intelligence is working to figure things out, varying strategies until a workable solution is found. Intelligence is knowing what one does (and doesn't) know, seeking information, and organizing that information so that it makes sense and can be remembered. In short, one's intelligence is the sum of one's habits of mind (Brown & Palincsar, 1989; Resnick & Nelson-Le Gall, 1997).

Being Smart and Getting Smart

Here is where the research by social psychologists comes in. Two decades of studies have shown that what people believe about the nature of talent and intelligence—about what accounts for success and failure—is closely related to the amount and kind of effort they put forth in situations of learning or problem solving (Dweck & Leggett, 1988).

Some people believe that intelligence and other forms of talent are fixed and unchangeable. Intelligence is a thing, an entity that is displayed in one's performance. Doing well means that one has ability; doing poorly means that one doesn't have ability. According to this belief, people who are very talented perform easily; they don't need to work hard to do well. Hence, if you want to appear to *be smart*, you should not appear to be working very hard. Any educator working with adolescents knows how this belief can drive some students away from schoolwork.

Other people believe that intelligence is something that develops and grows. These people view ability as a repertoire of skills that is continuously expandable through one's efforts. Intelligence is incremental. People can *get smart* (see Howard, 1995). When people think this way, they tend to invest energy to learn something new or to increase their understanding and mastery.

But it is not just brute effort that distinguishes these learners from people who think of intelligence as an entity. Incremental thinkers are particularly likely to apply self-regulatory, metacognitive skills when they encounter task difficulties, to focus on analyzing the task and generating alternative strategies. Most important, they seek out opportunities to hone their skills and knowledge, treating task difficulty (and thus occasional setbacks) as part of the learning challenge rather than as evidence that they lack intelligence. They get on an upward spiral in which their intelligence is actually increasing. Meanwhile, their peers who think of intelligence as fixed try to avoid difficult tasks for fear of displaying their lack of intelligence. They enter a downward spiral by avoiding the very occasions in which they could learn smarter ways of behaving.

Effort-Based Education and Learnable Intelligence

The good news is that people's beliefs about intelligence aren't immutable. They respond to the situations in which people find themselves. This means that it is possible to help students develop learning-oriented goals and an incremental view of intelligence and thus set them on the upward spiral by which they can become smarter and deliver the kinds of high-level academic achievement everyone is hoping for. To do this, we need to create effort-based schools in which academic rigor and a thinking curriculum permeate the school day for every student.

For several years the Institute for Learning at the University of Pittsburgh has been working with school systems across the country to set students—and whole school faculties—on the upward, getting-smarter spiral. A core set of principles guides this work, principles that educators have found both inspiring and practical. These principles, which can be illustrated in multiple examples of specific school and classroom practice, are based on cognitive research and research on learning organizations (Resnick & Hall, 2001). Here they are in a nutshell:

• **Organize for Effort.** An effort-based school replaces the assumption that aptitude determines what and how much students learn with the assumption that sustained and directed effort can yield high achievement for all students. Everything is organized to evoke and support this effort, to send the message that effort is expected and that tough problems yield to sustained work. High minimum standards are set and assessments are geared to the standards. All students are taught a rigorous curriculum, matched to the standards, along with as much time and expert instruction as they need to meet or exceed expectations.

• **Clear Expectations.** If we expect all students to learn at high levels, we need to define explicitly what we expect students to learn. These expectations need to be communicated clearly in ways that get them into the heads of school professionals, parents, the community, and, above all, students themselves. Descriptive criteria and models of work that meet standards should be publicly displayed, and students should refer to these displays to help them analyze and discuss their work. With visible accomplishment targets to aim toward at each stage of learning, students can participate in evaluating their own work and setting goals for their own effort.

• **Recognition of Accomplishment.** If we expect students to put forth and sustain high levels of effort, we need to motivate them by regularly recognizing their accomplishments. Clear recognition of authentic accomplishment is a hallmark of an effort-based school. This recognition can take the form of celebrations of work that meets standards or intermediate progress benchmarks en route to the standards. Progress points should be articulated so that, regardless of entering performance level, every student can meet real accomplishment criteria often enough to be recognized frequently. Recognition of accomplishment can be tied to opportunity to participate in events that matter to students and their families. Student accomplishment is also recognized when student performance on standards-based assessments is related to opportunities at work and in higher education.

• **Fair and Credible Evaluations.** If we expect students to put forth sustained effort over time, we need to use assessments that students find fair, and that parents, community, and employers find credible. Fair evaluations are ones that students can prepare for; therefore, tests, exams, and classroom assessments must be aligned to the standards and the curriculum being taught. Fair assessment also means grading against absolute standards rather than on a curve, so that students can clearly see the results of their learning efforts. Assessments that meet these criteria provide parents, colleges, and employers with credible evaluations of what individual students know and can do.

• **Academic Rigor in a Thinking Curriculum.** Thinking and problem solving will be the "new basics" of the 21st century. But the common idea that we can teach thinking without a solid foundation of knowledge must be abandoned. So must the idea that we can teach knowledge without engaging students in thinking. Knowledge and thinking are intimately joined. This implies a curriculum organized around major concepts that students are expected to know deeply. Teaching

must engage students in active reasoning about these concepts. In every subject, at every grade level, the instruction and learning must include commitment to a knowledge core, high thinking demand, and active use of knowledge.

○ **Commitment to a Knowledge Core.** The ability to think well goes hand-in-hand with rich stores of knowledge. In each field of learning, there is a core of knowledge and conceptual understanding that all students should learn. This knowledge core should be specified in rigorous academic standards. The standards can then serve as the basis for an articulated curriculum in which core concepts are taught and learned in considerable depth, along with skills and tools of the discipline.

○ **High Thinking Demand.** Students will learn thinking abilities best when thinking is infused throughout the curriculum. Each subject should be taught in ways that press students to pose and solve problems; to formulate conjectures and hypotheses and to justify their arguments; and to construct explanations and test their own understanding. These high thinking demands, normal in programs for the gifted and talented, should be the daily fare of all students.

○ **Active Use of Knowledge.** People acquire robust, lasting knowledge only if they themselves do the mental work of making sense of it. Good teaching is a matter of arranging for students to do their own knowledge construction, while ensuring that the ideas students develop will be in good accord with known facts and established concepts.

• **Accountable Talk.** Talking with others about ideas and work is fundamental to learning. But not all talk sustains learning. For classroom talk to promote learning, it must be accountable: to the learning community, to accurate and appropriate knowledge, and to rigorous thinking. Accountable talk seriously responds to and further develops what others in the group have said. It puts forth and demands knowledge that is accurate and relevant to the issue under discussion. Accountable talk uses evidence appropriate to the discipline (e.g., proofs in mathematics, data from investigations in science, textual details in literature, documentary sources in history) and follows established norms of good reasoning. Teachers should intentionally create the norms and skills of accountable talk in their classrooms.

• **Socializing Intelligence.** Intelligence is much more than an innate ability to think quickly and stockpile bits of knowledge. Intelligence is a set of problem-solving and reasoning capabilities, along with the habits of mind that lead one to use those capabilities regularly. Intelligence is equally a set of beliefs about one's right and obligation to understand and make sense of the world and about one's capacity to figure things out over time. Intelligent habits of mind are learned through the daily expectations placed on the learner. By calling on students to use the skills of intelligent thinking—and holding them responsible for doing so—educators can "teach" intelligence. This is what teachers normally do with students they expect much from; it should be standard practice with all students.

• **Self-Management of Learning.** If students are going to be responsible for the quality of their thinking and learning, they need to develop—and regularly use—an array of self-monitoring and self-management strategies. These *metacognitive* skills include noticing when one doesn't understand something and taking steps to remedy the situation, as well as formulating questions and inquiries that let one explore deep levels of meaning. Students also manage their own learning by evaluating the feedback they get from others; bringing their background knowledge to bear on new learning; anticipating learning difficulties and apportioning their time accordingly; and judging their progress toward a learning goal. These are strategies that good learners use spontaneously and that all students can learn through appropriate instruction and socialization. Learning environments should be designed to model and encourage the regular use of self-management strategies.

• **Learning as Apprenticeship.** For many centuries, most people learned by working alongside an expert who modeled skilled practice and guided novices as they created authentic products or performances for interested and critical audiences. This kind of apprenticeship allowed learners to acquire complex interdisciplinary knowledge, practical abilities, and appropriate forms of social behavior. Much of the power of apprenticeship learning can be brought into schooling by organizing learning environments so that complex thinking is modeled and analyzed, and by providing mentoring and coaching as students undertake extended projects and develop presentations of finished work, both in and beyond the classroom.

As we enter a new century, it is increasingly evident that the educational methods we have been using for the past 80 years no longer suffice. They are based on scientific assumptions about the nature of knowledge, the learning process, and differential aptitude for learning that have been eclipsed by new discoveries. Yet changing them has been slow, because the nature of educational reform in this country is largely one of tinkering with institutional arrangements. Rarely has reform penetrated the "educational core."

But that is now happening. With the movement for standards-based education, America has begun to explore the potential of designing policy structures explicitly to link testing, curriculum, textbooks, teacher training, and accountability with clearly articulated ideas about what should be taught and what students should be expected to learn. Our hopes for breaking this century's pattern of disappointing cycles of reform—and of enabling our children to function effectively in a complex new century—rest with this vision of creating effort-based systems grounded in knowledge-based constructivism, systems that allow all students to reach high standards of achievement.

REFERENCES

Brown, A. L., & Palincsar, A. S. (1989). Guided, cooperative learning and individualized knowledge acquisition. In L. B. Resnick (Ed.), *Knowing, learning, and instruction: Essays in honor of Robert Glaser* (pp. 393–451). Hillsdale, NJ: Erlbaum Associates.

Dweck, C. S., & Leggett, E. L. (1988). A social-cognitive approach to motivation and personality. *Psychological Review, 95,* 256–273.

Howard, J. (1995). You can't get there from here: The need for a new logic in education reform. *Daedalus, 124,* 85–92.

Resnick, L. B. (1995). From aptitude to effort: A new foundation for our schools. *Daedalus, 124,* 55–62.

Resnick, L. B., & Hall, M. W. (1998, Fall). Learning organizations for sustainable education reform. *Daedalus, 127,* 89–118.

Resnick, L. B., & Hall, M. W. (2001). *The Principles of Learning: Study tools for educators.* [CD-ROM, Version 2.0]. Available: www.instituteforlearning.org

Resnick, L. B., & Nelson-Le Gall, S. (1997). Socializing intelligence. In L. Smith, J. Dockrell, & P. Tomlinson (Eds.), *Piaget, Vygotsky and beyond* (pp. 145–158). London: Routledge.

2

Thinking Skills for the Information Age

LeRoy Hay

As an educational futurist, I study societal trends and projections and then analyze their potential impact on what and how we teach in our K–12 schools. Thus I am glad to share my vision of how thinking skills might change in the information age, and what schools might need to do to prepare students for this new era.

As futurists are wont to do, I begin by looking at the past, to see how education has evolved to bring us to the current focus on thinking skills. Then I project the trend into the future and, finally, discuss three major challenges that K–12 educators will face as thinking skills change.

THINKING IN THE INDUSTRIAL AGE

During my undergraduate preparation for teaching in the 1960s, I do not remember any instruction in how to teach higher-level thinking skills. Certainly I was aware of the need to foster comprehension and analysis; after all, I planned to be an English teacher, and my primary obligation would be to ensure that my students could comprehend and analyze the great works of literature. But it was much later in my teaching career that teaching higher-level thinking skills suddenly became the "hot" topic of education conferences and workshops. Overnight, I was expected to be overtly instructing my students in evaluating evidence, making inferences, synthesizing information, and applying other critical thinking skills. In retrospect, I can easily understand why this occurred.

I began teaching while the United States was still in its industrial age. The majority of citizens were employed in producing goods in factories, using an assembly-line mode of work. These blue-collar workers were trained to do the same task over and over, and the last thing wanted on an assembly line was a person thinking at high levels. That would slow down the line and decrease production.

When children went to school to prepare for that factory environment, the instruction emphasized rote, repetitive work.

The primary assessment mode was testing for recall of information—the lowest of the levels in Bloom's taxonomy of thinking, published late in the industrial age (Bloom, Englehart, Furst, Hill, & Krathwohl, 1956). Admittedly, most students did have some experience with higher levels of thinking in high school, but that was serendipitous, not a goal of K–12 education.

The "thinkers" of the industrial age—the white-collar workers—were clearly the minority during this era. Children who were expected to eventually join their ranks were normally identified early in their schooling and treated as the college-bound group. After all, college was where higher-level thinking was taught and practiced.

In reality, as the United States became the preeminent producer of goods in the world, the high school diploma was not even a requirement to earn a middle-class wage in the factory. According to the U.S. Department of Education (1993), in 1950 only about one-third of Americans 25 or older had earned a high school diploma, and only a little over 13 percent had gone to college. But this level of education sufficed for the industrial age.

THINKING IN THE INFORMATION AGE

Somewhere in the latter part of the second millennium, the United States began to transition from its industrial age into what is now usually referred to as the information age. Simply put, the majority of Americans started to make their living not by producing goods from raw materials but rather by manipulating data and helping to create information. The country continued to produce large amounts of goods and food, but this was accomplished with a steadily decreasing portion of the work force.

Further, the nature of the production sector began to change, as technological advances began to transform the factory. It went from a low-tech environment in which workers could be trained even if they had only a minimal education (high school diploma or less), to a high-tech world where computers began to run the machines and workers needed at least two years of postsecondary education to function successfully. We rapidly learned that "smart" (that is, high-tech) machines work best when they are run by smart (well-educated) people.

Fewer and fewer unskilled and low-skilled jobs were available. These jobs were being replaced by technology or exported to countries where the cost of labor was significantly less.

The thinking needs of the United States began to change rapidly, but American public education was not designed to produce a nation of higher-level thinkers. A hue and cry arose, beginning with the publication of *A Nation at Risk,* a report from the National Commission on Excellence in Education (1983) demanding reform of American schools. The hue and cry soon became a flood of attacks on public schools, condemning them as failing institutions.

What critics overlooked during this period was that schools were doing exactly what they were designed to do: provide the nation with industrial workers who were comfortable performing rote, repetitive work. I contend that schools were not doing a bad job, but the wrong job. The needs of society had changed dramatically in a very short period of time, and schools had not kept up with those changes.

And so the push for higher-level thinking skills began in earnest. The pendulum swung toward more schooling, and the college degree replaced the high school diploma as the mark of an educated person. In addition, an entirely new level of education emerged, as community colleges arose to provide postsecondary education for those students who did not have the appropriate literacy, numeracy, and thinking skills to succeed in a traditional four-year college or university.

THE INFORMATION AGE

Today, as we move into the third millennium, we have entered the age of information. The largest segment of the work force manipulates data or analyzes information to make a living. Industrial and agricultural work now relies heavily on information technologies. More and more of those employed in human service industries (the sector where low-skilled or semi-skilled jobs can still be found) also frequently work with computerized technology and thus need the ability to think beyond rote memorization of procedures.

An ever-increasing portion of society uses technology in their daily lives. The computer chip has become ubiquitous; it controls our automobiles, microwave ovens, banking machines, cell phones, and so forth. We "talk" to friends and fam-

ily members living hundreds of miles away via e-mail, and we bank and shop on the Internet.

The computer itself, whether sitting on a desk or on our laps, is rapidly becoming a household appliance. By 2025, it will likely be as common in American homes as the television is today. It will become easier to use—thanks to voice-in, voice-out activation—and simpler to understand as it is designed to respond in everyday language to a vast array of everyday tasks.

Furthermore, the Internet has had a phenomenal impact. Almost overnight, access to information was democratized. Consider that in June 1993 only 130 Internet sites existed; by June 2000 there were more than 17 million sites worldwide according to *Hobbes' Internet Timeline* (Zakon, 2000). No longer did anyone need access to a research library to tap the world's information base. All one had to do was to jump online, and people did exactly that in unprecedented numbers.

The fascination with the Internet and all its resources has not been limited to adults. Indeed, children have embraced the Internet more readily than adults, often preferring it to television. An ever-increasing number of children are now spending their spare time online—playing games, accessing and reading information, shopping, and communicating with people all over the world.

In sum, tomorrow most Americans will regularly use the computer as an appliance at home and as a tool at school or work. Learning to use the computer will be very easy. Anyone who is able to read and follow simple directions will be able to use almost any hardware or software. Computer courses, per se, will be less and less necessary at school. Children will come to school already comfortable with using the computer and maneuvering around the Internet. However, these information technologies will have a significant impact on what children need to learn in school.

CHANGING THINKING SKILLS: WHAT DO SCHOOLS NEED TO DO?

So what does all this mean as far as teaching thinking skills in schools in the future? I believe it presents three overriding challenges.

APPLYING SOFTWARE TO PROBLEM SOLVING

Almost all citizens will need to leave high school with the ability to analyze the problems they encounter in their daily and work lives and to apply the logic of technology systems to help solve those problems. Admittedly, American schools have already increased the emphasis on problem-solving skills throughout the curriculum, but most particularly in mathematics and science. They have not, however, universally embraced the computer as a tool for problem solving.

Too often, computer technology in schools today is limited to word processing and accessing information electronically. Although both of these uses are important, students must also be comfortable using the computer as a problem-solving tool. The challenge, then, is to integrate the computer into teaching and learning so that it takes its place right alongside textbooks and class discussions.

Accomplishing this presupposes that teachers are comfortable using the computer as a problem-solving tool. We will need to be certain that new teachers have this comfort level, and we will need to reeducate current teachers to help them understand and appreciate the power of the computer in solving problems.

RETHINKING THE ROLE OF MEMORIZATION

With the democratization of information, we no longer have to rely on our memories or printed sources, because we have easy access to information stored electronically in computer memories that are infinitely larger than our own. But does that mean we no longer need to memorize anything? Is recall of information, the lowest level of thinking in Bloom's taxonomy, becoming passé? Will memorized facts be useful in the future only on game shows?

I contend that memorization has become a tool of convenience rather than a tool of necessity in our information-age society. For example, having the multiplication tables in our memory banks proves useful when we need to make a quick cost calculation or evaluate whether our calculators have given us reasonable answers. I also believe that information stored in our memories provides the cultural framework for our understanding of the world and for our vision of the future.

The problem is to decide how much learning time should be spent on memorization. In 1984, noted educator John Goodlad and his researchers found that although teachers across the United States recognized the importance of higher-level thinking skills, when they assessed students they tested for recall of information about 75 percent of the time (Goodlad, 1984). I suspect that few educators today would accept such a high figure as appropriate, but how much is enough? What role should recall of information play in assessing students today—and tomorrow?

As an extension of the memorization issue, we also need to confront the question of what is worth knowing, in the sense of memorizing, as the world's information base continues to grow exponentially. We must also consider the implications of the e-book, which in the not-too-distant future could allow teachers to customize their textbooks to include the information they believe is most important for their students. Answering the questions of "What is worth knowing?" and "Who should determine that?" is beyond the scope of this chapter, but these are keystone issues that must be addressed as we reshape American schools for the information age.

FOCUSING ON INFORMATION LITERACY

Americans have been talking about reforming schools since 1983, but I believe there has been more tinkering than reforming. Nevertheless, the undeniable catalyst for change is upon us—the Internet.

In its October 4, 1999, issue (p. 74), *Business Week* labeled the Internet as the "disruptive technology" of the third millennium. "Disruptive" reflected the magazine editors' belief that the Internet will change the way we live and the way our societal institutions function as much as electricity, the internal combustion engine, railroads, radio and television, and jet travel changed the world in the past.

The impact of the Internet on what we teach and how we teach is just beginning to be felt. Because the Internet brings easy access to information in quantities that can boggle the mind, educators have begun to recognize that the relationship between education and information must change. This has led to the rise of a concept known as information literacy.

I define information literacy as the skills necessary to efficiently access information that is accurate and relevant, to apply that information to solving a problem, and to effectively communicate the results in a format that combines language and graphics. Many other definitions have been published recently, but they all seem to have in common the need to process information in ways that require high-level thinking skills.

In the industrial-age model of education, all students were expected to master the ability to recall and comprehend information. In recent years, we have added the expectation that students should be able to apply information to problem solving. But mastery of analysis, synthesis, and evaluation skills has been, and for the most part remains, the focus of learning for only the best and brightest. That must change if most of our students are going to be information service workers in the future.

No longer can we rely on a small segment of our population with college degrees to be the thinkers of society. The crème de la crème of our students leave our schools better educated than ever before, with the high-level thinking skills that will serve them well in the information age. The problem is that there isn't enough cream in the graduating crop to meet the rapidly growing need for information workers. So the real challenge lies with the students in the middle. How can we improve their thinking skills so that they are prepared to succeed in the information-based society of the third millennium?

ON TO THE FUTURE

All educators are really futurists, because they are trying to prepare students for a time that does not yet exist. To do that well, they need a vision of that future so they can anticipate what skills and knowledge students will need for success.

Certainly educators have differing views about how much information technology our schools will require and how to best integrate that technology into teaching and learning. But

I believe that most would agree that the information age is real and that schools must be transformed into institutions of higher-level thinking. The challenge is before us.

REFERENCES

Bloom, B. S., Englehart, M. D., Furst, E. J., Hill, W. H., & Krathwohl, D. R. (Eds.). (1956). *Taxonomy of educational objectives: The classification of educational goals. Handbook I: Cognitive domain.* New York: David McKay.

Business Week (1999, October 4). The Internet age (A thumbnail history of disruptive technology).

Goodlad, J. I. (1984). *A place called school: Prospects for the future.* New York: McGraw-Hill.

National Commission on Excellence in Education (1983). *A nation at risk: The imperative for educational reform.* Washington, DC: Author.

Snyder, T. D. (1993). *120 years of American education: A statistical portrait.* Washington, DC: U.S. Department of Education.

Zakon, R. H. (2000). *Hobbes' Internet timeline, v5.2* [Online document]. Available: http://www.isoc.org/guest/zakon/Internet/History/HIT.html

3

Thinking in Context: Teaching for Open-Mindedness and Critical Understanding

SHELDON BERMAN

Solutions to the significant problems facing modern society demand a widespread, qualitative improvement in thinking and understanding. We are slowly and painfully becoming aware that such diverse contemporary challenges as energy, population, the environment, employment, health, psychological well-being of individuals and meaningful education of our youth are not being met by the mere accumulation of more data or the expenditure of more time, energy or money. In view of the increasing pressures imposed on our society by these problems, many responsible thinkers have realized that we cannot sit back and hope for some technological invention to cure our social ills. We need a breakthrough in the quality of thinking employed both by decision-makers at all levels of society and by each of us in our daily affairs.
— *Robert Ornstein*

Many programs teach thinking as a set of isolated skills. The skill-oriented thinking programs often assume that students will draw upon these skills to improve the way they think through a problem. Although these individual skills are useful in themselves, thinking is more than developing a collection of isolated skills; it is an integrative process that happens when one is confronted with a real problem. Building isolated skills does not necessarily mean that one will be able to think well in the context of a real situation. The debate surrounding these two approaches to teaching thinking is analogous to the whole-language versus basic skills debate surrounding the teaching of reading.

Working with teachers and students to develop students' critical thinking abilities and their open-mindedness, Educators for Social Responsibility (ESR) has developed what could be called a "whole-language" approach to thinking. What we want to encourage is a love of thinking, an ability to reflect on one's thinking and be open to new ideas, an interest in contributing one's thinking to help others and to improve society, and the courage to think through the most difficult and complex problems. Although there is merit and utility in teaching component skills, the art and love of thinking are best nurtured holistically in the context of meaningful problems.

THE VEHICLE FOR TEACHING THINKING: PARTICIPATION IN MEANINGFUL PROBLEMS

As an organization, ESR began by exploring the question of how we can best help students develop a sense of social responsibility—that is, a personal investment in the well-being of others and of the planet—and encourage their confidence that they can make a difference. We observed, and recent research confirmed, that young people are finding it increasingly difficult to assume a sense of social responsibility and to believe that they can create a better world (Bachman, 1987; Berman, 1997; Hart Research Associates, 1989; Sax, Austin, Korn and Mahoney, 1997; Times Mirror Center, 1990). The world's problems—destruction of the environment; issues of social injustice, hunger, and homelessness on a mass scale; the nuclear threat; drug abuse; and violence—seem overwhelming to them. Many feel powerless and are cynical about the future. They believe that the odds of solving these problems are slim, the personal costs of participation are high, the disappointments inevitable.

This chapter is adapted from *Developing Minds: A Resource Book for Teaching Thinking*, Rev. ed., 1991.

The powerlessness students feel is exacerbated by their lack of preparation in the thinking skills necessary to understand the complexity of these issues, their root causes, and the many divergent points of view about solutions. The result is that they often either withdraw from active participation in our society or fall prey to simple and inadequate solutions to complex problems. We found, however, that when we used a particular methodology with issues of real concern to students, students not only acquired these thinking skills, but also developed a sense of their own power to influence change.

The key qualities that made this methodology work were that the problems were meaningful to students and their decisions were translated into some form of action. Lawrence Kohlberg found this to be true in the area of moral development. After years of presenting students with fictional moral dilemmas in order to foster moral development, Kohlberg shifted to an approach he found far more effective—setting up "just communities" in schools where students confronted the real moral dilemmas of day-to-day school life (Kohlberg, 1985). Similarly, the development of thinking skills is far more effective when students' thinking is challenged by real problems and real decisions. These can be classroom issues that are raised at a class meeting, curriculum content that is meaningfully related to the students lives or to the larger society, or global issues about which students express concern.

A thinking skills curriculum is not a special add-on. It uses the opportunities already existing in the classroom and the curriculum, but uses them in a new way. The basic strategy is to involve students in making decisions about circumstances that affect their lives or the lives of others. For example, the classroom can provide an excellent context for decision making by involving students in the ongoing decisions involving classroom management—class rules or guidelines, classroom appearance, homework policies, and interpersonal behavior and conflict. Although this is most easily done through class meetings in the elementary grades, a number of high school teachers have had their students write a constitution for the class, thinking through the issues of rights and responsibilities, authority and power, and structure and discipline. They then use this constitution as a vehicle to think through problems that emerged throughout the year.

The curriculum also provides numerous opportunities. Several middle school math teachers who worked with ESR on new curriculum materials are teaching thinking in mathematics by focusing on how numbers are used, and misused, in the political process and involving students in social issues where they can consider the implications of statistical data. Many science teachers have integrated the consideration of science-related social issues so that students can understand basic science concepts in the context of implications for society. In one elementary school, students had expressed concern about starvation in Africa, and this topic became the focus of the social studies curriculum for the year, with students not only studying Africa and hunger, but making decisions about how they could best help and what actions they would take.

This "thinking in context" gives students the opportunity to use their thinking purposefully and to experience the consequences of their decisions. Yet equally important to dealing with real problems and real decisions is the way we work with young people's thinking. Because ESR's focus has been holistic in nature, we have developed a methodology that teachers can use in their classrooms to nurture the ability to think clearly and independently. Because it is a "whole-language" approach, ESR's methodology is more about how we teach than what we teach. We believe that specific skill instruction as outlined in many of the other thinking skills programs can be useful within this larger context.

AN EMPOWERING METHODOLOGY

Underlying the methodology outlined below is a basic principle: *Students will feel more confident in their thinking and become more skilled when their thinking is valued and taken seriously, and when their thinking makes a difference by improving their own lives or by influencing or helping others.* The following nine strategies build on this principle and encourage students' confidence and empowerment. These strategies have been used by teachers to create an environment that effectively nurtures students' thinking abilities. Like the classroom and teaching changes that are entailed in cooperative learning, this approach to teaching takes time, attention, and practice. As we have learned from the work in cooperative learning, it is far easier to describe what needs to be done than it is to put this methodology into practice. To support the implementation of this approach, ESR has been providing individual teachers, schools, and school districts with inservice and summer institute opportunities.

STRATEGY 1: CREATE A SAFE ENVIRONMENT

Students cannot develop their thinking abilities unless they feel safe. They need to know that they can share their feelings and their thoughts without being ridiculed. They need to know that they can take risks, and even make mistakes, without feeling embarrassed. This safety allows students to put their energy into exploration rather than spending it being overcautious, self-conscious, and defensive. A safe classroom does not mean a risk-free classroom. In fact, within the context of a safe environment, students can and should be encouraged to take risks.

There are many ways to create the experience of a safe classroom. Building a sense of the class as a community, providing clear structure and goals, acknowledging and affirming risk taking, and demonstrating that classroom conflicts can be resolved equitably are only a few of these. One of the best ways of creating an environment that provides safety but also encourages risk taking is to involve students in collaboratively setting guidelines for the class and monitoring how well the class is working together.

In my own classes, I began the year by asking students, "What guidelines could we establish for ourselves that would not only make this a productive class, but would also make this a safe place for people to share what they are thinking and feeling, and a safe place for people to make mistakes and learn from them?" The guidelines that emerge are ones we would continually refer to throughout the year to make sure that we had a trusting, supportive, and productive environment. The discussions that resulted as we monitored our work together provided opportunities for students to resolve conflicts, think through problem situations, participate in making decisions that have an impact on the classroom, assume responsibility for their own behavior, and build a sense of community and shared values.

STRATEGY 2: FOLLOW STUDENTS' THINKING

Thinking skills develop as students make explicit their ways of thinking, hear alternative ways of thinking, and reflect on their thinking; therefore, the focus of our attention should not be on teaching students to think in a particular way, but on helping them explore and reflect on thinking processes they already use. As teachers, our challenge is to come to understand the way students are making sense of things, the logic they are using, and the sources of information they are drawing upon. As we understand these ways of thinking and make them explicit to a class, students can begin to choose those styles that seem most effective.

A 2nd grade teacher taught me a simple and effective way of following students' thinking that I later used in my high school social studies classes. She began each unit by asking students to brainstorm the answers to four questions—What do you know about this? What do you think you know but are not sure about? Where did you get your information? What questions do you have?—and then structured the unit around the questions the students indicated were most pressing for them. Teaching this way not only helped me understand my students better, but developed in them a respect for their knowledge, their thinking ability, and their power to guide their learning.

There are numerous ways that we can create an atmosphere that allows students to reflect on their own thinking. We can talk with them about how they can distinguish good thinking from poor thinking and work with them to set such standards as incisiveness, coherence, and open-mindedness. We can have students keep thinking journals in which they note and reflect on their thinking. We can have reflective writing times in class. We can allow open-ended time in class for students to talk about their thoughts and reactions to the topic being considered. We can ask them to consider such self-reflective questions as, "How do we know what we know about this?" and "What are the biases in the way we are socialized and in what we are told about this?" In my classes, I set aside a time called "connections" to communicate that this is a time for people to talk about the connections they are making with the subject material and the insights they have been having about their own thinking processes. The goal of all these is to make the thinking process explicit and available for review and examination.

STRATEGY 3: ENCOURAGE COLLABORATIVE THINKING

We tend to think about thinking as an internal and individual process, yet we know from the studies of creativity and from the field of organizational development that new ideas often emerge out of collaborative processes. Vera John-Steiner (1985) found that individual creativity was built on the scaffolding of collegial interactions. Just as we need to teach students how to think clearly and independently, we need to teach them how to think collaboratively. Whether we use brainstorming, synectics, cooperative activities, or any of a variety of discussion techniques, we need to help students learn how to submit ideas for group consideration, build on each other's ideas, and come to consensus on the ideas that seem most productive, coherent, attractive, and so on. But we can also take the additional step of processing these conversations with students so that they can better understand how people contribute to the thinking of the group.

STRATEGY 4: TEACH THE QUESTIONS RATHER THAN THE ANSWERS

Critical thinking skills rest on our ability to ask incisive and penetrating questions that get beneath the surface of a topic and reveal its complexity and subtlety. Developing this skill means paying close attention to students' questions and modeling questioning ourselves. We teach questioning by giving students the opportunity to articulate their questions. By talking about and categorizing these questions, the class then collectively hones them into broader and deeper questions. As mentioned in strategy 2, allowing students' questions to guide instruction is another powerful tool for teaching them how to ask good questions.

But we also need to help them ask the hardest questions, those that get at underlying assumptions, root causes, and internal contradictions, and those that ask students to examine their own beliefs and attitudes. If we encourage this deeper level of questioning, we will begin to hear students question things we often take for granted. Adolescents, especially, see the contradictions we have justified or ignored and ask us about the integrity of our beliefs and questions. They question beliefs and practices we may accept, such as nationalism, capitalism, religion, patriarchy, and the like. This questioning is not only natural but important because they are really attempting to create a coherent belief system for themselves. They are essentially asking if there is the possibility of living with integrity in their own lives. Although we should not dismiss any question, we do not need to answer all these questions. We can acknowledge the importance of the question and encourage students to explore it for themselves as deeply as possible.

STRATEGY 5: TEACH ABOUT INTERCONNECTEDNESS

During the last two decades we have become far more conscious of our social and ecological interdependence. We have begun to see things less in a cause-effect or linear mode and more in a systems mode. Systems thinking is a distinctly different way of thinking. It views situations holistically, examines the interconnections between parts of a system, and looks for interventions that can have a corrective influence on the system as a whole. Rather than focusing on one cause and one effect, it focuses on a continual stream of cause-effects, with effects becoming new causes in other parts of a loop that goes back on itself. Taking a systems perspective gives students an appreciation for interdependence and helps them explore problems much more comprehensively. They can also begin to see their role in the systems they are part of and appreciate more fully the consequences of their actions on others.

STRATEGY 6: PRESENT AND HAVE STUDENTS ENTER MULTIPLE PERSPECTIVES

One of the most important means of helping students reflect on their own thinking is to have them listen to and appreciate alternative perspectives. Entering the perspective of another is difficult, especially if it is in conflict with our own.

In those situations we tend to listen in ways that discount other points of view. Imagine, for example, attending a series of lectures on a controversial topic. If the speakers present positions with which we agree, we tend to listen for the cogent arguments they present—almost as if we were building our own case in preparation for our next debate with a friend or colleague. When we listen to someone with whom we disagree, on the other hand, we listen for the flaws in logic, the misinformation, and the things left unsaid. By listening this way we only affirm our own positions.

Our challenge is to help students reach beyond the limits of their own experience and enter the experience of others. To accomplish this, ESR has adapted Peter Elbow's (1983) technique for teaching writing, called methodological belief. I have had the opportunity to use methodological belief in teaching about controversial issues. Prior to any criticism of various positions on the issue, I ask students to suspend their disbelief temporarily and to attempt to understand how advocates of each position view the problem. We then try to identify the truth in each position with which we can all agree. At first it is very difficult for students to allow themselves to try to appreciate positions with which, in reality, they disagree. With each successive perspective we take, however, the issue becomes more complex and the "right" answer less clear. Each position becomes a personal statement of the truth as one individual sees it. Examining each position from the perspective of the person holding it personalizes the position and makes it more available for consideration. The emphasis on looking for common agreements allows students to find some new paths to their own answers.

The work of William Perry (1968) on the forms of ethical and intellectual development and the work of Robert Selman (1980) on perspective taking are particularly revealing in how powerful and productive this effort can be. Perry, in his study of students confronted with multiple, competing perspectives, found that students moved from either/or thinking through relativism to a commitment to a point of view with an openness to change. Selman, who studies interpersonal perspective taking, found that by teaching perspective-taking skills, students could move from egocentric and impulsive interpersonal negotiation strategies to mutual and collaborative strategies.

Entering the perspective of others compels us to tolerate ambiguity and to be continually open to change. This does not mean that we avoid taking positions, but that we take them knowing that we must allow for the possibility that we may be wrong. It does not mean that we lack criticalness or ethical standards, but that through our humility and openness we are able to evaluate and act in situations of social conflict with compassion and insight.

STRATEGY 7: BUILD ON SENSIBILITIES

When we place our primary focus on thinking, we tend to forget that thinking, feeling, and intuition are not separate but integrated. In fact, it is our feeling that something is wrong that often moves us to think about it. When teaching thinking to students, we need to help them pay attention to intuition, to feelings, and to ethical considerations. We need to ask them not only how they think about something, but how it feels to them. We want to nurture a trust of that intuitive sense that something is or isn't right.

STRATEGY 8: HELP STUDENTS SET STANDARDS AND WORK FROM A POSITIVE VISION OF THE FUTURE

We need standards by which to measure the product of our thinking, and we can help students construct these measures. In dealing with a conflict situation, students could consider the criteria for a good outcome. In dealing with a social or political issue, students could consider how people 100 years from now would be affected by their recommendations. In dealing with a classroom decision, students could consider its impact on them years later or its impact on the school as a whole. These standards not only help students evaluate their own thinking, but help them consider and construct a positive vision of what they would like the future to be.

STRATEGY 9: PROVIDE STUDENTS WITH OPPORTUNITIES FOR ACTING ON THEIR THINKING

Thinking remains abstract until it is embodied in action. Through observing the impact of their actions, students experience the power and quality of their thinking. The feedback they get allows them to further refine their thinking. Student projects and presentations and students teaching other students what they have learned are typical ways that we can have students act on their own knowledge. If we are building a relationship between what we teach and the larger social and political environment, students can also be appropriately involved in taking actions on classroom, school, community, national, or global problems. This kind of social action/community service learning effort is empowering to young people because it calls on them to contribute their talents and care to helping others and creating a better environment for everyone.

These actions need to be learning opportunities integrated into the curriculum so that they can see and learn from the feedback they get. If students are tackling a classroom problem the actions they take may have a highly visible impact and offer them direct feedback. If, on the other hand, students choose to tackle such larger social or global issues as the environment or hunger, it is important that the actions they take be specific and concrete, possibly local in nature, so that they can track their impact. Above all, it is not appropriate for teachers to enlist students in their own positions or causes. Propagandistic education only leads to compliance, not conviction and commitment. The causes need to be ones that come from the concerns of the students, and the actions need to be the result of their thinking and planning.

Not all actions will end well. Students will make mistakes. Sometimes the issue will be too large for them to see their impact. Yet in taking action, even in these circumstances, they begin to understand the complexity of problem situations and experience themselves as part of the larger network of people who are helping to create a better world.

Providing opportunities to contribute and have influence not only improves the quality of their thinking, but builds self-esteem and a sense of connection with the world around them. It demonstrates that their thinking is valued and that what they think can make a difference.

QUALITIES OF MIND: CRITIQUE AND SYNTHESIS

In working with students' thinking ability, we have observed that students develop both critical understanding and open-mindedness. We have come to identify these two elements as two complementary qualities of mind—critique and synthesis. I call these qualities of mind because each takes on a different frame of reference, approach, and attitude. Our goal in working with young people's thinking is to help them develop both of these qualities. And we can track our success by how well students are able to draw upon both of these qualities.

When we think of the critical thinker, it is very likely that we see an individual, at heart doubting, cautious, and logical, who approaches information with intelligent skepticism about the truth. The critical thinker stands apart from the world, evaluating, assessing, judging. The world appears polarized into competing ideas and interests, each of which is incomplete. Some of these ideas are right and some are wrong; and through the process of questioning, the critical thinker finds the inaccuracy and faulty logic in any position, as well as its valid points. The critical thinker discerns the truth by looking carefully through the close-up lens of logic.

The intelligence of critical thinkers is measured by their skill in dissecting arguments or "knowledge claims" in order to truly understand them, in searching for hidden meanings and assumptions, in comparing the arguments to what is known in order to examine their validity, and in making sure the information is logically consistent. Intelligence, in the critical mode of thinking, means discernment, discrimination, penetration, and precision in logical thought.

But there are vulnerabilities to the critical quality of mind. Because of its skepticism, it tends to question new information with far greater rigor than it questions already held positions and benefits. A classic example of this in classroom practice is, in fact, the formal debate—a superb tool for stimulating critical analysis. Each side submits its own best thinking and defends it against challenges. Each side searches for flaws and weaknesses in the other side's position. Yet in the end, each side usually remains as convinced of its original position as when it started. Through the process of debate, often the differences are highlighted and the issue is polarized. Each side stands in its solitary "rightness," closed to other alternatives. Each side has affirmed its strength in opposition to the other's point of view.

Critique is familiar to us. In fact, this skeptical and questioning attitude is the prominent one in our culture. Yet the skeptical side of thinking illuminates only part of the picture. By its nature, it encourages disbelief rather than empathy, debate rather than collaboration. It stresses the use of the close-up lens of logic rather than the wide-angled lens of vision and imagination.

The less familiar quality of mind, and therefore the more difficult to teach, is synthesis—the ability to draw connections and take larger and larger perspectives. It is a process that combines the disparate elements of a variety of positions or arguments into new and higher forms. It finds ways that ideas, elements within a system, or positions are interrelated. It looks for increasingly larger systems of organization and ways those systems affect one another. Rather than closing in on a narrowly focused critique, it seeks to broaden the focus and enlarge the vision.

Synthesis thinking focuses on interrelationships. The world is seen as a complicated network, open in nature and changing in character. Synthesis thinking assumes that all knowledge is limited. It assumes that each of us has a "window" on the truth and that we need to look through each other's windows as well as our own in order to broaden our understanding of that truth. Synthesis thinking seeks to find the value in

each position or idea irrespective of its "rightness" or "wrongness." Essentially, synthesis thinkers look for common agreements as well as differences. They are open to new information, new points of view, and new experiences in order to enlarge their perspectives. Intuition, imagination, and an ability to conceptualize relationships among systems are important tools. The lens through which synthesis thinkers view the world is a wide-angled lens.

The critical and synthesis qualities, therefore, employ different but complementary skills. Critical thinking stresses logic, dissection, and organization along linear or hierarchical lines; synthesis stresses integrative, global, intuitive, and creative thinking. Critical thinking encourages skepticism; synthesis encourages openness to new and different ideas. Both can work together in judicious harmony. Through the methodology outlined above, both are nurtured.

PUTTING THE METHODOLOGY INTO PRACTICE

Although many teachers already use some of these strategies, many find that this is a new approach to classroom instruction. Using it well means taking time to learn about and practice these strategies. It also means modeling critical questioning and open-mindedness for students.

To help teachers become better able to use these strategies, ESR has created a wide range of professional development programs. These include in-depth inservice programs for schools or school districts, day-long seminars, and week-long summer institutes that are open to all educators. Because modeling is so important in learning, our professional development programs are structured to not only teach about these strategies, but to put them into practice in the course of the program. For more information on ESR's professional development opportunities, you can contact us at 23 Garden Street, Cambridge, MA 02138; phone: 617-492-1764; e-mail: educators@esrnational.org; Web site: www.esrnational.org.

THE CONTEXT FOR THINKING

Just as the first strategy for developing thinking was to create a safe classroom environment, we have to realize that the structure and climate of our schools produce their own "hidden curriculum" that influences the cultivation of thinking skills. Are students' contributions to the school welcomed and valued? Do students participate in the problems and decisions of the school community? Does the curriculum of the school place the school in an ongoing relationship with the local community and the larger world? Is the faculty encouraged to think together and work together? Is the thinking of teachers valued and do teachers have an influence on school decision making? As I indicated earlier, students will feel more confident in their thinking and become more skilled when their thinking is valued and taken seriously, and when their thinking makes a difference by improving their own lives or by influencing or helping others. Likewise, teachers will teach thinking more effectively when their own thinking is valued and taken seriously. To effectively nurture thinking, we may need to change the way we think about our schools. Rather than see them as vehicles for producing some end product, we need to see them as participatory communities in themselves. They also need to be safe, collaborative environments.

A true community is a group of people who acknowledge their interconnectedness, have a sense of their common purpose, respect their differences, share in group decision making and responsibility for the actions of the group, and support each other's growth. Classrooms and schools can be communities of this kind, but it takes time, intention, and new forms of shared leadership. Schools that are healthy communities can more effectively foster thinking skills because they offer natural opportunities for "thinking in context."

REFERENCES

Bachman, J. (1987). *Monitoring the future, 1975–1986.* Ann Arbor: University of Michigan.

Berman, S. (1997). *Children's social consciousness and the development of social responsibility.* Albany, NY: SUNY Press.

Elbow, P. (1983, April). *Critical thinking is not enough.* Reninger Lecture at the University of Northern Iowa. (Available through Educators for Social Responsibility, 23 Garden St., Cambridge, MA 02138)

Hart Research Associates. (1989). *Democracy's next generation: A study of youth and teachers.* Washington, DC: People for the American Way.

John-Steiner, V. (1985). *Notebooks of the mind.* Albuquerque, NM: University of New Mexico Press.

Kohlberg, L. (1985). The just community approach to moral education in theory and practice. In M. Berkowitz & F. Oser (Eds.), *Moral education: Theory and application.* Hillsdale, NJ: Lawrence Erlbaum.

Perry, W. G. (1968). *Forms of intellectual and ethical development in the college years.* New York: Holt, Reinhart and Winston.

Sax, L. J., Austin, A. W., Korn, W. S., & Mahoney, K. M. (1997). *The American freshman: National norms for fall 1997.* Los Angeles: Higher Education Research Institute, UCLA Graduate School of Education, 3005 Moore Hall, Box 951521, Los Angeles, CA 90095-1521.

Selman, R. (1980). *The growth of interpersonal understanding: Developmental and clinical analysis.* New York: Academic Press.

Times Mirror Center for the People and the Press. (1990). *The age of indifference: A study of young Americans and how they view the news.* Washington, DC: Author.

4

Five Human Passions: The Origins of Effective Thinking

ARTHUR L. COSTA AND ROBERT J. GARMSTON

There is a dimension of the universe unavailable to the senses.

—Joseph Campbell

Scientists know there are forces in the universe: gravitational, electromagnetic, and electrostatic fields; inertia; centrifugal forces; and so forth. Although they cannot be observed directly, they are known through their effects. We believe there are unseen forces in humans as well. These basic human forces are the passions that drive, influence, motivate, and inspire our intellectual capacities. They also are known by their effects: productive human thought and action.

We categorize and define five central passions (Costa & Garmston, 1994):

• *Passion for efficacy.* Humans quest for continuous, lifelong learning, self-empowerment, mastery, and control.
• *Passion for flexibility.* Humans endeavor to change, adapt, and expand their repertoire of response patterns.
• *Passion for craftsmanship.* Humans yearn to become clearer, more elegant, precise, congruent, and integrated.
• *Passion for consciousness.* Humans uniquely strive to monitor and reflect on their thoughts and actions.
• *Passion for interdependence.* Humans need reciprocity and are inclined to become one with the community.

We believe these five passions to be the generators of effective thought and action. In this chapter, we elaborate on them, describe their intellectual manifestations, and draw educational implications for their continuous development.

This chapter is adapted with permission of the publisher from "Five Human Passions," by A. Costa and R. Garmston, October 1998, in *Think*, 9(1), 14–17.

EFFICACY

Efficacious people have an internal locus of control. They produce new knowledge. They engage in causal thinking. They pose problems and search for problems to solve. They are optimistic and resourceful. They are self-actualizing and self-modifying. They are able to operationalize concepts and translate them into deliberate actions. They establish feedback spirals and continue to learn how to learn.

Efficacy involves the ability and willingness to make a difference. It is a particularly catalytic state of mind because a sense of efficacy is a determining factor in the resolution of complex problems.

If a person feels little efficacy, then blame, withdrawal, and rigidity are likely to follow. With robust efficacy, people are likely to expend more energy in their work, persevere longer, set more challenging goals, and continue in the face of barriers or failure. Efficacious people regard events as opportunities for learning. They believe that personal action produces outcomes, they rely on personal resources to control performance anxiety, and they recognize and draw upon previous experiences. They are aware of what they do not know and seek to be in a state of continuous learning.

One value of efficacy and its by-product, self confidence, is that the more effective we feel, the more flexibly we can engage in critical and creative work. Developing effective thinking, therefore, requires becoming increasingly self-referencing, self-evaluating, self-initiating, and self-modifying.

FLEXIBILITY

Flexible thinkers are empathic. They are able to appreciate the diverse perspectives of others. They are open and comfortable with ambiguity. They create and seek novel approaches and have a well-developed sense of humor. They envision a range of alternative consequences. They have the capacity to change their mind as they receive additional data. They engage in multiple and simultaneous activities, draw upon a repertoire of problem-solving strategies, and shift styles as appropriate, knowing when to be broad and global in their thinking and when a situation requires detailed precision.

Flexibility requires a supple mind, receptivity to alternatives, and adaptable response patterns. Flexible thinkers know that they have and can develop options in their work, and they are willing to acknowledge and demonstrate respect and empathy for diverse points of view.

Flexible people also understand means-ends relationships. They are able to work within rules, criteria, and regulations, and they can predict the consequences of flouting them. They not only understand the immediate reactions but also perceive the bigger purposes that such constraints serve. Thus, flexibility of mind is essential for working in socially diverse settings, enabling individuals to recognize the wholeness and distinctness of other people's ways of experiencing and making meaning.

Flexible thinkers are capable of shifting at will through multiple perceptual positions. One position is what Jean Piaget called egocentrism—perceiving from our own point of view. By contrast, allocentrism is perceiving through another person's orientation. We operate from this second position when we empathize with others' feelings, predict how others are thinking, and anticipate potential misunderstandings.

Another perceptual position is macrocentric. It is similar to looking down from a balcony at ourselves and our interactions with others. Macro attention, the bird's-eye view, is useful for discerning themes and patterns from assortments of information. It is intuitive, holistic, and conceptual. Because we often need to solve problems with incomplete information, we need the capacity to perceive general patterns and jump across gaps in present knowledge. Macrocentric thinking is necessary for bridging the gaps and enabling us to perceive a pattern even when some of the pieces are missing.

Yet another perceptual orientation is microcentric—examining the discrete and sometimes minute parts that make up the whole. A micro mode is the worm's-eye view, without which science, technology, and complex enterprise could not function. Micro attention involves logical, analytical computation and searching for causality in methodical steps. It encompasses attention to detail, precision, and orderly progressions.

Flexible thinkers display confidence in their intuition. They tolerate confusion and ambiguity up to a point and are willing to let go of a problem, trusting their subconscious to continue creative and productive work on it. Flexibility is the cradle of humor, creativity, and versatility.

Flexibility is interrelated with consciousness. Although there are many possible perceptual positions—past, present, future, egocentric, allocentric, macrocentric, visual, auditory, kinesthetic—the flexible mind knows when to shift from one to another. Because the most flexible person is the one with the most control, developing effective thinking requires the continuous expansion of repertoire.

CRAFTSMANSHIP

Craftspersons seek perfection and pride themselves on their artistry. They yearn for precision and mastery. They value refinement and specificity in communications and use precise language to describe their activities. They generate and hold clear visions and goals. They strive for exactness of critical thought processes. They make thorough and rational decisions about actions to be taken. They test and revise, constantly honing strategies to reach goals.

Craftsmanship involves striving for mastery, grace, and economy of energy to produce exceptional results. It is based on the knowledge that we can continually perfect our craft and on a willingness to work to attain our own high standards and pursue ongoing learning.

Craftsmanship includes exactness, accuracy, flawlessness, and fidelity—but not in all things. The craftsperson also works flexibly. Craftsmanship without flexibility is perfectionism.

Because language and thinking are closely entwined, precision of language is an important characteristic of the craftsperson. Language acquisition plays a critical role in enhancing one's cognitive maps, the ability to think critically, and the knowledge base for efficacious action.

Precision and mastery across six temporal dimensions are also the mark of effective thinkers. Every thought, event, occurrence, or situation is definable in terms of

• *Sequence* (how events are ordered: 1st, 2nd, 3rd, and so on).
• *Duration* (how long the event lasts).
• *Rhythm* (how often the event occurs).
• *Simultaneity* (what other events are happening at the same).
• *Synchronization* (how events coordinate with other events).
• *Time perspectives, or temporal logic* (keeping both short-range and long-range events in mind).

As people acquire more exact language for describing their activities, they begin to recognize concepts, identify key attributes, distinguish similarities and differences, and make more thorough and rational decisions. Developing craftsmanship, therefore, enriches the complexity and specificity of language and simultaneously produces effective thinking.

CONSCIOUSNESS

Conscious thinkers metacogitate. They monitor their own values, intentions, thoughts, behaviors, and effects on others and the environment. They are aware of their own and others' progress toward goals. They have well-defined value systems that they can articulate. They generate, hold, and apply internal criteria for the decisions they make. They practice mental rehearsal and edit mental pictures in the course of seeking improved strategies.

Consciousness means knowing what and how we are thinking in the moment and being aware of how our actions affect others and our surroundings. Consciousness is the central clearinghouse in which varied events processed by different senses can be represented and compared. It therefore has catalytic properties for the other passions. It is *the* state of mind prerequisite to self-control and self-direction.

The function of consciousness is to represent information about what is happening outside and inside the organism in such a way that it can be evaluated and acted upon. Without consciousness we would still "know" what is going on, but we would have to react in a reflexive, instinctive way. It is because we have consciousness that we can daydream, change our perceptual position, write beautiful poems, and develop elegant scientific theories.

Consciousness provides a distinctive characteristic of the human nervous system in that we are able to affect our own emotional or mental states. We can make ourselves happy or miserable regardless of what is actually happening "outside," just by changing the contents of our consciousness.

Intentionality keeps information in consciousness ordered. Intentions arise whenever we become aware of wanting to accomplish something. They may be shaped by biological needs, personal interests, or internalized social values. Our intentions are organized in hierarchies of goals that specify the priorities among them.

Attention is psychic energy. What we allow into consciousness determines the quality of our lives. At any one time, human beings can attend to seven (plus or minus two) bits of information, such as differentiated sounds, visual stimuli, and recognizable nuances of emotion or thought (Miller, 1963). In-

formation enters consciousness either because we intend to focus attention on it or because of attentional habits based on biological or social instructions. It is attention that selects the relevant bits of information from the potential millions of bits available.

The mark of a person who is in control of consciousness is the ability to focus attention at will, to be oblivious to distractions, to concentrate for as long as it takes to achieve a goal. Developing effective thinking, therefore, requires the development of this priceless resource, consciousness.

INTERDEPENDENCE

Interdependent people have a sense of community: "we-ness" as much as "me-ness." They are altruistic. They value consensus, managing to hold their own values and actions in abeyance in order to lend their energies and resources to the achievement of group goals. They contribute to a common good, seek collegiality, and draw on the resources of others. They regard conflict as valuable, trusting their abilities to manage group differences in productive ways. They continue to learn from the feedback of others and from their consciousness of their own actions and effects on others. They seek engagement in part-whole relationships, knowing that all of us are more efficient that any one of us.

Interdependence means participating in, contributing to, and receiving from relationships and being willing to create and change relationships to our benefit. The human intellect grows in reciprocity with others. The individual interacts with others to construct shared knowledge. There is a cycle of internalization of what is socially constructed as shared meaning, which is then externalized to affect the learner's social participation. Learning, therefore, is viewed as a reciprocal process in that the individual influences the group and the group influences the individual (Vygotsky, 1978).

Vygotsky suggests that intelligence grows in two ways. One is the intelligence that develops through our own experience. But intelligence also gets shaped through interaction with others. Justifying our thoughts and actions, resolving differences, actively listening to another person's point of view, achieving consensus, and receiving feedback actually increase our intelligence.

As humans develop cognitively, they value and more consistently view situations from multiple perspectives. As stated earlier, flexibility is a prerequisite to interdependence, for flexibility allows one to see other points of view and to change and adapt based on feedback from others.

Developmentally, intellectual interdependence may be a latecomer. Although one may work interdependently, play on teams, live in a community, or take part in family or workplace dialogues, reasoning interdependently is quite different from merely being a member of a group. This is because, at the highest stage of cognitive thinking, we are psychically less and less attached to egocentric orientations and more capable of advanced reasoning.

Interdependent thinkers can interpret conflict as valuable, recognizing the potential benefits of solving problems or finding new and different ways to approach them. People endowed with the passion for interdependence can focus on ways to let a conflict-ridden relationship transform their thinking, rather than stubbornly clinging to their original positions.

As people become more interdependent, they may experience a sense of interconnectedness and kinship that comes from a unity of being—a sense of sharing a common habitat (class, school, neighborhood) and a mutual bonding to common goals and shared values. The interdependent individual's sense of self is enlarged from a conception of "me" to a sense of "us." Interdependent thinkers do not lose their individuality but rather their egocentricity (Sergiovanni, 1994).

As interdependence develops, it is characterized by altruism, collegiality, and the giving of oneself to group goals and needs. Interdependent people value dialogue and are able to place the interests of the group above their own interests. Just as they contribute to a common good, they also draw on the resources of others. They appreciate what others have to offer and can envision the expanding capacities of the group and its members.

Interdependence facilitates "systems thinking," which recognizes that many variables are constantly interacting. Each variable affects another, which affects another, and so on. Families, weather systems, and national economies are examples of systems. Their dynamics are such that tiny inputs can reverberate throughout the system, producing dramatic consequences. Interdependent thinkers understand these dynamics and their own potential to significantly influence the direction of the community they are part of.

Developing effective thinking, therefore, requires interdependence. Interdependence, along with the other four passions—efficacy, flexibility, craftsmanship, and consciousness—makes possible the most complete and effective intellectual functioning of human beings.

IMPLICATIONS FOR EDUCATION

If nurtured, the five passions can become habituated. When confronted with problematic situations, students and teachers might habitually ask themselves the following questions:

• What is the most *efficacious* thing I can do right now? What do I already know about the problem? What resources do I have available or need to generate? How can I draw on my past experience with problems like this? How can I learn from this?

• How can I approach this problem *flexibly*? How might I look at the situation in another way, from a fresh perspective (lateral thinking)? How can I utilize my repertoire of problem-solving strategies?

• What is the most *craftsman-like* thing I can do? How can I illuminate this problem to make it clearer, more precise? Do I need to check out my data sources? How might I break this problem down into its component parts and develop a strategy for understanding and accomplishing each step?

• How can I bring *consciousness* to bear on this problem? What do I know or not know? What questions do I need to ask? What strategies are in my mind now? What beliefs, values, and goals are informing my thinking? What feelings or emotions am I aware of that might be blocking or enhancing my progress?

• How can *interdependence* help me solve this problem? How does this situation affect others? How can we work together to find a solution? What can I learn from others that would help me become a better problem solver?

The five passions are all situational and transitory. They are utopian states toward which we constantly aspire, but their perfect realization is impossible. Csikszentmihalyi (1993, p. 23) states, "Although every human brain is able to generate self-reflective consciousness, not everyone seems to use it equally." Few people, notes Kegan (1994), ever fully reach the stage of cognitive complexity, and rarely before middle age.

The five passions may serve as diagnostic tools—constructs with which we can assess the cognitive development of ourselves, other individuals, and groups. We can then use those assessments to plan interventions for the continual refinement of the passions. Taken together, the passions are a force directing us toward increasingly authentic, congruent, ethical behavior; they are the touchstones of integrity.

The goal of education, therefore, should be to support ourselves and others in liberating and developing these passions more fully. They are the tools of disciplined choice making. They are the primary vehicles in the lifelong journey toward integration.

REFERENCES

Costa, A., & Garmston, R. (1994). *Cognitive coaching: A foundation for renaissance schools.* Norwood, MA: Christopher Gordon Publishers.

Csikszentmihalyi, M. (1993). *The evolving self: A psychology for the third millennium.* New York: HarperCollins.

Kegan, R. (1994). *In over our heads: The mental complexity of modern life.* Cambridge, MA: Harvard University Press.

Miller, G. A. (1963, March). The magical number seven, plus or minus two: Some limits to our capacity for processing information. *Psychological Review,* 81–97.

Sergiovanni, T. J. (1994). *Building community in schools.* San Francisco: Jossey-Bass.

Vygotsky, L. (1978). *Society of mind.* Cambridge, MA: Harvard University Press.

5

Learning and Thinking in the Workplace

John Edwards

M ost companies, like most educational institutions, are rife with unproductive myths about their practice. This chapter focuses on what research and industrial experience have taught us about learning and thinking in the workplace. Peter Senge and colleagues (1999, p. 6) sum up the situation well in their discussion of difficulties encountered during organizational change efforts:

> The sources of these problems cannot be remedied by more expert advice, better consultants, or more committed managers. The sources lie in our most basic ways of thinking. If these do not change, any new "input" will end up producing the same fundamentally *unproductive types of actions.*

What does Senge mean by "The sources lie in our most basic ways of thinking"? I have spent 30 years doing research on how people think, generate knowledge, and turn knowledge into action. For the last 10 years, my research colleagues and I have focused on thinking and learning in business and industry. We have been able, by working cooperatively with people in a range of companies, to convert our research into award-winning industrial practice. Nine of the major findings from this research are discussed here.

PERSONAL PRACTICAL KNOWLEDGE: THE MOST UNDERUTILIZED RESOURCE

In every organization where our research team has worked, the single greatest underutilized resource is the personal, practical knowledge (PPK) of the work force (Butler, 1994). What do we mean by PPK? We mean the knowledge acquired from leading a thoughtful work life. It is personal to you, it is practical in that it drives your practice, and it has a character that is recognizably different from "book learning."

PPK involves reflection, a habit that few use skillfully in the workplace. If people do not reflect on their experience, they do

not generate PPK. Many do not know how to put their PPK into words, or into any form usable by anyone apart from themselves. So this knowledge is lost to colleagues, to teams, to the wider company, and even to the persons themselves over time. We are currently researching how best to capture this knowledge.

I could share many examples from our research, but here is just one. A quiet, shy operator on the night shift in a small industrial plant suggested to his supervisor what he thought would be a better way for his furnace to operate. He was told to get on with his work. When we entered the company to help staff members improve their performance, we asked each person to design an improvement strategy. You can guess what this operator chose! With the help of engineers, he redesigned the way the furnaces operated. This single application of PPK saved the company 500,000 Australian dollars per year, every year—much more than the full cost of having the whole 150-person staff complete a jointly designed, three-year, professional growth program. There were many more such initiatives by this young man, whose career was transformed, and by many other staff members. The effect on the company has been dramatic (Hill, 1994, 1999).

WEAK MODELS OF LEARNING

To encourage knowledge generation and organizational learning, one has to understand how people grow professionally and how they learn in the workplace. Most companies work with outdated transmission models of learning, which manifest themselves in the language, systems, and structures of the organization. Many schools and universities are the same.

Butler has developed a powerful new model of personal action (Edwards, Butler, Hill, & Russell, 1997) that he and I have used successfully in Australian business, industry, and education. The model is diagrammed in Figure 5.1.

—*Figure 5.1*—
A Model of Personal Action

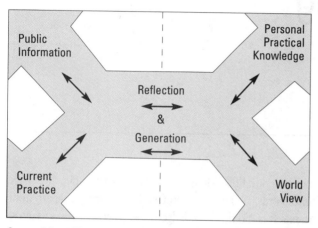

Source: Adapted from *People Rules for Rocket Scientists* (p. 175), by J. Edwards, J. Butler, B. Hill, & S. Russell, 1997, Brisbane, Australia: Samford Research Associates. Reprinted with permission.

The public information element of the model refers to information available in the public domain through print and other media, the Internet, training programs, and lectures. It is commonly believed that providing people with information will cause them to change their current practice.

This is too simplistic. Rather than translating directly into behavioral change, public information is first processed by individuals and matched against their PPK and world views. Then they determine what action, if any, to take.

Both public information and current practice are external to the self. By contrast, an individual's PPK and world view come from within and are not freely available to others. Because they drive one's actions, the major leverage for learning lies in one's PPK and world view. A world view arises from an individual's culture, traditions, and life experience, and is made up of rules, assumptions, values, and belief structures. It forms the foundation for personal behavior, washing through everything one does. It takes many years to form and is largely subconscious.

So how does one connect the inside of the self with the outside? We argue that at least two powerful processes can provide the link: reflection and generation. Reflection involves internally processing one's experiences, finding meaning in them, and relating them to one's existing PPK and world view. Although many people are reluctant to make time for reflection, few deny its power. Helping people focus on how they reflect currently, and then giving them experience with more

effective alternatives, can dramatically improve their practice (Rigano & Edwards, 1998). Bruner sees reflection as crucial to opening up possibilities: "a metacognitive step of huge import" (1986, p. 133).

We each choose to switch reflection "on" or to leave it "off" in any situation. Think for a moment about areas in your life where you switch on, and areas where you switch off or pay little attention. Successful leadership, coaching, and teaching involve awareness of the particular switches for members of the team or class.

Generation or design of new ideas is also a critical linking process for learning and change. Generation involves forming ideas that you would never have had otherwise and planning your way into new mental territory. We have found de Bono's thinking tools (1993) very powerful in this respect.

Hill (1994, 1999) outlines the type of program that has emerged in industrial practice when conscious attention is paid to the processes shown in Figure 5.1 and the ways they interact to help work teams. The results are impressive at the individual, team, and corporate levels.

LINEAR MANAGEMENT VS. ACTION LEARNING

Linear project management models are commonly used in most organizations. They presume an orderly, sequenced set of steps through which one passes.

Our research suggests that Revans's (1982) concept of action learning is much more effective. This involves spinning oneself through iterative spirals of acting, gathering data, reflecting, designing, and taking new action. Learning is not linear; it requires constantly revisiting and redefining where one is going and constantly seeing the links between the phases in the spiral.

Having this model clearly in mind is a strong aid to workplace learning. At any stage, workers can ask: Which phase am I in at present? How does this link to the associated phases? How long has it been since I shifted phases? For example, when workers are in the prototyping, experimental period of a project, they may spin through many action learning spirals in one day. In later stages of a project, the spiral may become longer.

Linear models can often lead to "analysis paralysis"—people become stuck in a particular thinking mode, frozen into inaction. They do not see the need to move on, redesign, act anew, generate more data, or provide a new basis for improved reflection.

The concept of action learning is fundamental to designing for workplace learning. Sending staff to workshops that do not link the training to the workplace is a waste of valuable human and financial resources. Most companies we encounter do not believe they are getting a good return on their training dollars. Similarly, most have no effective link from their training to their practice, and no long-term plan or structures to facilitate this. People should leave every workshop with a plan of action that is well-aligned to their career goals or the goals of the organization. One must act to learn.

UNDERSTANDING SKILL ACQUISITION

To generate collective competence with any new skill takes time and attention. Not allowing for this is a critical problem in many companies. Collective competence must be learned and practiced. Too often, organizations implement changes without thought for how their people are to learn the new forms of collective competence within the new structures.

The Dreyfus model of skill acquisition (Dreyfus & Dreyfus, 1986; Benner, 1984; Benner, Tanner, & Chesla, 1996) postulates a series of levels in skill acquisition:

• At the novice level, behavior is governed by rules. With no PPK, novices needs structures and rules to guide their performance. Even seasoned employees may become novices if they are transferred to a new area of work, and they need job descriptions and guidelines to support them. Houldsworth, O'Brien, Butler, & Edwards (1997) provide an Australian case study of the learning of a novice.

• At the advanced beginner level, workers recognize patterns but find it hard to know what is salient in any situation. They hunger for predictability and certainty, assume there is one best or right way to do things, and believe that someone will know this. They typically search for books and experienced people with "the answers."

• At the competent level, which commonly takes two to three years of relevant experience to reach, performance is efficient, organized, and analytical. Workers make conscious goals and plans and take personal responsibility for the outcomes of their work. Competent people make excellent coaches for both novices and beginners because their analytical understanding of their work provides a clear set of steps, rules, or guidelines for learners.

• Proficiency involves learning to trust one's great store of PPK and intuition. To make the transition from competent to proficient involves moving beyond analysis. This is extremely difficult for some people who have an unshakable faith in analysis. Proficient workers let the context determine their behavior, see things as wholes, and focus on synthesis.

• Expert performance is highly intuitive and characterized by doing the right thing at the right time. At this level, workers have a great capacity for handling the unexpected. Expert knowledge is highly linked to nuance and context. It is thus difficult to assess using common staff appraisal procedures, and difficult to codify into written quality standards and qualifications frameworks. The contextual rules of experts are not those needed by novices; indeed they will confuse novices. So unless the experts can remember the generalized rules that help novices, they make very poor teachers of novices. However, they often make excellent teachers for competent workers, challenging their faith in analysis by sharing complex realities.

The Dreyfus model is helpful for understanding people's level of development in different work-skill contexts, for identifying training needs, and for targeting training more closely to the skill levels of the participants. The needs of novice workers entering business and industry are commonly ignored. Our latest book (Edwards, Butler, Hill, & Russell, 1997), based on our research and experience with people entering the world of work, is aimed at meeting this need.

THE VALUE OF TEACHING THINKING SKILLS

Learning to think has been treated as a byproduct of mastery of academic disciplines. Teachers, lecturers, trainers, and consultants seldom make their own thinking explicit and seldom focus directly on thinking. Within companies, little is different. People focus on the product or output, not on the thinking process. Currently companies recognize the need to change this, but they do not know how.

A wealth of research exists on the powerful benefits of directly teaching thinking skills—collected, for example, in this volume and in *Thinking: International Interdisciplinary Perspectives* (Edwards, 1994c). Yet this research has had little general impact on education systems or company functioning. Most people are locked into familiar thinking strategies and ways of identifying and solving problems. These may work well for them. However, many years of research (Edwards, 1991a, 1991b, 1994a, 1994b, 1995, 1996) have shown me the value of teaching people new thinking techniques. The strategies of de Bono (1987, 1993, 1994a, 1994b) provide a practical basis for teaching generative thinking. Books such as *Serious Creativity* (de Bono, 1992) contain a wide range of examples detailing how these strategies have benefited the companies using them. This current volume is another excellent resource for people wanting to broaden their repertoire of thinking strategies.

CONFUSION AND FRUSTRATION AS A PRECURSOR TO LEARNING

Deep learning—transformational learning—requires struggle and periods of getting worse before getting better. The transformational learning curve involves an initial dip into "the pit." This is the period of confusion and frustration that is central to most learning. Unfortunately many designers of learning try to design this period out of the process.

There are those who know well the mixed feelings of uneasiness and anticipation as they approach the pit and do so with confidence. There are others whose life experience has taught them that "yet another failure" lies ahead. They need people and systems to support them. One great leadership skill is to know how to stand with colleagues while they go through the pit. This does not mean telling them what to do, fixing their mistakes, or taking over. It means being there in whatever way helps those individuals hold onto their nerve, push through the pit, and achieve deep learning.

Our experience has been that once people start to have successful experiences and develop their "learning courage," they often become hooked on growth and learning. This is a wonderful thing to behold.

Making the time and space for growth can be difficult, however, particularly in manufacturing organizations, where output figures must be maintained. The secret lies in understanding that most pits are contextual, and entering one does not mean losing skills in other areas. Nonetheless, companies planning for organizational learning need to consider how many are likely to enter the pit and how long they are likely to be there.

LISTENING AND TALKING IN PRODUCTIVE WAYS

To think differently, to assess oneself or one's peers, and to work reflectively all require a new language. We need new ways of communicating internally with ourselves, and new ways of communicating in teams. One worker described it to me as "seeing the world through new spectacles" and then being able to talk about it to yourself and others. For maximum effect, the language needs to be shared across the organization and tied to powerful processes that can turn concepts into action.

Fundamental to all of our work in this area is a strong emphasis on facilitative questioning—a technique for questioning other people in a deeply respectful way. It involves helping others find their own answers to their own questions. This is totally different from the "judge and fix them up" mentality that underlies much educational and workplace questioning. It means ignoring one's own agenda and turning the other parties back to their own resources, by listening carefully and genuinely seeking to understand what they are experiencing. Some people have natural skills in this area, but most need extensive practice to add facilitative questioning to their repertoire. Costa has done powerful work helping people acquire this skill, particularly through his cognitive coaching technique (see, for example, Baker, Costa, & Shalit, 1997).

When we work with an organization, we spend considerable time helping team members learn facilitative questioning. For most people, this is a new way of talking with one another. The careful listening and asking of genuine questions helps people look at the beliefs, values, and assumptions that underlie and drive their behavior. Examining these forces provides maximum leverage on performance.

Argyris (1982); Senge, Kleiner, Roberts, Ross, & Smith (1994); and Senge et al. (1999) discuss a variety of other useful tools. One is the "ladder of inference," which helps people see how they develop their own version of an event based on their beliefs, values, and assumptions. This is a very effective model for people to use to identify the sources of their beliefs and actions.

People tend to look for quick-fix or temporary solutions to problems. Argyris (1982) calls this "single-loop" learning. He argues that more effective action comes from "double-loop" learning, which involves deeper processing to find root causes. Unless people and companies can get to this level of systemic structures and underlying beliefs, values, and assumptions, they set themselves up for recurring problems. We use a range of strategies, including double looping, de Bono's (1993) "define the problem" technique, and Senge's (1994) "five why's," to generate deep processing.

Another powerful contribution from Argyris is the distinction he draws between espoused theories (what we say we do) and theories in use (what we actually do). These never match, but we are unable to see the mismatches in ourselves. Few of us ever receive honest feedback about how we may "talk the talk" but not "walk the walk." There are many reasons for this: some people send clear messages that they do not want feedback, some are afraid of the consequences of being honest, and few are adept at offering constructive critiques. But giving and receiving feedback are learnable skills. Our results in companies show that introducing these skills as a part of everyday work life can profoundly affect the atmosphere and efficiency of a workplace.

Argyris (1994) believes that too many managers do not encourage people to reflect on their work and behavior, do not encourage individual accountability, and do not surface the kinds of deep and potentially threatening or embarrassing information that can produce real learning and change. In some workplaces, openness and trust already exist. In others they must be developed. People need safe places to practice and sharpen new thinking and learning skills. Senge and his team (1994) describe ways to set up such practice fields.

CHALLENGE-AND-SUPPORT STRUCTURES

Although people can improve their workplace performance and their thinking on their own, most benefit from both challenge and support. When my colleagues and I work with organizations, we pay great attention to establishing learning-support teams. Our experience suggests that it is best to set up such structures within the existing power structure of the company. Otherwise, if the challenge-and-support structure comes up against the existing power structure, it will be crushed (Balatti, Edwards, & Andrew, 1997; Schein, 1995).

Mentoring, supporting, empowering, and facilitating come naturally to some people, but not to others. Furthermore, learning-support skills are contextual; someone who can help in technical matters may be unable to help in other areas. Some requisite skills may be well known already, but others may require a shift in beliefs or workplace culture.

Figure 5.2 shows the typical responses people give when asked to reflect on their professional learning in different challenge-and-support environments. No two people have the same challenge and support needs, and sharing these openly within the team promotes more effective operation of the team and the individuals in it. The keys are listening to people to learn their particular needs and helping them get in touch with their personal power.

By expecting people to make decisions at their own level, where they are best made, companies empower the work force, give them much more professional satisfaction, and allow the managers and leaders to do what they are really paid to do, instead of shouldering everyone else's work. By personally coaching managers to delegate decision making, my colleagues and I have been able to help them and their staffs make remarkable turnarounds in quite short periods.

THINKING AND LEARNING: LEGITIMATE BUSINESS ACTIVITIES

Unless learning and knowledge generation are clearly seen as legitimate business activities, they will be relegated to something people do in their spare time, when they are not doing their real work. This generally means that the company slips into maintaining its status quo, while "smarter" companies continue to move ahead of them.

The most successful organizations have a vision and organizational architecture that align their staff to growth and learning at all levels. As Fullan (1993) explains, change is compulsory; growth is optional.

—*Figure 5.2*—

Perceived Benefits and Drawbacks of Different Work Environments

	High Challenge	**Low Challenge**
High Support	*Positives:* Sense of accomplishment; synergy; feeling of being valued; high growth potential *Negatives:* Stress from high expectations; draining work days; tendency to force narrow focus on "success"	*Positives:* Chance to "cruise"; good starting point; chance to initiate; opportunity to "nail it" *Negatives:* Perception that others see me as incapable; insecurity that I am missing something; low self-esteem; tendency to get lazy
Low Support	*Positives:* Deepest learning; development of survival skills; self-responsibility; unforgettable experiences *Negatives:* Shattered confidence; feeling of abandonment; inclination to give up	*Positives:* Time for reflection, recovery, and creative work; freedom *Negatives:* Boredom; demoralized spirit; sense of wasted time; little learning

CHANGING CORPORATE CULTURE

Companies have inherited many of the views of learning and thinking that have long hindered schools and universities. But interactions among researchers, learning institutions, and business and industry are changing corporate culture, as evidenced by the success of Senge and his colleagues, for example. Learning organizations are emerging where people know how to generate knowledge, how to articulate and share it, and how to manage it in ways that produce powerful practice.

REFERENCES

Argyris, C. (1982). *Reasoning, learning and action.* San Francisco: Jossey-Bass.

Argyris, C. (1994, July–August). Good communication that blocks learning. *Harvard Business Review,* Reprint 94401.

Baker, W., Costa, A. L., & Shalit, S. (1997). The norms of collaboration: Attaining communicative competence. In. A. Costa & R. Liebmann (Eds.), *The process centered school: Sustaining a renaissance community.* Thousand Oaks, CA: Corwin Press.

Balatti, J., Edwards, J., & Andrew, P. (1997). Mentoring structures within a professional development program. *Training and Development in Australia, 24*(5), 8–14.

Benner, P. (1984). *From novice to expert: Excellence and power in clinical nursing practice.* Menlo Park, CA: Addison-Wesley.

Benner, P., Tanner, C., & Chesla, C. (1996). *Expertise in nursing practice: Caring, clinical judgment, and ethics.* New York: Springer.

Bruner, J. (1986). *Actual minds: Possible worlds.* Cambridge, MA: Harvard University Press.

Butler, J. (1994). From action to thought: The fulfillment of human potential. In J. Edwards (Ed.), *Thinking: International interdisciplinary perspectives* (pp. 16–22). Melbourne: Hawker Brownlow.

de Bono, E. (1987). *CoRT thinking program. Workcards and teachers' notes.* Chicago: Science Research Associates.

de Bono, E. (1992). *Serious creativity.* London: HarperCollins.

de Bono, E. (1993). *Teach your child how to think.* New York: Penguin.

de Bono, E. (1994a). *Parallel thinking.* London: Viking.

de Bono, E. (1994b). The teaching of thinking: Why and how? In J. Edwards (Ed.), *Thinking: International interdisciplinary perspectives* (pp. 45–55). Melbourne: Hawker Brownlow.

Dreyfus, H. L., & Dreyfus, S. E. (1986). *Mind over machine.* New York: Free Press.

Edwards, J. (1991a). The direct teaching of thinking skills. In G. Evans (Ed.), *Learning and teaching cognitive skills* (pp. 87–106). Melbourne: Australian Council for Educational Research.

Edwards, J. (1991b). Research work on the CoRT method. In S. Maclure & P. Davies (Eds.), *Learning to think: Thinking to learn* (pp. 19–30). Oxford: Pergamon.

Edwards, J. (1994a). Thinking and change. In S. Dingli (Ed.), *Creative thinking: A multifaceted approach* (pp. 16–29). Msida, Malta: Malta University Press.

Edwards, J. (1994b). Thinking, education and human potential. In J. Edwards (Ed.), *Thinking: International interdisciplinary perspectives* (pp. 6–15). Melbourne: Hawker Brownlow.

Edwards, J. (Ed.). (1994c). *Thinking: International interdisciplinary perspectives.* Melbourne: Hawker Brownlow.

Edwards, J. (1995). Teaching thinking in schools: An overview. *Unicorn, 21*(1), 27–36.

Edwards, J. (1996). The direct teaching of thinking in education and in business. In S. Dingli (Ed.), *Creative thinking: New perspectives* (pp. 82–95). Msida, Malta: Malta University Press.

Edwards, J., Butler, J., Hill, B., & Russell, S. (1997). *People rules for rocket scientists.* Brisbane, Australia: Samford Research Associates.

Fullan, M. (1993). *Change forces.* London: Falmer Press.

Hill, B. (1994). Growing people, growing crystals. In S. Dingli (Ed.), *Creative thinking: A multifaceted approach* (pp. 215–223). Msida, Malta: Malta University Press.

Hill, B. (1999, July 4–9). Creative thinking, education and experience in a major Australian mineral processing plant. Paper presented at the 8th International Conference on Thinking, Edmonton, Alberta, Canada.

Houldsworth, B., O'Brien, J., Butler, J., & Edwards, J. (1997). Learning in the restructured workplace: A case study. *Education & Training, 39*(6), 211–218.

Revans, R. W. (1982). *The origins and growth of action learning.* Lund, Sweden: Studentlitteratur.

Rigano, D., & Edwards, J. (1998). Incorporating reflection into workplace practice: A case study. *Management Learning, 29*(4), 431–446.

Schein, E. H. (1995). *Learning consortia: How to create parallel learning systems for organization sets* [working paper]. Cambridge, MA: MIT Center for Organizational Learning.

Senge, P., Kleiner, A., Roberts, C., Ross, R. B., & Smith, B. J. (1994). *The fifth discipline fieldbook: Strategies and tools for building the learning organization.* New York: Currency Doubleday.

Senge, P., Kleiner, A., Roberts, C., Ross, R., Roth, G., & Smith, B. J. (1999). *The dance of change.* New York: Nicholas Brealey.

6

Standards-Based Thinking and Reasoning Skills

Robert J. Marzano and Jane E. Pollock

The teaching of thinking and reasoning received proba-bly its strongest endorsement in the United States at the first Education Summit in September 1989, when President Bush and the nation's governors came together in Charlottesville, Virginia. These leaders, including then-gover-nor Bill Clinton, pledged to improve schooling in the United States. Their efforts resulted in six far-reaching goals for Amer-ican education, published in *The National Education Goals Re-port: Building a Nation of Learners* (National Education Goals Panel [NEGP], 1991). Goal Three specifically addressed the enhancement of thinking and reasoning: "and every school in America will ensure that all students learn to use their minds, so they may be prepared for responsible citizenship, further learning, and productive employment in our modern econ-omy" (p. 4).

The endorsement by the NEGP was not the first. Strength-ening thinking and reasoning skills had been recommended earlier by a host of prestigious organizations, including the National Education Association (Futrell, 1987), the American Federation of Teachers (1985), the Panel on the General Pro-fessional Education of the Physician and College Preparation for Medicine (1984), the National Science Board Commission on Precollege Education in Mathematics, Science, and Tech-nology (1983), the College Board (1983), and the Commission on the Humanities (1980). Many of the calls for focusing on thinking and reasoning have been kindled by reports that U.S. students, while demonstrating improved basic skills, have regularly performed poorly when asked to analyze a situation, explain their reasoning, or apply their knowledge (see, for example, Applebee, Langer, & Mullis, 1986a & 1986b; Dossey, Mullis, Lindquist, & Chambers, 1988).

Although there is a general consensus that the teaching of thinking and reasoning is worthwhile, a fair amount of contro-versy surrounds the specifics of which skills should be taught.

WHAT ARE THE SKILLS OF THINKING AND REASONING?

Some educators, like Beyer (1988), de Bono (1985), Marzano (1992), and Quellmalz (1987), have developed programs to teach and reinforce general thinking and reasoning skills that reportedly pertain to all content domains. Some psycholo-gists, however, consider it erroneous to talk about thinking and reasoning in isolation of subject matter. Resnick (1987) supports this position in a popular monograph titled *Education and Learning to Think*. In another compelling article, Glaser (1984) theorizes that there are no general thinking and reasoning skills that cross the boundaries of specific subject areas—in other words, no interdisciplinary thinking and rea-soning skills.

To date, the debate regarding the existence of such skills has involved more theory than fact; each side has provided conflicting arguments and opinion. Although these arguments are compelling, they do not resolve the issue. To provide an empirical perspective, a team of researchers at Mid-continent Research for Education and Learning (McREL) in Aurora, Colorado, led by John Kendall, turned to national standards documents that identify what students should know and be able to do in specific content areas (see Kendall & Marzano, 2000). If interdisciplinary thinking and reasoning skills do exist, posited the researchers at McREL, then logically they would be stated explicitly or implicitly in the national stan-dards documents. For example, if the national standards doc-uments for geography, science, and mathematics all mention the importance of argumentation, then one might conclude that argumentation is an interdisciplinary thinking and rea-soning skill, or a skill that cuts across these content areas. The national standards documents, then, represent a source from which general thinking and reasoning skills can be derived, if they in fact exist.

To fully understand McREL's efforts, it is necessary to briefly consider the genesis and development of the national standards documents. The National Council of Teachers of Mathematics (NCTM) led the way by publishing the *Curriculum and Evaluation Standards for School Mathematics* in 1989. This document, and the national goals established at the Education Summit during the Bush administration, spawned intense activity by national subject-matter organizations to establish rigorous standards in their respective areas. Furthermore, in June 1991, Congress established the National Council on Education Standards and Testing (NCEST) to make recommendations on the desirability and feasibility of voluntary national standards. Six months later, NCEST (1992) proposed that Congress create an oversight board, the National Education Standards and Assessment Council (NESAC), to prescribe guidelines for setting standards.

As a result of the attention given to creating voluntary national standards in the early 1990s, standards documents were developed in almost every subject area. A vast range of experts in their respective fields convened throughout the nation to draft and revise the documents. For example, some 18,000 science teachers and 250 groups reviewed the *National Science Education Standards* prior to their release (National Research Council [NRC], 1996). Similarly, more than 3,000 geography experts and teachers designed the standards for that subject (Geography Education Standards Project, 1994).

The national standards documents, then, represent consensuses regarding the cardinal knowledge within basic subject areas. The task undertaken by McREL researchers, as part of their funding from the U.S. Office of Educational Research and Improvement (OERI), was to use this unprecedented database to identify the general thinking and reasoning skills—if they do exist—that cut across subject areas. To this end, McREL researchers analyzed national standards documents and other relevant publications in 12 subject areas (see Figure 6.1). Areas 1–11 are those that most educators consider basic; they are commonly identified as the focus of state-level standards documents. Area 12, called the world of work, addresses the expectations of employers.

It is important to recognize that the McREL team studied multiple documents for a few subject areas. In science, for example, the "official" standards document is decidedly the *National Science Education Standards* (NRC, 1996). However, the McREL researchers also examined *Benchmarks for Science Literacy* (Project 2061, 1993), because of its broad acceptance as a reference in the field. For different reasons, McREL analyzed multiple documents in English language arts as well. At the suggestion of the National Council of Teachers of English

—Figure 6.1—
Subject Areas and Standards Documents in the McREL Study

1. **Science**
   - *Benchmarks for Science Literacy* (Project 2061, 1993)
   - *National Science Education Standards* (National Research Council, 1996)

2. **Mathematics**
   - *Curriculum and Evaluation Standards for School Mathematics* (National Council of Teachers of Mathematics, 1989)

3. **Social Studies**
   - *Expectations of Excellence: Curriculum Standards for Social Studies* (National Council for the Social Studies, 1994)

4. **Geography**
   - *Geography for Life: National Geography Standards* (Geography Education Standards Project, 1994)

5. **History**
   - *National Standards for History: Basic Edition* (National Center for History in the Schools, 1996)

6. **Civics**
   - *National Standards for Civics and Government* (Center for Civic Education, 1994)

7. **Physical Education**
   - *Moving into the Future: National Standards for Physical Education: A Guide to Content and Assessment* (National Association for Sport and Physical Education, 1995)

8. **Health**
   - *National Health Education Standards: Achieving Health Literacy* (Joint Committee on National Health Education Standards, 1995)

9. **The Arts**
   - *National Standards for Arts Education: What Every Young American Should Know and Be Able to Do in the Arts* (Consortium of National Arts Education Associations, 1994)

10. **Foreign Language**
    - *Standards for Foreign Language Learning: Preparing for the 21st Century* (National Standards in Foreign Language Education Project, 1996)

11. **English Language Arts**
    - *Standards in Practice: Grades K–2* (Crafton, 1996)
    - *Standards in Practice: Grades 3–5* (Sierra-Perry, 1996)
    - *Standards in Practice: Grades 6–8* (Wilhelm, 1996)
    - *Standards in Practice: Grades 9–12* (Smagorinsky, 1996)

12. **The World of Work**
    - *What Work Requires of Schools: A SCANS Report for America 2000* (Secretary's Commission on Achieving Necessary Skills, 1991)
    - *Workplace Basics: The Essential Skills Employers Want* (Carnevale, Gainer, & Meltzer, 1990)

(NCTE), the researchers reviewed four documents focusing on different grade levels, instead of the more general *Standards for the English Language Arts* (NCTE and the International Reading Association, 1996). They took this approach because the latter document does not articulate the specific skills and abilities expected of students. (For more details on McREL's document selection process, see Kendall & Marzano, 2000.)

The researchers examined each document for thinking and reasoning skills that were stated explicitly or implicitly. (For a detailed discussion of the protocols used in the analysis, see Kendall & Marzano, 2000.) Six general thinking and reasoning skills were identified in a majority of the content areas:

1. Identifying similarities and differences (found in all subjects).

2. Problem solving and troubleshooting (found in 83 percent of the subjects).

3. Argumentation (found in 83 percent of the subjects).

4. Decision making (found in 75 percent of the subjects).

5. Hypothesis testing and scientific inquiry (found in 58 percent of the subjects).

6. Use of logic and reasoning (found in 50 percent of the subjects).

For each of these skill areas, the researchers defined benchmark measures of the more specific knowledge and skills students should have at four intervals: Level 1 (grades K–2), Level 2 (grades 3–5), Level 3 (grades 6–8), and Level 4 (grades 9–12). To illustrate, Figure 6.2 presents the Level 3 benchmarks for the skill of hypothesis testing and scientific inquiry.

The benchmarks for all six thinking and reasoning areas are available on the World Wide Web (http://www.mcrel.org/compendium/browse.asp) and in Kendall and Marzano's *Content Knowledge* (2000). Each benchmark is accompanied by a detailed code, called a citation log, that indicates which documents include the benchmark and whether they do so explicitly or implicitly. For example, consider the citation log for the fourth benchmark in Figure 6.2: (2E,299;NSI,171). The numeral 2 indicates that the benchmark is found in *Benchmarks for Science Literacy* (Project 2061, 1993). The letter E indicates that the benchmark is explicitly stated; the number 299 designates the page on which it is found. The letters NS indicate that the information was also found in the *National Science Education Standards* (NRC, 1996). The letter I means that it is implicit, and the number 171 identifies the relevant page.

McREL researchers also determined the extent to which different subject areas emphasize the various thinking and reasoning skills. Figure 6.3 presents these findings. The 12 subject

—*Figure 6.2*—

Level 3 (Grades 6–8) Benchmarks for Hypothesis Testing and Scientific Inquiry

(2I,233;NHI,66;NSI,145)
1. Understands that there are a variety of ways people can form hypotheses, including basing them on many observations, basing them on few observations, and constructing them on only one or two observations.

(MI,75;NSI,148,171)
2. Verifies results of experiments.

(2E,299;NHI,66;NSI,145)
3. Understands that there may be more than one valid way to interpret a set of findings.

(2E,299;NSI,171)
4. Questions findings in which no mention is made of whether the control group is very similar to the experimental group.

(SSE,149;NSE,145;NSI,171)
5. Reformulates a new hypothesis for study after an old hypothesis has been eliminated.

(MI,78,81,143;NSI,145,171)
6. Makes and validates conjectures about outcomes of specific alternatives or events regarding an experiment.

Source: From *Content Knowledge: A Compendium of Standards and Benchmarks for K–12 Education* (3rd ed., pp. 641–642), by J. S. Kendall & R. J. Marzano, 2000. Alexandria, VA: Association for Supervision and Curriculum Development.

areas are listed in rank order by their percentage share of all the references to thinking and reasoning. For example, the science documents accounted for 27.2 percent of all the references to thinking and reasoning; history, 13 percent; mathematics, 11.3 percent; and so on. Because documents varied in length and because more than one document was analyzed in some subject areas, it is probably wise not to make too much of these percentages. It is interesting, however, to identify some patterns. More than half (51.5 percent) of all references made to thinking and reasoning came from three subject areas—science, history, and mathematics. And language arts, which had the most documents, accounted for the lowest percentage of references to thinking and reasoning.

More defensible inferences can be made by studying the patterns of emphasis within individual subject areas. For each area, the columns in Figure 6.3 show how the references to thinking and reasoning skills are distributed among each of the six skills. For example, science seems to stress hypothesis testing and scientific inquiry; 32.3 percent of the science documents' references to thinking and reasoning

—Figure 6.3—

Subject Matter Emphases on Various Critical Thinking and Reasoning Skills

Subject Areas	Share of All Subjects' References to Thinking and Reasoning	Share of Each Subject Area's References by Skills					
		Identifying Similarities and Differences	Problem Solving and Troubleshooting	Argumentation	Decision Making	Hypothesis Testing and Scientific Inquiry	Use of Logic and Reasoning
Science	27.2%	8.3%	11.5%	22.9%	3.1%	32.3%	21.8%
History	13.0%	32.6%	26.1%	15.2%	15.2%	8.7%	2.2%
Mathematics	11.3%	17.5%	50.0%	7.5%	0.0%	20.0%	5.0%
Social Studies	9.1%	28.1%	6.3%	28.1%	28.1%	3.1%	6.3%
The Arts	8.2%	46.4%	32.1%	7.1%	14.3%	0.0%	0.0%
Civics	7.4%	23.1%	38.5%	7.7%	30.8%	0.0%	0.0%
World of Work	6.8%	12.5%	54.2%	20.8%	0.0%	4.2%	8.3%
Foreign Language	4.0%	92.9%	0.0%	7.1%	0.0%	0.0%	0.0%
Geography	3.7%	30.8%	7.7%	7.7%	30.8%	23.1%	0.0%
Health	3.7%	46.2%	15.4%	7.7%	30.8%	0.0%	0.0%
Physical Education	3.1%	45.5%	18.2%	0.0%	36.4%	0.0%	0.0%
Language Arts	2.8%	50.0%	0.0%	0.0%	10.0%	20.0%	20.0%

Source: Mid-continent Research for Education and Learning (McREL). Adapted with permission.

relate to this one skill area. Additionally, science places heavy emphasis on argumentation and the use of logic, some emphasis on problem solving and identifying similarities and differences, and relatively minor emphasis on decision making.

The patterns of emphasis across subject areas for the six thinking and reasoning skill areas might be summarized as follows:

1. Identifying similarities and differences receives some attention in all subject areas and is stressed in history, social studies, the arts, foreign language, geography, health, physical education, and language arts.

2. Problem solving is mentioned in all subject areas except foreign language and language arts. It is particularly emphasized in mathematics and the world of work.

3. Argumentation receives some attention in all subject areas except physical education and language arts. It is stressed in science, social studies, and the world of work.

4. Decision making is addressed in all subject areas except mathematics, the world of work, and foreign language. It is stressed in social studies, civics, geography, health, and physical education.

5. Hypothesis testing and scientific inquiry are emphasized in science, mathematics, geography, and language arts. They receive modest attention in history, social studies, and the world of work, but they are not covered in the arts, civics, foreign language, health, and physical education documents.

6. The use of logic is emphasized in science and language arts. It receives modest attention in history, mathematics, social studies, and the world of work, but it is not covered in the arts, civics, foreign language, geography, health, and physical education documents.

These findings can contribute to future curriculum design. Educators can use them to integrate the teaching of thinking and reasoning into nearly all subject areas in a deliberate manner consistent with the basic structure of those subjects.

HOW SHOULD GENERAL THINKING AND REASONING SKILLS BE USED?

Almost every standards document analyzed in the McREL study made explicit or implicit reference to the fact that thinking and reasoning should be reinforced in the context of authentic tasks within each content area. For example, the *National Science Education Standards* (NRC, 1996, p. 31) notes that the use of "authentic questions, generated from student experience" is the most pertinent strategy for strengthening scientific thinking and reasoning. The *National Standards for History: Basic Edition* (National Center for History in the Schools, 1996, p. 15) notes that thinking and reasoning skills should not be "practiced in a vacuum."

To those ends, teachers in all subject areas should make use of assignments with real-world applications. As an example, consider the following task designed for high school science students (Marzano, Pickering, & McTighe, 1993):

The increase of waste material is a global issue. Waste materials can be toxic, dangerous to dispose of, bulky, reeking, and offensive. Your team of four must prepare a report for a task force created by the federal government. In that report, you should classify various types of waste materials and propose a plan to address the problem of waste management. Use information gathered from classroom lessons and from sources on reserve in the school media center to do the classification work. Select one category of waste materials and present a plan for resolving the problem of accumulation and disposal, and rethinking current practices in relation to that type of waste. Your plan should be prepared as a research report to the task force and should include the following elements:

1. Your classification of all waste materials and how you determined the categories.

2. An explanation of the effect on the environment caused by your selected category of waste material.

3. Your plan to address the specific problems created by your category of waste material.

4. The anticipated effect of your plan.

This classroom activity, commonly referred to as a performance task (Marzano, Pickering, & McTighe, 1993), requires students to employ at least two of the thinking and reasoning skills: identifying similarities and differences (for element 1) and problem solving (for element 3). The task also addresses students' competence in at least two other areas: their knowledge of waste management and their ability to write a research-based document.

As an aid to designing tasks that involve thinking and reasoning, Figure 6.4 lists a number of stimulus questions that correspond to the six thinking and reasoning skills. To understand how these questions might be used, consider the situation of a science teacher planning a unit on the cell. To infuse the teaching of thinking and reasoning into the unit, the teacher might want to develop a performance task with the cell as the focal topic and one or more of the six thinking and reasoning skills embedded in the methodology. To brainstorm ideas, the teacher would apply the suggested stimulus questions to the

—Figure 6.4—

Stimulus Questions for the Six Thinking and Reasoning Skills

Skill 1: Identifying similarities and differences
- Do I want to determine how things are similar and different?
- Do I want to organize things into groups? Can I identify the rules or characteristics that have been used to form groups?
- Do I see a relationship that no one else sees? Can I identify an abstract pattern or theme at the heart of the relationship?

Skill 2: Problem solving and troubleshooting
- Do I want to describe how some obstacle can be overcome?
- Do I want to improve on something?

Skill 3: Argumentation
- Is there a position I want to defend on a particular issue?
- Are there differing perspectives on an issue I want to explore?

Skill 4: Decision making
- Is there an important decision that should be studied or made?

Skill 5: Hypothesis testing and scientific inquiry
- Is there a prediction I want to make and then test?
- Do I have a hypothesis about a past or future event that I want to explore?
- Do I have a new theory or idea that I want to explore?

Skill 6: Use of logic and reasoning
- Do I want to identify the rules operating in this situation?
- Is there a conclusion I can draw based on these rules?
- Do I want to identify rules that are not being followed in this situation?

Source: Adapted with permission of Mid-continent Research for Education and Learning (McREL), from *Transforming Classroom Grading* by R. J. Marzano, 2000, p. 95. Alexandria, VA: Association for Supervision and Curriculum Development. Copyright McREL Institute.

focal topic: Do I want students to determine how things are similar to and different from the cell? Do I want students to organize aspects of the cell into groups and then identify the rules or characteristics they used to form groups? As the teacher went down the list, a "yes" answer to any question would indicate that the relevant thinking and reasoning skill is a good candidate for integrating into the performance task.

MOVING FORWARD

According to McREL's analysis, interdisciplinary thinking skills do exist. The research shows that national standards documents expect six general thinking and reasoning skills to be taught in most subject areas. What remains now is for educators to address those six skills in a systematic and explicit way as they design curriculum.

REFERENCES

American Federation of Teachers. (1985, September). Critical thinking: It's a basic. *American Teacher*, 21.

Applebee, A. N., Langer, J. A., & Mullis, I. V. S. (1986a). *The reading report card: Progress toward excellence in our schools: Trends in reading over four national assessments, 1971–1984.* Princeton, NJ: Educational Testing Service.

Applebee, A. N., Langer, J. A., & Mullis, I. V. S. (1986b). *The writing report card: Writing achievement in American schools.* Princeton, NJ: Educational Testing Service.

Beyer, B. K. (1988). *Developing a thinking skills program.* Boston: Allyn & Bacon.

Carnevale, A. P., Gainer, L. J., & Meltzer, A. S. (1990). *Workplace basics: The essential skills employers want.* San Francisco: Jossey-Bass.

Center for Civic Education. (1994). *National standards for civics and government.* Calabasas, CA: Author.

College Board. (1983). *Academic preparation for college: What students need to know and be able to do.* New York: College Entrance Examination Board.

Commission on the Humanities. (1980). *The humanities in American life.* Berkeley: University of California Press.

Consortium of National Arts Education Associations (1994). *National standards for arts education: What every young American should know and be able to do in the arts.* Reston, VA: Music Educators National Conference.

Crafton, L. K. (1996). *Standards in practice: Grades K–2.* Urbana, IL: National Council of Teachers of English.

de Bono, E. (1985). The CoRT thinking program. In J. W. Segal, S. F. Chipman, & R. Glaser (Eds.), *Thinking and learning skills: Vol. 1. Relating instruction to research* (pp. 363–388). Hillsdale, NJ: Lawrence Erlbaum.

Dossey, J. A., Mullis, I. V. S., Lindquist, M. M., & Chambers, D. L. (1988). *The mathematics report card.* Princeton, NJ: Educational Testing Service.

Futrell, M. H. (1987, December 9). A message long overdue. *Education Week, 7*(14), 9.

Geography Education Standards Project. (1994). *Geography for life: National geography standards.* Washington, DC: National Geographic Research and Exploration.

Glaser, R. (1984). Education and thinking: The role of knowledge. *American Psychologist, 39*, 93–104.

Joint Committee on National Health Education Standards. (1995). *National health education standards: Achieving health literacy.* Reston, VA: Association for the Advancement of Health Education.

Kendall, J. S., & Marzano, R. J. (2000). *Content knowledge: A compendium of standards and benchmarks for K–12 education* (3rd ed.). Alexandria, VA: Association for Supervision and Curriculum Development; Aurora, CO: Mid-continent Research for Education and Learning.

Marzano, R. J. (1992). *A different kind of classroom: Teaching with dimensions of learning.* Alexandria, VA: Association for Supervision and Curriculum Development.

Marzano, R. J. (2000). *Transforming classroom grading.* Alexandria, VA: Association for Supervision and Curriculum Development.

Marzano, R. J., Pickering, D., & McTighe, J. (1993). *Assessing student outcomes: Performance assessment using the dimensions of learning model* (p. 51). Alexandria, VA: Association for Supervision and Curriculum Development.

National Association for Sport and Physical Education. (1995). *Moving into the future. National standards for physical education: A guide to content and assessment.* St. Louis, MO: Mosby.

National Center for History in the Schools, UCLA. (1996). *National standards for history: Basic edition.* Los Angeles: Author.

National Council for the Social Studies. (1994). *Expectations of excellence: Curriculum standards for social studies.* Washington, DC: Author.

National Council of Teachers of English and the International Reading Association. (1996). *Standards for the English language arts.* Urbana, IL and Newark, DE: Authors.

National Council of Teachers of Mathematics. (1989). *Curriculum and evaluation standards for school mathematics.* Reston, VA: Author.

National Council on Education Standards and Testing. (1992). *Raising standards for American education: A report to Congress, the Secretary of Education, the National Education Goals Panel, and the American people.* Washington, DC: Government Printing Office.

National Education Goals Panel (1991). *The national education goals report: Building a nation of learners.* Washington, DC: Author.

National Research Council (NRC). (1996). *National science education standards.* Washington, DC: National Academy Press.

National Science Board Commission on Precollege Education in Mathematics, Science and Technology. (1983). *Educating Americans for the 21st century.* Washington, DC: National Science Board Commission.

National Standards in Foreign Language Education Project. (1996). *Standards for foreign language learning: Preparing for the 21st century.* Lawrence, KS: Allen Press.

Panel on the General Professional Education of the Physician and College Preparation for Medicine. (1984). *Physicians for the twenty-first century: The GPEP report.* Washington, DC: Association for American Colleges.

Project 2061, American Association for the Advancement of Science. (1993). *Benchmarks for science literacy.* New York: Oxford University Press.

Quellmalz, E. S. (1987). Developing reasoning skills. In J. B. Baron & R. J. Sternberg (Eds.), *Teaching thinking skills: Theory and practice.* New York: W. H. Freeman.

Resnick, L. B. (1987). *Education and learning to think.* Washington, DC: National Academy Press.

Secretary's Commission on Achieving Necessary Skills. (1991). *What work requires of schools: A SCANS report for America 2000.* Washington, DC: U.S. Department of Labor.

Sierra-Perry, M. (1996). *Standards in practice: Grades 3–5.* Urbana, IL: National Council of Teachers of English.

Smagorinsky, P. (1996). *Standards in practice: Grades 9–12.* Urbana, IL: National Council of Teachers of English.

Wilhelm, J. D. (1996). *Standards in practice: Grades 6–8.* Urbana, IL: National Council of Teachers of English.

7

Teaching Thinking Skills— Defining the Problem

BARRY K. BEYER

The teaching of thinking skills is a lot like the weather. Almost everybody talks about it, but few seem able to do much to improve it. Yet this failure has not been for want of trying.

Ever since the turn of the century, U.S. schools have considered mastery of thinking skills a major goal of instruction in almost all subject areas.[1] Considerable evidence suggests that we still have a long way to go in achieving this goal.[2] Why haven't we been as successful as we would like? What can we do to improve the teaching and learning of thinking in our schools?

Clearly, we can do a better job than we now do of helping students learn thinking skills. But we will *not* accomplish this goal simply by spending more time delivering the same kind of instruction as we now provide. Instead, we must constructively confront the major obstacles that stand in the way of effective teaching of thinking skills. I wish to point out here some of the more significant of these obstacles.

DEFINING THE PROBLEM

Observers have attributed poor student achievement in thinking skills to just about everything from atomic fallout to video games and television.[3] However, I believe that the primary explanation for poor achievement is that most teachers do not teach these skills.[4] Even among teachers who do, the problem is more complex than simply too little time on task. It has to do with *how* we use our teaching time and with *what* we choose to teach.

There are at least five major reasons why we educators have not put to better use the time that we devote to teaching thinking skills. First, we do not agree among ourselves which thinking skills we should teach. Second, too many educators

and developers of instructional materials do not understand— or have not defined precisely—the skills that they have elected to teach. Third, despite their best intentions, most teachers never actually provide the kinds of instruction that research suggests are most productive in developing competent thinkers. Fourth, school curricula too frequently suffer from "skills overload"; they bombard students with one-shot exposures to literally dozens of skills at each grade level, apparently on the assumption that children can master these skills on first introduction. Finally, the assessment instruments currently in use in many schools may actually inhibit the teaching and learning of thinking skills; at the very least, they hinder the consistent evaluation of students' competence in these skills. Until we understand the influence of these five factors, efforts to improve the teaching and learning of thinking skills are not likely to succeed.

LACK OF CONSENSUS

Most educators agree that thinking skills (unlike social or psychomotor skills) are essentially mental techniques or abilities that enable human beings to formulate thoughts, to reason about, or to judge. The frequently used synonyms for thinking suggest the wide range of skills that thinking includes. We use the word *think* to mean, among other things, to form in the mind, ponder, decide, recall, invent, weigh, imagine, believe, and anticipate. Teaching thinking skills consists of teaching students how to engage in these behaviors.

Unfortunately, agreement seems to end at this point. Little has happened in the last 15 years to remedy what Hilda Taba once referred to as "the haziness about what is meant by thinking."[5] In what they choose to discuss or to teach as thinking skills, educators today continue to exhibit both haziness and great diversity.

Some teachers teach skills they describe as reasoning or logical analysis, which include syllogistic reasoning, spotting

Adapted with permission of author from *Phi Delta Kappan*, 65(7), March 1984, 486–490. Copyright © by 1984 Barry K. Beyer.

contradictions, deductive logic, sequential synthesis, and making inferences.[6] Others focus on the hierarchy of cognitive skills that Benjamin Bloom and his colleagues have described.[7] Some school systems teach inquiry; others emphasize problem solving, decision making, or conceptualizing. Some schools teach taxonomies of skills; others focus on discrete skills almost at random: mnemonics as well as creative thinking, Socratic reasoning as well as critical thinking. Some school systems even seek to teach their own sets of thinking skills. One such system labels these skills as clarifying issues, giving one's opinion, explaining, predicating, generalizing, and concluding.[8] Commercial publishers also offer instructional materials focused on a wide variety of thinking skills. One publisher, for example, has chosen to focus on "qualification, structure analysis, operation analysis, and seeing analogies."

This diversity might not be quite so serious a problem were it not for two related factors. First, we frequently tend to consider all thinking skills as similar in terms of complexity, utility, and function. Locally developed instructional programs often give such skills as classifying data equal status with such skills as decision making; one curriculum guide puts "locating information in an index" on a par with "choosing from alternatives based on one's values." Obviously, with each of these two pairs, the cognitive operations are not equally complex, nor do these skills serve the same kinds of purposes. Yet we often devote equal teaching time to each skill, regardless of its complexity or its relationship to other thinking skills or procedures.

Second, considerable confusion exists among teachers regarding the definitions of these skills. Thus, although many school systems may claim to teach the same skill, we cannot be certain that the skill—as taught—is identical everywhere. Teachers vary considerably in the meanings that they assign to even the most common thinking skills. This confusion over definition manifests itself in three ways.

First, many definitions of thinking or of thinking skills are so vague that they fail to explain—and sometimes even mislead. Consider, for example, the definition of thinking as "the operating skill with which intelligence acts upon experience." Or witness the way this recently published explanation misleads: "Inquiry deals almost entirely with the convergent aspect of thinking." How helpful can such statements be in guiding the teaching of these skills?

Second, educators often define thinking skills inaccurately. For example, one prominent school system has developed a continuum of skills that lists "inquiry or recall" as a thinking skill, defines it as "to remember previously gained material," and further gives as its operational definitions "to differentiate between facts and opinions" and "to locate factual information

on a time line to answer specific questions." To equate inquiry with recall flies in the face of 80 years of thinking and research in education and psychology. To equate the processes involved in distinguishing fact from opinion with those involved in matching events with dates is inaccurate, to say the least.

Nor are the descriptions of thinking skills that have been devised by state education departments immune from similar confusion and error. One such agency lists the following behaviors as geographic skills: "describes the routes, reasons, and results of exploration at various historical times and places" and "describes the cultural contributions of an area studied and how they have affected the way things are done now in the area or other parts of the world."

One wonders what particular cognitive skills these behaviors are supposed to represent. Clearly, many educators would view them as examples of recall, not of higher-order thinking.

All too commonly, educators confuse skills with substantive generalizations, mistake simple recall for higher-order thinking, or focus on inappropriate behaviors as indicators of a particular skill. It is not surprising that students taught these "skills" may not do well on standardized tests of thinking skills; nor is it surprising that they may be befuddled when first exposed to programs that derive their scope and sequence from the thoughtful work of such scholars as Benjamin Bloom, J. P. Guilford, and Reuven Feuerstein.

The conflicting terminology we often use to describe the thinking skills we teach also demonstrates our confusion. Often we use the same word to denote different skills. For example, one widely used social studies textbook defines a conclusion as a generalization. However, a science textbook used at about the same grade level defines a conclusion as an explanation of similarities and differences; yet another textbook describes a conclusion simply as a summary. Moreover, we sometimes use labels with different meanings to stand for a single skill. For instance, many educators equate problem solving with decision making, and many others also equate reflective thinking with either or both of these—despite the fact that each phrase describes a particular set of subskills that are used in a unique order to accomplish a different kind of task. Meanwhile, the term *inquiry* seems to mean just about anything we stipulate it to mean.

Our inability to agree on the thinking skills that are essential for learning and our inability to arrive at commonly held definitions of the skills we do attempt to teach are both obstacles to professional dialogue, research, teaching, and assessment in this area. Students taught a given thinking skill by one teacher may not be able to perform that same skill as it is presented by another teacher—even one in the same district—or as it appears on a district, state, or national test. Clearing up the ambiguities regarding which thinking skills to teach and how we define each is an important first step toward improving the thinking skills of students. (See Appendix A of this book for a glossary of thinking skill names and related thinking terms.)

LACK OF KNOWLEDGE

A second obstacle to effective teaching and learning of thinking skills lies in our failure to identify with precision those cognitive operations that constitute the individual skills we choose to teach. For example, in what cognitive procedures do we engage when we compare two or more things? What goes on in our minds when we distinguish fact from opinion, apply a previously learned concept to new information, or generalize from specifics? If we knew the essential components of these thinking skills, we could devise better ways to teach these skills to students.

Unfortunately, there is a significant gap in the literature when it comes to specifying the cognitive components of many thinking skills. The work of such scholars as Hilda Taba, Louis Raths, and Benjamin Bloom could serve as a starting point for this task. However, until we can specify at least some of the cognitive steps involved in any given thinking skill, the teaching of that skill will remain largely hit or miss—a nebulous exercise with imprecise learning outcomes.

Unfortunately, many educators continue to view skills of all kinds as performances only, ignoring the fact that skills involve certain kinds of knowledge as well.[9] This knowledge includes rules that govern the use of a given skill and criteria or other information that enable us to use the skill more effectively. Such knowledge *informs* our execution of a specific skill. It is as much a part of that skill as are the procedures by which we operationalize the skill.

For example, one basic thinking skill is that of establishing relationships. In social studies, science, and language arts classes, we frequently ask students to identify or explain relationships among given pieces of information, events, conditions, people, and so on. Students often find it difficult to do so, largely because they don't know either the wide range of relationships that could exist among data or the distinguishing clues to and features of such relationships. Students have a better chance to make connections if they know how things might be connected (e.g., spatially, functionally, comparatively, temporally) and if they know the clues that distinguish each kind of relationship. But we often fail to teach the knowledge that enables students to use this and other thinking skills— largely because we do not clearly understand what knowledge and which procedural components underlie the thinking skills we seek to teach.

INAPPROPRIATE INSTRUCTION

Much (if not most) of what teachers do under the guise of skills teaching is really skills testing. Instead of providing explicit instruction on how to perform a given skill, teachers generally put students into situations that require them to perform that skill to the best of their ability.[10] This strategy assumes that, by requiring students to use a skill (however well or poorly they understand what they are doing), they will automatically learn to perform that skill correctly—a fallacious assumption.[11] Instead, such "teaching" is likely to reinforce inappropriate or incorrect executions of the skill, to lead students to develop alternative methods of arriving at correct answers without using the skill, and to frustrate some students.

Probably the most widely used approach to the teaching of thinking skills involves the use of structured hierarchies of teacher-generated questions, either written or oral. Most teachers and developers of instructional materials who use this teaching approach assume that, in their struggles to answer the questions, students will be forced to use the kinds of thinking skills that the questions are believed to elicit. And, if such questions are asked often enough, these educators believe, students will learn the skills that the questions force them to practice.

The most common kinds of questions used to teach thinking skills appear on printed worksheets or at the end of textbook chapters. Although these questions may seem to require students to use specific thinking skills, they are just as likely to encourage students simply to copy or to guess. Moreover, these written exercises rarely (if ever) provide step-by-step instructions on how to use specific thinking skills. Most important, too many of the questions in these exercises do not even evoke the thinking skills their authors intended them to elicit.

A sample "thinking skills" exercise published by a state education agency exemplifies the dimensions of this problem. Given a time line marked at intervals of 500 years, students are asked, "During which time period did people begin to use such things as steel, factories, and electric power?" The authors of this question claim that it evokes the skill of identifying a century during which a given event occurred. Of course, whether this is really a *thinking* skill is highly questionable. That issue aside, the question relates only peripherally to the "skill," since the accompanying time line is not even divided into centuries, nor does the question specify which people. If the question involves any skill at all, it is recall—remembering previously learned facts or generalizations. More likely than not, to answer this question a student must know when steel, factories, and electric power were first used by people in many different societies. This question may validly measure a number of skills—but not the skill that its authors intended. Incorrect responses to this question can be interpreted in many different ways, but they can scarcely be seen as reflecting only a student's inability to match an event with a century.

Such a question is not atypical of those presented by most instructional materials that purport to "teach" thinking skills. The fact that this question came from materials developed by a state education agency only serves to underscore the extent to which such poorly conceived items have permeated all levels of education. By accepting such questions as models and copying or imitating them, teachers believe that they are teaching specific thinking skills, when in fact they almost certainly are not.

Textbooks are also guilty of mixing teaching and testing, of not defining clearly the skills they purport to teach, and of failing to relate learning activities to specific thinking skills. Frequently, the guides that accompany textbooks suggest that teachers ask questions that require only yes/no answers, at best. For example, the guide for a textbook that seeks to teach the "skill" of distinguishing between evidence and hypotheses suggests such questions as, "Is the idea that the people of the Southwest were farming 5,000 years ago evidence of a hypothesis?" The specific thinking skills that a student would have to employ to answer such a question correctly are left unstated—for teachers as well as for students. More to the point, the textbook never tells readers, either directly or by example, how to engage in the skills that are needed to answer this question and others like it.

In these instructional omissions, this textbook is no different from most textbooks. Rare, indeed, is the textbook in any subject that provides instructional guidelines to students on how to engage in thinking. Even the most useful textbooks provide little more than a definition of each skill and examples of its use, often only in the form of multiple-choice questions. Students are generally left to infer whatever they can about exactly how to execute a skill. Virtually all textbooks omit the most crucial part of teaching a skill, i.e., making explicit its operational procedures. Because of this omission, textbooks create and reinforce the erroneous impression that we can best teach thinking skills by forcing students to answer questions that purport to be skill-related without giving them any direct instruction on how to answer such questions.

Teacher-generated "discussion" questions are a second device commonly employed to "teach" thinking skills. More than one school system has developed elaborate questioning strategies through which teachers are expected to elicit from students increasingly sophisticated thinking. This technique suffers from all the faults that characterize written questions, however. There is little evidence to justify the assumption that students who correctly answer "higher-level" questions also understand the cognitive tasks implied by the questions. For every research study that suggests that certain patterns of questioning by teachers improve students' thinking, there is another study that suggests no connection between teachers' questioning patterns and students' mastery of thinking skills.[12]

Without direct instruction on how to answer questions, students commonly try to guess what the teacher wants them to say. Thinking undoubtedly occurs in response to such questioning—but not always the type of thinking that the questioners intended. Nor is such thinking at a level of consciousness that allows students to capture, analyze, and learn the operations involved. Moreover, the use of hierarchies of teacher-initiated questions as the primary method of instruction in thinking skills contradicts the basic goal of such instruction, for it inhibits the development of learner autonomy that such instruction seeks to foster. Instruction that leads to systematic question-asking *by students* would be more appropriate, but such an approach is rare indeed.

Questions—whether on worksheets, in textbooks, or asked by teachers—do not, in and of themselves, teach thinking skills. At best, they provide only practice. At worst, they test. Educators and authors of instructional materials who persist in using such activities as the core of instruction in thinking skills simply delude themselves and others into believing that they are teaching thinking skills to students. In fact, they are not.

SKILLS OVERLOAD

A fourth obstacle to the effective teaching of thinking skills lies in what can best be described as skills overload: attempting to teach too many skills in too little time. This overload customarily manifests itself in three related ways.

The first symptom is the sheer number of skills that teachers attempt to teach. In an effort to remedy perceived deficiencies in skills, many authors of instructional materials and curriculum developers have emphasized the quantity of skills to be taught, not the quality of the teaching. It is not unusual to find science, language arts, and social studies curricula and textbooks today that claim to provide instruction in dozens of thinking skills within the span of a single school year. For example, in addition to offering instruction in 17 different thinking skills—from "conveying personal opinions" to "creating novel solutions"—one social studies textbook also claims to teach almost three dozen other geography, study, and research skills.

Second, as a consequence of seeking to "teach" a great many thinking skills in a relatively short time, most curricula and textbooks provide students with little more than one formal encounter with each skill. These encounters are often referred to in teachers' guides or in statements of objectives as "exposures." The implied hope is that such exposures will cause students to "catch" the target skills. But faith in happy accidents is no substitute for purposeful teaching. Learning a skill to any significant level of competence takes more than a single, vague encounter.

Finally, skills overload manifests itself by a general absence in school systems and in textbook series of developmental, sequential, or integrated curricula for teaching thinking skills. Most courses or textbooks—especially at the secondary level—seem to have been developed independently of one another. All too often, thinking skills that are introduced at one grade level are never reinforced or practiced in subsequent grades. Moreover, thinking skills that are introduced in one content area are rarely reinforced deliberately in other content areas at the same grade level. One sequence of skills in social studies, recently proposed by a state education agency, introduces the skill of problem identification in the third grade, mentions it again in the sixth grade, and ignores it thereafter. Unfortunately, such a skills program—whether developed by a state agency, a local school district, or a textbook publisher—is not atypical. Because coherent, sequential instructional programs that focus on thinking skills are not widely available, teachers usually find it impossible to relate their teaching efforts to those of teachers in previous or subsequent grades. Instead, the thinking skills that are introduced or taught in any given classroom reflect the idiosyncrasies of the individual teacher—and students may or may not learn them.

INAPPROPRIATE ASSESSMENT

As unlikely as it may seem, tests of thinking skills, as they currently exist and are used, may actually be a fifth obstacle to the effective learning of thinking skills. At the moment, these tests seem to determine the teaching that goes on in most of our schools. And the quality of these tests leaves much to be desired.

Many school systems launch their teaching programs by creating or adopting tests to measure what they believe is proficiency in the thinking skills they want students to master. Such decisions are often made without carefully evaluating the nature and appropriateness of the skills covered by the tests, without communicating to teachers precise descriptions of these skills, and without developing instructional programs to teach these skills systematically.

Tests of thinking skills suffer from at least two general flaws. First, almost all of them suffer from conceptual inadequacy. They measure discrete skills in isolation, ignoring, by and large, students' ability to engage in sequences of cognitive operations. Years ago, Harold Berlak pointed out the dangers in assuming that measures of students' performance of isolated thinking skills adequately measure such basic processes as critical thinking or problem solving.[13] Yet test makers continue to offer tests that measure almost exclusively students' performance of discrete thinking skills.

Specific items—especially in locally developed tests of thinking skills—are also suspect. For example, some school systems have developed tests that use students' recall to evaluate their proficiency in inquiry. This is merely a symptom of the larger problem: inadequate definition of the components of the skills that are tested. In many instances, items on tests of thinking skills bear no relation to the skills these tests purport to evaluate.

The problems with such tests are exacerbated by the uses to which the tests are often put. Teachers often use test items designed to measure competence in particular thinking skills as prototypes for the instructional materials they prepare to help their students learn these skills. Much so-called teaching of thinking skills consists largely of giving students practice in answering old test questions, a procedure that probably focuses students' attention more on question-answering techniques than on the specific cognitive skills that are the intended outcomes of such activities.

An even more serious problem with the testing of thinking skills is that professional test developers fail to share with teachers the descriptions or models of skills that they use (if indeed they use any) in developing test items. Nor do they say which specific behaviors indicate competence in these skills. Lacking such information, teachers can only try to teach prescribed skills as best they know how. Two of the most popular tests of critical thinking measure quite different skills—and neither measures those skills that most classroom teachers try to teach as critical thinking skills.[14] Without a common awareness of and agreement on the components of skills selected for testing, teachers are bound to provide hit-or-miss instruction at best.

Finally, the whole aura surrounding tests of thinking skills seems likely to weaken instruction in these skills. Once it has developed and implemented an achievement test devoted to thinking skills, a school system may be lulled into believing that students' scores on this instrument are the only valid measures of the learning and teaching of these skills. In reality, such tests may not even measure the competencies they are intended to measure.

In fact, commercial or teacher-made tests using multiple-choice items may be the *least useful* way to measure students' thinking skills. The best measure of students' ability to think may be their behavior as they sift through data to arrive at a conclusion or as they go about solving a problem. The development of instruments or observation techniques that can measure such behavior ought to be a major priority of test makers. Using carefully constructed and valid instruments to evaluate students' competence for both diagnostic and summative purposes is to be applauded. But it seems reasonable to expect congruence between the skills being tested, the techniques used to measure competence in these skills, and the nature of the skills being taught. Too often, such congruence is lacking in programs intended to teach and test thinking skills.

WHAT NEXT?

If we are to improve the thinking skills of our students, as some national leaders and a significant proportion of the public now demand that we do, then we must clearly identify the changes that we must make in our teaching. This requires first an honest appraisal of what we now do with regard to the teaching of thinking skills. I have attempted here to describe the "state of the art" of teaching thinking skills and to identify and clearly define the things we do that may keep our students from learning to think better.

NOTES

[1] See, for example, John Dewey, *How We Think* (Boston: D. C. Heath, 1910); *The Study of History in the Schools* (New York: American Historical Association, 1899); "ED Calls for 'No-Nonsense' Approach to Education," *Higher Education Daily*, 24 November 1981, p. 5; and National Commission on Excellence in Education, *A Nation at Risk* (Washington, DC: U.S. Government Printing Office, 1983).

[2] "Students Lack Analytical Skills, NAEP Says," *Report on Education Research*, 25 November 1981, pp. 1–2; *Reading, Thinking, and Writing: Results* from the *1979–80 National Assessment of Reading and Literature* (Denver: National Assessment of Educational Progress, 1981); Susan Walton and Thomas Toch, "Competency Tests Linked to Decline in Analytic Skills," *Education Week*, 8 December 1982, pp. 1, 17; Gene Maeroff, "Teaching to Think: A New Emphasis in Schools and Colleges," *New York Times Magazine*, 9 January 1983, pp. 1, 37; and Thomas Toch, "That Noble and Most Sovereign Reason—States, School Districts Display Growing Interest in the Teaching of Thinking Skills," *Education Week*, 9 June 1982, pp. 7, 16.

[3] Ernest J. Sternglass and Steven Bell, "Fallout and SAT Scores: Evidence for Cognitive Damage During Early Infancy," *Phi Delta Kappan*, April 1983, pp. 539–45; and Maeroff, "Teaching to Think."

[4] See, for example, Lynne Ames, "The Need: Teachers Who Can Make Them Think," *New York Times Magazine*, 9 January 1983, pp. 40–41; and Catherine Cornbleth and Willard Korth, "If Remembering, Understanding, and Reasoning Are Important . . .," *Social Education*, April 1981, pp. 276, 278–79.

[5] Hilda Taba, "Implementing Thinking as an Objective in Social Studies," in Jean Fair and Fannie R. Shaftel, eds., *Effective Thinking in the Social Studies* (Washington, DC: National Council for the Social Studies, 1967), p. 26.

[6] See, for example, the materials produced by the Institute for the Advancement of Philosophy for Children, Montclair State College, Upper Montclair, NJ.

[7] Benjamin Bloom et al., *Taxonomy of Educational Objectives—Handbook I: Cognitive Domain* (New York: David McKay, 1956).

[8] This school system will remain nameless, as will all other sources of specific examples that I cite here. The intent of such examples is not to embarrass; similar examples could as easily be found in the instructional materials produced by dozens of other school systems, state education agencies, or commercial publishers. I present these particular examples simply to demonstrate that my assertions are based on hard evidence, not on supposition. By providing such examples, I also hope to encourage educators to examine their own practices for similar flaws.

[9] See, for example, David Pratt, *Curriculum Design and Development* (New York: Harcourt, Brace, Jovanovich, 1980), pp. 312–14; and Robert H. Ennis, "A Concept of Critical Thinking," *Harvard Educational Review*, Winter 1962, pp. 81–111.

[10] Catherine Cornbleth and Willard Korth, "In Search of Academic Instruction," *Educational Researcher*, May 1980, p. 9; and Cornbleth and Korth, "If Remembering, Understanding, and Reasoning Are Important . . . ."

[11] Edward de Bono, *Teaching Thinking* (London: Maurice Temple Smith, 1976), p. 104.

[12] Meredith D. Gall, "The Use of Questions in Teaching," *Review of Educational Research*, December 1970, pp. 707–21; Philip H. Winne, "Experiments Relating Teachers' Use of Higher Cognitive Questions to Student Achievement," *Review of Educational Research*, Winter 1979, pp. 13–49; and Doris L. Redfield and Elaine Weldman Rousseau, "A Meta-Analysis of Experimental Research on Teacher Questioning Behavior," *Review of Educational Research*, Summer 1981, pp. 237–45.

[13] Harold Berlak, "New Curricula and Measurement of Thinking," *Educational Forum*, March 1966, p. 309.

[14] John E. McPeek, *Critical Thinking and Education* (New York: St. Martin's Press, 1981), pp. 132–50.

II

Thinking: Building Common Understandings

The efficient man is the man who thinks for himself.

—*CHARLES W. ELIOT*

Introduction

ARTHUR L. COSTA

Teachers often say to students, "Now think about it," "Think hard," or "Let's put on our thinking caps." Teachers rarely agree, however, about exactly what they expect to go on inside a student's head. Often, students don't have a clear idea of what it means to think, and, as they progress from teacher to teacher over the elementary years or as they pass from teacher to teacher during a secondary school day, they find that each teacher means something different by "think about it."

Senge (1990) suggests that a culture is people thinking together. As individuals share meaning, and as they become more skillful in employing thinking operations and habits, they renegotiate the organization's value system, changing the practices and beliefs of the entire organization. By employing thinking skills, the group mind illuminates issues, solves problems, and accommodates differences. The shared focus on thinking helps create a common vision.

As individuals, we organize ourselves around identities and beliefs. When we voluntarily join groups, it is usually because we want to ally ourselves with the causes and values those groups represent. Similarly, schools organize into communities in the process of determining purpose, values, and vision. A shared identity creates a powerful sense of direction. Without a common purpose, values, and vision, the school will be fragmented and lacking congruence and integrity. Pettiness, competition, and self-serving behavior will be prevalent. However, with a shared focus on thinking and intellectual development as outcomes, the school creates partnerships that transcend traditional boundaries, roles, and grade levels and make stakeholders feel responsible for the whole. Staff, parents, and students become committed to a shared destiny—for the students, for themselves, and for the organization.

Bohm (1990, pp. 7–8) writes insightfully about the importance of coherent, unified thinking:

The power of a group . . . could be compared to a laser. Ordinary light is called "incoherent," which means that it is going in all sorts of directions, and the light waves are not in phase with each other so they don't build up. But a laser produces a very intense beam that is coherent. The light waves build up strength because they are all going in the same direction. This beam can do all sorts of things that ordinary light cannot.

. . . Ordinary thought in society is incoherent—it is going in all sorts of directions with thoughts conflicting and canceling each other out. But if people were to think together in a coherent way, [the organization] would have tremendous power.

To live and learn in an incoherent organization, people must devote considerable energy to staying out of one another's way. By contrast, when people are standing "shoulder to shoulder" and heading in the same direction, they can focus their energy on moving forward. If educators can collectively agree on the thinking behaviors they value, they have a better chance of realizing the ultimate goal of building a learning organization for all members of the school community.

The purpose of this section is to bring coherence to our views of thinking to learn and learning to think. Toward that end, the chapters illuminate, define, and describe various thinking skills, processes, and dispositions. The glossary at the end of this book provides additional definitions of terms associated with cognition, teaching for thinking, and intellectual development.

Robert Ennis opens this section with a chapter that clearly categorizes critical thinking dispositions and abilities and outlines the goals of a critical thinking curriculum. Barbara Presseisen then analyzes and clarifies a range of thinking terms and processes. The following chapters explore in depth three tasks that require skillful thinking: Jack Lochhead and Aletta Zietsman discuss problem solving, Robert Swartz covers decision making, and Gerard Puccio and Mary Murdock address creative thinking.

Teaching students the steps and procedures of particular thinking skills, of course, is not enough to ensure their success. Students must also possess the desire and capacity to persevere when confronted with problems that require sustained mental effort over time. Shari Tishman believes that educators should try to foster thinking dispositions—intellectual character traits—rather than focusing on skills. Jonathan Baron argues that open-mindedness is one key trait. Arthur Costa describes 16 "habits of mind" that characterize effective thinkers in many walks of life. Finally, Barry Beyer closes this section by exploring the role of philosophy and its contribution to the teaching of thinking.

The purpose of this section is not only to provide definitions, but also to encourage all those involved in education to seek more congruence about what "teaching for effective thinking" means. By reaching a common understanding, standards and expectations become more precise, a shared vision develops about the attributes of effective thinkers, stakeholders agree on their goals, and teachers, parents, and community members can monitor and model desirable thinking behaviors.

REFERENCES

Bohm, D. (1990). *On dialogue*. Dayton, OH: Institute for the Development of Educational Activities.

Senge, P. (1990). *The fifth discipline: The art and practice of the learning organization*. New York: Doubleday Currency.

8

Goals for a Critical Thinking Curriculum and Its Assessment

Robert H. Ennis

Critical thinking, as the term is generally used these days, roughly means reasonable and reflective thinking focused on deciding what to believe or do. In doing such thinking, it is helpful to employ the dispositions and abilities outlined in this chapter. These can also serve as a set of comprehensive goals for a critical thinking curriculum and for guiding its assessment.

This chapter is intended to be pedagogically and psychometrically useful, not theoretically elegant. The categories overlap on occasion. It outlines critical thinking content only, without specifying grade level, curriculum sequence, emphasis, teaching approach, or type of subject matter involved (such as standard content in a given discipline, content for everyday living, and vocational content). Qualifications and more detail can be found in *Critical Thinking* (Ennis, 1996).

DISPOSITIONS

Ideal critical thinkers are characterized by three broad dispositions. First, they tend to care that their beliefs be true[1] and their decisions be justified; that is, they care to "get it right" to the extent possible. This disposition involves the subdispositions to (a) seek alternative hypotheses, explanations, conclusions, plans, sources, and so forth, and be open to them; (b) endorse a position to the extent that, but only to the extent that, it is justified by the information available; (c) be well informed;[2] and (d) consider seriously other points of view besides their own.

Second, ideal critical thinkers tend to care about presenting a position honestly and clearly, whether theirs or another's. This involves the subdispositions to (a) be clear about the intended meaning of what is said, written, or otherwise communicated, seeking as much precision as the situation requires; (b) determine and maintain focus on the conclusion or question; (c) seek and offer reasons; (d) take into account

the total situation; and (e) be reflectively aware of their own basic beliefs.

These first two major dispositions are *constitutive* dispositions. That is, they are by definition part of this conception of critical thinking. The third major disposition is a *correlative* one—not integral to critical thinking, but a desirable accompaniment whose absence would make critical thinking less valuable, or even dangerous. This third broad disposition involves concern for the dignity and worth of every person.[3] This includes the subdispositions to (a) discover and listen to others' views and reasons; (b) avoid intimidating or confusing others with one's own critical thinking prowess, taking into account others' feelings and level of understanding; and (c) be concerned about others' welfare.

ABILITIES

In addition to the three broad dispositions outlined above, ideal critical thinkers have 15 key abilities. These fall into two main categories: *constitutive* abilities that are at the very core of critical thinking, and *auxiliary* abilities that are helpful but not intrinsic.

THE CONSTITUTIVE ABILITIES

Twelve critical thinking abilities are classified as constitutive. The first three involve elementary clarification skills. They are

- The ability to *focus on a question*, including identifying or formulating a question, identifying or formulating criteria for judging possible answers, and keeping the situation—including the question—in mind.
- The ability to *analyze arguments*, including identifying conclusions, identifying both stated and unstated reasons,

identifying and handling irrelevance, seeing the structure of an argument, and summarizing.

- The ability to *ask and answer questions of clarification or challenge*. These might include: Why? What is your main point? What do you mean by . . . ? What would be an example? What would come close but not qualify as an example? How does that apply to this case? What difference does it make? What are the facts? Are you saying that . . . ? Would you tell me more about that?

Two other critical thinking abilities address the basis for a decision:

- The ability to *judge the credibility of a source*. Major criteria (but not necessary conditions) for credibility include expertise, reputation, known risk to reputation,[4] lack of conflict of interest, agreement with other sources, use of established procedures, ability to give reasons, and careful habits.
- The ability to *make observations and judge observation reports* is a related characteristic of the ideal critical thinker. Major criteria (but not necessary conditions) for strong performance include minimal inferring in making the observation, a short time interval between the observation and the report, first-hand observation rather than hearsay, provision of records, corroboration (or at least the possibility of such), good access, competent use of technology, if applicable, and satisfaction by the observer and the reporter (if a different person) of the criteria for the credibility of sources (using the criteria noted above).

The third group of abilities involve inference:

- The ability to *deduce and to judge whether an argument is deductively valid*. Ideal critical thinkers understand elementary class logic (which deals with sets or groups) and conditional logic (including "if-then" reasoning). Furthermore, they can employ and interpret logical terminology in statements, including negation and double negation, references to "necessary and sufficient conditions," and such words as "only," "if and only if," "or," "some," "unless," and "not both."
- The ability to *induce and to judge whether an argument is inductively valid*. This may take the form of reasoning from particulars to generalizations. In such cases, broad consideration is given to the likely typicality of the data—including sampling where appropriate—and to the breadth of coverage.

Another form of inductive thinking leads to and evaluates explanatory conclusions (including hypotheses). The major types of explanatory conclusions and hypotheses are causal claims, scientific laws, claims about the beliefs and attitudes of people, interpretation of authors' intended meanings, historical claims that certain things happened (including criminal accusations), reported definitions, and claims that a given proposition is an unstated reason. This form of induction often involves certain investigative activities: designing experiments (including planning to control variables); seeking evidence and counterevidence; and seeking other possible explanations. There are three essential criteria for a conclusive explanatory argument: (a) the proposed conclusion explains the evidence; (b) the proposed conclusion is consistent with all known facts; and (c) competing explanations are inconsistent with the facts. An additional criterion, while not essential, is desirable: the proposed conclusion seems plausible.

- The ability to *make and evaluate value judgments*. Important factors in this thinking process are an understanding of the situation, including the background facts, and the consequences of accepting or rejecting the judgment; prima facie application of acceptable principles; the existence of alternatives; and skill in balancing, weighing, and deciding.

Recall that the first group of abilities discussed at the beginning of this section involved elementary clarification. The next two involve advanced clarification:

- The ability to *define terms and judge definitions*. Three dimensions of definitions are form, strategy, and content. The major forms are synonym, classification, range, equivalent expression, and operational and example-nonexample definition. Definitional strategy involves a choice among possible definitional acts. Three types of acts are reporting a meaning, stipulating a meaning, or expressing a position on an issue (including "programmatic" and "persuasive" definitions). But identifying and handling equivocation is also part of the strategy for judging definition and word usage. The content of a definition should responsibly suit the definitional act being performed. For example, the content of a reported definition should accurately reflect usage.
- The ability to *attribute unstated assumptions*. Although this is an advanced clarification skill, it also relates to inference. Often one attributes the assumption that produces the strongest overall argument (the principle of charity).

Ideal critical thinkers demonstrate two other notable abilities:

- The ability to *engage in "suppositional thinking"*—to consider and reason from premises, reasons, assumptions, positions, and other propositions that they doubt or disagree with, without letting the doubt or disagreement interfere with their thinking.

- The ability to *integrate the other critical thinking abilities and dispositions* in making and defending a decision.

THE AUXILIARY ABILITIES

The next three critical thinking abilities are the auxiliary ones. They are very helpful to have, but not constitutive of being a critical thinker:

- The ability to *proceed in an orderly manner appropriate to the situation*. This includes, for example, following problem-solving steps, monitoring one's own thinking (that is, engaging in metacognition), and employing a reasonable critical thinking checklist.
- The ability to *be sensitive to the feelings, level of knowledge, and degree of sophistication of others*.
- The ability to *employ appropriate rhetorical strategies* in discussion and presentation (both oral and written). This includes understanding "fallacy" labels such as "circularity," "bandwagon," "post hoc," "equivocation," "non sequitur," and "straw person." These labels are useful to know and understand (at least as shorthand), but because they can be intimidating and easy to misapply, they are dangerous when used by, or in the company of, people who do not understand them fully.[5]

SUMMARY AND COMMENTS

In brief, the ideal critical thinker is disposed to care to "get it right," to care to present a position honestly and clearly, and to care about the worth and dignity of every person. Additionally, the ideal critical thinker has the ability to clarify, to seek and judge well the basis for a view, to infer wisely from the basis, to suppose and integrate imaginatively, and to do these things with dispatch, sensitivity, and rhetorical skill.

In outlining these critical thinking dispositions and abilities, I have attempted only to depict, and not defend, them. The defense would require much more space than is available, but would follow two general paths: (a) examining the traditions of good thinking in successful disciplines of inquiry, and (b) seeing how we go wrong when we attempt to decide what to believe or do.

In every teaching situation, all of the critical thinking dispositions, as well as the abilities involving supposition and in-

tegration and the auxiliary abilities, are applicable all the time. This holds true whether the setting is a separate critical thinking course or module, one in which the critical thinking content is embedded in standard subject-matter content, or some mixture or variant of these two.

There is much more to all of these topics, but here my intention was to outline a usable, comprehensive, and defensible set of critical thinking goals, including criteria for making judgments. Goals are the place to start. I hope that this outline provides a useful basis on which to build curricula and assessment procedures.

NOTES

This chapter is based on a presentation at the Sixth International Conference on Thinking at the Massachusetts Institute of Technology, Cambridge, MA, July, 1994. I have revised the structure and added information from Ennis (1985, 1996). Readers will find further thoughts on the nature of critical thinking and the issues of curriculum and assessment on my academic Web site, http://faculty.ed.uiuc.edu/rhennis/.

[1]Epistemological constructivism holds that truth is constructed. In suggesting that critical thinkers care about true beliefs, I accept the view that we construct our concepts and vocabulary, but I also maintain (to oversimplify somewhat) that we do not construct the relationships among the referents of our concepts and terms. We can have true or false beliefs about these.

Pedagogical constructivism is the view that students learn best when they construct their own answers to problems and questions. For some (but not all) goals and types of learning, this view has empirical support, but it should not be confused with epistemological constructivism. In particular, the validity of pedagogical constructivism (insofar as it is valid) does not imply the validity of epistemological constructivism. They are totally different ideas.

[2]Several other subdispositions (specifically, the willingness to consider other viewpoints, awareness of one's basic beliefs, and the inclination to discover and listen to others' positions) contribute to being well-informed, but they are distinct and important enough to be listed separately.

[3]Some people might argue that critical thinking should, by definition, include caring for the worth and dignity of every person, apparently assuming that critical thinking encompasses every positive form of thought. This is an overwhelming and unreasonable requirement indeed.

[4]The source should be aware that his or her reputation could and would be diminished by being shown to be wrong.

[5]The constitutive abilities involve appropriate competence in applying fallacy labels; this is not solely a rhetorical skill.

REFERENCES AND OTHER SOURCES

Ennis, R. H. (1985). A logical basis for measuring critical thinking skills. *Educational Leadership, 43*(2), 44–48.

Ennis, R. H. (1987). A taxonomy of critical thinking dispositions and abilities. In J. B. Baron & R. J. Sternberg (Eds.), *Teaching thinking skills: Theory and practice,* (pp. 9–26). New York: W. H. Freeman.

Ennis, R. H. (1996). *Critical thinking.* Upper Saddle River, NJ: Prentice Hall.

9

Thinking Skills: Meanings and Models Revisited

Barbara Z. Presseisen

It is not best that we should all think alike: it is difference of opinion which makes horse races.

—*Mark Twain*

Many tasks confront educators as they plan for teaching thinking in the curriculum. Few are more critical than determining what is meant by thinking and developing a model of the thinking process.

Essential Thinking Skills

Thinking is generally assumed to be a cognitive process, a mental act by which knowledge is acquired. Although cognition may encompass several ways of knowing something—including perception, reasoning, and intuition—the current emphasis in thinking skills is on *reasoning* as a major cognitive skill. Consider, for example, the following definitions of thinking:

- "The mental derivation of mental elements (thoughts) from perceptions and the mental manipulation/combination of these thoughts" (Cohen, 1971, p. 5).
- "The mental manipulation of sensory input to formulate thoughts, reason about, or judge" (Beyer, 1984).
- "The extension of evidence in accord with that evidence so as to fill up gaps in the evidence: and this is done by moving through a succession of interconnected steps which may be stated at the time, or left till later to be stated" (Bartlett, 1958, p. 75).

Several interesting aspects underlie these definitions of thinking. Thinking processes are related to other kinds of behavior and require active involvement on the part of the thinker. Notable products of thinking—thoughts, knowledge, reasons—and higher processes, like judging, problem solving, and critical analysis, can also be generated. Complex relationships are developed through thinking, as in the use of evidence over time. These relationships may be interconnected to an organized structure and may be expressed by the thinker in a variety of ways. If anything, these definitions indicate that thinking is a complex and reflective endeavor as well as a creative experience. Such meanings are highly reminiscent of Dewey's original 1910 writing (see Dewey, 1933).

Current literature on thinking offers multiple lists of cognitive processes that can be considered thinking skills. It is dangerous to confuse one level of thinking with another in terms of its power or significance. In Chapter 7 of this volume, Barry Beyer stresses the importance of defining skills accurately and suggests reviewing the work of researchers like Bloom, Guilford, and Feuerstein to find useful definitions. Clear definitions, Beyer maintains, do not confuse distinctly different processes like inquiry and simple recall. Furthermore, consistent with other researchers of cognitive processes, Beyer distinguishes between lower, essential skills and complex, multiple-process strategies. For example, there is great difference between picking identical examples of a particular insect and finding the antidote to the sting of the same insect. One task involves the basic processes of identification and comparison; the other requires multiple, sophisticated, replicable, and sequential steps of problem solving.

What are the basic, essential skills of thinking? Nickerson (1981) suggests that no one taxonomy exists. Educators would be wise, he advises, to decide what they want students to be able to do and incorporate these particular skills into their curricula and school programs. Researchers' lists can be the basis of such selections, and a number of such resources are now available (Marzano et al., 1988). Consider, for example, the categories of skills suggested by Bloom, Englehart, Furst, Hill, and Krathwohl (1956) and Guilford (1967).

Bloom's Taxonomy	Guilford's Structure of Intellect
Knowledge	Units
Comprehension	Classes
Application	Relations
Analysis	Systems
Synthesis	Transformations
Evaluation	Implications

Each of Bloom's cognitive categories includes a variety of thinking skills and indicates the kind of behavior students are to perform as the objectives or goals of specific learning tasks. For example:

- **Knowledge:** Define, recognize, recall, identify, label, understand, examine, show, collect.
- **Comprehension:** Translate, interpret, explain, describe, summarize, extrapolate.
- **Application:** Apply, solve, experiment, show, predict.
- **Analysis:** Connect, relate, differentiate, classify, arrange, check, group, distinguish, organize, categorize, detect, compare, infer.
- **Synthesis:** Produce, propose, design, plan, combine, formulate, compose, hypothesize, construct.
- **Evaluation:** Appraise, judge, criticize, decide.

Some of these tasks are also evident in Guilford's six categories. For example:

- Recognizing a particular object is a *units* skill.
- Showing a group of similarly colored or shaped objects is a *classes*-based task.
- Forming a geometric structure out of six matchsticks is a *systems* task.

In both researchers' work, there are some unstated dimensions to the thinking skills sequence. Tasks generally move from simpler to more complex operations, from observable and concrete to abstract dimensions, and from an emphasis on working with known materials toward an emphasis on creating or inventing new, previously unknown approaches or materials. Guilford is interested in both convergent and divergent operations, and his ultimate goal is a thorough exposition of the nature of intelligence.

Since the initial work of Bloom and Guilford, a greater concern for the developmental appropriateness of tasks or thinking skills has emerged. Hudgins's (1977) study of thinking and learning emphasizes Piaget's research on the develop-ment of thinking processes as children grow intellectually. This research assumes that children's cognitive development will follow a regular sequence, but not precisely correlated to age. Piaget (1970) suggests that youngsters first entering school are mostly "preoperational," or dominated by their perceptions. Gradually, and depending on the quality of their mental interactions, students develop systematic explanations or concrete rules for resolving conflicts or explaining diverse phenomena; they form conceptualizations. By their early teens, most students develop the ability to perform higher forms of cognitive operations: they learn to vary interpretations or descriptions in abstract form and to construct formal explanations of cause and effect. Goleman (1995) and Elias and colleagues (1997) stress that such cognitive operations also relate to social and emotional learning occurring during the same period. Somehow, says Hudgins, the scope of thinking skills expressed in a K–12 curriculum needs to relate to this developmental and cumulative sequence, as well as to the empirical research it represents. The relationship of particular subject matter to the specific skills to be learned also may be of developmental consequence.

Despite American educators' interest in teaching thinking, many students do *not* learn to think effectively (Presseisen, 1988). They do not become proficient in the essential, or basic, thinking skills. Some students fail to complete their schooling and either are pushed out or drop out of school before graduation. Others continue through the system but do not learn to use their minds independently or are unable to perform the higher-order thinking skills associated with adult behavior. This is a population at risk, whether they have failed to be "mediated," as Feuerstein (1980) suggests, or whether they cannot master the tasks of complex information demands, as Sternberg (1983) sees the problem. These students face great obstacles in a world that increasingly requires them to think. In addition, suggest Comer, Haynes, Joyner, and Ben-Avie (1995), young people are particularly dependent on schools for learning such skills.

Another issue concerns the various models of thinking and types of symbol systems that are available to learners. Much school learning involves linguistic or verbal abilities as well as quantitative, numerical skills. Spatial or visual depictions of mental processing are becoming more significant to instruction, especially with the advent of video and computer technologies in the classroom. How do these different modes of thinking influence cognitive development? How can different approaches to learning be incorporated into instruction to enhance skill development for every youngster, regardless of cultural or socioeconomic background? Today these are open research questions in teaching thinking and expanding intelligence (Presseisen, 1999).

The testing of basic cognitive ability is another field currently in flux. Although lower-level skills of memorization and recall are still part of nearly every standardized test battery, researchers generally agree that it is equally important to assess more complex cognitive operations and creative relationships, like the use of metaphors and analogies. Differing modalities appear on student tests. For example, the Developing Cognitive Abilities Test (1980) is designed around a content format that uses Bloom's taxonomy and a three-mode organization of content—verbal, quantitative, and spatial—for students in grades 2–12. Other emergent thinking assessments, including statewide and national standardized tests in the United States, now stress performance rather than mere information acquisition and emphasize the use of thinking skills in various modalities within an integrated content approach (Baron, Forgione, Rindone, Kruglanski, & Davey, 1989). Formats of continuous progress and the gradual building of portfolio collections of student work are yet other current directions for assessing students' thinking in essential skills (Wolf, 1989).

There are a host of candidates, then, for a taxonomy of basic thinking skills. In planning a curricular sequence, teachers should consider the developmental level of the learners, the mode of presenting information to them, the subject matter involved, and the testing program to assess mastery. At least five categories of thinking skills merit consideration: qualifying, classifying, finding relationships, transforming, and drawing conclusions. Figure 9.1 elaborates on each of these. This taxonomy of essential thinking skills is not the only one possible, of course; Marzano and his colleagues (1988, p. 69) present an alternative that includes 21 core skills in eight categories. What is important is that educators develop and use a common design to link essential skills to higher-order, more complex operations.

COMPLEX THINKING PROCESSES

The five categories suggested in figure 9.1 are essential thinking skills. The complex processes involved in thinking skills programs—the "macro-process strategies"—incorporate essential skills but use them for a particular purpose. Cohen (1971, p. 26) distinguishes processes that rely on external stimuli and seek to be productive, such as making judgments or resolving problems, from processes that depend about equally on exter-

—Figure 9.1—
A Taxonomy of Basic Thinking Skills

From simple to complex development

Qualifying (finding unique characteristics)
- Recognizing units of basic identity
- Defining
- Gathering facts
- Recognizing tasks/problems

Classifying (determining common qualities)
- Recognizing similarities and differences
- Grouping and sorting
- Comparing
- Making "either/or" distinctions

Finding Relationships (detecting regular operations)
- Relating parts and wholes
- Seeing patterns
- Analyzing
- Synthesizing
- Recognizing sequences and order
- Making deductions

Transforming (relating known to unknown)
- Making analogies
- Creating metaphors
- Making initial inductions

Drawing Conclusions (assessing)
- Identifying cause and effect
- Making distinctions
- Inferring
- Evaluating

nal and internal stimuli and seek to be creative. He suggests at least four different complex thinking processes:

• **Problem solving:** Using basic thinking processes to resolve a known or defined difficulty; assemble facts about the difficulty and determine additional information needed; infer or suggest alternate solutions and test them for appropriateness; potentially reduce to simpler levels of explanation and eliminate discrepancies; provide solution checks for generalizable value.

• **Decision making:** Using basic thinking processes to choose the best response among several options; assemble information needed in a topic area; compare advantages and disadvantages of alternative approaches; determine what additional information is required; select the most effective response and be able to justify it.

• **Critical thinking:** Using basic thinking processes to analyze arguments and generate insight into particular meanings and interpretations; develop cohesive, logical reasoning patterns and understand assumptions and biases underlying particular positions; attain a credible, concise, and convincing style of presentation or argument.

• **Creative thinking:** Using basic thinking processes to develop or invent novel, aesthetic, constructive ideas or products from percepts as well as concepts. Stresses the initiative aspects of thinking as much as the rational. Emphasis is on using known information or material to generate the possible, as well as to elaborate on the thinker's original perspective or design.

These complex processes obviously draw on and expand the underlying essential skills. Certain of the essential skills may be more significant to one complex process than another, but current research has not clarified such relationships. What seems most important to developing effective thinkers is building on an appropriate foundation. Learners should develop early competence, and then in middle or junior high school be introduced to the more complex processes in specific content matter that is closely related to the use of such skills.

Middle school or early junior high school is an appropriate time for beginning instruction about higher-order skills or complex thinking processes. The adolescent learner's growing cognitive capacities are ripe for the challenges of more complex thinking (Presseisen, 1982). Elementary students can benefit from early exposure to varied thinking processes and different modes of presentation, but they probably can approach more complex sequences only as they gain experience and apply similar skills in multiple content areas. In Chapter 7 of this volume, Beyer suggests that an effective thinking skills curriculum will introduce only a limited number of skills at a particular grade level, will teach these across all appropriate content areas, and will vary the modes and content of presen-

tation. Subsequent grades should enlarge the thinking skills base and provide additional, and more elaborate, applications of skills already introduced.

Some complex thinking processes may be more relevant to certain subject areas than to others. For example, problem-solving skills seem ideal for mathematics or science instruction. Decision making might be especially useful for social studies and vocational studies; critical thinking might be more relevant for the debate team, language arts class, and courses in democracy or American government. Creative thinking might enhance all subjects but be particularly meaningful in art, music, or literature programs. Most important, the goals of the specific complex process and the objectives for learning in a given subject area should be parallel and reinforcing.

Figure 9.2 presents a suggested model of complex thinking processes, noting the essential skills that underlie each. This model is not necessarily comprehensive; potential additions might be examined in terms of how they compare to these four complex processes, the underlying skills, and the ultimate outcomes. Kuhn's (1999) recent work, for example, elaborates extensively on critical thinking.

METACOGNITION AND THINKING

A useful taxonomy of thinking must somehow account for metacognitive aspects of the current thinking skills movement. According to Flavell (1976, p. 232), " 'metacognition' refers to one's knowledge concerning one's own cognitive processes and products." Learners must actively monitor their use of thinking processes and regulate them according to their cognitive objectives. Henle (1966) considers such regulation the essence of autonomous self-education. Costa (1991) sug-

—*Figure 9.2*—
A Model of Complex Thinking Skills

	Problem Solving	**Decision Making**	**Critical Thinking**	**Creative Thinking**
Task:	Resolve a known difficulty	Choose the best alternative	Understand particular meanings	Create novel or aesthetic ideas or products
Essential Skills Emphasized:	Transforming Conclusions	Classifying Relationships	Relationships Transforming Conclusions	Qualifying Relationships Transforming
Yields:	Solution Generalization (potentially)	Assessment	Sound reasons Proof Theory	New meanings Pleasing products

gests that this ability to "know what we know and what we don't know" is a uniquely human trait, but not necessarily one that all adults acquire. He proposes metacognitive skills as a key attribute of formula thinking or higher-process skills instruction, and stresses that the teacher's classroom methodology must constructively deal with metacognition. Other researchers maintain that metacognitive skills are also significant factors in developing subject-skilled performers.

One of the most salient characteristics of metacognition is that it involves growing consciousness. One becomes more aware of the thinking processes themselves and their specific procedures, as well as more conscious of oneself as a thinker and performer. As learners acquire understanding of what the various thinking processes are, they can better understand and apply them. Thus, some researchers, such as Beyer and Feuerstein, suggest that, initially, thinking skills be taught directly and in relatively content-free situations.

Metacognitive thinking has two main dimensions. The first is task-oriented and relates to monitoring the actual performance of a skill. The second dimension is strategic: It involves selecting a strategy appropriate to the circumstances and seeking feedback to affirm or alter that choice. Figure 9.3 illustrates these dimensions of metacognition.

Monitoring task performance requires learners to be aware of their own activities. Students cannot tell if they are at the right place if they do not know the assigned task, the directions for completing it, and the sequence of steps they should follow. They might be advised to discriminate subgoals of a task and relate them to ultimate objectives. In a mathematics reading problem involving averaging, for example, students might identify addition as the first step and division as the second step in determining the answer. Detecting errors while working may involve checking or proofreading, rereading passages, or recalculating or retranslating material. Allocating time for specific tasks and checking coverage in qualitative dimensions ("Is my outline extensive enough?") are aspects of pacing the completion of an assignment. The metacognitive thesis is that any and all of these behaviors can enhance performance of the task. Often these same behaviors are also characteristic of sound study skills.

With regard to selecting appropriate strategies to work by, metacognitive theory suggests that the first order of learning is to recognize the particular problem and determine what information is needed to resolve it and where to obtain such data. Through such consideration, the student comes to recognize the limitations of the learning and the ultimate boundaries of the solution being sought. Sternberg (1984) considers these the "executive processes" of sound reasoning. Flavell (1976,

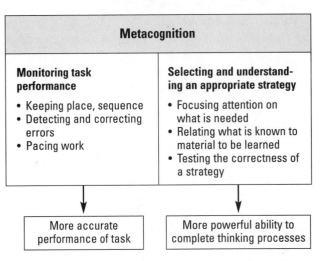

—Figure 9.3—

A Model of Metacognitive Thinking Skills

Metacognition	
Monitoring task performance	**Selecting and understanding an appropriate strategy**
• Keeping place, sequence • Detecting and correcting errors • Pacing work	• Focusing attention on what is needed • Relating what is known to material to be learned • Testing the correctness of a strategy
More accurate performance of task	More powerful ability to complete thinking processes

p. 234) refers to the various aspects of information retrieval in learning to think—remembering, monitoring, and updating information—and draws parallels between classroom learning and experiences involving thinking in the world outside school. Henle (1966, p. 57) suggests that recognizing what is understood and to what degree ultimately helps learners come to terms with the power of their own thoughts. Consider, for example, the importance of knowing the difference between a wild guess, an informed guess, a hypothesis, an intuition, and a fact. Finally, testing the accuracy of a strategy means applying various evaluative criteria and determining if, in fact, the right approach is being employed. The learner has an opportunity to assess the initial selection of strategy, as well as to develop insight into a potentially better choice. The result is a more holistic understanding of strategy and the development of fluency or competence in a particular strategy. From the metacognitive viewpoint, the thinker becomes more autonomous as these strategic skills are developed and refined.

CONATION AND THE IMPORTANCE OF AFFECT AND ENVIRONMENT

Recent research has emphasized the influence of the more affective aspects of thinking on students' cognitive performance (see, for example, McCombs & Marzano, 1989). What researchers call "conation"—an inclination to think clearly and to develop and consistently use rational attitudes and practices—may be crucial to the fostering of thoughtful learners. Metacognitive understanding assumes a relationship between skill and will that enables a problem solver to stick to a task, keep searching for an adequate solution, and check that an answer continues to fit. Ennis (1986) has developed a list of dispositions that are essential to critical thinking and analytical pursuit, and he emphasizes the importance of developing these personal inclinations throughout a lifetime. Beyer (1984) stresses the significance of learning such thinking behaviors through modeling in the classroom and through practice guided by a cognizant coach.

Currently, the research of Soviet psychologist Lev Vygotsky has begun to influence the development of a theory of teaching and schooling (Wertsch, 1985). Taking social and behavioral views of human development; a number of social scientists propose that higher-order thinking develops out of social interaction; they emphasize the importance of context and interaction in cognitive instruction (Tharp & Gallimore, 1988). The conditions of the classroom as a supportive environment for learning, as well as the teacher's role as a thoughtful mediator and model of thinking and disposition, are key aspects of this emergent theory. These researchers emphasize the need for user-friendly settings for learning, particularly for children from multicultural backgrounds. At the same time, these researchers state, the environment should be carefully planned for gradual and steady cognitive improvement.

The Vygotskian model also has implications for teaching thinking in specific contexts. "Hands-on learning," an approach parallel to the Russian researcher's "zone of proximal development," involves the interplay of concrete experience and theoretical abstraction. By manipulating objects in science class, for example, students may actively test their own hypotheses while the teacher seeks to explain related scientific principles and concepts. Such social interaction in the classroom, coupled with discovery and evaluative feedback, provides for the mediation of learning. Research seems to indicate that both metacognition and conation contribute to the real transfer of knowledge. Students experience the excitement of the creation of knowledge. Not only is this excitement contagious, it also has a long-term influence on a student's self-image, personal learning behavior, and understanding of such behavior.

TOWARD A COMMON UNDERSTANDING

When we focus on what we mean by thinking, we need to consider the various levels of thought that humans are capable of. The complexity of the cognitive process becomes evident. Figure 9.4 depicts a global view of thinking with four components:

• **Cognition:** The skills associated with essential and complex processes.

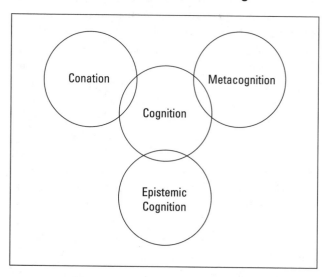

—*Figure 9.4*—
A Global View of Thinking

• **Metacognition:** The skills associated with the learner's awareness of his or her own thinking.

• **Epistemic cognition:** The skills associated with understanding the limits of knowing, as in particular subject matter and the nature of the problems that thinkers can address.

• **Conation:** The striving to think clearly, including personal disposition, and to develop and consistently use rational attitudes and practices.

Considering this four-part model can help educators examine the kinds of material available to them for enhancing thinking instruction in the classroom. They may also see a need to clarify understanding of what thinking is, to determine how it ties in with student development and classroom instruction, and to relate the teaching of thinking to current school programs. A supportive school environment and the quality of interaction in the classroom are other pertinent concerns. Additionally, educators must consider how to assess student achievement in various thinking skills.

Without a common understanding of what we mean by "thinking," we cannot even begin to address such educational issues. Improving students' cognitive performance thus starts with building consensus about the cognitive processes we expect them to master.

REFERENCES

Baron, J. B., Forgione Jr., P. D., Rindone, D. A., Kruglanski, H., & Davey, B. (1989). *Toward a new generation of student outcome measures: Connecticut's common core of learning assessment.* Hartford: Connecticut State Department of Education.

Bartlett, F. C. (1958). *Thinking: An experimental and social study.* London: Allen & Unwin.

Beyer, B. K. (1983, November). Common sense about teaching thinking skills. *Educational Leadership, 41*(3), 44–49.

Beyer, B. K. (1984, February). Practical approaches to teaching thinking skills in every classroom. Program presented at a National Curriculum Study Institute of the Association for Supervision and Curriculum Development, San Francisco.

Bloom, B. S., Englehart, M. D., Furst, E. J., Hill, W. H, & Krathwohl, D. R. (Eds.). (1956). *Taxonomy of educational objectives: The classification of educational goals. Handbook I: Cognitive domain.* New York: David McKay.

Cohen, J. (1971). *Thinking.* Chicago: Rand McNally.

Comer, J. P., Haynes, N. M., Joyner, E. T., & Ben-Avie, M. (Eds.). (1996). *Rallying the whole village: The Comer process for reforming education.* New York: Teachers College Press.

Costa, A. L. (1991). Mediating the metacognitive. In A. L. Costa, *The school as a home for the mind,* (pp. 87–94). Palatine, IL: SkyLight.

Developing cognitive abilities test (teacher's manual). (1980). Glenview, IL: Scott Foresman.

Dewey, J. (1933). *How we think.* Boston: D. C. Heath.

Elias, M. J., Zins, J. E., Weissberg, R. P., Frey, K. S., Greenberg, M. T., Haynes, N. M., Kessler, R., Schwab-Stone, M. E., & Shriver, T. P. (1997). *Promoting social and emotional learning: Guidelines for educators.* Alexandria, VA: Association for Supervision and Curriculum Development.

Ennis, R. H. (1986). A taxonomy of critical thinking dispositions and abilities. In J. B. Baron & R. J. Sternberg (Eds.), *Teaching thinking skills: Theory and practice.* New York: W. H. Freeman.

Feuerstein, R. (1980). *Instrumental enrichment: An intervention program for cognitive modifiability.* Baltimore: University Park Press.

Flavell, J. H. (1976). Metacognitive aspects of problem solving. In L. B. Resnick (Ed.), *The nature of intelligence.* Hillsdale, NJ: Lawrence Erlbaum.

Goleman, D. (1995). *Emotional intelligence.* New York: Bantam.

Guilford, J. P. (1967). *The nature of human intelligence.* New York: McGraw-Hill.

Henle, M. (1966). Cognitive skills. In J. S. Bruner (Ed.), *Learning about learning: A conference report.* Washington, DC: U.S. Department of Health, Education, and Welfare.

Hudgins, B. B. (1977). *Learning and thinking: A primer for teachers.* Itasca, IL: F. E. Peacock.

Kuhn, D. (1999, March). A developmental model of critical thinking. *Educational Researcher, 28*(2), 16–25, 45.

Marzano, R. J., Brandt, R. S., Hughes, C. S., Jones, B. F., Presseisen, B. Z., & Suhor, C. (1988). *Dimensions of thinking: A framework for curriculum and instruction.* Alexandria, VA: Association for Supervision and Curriculum Development.

McCombs, B. L., & Marzano, R. J. (1989, September–October). Integrating skill and will in self-regulation. *Teaching Thinking and Problem Solving, 11,* 1–4.

Nickerson, R. S. (1981, October). Thoughts on teaching thinking. *Educational Leadership 39*(2), 21.

Piaget, J. (1970). Piaget's theory. In P. H. Mussen (Ed.), *Carmichael's manual of child psychology* (Vol. 1). New York: John Wiley and Sons.

Presseisen, B. Z. (1982). *Understanding adolescence: Issues and implications for effective schools.* Philadelphia: Research for Better Schools, Inc.

Presseisen, B. Z. (1988). *At-risk students and thinking: Perspectives from research.* Washington, DC: National Education Association Publications and Research for Better Schools, Inc.

Presseisen, B. Z. (Ed.). (1999). *Teaching for intelligence: A collection of articles.* Arlington Heights, IL: SkyLight.

Sternberg, R. J. (1983, February). Criteria for intellectual skills training. *Educational Researcher, 12*(2), 6–12, 26.

Sternberg, R. J. (1984, January). What should intelligence tests test? Implications of a triarchic theory of intelligence for intelligence testing. *Educational Researcher 13*(1), 5–15.

Tharp, R. G., & Gallimore, R. (1988). *Rousing minds to life: Teaching, learning, and schooling in social context.* New York: Cambridge University Press.

Wertsch, J. V. (Ed.). (1985). *Culture, communication, and cognition: Vygotskian perspectives.* New York: Cambridge University Press.

Wolf, D. P. (1989, April). Portfolio assessment: Sampling student work. *Educational Leadership, 46*(7), 35–39.

10

What Is Problem Solving?

Jack Lochhead and Aletta Zietsman

Problem solving has always been easier to talk about than to investigate.

—Bert F. Green Jr., Problem Solving:
Research, Method, and Theory

Problem solving is a bit like beauty . . . we know it when we see it, but we cannot define it.

—Earl Hunt, "Problem Solving," in
Thinking and Problem Solving

Problem solving is an activity we encounter every day of our lives. It might involve finding a parking space, evading unpleasant responsibilities, or deciphering this sentence. These kinds of problems are so ordinary we rarely notice them. We tend to become aware that we are solving problems when the consequences are dramatic: bailing a child out of prison, putting parents in a nursing home, paying a huge and unexpected bill. Because everyone is familiar with problem solving, it may seem surprising that the experts cannot agree on what it is.

Although there is no universal definition of problem solving, experts do agree that it is strongly related to context. Problem solving always entails the appropriate application of knowledge in a specific situation. The context often determines what types of action are appropriate and what impact those actions have. For example, dealing with a major illness and finding the factors of 71 may both involve the enumeration of possibilities, but they are very different experiences.

In this book, "problem solving" refers mostly to those classroom-based activities that are intended to accomplish two goals: to improve how students think and to link school-learned knowledge with everyday contexts outside of school. Despite this narrow view of problem solving, there is still more ground here than we can fully survey in a single chapter.

Why Teach Problem Solving?

Problem solving has become an increasingly important part of schooling as computers have gradually changed the way we live. In the words of Tuma and Reif (1980, p. ix), "There is an increasing need to teach improved problem-solving skills to students who must be adequately prepared to cope with a world characterized by growing complexity, rapid change, and vastly expanding knowledge."

Early teaching efforts stressed the difference between "exercises" and "problem solving." The former are tasks that can be readily accomplished with knowledge at hand (for example, finding the factors of 71); the latter require consideration of the context as well as the facts. Schoenfeld (1991) provides an example:

> An Army bus holds 36 soldiers. If 1,128 soldiers are being bused to their training site, how many buses are needed?

The context implies that a fractional answer is not appropriate. But 36 does not divide 1,128 evenly; it yields a quotient of 31.333. Thus 32 buses will be required—31 that are fully loaded and an extra bus carrying fewer than 36 passengers. Despite the simplicity of this problem, the vast majority of students give answers with fractions or remainders, suggesting that their schooling has not prepared them well for problem solving.

For centuries, schools have been very effective in teaching algorithms. These algorithms call for a specific set of steps to be taken under clearly specified circumstances. Such an approach works fine when context is not a concern, as when finding the factors of a number. Today most algorithms can be preprogrammed into a computer, and there is much less need to teach students to perform them. What is needed instead is schooling that prepares students to apply algorithms in a rich context. The issue is no longer how to perform the algorithm but whether to perform it, when to perform it, and with what modifications.

SUBJECT-SPECIFIC PROBLEM SOLVING

Much of the literature on problem solving concerns how to solve problems within a particular discipline. One of the best-researched areas is mathematics.

The literature on mathematical problem solving has been heavily influenced by Pólya (1957) and Schoenfeld (1985). It has tended to stress general-purpose strategies that can be applied across a range of mathematical contexts. For example, one strategy is to look at a specific case that is relatively easy to conceptualize. If 40 soldiers wanted a ride, how many buses would be needed then? How might that situation help us analyze the case when there are 1,128 soldiers?

A considerable amount of research also exists on computer assisted problem solving. Some common examples include using the computer as a tool, working within a computer-generated environment, and using the computer to model problem solving itself. Hafner and Stewart (1995) describe a Mendelian genetics problem-solving package that allows students to manipulate large numbers of variables to predict changes in populations of fruit flies. By using the computer as a tool in this manner, students can tackle core conceptual problems in the subject without being overwhelmed by the calculation of complex probabilities. Frederiksen, White, and Gutwill (1999) describe a computer-simulated world of electric circuits where students can manipulate physical variables such as current flow. Here students solve problems within the simulation and thereby come to understand that environment. Tabachneck-Schiff, Leonardo, and Simon (1997) describe a computer program that models teaching economics (a highly complex problem-solving behavior). Their article stresses the importance of multiple representations.

GENERAL-PURPOSE PROBLEM SOLVING

Mathematical problem solving is one example of subject-specific problem solving. Several other fields, such as physics, also have a literature on discipline-specific problem solving. In schools, however, the issue of teaching problem solving usually arises from a broader concern. Students are found to be doing poorly in contexts where the faculty believe they have already taught the basic knowledge needed to succeed. If students have the facts but do not know how to use them, the culprit is often seen to be poor problem-solving skills. These skills (often

ill-defined) are believed to be broad in scope; they might explain poor performance on a mathematics problem or failure to get a history assignment read before the quiz.

The value of general-purpose problem-solving skills continues to be hotly debated among the so-called experts in problem solving. The enumeration of possible options would seem to be a useful general-purpose skill. But is the ability to enumerate the factors of 71 in any way related to facility at enumerating the options facing a sick patient (especially when the sick patient is a relative or oneself)? We do not know. It seems intuitively obvious that general skills must exist, and equally obvious that they may not. Further, if such skills do exist, can they be taught?

The best candidates for broadly applicable problem-solving skills are two characteristics not often thought of as skills: attitude and awareness. Good problem solvers tend to have a positive and determined attitude about problem solving. They show persistence in the face of failure and confidence despite uncertainty. Several such attitudinal variables were described by Bloom and Broder (1950) and more recently expanded by Whimbey and Lochhead (1999). The role of awareness in successful problem solving is a little more complicated. Although all successful problem solvers must be determined, not all appear to be fully aware of how they solve problems. Nevertheless, problem solvers who are aware of their actions are clearly in a strong position to learn from their mistakes or triumphs.

Closely linked to awareness is the concept of metacognition—essentially thinking about thinking. A large literature on the subject began with Dewey (1933) and was reviewed recently by Hacker, Dunlosky and Graesser (1998).

"THAT'S NOT MY PROBLEM"

In studying the attitude of problem solvers, one quickly becomes aware of the issue of ownership. Unless those confronting a question perceive it as a problem, they will not be interested in solving it. Some students might be delighted that 1,128 soldiers cannot get to their training program, and they might prefer to sabotage the transportation system than find the right number of buses.

It is common for students to perceive the context of a problem in ways quite different from those expected by their teachers. A student who has been asked to find the factors of 71 might decide that the problem is how to get out of the classroom as quickly as possible. An old story tells of a physics student answering an exam question about the way to find the height of a tall building using a barometer. The teacher had only one solution in mind, but the student found about 10. One involved throwing the barometer off the top of the building and timing its fall.

Problems always include a context, and contexts are never absolute. Contexts inevitably are perceived in different ways by different people. For this reason, one cannot teach problem solving without carefully listening to students. The appropriateness of a problem solution depends on the student's stated perception of the context. If this perception is ignored, then no matter how much the students may learn, they are not learning about problem solving.

HOW DO WE SOLVE PROBLEMS?

A vast literature now exists on problem solving. For a comprehensive review of issues relevant to teaching, see Nickerson (1994). Teaching problem solving, however, is but a small part of the total literature. Most work focuses on how problem solving is accomplished. Particularly noteworthy is the computer-based cognitive science orientation to problem-solving research. This approach is most closely associated with Herb Simon and Carnegie-Mellon University (Newell & Simon, 1972). It has consisted of studying computer programs to learn how people might solve problems, and studying how people solve problems to learn how to build better computer programs. The victory of the computer Deep Blue over a grand chess master is perhaps the current culmination of this work. Many of the details are far too intricate to be useful in the classroom. The following core ideas, however, may prove valuable.

It is useful to imagine problem solving as metaphorically equivalent to finding your way in a strange new territory. The problem solution is some distant location. Many possible paths radiate from your initial position, but you cannot tell which lead to the goal. Some paths are blocked; others lead in nonproductive directions. The terms "problem space" and "solution paths" come from this analogy and are useful concepts in discussing the steps involved in problem solving. Various search strategies have been described for finding suitable paths to a solution: working backwards, hill climbing, means-ends analysis, forward chaining.

Another key concept coming out of the spatial metaphor is that of problem representation. To navigate in a new environment, or to solve a problem, you must devise some kind of map to keep track of things in your head. For some people, the map is visual; for others, it is more like a verbal list of landmark descriptions and movements. Success in negotiating the territory has a great deal to do with the mental representations you create to remember paths already traversed. Many of the differences between experts and novices stem from the expert having a mental representation that fits well with the terrain. Hence, problem solving is not simply a search through a predetermined problem space; it is also a search for an appropriate representation of the problem. Finding a helpful representation can often be the most important step.

The spatial metaphor for problem solving has deep roots. The ability to solve problems first appeared in animals when they evolved strategies to search their environment for food. It is likely that higher forms of problem solving are accomplished using the same basic routines that evolved for that purpose. Psychologists employed the connection when they ran rats through mazes to learn how those animals solved problems. Unfortunately, they then attempted to generalize their findings to education theory, without recognizing that the rat's representation of space is quite different from our own.

A COMPLEX CHALLENGE

Problem solving is a complex activity. Skinner (1966, pp. 225–226) described it this way:

> A question for which there is at the moment no answer is a problem. It may be solved, for example, by performing a calculation, by consulting a reference work, or by acting in any way which helps in recalling a previously learned answer. Since there is probably no behavioral process which is not relevant to the solving of some problem, an exhaustive analysis of techniques would coincide with an analysis of behavior as a whole.

The teaching and learning of problem solving are even more complex. They are among the most challenging problems anyone might choose to work on. There are no clear routes to a solution; we do not even know what representation would produce an appropriate map. As Nickerson (1994, pp. 440–441) points out,

> Designing an educational process that will develop competent thinkers and problem solvers is ambitious and something we do not yet know how to do as well as we would like. . . . Teaching problem solving, or skillful thinking toward given ends, important as it is, is surely not enough. It does not suffice to be able to bring effective strategies to bear on problems as given; one should be able also to make reasonable judgments about which problems are worth solving and which are not.

But despite all these difficulties we must persevere. For what could be more worthwhile than solving the problem of teaching problem solving?

REFERENCES

Bloom, B., & Broder, L. (1950). *Problem-solving processes of college students.* Chicago: University of Chicago Press.

Dewey, J. (1933). *How we think.* Boston: D. C. Heath.

Frederiksen, J. R., White, B. Y., & Gutwill, J. (1999). Dynamic models in learning science: The importance of constructing derivational linkages among models. *Journal of Research in Science Teaching, 36*(7), 806–836.

Green, B. F., Jr. (1966). Introduction: Current trends in problem.solving. In B. Kleinmuntz (Ed.), *Problem solving: Research, method, and theory* (pp. 3–18). New York: John Wiley & Sons.

Hacker, D. T., Dunlosky, J., & Graesser, A. C. (1998). *Metacognition in educational theory.* Mahwah, NJ: Lawrence Erlbaum Associates.

Hafner, R., & Stewart, J. (1995). Revising explanatory models to accommodate anomalous genetic phenomena: Problem solving in the context of discovery. *Science Education, 79*(2), 111–146.

Hunt, E. (1994). Problem solving. In R. J. Sternberg (Ed.), *Thinking and problem solving* (pp. 215–228). San Diego, CA: Academic Press.

Newell A., & Simon, H. A. (1972). *Human problem solving.* Englewood Cliffs, NJ: Prentice Hall.

Nickerson, R. S. (1994). The teaching of thinking and problem solving. In R. J. Sternberg (Ed.), *Thinking and problem solving* (pp. 409–449). San Diego: Academic Press.

Pólya , G. (1957). *How to solve it: A new aspect of mathematical method* (2nd ed.). Garden City, NY: Doubleday.

Schoenfeld, A. (1985). *Mathematical problem solving.* New York: Academic Press.

Schoenfeld, A. (1991). What's all the fuss about mathematical problem solving? In A. L. Costa (Ed.), *Developing minds: A resource book for teaching thinking* (pp. 144–146). Alexandria, VA: Association for Supervision and Curriculum Development.

Skinner, B. F. (1966). An operant analysis of problem solving. In B. Kleinmuntz (Ed.), *Problem solving: Research, method, and theory* (pp. 225–257). New York: John Wiley & Sons.

Tabachneck-Schiff, H. J. M., Leonardo, A. M., & Simon, H. A. (1997). CaMeRa: A computational model of multiple representations. *Cognitive Science, 21*(4), 305–330.

Tuma, D. T., & Reif, F. (Eds.). (1980). *Problem solving and education: Issues in teaching and research.* Mahwah, NJ: Lawrence Erlbaum Associates.

Whimbey, A., & Lochhead, J. (1999). *Problem solving and comprehension* (6th ed.). Mahwah, NJ: Lawrence Erlbaum Associates.

11

Thinking About Decisions

Robert J. Swartz

When we think about decision making, we often only think of "big" choices like buying a car, choosing a college, or deciding whom to vote for. However, opportunities for decision making are much more plentiful. Our decisions may also be about "little" things, like which route to take on a trip or what clothing to wear to work. Whenever we want to do something and believe we have a choice, we strive to make a decision. And we are usually in this position almost every moment of our lives.

The importance of good careful decision making cannot be underestimated. Of all the intellectual activities we engage in, decision making, by its very nature, has the most immediate practical consequences. These consequences may, of course seem benign. Whether I put the toothpaste on my toothbrush before or after I wet it may not have many important consequences. But such decisions are few and far between. When I decide what shirt to wear my choice usually doesn't seem earth shattering either. But even such a "little" decision may, on occasion, have its share of practical consequences. Which shirt I wear to a job interview may contribute to the interviewer's overall impression of me and that, in turn, may make a difference in whether I am offered the job or not.

The importance of thinking carefully about decisions before they are made is more obvious in the case of more "global" choices. President Truman's decision to drop an atomic bomb on the city of Hiroshima to try to end World War II was earth shattering. Of course, such decisions can result in consequences that are viewed as benefits as well as in consequences viewed as disadvantages. "Earth shattering" may be the wrong word here; perhaps "momentous" would be better. But which-

ever word is used, the point is that the potential for such consequences underscores the need for care in thinking through decisions before they are made.

Unfortunately, much decision making is not something that people engage in thoughtfully. Sometimes unwanted and even disastrous consequences result that were not anticipated. Regret, surprise, and even a sense of failure often result. Purchasing an older car that breaks down frequently can be more costly than buying a new one. Choosing the wrong street on the way to work can cause a delay that could be embarrassing and put you at risk of losing your job.

Everyone makes decisions, even small children. But not everyone makes them as carefully and well as they could be made. So how can they do better? Recognizing the multitude of circumstances in which we make decisions is the first step in making them better.

PROBLEMS WITH OUR THINKING ABOUT DECISIONS

Sometimes things beyond our control make our decisions work out poorly. A water main may break on the street we decide to take to work. A car purchased may be the one in 10,000 that is a lemon.

Sometimes the fault is ours, however. We may not consider everything that we might in making a decision. Suppose that there is readily available information showing that a car I am considering for purchase has a very bad repair record, but I don't think to seek that information. Then, if the car needs frequent repairs and I regret having purchased it, the fault is mine. I could have taken the time to get sufficient information in order to make a better decision. We can all recall situations in which we might have thought about a choice more carefully.

A number of common shortcomings limit our decision making. One is that we often make snap decisions—we decide to do the first thing that comes to mind. We may have more

Adapted with permission of the publisher from Chapter 2, "Decision Making," by R. Swartz and S. Parks, 1994, in *Infusing the Teaching of Critical and Creative Thinking into Content Instruction: A Lesson Design Handbook for the Elementary Grades*, pp. 31–38. Pacific Grove, CA: Critical Thinking Books and Software.

options than we realize, however. Some of these options may work out better than others. For example, someone might say, "I stained my blouse; I'll put water on it to get the stain out." The water may set the stain; cleaning fluid may do a better job. If we don't stop to think about other options, we'll never find out whether there are any alternatives that might be better.

Sometimes we fail to consider alternatives, not because we are hasty in our decision making, but because we think that our decisions are "black or white." We sometimes hear, "I can either do x or not x." Choices are seldom so simple. I may believe that I must either pay the asking price for a car or not buy it at all. Usually, though, "not doing x" masks a variety of other options. I might negotiate with the seller for a better price, trade in my old car, or wait for a special sale. Thinking about the different ways of not doing something may reveal choices we didn't realize we had.

A second common problem in decision making arises when we don't take the time to think about all the important consequences of our choices before we make them. Carefully considering outcomes can show us whether a decision is a wise one. Often, however, we consider only the most immediate and obvious consequences. I may just think about the initial cost of the car I am interested in and not consider other important factors like gas mileage, reliability, availability of service, and so on. If I find out after I purchase the car that it gets very low gas mileage, it is too late for this consequence to influence my decision. Knowing about this outcome beforehand might have deterred me from buying the car.

There are other examples of consequence-related problems that often creep into our decision making. For example, we often think of results only in terms of ourselves. A person may decide that the best place to go on a family vacation is to the lake because he likes fishing and the lake is a great place to fish. But his family may have no interest in fishing and may have preferred to go elsewhere. This has been called a "myside bias" in decision making (Baron, 1990).

When these two limited forms of thinking about decisions are put together, we get what is perhaps the most common fault in decision making: considering only immediate self-gratification. Often when a decision maker judges that he will derive some pretty immediate benefit from a certain decision, that's enough to prompt that decision without thought about other factors. This can result in unexpected long-term negative consequences for the decision maker herself. People who smoke cigarettes often make the choice based on immediate gratification and do not stop to consider the health risks. Earlier writers have referred to this fault as decision making based on "immediate self interest" without taking into account our

long-term self interest. Giving adequate weight to long-term self interest has been called deciding on the basis of "enlightened self-interest."

Making decisions on the basis of enlightened self-interest, however much an advance this is over deciding about things based on one's immediate self-interest, still exhibits myside bias. So, as one might expect, these two forms of self-interest are contrasted with decision making that takes into account and gives appropriate weight to the interests of others. When the interests of others always override the self-interest of the decision maker this can be called altruistic decision making. Obviously, a balance is preferable.

Finally, as often happens when a person has a predisposition toward (or away from) a particular option, sometimes only consequences that count in favor of the decision—"pros"—are taken into account (or vice versa), whether they involve the interests of the decision maker only or also include the interests of others. When this happens the decision making is often considered one-sided.

COMMON FAULTS IN THINKING

These problems with decision making can be viewed as instances of two common and generic faults in thinking: *hastiness* and *narrowness* (Perkins & Swartz, 1992; Swartz & Perkins, 1989). Two other generic faults with thinking manifest themselves during decision making.

Sometimes I may miss important options or consequences because my thinking is *scattered and sprawling*. I may jump from one idea to another without exploring any fully. I may think about going to the mall, and that may generate images of some of the stores at the mall. That, in turn, may make me think about how much I like to find bargains. It may not enter my mind to think about whether I have the time to make this shopping trip, whether I have other more important things to do, or whether I really need anything at the mall. I may simply not be aware that I am missing important factors.

I also may make poor decisions because my thinking is *fuzzy*. I may blur together distinct options, not being aware of their differences. I may think that traveling to Florida means a trip to Miami, because the people I know who go to Florida always go to Miami. Thus, fuzziness in my thinking can limit an appreciation of my range of choices and their different implications.

In summary, these four habits of thought may limit our decision making. Hastiness in our thinking, narrowness, scattered and sprawling thinking, and fuzzy thinking can become powerful habits that affect all of the thinking we do, not just decision making. In the case of decision making, however, such faults can lead us to be unaware of our options or overlook important consequences. Being aware of these faults can motivate us to develop better decision-making habits.

STUDYING GOOD DECISION MAKERS

In order to develop better habits, we can think about the habits of good decision makers. We can do this by studying actual situations of careful decision making, such as during the Cuban missile crisis of the 1960s. Or we can all think of times when we have made poor decisions. If we ask how good decision makers might have made decisions in those circumstances, various remedies may come to mind.

First, good decision makers understand why a decision is needed. Understanding what creates the need for a decision can help us set our standards for a good choice—one that meets the need. For example, if I am regularly late for work, I may think that I have to choose a better route to get to work in the morning. When I realize getting to work on time may also depend on when I leave home, I expand my options to include leaving earlier.

Second, it is always important to consider as many options as possible. I might ask myself, What are some different ways to get to work? At what different times can I leave home? An effective way to answer these questions is to engage in brainstorming—to practice creative thinking. By generating many ideas, we increase our chances of finding a really good option. We should try to come up with some unusual options for our decision, as those sometimes provide us with the best ideas.

A number of different dimensions of the thinking involved in brainstorming have been identified, sometimes described as fluency, flexibility, originality, and elaboration. Many good decision makers deliberately attend to each of these. They ask not only how many ideas can they come up with, but what different kinds of ideas can they generate, what original ideas they can come up with, and what details they can fill in as they think about these ideas.

There are three other matters that good decision makers attend to before they make a decision:

• They consider a range of consequences of their options—including short- and long-term consequences, consequences for others as well as themselves, and cons as well as pros.
  • They consider how likely these consequences are.
  • They consider how significant the consequences are.

Considering a range of consequences prevents narrowness in our thinking. It is often important to note short- and long-term consequences for ourselves and for others who might be affected by our actions. If leaving for work earlier in the morning will create a conflict because my children and I will have to use the same bathroom before they catch an early school bus, I should certainly take this into account.

To counter the kind of narrowness that infects decision making when a person already has a predisposition toward a specific option, it is important to lean over backward and search for consequences that are cons as well as pros. Acknowledging that both are relevant and important makes for a well-considered decision. Good decision makers often jot down pros and cons using a simple T-bar on a sheet of paper, for example with the left-hand column for pros and the right for cons.

It is also important to consider how likely a projected outcome may be. If I don't, I may exaggerate the significance of consequences that are unlikely or far-fetched. I may initially think that there will be a conflict with my children over using the bathroom if I leave for work earlier, but then I might remember that they usually get up early to review their homework. They are often out of the bathroom before I would want to use it.

Good decision makers are alert to how much support independent and reliable information lends to the likelihood of the predicted occurrence. They consider the frequency of past occurrences in similar circumstances. Let's say I search for information and find that a car I am considering for purchase typically has a poor repair record, and I determine that the source of this information is reliable. Then I can say it is likely that if I bought one I would have to get it repaired a lot also. If we judge that a consequence is likely, we should take this potential outcome more seriously than those we judge less likely to occur. Our hopes and fears often play a role in the predicted consequences we consider when making a decision. By relying on hard evidence, we can engage in a reality test of these predictions and guard against basing decisions on emotions or mere guesses. Of course, evidentiary support for our predictions is not a guarantee. But such critical thinking about the likelihood of a consequence is important to the process.

Good decision makers also think about how important the consequences are. Are they a cost or a benefit? How serious is that cost or benefit? In leaving earlier for work, I may have to sacrifice watching the morning news. Is that serious? Should I weigh it heavily in my decision making? I may realize that while I like watching the morning news, it is not as significant as the stress of rushing to get to work on time. In addition, if continuing to be late is likely to result in losing my job, I should take that outcome even more seriously.

These are questions about *values*. It is interesting that some of the great moral theories—like classical utilitarianism, "we ought to do what will lead to the greatest happiness for the greatest number of people," or Kant's famous dictum "we ought to follow the categorical imperative"—were designed to facilitate rational decision making (Bentham, 1789; Kant, 1785).

Finally, open-mindedness is also an important mark of a good decision maker. Good decision makers always allow for the possibility of changing their minds when new information comes along that significantly shifts the balance of pros and cons. Practicing open-mindedness is part and parcel of good decision making, and as important as considering questions like "What are my options?" and "What are the consequences of these options?"

When we reflect on all of these attention points for a well-thought-out decision, we are reminded that skillful decision making is a complex task involving a number of thinking skills. Good decision making blends skills of creative thinking and critical thinking, but also involves the need for skill at clarifying the options and consequences. These are the three domains often referred to using the categorization introduced by Benjamin Bloom and his colleagues as "higher-order thinking" (1956). Specific thinking skills like comparing and contrasting, prediction, and determining the reliability of a source of information fall within three domains best categorized as skill at generating ideas (synthesis), clarifying ideas (analysis), and assessing the reasonableness of ideas (evaluation). (See Swartz & Parks, 1994, p. 8, for an elaboration of this thinking skills framework.) Figure 11.1 sketches the overall questions that prompt good decision making, and, in the boxes at the bottom of the diagram, the specific thinking skills needed to determine their answers. When making specific decisions, some of these focal points and skills may be more important than others because of the background and the context within which the specific decision-making task is called for.

—*Figure 11.1*—

Thinking Skills Involved in the Decision-Making Process

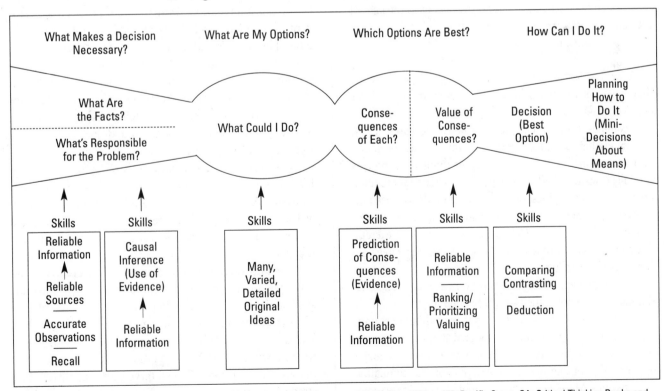

Source: Adapted from *Teaching Thinking: Issues and Approaches,* by R. Swartz and D. Perkins, 1989, p. 158. Pacific Grove, CA: Critical Thinking Books and Software.

MONITORING OUR DECISION MAKING

How do people who are skillful decision makers make sure they attend to all of these issues? One way is to explicitly remind ourselves of key questions and the order in which we should answer them. We can metacognitively monitor our progress to make sure that we are not forgetting anything. Good thinkers consider the following:

- What makes this decision necessary? What is creating the need for a decision?
- What are my options? Are there unusual ones that I should consider in this circumstance?
- What consequences would result if I took these options? Are there long-term consequences, consequences for others, or consequences that I might not ordinarily consider?
- How likely are these consequences? Why? What evidence or reasons are there for thinking that they are likely? Is this information reliable?
- Do these consequences count in favor of or against the options being considered?
- How important are these consequences—not just for me, but for all those affected by them? Are there some consequences that are so important that they should count more in my thinking than others? Why?
- When I compare and contrast the options in the light of the consequences, which option is best?
- How can I carry out this decision?

A written list of these questions can guide people when they have not yet internalized the strategies and when their decision making is habitually prone to one or more of the shortcomings I mentioned above (Swartz & Parks, 1994; Swartz, Fischer, & Parks, 1998). I call this a "map" of skillful decision making because it can guide us through the process carefully (Swartz & Parks, 1994, p. 27). It is important to note, however, that other questions or a different order of questions may be appropriate for skillful decision making on specific occasions. In using this model, good decision makers exercise flexibility of thought that allows them to adapt the strategy depending on the circumstances.

A second practice, especially in the case of complex decisions, is to write down the answers or other information these questions yield to ensure that we take everything important into account. Using two columns for pros and cons is one version of this practice. People often also write down the major options, relevant information, and sources of the information on note cards. More-sophisticated graphic organizers are sometimes used (Swartz & Parks, 1994).

A final practice well worth mentioning is to think through a decision, attending to all of these points, with one or more people. Other people bring different perspectives to situations that call for skillful thinking. They may notice things that we miss. But more important, they may disagree with us about how likely a consequence is, how important it is, or which option has the best balance of pros and cons. In a variant of this practice, decision makers can role-play people who disagree with them. Listening to others may help us broaden our perspectives, see other points of view, and even change our minds: it fosters open-mindedness.

Thinking about our decisions in these ways counters each of the thinking defaults. Organizing our thinking by following this sequence of questions prevents our decision making from being sprawling. Considering a wide range of options and consequences prevents it from being either narrow or hasty, as does considering the points of view of others. And systematically thinking about our options and their consequences prevents our thinking from being fuzzy.

TEACHING STUDENTS TO BE SKILLFUL DECISION MAKERS

Where and when is it best to teach skillful decision making? Classroom interventions with the purpose of helping students think more carefully about decisions are not uncommon. The most effective ones incorporate direct instructional practices that speak to each of the tips mentioned previously. Those that simply have students respond to decision problems with no instruction that speaks to these tips tend to be the least effective in helping students modify the way they think about decisions. In addition, many educators agree that the degree of care and skillfulness students practice in their decision making is proportionate to the level of articulation teachers provide as they introduce the strategies. At the same time, the level of articulation should, at least in part, depend on the age and grade level of the students and should increase as students move up through the grades.

Direct instruction in ways of improving decision making can range from separate programs and courses to the infusion of skillful decision making into content instruction (Swartz & Perkins, 1989; Swartz, Reagan, & Kiser, 1999; Wales, 1983). There is also some variation in the degree to which a strategy for skillful decision making is articulated in these interventions. Some interventions simply rely on a strategy of considering pros and cons, perhaps making use of a T-bar as a tool to support student thinking. Others are more complex, involving the explicit use by students of the skillful decision-making strategies I mentioned above. Care and thought should obviously go into the selection (and perhaps modification) of these to meet individual classroom needs.

A commonly practiced intervention is used to help students temper their behavioral impulsivity in interpersonal relationships—for example, when a student starts a fight with another student. In that case, a counselor or teacher might let the student who initiated the fight cool down and then focus on a two-pronged strategy: "What other things might you have done instead?" and "What do you think might have happened if you did those things rather than what you did?" Students are sometimes asked to write these ideas down rather than just discuss them with the counselor or teacher. The idea is to get the student familiar with asking and trying to answer these questions. Ideally, in the next emotionally laden situation the student will be more likely to think about what to do rather than just react.

A variant on this approach involves having students in the classroom role-play children in similar situations (Shure, 1996). They are then asked to think about the same questions. Such activities are often used with children in the early grades. More sophisticated simulations can be employed with older children all the way up through much more specialized programs such as in business schools or medical schools (Wales, 1983).

When skillful decision-making instruction is infused into content instruction, lessons often are designed so that students will attain a deeper understanding of the content they are studying as well. For example, in a 12th grade history lesson students "become" President Truman in July of 1945. They use a decision-making strategy like the one shown in Figure 11.2 to think carefully about the best way to end World War II, knowing that the United States has an atomic bomb and can use it to destroy a Japanese city.

In this lesson, students do not presume that the decision made by President Truman to bomb Hiroshima was the best decision. After the activity, however, there is usually a sizeable group of students who agree that dropping the bomb is the best thing to do. In this lesson, they follow the steps for skillful decision making listed in Figure 11.2, and they often use a graphic organizer like the one in Figure 11.3 to write down their thoughts. Then they must defend their choices, referring to the consequences they have projected for the various options. Many teachers also have students do writing activities in which they are guided to write persuasive letters or recommendations about how to end the war. Writing templates that

—Figure 11.2—
Skillful Decision Making

1. What makes a decision necessary?
2. What are my options?
3. What are the likely consequences of each option?
4. How important are the consequences?
5. Which option is best in light of the consequences?

Source: From *Infusing the Teaching of Critical and Creative Thinking into Content Instruction: A Lesson Design Handbook for the Elementary Grades*, by R. Swartz and S. Parks, 1994, p. 39. Pacific Grove, CA: Critical Thinking Books and Software.

guide them to expose their thinking is often effective in producing very well organized and articulate pieces (Swartz, Reagan & Kiser, 1999).

During this lesson, students need to "get the facts" of this historical period to back up their projections of consequences as they go through the decision making process. For example, they often have to study the type of fighting that was going on in the battles of Iwo Jima and Okinawa. This helps them get a sense of how viable an invasion of the Japanese mainland would have been as a tactic to end the war. In this way, students can gain a richer and deeper understanding of the historical content than they can glean by simply reading their textbooks as they think through this decision.

The curriculum abounds with opportunities for such dual-goal lessons. Other well-crafted infusion lessons can focus on the choices characters have to make in stories or novels, on decisions students make about ways of solving math problems, and on decision issues that arise in applied science. One middle school teacher, for example, asked students to investigate energy sources and recommend one for the United States to rely on as its dominant energy source. They then wrote to legislators explaining why they supported a particular source. In these kinds of infusion lessons, teachers find the use of graphic organizers very helpful for students in articulating their thinking (Swartz, Fischer, & Parks, 1998).

A beginning version of this decision-making strategy can even be used in the primary grades. For example, some teachers have used the Dr. Seuss book *Horton Hatches the Egg*, asking students to become the little elephant Horton trying to

—Figure 11.3—
Graphic Organizer for Skillful Decision Making

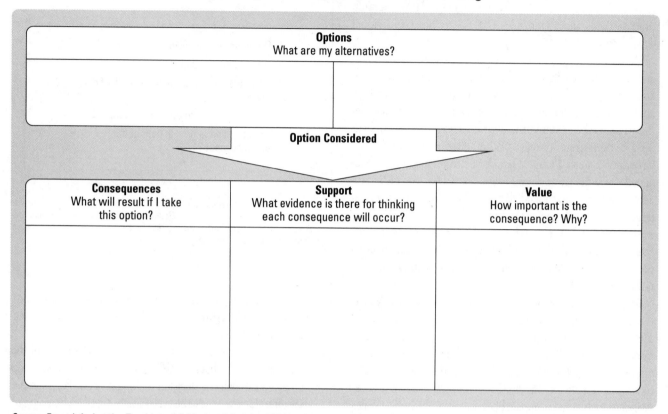

Source: From *Infusing the Teaching of Critical and Creative Thinking into Content Instruction: A Lesson Design Handbook for the Elementary Grades,* by R. Swartz and S. Parks, 1994, p. 42. Pacific Grove, CA: Critical Thinking Books and Software.

decide the best thing to do when he first faces the hunters. In this case, the content objective is better listening skills. But decision making is also an objective, even for these younger students. The simpler decision-making strategy is shown in Figure 11.4.

—Figure 11.4—
Choosing

1. What things could I do?
2. What would happen if I did each of these things?
3. What is the best thing to do?

Source: From *Infusing the Teaching of Critical and Creative Thinking into Content Instruction: A Lesson Design Handbook for the Elementary Grades,* by R. Swartz and S. Parks, 1994, p. 40. Pacific Grove, CA: Critical Thinking Books and Software.

MAKING SKILLFUL DECISION MAKING STICK

When lessons such as these are taught, teachers usually engage in some form of explicit instruction that also involves metacognition as well as teaching for transfer. The idea is to have students incorporate such careful decision-making strategies in their way of thinking *before* they make decisions. Here is a list of some of these techniques:

• Making explicit the strategy for skillful decision making you use in the lesson by writing it on the board, on a flip chart, on a poster, etc.

• Guiding students through the strategy by asking these questions orally as students think through a decision.

• Having students work on a decision-making task collaboratively.

• Using a graphic organizer for skillful decision making as a way for students to record their thoughts.

• Asking students to describe and evaluate their thinking while doing the thinking or after it.

• Asking students to develop a plan for future skillful decision making after they think through their decisions.

• Prompting students to think through other decision-making issues using the same strategy they were introduced to in the lesson or using the plan for decision making they developed.

ASSESSING STUDENTS' DECISION-MAKING ABILITIES

Attending to what students have decided after going through a decision-making process is not enough to reveal to us their thinking in arriving at their decisions. While such products are not irrelevant, much more to the point is an answer to the question "Why do you think this is the best choice?" The most natural way to prompt an answer to this question that will reveal the thinking that goes into a choice is to ask students to write a persuasive letter or a report and recommendation (Mirman, Swartz, & Barell, 1988). Oral reporting is also a possible vehicle for assessment, but it is much more time consuming in classrooms of 25 or more students.

What standards should we use to judge how carefully students are thinking through their decisions when we read such pieces of persuasive prose or hear such oral reports? That depends on what our objectives are in teaching students to be more thoughtful decision makers. The simplest and most straightforward approach is to base the assess-

—Figure 11.5—
Rubric for Persuasive Decision-Making Essays

Indicators	Expert	Practitioner	Apprentice	Novice
Main Idea	Starts essay with a strong recommendation that is chosen from at least three other options and does not repeat the consequences used as support.	Starts essay with a strong recommendation that is chosen from at least three other options and does not repeat the consequences used as support.	Starts essay with a recommendation that is chosen from fewer than three other options and does not repeat the consequences used as support.	Does not start essay with a recommendation or starts by repeating consequences used as support. Does not mention options considered.
Evidence	Cites at least three positive and negative consequences, each relevant to the recommendation as evidence for and against the recommendation.	Cites some, but less than three, positive and negative consequences, each relevant to the recommendation as evidence for and against the recommendation.	Cites some consequences as evidence for the recommendation, some of which are not relevant.	Cites few positive and/or negative consequences in the main body of the essay.
Examples	Supports each consequence with at least one example. Provides details in the examples. Well organized.	Supports some, but not all, consequences with at least one example. Provides some detail in the examples. Organized.	Rarely uses examples to support the consequences cited.	Uses no examples to support the consequences cited.
Concluding Paragraph	Returns to recommendation and, based on the body of the essay, explains why it is best despite the negative consequences.	Returns to thesis, elaborates it, but does not explain why it is best despite the negative consequences.	Returns to thesis but merely repeats main idea.	No concluding paragraph.
Conventions of Writing	Has few, if any, errors and follows appropriate conventions, including spelling, paragraphing, and punctuation.	Has some errors and mainly follows conventions, including spelling, paragraphing, and punctuation.	Has some errors in spelling and punctuation.	Has many errors in spelling and punctuation.

ment standards on the specific strategy that is being taught in decision-making instruction (e.g. Figures 11.2 and 11.4). For example, if we are teaching students to slow down in their decision making and think about options and their consequences, then we can set our standards based on these focal points. We will, simply, want to ascertain whether students are considering a variety of options and taking account of the positive and negative consequences in making their decisions.

More elaborated thinking strategies for decision making will yield more articulated standards. And in fact, once these focal points are isolated, more subtle questions need to be asked and answered relating to the degree of skillfulness a student manifests in considering options and consequences. For example, how many, and what kinds of options count as really good thinking, what number and kind will count for more superficial thinking, etc.? This can yield a rubric for assessing students' decision-making abilities. Figure 11.5, p. 65, is one example of a guide for assessing students' decision-making abilities as expressed in a piece of persuasive writing. The writing in this example is supposed to expose the way students thought through a decision issue to arrive at their conclusions. It should answer the question "Why do you think that what you recommend is the best thing to do?"

Decision making is something that every human being does every day. Not everyone thinks as carefully about their decisions as they could, however. It is important that we work to enhance our students' skillful decision making and all of its concomitant skills. The quality of a person's life—indeed, that life itself—may depend on exercising this kind of careful thinking about decisions.

REFERENCES

Baron, J. (1990). *Thinking and deciding.* Cambridge, England: Cambridge University Press.

Bentham, J. (1789). *Introduction to the principles of morals and legislation.*

Bloom, B., Englehart, M. D., Furst, E. J., Hill, W. H, & Krathwohl, D. R. (Eds.). (1956). *Taxonomy of educational objectives: The classification of educational goals. Handbook 1: Cognitive domain.* New York: David McKay.

Kant, I. (1785). *Fundamental principles of the metaphysics of morals.*

Mirman, J. A., Swartz, R., & Barell, J. (1988). Strategies to help teachers empower at-risk students. In B. Presseisen (Ed.), *At-risk students and thinking,* (pp. 138–156). Washington, DC: National Education Association.

Perkins, D. N., & Swartz, R. (1992). The nine basics of teaching thinking. In A. Costa, J. Bellanca, & R. Fogarty (Eds.), *If minds matter: A foreword to the future* (pp. 53–69). Palatine, IL: Skylight Publishing Co.

Seuss, D. (1940). *Horton hatches the egg.* New York: Random House.

Shure, M. (1996). *Raising a thinking child workbook.* New York: Henry Holt & Co.

Swartz, R., Fischer, S. D., & Parks, S. (1998). *Infusing the teaching of critical and creative thinking into secondary science.* Pacific Grove, CA: Critical Thinking Books and Software.

Swartz, R., & Parks, S. (1994). *Infusing the teaching of critical and creative thinking into content instruction: A lesson design handbook for the elementary grades.* Pacific Grove, CA: Critical Thinking Books and Software.

Swartz, R., & Perkins, D. N. (1989). *Teaching thinking: Issues and approaches.* Pacific Grove, CA: Critical Thinking Books and Software.

Swartz, R., Reagan, R., & Kiser, M. A. (1999). *Teaching critical and creative thinking in language arts: A lesson book, grades 5 & 6.* Pacific Grove, CA: Critical Thinking Books and Software.

Wales, C. (1983). *Guided design.* Morgantown, WV: Center for Guided Design.

12

Creative Thinking: An Essential Life Skill

GERARD J. PUCCIO AND MARY C. MURDOCK

"One can't," declared Alice, "believe impossible things."
"I daresay," replied the Queen, "you haven't had much
practice. Why, sometimes I've believed as many as ten
impossible things before breakfast."

—Lewis Carroll, Alice's Adventures in Wonderland

Homing in on the essence of creativity can be as bewildering as Alice's conversation with the Queen. Some people insist that creativity is impossible to define; others offer a dizzying array of definitions that can make one wonder which to believe or use. For example, Rhodes's (1961) synthesis of definitions was based on an examination of more than 50 definitions of creativity and imagination. More recently, Treffinger (1995) compiled more than 100 definitions of creativity, creative thinking, and critical thinking.

Torrance and Safter (1999, p. 98) comment that "many highly creative people fail to solve problems or produce really worthwhile creative products because they lose sight of what is important or essential. They do not 'highlight the essence.'" Torrance and Safter further note that this is especially likely to occur when there are a large number of problems or many alternative solutions. Given the variety of definitions and approaches to understanding creativity, getting to its essential nature presents such a risk (Isaksen, Murdock, Firestien, & Treffinger, 1993).

Making sense of the many perspectives on the subject requires patience and a genuine interest in finding the one that is best-suited for a given aim. Somewhere between Alice's logic and the Queen's irrationality lies what we have previously described as a "productive range" of abstraction that can allow terms to be appropriately defined according to function and purpose (see Murdock & Puccio, 1993). Thus, in this chapter, before focusing on creative thinking, we believe it is important to briefly examine the broader construct of creativity.

THE BASIC NATURE OF CREATIVITY

Many use the terms "creative thinking" and "creativity" as if they were interchangeable, but they are not (Treffinger, 1996). Creativity and creative thinking are conceptually related but not identical. Creativity is an umbrella construct that subsumes creative thinking.

Although there is no universally accepted definition of creativity, most scholars agree on some general principles and characteristics. In our own work on teaching and studying creativity, we have articulated some basic elements to help teachers and trainers identify the conceptual essence of creativity. Figure 12.1 proposes two characteristics to support the assumption that creativity can be taught. Figure 12.2 presents two basic principles, along with corollaries, that identify critical points to understand when teaching creativity. The first principle holds that creativity is best understood through a multifaceted perspective; the second principle states that the generation of novel perspectives is a fundamental element of creativity.

In maintaining that the multifaceted principle is as important as its more obvious novelty counterpart, we are not trying to avoid defining creativity. Instead, we wish to highlight the necessity for dealing realistically with the complex and dynamic interactions behind a creative act. A simple, brief definition cannot serve well in all circumstances; however, frameworks and schemas that classify definitions by their common characteristics can be very useful in understanding what definition to use for a particular purpose (see Dacey, 1989; Davis, 1998; Gowan, 1972; Treffinger, 1996; Treffinger, Isaksen, & Firestien, 1983).

For example, many scholars (MacKinnon, 1978; Mooney, 1963; Rhodes, 1961; Stein, 1968) agree that the multifaceted nature of creativity involves at least four discrete elements. These are (a) the characteristics and skills associated with the creative *person*; (b) the stages of thinking that comprise the creative *process*; (c) the qualities of the creative *product*; and

—Figure 12.1—
The Teachability of Creativity

Assumption: *Creativity involves sustained, deliberate application of definable and generalizable methods and techniques that can be observed, identified, evaluated, and assessed for deliberate learning and teaching.*

Integrative characteristics: Creativity can be described as a content and/or a process whose teaching should contain a balance of theoretical and applied models and approaches. Content and process in creativity can be taught separately and prescriptively or integrated descriptively with experiential and metacognitive strategies.

Disciplinary characteristics: The content of creativity contains identifiable concepts, definitions, and principles that can be simplified, coordinated, and changed with the addition of new knowledge. The application of this content is not limited to any one discipline or perspective. Its basic principles may be applied in inter-, intra-, multi-, or trans-disciplinary situations, allowing for similarities and differences to be examined, articulated, and developed.

Source: From *Key Principles and Assumptions of Creative Teaching and Learning in the Educational Program at the Center for Studies in Creativity* (p. 1), by M. C. Murdock, 1995, Buffalo, NY: Center for Studies in Creativity, Buffalo State College [unpublished manuscript].

—Figure 12.2—
Basic Principles About the Nature of Creativity

Multifaceted principle: The content that defines the domain of creativity is not limited to one theory, model, definition, concept, or approach. The most effective understanding of it is obtained through a dynamic, multifaceted perspective.

- *Contextualization corollary:* Recognizing, nurturing, and applying the multifaceted phenomenon of creativity requires awareness and understanding between novel or useful information in relation to past and current knowledge and practice in particular settings. Contextualizing is a dynamic, social operation that provides a perspective on what works for whom under what circumstances.
- *Explicitness corollary:* Despite multiple definitions, theories, and approaches, it is possible and beneficial to identify, construct, and use concrete frameworks that organize the understanding of the parts of creativity in relation to its whole and to examine and use specific definitions within these categories.

Novelty principle: The production of new and different perspectives is an essential element associated with creativity.

- *Usefulness corollary:* There is potential value in what may initially appear to be unique, original, or irrelevant. Obtaining novelty and making it useful is a dynamic process that requires the deliberate management of judgment in selecting and developing ideas and in implementing them.
- *Diffusion corollary:* It is possible to communicate novel outcomes in such a way as to gain external understanding of and acceptance for them.

Source: From *Key Principles and Assumptions of Creative Teaching and Learning in the Educational Program at the Center for Studies in Creativity* (p. 2), by M. C. Murdock, 1995, Buffalo, NY: Center for Studies in Creativity, Buffalo State College [unpublished manuscript].

(d) the nature of an *environment* that is conducive to creative thought. So, like the parable of the four blind men and the elephant, there are at least four distinct ways of describing creativity (Ornstein, 1972). Taken independently, these four elements provide a glimpse into creativity, but they do not illuminate the full image nor depict the interactions that facilitate or inhibit the appearance of creative behavior. To truly understand the nature of creativity, one must consider the whole elephant.

WHAT IS CREATIVE THINKING?

The term "creative thinking" is perhaps most closely associated with the process facet of creativity, and thus relates to the steps and cognitive skills associated with a person's progression from a problem or need to a creative solution or outcome. Torrance's (1974) classic definition of creative thinking also provides a clear description of some behaviors that are illustrative of creative thinking:

A process of becoming sensitive to problems, deficiencies, gaps in knowledge, missing elements, and so on; identifying the difficulty; searching for solutions, making guesses, or formulating hypotheses about the

deficiencies; testing and retesting these hypotheses and possibly modifying and retesting them; and finally communicating the results. (p. 8)

Torrance's definition outlines the stages people go through as they engage in creative thinking. This process is tacitly supported by the abilities and skills necessary to do what is being described; it leads to outcomes and results that will be communicated; and, because nothing takes place in a vacuum, it is linked to the environment as well.

THE NECESSITY OF CREATIVE THINKING

The need for creative thinking occurs on several levels: individually, in organizations, and in societies or cultures. In various ways and throughout our lives, we are all called upon to use our creative thinking skills to address open-ended questions. Every problem that has no preset solution, and every opportunity that has no prescribed pathway to success, demands creative thinking. To survive and thrive in a complex world, professionally and personally, we need to think creatively. Creative thinking permeates all facets of our lives, from household planning to leisure and recreation to work. Given its centrality, we believe creative thinking is an essential life skill.

To use one's capacity to think creatively is natural and healthy. Creative thinking and problem solving enable us to cope with life's challenges (Torrance, 1962), as well as to actualize our fullest potential (Rogers, 1959). Individuals who are caught in situations that do not allow them to use their creative talents can become frustrated and dissatisfied. Using one's creative thinking skills promotes well-being and good mental health, and some researchers suggest it may even counteract the mental decline associated with aging (Warshofsky, 1999).

Our work lives, in particular, demand creative thinking. Carnevale, Gainer, and Meltzer (1990) conducted an extensive 30-month investigation to identify basic skills required in today's workplace. They found that "increasingly, employers have been discovering that their work forces need skills that seem to be in short supply, skills over and above the basic academic triumvirate of reading, writing, and computation" (p. xiii). One of the seven skill categories the researchers identified as essential in the workplace was creative thinking and problem solving.

The importance of creative thinking in the workplace is not surprising. In an increasingly competitive economic environment, it is essential for organizations to tap the creative potential of their employees. An organization's ability to do so often means the difference between success and failure. VanGundy (1987, p. 358) argues that "organizational growth and survival can be tied directly to an organization's ability to produce (or adopt) and implement new services, products, and processes."

Organizations have come to emphasize participative management styles and to expect all employees to improve product and service quality. Concomitantly, they see an increased need for creative thinking throughout the organizational structure. Creative thinking is no longer the bastion of research and development. Employees within all functions and levels are now expected to creatively solve problems.

To help organizations stay competitive and to prepare individuals to join the work force, it is imperative that schools nurture the creative thinking skills of all students. Whether students go on to become engineers or secretaries, machinists or

accountants, doctors or nurses, computer technicians or software designers, bankers or teachers, they will have at least one thing in common. They will need to use their creative thinking skills to solve problems.

Creative thinking is not only necessary for individuals and organizations, but also for society as a whole. Creative thinking plays a critical role in the preservation and growth of a society. As the historian Arnold Toynbee (1964, p. 4) noted, "To give a fair chance to potential creativity is a matter of life and death for any society." Toynbee went on to argue that when nations nurture creative thinking, they have a greater chance of making history, and conversely, those nations that ignore the creative talents of their people will be surpassed by others.

NURTURING CREATIVE THINKING SKILLS

The preceding section underscored the central importance of creativity in the individual's personal and professional life and in society as a whole. (For more elaboration, see Puccio, 1995.) Clearly, creative thinking is a life skill. We maintain that it can be nurtured and developed. The Creative Problem Solving (CPS) process developed by Osborn (1953) is one model for doing so.

Osborn's (1953) pioneering work led to the founding of the graduate and undergraduate programs we teach in at the Center for Studies in Creativity at Buffalo State College in Buffalo, New York. Interest in the continued development, research, and application of the CPS model has remained strong for decades (Firestien, 1996; Isaksen, Dorval, & Treffinger, 1994; Isaksen & Treffinger, 1985; Parnes, 1967; Parnes, Noller, & Biondi, 1977).

As one of the most widely used and well-researched processes for nurturing creative thinking (Torrance, 1972), the CPS model continues to be useful for practicing many skills identified with creative thinking. Our 30-hour master's degree program includes four courses that focus on developing creative thinking skills through CPS. The introductory course emphasizes the use of basic CPS principles and tools by individuals; the next courses move through the use of these principles and tools with groups.

The CPS framework parallels Torrance's definition of the creative thinking process presented earlier. The CPS process comprises three basic elements: problem defining, idea generation, and solution development and implementation (Osborn, 1963). Two basic operations are used throughout these elements—divergent and convergent thinking. Divergent thinking involves a broad search for many diverse options; convergent thinking involves focused search and selection. In addition, there is a metacognitive aspect to selecting and applying the basic elements. Metacognition entails awareness of one's own thinking processes and the ability to articulate the information that results (Costa, 1984). This executive function is used to diagnose tasks for appropriate entry into the CPS model and then plan for appropriate action (Isaksen, Dorval, & Treffinger, 1994; Vehar, Firestien, & Miller, 1997).

From our experience and research in teaching and training, we know that working with CPS develops particular skills (Keller-Mathers, 1990; Lunken, 1990; Neilson, 1990; Parnes, 1985; Puccio, 1994; Vehar, 1994). As people learn the CPS process, they develop three types of skills: cognitive, affective, and metacognitive. Cognitive skills relate to or focus on thinking (Bloom, 1956); affective skills relate to or focus on feelings (Krathwohl, Bloom, & Masia, 1964); metacognitive skills, as noted earlier, involve thinking about thinking. Taken together, these three groups provide a multifaceted way of organizing and simplifying the diverse creative thinking skills used in applying the Creative Problem Solving process.

Figure 12.3 lists sample skills in each of the three areas. The cognitive skills are closely aligned with the steps and stages of the CPS process and build on the initial set of skills that Parnes

described in 1985. The skills in this group identify some of the knowledge base or content needed to master CPS. The affective skills reflect the functions described by Krathwohl, Bloom, and Masia (1964). They help people to internalize knowledge about the CPS process and make meaning of it in their lives. For example, based on our experience and data about the impact of CPS on our students, a common theme is that CPS training "changed my life." The metacognitive skills make people aware of the processes necessary for successful application of CPS and provide a means of transferring process knowledge to other contexts. The metacognitive skills provide insights about the breadth and magnitude of CPS applications.

DEFINITION OF CREATIVE THINKING

Creative thinking is an essential life skill. It is a rational process that enables people to successfully produce novel and useful responses to open-ended challenges and opportunities. Creative thinking involves specific cognitive, metacognitive, and affective skills. Once internalized, these skills can be readily applied to all areas of life. Creative thinking is subsumed within the domain of creativity and reflects the inherent mul-

—*Figure 12.3*—

Sample Creative Thinking Skills Developed Through CPS Training

Cognitive Skills	Affective Skills	Metacognitive Skills
• Identifying problems and opportunities • Asking better and different questions • Judging relevant from irrelevant data • Isolating productive problems and opportunities • Prioritizing competing options and information • Increasing the amount of idea production (fluency) • Increasing the production of different categories and kinds of ideas (flexibility) • Increasing production of new or different ideas (originality) • Seeing relationships among options and alternatives • Breaking old thinking patterns and habits • Making new connections • Elaborating, extending, or refining ideas, situations, or plans • Discerning criteria • Evaluating options	• Sensing problems and opportunities • Developing tolerance for ambiguity • Increasing awareness of one's environment • Becoming aware of one's creativeness • Encouraging attention to intuition • Being open-minded • Taking risks • Building self-confidence • Operating from an internal locus of control • Engaging in playful thought and behavior • Expressing feelings and emotions • Being curious • Responding to emotions • Anticipating the unknown	• Strategic planning • Goal setting • Decision making • Predicting from limited information • Developing understanding of one's creativeness • Knowing what one doesn't know • Applying judgment when appropriate • Diagnosing missing parts or incomplete information • Juxtaposing opposites • Reconciling opposites • Considering multiples (parallel processing) • Balancing positive and negative feedback through affirmative judgment • Managing emotions through deferred and affirmative judgment • Improving elaboration by strengthening solutions and planning

tifaceted nature of this broader construct. Thus, although creative thinking is at first an individual process, it is affected by such factors as the surrounding environment and the task at hand. Finally, creative thinking is not rare. All normally functioning people have the ability to think creatively. Moreover, this ability can be taught and enhanced through such methods as Creative Problem Solving.

REFERENCES

Bloom, B. S., Englehart, M. D., Furst, E. J., Hill, W. H., & Krathwohl, D. R. (Eds.). (1956). *Taxonomy of educational objectives: The classification of educational goals. Handbook I: Cognitive domain.* New York: David McKay.

Carnevale, A. P., Gainer, L. J., & Meltzer, A. S. (1990). *Workplace basics: The essential skills employers want.* San Francisco, CA: Jossey-Bass.

Costa, A. L. (1984, November). Mediating the metacognitive. *Educational Leadership, 42,* 57–62.

Dacey, J. S. (1989). *Fundamentals of creative thinking.* Lexington, MA: Lexington Books.

Davis, G. A. (1998). *Creativity is forever* (4th ed.). Dubuque, IA: Kendall-Hunt.

Firestien, R. L. (1996). *Leading on the creative edge: Gaining competitive advantage through the power of Creative Problem Solving.* Colorado Springs, CO: Piñon Press.

Gowan, J. C. (1972). *The development of the creative individual.* San Diego, CA: Knapp.

Isaksen, S. G., Dorval, K. B., & Treffinger, D. J. (1994). *Creative approaches to problem solving.* Dubuque, IA: Kendall-Hunt.

Isaksen, S. G., Murdock, M. C., Firestien, R. L., & Treffinger, D. J. (Eds.). (1993). *Understanding and recognizing creativity: The emergence of a discipline.* Norwood, NJ: Ablex.

Isaksen, S. G., & Treffinger, D. J. (1985). *Creative problem solving: The basic course.* Buffalo, NY: Bearly Limited.

Keller-Mathers, S. (1990). *Impact of creative problem solving training on participants' personal and professional lives: A replication and extension.* Unpublished master's project, Center for Studies in Creativity, Buffalo State College, Buffalo, NY.

Krathwohl, D. R., Bloom, B. S., & Masia, B. B. (1964). *Taxonomy of educational objectives: The classification of educational goals. Handbook II: Affective domain.* New York: David McKay.

Lunken, H. P. (1990). *Assessment of long-term effects of the master of science degree in creative studies on its graduates.* Unpublished master's project, Center for Studies in Creativity, Buffalo State College, Buffalo, NY.

MacKinnon, D. W. (1978). *In search of human effectiveness.* Buffalo, NY: Creative Education Foundation.

Mooney, R. L. (1963). A conceptual model for integrating four approaches to the identification of creative talent. In C. W. Taylor & F. Barron (Eds.), *Scientific creativity: Its recognition and development* (pp. 331–340). New York: Wiley.

Murdock, M. C., & Puccio, G. J. (1993). A contextual organizer for conducting creativity research. In S. G. Isaksen, M. C. Murdock, R. L. Firestien, & D. J. Treffinger (Eds.), *Nurturing and developing creativity: The emergence of a discipline* (pp. 249–280). Norwood, NJ: Ablex.

Neilson, L. (1990). *Impact of CPS training: An in-depth evaluation of a six-day course in CPS.* Unpublished master's project, Center for Studies in Creativity, Buffalo State College, Buffalo, NY.

Ornstein, R. E. (1972). *The psychology of consciousness.* San Francisco: W. H. Freeman.

Osborn, A. F. (1953). *Applied imagination: Principles and procedures of creative thinking.* New York: Scribner.

Osborn, A. F. (1963). *Applied imagination: Principles and procedures of creative problem-solving* (3rd rev. ed.). New York: Scribner.

Parnes, S. J. (1967). *The creative behavior guidebook.* New York: Scribner.

Parnes, S. J. (1985). Creative problem solving. In A. L. Costa (Ed.), *Developing minds* (pp. 230–232). Alexandria, VA: Association for Supervision and Curriculum Development.

Parnes, S. J., Noller, R. B., & Biondi, A. M. (1977). *Guide to creative action* (rev. ed.). New York: Scribner.

Puccio, G. J. (1995). Why study creativity? In M. Joyce, S. Isaksen, F. Davidson, G. Puccio, & C. Coppage (Eds.), *An introduction to creativity: An anthology for college courses in creativity which provides historical and current thinking from interdisciplinary perspectives* (pp. 49–56). Acton, MA: Copley.

Puccio, K. G. (1994). *An analysis of an observational study of creative problem solving for primary children.* Unpublished master's project, Center for Studies in Creativity, Buffalo State College, Buffalo, NY.

Rhodes, M. (1961). An analysis of creativity. *Phi Delta Kappan, 42,* 305–310.

Rogers, C. (1959). Toward a theory of creativity. In H. H. Anderson (Ed.), *Creativity and its cultivation* (pp. 69–82). New York: Harper & Brothers.

Stein, M. I. (1968). Creativity. In E. F. Boragatta & W. W. Lambert (Eds.), *Handbook of personality theory and research* (pp. 900–942). Chicago: Rand McNally.

Torrance, E. P. (1962). *Guiding creative talent.* Englewood Cliffs, NJ: Prentice Hall.

Torrance, E. P. (1972). Can we teach children to think creatively? *Journal of Creative Behavior, 6,* 114–143.

Torrance, E. P. (1974). *Norms and technical manual for the Torrance Tests of Creative Thinking.* Bensenville, IL: Scholastic Testing.

Torrance, E. P., & Safter, H. T. (1999). *Making the creative leap beyond.* Buffalo, NY: Creative Education Foundation.

Toynbee, A. (1964). Is America ignoring her creative minority? In C. W. Taylor (Ed.), *Widening horizons in creativity* (pp. 3–9). New York: Wiley.

Treffinger, D. J. (1995). *Creativity, creative thinking, and critical thinking: In search of definitions* [Idea capsule report 5001]. Sarasota, FL: Center for Creative Learning.

Treffinger, D. J. (1996). *Dimensions of creativity* [Idea capsule report 9004]. Sarasota, FL: Center for Creative Learning.

Treffinger, D. J., Isaksen, S. G., & Firestien, R. L. (Eds.). (1983). *The handbook of creative learning* (Vol. 1). Williamsville, NY: Center for Creative Learning.

VanGundy, A. (1987). Organizational creativity and innovation. In S. G. Isaksen (Ed.), *Frontiers of creativity research: Beyond the basics* (pp. 358–379). Buffalo, NY: Bearly Limited.

Vehar, J. (1994). *An impact study to improve a five-day course in facilitating creative problem solving.* Unpublished master's project, Center for Studies in Creativity, Buffalo State College, Buffalo, NY.

Vehar, J., Firestien, R. L., & Miller, B. (1997). *Creativity unbound: An introduction to creative problem solving.* Williamsville, NY: Innovation Systems Group.

Warshofsky, F. (1999). *Stealing time: The new science of aging.* New York: TV Books.

13

Added Value:
A Dispositional Perspective on Thinking

Shari Tishman

Imagine a cluster of students huddled around a picture of animal footprints. The picture shows two sets of tracks proceeding toward each other from opposite sides and meeting in the middle, where they blend together in a chaotic, slightly circular pattern. Only one set of tracks emerges from the circle. Has there been a fight? Has one of the animals been eaten? Students discuss what they think is going on. Eventually, everyone concludes that there has indeed been a fight to the death. Everyone, that is, except Genella.

"How do we know these footprints were made at the same time?" Genella asks. "What if the first animal was wounded or sick and walked to this place and just died? And then later another animal came along and ate the remains." Genella squints again at the picture and then gets out of her seat to walk in long, loping steps across the room, trying to imitate the pattern of footprints. "No, wait," she says, stopping herself. "That's wrong." She looks at the picture again and repeats the walk, this time moving her body more awkwardly. "See?" she says to her classmates. "When you imitate the footsteps, it feels like the animal was limping before it got there."

What teacher wouldn't be pleased with Genella's behavior? Not satisfied to accept an explanation at face value, she proposes and tests an alternative theory. One way of describing Genella's behavior is to say that she has a certain sort of thinking disposition: She is disposed to critique and test explanations.

What Are Thinking Dispositions?

Why characterize Genella's behavior in terms of thinking dispositions rather than thinking skills? Thinking dispositions are broad intellectual behaviors that include skill but also include attitudes, motivations, emotions, and other elements typically left out of ability-centered accounts of good thinking. Recall what Genella did. To be sure, she was displaying skill in theory-

testing, an important area of critical thinking. But to characterize her behavior in terms of thinking skills is to capture only a piece of it. Beyond skill, she was also demonstrating behavior that was self-initiated and self-sustained. She recognized that a theory was being proposed, took issue with it, and then invested herself in testing an alternative theory.

Thinking dispositions are a part of a person's character, and a shorthand way to define them is to call them intellectual character traits. Like character traits in general, thinking dispositions can be positive, negative, or neutral. They can be described with a variety of everyday adjectives: detail-oriented, open-minded, close-minded, curious, skeptical, impulsive, and so on. Following the title of this book, *Developing Minds*, this chapter is concerned with positive thinking dispositions—patterns of intellectual behavior that yield insight, rational action, innovation, and understanding.

What Kinds of Dispositions Exist?

What sorts of thinking dispositions would we like young minds to develop? Many educators and psychologists have turned their attention to this question and, over the last decade or so, have put forth several definitions and lists. Some scholars emphasize a single broad disposition toward good thinking, such Peter and Noreen Facione's notion of the disposition to think critically (Facione & Facione, 1992), or psychologist Ellen Langer's notion of mindfulness (Langer, 1989). Other researchers identify a range of distinct behaviors. For example, Art Costa proposes several habits of mind (Costa & Kallick, 2000). Robert Ennis (1986) identifies several critical thinking dispositions. Naturally, my colleagues and I have discussed several key thinking dispositions (Perkins, Jay, & Tishman, 1993). Although these lists differ in many respects, by and large they all emphasize such tendencies as open-mindedness, reasonableness, curiosity, and metacognitive reflection.

Copyright © 2001 Shari Tishman

Rather than providing a comprehensive synthesis of these lists, let me suggest four broad thinking dispositions that capture the spirit, if not the detail, of the kinds of intellectual behaviors celebrated in most of the literature on thinking dispositions:

1. The disposition to pose and explore problems.
2. The disposition to critique and test theories and explanations.
3. The disposition to seek multiple perspectives and possibilities.
4. The disposition to be judicious and reflective.

To readers familiar with the thinking skills movement, these dispositions may sound suspiciously like broad thinking skills. After all, considering other perspectives, reasoning, and so forth have long been encouraged by advocates of thinking skills. So why talk about dispositions instead of skills? The answer depends on showing that intellectual character involves more than the exercise of skill. The following section tries to do this.

HOW DO YOU RECOGNIZE DISPOSITIONS?

Consider the tendency to seek multiple perspectives and possibilities. People who have this tendency are inclined to see several sides of a situation, rather than taking just one point of view. They also tend to explore several options in response to a decision or a problem, rather than immediately settling on the obvious course of action.

Suppose you want to determine whether someone has this tendency. What psychological components will you look for? It won't be enough to look for cognitive ability. People often display cognitive abilities in test-taking situations and other artificial settings, but they don't use the same abilities in their daily lives. For example, people who can brainstorm alternative solutions to a problem when asked may not do the same when faced with everyday problems of their own. Possessing certain thinking skills is a necessary condition of having a thinking disposition, but it is not a sufficient one. Thinking dispositions are abiding intellectual character traits rather than "special occasion" displays of skill. So, if someone has a thinking disposition, you will see not only skill but also the psychological components that spark the use of that skill.

From a logical point of view, there are three distinct and necessary components of thinking dispositions: ability, sensitivity, and inclination. Ability concerns the basic capacity to carry out a behavior. Sensitivity involves alertness to opportu-

nities to initiate the behavior. Inclination is the motivation or impulse to engage in and sustain the behavior. For example, consider the disposition under discussion, the disposition to seek multiple perspectives. People who have it (a) have the capacity to see a situation from more than one perspective, (b) recognize, on their own, occasions to explore alternative perspectives, and (c) feel inclined to invest the energy in doing so.

These components may sound good in theory, but do they really exist as separate functions in the mind? Research seems to show that they do. All three elements—inclination, sensitivity, and ability—are separable and measurable (Perkins, Tishman, Donis, Ritchart, & Andrade, 2000). Each one makes its own distinct contribution to thinking, and weaknesses in any of the three elements hinder good thinking. For example, for any particular disposition, some people are strong in ability but weak in inclination and sensitivity; some are strong in inclination but weak in the other elements; and so on. Interestingly, although all three elements must be present to produce a thinking disposition, there is a surprising story to tell about the relative importance of these elements—a story that has direct relevance for the teaching of thinking.

SENSITIVITY AND ITS SURPRISING IMPORTANCE

Typically, when we think about cultivating students' intellectual behavior, we focus on two dimensions—ability and motivation, or "skill and will." We need to teach the right intellectual skills, the thinking goes, but we also must motivate students to use them. Sensitivity is taken for granted.

Motivation is important, of course, as are intellectual skills. But research reveals that sensitivity plays a surprisingly large role in effective thinking. Sensitivity, as we have said, involves recognizing opportunities to engage in certain patterns of intellectual behavior—for example, to think flexibly, to ask questions, to probe and test theories, to be self-reflective. Students often have difficulty perceiving these sorts of opportunities when they are embedded in the everyday stream of life, even when they possess the skills and the will to respond to them. Research shows that low sensitivity is more frequently a roadblock to good thinking than low inclination or even low ability. In other words, students very often fail to do their best thinking not because they aren't able to, and not because they don't want to, but because they simply don't recognize occasions to do so (Perkins et al., 2000).

Furthermore, correlation studies show that sensitivity is not as strongly correlated with IQ as is ability, which *is* highly correlated. This means that when we measure students' thinking dispositions, high scores on ability are not necessarily accompanied by high scores on sensitivity. The reverse is also true: high scores on sensitivity don't necessarily reflect high ability. This finding underscores what many educators already believe—that traditional intelligence measures such as IQ tests (and standardized tests, whose scores are highly correlated with IQ) don't tell the whole story of intelligent behavior.

ADDING VALUE: WHY A DISPOSITIONAL PERSPECTIVE MAKES A DIFFERENCE

What are the implications of thinking dispositions for teaching thinking? In a moment, we'll take a closer look at the implications of sensitivity and inclination specifically. But first a general caution against throwing out the baby with the bath water. Taking a dispositional approach to the teaching of thinking doesn't mean throwing away all the fine work that has been done on thinking skills. Plenty of good thinking skills programs exist, with lots of experience and expertise invested in them. Chances are, if a program is working well, it's because the program is also paying attention to inclination and sensitivity, even if its explicit focus is on abilities.

CULTIVATING SENSITIVITY

The value of being sensitive to thinking opportunities seems obvious and uncontroversial. Who would argue with the idea that it's important to notice occasions to think? But teaching sensitivity means training students to seek and recognize thinking occasions on their own. And this is harder than it sounds. Most instruction acts as a surrogate for sensitivity by providing students with the thinking opportunities, usually in the form of questions or problems, rather than challenging them to find them on their own.

Accordingly, one approach is to design activities that straightforwardly ask students to look for thinking opportunities. For example, students can be asked to seek out theories and generalizations in texts (e.g., newspapers, textbooks, and other information sources—including the Internet). They can be asked to keep a problem-finding journal in which they track questions and enigmas they encounter in everyday life.

Another approach is to increase students' awareness of their own emotional and perceptual reactions to thinking opportunities. For example, teachers might encourage students to be alert to feelings of puzzlement or curiosity, which can signal opportunities to question and probe. They can be urged to note feelings of doubt and of certainty, which can signal opportunities to test and critique. And they can be helped to be more aware of feelings of empathy, which can signal opportunities to explore alternative perspectives.

CULTIVATING INCLINATION

Inclination is the leaning, or urge, to act in a certain way. It is akin to motivation, and, like motivation, it is cultivated through a combination of extrinsic and intrinsic support. Extrinsic support comes when others reward students for displaying thinking dispositions. Intrinsic support comes from the internal payoff students feel when a behavior genuinely increases their pleasure, insight, or understanding.

One needs to be careful about extrinsic rewards, of course. But most teachers recognize that two powerful rewards for students are attention and recognition. Paying mind when students display positive thinking dispositions—for example, when they notice alternative perspectives, go beyond an obvious solution, or critique a theory—serves a twofold purpose. It provides a reward in the form of increased attention. And, by singling out such behaviors for praise, it points out models of good thinking for students to emulate.

As useful as extrinsic support is, intrinsic support is better—more satisfying, more durable, less coercive. So what can be done to increase students' intrinsic inclination toward positive thinking dispositions? Intrinsic inclination is stronger when tasks involve pleasurable cognitive engagement. For students, this means using thinking dispositions in contexts that interest them. Of course, one of the challenges of teaching is to get students interested in things that are new or difficult, and the trick is to find ways to make new material engaging. This is what good teaching is all about. There are as many ways of doing this as there are good teachers, but here are a couple of general principles.

First, cognitive engagement is increased when students have a chance to choose intellectual directions and influence outcomes. So, for example, if one wants to increase intrinsic inclination toward problem-finding, give students the opportunity to choose and explore problems of their own choice.

Another general principle concerns making room for students' individual learning styles or preferences. Much has been written about multiple intelligences and multiple ways of knowing. Regardless of which particular theory about learning styles may be most compelling, it is certainly true that every student finds certain learning modalities more engaging than others. This chapter opened with an example about a girl who used a kinesthetic modality, making her own body a tool to test a theory. Would she have done this if the physical setup of the classroom were different, or if the teacher were unacccepting of such behavior? Perhaps not. Cultivating intrinsic inclination means giving students plenty of choices, and providing them with opportunities to engage in a variety of learning modalities.

WHERE TO START WHEN YOU'VE ALREADY STARTED

Many teachers, especially those reading this book, are already using thinking-centered practices in their classrooms, often with considerable success. So how can the ideas presented here be useful to educators who are already teaching thinking? Their greatest value may lie in suggesting criteria to assess and refine what is already being done.

As mentioned earlier, thinking skills programs that work well probably already pay implicit attention to inclination and sensitivity. The three components of thinking dispositions—ability, sensitivity, and inclination—are useful lenses for evaluating program effectiveness. For example, suppose you are using a critical thinking program designed to teach reasoning skills. The program probably adequately targets the skill side of good thinking, since that is its intent. But beyond ability, does it develop and support students' inclination to reason? Can it be strengthened by finding additional ways to provide extrinsic and intrinsic support for reasoning—for example, by increasing positive attention to reasoning behaviors in the classroom and by increasing students' opportunities for choice? Can it be strengthened by increasing attention to

sensitivity? For example, can more ways be found to encourage students to recognize reasoning opportunities on their own, opportunities such as the overgeneralizations and undersupported theories that are often embedded in written and oral language?

Adopting a dispositional perspective on teaching thinking needn't undermine other approaches that are already under way. Rather, it can add value, both as an evaluative tool and as a design tool. As an evaluative tool, it can help teachers understand what's working, and why. As a design tool, it can provide a framework for crafting thinking-centered instruction that reaches beyond the development of skill to cultivate students' intellectual character.

REFERENCES

Costa, A. L., & Kallick, B. (Eds.). (2000). *Discovering and exploring habits of mind.* Alexandria, VA: Association for Supervision and Curriculum Development.

Ennis, R. H. (1986). A taxonomy of critical thinking dispositions and abilities. In J. B. Baron & R. S. Sternberg (Eds.), *Teaching thinking skills: Theory and practice* (pp. 9–26). New York: W. H. Freeman.

Facione, P. A., & Facione, N. C. (1992). *The California Critical Thinking Dispositions Inventory (CCTDI) and the CCTDI test manual.* Millbrae, CA: California Academic Press.

Langer, E. (1989). *Mindfulness.* Reading, MA: Addison-Wesley.

Perkins, D. N., Jay, E., & Tishman, S. (1993). Beyond abilities: A dispositional theory of thinking. *The Merrill-Palmer Quarterly, 39*(1), 1–21.

Perkins, D. N., Tishman, S., Donis, K., Ritchart, R., & Andrade, A. (2000). Intelligence in the wild: A dispositional view of intellectual traits. *Educational Psychology Review, 12*(3), 269–293.

14

Actively Open-Minded Thinking

JONATHAN BARON

We can more effectively improve thinking if we have standards for what good thinking is. "We" means students as well as educators; students apply standards of thinking to one another, just as teachers apply them to students and to other teachers. In early universities, the standards came from Aristotle. Logic was an essential part of the curriculum. We still criticize answers that beg the question, non sequiturs, and other Aristotelian fallacies. Recent scholarship has given us a clearer idea of what good thinking is, where thinking goes wrong, and how education can help.

The most important standards concern active open-mindedness about arguments on all sides of a question. We need to enforce these standards because many people tend to think in ways that reinforce their current views. Few people make the opposite mistake.

Teachers can encourage active open-mindedness by making these standards explicit and by taking them seriously when we assign grades. We should not, for example, give high marks to papers that ignore obvious arguments that fly in the face of the point being made. We can also support the standards by showing, across the curriculum, how good thinking is the only path to true knowledge.

WHAT IS THINKING?

Thinking concerns the resolution of doubt about what to do, what to believe, or what to value. It consists of search and inference. (Logic concerns inference only.) When we think, we search for possibilities, which are ways of resolving the doubt; for evidence, which bears on the merit of the possibilities; and for relevant values, which allow us to evaluate the possibilities in the light of the evidence. In buying a car, for example, the possibilities consist of particular cars (and perhaps other options such as not buying the car and taking the train instead). The evidence is information about quality, safety, price, alternatives, and so forth. And the values are what we care about,

from avoiding hassle to minimizing pollution. During and after our search, we make inferences from what we have found. Possibilities strengthen and weaken, sometimes getting rejected from the set under consideration or being adopted as our provisional or final choice.

Buying a car involves thinking about a decision, but we also think about beliefs and values. We think about beliefs by gathering evidence from our own pre-existing beliefs and from other sources. For example, we may recall things we've heard about the effects of gasoline combustion on the environment and the economy, and we may read more or ask others. Thinking about values relies more heavily on pre-existing values (as evidence) rather than external ones. We can, for example, think about how our choice of cars bears up in light of our deepest values about what matters in life, including such things as enjoying ourselves and protecting the environment. Here, the evidence consists of these other values, brought to bear on the values we form for a particular kind of decision (Keeney, 1992.)

The examples so far involve mostly search. We also make inferences from what we find as we search. Many times, we simply weigh arguments against one another in light of our relevant values. In other cases, we follow rules or principles of inference. These rules themselves are often the results of prior decisions to adopt or try to follow them. Thinking well or badly about our rules can affect how good they are.

For example, some people follow a rule to "do no harm." They take care not to cause harm through action (but harm caused by inaction may be acceptable, especially if the person does not think about the consequences). In general, this is a good rule that is consistent with people's personal and moral values. Sometimes, however, it causes trouble, as when people resist reforms that are largely beneficial but harmful to a few (even though blocking the reforms would hurt more people to a greater extent), or when they resist potentially worthwhile actions that carry some risks, such as giving a child a vaccine that, in rare cases, causes rather than prevents a disease (Baron, 1994a). If people reflected on this rule, they might realize that the consequences are what they really care about, and they might modify it.

NORMATIVE, DESCRIPTIVE, AND PRESCRIPTIVE MODELS

The study of thinking implicitly or explicitly involves three kinds of models. Normative models describe the standard we use to evaluate thinking. Descriptive models tell us how thinking usually is done, in terms that we can compare to the normative models. Prescriptive models tell us how we need to push one another to make our thinking better according to the normative standard. Actively open-minded thinking is a prescriptive standard.

The normative standard is derived from the goals of thinking itself. We think because we want to reach the best decision or conclusion, given our other values (Baron, 1985, 1994a, 1994b). One aspect of that standard concerns fairness to possibilities.

Ideally, thinking should be impartial, giving both old and new possibilities an equal chance. If we are looking only for reasons our initial opinion was right all along, we are just wasting time. In fact, people are biased toward what they already favor. This happens in both search and inference. We search for evidence that supports the favored possibilities, and when we find contradictory evidence we give it too little weight (Baron, 1994b). Perkins, Allen, and Hafner (1983) aptly call this "myside bias." There may not be an adversary on the opposing side, but that other view still deserves fair consideration. Myside bias exists in part because some people confuse good thinking with being committed to a prior position. They regard open-minded thinking as wishy-washy and weak (Baron, 1995; Kuhn, 1991; Stanovich & West, 1998). Prescriptively, to avoid this bias, we must learn to consider the other side (Nickerson, 1989).

Examples of the effects of myside bias are easy to find. Janis (1982), for example, has shown how this sort of thinking led to such fiascos as the Bay of Pigs invasion. Herek, Janis, and Huth (1987) found that such bias is correlated with bad outcomes in major foreign policy decisions of the U.S. government. Ethno-political conflicts such as those in India and the Balkans are rife with myside bias (Baron, 1998b).

Myside bias leads to, and stems from, overconfidence. It is often thought that confidence is an unalloyed good. People who are confident take risks for the sake of achievement, and, as a result, they achieve more. Note, however, that this confidence involves one's expectations for the future. Confidence in one's past efforts, especially past thinking, can have exactly the opposite effect, making people less inclined to take risks and reluctant to question their conclusions. "If I have the right answer," one might think, "then any evidence against it must be incorrect." Extremely high confidence is typically unwarranted (Baron, 1994b; Gilovich, 1991). For example, people who judge that they are absolutely correct on difficult test items are typically wrong on more than 20 percent of those items. Asking people to think of reasons why they might be wrong reduces this bias (Koriat, Lichtenstein, and Fischhoff, 1980).

Another impediment to good thinking is misapplication of rules and principles. An example would be applying the "do no harm" rule, mentioned earlier, to cases in which it is not appropriate. By "appropriate" I mean consistent with the values that motivate the rule in the first place. Another example is the prescript against wasting money. People try not to spend money on things they will not use. But they also do the reverse, making it a rule to use what they have already spent money on. Thus, on a beautiful April day when plenty of outdoor tennis courts are available at the local YMCA, we see people trudging inside to use the indoor court they have paid for through the end of the month. They don't want their money to go to "waste," even though they would prefer to be outdoors. If they thought in an actively open-minded way about the rules guiding their behavior, they might play outside and enjoy themselves more.

Actively open-minded thinking is the name I give to the prescriptive model. To correct myside bias, we must bend over backward the other way. When we hear arguments that contradict our favored position, we should listen. Beyond that, we should seek out counterarguments. That is where being "active" comes in.

HOW EDUCATORS CAN HELP

Educators can improve thinking skills by insisting on thorough and fair search, fair inference, and appropriate confidence. I call this actively open-minded thinking because we must work actively against wishful thinking and bias toward pet possibilities. Because good thinking involves competition among possibilities, evidence, and values, it is almost always quantitative, in the sense of weighing things against one another. When we pit safety against price, we must ask how much safety, what price, and how much we care about each. Sometimes it may help to make the quantitative aspects explicit.

Actively open-minded thinking is fundamental to academic inquiry. When professors submit papers to journals, they

77

might be criticized for their search techniques—for failing, for example, to seek opposing views in the literature or alternative interpretations of their findings; they might also be faulted for biased inferences, such as dismissing discrepant results. Students receive the same sorts of criticism of their work. Colleges and universities are thus well-situated to teach actively open-minded thinking. Tenure and promotion of faculty are based to a large extent on candidates upholding these scholarly values in their own work.

In some of my classes, I explicitly try to encourage actively open-minded thinking. For example, I assign a reflective essay with the following suggested outline (Baron, 1998a):

1. Explain your question and why it is important.
2. Present the most obvious answer or answers.
3. Consider less obvious alternatives, or objections to the obvious answers.
4. Rebut the criticisms, or explain how the original answers can be modified to deal with them.

Many students have trouble with this exercise. Yet some who are not otherwise the best students take to it easily. Those who fail usually err by making a case for one side, like a lawyer, but neglecting the other side. In the 1970s, when students were more rebellious, I used to get essays that made a one-sided attack on, for example, me. It was particularly easy in these cases to point out the students' failures to consider arguments on the other side.

Another way to promote actively open-minded thinking is to have students retrace the thinking that led to a particular piece of knowledge. Rather than just teach about the solar system as a given, why not take students through the history of knowledge about it: the ancient Greek discovery that the Earth is spherical; the continuing resistance to that idea; Ptolemy's theory of the solar system; Copernicus's not-so-obviously correct alternative to it; Galileo's observations of the moons of Jupiter; and (in advanced high school math) Kepler's laws and Newton's reconstruction of them. The same can be done in other fields (Baron, 1993).

Educators can encourage good thinking in other ways—for example, by encouraging discussion in which alternative points of view are requested and debated. Even in grading exams, we can give credit for bringing up an alternative or a criticism. Most importantly, we can help students learn to think by telling them explicitly what our standards are and then acting consistently with these standards, both in the classroom and when assigning grades.

IS ACTIVELY OPEN-MINDED THINKING ALWAYS GOOD?

Let me try a little active open-mindedness myself. Is being actively open-minded the best thing to do when we are confronted with the arguments of, say, Hitler or Milosevic (Tetlock, 1993)? In hindsight, it is easy to see that the Nazis were completely wrong. Even at the time, it should not have taken a thoughtful person long to grasp this. However, clear-cut cases are rare. If we always "know" that certain views are unworthy of a hearing, we will reject the good along with the bad. Those who dismissed Nazi ideology without a moment's thought might also reject more reasonable ideologies in the same way. How would they distinguish the deserving from the undeserving unless they spend a little time searching for evidence on both sides?

In fact, we see such rejections all the time in various polarized debates. Each side, without thinking, is convinced of its rightness, but both cannot be right. Perhaps even the American abolitionists would have failed a course in thinking, although in opposing slavery they were on the side of the angels. The wisdom of hindsight is great, but until the time machine is invented, we cannot depend on it at the moment of decision.

Of course, public expression is very different from private thinking. In many situations, one-sided arguments are more persuasive. Under some conditions, it is necessary to rally the troops rather than inspire a reflective search for truth and good. At such times, it is still prudent to be familiar with the arguments on the other side, even if we must suppress this knowledge in the present.

But this chapter concerns thinking skills, not public expression. When educators assign writing topics or encourage classroom discussion, we must be clear about our standards. If our standards are scholarly, we will favor active open-mindedness and not accept one-sided arguments. Students should understand what scholarly standards are about, for they are the backbone of education.

REFERENCES

Baron, J. (1985). *Rationality and intelligence.* New York: Cambridge University Press.
Baron, J. (1993). Why teach thinking? An essay. *Applied Psychology: An International Review, 42,* 191–237.
Baron, J. (1994a). Nonconsequentialist decisions. *Behavioral and Brain Sciences, 17,* 1–42.
Baron, J. (1994b). *Thinking and deciding* (2nd ed.). New York: Cambridge University Press.
Baron, J. (1995). Myside bias in thinking about abortion. *Thinking and Reasoning, 1,* 221–235.

Baron, J. (1998a). Intelligent thinking and the reflective essay. In R. J. Sternberg & W. Williams (Eds.), *Intelligence, instruction, and assessment* (pp. 133–147). Hillsdale, NJ: Erlbaum Associates.

Baron, J. (1998b). *Judgment misguided: Intuition and error in public decision making.* New York: Oxford University Press.

Gilovich, T. (1991). *How we know what isn't so: The fallibility of human reason in everyday life.* New York: Free Press.

Herek, G. M., Janis, I. L., & Huth, P. (1987). Decision making during international crises: Is quality of process related to outcome? *Journal of Conflict Resolution, 31,* 203–226.

Janis, I. L. (1982). *Groupthink: Psychological studies of policy decisions and fiascoes.* Boston: Houghton Mifflin.

Keeney, R. L. (1992). *Value-focused thinking: A path to creative decision-making.* Cambridge, MA: Harvard University Press.

Koriat, A., Lichtenstein, S., & Fischhoff, B. (1980). Reasons for confidence. *Journal of Experimental Psychology: Human Learning and Memory, 6,* 107–118.

Kuhn, D. (1991). *The skills of argument.* New York: Cambridge University Press.

Nickerson, R. S. (1989). On improving thinking through instruction. *Review of Research in Education, 15,* 3–57.

Perkins, D. N., Allen, R., & Hafner, J. (1983). Difficulties in everyday reasoning. In W. Maxwell (Ed.), *Thinking: The expanding frontier* (pp. 177–189). Philadelphia: Franklin Institute.

Stanovich, K. E., & West, R. F. (1998). Individual differences in rational thought. *Journal of Experimental Psychology: General, 127,* 161–188.

Tetlock, P. E. (1993). Flattering and unflattering personality portraits of integratively simple and complex managers. *Journal of Personality and Social Psychology, 50,* 819–827.

15

Habits of Mind

Arthur L. Costa

By definition, a problem is any stimulus, question, task, phenomenon, or discrepancy whose explanation is not immediately known. We are interested in student performance under those challenging conditions that demand strategic reasoning, insightfulness, perseverance, creativity, and craftsmanship to resolve a complex problem. Not only are we curious about how many answers students know, but also about how they behave when they *don't* know—in particular, what habits of mind they fall back on. We are interested in observing how students produce, rather than merely reproduce, knowledge. The critical attribute of intelligent human beings is not only having information, but also knowing how to act on it.

By "habit of mind," I mean a disposition toward behaving intelligently when confronted with problems. When humans experience dichotomies, are confused by dilemmas, or come face to face with uncertainties, effective action depends on following certain patterns of intellectual behavior. When we draw upon these resources, the results are more powerful, of higher quality, and of greater significance than if we fail to perform these intellectual behaviors.

Employing habits of mind requires a composite of many skills, attitudes, cues, past experiences, and proclivities. It obliges us to choose among patterns of thinking and therefore implies that we value certain patterns over others. It includes alertness to the contextual cues that signal the appropriate time and circumstance to adopt a particular pattern. It requires a level of skillfulness to execute the behaviors and follow through effectively over time. It suggests that as a result of each experience in which the behaviors were employed, the effects of their use are reflected upon, evaluated, modified, and carried forth to future applications.

This chapter is adapted from *Discovering and Exploring Habits of Mind*, edited by A. L. Costa and B. Kallick, 2000. Alexandria, VA: Association for Supervision and Curriculum Development.

People who employ habits of mind thus have five key characteristics:

- **Inclination:** They feel a tendency to employ patterns of intellectual behaviors.
- **Value:** They choose to value and employ the most effective patterns of intellectual behaviors, rather than other, less productive patterns.
- **Sensitivity:** They perceive opportunities for, and the appropriateness of, employing a particular pattern.
- **Capability:** They possess the basic skills and capacities to carry out the intellectual behaviors.
- **Commitment:** They constantly strive to reflect on and improve their performance of the behaviors.

SIXTEEN HABITS OF MIND

What behaviors are indicative of the efficient, effective problem solver? Just what do human beings do when they behave intelligently? Research on effective thinking and intelligent behavior reveals some identifiable characteristics of effective thinkers (Feuerstein, Rand, Hoffman, & Miller, 1980; Glatthorn & Baron, 1985; Sternberg, 1986; Perkins, 1985; Ennis, 1985; Goleman, 1995). It is not necessarily scientists, artists, mathematicians, or the wealthy who demonstrate these behaviors. They have been found in mechanics, teachers, entrepreneurs, salespeople, and parents—people in all walks of life.

Following are descriptions of 16 habits of mind—specific behaviors that human beings engage in when we respond intelligently to problems. We seldom practice these habits in isolation. Instead, we draw together clusters of such habits to use in various situations. When listening intently, for example, we employ flexibility, metacognition, precise language, and perhaps questioning. There are, of course, more than 16 ways in which people display intelligence. This list is not meant to be complete, but rather a starting point for the collection of additional attributes.

1. PERSISTING

Efficacious problem solvers stick to a task until it is completed. They don't give up easily. They are able to analyze a problem and develop a system, structure, or strategy to attack it. They have a repertoire and employ a range of alternative approaches. They collect evidence that their strategy is working, and if one strategy doesn't work, they know how to back up and try another. They recognize when a theory or idea must be rejected and replaced with another. They have systematic methods of analyzing a problem, which include knowing how to begin, what steps to perform, and what data need to be generated or collected. Because they are able to sustain a problem-solving process over time, they are comfortable with ambiguous situations.

Students who lack persistence often give up in despair when the answer to a problem is not immediately known. They sometimes crumple their papers and throw them away, saying, "I can't do this; it's too hard," or they write down any answer to get through the task as quickly as possible. Some students have attention deficits; they have difficulty staying focused for any length of time, and they are easily distracted. Others lack the ability to analyze a problem or develop a way of attacking it. They may give up because they have a limited repertoire of problem-solving strategies, and if their strategy doesn't work, they have no alternatives.

2. MANAGING IMPULSIVITY

Effective problem solvers have a sense of deliberativeness: They think before they act. They intentionally form a vision of a product, a plan of action, a goal, or a destination before they begin. They strive to clarify and understand directions, develop a strategy for approaching a problem, and withhold value judgments until they fully understand an idea. Reflective individuals consider alternatives and the consequences before taking action. They increase their chances of success by gathering information, taking time to reflect before giving answers, making sure they understand directions, and listening to alternative points of view.

Often students blurt the first answer that comes to mind. Sometimes they start to work without fully understanding the directions, or lack an organized plan for approaching a problem. They may take the first suggestion given or operate on the most obvious and simple idea that occurs to them, rather than considering more complex alternatives and consequences of several possible directions.

3. LISTENING TO OTHERS WITH UNDERSTANDING AND EMPATHY

Highly effective problem solvers spend an inordinate amount of time and energy listening (Covey, 1989). Some psychologists believe that the ability to listen to others, empathize with them, and understand their points of view is one of the highest forms of intelligent behavior. Accurately paraphrasing other people's statements, detecting indicators of their feelings or emotional states (perceiving cues) in their oral and body language, and correctly interpreting their ideas, emotions, or problems are all indications of listening behavior (Piaget called it "overcoming egocentrism"). People with this habit of mind are able to take on the diverse perspectives of others. They gently demonstrate their understanding and empathy by recapping, building on, clarifying, or giving examples.

Senge, Ross, Smith, Roberts, and Kleiner (1994) suggest that to listen fully means to pay close attention to what is being said between the words. You listen not only for what someone knows, but also for what he or she is trying to represent.

Listening is one of the least-taught skills in schools. Some students laugh at others' ideas, interrupt, or are unable to consider the merits of someone else's views. When they think they are listening, they often are rehearsing in their heads what they are going to say next.

We want our students to learn to devote their mental energies to listening to other speakers and thinking through their positions. We wish students to hold in abeyance their own values, judgments, opinions, and prejudices in order to entertain another person's ideas. This is a very complex skill, requiring the ability to monitor one's own thoughts while attending to someone else's words. This does not mean that one must agree; a good listener simply tries to understand what the other person is saying.

4. THINKING FLEXIBLY

An amazing discovery about the human brain is its plasticity—its ability to "rewire," change, and even repair itself to become smarter. Flexible people draw upon a repertoire of problem-solving strategies and tailor their style to the situation, knowing when to be broad and global in their thinking and when to apply detailed precision. They can approach a problem from a new angle using a novel approach—what de Bono (1970) refers to as lateral thinking. They consider alternative points of view and are comfortable dealing with multiple sources of information simultaneously. Their minds are open to change, based on additional information or reasoning that contradicts their beliefs.

Flexible thinkers nonetheless display confidence in their intuition. They tolerate confusion and ambiguity up to a point and are willing to let go of a problem, trusting their subconscious to continue creative and productive work on it.

Students who lack flexibility as a habit of mind perceive situations from a very ego-centered point of view. They regard their approach to solving a problem as the only acceptable one.

5. THINKING ABOUT OUR THINKING (METACOGNITION)

Metacognition, a mental processing that occurs in the neocortex, involves knowing what we know and what we don't know. It is our ability to devise a plan for producing whatever information is needed, to be conscious of our own steps and strategies during the act of problem solving, and to reflect on and evaluate the productiveness of our thinking. Metacognition is a key attribute of formal thought, flowering about age 11.

Probably the major components of metacognition are developing a plan of action, keeping that plan in mind over a period of time, and then evaluating the plan upon its completion. Mapping out a strategy before embarking on a course of action helps us consciously track the steps in the sequence of planned behavior for the duration of the activity. It facilitates making temporal and comparative judgments, assessing readiness for more or different activities, and monitoring our interpretations, perceptions, decisions, and behaviors. Superior teachers practice metacognition daily when they develop a teaching strategy for a lesson, keep that strategy in mind throughout the instruction, and then reflect later on its effectiveness in producing the desired outcomes.

Intelligent people plan for, reflect on, and evaluate the quality of their own thinking skills and strategies.

6. STRIVING FOR ACCURACY AND PRECISION

Embodied in the stamina and skill of a ballerina or a shoemaker is the desire for craftsmanship, mastery, flawlessness, and economy of energy to produce exceptional results. Being craftsmanlike means taking pride in one's work, seeking continually to perfect it, trying to attain the highest possible standards, and pursuing ongoing learning in order to bring a laser-like focus to accomplishing a task.

People who value accuracy, precision, and craftsmanship take time to check over their products. They review the rules by which they are to abide, the models and visions they are to follow, and the criteria they are to employ and confirm that their finished product conforms exactly. For some people, craftsmanship requires continuous reworking. Mario Cuomo, a great speechwriter and politician, once said that his speeches were never done—only a deadline made him stop working on them.

Students who lack this habit of mind may turn in sloppy, incomplete, or uncorrected work. They are more anxious to be done with an assignment than to check it over for accuracy and precision. Minimal effort suffices, because expedience is more highly valued than excellence.

7. QUESTIONING AND POSING PROBLEMS

One of the characteristics that distinguishes humans from other forms of life is our inclination and ability to *find* problems to solve. Effective problem solvers know how to ask questions to fill in the gaps between what they know and what they don't know.

Inquirers recognize discrepancies and phenomena in their environment and probe for explanations and information: "Why do cats purr?" "What would happen if we put saltwater fish in a freshwater aquarium?" "What are some alternative solutions to international conflicts, other than wars?"

Effective questioners are inclined to ask a range of questions. For example, they request data to support others' conclusions and assumptions, asking questions like, "What evidence do you have? How do you know that's true? How reliable is this data source?" They inquire about point of view: "From whose perspective are we seeing, reading, or hearing? Can we view this situation from other angles?" They pose questions that make causal connections and relationships: "How are these people, events, or situations related? What produced this connection?" And they pose hypothetical scenarios characterized by "if" questions: "What do you think would happen if . . . ?"

Some students may not realize that questions vary in complexity, structure, and purpose. When their questions do not elicit the desired information, they may lack strategies for rephrasing to find solutions.

8. APPLYING PAST KNOWLEDGE TO NEW SITUATIONS

Intelligent human beings learn from experience. When confronted with a new and perplexing problem, they will often turn to the past for guidance. They call upon their store of knowledge and experience for sources of data and for processes that will help them solve each new challenge. Furthermore, they are able to abstract meaning from one experience, carry it forth, and apply it in new and novel situations. They explain what they are doing now by making analogies or references to previous experiences: "This reminds me of . . ." or "This is just like the time when . . . ."

Too often, students begin each new task as if they were blank slates. Teachers feel dismay when they invite students to recall how they solved a similar problem previously and students don't remember. It is as if each experience is encapsulated and has no relationship to what has come before or what comes afterward. Such thinking is what psychologists refer to as an "episodic grasp of reality" (Feuerstein, Rand, Hoffman, & Miller, 1980). People who see events as separate, discrete, and unrelated to others seem unable to learn from one experience and apply that learning to another context.

9. THINKING AND COMMUNICATING WITH CLARITY AND PRECISION

Language refinement plays a critical role in enhancing people's cognitive maps and their ability to think critically, which is the basis for efficacious action. Enriching the complexity and specificity of language simultaneously produces more effective thinking.

Language and thinking are closely entwined. Fuzzy language reflects fuzzy thinking, just as clear language reflects clear (though not necessarily correct) thinking. Intelligent people strive to communicate accurately in both written and oral form, taking care to define terms and to use precise language, correct names, universal labels, and apt analogies. They strive to avoid overgeneralizations, distortions, and omissions. Instead they support their statements with explanations, comparisons, quantification, and evidence.

10. GATHERING DATA THROUGH ALL SENSES

The brain is the ultimate reductionist. It reduces the world to its elementary parts: photons of light, molecules of smell, sound waves, vibrations of touch—which send electrochemical signals to individual brain cells that store information about lines, movements, colors, smells, and other sensory inputs.

Intelligent people know that all information gets into the brain through the sensory pathways: gustatory, olfactory, tactile, kinesthetic, auditory, and visual. Most linguistic, cultural, and physical learning is derived from the environment by observing or taking in through the senses. To be known, a wine must be drunk, a role must be acted, a game must be played, a dance must be moved, a goal must be envisioned. Those whose sensory pathways are open, alert, and acute absorb more information from the environment than those whose pathways are withered, immune, and oblivious to sensory stimuli.

Some people, unfortunately, go through school and life oblivious to the textures, rhythms, patterns, sounds, and colors around them. They operate within a narrow range of sensory strategies for problem solving, wanting perhaps to "describe it but not illustrate or act it," or to "listen but not participate."

11. CREATING, IMAGINING, AND INNOVATING

All human beings have the capacity to generate novel, original, clever, or ingenious products, solutions, and techniques. Creative human beings develop that capacity, trying to conceive different problem solutions by examining alternative possibilities from many angles. They tend to project themselves into various roles using analogies.

Creative people take risks and frequently push the boundaries of their perceived limits (Perkins, 1985). They are intrinsically rather than extrinsically motivated, working on tasks because of the aesthetic challenge rather than the material rewards. Creative people are open to criticism. They hold up their products for others to judge and seek feedback in an ever-increasing effort to refine their technique. They are uneasy with the status quo.

12. RESPONDING WITH WONDERMENT AND AWE

Describing the 200 best and brightest of the All USA College Academic Team identified by USA Today, Tracey Wong Briggs (1999, pp. 1A–2A) states, "They are creative thinkers who have a passion for what they do." Efficacious people have not only an "I can" attitude, but also an "I enjoy" feeling. They seek challenges for themselves and others. They delight in making up problems to solve on their own, and they request enigmas from others. They enjoy figuring things out by themselves and continue to learn throughout their lifetimes.

Some children and adults avoid problems and are "turned off" to learning. They make such comments as, "I was never good at these brainteasers," "It's boring," "When am I ever going to use this stuff?" or "Who cares?" Many people perceive of thinking as hard work and therefore recoil from situations that demand "too much" of it. Students might never enroll in another math class, for example, or pursue other "tough" academic subjects after they complete the basic requirements.

We want our students, however to be curious and to commune with the world around them—to marvel at the intricate geometry of a spider web, feel charmed by the opening of a bud, or exhilarate at the iridescence of a hummingbird's wings. Students can find power in a poem, elegance in a mathematical equation, mystery and orderliness in a chemical change, serenity in a distant constellation. By encouraging wonderment and awe as a habit of mind, we help our students to feel compelled, enthusiastic, and passionate about learning, inquiring, and mastering.

13. TAKING RESPONSIBLE RISKS

Flexible people tend to go beyond established limits; they "live on the edge" of their competence. They accept confusion, uncertainty, and the higher risks of failure as part of the norm, and they view setbacks as interesting, challenging, and growth-producing. However, they do not behave impulsively. Their risks are calculated. They draw on past knowledge, are thoughtful about consequences, and have a well-trained sense of which risks are worthwhile.

Risk takers tend to focus on a venture or an adventure. Those who focus on a venture seek some kind of tangible gain. For example a venture capitalist seeks economic gain and studies the risks carefully. Those who focus on adventure seek to test their own responses and experience new vistas, physically or emotionally. But they too must study the risks carefully and be confident that their actions will not be life-threatening or otherwise harmful.

It is only through repeated experiences that risk-takers learn to make sound decisions. They often draw on a mix of intuition, past knowledge, and passion for new challenges. As Bobby Jindal, executive director of the National Bipartisan Commission on the Future of Medicare, stated, "The only way to succeed is to be brave enough to risk failure" (Briggs, 1999, p. 2A).

People who hold back from taking risks constantly miss opportunities. Some students shy away from games, new learning, and new friendships because their fear of failure is far greater than their longing for venture or adventure. They get reinforcement from the mental voice that says, "If you try it and stumble, you will look stupid. If you don't even try, there's

no danger of failing." The other voice that might say, "You will never know what you can do unless you try," is silenced by fear and mistrust. Risk-averse people care more about finding the correct answer than about being challenged as they explore the question. They are unable to sustain a process of problem solving over time and therefore avoid ambiguous situations.

We hope that students will learn how to take intellectual as well as physical risks. In an era of innovation and rapid change, students who are comfortable going against the common grain, thinking of new ideas, and testing them with peers as well as teachers are more likely to succeed than are timid thinkers.

14. FINDING HUMOR

Another unique attribute of human beings is our sense of humor. Laughter is universal medicine. Its positive effects on physiological functions include a drop in the pulse rate, the secretion of endorphins, and increased oxygen in the blood. It has been found to liberate creativity and provoke such higher-level thinking skills as anticipating, finding novel relationships, using visual imagery, and making analogies. People who engage in humor generally have the ability to perceive situations from original and often interesting vantage points. They tend to appreciate and understand others' humor and to be verbally playful when interacting with others. Having a whimsical frame of mind, they thrive on catching incongruities; perceiving absurdity, irony, and satire; and being able to laugh at situations and themselves.

Some students find humor in all the wrong places—human differences, ineptitude, injurious behavior, vulgarity, violence, and profanity. We want our students to distinguish between those situations of human frailty and fallibility that call for compassion and those that are truly funny (Dyer, 1997). If they can use humor not as a weapon but as a tool—a means of relieving tension, winning allies, boosting group morale—they can be more effective problem solvers.

15. THINKING INTERDEPENDENTLY

Human beings are social beings. We congregate in groups, find it therapeutic to be listened to, draw energy from one another, and seek reciprocity. In groups we contribute our time and energy to tasks that we would quickly tire of when working alone. In fact, we have learned that one of the cruelest forms of punishment possible is solitary confinement.

Most people realize that all of us together are more powerful, intellectually and physically, than any one individual. We find ourselves increasingly more interdependent and sensitive to others' needs. Problem solving has become so complex that no one has access to all the data needed to make critical decisions; no one person can consider as many alternatives as several people can.

Students with underdeveloped social skills may not have learned to work cooperatively in groups. Some feel isolated and prefer their solitude: "Leave me alone—I'll do it by myself." Others make poor group members either because they are "job hogs" or because they let others do all the work.

Contributing to groups requires the ability to justify ideas and to test the feasibility of solution strategies on others. It also requires a willingness and openness to accept critical feedback from friends. Through such interaction, the group and the individual both continue to grow. Listening, seeking consensus, giving up an idea to work with someone else's, feeling empathy and compassion, leading, supporting group efforts, acting altruistically—all are behaviors indicative of cooperative human beings and intelligent problem solvers.

16. LEARNING CONTINUOUSLY

Intelligent people are in a continuous learning mode. Their confidence, in combination with their inquisitiveness, allows them to constantly search for new and better ways. People with this habit of mind are always striving for improvement, always growing, always learning, always modifying and improving themselves. They seize problems, situations, tensions, conflicts, and circumstances as valuable opportunities to learn.

A great mystery about humans is that we often confront learning opportunities with fear instead of enthusiasm and curiosity. We seem to feel better when we know than when we learn. We tend to defend our biases, beliefs, and storehouses of knowledge, rather than inviting the unknown, the creative, and the inspirational.

From an early age, following traditional, fragmented, reactive curricula, students have been trained to believe that deep learning means figuring out the truth rather than developing capabilities for effective and thoughtful action. They have been taught to value certainty rather than doubt, to give answers rather than to inquire, to know which choice is correct rather than to explore alternatives.

Our wish is for creative students who are eager to learn and humble enough to realize they don't have all the answers. Knowing what we don't know is the first step in the quest for knowledge; paradoxically, it is also the highest form of thinking possible.

THOUGHTFUL, EFFECTIVE HABITS

Based on research on human effectiveness, descriptions of remarkable performers, and analyses of the characteristics of efficacious people, I have described 16 habits of mind. As I stated at the outset, this is not an exhaustive list but a starting point for further elaboration and discussion.

When confronted with problematic situations, students—indeed, all of us—might profitably ask, "What is the most *intelligent* thing I can do right now?" Taking a reflective stance in the midst of active problem solving is often difficult. But consciously thinking about the habits of mind discussed here can be productive. We might first try to identify which habits will be most useful in the situation at hand: "Does this problem demand persistence? Should I listen empathetically to others? Do I need to raise questions? Is risk taking an appropriate response? Will it be helpful to look for humor?" After reviewing various possibilities, the next step is to consider how to apply those habits of mind that seem most beneficial: "How can I approach this problem flexibly? What questions should I ask? What past knowledge can I bring to bear? How can I illuminate this problem to make it clearer, more precise? Who should I turn to for help?"

The 16 habits of mind exhibited by intelligent problem solvers cut across all subject matters commonly taught in school. They are characteristic not only of superior students but also of peak performers at home, on the athletic field, in organizations, in the military, in the government, at church, and in corporations. They are what make marriages successful, learning continual, workplaces productive, and democracies enduring. The goal of education, therefore, should be to develop and reinforce these habits of mind. As Aristotle said, "We are what we repeatedly do. Excellence, then, is not an act but a habit." Only by routinely practicing these habits of mind can we assure ourselves that we are thinking clearly, confronting problems intelligently, and making wise decisions.

REFERENCES

Briggs, T. W. (1999, Febrary 25). Passion for what they do keeps alumni on first team. *USA Today*, pp. 1A–2A.

Chiabetta, E. L. (1970). A review of Piagetian studies relevant to science instruction at the secondary and college levels. *Science Education, 60*, pp. 253–261.

Costa, A. L. (1991). The search for intelligent life. In A. L. Costa (Ed.), *Developing minds: A resource book for teaching thinking* (pp. 100–106). Alexandria, VA: Association for Supervision and Curriculum Development.

Covey, S. (1989). *The seven habits of highly effective people.* New York: Simon & Schuster.

de Bono, E. (1970). *Lateral thinking: Creativity step by step.* New York: Harper Row.

Dyer, J. (1997). Humor as process. In A. L. Costa & R. Liebmann (Eds.), *Envisioning process as content: Toward a renaissance curriculum* (pp. 211–229). Thousand Oaks, CA: Corwin Press.

Ennis, R. (1985). Goals for a critical thinking curriculum. In A. L. Costa (Ed.), *Developing minds: A resource book for teaching thinking* (pp. 68–71). Alexandria, VA: Association for Supervision and Curriculum Development.

Feuerstein, R., Rand, Y. M., Hoffman, M. B., & Miller, R. (1980). *Instrumental enrichment: An intervention program for cognitive modifiability.* Baltimore: University Park Press.

Glatthorn, A., & Baron, J. (1985). The good thinker. In A. L. Costa (Ed.), *Developing minds: A resource book for teaching thinking* (pp. 63–67). Alexandria, VA: Association for Supervision and Curriculum Development.

Goleman, D. (1995). *Emotional intelligence: Why it can matter more than IQ.* New York: Bantam Books.

Perkins, D. (1985). What creative thinking is. In A. L. Costa (Ed.), *Developing minds: A resource book for teaching thinking* (pp. 85–88). Alexandria, VA: Association for Supervision and Curriculum Development.

Senge, P., Ross, R., Smith, B., Roberts, C., & Kleiner, A. (1994). *The fifth discipline fieldbook: Strategies and tools for building a learning organization.* New York: Doubleday/Currency.

Sternberg, R. (1986). *Intelligence applied: Understanding and increasing your intellectual skills.* New York: Harcourt Brace Jovanovich.

16

What Philosophy Offers to the Teaching of Thinking

BARRY K. BEYER

The true test of character is . . . how we behave when we don't know what to do.

—*John Holt*

M uch of what is written and done about the teaching of thinking reflects the influence of psychology. This is hardly surprising. In recent years, psychologists have taken major strides toward a fuller understanding of how we generate, process, store, and retrieve information and knowledge. Furthermore, because the training of educators often includes study in psychology or some subject closely related to it, we seem quite receptive to what psychologists have to tell us.

As important as psychology is in improving student thinking, however, it provides only one perspective for analyzing and understanding thinking. Philosophy offers another equally valuable, but too often ignored, perspective. Philosophy neither competes with nor negates the findings of psychology, but goes beyond them, adding unique insights into the cognitive processes we use to establish meaning.

Essentially, psychology offers insights into process, into *how* thinking occurs and thus how thinking procedures might be effectively taught. Philosophy, on the other hand, offers substance: it offers insights into *what* ought to be included in any worthwhile thinking skills program. If we fail to include insights from *both* psychology and philosophy in teaching thinking, we are likely to restrict ourselves to a one-dimensional understanding of thinking and to seriously limit our efforts to improve student thinking. I wish here to call attention to what philosophy offers about thinking that psychology does not so

This chapter is adapted from "What Philosophy Offers to the Teaching of Thinking," by Barry K. Beyer, in *Educational Leadership*, 47(5), February 1990, 55–60. Reprinted with permission. Copyright © 1990 Barry K. Beyer.

that these important dimensions of thinking can be incorporated into our classroom curriculums and teaching.[1]

PHILOSOPHY IS THINKING

Probably no discipline has more to do with thinking than does the discipline of philosophy, for philosophy and thinking are inextricably interwoven. Experts define philosophy as inquiry based on logical reasoning—it is the love and pursuit of wisdom (Morris 1973, p. 985). Unlike other disciplines, which generally apply thinking in specific contexts to particular data or problems, philosophy is thinking, the thinking that underlies all assertions, claims, and principles. It is the only discipline that has thinking as both its *subject* and its *method* of inquiry.

Philosophers study, apply, and evaluate rules and standards for thinking and for judging the substance of thinking. By focusing on the *standards* of good thinking, philosophy brings to us a different—and philosophers think more sophisticated—conception of thinking.

At the risk of oversimplifying a complex discipline, I would suggest that six concepts in philosophy have immediate relevance to improving student thinking. A brief analysis may clarify how each can contribute to classroom efforts to improve this thinking.

Reasoning. Reasoning, the most distinctive feature of philosophy, is the systematic inferring of information according to rules of logic so as to demonstrate or ascertain the validity of a claim or an assertion. It is the process by which we draw conclusions from observations or invent hypotheses and beliefs. The use of reasoning gets us from given, perhaps fragmentary, evidence to a conclusion. Indeed, we reason for many purposes, including the need to find unstated assumptions, to distinguish the relevant from the irrelevant, to justify claims, to determine the validity of others' claims, and so on.

Reasoning usually presents itself in the form of arguments, or sequences of statements presented to demonstrate the truthfulness of some assertion. This, for example, is an argument: "It's my turn to use the hall pass. I'm done with my work, and everyone else who has finished has already used it." By itself, the assertion "it's my turn to use the hall pass" is not an argument; it is simply a claim with no supporting reasons.

Argumentation can be thought of as a structure within which the various skills and dispositions of thinking are exercised. Levels of argumentation, from the simple to the complex, include recognizing arguments, analyzing arguments, evaluating arguments, and producing arguments.

Argument recognition consists of the ability to distinguish a communication that presents a claim with one or more supporting reasons from a communication that simply describes or explains. *Argument analysis,* as defined by philosophers Michael Scriven, Steven Toulmin, and others, involves examining a communication to identify (1) the claim (what the author is trying to make one believe or accept), (2) the stated reasons that are invoked to support this claim, and (3) the stated and unstated premises or assumptions that underlie the given reasons (the claimant may not prove or even state these but ofttimes implicitly asks that they be accepted as true) (Scriven 1976, pp. 39–45; Toulmin, Ricke, and Jarik 1984). In *argument evaluation,* the extent to which the argument works or does not work is judged. In *argument making,* lines of valid reasoning must be produced to support an assertion. This generative process applies argument analysis and evaluation, as well as other cognitive skills.

The abilities to recognize, analyze, judge, and formulate valid arguments through the application of reasoning and rules of logic are central to critical thinking.

Critical judgment. Philosophical thinking is critical thinking, which means a willingness (indeed, a predisposition) and an ability to scrutinize and evaluate thinking—one's own as well as others'—to determine truth, accuracy, or worth, and to construct logical arguments to justify claims or assertions (Paul, 1984b, 1987). Such thinking is called critical because it judges according to prescribed criteria, not because it is negative or accusatory. The results of critical thinking can be positive or negative, depending on whether or not the criteria are met.

Critical thinking is discriminating, disciplined, and questioning. We often naively assume that the opposite of critical thinking is creative thinking, but its actual opposite, as Matthew Lipman points out, is undiscriminating, undisciplined, and unquestioning thought—in short, the gullible acceptance of claims without careful analysis of their bases in evidence, reasons, and assumptions (Lipman, 1987).

One of the most essential aspects of critical thinking is critical judgment, which to philosophers means the inclination to evaluate objectively rather than to accept blindly (Lipman 1988). Philosophers examine reasoning to judge the extent to which it meets accepted standards of reasonableness and logic (Paul 1984b, 1987). Critical judgment consists of applying appropriate criteria to any sort of communication—an oral statement, a written document, a film, a painting, an action, or an event.

Philosophers have identified many specific critical judgment skills that good thinkers are able to execute. These include, for example, the ability to make logical inferences, to identify logical fallacies, and to judge the logical consistency of arguments.

Because critical thinking is concerned with what is reasonable to accept, critical judgments must also be made about the accuracy and reliability of information in the premises of arguments and in the evidence offered in support of claims. Matthew Lipman, Robert Ennis, and Richard Paul have identified a number of critical thinking skills that can be employed to judge the quality of such reasoning (Ennis, 1962; Paul, Binker, Jensen, & Kreklau, 1987). Among the skills they believe all of us should master are

- Determining the credibility of a source.
- Distinguishing the relevant from the irrelevant.
- Distinguishing facts from value judgments.
- Identifying and evaluating unstated assumptions.
- Identifying bias.
- Identifying point of view.
- Evaluating evidence offered in support of a claim. (Beyer, 1985)

For philosophers, being able to think means being able to execute these and other thinking operations within the context of searching for truth. For Lipman, reasoning at the lowest level means being able to execute each of these critical judgment skills. The highest level of reasoning demands the ability to combine these skills in a concerted, simultaneous fashion for highly sophisticated purposes (Lipman, 1984, 1987).

Criteria. Philosophy, as Lipman and others frequently point out, is unlike other disciplines in that it provides criteria for judging the quality of thinking (Lipman, 1988). More important, philosophers continuously submit these criteria to intensive critical analysis in an effort to devise the best criteria to use in their search for truth.

To examine the claims and arguments with which we are bombarded (and which we ourselves devise), we must understand and be able to apply criteria for determining the reasonableness of given claims and arguments. Experts generally agree, for example, on the criteria for identifying bias, the criteria that a line of reasoning must meet to be considered valid, and the criteria that a written document must meet to be considered credible. For instance, to be considered credible, an author must be recognized as expert on the subject, must have a reputation for accuracy, and must have no vested interest in distorting the truth in what has been written (Ennis, 1985a, 1985b). The criteria used in critical thinking are a knowledge dimension unique to this kind of thinking.

Philosophers have formulated (or, some would say, discovered) rules of reasoning that have come to constitute logic. These rules serve as guidelines for producing reasoned arguments as well as criteria for judging the quality—the reasonableness—of any claim or argument. One such rule, for example, is often expressed as

1. If A, then B.
2. If B, then C.
3. Therefore, if A, then C.

Translated into an everyday example, such a statement might read:

1. If Jane gets a 90 on this exam, she gets an A as her average in this course for this semester.
2. If Jane gets an A average for this course for this semester, she makes the honor roll for this semester.
3. Therefore, if Jane gets a 90 on this exam, she makes the honor roll for this semester.

This argument is perfectly logical according to this rule, which holds that the truth of premises 1 and 2 *necessarily* leads to a true conclusion (as stated in number 3).

Logic, it should be noted, deals not with the substance of what is said, but with its structure, with the rules of how to put statements together so that one leads invariably to the next. These rules help us determine the validity of conclusions in terms of the reasons upon which they are based. Generating and judging valid arguments calls for knowledge of the rules of logic as well as the skills and inclination to apply them. Critical thinkers think critically about the criteria and standards on which thinking is based and use these standards to judge thinking and its products.

Point of view. When philosophers think about the substance of thinking, they focus not only on its elements,

process, and structure, but also on the context in which thinking occurs. One important feature of this context is the point or points of view taken, represented, or expressed by the individuals involved.

The phrase *point of view* means different things to different people. To some, it simply means one person's opinion. For philosophers, however, it is a much more complicated and sophisticated concept. In terms of critical thinking, a point of view is the position from which one views things; that position, in turn, is a product of one's accumulated experience (Paul, 1987). An individual standing on the rim of the Grand Canyon, for example, sees a different scene than does one standing along the riverbed at the bottom of the canyon. Although both observers see the Grand Canyon, each sees it from a different point of view. Furthermore, what is viewed differently is interpreted differently, according to each viewer's prior knowledge, interests, motives, assumptions, biases, predilections, and similar variables. So, in examining ideas, events, or experiences, different individuals often see altogether different aspects of the subject, depending on where they are and where they have been. Only when different viewpoints are put together is the whole comprehensible.

Full understanding of an explanation or a description requires an understanding of the point of view that produced it. Thus, detecting points of view and taking them into account are important aspects of philosophical thinking, as is the ability to look at a subject from different points of view. It should be noted, however, that the rules of logic are valid for all persons regardless of their points of view.

Dialogue. One major method by which individuals exercise their critical thinking abilities is dialogue. Dialogue has been defined as an interchange among two or more individuals or points of view on a given topic, claim, or subject in an effort to ascertain the truth (Lipman 1984; Paul, 1987). Such an interchange involves giving and analyzing evidence, reasoning logically, identifying assumptions, looking at consequences, and representing differing points of view. This dialogue may be conducted between or among people, or it may even be carried on by an individual through critical self-reflection.

Asking and answering questions is one way that dialogue is stimulated, directed, and critically evaluated. Of course, not all questions call for critical thinking. Some simply call for a literal report of what some source has asserted or what appear to be the attributes of an object, a scene, a process, or a claim. Questions that require critical thinking, on the other hand, call for sustained efforts to reason and to evaluate reasoning. Such questions require respondents to clarify statements, define terms, and judge the relevance, accuracy, and nature of statements (Lipman, 1984; Paul, 1984a, 1987). A typical line of questioning that activates critical thinking might include the following questions:

- Why is your claim true?
- What reasons or evidence can you give for saying what you said?
- If that is so, what is likely to follow?
- What are you assuming? If that is so, aren't you also assuming that . . . ?
- What are other ways of looking at this?

This line of questioning (sometimes called Socratic questioning) provides an opportunity, a stimulus, and a guide for applying critical thinking. The process probes the thinking by which an individual makes and justifies assertions. Socratic questioning does not teach anyone how to do critical thinking, but it provides a device for *exercising* critical thought. Engaging in dialogues guided by questions like these moves a thinker closer to understanding a particular claim or topic and to ascertaining what is true. Many philosophers assert that the ability to think rationally is thereby enhanced.

Dispositions. Some philosophers emphasize that thinking is much more than simply technique or skill, that in addition to criteria, rules, and procedures, critical thinking is a particular mental set that calls for distinct, habitual ways of behaving. These ways—called dispositions by Ennis, passions by Paul—constitute the spirit, or affective dimension, of critical thinking, making it much less mechanistic than it is customarily portrayed to be.

Paul asserts that skilled thinkers are driven by a passion for getting to the bottom of things, are devoted to seeking the truth rather than to self-aggrandizement, are inclined to ask probing questions about why things are believed to be as they are asserted to be, are persistent in thinking their way through perplexing problems, and are deeply averse to sloppy, ambiguous thinking (Paul, 1987).

Ennis claims that skilled thinkers are also disposed to continually seek more information, to use credible sources, to volunteer and seek reasons and evidence in support of claims, to suspend judgment, to examine issues from different points of view, and to be willing to change their positions when evidence and reasoning warrant (Ennis, 1962, 1985a).

Notice the words used to describe these operations: *drive, devoted, persistent, disposed, seek,* and *be willing.* These attributes of dispositions, which reflect emotions and feelings, show that while critical thinking is objective, it is hardly value-free. Crit-

ical thinkers attach great value to seeking understanding, determining worth, and searching out truth. The continuing persistent disposition to know what is true motivates critical thinking and guides it by basing its execution on a clear underlying value.

PHILOSOPHY AND TEACHING THINKING

Of course, philosophers deal with concepts other than the six just highlighted. Some, such as matters of free will and determinism, however, do not seem especially relevant to efforts to improve critical thinking or its teaching.

Others may be relevant but are at the moment receiving attention from philosophers interested in furthering the teaching of critical thinking. One of these is reasoning about moral and ethical issues and principles. Another is the analysis and conceptualization of concepts such as *truth, fairness,* and *equality,* which are central to our democratic way of life. Indeed, the conceptual repertoire of philosophy is one of the treasure houses of the humanities. Only a portion of these riches has yet been uncovered or applied to the teaching of thinking.

Regardless of the kind of "thinking curriculum" educators might develop, it should include at the very least the six basic concepts of philosophy outlined here. Moreover, no matter which cognitive skills are selected as learning objectives, reasoning—inductive, deductive, analogical—ought to be included, for this skill is foundational to all thinking, including recall.

Critical judgment and the specific operations by which it is carried out should also be included because of the crucial role they play in generating and evaluating the hypotheses, theories, and conclusions that thinking produces.

In addition, any viable thinking skills curriculum should provide instruction in the criteria by which we judge the worth, accuracy, and truth of our own thoughts and those of others, especially the rules of reasoning, the principles of logic, and the evaluative criteria used in critical thinking. Identifying, analyzing, and evaluating point of view should be included among those concepts.

Finally, to be worthwhile and effective in producing skillful thinkers, a K–12 thinking skills curriculum should attend to the methods philosophers use to stimulate and guide thinking as well as to the dispositions that support and motivate this thinking.

Such a curriculum should employ dialogue and structured, *student-generated* critical thinking questioning, not simply as devices for exercising thinking, but as frameworks for instruction and as devices for guiding practice and application following instruction. The values and attitudes that support critical thinking should also be explicit goals of instruction, for such dispositions, as much as skill with cognitive operations and critical knowledge, carry thinking forward.[2]

Those of us who want to improve student thinking ignore these six *qualitative* attributes of philosophic thinking at some peril. Unfortunately, in our desire to infuse thinking skills into the K–12 curriculum, many of us have been focusing almost exclusively on information processing skills and cognitive strategies (such as decision making, problem solving, and creative thinking) to the exclusion of reasoning and the other thinking skills and dispositions associated with philosophy. We should do more.

If we do not begin to incorporate the concepts of philosophy into programs to improve thinking, we run the risk of producing form without substance, technique without purpose, performance without measures of quality. If we do incorporate what philosophy has to offer, however, we can enable students to claim, as Descartes did, "I think, therefore I am."

NOTES

[1] A small number of philosophers, deeply committed to the teaching of thinking, have made cogent efforts to refine, clarify, and interpret aspects of philosophy that relate to thinking. Three who have made especially noteworthy contributions are Matthew Lipman, Robert Ennis, and Richard Paul.

From Lipman's incisive interpretations of critical thinking came his ingenious invention of very specific classroom approaches for teaching children to sharpen their thinking skills and dispositions (see Lipman & Sharp, 1980).

Ennis's ground-breaking analyses of the nature of critical thinking and his exploration of ways to assess it have made an immense contribution to our understanding of this complex mental phenomenon (see Ennis 1962, Ennis 1987).

Paul's analysis and advocacy of philosophical thinking have inspired appreciation of philosophy as a tool for improving thinking (see Paul, 1984b).

The points in this paper distill the work of Lipman, Ennis, and Paul, as well as that of Steven Toulmin, John Chafee, Vincent Ruggerio, Tony Blair, Ralph Johnson, and Philip Percorino. Along with their thoughts and claims are insights I have derived from applying their ideas to the teaching of writing.

[2] For detailed approaches to developing such a curriculum, see, for example, Beyer, 1988.

REFERENCES

Beyer, B. K. (1985, April). Critical thinking—What is it? *Social Education, 49*(4), 270–276.

Beyer, B. K. (1988). *Developing a thinking skills program.* Boston: Allyn and Bacon.

Ennis, R. (1962, Winter). A concept of critical thinking. *Harvard Educational Review 32*(1), 81–111.

Ennis, R. (1985a, October). A logical basis for measuring thinking skills. *Educational Leadership, 43*(2), 46.

Ennis, R. (1985b, Winter). Critical thinking and the curriculum. *National Forum, 65*(1), 28–31.

Ennis, R. (1987). A taxonomy of critical thinking dispositions and abilities. In J. Baron & R. Sternberg (Eds.), *Teaching thinking skills: Theory and practice.* New York: W. H. Freeman.

Lipman M. (1984, September). The cultivation of reasoning through philosophy. *Educational Leadership, 42*(1), 51–55.

Lipman, M. (1987, September 25). *What is the thinking skills movement doing to American schools?* Address at the Conference on Thinking and Education of the Virginia Department of Education, Williamsburg, VA.

Lipman, M. (1988, September). Critical thinking—What can it be? *Educational Leadership, 46*(1), 38–43.

Lipman, M., & Sharp, A. M. (1980). *Philosophy in the classroom* (2nd ed.). Philadelphia, PA: Temple University Press.

Morris, W. (Ed.). (1973). *American heritage dictionary of the English language.* Boston: American Heritage Publishing Company/Houghton Mifflin.

Paul, R. (1984a, Winter). The critical thinking movement: A historical perspective. *National Forum, 65*(1), 23, 12.

Paul, R. (1984b, September). Critical thinking: Fundamental to education for a free society. *Educational Leadership, 42*(1), 4–14.

Paul, R. (1987). Dialogical thinking: Critical thought essential to the acquisition of rational knowledge and passions. In J. Baron & R. Sternberg (Eds.), *Teaching thinking skills: Theory and practice.* New York: W. H. Freeman.

Paul, R., Binker, A. J. A., Jensen, K., & Kreklau, H. (1987). *Critical thinking handbook: 4th–6th grades.* Rohnert Park, CA: Center for Critical Thinking and Moral Critique.

Scriven, M. (1976). *Reasoning.* New York: McGraw-Hill.

Toulmin, S., Ricke, R., & Jarik, A. (1984). *An introduction to reasoning* (2nd ed.). New York: Macmillan.

III

Creating Thought-Full Environments

Just as a picture is drawn by an artist, surroundings are created by the activities of the mind.

—BUDDHA

Introduction

ARTHUR L. COSTA

I have a theory: It is more likely that teachers will teach for thinking, intellectual development, cooperation, and creativity if they are in a thoughtful, intellectually stimulating, cooperative, and creative environment themselves. Furthermore, it has been shown that teachers who are higher-level thinkers produce students who are higher-level thinkers. It behooves us, therefore, to ensure that the environments in which children grow and learn and in which teachers teach are conducive to enhancing the intellectual functioning of all the inhabitants of the organization.

This section opens with a chapter by noted cognitive educators and organizational researchers Geoffrey and Renate Nummela Caine, who cite certain conditions in an organization that promote intellectual development, professional growth, and organizational adaptiveness.

The development of a child's intellectual capacities, however, does not begin in school or even at birth; it starts long before. In fact, much of a child's intellectual development is predicated on the quality of life in the mother's womb. Not only does a fetus need proper nutrition, it also needs an environment that is drug-free, tobacco-free, alcohol-free, and stress-free. Because parents are the first teachers and because much of a child's values, vocabulary, behavior, and intellectual potential is determined by the home environment, Dee Dickinson helps parents understand their roles in providing a home environment that maximizes the development of a child's intellectual potential.

Sensitive to the need for positive human interaction, John Barell describes the kind of classroom environment that provides a safe haven for students to exercise and grow their mental capabilities. Teacher-training institutions have a responsibility to prepare teachers to create such environments. David Martin and Nicholas Michelli describe a teacher-education program that focuses on the requisite knowledge, skills, and attitudes for teachers to teach for thinking.

Ongoing professional development also must sustain the intellectual focus of the school environment. Laura Lipton and Bruce Wellman describe many ways in which school staffs grow more thoughtful by engaging in job-embedded activities that require creativity, intellectual stimulation, and collaboration.

Leadership is essential to maintaining a thought-full school environment. It is easy for school administrators to lose their focus on the development of complex thought processes and long-range habits of mind when they are admonished by well-meaning parents, community members, and politicians who make immediate, short-term, politically expedient decisions without regard to essential and enduring life-span learnings. David Martin helps administrators stay focused on the development of higher-order problem-solving skills and critical and creative strategies amid such pressures.

How does a school become thought-full? In Michigan, Monroe High School Principal Bill Martin, drawing on personal experience, describes how a staff transforms itself into a nationally recognized, award-winning school by engaging in an electrifying process of school improvement.

Schools, however, cannot do it alone. They need support, encouragement, and resources from the community and district administration. Sherry King next describes how, as a school superintendent, she works to create a climate for reflection among the staff, the board of education, and the community. By using processes of self-reflection and self-monitoring, King seizes opportunities in the day-to-day operation of the school for all the stakeholders to become more thoughtful through structured reflection.

The home, classroom, school, school district, and community—all are working toward common goals. Wheatley (1992) defines this as a fractal quality. She says:

> The very best organizations have a fractal quality to them. An observer of such an organization can tell what the organization's values and ways of doing busi-

ness are by watching anyone, whether it be a production floor employee or a senior manager. There is consistency and predictability to the quality of behavior. No matter where we look in these organizations, self-similarity is found in its people, in spite of the complex range and levels. (p. 132)

Thoughtfulness, therefore, pervades the entire enterprise. Thus, the entire school and community become environments that mediate intellectual growth. In the final chapter, Arthur Costa likens the intellectual ecology of a school to an environmental protection agency in which leaders must ensure that thinking, collaboration, and creativity become neither endangered, nor worse, extinct.

REFERENCES

Wheatley, M. (1992). *Leadership and the new sciences.* San Francisco: Berrett Koehler Publishers.

17

Capitalizing on the Invisible Dimension of Organizational Learning

Geoffrey Caine and Renate Nummela Caine

Every organization and every human being is like an iceberg or a volcano. The visible tip is only a small fragment of a much larger system. When we look at new ways to function and do things, our action tends to be on the surface, but most activity occurs in a vast, invisible, implicit realm. Indeed, we can rearrange the elements on the surface all we like, but the real task is to spur the unconscious (in a person) and the invisible culture (in an organization) to begin to function differently. Change is always the byproduct of the interaction between the surface and the hidden, the visible and the invisible.

In our view, the key to real change is to work intentionally at the visible level to enliven those invisible layers or elements. So the challenge is to learn our way into mastering the invisible—the deep levels at which individuals and organizations function. In fact, we suggest that it is the process of learning itself that both makes the invisible visible and drives the way in which the two levels interact. Thus, in our work with schools, it is not our objective to try to force everyone into a new mode of organization. Rather, we seek to build a climate and culture that is both orderly and dynamic, reflective and action oriented, and realistic and true to principle in every aspect of what is done, so that invisible needs and new solutions have an opportunity to express themselves.

REAL LIFE

The two of us are gaining additional experience implementing our ideas in the early stages of a charter high school we have helped establish in our small mountain community. Three full-time teachers and about 50 students in an idyllic physical environment would seem to be a dream. Yet the demands, most

of which have fallen on the principal—ranging from the legal issues of incorporation to the intricacies of working with a district and engaging the local community—are exhausting. And that is without considering curriculum development, building community with students, teaching, soliciting funds, managing crises, integrating part-time teachers, coping with a small building, and more.

We are all immersed in layer upon layer of learning. One of us (Renate) is teaching an introductory course in psychology and a course for teachers at the school who are seeking California credentials. The other (Geoffrey) is one of nine board members and is setting up a separate nonprofit entity, one purpose of which is to raise money for this and similar brain-based ventures. The students range from the sophisticated and well-prepared to those with a limited academic and social foundation. The two teachers and the teacher-principal are working to become a team. Members of the board need to find their feet and grasp their roles. All of this must be done within the constraints of the system, and, notwithstanding that this is a charter school, its constraints are substantial. The school clearly is a learning organization.

A WORD ON DEFINITIONS

There are at least two meanings of "learning organization." First, the organization creates opportunities and challenges for its members to learn. Thus, individuals are thrust into roles and functions that call for considerable personal learning. At a basic level, there is information to acquire such as names to go with faces, community and district needs with which to deal, and state frameworks and credentialing requirements to meet. Next, new skills are being called for in real time. It is simply different, for instance, to walk into a system that is up and running than to actually set it up. Third, professional knowledge is continually updated and tested, even in subjects and domains

Copyright © 2001 Geoffrey Caine and Renate Nummela Caine

where teachers are already proficient. And, finally, personal identity is on the line because the actions and beliefs of all adults and students are being made public. In this school, there is no way to retreat into private classrooms that are personal and secret domains. All this change has more subtle effects. Every adult in the school is growing as a human being: Attributes are being tested, qualities are being called for, and greater maturity is being required. Patience, for example, is being sorely tested at every level from community relations to working with rebellious students. And through all this, the conscious, planned-out, and necessary specifics are interacting with the more unarticulated personal assumptions and perceptions.

Second, the organization itself is coming into being. In the language of complex adaptive systems, we are watching self-organization first-hand and are party to the emergence of an organizational identity that is much more than the sum of its parts. We can see the organization taking on its own identity. We can see it responding and adapting to the exigencies of the moment and the context, such as the unexpectedly large number of students with special needs. And we can see it reframing its actions and goals to comply with district requirements, while seeking to engage the vision through which it was founded. There already are networks of interaction and types of relationships that differ significantly from anything found on any organizational chart. The organization as a whole is beginning to take shape and learn its way into existence.

One of the key features that drive self-organization is self-reference (Abraham and Gilgen, 1995). That is, each person, each player, interprets events through her own eyes and values and reacts accordingly. Even with the best will in the world, most individuals do not have a deeply held common vision, even if they speak the same language and have worked together. And the differences persist in any organization where individuals come and go. They will have different mental models of teaching and learning and doing their jobs, adhere to different views of how the world works and what causes what, and be at different places on a developmental continuum—whether as teachers, administrators, or community members.

It is through self-reference that all aspects of personal and organizational learning which we have mentioned come into play interactively. Individuals act on the surface but are driven by the vast unconscious sets of their own unarticulated beliefs, assumptions, and patterns. And their overt interactions lead to the creation of an implicit culture and an organizational way of being. What emerges—the organization itself—is the sum total of the dynamic network of self-referring interactions within the larger context.

LESSONS FOR LEARNING ORGANIZATIONS

Our goal is to work with schools and districts by influencing self-reference, and what follows is some of what we have been learning in this area:

1. Individuals learn what they believe they have to learn. We wrote in *Making Connections* (1994) that real learning is driven by deep meanings—the issues and values that are important to an individual. We experienced that with the charter school. Survival and relationship, for example, were paramount for the staff. Survival became a problem when state money did not become available until eight months after teachers had come on board and six months after school had begun. We had to learn where to look for funds and how to generate short-term loans. We learned what other schools and districts do before their regular funds are released. The problem persisted when the school opened and found itself with many students who were shell-shocked from previous school experiences. Many had come from families where a parent had walked out or died recently, and the academic and social foundations of at least half the students were substantially lower than expected.

These survival issues began to drive and focus energy. Our observation was that personnel downshifted—they lost some flexibility in their thinking and hunkered down, sometimes not even availing themselves of help and support. Their perceptual field literally narrowed as a natural response to the need to survive. Survival became a major influence, driving self-reference and, therefore, the self-organization of the school.

2. A foundation of relationship and positive affect is essential. We have argued for some time that strengthening relationship and building community are indispensable to successful change, both in the wider school and the classroom. This is supported by research that positive affect—the pleasant feeling associated with safety, comfort, and interest—is highly correlated with flexibility, creative problem solving, and cooperation (Ashby, Isen, & Turken, 1999). Therefore, it counteracts downshifting to some extent.

The three full-time and the half-dozen part-time teachers were dedicated to building relationship with each other and the students, and this became vital. In the early weeks, many of the students came to the school at the strong behest of their parents. They were not invested in it and did not care. In those early days, however, it became clear that the staff really did care about them, that there was time to stop and talk, that even when discipline became necessary because of unacceptable substance abuse, there really was no hostility or animosity involved. In this school, students and staff were on a first-name basis from the beginning, and the school soon became a place where most of the students felt relatively safe and at home with the staff. This, it seems to us, has translated into greater student and parental acceptance of the school, has buoyed the staff during difficult early times, and has become an essential part of the platform from which the school can build. An implicit culture in which relationship was genuinely appreciated began to form.

3. The context constrains what is possible. Capra (1996) has tried to frame a way of thinking about complex adaptive systems. He suggests that every such system is based on a pattern or blueprint (the traditional model of a school being a good example). A structure, therefore, is the physical manifestation of that pattern (seen in school buildings, employment practices, class schedules, and the like). Self-reference occurs within this context because, as previously mentioned, perceived constraints and possibilities always influence plans and actions.

The school confirms this beautifully. The charter had to be approved by the local school district, which insisted on provisions for core courses, a grade-level progression of students, and a schedule that reflected some relatively discrete blocks of time for different subjects. These needs determined how we framed the charter—the pattern or blueprint for the school. Implementation then occurred in a small building with modest funding and very little time to move in. These were some of the parameters within which each participant viewed and interpreted his role and reactions.

In effect, these and other constraints made it impossible to adopt some of what we knew would work for the students. For example, students who take things literally or have difficulty in delaying gratification, and who are easily distracted, need to be physically involved in ongoing projects that are related, if at all possible, to something in which they take a real interest. Although it became apparent that such projects were needed, the constraints described previously made some actions unfeasible. In addition, this type of learning was unfamiliar to students who had come from more traditional educational environments. In fact, one of the real barriers to innovation turned out to be student expectations for traditional classes, teachers, periods, and segregated teacher-student responsibilities. These were the self-referential aspects of students that deeply influenced any attempt at innovation.

4. Leadership is pivotal. The school has taken on many of the characteristics of the principal. For instance, she is on-the-go all the time at a very fast pace. This makes it difficult to in-troduce a more rhythmic balance between activity and real breaks. We had never before so fully appreciated the effect a central person or core team could have on an emergent system. In this school, lines of communication—from staff, board, and community—course through the principal. The key players wield enormous influence, irrespective of their leadership styles. In addition, adapting a term from Arthur Costa, the habits of mind of the leader are critical. Is the person a doer, a delegator, or both? Can he generate support and inspire participation? Can the leader stay the course and handle the details and bureaucracy? Does the person have dual planeness; that is, does he exemplify the vision that is articulated? To what extent is there a grasp of process—of the ups and downs, a sense of appropriate timing and rhythm, and a capacity to both persist and let go? How authentic is communication and relationship?

Such questions are key because the qualities of the leaders are among the most powerful of all factors in determining an organization's eventual shape. Indeed, the view that each participant holds about what it means to be a leader, a follower, or a supporter is crucial. In our view, ongoing process groups (see point 6) that deal with real tasks and also open up discussion on core assumptions about leadership, communication, and roles can have an enormous positive effect on capitalizing on, and distributing, leadership.

5. Rhythm and orderliness are essential in chaos and turbulence. We ultimately chose to move quickly with this school. We conceived of the idea for the school in October 1998 and opened its doors Sept. 5, 1999. The preparation work was demanding, and the load fell primarily on the intended principal. It included a demonstration week for students in July, and we weren't able to move into the facility—which had been and continues to be an underused community center—until a month before school started. The pace did not let up when students arrived. Even though there has been considerable fulfillment for the staff, the stress is still palpable.

One obvious lesson for our school is that a constant rush was enormously stressful. The larger lesson is that orderliness must be maintained in the midst of turbulence even if it is extremely difficult. Individuals who are under constant deadlines, who face multiple new and competing demands, and whose very careers may be on the line do not, as a matter of course, take time to stop and smell the roses, neither individually nor collectively. For this to occur, there must be automatic, built-in routines that are taken for granted and that regularly bring people back to a sense of coherence and orderliness. In effect, most of us need to work the system so that a rhythm is established that allows us to feel less hurried.

6. Processing, and small group processes, are powerful, and perhaps indispensable, for building community and establishing orderliness. For the past 10 years, we have been developing and refining what we call our "mindshifts" process. This is a way to bring together seven to twelve people, at least once a week, in what we call a process group. We cannot describe it in detail (Caine, Caine, & Crowell, 1999) but can highlight specific elements.

Each process group begins with a brief ordered sharing, in which each person shares, in sequence, an opinion about a complex system idea—for example, "the whole is greater than the sum of its parts." The process and guidelines begin to create an atmosphere in which individuals listen to each other fully, do not compete for space and time, experience orderly interactions on a regular basis, have a growing awareness of how learning organizations function, and learn how to listen to themselves in order to become aware of the assumptions, values, and hidden agendas they carry. We now begin each business day with a similar process.

We also use a related process to conclude business. At the end of every meeting and every work day, we take time to gather and reflect, in an orderly way, about what transpired, what we did or did not accomplish, and what we learned. Thus, we make a point of publicly and consciously learning from our moment-to-moment experiences. Over time, we have sensed that a spirit is evoked that makes communication and conflict resolution easier and makes work much more productive and joyful.

The small group process is one of the primary tools we use to support teacher development, the creation of community, and system change. When it has been used systematically and with commitment—for example, in the first two years of our work with Dry Creek Elementary (Caine & Caine, 1997)—we sense that a pervasive and subtle, but very powerful, field effect has been created that manifests itself in a marvelous spirit of cooperation and learning.

For reasons spelled out below, the group process has not been used in the charter school. We strongly believe that much of the pressure, turbulence, and lack of order in the school could have been alleviated had this or a similar process been adopted as a matter of routine.

7. There probably are windows of opportunity for influencing systems. It never was our intention for the school to be our school. This is a community school that we have only some capacity and opportunity to influence. However, the charter is based on our writing, and we did want it to reflect some of our core processes. Nevertheless, in the early months of planning and preparation, we were spending most of our time traveling across the country, meeting obligations we had incurred before the decision was made to set up a school. In retrospect, that was the critical time to be more active and involved. For example, our consulting work is organized around the small group process discussed above. However, none of the staff and none of the board members were familiar with such a process, and we were not available to install it as a regular practice. As a result, although we believe in it deeply, it is not central to the school process. One inference is that there may be windows of opportunity to influence a system, in much the same way there are windows of opportunity to influence growing brains. Just as with a new class at the beginning of a school year, processes must be introduced and find their place at the right time. If such windows are not availed of, other opportunities may arise. However, when patterns have been established, they can become difficult but not impossible to dislodge. And, just as the first few days of a class need to be used for building this atmosphere, the early days of a system need to be focused to a large extent on generating that order.

A FOCUSED LEARNING CULTURE

Learning and change happen—in people and in organizations. They may not, however, be effective or appropriate. In a learning culture, people learn at several levels. On the one hand, they have to master facts and skills and the way the system works. On the other hand, they must constantly reflect on their own strengths and weaknesses so that they can grow and become more effective. How well we deal with change depends largely on what we learn and how well we learn.

Experience suggests to us that some of our learning should be done publicly and consistently. We learn from each other's learning, and sometimes we learn best in dialog with others. When we learn together consistently, we establish a commitment to ongoing learning that is vital. All of this cumulatively releases energy, enriches relationship, and builds community. Thus, the invisible realm is engaged and enlivened, and we and the organization benefit. The art of collective learning is difficult to master. Although readily accepted by some, it is challenging and unfamiliar to many. In fact, most people, in our experience, regard learning about self as a luxury and an indulgence to be partaken of, if at all, when everything else is going smoothly and time is available. Precisely the opposite is needed. When times are tough and demands urgent, a learning community becomes immensely valuable. For this to be possible, participation in small process groups—where participants feel safe enough to unveil their issues, struggles, leanings, and achievements—is indispensable.

When we learn well together, we can come to terms with each other in a way that is productive and responsive to the needs of body, mind, and soul. And we create the conditions that allow for the emergence of an effective mode and form of organization—one that is capable of actually giving voice to shared purpose and vision and where work and learning is a joy.

FINAL NOTE

The Idyllwild charter high school opened its doors in September 1999, and had its charter revoked June 30, 2000. A subsequent performance audit showed that both grounds for revoking the charter were unfounded. The audit said that "the operation was a success but the patient died." The lessons were much tougher than expected; the system as a whole is more brutal than we had realized. But the essential ideas developed in this chapter have been strongly reinforced.

REFERENCES

Abraham, F. D., & Gilgen, A. R. (Eds.). (1995). *Chaos theory in psychology.* Westport, CT: Praeger.

Ashby, G. F., Isen, A. M., & Turken, U. (1999, July). A neuropsychological theory of positive affect and its influence on cognition. *Psychological Review, 106*(3), 529–550.

Caine, G., Caine, R., & Crowell, S. (1999). *Mindshifts* (2nd ed.). Tucson, AZ: Zephyr Press.

Caine, R., & Caine, G. (1994). *Making connections: Teaching and the human brain.* Menlo Park, CA: Addison Wesley Longman.

Caine, R., & Caine, G. (1997). *Education on the edge of possibility.* Alexandria, VA.: Association for Supervision and Curriculum Development.

Capra, F. (1996). *The web of life.* New York: Anchor Books.

18

Thoughtful Parenting

Dee Dickinson

How can we help children develop to their fullest potential? What kinds of environments and experiences in the home, school, and community are essential for such development? What insights do new research in the neurosciences and studies in human development offer parents and teachers? Considering what is now known about human development, it should be the right of every human to discover his innate strengths, develop new ones, and use these strengths to learn, unlearn, and relearn in this rapidly changing world. Through developing the fullest potential in mind, body, and spirit, our children can become adults who continue to develop the wisdom the world needs so desperately.

THE COMPLEX ADULT

Although different groups can describe the mature adult in many different ways, there are certain characteristics that appear consistently. For example, most parents want their children to grow up to be caring, well educated, self-confident, responsible, and ethical and moral contributing members of society. Schools identify the following character traits as ideal for young people moving into the adult world: accountability, integrity and honesty, self-esteem, loyalty, empathy, self-motivation, respect, responsibility, independence, and the ability to work cooperatively.

The well-known Secretary's Commission on Achieving Necessary Skills (SCANS) report, published in 1992 by the U.S. Department of Labor, suggests that beyond basic education, adult workers need to have developed the ability to think creatively, make good decisions, work well with others, solve problems, see things in the mind's eye, and know how to learn and reason. They should demonstrate individual responsibility, self-esteem, sociability, self-management, and integrity.

Abraham Maslow (1962) described self-actualizing adults as, "without a single exception, involved in a cause outside of themselves. They are devoted, working at something precious to them. . . . They are working at something fate has called them to somehow, and which they love, so that the joy-work dichotomy in them disappears. Self-actualization means experiencing life fully, vividly, with full concentration and total absorption."

Maslow notes that a healthy individual is motivated by a need to develop and actualize her potential and abilities. Some of these traits include spontaneous ethical behavior; independent stability in the face of hard knocks; freshness of appreciation; profound personal relationships; a philosophical, unhostile sense of humor; creativity; and the ability to continue to develop their capacities.

Mihaly Csikszentmihalyi and Kevin Rathunde (1998) describe a healthy, well-developed person as having developed psychological complexity. They suggest that there are six conditions for complex adulthood that seem to provide guidelines for optimal development throughout life. These conditions are: health and fitness, the ability to preserve an alert and vital mind, continuity of vocation, keeping up relationships with family and friends, continued involvement in the community, and becoming a wise person. Csikszentmihalyi and Rathunde define wisdom as having the ability to get at the essence of problems. The wise have learned much throughout life. They think globally and holistically, behave in line with the common good, and develop a serene acceptance of their lot in life.

Clearly, it is a tall order to suggest that everyone can become such an exemplary adult as described previously, but these are goals to which we all can aspire. These goals also may be considered in discussing how parents and other caregivers can create appropriate conditions for facilitating the optimal development of their children. Although this book is called *Developing Minds*, it is clear that every human is a complex system in which cognitive, physical, emotional, and social development are interdependent.

THE BRAIN, THE MIND, AND INTELLIGENCE

The research of Marian Diamond, one of the nation's foremost neuroscientists at the University of California, Berkeley, has revealed the phenomenal ongoing plasticity of the brain. She points out that the brain changes structurally and functionally as a result of learning and experience—for better or worse— and that optimal environments for healthy development are "positive, nurturing, stimulating, active, and interactive" (Diamond & Hopson, 1998). She and other neuroscientists are now confident that providing children with enriched environments in the first three years of life offers the greatest opportunities for healthy cognitive, physical, emotional, and social development. Such environments are diametrically opposed to those in which children are passively occupied, for example, watching too much TV at the expense of playing games or doing creative work. Diamond also stresses the role of emotion in learning and human development, and she does not hesitate to point out the critical need of all humans, from the beginning of life, for love.

Not only does the brain have plasticity, it also appears that intelligence in the broadest sense can continue to develop throughout life. The pioneering work of Reuven Feuerstein, director of the Center for the Development of Learning Potential in Israel, shows that intelligence is not just a static structure but also, rather, an open and dynamic system that can continue to develop throughout life (Feuerstein & Rand, 1974). Parents who interact sensitively and observe carefully can learn much about their child's kind of intelligence that goes far beyond I.Q.

Howard Gardner, director of Project Zero at Harvard University and author of *Frames of Mind* (1983), suggests that there are at least eight kinds of intelligence. They are verbal, logical/mathematical, visual/spatial, kinesthetic, musical, interpersonal, intrapersonal, and naturalistic. Most humans have all these intelligences available to develop to different degrees and in different combinations. They cut through differences in ability, culture, and economic and educational backgrounds. They offer the means for communication and self-expression, and they provide tools for learning. The more we develop the spectrum of intelligences, the more we develop our possibilities.

Parents and other caregivers can help children develop their intelligences by playing musical games together, doing creative artwork, dancing, participating in sports and other physical activities, exploring the natural world and their communities, learning to play cooperatively, setting and achieving realistic goals, and reflecting on their experiences through discussion or writing. Parents also would do well to help their children find practical applications for what they have learned at home and in the classroom. In this way, parents can help consolidate learning, moving it into a deeper understanding. Gardner (1999) points out that "an individual understands a concept, skill, theory, or domain of knowledge to the extent that he or she can apply it appropriately in a new situation." Humor and conversation in the home covering a range of topics are other effective ways to develop the intelligence of children as well as to strengthen the parent-child bonding.

In creating rich environments for their children, parents can draw on the understanding of "distributed cognition" (Salomon, 1993); that is, that intelligence is not just in the head but also throughout the human body. We not only remember better what we do physically, but many learners more easily understand complex abstractions when they take a concrete form in their hands. Parents can help their children develop their "body intelligence" by filling their environment with a rich array of materials with which to play, create, and learn. We might keep in mind that more than 100 years ago, Maria Montessori took objects from the junk piles of Rome for her students to experiment with, and the result was the "explosions of learning" that are the hallmarks of her work.

Part of our intelligence also is revealed in our interactions with others. Some of the most powerful learning is social and activated through discussion, dialogue, and debate. Social interaction provides rich opportunities, not only to learn from others, but also to learn about our own inner resources as we hear ourselves talk about our ideas. It can catalyze reflective thinking and help consolidate learning.

Some of our intelligence lies in resources in nature, which offers continual opportunities for new learning, and in those resources that humans have created, such as books and libraries, films and TV, databases, and the Internet. This kind of intelligence knows how to explore such resources and where to find what we need to know.

Much of our intelligence is developed by and revealed in the cognitive tools we use, such as words, numbers, and mental images. It also is revealed in the tools we have created, such as hammers and chisels, pens and paper, printing presses, paintbrushes and musical instruments, and calculators and computers. Yale psychologist Sternberg suggests that "a major factor behind the massive I.Q. gains in each generation is an important force that has penetrated all but the most remote regions of the globe—technology" (Sternberg, 1997). This is seen in students who use computers to go beyond drill and practice to explore the world of ideas on the Internet and to create complex multimedia projects. The computer is only one of many tools that can help students develop higher-order thinking skills, such as questioning, analysis, synthesis, logic, creativity, and informed decision making. Like other tools, including TV, the computer should be used in moderation, with parents recognizing the critical importance of active learning in a social context.

The ability to learn and become broadly intelligent is not sufficient without the development of other highly human qualities. Every day in the media, one can see examples of highly intelligent, well-educated people who lack altruism and sensitivity to others' needs. At the extreme are those who are capable of hostile and violent acts against humanity. We might do well to reflect on how self-actualization, which appears in the later years, develops. Certainly, empathy, compassion, generosity, integrity, and understanding of others do not develop spontaneously at the age of 60. Such qualities begin developing early in life through the observation of role models, and they are learned by doing. Community service and collaborative projects in the home can help develop the qualities desperately needed in the world today.

Csikszentmihalyi and Rathunde have explored the kinds of early experiences that can predispose a person to be wise in old age. They suggest that an environment that encourages empathy, integrity, responsibility, and sensitivity to intrinsic rewards, along with an ability to set long-range goals, is more likely to lead to the development of wisdom. According to these researchers, an optimal home environment offers many opportunities for choice and creativity within a solid, dependable structure where high expectations are clearly and supportively communicated. They note that "extremes either of disorganization or rigidity in structure or function represent danger signs for psychological growth, with some intermediate degree of system flexibility constituting the optimal condition for human development" (1998).

IN THE BEGINNING

It is now well understood that the nine months after conception are crucial for laying the foundations of a child's healthy development. A pregnant mother's smoking, use of alcoholic beverages and drugs, inadequate nutrition, and negative emotions can have detrimental effects on her baby. On the other hand, a mother who is careful about her diet, exercises moderately, gets plenty of fresh air, and is as happy and emotionally stable as possible gives her child a head start. There also is substantial evidence that babies hear and feel physical sensations in utero. Playing soft, pleasant music, reading children's stories out loud, and talking with the unborn child appear to have pos-

itive cognitive and emotional effects. It also seems that babies who are read to before birth even get a head start on literacy.

Knowing how to parent doesn't happen magically when a baby is born. Good parenting is something every parent must learn. It is important, for example, to understand the rapid mental development during the crucial first year of life. During that time a baby develops 70 percent of his brain. Three things are crucial to this spectacular growth and development: love, good nutrition, and stimulation of the senses in a relaxed, playful manner that is responsive to the baby. These are the characteristics of the enriched environments recommended by Diamond as well as such prominent neonatologists as T. Berry Brazelton.

It is never too soon for parents to get to know their child, to learn how to understand and respond to each other. Babies develop a sense of security when there are appropriate responses to their needs and when they are held, nurtured, and comforted affectionately. Positive stimulation at appropriate times that takes into consideration a baby's mood and alertness includes offering opportunities to hear classical music, see brightly colored designs and pictures, feel different textures, and smell the fragrances of foods and flowers. Contrary to the general belief that babies are not aware of much besides being fed and kept dry, there is clear evidence that the foundations of cognition, language, and learning are being laid as parents and other caregivers talk with their babies, tell them stories, and introduce them to the world.

PRESCHOOL YEARS

During a child's early years, parents have ongoing opportunities to learn more about their child as language and thought develop. Children's behavior also gives clues to their predispositions, talents, and emerging personalities. Parents learn to be patient with the seemingly endless questions that children ask, knowing that being responsive can help encourage curiosity. This is a wonderful time to help a child learn about the world by experiencing the natural environment, creative activities, trips to the store, and trying on make-believe roles. Some of the best toys—many of which can be made from materials at home—can stimulate creative play and help develop different skills. Simple board games that a family can play together offer meaningful opportunities for developing verbal fluency, understanding numbers and counting, problem solving, learning to take turns, and other cognitive and social skills.

Children might enjoy dictating little stories, making up songs, playing games, and experimenting with different tools and art supplies. When the results of their efforts are valued openly, shared with others, and displayed on walls or the refrigerator, children begin to develop self-esteem. Sometimes a child's experiments or behavior may go awry, but sensitive parents make it clear that it is the behavior and not the child that has gone wrong.

In well-meaning attempts to give children a strong foundation for successful learning and cognitive development, programs focusing on basic academic skills are being started earlier and earlier. However, according to Meyerhoff, a researcher with the Harvard Preschool Project and the author of *The Complete Book of Parenting,* having fun and learning are one and the same for infants, toddlers, and preschoolers. He and other early childhood specialists, including those at the National Association for the Education of Young Children, urge parents to never underestimate the power of play in promoting healthy, well-balanced development in the early years. Meyerhoff notes that "developmentally appropriate play involves freedom, flexibility, fascination, and fun; and it is these elements that inspire a young child to develop the unbounded imagination and unbridled creativity which will enable him/her not only to function, but flourish too" (1998).

ELEMENTARY SCHOOL YEARS

Children thrive when they are offered positive challenges in a safe environment. For example, it is important not to intervene when a child can be successful on her own and to acknowledge successful achievements. Thoughtful parents will have already created such an environment at home, and it is important that they seek out other learning environments for their child with such characteristics. By the time their child enters school, he will have learned much about his unique strengths, which may differ from their own. Parents can observe early on that some children learn best with an oral explanation while others are clearly more kinesthetic or visual in how they perceive and process experience. When parents are sensitive to these traits, they can offer appropriate help to their child as she learns in the home and in the classroom.

Parents who are keenly aware of their child's talents, abilities, and kinds of intelligence can offer rich opportunities to develop such qualities without going overboard in programming their life. A child-centered approach is sensitive to the need for quiet time and "just to be." Well-balanced experiences can include various indoor and outdoor activities; field trips to museums, plays, and musical programs; playing with friends; quiet times for stories; and even selected TV programs, with meaningful discussion. Family trips and experiences away from home can offer rich opportunities for children to write about and illustrate. More challenging board games, such as

chess or Monopoly, or carefully selected computer games can help children develop strategy, restraint of impulsivity, planning skills, and an ability to manipulate mental images.

ADOLESCENCE

A combination of parental love and discipline continues to be crucial to the developing human during adolescence. As in the early years, adolescents must be offered challenges slightly beyond their skill level yet within the possibility of achieving success—a balance that prevents boredom and frustration. Lev Vygotsky (1978) calls this the "zone of proximal development" and notes the critical importance of "scaffolding"; that is, making sure the young person has developed the skills and abilities to achieve his goals. Parents who have come to know their child well are in the best position to make sure these skills are in place throughout their child's development and to help adolescents take on more mature responsibilities, learn new age-appropriate skills, and meet new challenges.

At a time when hormones, emotions, and physical development cause confusion and disturbing feelings, parents can offer support by simply listening nonjudgmentally and with empathy. They also can make sure their teenagers have a variety of socially acceptable outlets for their energy through sports, music, drama, and other creative-arts programs. Youngsters also feel more secure when parents communicate clear expectations and set dependable, consistent limits—although, with encouragement and support, adolescents will internalize and take increasing responsibility for their own behavior. Creating such "complex" environments keeps the crucial parent-child relationship thriving, making it possible for young people to turn boredom and anxiety into positive experiences.

Parents can help their children develop maturity by offering meaningful choices from the early years on and by dealing with problems in all-family meetings where they can feel there isn't anything they can't discuss. As parents, even though we try our best, we all make mistakes. What parent does not look back and think about what he or she might have done differently? Acknowledging our mistakes honestly keeps communication lines open and makes it easier for youngsters to deal with their own imperfections as they explore and develop their capacities as fully as possible. A good sense of humor also helps!

BECOMING A SUCCESSFUL ADULT

Returning to Maslow's hierarchy of human needs, developed long ago yet still relevant, there are certain preconditions for optimal human development:

• In the external environment, there is a basic need for freedom, justice, orderliness, and challenge. These are indeed the characteristics of the complex environment previously discussed. Freedom without discipline can lead to chaos. Discipline without freedom of choice can lead to a demeaning of the human spirit, as well as to a stifling of creativity and other higher-order thinking skills.

• Physical needs for fresh air, clean water, adequate food, shelter, sleep, and sensory stimulation must be satisfied. Without meeting these needs, it is difficult to grow and learn. Meeting them as fully as possible helps the whole interdependent human system function well.

• There also is the need for safety and security, which many homes, schools, and communities do not always provide and without which psychological, physical, emotional, and social development suffer. When we don't feel secure, fearing not only physical harm but also rebuke or sarcasm, it is difficult to take the risks associated with learning and growing.

• A sense of belonging also is crucial. When we're not recognized for who we are—for our unique differences—it is difficult to be part of any group. Social context and communion is for most people an essential part of human life, without which one can become insecure, hostile, and even violent.

• We must also develop self-esteem and feel that others value us. This does not result from self-esteem programs that help us feel good about ourselves even when we are failing. Self-esteem is accomplished by mastering a succession of challenges through the development of our skills, abilities, and intelligences, ideally in supportive and nurturing environments.

Homes and schools alone cannot meet all these needs today, so total community involvement and support is critical. Many fine programs are available to help parents in nearly every community through local schools, park departments, YMCA's or YWCA's, and other cultural organizations, churches, and community centers. Even more resources will emerge as there is a growing recognition of the critical role parents and caregivers or mentors play in helping young people meet basic needs and making it possible for them to develop the qualities of a mature, complex adulthood.

REFERENCES

Ben-Hur, M. (1994). *On Feuerstein's instrumental enrichment.* Arlington Heights, IL: SkyLight.

Bredekamp, S. (Ed.). (1986). *Developmentally appropriate practice in early childhood programs serving children from birth through age 8.* Washington, DC: National Association for the Education of Young Children.

Campbell, B., Campbell, L., & Dickinson, D. (1996, 1999). *Teaching and learning through multiple intelligences.* Needham Heights, MA: Allyn and Bacon.

Csikszentmihalyi, M., & Rathunde, K. (1998). The development of the person. In R. M. Lerner (Ed.), *Theoretical models of human development, 1. Handbook of psychology.* New York: Wiley.

Diamond, M., & Hopson, J. (1998). *Magic trees of the mind.* New York: Dutton.

Feuerstein, R., & Rand, Y. (1974). *Mediated learning experience.* Jerusalem: Hadassah Wizo Canada Child Research Institute.

Gardner, H. (1983). *Frames of mind.* New York: Basic Books.

Gardner, H. (1999). *The disciplined mind.* New York: Simon and Schuster.

Maslow, A. (1962). *Toward a psychology of being.* New York: Van Nostrand.

Meyerhoff, M. (1998). *The power of play.* Lindenhurst, IL: The Epicenter.

New Horizons for Learning. (1983, 1998). *Day one: A positive beginning for parents and their infants.* [Videotape]. Seattle, WA: Author.

Salomon, G. (Ed.). (1993). *Distributed cognitions.* New York: Cambridge University Press.

Sternberg, R. (1997, Summer). Technology changes intelligence: Societal implications and soaring I.Q. *Technos, 6*(2), 12–14.

U.S. Department of Labor (1992). Secretary's Commission on Achieving Necessary Skills (SCANS) report. Washington, DC: Author.

Vygotsky, L. (1978). *Mind in society.* Cambridge: Harvard University Press.

19

Designing the Invitational Environment

JOHN BARELL

Several years ago, I learned just how powerful a teacher's words could be in creating an environment that invites students to participate mindfully and soulfully. Huong Tran was a student in my Introduction to Literature class. She was an excellent student who enthusiastically read all the assigned readings, from *Othello* to Joyce Carol Oates. One day, I asked her and her peers to write their own stories, and I learned about the life she had led before attending our class in Upper Montclair, N.J. Here is a portion of Huong's story:

> I have been blessed with many riches in life. First, I was born into a loving home with caring parents. Second, I had brothers and sisters who loved to play with me on a daily basis without complaining. Third, I had good food and clothes to eat and wear each day. Finally to top it off, I also had a nanny who took care of my every need. It was a perfect life for me.
>
> Unfortunately, this life shattered into pieces when the Communists took over Vietnam April 30, 1975. At the time, I was at the age of eight. Although I was a child, I could still remember how the changes destroyed my family. (Barell, 1995, p. 70)

Huong went on to tell of the horrors of the boat ride from Vietnam and of the Communists opening fire on them, hitting her sister in the ear and killing one of the passengers. They were starving, and a passing merchantman made them give up their jewelry and valuables for a few scraps of food.

> I wondered why life can be so cruel to someone like my sister who is young, smart and full of energy to get shot and now trying to fight for her life. At first, I blamed my parents for wanting to leave, but then I realized this was all the Communists' fault. (p. 71)

Fifteen days later, they arrived at their first destination, Hong Kong. Months later, Huong was sent to an elementary school in New Jersey. There, her classmates taunted her because she was different. She did not look like the other children, and she felt miserable again. Huong avoided school, until one day, a teacher changed her life.

> I was bothered by the fact that I didn't feel I belonged there. . . . I thought it was punishment on my part. . . . [Then] my teacher said, "You are a very special person with looks that come from your parents at birth. Your looks—your dark eyes and black hair—make you stand out. Your appearance makes you unique, and that makes you very special! I think you are lovely to look at, and you can be very proud of who you are!" (p. 71)

Just imagine if Huong had not met that teacher! What if the cruelties visited upon her had continued?

I retell this story (Barell, 1995) because it shows that if I hadn't given each student an opportunity to tell a story, I never would have learned about the power of this teacher in Huong's life. I want to emphasize how one teacher's words transformed a life. Those words communicated such love and caring; the words emerged from one person's deep commitment to the children in her care. Such stories will abound in classrooms that are powerfully organized to invite thoughtfulness in students.

THE POWER OF STORIES

When we tell stories, we share our lives with students. How well I remember Harry Passow of Teachers College, Columbia University, telling stories of his work on the lower east side of Manhattan in poverty programs during the 1960s. How well I recall stories that my high school English teacher, Wilbury A. Crockett, told us during my senior year—stories about working two jobs in order to make a decent living as a teacher.

Stories reveal who we are as teachers and as individuals with a past. They also help us connect with our students. Bruner (1986) suggests that our minds are specially equipped to respond to narrative structures and Pagano reminds us that "teaching is textual. When we teach, we tell stories about the world. Some stories are scientific, some historical, some philosophical, some literary, and so on" (1991, p. 197). This suggests that as we introduce students to our subject matter, we can share stories of how that subject, for example, mathematics or history, came to be, who the major characters were, and the conflicts or problems they faced. In other words, each subject has the structure of a good story with characters, plot, tensions, and resolutions.

When we teach and tell stories, we also are sharing our passion for the subject; that is, how we came to be so involved in it that we wanted to share this part of our lives with students like Huong. Thus, stories help us connect with our students. They are powerful tools in the invitational environment because each of us, like Huong, wants to feel important, to be recognized and empowered to grow beyond the textbooks before us. We all have stories, and when a teacher shares his own stories, we feel invited to witness another person's growing up, with vulnerabilities and strengths. We feel welcome, as if at a party hosted by a friend.

There are many ways we can work with our students to create an invitational environment. These elements include setting high expectations, responding to students' answers and questions with sensitivity, having a desire to learn more from them, and being willing to risk asking good questions. Let's examine these elements.

"SHE WILL DO EXACTLY WHAT SHE WANTS TO DO"

Pam Lowry was a teacher in Greensboro, N.C., when I met her. I had been invited to a teachers' conference there by my friend and colleague Jan Williamson to share a story. As a young man, I had become immersed in the tales of Antarctica during the pioneering days of polar exploration. Narratives by Captain Robert Falcon Scott and Admiral Richard E. Byrd thrilled my 13-year-old imagination and led to meeting Byrd and sailing to Antarctica myself on the "free world's most powerful icebreaker."

Modeling this experience led to several teachers writing their own stories. Here is Lowry's, which appeared in a writing center newsletter (Lowry, 1993):

As a 12-year-old girl growing up in rural South Carolina, the highlight of any summer's day was eavesdropping on unsuspecting victims whenever the opportunity blossomed . . . . Daddy (for all southern male parents were thusly called) was earnestly saying that he had to make more money . . . . He [was] talking to Lee Roy (for most men in my hometown were Lee Roy or

Jim Bob or Joe Dean). He remarked in his solemn voice that he was determined to make more money so that college tuitions would be available for my brother and me . . . . Lee Roy casually drawled, "Why would you want to waste money on sending Pamela Lea (for females were always called Pamela Lea or Vera Sue or Deborah Jean) to college? She'll just get married and have babies; she won't need a college education for that."

Daddy, a soft-spoken, hard-as-rock, no-nonsense kind of fellow, replied in a voice I didn't recognize, "She deserves the same chance as her brother. She will do exactly what she wants to do as an adult . . . maybe teach school. But she will go to college and she will decide! Being a girl has nothing to do with whether or not I spend money on giving her a chance for an education."

Daddy seemed almost angry, fanatical, passionate. At that precise moment in time, I accepted the value of an education. If my daddy wanted me to have one at all costs, then surely it must be worthwhile (p. 10).

Pam's father had high expectations for both of his children. It is through such expectations that we show respect, appreciation, and concern for individual differences in language, ethnicity, and experiences. This is where we acclaim our commitment to the premise that all children and adolescents can succeed and that each has equal access to the knowledge and wisdom of our varying cultures.

How do we manifest these expectations in our classrooms? There are many ways:

• **Problem-based learning.** We present our students with complex, authentic tasks worth investigating or encourage them to help us develop such tasks together (Barell, 1998). For example, in high school science, we hypothesize about the location of the most intense concentrations of bacteria, investigate, and draw conclusions. In math, we design a house using 15 geometric concepts and explain why such concepts are important. In social studies, we investigate different regions of Africa and make a proposal to the World Bank seeking funds for economic development (see Chapter 43 in this volume). And in literature, we make a film from the text of *Crime and Punishment* and have all students volunteer for roles. In all these situations, we are like Pam's daddy: We have high expectations for our students, knowing that each can participate in her own way, thereby making the content meaningful. What we know about brain functioning (Caine & Caine, 1997; Jensen, 1998; Diamond & Hopson, 1999) suggests that we relish engaging complex, authentic and ill-structured problematic situations. "The single best way to grow a better brain is through challenging problem solving" (Jensen, 1998, p. 35).

• **Complex questions.** Posing what have come to be known as higher-order questions of *all* students, we communicate our expectations that everyone in class can think productively. Rather than limiting ourselves to a definition of kinetic energy, we challenge students to define, explain, and relate the concept to their own experiences, and, perhaps, create authentic problems using the concept for their peers to figure out.

• **Waiting.** We wait equally for all students to think through these complex ideas, and we will expect girls as well as boys to participate equally. Research by Sadker and Sadker (1994) suggests that differentiated treatment of boys and girls sends the message that girls "are educational second-class citizens." Listening to all students is important in the invitational classroom, and Rowe (1986) has demonstrated the very practical results from extending our listening time: We hear more inferential thinking, more student questions, and more speculative reasoning.

• **Responding.** How we probe for clarification and elaboration of students' ideas communicates powerful messages about our interest in students' thoughts and feelings. Irving Sigel of the Educational Testing Service told me long ago that how we respond to students' questions and answers might be more important than the questions we ask. For example, are we attending to their ideas with our bodies, our eyes, and an accepting, inviting tone of voice?

Here is another story about quality responding.

QUALITY RESPONDING

Madeline Swaney is another teacher from Greensboro. After sharing my story about meeting Byrd, the first person to fly over the South Pole in 1929, and his respectful letters answering all my questions about his four expeditions to Antarctica, Madeline told us about a short story she had written based on her love of science fiction and her favorite TV shows, "The Twilight Zone" and "The Outer Limits":

> "I knew I'd done well. I'd never before written as I did that afternoon and night. I could barely contain myself as I turned in my final draft. I knew the teacher would love the story, read it to the class, and give me the coveted A! The fever of that writing experience is still warm in my heart.
>
> "The day finally arrived when the stories were returned. My hand trembled and my heart pounded as I reached for my paper. It continued to tremble as I realized what a fool I'd been. I was ashamed and embarrassed. My paper, that had been so alive to me a few

nights before, lay bleeding to death in my hands. The wounds on every line supported the C minus in the margin. The intense pain of the grade would have been more easy to bear, if only some comment had been made about the story itself. Some word of encouragement or acknowledgment of my effort; but there was none. No words were written to me, the insecure, less-than-successful student, writer, human being! Communication about my paper wasn't to me, but to a *machine* that had malfunctioned on paragraphing, punctuation, and spelling—definite error in programming."

This was an experience that seared like a burning coal in Madeline's soul. Now, years later, Madeline is a teacher of writing who sees herself as an "encourager, even of weak writing. The potential is there, if the flame can be sparked, the desire intensified, and the child viewed as a valuable human being" (Swaney, 1993).

The power of our responses to students' inquiries, answers, and projects can do so much. We should express appreciation, validate ideas, ask for elaboration and clarification, and encourage students to go beyond whatever they or we think their limits are. Madeline's inner flame was almost extinguished by an adult response. To call it a "teacher's response" really only says that the individual with the authority gave the paper a C minus. A *teacher* would have found a way to help Madeline develop her story into something worth putting in the portfolio.

There are so many ways to respond to students' initiatives. Some of the most important include

• **Validating students' thinking.** "All your ideas are important, and we want to hear them."

• **Seeking clarification.** "Could you help us understand . . . ?"

• **Asking for elaboration.** "Please tell us more about your thinking here."

• **Sharing feelings.** "How did that make you feel? Perhaps others felt the same way?"

• **Reflecting on thought processes.** "Very interesting. How did you arrive at that conclusion? Could you share your mental steps with us?"

• **Searching for good reasoning.** "Can you tell us what evidence you have to support your conclusions? How did you reason this out?"

• **Asking for counter evidence.** "What evidence contradicts your point of view, and how does this affect your conclusions?"

• **Seeking transfer and application.** "How can you apply these ideas to what we have studied? To other subjects? To your personal life?"

• **Reflection.** "What have you learned from these experiences? About yourself? Others? The subject?"

Imagine how Madeline would have felt if her teacher had been open to the thinking and feeling of her students and could respond in this fashion. Evidently, Madeline's instructor felt that mechanics were more important than the identity of the student, that precision was more important than feelings, and that accountability was more significant than development. Mechanics, accountability, and precision are, indeed, important, but there are times when we decide that it's equally (or more) important to communicate encouraging expectations that imply: "This is a good start. Now, let's see if we can make this the kind of story you'd be even more proud of!"

Finally, there is another story. One that emphasizes what every invitational environment needs—an inquiring mind.

LEAH'S STORY

When we shared our stories, Leah Kraus was a teacher of business education in Greensboro. Her story illustrates what it means to internalize various language patterns from our parents. We listen and, over time, develop mental scripts that deeply affect our adult lives. Some of these scripts (or "self-talk") relate to success: "I can do anything I set my mind to." Some deal with difficulties: "I'll never be good at this subject." Leah's self-talk deals with another significant element in the invitational environment: inquiry.

> From a very young age I can remember listening to my father and trying to understand and interpret what he was saying. He was talking about what it means to be a Jew. I can remember one of the most important qualities is that Jews question, ask, and learn as much as we can. My father and mother are very religious; so it was not unusual for our discussions to be about what being a Jew means. However, I did not know at that time how these discussions would affect me, my career choice and my lifestyle. . . .
>
> As I got older my questions began to address philosophical issues. I needed to find answers to questions that were about ideals and interpretations. I needed to find my own answers to universal questions. My parents and the Jewish interpretations were no longer satisfying my curiosities. Unfortunately, as I found my answers, problems and conflicts and even more questions arose. The conflicts have followed me over the past 15 years. My love and respect for my parents and their beliefs somehow conflict with some of my life's choices. These choices have come from my own beliefs and morals. My interpretations have led me to the understanding that there is very little black and white or good and evil, but

> there is a lot of gray. I try to live by the interpretations I have developed while continuing to reexamine the gray. (Kraus, 1993, p. 12)

Leah realizes now that she has some answers but "so many more questions."

After hearing a story like this, I wonder how we can foster this kind of inquiry within families and classrooms. Leah's story reminds me of another one, about a boy growing up in Brooklyn, N.Y., whose mother would greet him every day after school—not with what every other mother asked, "So, did you learn anything today?"—but with, "Izzy, did you ask a good question today?" Isidore I. Rabi grew up to be a world class scientist and Nobel Prize winner in atomic physics, and he attributes his success to asking good questions.

Izzy's mother and Leah's parents knew something: At the heart of our development as civilized humans is our curiosity about the world and our lives therein.

> "Beneath humanity's raging debates, there is a common element that unites us all. We're curious" (AltaVista advertisement, 1999).

Without curiosity, we become passive, accepting individuals ripe for submission to any passing autocrat or dictator. Asking good questions is at the heart of being a citizen in our democracy.

How do we foster this in our classes? Options include

• **Setting expectations early.** "In this class, we expect you to develop your own questions about the subject. I'm not the only one who asks questions here."

• **Using thinking journals.** We can start by giving students such stems as: "I wonder . . . . What I'm curious about is . . . . I do not understand . . . . What I want/need to know more about . . . . I feel . . . . I can relate this to . . . . What's important here is . . . ." and so on (Barell, 1995).

• **Challenging students to develop their own questions through problem-based learning strategies.** For example, using the KWHLAQ strategy—which is an acronym created from the italic words in the following questions (Barell, 1998)—students ask: What do we think we *know* about the subject? What do we *want* or need to find out? *How* will we go about finding out? What do we expect to *learn* (and what have we learned) about the subject? How can we *apply* our learnings and findings? And what new *questions* do we have? These strategies allow students to share some control over their own learning (McCombs, 1991; Good & Brophy (1997).

• **Offering quality responses when students ask questions** and honoring and validating them and, occasionally, redirecting them to other students for a response: "What do you all think of Leah's question?"

Posing good questions is at the heart of learning how to learn and can be seen as a foundational element in the invitational classroom. As France said in 1890, "The whole art of teaching is only the art of awakening the natural curiosity of young minds for the purpose of satisfying it afterwards." We might add that the art of teaching involves structuring learning situations so students can satisfy their own curiosities. Indeed, inquisitiveness is the beginning of meaningful learning.

Huong's third-grade teacher, Pam's Daddy, Izzy's mother, and Leah's parents all recognized that every child deserves, needs, and should pursue a lifelong adventure of posing and resolving their own questions. Thankfully, each had a mentor who recognized this most fundamental human characteristic and need and communicated it.

NURTURING CLASSROOMS

All the teachers whose stories we have shared have developed environments in their classrooms that nurture and are full of what Diamond and Hopson (1999) call challenge, choice, and curiosity. Such environments invite students to pose good questions, take risks, learn and grow, and feel good in the process.

In Alice Walker's book *The Color Purple*, a character known only as "Mr." abuses young Celie. But at the end of the book, they reconcile. In a most reflective moment, Mr. says, "I think us here to wonder . . . to ast. . . . The more I wonder . . . the more I love." (1982, p. 290).

Amen!

REFERENCES

AltaVista. (1999, November 1). [Advertisement]. *The New Yorker.*

Barell, J. (1995). *Teaching for thoughtfulness: Classroom strategies to enhance intellectual development* (2nd ed.). New York: Longman.

Barell, J. (1998). *Problem based learning: An inquiry approach.* Arlington Heights, IL: SkyLight.

Bruner, J. (1986). *Actual minds, possible worlds.* Cambridge, MA: Harvard University Press; and Alexandria, VA: Association for Supervision and Curriculum Development.

Caine, R., & Caine, G. (1997). *Education on the edge of possibility.* Alexandria, VA: Association for Supervision and Curriculum Development.

Diamond, M., & Hopson, J. (1999). *Magic trees of the mind: How to nurture your child's intelligence, creativity, and healthy emotions from birth through adolescence.* New York: Penguin/Plume.

France, A. (1890). *The crime of Sylvestre Bonnard.* New York: Harper and Brothers.

Good, T., & Brophy, J. (1997). *Looking in classrooms* (7th ed.). New York: Longman.

Jensen, E. (1998). *Teaching with the brain in mind.* Alexandria, VA: Association for Supervision and Curriculum Development.

Kraus, L. (1993). Leah's story. *Network, 5*(9). Greensboro, NC: Reasoning & Writing Center.

Lowry, P. (1993, May). Daddy. *Network 5*(9). Greensboro, NC: Reasoning & Writing Center.

McCombs, B. (1991). *Metacognition and motivation for higher level thinking.* Paper presented at the annual meeting of the American Educational Research Association, Chicago.

Pagano, J. (1991). Moral fictions: The dilemma of theory and practice. In C. Witherell & N. Noddings (Eds.), *Stories lives tell: Narrative and dialogue in education* (pp. 193–206). New York: Teachers College Press.

Rowe, M. B. (1986, Spring). Wait time—Slowing down may be a way of speeding up. *American Educator, 2*(1).

Sadker, M., & Sadker, D. (1994). *Failing at fairness: How America's schools cheat girls.* New York: Charles Scribner's Sons.

Swaney, M. (1993). Madeline's story. *Network, 5*(9). Greensboro, NC: Reasoning & Writing Center.

Walker, A. (1982). *The color purple.* New York: Harcourt Brace Jovanovich.

20

Preparing Teachers of Thinking

David S. Martin and Nicholas M. Michelli

To waken interest and kindle enthusiasm is the sure way to teach easily and successfully.

—*Tyrone Edwards*

For a long time, curriculum innovators have believed in and acted upon the idea of a strong relationship between curriculum change and teacher change. In fact, curriculum change cannot truly occur without teacher change. In this chapter, we address the question of how to prepare *new* teachers as teachers of thinking. According to R. Nickerson (1988)

> It is no more reasonable to expect an individual who does not know a lot about thinking to teach thinking effectively, than to expect one who does not know a lot about math, or physics, or literature to be an effective teacher in any of these areas. In the long run, how successful institutionalized education will be in incorporating effective teaching of thinking in the typical classroom will depend to no small degree on how much emphasis teacher-training programs put on thinking in their curricula. (p. 6)

Although Nickerson made his statement years ago, it is only recently that teacher-education programs have begun to systematically incorporate the dimension of teaching thinking into the curriculum for preparing new teachers.

How can we ensure that new teachers become teachers of thinking? We will begin with the need to incorporate thinking skills into teacher education and related background, and continue by discussing models for teacher preparation, the results achieved by teachers who have been prepared to be teachers of thinking, a status report on the incorporation of cognitive strategy development within teacher-preparation programs, a proposed vision, and recommendations for action and research by teacher educators.

The curriculum in many schools emphasizes easily measured and sometimes superficial standards—with the simultaneous compartmentalization of subject matter, it becomes all the more essential to maintain a focus on critical thinking. In fact, a few states such as Maryland have actually returned to an emphasis on thinking skills—as was more common in the 1960s—in their state-mandated student tests through constructed-response items. We hope that this resurgence spreads.

The Need

The movement to formally incorporate the teaching of thinking into elementary and secondary schools in the United States began to gain momentum in the early 1980s. The essential element in the methodology is the explicit discussion of cognitive and metacognitive processes within many of the thinking skills programs. Some, but not all, programs require some form of teacher preparation, usually in an inservice context. Preservice teacher-education programs, on the other hand, have been slower to respond to the need for the explicit preparation of teachers of thinking. However, preservice programs need to meet the expectations created by the thinking skills programs in schools hiring new teachers.

Goodlad (1999) reminds us that the people in the United States make up a nation of "non-voters and non-listeners," and, therefore, teachers "must be about much more than merely preparing youth for a job." He endorses the idea of developing a student's intelligence in a variety of ways, including the use of narratives. A recent report found that students of math teachers who studied and taught for higher-order thinking skills outperformed students of math teachers who had *not* studied pedagogy using higher-order thinking skills (Wenglinsky, 2000, p. 7).

A BRIEF HISTORY

Just as Costa's distinction among teaching for thinking, teaching of thinking, and teaching about thinking (see Section VIII and Chapter 57 in this volume) is useful in elementary and secondary education, it also is useful in teacher education. That is, many teacher-education programs have prepared teachers to teach *for* thinking by emphasizing that teachers incorporate challenging questions and special activities within, for example, science and social studies. However, preparing teachers to teach thinking as an explicit part of the curriculum (*of* thinking) or teaching students to explicitly reflect on their own mental processes (*about* thinking) has been, until recently, neglected in the teacher-preparation curriculum. In addition, preparing teachers to include specific thinking-strategy programs in their teaching has not been part of pre-service programs.

In the early 1980s, the Association Collaborative for Teaching Thinking (ACTT) was formed, bringing together leaders and representatives from professional associations, including the Association for Supervision and Curriculum Development (ASCD) and the American Association of Colleges for Teacher Education (AACTE). AACTE's participation was one of the first acts of official recognition by the teacher-education community that the teaching of thinking is important. The participants developed standards to propose for adoption by the National Council for Accreditation of Teacher Education (NCATE). The proposed standards said that teacher-preparation programs would be assessed for accreditation on the basis of evidence that their programs actively promoted

• An attitude of thoughtful consideration of the problems, topics, and issues of their professional experience.
• An active working knowledge of the methods of effective inquiry, using all levels of thinking.
• The application of methods of inquiry to classroom teaching.
• Explicit opportunities for candidates to reflect on, analyze, and apply higher-order thinking operations to real-world issues and problems and to subject matter.
• An actively supportive climate that promotes the exercise, application, teaching, and learning of thinking dispositions and cognitive operations.

NCATE subsequently adopted standards in 1995 under Professional and Pedagogical Studies for Initial Teacher Preparation, including having candidates complete a well-planned sequence of courses and/or experiences in pedagogical studies that help develop understanding and use of a variety of instructional strategies for developing critical thinking and problem solving (NCATE, 1995).

Although the language of the standard, paraphrased above, is not precisely as proposed by the collaborative, its incorporation gives national recognition to the importance of preparing teachers of thinking.

In the fall of 1987, AACTE called a special task force meeting to discuss directions for the association concerning the preparation of teachers of thinking. This meeting brought together 12 individuals representing the fields of psychology, teacher education, curriculum, and related fields. As a result of that meeting, 65 teacher educators met in 1988 to examine possible models for including thinking skills programs into teacher education. Later in 1988, a one-week seminar was held for teacher educators representing eight teacher-education institutions to examine in-depth models for program revision and course revision in teacher preparation. The seminar was part of a larger annual institute at the University of Massachusetts, Boston, on thinking skills. Out of that seminar grew a network of interested individuals, as well as a special resolution for AACTE as a whole. (The network has evolved into the Special Study Group for the Infusion of Critical Thinking.)

The AACTE resolution called for all programs in teacher education to incorporate preparation for teaching thinking, and it was approved by a large margin at the association's 1989 annual meeting. The association also approved the formation of a special study group (SSG) to enable interested institutional representatives to exchange ideas and models on implementing thinking skills within their programs. Some examples of specific implementations and models from current SSG members are provided later in this chapter.

COGNITIVE EDUCATION AND THE TEACHER-EDUCATION KNOWLEDGE BASE

Much is known about the ways in which a learner constructs and manipulates ideas effectively, given appropriate classroom methodologies. Costa (1991) provides a useful list and explication of teacher behaviors that lead to student thinking. They include praise, the use of silence or wait time, clarifying statements, acceptance of student responses, use of questioning, and giving students opportunities to apply and evaluate actions in novel situations. We add other effective behaviors for teachers, such as

• Asking questions that demand "why" and "how" responses.

• Identifying the specific strategies that students have used to solve a problem (metacognition).

• Reminding students of the cognitive strategies they may apply while solving a subject-matter problem.

• Establishing an atmosphere in which thinking is valued.

• Modeling reflective thought by the teacher.

• Developing evaluation techniques that are consistent with teaching for thinking.

Many pathways are possible to incorporate such behaviors into a new teacher's repertoire. Some may be part of the natural behavior of future teachers, while others may require specific cultivation.

An exciting and burgeoning area of the knowledge base comes from ongoing research on the brain. Teacher educators are well aware of the attention given to the possible connections between ongoing physiological and psychological brain research and classroom learning. Some have even called the 1990s "the decade of the brain" (Bruer, 1999). Much, of course, remains to be done before clear connections can be understood. Such important technologies as CAT scans and MRIs are leading to greater insights about the brain's operation. However, as Bruer indicates, despite significant theoretical progress on "neural hardware" and the relationship between brain structures and mental functions, "we know relatively little about learning, thinking, and remembering at the level of brain areas, neural circuits, or synapses; we know very little about how the brain thinks, remembers, and learns" (p. 650).

We can say, however, that nothing thus far in neurological brain research diminishes the view that teaching for thinking must be an important part of U.S. education. Research to date is easily interpreted to support a classroom focus on more complex learning rather than on simplistic basic skills, on the importance of meaning-making rather than imposed knowledge, and on constructivist approaches to teaching. Until more is known about neurological research, we can rely on our understanding of learning from psychological and philosophical inquiry to make a case for the importance of teaching for thinking.

A related body of research includes investigations of teaching itself as a cognitive activity for adults. The work of Morine-Dershimer (1982) establishes methods for researching the thinking of teachers. Carbone (1980) observed the need for a teacher to diagnose the causes of student difficulties and to prescribe beyond trial and error. In addition, Renner (1975) demonstrated positive cognitive growth in teacher candidates as a result of preservice preparation for the teaching of science using reasoning activities.

Clark and Yinger (1979) and others have studied teaching as a cognitive activity. Clark and Lampert (1986) provide an excellent summary of those aspects of the research on teacher thinking that belong in the knowledge base of teacher education. Peterson (1988) conceptualizes how teacher and student cognitions and knowledge can mediate effective teaching. Shulman (1986) calls for a "paradigm shift" in research on teacher education, away from the process-product approach and toward a cognitive paradigm that examines the effects of the thinking and decision making that teachers do while interacting with students (see also Clark & Peterson, 1986; Peterson, Swing, & Stolber, 1986).

Martin (1998) looks at the effects of teaching thinking on the thinking of teachers themselves. A comparison of teachers in Costa Rica and the United States who had been trained in and had implemented a program of teaching thinking found that teachers in both cultures reported changes in their teaching styles. The changes were an increased use of discussion and cognitive vocabulary, and more frequent preplanned problem-solving tasks in their classrooms. According to the teachers, their personal adult problem-solving styles also evolved toward a more systematic use of strategies, such as personal planning, sequencing, and the application of logic.

Although the study involved inservice rather than preservice teachers, we may infer that preservice teachers require special preparation for teaching thinking and will also change personally as they transform into well-prepared teachers of thinking.

MODELS OF TEACHER-PREPARATION PROGRAMS

Knowledge base alone is not sufficient for preparing proactive teachers of thinking. The infusion of thinking skills must cut across the teacher-education curriculum not only into coursework but also into practicum work. Some teacher-education programs already have thinking skills as part of their curriculum.

One model requires faculty development for the teacher-education faculty. The faculty would infuse thinking within the teacher-preparation curriculum. The faculty would become proficient with a body of higher-order thinking skills and their classroom applications (e.g., categorization, sequencing, logic, comparison, and pattern identification). Then each component of the teacher-education program (foundations, curriculum, methods, and practicum) would share responsibility for infusing particular cognitive skills. For example, the foundations course in educational psychology would emphasize not only the knowledge base about cognition but also the cognitive skill of analysis, and would have candidates apply analysis to the diagnostic activities that a teacher must carry out with students. The curriculum course, among other emphases, would teach future teachers the skill of logical reasoning and apply it to an examination of the logic behind different theories of curriculum. A practicum experience would emphasize synthesizing as a skill needed to put together the components of the program, as well as how to teach synthesis to students (Martin, 1984a, 1984b).

Naturally, teacher preparation models vary. The Institute for the Advancement of Philosophy for Children administers a special fifth-year program for K–8 preservice teachers that focuses on the teaching of thinking. The University of Massachusetts, Boston, has a master's degree program in thinking skills for the experienced teacher. The preservice preparation program at the University of Virginia integrates reasoning skills across a block of method courses in social studies, science, and math.

Hayes, Grace, and Pateman (1998) describe a reconfiguration of the preservice teacher-education program to incorporate an inquiry-based approach. They have done away with traditional forms of teacher-education coursework and work instead to prepare teachers who will effect change. Specifically, candidates participate in seminar dialogues and inquiry projects, explore teaching as a "complex and ambiguous act," and apply the triad of dialogue, inquiry, and critique throughout all the teacher-preparation experiences at their institution.

AACTE's Special Study Group for the Infusion of Critical Thinking meets regularly at the organization's annual meeting. Representatives of teacher-education institutions involved with the group assemble and share plans and issues related to the explicit incorporation of thinking into their programs. At the 1999 meeting of this group, the following models were reported in use.

• Marshall University (West Virginia) uses the theme of critical thinking in their teacher-education program and investigates methods of assessment for it.

• Marymount University (Virginia) is implementing an Ethics Across the Curriculum program, identifying its theme as "Habits of Mind" and applying it to such areas as reflection and analysis of candidates' portfolios.

• The University of Northern Iowa has a required course in deductive and inductive reasoning for its candidates, which is offered by its Psychology Department. The university also uses the Watson-Glaser Critical Thinking Appraisal in its program (Watson & Glaser, 1980).

• Steven Foster State University (Texas) is addressing new state curriculum standards that include critical thinking by changing their teacher-education program.

• Lehman College (New York) is pursuing a critical thinking approach in its general education component for candidates.

• Wake Forest University (North Carolina), during its prepracticum experiences, requires a parallel seminar to compare four classrooms observed by candidates.

• Tuskegee University (Alabama) has infused critical thinking into its professional education courses, and the program collaborates with the university's College of Arts and Sciences along this theme. The university's president has spoken publicly in favor of critical thinking in all university programs. The school requires that candidates' portfolios show evidence of critical thinking, and during coursework, candidates must solve critical-thinking problems.

• The University of Georgia prepares candidates to succeed on the new state teacher test, which requires constructed responses.

• Mitchell State College (Colorado) has a partnership, similar to Tuskegee's, with its College of Arts and Sciences in incorporating critical thinking.

Quite possibly, in terms of comprehensive infusion, the most fully developed model now is at Montclair State University in New Jersey. In place since the early 1980s, the model has evolved significantly. Its focus is on critical thinking that is conceptualized as "thinking that leads to good judgment" because it is based on identified criteria, sensitive to context, and derived from a "community of inquiry." The concept is based on the work of Lipman and the Institute for the Advancement of Philosophy for Children at the university, which conducts extensive international teacher-education programs to prepare teachers to teach critical thinking through philosophy to children, beginning at the elementary level (Lipman, 1988).

Since the early 1990s, through membership in Goodlad's National Network for Educational Renewal, Montclair's teacher-education program has evolved through the application of a program titled Agenda for Education in a Democracy. The program uses critical thinking as a way to enable students to become effective, functioning citizens in a political and social democracy. This focus, of course, includes a strong emphasis on providing access to knowledge through the study of the disciplines but with critical thinking as its organizing theme (Michelli, Jacobowitz, & Pines, 1994). Further, the program has introduced a focus on the moral dimensions of a teacher's work, again using critical thinking as a vehicle for examining such dimensions. Over the years, the New Jersey Network for Educational Renewal, a partnership between Montclair and 20 neighboring school districts, has evolved to bring about significant changes in the schools and to prepare teachers to work with teacher candidates from the university.

Critical thinking is deeply infused into many of the professional sequences of courses in Montclair's teacher-education program. In addition, a specific course, Teaching for Critical Thinking, is required of all candidates. Critical thinking also is found in many of the university's arts and sciences programs, and, in 1999, the university's faculty approved a new general-education program with an explicit goal of teaching for critical thinking.

The entire teacher-education program at Montclair is embodied in *The Portrait of a Teacher* (Jacobowitz & Michelli, 1999), which describes expectations for excellent teachers and includes critical-thinking attributes as important elements. The document is used to assess the dispositions, skills, and knowledge of candidates for admission to and graduation from the program and as a basis for curriculum design.

In addition, the university offers a master's degree in education in critical thinking, along with a doctoral program designed for teachers who are committed to remaining in the classroom rather than preparing to become school administrators. Critical thinking is a core theme of the master's program, and one of the first specializations within it is philosophy for children.

Sharing a Vision

Upon considering the descriptions of the models, it becomes clear that many institutions view preparing future teachers of thinking as an important responsibility. It is also clear that the variety of definitions of and approaches to the teaching of thinking are as diverse as the number of institutions.

Some institutions conceptualize the teaching of thinking as a discrete set of thinking skills that take students beyond simply receiving knowledge. Thinking-skills programs of this type expect students to integrate, analyze, compare, use deduction and induction, and otherwise use knowledge to go beyond simple memory. The influence of Benjamin Bloom's cognitive taxonomy is reflected in such programs.

Other institutions approach the teaching of thinking as a developmental process, using either sequential stages or definitions of prerequisites for each level of the ability to engage in thinking. Much of this work has evolved from psychology and cognitive science and reflects the work of Jean Piaget, Reuven Feuerstein, and Lawrence Kohlberg.

Thinking may also be conceptualized as problem solving, and this approach often emerges in programs to prepare teachers of science and mathematics. Those who see teaching thinking as critical thinking may use the concept of critical thinking leading to good judgment based on explicit criteria and derived from discussions within communities of inquiry. This concept is derived from the field of philosophy and reflects the work of Lipman (1988).

And others see critical thinking as central to their view that, as one of the primary purposes of public education, schools prepare young people to be active, questioning citizens in a political and social democracy. Goodlad (1999) puts forth such an argument. Those using the perspective of critical pedagogy see all critical thinking as focusing on significant social issues and as potentially transforming the individual and society.

Thus, significantly different approaches to teaching thinking abound, and they, in turn, have different implications for the preparation of teachers of thinking. Not all the approaches mentioned are mutually exclusive, and it is clearly possible to envision a program that combines some of these concepts. However, for teacher-education programs to effectively prepare teachers to teach thinking, teacher educators must confront what they mean by "teaching thinking." Failing to take a programmatic perspective on teaching for thinking may well lead to candidates' experiencing miscellaneous approaches in a variety of courses without seeing connections or developing a clear viewpoint on teaching for thinking. Coming to an agreement on the meaning of teaching thinking can be an important part of developing a shared vision, not only of education, but also of teacher preparation. The approach to teaching thinking will be enhanced if the concept of teaching for thinking that evolves is shared with those teaching in a university's arts and sciences program, as well as with those with whom candidates work in practicum experiences in the schools.

The process of exploring different meanings of thinking and developing a coherent approach also can be an important activity for partnerships between universities and schools. Consider the power of the learning experience of a future teacher who finds that, within his discipline, university arts and sciences faculty recognize and identify the meaning of thinking within the discipline (e.g., what it means to "think" like a historian, a chemist, or a mathematician). If that same candidate compared thinking across disciplines, within a sequence of professional courses, it would expand his understanding of knowledge and offer an important perspective on learning. For example, the candidate learns that the questions asked by a biology professor and an English professor vary because the disciplines are different.

The teacher candidate then learns the relationship between thinking and cognitive development in children, including the implications of recent brain research. Now imagine that this same candidate enters a school for structured field experiences, culminating in student teaching, and encounters teachers there who understand the same perspective on teaching and thinking that is taught at the university. Such an understanding would be the result of the university's prior efforts to work with the school system to agree on a concept of teaching for thinking, leading to a truly shared vision of the place of thinking in U.S. education and a sense of how teachers should be prepared for their roles. Candidates in this position would not have their prior work deemed useless by their mentor teachers, but would find that the mentors embrace thinking within their own classrooms.

Working to develop unambiguous meanings of teaching for thinking that are shared by faculty in education, arts and sciences, and the schools is difficult but achievable. And the idea that thinking should be the vehicle for building school-university partnerships is not the result of choosing just any one of dozens of themes. Thinking has always been and will continue to be the most basic and enduring outcome of education. Facts learned in the course of education are likely to have less validity as time goes on, but the ability to think about ideas and to evaluate facts is the critical essence of education. So, too, should it be the essence of how we prepare teachers. Further, we need to see the preparation of teachers as not only the responsibility of schools, academic departments, and colleges of education; it is also the responsibility of an entire university and of prekindergarten to 12th grade teachers. Ideally, faculty in these institutions would foster dialogue to lead to consensus, coordinate and integrate cross-disciplinary meaning, promote conversations to clarify the place of thinking in U.S. education, and refine the appropriate pedagogies that must be mastered in order to teach thinking. (See also Patterson, Michelli, & Pacheco, 1999, for further exploration of such partnerships.)

RECOMMENDED ACTION STEPS FOR TEACHER EDUCATORS

In addition to the development of full programs in the teaching of thinking within teacher-preparation curricula, individual teacher educators may initiate and foster the teaching of thinking by

• Broadening course objectives to include certain higher-order cognitive strategies that are relevant to the topic of the course. For example, in a philosophy of education course, an objective could be learning to take a position on an issue and defend it logically in front of peers.

• Building into a course some activities in which teacher candidates identify a relevant cognitive skill (such as categorization), apply it during the course, reflect on the cognitive strategies used, and discuss ways to apply that skill to the teaching of children.

• Adding to the course a view of the *structure* of the discipline as well as its content (e.g., the structure of the curriculum field, the structure of history).

• Fostering regular dialogue, modeling higher-order questioning and wait time, and reflecting on those strategies with candidates.

• Connecting activities with parallel observation experiences in classrooms of teachers whom teacher educators have identified as models of teachers of thinking.

• Revising course-assessment tools to include not only memory and comprehension of course ideas but also higher-level analysis, reasoning, and manipulation of course ideas.

• Initiating conversations with colleagues and teacher-education leaders in the institution to begin a dialogue with arts and sciences faculty, and school faculty, about developing the shared vision described in the previous section. (See Martin, 1989, for more ideas about models for changing teacher-education programs.)

NEEDED RESEARCH

Several important research questions about the relationship between teacher education and student thinking remain to be investigated. They offer fertile opportunities for action-research projects shared by university and school faculty within institutional partnerships. Such topics include

• Which cognitive education strategies from schools are most applicable to teaching the teacher candidate as a learner?

• To what degree do infused cognitive skills in teacher-education pedagogy courses truly transfer into the student-teaching experience of a candidate?

• What effects do infused cognitive education elements in a teacher-education program have on a candidate's view of the classroom reality when he encounters it as a student teacher or as a regular classroom teacher?

• What is the impact of a student teacher's use of cognitive skills on children's views of that student teacher, compared with children's views of student teachers who do not employ thinking strategies?

• What assessment tools are most sensitive to the effects of a teacher-education program's infusion of thinking skills on candidates, both as adult learners and new teachers? What is the effect of a thinking-skills program on a student teacher's self-concept?

• When a student teacher works with a cooperating teacher who has been identified as a teacher of thinking, what influence will that teacher have on the candidate's thought processes and teaching strategies during the student teaching period?

The exploration of these questions and others will lead to additional questions and to an accumulation of the necessary knowledge base.

PREPARING THE NEXT GENERATION

The teacher-education community has made important strides in embracing the movement to focus teaching and learning on thinking. Many options are available to teacher educators who are serious about preparing teachers of thinking. Only through a systematic approach, with careful attention to infusion, can we expect the next generation of teachers to regard the teaching of thinking as a fundamental part of their activities with students.

Employers of high school graduates now are saying they want to hire individuals who exhibit three characteristics: writing skills, interpersonal skills, and critical thinking skills; the employers say they will teach the rest of what is needed on the job. In addition, society needs citizens who can think effectively and make sound judgments on all issues. Clearly, teachers of thinking are necessary to meet this demand and enable the young to become effective problem solvers. Let us move forward to implement the principle that teacher change is essential to curriculum change, so we may, in turn, prepare the next generation of graduates to make us into a nation of thinkers.

REFERENCES

Bruer, J. T. (1999, May). In search of brain-based education. *Phi Delta Kappan, 8*(9), 648–657.

Carbone, P. F. (1980, May–June). Liberal education and teacher preparation. *Journal of Teacher Education 31*(3), 7–12.

Clark, C. M., & Lampert, M. (1986). The study of teacher thinking and implications for teacher education. *Journal of Teacher Education, 37*(5), 27–31.

Clark, C. M., & Peterson, P. L. (1986). Teachers' thought processes. In M. C. Wittrock (Ed.), *Handbook of research on teaching.* New York: Macmillan.

Clark, C. M., & Yinger, R. L. (1979). Teacher thinking. In H. J. Walberg & P. L. Peterson (Eds.), *Research in teaching: Concepts, findings, and implications.* Berkeley, CA: McCutchan.

Costa, A. L. (1991). Teacher behaviors that enable student thinking. In A. L. Costa (Ed.), *Developing minds.* Alexandria, VA: Association for Supervision and Curriculum Development.

Goodlad, J. (1999). *Teachers for the teaching of intelligence.* Presentation at the 5th Annual Conference for the Teaching of Intelligence, San Francisco.

Hayes, M. T., Grace, D., & Pateman, N. (1998, Winter). Reconfiguring the preservice curriculum: A proposal for an inquiry-based teacher education program. *Inquiry: Critical Thinking Across the Disciplines, 18*(2), 65–79.

Jacobowitz, T. & Michelli, N. (1999). Montclair State University and the New Jersey Network for Educational Renewal. In W. F. Smith & G. D. Fenstermacher (Eds.), *Leadership for educational renewal: Developing a cadre of leaders.* San Francisco: Jossey-Bass.

Lipman, M. (1988, September). Critical thinking—What can it be? *Educational Leadership, 46*(1), 38–43.

Martin, D. S. (1984a). *Can teachers become better thinkers?* [Occasional paper No. 12]. Oxford, OH: National Staff Development Council.

Martin, D. S. (1984b). Infusing cognitive strategies into teacher preparation programs. *Educational Leadership, 42*(3), 68–72.

Martin, D. S. (1989, May/June). Restructuring teacher education programs for higher-order thinking skills. *Journal of Teacher Education, 40*(3), 2–8.

Martin, D. S. (1998). *Teaching of thinking: A cross-cultural study of effects on professionals.* (Eric Clearinghouse on Teacher Education, Document No. SP 038 049).

Michelli, N. M., Jacobowitz, T., & Pines, R. (1994, Spring/Summer). Renewing teacher education through critical thinking. *Record in Educational Leadership,* 45–48.

Morine-Dershimer, G. (1982, March). *Tying threads together: Some thoughts on methods for investigating teacher thinking.* New York: American Educational Research Association.

National Council for Accreditation of Teacher Education (NCATE). (1995). *Standards, procedures, and policies for the accreditation of professional education units.* Washington, DC: Author.

Nickerson, R. (1988). On improving thinking through instruction. *Review of Research in Education, 15,* 3–57.

Patterson, R., Michelli, N., & Pacheco, A. (1999). *Centers of pedagogy: New structures for educational renewal.* San Francisco: Jossey-Bass.

Peterson, P. L. (1988, June/July). Teachers' and students' conditional knowledge for classroom teaching and learning. *Educational Researcher, 17*(5), 5–14.

Peterson, P. L., Swing, S. R., & Stolber, K. D. (1986). *Learning time vs. thinking skills: Alternative perspectives on the effects of two instructional interventions.* Program Report 86-6. Madison, WI: Wisconsin Center for Education Research.

Renner, J. W. (1975). Determination of intellectual levels of selected students: Final report to National Science Foundation. Washington, DC: National Science Foundation. (Eric Document No. 75-SP-0517).

Shulman, L. S. (1986). Paradigms and research programs in the study of teaching: A contemporary perspective. In M. C. Wittrock (Ed.), *Handbook of research on teaching.* New York: Macmillan.

Watson, G., & Glaser, E. M. (1980). *Watson-Glaser critical thinking appraisal.* San Antonio, TX: The Psychological Corporation.

Wenglinsky, H. (2000). *How teaching matters: Bringing the classroom back into discussions of teacher quality.* Princeton, NJ: Educational Testing Service.

21

From Staff Development to Professional Development: Supporting Thoughtful Adults for Thinking Schools

Laura Lipton and Bruce Wellman

Different approaches to learning and different forms of instruction—from imitation, to instruction, to discovery, to collaboration—reflect differing beliefs and assumptions about the learner—from actor, to knower, to private experiencers, to collaborative thinkers.

—J. Bruner, The Culture of Education

Knowing the names of things and understanding their meanings reveal the underlying structures and beliefs shaping our world. Unexamined words exert invisible forces that confine and constrain individuals and organizations.

In the field of education, the term "staff development" carries several hidden meanings that bind teachers to unproductive patterns of adult learning in schools and districts. Exploring the roots of the word "staff" provides insight into the tenacity of many outmoded approaches and programs.

The most direct meaning of the word "staff" is as a rod, a pole, or a baton. In the 18th century, an officer's baton or staff of office symbolized the idea of command. The word came to mean a group of military or naval officers serving a commander. The staff officers did not participate in combat and had no authority to command. In German the phrase "den regiment oder colonel stab" means the colonel's staff with which he rules. In educational practice, this definition suggests that a staff follows orders, makes few decisions, and learns at the command of others. This definition includes rewards and sanctions, rules and procedures, and record keeping and ranking. The hidden metaphor subtly manages systems and individuals, with many undesirable consequences.

In contrast, the word professional implies "one who has an assured competence in a particular field or occupation," is capable of making decisions, and is a self-directed learner. This definition suggests that developing professionals is profoundly different from developing a staff.

The following vignettes illustrate this contrast. Imagine School A:

The *District Staff Development Catalog* has just been delivered. The catalog includes courses and workshops sponsored by the school district, as well as some from local universities and regional agencies. The principal has provided a faculty meeting time for exploring the offerings. If we listen in, we might hear:

"I'm free on Thursdays; what's offered for fall?"
"This one has a really great presenter; I've used lots of her stuff for reading instruction."
"I need two inservice credits; what looks good?"
"What are the requirements for that hands-on math course?"

Now, consider School B:

Cross-grade teams are gathered in the school conference room. Large displays of bar graphs cover the walls, and student work samples lie on the tables. The state assessment scores in writing serve as a catalyst for motivating a schoolwide focus on expository writing. These teams, as well as grade-level teams, have been meeting to explore a variety of data and determine ways to improve students' skills. In this case, if we listen in, we might hear:

Copyright © 2001 by MiraVia LLC

"What connections do you see between the work samples and the test scores?"

"How do the work samples differ from grade to grade? How do they compare to what we're expecting to see?"

"Let's go online to search for other resources."

"Let's look at the work samples for 4th grade, and compare them to our rubric."

NEW MODELS FOR TEACHER LEARNING

As these scenarios illustrate, current notions of teacher learning reflect a belief that autonomous individuals, pursuing personal interests, can produce significant improvements in student performance. They rely on staff development programs organized by courses, credits, and rewards that are not linked to student learning. Individuals must establish specific, purposeful learning agendas that serve their professional needs while supporting the improvement efforts and direction of the organization. We suggest that it is time to move beyond staff development as an activity—something done on "special" days and, worse, something done *to* teachers but chosen and planned by someone else.

Although approaches to growth and development for educators have changed during the last 20 years, the enormous challenge for professional development has remained fairly constant. That is, the goal of developing a collaborative, learning-oriented school culture is constrained by the prevailing context of teachers' work. Such environments do not foster thoughtful practitioners in thoughtful schools and do not produce continual refinement of practice and increased success for students. Promoting schools as places of learning for all members is not currently reflected in the daily routines, job expectations, supervisory practices, or even programs for professional growth.

New models for teacher learning align personal responsibility with collective goals. When practitioners view themselves as continual learners, as well as contributors to the learning of others, they become thoughtful teachers in thoughtful schools. To reap the learning benefits of such a workplace, we propose three attributes for professional development: It should be learning-focused, authentic, and collaborative.

LEARNING-FOCUSED

For professional development to be effective, it must be relevant to students' needs and be part of the continual, data-driven refinement of professional practice. Successfully learn-ing any educational innovation requires *frequency* of involvement with new ideas and strategies. It also demands *duration* of exposure to these techniques in classroom settings for integration of essential patterns and context-based adaptations (Little, 1986). Job-embedded learning offers concrete opportunities for applying and practicing new skills, with immediate feedback from students and peers.

Further, methods to mark progress, make errors, and gather feedback necessary for cumulative discovery have to be part of professional development. A prescriptive approach to school improvement—purchasing a program or adopting "teacher friendly" materials—will not yield thinking practitioners or thoughtful students. Single course offerings or traditional models of staff development tend to limit the "how" of learning, focusing only on the "what."

The differences between School A and School B illustrate this point. Notice that in School A, the choices are directed by personal concerns and unaligned interests. In School B, the motivation to learn arises from a perceived need or a value that the learning will satisfy. The learning needs of students frame the learning focus for the adults that serve them. Practitioners should be able to choose learning opportunities that are relevant and specific to their own learning agendas, while being congruent with the overall school or district focus for improvement.

AUTHENTIC

Opportunities to learn in schools are numerous. "Teachers participate in decisions, redefine their roles, reflect on their own competence, converse with peers, advocate designing new programs or schedules, pose questions about their work, or give guidance to new teachers, thereby eliciting and articulating their own knowledge" (Lambert, 1989, p. 80). Authentic professional development derives from these daily activities and is an integral part of the workplace, not a separate function. When professional development is authentic, collaborative endeavors that support learning emerge out of need and desire, not formal procedures or artificial expectations.

Organizational contrivances, such as shared planning periods, prescriptive or prepackaged training programs, or assigned learning partners, will keep collegiality bounded to a specific, predetermined purpose. While potentially useful as an initial phase toward a culture of colearning, this quick-fix practice can dilute the effort necessary to cultivate and nurture genuine learning communities. The result? Hargreaves and Fullan (1992) label the resulting activities as "contrived collegiality."

Again, our two schools provide a vivid contrast. In School A, the options for learning are episodic, scattered across multiple venues, topics, and purposes. In School B, professional development is ongoing, centered on specific school improvement initiatives, and embedded within daily work life.

COLLABORATIVE

Craft knowledge is constructed through collaborative experimentation and reflection. The essence of collaboration is colearning and the coconstruction of new understandings. Collaborative professional development creates opportunities to build a shared language for describing, analyzing, and continually improving practice, thus producing cultural shifts toward shared responsibility for all students' success. School B clearly exemplifies this practice.

In collaborative cultures, uncertainty is not defended, but valued as a source of problem posing and potential problem solving. Collaborative cultures embody broad agreement on fundamental educational issues, with high tolerance for divergent views. In fact, disagreement and alternative perspectives are vital to sustaining energy and attention. School communities that grapple thoughtfully with educational issues are composed of thoughtful practitioners who are better able to engage thoughtful students.

SUPPORTING THE SHIFT: NEW MODELS, NEW POSSIBILITIES

> To the extent that we can develop views of knowledge as emergent, views of the profession as changing, and views of the individual as growing, we will have provided the conditions that enable teachers to experiment with the process and content of their craft. (Joyce & Showers, 1988, pp. 77–78)

As a result of current knowledge about learning and school culture, multiple new models for professional development are emerging. These nontraditional examples are process oriented, incorporating the three qualities previously described. In these novel configurations, formats are varied, providing a high degree of choice in the *when*, *where*, and *how* of learning. They incorporate flexible use of time, take advantage of shared resources, and, most important, place professional practice at the center. Four categories of configuration—networks, professional learning partnerships, study groups, and dialogue—

illuminate some of the possibilities for supporting thoughtful adults in thinking schools.

NETWORKS

Networks are groups of practitioners with common interests, needs, or beliefs that work across school sites, districts, states, or even countries. Some examples of networks in the United States include the Coalition of Essential Schools; Impact II; Arthur Costa's Intelligent Behaviors Network and ASCD's Teaching Thinking Network, led by Esther Fusco and Sandra Parks. Networks offer purpose and direction, collaboration and commitment, and relationship and representation (Lieberman & Grolnick, 1996). Network membership is voluntary; thus, the commitment to a shared purpose is built in. Network members receive both information and—often—emotional support, as their own needs dictate. Networks are built upon respect for teachers' practical experience and knowledge bases, as well as the knowledge base of academic research and practical reform efforts. As a forum for professional development, membership in a network respects the individual practitioners' knowledge and time and is relevant to their learning needs and interests.

In School B, for example, information flows in and out of the school in several different ways. In one instance, lead teachers serve on District Learning Academy teams, which become formal and informal conduits for new ideas. In another, several teachers participate in a regional literacy network devoted to resource sharing and exploration of classroom practices and shared issues. Major learnings from these sessions trickle into conversations back at school, and new resources find their way into classrooms.

In many cases, technology serves to enhance the power of networks. At School B, there is a physical education teacher who contributes to school improvement by searching the Internet for resources relevant to improving writing, thereby connecting the district to the vast electronic community. In other instances, international communities are organized around specific interests via the Internet, making use of chat rooms, forums, and bulletin boards to exchange information, share resources, and support learning.

PROFESSIONAL LEARNING PARTNERSHIPS

Professional learning partnerships are formal and informal paired relationships that support the growth and development of individuals in a school. These can be peers working together on common issues, mentors or support teachers working with novices or those new to a building, and supervisors working directly in one-on-one relationships with selected teachers. The common element is a focus on the individual's learning to support planning, problem solving, and reflecting on practice. This is done through coaching, collaborating, and consulting by the supportive partner.

At School B, many such partnerships operate throughout the building. A number of teachers are involved in peer coaching relationships, in which partners support each other's investigations of new approaches to literacy development. This involves planning lessons, observing each other teach, reflecting on those experiences, and determining both major learnings and next steps for that classroom (Costa & Garmston, 1994). Several novice teachers have formal mentors to guide and support their growth as emerging professionals. The mentors model lessons, offer advice, collaboratively plan lessons, and coach the novices along their learning journey.

The principal also has a learning focus as a supervisor. Over time, she is spending less time in formal classroom observations and more time sitting with teachers examining student work, analyzing data, and sharing research highlights that apply to the challenges they have collectively identified. This is especially important with low-performing teachers, who often lack confidence during collaborative sessions with peers. The principal's goal with these individuals is to make it safe to "not know" and unsafe to persist in "not knowing."

STUDY GROUPS

A study group is a shared learning experience in which a group of practitioners meets regularly to explore a topic of choice. These groups often focus on new research studies (or other external information) in light of their own experiences, reflect upon a specific problem or practice, or other collaborative learning issues. Most important, the choices of group members, topics, meeting time, and place are the domains of the study group.

Study groups are powerful, authentic opportunities for collaborative learning. Among the many possibilities that focus a study group's attention and energy are conducting action research, exploring case studies, and examining student work.

Conducting Action Research. Action research offers a powerful opportunity for the collaborative examination and analysis of classroom- and school-based issues, and for a data-driven exploration of potential paths of inquiry and action. Action research can be highly structured or somewhat informal, and it can involve one or two practitioners exploring their specific work setting, or research teams examining wider issues within a school or across a district.

At School B, the primary teachers are actively engaged in two different action research projects. One explores methods to enhance oral language development as a foundation for vocabulary building. The other project targets expanding approaches to teaching writing from nonfiction texts. They will share the results of their studies with the greater school community, and the impact of their findings will be considered in the ongoing efforts to improve student success.

As a professional development activity, action research offers several key features:

- A *problem-solving focus.* The questions to be studied emerge from the context of the school situation.
- A *collaborative spirit.* The study group collaboratively determines choices regarding the research topics, data sources and collection procedures, and analysis process.
- A *rigorous application of research to improved practice.* External data (current literature and academic research) and internal data (specific site-based sources collected through the action research process) support inquiry, analysis, action planning, and continued inquiry.

Exploring Case Studies. Case studies are usually written narratives or videotapes (or both), developed to provide a stimulus for exploring school-based issues. An effective case study illuminates critical issues from which learners can generalize, apply the new knowledge, and continue the learning journey. These cases create opportunities to generate theories of practice through the participants' inquiry and analysis. Skillful facilitation or a structured protocol increases the learning power of a case study.

Examining Student Work. When expectations for student learning are driven by clear and rigorous standards, a team focus on comparing student work with the standards is a powerful method for team learning and school improvement. When focused directly on student learning, examining students' written products clarifies and creates a shared understanding of district (or state, provincial, or national) expectations, while exploring the current methods for achieving them and their relationship to supporting student success.

As a result of shared examination of student work, an ad hoc committee emerged at School B. This group of volunteers unified the school's use of proofreading marks, creating consistency across grade levels.

Tuning Protocols. Tuning protocols (Allen, 1995) are highly structured experiences of approximately 60 minutes within which a group of critical friends builds and refines professional practice. In a collaborative setting, an individual practitioner presents some aspect of teaching to be discussed. The brief presentation is usually enhanced by student work or audio- or videotapes and focuses on one or two presenter-generated questions. Subsequent steps include several minutes of nonjudgmental, clarifying questions, individual writing by each participant in response to the initial focusing questions, participant discussion, presenter reflection and group debriefing. Critical to the process are clear protocols, respect for time parameters, a nonjudgmental, supportive environment, and the shared intention to support growth and development of professional practice.

DIALOGUE

Dialogue builds reciprocal relationships, deepens understandings, and creates shared meaning. To commit to collective action, group members need a space within which to express personal viewpoints, perspectives, and assumptions. This way of talking is not for the purpose of making decisions. It is a conversational form designed to connect individuals to their underlying motivations and mental models (Garmston & Wellman, 1999). As groups and group members explore alternative viewpoints, they come to appreciate and validate a variety of frames of reference and a variety of approaches to issues. Well-crafted dialogue creates an emotional and cognitive safety zone in which ideas flow for examination without group members judging them (Wellman & Lipton, 2000).

The staff at School B has worked hard to cultivate norms of dialogue in its culture. This is the basis for the spirit of collaborative inquiry that pervades the school. This inquiry not only delves into options and ideas, but also into the sources within individuals who offer those options and ideas—an inquiry into the very act of thinking. As teachers here practice these habits with each other, they notice that the habits extend into their practices with students. One current focus of exploration is how these habits of thought and of exploring thoughts are the roots of the literacy issues that have energized their work together.

FORM AND FUNCTION IN PROFESSIONAL DEVELOPMENT

Industrial and graphic designers constantly balance the dual demands of form (the shape of an object or piece of work) and function (its purposes). Each drives the other as aesthetics interact with practical outcomes.

Designers of professional development for teachers face similar form and function challenges. The form of teacher learning matters greatly if the function is to produce meaningful changes in school and classroom practice. *How* teachers learn cannot be separated from *what* teachers learn. Journey and destination intertwine, just as individual questions and insights become inseparable from collective exploration and discovery.

> Probably nothing within a school has more impact on children, in terms of skill development, self-confidence, and classroom behavior, than the personal and professional growth of teachers. When teachers individually and collectively examine, question, reflect on their ideals, and develop new practices that lead toward those ideals, the school and its inhabitants are alive. When teachers stop growing, so do their students. (Barth, 1980, p. 147)

REFERENCES

Allen, D. (1995). The tuning protocol: A process for reflection. *Studies on exhibitions No. 15.* Oakland, CA: Coalition of Essential Schools.

Barth, R. (1980). *Run, school, run.* Cambridge, MA: Harvard University Press.

Bruner, J. (1996). *The culture of education.* Cambridge, MA: Harvard University Press.

Costa, A., & Garmston, R. (1994). *Cognitive coaching: A foundation for renaissance schools.* Norwood, MA: Christopher-Gordon.

Garmston, R., & Wellman, B. (1999). *The adaptive school: A sourcebook for developing collaborative groups.* Norwood, MA: Christopher-Gordon.

Hargreaves, A., & Fullan, M. (1992). *Understanding teacher development.* New York: Teachers College Press.

Joyce, B., & Showers, B. (1988). *Student achievement through staff development.* New York: Longman Publishing.

Lambert, L. (1989). The end of an era of staff development. *Educational Leadership, 47*(1), 78–81.

Lieberman, A. & Grolnick, M. (1996). Networks and reform in American education. *Teachers College Record, 98*(1), 7–45.

Little, J. W. (1986). Seductive images and organizational realities in professional development. In Lieberman, A. (Ed.), *Rethinking school improvement: Research, craft and concept* (pp. 26–44). New York: Teachers College Press.

Wellman, B., & Lipton, L. (2000). Navigation: Charting a path through a sea of information. *Journal of Staff Development, 21*(1), 47–50.

22

For Administrators: Keeping the Focus

David S. Martin

Responsible school administrators in the 21st century find themselves buffeted by many forces and demands. Beginning in the late 1990s, these intense pressures have included calls for increased attention to state and national curriculum standards, along with the attendant mandated tests. Many career administrators are facing unprecedented demands. We don't have to look back far into the history of U.S. education, however, to find similar movements—in the 1970s, 1950s, and earlier. The cyclical nature of these pressures is notable and sometimes corresponds with economic trends, as well as other social influences.

Whatever the cause, school administrators who are intent on demonstrating strong achievement results from their students often focus on test results—on an ever-expanding amount of material. After all, many segments of the public overtly judge schools by their students' test scores alone. Has there ever been a time in U.S. education when such pressures were not evident? Probably not, although they have taken different forms. The curriculum revolution of the 1960s, for example, emphasized cognitive development and the incorporation of concepts from the academic disciplines into the curriculum with a concomitant moving away from a focus on test results in the narrow sense.

Within this context, then, how can administrators encourage students to develop higher-order problem-solving skills and strategies, both critical and creative, amid these other pressures? The answer is complex, but here's a simple response: We *must* incorporate the developing mind as a focus for the curriculum. We can't afford not to. Why? Developing students' problem-solving skills and other strategies is a means—sometimes apparently indirect—to achieving higher test scores, higher standards, and improved achievement. Let us look at some aspects of the rationale and how administrators might be able to legitimately initiate and maintain a focus on thinking.

RATIONALES

Ask any group of dedicated teachers why incorporating higher-order thinking skills into the curriculum is an important goal, and they will offer many reasons. Such reasons often include

- The need for strategies to solve complex world and national problems.
- The need for strategies to solve personal problems.
- The rapidly changing face of information.
- The importance of reflection in relation to difficult ethical dilemmas.
- The fundamental demand for the careful use of the vote in a democracy.

At the same time, teachers frequently will say that although such needs are important, they don't know how they could possibly find time to focus on such areas because they, too, feel pressure for their students to do well on state- or locally mandated tests. Let us look at some of these arguments in favor of thinking skills and then address the time question.

Futurists are fond of making predictions about trends, and among those is the explosion of knowledge. One rather disturbing projection indicates that if we trace the doubling of knowledge in recent centuries, we can observe the following events: Between 1750 and 1900, knowledge in the world doubled once; it doubled again between 1900 and 1950; it doubled again between 1950 and 1960; and since 1960, knowledge has doubled at least every 5 years and more quickly in recent years. By the year 2020, it is projected that knowledge will double every 73 days (Teacher Education for the 21st Century, 1992).

Of course, one may choose to be skeptical of this projection. But even if we assume that it is only half-correct, the trend is apparent: It is already impossible for anyone to know everything about everything, and that has been true for many centuries. With the incorporation of the Internet into everyday life and into most schools, as well as into laboratories and other areas where knowledge is created, we must accept this trend even if we are uncertain about the actual numbers. But what does such a projection mean in relation to thinking skills? At the least, it means that instead of an emphasis on acquired knowledge of facts alone—although facts continue to be important because we must think *with* something—it is equally or more important for tomorrow's graduates to know how to find information, how to create it, how to criticize it, and how to evaluate it.

Another less-recognized rationale for the incorporation of thinking skills into the curriculum relates to its effect on academic achievement in academic school subjects. Several studies on the effects of a focus on thinking-strategy activities throughout the school year have examined test results in such areas as reading and mathematics. In the schools tested, teachers had used thinking exercises that, on the surface, did not appear to relate to any specific content in the curriculum. Here are examples of such instruction:

• Exercises using diagrams, drawings, or words for comparison.
• Activities involving classification of objects or ideas.
• Activities involving the sequencing of pictures or items that appear not to have any specific "content" other than the thinking strategy itself.

On measures of academic achievement, students involved with trained teachers in such activities appear not only to improve in their abilities to discuss these strategies but also to do well on examinations in such areas as literacy and computation.

How could this be true? Here's part of the answer: *More of the same is not necessarily better.* In other words, many of the activities in thinking-skills programs provide students with the important cognitive *prerequisites* for achievement in these basic areas. More math problems for homework will not necessarily boost a student's achievement in the subject, particularly if the student needs to improve in the cognitive prerequisites for performing better in math (areas such as sequencing, finding alternative solutions to a problem, and so forth).

Studies of such thinking programs also indicate positive effects in the more overt aspects of the programs—namely, habits of reflection, finding alternatives, making reasoned choices, and the like. Other positive effects are mentioned elsewhere in this volume, but the case is clear: A systematic incorporation of thinking strategies not only results in the obvious direct benefits but also in the indirect area of achievement in academic domains.

In addition, a number of standardized and mandated tests (for example, the Maryland state tests for schools, known as the Maryland State Performance Assessment Program [MSPAP], 2001, and the Terra Nova tests published by McGraw-Hill, 2000) now have begun to incorporate overt and explicit critical-thinking items. Mid-continent Research for Education and Learning (McREL) in Colorado also is actively helping school districts incorporate thinking items into their locally mandated school tests. McREL has listed six thinking and reasoning standards for grades K–12 on its Web site (http://www.mcrel.org/compendium/browse.asp). Thus, in addition to the indirect benefits on achievement from thinking programs, now the tests themselves have begun to incorporate the relevant items for higher-order thinking, indicating that society in general has begun to place an explicit importance on this domain.

TAKING THE INITIATIVE

In light of such evidence, the question should not be *whether* thinking skills should be part of school life but rather *how*. The question of "making time" is still uppermost in many teachers' minds because many curricula do not explicitly incorporate higher-order thinking strategies, and teachers understandably expect that their students will be tested on that curriculum. Ironically, once again, we have tests driving the curriculum. But in this instance, if mandated tests are only beginning to include items on thinking strategies, it is unlikely that such tests will have a positive effect on curricula. The challenge now is how to help teachers make the leap into infusing thinking strategies into the curriculum.

Elsewhere in this volume, other authors discuss the need for preservice teacher education programs to include cognitive-strategy instruction. Although preservice education may appear beyond the direct influence of school administrators, in this era of professional development–school partnerships, school administrators have opportunities to influence the preservice curriculum.

But school administrators also have a direct opportunity to influence *inservice* education in this arena. Because many of today's teachers are products of teacher-preparation programs that have not explicitly valued or incorporated higher-level cognitive strategies, the need for inservice opportunities is clear. But what kinds of inservice opportunities are most productive?

Many published programs and inservice preparation plans are available to a school administrator who is truly committed to the infusion of thinking strategies into the curriculum. But some important principles must remain paramount for such inservice education to be effective. These principles include the following:

• The one-shot approach is probably better than nothing but will likely produce little change, in comparison with a *series* of opportunities for a group of teachers to learn about and practice.

• Facilitators and staff developers in such sessions must employ a careful blend of both theory and practice. Teachers must understand the cognitive foundation of the thinking-skills movement if they are to create additional opportunities beyond whatever program they use in their own classrooms.

• As with most inservice education opportunities, hands-on activities are essential to making teachers fully comfortable with the strategies and knowledgeable about how they will actually work.

• Facilitators of inservice sessions must respect the participating teachers as adults and should not ask them to role-play children. Facilitators need to conduct thinking-strategies activities on an adult level. These activities can be highly stimulating and can allow the transfer to students.

• Administrators and staff developers must invite inservice teachers to participate in action research to investigate the result of such infusions. Such involvement also provides teachers with a level of professionalism and appropriate control that is highly valued and will ensure that innovations endure.

• A powerful presence by the school administrator during the inservice sessions will provide two advantages: It will serve as a strong indicator of the administrator's commitment by example, and the administrator can assist in the adaptation of the program and be an informed source to whom the teachers can turn as they start to implement the thinking-skills aspect of their programming.

None of these principles is unique to inservice education for teachers in thinking strategies; they apply across topic areas. But in a domain that is new, cuts across all disciplines, and is not a part of any traditional curriculum-content area, these principles become even more essential.

MOVING FORWARD

The best first step for a change of this magnitude frequently is the involvement of a subgroup of teachers in an examination of possible thinking programs, including a review of material and observation of programs in action. A set of careful criteria is always important in making a decision for a school-level adoption or adaptation of this kind. Such criteria for a thinking-skills program decision could include the following:

• The program is comprehensive in that it would apply a variety of thinking strategies, rather than one or two.

• The program is tested, and evaluation reports are available.

• The approach is grounded in some defensible cognitive theory.

• The approach requires or strongly recommends some form of inservice education, rather than simply being a product that one purchases and implements. This feature reflects the fact that teaching thinking is truly a different way of teaching in that the teacher is a constructivist rather than a giver of knowledge.

Multiple examples and models are available to the committed school leader. Taking this step recognizes the truth of the often-quoted Confucian proverb:

> Give me a fish and I shall eat tomorrow; teach me how to fish, and I shall eat for a lifetime.

For too long, we have been content with "giving fish," and now it is time to teach lifelong strategies of "how to fish" so that our students become reflective and independent thinkers. It would be difficult to think of a more important goal for any school leader.

REFERENCES

Maryland, State of (2001). Maryland State Performance Assessment Program.
Teacher Education for the 21st Century [chart]. (1992). Washington, DC: American Association of State Colleges and Universities.
Terra Nova Tests (2000). (2nd ed.). Monterey, CA: CTB McGraw-Hill Co.

23

Building a Thoughtful High School

WILLIAM C. MARTIN

The 21st century requires leaders willing to spark permanent and positive organizational change. Systems thinking motivates organizational improvement by identifying areas of highest leverage. This often involves mental model transformations leading to new patterns of behavior. Mental models are resistant to change. However, the right ensemble of change tools can create an environment for thinking that fosters personal and collective "mindshifts." The change tools used to generate such dramatic transformations blend the personal, practical knowledge of the workforce with the research of Arthur Costa and Robert Swartz in the thinking domain and Peter Senge and John Edwards in organizational learning.

Pictures of wondrous places to learn are inside our hearts and are unique to each individual. Ironically, they are similar in many ways. Extracting such a portrait allows a school community to begin electrifying school improvement. Fueling this path is the intentional application of change tools:

- *A Climate for Thinking* (Costa, 1985)
- *Disciplines of a Learning Organization* (Senge, 1990)
  a. Systems Thinking
  b. Shared Visioning
  c. Mental Models
  d. Personal Mastery
  e. Team Learning
- *Model of Human Action and Change* (Butler, 1994)

All of these together work to create the most powerful tool of all—a climate for thinking (Costa, 1985), which encourages people to

- Solve problems
- Take risks
- Experiment
- Identify rich data sources
- Collaborate
- Use structures of thinking

- Trust
- Raise questions
- Pose paradoxes
- Raise discrepancies
- Create dilemmas
- Value ideas
- Listen nonjudgmentally
- Model the thinking dispositions

This thinking environment is essential to the school renewal process because questions become more important than answers and problems are viewed with relish. Community members respond to ideas in such a way that trust, risk taking, and empowerment become the guiding forces of daily life. Each change tool nurtures personal, practical knowledge in adults, individually and collectively. The change tools spark mental model transformations that result in new patterns of behavior. These new mental models and accompanying behavior become the true essence of positive school improvement. Impressive data are surfacing indicating that new mental models always emerge if a school community engages collaboratively in these five improvement tasks using the change tools:

1. Collect "heart" data to create shared vision.
2. Write and affirm shared vision.
3. Engage in collective research.
4. Describe and sequence organizational improvement tasks into long–term improvement plan.
5. Implement long-term improvement plan.

SHARED VISIONING

A shared vision is not an idea. It is a force in people's hearts, a force of impressive power. . . . It is palpable. People begin to see it as if it exists. Few, if any, forces in human affairs are as powerful as a shared vision.

— *Peter Senge, The Fifth Discipline*

Shared visioning immediately allows a school community to make the thinking disposition of raising questions a cultural attribute. It creates a powerful answer to the question: What do we want to create together? Shared visioning encompasses a school community that collaboratively completes such tasks as:

- Answering inquiry probes.
- Writing a shared vision.
- Publicly affirming acceptance of the vision.
- Making a personal commitment to be accountable for constructing the vision through a series of stewardship conferences.

Besides raising questions, the shared visioning process is rich in other thinking dispositions. The entire process allows a school to organize for collaboration and implement a structure for thinking that places great value on all ideas. The first step is to engage community members in "heart surgery." Using the set of questions or "inquiry probes" shown below, a facilitator gets participants to look inside their hearts to describe what they want their school to be like as a place to work and learn:

- What habits must teachers seek to instill in students?
- What five attitudes do the local community most prize in young adults?
- How shall we spend our days in school?
- What should we confront 100 percent of the time?
- How is engagement stimulated?
- Why do you want to teach/work at this high school?
- What makes a good school?
- What makes a good staff member?
- What are the most critical issues facing us?
- What skills should students leave our school being able to demonstrate?
- What are our biggest challenges?
- What opportunities do you see for us?
- What should we never tamper with?
- What would you like our school to be like five years from now?

This experience is accomplished in a one-day cooperative learning format that uses classic brainstorming and a simple voting format. By engaging in brainstorming and voting activities, the participants bring from within their hearts the consensus answers to each inquiry probe. The answers are the rich "heart data" that serve as the foundation of a shared vision.

A writing team is then established and given the responsibility of creating a shared vision. A first draft is written, initiating a four- to six-month approval process. During this time, the vision is continually critiqued, rewritten, and critiqued again. Throughout the process, community members engage in positive dialogue about schooling and learning. Finally, at a public meeting, a visible affirmation of the vision occurs. One dramatic way to accomplish this public affirmation is by showing the vision on an overhead projector and explaining that it is the school inside everyone's heart. Also, ask community members to stand, affirming this shared vision. This public affirmation motivates a powerful commitment to the future.

SYSTEMS THINKING

At the same time as the shared visioning process, systems thinking (Senge, 1990) should be introduced to the school community to provide instant energy and action. Systems thinking teaches that quality evolves over time and that there are no quick fixes. Applying systems thinking shows how to identify the "areas of highest leverage" in anything we do. By creating a strategy and action plan in an area of highest leverage, improvement will occur. It is important to understand that in quality improvement, there will always be a gap—a delay between when one applies an action and when one sees the results that are desired. Although systems thinking is a complex domain of learning, if it is applied in even its simplest forms, a school community has a powerful tool to build a climate for thinking through problem solving, experimenting, raising questions, posing paradoxes, raising discrepancies, and creating dilemmas. To jumpstart school improvement while constructing a shared vision, three or four schoolwide problems should be identified to address immediately. Such problems will surface in the inquiry probes dialogue. In a workshop format, the school community should be introduced to the four story characters of systems thinking (Senge, 1994):

1. **Events or Actions.** An event or an action is something we can physically see take place.
2. **Systemic Structures.** Systemic structures are physical or human components created to support the work of the organization.
3. **Patterns of Behavior.** Patterns of behavior are trends that continue to occur over time. These patterns can be human behaviors or our internal thinking, our processes, our practices, our procedures.

4. Mental Models. Mental models are assumptions, images, and stories that we carry in our minds about ourselves, others, institutions, and every aspect of the world. Mental models determine what we see. All our mental models are flawed in some way.

The workshop will show that any problem, process, or, in reality, any aspect of school life can be depicted as a story using these characters. The workshop participants should be divided into teams with each team given a problem. They become "Problem Story Teams." A room with white paper affixed over one entire wall should be provided for each team. Each team then should use a set of questions to draw forth the problem story's characters (Senge, 1994):

• How would this problem look from a school board member's view?
• How would the problem look from a central administrator's view?
• What "characters" would be visible from these levels?
• How would the problem look from a school administrator's view?
• How would the problem look from a teacher's view?
• How would the problem look from a support person's view?
• What characters would be visible from these levels?
• How would students view this problem?
• How would parents view this problem?
• What would parents and students consider the key characters?

The team then should divide into subgroups to complete the lengthy first reflection stage. Each subgroup identifies as many characters as possible and, when finished, come back together as a team and build their story wall. Each team should be provided with symbols and drawing tools to use in story construction. First, they should simply make sure that all story characters are on the wall. Second, on another section of the wall, the team should organize the characters so they can be constructed together to tell the problem story from beginning to end. Now the team becomes a group of systems sleuths. Team members investigate their story, looking for patterns, interrelationships, connections, important sequences, time frames, and so forth. Next, another reflection stage takes place. A set of story questions fuels reflection (Senge, 1994):

• What is the vision of this problem?

• What does the school community want to achieve by interacting with this problem?
• Where is this problem going?
• What needs to be changed?
• What crutches or dependencies exist in this problem?
• To achieve a fundamental solution, who would have to be the primary actors?
• Is there a delay that makes it difficult to see the value of your fundamental solution to this problem or a lack of delay that makes the "quick fix" appealing?
• To achieve your most desired goal, what parts of the problem would have to be changed further?

The team then identifies consensus answers for each question and records them on flip-chart paper. The teams add these answers to their story walls to complete their problem stories. The final stage requires the teams to construct fundamental solutions. Areas of highest leverage are most often found in mental models. A key to breaking organizational gridlock is mental model transformation, which creates new patterns of behavior. The final stage begins with an eight-step reflection activity to identify the areas of highest leverage by thinking "outside of the box":

1. Identify constraints. Constraints are unchangeable factors (characters) that will limit the options you can realistically consider.
2. Identify original problem symptoms. Identify all the different classes of symptoms that have been recurring.
3. Map all quick fixes. Map all the fixes that have been used to tackle this problem.
4. Identify undesirable impacts. Identify characters that have had a negative impact on the problem.
5. Identify fundamental solutions. Identify solutions that will more fundamentally address the problem.
6. Map addictive side effects of quick fixes. Compare and contrast your quick fix maps, your undesirable impacts, and your fundamental solutions. Map all quick fix addictions that become apparent.
7. Find interconnections. Make a plot of any interconnections in your story that contribute to the problem.
8. Identify high-leverage actions. Identify the areas of highest leverage that will allow you to sustain your fundamental solutions.

This reflection exercise leads the problem story team to the most crucial stage associated with this simple form of systems thinking—the fundamental solution. Each team creates one or more fundamental solutions to their problem by following a script provided. These solutions reside in the areas of highest leverage. Normally, this is a place in the story where an action can transform a mental model so a new pattern of behavior is generated. The team brainstorms and prioritizes strategies to implement each fundamental solution.

Each strategy requires the construction of an action plan. The story problems, fundamental solutions, strategies, and action plans become start-up improvement plans while institutionalizing systems thinking as a permanent change tool.

While shared visioning and systems thinking are applied in concert during these initial stages (six to eight months), the discipline of team learning is introduced to the school community (Senge, 1990). In order to begin mastering team learning, the community must understand the difference between discussion and dialogue. Discussion is about winning one's point of view even if it is not the best one. Power and politics are attributes of discussion. Dialogue is used in learning organizations to promote a free and creative exploration of complex and subtle issues, a deep listening to one another, and the suspension of one's own view. Dialogue should always proceed discussion, but to engage in dialogue takes practice. Every time one collaborates, constructs a shared vision, or tells a story problem, a fertile field for dialogue is created. As one travels through this time frame, which includes shared visioning, systems thinking, and team learning, one can begin to see people taking risks to implement innovations, and one can begin to see new patterns of behavior. Adding Butler's Model of Human Action and Change (see Figure 23.1) to this ensemble of tools can cement a schoolwide climate for thinking and fertilize community members' readiness and willingness to engage in personal and collaborative learning (Butler, 1994).

Public knowledge is the knowledge available through a rich research base. Individuals can obtain such knowledge by reading, going to conferences, taking classes, and accessing the Internet and other media sources.

Personal, practical knowledge is knowledge that is owned by each individual—the knowledge within the reality of living his or her life. Such knowledge is the essence of their humanness and may be the essential element of the change process. It is everything one knows and believes about life. Assumptions that determine mental models and patterns of behavior reside in such knowledge, which resists change.

World view encompasses the rules of culture, tradition, and experiences people have encountered throughout their lives. This view determines how an individual behaves and is largely

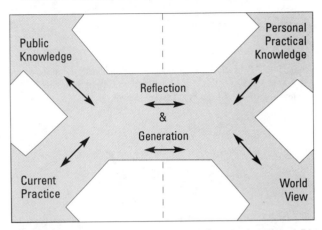

—Figure 23.1—
Butler's Model of Human Action and Change

Source: Adapted from *People Rules for Rocket Scientists* (p. 175), by J. Edwards, J. Butler, B. Hill, & S. Russell, 1997, Brisbane, Australia: Samford Research Associates. Reprinted with permission.

subconscious. Change is aligned with an individual's ability to bring world view to the surface. Surfacing world view allows people to determine how applicable the rules are to their lives. Current practice has to do with how the world currently views any issue.

Reflection is the trigger mechanism for human change and may be the most powerful learning tool. Reflection allows individuals to connect internal and external knowledge to themselves. In any given situation, a person decides whether to turn reflection on or off (Edwards, 1999). Generation is the creative design process. This is the action stage, where individuals engage in many critical-thinking processes.

According to Edwards, powerful human change occurs when individuals take an issue and put it into the model. Each person washes the issue with what he or she knows in terms of public knowledge, current practice, world view, and personal, practical knowledge. Then he or she spins it all together by turning on their reflection mechanism and generates an action regarding the issue. The sum total of this powerful "wash" cycle is to increase each person's store of personal, practical knowledge. This is how people change. As such knowledge increases, individuals develop new mental models and patterns of behavior.

The climate for thinking that evolves from the practical application of this ensemble of change tools becomes the driving force that can allow a school community to engage in collective research. This, in turn, can result in a long-term school improvement plan. Implementing the plan becomes the cohesive vehicle for application of the tools, motivating continual collective learning and the accomplishment of a vision.

REFERENCES

Butler, J. (1994). From action to thought: The fulfillment of human potential. In J. Edwards (Ed.), *Thinking: International interdisciplinary perspectives* (pp.16–22). Melbourne: Hawker Brownlow.

Costa, A. (1985). Teaching for, of, and about thinking. In A. Costa, *Developing minds* (pp. 20–23). Alexandria, VA: Association for Supervision and Curriculum Development.

Edwards, J. (1999). *Learning, thinking and assessment*. North Queensland: University of North Queensland.

Senge, P. M. (1990). *The fifth discipline*. New York: Doubleday Currency.

Senge, P. M. (1994). *The fifth discipline fieldbook*. New York: Doubleday Currency.

24

Managing for Reflection: A Superintendent's Dilemma

Sherry P. King

In her book *Leadership and the New Science,* Wheatley (1992) offers an image of running water that is clear about its purpose, which is to get to the next largest body of water. Sometimes that means moving over logs or underground, but these apparent diversions are just the water's way of reaching its goal.

Contrast that vision to schools in which the goal is student achievement, but their structures often dam the flow toward learning. Block scheduling is one example. Schools across the United States have been intent on expanding blocks of instructional time—often without a clear sense of what a math teacher might do differently to make 90 minutes more valuable to students than 40 minutes. Somehow, time-on-task became longer blocks of time—a structure that may, but does not necessarily, support enhanced student achievement.

To ensure that the structures and the work of schools are moving toward a clear goal, the organization itself must be one that supports thinking. We need to have processes in place that insist on links between structures and student learning. Decisions about priorities, the work a school is willing to undertake, and the ways in which the work will be assessed against the goal of student learning require continual feedback and thought.

Role of the Superintendent

In some ways, the school superintendent is in a difficult position, expected to fulfill the tasks of a CEO heading an organization that may be the largest employer in a community and to serve as an educational leader. Compound that with elected boards of education that may have different and changing agendas, producing a climate where the complex work of schools is reduced to simple numbers published in the press, and it is easy to see how one could simply try to manage the system. The challenge of building a reflective culture requires that a system move from reacting to each event—the publication of

test scores, a new educational fad—to maintaining commitment over time, using data to examine student achievement, and rethinking direction based on that information. Leadership toward this kind of systemic thinking is complicated and takes the long-term commitment of all the stakeholders.

As the chief executive officer of a school system and the link between the professional staff and the community, the superintendent is uniquely positioned to support a culture of thinking and inquiry toward the goal of enhanced student performance. In this chapter, I focus on two aspects of that leadership work that have ripple effects at all levels of the system: (1) transforming board of education study sessions into systemic opportunities for reflection and (2) sustaining work over time in a way that allows assessment data to become an instructional tool.

Reflective Study Sessions

Board of education study sessions provide a structure that has been evolving in my own practice for the past five years; each iteration deepens the possibilities for thinking about the work of the schools. In the first study sessions (King, 1995), we had hoped to provide an opportunity to talk in depth about complicated issues of education without the board taking any action. For example, in some meetings, the board engaged in discussion with staff members about the relative benefits and challenges of homogeneous and heterogeneous grouping of students. In other sessions, the board explored the principles of the Coalition of Essential Schools, paralleling the work of the faculties within the district.

Although the meetings provided new opportunities for sharing, with Bena Kallick's help (King, 1999), we also developed a protocol for board of education study sessions that helped us move beyond sharing toward greater reflection. By framing essential questions, the board could ask more thoughtful questions; and the presenters could be more thoughtful about their work. This protocol also encouraged presenters to keep in mind that their audience was a policy-making body; thus, we encouraged presenters to consider research that supported their practices, what kinds of questions the board might expect to hear from the public, and possible fiscal implications. The protocol also reminded the board that its role was not to micromanage but to support the policies and mission of the district. Important to the board, the protocol also asked presenters to consider how their initiative or program would be evaluated and how that would be reported in an effort to build a feedback loop into the system.

The protocol for school board study sessions includes the following:

- Research process.
- Criteria—How will the school define success?
- Public engagement—How have parents been involved? Questions the public might need to answer.
- Teachers—Where do they stand on the proposed changes?
- Evaluation—Time line.
- Financial implications.
- Next steps—What kind of support can or should the board provide? Public comments, questions, or concerns the board might hear.

For the past two years, the Mamaroneck (N.Y.) Board of Education, again with Kallick's support, has taken the framework of study sessions to a new level of thinking and reflection. We have devised a new format for study sessions, as follows:

- Frame session with goals and policy implications in mind.
- Conduct study session as an inquiry about the goals, including the following questions:
  ○ How do approach, implementation, and results align with goals?
  ○ What is the measurable evidence of achievement (assessment)?
  ○ Does this program have coherence throughout the system?
  ○ Do all children have equal access to achieving our goals?
  ○ How do we provide for each child at each level, including extra support for those who are struggling and extra challenges for those who are high achievers?
  ○ How has this information been communicated to students, parents, and community?
  ○ What are the next steps?

A CREATIVE BOARD OF EDUCATION STUDY SESSION

A description of one study session shows how creating priorities, framing the essential questions for all stakeholders, and insisting on a feedback process can help support a learning organization.

Each year, the Mamaroneck Board of Education goes on a retreat and establishes priorities for the forthcoming year. Those decisions grow out of a careful assessment of progress toward goals established the previous year. The process also is predicated on a belief that less is more: The staff members of the system cannot do work deeply and well if they are asked to focus on too much. Also, much of a school's most important work is complex and must be sustained over time. Therefore, the board has resisted the temptation to adopt an "innovation du jour." The clarity of focus also allows for a kind of accountability that is based on continual learning. The board can, and does, ask for regular progress reports toward the goals to which it has committed time and resources.

In 1999–2000, the issue of whether all students had access to the most rigorous classes within the district was among the board's curriculum goals. Despite a process by which goals are set and the presence of a protocol for study sessions, ensuring that the meetings provide opportunities for thinking and reflection is not easy. Individuals, whether they are staff members, parents, students, or board members, tend to come to meetings with a position they already hold. In this case, some people clearly wanted the most selective courses open to more students. Others said they thought that opening the gates would water down the courses' level of rigor. Sometimes the positions were more individual, as in questions about why a particular child was not accepted into a particular course. In cases like these, the superintendent's challenge is to transform the meeting from one that puts forth differing positions to one that helps all participants consider the multiple perspectives and reflect on their meanings. Without a reason to rethink positions, there may be informative presentations, but not a true sharing of ideas, which can lead to even better practices than those each person or group held when they entered the room.

One way to work toward this way of thinking about board study sessions has been by supporting the board in framing their questions around policy, which is its domain. This helps ensure that the board doesn't become managers of the system. It also prevents the teacher presenters at the sessions from feeling they are expected to do a show-and-tell. The board's questions signal that it understands the complexity of the issues at hand and wants to use the meetings as opportunities to think deeply about such issues from the advantage of different perspectives: the staff, data (often including examples of students' work), parents (whom the board represents and who call with their concerns), and the board itself as the policy arm of the district.

As in other districts struggling to ensure that all students are reaching the highest standards, the question of who has access to which courses emerged as an important policy concern. The board framed three questions for the meeting called "Proper Placement Versus Gate Keeping: The Perceptions and the Reality":

• How do we ensure that the system we use is as fair as possible to all parties (advanced and nonadvanced students)?

• How do we balance the twin goals of encouraging students to pursue advanced work with maintaining high standards (for course content, teaching, and student participation and achievement) in both advanced and standard courses?

• The (high school) catalogue shows a wide range of criteria for admission into advanced courses. Who defines those qualifications, and what voices are included in those decisions?

BASING DECISIONS ON THE DATA

Aside from using framing questions designed to steer participants away from a show-and-tell format, the district is committed to data-based decision making. By gathering and analyzing data on our ongoing processes, the system is moving from relying on anecdotal and highly personal information to a more systematic view of what decisions mean for all students in the schools, whether that applies to allocation of resources, creation of priorities, or in this case the criteria for entrance into advanced classes.

For this particular study session, the middle and high school staff members did not begin by showing off what they do well but by examining their own practices to see where they were truly excelling and where they had work to do. For example, the number of students in advanced classes at the high school has been consistently high over the past five years, with the number of advanced placement exams taken increasing consistently. At the middle school, the number of students in advanced science was higher than those in accelerated math classes. Given the high performance of both groups on state tests, the middle school math teachers were left with the question of whether they could challenge even more students with a more rigorous curriculum. Beyond the data, each stakeholder group in the school—board members, administrators,

teachers, and parents—had questions they could explore in the study session. In essence, the board members wanted to know whether the district's policy was being implemented and whether the system was fair and open. Not only did they see that as their job, but they also needed accurate information for the occasions when they were called on to respond to a parent who might call when a child is not accepted into a selective course.

For administrators, the compelling questions revolved around what would happen to the instructional experience if they opened the opportunity to more students. The administrators wanted to know whether the board would continue to support the school if the average score decreased because a wider range of students was taking the more rigorous courses. They were concerned about the quality of the courses for students not in advanced sections if the vast majority were placed in the higher courses.

For teachers, the conversation turned to the effect of opening the gates on classroom practice. Could they maintain the high standards that have brought about such strong results if they included more students? Creating a learning organization means framing meetings so that these complicated questions can be at the core of the discussion. In this case, the meeting led to renewed discussions at the middle school about student placement in math classes and the need for a common curriculum. At the high school, the principal reviewed effects from the previous year for a more open and inclusive appeal process for students who want to enter the most selective courses.

AN EXAMPLE OF REFLECTIVE DECISION MAKING

The second example that illustrates ways in which school districts can become more reflective concerns our district's approach to literacy curriculum, instruction, and assessment. Like the work with the board, the professional development commitment is consistent with Costa and Kallick's (1995) "Feedback Spiral" and demonstrates how maintaining a focus in a single area over time can deepen work for teachers and, therefore, for students. In this arena, as in the board goal-setting process, setting priorities that grow out of data analysis of prior work is central.

Four years ago, an item analysis of reading scores and an examination of students who were achieving at the highest levels, as well as those in need of extra support to meet state standards, led the district to define the need to implement a balanced approached to literacy—one incorporating phonics, enriched reading programs, and a range of instructional practices. Over the next three years, the district held summer workshops and publishers' fairs, and the district purchased new instructional materials. All these actions helped teachers expand their teaching practice to include the components of a balanced approach to literacy. In addition, the board has held study sessions to better understand what a balanced approach to literacy means. The PTA held meetings to help parents work as partners in supporting their children as readers and writers. Perhaps most important, however, is that the levels of support and accountability are as strong in the fourth year of work as in the first year. That commitment over time has moved the literacy work from an initiative to a thoughtful way of doing work. A few anecdotes may help illustrate the difference.

In the first year of our work, teachers were involved in workshops for particular elements of a balanced literacy curriculum. They learned or refined their skills in techniques like shared and guided reading. Many teachers assigned reading levels to the books in their classroom libraries and began to provide more direction for students in the selection of individual reading materials. The teachers also expanded "word walls," which display familiar words according to the first letter of each word. Even with the expansion and sharing of good practices, however, the activities felt isolated to teachers, often connected only to the presence of a consultant and separate from the practices of reading that are central to classroom experiences. Over time, however, this has begun to change. The district released a teacher from her classroom to support colleagues in literacy work. Listening to the confusion about integrating instructional and assessment practices, she worked with teachers to develop a detailed explanation of the components of a balanced literacy program, which allowed teachers to identify particular areas where they wanted help in strengthening their practices.

As the pieces became clearer, teachers gained insights into the strength of their own practices and also could identify the particular areas where they needed more support. After four years of literacy work, 1st grade teachers throughout the district developed their own literacy assessment tool. They now examine the results to understand what they mean to their classroom practices, and they meet with kindergarten teachers to review examples of student work and their expectations for student performance. Instead of teachers maintaining their individual classroom libraries, teams of grade-level teachers have begun to order and share books after discussing the kinds of materials that would best challenge all students at a particular grade level. The staff-development model has been modified at the request of teachers to become more focused on the needs they have identified in their own practices.

In sum, by constantly reviewing student-achievement data in a timely fashion and not just in individual classrooms but also across a grade or a building; by discussing what the assessment data mean for practice; and by providing staff development in direct response to those needs, teachers have become even more reflective about their practice. We know this because even veteran and highly respected staff members have been seeking support in expanding their teaching repertoire, because reading scores at all levels continue to rise, and because, after four years, we have more requests for support than ever before.

* * *

The process of encouraging reflective practice as the norm for a school system is hard work. But it is also the most important work a superintendent can do. It does not produce the quick fixes that politicians and the press seem to seek. But my experience in several school systems convinces me that the public is smarter than the media would allow. Our communities want to be brought together for genuine, thoughtful discourse that grows out of stated goals, is based on meaningful data, results in specific actions, and guarantees ongoing assessment. This is a structure that, like the stream seeking its next destination, will not be thrown off course by new state mandates or the newest innovative fad. Instead, thoughtful practice and evidence of student achievement will define the way.

REFERENCES

Costa, A. L., & Kallick, B. (Eds.). (1995). Process design: Feedback spirals as components of continued learning. *Assessment in the learning organization.* Alexandria, VA: Association for Supervision and Curriculum Development.

King, S. P. (1995). Even a superintendent needs critical friends. In A. L. Costa & B. Kallick (Eds.), *Assessment in the learning organization: Shifting the paradigm.* Alexandria, VA: Association for Supervision and Curriculum Development.

King, S. P. (1999). Leadership in the 21st century: Using feedback to maintain focus and direction. In D. Marsh (Ed.), *Preparing our schools for the 21st century: 1999 ASCD yearbook.* Alexandria, VA: Association for Supervision and Curriculum Development.

Wheatley, M. J. (1994). *Leadership and the new science.* San Francisco: Berrett-Koehler.

25

Mediative Environments

ARTHUR L. COSTA

Many out-of-conscious factors influence teachers' thinking as they make daily decisions about curriculum and instruction. Their own culture, knowledge of content, cognitive style, knowledge about their students, and their professional values and beliefs about education influence their judgments about when to teach what to whom. Frymier (1987), however, states

> In the main, the bureaucratic structure of the workplace is more influential in determining what professionals do than are personal abilities, professional training or previous experience. Therefore, change efforts should focus on the structure of the workplace, not the teachers. (p. 10)

Frymier suggests that less obvious, but vastly more persuasive, influences on teacher thought are the norm and culture of the school setting. Hidden, but powerful, cues emanate from the school environment. These subtle cues signal the institutional value system that governs the operation of the organization.

Efforts to infuse thinking, creativity, and intellectual development will prove futile unless the school environment signals the staff, students, and community that the development of the intellect and cooperative decision making are the school's basic values. Although efforts to enhance the staff's instructional competencies, raise standards, and adopt high-stakes accountability may be important, it also is crucial that the climate in which parents, teachers, and students make their decisions be aligned with these goals of development of intellectual potential. Teachers will more likely teach for thinking, creativity, and cooperation if they are in an intellectually stimulating, creative, and cooperative environment themselves.

This chapter is adapted from "Constructing a Home for the Mind," by A.L. Costa and B. Kallick, 2000, in *Integrating and Sustaining Habits of Mind* (pp. 11–29), edited by A.L. Costa and B. Kallick, Alexandria, VA: Association for Supervision and Curriculum Development.

EDUCATIONAL STRESSORS

Research by Harvey (1966) found that teaching is the second most stressful profession! Goodlad (1984), Rosenholtz (1989), Sarason (1991), Fullan (1993), and other authors have identified several sources of stress:

- Teachers may lack a sense of power and efficacy. They often are cast at the bottom of a hierarchy while decisions about curriculum, staff development, assessment, instructional materials, and evaluation—decisions that affect them directly—are handed down from "above."

- Teachers feel isolated. Ours is probably the only profession that performs a most beautiful and creative craft behind closed doors. Contributing to this situation is the inadequate amount and inflexibility of time for teachers to reflect and meet, plan, observe, and talk with one another.

- The complex, creative, and intelligent act of teaching is often reduced to a rubric, a simplistic formula, or a list of competencies, the uniform performance of which naively connotes excellence and elegance in the art of teaching.

- The feedback of data on student achievement is for political, competitive, evaluative, or coercive purposes. It neither involves nor instructs the school staff in reflecting on, evaluating, and improving their curriculum and instructional decisions.

- Educational innovations often are viewed as mere "tinkerings" to the instructional program. They are so frequent and limited in impact that frustrated teachers sometimes feel that "this, too, shall pass." Instead of institutionalizing the change, deeply entrenched traditional practices and policies in the educational bureaucracy—such as assessment, reporting, securing parent understanding and support, teacher evaluation, scheduling, school organization, and discipline procedures—are seldom revised to be in harmony with the overall innovation.

The effects of excessive stress on cognition, creativity, and social interaction are well documented (Caine & Caine, 1997;

MacLean, 1978). In such barren and intellectually polluted school climates, some teachers understandably grow depressed. Teachers' vivid imagination, altruism, creativity, and intellectual prowess can soon succumb to the humdrum daily routines of unruly students, irrelevant curriculum, impersonal surroundings, and equally disillusioned coworkers. In such an environment, the likelihood that teachers will value the development of students' intellect and imagination is marginal.

Toward an Ecology of the Intellect

The level of teachers' intellectual development has a direct relationship to student behavior and performance. Higher-level intellectually functioning teachers produce higher-level intellectually functioning students (Sprinthall & Theis-Sprinthall, 1983). Characteristic of these teachers is their ability to empathize, symbolize experience, and act in accordance with a disciplined commitment to human values. Such teachers employ a greater range of instructional strategies, elicit more conceptual responses from students, and produce higher-achieving students who are more cooperative and involved in their work. Glickman (1985) concluded that thoughtful teachers stimulate their students to be thoughtful as well.

To realize our desire to develop students' intellectual capacities, the intellectual ecology of the school community must be constantly monitored and managed—like an "environmental protection agency"—to ensure that intellectual growth, creativity, and cooperation are continually sustained and regenerated.

Systems analysts believe in "leverage points"—places within a complex system where a small shift in one condition can produce big changes in the rest of the system. Studies by Louis, Marks, and Kruse (1996) identified five norms that characterize a professional learning culture in a school. These norms may serve as interventions to enhance continual intellectual growth and sustain the professional zest of the stakeholders in the educational enterprise. The intent is not to alleviate stress entirely but to shift from *distress to eustress* (*eu* is taken from the word "euphoria"). The five characteristics are

1. Shared norms and values. There is a sense of common values and expectations of and for each other.

2. A collective focus on student learning. Teachers' professional actions focus on choices that affect students' opportunities to learn and to provide substantial student benefit.

3. Collaboration. Professional communities foster the sharing of expertise, and faculty members call on each other to discuss the development of skills related to the implementation of practice.

4. Deprivatized practice. Teachers come to know one another and their craft by sharing and trading off the roles of mentor, advisor, specialist, peer coach, and coteacher.

5. Reflective Dialogue. Reflection on practice leads to a deepened understanding of the processes of learning and instruction by engaging in in-depth public conversations about quality learning, standards, concerns of schooling, and questions of student development.

Let us examine each of these characteristics in greater depth and describe how they contribute to a teacher's sustained intellectual growth.

1. Shared Norms and Values

If your vision statement sounds like motherhood and apple pie, and is somewhat embarrassing, you're on the right track. You bet the farm.

—Peter Block, The Empowered Manager

Senge (1990) believes that in a learning organization, there is "creative tension" that emerges from seeing clearly where we want to be—the vision—and describing truthfully where we are now—our current reality. The gap between the two generates creative tension, as in Figure 25.1.

This principle has long been recognized by such leaders as Martin Luther King Jr., when he proclaimed, "I have a dream." King talked about productive tension in that speech.

> Just as Socrates felt that it was necessary to create a tension in the mind, so that individuals could rise from the bondage of myths and half truths . . . so must we create the kind of tension in society that will help men rise from the dark depths of prejudice and racism.

This tension can be resolved by raising current reality toward the vision. Intellectual growth is caused by creative organizational tension between present practices and the community's visions of what could be, images of desired states, valued aspirations, outcomes, and scenarios of more appropriate futures.

—Figure 25.1—

Tension Between Vision and Reality

What gives an organization integrity is how staff members perceive the congruence between their policies, vision, and mission and their daily practices.

2. FOCUSING ON STUDENT LEARNING

Senge (1990) emphasizes that a characteristic of the learning organization is that it challenges existing mental models. The staff, in an atmosphere of trust, challenges existing practices, assumptions, policies, and traditional ways of delivering curriculum. Intellectual growth is found in disequilibrium, not balance. It is out of chaos that order is built, that learning takes place, that new understandings are forged, that new connections are bridged, and that organizations function more consistently with their mission, vision, and goals.

The purpose of this book is to publicly admit that the process of thinking and intellectual development *is* the content. The core of our curriculum focuses on such processes as thinking, learning to learn, knowledge production, metacognition, transference of knowledge, decision making, creativity, group problem solving, and knowing how to behave when correct answers are not readily apparent. These *are* the subject matters of instruction. Content, selectively abandoned and judiciously selected because of its fecund contributions to the thinking/learning process, becomes merely the vehicle in which to experience the joyride of learning. The focus is on learning *from* the objectives instead of learning *of* the objectives.

Since these process-oriented goals cannot be assessed using product-oriented assessment techniques, our existing evaluation paradigm must shift as well. Thus, assessment of students' thinking will focus on students becoming more conscious, more reflective, more efficient, more flexible, and more transferable (Costa & Kallick, 1995, 2000; Costa & Liebmann, 1997).

Frymier (1987) goes on to state

> The solution is to empower teachers, to help them develop an internalized locus of control. Teachers and principals, supervisors and superintendents, boards of education and state legislators all must appreciate the possibilities of school improvement efforts that marshal the motivations and unleash the talents of those who work directly with children day after day. (p. 50)

For too long, the process of assessment has been external to teachers' goal setting, curriculum, and instructional decision making. School effectiveness, student achievement, and teachers' competence have often been determined by a narrow range of standardized achievement test scores in a limited number of content areas. Rank-order test results are published in newspapers, awards of excellence have been granted to schools that show the highest gains in scores, and merit pay is awarded to teachers whose students excel in test-taking skills.

In the process, teachers have become disenfranchised. Educators have had little say about what the test measured; what tests do measure is often irrelevant to the curriculum; and the results of testing disclose little about the adequacy of teachers' curriculum and instructional decisions. In many ways, the desire for measurable outcomes has signaled to teachers that they are incompetent to assess student achievement. They, in effect, have been told they cannot be trusted to collect evidence of students' growth—that their daily observations in the classroom are suspect and of little worth.

High-stakes accountability causes educators to search for hard data by which to assess their efforts. Therefore, what teachers observe, by inference, is soft data. The "hardest," most objective data available may be that collected by an *enlightened teaching team* that systematically and collectively gathers data over time in the real-life, day-to-day interactions and problem solving of the classroom. Conversely, the "softest," most suspect data may be that which is designed and collected by testing "experts" outside the school setting and ignorant of the school's mission, values, and goals; the community's culture and socioeconomics; and the classroom's mix of learning styles, teaching strategies, and group dynamics in which their tests are administered.

Staff-collected data can be an energy source for intellectual growth. The teaching staff designs strategies for collecting data and for using assessment data as feedback to guide informed and reflective practice (Costa & Kallick, 1995; Garmston & Wellman, 1999). Staff members design feedback spirals, including multiple ways to gather such data; establish criteria for judgment; work together to develop their common understanding and reliability of observations; and report results.

3. COLLABORATION

It is acceptance and trust that make it possible for each bird to sing its own song—confident that it will be heard—even by those who sing with a different voice.

—*Barbara Hateley and Warren Schnidt,*
A Peacock in the Land of Penguins

Humans are made to be different. Diversity is the basis of biological survival. Each of us has a different genetic structure; unique facial features; a distinguishing thumb print; a distinctive signature; diverse backgrounds of knowledge, experience, and culture; and a preferred way of gathering, processing, and expressing information and knowledge. We even have a singular frequency in which we vibrate (Leonard, 1978). In mediative environments, we are sensitive to and capitalize on these differences to enhance intellectual growth.

Organizational life might seem easier if all members of a learning community thought and acted in a similar fashion and remained in their own departments and grade levels. Limitations of time, isolation, and our obsession with the archaic compartmentalization of the disciplines and grades keep school staffs separated. Thus, opportunities for teachers' intellectual growth are limited. Humans grow intellectually through resolving differences, achieving consensus, and stretching to accommodate dissonance. They realize there is a greater possibility for making connections, stimulating creativity, and growing the capacity for complex problem solving when such differences are bridged. (In some businesses, this is referred to as "skunkworks"—deliberately bringing together personnel from different departments, positions, and grade levels to make connections and find new and divergent ways to solve problems.)

Interdependent learning communities are built not by obscuring diversity but by valuing the friction those differences bring and resolving them in an atmosphere of trust and reciprocity. Therefore, in mediative environments, this diversity is valued by deliberately bringing together people of different political persuasions, cultures, gender, cognitive styles, belief systems, modality preferences, and intelligences. Groups are purposely composed of representatives from different schools, diverse departments, community groups, and grade levels in order to envision, describe learning outcomes, plan curriculum and staff-development activities, and allocate resources.

4. DEPRIVATIZED PRACTICE

The current management culture, with its focus on controlling behavior, needs to be replaced by a management culture in which skillful coaching creates the climate, environment, and context that empowers employees and teams to generate results.

—R. D. Evered and J. C. Selman, "Coaching and the Art of Management," Organizational Dynamics

Peer coaching is one of the most powerful means to overcome the extreme isolation and intellectual depression of teachers. Coaching produces intellectual growth for a variety of reasons:

1. Observing each other enhances instructional thought. The act of teaching is, itself, an intellectual process. Jackson (1968) found that teachers make more than 1,300 decisions a day. The behaviors observed in the classroom are artifacts of decisions that teachers make before, during, and after instruction (Shavelson, 1976). The purpose of coaching, therefore, is to enhance teachers' capacities to plan, monitor, and reflect upon their own instructional decision making, perceptions, and the intellectual functions. Costa and Garmston (1994) note that the purpose of coaching is to modify teachers' capacities to modify themselves.

2. Humans who desire to continually improve their craft, seek and profit from being coached. Skillful artists, athletes, and musicians never lose their need for coaching. Likewise, to continually perfect their craft, teachers profit from coaching as well.

3. To work effectively as a member of a team requires coaching. We are the only profession that is expected to work as a team but practice our craft in isolation. Combining the efforts of individual team members into a well-organized and efficient unit requires that we make public our craft of teaching.

4. Few educational innovations achieve their full impact without a coaching component. Joyce and Showers (1988) found that efforts to bring about changes in classroom practice are fruitless unless the teacher is coached in the use of the innovation. Only when the component of coaching was added was the innovation internalized, valued, and transferred to classroom use.

5. Deprivatization enhances the intellectual capacities of teachers, which, in turn, produces greater intellectual achievements in students.

Vygotsky (1978) helps us understand that the human intellect grows and develops not only from the inside of us on the individual level, but also through interactions and relationships with others.

It is through social interaction that new concepts and intellectual behaviors are formed and grown, which, in turn, influences the student's level of intellectual development (Witherall & Erickson, 1978).

5. REFLECTIVE DIALOGUE

Teamwork is the ability to work together toward a common vision. The ability to direct individual accomplishment toward organizational objectives. It is the fuel that allows common people to accomplish uncommon results.

—George Land and Beth Jarman, Break-Point and Beyond: Mastering the Future Today

Trust is a vital element in enhancing cognition. We know that higher-level, complex, and creative thinking closes down when trust is lacking in the environment or in the relationship with others. Teachers will be encouraged to inquire, speculate, construct meanings, experiment, self-evaluate, and self-prescribe when there a trusting environment.

Humans, as social beings, mature intellectually in reciprocal relationships. Collaboratively, individuals generate and discuss ideas, eliciting thinking that surpasses individual effort. Together and privately, they express different perspectives, agree and disagree, point out and resolve discrepancies, and weigh alternatives. Because individuals grow their intellect through this process, collegial interaction is a crucial factor in the intellectual ecology of a school.

The essence of building trust and collegiality is established when teachers work together to better understand how to co-operate. Trust requires a nonjudgmental atmosphere in which information can be shared without fear that it will be used for evaluative purposes.

Baker, Costa, and Shalit (1997) identify eight norms that may serve as standards that are understood, agreed upon, adopted, monitored, and assessed by each participant when working as a facilitating and contributing member of a group. They are the glue that enables school and community groups to engage in productive and satisfying discourse:

1. Pausing. Taking turns is the ultimate in impulse control (Kotulak, 1997). In discourse, space is given for each person to talk. Time is allowed before responding to or asking a question. Such silent time allows for more complex thinking, enhances all forms of discourse, and produces better decision making. Pausing is the tool that facilitative group members use to listen to each other respectively.

2. Paraphrasing. Covey (1989) suggests we seek to understand before being understood. Paraphrasing lets others know that you are listening, that you understand or are trying to understand, and that you care.

3. Probing and clarifying. This is an effective inquiry skill when the speaker expresses vocabulary, uses a vague concept, or employs terminology that is not fully understood by the listener. The use of probing and clarifying is intended to help the listener better understand the speaker and increases the clarity and precision of the group's thinking by clarifying understandings, terminology, and interpretations.

4. Putting your ideas on and pulling them off the table. Groups are most productive when everyone shares their thoughts, dreams, mistakes, assumptions, and opinions. While they offer ideas, opinions, information, and positions, they try to keep their suggestions relevant to the topic at hand. Because there are times when continuing to advocate a position

might block a group's functioning, group members also volunteer to withdraw their ideas.

5. Paying attention to self and others. Meaningful dialogue is facilitated when each group member is sensitive to and conscious of the subtle cues inside themselves and within the group. Paying attention to learning styles, modalities, and beliefs when planning for, facilitating of, and participating in group meetings enhances group members' empathizing with each other as they converse, discuss, deliberate, dialogue, and make decisions.

6. Presuming positive intentionality/positive presuppositions. Individuals operate on internal maps of their own realities, and, therefore, we assume that they act with positive intentions. This assumption promotes and facilitates meaningful dialogue. Because our language contains overt and covert messages, deeper meanings may be misinterpreted. The subtle (and often not so subtle) way in which we embed presuppositions in our language can be hurtful or helpful to others. The deliberate use of positive presuppositions assumes and encourages positive actions (Costa & Garmston, 1994).

7. Providing data. Groups exercising high levels of communication act on information rather than on hearsay, rumor, or speculation. Data serve as the energy source for group action and learning. Seeking, generating, and gathering data from group members as well as from a variety of other primary and secondary sources enhances individual and group decision making.

8. Pursuing a balance between advocacy and inquiry. Advocating a position as well as inquiring into another's position assists a group in continuing learning. Senge, Ross, Smith, Roberts, and Kleiner (1994) suggest that balancing advocacy and inquiry is critical for an organization in order to grow and learn.

Groups may monitor and assess their own use of these eight norms of collaboration. During and upon completion of meetings, group-process observers provide feedback to the group about its performance of the norms. These data are discussed, the effects of their use on group effectiveness are illuminated, and strategies for individual and group improvement planned (Costa & Kallick, 1995).

BUILDING A HOME FOR THE MIND

The development of thinking, individuality, and collegiality as goals of education is not just kid stuff. Education will achieve an intellectual focus when a school becomes an intellectually stimulating environment. It can become a home for the mind for all who dwell there when all the schools' inhabitants realize that freeing human intellectual potential is the goal of education; when staff members strive to get better at it themselves; and when they use their energies to enhance the intelligent behaviors of others. School staffs become an "environmental protection agency," constantly monitoring the intellectual ecology of the school. Their chief purpose is to ensure that thinking, creativity, and collaboration do not become either endangered or, worse, extinct.

REFERENCES

Baker, W., Costa, A. L., & Shalit, S. (1997). The norms of collaboration: Attaining communicative competence. In A. L. Costa & R. Liebmann (Eds.), *The process centered school: Sustaining a renaissance community.* Thousand Oaks, CA: Corwin Press.

Block, P. (1987). *The empowered manager.* San Francisco: Jossey-Bass.

Caine, R. N., & Caine, G. (1997). *Unleashing the power of perceptual change: The potential of brain-based teaching.* Alexandria, VA: Association for Supervision and Curriculum Development.

Costa, A. L., & Garmston, R. (1994). *Cognitive coaching: A foundation for the renaissance school.* Norwood, MA: Christopher Gordon.

Costa, A. L., & Kallick, B. (1995). *Assessment in the learning organization: Shifting the paradigm.* Alexandria, VA: Association for Supervision and Curriculum Development.

Costa, A. L., & Kallick, B. (2000). *Assessing and reporting on habits of mind.* Alexandria, VA: Association for Supervision and Curriculum Development.

Costa, A. L., & Liebmann, R. (1997). *Process as content: Envisioning a renaissance curriculum.* Thousand Oaks, CA: Corwin Press.

Covey, S. (1989). *The seven habits of highly effective people.* New York: Simon and Schuster.

Evered, R., & Selman, J. (1989, Autumn). Coaching and the art of management. *Organizational Dynamics, 18,* 16–32.

Frymier, J. (1987, September). Bureaucracy and the neutering of teachers. *Phi Delta Kappan, 69*(1), 10.

Fullan, M. (1993). *Change forces.* New York: Falmer.

Garmston, R., & Wellman, B. (1999). *Adaptive schools: A sourcebook for developing collaborative groups.* Norwood, MA: Christopher Gordon.

Glickman, C. (1985). *Supervision of instruction: A developmental approach.* Newton, MA: Allen and Bacon.

Goodlad, J. I. (1984). *A place called school: Prospects for the future.* New York: McGraw-Hill.

Harvey, O. J. (1966). System structure, flexibility and creativity. In O. J. Harvey (Ed.), *Experience, structure, and adaptability.* New York: Springer.

Hateley, B., & Schnidt, W. (1995). *A peacock in the land of penguins.* San Francisco: Berrett-Koehler.

Jackson, P. (1968). *Life in classrooms.* New York: Holt Rinehart Winston.

Joyce, B., & Showers, B. (1988). *Student achievement through staff development.* New York: Longman.

Kotulak, R. (1997). *Inside the brain: Revolutionary discoveries of how the mind works.* Kansas City, MO: Andrews McMeel Publishing.

Land, G., & Jarman, B. (1992). *Break-point and beyond: Mastering the future today.* New York: Harper Business.

Leonard, G. (1978). *The silent pulse: A search for the perfect rhythm that exists in each of us.* New York: Bantam Books.

Louis, K., Marks, H., & Kruse, S. (1996). Teacher's professional community in restructuring schools. *American Educational Research Journal, 33*(4), 757–798.

MacLean, P. (1978). A mind of three minds: Educating the triune brain. In J. E. Chall & M. Mursky (Eds.), *Education and the brain.* Chicago: University of Chicago Press.

Rosenholtz, S. (1989). *Teacher's workplace: The social organization of schools.* New York: Longman.

Sarason, S. (1991). *The predictable failure of educational reform.* San Francisco: Jossey-Bass.

Shavelson, R. (1976). Teacher decision making: The psychology of teaching methods. *1976 Yearbook of the National Society for the Study of Education. Part 1.* Chicago: University of Chicago Press.

Senge, P. (1990) *The fifth discipline.* New York: Doubleday.

Senge, P., Ross, R., Smith, B., Roberts, C., & Kleiner, A. (1994). *The fifth discipline fieldbook.* New York: Doubleday/Currency.

Sprinthall, R., & Theis-Sprinthall, L. (1983). The teacher as an adult learner: A cognitive developmental view. *Staff development: 82nd yearbook of the National Society for the Study of Education. Part 2.* Chicago: University of Chicago Press.

Vygotsky, L. (1978). *Society of mind.* Cambridge, MA: Harvard University Press.

Witherall, C. S., & Erickson, V. L. (1978, June). Teacher education as adult development. *Theory into Practice, 17*(4), 17.

IV

Our Changing Perspectives on Thinking

One ideology, one system is not sufficient. It is helpful to have a variety of different approaches. We can then make a joint effort to solve the problems of the whole of humankind.

—DALAI LAMA

Introduction

ROBIN FOGARTY

"The times they are a-changin' " is the way Bob Dylan described the 1960s. The times and the thinking did change. Indeed, in the decades that followed the political turbulence of the '60s, the thinking about human intellectual potential produced a turbulence of its own. Traditional theories about intelligence were questioned and previously accepted theory eventually was turned upside down—and inside out.

In turning the theory *upside down*, thinking shifted from the view of a genetically programmed intelligence that is inherited and unchanging, to a radically different view that held that the inherited genetic code for intelligent behavior is significantly affected by the environment and is constantly changing based on the sensory stimuli received. This emergent theory advocated that the learning experiences of each human being help shape the cognitive capacities of that individual. The contemporary view is that while some aspects of intelligence are determined by the genetic makeup of the person, in the end, intelligence can be modified.

In turning the thinking about human potential *inside out*, recent theories suggest that intelligence is not a single, fixed entity, but rather a plurality of talents and gifts, profiled differently in each person. Emerging theories suggest that intelligence is far more expansive than previously believed, that in addition to the cognitive realm, it involves the social, emotional, and even the moral realms of the individual. The prevailing theories suggest intelligence is comprised of a profile of capabilities. This profile is different for each human being and can be affected by environment and education opportunities. Intelligence can be learned!

In this section, seven essays portray the emerging perspectives of human potential called "intelligence." In the first discussion, Robin Fogarty profiles 13 theories advocated by recent and current "architects of the intellect." Included are the

theories of Dewey, Montessori, Piaget, Vygotsky, Feuerstein, Costa, Gardner, Sternberg, Perkins, Diamond, Pinker, Goleman, and Coles. Fogarty describes how these theories affect educational practice today as the legacy of these master "architects of the intellect" plays out in classrooms around the world.

Then, building on the work of Jean Piaget, Jacqueline Grennon Brooks and Martin Brooks discuss the theory of constructivism. This insightful and practical essay suggests that the quest for understanding is at the center of the educational enterprise. The authors present five overarching principles to enhance the classroom teaching/learning process, ranging from accepting student autonomy and initiative to inquiring about students' understandings prior to presenting the accepted wisdom on the topic.

In the third article, David Perkins presents an inspired essay about the social side of thinking. Citing the work of Vygotsky, who proposes that human development appears first on a social level and then on an individual level, Perkins dissects the theory into three areas: abilities, inclinations, and sensitivities. Social interaction helps the learner pool information, explore ideas, and detect opportunities for group interaction.

While Perkins promotes the concept of the "social side of thinking," Robert Swartz presents a compelling discussion about emotions and intelligence titled, "In the Grips of Emotion." He explores two ideas: emotions are a part of us and must be accepted as such, and emotions lead us to some sort of action. Swartz contends that this emotional arena is fertile ground for reflective decision making and suggests that emotional states are cognitive states in which particular attitudes are adopted in specific situations. He calls for early interventions in the areas of emotions and thinking to prepare youngsters with appropriate habits of mind for dealing with the real world.

The next two essays present a fascinating discussion that links biological and biochemical findings of the neurological

Copyright © 2001 by Robin Fogarty

sciences to the cognitive and psychological findings of the behavioral sciences. First, Ron Brandt interviews Robert Sylwester, a former biology teacher and education professor emeritus, to discern the state of affairs between the emerging brain research and the practical concerns of educators. Next, Lawrence Lowery extends our inquiry into how the brain learns and processes information, asking, Is it too early to find biological correlates to educational practice? Is metacognition a uniquely human trait? Do emotions drive thinking? What is the role of evolution in shaping the modern mind? Does the research inform our practice to the extent that we can advocate the teaching of thinking?

These theoretical stances influence our curriculum design and instructional strategies for teaching thinking, as illustrated by Bloom's Taxonomy (1956), which for many years provided educators with a structure on which to design curriculum, compose classroom questions, and construct assessment instruments. Robert Marzano provides some intriguing new insights based on research in brain functioning and the role of emotions on thinking and offers a new taxonomy for our consideration.

This section presents a display of cognitive fireworks for the reader to read, to enjoy, and to ponder. "The times they are a-changin'," that's for sure.

REFERENCE

Bloom, B. S., Englehart, M. D., Furst, E. J., Hill, W. H., & Krathwohl, D. R. (Eds.). (1956). *Taxonomy of educational objectives: The classification of educational goals. Handbook I: Cognitive domain.* New York: David McKay.

26

Our Changing Perspective of Intelligence: Master Architects of the Intellect

ROBIN FOGARTY

As we reflect on how the view of human intelligence has expanded during the past 20 years, we can truly say, "We've come a long way." The notion that intelligence is a static, known, and quantifiable entity (Gould, 1981) that can be represented by a little-changing intelligent quotient (IQ) is under scrutiny. The concept of an unchanging IQ seems to educational psychologists as archaic as bloodletting does to medical practitioners.

This limiting view of intelligence is yielding to an expansive and more encompassing perspective of human potential (Perkins, 1995). We understand intelligence to be a function of both genetics and the surrounding environment (Pinker, 1997; Sylwester, 1995). True, nature provides an inherited genetic code, but environment nurtures that natural potential in dramatic and dynamic ways. Environment, if rich, nourishes the intellect; if impoverished, it diminishes intellectual capacity (Diamond & Hopson, 1998).

The prevailing belief that intelligence encompasses the cognitive and the metacognitive (Perkins, 1995; Piaget, 1970; Sternberg, 1986), the creative and the critical (Perkins, 1995; Sternberg, 1986), the academic and the practical (Gardner, 1983; Sternberg, 1986), the personal and the social (Diamond & Hopson, 1998; Gardner, 1983; Montessori, 1955; Vygotsky, 1978) and the moral and the emotional (Coles, 1997; Goleman, 1995; Pinker, 1997), suggests the wide variance of human potential today's society acknowledges and values. This chapter discusses the spectrum of theories of the master "architects of the intellect" so we may understand their influence in the classroom and on the policies and practices of schooling.

ARCHITECTS OF THE INTELLECT

Architects of the intellect envision exquisite kinds of learning for eager and fertile minds, and their theories are designed with the brain in mind. Their mission is a daunting one, as their designs invite students to construct knowledge and make their own meaning of the world. The human mind innately strives to make sense of things through intricate connections in the neural pathways. Yet, these neural connections are inextricably linked to the learner's past experiences, prior knowledge, and subjective perspectives. How do the theories of these master architects accommodate each learner's unique schema?

As one might suspect, the theoretical designs are robust, rigorous, and often interrelated. Drawing on fields ranging from cognitive psychology to neurobiology, these architects of the intellect have set the foundation for sound pedagogy and a teaching repertoire of best practices. At the heart of the expanded and emerging view of human potential are theories by an impressive field of researchers, writers, and thinkers. The seminal works of a constructivist theory of learning include the legacies of Dewey, Montessori, Piaget, Vygotsky, Feuerstein, Costa, Gardner, Sternberg, Perkins, Diamond, Pinker, Goleman, and Coles (see Fig. 26.1). The influence of each of these architects is evident in classrooms throughout the world.

DEWEY: EXPERIENTIAL LEARNING

Dewey's designs (1938) embed learning in experience. In his concept, curriculum and instruction expand far beyond the classroom walls into life experiences. He advocates field studies and immersion in the experience itself to stimulate learning.

Dewey's influence is seen in community service and in civic projects such as reading to the blind, cleaning up the neighborhood graffiti, or partnering with village agencies to protest the pollution of the nearby river. His influence is seen as the class sets up a real store to manage consumer products, work with currency, and understand the theory of supply and demand. The influence of his architectural design is evidenced in outdoor education experiences and field trips to local museums and historic county court houses. Dewey's theory is prac-

Copyright © 2001 by Robin Fogarty

—Figure 26.1—
Architects of the Intellect

Master Architect	Theory
Dewey:	Experiential Learning
Montessori:	Discovery Learning
Piaget:	Constructed Learning
Vygotsky:	Social Interactions
Feuerstein:	Cognitive Modifiability
Costa:	Habits of Mind
Gardner:	Multiple Intelligences
Sternberg:	Successful Intelligence
Perkins:	Learnable Intelligence
Diamond:	Enriched Environments
Pinker:	Computational Theory of Mind
Goleman:	Emotional Intelligence
Coles:	Moral Intelligence

ticed as students simulate a real archaeological dig by examining the layers of artifacts found in a classroom wastebasket, reconstructing the imagined scene.

MONTESSORI: DISCOVERY LEARNING

Montessori's (1955) concept of a prepared learning environment emphasizes practical, sensory, and formal skills. Success-oriented and self-correcting, hands-on manipulatives accommodate the holistic nature of the child, including physical, mental, and moral aspects. These materials are inviting and pleasing to children and foster their competence in practical life skills. Sensory and motor skills develop through repetition of exercises and lead to formal skills of reading, writing, and mathematics. Throughout the process, the teacher facilitates, providing the didactic materials for growth and development without dictating direction. This is a form of auto-education in which the student chooses the learning experiences and the teacher respects the internal, individual nature of the learner.

The influence of Montessori's methods is seen in the richness of sensory materials and self-correcting manipulatives that crowd the early childhood classrooms. These highly motivating, structured environments are overflowing with books, booklets,

pamphlets, and papers. An abundance of specifically designed toys, games, and puzzles invite playful discovery. Throughout the learning experience, the teacher's observation and direction lead the child toward meaningful, ongoing progress. While Montessori schools primarily target children in the early grades, when, according to Montessori, the propensity for learning is at its highest, they also address students in the elementary years and even the transition years of middle school.

PIAGET: CONSTRUCTED LEARNING

Piaget theorized that the learners' interactions lead to structural changes in how they think about something as they assimilate and accommodate incoming data (1970). His work influences today's classroom through constructed learning designs in which students manipulate subject matter and objects representing the subject matter content as they interpret their findings and form ideas and concepts about the experience.

The influence of Piaget's designs is easy to spot in K–12 classrooms as students work with an assortment of objects and magnets or experiment with the idea of buoyancy as they test various items in a water basin. Students might be stringing and restringing electrical circuitry or manipulating Cuisenaire rods as they master the concept of fractions. Constructed learning is evident in much of the hands-on activities seen in classrooms, including the discovery and feedback loop of complex computer software programs. Constructing meaning based on one's interpretation of the data, as Piaget postulates, is at the heart of scientific inquiry.

VYGOTSKY: SOCIAL INTERACTIONS

Vygotsky (1978) suggests that one learns first through a social setting of person-to-person interactions and then personally through an internalization process that leads to deep understanding. This belief in the socialization process of idea making permeates the essence of the interactive classroom. Student-to-student engagement ranges from small groups of children bent over a map of Antarctica, deep in discussion of human survival, to pairs of students going head-to-head as they debate the most efficient way to solve the "tower problem," which requires, first, recognition that this is a certain type of problem. With that understanding, a certain procedure falls into place.

To see the incredible influence of Vygotsky's designs, one need only look at the innumerable studies focused on classroom interaction patterns. Teacher-to-student interactions bridge the spectrum from a teacher-directed whole group discussion on the changes in Pip's character as he evolves in *Great Expectations* to the skillful questioning orchestrated by the teacher as one student illustrates her understanding of the Pythagorean theorem. The teacher's reflective probing guides the social interactions in the classroom and is evidence of the influence of Vygotsky's thinking.

FEUERSTEIN: COGNITIVE MODIFIABILITY

The portraits of these architects of the intellect would be incomplete without acknowledging the influence of Feuerstein (1990). This Israeli psychologist performed groundbreaking work with cognitive modifications with traumatized children of the Holocaust. As a result of his success through mediated learning experiences (MLE) with these children, Feuerstein transformed thinking about intelligence and human potential. His theory of cognitive modifiability refutes the concept of a static and unchanging IQ and opens the metacognitive realm of the classroom to intense examination.

Feuerstein believes the "construction of knowledge" requires that teachers intervene to guide students' learning. For example, witness a student deeply engaged in a cognitive task of searching for a pattern that connects a seemingly random series of dots and listen closely to the expert intervention of the teacher-coach: "Why did you do that?" "What were you thinking just now?" "How does this remind you of another problem we did, yesterday?" "Do you have you a good reason for doing what you did here? Tell me about it."

Then, shift to a classroom scene in which youngsters are asked to think about their teamwork after completing a large mural depicting the Oregon Trail. "What were you supposed to do?" "What did you do well?" "What might you change if you work together again?" "Do you need any help?" Notice how the teacher goes beyond the cognitive and into the realm of the metacognitive by prompting students to think about their thinking and learning through guided reflection. These teachers put Feuerstein's theory into practice as they capture "teachable moments" and lead students toward deeper understanding and reflective transfer.

COSTA: HABITS OF MIND

Costa's theory focuses on 16 habits of mind that he believes characterize how human beings behave when they intelligently deal with problems (Costa & Kallick, 2000). Those 16 intelligent problem-solving behaviors are persisting; managing impulsivity; listening to others with understanding and empathy; thinking flexibly; thinking about our thinking; striving for accuracy and precision; questioning and posing problems; applying past knowledge to new situations; thinking and communicating with clarity and precision; gathering data through all senses; creating, imagining, and innovating; responding with wonderment and awe; taking responsible risks; finding humor; thinking interdependently; learning continuously. According to Costa, these habits of mind have been identified in effective thinkers across the spectrum of vocations and avocations, including mechanics, teachers, salespeople, entrepreneurs, and corporate business leaders.

To realize the influence of Costa's synthesis of what intelligent people do when faced with problems, we need only look in the classrooms. Students are asked to think critically about the news headlines on school violence; to analyze the stock market and use their findings to create their own financial portfolios; to understand and empathize with the victims of hate crimes; to inquire about service to the community; to draft a political cartoon that sends an important message through humor; to work collaboratively on a school project; or to think reflectively about their own learning. The focus on higher-order thinking, spelled out explicitly in national and state standards, is emphasized in Costa's intelligent behaviors.

GARDNER: MULTIPLE INTELLIGENCES

Gardner's gift to the classroom is in his conceptualization of intelligence as multifaceted and multidimensional (1983). He defines human potential in terms of the ability to solve problems in a culturally valued setting. In light of this broad perspective, Gardner identified eight realms of intelligence: verbal, logical, visual, musical, bodily, interpersonal, intrapersonal, and naturalist. As seen in countless classrooms, these multiple intelligences work in various combinations as students interact and connect in the execution of complex tasks.

For example, envision a youngster planting a summer garden and think of the many intelligences that must come into play. The gardener may think logically in the planning, interpersonally in getting advice about the proper seeds, visually in laying out the rows, as a naturalist in understanding the gestation periods of the seedlings, and intrapersonally in reflecting on the results. In another situation, as high school boys build a rocket in physics class, they may tap into logical thinking as they sequence the parts, into visualization as they design the rocket, into interpersonal skills as they cooperate as a team, and into intrapersonal competence as they celebrate their success.

The influence of Gardner's genius is felt in the understanding that not only are there many ways of knowing about the world and making personal meaning, but also that there are many ways of expressing what one knows and is able to do. The impact of this theory permeates the movement in educational evaluation. For example, performance assessment is valued as an authentic measure of what students know and are able to do.

Students might perform in terms of driving a car in a simulated experience, executing a dance number, demonstrating a basketball move, or playing "Peter and the Wolf" on the flute. Yet, performance can be more subtle than that. Students might also perform by completing a persuasive essay on banning smoking in public buildings or by demonstrating the proper procedures for a lab setup in chemistry class.

STERNBERG: SUCCESSFUL INTELLIGENCE

Sternberg and Grigorenko (2000) propose successful intelligence—originally introduced as the triarchic theory on intelligence (Sternberg, 1986)—as a factored model. They argue for three types of intelligence: analytical (compare, analyze, judge, evaluate); creative (invent, imagine, suppose, design); and practical (practice, implement, show, use). Based on this theory, analytical intelligence involves verbal abilities; creative, quantitative thinking; and practical, spatial thinking. The interaction of the three is necessary for problem solving, decision making, and creative ideation. It is the interactive nature of the three intelligences that creates what Sternberg calls "successful intelligence."

To see the influence of Sternberg's theory in the classroom, think about the traditional fact-oriented tasks in which students are expected to quantify their answers by finding mathematical solutions for a statistical analysis or to qualify their opinions about space exploration by justifying those opinions with supporting evidence. Think of a project-oriented curriculum in which students must fashion practical solutions for the impending teacher shortage. Think of community service projects that require all the practical, commonsense kinds of thinking used in the real world of work. Think of life situations, sometimes experienced through case study approaches, in which all aspects of successful intelligence come into play in an examination of one's values and practical implications to real life circumstances. And, finally, think of the students who have "street smarts" and are the informal leaders in the class-

room. Successful intelligence honors their pragmatism and provides the framework to further their learning.

PERKINS: LEARNABLE INTELLIGENCE

Perkins (1995) presents one of the more palpable views of intelligence when he argues for what he calls "learnable intelligence." Perkins poses the idea of a neural intelligence that contributes to efficiency; an experiential intelligence that stores personal experience in diverse situations; and a reflective intelligence that contributes knowledge, understanding, and attitudes about how to use the mind in intelligent behavior. In brief, Perkins makes the case for "knowing your way around the good use of your brain," just as you know your way around the supermarket, airport, or an opera. His theory focuses on the metacognitive realms of intelligent behavior.

A look inside a classroom shows the noticeable influence of Perkins's theory of a learnable intelligence. There is a focus on reflection through dialogue, journals, and discussions, with reference to metacognitive "thinking about thinking" activities. Perkins's assertion that learning is a function of experience shows in the authentic kinds of learning seen in the use of field trips, outdoor education, simulations, virtual field trips, and the concept of schools without walls—the whole community as the school.

DIAMOND: ENRICHED ENVIRONMENTS

In the 1990s, the explosion of research on the brain and learning brought the pioneering work of neurobiologist Marian Diamond to the forefront. Describing the growth of dendrites in the brain as "magical trees of the mind," she shows a closed hand opening to demonstrate the flowering of the dendrites with stimuli-rich environments. As she speaks of an impoverished environment, she shows how the dendrites shrivel by slowly closing her hand into a small circle. The influence of this research on enriched environments speaks to the same theory base as constructivism. In both domains, the learner is mindfully managing the input and making sense of things in the ever-changing environment.

Hallways overflowing with posters, writings, mobiles, sculptures, and paintings; classrooms with bean bag chairs, rugs and fluffy pillows, books, magazines, newspapers, and journals; science corners filled with greenery, tanks of fish, gerbil cages, rock collections, and classifications charts of sea shells; the listening station alive with classical music, pop songs, ballads, and the blues; the art center crammed with paint tubes, brushes, clay, sand, beads, construction paper, scissors, glue, and markers; the classroom lab stocked with beakers, microscopes, electrical circuitry, chemicals, and formaldehyde; the computer room with clicking keyboards, graphics software, CD-ROMs, modems, and Internet phones lines buzzing—these are the sights and sounds of the enriched environment.

PINKER: COMPUTATIONAL THEORY OF MIND

Relying on the work of Newell, Simon, Minsky, Putnam, and Fodor, Pinker (1997) envisioned the "computational theory of mind" what the brain does to allow us to see, feel, think, choose, and act. Pinker explains the mind by "reverse-engineering" it, by tracing the process of natural selection to see what nature intended the mind to be able to do as it evolved.

The mind, according to Pinker, allowed our ancestors to understand and outsmart other plants and animals through a system of "organs of computation." In his view, intelligence is the ability to attain goals in the face of obstacles, through decisions based on rational rules. We have desires and we pursue them using beliefs that, if we are lucky, are approximately true. In short, Pinker's computational theory of mind is based on the idea that information processing is the fundamental activity of the mind and is the function that makes human beings intelligent.

To see the influence of this theory of computation in relationship to intelligence, look to the field of artificial intelligence or "natural computation," as Pinker prefers to call it. This is the study of computers as a way to understand how the mind works. Computer programming for information processing is the best example of this theory applied to schools at the highest level of curriculum work. Yet, to appreciate Pinker's computational theory of mind, one must understand the biological theory of evolution.

GOLEMAN: EMOTIONAL INTELLIGENCE

Goleman (1995) developed his idea of an emotional intelligence in the mid-1990s. Within his theory, he delineates five distinct domains: self-awareness (self-confidence and self-decisiveness); self-regulation (controlling impulsivity and handling emotions); motivation (hope, initiative in goal setting, zeal); empathy (reading others' feelings, caring); and social skill (influence, leadership, team building). Goleman argues that this emotional intelligence may be more important than IQ in terms of life success, encompassing things such as happiness and fulfillment on the job and at home.

Evidence of Goleman's work often centers on curriculum and instruction in the affective domain. Attention to self-esteem issues, self-knowledge in terms of decision making about drug and alcohol use, and discussion and practice in using social skills in small and large groups are examples of how the theory of emotional intelligence is affecting learning in the classroom. While the affective domain has always been a part of the curriculum, there are signs that this domain is coming into more intense focus. Considering the research on the brain and the link between memory and the emotional system, Goleman's theory is ripe for sustained attention in the future.

COLES: MORAL INTELLIGENCE

Using character development as the basis of intelligence, Coles (1997) contends that moral intelligence is a valid theory. Coles shows how children can become "smarter" in their inner characters and can learn empathy, respect, and how to live by the golden rule. He suggests that, through the example of others and through explicit dialogue about moral issues, children can become more skilled, more thoughtful, and more caring. The theory is founded on how values are born and shaped through the "moral archeology of childhood."

Much like emotional intelligence, a first cousin of this theory, the evidence of Coles's theory at work in the schools is epitomized by the public cry for character education. Evidence of programs that focus on moral issues are seen in the increasing use of case studies and in the ethical issues that arise in problem-based learning units. From the early grades through middle school and into the high school years, attention to social skills and social responsibility is part of the cooperative learning agenda. Character education is prominent in the curriculum of today's schools.

A SYNTHESIS OF THE CHANGING PERSPECTIVE OF INTELLIGENCE

Yes, we've come a long way in our thinking about human intelligence. If we examine the varied work of the masters and try to crystalize the critical elements of the constructivist architecture, an array of complex tools emerges. These tools include a learner-centered/life-centered curriculum, enriched environments, interactive settings, differentiated instruction, inquiry, experimentation, investigation, computation, mediation, facilitation, and metacognitive reflection. These theoretical designs resonate with the emerging perspective of what comprises the human intellect. They embrace the cognitive and the metacognitive, the creative and the critical, the academic and the practical, the personal and the social, and the moral and the emotional.

The intellectual structures of today's classroom architects vibrate with the sounds of Dewey, Montessori, Piaget, Vygotsky, Feuerstein, Costa, Gardner, Sternberg, Perkins, Diamond, Pinker, Goleman, and Coles. Emerging curriculum designs capture the cognitive genius of these visionaries. And, these master architects willingly pass their legacies to the teachers in our schools today, for these architects design with the brain in mind.

REFERENCES

Coles, R. (1997). *The moral intelligence of children: How to raise the moral child.* New York: Random House.

Cooney, W., Cross, C., & Trunk, B. (1993). *From Plato to Piaget: The greatest educational theorists from across the centuries and around the world.* New York: University Press of America.

Costa, A. L., & Kallick, B. (Eds.). (2000). *Discovering and Exploring Habits of Mind.* Alexandria, VA: Association for Supervision and Curriculum Development.

Dewey, J. (1938). *Experience and education.* New York: Collier.

Diamond, M., & Hopson, J. (1998). *Magical trees of the mind: How to nurture your child's intelligence, creativity and healthy emotions from birth through adolescence.* New York: Penguin Putnam.

Feuerstein, R. (1990). *Instrumental enrichment.* Baltimore: University Park Press.

Fogarty, R. (1998). *Brain compatible classrooms.* Arlington Heights, IL: Skylight Training and Publishing.

Gardner, H. (1983). *Frames of mind: The theory of multiple intelligences.* New York: Basic Press.

Goleman, D. (1995). *Emotional intelligence: Why it can matter more than IQ.* New York: Bantam.

Gould, S. J. (1981). *The mismeasure of man.* New York: W.W. Norton.

Montessori, M. (1955). *Childhood education* (A. M. Joosten, Trans.). New York: New American Library.

Perkins, D. (1995). *Outsmarting IQ.* New York: The Free Press.

Piaget, J. (1970). Piaget's theory. In P. Mussen (Ed.), *Carmichael's manual of child psychology.* New York: Wiley.

Pinker, S. (1997). *How the mind works.* New York: W. W. Norton.

Sternberg, R. J. (1986). *Intelligence applied: Understanding and increasing your intellectual skills.* Orlando, FL: Harcourt Brace Jovanovitch.

Sternberg, R. J., & Grigorenko, E. (2000). *Teaching for successful intelligence: To increase student learning and achievement.* Arlington Heights, IL: Skylight Training and Publishing.

Sylwester, R. (1995). *A celebration of neurons: An educator's guide to the human brain.* Alexandria, VA: Association for Supervision and Curriculum Development.

Vygotsky, L. (1978). *Mind in society: The development of higher psychological processes.* Cambridge, MA: Harvard University Press.

27

Becoming a Constructivist Teacher

Jacqueline Grennon Brooks and Martin G. Brooks

You cannot teach a man anything; you can only help him find it within himself.

—*Galileo*

Constructivism is a theory of learning that places the quest for understanding at the center of the educational enterprise. When presented with new information, whether theoretical, objective, or interpersonal, humans seek to make sense of it. The process of making sense is enhanced in classroom settings when teachers practice five overarching principles:

1. Seeking and valuing students' points of view.
2. Challenging students' suppositions.
3. Posing problems of emerging relevance for students.
4. Structuring lessons around "big" concepts and ideas.
5. Assessing students' learning within the context of teaching.

When we first wrote *In Search of Understanding: The Case for Constructivist Classrooms* in 1993, most teachers with whom we met believed that constructivism was the way they had "always known people learn" and the way in which they wanted to teach. In the ensuing years, this view has been reinforced time and time again through discussions with many more teachers.

Yet, many of these same teachers acknowledge that they have not changed their teaching practices accordingly. They offer several reasons for this, most prominently these four:

1. Their school districts' educational approaches require them to focus primarily on test preparation.

2. Irrespective of their districts' educational approaches, they teach in a high-stakes grade level or subject area and are worried about how well their students perform on examinations.
3. Their school administrators do not support constructivist pedagogy.
4. They simply don't know how to do it.

The politics of education have certainly changed since 1993. Most states have developed standards for learning, implemented new assessments tied to these standards, and linked high school graduation to passage of these new assessments. Students in some states cannot graduate if they fail certain exams, and schools that fall below state guidelines are placed on lists of "failing schools" and required to develop local improvement plans approved by their boards of education and state education departments.

In today's climate, the key to student and school success is higher test scores, and that focus naturally breeds the impulse to teach to the tests. It is difficult for teachers to embrace teaching practices designed for the construction of meaning in such a regressive educational climate, even though it is our experience that students educated in constructivist classrooms do at least as well on high-stakes assessments as students educated in more traditional classrooms.

Many courageous teachers continue to structure their lessons around the search for understanding, exhibiting the teaching behaviors described in Chapter 9 of our book *In Search of Understanding: The Case for Constructivist Classrooms* (Brooks & Brooks, 1999). They do so in the belief that true learning is rooted in understanding, not memorization, and that students who truly understand important concepts will succeed on their high-stakes examinations and will seek to know even more than that which is required to pass the tests.

Most teachers with whom we've met who view constructivism as the way they've "always known people learn" believe they have been prevented from teaching in accord with that

This chapter is adapted from "Becoming a Constructivist Teacher" in *In Search of Understanding: The Case for Constructivist Classrooms*, by J. G. Brooks & M. G. Brooks, 1999, (pp. 101–118). Alexandria, VA: ASCD.

knowledge by a combination of rigid curricula, unsupportive administrators, and inadequate preservice and inservice educational experiences. Once offered the opportunity to study and consider the role of constructivism in educational practice, they tend to view the inclusion of such teaching practices as natural and growth producing. Once teachers are exposed to these practices, they enthusiastically experiment with constructivist pedagogy until it becomes part of the very fabric of their classrooms.

Teachers who resist constructivist pedagogy usually do so for one of three reasons: commitment to their present instructional approach, concern about student learning, or concern about classroom control. Some teachers have told us that although they are compelled by the power and promise of constructivist teaching, they are too deeply into their teaching careers to consider tearing down and rebuilding their instructional practices. Others see no reason to change because their current approaches seem to work well for their students. In other words, their students take comprehensive notes and pass important tests, perform well on worksheets, complete assignments neatly and on time, write well-structured and well-researched individual or group reports, and receive good grades for their work. Still other teachers, while focused to varying degrees on how well they perceive their approaches have worked for students, are more concerned about how well their approaches have worked for themselves. These teachers tend to be more concerned with behavior management issues than with student learning and are fearful that the constructivist approach to teaching will erode some of their control.

When teachers arrange classroom dynamics so they are the sole determiners of what is "right" in the classroom, most students learn to conform to expectations without critique, to refrain from questioning teacher directives, to seek permission from the teacher to move about the room, and to look to the teacher for judgmental and evaluative feedback. The rest disengage. Therefore, these teachers perceive empowering students to construct their own understandings as a threatening break from the unwritten but widely understood hierarchical covenant that binds teachers and students.

Becoming a teacher who helps students search rather than follow is challenging and, in many ways, frightening. Teachers who resist constructivist pedagogy do so for understandable reasons: most were not themselves educated in these settings nor trained to teach in these ways. The shift, therefore, seems enormous. And, if current instructional practices are perceived to be working, there is little incentive to experiment with new methodologies—even if the pedagogy undergirding the new methodologies is appealing.

But becoming a constructivist teacher is not as overwhelming as many teachers think. The following set of descriptors of constructivist teaching behaviors provides a useable framework within which teachers can experiment with this new approach. This set of descriptors presents teachers as mediators of students and environments, not simply as givers of information and managers of behavior. The development of these descriptors is based on our own interactions with students and our classroom observations, and has been informed by the work of several researchers and theoreticians, including Sigel (1968), Elkind (1974), Kuhn (Kuhn & Brannock, 1977), and Arlin (1985).

1. CONSTRUCTIVIST TEACHERS ENCOURAGE AND ACCEPT STUDENT AUTONOMY AND INITIATIVE.

While the philosophies and mission statements of many schools purport to want students to be thinking and exploring individuals who generate hypotheses and test them, the organizational and management structures of most schools militate against these goals. So, if autonomy, initiative, and leadership are to be nurtured, that nurturing must take place in individual classrooms.

Autonomy and initiative prompt students' pursuit of connections among ideas and concepts. Students who frame questions and issues and then go about answering and analyzing them take responsibility for their own learning and become problem solvers and, perhaps more important, problem finders. These students—in pursuit of new understandings—are led by their own ideas and informed by the ideas of others. These students ask for, if not demand, the freedom to play with ideas, explore issues, and encounter new information.

The way a teacher frames an assignment usually determines the degree to which students may be autonomous and display initiative. For example, students in a 12th grade English class read *Oedipus Rex*. The teacher asked the students to write an essay describing the book as Oliver Stone, the controversial film director, might think about it, and then to compare that interpretation to their understandings of Sophocles's views. To pique their interest, the teacher asked one group of students if they could find proof in the text that Oedipus had actually slept with his mother. After poring over the text, this group concluded that, according to the chronology of events, Oedipus could not possibly have done so. The students then wrote essays defending their positions and retold the story as they imagined Oliver Stone might have.

Conscientious students who are acculturated to receiving information passively and awaiting directions before acting will study and memorize what their teachers tell them is important. Robbing students of the opportunity to discern for themselves importance from trivia can create a well-managed classroom at the expense of a transformation-seeking classroom.

2. CONSTRUCTIVIST TEACHERS USE RAW DATA AND PRIMARY SOURCES, ALONG WITH MANIPULATIVE, INTERACTIVE, AND PHYSICAL MATERIALS.

Concepts, theorems, algorithms, laws, and guidelines are abstractions that the human mind generates through interaction with ideas. These abstractions emerge from the world of phenomena such as falling stars, nations at war, decomposing organic matter, gymnasts who can hurl their bodies through space, and all the other diverse happenings that describe our world. The constructivist approach to teaching presents these real-world possibilities to students, then helps the students generate the abstractions that bind these phenomena together. When teachers present to students the unusual and the commonplace and ask them to describe the difference, they encourage students to analyze, synthesize, and evaluate. Learning becomes the result of research related to real problems—and is this not what schools strive to engender in their students?

For example, students can read historical accounts of the effects of the social policies of the early 1980s on the economic and educational profile of the black population in the United States. Or, students can be taught to read the census reports and allowed to generate their own inferences about social policies. The former relies on the authority of a stranger; the latter relies on the ingenuity of the individual student.

3. WHEN FRAMING TASKS, CONSTRUCTIVIST TEACHERS USE COGNITIVE TERMINOLOGY SUCH AS "CLASSIFY," "ANALYZE," "PREDICT," AND "CREATE."

The words we hear and use in our everyday lives affect our way of thinking and, ultimately, our actions. Asking students to select a story's main idea from a list of four possibilities on a multiple-choice test is a very different task than asking students to analyze the relationships among three of the characters or predict how the story might have proceeded had certain events not occurred. Analyzing, interpreting, predicting, and synthesizing are mental activities that require students to make connections, delve deeply into texts and contexts, and create new understandings.

In a 3rd grade classroom, a teacher read a story to her students about three children who became lost in a forest. After struggling mightily, yet unsuccessfully, to find their way, one of the three children, a brave and daring youngster, volunteered to go off alone in search of help while the other two waited in a clearing. At this point, the teacher stopped and asked the students to predict how the story is likely to end and to reveal the reasons behind their predictions. The overwhelming majority of students predicted that all three would be rescued and they explained their predictions by pointing to the competence of the child who went in search of help. The students used information and impressions garnered from the text to predict how the story was likely to end.

Framing tasks around cognitive activities such as analysis, interpretation, and prediction—and explicitly using those terms with students—fosters the construction of new understandings.

4. CONSTRUCTIVIST TEACHERS ALLOW STUDENT RESPONSES TO DRIVE LESSONS, SHIFT INSTRUCTIONAL STRATEGIES, AND ALTER CONTENT.

This descriptor does not mean that students' initial interest, or lack of interest, in a topic determines whether the topic is taught; nor does it mean that whole sections of the curriculum are to be jettisoned if students wish to discuss other issues. However, students' knowledge, experiences, and interests occasionally do coalesce around an urgent theme. Such was the case during the Persian Gulf War. Students at all grade levels were compelled by the images they saw, the reports they heard, and the fears they experienced. The social studies teacher attempting to continue discussions on the Renaissance, the science teacher moving ahead with the Krebs cycle, and the art teacher in the middle of a unit on symmetry all experienced a similar phenomenon—the students were preoccupied with the war. When magnetic events occur that exert an irresistible pull on students' minds, continuing with preplanned lessons is often fruitless.

This descriptor does address the notion of "teachable moments" throughout the school year. As educators, we have each experienced moments of excitement in the classroom, moments when the students' enthusiasm, interest, prior knowledge, and motivation have intersected in ways that made a particular lesson transcendental and enabled us to think with pride about that lesson.

It's unfortunate that much of what we seek to teach our students is of little interest to them at that particular point in their lives. Curricula and syllabi developed by publishers or state-level specialists are based on adult notions of what students of different ages need to know.

Although some teachers may not have much latitude regarding content, all generally have a good deal of autonomy in determining the ways in which the content is taught. For example, an elementary science curriculum called for students to begin learning about the "scientific method" and to conduct some rudimentary experiments using this method: ask a question (develop a hypothesis), figure out a way to answer the question (set up an experiment), tell what happens (record your observations), and answer the question (support or refute the initial hypothesis). One 5th grade teacher asked her students, in preparation for this assignment, to talk about their favorite things at home. One student, Jane, spoke about her cat. The teacher asked Jane to think of questions she had about the cat. Jane wanted to know if her cat would like other cat foods as much as he liked the brand he normally ate.

Through the teacher's mediation, Jane organized an experiment to answer her question about cat food. She arranged four different brands of cat food in four different bowls and placed them on the floor. When the cat entered the room, she observed which bowl he went to initially and from which bowl he ate. Jane changed the positions of the bowls and tried the experiment again. Ultimately, she concluded that her cat preferred one brand over the others.

The student's thinking drove these experiments, and the teacher's mediation framed the processes that followed. The curriculum content—exploration of the scientific method—was addressed faithfully in a different manner for each student.

5. CONSTRUCTIVIST TEACHERS INQUIRE ABOUT STUDENTS' UNDERSTANDINGS OF CONCEPTS BEFORE SHARING THEIR OWN UNDERSTANDINGS OF THOSE CONCEPTS.

When teachers share their ideas and theories before students have an opportunity to develop their own, students' questioning of their own theories is essentially eliminated. Students assume that teachers know more than they do. Consequently, most students stop thinking about a concept or theory once they hear "the correct answer" from the teacher.

It's hard for many teachers to withhold their theories and ideas. First, teachers often have a "correct answer" that they want to share with students. Second, students themselves are often impatient. Some students don't want to "waste their time" developing theories and exploring ideas if the teacher already knows that they are "on the wrong track." Third, some teachers struggling for control of their classes may use their knowledge as a behavior management device: when they share their ideas, the students are likely to be quiet and more attentive. And fourth, time is a serious consideration in many classrooms. The curriculum must be covered, and teachers' theories and ideas typically bring closure to discussions and move the class on to the next topic.

Constructivist teachers, the caveats presented in the preceding paragraph notwithstanding, withhold their notions and encourage students to develop their own thoughts. Approximated (or invented) spelling is a good example of this approach. As very young students are learning how to put words into writing, they begin to approximate the conventional spellings of words. A kindergarten student titled a sign language book she had illustrated by writing on the cover "My sin lnge bk." The teacher chose not to correct her spelling but, instead, to permit her to continue approximating the spelling of words. Interestingly, when reading the book at home to her parents only one day after writing this title, the girl said, "Oh, I left the two o's out of book." No one told the girl that her spelling was incorrect. She reformulated her own work in the process of sharing it. The teacher's plan to share her understanding of the conventional spelling, in this case, became unnecessary.

6. CONSTRUCTIVIST TEACHERS ENCOURAGE STUDENTS TO ENGAGE IN DIALOGUE, BOTH WITH THE TEACHER AND WITH ONE ANOTHER.

One powerful way students change or reinforce conceptions is through social discourse. Having an opportunity to present one's own ideas and being permitted to hear and reflect on the ideas of others is an empowering experience. The benefit of discourse with others, particularly with peers, facilitates the meaning-making process.

Over the years, most students come to expect their teachers to differentiate between "good" and "bad" ideas, to indicate when responses are "right" and "wrong," and to transmit these messages in a fairly straightforward fashion. Dialogue is not a tile in the mosaic of school experienced by most students. Consequently, most students learn to offer brief responses to questions and to speak only when they are reasonably certain that they are supporting either a "good" idea or the "right" answer. This may help teachers move speedily through the curriculum, but it doesn't help students construct new understandings or reflect on old ones.

A group of 8th grade teachers decided to offer a wider literature selection to students and to engage the students in more thorough analyses of important ideas. The teachers organized a series of "booktalks." In a booktalk, a group of about eight students and an adult read and discuss the same book.

The students select the book they wish to read from a master list compiled by the teachers, and the school's schedule is altered so the groups can meet twice for 45 minutes during a three-week period.

In one booktalk, students had read John Steinbeck's *Of Mice and Men*. The issues raised by students during the post-reading discussion, issues generated by questions and contradictions posed by the teacher, included treatment of people with disabilities, sexism, the distribution of wealth and power in our nation, friendship, and death. The teacher orchestrated the discussion so that quiet students also had a chance to speak, but the ideas that drove the discussion belonged to the students and were fueled by student-to-student dialogue.

Student-to-student dialogue is the foundation upon which cooperative learning (Slavin, 1990) is structured. Cooperative learning experiences have promoted interpersonal attraction among initially prejudiced peers (Cooper, Johnson, Johnson, & Welderson, 1980), and such experiences have promoted interethnic interaction in both instructional and free-time activities (Johnson & Johnson, 1981).

7. CONSTRUCTIVIST TEACHERS ENCOURAGE STUDENT INQUIRY BY ASKING THOUGHTFUL, OPEN-ENDED QUESTIONS AND ENCOURAGING STUDENTS TO ASK QUESTIONS OF EACH OTHER.

If we want students to value inquiry, we, as educators, must also value it. If teachers pose questions with the orientation that there is only one correct response, how can students be expected to develop either the interest in or the analytic skills necessary for more diverse modes of inquiry? Schools too often present students with one perspective—Columbus was a courageous explorer who discovered America. But what does that imply about the Native Americans here when he came ashore? Complex, thoughtful questions challenge students to look beyond the apparent, to delve into issues deeply and broadly, and to form their own understandings of events and phenomena. For example, students could benefit from knowing that Columbus's ships carried with them diseases for which Native Americans had no antibodies. Information about Columbus and his men enslaving Native Americans for the return voyage home also adds food for thought. By thinking about these details, students could view the historical development of our nation in terms of Columbus's calculated and uncalculated risks and the Native Americans' subsequent oppression. Fostering appreciation for a multiplicity of truths and options is the "real" mission of education because "real" problems are rarely unidimensional.

In one 3rd grade classroom, a teacher formed "consultant groups." Each student became a consultant on a self-selected topic and was responsible for keeping the rest of the class informed about that topic. Each consultant belonged to a small group of students who were charged with questioning each other in order to learn about the chosen topics.

One student became quite knowledgeable about volcanoes and gave "lectures" on the topic to other classes. One day, the student was describing to his group how volcanoes develop in certain regions. One student asked him whether a volcano could be developing underneath the school. The student-consultant carefully pondered this question and said, "I don't think that volcanoes could develop here, but I'm not sure." When asked how they would know if one were developing, the student-consultant responded, "If a volcano were under the school, the grass would be turning brown from the heat. As long as the grass is green, I think we're safe."

Discourse with one's peer group is a critical factor in learning and development. Schools should create settings that foster such interaction.

8. CONSTRUCTIVIST TEACHERS SEEK ELABORATION OF STUDENTS' INITIAL RESPONSES.

Initial responses are just that—initial responses. Students' first thoughts about issues are not necessarily their final thoughts nor their best thoughts. Through elaboration, students often reconceptualize and assess their own errors. For example, one middle school mathematics teacher assigned his class problems in a textbook. A student, looking quite confused, asked the teacher if her approach to solving one of the problems was appropriate. The teacher asked the student to explain what she had done. As she was explaining her approach in a step-by-step manner, she recognized her own procedural error. The teacher based his responses to the student on the premise that he could learn more about what teaching steps to take in subsequent lessons with the student than he could learn from simply fixing the mistake for her.

9. CONSTRUCTIVIST TEACHERS ENGAGE STUDENTS IN EXPERIENCES THAT MIGHT ENGENDER CONTRADICTIONS TO STUDENTS' INITIAL HYPOTHESES AND THEN ENCOURAGE DISCUSSION.

Individuals grow cognitively when they revisit and reformulate a current perspective. Therefore, constructivist teachers engage students in experiences that might lead students to question their initial hypotheses. Teachers then encourage discussions of hypotheses and perspectives. Teachers cannot know what students will perceive as a contradiction to their hypotheses, as this is an internal process. But teachers can and must challenge students' present conceptions and use information about the students' present conceptions, or points of view, to help them understand which notions students may accept or reject as contradictory.

Students of all ages develop and refine ideas about phenomena and then tenaciously hold onto these ideas as eternal truths, even in the face of "authoritative" intervention and "hard" data that challenge their views. Through experiences that might engender contradictions, the frameworks for these notions weaken, causing students to rethink their perspectives and form new understandings. Consider the following example:

During an 11th grade discussion about the causes of World War I, one student contended with great conviction that the assassination of the Archduke Ferdinand of Austria caused the war. The teacher asked the student what would have happened with the economy and politics of the region if the Archduke had not been assassinated. After a moment's thought, the student said, "I guess they wouldn't have changed that much."

The teacher then asked, "Would anything else have changed? How about Germany's quest to rule Europe?"

The student replied, "I can't think of anything that would have changed, except that maybe the Archduke would still be alive."

"Then," continued the teacher, "what was it that made this event the cause of the war?"

The student, now quite enmeshed in thought, said, "I guess that maybe it [the war] could have happened anyway. But, the killing of Austria's Archduke gave the Germans an excuse to begin their plan to conquer all of Europe. When Russia and France jumped in to help Serbia, the Germans declared war on them, too. But, I think I see what you mean. It was probably going to happen anyway. It just happened sooner."

Note that this elaborate explanation didn't come from the teacher, but from the student. Note also that the student said, "I think I see what you mean," as if the meaning came from the teacher. But it did not. The meaning was constructed by the student who was ready and able to understand a different point of view. When the student revealed his original perspective, the teacher was presented with the opportunity to intervene; but the contradiction was constructed by the student.

In this example, the teacher challenged the student's thinking with questions. The questions provided a mechanism for the student to reveal very sophisticated understandings of the events and political subcurrents. The teacher never directly told the student to look at the assassination as a catalyst rather than a cause. She simply wanted to present a way for the student to consider this perspective as an option. The student quickly embraced this view. The teacher then directed the class discussion to other students with subsequent questions such as: "Who also thinks that war would have just happened sooner?" "Why?" "Who disagrees?" "For what reason?" Without acknowledging one answer as better than another, everyone can participate and listen to others.

10. CONSTRUCTIVIST TEACHERS ALLOW WAIT TIME AFTER POSING QUESTIONS.

Several years ago, as part of its professional development efforts, a school district hired a graduate student to record lessons in individual classrooms to provide feedback to teachers about their instructional practices. Several one-minute snippets were tape recorded during a lesson and then transcribed into writing for the teachers' reflection. One teacher, generally acknowledged to be highly skilled, was appalled to discover that she asked and answered questions in virtually the same breath. Students had no time to think about the questions she asked and quickly learned simply to wait for her to answer her own questions.

Similarly, another teacher found out that she had inadvertently orchestrated competition in her classroom. The first two or three students to raise their hands were, by and large, the only ones ever called on. If students didn't get their hands in the air immediately, they were effectively locked out of the "discussion."

These two examples illustrate the importance of wait time. In every classroom, there are students who, for a variety of reasons, are not prepared to respond immediately to questions or other stimuli. They process the world in different ways. Classroom environments that require immediate responses prevent these students from thinking through issues and concepts thoroughly, forcing them, in effect, to become spectators as their quicker peers react.

Another reason students need wait time is that, as we have discussed, the questions posed by teachers are not always the questions the students hear. The rapid fire approach to asking and answering questions does not provide an opportunity for the teacher to sense the manner in which most of the students have understood the questions.

In addition to increasing wait time after questioning in large-group formats, we have had success with posing questions and then encouraging small groups of students to consider them before the whole group is invited back together to report on the deliberations. This format provides opportunities for all students to participate in different ways while encouraging students' intellectual autonomy with regard to concept formation.

11. Constructivist Teachers Provide Time for Students to Construct Relationships and Create Metaphors.

In one 2nd grade classroom, students were given magnets to explore. Almost all of the students quickly discovered that one end of a magnet attracted the other magnet while the opposite end repelled it. Most also discovered that if one of the magnets were turned around, the magnets that had attracted each other now repelled each other. This activity took nearly 45 minutes, during which time some students went beyond these initial relationships and joined forces with their peers to create magnetic "trains" and patterns with iron filings. The students themselves generated a number of relationships, patterns, and theories during this activity. The teacher structured and mediated the activity and provided the necessary time and material for learning, but the students constructed the relationships themselves.

Encouraging the use of metaphor is another important way to facilitate learning. People of all ages use metaphors to bolster their understandings of concepts. One kindergarten student, after a field trip to pick strawberries at a local farm, ran home to his parents saying "You should have been there. It was a red heaven."

Metaphors help people understand complex issues in a holistic way and tinker mentally with the parts of the whole to determine whether the metaphor works. And all of this takes time.

12. Constructivist Teachers Nurture Students' Natural Curiosity Through Frequent Use of the Learning Cycle Model.

The learning cycle model has a long history in science education. The most popular description of this model was published by Atkin and Karplus (1962). Highlighting the important role of self-regulation in the learning process, the model describes curriculum development and instruction as a three-step cycle.

First, the teacher provides an opportunity for students to interact with purposefully selected materials. The primary goal of this initial lesson is for students to generate questions and hypotheses from working with the materials. This step is often called "discovery." Next, the teacher provides the "concept in-

troduction" lessons aimed at focusing the students' questions, providing related new vocabulary, framing with students their proposed laboratory experiences, and so forth. The third step, "concept application," completes the cycle after one or more iterations of the discovery–concept introduction sequence. During concept application, students work on new problems with the potential for evoking a fresh look at the concepts they studied previously.

Note that this cycle stands in contrast to the ways in which most curricula, syllabi, and published materials present learning and the ways in which most teachers were taught to teach. In the traditional model, concept introduction happens first, followed by concept application activities. Discovery, when it occurs, usually takes place after introduction and application, and with only the "quicker" students who are able to finish their application tasks before the rest of the class.

Let's take a look at how this cycle evolved in a 9th grade earth science classroom. In this classroom, the teacher told the students about the chinooks, the warm, dry, fast winds that blow down from the Rocky Mountains into the region just east of the mountains. The winds can be 40–50 degrees Fahrenheit warmer than the surrounding air. For discovery purposes, the teacher asked the students to work in small groups to generate a diagram that could explain why this occurrence might happen. As the groups began to work, the teacher listened to the students' deliberations, intervening in different ways depending on the course of the dialogue among the students. He asked a group that was "stuck" to begin by drawing the vegetation on the sides of the mountain. While drawing, the students began to talk about rainfall, where it comes from, the patterns of cloud movement, and so on. At that point, the teacher moved to a group of students talking about how hot air rises. The teacher asked another group, "Why does the warm wind move down if hot air rises?"

One girl in the group said emphatically, "That's what I don't understand." Music to a constructivist teacher's ears!

The teacher said, "You know what your problem is now. Don't forget that the wind is fast, too." And the teacher moved on to students with whom he had not yet interacted that day.

What was the concept introduction to follow this discovery opportunity? The teacher wanted to introduce the concept of adiabatic pressure—a most sophisticated concept that without consideration of heat gain and heat loss, wind speed, and moisture conditions is largely inaccessible. The chinook winds activity allowed the teacher to assess what elements of the concept are within the students' intellectual reach.

These 12 descriptors highlight teacher practices that help students search for their own understandings rather than follow other people's logic. The descriptors can serve as guides that may help other educators forge personal interpretations of what it means to become a constructivist teacher.

REFERENCES

Arlin, P. K. (1985). Teaching thinking: A developmental perspective. *IMPACT on Instructional Improvement, 19*(3), 25–29.

Atkin, J. M., & Karplus, R. (1962). Discovery or invention? *Science Teacher, 29*(5), 45.

Brooks, J. G., & Brooks, M. G. (1999). *In search of understanding: The case for constructivist classrooms.* Alexandria, VA: Association for Supervision and Curriculum Development.

Cooper, L., Johnson, D., Johnson, R., & Welderson, F. (1980). The effects of cooperative, competitive, and individualistic experiences in interpersonal attractions among heterogeneous peers. *The Journal of Social Psychology, 111,* 243–252.

Elkind, D. (1974). *Children and adolescents: Interpretive essays on Jean Piaget.* New York: Oxford University Press.

Johnson, D., & Johnson, R. (1981). Effects of cooperative and individualistic learning experiences on interethnic interaction. *Journal of Educational Psychology 73*(3), 444–449.

Kuhn, D., & Brannock, J. (1977). Development of the isolation of variables scheme in experimental and "natural experiment" contexts. *Developmental Psychology, 13*(1), 9–14.

Sigel, O. E., & Hooper, F. H. (1968). *Logical thinking in children.* New York: Holt, Rinehart, and Winston.

Slavin, R. (1990). *Cooperative learning theory, research and practice.* Englewood Cliffs, NJ: Prentice-Hall.

28

The Social Side of Thinking

DAVID PERKINS

"Please place your booklets face down on your desks and do not turn them over until I say to. When I say 'go,' turn over the booklets and begin to work. You may use the blank piece of paper provided for scratch work, but no other papers or books. Please keep your eyes focused on your own work."

Such a scene is enough to awaken posttraumatic stress syndrome in many a survivor of schooling. It evokes a world of tests and time pressure, grades and cramming. Yet, if we take a moment to reflect on such experiences, it's striking how strange they are. Formal tests ask us to remember and even think, but in ways quite removed from remembering and thinking as they play out in the everyday world of making decisions, formulating plans, solving problems, sustaining personal relationships, and so on.

One especially strange characteristic of the test experience is its solitary character. Help is forbidden. Teamwork is out of the question. One is asked to eschew even the indirect help that others might give through what they have written—keep your books closed! To be sure, the aim is to test individual mastery, and that has its importance. Still, the solitary confinement of the test is a singular reminder that, once we escape into a larger world, things generally work differently. Thinking is a profoundly social activity.

How is thinking socially distributed? How is thinking cultivated by social interactions of various kinds—between parent and child, teacher and child, and among peers? And how is thinking socially manipulated and repressed? A better understanding of such matters points to a central opportunity for those concerned with educating children and adults to think better: the systematic use of social resources to foster the development of thinking.

HOW TO THINK ABOUT THINKING

Scholars have offered many perspectives on thinking in general and on the social side of thinking in particular. For example, one might view good or not-so-good thinking as a matter of intelligence quotient (IQ), strategic repertoire, or the activation of different parts of the brain (see Perkins, 1995). For several years, my colleagues and I have found it especially useful to adopt a *dispositional* perspective on thinking (Perkins, Jay, & Tishman, 1993). When people speak of dispositions in the ordinary sense—"Nancy has a sweet disposition"—they point to trends in the way people conduct themselves. Nancy generally shows kindness and optimism. Over the past decades, several philosophers and psychologists interested in thinking have employed this idea (e.g. Baron, 1985; Cacioppo, Petty, Feinstein, & Jarvis, 1996; Ennis, 1986; Facione & Facione, 1992; Stanovich, 1999).

Thinking dispositions refer to trends in the way different people think. Roger is open-minded, but Randy is closed-minded. Alice is curious, but Andrea is indifferent. The basic observation urging attention to the dispositional side of thinking is strikingly simple: In real world situations, what's important is not just what you are able to do as a thinker but what you tend to do. Roger, Randy, Alice, and Andrea may have the same IQ, thinking strategies, and brain modules, but they will think in very different ways because of their dispositions.

It's especially valuable to make a distinction among *sensitivity, inclination,* and *ability* (Perkins, Jay, & Tishman, 1993). To function in an open-minded way, Roger has to be *sensitive* to occasions that call for open mindedness, such as in instances surrounding the civil rights of minority groups or the attitudes of people from different cultures. After Roger detects such a situation, he should be *inclined* to look at it from various viewpoints—motivated, ready to make the investment of effort. And, if so inclined, he needs to have the *ability* to do so. These distinctions are important because sensitivity, inclination, and

Copyright © 2001 by David Perkins.

ability do not always go together. You can have one without the others. But to behave regularly in an open-minded way, you need all three.

Let us step back into the world of tests for a moment. Just as the setting of tests does not reflect the social character of thinking very well, it also does not reflect the dispositional character of thinking very well. Sensitivity and inclination have to do with what challenges of thinking you detect as you go about your daily activities and what you feel you should do about them. In contrast, a well-designed test usually tells you exactly what the problem is, and, if you care at all about performing well, you invest yourself. In fact, good conventional tests are deliberately designed to foreground abilities and factor out the contributions of sensitivity and inclination.

Of course, abilities are an important part of the story. However, in everyday situations, sensitivity and inclination influence how well people think as much as abilities do (Perkins & Tishman, in press; Perkins, Tishman, Ritchhart, Donis, & Andrade, in press). My colleagues and I have conducted several studies that involve open-ended thinking tasks where a participant might, for example, invent alternative options for a decision or look at evidence on both sides of an issue. We found that usually the participants did not make such moves unprompted, although they were almost always able to invent alternatives or look at both sides if asked. However, they did not notice or feel the need in the first place—problems of sensitivity and inclination.

Accordingly, a dispositional perspective on thinking provides a richer view of what good thinking demands and therefore is a useful instrument for examining the social side of thinking.

THE SOCIAL DISTRIBUTION OF THINKING

Once we step outside the solitary confinement of test taking and a few other similarly specialized activities, we encounter the social side of thinking. It may be a husband and wife discussing a purchase decision, or members of the board of a corporation planning a shake-up in management, or children arguing about the rules of playing marbles, or a NASA development team designing a new mission. All such occasions invite what has been called *distributed cognition* or *distributed intelligence* (Salomon, 1993).

The dispositional perspective allows us to analyze broadly how social configurations contribute to the collective thinking process. It's easiest to begin with the most familiar of the dispositional triad: abilities. When all goes well, people pool their abilities as they think together. Perhaps the simplest form of

this is dividing up the work: You tackle this part and I'll tackle that part. But dividing up the work is only part of the story. As people discuss and argue, they pool information, experiences, and ideas to form a richer mix. They also provide critical checks on one another's thinking.

The discourse also produces more metacognition—more explicit recognition of the thinking moves in play—simply because the participants need to articulate their thoughts to communicate and thus make their patterns of thinking more salient and subject to examination. Of course, efforts to join together in thinking can also be acrimonious and chaotic, but often the result is a collective process of thought more potent than any one contributor's thinking.

Ability is hardly the end of the story. The social distribution of thinking has implications for how people are *inclined* to think. Bringing diverse views to the table tends to stimulate exploratory thinking if the discussion does not degenerate into participants taking positions. Competing views can stimulate a search for evidence. When people work together, the social interplay generates greater investment in the matter at hand. Cooperative learning environments help children be aware of their ongoing academic improvement (Bempechat, 1998).

Sensitivity refers to the detection of occasions that call for thinking. Here, too, the social context matters. When people work together, any individual may detect a situation that calls for the attention of the group. The different participants, bringing with them their distinctive personal histories, are likely to be sensitive to different things, thus expanding the overall alertness of the group. Beyond groups of people specifically working together, challenges of importance can arise and be passed around within a culture or subculture, so many people have a chance to work on them. For example, Edison invented the electric light, but he did not invent the *idea* of the electric light. Several other inventors already had recognized that such a device might be designed. Edison, master that he was, made it work through an ingenious and arduous development process (Baldwin, 1995).

THE SOCIAL CULTIVATION OF THINKING

If thinking is commonly distributed across social groups, it is easy to imagine that socialization plays an important role in the development of thinking. Russian psychologist Lev Vygotsky, who pioneered the role of social interactions in the development of individual cognitive competencies, expressed the essence of his view in a notable quote: "Every function in . . . cultural development appears twice: first, on the social level, and later on the individual level. . . . All the higher functions originate as actual relationships between individuals" (Vygotsky, 1978).

Vygotsky elaborated on this idea through his concept of the "zone of proximal development." Imagine a learner on the verge of considering arguments from multiple perspectives or understanding the idea of a formal logical proof. The learner cannot sustain such patterns of thinking alone, but she can do so with help, the patterns are within her zone of proximal development. For example, a learner's participation in a conversation with parents or students helps him internalize the patterns and develop autonomous use of them. Relating all this to the dispositional perspective, the internalization of patterns fosters sensitivity (by becoming familiar with the contexts in which the patterns are used), inclination (by forming rationales and habits of use), and ability (by developing facility with the use of the patterns).

Language usually figures centrally in social interactions that involve thinking. Moreover, language itself is a powerful resource for supporting the development of thinking. Tishman and Perkins (1997), Olson and Astington (1993), and others note that there is what might be called a "language of thinking." Terms like "claim," "evidence," "possibility," "speculation," "imagination," and "inkling," for example, carry with them patterns of thinking. A claim calls for evidence. An inkling calls for elaboration. English and other languages are rich in words that refer to different kinds of thinking, and their use in social contexts fosters the development of thinking. Olson and Astington (1990) contend that not only language generally but literacy specifically adds to the mix. Putting ideas down on paper, where they can be examined, critiqued, and revised, fosters better thinking on paper, but also better thinking in general, because the practices supported by thinking on paper migrate to some extent to thinking in oral contexts. Again, the contributions of language and literacy seem to touch all three aspects of thinking: sensitivity, inclination, and ability.

Another social force focuses on inclination in the form of students' commitment to learning. Bempechat (1998) examined the difficulties underprivileged children often experience in school. In years past, she notes, it was believed that underprivileged children suffered from cognitively impoverished home settings and entered school without the cognitive repertoire of more privileged children. From a dispositional perspective, this view diagnoses the problem as an abilities shortfall. However, further research has questioned such a diagnosis. At the time they enter school, underprivileged children do not generally show deficits in basic cognitive functioning. In-

stead, the problem seems to be a matter of *inclinations*. Some children see intellectual ability as more fixed, others as more malleable. The latter strive harder and select more challenging tasks when they have a choice. However, social stereotypes can lead children from underprivileged groups to see themselves as intellectually limited. Also, there appear to be differences in children's sense of responsibility. Some children do not accept good performance as a responsibility to themselves, their families, and communities. Certain cultures, such as Asian cultures, encourage the pattern of social responsibility more than others. The culture of the school can also foster social responsibility.

In summary, at least three social forces foster the development of thinking: social interactions that support learners in thinking activities they are not quite up to individually, the sea of language and literacy in which we swim, and socialization into responsibility as a learner. Assuredly, there are more.

THE SOCIAL INHIBITION OF THINKING

In the story so far, the social side of thinking appears as a positive force, supporting the development of sensitivity, inclination, and ability. However, in the Star Wars spirit, there is a dark side to the force. One cannot live in a social mix for long without realizing that not all thoughts or kinds of thinking are welcome.

Doctrine is one social antagonist of thinking. A doctrine is an official stance of a group—what you as a member of the group are supposed to believe in and remain committed to. Doctrines can be benign or vicious, liberal or conservative. They can certainly serve good social purposes, fostering group cohesiveness. However, doctrines are not good for thinking as such, especially when part of the doctrine says that it should not be questioned.

Authoritarianism is another social force that works against thinking. Authoritarianism should be distinguished from legitimate authority, both political and intellectual. Authoritarianism refers to the exercise of authority beyond its proper boundaries. Characteristically, authoritarianism does not welcome thinking outside the authority group. Members are supposed to follow in line, not think for themselves. Thinking is a disruptive force, not just because it might introduce new ideas, but also because contributions from below challenge the authority structure.

References to doctrines and authoritarianism place the problem outside the individual thinker, blaming it on the "oppressors." However, it's important to recognize that individuals often hunger for doctrine and authority. When there is no clear doctrine or authority, they find one or create one. Indeed, most models of cognitive and social development include a stage in which truth is viewed as a matter of others' authority rather than evidence. It is naïve to view problems of doctrine and authoritarianism in thinking as born entirely of intellectual aggression. They come also from willing and sometimes ardent intellectual submission.

Prejudice is another familiar social antagonist of thinking. Prejudice—prejudgment in its etymology—typically involves socially sustained and amplified stereotypes regarding other individuals and groups. Prejudice often receives reinforcement from doctrines and authority figures, but it need not. The stereotypes may simply be "in the air." Their presence relieves people of the need to seek evidence and form judgments on subtle matters. Like doctrine, prejudices have useful individual and social functions: They simplify things and foster group cohesiveness. But again, like doctrines—indeed, prejudices operate very much like unofficial doctrines—prejudices work against thinking. Why think when you already know?

Doctrine, authoritarianism, and prejudice all name social forces that narrow people's thinking. However, sometimes social factors can open up thinking too much. When people discover that opinions about matters like art and politics differ a great deal, they often adopt a relativist stance. Anything goes. Truth is what you believe. My truth is different from your truth. As with reliance on authority, many social developmental theories recognize relativism as a characteristic stage. Moreover, some cultural mindsets encourage a relativist stance. It can become politically correct to treat all value systems and cultural practices as equally precious and legitimate when some are incoherent, maladaptive, or cruel. The problem, of course, is that extreme relativism undermines thinking just as much as do doctrines, authority, and prejudice. While the latter three say, "Think this!" relativism says, "Think anything you please!"

All these points affirm the argument that thinking has an important social side, but they warn that the social side includes forces in opposition to good thinking. Recalling the dispositional perspective, such social threats to thinking have very little to do with thinking *ability*. Rather, they shape sensitivity and inclination—the kinds of situations that are detected as worth thinking about and the readiness to invest in thinking about them. Authority, doctrine, and prejudice tell us not to notice exceptions or anomalies and, if we do, not to think about them seriously. Relativism tells us not to worry about differences and try to puzzle out what's right.

TEACHING THINKING THROUGH SOCIALIZATION

The mission of teaching thinking is challenging, and a dispositional perspective ups the ante. If the development of thinking were just a matter of fostering skills, one could focus on teaching and practicing strategies. However, developing sensitivities and inclinations is a different matter. Sensitivities by definition operate on the fly, in the mixed and messy flow of events. It is not so easy to provide either strategies or authentic occasions to practice sensitivity. Inclinations are a matter of motivation and in-context habits. These also are not so readily installed.

Given such challenges, a social perspective on thinking offers a valuable resource that can be stated in a single word: enculturation. When people become enculturated, they become socialized into the values and practices from the culture that surrounds them (Costa, 1991; Tishman, Jay, & Perkins, 1993; Tishman, Perkins, & Jay, 1995). Culture teaches, not in the direct manner of a text or a lecture, but by surrounding learners with particular sets of values and styles of action. Culture does not substitute for laying certain things out explicitly, but does a job that didactic instruction cannot readily accomplish.

This creates an important opportunity in classrooms and other settings, where we can foster the development of thinking by creating microcultures around learners. Several aspects of the social side of thinking point the way to how this might be done—and indeed how it has been done by many teachers and thought leaders throughout history.

TAKE THINKING OUT OF SOLITARY

The first lesson that follows from the social nature of thinking is simple: Take thinking out of solitary. In formal educational settings, learners should spend less time thinking and learning by themselves and more time thinking and learning together. This can mean small group collaborative learning, whole-class probing discussions, projects where learners work together over time to investigate an issue, and many other situations. Configurations can vary, but the key ingredient is intense and frequent thoughtful interaction around intellectually challenging matters. It will help the development of sensitivity if the tasks are somewhat open ended, so learners need to find their own way, thereby learning to navigate in complex intellectual terrains.

COACH THINKING

Research and experience on collaborative learning tell us that learners do not necessarily fall into productive patterns of interaction. They need some coaching about how to think and work well together. More generally, coaching is a key social element in the learning of thinking (Costa & Garmston, 1994). Coaching can range from coaching as a participant—for instance a teacher both guiding a complex conversation and joining in—to coaching from the outside, as when a teacher cruises a classroom full of collaborative groups, helping here and there. In the spirit of Vygotsky, artful coaching keeps learners in their zones of proximal development, lifting them to manage processes of thinking that are a bit ahead of what they can do alone.

USE PEER SUPPORT

In typical classroom situations, teacher-student ratios make it difficult for students to receive as much coaching as might be desirable, even in groups. Fortunately, various methods of providing peer support can also lift learners into their zones of proximal development. One such technique is *pair problem solving*, developed by Arthur Whimbey and Jack Lochhead (1982). In this method, learners work in pairs, one addressing a problem while thinking aloud, the other not helping but asking questions: "Why are you doing that?" "Why did you reject that answer?" "What's your plan?" For the next problem, the two switch roles. By giving the participants specific roles, pair problem solving lets each one focus more while benefiting from the other's comments, raising the overall cognitive level.

Another basic technique is to form groups mixed in ability and experience, rather than homogenous groups. The more able or knowledgeable students, with appropriate guidance, inform and coach their peers while becoming more explicit and articulate about what they know themselves.

USE THE LANGUAGE OF THINKING

The language of thinking cannot be taken for granted. Although available, it often does not see much use. Research on science classrooms and texts has disclosed that terms like "hypothesis," "evidence," "theory," "model," and so on appear relatively rarely (Astington & Olson, 1990). It is as though teachers and texts have shied away from the language of thinking for fear that it would challenge learners too much. To the contrary, the appropriate use of such language in context is a powerful social mechanism for enculturating learners into the patterns of thinking of science—or any other discipline.

FOSTER RESPONSIBILITY FOR THINKING AND LEARNING

Recalling the synthesis by Bempechat (1998), students' inclinations to think and learn reflect their sense of responsibility and commitment to themselves, parents, and others. Teachers, parents, and other community figures do well to project expectations and adopt practices that do not just ask students to do well, but ask them to accept responsibility and develop commitment in their and others' behalf.

AVOID THE SOCIAL ANTAGONISTS OF THINKING

All the above will come to nothing if the social antagonists of thinking stand in the way. Doctrines, authoritarianism (in contrast with appropriate authority), prejudice, and extreme relativism have no place in the thinking classroom, except as problems worthy in themselves of examination. This does not, of course, mean that there are no doctrines of conduct, just no doctrines about what you must believe and think.

THE HIDDEN CURRICULUM

I profiled these six principles as they might apply in classroom settings. But just as culture is everywhere, the social forces that foster or undermine the development of thinking are everywhere. Parents, for example, can take thinking out of solitary by involving their children in family decision making and coaching at the same time. They can use the language of thinking and foster responsibility for thinking and learning—one of their most important roles, according to Bempechat. And they can certainly keep the social antagonists of thinking at bay within the family. The same can be said for the workplace. A principal or president or CEO can encourage collaboration around difficult issues, can coach his or her peers even while participating, can foster responsibility for thinking and learning, and above all, from a position of power, can strive to sweep away the social antagonists of thinking.

The social side of thinking can foster thinking, undermine it, or not do much one way or the other. This depends most directly not on national or ethnic cultures, but on the microculture around the potential learner in family, classroom, workplace, and other settings. Although that microculture is certainly influenced by national and ethnic cultures, in large part it gets its character from the styles of key figures, such as parents, teachers, and bosses, who support particular patterns of thinking by what they model and reward. Culture is the hidden curriculum about thinking as about so much else, but key figures can, through their actions, write the hidden curriculum to foster better thinking.

REFERENCES

Astington, J. W., & Olson, D. R. (1990). Metacognitive and metalinguistic language: Learning to talk about thought. *Applied Psychology: An International Review, 39*(1), 77–87.

Baldwin, N. (1995). *Edison: Inventing the century.* New York: Hyperion.

Baron, J. (1985). *Rationality and intelligence.* New York: Cambridge University Press.

Bempechat, J. (1998). *Against the odds: How at risk students exceed expectations.* San Francisco: Jossey-Bass.

Cacioppo, J. T., Petty, R. E., Feinstein, J. A., & Jarvis, W. B. G. (1996). Dispositional differences in cognitive motivation: The life and times of individuals varying in need for cognition. *Psychological Bulletin, 119,* 197–253.

Costa, A. (1991). *The school as a home for the mind.* Palatine, IL: Skylight Publishing.

Costa, A., & Garmston, R. (1994). *Cognitive coaching: A foundation for renaissance schools.* Norwood, MA: Christopher Gordon.

Ennis, R. H. (1986). A taxonomy of critical thinking dispositions and abilities. In J. B. Baron & R. S. Sternberg (Eds.), *Teaching thinking skills: Theory and practice* (p. 926). New York: W. H. Freeman.

Facione, P. A., & Facione, N. C. (1992). *The California critical thinking dispositions inventory (CCTDI) and the CCDTI test manual.* Millbrae, CA: California Academic Press.

Olson, D. R., & Astington, J. W. (1990). Talking about text: How literacy contributes to thought. *Journal of Pragmatics, 14*(15), 557–573.

Olson, D. R., & Astington, J. W. (1993). Thinking about thinking: Learning how to take statements and to hold beliefs. *Educational Psychologist, 28*(1), 7–23.

Perkins, D. N. (1995). *Outsmarting IQ: The emerging science of learnable intelligence.* New York: The Free Press.

Perkins, D. N., Jay, E., & Tishman, S. (1993). Beyond abilities: A dispositional theory of thinking. *The Merrill-Palmer Quarterly, 39*(1), 1–21.

Perkins, D. N., & Tishman, S. (In press). Dispositional aspects of intelligence. In S. Messick & J. M. Collis (Eds.), *Intelligence and personality: Bridging the gap in theory and measurement.* Mahwah, NJ: Erlbaum.

Perkins, D. N., Tishman, S., Ritchhart, R., Donis, K., & Andrade, A. (In press). Intelligence in the wild: A dispositional view of intellectual traits. *Educational Psychology Review.*

Salomon, G. (Ed.) (1993). *Distributed cognitions: Psychological and educational considerations.* New York: Cambridge University Press.

Stanovich, K. E. (1999). *Who is rational? Studies of individual differences in reasoning.* Mahwah, NJ: Erlbaum.

Tishman, S., Jay, E., & Perkins, D. N. (1993). Thinking dispositions: From transmission to enculturation. *Theory Into Practice, 32*(3), 147–153.

Tishman, S., & Perkins, D. N. (1997). The language of thinking. *Phi Delta Kappan, 78*(5), 368–374.

Tishman, S., Perkins, D. N., & Jay, E. (1995). *The thinking classroom.* Boston: Allyn and Bacon.

Vygotsky, L. S. (1978). *Mind in society: The development of higher psychological processes.* Cambridge, MA: Harvard University Press.

Whimbey, A., & Lochhead, J. (1982). *Problem solving and comprehension.* Hillsdale, NJ: Lawrence Erlbaum Associates.

29

In the Grips of Emotion

Robert J. Swartz

The sign of intelligent people is their ability to control emotions by the application of reason.

—*Marya Mannes, author, in* More in Anger

In the dialogue *Phaedrus*, Plato describes the human condition as analogous to a chariot being pulled headlong through the sky by two horses, a dark horse and a light horse. The dark horse has a natural tendency to pull the chariot downwards toward the earth while, at the same time, the light horse has a natural tendency to ascend toward the heavens and free itself of the grips of earthly things. We, too, are constantly caught in that tension Plato suggests. Our bodies, through our emotions, pull us in one direction, while our minds, through our ability to think and reason, direct us to more lofty things: true knowledge, untainted by the fluid and murky tide of emotional energy, yet only really attainable when that light horse in us can break free of the pull of the dark horse and carry us to the world of pure thought where we can contemplate things as they are.

The idea that emotions and thought are two independent forces in our conscious lives that often are in conflict has persisted through the ages. Emotions such as anger, fear, and hatred often lead people to do things that they themselves think they shouldn't do. Yet they seem to lose control to these powerful forces that play themselves out in actions. If ever there was a recurring theme that displays the underpinnings of human history, this is it.

Author's Note: This chapter has grown out of a yearlong research seminar on thinking and the emotions conducted during 1997 and 1998 under the auspices of the National Center for Teaching Thinking. The ideas in the article are, in many instances, the collective efforts of the seminar paticipants, who were Joyce Dawson, Lori Hyde, Yunja Lassek, Janet Moss, Sally Selig, and Kathleen Moran.

Copyright © 2001 by Robert J. Swartz

Banish or Celebrate Emotions?

Mr. Spock, the Vulcan who feels no emotions in the TV series *Star Trek*, or Data, the android in more recent versions of this series who wonders what it is like to feel things, are near-perfect thinking machines. Yet both are, in their own ways, appealing. Are they models that we should emulate? Should we suppress our emotions? Is that the way we can underscore the importance of thought in our lives? While some people try not to let their emotions surface, it is not easy. Emotions erupt in many ways, causing physical problems like ulcers or emotional outbursts like child or spouse abuse.

The extreme position that all emotions be banished is based on an over-exaggeration of the role of strong emotions that sometimes misguide us in our lives. Our lives are constantly charged not with extreme anger or rage or hatred, but with a myriad of likes, dislikes, satisfactions, and displeasures, that not only guide us successfully but also enrich the quality of our experiences. Even strong emotions like fear and panic have a clear function—self-protection.

Respect for emotions and the important role they play in our lives was not born with Charles Darwin, but certainly his work, *The Expression of the Emotions in Man and Animals* (1873), illustrates this point of view, as does *Emotional Intelligence* by Daniel Goleman (1995). We can now add to this list of those supporting and appreciative of the important role of emotions in our lives many brain researchers who have charted the development of and central role of the neural pathways that control our emotions.

New discoveries about the emotional side of our brains are being made every day based on sophisticated new technological advances that enable us to "see" inside our brains (Sylwester, 2000). (See also Chapter 30 in this book, by Ron Brandt.) One of the most distinguished brain researchers who has focused on the emotions is Joseph LeDoux, whose major work, *The Emotional Brain*, was published in 1996. This research points to a vast network of "emotionally charged" neural pathways in the brain that can manifest themselves in emotional states like strong fear and anger. When we realize the vast involvement of activity in these networks every day, we must appreciate the functional role of emotions in our lives.

The great medieval thinker Saint Thomas Aquinas embraced the idea that without these emotional charges, our thoughts alone would be incapable of moving us to action. It takes knowledge that radishes are bitter (thought) and dislike of bitter things (emotion) to cause us to avoid eating radishes. Thought without emotion is dormant; emotion without thought is blind. In fact, the debate over this issue is many centuries older, appearing in the works of Plato and Aristotle, who disagreed on this point.

However one might feel about the connection between thought and action, there are two fundamental tenets about our emotional life that most contemporary thinkers embrace. First, we have emotions, they have a function in our lives, and we should accept them. Second, we need thought to reflect about what we should do based on the emotions we feel. Most present educational interventions are based on these two views (Elias et al., 1997).

TEACHING STUDENTS TO COPE WITH THEIR EMOTIONS

A lesson book for young children on thinking and the emotions presents various vignettes mirroring situations in which students often find themselves. Students are directed to think about what emotions the children in the vignettes are feeling and the best thing to do about each situation (Shure, 1996). For example, in one vignette, a child is playing with a ball. A second child takes the ball the first child is playing with and starts to play with it himself. The first child gets angry and starts punching the second child. A fight results and both children are hurt.

The teacher might ask, "What was the first child feeling when the ball was taken away by the second child?" "What does that feel like?" "Have you ever felt that way?" The purpose of these questions is to enhance the students' awareness of emotions and, by extension, help them become more aware of their own emotional lives.

The second set of questions, however, deals with the actions that follow emotions. Students are asked to identify what the first child did and then to think about what other options he had. They discuss and list these options. Then the teacher asks them to think about the consequences of these other options, whether the child should have acted differently, and why. This is a fairly standard decision-making strategy used to

—**Figure 29.1**—

Skillful Decision Making

1. What makes a decision necessary?
2. What are my options?
3. What are the consequences of these options?
4. How important are these consequences?
5. What is the best thing to do in light of the consequences?

Source: From *Infusing the Teaching of Critical and Creative Thinking into Content Instruction: A Lesson Design Handbook for the Elementary Grades,* by R. Swartz and S. Parks, 1994, p. 39. Pacific Grove, CA: Critical Thinking Books and Software.

teach students to think more carefully about their decisions before they make them. Teachers of older children often do well to supplement what are often basic decision-making strategies with more sophisticated strategies like those presented in Figure 29.1. More sophisticated graphic organizers can also be used (Swartz & Parks, 1994).

This type of intervention has two important features that distinguish it from other more or less straightforward decision-making lessons. First, it is important that the situation be one in which strong emotions precede actions prompted by these emotions without (much) thought. Second, it is important that the students reflect on the situation after the actions. The first of these needs little comment. Let's think about the second.

Having students reflect about behavior after the fact is not uncommon in schools. Students who "get into trouble" are sometimes asked to think about what they did and what they could have done instead. The purpose of such questions is not just intellectual, it is to try to influence the students' future behavior if something similar happens again.

Attempting to get someone to think about what they are about to do—or even are in the midst of doing—while they are in the grips of emotion is like trying to reverse the flow of a river. When we do this we are trying to prompt the individual to exercise some internal constraint on powerful forces that come from within—the forces of strong emotion. But, while the flow is often against the direction thinking may take a person, sometimes we are successful in reversing the flow. So the effort is often worthwhile.

The intervention that I am describing is built on the idea that reflection about actions is more effective when the person who is reflecting is "cool" rather than in the grips of "hot" emotional forces. If we can prompt cool reflection and build up a person's internal mental habit of reflecting before acting, then even when in the grips of emotion, we won't need to be there to prompt such reflection.

Of course, strong emotions are powerful forces and often make it very difficult to reflect, let alone follow the dictates of reason in hot situations. But this may be a matter of degree; maybe we should not hope for 100 percent success, but accept some success as success and strive for more.

Reflection after the fact is often easier because people usually "cool down" after an emotional outburst. Using simulations such as the one in the intervention described earlier, gives us a broad array of examples with which to help students practice, rather than waiting for emotional outbursts for after-the-fact reflection.

I recommend this approach to bringing thinking to bear on emotion-laden situations with the following provisos: that the decision-making strategy used as a basis for instruction be as sophisticated as the students can be challenged to use, and not just restricted to "what is in the book"; and that if your goal is to help students develop strong habits of reflective thought, students be given continued practice in this approach with curricular as well as noncurricular examples.

DEEPER CONNECTIONS BETWEEN THINKING AND THE EMOTIONS

In the second half of the 20th century, the "philosophy of mind" became a central focus of much investigation. This tendency occurred in part because of the growing evidence that seemed to contradict any kind of spiritualism in approaching the traditional mind-body problem, and in particular because investigations of brain physiology seemed to point in the direction of identifying mental processes with specific brain processes. While this debate still goes on, one interesting line of investigation focused on the emotions and their relation to thought (Kenny, 1963).

According to this line of investigation, the idea that emotion and thought are diametrical opposites is replaced by the idea that emotion and thought are intimately connected. In fact, emotional states are fundamentally cognitive states in which various attitudes are adopted toward specific states of affairs that are their cognitive "object," much as beliefs are cognitive states focused on a state of affairs or object.

From this viewpoint, any bodily states like increased heart beat, getting flushed, and muscle tension should not be identified with an emotional state. Rather, these are usually caused

by and accompany such states. Sometimes, in fact, people experience emotions without these bodily changes, for example, being happy that two friends are getting married.

Let us consider one of those extreme emotions that we seem most concerned about: anger. Suppose Ralph, a young student, is angry. At first blush, this seems simple: a condition, anger, has overcome Ralph, and he is in that condition, much like being overweight. It has happened and that's it. Of course there are various things that Ralph might do to get rid of the anger, just as he might do various things to overcome the condition of being overweight. In the one case a diet might help relieve Ralph's condition of being overweight; in the other case, some sort of aggressive behavior may relieve his anger.

However, the way we talk about anger often masks its true structure. Anger is often directed at someone or something specific. Ralph isn't angry at anyone who comes along. Rather, he is angry *at Sally*. So maybe Ralph's anger isn't really a condition like being overweight, but rather is relational in character, just as being Sally's brother is relational. In this instance, his anger includes another person, Sally, just as being the brother of Sally is a condition that includes Sally. This, indeed, helps us understand why Ralph pulls Sally's hair, not Jane's hair. Ralph is not angry at Jane.

According to the view of the emotions we are describing, this explanation is not enough. "Ralph is angry at Sally" also masks something, and that is what it is about Sally that Ralph is angry about. When Ralph is angry at Sally it is not everything about Sally that Ralph is angry about. For example, Sally's desk is right next to Ralph's. Ralph is not angry at that. In fact, he sort of likes it. Rather, Ralph is angry that Sally opened his desk and took his pencils, leaving him with nothing to write with. Ralph is angry *that Sally took his pencils*. It is this state of affairs that is the object of Ralph's anger. It is because Sally plays the role she does in this state of affairs that we say that Ralph is angry at Sally, but the true situation is that Ralph is angry that Sally took his pencils!

Of course, Ralph could have several different attitudes toward that state of affairs. Ralph could be happy that Sally took his pencils because he likes Sally and is glad she would want to use his pencils. Or he could be neither happy nor angry, but simply accept the fact that Sally took his pencils. However, in this case he is *angry*, and that means he has a certain attitude toward that state of affairs: he thinks that it is wrong and that something should be done about it. Without the thought in his mind that Sally took his pencils, he would not be angry at Sally and perhaps not think that anything she did was wrong and should be corrected.

How well does this view of emotions extend to other emotions like fear, hatred, and love? What about the obvious challenge that sometimes people are just angry, but not angry at anything in particular? For further discussion of these questions, I refer you to Thalberg (1966).

Of great interest about this view is that the viability—indeed the very existence of—the emotions in question seems to depend on our accepting the *truth* of the state of affairs that they are predicated on. We can have beliefs regardless of whether or not what we believe is true. While I may believe that it will rain tomorrow, we could be in store for a sunny day. At the same time, if I know that it will not rain tomorrow I shouldn't believe it will. We have an obvious and interesting consequence when we recognize this about emotions. Emotions are *appropriate* only if the states of affairs that are their objects are true. We say to children, for example, "Don't be afraid; there are no monsters in your closet." We tell a friend, "You shouldn't love her; she's just after your money."

Let's return to Ralph and Sally. Ralph is angry at Sally and pulls her hair because of his anger. According to this account of the emotions, Ralph's being angry at Sally amounts to Ralph being angry *that* Sally took his pencils. Ralph should, of course, think about what he should do next before he pulls Sally's hair. But he should also think about whether or not Sally really did take his pencils. Suppose Sally didn't take Ralph's pencils and you, their teacher, know it. Suppose you know, in fact, that Ralph's pencils are still in his desk, but hidden under some books, and that Ralph has not seen them there. You might well say to Ralph, "You shouldn't be angry at Sally. She didn't take your pencils." When Ralph finds this out, he will, in all likelihood, no longer be angry at Sally. He might even, we hope, apologize to Sally for making this mistake.

Now, of course, emotions are complex phenomena and there may be other things, not so obvious, that Ralph is angry about connected with Sally, and that may sustain his anger even if he finds out that she didn't take his pencils. (Or Sally may remind Ralph of someone he is angry at for some other reason, giving rise to a situation of misplaced anger.) So maybe we have to say that his anger would *probably* dissipate, "all other things being equal." But the connection I have sketched here between emotions and beliefs is an extremely important one despite this complexity. For while it is clear that we shouldn't expect anything like a guarantee that a person's emotions will follow his beliefs when they are subject to his careful critical scrutiny, there are many cases in which they will, and in those in which they don't, the difference may just be a matter of degree. Recognizing this important connection

—Figure 29.2—
Thinking Skillfully About Emotions

1. What is the emotion that the person is experiencing? To what degree is the person experiencing this emotion?

2. What is the emotion about?

3. Is what the person thinks the emotion is about accurate?

   3a. What information is there for and against this belief?
   3b. What does this information show about the accuracy of the belief?

4. If accurate, does the belief justify the person's emotion?

5. What is the best thing for the person to do given that he or she is experiencing that emotion on that occasion?

   5a. What options are there?
   5b. What are the consequences of these options and which are pros and cons?
   5c. Which option is best in light of the consequences?

If the person is you, then the pronouns should be changed to the first person and the verbs changed accordingly.

may well give us a further direction to go in to get a person like Ralph to think more deeply about his emotions.

This is a clear example of where some thinking can have a dramatic impact on our emotions, not just on what we should do once we have these emotions, *but on the emotions themselves*. And the interesting thing about this is, philosophical investigations aside, that we all, in one way or another, seem to recognize this.

HELPING STUDENTS THINK ABOUT THEIR EMOTIONS

Here is what I like to call a "thinking strategy map" for our emotional lives that grows out of our discussion of our emotions so far (see Fig. 29.2).

Like other thinking strategy maps for other activities like comparing and contrasting or decision making, this can guide us through a series of thought-prompting questions that can make our approach to our emotions more intelligent. Notice how the "traditional" set of questions about what should be done when a person is in an emotional state (#5) appears at the end of this list, preceded by the questions in (#1) and (#2) about what the emotion is that is being experienced and what the state of affairs is that is stimulating the emotion, and in (#3) and (#4) about whether the beliefs it is founded on are acceptable. These are all thought questions requiring various thinking abilities, both analytical and critical, to answer effectively. Imagine how thoughtful and intelligent our emotional lives would be if we were in the habit of thinking this way about our emotions as they arose. This thinking strategy map can give new and enriched meaning to the term "emotional intelligence."

We can, of course, get students thinking about these questions in relation to their own emotional lives. The paradigm of this kind of intervention described earlier can certainly be expanded to encompass not only violent emotions like anger, hatred, and fear, but also positive emotions like love, empathy, and happiness. Real case studies like that of Ralph and Sally can be used to expand and enrich such a program, and students can be asked to role-play Ralph guided by this thinking strategy map. Indeed, teachers might develop their own simulations of emotional situations like the situation of Ralph and Sally.

The way such interventions might work would be guided by the explicit use of the thinking-about-our-emotions thinking strategy map. Teachers could also use an array of other tools and techniques used in other thinking programs, such as collaborative learning groups, "think-pair-share" teams, graphic organizers, thinking logs, etc. And, of course, students could also be engaged in metacognitive activities around thinking about their emotions and those of others. Their new ways of thinking about their emotions can be reinforced through reflective repeated practice for transfer.

But what of the regular curriculum? Where, in the context of what we already teach, are there opportunities for the design of what I have called "infusion lessons" based on this thinking strategy map (Swartz & Parks, 1994)? (See also Chapter 50, by Robert J. Swartz and Stephen Fischer, in this book.)

I once worked with a high school teacher of English, a Shakespeare enthusiast, who decided to tackle the question of emotions using the traditional approach I described above. His method involved asking students to simulate one of the many highly emotional vignettes that one finds so well-portrayed in Shakespeare and then to think about the best action for the person feeling those strong emotions to take.

This teacher chose the play *Othello* as his vehicle, and put his students in the position of Othello, wildly jealous of Des-

demona's alleged amorous adventures, now about to kill her, as he does in the play. The students were to stop, imagine that they had "cooled down," and think about what other actions might be better for Othello to take.

I watched as this teacher struggled to get his students into the spirit of this decision-making lesson. They just wouldn't go there. The reason they were having trouble with the task at hand was that they were preoccupied with another issue: what Othello could have done to verify the story that Desdemona had, indeed, been unfaithful to him. For it was the scheming Iago who deceived Othello into thinking that Desdemona had betrayed him, and the students in this classroom were all worked up about how "stupid" Othello was to believe Iago. They thought of many ways that Othello could have thought about what Iago was telling him and checked up on his story. And, of course, they knew that if Othello had found out that what Iago was telling him was not true his jealousy of Desdemona would have dissipated and he would never have been in the position of considering killing Desdemona in a jealous rage.

At the time, the teacher and I both thought the lesson planned had simply failed. What we didn't realize was that the students were 10 steps ahead because they were focusing on the real issue—the appropriateness of Othello's emotions of jealousy and what a little more careful thinking might have accomplished. Now that I think back on this incident I see how that was the right center of gravity for this lesson, not what *we* planned for the students. And it is the kinds of reflections I have shared in this chapter, and the thinking strategy map for thinking about emotions, that makes this ever so clear. In fact, what the students in this classroom were reacting to was what Shakespeare, in his deep poetic wisdom, *wanted* his readers to realize and react to. Shakespeare was not the first champion of bringing thinking to bear on our emotional lives, but he certainly was one of its most articulate spokespeople. It is as important, if not more important, to help students get in the habit of thinking about questions 2 and 3 on the thinking strategy map for the emotions as it is to think about question 4.

So what is the moral of this story? Well, think of the variety and range of emotions and emotional circumstances portrayed in the literature students are exposed to as they move from the primary grades through high school. *Othello* is there waiting in grades 11 and 12, but before that there is *Franklin in the Dark* in the primary grades, along with *Jack and the Beanstalk*, and, as we move up through the elementary grades, books like *The Sign of the Beaver*, a study in prejudice and the hatred it spawns, and in middle school books like *My Brother Sam Is Dead*. You don't have to wait until *Othello* to start students thinking about emotions, and what better way to do that than through the characters in the literature that they read about and identify with.

Habits of mind can be developed early, but the harder habits of subjecting our emotions to the life of reason and thought cannot catch hold if we wait until *Othello*. And where else can students learn to develop these habits in a sustained way than in school? Our curriculum already contains opportunities to do this, and we should all take advantage of that.

REFERENCES

Darwin, C. (1873). *The expression of the emotions in man and animals.* New York: D. Appleton.

Elias, M. J., Zins, J. E., Weissberg, R. P., Frey, K. S., Greenberg, M. T., Haynes, N. M., Kessler, R., Schwab-Stone, M. E., & Shriver, T. P. (1997). *Promoting social and emotional learning: Guidelines for educators.* Alexandria, VA: Association for Supervision and Curriculum Development.

Goleman, D. (1995). *Emotional intelligence.* New York: Bantam Books.

Kenny, A. (1963). *Action, emotion, and will.* London: Routledge & Kegan Paul.

LeDoux, J. (1996). *The emotional brain.* New York: Touchstone.

Shure, M. (1996). *Raising a thinking child workbook: Teaching young children how to resolve everyday conflicts and get along with others.* New York: Henry Holt.

Swartz, R., & Parks, S. (1994). *Infusing the teaching of critical and creative thinking into content instruction: A lesson design handbook for the elementary grades.* Pacific Grove, CA: Critical Thinking Books and Software.

Sylwester, R. (2000, November).Unconscious emotions, conscious feelings. *Educational Leadership, 58*(3), 20–24.

Thalberg, I. (1966). Emotion and thought. In S. Hampshire (Ed.), *Philosophy of mind.* New York: Harper & Row.

30

On Teaching Brains to Think:
A Conversation with Robert Sylwester

RON BRANDT

Robert Sylwester is one of the foremost interpreters of brain research for educators. A biologist and emeritus professor of education at the University of Oregon, Sylwester is the author of numerous articles and several books about the human brain, including his well-known 1995 book *A Celebration of Neurons*.

Brandt: Brain research is producing a lot of fascinating information, but it isn't necessarily related to the practical concerns of educators. What can we say at this point about how our growing knowledge of the human brain applies to teaching thinking?

Sylwester: Well, let's give it a try. I know some scientists say it's too early for such specific questions. But why is it surprising that educators want to look for biological correlates to the things they've learned over the centuries by teaching students and by doing educational research? Why wouldn't we want to know how our folklore knowledge of teaching and learning relates to biological knowledge, now that such information is emerging?

It's important to realize that Frances Crick (1994) wasn't just being cute when he wrote in *The Astonishing Hypothesis* that we're nothing but a pack of neurons. Biology explores physical realities—not the sort of floating-about-essences we call "mind." Mind folks explore functional realities; cognitive neuroscientists explore the behavior of neuron assemblies and the distribution and effects of chemicals. They both explore the same phenomena, but in very different ways, and they describe things differently. If nonmaterial cognition exists, it's something for philosophers and theologians to explore, not biologists. Thus, reducing cognition to physical realities is biologically sound.

This chapter is adapted, with permission, from "On Teaching Brains to Think: A Conversation with Robert Sylwester" by R. Brandt, April 2000, in *Educational Leadership*, 57(7), 72–75. Alexandria, VA: Association for Supervision and Curriculum Development.

Brandt: Your mention of philosophers reminds me that when I began looking into the teaching of thinking I found there were different camps. Two that stood out were the philosophical approach, with a heritage of thousands of years, and the psychological approach, which is newer and more scientific. But biology presents a third approach, the newest of all. I've come across accusations from neuroscientists, including Crick (1994), who charge that until recently, cognitive scientists ignored the physiological basis of what they were studying. Is that a fair criticism?

Sylwester: I think it is. I've often said that education must change from relying mostly on social and behavioral science to being a profession based more on biology. In fairness, though, we should recognize that until the last decade it wouldn't have done cognitive scientists much good to worry about biology because research tools such as functional magnetic resonance imaging didn't exist. These new tools allow scientists to directly study brain activity in human beings, so imaging played a key role in many of the recent spectacular advances in the brain sciences.

Brandt: I want to hear your views about how the new knowledge these tools are producing relates to educators' desire to help students become better thinkers. But thinking is a big subject. Maybe this will help.

When some of us got together in the 1980s to try to make sense of the exciting developments in teaching thinking, we cobbled together a framework meant to incorporate various perspectives on thinking, ranging from particular skills to broad concepts like critical thinking (Marzano et al., 1988; Marzano et al., 1997). To see how the various aspects of thinking might relate to one another, we proposed five "dimensions." So although there are lots of other formulations, I tend to conceptualize thinking in five categories: 1) having positive attitudes toward learning, such as seeing the value of learning something and believing you can learn it; 2) acquiring and integrating two main types of knowledge: declarative (knowing what) and procedural (knowing how); 3) refining and extending knowledge, such as finding analogies; 4) using knowledge for meaningful purposes such as solving problems; and 5) having productive habits of mind, such as thinking creatively. This is clearly a mixed bag and it's just one of many ways to conceptualize "thinking."

Sylwester: The many facets of thinking may be something like grammar. A child learns to speak grammatically correct English without having a clue about what a prepositional phrase is. Then, several years later, we explain grammar in school. When the now grammatically astute child speaks, there's still a very good chance that he or she doesn't consciously consider syntactical formulations. But when I'm writing something and it doesn't read well, I examine it grammatically and often discover the problem. So having a conscious grasp of grammar is quite useful to me, although most of the time I'm not aware of how I'm using it automatically.

Thinking may be similar. We probably have a lot of problem-solving heuristics in our heads that thinking theorists have made more explicit in thinking strategy programs. They're useful when one takes the time to think through a difficult problem—consciously identify and consider alternatives, and so on. So it can be useful to have explicit knowledge of both grammar and thinking, although outside the classroom we may not use either one very often.

Brandt: I'll suggest what may be an example. One of the most intriguing themes addressed in some school programs is metacognition, the awareness of one's own thinking and the ability to "control" it to some degree. Can brain research help us understand that?

Sylwester: Metacognition, like imitation, is probably a unique human ability. It's deeply grounded in the concept of consciousness—currently the holy grail in the cognitive neurosciences—so at this point who knows exactly what it is. We human beings do a lot of introspection; as I think about your questions I'm carrying on a conversation with myself right now. I suppose it helps me consciously understand what I'm unconsciously doing (and have been doing since early childhood), and I suppose that metacognitive programs and meditation and so on may be able to enhance the process. But even though brain researchers hope eventually to understand it better, I'm afraid they can't be of much help at this point.

Brandt: Well, then, what about "self-regulation"? One of the goals of Reuven Feuerstein's Instrumental Enrichment program, for example, is "restraining impulsivity." Knowledge of brain functioning should be helpful here, I think, because we're getting into the relationship between thinking and emotions.

Sylwester: Right. We seem to have a fast and a slow response system. The fast reflexive system emerged to deal with dangers and opportunities that were clearly immediate: act quickly or die, or lose a fleeting opportunity for resources. The slower reflective system solves challenges that permit time for rational consideration of alternate responses. Thinking programs encourage greater use of reflective thought. Impulsivity is inappropriate activation of the fast reflexive system in response to a minor danger or opportunity that doesn't require immediate action.

The reflexive system is obviously triggered by a strong emotional impulse and it proceeds hell-bent without checking things out with our rational reflective cortical systems. It's what has been called—mistakenly, in my view—"downshifting." It's not that we can't think under threat; it's a different but equally valuable form of thinking. The fast reflexive system is obviously the default system, since it (admirably) keeps us alive and well-fed, while the reflective system may only help us decide which necktie to purchase. Prisons are full of folks who wished they had counted to 10 and might have benefited from a thinking skills program.

Brandt: You've said the reflexive system is triggered by an emotional impulse, but both types of responses have an emotional element, don't they?

Sylwester: True, even though we may not be conscious of it. Researchers have found that stored memories of our experiences include an emotional component, so even reasoned choices are probably influenced by associations we're not aware of. What we call emotions are at the heart of an unconscious arousal system that triggers all sorts of conscious cognitive activity. It's a sort of biological thermostat that activates attention (our focusing system), which then activates a rich set of problem-solving and response systems. The various emotions (such as fear and pleasure) probably provide an important initial response bias that speeds up and enhances the response.

Brandt: I recently came across the work of Stanley Greenspan (1997), a child psychiatrist who is worried about the emotional well-being of children in today's society. He and his colleagues have been able to help a number of autistic children by concentrating on their emotional needs.

I may be going way beyond Greenspan's ideas, which themselves are ground-breaking, but I'll invite you to speculate along with me for a moment. A classic conflict among researchers interested in teaching thinking is over the value of teaching conscious strategies. Because strategies (such as step-by-step protocols for making decisions) are basic to the thinking skills movement, it's an important issue. Some researchers report success in getting students to use strategies that were taught directly, while others have concluded that, in general, it's not effective (Brandt, 1989).

Greenspan contends that good thinking depends not just on pure rationality, but on emotional overtones. He encourages parents to make sure young children see the connections between their feelings and appropriate actions. If he's right, his findings may provide a clue to how people learn to think strategically, and therefore how we might be more successful teaching various thinking strategies.

Sylwester: Emotion drives everything. We only attempt to solve problems that are emotionally important to us. Emotion is an unconscious arousal system that informs our body and brain that something has occurred, or will occur shortly, that may be important to us. Feelings are our conscious awareness of this unconscious emotional arousal, so it's really feelings that get us into conscious attentive and problem-solving behaviors.

Greenspan's marvelous book certainly provides excellent advice to parents and educators on how to guide this process. So the "getting in touch with your feelings movement" that started a couple of decades ago has some serious biological substance to it, even though lots of rationally driven folks laughed it off. Think of emotion as the unconscious ignition system that starts the car and feelings as our getting-in-an-idling-car-and-driving-it behavior that provides cognitive control to an otherwise unconscious process. Folks with no conscious understanding of their emotional state often do foolish things, so it's important to help children understand how emotions and feelings affect their behavior.

Brandt: Some of your comments imply that evolution has played a big role in shaping human characteristics, including the structure of our brains. Most neuroscientists apparently assume an evolutionary perspective and some—Stephen Pinker (1997), Michael Gazzaniga (1998), and Henry Plotkin (1998), for example—go so far as to insist that, through evolution, many aspects of our brains are "hard-wired." They contend

that our brains couldn't possibly develop capabilities like using language and recognizing faces if we weren't born with systems of neurons pre-designated for that purpose. That makes me reconsider the idea of "teaching" thinking skills, because they are undoubtedly a basic part of our intellectual inheritance. Leslie Hart (1975), who was a pioneering interpreter of brain research, used to argue that, "The brain doesn't have to be taught to think any more than the stomach has to be taught to digest food. That's what it does!"

Sylwester: Organisms have to stay alive long enough to procreate, so they certainly have to develop strategies to do that (and to initially protect their vulnerable young in wombs, eggshells, nutcases, and so on). Further, humans have a very long childhood, so they have to learn how to communicate and connect emotionally with older kin and others who will protect them and solve problems for them during their immaturity.

The way I look at it, we go through two decade-long childhoods. One is from birth to about 10, when children have to develop three essential properties of human beings: an efficient motor system, mastery of the local language, and a knowledge of the social rules and conventions that their local group espouses (good manners). The second childhood is from age 10 to about 20, during which a person has to learn how to be a productive, reproductive human being. This involves a gradual weaning from dependency on parents and the maturation of the frontal lobes and the concomitant gradual weaning from dependency on parents' problem-solving abilities. This allows us to assume the more independent roles expected of adults: pulling your own economic weight in a highly interdependent society and rearing the next generation (directly through parenting and indirectly through financial support of public institutions, including schools).

Genetics being what it is, any capabilities a person could develop that would enhance these important tasks would be adaptive (genetically beneficial). Our brains may have several hundred distinct processing systems that enable us to address the myriad dangers and opportunities we confront. Some are on line and functioning well at birth: circulation, respiration, suckling, and so on. Some function at a beginning but basically dysfunctional level: the ability to move fingers and legs but not to grasp or walk. Some may emerge years later: handwriting, tap dancing. The really important survival skills seem to emerge effortlessly and without formal instruction—articulate speech, grasping, walking—so we probably have some kind of innate system to quickly get the important things going. The biologically less important (tap dancing, learning the multiplication tables and calculus) must be explicitly taught, and are mastered with effort. There's probably also an upper biological limit in many of these skills beyond which normal human beings generally don't go (memorizing hundreds of phone numbers, mentally multiplying large numbers, running 50 miles an hour) and so we off-load such tasks to technologies (phone books, calculators, automobiles). Some folks (virtuosos and savants) can go way beyond normality in a skill—and the rest of us tend to be impressed by such feats—but these are special cases that require an intense focus on a small segment of human capability, often to the detriment of other capabilities (often social capabilities).

How would we go about developing a capability if our brain didn't have the essence of it hardwired? For example, the human visual system can't process the infrared segment of the electromagnetic spectrum, but insects can. We can experience it only as heat. It's vital for the insect visual system to have this capability, since infrared provides it with important information about food sources. Since we don't seek the same food sources, we don't need the capability. Thus, the best teacher in the world couldn't teach a person to see infrared. It's possible to improve an existing innate system, but not to create a new one. We typically go outside of evolutionary processes into technology when we seek information beyond our capabilities—such as to develop an oscilloscope to see the visual representation of sounds that we can't hear.

I guess this is a long way to simple agreement with the idea that all human capabilities exist at birth, at least at a proto-level, and that experience, instruction, and practice move these capabilities from dysfunctional to functional. Further, humans have the almost unique capability of imitating the behavior of others, so we observe how others mix and match a set of basic capabilities into a problem-solving strategy, and then we try it—often in play activities, but also in school.

In short, the idea that aspects of thinking may be inherent in the structure of our brains is not an argument against bringing these processes to consciousness and practicing to improve them. Thinking skills probably emerge like the structure of language—which we master unconsciously before we consciously understand it.

Brandt: That's reassuring, but I want to push a little further. Some thinking skills programs call for students to practice such mental abilities as comparing and classifying. Students compare familiar things, like forks and spoons, so that when they encounter more complex matters, they'll be able to compare and classify those. The idea makes sense when you understand that "neurons that fire together wire together" (neu-

rons that often fire at the same time as certain other neurons become more likely to fire whenever those other neurons fire). In other words, we use less brain energy to perform familiar functions, like tying shoestrings or driving a car, than when we're learning new skills. But does that apply to mental functions like comparing, do you think?

Sylwester: Comparison and classification are monumental cognitive capabilities. They're at the absolute heart of language (our language being nothing more than the verbalization of 500,000 categories). Put 50 maple leaves and one oak leaf on a table and ask 4-year-olds to indicate which one is different. They will typically point to the oak leaf, which is the wrong answer, because all 51 leaves differ from each other. The remarkable thing is that the children are humanly correct, since the oak leaf is more different from the maple leaves than the maple leaves are from each other. It just blows me away to realize that no one really teaches young children to make that kind of discrimination—and it's so essential to everything we do cognitively.

Another excellent illustration of this ability is the current Pokémon trading cards and video game phenomenon that so fascinates young children. Pokémon requires players to quickly classify and match more than 150 complex cartoon characters that can constantly change their configurations during the game. My preschool grandchildren are way ahead of me in Pokémon capabilities, so it wasn't adults who helped them to develop their amazing classification proficiency. It makes me wonder whether we're seriously underestimating the classification capabilities of primary age students with some of the simple static classification tasks in some current curriculums. And it's similar to our immune system's amazing ability to quickly recognize and respond to myriad constantly changing molecular invaders.

I'm still awestruck by the 4-year-old who has never been enrolled in a thinking skills program, but already has amazing mental capabilities. There simply must be a powerful innate system already on line as language emerges. Educators need to be aware of that and respectful of it. We mustn't assume that children will never be able to think if we don't give them workbook exercises in thinking skills.

Nevertheless, all brain systems move from a slow, awkward functional level to a fast, efficient level—crawling to toddling to walking to running, and so on. It's to be expected that the ability to classify any set of objects, events, qualities, and so on into categories would begin with an ability to only recognize gross differences, and then with more experience and instruction move to a level at which the discriminations would be quite sophisticated and quickly made. And it requires much less cognitive energy to make a classification decision if the person has a lot of experience with the problem.

So I believe it makes sense to focus on thinking skills such as comparing and classifying. I'm on the side of those who believe latent abilities can be enhanced by the right kind of learning experiences.

REFERENCES

Brandt, R. (1989, December). On learning research: A conversation with Lauren Resnick. *Educational Leadership* 46(4), 12–16.

Crick, F. (1994). *The astonishing hypothesis: The scientific search for the soul.* New York: Charles Scribner's Sons.

Gazzaniga, M. S. (1998). *The mind's past.* Berkeley: University of California Press.

Greenspan, S. I. (1997). *The growth of the mind and the endangered origins of intelligence.* Reading, MA: Addison-Wesley.

Hart, L. A. (1975). *How the brain works.* New York: BasicBooks.

Marzano, R. J., Brandt, R. S., Hughes, C. S., Jones, B. F., Presseisen, B. Z., Rankin, S. C., & Suhor, C. (1988). *Dimensions of thinking: A framework for curriculum and instruction.* Alexandria, VA: Association for Supervision and Curriculum Development.

Marzano, R. J., Pickering, D. J., Arredono, D. E., Blackburn, G. J., Brandt, R. S., Moffett, C. A., Paynter, D. E., Pollock, J. E., & Whisler, J. S. (1997). *Dimensions of learning* (2nd ed.). Alexandria, VA: Association for Supervision and Curriculum Development.

Pinker, S. (1997). *How the mind works.* New York: W. W. Norton.

Plotkin, H. (1998). *Evolution in mind.* Cambridge, MA: Harvard University Press.

Sylwester, R. (1995). *A celebration of neurons: An educator's guide to the human brain.* Alexandria, VA: Association for Supervision and Curriculum Development.

31

The Biological Basis for Thinking

Lawrence F. Lowery

Humans, for the most part, are pattern seekers. Sometimes they are playful pattern seekers, as when they doodle, work puzzles, or daydream. Sometimes they are purposeful pattern seekers, as when they plan ahead or resolve problems. As humans use their pattern-seeking capabilities, they learn about and better understand their surroundings.

All of us by nature are pattern seekers. It is natural that much of our world today is best understood through the sciences, because nature has prepared us to seek patterns in what we see and do, and the patterns we discover enable us to cope with, understand, appreciate, and predict events in our environment. Scientists, whether they are biologists, physicists, or astronomers, are simply experienced pattern seekers.

We know of no other organism aside from ourselves that can contemplate the outer edges of the universe or the inner workings of the atom. No other creature can imagine the future or reconstruct the past beyond the limits of its own life. How have humans, alone, been able to attain such thinking capabilities? As we look to the future of schooling, what should we, as educators, know and consider about how humans reason.

THE GENESIS OF PATTERN-SEEKING CAPABILITIES

Humans' inquisitiveness about the world around us is different and greater than the inquisitiveness of other animals. We've explored deep caves and high mountains. We've examined the coldest regions of the Antarctic and the hottest deserts of Africa. We have seen the bottom of the deepest ocean and the surfaces of planets we have not yet visited. We have the urge to explore every nook and cranny of our environment.

This chapter is adapted with permission from *The Biological Basis of Thinking and Learning*, University of California, Berkeley. Copyright © 2001 by Lawrence F. Lowery.

Although other animals explore and exhibit curiosity, the driving force that leads us into and through investigations is unique to humans—the desire to seek patterns.

Pattern seeking is a fundamental component of good thinking. To best understand the nature of such thinking, it is helpful to know how it developed in humans. This knowledge is useful for educators, who are responsible for teaching students to learn and who must know about the complex set of natural processes of which thinking is comprised. Biologists have theorized that our ability to inquire and develop pattern-seeking capabilities stemmed from our adaptation to being a nonspecialist animal. Some animals are adapted to survive in a particular environment; humans may adapt to live in almost any environment (National Research Council, 2000).

Biologists have learned about the adaptive similarities and differences among animals by applying their own capability to seek patterns. For example, a biologist who is curious about a particular survival characteristic, such as an animal's evolutionary adaptation that enables it to gather food, could sequentially compare all animals, from those that have specialized adaptations to those that have nonspecialized adaptations.

The biologist would place animals that are dependent on the environment in which they live at the specialized end of the arrangement. The koala bear is one such animal. It lives most of its life in the branches of gum trees in Australia, getting all of its sustenance—both water and nutrients—from the gum leaves. As long as it stays in the trees, food gathering is comparatively easy.

Animals at the specialized end of the spectrum are at risk if something happens to drastically change their environment. If a disease infects the gum trees and they die out, so does the koala bear. It is so specialized that it cannot survive elsewhere. A major change in an environment has a direct effect on the survival of specialized animals.

At the other end of the arrangement are the nonspecialized animals—those that can adapt to different environments or changes in environmental conditions. Primates are among the nonspecialists. If the nuts and fruits eaten by monkeys disappear, the monkeys search out another food source such as roots, shoots, worms, or grubs.

Along the continuum, the pattern seeker would note that all animals exhibit a natural tendency to explore, but toward the nonspecialist end, the need to explore is of greater importance. Nonspecialists live in changing environments. They are never sure where their next meal is coming from; thus they must always be alert for opportunities and learn about an environment in order to survive in it. Determining patterns is important to survival in varied environments.

Humans are the most nonspecialized food gatherers of all animals. They have learned to examine every niche in every environment, exploring, testing every possibility, rechecking if necessary, always looking for an opportunity. Compared to animals toward the opposite end of the spectrum, humans exhibit a constant, high level of curiosity and thinking capacities.

Unlike the other nonspecialists, humans have become specialists at being nonspecialists. Curious, stimulated by the unknown, we continually explore, investigate, and test. We use trial-and-error techniques when we don't know what to do. We speculate when we have some prior knowledge, perhaps hypothesizing and predicting as we proceed. We reflect on what happens, sometimes by observation, sometimes by gathering, assembling, and synthesizing data. We check and recheck what we think happens as it relates to our prior experiences. We incorporate the new experiences in a way that is understandable with what we knew before. This complex set of thinking processes that first enabled humans to gather food or escape danger has evolved further into a unique human adaptation of its own. Thus, in recent human history, some humans in cooperative societies have been freed to redirect their pattern-seeking capacities toward other interests—perhaps the nature of sounds, scratches on surfaces, moving objects, and so on. When enough knowledge (patterns) coalesced, fields of study appeared, such as music, art, and physics (National Research Council, 2000).

The wonderful mix of thinking processes that developed to enable us to seek and learn patterns has become the greatest survival capacity of our species.

THE BRAIN AND THINKING

Most people consider thinking and the brain as synonymous. A fine thinker is often referred to as "brainy." A "brainless" person is one who lacks intelligence. However, the brain and thinking are not synonymous. In fact, they are quite distinct.

The human brain is a physical organ that is estimated to contain about 100 billion cells at birth. At birth, the brain is about one-third of its eventual mass; within two years it doubles in size. During the next 15 years, many of its cells develop up to 600,000 connections between themselves and other cells (Maranto, 1984).

In the past 10 years we have learned much about the physiology of the brain—its electroconductivity, chemistry, and anatomy. Thinking, however, is like a ghost in the machinery. It is something beyond the physiological attributes. Imagine looking at a chessboard at mid-game. The physical placements of the pieces can be described, but where are the strategies of offense and defense? Similarly, imagine visiting a school classroom. Can you point to the "education" that takes place there? Thinking is to the brain as time is to a watch. The watch has hands and numerals, but where is the time? Time in a watch, strategies in a game, and education in a classroom are processes within physical configurations. And so, too, is thinking within the brain. Neurobiologists may identify activity among cells during a thought process, but with the billions of interactions that are possible within our heads, it is the process of thinking that is of prime importance, not the physiological components (Bransford, Brown, & Cocking, 1999).

In the past 10 years, neurobiologists have made significant breakthroughs in discovering what happens within the brain as it processes information. They are discovering what parts of our brains are used for what kinds of thought through inventive techniques that provide instantaneous, well-localized sig-

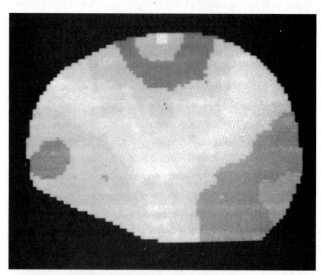

EEG: This technique detects electrical activity in the brain. The photo shows the brain activity in response to touch.

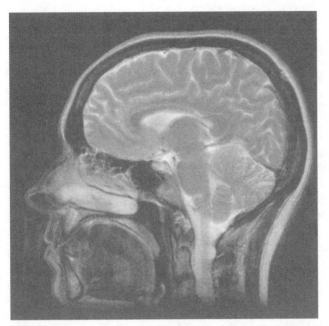

MRI: This technique takes a detailed image of the brain. It cannot detect function, but it can distinguish structures that are 1 centimeter apart.

nals of brain activity. Each technique provides a different view of the brain's processes.

The EEG (electroencephalograph) and MEG (magneto-encephalograph) were the earliest techniques developed for observing brain function. They record the brain's electrical impulses as fast as they happen, but they do not reveal where the event originates.

The EEG produces an image of the brain on a computer screen. The computer displays and records localized brain activity as the person performs tasks. The MEG measures both the positions of activities in the brain and the intensity of these activities.

Recently, EEG and MEG techniques were combined with magnetic resonance imaging (MRI), which provides detailed views of brain structures, to construct a computer-generated, three-dimensional picture of the brain from a set of two-dimensional magnetic resonance images. The program is able to trace precisely the boundaries of each cortical area of the brain. This non-invasive technique is called functional magnetic resonance imaging (fMRI). Positron emission tomography (PET) is a brain scan that measures blood flow in the brain. Increased blood flow indicates increased metabolic activity. Such scans are used to identify which areas of the brain carry out particular tasks. Much of the following information is based on findings from studies that used these techniques.

EARLY BRAIN DEVELOPMENT

Soon after conception, brain cells begin to divide and redivide at an astonishing rate. Beginning with just a few cells at the tip of the embryo, as many as 250,000 are reproduced every minute by the 20th week, and by the time of birth, some 200 billion have been created.

The number of brain cells produced is more than any individual needs. Overproduction is nature's way of making sure there are enough cells to handle the development of the numerous complex skills needed for survival. Before birth, the job of the brain cells is to get acquainted with the body that is developing around them. Cells do this by sending out connectors—axons and dendrites—that branch and connect with other brain cells. About half of these cells die before birth—many because they fail to connect to some part of the developing body and others through a pruning process that eliminates flawed neural connections (Begley, 1996; Marcus, Mulrine, & Wong, 1999).

During pregnancy, especially around the 20th week, risk factors such as vitamin deficiency, smoking, alcohol, certain chemicals, or excessive heat can prevent proper neural development or cause damage to neurons and their connections.

Brain cells continue to multiply after birth, but the production ceases before the end of the first year of life. After the first year, humans will generate some brain cells in certain parts of the brain, but essentially all they will ever have is in place. The mass of the brain, however, is only about one-third that of the adult brain. The brain becomes bigger after birth because brain cells grow in size and because the webbing of connections between and among cells increases. The number of new connections in the brain increases as a result of experience throughout one's life (Nash, 1997; *Newsweek*, 1997).

THE BRAIN'S FILING SYSTEM

By birth, the brain has organized itself into more than 40 different functional regions that broadly govern such things as vision, hearing, language, and muscle movement. The brain processes incoming sensory data into and through the functional regions as the sensory data enter through the avenues of the five senses: all that we see, hear, feel, smell, and taste. The five senses are the brain's only way to obtain data about the "outside" world.

To enhance the input, the brain constructs motor mechanisms that improve the gathering of information. This enhancement ranges from simple and automatic reflexes to thoughtful and deliberate explorations. When an event in the environment surprises us (e.g., something is seen that was never seen before or something happens that cannot be explained easily), our eyebrows rise and eyes widen. Raising the eyebrows is like opening the windows. It is the brain's way to let more light into the eyes and to increase the range of view. Widening of the eyes allows more visual information to enter the brain.

When something attracts the brain's attention, the brain may command the arm and hand muscles to grasp the object, turn it, feel it, and test it in other ways. The reception of these thoughtful and deliberate exploratory actions is processed into the brain's mapping systems.

As the perceptual sensory data enter the brain, the data are fragmented and distributed to the functional regions according to the general type of data the region records. For example, the non-language, sensory perceptions of the world are categorized in many different places: shapes are stored in one place, color in another; movement, sequence, and emotional states are all stored separately.

The neural processes that record the interaction between the brain and the event constitute a rapid sequence of numerous microperceptions (input) and microphysical actions (output) that take place almost simultaneously. Each occurs in separate functional regions of the brain and each is comprised of additional subdivisions. Visual input, for example, is segregated within the visual mapping region near the back of the brain into smaller systems that specialize for color, shape, and movement. These subsystems also subdivide. At the molecular level, one set of brain cells recognizes perpendicular lines, another only lines slanted at a one o'clock angle, another at two o'clock, and so on (Restak, 1980).

As a data storage system, the brain disassembles countless images into their parts and stores the parts in specialized brain cells. The benefit of this reduction strategy is that one cell can be called upon many times to identify a similar factor (e.g., whether something is horizontal or vertical) in other diverse objects. Each brain cell has the capacity to store fragments of many memories. These memories or characteristics of the world are broken down into their elemental parts—photons of light, molecules of smell, vibrations of sound waves—ready to be called up when a particular network of connections needs to be activated (The Diagram Group, 1983).

Aspects of language are also stored in various parts of the brain. Auditory, oral, visual (reading), and writing capacities are stored separately. The names of natural things, such as plants and animals, are recorded in one part of the brain; the names of objects, machines, and other human-made items are stored in another. Nouns are separated from verbs and phonemes from words (Jackendoff, 1994).

As the brain files away the perceptual information, it also constructs connections among the cells in the storage areas. The connections provide an organization of the relationships among different storage areas and are activated as systems and subsystems: *objects*, including their individual characteristics; *events*, the sequences of movements in time and space; and *actions of the learner*, what was done to an object and what happened as a result. An activated system is a construct of a concept, principle, or other idea (Swerdlow, 1995).

Neurobiologists have learned that pictures are not stored anywhere in the brain. The brain is not a camera-like device that stores detailed pictures of what is seen. There is no such thing as a photographic memory. Nor is the brain a recording device that stores and plays back what it hears. There are only patterns of connections within the brain, as changeable as they are numerous. When triggered, the connections that have been constructed reassemble the parts into the patterns that make up a memory (a concept, event, etc.). The quality of the reassembly depends on the quality of the original input.

MAKING CONNECTIONS

In general, enriched environments increase the number of brain connections. Connections are created when an individual becomes curious about something and is free to explore that curiosity. At such times, brain cells sprout thousands of new connectors—dendritic spines that grow out like tree branches. Any one cell can generate hundreds of thousands of connectors during its lifetime. The brain makes the new connectors available for the processing of sensory data and for incorporating that data into prior knowledge constructions (Wright, 1997).

Enriched environments, varied experiences, and piqued interest around a central topic stimulate the production of connectors, thus allowing for more storage options in response to the experience. Even a slight change for a learner, such as changing to a new seat in the classroom, will cause the brain to generate new dendritic branches and spines as it attempts to incorporate the new viewpoint and new relationships that the learner experiences among objects and people in the classroom. The brain adapts itself to cope with changes it encounters in its environment (Case, 1974).

New connectors are not necessarily permanent. They may gradually become permanent by being revisited—repeating the activity (practice), exploring the activity with some variation (rehearsal), or reflecting on the activity by talking about it. If the connections are not revisited, they may disintegrate and be lost forever. The adage "use it or lose it" applies most certainly to the establishment and retention of connectors within the brain (Diamond & Hopson, 1998).

The quality and extensiveness of the connections within the brain's systems constitute how well a person understands something or how well an individual can perform. Evidence indicates that the more connections you have, the better you are able to solve problems, think clearly, and understand events. The number of connections the brain constructs depends on the individual's interest in participating in an experience.

Generating the growth of dendrites, the threadlike extensions that grow from neurons (brain cells), is important. When dendrites grow, neurons make more connections to other neurons. When information within a dendritic system is reinforced through practice or rehearsal, the connections gradually become stable, permanent, and usable (*Scientific American*, 1992).

Increasing proper connections among the brain's neurons results in a better functioning brain. These connections result, in part, through inherited growth patterns within the genetic makeup of a person. They also develop in response to stimuli in the environment that the brain encodes as nerve impulses. This information is important for educators to know. Since brains increase dendritic growth as a result of new, enriching experiences, and since practice and rehearsal stabilize growth, the school environment can and should provide such experiences. Doing so will help students retain what they have experienced and increase the likelihood of their being able to apply that learning to new situations (Lowery, 1998).

As people climb the educational ladder, the number of branching connectors between and among brain cells (dendritic material) dramatically increases. Autopsy studies of brains found that very young children have fewer connectors than do school-age children. The brains of university graduates who remained mentally active had up to 40 percent more dendritic material than did the brains of high school dropouts. The brains of university graduates who were mentally inactive had fewer connectors than did those of graduates who were mentally active (Kotulak, 1996).

Some studies have shown that whenever the brain is challenged, brain cells sprout new dendrites (Diamond & Hopson, 1998). Healthy people can learn something new at any age by generating new connectors and integrating them into prior structures.

By piecing together research information from anthropologists, biologists, neurobiologists, psychologists, and psychobiologists, we know that learning depends on how we use our physical attributes: how our hands manipulate objects to find out about them, how our head tilts and turns to let our eyes and ears take in information, and how our body shifts and moves through space. These pattern-seeking gifts that distinguish us from other animals evolved from the need to survive in a changing environment. The pattern-seeking gifts are fundamental in the construction of knowledge.

CONSTRUCTING KNOWLEDGE

To construct knowledge, the brain takes in data through the sensory perceptions that enter through the body's five senses. Anything that a person does, perceives, thinks, or feels while acting in the world is processed through the complex systems of storage and pathways. If a student picks up a magnet, brings it toward another object, and feels the effect as that object is repelled or attracted by the magnet, that action is processed through the systems in the student's brain.

Although individuals construct basic knowledge through experience, the quality of the construction depends on how well the brain organizes and stores the relationships between and among aspects in the event—how the arm and hand are positioned to hold the magnet (the relationship of the learner to the object), how the magnet can be moved and manipulated (cause and effect relationships between the learner's actions and the observed results), and how other objects behave in the presence of the magnet (cause and effect relationships in an interaction between objects in the environment). While further exploring with magnets, learners link new perceptions to what they have already constructed in the brain's storage systems. They use this prior knowledge to interpret the new material in terms of the established knowledge. Without such connections, bits of information are isolated from the prior knowledge and are forgotten (Cowley & Underwood, 1998).

Educators have long praised the hands-on approach to teaching, but in spite of the praise, books replace experience very early in the education process and are almost the exclusive way by which students are taught from grade 4 through grade 12. Classrooms primarily are environments in which symbols are manipulated and substituted for experience (Lowery, 1989). When not doing assignments in books, students spend time listening to teachers or responding to their questions.

We can learn from books if our experiential foundation is well established. To learn geometry, we must have experience handling geometric forms and comparing them for similarities and differences. To learn about electricity, we must explore relationships among cells, wires, and bulbs. To read a word on a page, we must first have a concept for the word within ourselves. The power of well-written books is that they lead us beyond direct experiences and into abstractions of thought that cannot be reached directly.

Expert teachers never forget that it is only by using the senses while interacting with an environment that students come to recognize patterns and learn about the world around them.

REFERENCES

Begley, S. (1996, February 19). Your child's brain. *Newsweek*, 54–60.

Bransford, J. D., Brown, A. L., & Cocking, R. R. (Eds). (1999). *How people learn: Brain, mind, experience, and school.* Washington, DC: National Academy Press.

Case, R. (1974). "Structures and strictures, some functional limitations on the course of cognitive growth." *Cognitive Psychology, 16,* 544–573.

Cowley, G., & Underwood, A. (1998, June 15). Memory. *Newsweek,* 49–54.

Diagram Group, The. (1983). *The brain: A user's manual.* New York: Berkeley Books.

Diamond, M., & Hopson, J. (1998). *Magic trees of the mind: How to nurture your child's intelligence, creativity, and healthy emotions from birth through adolescence.* New York: Penguin Putnam.

Jackendoff, R. (1994). *Patterns in the mind: Language and human nature.* New York: Basic Books.

Kotulak, R. (1996). *Inside the brain: Revolutionary discoveries of how the mind works.* Kansas City, MO; Andrews & McMeel.

Lowery, L. F. (1989). *Thinking and learning.* Pacific Grove, CA: Critical Thinking Press.

Lowery, L. F. (1998, November). How new science curriculums reflect brain research. *Educational Leadership,* 26–30.

Maranto, G. (1984, May). Neuroscience: The mind within the brain. *Discover, 5*(5), 34–37, 40–43.

Marcus, D., Mulrine, A., & Wong, K. (1999, September 13). How kids learn. *U.S. News and World Report,* 44–52.

Nash, M. (1997, February 3). The brain. *Time Magazine,* 49–56.

National Research Council. (2000). *Inquiry and the National Science Education Standards.* Washington DC: Author.

Newsweek (1997, Spring). The brain (special issue).

Pinker, S. (1994). *The language instinct: How the mind creates language.* New York: William Morrow.

Restak, R. M. (1980). *The brain, the last frontier.* New York: Warner Books.

Scientific American (1992, September). The decade of the brain (special issue).

Swerdlow, J. L. (1995, June). Miracles of the brain. *National Geographic,* 2–40.

Wright, K. (1997, October). Babies, bonds, and brains. *Discover, 18*(10), 75–78.

32

A New Taxonomy of Educational Objectives

Robert J. Marzano

In the more than 40 years since the publication of *The Taxonomy of Educational Objectives, The Classification of Educational Goals* (Bloom, Engelhart, Furst, Hill, & Krathwohl, 1956), Bloom's Taxonomy, as it is frequently called in deference to Benjamin Bloom, the work's editor, has been used by educators in virtually every subject area at every grade level.

The expressed purpose of the taxonomy was to develop a codification system whereby educators could design learning objectives that have a hierarchic organization. That Bloom's Taxonomy is still used after four decades is a testament to its contribution to education. Indeed, it has been referred to as "arguably, one of the most influential educational monographs of the past half century" (Anderson & Sosniak, 1994, vii).

As influential as Bloom's Taxonomy has been, it is not without its critics (for a review, see Kreitzer & Madaus, 1994). One of the most common criticisms is that the taxonomy oversimplifies the nature of thought and its relationship to learning (Furst, 1994). Bloom's Taxonomy certainly expanded the conception of learning from a simple, unidimensional, behaviorist model to one that was multidimensional and more constructivist in nature. However, it assumed that a rather simple construct—difficulty—was the primary characteristic separating one level from another. Superordinate levels involved more difficult cognitive processes than did subordinate levels. The research conducted on Bloom's Taxonomy simply has not supported this structure. For example, educators who consistently were trained in the structure of Bloom's Taxonomy were not able to recognize questions at higher levels as more difficult than questions at lower levels of the taxonomy (see Fairbrother, 1975; Poole, 1972; Stanley & Bolton, 1957).

The problems with Bloom's Taxonomy were indirectly acknowledged by its authors, as indicated in their discussion of analysis: "it is probably more defensible educationally to consider analysis as an aid to fuller comprehension (a lower class level) or as a prelude to an evaluation of the material" (p. 144).

The authors also acknowledged problems with the taxonomy's structure in their discussion of evaluation:

> Although evaluation is placed last in the cognitive domain because it is regarded as requiring to some extent all the other categories of behavior, it is not necessarily the last step in thinking or problem solving. It is quite possible that the evaluation process will in some cases be the prelude to the acquisition of new knowledge, a new attempt at comprehension or application, or a new analysis and synthesis. (p. 185)

In short, the hierarchical structure of Bloom's Taxonomy simply does not hold together well from logical or empirical perspectives. As Rohwer and Sloane (1994) note, "The structure claimed for the hierarchy, then, resembles a hierarchy" (p. 47).

Recognizing the incredible contribution of Bloom's Taxonomy, it is time to design a new taxonomy of educational objectives—one that incorporates the best of what Bloom's work has to offer with what has been learned during the more than 40 years since Bloom's Taxonomy was published. This chapter briefly describes one effort to design a new taxonomy. For a more detailed discussion, consult *Designing a New Taxonomy of Educational Objectives* (Marzano, 2000).

As mentioned earlier, the major problem with the approach Bloom and his colleagues took is that it attempted to use degrees of difficulty as the basis for the differences between levels of the taxonomy. *Evaluation* activities were assumed to be more difficult than activities that involved *syntheses*, which were assumed to be more difficult than activities involving *analysis*, and so on. Any attempt to design a taxonomy based on difficulty of mental processing is doomed to failure. This is because of the well-established principle in psychology that even the most complex process can be learned to a level at which it is performed with little or no conscious effort (for discussions, see Anderson, 1983, 1990b, 1995; LaBerge & Samuels, 1974). The difficulty of a mental process is a function of at least two factors: the inherent complexity of the process in terms of steps involved, and the level of familiarity one has with the process. The complexity of a mental process is invariant—the number of steps and their relationship do not change. However, familiarity with a process changes over time. The more familiar we are with a process, the more quickly we execute it, and the easier it becomes.

Where mental processes cannot be ordered hierarchically in terms of difficulty, they can in terms of control; some processes influence control over the operation of other processes. The model used to develop the New Taxonomy as described in this chapter is presented in Figure 32.1.

The model depicted in Figure 32.1 not only describes how human beings decide whether to engage in a new task at any point in time, it also explains how information is processed once a decision to engage has been made. The model depicts three mental systems: the self-system system, the metacognitive system, and the cognitive system, all of which operate on the fourth component of the model: knowledge.

In this theory, a "new task" is defined as an opportunity to change whatever one is doing or attending to at a particular time. For example, assume that a student in a history class is daydreaming about an upcoming social activity. At that point in time, her energy and attention are on the upcoming social ac-

tivity—she is engaged in the task of daydreaming. However, if her teacher asks her to pay attention to some new information that is being presented about history, she is confronted with a decision regarding a new task. The decision the student makes and her subsequent actions will be determined by the interaction of her self, metacognitive, and cognitive systems, as well as her knowledge. Specifically, the self-system is engaged first, then the metacognitive system, and then the cognitive system. All three systems reference the student's store of knowledge.

THE THREE SYSTEMS AND KNOWLEDGE

The self-system includes a network of interrelated beliefs and goals (Harter, 1980; Markus & Ruvulo, 1990) that are used to make judgments about the advisability of engaging in a new task and determining the level of motivation one brings to a task (Garcia & Pintrich, 1991, 1993, 1995; Pintrich & Garcia, 1992). If a task is judged as important, the probability of success is high, and if positive emotion is generated or associated with the task, the individual is motivated to engage in the task (Ajzen, 1985; Ajzen & Fishbein, 1977, 1980; Ajzen & Madden, 1986). If the new task is evaluated as having low relevance and/or low probability of success and has an associated negative emotion, motivation to engage in the task is low. To be motivated to attend to the new history information, then, the student in the history class would have to perceive the information as more important than the social event, believe she can comprehend the information, and have no strong negative emotions associated with it.

If a new task is selected, the metacognitive system is engaged. One of the initial jobs of the metacognitive system is to set goals relative to the new task (Schank & Abelson, 1977). For example, the student in the history class might set a goal to understand the new content just enough to pass a test on it. The metacognitive system is also responsible for designing strategies for accomplishing a set goal (Sternberg, 1977, 1984a, 1984b, 1986a, 1986b). In terms of the student in the history class, then, the metacognitive system is responsible for setting learning goals relative to the new information and designing strategies to accomplish those goals. Once engaged, the metacognitive system continually interacts with the cognitive system.

The cognitive system is responsible for effectively processing the information used to complete a task. It involves analytic operations such as making inference, comparing, and classifying. For example, as the student in the history class listens to the new information, she undoubtedly makes inferences about it, compares it with what she already knows, and so on.

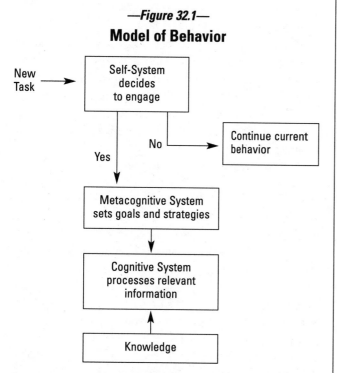

—*Figure 32.1*—
Model of Behavior

Reprinted by permission of the publisher from *Designing a New Taxonomy of Educational Objectives* by Robert Marzano. © 2000 by Corwin Press.

Finally, relative to any new task, success depends on the amount of knowledge an individual has about that task (Anderson, 1995; Lindsay & Norman, 1977). For example, the extent to which the history student achieves her learning goals would depend to a great extent on her prior knowledge about the history topic.

The various components of the three systems and the various domains of knowledge are depicted in Figure 32.2.

IMPROVING ON BLOOM'S TAXONOMY

How, then, does the model depicted in Figures 32.1 and 32.2 improve on Bloom's efforts? It does so in at least two ways. First, it presents a "model" or a "theory" of human thought rather than a "framework." Technically, models and theories are systems that allow one to predict phenomena; frameworks are loosely organized sets of principles that describe characteristics of a given phenomenon, but do not necessarily allow for the prediction of phenomena. (For a discussion of models, theories, and frameworks, see Anderson, 1990a.) By defini-

tion, Bloom's Taxonomy is a framework in that it describes six general categories of information processing. They are useful categories in helping educators understand the multifaceted nature of learning. Indeed, in his 1977 edition of *The Conditions of Learning*, Gagne commented on the taxonomy authors' "ingenious" contributions to an understanding of the various categories of learning. However, Bloom's Taxonomy was not designed to predict specific behaviors (Rohwer & Sloane, 1994) and is, therefore, not a model or theory. The depiction in Figures 32.1 and 32.2 allows for the prediction of specific behaviors within specific situations. For example, given an understanding of an individual's beliefs within the self-system, one can predict the attention that will be paid to a given task and the motivation that will be displayed.

Second, (and more important relative to the discussion here), the theory presented here improves on Bloom's effort in that it allows for the design of a hierarchical system of human thought from the perspective of flow of information.

In terms of flow of information, processing always starts with the self-system, proceeds to the metacognitive system,

—*Figure 32.2*—
The Three Systems and Knowledge

Self-System		
Beliefs about the importance of the knowledge	Beliefs about efficacy (ability to learn)	Emotions associated with knowledge
Overall Motivation to Learn		

Metacognitive System			
Specifying learning goals	Monitoring the execution of knowledge	Monitoring clarity	Monitoring accuracy

Cognitive System											
Retrieval		Comprehension		Analysis					Knowledge Utilization		
Recall	Execution	Synthesis	Representation	Matching	Classifying	Error Analysis	Generalizing	Specifying	Decision Making	Problem Solving	Experimental Inquiry	Investigation

Knowledge Domain		
Information	Mental Procedures	Physical Procedures

© 2000 by R. J. Marzano, unpublished workshop materials. Reprinted by permission.

then to the cognitive system, and finally to the knowledge domains. In addition, the status of the various factors within one system affects the status of the various factors within lower systems. For example, if the self-system includes no beliefs that would render a given task important, then the individual will not engage in the task or will engage with low motivation. If the task is deemed important but a clear goal is not established by the metacognitive system, execution of the task will break down. If clear goals have been established and effectively monitored but the information processing functions within the cognitive system do not operate effectively, the task will not be carried out. The three systems, then, represent a true hierarchy in terms of flow of processing.

APPLYING THE NEW TAXONOMY MODEL

The three systems of thought as they relate to knowledge make for a fairly straightforward taxonomy of educational objectives as depicted in Figure 32.3.

The six levels depicted in Figure 32.3 are produced by considering the four components of the cognitive system as four taxonomic levels below the level of metacognition. The explanation for this goes beyond the scope of this chapter (see Marzano, 2000, for a detailed discussion). Briefly, however, retrieval of knowledge (Level 1) is a prerequisite for the comprehension of knowledge (Level 2). Similarly, individuals must have a firm comprehension of knowledge (i.e., be able to synthesize and represent it) to be able to analyze (Level 3) the knowledge. Finally, the ability to utilize the knowledge (i.e., to solve problems with it, make decisions using it, and the like) (Level 4), requires the use of analysis skills (Level 3). Given that the metacognitive and self-systems are superordinate to the cognitive system, the hierarchic levels of the cognitive system constitute four subordinate levels to the metacognitive and self-systems.

To illustrate how the taxonomic objectives depicted in Figure 32.3 might be applied to school content, consider the example of information about the heart that might be taught in a health class. At Level 1 (retrieval) learners would be expected to remember or recognize critical features of the heart but would not be expected to differentiate critical from noncritical elements. At Level 2 (comprehension) learners would be expected to know the critical versus noncritical elements of the heart and identify the basic structure of information about the heart—superordinate versus subordinate ideas (synthesis). At Level 2, learners would also be expected to construct an accurate symbolic representation of information about the heart (representation). At Level 3 (analysis), learners would be ex-

pected to accurately complete tasks such as identifying how the heart is similar to and different from other organs like the liver (matching); identifying the general category of organs to which the heart belongs (classifying); and constructing generalizations about the heart based on known facts (generalizing). At Level 4 (utilization), learners would be expected to accurately complete tasks such as making decisions about healthy and unhealthy physical habits based on knowledge of the heart (decision making) and generating and testing hypotheses about the heart (experimental inquiry). At Level 5 (metacognition), learners would be expected to examine their goals relative to learning about the heart and examine the clarity and accuracy of their understanding of the heart. Finally, at Level 6 (self), learners would be expected to successfully engage in tasks such as identifying and analyzing how important knowledge about the heart is to them (examining importance) and their overall level of motivation for learning about the heart (examining motivation).

Knowledge about the heart is informational. As depicted in Figure 32.2, knowledge can also be in the form of mental and physical procedures. To illustrate how the New Taxonomy might apply to mental procedures, consider the process of using a specific search engine on the Internet. At Level 1 (retrieval), learners would be able to find information via the search engine without significant error (execution). At Level 2 (comprehension), learners would be able to identify the basic steps involved in using the search engine and their order of execution (synthesis) and represent the flow of execution in some graphic form like a flow chart (representation). At Level 3 (analysis), learners would be able to identify common errors made during the use of the search engine (error analysis) and make predictions based on their knowledge of the process (specification). At Level 4 (knowledge utilization), learners would be able to use the search engine as an aid in solving problems (problem solving) or investigating a past event (investigation). At Level 5 (metacognition), learners would be able to monitor the effectiveness of their use of the search engine (process monitoring) and determine how clear they are about its use (monitoring clarity). At Level 6 (self), learners would be able to identify and analyze beliefs about their skill at using the search engine (examining efficacy) and identify and analyze their emotional response to its use (examining emotional response).

Finally, to illustrate how the New Taxonomy might apply to physical procedures, consider the skill of throwing a baseball. At Level 1 (retrieval), learners would be able to throw a baseball without making significant errors (execution). At Level 2

—*Figure 32.3*—

Objectives for the Levels of the New Taxonomy

Level 6: Self	Examining Importance	The learner can identify how important the knowledge is to him or her and the reasoning underlying this perception.
	Examining Efficacy	The learner can identify beliefs about his or her ability to improve competence or understanding relative to the knowledge and the reasoning underlying this perception.
	Examining Emotional Response	The learner can identify emotional responses to the knowledge and the reasons for these responses.
	Examining Motivation	The learner can identify his or her level of motivation to improve competence or understanding relative to the knowledge and the reasons for this level of motivation.
Level 5: Metacognition	Goal Specification	The learner can set and plan for goals relative to the knowledge.
	Process Monitoring	The learner can monitor the execution of the knowledge.
	Monitoring Clarity	The learner can determine the extent to which he or she has clarity about the knowledge.
	Monitoring Accuracy	The learner can determine the extent to which he or she is accurate about the knowledge.
Level 4: Utilization	Decision Making	The learner can use the knowledge to make decisions or can make decisions about the use of knowledge.
	Problem Solving	The learner can use the knowledge to solve problems or can solve problems about the knowledge.
	Experimental Inquiry	The learner can use the knowledge to generate and test hypotheses or can generate and test hypotheses about the knowledge.
	Investigation	The learner can use the knowledge to conduct investigations or can conduct investigations about the knowledge.
Level 3: Analysis	Matching	The learner can identify important similarities and differences between knowledge.
	Classifying	The learner can identify superordinate and subordinate categories related to the knowledge.
	Error Analysis	The learner can identify errors in the presentation or use of the knowledge.
	Generalizing	The learner can construct new generalizations or principles based on the knowledge.
	Specifying	The learner can identify specific applications or logical consequences of the knowledge.

(continued)

—Figure 32.3—
Objectives for the Levels of the New Taxonomy *(Continued)*

Level 2: Comprehension	Synthesis	The learner can identify the basic structure of the knowledge and the critical as opposed to noncritical characteristics.
	Representation	The learner can construct an accurate symbolic representation of the knowledge differentiating critical from noncritical elements.
Level 1: Retrieval	Recall	The learner can identify or recognize features of information but does not necessarily understand the structure of knowledge or cannot differentiate critical from noncritical components.
	Execution	The learner can perform a procedure without significant error but does not necessarily understand how and why the procedure works.

Reprinted by permission of the publisher from *Designing a New Taxonomy of Educational Objectives* by Robert Marzano. © 2000 by Corwin Press.

(comprehension), learners would be able to describe the basic process of throwing a baseball (synthesis) and depict the process in graphic or flow chart form (representation). At Level 3 (analysis), learners would be able to successfully engage in tasks such as making deductive predictions about throwing a baseball (specifying) and identifying the general category of physical activity to which throwing a baseball belongs (classifying). At Level 4 (knowledge utilization), learners would be able to use the skill of throwing a baseball to help solve problems (problem solving) and to generate and test hypotheses (experimental inquiry). At Level 5 (metacognition), learners would be able to establish and carry out goals relative to increasing their skill at throwing a baseball (goal specification) and monitor how well they are executing the skill (process monitoring). Finally, at Level 6 (self), learners would be able to identify and analyze their beliefs about their ability to throw a baseball (examining efficacy) and their motivation to increase their skill at throwing a baseball (examining motivation).

The New Taxonomy can be used to construct tasks that actively engage learners in thought processes along the various levels of the taxonomy. Figure 32.4 on the next page provides questions or cues a teacher might use to construct these tasks.

USING THIS TAXONOMY FOR DEEPER UNDERSTANDING

While Bloom's Taxonomy has served educators and education well for almost five decades, it is time to update the taxonomy with new information about the nature of thinking and the nature of knowledge. This chapter has briefly described a New Taxonomy of educational objectives that is organized around three systems of thought that appear to have a hierarchical structure (the self-system, the metacognitive system, and the cognitive system). The various components of these three systems can be organized into six levels of thought (retrieval, comprehension, analysis, utilization, metacognition, self) that apply to three types of knowledge (information, mental procedures, and physical procedures). Educators can use this New Taxonomy to structure classroom tasks that will challenge students and deepen their understanding of knowledge along with their understanding of themselves as learners.

REFERENCES

Ajzen, I. (1985). From intentions to actions: A theory of planned behavior. In J. Kuhl & J. Beckman (Eds.), *Action-control: From cognition to behavior.* Heidelberg: Springer.

Ajzen, I., & Fishbein, M. (1977). Attitude-behavior relations: A theoretical analysis and review of empirical research. *Psychological Bulletin, 84,* 888–918.

Ajzen, I., & Fishbein, M. (1980). *Understanding attitudes and predicting social behavior.* Englewood Cliffs, NJ: Prentice Hall.

Ajzen, I., & Madden, T. J. (1986). Prediction of goal-directed behavior: Attitudes, intentions, and perceived behavioral control. *Journal of Experimental Social Psychology, 22,* 453–474.

Anderson, J. R. (1983). *The architecture of cognition.* Cambridge, MA: Harvard University Press.

Anderson, J. R. (1990a). *The adaptive character of thought.* Hillsdale, NJ: Lawrence Erlbaum.

—Figure 32.4—

Cues and Questions for the Levels of the New Taxonomy

Level 6: Self	Examining Importance	How important is this to you? What is your reasoning? How logical is your reasoning?
	Examining Efficacy	How capable are you to learn this? What is your reasoning? How logical is your reasoning?
	Examining Emotional Response	What is your emotional response to this? What is the reasoning behind your response? How logical is your reasoning?
	Examining Motivation	What is your level of motivation to learn this? What is your reasoning? How logical is your reasoning?
Level 5: Metacognition	Goal Specification	What is your goal relative to learning this? What is your plan for accomplishing this goal?
	Process Monitoring	What is working well and what is not working well relative to your use of this skill or process?
	Monitoring Clarity	About what are you clear and about what are you not clear in terms of this knowledge?
	Monitoring Accuracy	About what are you accurate and about what are you not accurate in terms of this knowledge?
Level 4: Utilization	Decision Making	How can this knowledge be used to help make a decision? What decision can be made about the knowledge?
	Problem Solving	How can this knowledge be used to help solve a problem? What problem can be solved about the knowledge?
	Experimental Inquiry	How can this knowledge be used to help generate and test a hypothesis? What hypotheses can be generated and tested about the knowledge?
	Investigation	How can this knowledge be used to help investigate something?
Level 3: Analysis	Matching	How is this knowledge similar to and different from other knowledge?
	Classifying	To what general category does this knowledge belong? What are subcategories of this knowledge?
	Error Analysis	What errors (if any) have been made in the presentation or use of this knowledge?
	Generalizing	What generalizations can be inferred from this knowledge?
	Specifying	What predictions can be made and proven based on this knowledge?

(continued)

—*Figure 32.4*—

Cues and Questions for the Levels of the New Taxonomy *(Continued)*

Level 2: Comprehension	Synthesis	What is the basic structure of this knowledge—main ideas versus supporting ideas, sequence of information, relationship between the parts?
	Representation	How can the basic structure of this knowledge be represented symbolically or graphically?
Level 1: Retrieval	Recall	Is this accurate about the knowledge?
	Execution	Perform this skill or process.

© 2000 R. J. Marzano, unpublished workshop materials.

Anderson, J. R. (1990b). *Cognitive psychology and its implications* (3rd ed.). New York: W. H. Freeman.

Anderson, J. R. (1995). *Learning and memory: An integrated approach.* New York: John Wiley & Sons.

Anderson, L. W., & Sosniak, L. A. (Eds). (1994). *Bloom's taxonomy: A forty-year retrospective: Ninety-third yearbook of the National Society for the Study of Education.* Chicago: University of Chicago Press.

Bloom, B. S., Engelhart, M. D., Furst, E. J., Hill, W. H., & Krathwohl, D. R. (Eds.). (1956). *Taxonomy of educational objectives: The classification of educational goals. Handbook I: Cognitive domain.* New York: David McKay.

Fairbrother, R. W. (1975). The reliability of teachers' judgments of the ability being tested by multiple-choice items. *Educational Researcher, 17*(3), 202–210.

Furst, E. J. (1994). Bloom's taxonomy: Philosophical and educational issues. In L. W. Anderson & L. A. Sosniak (Eds.), *Bloom's taxonomy: A forty-year retrospective: Ninety-third yearbook of the National Society for the Study of Education* (pp. 28–40). Chicago: University of Chicago Press.

Gagne, R. M. (1977). *The conditions of learning* (3rd ed.). New York: Holt, Rinehart & Winston.

Garcia T., & Pintrich, P. R. (1991). *The effects of autonomy on motivation, use of learning strategies, and performance in the college classroom.* Paper presented at the annual meeting of the American Psychological Association, San Francisco, CA.

Garcia, T., & Pintrich, P. R. (1993). *Self-schemas as goals and their role in self-regulated learning.* Paper presented at the annual meeting of the American Psychological Association, Toronto, Canada.

Garcia, T., & Pintrich, P. R. (1995). *The role of selves in adolescents' perceived competence and self-regulation.* Paper presented at the annual meeting of the American Educational Research Association, San Francisco, CA.

Harter, S. (1980). The perceived competence scale for children. *Child Development, 51,* 218–235.

Kreitzer, A. E., & Madaus, G. F. (1994). Empirical investigations of the hierarchial structure of the taxonomy. In L. W. Anderson & L. A. Sosniak (Eds.), *Bloom's taxonomy: A forty-year retrospective: Ninety-third yearbook of the National Society for the Study of Education* (pp. 64–81). Chicago: University of Chicago Press.

LaBerge, D., & Samuels, S. J. (1974). Toward a theory of automatic information processing in reading. In H. Singer & R. B. Riddell (Eds.), *Theoretical models and processes of reading* (pp. 548–579). Newark, DE: International Reading Association.

Lindsay, P. H., & Norman, D. A. (1977). *Human information processing.* New York: Academic Press.

Markus, H., & Ruvulo, A. (1990). Possible selves: Personalized representations of goals. In L. Pervin (Ed.), *Goal concepts in psychology* (pp. 211–241). Hillsdale, NJ: Lawrence Erlbaum.

Marzano, R. J. (2000). *Designing a new taxonomy of educational objectives.* Thousand Oaks, CA: Corwin Press.

Pintrich, P. R., & Garcia, T. C. (1992, April). *An integrated model of motivation and self-regulated learning.* Paper presented at the annual meeting of the American Educational Research Association, San Francisco, CA.

Poole, R. L. (1972). Characteristics of the taxonomy of educational objectives, cognitive domain: A replication. *Psychology in the Schools, 9*(1), 83–88.

Rohwer, W. D. & Sloane, K. (1994). Psychological perspectives. In L. W. Anderson & L. A. Sosniak (Eds.), *Bloom's taxonomy: A forty-year retrospective. Ninety-third yearbook of the National Society for the Study of Education* (pp. 4–63). Chicago: University of Chicago Press.

Schank, R. C., & Abelson, R. (1977). *Scripts, plans, goals and understanding.* Hillsdale, NJ: Lawrence Erlbaum.

Stanley, J. C., & Bolton, D. (1957). A review of Bloom's taxonomy of educational objectives and J. R. Gerberich's specimen objective test items: A guide to achievement test construction. *Educational and Psychological Measurement, 17*(4), 631–634.

Sternberg, R. J. (1977). *Intelligence, information processing and analogical reasoning: The componential analysis of human abilities.* Hillsdale, NJ: Lawrence Erlbaum.

Sternberg, R. J. (1984a). *Beyond IQ: A triarchic theory of human intelligence.* New York: Cambridge University Press.

Sternberg, R. J. (1984b). Mechanisms of cognitive development: A componential approach. In R. J. Sternberg (Ed.), *Mechanisms of cognitive development* (pp. 163–186). New York: W. H. Freeman.

Sternberg, R. J. (1986a). Inside intelligence. *American Scientist, 74,* 137–143.

Sternberg, R. J. (1986b). *Intelligence applied.* New York: Harcourt Brace Jovanovich.

V

Human Variability and Thinking

It is acceptance and trust that make it possible for each bird to sing its own song — confident that it will be heard, even by those who sing with a different voice.

— BARBARA HATELEY &
WARREN H. SCHMIDT
A Peacock in the Land of Penguins:
A Tale of Diversity and Discovery

Introduction

Sandra Parks

Throughout history, humankind has pondered how people think, learn, create new products, derive meaning, make decisions, and solve problems. Various psychological, philosophical, and scientific theories have proposed cultural, biological, social, and spiritual explanations for differences in thinking.

During the last 50 years, cognitive scientists and medical investigators have conducted unprecedented research on how people process information. Educators have attempted to use brain research, inventories of learning styles, multiple intelligences, social and emotional learning activities, critical thinking strategies, and problem-based learning to improve the quality of students' thinking.

In addition to physiological and cognitive differences among individuals, the influences of gender and culture on thinking, learning, and problem solving are increasingly acknowledged. Gender studies underscore social and emotional influences that affect how boys and girls perceive and conceptualize new learning and how well they achieve in various disciplines and at various stages of development.

As multicultural education has become better defined and more widely practiced, educators have recognized cultural influences on constructing knowledge. Teachers now employ a variety of instructional methods to increase learning capacities of all their students. Varying teaching techniques to account for cognitive diversity assures that each student experiences some learning activities well suited to the individual's learning preferences.

The more we know about human variability in thinking and learning, the more complex teachers' decision making becomes. As educators ponder the interaction of physical functioning, language, culture, gender, and class for individual students—and try to account for such differences among individuals in the classroom—several practical and philosophical issues emerge:

- To what extent should curriculum content, organization, and assessment procedures be modified to account for these differences?
- To what extent should instructional methods be modified if a substantial number of students share similar cognitive traits based on physical functioning, language, culture, gender, and class?
- To what extent should students' natural cognitive traits be mediated to promote school achievement as they learn bodies of knowledge whose structure, procedures, and performances of understanding may differ noticeably from students' own cultural preferences?
- When we teach students to use the thinking and learning strategies based on European theories of knowledge and analytical thinking, do these newly acquired cognitive skills supplement—not supplant or diminish—the mental habits and dispositions that are valuable in students' own social contexts?

To resolve such complex instructional dilemmas, teachers, curriculum specialists, and staff development coordinators are becoming increasingly familiar with the insights into human diversity offered by specialists in cognitive psychology, cross-cultural communication, and brain research. Educators then are modifying instructional practices based on the relevance of such information to each learning community. In the process, teachers and school administrators are carrying out action research, however informal, to decide whether translating insights about human variability into classroom practice improves students' understanding and achievement.

Translating educational theory into practice is seldom a straight line from principles to program development to professional development, to classroom implementation to improved student performance. During the last two decades school districts' efforts to improve students' thinking have demonstrated that incorporating insights about variability in thinking into classroom practice requires long-term commitment. Successful programs feature some common characteristics:

• Teachers, administrators, school boards, and parents believe that improving students' thinking and learning is valuable and that the proposed intervention is likely to be effective.

• Modifying curriculum and instruction to reflect cognitive diversity requires time and reflective practice.

• A commitment of five to eight years is a realistic time frame to demonstrate effective practice in program development, professional development, and initial implementation.

• All stakeholders are clear about the benefits to students of putting cognitive theories into classroom practice and agree on how student gains will be evaluated.

• Staff development parallels teachers' own intellectual and professional growth and incorporates their practical knowledge of effective teaching.

• Modifications in instructional methodology are consistent with both the structures of the academic disciplines and the thinking and learning preferences of students.

• Teachers and students understand standards of effective thinking and learning, use the language associated with selected thinking or learning processes, and demonstrate the behavioral dispositions, as well as the cognitive principles, associated with them.

• All stakeholders respect the reflective thinking of individuals and the reflective practice of teachers, creating school cultures that are truly communities of inquiry and respect.

• Successful initiatives promote the social, emotional, moral, and spiritual growth of students and teachers, as well as the intellectual development involved in learning.

This section focuses on recognizing differences among students and suggesting ways of responding flexibly to the human variability found within each family, classroom, school, and community. The section opens with Armando Lozano's overview of stylistic differences, as described by a wide range of theoreticians. Next, Robert Sternberg explains differences in thinking styles. David Lazear, building on Howard Gardner's theory of multiple intelligences, acquaints us with eight forms of intelligence and how to appreciate and develop them in the classroom. David Martin describes the contributions of thinking skills programs to special-needs youngsters.

The influence of culture on thinking, problem solving, and decision making is explored from a variety of viewpoints. Douglas Brenner and Sandra Parks describe how culture affects thinking. Next Yvette Jackson provides strategies for working with those cultural differences. Ruby Payne describes the impact on thinking of growing up in an environment of poverty, with suggestions for ways of working with those children. Finally, Lawrence Lowery helps us understand why developmental differences in learning rates must also be considered in planning for curriculum, instruction, and assessment.

Improving instruction by addressing human intellectual variability is an approach to school reform that moves beyond the faddishness of present educational practice. It calls on teachers and students to demonstrate a degree of intellectual rigor, personal reflection, interpersonal awareness and respect, and community culture that is sought, but not yet realized, in schools and in the larger community.

33

A Survey of Thinking and Learning Styles

Armando Lozano

The shoe that fits one person pinches another; there is no recipe for living that fits all cases.

—Carl G. Jung

Identifying the various processes by which a student effectively acquires knowledge and develops skills is one of the most difficult tasks of the teacher, counselor, or anyone interested in promoting student learning. The overview of thinking styles presented here can help educators make sense of the differences in students' thinking processes and study ways of enhancing learning.

The thinking styles involve a series of indicators that affect learning situations in different, but equally important ways. The first indicator to consider is the understanding of and ability to face and resolve problematic situations in a way that depends mainly on the person's cognitive structure and particular kinds of experiences as well as the individual's own interpretation of the situation based on his or her personality structure (Hirsh & Kummerow, 1989). Another indicator is the learning attitude, from which acquisition, storage, and recovery of information depend in great measure (Woolfolk, 1996). A third indicator is the fact that each individual has a different way of assigning significance, independently from the academic group to which he or she belongs, in which motivation plays a very important role (Dunn & Dunn, 1978).

These indicators can help as a frame of reference for the construction of theories that explain, understand, and predict the differences between people with similar characteristics but different potentials.

Psychological investigation during the last decades has drawn explicit conclusions about why learning varies from one individual to another (Santos, 1992). People's individual differences give rise to diverse leanings and preferences in learning, and even in thinking, which can be considered "styles."

LEARNING STYLES AND OTHER TYPES

The concept of style is not new in educational psychology. Various authors have developed their own models about differences in the ways in which people perceive, process, and conceptualize information. Guild and Garger (1985) made an inventory of the theories about teaching and learning styles in the mid-1980s. For them, the term "style" designated a particular way of performing activities or behaving, such as speaking in public, writing, or practicing a sport. The same idea can be applied to learning and thinking.

Some authors have labeled these styles as cognitive (Witkin & Goodenough, 1981; Kagan & Kogan, 1970). Others have referred to them as learning styles (Kolb, 1982; Dunn & Dunn, 1978) or studying styles (Castañeda & López, 1992). Others have called these differences types of personality (Jung, 1923; Myers, 1987). And still others have considered them to be thinking styles (Sternberg, 1988). It's not our purpose in this paper to detail every model of these theories, but just to mention them as background in the field.

Among the theories of styles, Grigorenko & Sternberg (1997) have distinguished three principal approaches:

1. The cognition-centered approach, which deals with the characteristic ways in which people perform intellectually; the dependence or independence of the field, that is, the ability to differentiate an object from its context; and impulsiveness versus reflection as a way of reacting to various options. The works of Witkin, Kagan and Kogan, Klein, Fowler, and others are included in this category.

2. The personality-centered approach, going back to Carl Jung's initial work (1923) and later developed by Isabel Briggs Myers and Katharine Briggs. Besides Jung's first three dimensions, this approach includes a fourth—lifestyle—that refers to the attitude toward the external world and includes "judgment" and "perception." The three Jung initially focused on

were sensation and intuition, thinking and feeling, and extroversion and introversion. Authors such as Gregorc and Miller also focus on this personality-centered approach.

3. The activity-centered approach, which more specifically focuses on teaching and learning. Kolb (1982) outlines four styles: convergent, divergent, assimilating, and accommodating, each one formed by the union of two variables in a Cartesian plan. Dunn & Dunn (1978) alternate the styles based on certain elements present or absent in learning situations: environmental elements (sound, illumination, temperature, and design or physical distribution of the area); emotional elements (motivation, persistence, responsibility, and structure); sociological elements (partners, individualization, and small groups); and physical elements (perceptual, recesses, timing, and mobility). The work of Renzulli and Smith is also included in this approach.

As mentioned previously, the factors or elements of the styles identified by the various authors can be affected by the individual's environment or other external matters and the relationship between the person and the environment.

THINKING STYLES

With the expansion and diffusion of theories about learning styles over the last 10 years in the United States, Canada, and Mexico, it may not be strange that educators facing the new millennium know that their students can differ in their preferences or prejudices to learn or study. But are there also differences in the ways people think? What mechanisms of personality are involved in making a person think in a specific way? Do cognitive, attitudinal, and emotional aspects have to be combined to determine ways of thinking?

We can observe that beyond theories or models of learning, teaching, studying, or cognition styles, few known works actually attempt to explain the various ways in which people think.

But do we all think in the same way? Nickerson, Perkins, and Smith (1985) outline dichotomies in some authors' thinking. I will refer to only two pairs and try to illustrate them with fragments of well-known movies:

1. Guilford's convergent and divergent thinking. When a person tries to solve a problem, he or she can think in terms of just one solution (convergence) or of several possible solutions (divergence).

Let's think for a moment of a scene in Disney's cartoon movie *Hercules*, in which Hercules fights with a dragon to demonstrate to people watching him that he is a hero. In the first confrontation, Hercules cuts off the dragon's head, think-

ing that it is the only way to kill the creature. To everyone's surprise, the dragon generates two new heads every time one is cut, and there comes a moment in which the dragon has many heads. Then someone shouts at Hercules, asking whether cutting heads is the only thing he knows how to do. Hercules's convergence (in which killing the creature equates to cutting off its head) turns into divergence when he triggers an avalanche in the mountain to crush the dragon and finally beats him.

2. De Bono's vertical, or linear, and lateral thinking. In the framework of creativity, vertical or linear thinking is the conventional or logical approach, whereas lateral thinking is a leap from imagination that can fall into the absurd, but with novel results. Now let's think of another Disney cartoon movie: *The Sword in the Stone*. There is a confrontation between the magician Merlin and the witch. The rules are that they can turn into known animals and that no black dragons or disappearing acts are accepted. Time and again the opponents turn into various animals trying to beat their rival, until the witch cheats and turns into a purple dragon (although according to her, no rules have been broken because the prohibition was against black dragons). Merlin looks defenseless, and when the witch attacks, he disappears. The witch accuses him of cheating, and you can hear Merlin's voice saying that he did not disappear but turned into a tiny microorganism, and that he has infected her with a rare illness. Conclusion: Merlin wins the confrontation. Maybe the idea of turning into an infectious microorganism was unconventional, in the strictest sense, given the nature of the fight.

How do thinking styles fit in with the differences between convergent and divergent thinking? Between intuitive thinking and a more rational approach? To begin with, we could consider that just as with learning styles, some people lean toward thinking in a specific way without eliminating the possibility of exercising their thinking in the opposite direction or in line with other alternatives (as in the case of theories that propose more than two styles of thinking) or even multiple combinations. What factors determine thinking styles? Are creative thinkers different from critical thinkers? Do some people interchange these ways of thinking on purpose?

One of the experts in thinking that considers this to be so is de Bono (1986), who talks about six ways of thinking in his book *Six Thinking Hats*. These are six hats that the same person can interchange to think. Each hat has a color that symbolizes its essence and is generally associated with objects and situations that are easy to remember (see Figure 33.1).

—*Figure 33.1*—
De Bono's Thinking Hats

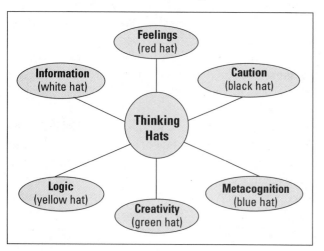

Information, logic, emotions, caution, creativity, and metacognition are six options that a person can handle in an alternating way. There might also be individuals who are more logical, whereas others might be more emotional, or perhaps more creative.

The first of de Bono's six hats is the white hat (representing virgin, pure, uncontaminated information). A person who wears this hat is neutral and objective when presenting information, and does not make interpretations or give opinions.

The red hat represents fire, anger, emotions, and feelings, as well as premonition and intuition. A person wearing this hat legitimizes emotions and feelings as an important part of thinking.

The black hat reflects what is bad, negative, the reason something won't work. A thinker with this hat points out what is wrong, incorrect, or mistaken. What's more, he points out why something will not work.

The yellow hat (sunlight, brightness and optimism, what is positive and constructive) is the counterpart of the black hat. The yellow-hat thinker is idealistic and gives hope. Her perspectives are generally positive; most things have a solution.

The green hat (fertility, creativity, generation from nothing, nature) symbolizes that its wearer is a person who offers creative solutions to problems, offers alternatives, and has an intense imagination.

The blue hat represents what is above—the sky, moderation and control, the orchestra conductor, the metacognitive aspect. A blue-hat thinker knows which hat to wear when needed. He thinks about thinking and is responsible for syn-

thesis, the global vision. He also is the one who has the last word.

De Bono (1986) highlights the idea of balance between white and red (rational versus emotional), black and yellow (negative versus positive), and green and blue (creativity versus metacognition). People who tend to polarize themselves by overusing one of the options can strive for better balance in these areas.

Sternberg (1988), in his triarchic theory of intelligence, mentions three variants: a person's internal and external worlds and the relationship between them. These three are part of his tridimensional approach to intelligence:

- Componential (analytical thinking)
- Experimental (creative thinking)
- Contextual (adaptive or successful thinking)

When Sternberg describes the roles personality and motivation play in the intellectual skills he identifies, he introduces his theory of mental self-regulation (1988, 1994). He refers to 11 intellectual styles that try to explain and predict aspects of thinking that are not directly ascribed to intelligence per se.

According to this theory, people can autoregulate their intellectual performance in daily life, that is, beyond the classroom. He organizes the functions of self-regulation in a way that mirrors the organization of a government in society.

The theory of mental self-regulation outlines functions, forms, levels, scopes, and leanings in people (see Figure 33.2).

Three kinds of functions are identified: legislative, executive, and judicial. Legislative refers to individuals who enjoy creating, formulating, and planning solutions to problems. Executive describes people who put ideas into practice, follow rules, and like to put their knowledge in action to solve problems. Judicial applies to those who like to evaluate rules and procedures.

The four kinds of forms—monarchic, hierarchic, oligarchic, and anarchic—can be combined, separately, with any of the previous functional styles. The first kind of form, monarchic, refers to people who have only one goal or necessity to strive for. They are relatively unaware of their actions, intolerant, and inflexible. They believe that their purpose justifies the means. The second style, hierarchic, includes people who follow priorities in reaching for their goals. They are relatively aware of their actions, tolerant, and moderately flexible. The third one, oligarchic, involves several goals of the same importance at the same time. The people characterized by this style are very versatile when attacking a problem. They do not believe the means justify their purposes, and they are very self-

—*Figure 33.2*—
Elements of Thinking Styles

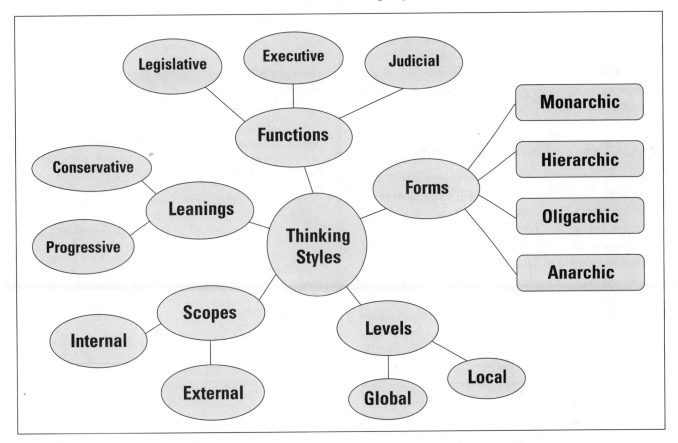

aware, tolerant, and extremely flexible. The last category, anarchic, refers to people reaching for many goals that are not clear. These people are not reflective. They believe that their purposes justify the means, and they are intolerant.

Sternberg identifies two levels of mental self-regulation: global and local. Global applies to people who like conceptualizing and working with ideas. Their thinking is diffuse; they see the forest but not the trees. People at the local level are detail-centered and focus on specifics. Their thinking is concrete; they see the trees more than the forest.

There are two kinds of scopes in Sternberg's theory: external and internal. The external scope refers to extroverted, easygoing, more socially adept persons. They like to work with people and are comfortable working in small groups. The internal scope applies to people who are introverted, reticent, less socially adept. They like to work individually.

We also have two leanings: conservative and progressive. The first reflects people who like to follow established rules. They do not like change and avoid ambiguous situations. The

second includes people who like to go beyond the rules; they like change. They prefer novel situations in their work and daily life.

Sternberg (1997) emphasizes that there is not a person with only one style, but that there is a profile of styles. In other words, one person could adopt a variety and combination of them.

The styles can be combined by function, form, level, scope, and leaning. A person can be, to state a possibility, judicial, oligarchic, local, external, and conservative. If we sum up the characteristics, we get a more precise profile of that person's intellectual style.

The previous styles show an important link between personality and intelligence. If it is certainly true that thinking carries emotion, the fact that context and experience play other roles that can influence a person's intellectual leanings is also true.

What can we do with information about thinking styles? First of all, we must realize that people learn, teach, behave, and think in different ways. As educators or administrators we can see thinking processes not in a linear form but as a manifestation of alternatives for solving problems, being creative, adopting attitudes, and so on. There is no one way to face situations.

Also, although theory in the field of thinking styles is younger than in the area of learning styles, there are more similarities than differences between them. Sternberg's approach is only a beginning. Other points of view can shed even more light on the ways people think.

APPLICATION TO INSTRUCTIONAL STRATEGIES

Many of the theories about learning styles have been shaped in operative models of the curricular environment in an attempt to improve learning among students whose individual differences had not been considered.

In the same way, there have been attempts to teach thinking that are oriented to the development of general intellectual skills. It might be necessary to identify differences among ways of thinking in order to propose instructional strategies that are more in harmony with intellectual preferences. Moreover, educators could use an explanatory and predictive framework of various ways of thinking in the curriculum and so help enhance or improve students' intellectual development.

Prejudice, attitude, personality, cognition, and motivation are some of the components that shape the thinking style. Even though cognition has an obvious role in thinking styles, we should not overlook the emotional charge in thinking that is conditioned by personality.

These components of thinking can help us develop students' intellectual potential within their environment, their community, and humanity.

REFERENCES

Castañeda, S., & López, M. (1992). La psicología instruccional Mexicana. *Revista Intercontinental de Psicología y Desarrollo, 5*(1), 46–61.

de Bono, E. (1986). *Six thinking hats.* London: Penguin Books.

Dunn, R., & Dunn, K. (1978). *Teaching students through their individual learning styles: A practical approach.* Englewood Cliffs, NJ: Prentice-Hall.

Grasha, A. (1997). *Teaching with style.* Pittsburgh, PA: Alliance Publishers.

Grigorenko, E., & Sternberg, R. (1997). Styles of thinking, abilities, and academic performance. *Exceptional Children, 63*(3), 295–312.

Guild, P., & Garger, S. (1985). *Marching to different drummers.* Alexandria, VA: Association for Supervision and Curriculum Development.

Hirsh, S., & Kummerow, J. (1989). *Life types: Understand yourself and make the most of who you are.* New York: Warner Books.

Jung, C. (1923). *Psychological types.* New York: Random House.

Kagan, J., & Kogan, N. (1970). Individual variation in cognitive processes. In P. H. Mussen (Ed.), *Carmichael's manual of child psychology, Vol. 1.* New York: Wiley.

Kolb, D. (1982). *Psicología de las organizaciones: Experiencias.* Madrid, Spain: Prentice-Hall.

McCarthy, B. (1987). *The 4MAT System: Teaching to learning styles with right/left mode technique.* Barrington, IL: Excel.

Myers, I. B. (1987). *Introduction to type.* Palo Alto, CA: Consulting Psychologists Press.

Nickerson, R., Perkins, D., & Smith, E. (1985). *The teaching of thinking.* Hillsdale, NJ: Erlbaum.

Santos Haliscak, M. E. (1992). *Impacto que han tenido los estilos de enseñanza-aprendizaje a través de los diferentes modelos que han surgido desde sus inicios hasta la actualidad.* Unpublished master's thesis, Universidad Regiomontana, Monterrey, Nuevo León, México.

Sternberg, R. (1988). *The triarchic mind: A new theory of human intelligence.* New York: Penguin Books.

Sternberg, R. (1994). Allowing for thinking styles. *Educational Leadership, 52*(3), 36–39.

Sternberg, R. (1997). *Thinking styles.* New York: Cambridge University Press.

Witkin, H., & Goodenough, D. R. (1981). *Cognitive styles: Essence and origin.* New York: International Universities Press.

Woolfolk, A. (1996). *Psicología educativa* (6th ed.). D. F., México: Prentice-Hall.

34

Thinking Styles

Robert J. Sternberg

Teaching that fully takes into account students' styles of thinking and learning will produce achievement superior to that produced by teaching that does not take their styles into account. Outcomes will be especially favorable when teachers match their instruction and assessment, at least part of the time, to a range of student styles. These superior outcomes should hold up regardless of the subject matter taught or the age or gender of the students. It is therefore to the advantage of every teacher to be familiar with the concept of thinking styles.

Styles are not a new field of study. In a brief essay, it is not possible to summarize all of the different approaches that might be taken to conceptualizing them. For a recent review, see Sternberg (1997). In this chapter, I will concentrate on one theory that has been found to be useful in classroom settings: the theory of mental self-government.

CONCEPTUALIZATION OF THEORY

The theory of mental self-government (Sternberg, 1988, 1990, 1994a, 1994b, 1997; Sternberg & Grigorenko, 1997) states that people have preferred ways of thinking, which metaphorically map onto different aspects of the organization of government. These preferred ways of thinking are styles rather than abilities—that is, they reflect not how well someone can do a class of tasks, but how much the person enjoys doing them. The styles specified by the theory are divided into functions, forms, levels, scopes and leanings of mental self-government. What are these styles?

THE STYLES

Functions. Just as governments carry out legislative, executive, and judicial functions, so does the mind.

• The *legislative* style characterizes people who enjoy creating and formulating. Such individuals like to create their own rules, do things in their own way, and build their own structures when deciding how to approach a problem. They prefer tasks that are not prestructured or prefabricated. Because students with legislative styles tend to be independent in their thinking, they sometimes get into trouble when their approach doesn't conform to the teacher's. These students tend to do best on independent projects, essays in which they can express their own point of view, and unstructured activities.

• The *executive* style characterizes people who are implementers. They prefer to follow rules, and they often rely on existing methods to master a situation. They prefer that activities be defined and structured for them. Students with this style often get along well with their teachers because they willingly accept direction and guidance. These students tend to do best on structured activities, such as multiple-choice tests, short-answer problems, and essays for which the topic is assigned.

• The *judicial* style characterizes people who like to evaluate rules and procedures; who like to judge things; and who like tasks in which they analyze and evaluate existing rules, ways, and ideas. Judicial students tend to get along well with teachers so long as they do not start evaluating the teachers' behavior in front of other students. These students tend to do well on critical essays and analyses.

Forms. There are four forms of mental self-government.

• The *monarchic* style characterizes individuals who like to focus on one task or aspect of that task until it is completed. People with a primarily monarchic style tend to focus single-mindedly on one goal or need at a time. Monarchic students tend to do well in school in their preferred subject-matter area, but less well in other areas. They can be helped by a teacher if the teacher is able to bring the students' areas of interest into the classroom, perhaps forming a bridge between what is being taught and what the student would like to learn.

• The *hierarchic* style characterizes individuals who allow for multiple goals, each of which may be given a different priority. People with a primarily hierarchic style enjoy dealing with many goals, although they recognize that some goals are more important than others; they tend to set priorities and to be systematic in their approach to solving problems. Hierarchic students tend to fit well into school settings if they set their priorities to match those of their teachers.

• The *oligarchic* style characterizes people who allow for multiple goals, all of which are roughly equal in importance. People with a primarily oligarchic style like to do multiple things within the same time frame but have difficulty setting priorities for getting the things done. Oligarchic students sometimes run into trouble in school because they have trouble allocating their time. They may allocate a lot of time to tasks the teacher considers unimportant and little time to tasks the teacher considers important. Thus they need help in allocating time.

• The *anarchic* style characterizes individuals who do not like to be tied down to systems, rules, or particular approaches to problems. Often they oppose existing systems, although not necessarily in favor of any clearly specified alternative. They tend to take a random approach to problems, thereby sometimes drawing connections that other people would not make. Anarchic students tend to have trouble in school and need help focusing. They are most at risk for antisocial behavior, but they also may have a creative streak because they are willing to combine ideas that others would see as having nothing to do with each other.

Levels. There are two levels of mental self-government.

• The *local* style characterizes individuals who prefer tasks that require engagement with specific, concrete details and that often require considerable precision to execute. Local students do well on detail-oriented tasks and tests—for example, picky multiple-choice tests. They may have trouble on more abstract essays, however.

• The *global* style characterizes individuals who prefer problems that are more general in nature and that require abstract thinking. The global person likes to conceptualize and work in the world of ideas. Global students tend to do well on broad-based tasks and to fall apart on detail-oriented types of assignments and tests.

Scope. There are two scopes of mental self-government.

• The *internal* style characterizes individuals who prefer tasks that allow them to work independently of others. Their preference is generally to be on their own. They generally do not take well to group work or other forms of cooperative learning.

• The *external* style characterizes individuals who prefer tasks that allow them to work with other people through interaction. Their preference is to be with others. They like group work and prefer it to working alone.

Leanings. There are two major leanings of mental self-government.

• The *liberal* style characterizes individuals who like to go beyond existing rules and procedures and who allow substantial change from the way things are currently done. Unlike in the legislative style, however, the new ideas do not have to be the individuals' own. Liberal students tend to be very receptive to new ways of doing things.

• The *conservative* style characterizes individuals who prefer familiarity in life and to follow traditions. Unlike in the executive style, they may like to come up with their own ideas, but these ideas are grounded in existing and accepted customs. Conservative students tend to resist new ways of doing things.

SOME GENERAL PROPERTIES OF THE THINKING STYLES

Whenever possible, people choose styles of managing themselves with which they are comfortable. Thus, people have sets of thinking styles that are more and less preferred. Still, people are at least somewhat flexible in their use of styles and try, with varying degrees of success, to adapt themselves to the stylistic demands of a given situation. The flexible use of the mind for mental self-government accounts for the variety of thinking styles.

Styles, like abilities, are not etched in stone at birth. They appear to be largely a function of a person's interactions with the environment, and they can be developed and socialized. An individual with one style in one task or situation may have a different style in a different task or situation. Moreover, some individuals may have one preferred stylistic profile at one stage of life and another preferred stylistic profile at another stage. Styles are not fixed, therefore, but fluid.

Thinking styles seem to be largely a function of people's interactions with tasks and situations. Certain tasks are more optimally performed with certain styles. For example, creative writing or composing music might draw more on the legislative style, whereas managing a plant might capitalize on the executive style. Rewarding students for using preferred styles on these tasks is likely to lead to greater display of the rewarded styles. More generally, a child's socialization into a value system will probably reward some styles more than other styles, leading to preferences for these styles. But the fact that some people retain less rewarded styles despite environmental pressures suggests that socialization does not fully account for the origins of styles and that there may be preprogrammed dispositions that are difficult to change.

USING STYLES IN THE CLASSROOM

It is important not to teach only to students' preferred styles of thinking. Students need to be able to capitalize on their preferred style some of the time, but they also need to learn how to develop nonpreferred styles at other times. It is unrealistic for students to expect instruction always to fit their preferred styles, and hence they must learn to be flexible. Teachers need to be flexible as well. If they always teach in their own preferred styles, then they systematically will favor students whose styles match their own and disfavor students whose styles do not.

Consider how the functions of mental self-government can be used in the classroom.

Executive instruction emphasizes didactic lecture, reading, and group recitation (for factual responses). Executive assessment will emphasize multiple-choice and short-answer responses. Executive instruction and assessment involve queries such as

- Who said . . . ?
- Summarize . . . .
- Who did . . . ?
- When did . . . ?
- What did . . . ?
- How did . . . ?
- Repeat back . . . .
- Describe . . . .

Judicial instruction emphasizes Socratic discussion, analytical essays and other activities, and group recitation (for analysis). Judicial assessment will emphasize critical essays and performances. Judicial instruction and assessment involve queries such as

- Compare and contrast. . . .
- Analyze. . . .
- Evaluate. . . .
- In your judgment. . . .
- Why did . . . ?
- What caused . . . ?
- What is assumed by . . . ?
- Critique. . . .

Legislative instruction emphasizes projects and creative essays and other activities. Legislative assessment will emphasize creative essays and performances. Legislative instruction and assessment involve queries such as

- Create . . . .
- Invent . . . .
- If you . . . .
- Imagine . . . .
- Design . . . .
- How would . . . ?
- Suppose . . . .
- Ideally . . . .

MEASUREMENT OF THINKING STYLES

We have developed a number of converging operations for measuring styles, both in adolescents and adults (see Sternberg, 1997; Sternberg & Grigorenko, 1995). Four of the main ones are described briefly below.

The Thinking Styles Inventory (Sternberg & Wagner, 1991) is a self-report measure in which students (or other examinees) rate themselves on a 9-point scale ranging from 1 (low) to 9 (high) on a number of preferences. Examples of items on the inventory are: "I like tasks that allow me to do things my own way" (legislative), "I like situations in which it is clear what role I must play or in what way I should participate" (executive), and "I like to evaluate and compare different points of view on issues that interest me" (judicial). The most recent version of this inventory can be found in Sternberg (1997).

The Thinking Styles Questionnaire for Teachers (Grigorenko & Sternberg, 1993c) measures teachers' preferences for thinking styles in students (for seven of the styles). These preferences may or may not correspond to their preferences for themselves. Examples of items, rated on a 1–9 scale, are: "I want my students to develop their own ways of solving problems" (legislative) and "I agree with people who call for more, harsher discipline and a return to the 'good old ways' " (conservative).

The Set of Thinking Styles Tasks for Students (Grigorenko & Sternberg, 1993a) measures students' preferences for styles in actual tasks. An example of an item is: "When I am studying literature, I prefer to (a) follow the teacher's advice and interpretations of authors' positions, and to use the teacher's way of analyzing literature" (executive), "(b) to make up my own story with my own characters and my own plot" (legislative), "(c) to evaluate the author's style, to criticize the author's ideas, and to evaluate characters' actions" (judicial), or "(d) to do something else (please indicate in the space below)."

The Students' Thinking Styles Evaluated by Teachers (Grigorenko & Sternberg, 1993b) has teachers evaluate the styles of individual students. Examples of items are: "S/he prefers to solve problems in her or his own way" (legislative) and "S/he likes to evaluate her or his own opinions and those of others" (judicial).

DOES THE THEORY WORK IN THE CLASSROOM?

We have tested the theory of mental self-government both in the United States (Grigorenko & Sternberg, 1997; Sternberg, 1994b, 1997; Sternberg & Grigorenko, 1995, 1997) and in China (Hong Kong and Nanjing) (Zhang & Sternberg, 1998a, 1998b). Detailed data are reported in original articles. Some of our main findings are as follows:

Structure of the inventories. The scales show good psychometric properties. Their internal-consistency reliabilities are generally satisfactory, with an average of about 0.8 (on a scale in which 0 is low and 1 is high). Most of the scale intercorrelations were low; the exceptions were ones that were anticipated. Substantial positive relationships exist for the legislative and liberal styles and for the executive and conservative styles. Substantial negative relationships exist for the global with local styles, conservative with legislative, and liberal with conservative. Factor analysis, which examines the basic structure underlying the questionnaires, generally supports the theory (for details, see Sternberg & Grigorenko, 1995).

Relation of the inventories to other measures. We looked at some correlates with other tests, both of styles and of abilities. Correlations were computed with the MBTI (Myers-Briggs Type Indicator) and Gregorc's (1982) measure of mind styles. The correlations are well above the levels that would be expected by chance and suggest that the various style measures partition a similar space of the intelligence-personality interface, but in different ways.

We also have assessed the usefulness of our measures in educational settings and have obtained some interesting findings (Grigorenko & Sternberg, 1997; Sternberg & Grigorenko, 1993, 1995).

Teachers at lower grade levels were more legislative and less executive than were teachers at higher grade levels. In other words, the teachers at the lower grade levels were more encouraging toward a style linked to creativity in their work with students (Sternberg & Lubart, 1995, 1996).

Older teachers were more executive, local, and conservative than younger teachers. Of course, we do not know whether this result was a cohort effect or whether it represented an aging process. But the study indicated that, on av-

erage, the younger teachers had styles that encouraged creativity more than the styles of the older teachers.

Teachers also showed some differences in styles across subject-matter areas. Science teachers tended to be more local, whereas humanities teachers tended to be more liberal.

There were large differences in stylistic patterns of teachers across schools, differences that seemed to make sense in terms of the kinds of education the schools were providing. Therefore, we decided to have an independent rater look at the ideology of each school for each of the style dimensions. The idea here was for the rater, who was unaware of our hypotheses, to rate the ideology of the school, using catalogs, faculty and student handbooks, statements of goals and purposes, curricula, and related information. Some schools, for example, were rated as ideologically more legislative or liberal than were others. We found that teachers' styles tended to match the ideology, or styles, of the school.

Students also tended to match their teachers in style. As students could not possibly have been placed in classes to achieve such a match, the results are consistent with the notion that styles are partially socialized.

Teachers tended to overestimate the extent to which their students matched them in styles. In other words, teachers are likely to think their students are more like them than they really are.

Students were more positively evaluated by and received better grades from teachers who matched their styles than from those who did not. In other words, teachers tend more to value students like themselves.

What was valued in one school sometimes was actually devalued in another. In other words, a given style could have a positive relationship to achievement in one school and a negative relationship in another.

There were consistent positive relationships between the judicial style and performance.

Styles predicted school performance over and above the prediction derived from abilities.

In sum, thinking styles are an important psychological attribute for school performance. They can be used to facilitate the teaching-learning process. And they can be measured. When they are taken into account, they improve students' academic performance and help teachers expand the repertoire of teaching strategies that they bring to bear in the classroom.

AUTHOR NOTES

Preparation of this article was supported under the Javits Act Program (Grant No. R206R000001) as administered by the Office of Educational Research and Improvement, U.S. Department of Education. Grantees undertaking such projects are encouraged to express freely their professional judgment. This article, therefore, does not necessarily represent the position or policies of the Office of Educational Research and Improvement or the U.S. Department of Education, and no official endorsement should be inferred.

REFERENCES

Gregorc, A. F. (1982). *Gregorc style delineator.* Maynard, MA: Gabriel Systems.

Grigorenko, E. L., & Sternberg, R. J. (1993a). *The set of thinking styles tasks for students.* Unpublished material, Yale University, New Haven, CT.

Grigorenko, E. L., & Sternberg, R. J. (1993b). *The students' thinking styles evaluated by teachers.* Unpublished material, Yale University, New Haven, CT.

Grigorenko, E. L., & Sternberg, R. J. (1993c). *Thinking styles questionnaire for teachers.* Unpublished material, Yale University, New Haven, CT.

Grigorenko, E. L., & Sternberg, R. J. (1997). Styles of thinking, abilities and academic performance. *Exceptional Children, 63,* 295–312.

Myers, I. B., & McCaulley, M. H. (1985). *Manual: A guide to the development and use of the Myers-Briggs type indicator.* Palo Alto, CA: Consulting Psychologists Press.

Sternberg, R. J. (1988). *The triarchic mind: A new theory of human intelligence.* New York: Viking.

Sternberg, R. J. (1990). *Metaphors of mind: Conceptions of the nature of intelligence.* New York: Cambridge University Press.

Sternberg, R. J. (1994a, November). Allowing for thinking styles. *Educational Leadership, 52*(3), 36–40.

Sternberg, R. J. (1994b). Diversifying instruction and assessment. *The Educational Forum, 59*(1), 47–53.

Sternberg, R. J. (1997). *Thinking styles.* New York: Cambridge University Press.

Sternberg, R. J., & Grigorenko, E. L. (1993). Thinking styles and the gifted. *Roeper Review, 16*(2), 122–130.

Sternberg, R. J., Grigorenko, E. L. (1995). Styles of thinking in school. *European Journal of High Ability, 6*(2), 1–18.

Sternberg, R. J., & Grigorenko, E. L. (1997). Are cognitive styles still in style? *American Psychologist, 52*(7), 700–712.

Sternberg, R. J., & Lubart, T. I. (1995). *Defying the crowd: Cultivating creativity in a culture of conformity.* New York: Free Press.

Sternberg, R. J., & Lubart, T. I. (1996). Investing in creativity. *American Psychologist, 51*(7), 677–688.

Sternberg, R. J., & Wagner, R. K. (1991). *Thinking styles inventory.* Unpublished material, Yale University, New Haven, CT.

Zhang, L., & Sternberg, R. J. (1998a). The pentagonal implicit theory of giftedness revisited: A cross-validation in Hong Kong. *Roeper Review, 21,* 149–153.

Zhang, L. F., & Sternberg, R. J. (1998b). Thinking styles, abilities, and academic achievement among Hong Kong University students. *Hong Kong Educational Research Association Educational Research Journal, 13,* 41–62.

35

Teaching For, With, and About Multiple Intelligences

David G. Lazear

Some Implementation Implications of the MI Theory

Without a doubt, one of the reasons that MI theory has attracted attention in the educational community is because of its ringing endorsement of an ensemble of propositions: we are not all the same; we do not all have the same kinds of minds; education works most effectively for most individuals if these differences in mentation and strengths are taken into account rather than denied or ignored.

— *Howard Gardner, "Reflections on Multiple Intelligences: Myths and Messages," Phi Delta Kappan*

One of the most hopeful and revolutionary theories impacting the dialogue on restructuring and renewing education is the theory of multiple intelligences as presented by Howard Gardner, codirector of Harvard's Project Zero. And yet, one of the curious things about this is that, in the first instance, the theory of multiple intelligences is not an educational theory. Rather, it is based primarily in the psychology of human development, the cognitive sciences, and in the findings of contemporary brain-mind research.

The heart of the theory is the notion that at the core of our cognitive or intellectual abilities every human being possesses the bio-, neuro-, and psychological potential for knowing, for acquiring information, for understanding, and for learning in *at least* eight distinct but interrelated ways—what Gardner called "intelligences" or "frames of mind" (also the title of the groundbreaking book that presents the findings of his original research into the multiplicity of human intelligence).

Briefly, the eight intelligences can be grouped into three overarching ways of knowing (Gardner, 1983). These broad classifications also correspond to three major survival systems within the human brain. These systems are concerned with space—our ability to maneuver around our environment and to sustain ourselves; time—the ability to recognize and deal with change and the passage of time; and identity—the need to establish a secure sense of individuality and the ability to work with others (Sylwester, 1998).

One of these groups is **object-related intelligences,** which are based on the concrete shapes, patterns, colors, images, designs, and objects in the external world that we come into contact with and interact with on a daily basis. It is the very existence of these so-called objects that "triggers" the related intelligences. In other words, without them the intelligences would have nothing to do. This group contains four intelligences:

- *Visual/spatial intelligence* deals with such objects as shapes, images, patterns, designs, colors, and textures that we observe with our eyes as well as those we can visualize in our "mind's eye."
- *Bodily/kinesthetic intelligence* deals with the "stuff" (or objects) of the human body: our extremities, internal organs, facial expressions, postures, and the ability to express thoughts and feelings in and through our bodies, for example in dance, drama, mime, and our "body language."
- *Logical/mathematical intelligence* deals with understanding the relationships of concrete patterns and objects observed in the world. Although math and logic often seem to be very abstract, their abstractions are always rooted in the concrete world of objects.
- *Naturalist intelligence* focuses on the objects of nature; the flora and fauna, the physical world, weather patterns and conditions—all of the "objects" of our environment as opposed to the humanly created world.

The **object-free intelligences,** unlike the object-related intelligences, do not rely on objects, real or imagined, that exist independently in the external world or that of the imagination.

• *Musical/rhythmic intelligence* deals with the auditory realms of tones, vibrational patterns, rhythms and beats, and music. In fact I have started to call this intelligence the *auditory/vibrational intelligence,* for I believe the term more accurately describes the cognitive process involved—the knowing that occurs through sound and vibration.

• *Verbal/linguistic intelligence* deals with the mystery and wonder of human language and communication. Written and spoken words can transport us to other times and places or to realms of fantasy. They can persuade us to change our opinions, values, and beliefs. They can move us to action. They can give expression to profound levels of our beings.

The **personal intelligences** are grounded primarily in our own "personhood" and in all the distinctive aspects of our lives as humans, namely our lives in relation to each other, on the one hand, and our lives as solitary individuals on the other. In some ways these intelligences are two sides of one coin, so to speak.

• *Interpersonal intelligence* deals with our capacities to work with others, to collaborate, to function effectively in a team effort, to empathize with others, to deeply communicate with each other, and to be sensitive and responsive to others' moods, motives, temperaments, and feelings.

• *Intrapersonal intelligence* is rooted in the unique capacity human beings possess to be introspective and reflective. These capacities allow us not only to engage in a full range of metacognitive processes, such as thinking about and improving our thinking and being aware of and taking charge of our emotional beings, but also to explore the so-called "big questions" of our existence—questions of meaning, purpose, significance, and what really matters ultimately.

The theory of multiple intelligences should not be confused with or equated to learning styles (Gardner, 1995). They are distinct and separate systems, albeit, in my own thinking, very compatible. When dealing with an intelligence, we are dealing primarily with a bio-neurological, cognitive process. The intelligences represent ways of knowing or acquiring knowledge, distinct capacities we can activate or trigger to help us learn and to more fully understand various kinds of information. I like to say that whatever one's own preferred learning style, within that style each of us has at least eight intelligences that we can develop and use to give us a more holistic perspective on all aspects of our lives.

The remainder of this chapter will look at some implications of the practical implementation of the theory for today's

educational tasks. However, a few words from Gardner (1995, p. 206) are in order before proceeding:

> MI theory is in no way an educational prescription. There is always a gulf between psychological claims about how the mind works and educational practices, and such a gulf is especially apparent in a theory that was developed without specific educational goals in mind. Thus, in educational discussions, I have always taken the position that educators are in the best position to determine the uses to which MI theory can and should be put.

Given these words of caution, I believe that the cutting edge of multiple intelligences research, as it applies to the task of educating, is the wide variety of practical implementations of the theory that are currently underway in hundreds of schools, school districts, and school divisions around the world. In my view, these locations are the new research laboratories for the next stage of MI's development, namely: *How can we use the findings of MI research to make a difference in the lives of the students who inhabit our classrooms day in and day out?*

It is important to recognize that MI is not a quick fix or a magic bullet. It will not provide answers to every problem or challenge we face in the renewal of our schools today. However, I believe that the findings about our many ways of knowing bring some very significant pieces to the larger discussion of educational restructuring. It is these contributions to which I turn in the remainder of this chapter.

Three key areas of "applied MI efforts" have concerned me over the years and have been the focus of my work with the implementation of the theory. In each of these areas my concern is that we "act on what we know" based on the findings of contemporary brain-mind research, the cognitive sciences, and research on multiple intelligences themselves. While, as Gardner points out above, there is no *a priori* educational application of this research, I will nonetheless suggest several practical implications for school restructuring.

TEACHING FOR MULTIPLE INTELLIGENCES: INTEGRATING THE CURRICULUM

I have often felt that if you want to see the natural learner, look at children when they show up on the doorsteps of our schools. Look at students in early childhood. Generally what you will see is all of the intelligences alive, awake, and bubbling, like a series of pots on the proverbial stove. Then also consider what tends to happen, year by year by year, as they proceed through their educational journey. I would suggest that what you will observe is the systematic shutdown of those many intelligences.

Have you ever noticed how early in a child's educational journey the "I can'ts" start appearing? I often ask workshop participants to imagine walking into any preschool or kindergarten classroom in almost any nation of our world and asking the children, "How many of you know how to sing? How many of you know how to draw? How many of you know how to dance? Who likes to work with others?" Generally, every hand will go up. Now go to your typical third-grade class and ask the same questions. How many hands will go up? Usually about half. Then go to the typical middle school or junior high and ask the same questions. Probably you will see two or three very hesitant hands being raised. And in the typical high school classroom, you find yourself having to ask whether anyone even knows how to raise their hands, for likely no hands will be raised.

• What if we could keep alive in students everything that is alive in them when they first appear in our schools, from K through 12 and beyond?

• What if we could prevent the intelligence shutdown I have described from occurring?

• What if there were a way to help students activate more and more and more of their full intellectual potential, year after year, as they go through their formal schooling?

In Gardner's original research on the theory of multiple intelligences, one of the so-called qualifying criteria for an intelligence was that it must possess a core set of operations (Gardner, 1983). In my work with MI theory, I have called these the core capacities of the various intelligences (Lazear, 1991). These capacities define the operation of an intelligence at the bio-neurological, cognitive level. One of the most exciting and revolutionary pieces of the research on multiple intelligences is that at almost any stage of our lives and at almost any ability level, these capacities can be awakened or triggered in the brain. They can be taught, learned, enhanced, and amplified. In other words, given the plasticity of the human brain, each of the intelligences can be strengthened and its knowing capacities vastly expanded (Gardner, 1983; Houston, 1982).

In my own thinking about the educational implications of these findings, I believe that, if we want students to reach their potential intellectually, the systematic development of the capacities of each intelligence (see Figure 35.1) must be integrated in and through the K–12 academic curriculum, regardless of the curricular content. And second, we must move beyond the biases of most of our current curricula, which value almost exclusively the development of the capacities of verbal/linguistic and logical/mathematical intelligence (Lazear, 1999).

If we are to take seriously the findings about multiple intelligences and act on them, what are some of the possible implications?

• *The various intelligence capacities should be integrated into the design of curricular units* so that students have ample opportunities to practice using them to gain knowledge, process information, and deepen their understanding of the required material. Students should be taught how to successfully access all of their own intelligences in and through the existing curriculum.

• *The so-called fine arts part of the curriculum should be expanded and incorporated into the traditional academic areas.* This should include instrumental and vocal music, art, dance, drama, poetry, storytelling, and creative writing, as well as physical education. This will provide all students with ample opportunities to develop the full spectrum of their intellectual capacities.

I believe that these dimensions of the curriculum should not be optional, nor be viewed as extracurricular. At the same time I believe that it is a cop-out to say, "Oh, visual/spatial intelligences is the job of the art teacher; bodily/kinesthetic intelligence is dealt with in physical education; musical/rhythmic intelligence is assigned to the music teachers," and so on. It is an error to equate these curricular areas or disciplines with certain of the intelligences (Gardner, 1995). The intelligences are ways of knowing, acquiring knowledge, processing information, learning, and understanding, and they must be addressed and dealt with in every area of the curriculum.

• *Curriculum guides should be written in such a way that the development of the full range of intellectual capabilities is clearly valued.* Teachers also should be held accountable for fostering students' capacities in each of the eight intelligence areas, much as we now do with the verbal/linguistic (language arts) and logical/mathematical (math and science) parts of the curriculum.

APPROACHES FOR INTEGRATING MI INTO THE CURRICULUM

In my most recent book, *The Intelligent Curriculum* (Lazear, 1999), I share four models that represent four different approaches to integrating these intelligences into the curriculum. The four models have been adapted from approaches used in

—*Figure 35.1*—
Multiple Intelligences Capacities Summary

Logical/ Mathematical	Abstract pattern recognition Inductive reasoning Deductive reasoning Discerning relationships and connections Performing complex calculations Scientific reasoning	**Musical/Rhythmic**	Structure of music Schemas for hearing music Sensitivity to sounds Creating melody and rhythm Sensing qualities of a tone
Intrapersonal	Concentration of the mind Mindfulness Metacognition Awareness and expression of different feelings Transpersonal sense of the self Higher-order thinking and reasoning	**Verbal/Linguistic**	Understanding the order and meaning of words Convincing someone of a course of action Explaining, teaching, and learning Humor Memory and recall Metalinguistic analysis
Interpersonal	Creating and maintaining synergy Discerning underlying intentions, behavior, and perspectives Passing over into the perspective of another Working cooperatively in a group Sensitivity to others' moods, motives, and feelings Verbal and nonverbal communication	**Visual/Spatial**	Accurate perception from different angles Recognizing relationships of objects in space Graphic representation Image manipulation Finding your way in space Forming mental images Active imagination
Naturalist	Communion with nature Caring for, taming, and interacting with living creatures Sensitivity to nature's flora Recognizing (and classifying) species Growing natural things	**Bodily/Kinesthetic**	Improved body function Miming abilities Mind/body connection Expanding awareness through the body Control of preprogrammed movements Control of voluntary movements

Source: Adapted from *Eight Ways of Knowing: Teaching for Multiple Intelligences,* Third Edition, by David Lazear. © 1991, 1999 by SkyLight Training and Publishing, Inc. Reprinted by permission of SkyLight Professional Development, www.skylightedu.com or (800) 348-4474.

various schools and districts in North America. The goal of each model is to embed the various capacities of the intelligences into the existing curriculum.

Yearlong MI curriculum journey. This approach works with a matrix in which the year's curriculum content is listed across the top of the matrix and the intelligences are listed down the side. The various capacities for each intelligence are then dragged across the curriculum, much akin to a whole-language approach to the language arts. The task is to find a home for the various capacities in all areas of the curriculum.

MI unit stretching. The fundamental intent of this approach is to work with the plans for an existing unit of study or for a theme that is to be explored. Begin with an inventory of the unit, using the screen of the multiple intelligences capaci-

ties. The goal of this approach is threefold: 1) to recognize the intelligence capacities that are already being addressed in the unit; 2) to note the intelligences that have a weak showing, have been avoided altogether, or are represented only superficially; and 3) to stretch the unit to incorporate the capacities of weak and neglected intelligence areas in teaching the content.

MI stations/learning centers. In this model, the teacher sets up learning centers, with intelligence-appropriate tasks in each station or center. The tasks provide students an opportunity to process the information in a unit in a variety of unique and creative ways. Students are provided with whatever introductory material is necessary to get them started. Then they are divided into teams, and the remainder of the unit (including the learning) takes place in a very hands-on fashion as the teams visit each of the stations, exploring, discovering, and interacting with the curricular material by performing the learning tasks.

Schoolwide or departmentwide MI focus. The goal of this model is to provide time for teachers and students to zero in on the development of the full range of capacities for targeted intelligences in and through a given unit of instruction. Within the allotted time frame, make sure students have ample opportunities to practice using the various capacities of the focal intelligence in their learning of the curricular material. Also, make sure that teachers are held accountable for using the capacities in their instruction throughout the week. This model is probably one of the best for implementing a project-based and a problem-solving-based approach to teaching and learning.

TEACHING WITH MULTIPLE INTELLIGENCES: MULTIMODAL INSTRUCTION

In some ways, the art of instruction is the heart of the teaching profession. I have often commented on the immense power classroom teachers have in effecting educational change, renewal, and reform. Almost any educational policy, regardless of its origin, happens or doesn't happen with what takes place in the classroom when teachers close their doors and begin the day's instruction. This may well be the place that the theory of multiple intelligences can have the most profound impact on our schools.

As a parent of two daughters, neither of whom was a traditional learner in school, I have learned a great deal about using multiple intelligences to help students succeed in an educational system that, for the most part, has very little understanding of how to deal with children who simply weren't reached by traditional instructional methods in the regular classroom. Far too often the first response, when we encounter these so-called nontraditional learners, is that they must have some kind of learning disability. In some of the early work done by Thomas Armstrong on translating Gardner's research on multiple intelligences for the public, he suggests that the term "LD" (usually meaning learning disability) should, from the perspective of MI, really mean learning different (Armstrong, 1987). I believe that MI, applied to the task of education, requires us to view students in more holistic ways and to take human differences in our classrooms very seriously.

In my own work in applying multiple intelligences theory to educational tasks, I have advocated multimodal approaches to both teaching and learning, and to assessment of students'

progress (Lazear, 1991, 1994). Current brain-mind research and the cognitive sciences have known for a long time that the more levels of the brain-mind-body system engaged in a given situation, the greater is the learning potential of people in that situation (Sylwester, 1995; Jensen, 1998; Caine & Caine, 1994; Diamond, 1998). In other words, increased neurological activity likewise increases the potential connections that the brain-mind can make with one's total life experience—past, present, and future. What this means for education is that instruction and learning should involve enough complexity, in structuring the tasks involved, that students' brains are put into highly activated states. They will thus draw on a much larger spectrum of sensory and cognitive possibilities than is usually the case (Houston, 1980).

• What if we could activate students' learning throughout their entire brain-mind-body system so they moved beyond mere memorization and regurgitation of various facts and figures in daily lessons to genuine understanding of the material?

• What if it were possible to catalyze a genuine love of learning in students by helping them make meaningful connections in their own lives for everything they study in school?

• What if all children could be served in the regular classroom, including special education and gifted students?

If we were to take seriously this multimodal approach to teaching and learning, some of the implications might include:

• **Daily lessons should be "multisensory" learning experiences** that provide students with chances to touch, see, hear, taste, dance, smell, write, discuss, draw, sculpt, paint, reflect, and sing about what they are learning. This not only creates more learning connections in the brain, but also tends to store learning in the brain's long-term memory system. Students should be encouraged to regularly use the full spectrum of their intelligences in the task of acquiring knowledge and to process information in daily lessons, as well as to deepen, amplify, and enhance their understanding. In my view, approximately 95 percent of current school curricula (including both teacher and student materials) comes already prepackaged, so to speak, in a verbal/linguistic or logical mathematical mode. Students must be asked to stretch beyond the traditional verbal/linguistic and logical/mathematical intelligences.

• **The various media and tools for stimulating the intelligences must be abundantly present in the classroom,** and students must be encouraged and taught how to use them for gaining knowledge, processing information from a lesson, knowing and learning, and for creating a range of products that demonstrate their understanding. Much research is available today on the importance of a sensory-rich environment for continued, lifelong dendritic growth in the brain (Diamond, 1998; Jensen, 1998; Sylwester, 1998).

• **Teachers should create "self-instructional tracking plans"** to ensure that they are teaching in intelligence-balanced ways. Most teachers tend to teach in the way they were taught and in ways that are most comfortable for them. It is important to reflect on the fact that one's own most comfortable and accustomed ways of teaching may block some students from learning. Likewise we often mistakenly assume that certain concepts can be taught only in certain ways. Multiple intelligences theory challenges this assumption. It does not suggest that everything can be taught using all the intelligences but does suggests that, in principal, everything can be taught using several intelligences. By stretching ourselves to find multiple ways to teach everything, not only will we likely help more students succeed more of the time, but we may also gain new and deeper understandings of the very concepts we are teaching.

• **Assessment of students' learning must likewise involve a range of intelligence performances** that go beyond paper-and-pencil tasks. Gardner has suggested that if we are concerned with students' genuine understanding of the curricular material (as opposed to their ability to recall memorized information), then we must require them to represent that understanding in at least three different ways (Gardner, 1997).

Just because students can write down the correct answer on paper does not mean they really understand the concepts at hand. And, vice versa, just because they can't write it does not mean they don't understand.

In my work with professional development workshops and seminars in many schools and districts around the world, I have focused on sharing a variety of lesson planning and unit design processes that tap students' many "ways of knowing," not as an add-on but as part and parcel of daily lessons. Key to this is the understanding that each intelligence has its own distinct language, vernacular, jargon, and *modus operandi*. This constitutes a unique symbol system for each intelligence (Gardner, 1983). The symbol systems are manifest in a variety of precise "notational forms" unique to each intelligence, including such things as written words, artistic forms, numbers, musical notes, dance steps, body language, visual symbols involving both internal and external seeing, and human relations or group processing forms. The *modus operandi* involves a

series of specific, intelligence-compatible tools, methodologies, techniques, and strategies.

Multiple intelligences lessons must, first of all, be couched in the unique language and symbol systems of the various intelligences, which include but go beyond the traditional "reading, writing, and 'rithmetic" biases of the existing curriculum. Teachers and students must learn how to speak the language of each intelligence and to interpret the symbols each employs. Second, MI lessons need to be staged so that they are intelligence-compatible—that is, in line with the operating mode of each intelligence. In some lessons it is possible to incorporate all or most of the intelligences in a single learning experience. Other lessons may focus the teaching and learning in one intelligence area. In any event, intelligence-awakening exercises, games, puzzles, and so forth should be employed at the beginning of a lesson to stimulate, activate, or trigger "focus intelligences"—the intelligences being given specific attention in that lesson. Then the ensuing information processing and knowledge acquisition should be designed around employing the specific tools, techniques, and strategies of the intelligence (Lazear, 1991). Figure 35.2 provides several practical examples of what this can look like when dealing with the traditional academic curriculum.

TEACHING ABOUT MULTIPLE INTELLIGENCES: RESTRUCTURING THE LEARNING PROCESS

There may be no area of educational research more important than the research on the various patterns of thinking, higher-order thinking, teaching students to be thinkers, and meta-cognition. All of this study applies equally well to what I have called "meta-intelligence"—consciously teaching students about their own multiple intelligences.

• What if students could find and use their own best ways of learning required material?

• What if parents were involved in nurturing their children's many intelligences at home?

• What if the school culture valued MI, promoted its use, and celebrated achievement in all the intelligence areas?

During the years I have been working to translate multiple intelligences theory into applied educational practice, I have over and over again been surprised, delighted, and amazed by students' capacity to understand the theory, and by their excitement when they are provided opportunities to learn about their many intelligences. These experiences, along with a deep

—Figure 35.2—
MI Lesson Ideas Matrix

	Language Arts	Mathematics	Global Studies and History	Science and Health	Fine Arts
Visual/ Spatial	Illustrate aspects of a piece of literature (scenes, plot line, characters).	Do a survey of students' likes and dislikes, then graph the results.	Study a culture through its visual art—painting and sculpture.	Pretend you are microscopic and can "go inside" a scientific process.	Listen to music with eyes closed and create a sculpture from clay.
Bodily/ Kinesthetic	Play "The Parts of a Sentence" game or vocabulary charades.	Make up a playground game that uses math concepts or operations.	Reenact great scenes or moments from history for today.	Have class members act out the rotation of the planets around the sun.	Design a "living painting" of a classical work.
Logical/ Mathematical	Use a story grid for creative writing activities.	Create a sequence ladder to show the thought processes for working on proofs for geometric theorems or other math problem solving.	Rank-order key socioeconomic factors that shaped a culture's development.	Rank-order key socioeconomic factors that shaped a culture's development.	Create a paint-by-numbers picture for another person to paint.
Naturalist	Write poetry or descriptive essays based on experiences in nature.	Create and work calculation problems based on nature or natural processes.	Grow, taste, and learn to recognize foods grown in different cultures.	Keep a diary of the natural processes of your own body.	Create dances that embody or demonstrate patterns, objects, and animals in nature.
Auditory/ Vibrational (Musical/ Rhythmic)	Illustrate a story or poem with appropriate sounds, music, rhythms, and vibrations.	Break a set of tones or rhythmic patterns into groups to learn division tables or fractions.	Listen to and analyze different kinds of music from various cultures.	Learn to use music, rhythm, sound, and vibrations to reduce stress.	Turn a nonmusical play into a musical or into an old-time radio show.
Verbal/ Linguistic	Create crossword puzzles or word jumbles for vocabulary words.	Explain to others how to work a problem while they follow along doing it.	Read and learn stories, myths, and poetry from other cultures.	Create a diary on the life of a red blood cell from the cell's perspective.	Turn a Greek or Shakespearean tragedy into a situation comedy.
Interpersonal	Analyze the message or moral of a story with a group and reach a consensus.	Have teams construct problems linking many math operations, then solve them.	Role-play a conversation with a historical figure.	Discuss controversial health topics and write team position papers.	Practice stopping the action and improvising while dramatizing a play.
Intrapersonal	Write a new poem each day for a week on: Who am I? and Where am I going?	Bridge math concepts beyond school into real life, asking What? So what? Now what?	Keep a journal on questions from life that history might be able to answer.	Write about the theme: If I could be any animal, what would I be and why?	Imagine yourself as each character in a play, noting different feelings, values, beliefs.

—*Figure 35.3*—
Activities for Teaching Students About Multiple Intelligences

1. To introduce multiple intelligence activities to students:	• *Intelligence scavenger hunt.* Create a list of eight "intelligence-specific" skills, capacities, activities, or tasks about which students must interview each other to identify and demonstrate. • *MI activity posters.* Design posters, with suggested activities, that ask students to exercise various intelligence skills to complete the activities. • *Observation checklist.* Make a list of behaviors, activities, skills, and so forth related to the various intelligences. Ask students to log observations about themselves and the various "intelligence behaviors."
2. To deepen awareness of students' own, and others', intelligences:	• *Each one teach one.* Design a process in which students who are strong in a certain intelligence teach the skills and capacities of that strength to fellow students. • *Eight-in-one activities.* Ask students to think of eight different MI ways to perform certain tasks that usually are considered from a more limited perspective. • *Self-analysis.* Create a set of questions asking students to evaluate their own intelligence strengths and weaknesses and to create plans for improving the weaker areas.
3. To help students develop appropriate strategies for using MI:	• *Multiple roles in cooperative groups.* Assign students to practice various multiple-intelligence skills as part of cooperative learning lessons. • *Intelligence triggers.* Create a self-evaluation screen whereby students learn how to access the eight ways of knowing to help them master classroom lessons and homework. • *Intelligence coaching.* Set up a process in which students become mentors to each other, seeking effective multiple-intelligence approaches for succeeding in school and beyond.
4. To help students incorporate MI into their repertoire for living:	• *Intelligence use and improvement planning.* Design a self-assessment that provides students an opportunity to reflect on "the state of development" of the eight intelligences in their own lives. • *Keeping an intelligence diary.* Set up a journal-keeping method to help students track their use of the various intelligences and to learn how to use them more fully in their daily lives. • *A few of my favorite MI things.* Help students create a portfolio of "intelligence artifacts" to remind them of their eight ways of knowing, including plans for nurturing them.

commitment to promoting metacognitive behavior anywhere possible, have made me a strong advocate of taking time to teach students about MI. I feel strongly that they need to "get to know themselves" intellectually. I advocate several dimensions of this MI curriculum:

• *Students need to recognize or discover the various intelligences in themselves.* They need to learn that they have at least eight ways of knowing but that not all eight ways are equally developed. Some tend to be stronger. Others may be in various states of latency. Nevertheless, since all of the intelligences are part of our biology and neurology as human beings, each of them can be further developed, enhanced, strengthened, and amplified (Gardner, 1983, p. 47).

In my experience, students are generally enthralled with knowing about the eight intelligences. The learning tends to open many new realms of self-understanding. Knowledge

about the intelligences is also a great boost to self-esteem. Some of the very areas in which students are feeling badly about themselves are those in which they attempted to use one of the so-called "nontraditional" intelligences and were put down by their peers, a parent, or a teacher. However, once they have the knowledge about the intelligences, they can often become advocates for themselves in such situations.

• *Students need to be taught to recognize, honor, respect—even celebrate—the various intelligences in their classmates.* The truth is that most students have intuitively known about the various ways of knowing, both in themselves and each other, for many years, but without consciously recognizing and naming them. Once they are named, however, they can be embraced and become a conscious part of students' regular daily repertoires, both in school and beyond.

• *Students need to be given regular opportunities to exercise all eight of the intelligences, along with many occasions that challenge them to use as many intelligences as possible.* As with any skill we have developed in our lives, "proper practice makes perfect." The same is true for the intelligences. Of course, anytime a person experiments with something new, a safe, low-risk classroom environment is essential. Both students and the instructor will stretch themselves to find more ways to activate the full spectrum of their intelligences.

Figure 35.3 on the preceding page shows several examples of learning experiences, lessons, and activities that can be used to achieve the goals I have mentioned. These can be used as mini-lessons, in and of themselves, or integrated into other content-based lessons. They represent a sampling of suggestions from *Seven Pathways of Learning* (Lazear, 1994b).

Another aspect of the intelligences that comes to bear when considering teaching students about MI is what Gardner calls the "development trajectory" of an intelligence. The intelligences tend to move through various developmental stages, from the acquisition and "raw patterning" of basic-level skills (usually in infancy and the early childhood years) to the development of a more complex repertoire of skills (generally in the elementary years), to the ability to use the intelligences in a more coherent and integrated way as part of one's repertoire for living (usually in the secondary years), to the level of mastery often evident in one's vocational and avocational pursuits (Gardner, 1993, pp. 27–29). One of the biggest implications of these developmental factors is that they challenge all of us, parents and teachers alike, to look at youngsters in totally different ways than we have in the past.

• *So-called "diagnostic evaluations" of students' abilities should be expanded to include a wide variety of "intelligence-fair" and "in-context" observations of students involved in meaningful, real-life activities and tasks.* This must not be limited to standard IQ or ability testing, which often occurs in a "decontextualized" setting biased toward paper and pencil.

The goal of all such intelligence or ability testing should be the creation of "student intelligence profiles" (Gardner, 1993), as opposed to the labeling of students. An intelligence profile should provide a whole picture of the various factors (strengths and weaknesses, likes and dislikes) that comprise the student's intellectual functioning and capabilities. These intelligence profiles should then be the basis for designing individualized, developmentally appropriate learning plans and capacity development opportunities for students that will fully harness their strengths toward working on developing capacity in their weaker areas (Lazear, 1994).

• *Parents should be offered school-based inservice training on the theory of multiple intelligences periodically.* There are many things they can do at home to nurture, encourage, even evoke the intelligences in their children. Parents know that their children are smart, even if not in the way school has traditionally valued. Likewise, inservice events can help them understand new efforts the school is making to address all the intelligences.

REFERENCES

Armstrong, T. (1987). *In their own way: Discovering and encouraging your child's personal learning style.* Los Angeles: J. P. Tarcher.

Caine, R., & Caine, G. (1994). *Making connections: Teaching and the human brain.* Menlo Park, CA: Addison-Wesley.

Caine, R., Caine, G., & Crowell, S. (1994). *Mind shifts: A brain-based process for restructuring schools and renewing education.* Tucson, AZ: Zephyr Press.

Diamond, M. (1998). *Magic trees of the mind: How to nurture your child's intelligence, creativity, and healthy emotions from birth through adolescence.* New York: Dutton.

Gardner, H. (1983). *Frames of mind: The theory of multiple intelligences.* New York: Basic Books.

Gardner, H. (1987). Developing the spectrum of human intelligences: Teaching in the eighties: A need to change. *Harvard Educational Review, 57,* 87–93.

Gardner, H. (1993). *Multiple Intelligences: The theory in practice.* New York: Basic Books.

Gardner, H. (1995). Reflections on Multiple Intelligences: Myths and messages. *Phi Delta Kappan 77*(3), 200–209.

Gardner, H. (1997). Keynote address at "Using Your Brain" conference, sponsored by Hawker- Brownlow Education, Melbourne, Australia.

Houston, J. (1980). *Life force: The psycho-historical recovery of the self.* New York: Delacorte Press.

Houston, J. (1982). *The possible human: A course in enhancing your physical, mental, and creative abilities.* Los Angeles: J. P. Tarcher.

Jensen, Eric. (1998). *Teaching with the brain in mind.* Alexandria, VA: Association for Supervision and Curriculum Development.

Lazear, D. (1991). *Eight ways of knowing: Teaching for multiple intelligences.* Palatine, IL: SkyLight Publishing.

Lazear, D. (1994a). *Multiple intelligence approaches to assessment: Solving the assessment conundrum.* Tucson, AZ: Zephyr Press.

Lazear, D. (1994b). *Seven pathways of learning: Teaching students and parents about multiple intelligences.* Cheltenham, Vic.: Hawker Brownlow Education.

Lazear, D. (1999). *The intelligent curriculum: Using MI to develop your students' full potential.* Tucson, AZ: Zephyr Press.

Sylwester, R. (1995). *A celebration of neurons.* Alexandria, VA: Association for Supervision and Curriculum Development.

Sylwester, R. (1998). How the arts enhance the development and maintenance of our brain. Keynote address at the Zephyr Press New Ways of Learning Conference, "Our Intelligent Brain," in Tucson, AZ.

36

Thinking and the Special-Needs Learner

David S. Martin

Since the publication of the first edition of this volume in the 1980s, many school districts have worked to adapt or adopt programs for the teaching of thinking, in many cases with an emphasis on inservice teacher education. Based on experience, I have found that teachers commonly respond to the ideas of teaching thinking and the styles that accompany it with the opinion, "All of these thinking ideas are wonderful, but they could never apply or be done with any children who have special needs." Another frequently heard response is, "These ideas are very stimulating, and they would be great for gifted children but probably not doable for other children."

Such responses, while understandable, could not be further from the truth. In fact, *all* learners, at all ages, need and benefit from active involvement with the explicit application of higher-level cognitive strategies. This chapter examines the questions of appropriate adaptation and sequencing of thinking strategies for a variety of special-needs learners, including learning-disabled, behavior-disordered, deaf or hard of hearing, and gifted students.

During discussions on cognitive skills, the question arises, "Are there any thinking skills that are basic or should be taught first?" Of course, various scholars will provide varying answers to that question. It is ultimately a question that all teachers need to answer for themselves, whether they are teaching in the general classroom or in a special-needs environment. Beyer (personal communication, November 1998), for example, indicates that the *basic* thinking skills are prediction, classification, and sequencing. Feuerstein (1980) suggests that the fundamental thinking skills are organizing, orientation in personal space, analysis, and comparison, followed closely by classification and following written instructions. These are not serious disagreements, and many would indicate that the *higher* level beyond the basic thinking skills would include such areas as synthesis, symbolic logic, and propositional logic, among others.

The danger in attempting to identify a "basic" set of thinking skills is to then lower the expectations for special-needs learners and to be satisfied with involving them only with those skills and not the higher-level skills, when, in fact, evidence indicates that there is not necessarily a ceiling for many special-needs learners.

Let us now examine each of several categories of special-needs learners in relation to the teaching of thinking.

LEARNING DISABILITIES

By far the largest number of literature citations for special-needs learners in regard to thinking strategies is found in the area of learning-disabled students. Swanson and Hoskyn (1998) in an experiment found that direct instruction and cognitive-strategy instruction were "pervasive" influences in remediating difficulties for children who have learning disabilities.

In a coaching environment using active reasoning strategies with students in grades 4 and 5, Sullivan (1995) found that learning-disabled students who had coaching in reasoning outperformed those who did not, in regard to the ability to make explanations.

Lins (1993) set up tasks for language-delayed students to make pictorial chart plans and other self-monitoring activities and found that these strategies increased students' critical thinking skills. Peterson (1994) used problem analysis and higher-order thinking through reading and writing, and found they resulted in improvements in reading level and in students' ability to communicate original ideas.

In an experiment with five primary-school age students, Ibler (1997) used problem-solving strategies on a regular basis; the outcome was improved student conduct, successful problem-solving applied to language and science, improvement in written and oral expression, and an increase in regular usage of the higher-order strategies.

Evaluators of the Instrumental Enrichment program and the Strategies Program for Effective Learning and Thinking (SPELT) found that both were effective in improving student thinking for learning-disabled students in reading comprehension and comprehension monitoring (Mulcahy, 1993). Researchers performed three-year longitudinal evaluations of the two cognitive education programs.

Several researchers describe techniques that they recommend using with learning-disabled students in thinking contexts, although no outcomes are reported. For example, Montague (1997) describes cognitive-strategy instructional techniques for use with middle-school age students with learning disabilities in mathematical problem solving. And a team at Johns Hopkins University (1993) developed a series of critical-thinking activities using computerized instructional modules and multimedia instruction for students with learning disabilities at the elementary level.

AUTISM

Apparently little systematic investigation has occurred in relation to thinking strategies as applied to autistic learners. It is known that autistic children have difficulty with the concept of object permanence, related to Piagetian cognitive strategies. Specifically, they have difficulty with maintaining "set" and tend to perseverate errors (Adrien, 1995). This area is one that demands further investigation.

BEHAVIOR DISORDERS

Teachers who work with students who present the challenge of behavior disorders often seek calming and nonstimulating activities within the learning context. But this approach, understandable in regard to the nature of these learners, militates against the use of potentially exciting and cognitively stimulating activities such as are found in many cognitive education programs.

Rider-Hankins (1992) investigated the effects of cognitive-strategy instruction with adolescents within a correctional institution. Her analysis indicates that a cognitive model has positive implications for both prevention and rehabilitation efforts in that context.

In a psychiatric treatment center, Peniston (1995) makes a strong case for the use of problem-solving strategies to help students comprehend new information and use thinking skills to overcome everyday obstacles. She particularly identifies the

teaching methods of guided questioning, heuristic problem solving, analysis of choice making, and brain-teaser activities as being promising in this regard. Research should follow up on this important assertion.

COGNITIVE DEFICITS

Children with cognitive deficits—classified variously at other times as "mentally retarded" or "cognitively challenged," among other terms—have been the subject of some study in regard to thinking skills. Mastropieri, Scruggs, and Butcher (1997) found that students with identified mental retardation were less likely than other students to make a correct induction or to answer transfer and application questions correctly. This implies a need for systematic cognitive-strategy instruction for such students.

Art procedures have been used to remediate deficits in cognitive skills. The association and representation of concepts through drawing from imagination, the ability to perceive and represent spatial concepts, and the ability to order sequentially were all enhanced by specially planned art activities (Silver, 1989).

Lombardi (1992) provides a strong rationale, without investigation as yet, for using a four-step model of teaching higher-order thinking skills with students having cognitive deficits, through the use of careful questioning. The four steps are: introduce the skill, explain it, demonstrate it, and apply it. Investigation would be useful to test this rationale.

EDUCATIONAL DISADVANTAGE

Much has been written about the value of systematic cognitive intervention for students who have a so-called educational disadvantage resulting from poverty. Feuerstein (1980), in his seminal work on instrumental enrichment, successfully tested a *systematic* cognitive intervention approach with students who had been so labeled, indicating that in the past they had only ·been deprived of appropriate adult mediation in the learning process and had at least normal cognitive potential.

Bryson and Scardamalia (1991) examined cognitively based writing instruction with disadvantaged students and found that a deliberate fostering of higher-order thinking skills brought students' writing significantly closer to the highest ranking of written work, on a holistic scale, than other methods.

A potentially large body of literature could be amassed in this area, in view of the adoption or adaptation by urban school districts of a number of published cognitive-education programs. However, data from such implementations are often limited to in-house reports and represent an as-yet-unfulfilled need for systematic and objective external evaluation.

BRAIN INJURIES

Students with brain injuries have only recently become the subjects of well-organized educational investigation, given that a medical focus has dominated the research until recently. Yet with the increase in medical technology, far more students with such injuries survive and return to school than in the past. Thus they need to be studied in this regard.

Jenison (1993) found that systematic cognitive instruction in a community college context with brain-injured learners resulted in greater internal locus of control, higher self-esteem, and improved critical thinking skills. These results are particularly illuminating in that they are among only a few instances in the cognitive education literature that address the *affective* benefits of cognitive instruction.

DEAF AND HARD OF HEARING

For centuries, researchers and educators posited that deaf learners had limited cognitive potential. Going back to the ancient world, Aristotle said that the ear is the organ of instruction, implying that deaf people are not capable of instruction or thought. As recently as the 1960s, Myklebust (1965) said that deaf learners are capable only of concrete thought. It was not until the late 1960s that Vernon (1968) did a meta-analysis of studies of deaf learners and thinking, finding that as a group they have the same range of cognitive potential as hearing learners.

At that point, the question in this field shifted from *whether* to *how* deaf learners could acquire higher-level cognitive strategies. Martin and Jonas (1985) found that after a systematic intervention program (instrumental enrichment), deaf learners indeed demonstrated significant achievement in a variety of cognitive skills including complex ones. That study was replicated by Craig (1987).

What adaptations are needed for deaf learners, if they are as fully capable as others in acquiring thinking skills? The experience of teachers and researchers in this field has indicated that only two adaptations are essential.

The first is that the fluent use of sign language as the medium of instruction is critically important as a natural first language for deaf learners in the discussion-based procedures that are fundamental to the acquiring of thinking strategies. In fact, this principle applies to other domains of instruction for deaf learners as well. The enabling aspect of this medium of instruction ensures that the deaf learner has complete access to all the nuances of cognitive strategies, no matter what type of program is used.

The second important adaptation for deaf and hard-of-hearing children is a somewhat slower pace of instruction, compared with "regular" hearing learners. Two reasons exist: (a) a need to teach some specialized vocabulary to which the deaf learner has not been exposed; and (b) a need to teach in more detail about certain applications of thinking strategies when deaf learners perhaps have not had the real-world experience that hearing learners have had and can bring to discussions of how thinking strategies might be applied to life outside the classroom.

Other than these adaptations, which are understood by most experienced teachers of deaf and hard-of-hearing learners, there is no reason to expect that thinking-strategy instruction will apply any less to these learners than to any group. (Of course, if secondary disabilities accompany deafness, a different kind of adaptation would be necessary.) Teachers of deaf and hard-of-hearing children, then, should move ahead with the incorporation of thinking strategies within their programs.

GIFTED AND TALENTED

At first sight, it may appear that gifted and talented students, no matter what definition is used to identify them, may be in even *less* need for explicit teaching of thinking strategies than other learners. Or, some will say that such students can be left to go quickly at their own pace through materials related to teaching thinking because it comes so naturally to them. Both of these points of view represent fallacies.

In relation to the first fallacy, gifted and talented students in some situations in fact have a *greater* need for some of these strategies than others. An example would be in the thinking habit of persistence in the search for a solution to a difficult problem. Many gifted and talented learners have found that other school tasks have come easily for them. Thus, when a true challenge is faced, they may impulsively turn aside, saying the task is not important. In fact, they need to work on slowing down and being less impulsive, because they will face problems that defy the easy solution, in both the curriculum and in their lives. They need the systematic approach that is frequently a part of some thinking-strategy programs.

In relation to the second fallacy, allowing such students to move ahead at their own pace denies them the opportunity for the valuable interactive dialogue and stimulation of elaboration that are important parts of becoming a high-level thinker.

Thinking strategies, therefore, have an important and fundamental place within programs for gifted and talented students.

THE INCLUSIVE CLASSROOM

The majority of identified special-needs learners today are in inclusive classrooms, where frequently their special needs may be ignored or insufficiently addressed. This situation may be both an advantage and a disadvantage for special-needs learners in regard to thinking skills. It can be a disadvantage if the teacher is unable to teach thinking skills in a way that is appropriate for such a variety of learners within a larger classroom. It can be an advantage because the adaptations necessary for special-needs learners in regard to thinking strategies are not significant; thus expectations can be maintained at an appropriate level for everyone. If thinking skills are tailored to a subgroup, this can implicitly mean differing expectations. In learning to think, the strong advantages of large-group discussion are important for everyone to experience, and that activity can benefit all learners in such classrooms, regardless of special needs.

Swartz, Reagan, and Kiser (1999) provide a useful perspective on the inclusive classroom and the teaching of thinking. They remind us that "all learners are special—all learners think, all reason, and all approach a task with a set of particular learning preferences and abilities." Infusion of thinking lessons in classrooms, particularly inclusive classrooms, allows for teachers to modify lessons as needed. Swartz and Reagan underscore the usefulness of "streamlining," in which a teacher diagnoses the degree of complexity and abstraction that special students can be expected to achieve and simplifies thinking tasks as needed, while still involving all students in the tasks. They also discuss a process called "diversification" in the same context. Here the teacher develops a repertoire of techniques for each thinking task in a lesson and includes a range of tasks of varying difficulties tailored to the individual student "in ways that complement each other while demanding quality thinking on the part of each student participating."

These generic approaches indicate a fundamentally egalitarian expectation for thinking in some important form by *all* learners. The special needs adaptations discussed above, of course, are challenging for any teacher with an inclusive classroom, but we are reminded that expectations frequently lead to achievement—an especially important point in the teaching of thinking.

HIGH EXPECTATIONS

Special-needs learners can be included in some form of thinking-strategy instruction in all classrooms. Thus, preparation for teaching thinking could be infused into various types of teacher preparation programs, as well as in staff development sessions for all kinds of settings. Most important, systematically involving special-needs learners in thinking strategies education holds promise for enabling them to move well beyond mistakenly identified learning goals. Everyone has limitations, of course, but educators should not presume to state those limitations for any learner, but rather to always provide one more opportunity for the "bar" to be raised still higher.

REFERENCES

Adrien, J. L. (1995, June). Disorders of regulation of cognitive activity in autistic children. *Journal of Autism and Development Disorders, 25*(3), 249–263.

Bryson, M., & Scardamalia, M. (1991). Teaching writing to students at risk for academic failure. *Resources in Education.* (ERIC Document Reproduction Service No. ED 338725)

Craig, H. (1987). Instrumental enrichment: Process and results with deaf students. *Thinking Skills Newsletter,* Pennsylvania State Department of Education.

Feuerstein, R. (1980). *Instrumental Enrichment.* Baltimore: University Park Press.

Ibler, L. S. (1997). Improving higher-order thinking in special education students through cooperative learning and social skills development. *Resources in Education.* (ERIC Document Reproduction Service No. ED 410732)

Jenison, M.E. (1993). Project ABLE: Academic bridges to learning effectiveness. *Resources in Education.* (ERIC Document Reproduction Service No. ED 359705)

Johns Hopkins University. (1993). Technology: Educational media and materials for the handicapped program. *Resources in Education.* (ERIC Document Reproduction Service No. ED 38511)

Lins, J. B. (1993). Developing critical thinking skills in young hearing-impaired students, using realia, practice sessions, and parent involvement. *Resources in Education.* (ERIC Document Reproduction Service No. ED 367080)

Lombardi, T. P., & Savage, L. (1992). Higher-order thinking skills for students with special needs. *Resources in Education.* (ERIC Document Reproduction Service No. ED 343351)

Martin, D. S., & Jonas, B. S. (1985). Cognitive improvement of hearing-impaired high school students through instruction in Instrumental Enrichment. *Resources in Education.* (ERIC Document Reproduction Service No. ED 247725)

Mastropieri, M. A., Scruggs, T. E., & Butcher, K. (1997). How effective is inquiry learning for students with mild disabilities? *Resources in Education.* (ERIC Document Reproduction Service No. EJ 552082)

Montague, M. (1997, March–April). Cognitive strategy instruction in mathematics for students with learning disabilities. *Journal of Learning Disabilities, 30*(2), 164–177.

Mulcahy, R. (1993). *Cognitive Education Project: Summary report.* Alberta, Canada: Department of Education. *Resources in Education.* (ERIC Document Reproduction Service No. ED 367682)

Myklebust, H.R. (1965). *Development and disorders of written language.* New York: Grune & Stratton.

Peniston, L. C. (1995). Study skills and critical thinking curriculum for adolescents in a psychiatric treatment center. *Resources in Education.* (ERIC Document Reproduction Service No. ED 401670)

Peterson, K. S. (1994). Integration of reading and writing strategies in primary level special education resource students to improve reading performance. *Resources in Education.* (ERIC Document Reproduction Service No. ED 371321)

Rider-Hankins, P. (1992). The educational process in juvenile correctional schools: Review of the research. *Resources in Education.* (ERIC Document Reproduction Service No. ED 349436.

Silver, R. A. (1989). Developing cognitive and creative skills through art: Programs for children with communication disorders or learning disabilities. *Resources in Education.* (ERIC Document Reproduction Service No. ED 410479)

Sullivan, S. G. (1995, Fall). Reasoning and remembering: Coaching students with learning disabilities to think. *Journal of Special Education, 29*(3), 310–322.

Swanson, H. L., & Hoskyn, M. (1998, Fall). Experimental intervention research on students with learning disabilities: A meta-analysis of treatment outcomes. *Review of Educational Research, 68*(3), 277–321.

Swartz, R., Reagan, R., & Kiser, M.A. (1999). *Teaching critical and creative thinking in language arts: A lesson book, grades 5 and 6.* Pacific Grove, CA: Critical Thinking Books and Software.

Vernon, M. (1968). Five years of research on the intelligence of deaf and hard-of-hearing children: A review of literature and discussion of implications. *Journal of Research on Deafness, 1*(4), 1–12.

37

Cultural Influences on Critical Thinking and Problem Solving

Douglas F. Brenner and Sandra Parks

Thinking occurs within a particular cognitive schema—a pattern that shapes how people seek and process information, the assumptions they make, and the guiding principles they apply to consider and solve problems. Because our habits of mind are influenced by our cultural and historical circumstances, the decision-making strategies that we seek to promote in students reflect our own culture. These schemata are not necessarily universal models that apply across all ethnic and cultural groups (Kim & Park, 2000; Paul, 1993).

During the last decade, critical thinking and problem solving have gained importance in educational reform. Standards adopted by professional education associations and articulated in curriculum guides and state assessment tests identify critical thinking and problem solving as significant goals of schooling. Problem-based learning, as an approach to organizing curriculum and as an instructional method, assumes that students have or will develop effective decision-making and problem-solving skills. Critical thinking is an essential aspect of moral reasoning and is employed in conflict resolution and interpersonal problem solving.

Although definitions of critical thinking vary, it can be described as "the intellectually disciplined process of actively and skillfully conceptualizing, applying, synthesizing, and evaluating information gathered from or generated by observation, reflection, reasoning, or communication, as a guide to belief and action" (Paul, Elder, & Bartell, 1997, p. 4). Critical thinking means consciously attending to the process and elements of thinking and thoughtfully assessing both our thinking process and its contents by specified standards. Thus research shows that critical thinking includes dispositions or critical attitudes, certain cognitive skills, metacognitive reflection, and supporting character or moral traits (Chaffee, 2000; Paul, 1993; Perkins, Goodrich, Tishman, & Owen, 1993).

As it is commonly defined or expressed, critical thinking has been characterized as favoring a masculine, instrumental, logical-rational, linear, objective, deductive, and Eurocentric viewpoint (Bailin, 1995; Norris, 1995; Wheary & Ennis, 1995). Clearly, standards of effective thinking expressed in Western habits of mind and construction of knowledge greatly influence curriculum design and instructional methodology. If Western epistemology creates cultural biases that limit some students' understanding and achievement, the effects of those influences are remediable (Bailin, 1995).

Expanding our knowledge of cultural perspectives enriches our understanding of the complex of traits, skills, habits, values, and abilities that individuals bring to the process of problem solving. It may also uncover the partiality or limits of any one perspective. All cultural practices may not be equally valuable or effective in enhancing critical thinking. However, within a culture's own context or perspective, what may be accepted as effective critical thinking may not be judged similarly in another culture. We can enlarge our understanding of the cognitive perspectives that students bring as members of their cultural or ethnic groups in order to adapt our teaching practices and create classroom communities where students feel supported.

What counts as good or effective critical thinking in solving problems or decision making in other cultures? How can educators use awareness of good thinking in various cultures to improve all students' thinking and learning? Answering these questions is a complex undertaking, since cultural study is inherently value-laden. Culture is a complex construct of influences that signals to the individual who he or she is, what constitutes a good and satisfying life, the resources available to achieve it, and the principles or guideposts (symbols, institutions, rituals, or values) that guide behavior (Hall & Hall, 1990).

INDIVIDUALIST AND COLLECTIVIST CULTURES

One useful way of describing differences between cultures involves the concepts of individualism and collectivism (Hofstede, 1991; Triandis, Chen, & Chan, 1998). Although individuals as well as cultures possess both individualistic and collectivistic tendencies to varying degrees, examining the distinctions between these cultural dimensions offers insight about the cultural frameworks that influence how people reason.

Individualistic cultures, such as Australia, Britain, Canada, Germany, and the United States, esteem the person as an individual. These cultures foster an autonomous self—a sense of each person as unique and separate from others—and emphasize independence, self-determination and self-reliance to achieve personal goals (Mpofu, 1994; Triandis et al., 1998; Watkins, Mortazavi, & Trofimova, 2000). In individualistic cultures, self-esteem is derived from what a person does or accomplishes. Although acting within social contexts, individualists' achievements are attributed to their own traits and choices, apart from relational or contextual matters. Focused on their plans, individualists' personal goals take priority over the goals of in-groups such as the family. Since individualism reinforces detachment from others, each person is largely emotionally disconnected from in-groups. Therefore, individualist cultures rely upon personal guilt for social control rather than shame or other social norms of conformity (Triandis, 1995; Watkins et al., 2000).

Individualism fosters a "low-context" communication style, which values direct self-expression, clarity, and speaking one's mind freely in a climate of competitiveness. Regardless of context, individualist communicators are expected to be verbally explicit, specific, and direct (Gudykunst & Kim, 1997; Neuliep, 2000). Considerable information is sought to direct the communication process, minimizing uncertainty and ambiguity. Individualists' messages include more self-referents such as "I" than other-referents such as "we" (Dodd, 1998).

Collectivistic cultures, such as Africa, China, Japan, Korea, Malaysia, Mexico, Pakistan, Peru, the Philippines, Thailand, or Native American cultures, foster a sense of the self as interrelated and interdependent with others (Ho, 1998; Moemeka, 1998; Singelis & Brown, 1995; Triandis, 1995). Goals and values that serve the in-group (the family, neighborhood, or community) are stressed along with mutual obligations and shared responsibility. Concepts of self and others are seen not as separate from, but as molded by, ongoing social contexts: "I am because we are" (Moemeka, 1998, p. 125). Harmony, social

reciprocity, obligation, dependence, and obedience are dominant values (Triandis, 1995).

Moemeka (1998) summarizes five characteristics that communal cultures share: (a) supremacy of the community; (b) sanctity of authority and hierarchy; (c) usefulness of the individual; (d) respect for the elderly; and (e) religion as a way of life. Collectivists are emotionally connected to their in-group through shared beliefs and values. Self-esteem is derived from maintaining harmonious interpersonal relationships while adapting to changing situations. Violating group harmony may be punished, often by shame.

Members of collectivistic cultures are expected to listen and infer the speaker's intention from what is not explicitly said (Ng, Loong, He, Liu, & Weatherall, 2000). Relying upon the context for communication cues is possible because members know each other and are expected to be sensitive to their respective social roles in varying contexts. Less reliance upon verbal communication and heightened use of nonverbal cues, as well as indirectness, ambiguity, and silence are therefore possible and valued. "Saving face" (avoiding criticism or the appearance of disagreement) is essential to help maintain harmony (Ng et al., 2000). This "high-context" communication is receiver-oriented. Sender and receiver focus on and are sensitive to each other. For example, "the Japanese value catching on quickly to another's meaning before the other must completely express the thought verbally or logically" (Ramsey, 1979, p. 142).

The features of individualistic and collective cultures remind us that, although we should not overemphasize differences, neither should we presume that other cultures share identical ways of knowing, being, and valuing (Banks, 1995, 1997). "Rather, the collectivistic mode has been more representative by far throughout the ages and in diverse parts of the world. In Chinese societies, for instance, the family, and not the individual, has been regarded as the basic social unit since ancient times" (Ho, 1998, p. 99). Wong & Tjosvold (1992) note that Chinese-Confucian culture values filial piety, emphasizing respect and obedience to parents, collective interdependence of people, and a code of conduct that guides appropriate behavior in view of people's hierarchical positions.

The Sioux (Native American) culture exemplifies a collectivist social order. The pervasive role of kinship is reflected in the Dakota/Lakota/Nakota salutation and prayer, "Mitakuye Oyasin," or "We are all related." This saying expresses the intimate connection they feel with others and the universe, reflecting their social identity and civic obligations to their relations (Brenner & Hoag, 1998). This sense of kinship, with accompanying appropriate attitudes and behaviors, developed in the dynamics of their demographics and the struggle to survive, and is intrinsically grounded in their spirituality (Bryde, 1970).

In Lakota culture, kinship changes the context of decision making and problem solving by emphasizing the responsibility members feel for each other and sensitizing them to the consequences of their behavior upon others. Civility and discipline are required; members must control their impulse to argue or disagree, both internally and externally. Deloria notes that "a socially responsible Dakota might not thoughtlessly indulge his moods, lest there be within range of his voice or presence a relative before whom his feelings must be suppressed as a matter of obligatory respect" (1983, p. 21). Moreover, silence is also highly valued because it encourages thorough, reflective, respectful, and deep listening in social exchanges. In varying ways, communal cultures cultivate those ways of communicating and thinking that inwardly and outwardly reflect thoughtful and behavioral regard for others, maintaining social harmony.

CRITICAL THINKING AND PROBLEM SOLVING

Differences in values, patterns of communication, and thinking dispositions in individualist and collectivist cultures influence the purposes, conduct, and standards for good thinking when one forms critical judgments or solves problems. Individualistic societies encourage direct, unambiguous statements. In Western culture, critical thinking and solving problems are intellectual tasks that each individual carries out independently, yielding consequences for which one usually is solely responsible. Thinking in various collectivistic cultures is socialized across group members. Communal cultures highlight the social dimension of thinking, a necessary dependence upon the informational and experiential resources offered by others. Thinking is not an entirely solitary activity but is strengthened through communication with others and through assessment and correction.

Paul and colleagues (1997) consider clarity as the "gateway" standard—a fundamental criterion to facilitate critical thinking, which may involve disagreement, correction, self-expression, or verbalization of one's inner beliefs and opinions, and may assume the importance of openly changing things or situations. However, communal cultures, in which saving face is paramount, find ambiguity and indirection essential to maintaining harmonious relationships. Argumentation and persuasion are devalued because they suggest that one has superior knowledge or that others must be corrected or con-

verted, potentially creating ill will or disharmony. Private conversations or intermediaries may be employed carefully in cases of significant disagreement; public forums are not considered appropriate venues for self-expression.

Critical thinking is characterized as utilitarian, focusing on dominating, controlling and computing information while seeking definite, unambiguous, and objective results and knowledge (Hvolbek, 1992). Accuracy is espoused as a standard to assess and uphold the value of critical thinking (Costa & Kallick, 2000; Paul et al., 1997). Yet accuracy or eliminating errors may enjoy less currency in those communal cultures where maintaining social harmony and respecting the wisdom of the group or elders is valued more highly.

In individualistic cultures, critical thinking tends to involve a strategy, a process of asking and answering with evidence the key questions that thoughtful people satisfy before making certain judgments. Swartz and Parks (1994) describe a five-step decision-making strategy: determine whether a decision is necessary; consider a number of options; gather information to predict each option's likelihood of positive and negative consequences; evaluate the importance of likely consequences; and choose the best option based on their significance. This approach reflects an individualist perspective that values thorough, systematic thought, inferences of likelihood, and prioritizing of values. In many collectivistic cultures, a more desired process would be to consider an issue carefully, frame a question, approach a wise elder for advice, and ponder it before making a thoughtful choice. If an issue is decided in a group forum, discourse may express many similar factors, but not through a step-wise, organized strategy.

Problem posing may vary across cultures. Individualist, action-oriented cultures presume the value of solving problems and doing things. A "problem" is often perceived as a barrier or negative condition to be overcome or abated, prompting a plan or device to accomplish a desired goal or outcome. However, in collectivist cultures one typically may accept things or situations as they are and simply "not enter into the problem-solving frame of mind" (Larson, 2001, p. 192). "In the traditional way, trying to control things or people is considered a waste of energy because it is believed that everything is as it should be at any given point in time. . . . Acceptance is a very important part of living in harmony and balance in a world view that emphasizes that everyone and everything has a reason for being" (Garrett & Wilbur, 1999, pp. 198–199).

Individualistic cultures may focus on short-term goals such as scoring a point, making oneself understood, winning an argument, or abating a problem. However, in collectivistic cultures, decision making involves considering long-term consequences that must be especially carefully weighed in terms of how decisions could affect the larger community. The Lakota, for instance, are exhorted to consider a decision's possible effect on "the seventh generation" from the present one.

Many cultures, including Native Americans, typically value holistic rather than analytical types of thinking. They view all things as connected and think in terms of general principles or seeing the big picture (see Gilliland, 1995; Lame Deer, Archie Fire, & Erdoes, 1992). In Chinese culture, dialectic tensions that Western thinkers see as opposites—for example, good versus evil and right versus wrong—are seen instead as complementary. The yin and yang illustrate not simply opposites, but the balance or harmony of the whole—the unity of the two (Chen, 1998). Ho (1998) draws attention to the Filipino concept of "pakapa-kapa," or groping, as a general way of problem solving that encourages approaching problems with no preconceived notions or questions, as a blank slate, "as if one were in a state of total ignorance" (p. 97). This approach, grounded in a sense of shared identity and connection with others, is similar to what Hvolbek (1992) describes as a meditative type of thinking, developing full awareness of the moment, and avoiding analysis and categorization, while being fully present and passively contemplative rather than actively investigative.

All cultures rely upon information, but data and credible sources may be defined differently. In Western culture evidence is drawn from scientific research, experts and authorities, or books. In collective cultures, wise elders—referred to by the Lakota as "living libraries of knowledge"—are sources of information. In oral cultures, decision making is informed by stories prized for reflecting the values and wisdom of generations (a coded wisdom). Polynesian navigators developed keen sensitivity and accuracy in reading patterns in seemingly unrelated signs, information that Western science traditionally regarded as chaotic (Witt-Miller, 1991). Meadows explains that American Indian traditions derived from "knowledge of the pulsating rhythm of life that could be seen and sensed all around in the Book of Nature, in the chapters of the seasonal cycles, in the passages of the Sun and the Moon, and whose words could be found among the trees and plants and animals and birds" (1996, p. 13).

The purposes and outcomes of critical thinking and problem solving also vary with culture. The desired result of critical thinking and problem solving in Western culture is well-founded knowledge or judgment. Degree of certainty, warranted inferences, and practical effectiveness are standards by which we judge whether thinking is sound. The intelligence modality favored in Western cultures focuses upon recalling, classifying, analyzing, or applying knowledge. Limited by the contexts in which it operates, this modality seeks efficiency, prediction, and control through logical, analytical reasoning and simple solutions (Hanna, Bemak, & Chung, 1999).

Collectivist cultures not only value group kinship; they cultivate spiritual wisdom as well. Hanna and colleagues (1999) define wisdom as the cognitive and affective traits reinforcing "life skills and understanding necessary for living a life of well-being, fulfillment, effective coping, and insight into the nature of self, others, environment, and interpersonal interactions" (p. 126). They argue that wisdom promotes an extraordinary holistic and affective "depth, fluidity, and richness of understanding" (p. 131), including awareness of its own limits and origins through dialectic, experiential and transcendent reasoning that accommodates ambiguity.

IMPLICATIONS FOR EDUCATORS

Since American education is based strongly on Western structures of knowledge and epistemology, individualist modes of critical thinking and decision making will remain the dominant thinking practices in schools. Students' academic achievement and understanding of important curriculum concepts and principles require thoughtful analysis and well-informed evaluation.

Adding collectivist decision-making practices to students' thinking repertoires addresses each of Banks's suggested five dimensions of multicultural education: content integration, knowledge construction process, prejudice reduction, an equity pedagogy, and an empowering school culture and social structure (1995). Curriculum content should include awareness that different cultures solve problems differently and that historical events and literary works are influenced by the intellectual dispositions of the culture in which they occur. Banks's notion of "the knowledge construction process" is closely linked to the practice of critical thinking and encourages divergent or expansive thinking. Collectivist decision making offers experiential techniques to show how events, issues, or concepts can be viewed from many points of view and arrived at by various ways of knowing.

Collectivist decision making employs social and emotional interactions that are promoted in the current interest in emotional intelligence. It provides techniques for prejudice reduction, creates a school culture of civility and respect, and offers students from collectivist culture families some school experiences that resemble their own cultural styles.

Enhancing critical thinking and problem solving across cultures requires educators to understand standards of good thinking, to clarify them for themselves and for students, and to practice sound thinking in the classroom, in one's personal experiences, and in the culture of the school. Teachers and students must evaluate the quality of thinking and acknowledge good thinking whenever it is demonstrated.

As educators, we are challenged to explore the implications of collectivist thinking styles:

• How can we create classroom cultures in which people take responsibility for each other—not just through occasional empathy and sympathy, but through natural, daily actions?

• What levels of trust, respect, civility, and humility are required and demonstrated when we fully listen to each other, with few if any interruptions?

• How can we address vital issues while de-emphasizing personal agendas and emotions?

• How can we use in schools the accumulated experience and wisdom of the elderly and experience the social and cultural value of good storytellers?

• How can we help students curb their typical rush to formulate a response in conversation? Do we truly possess and demonstrate the patience to listen to them before giving our opinions?

• In classroom interactions, have we evaluated the extent to which expediency has become more important than thinking and listening together?

Both individualist and collectivist thinking practices offer teachers and students increased intellectual richness, social poise, and personal efficacy and satisfaction. We are challenged to foster in students the traits we admire from communal cultures—humility, listening and silence, reflective thinking, responsibility, civility, respect, holistic and intuitive thinking—while at the same time honoring Western intellectual standards of accuracy, clarity, and rationality.

REFERENCES

Bailin, S. (1995). Is critical thinking biased? Clarifications and implications. *Educational Theory, 45,* 191–197.

Banks, J. A. (1995). Multicultural education: Historical development, dimensions, and practice. In J. A. Banks & C. A. M. Banks (Eds.), *Handbook of research on multicultural education* (pp. 3–24). New York: Macmillan.

Banks, J. A. (1997). *Educating citizens in a multicultural society.* New York: Teachers College Press.

Brenner, D. F., & Hoag, C. L. (1998, March). *Explorations in considering critical thinking from the perspective of Lakota/Native American culture.* Paper presented at the South Florida Thinking Skills Conference, Miami, FL.

Bryde, J. (1970, August 13–14). *Values and the [Sioux] American Indian.* Transcript of a speech given at Huron College, Huron, SD. [A copy of the transcript of this speech is available from the authors of this chapter.]

Chaffee, J. (2000). *The thinker's way: Create the life you want.* Boston: Little, Brown & Co.

Chen, L. (1998). Chinese and North Americans: An epistemological exploration of the intercultural communication. In J. N. Martin, T. K. Nakayama, & L. A. Flores (Eds.), *Readings in cultural contexts* (pp. 357–369). Mountain View, CA: Mayfield Publishing.

Costa, A. L., & Kallick, B. (Eds.). (2000). *Discovering and exploring habits of mind.* Alexandria, VA: Association for Supervision and Curriculum Development.

Deloria, E. C. (1983). *Speaking of Indians.* Vermillion, SD: State Publishing Co., University of South Dakota.

Dodd, C. H. (1998). *Dynamics of intercultural communication* (5th ed.). Boston: McGraw-Hill.

Garrett, M. T., & Wilbur, M. P. (1999). Does the worm live in the ground? Reflections on Native American spirituality. *Journal of Multicultural Counseling and Development, 27,* 193–206.

Gilliland, H. (1995). *Teaching the Native American* (3rd ed.). Dubuque, IA: Kendall/Hunt.

Gudykunst, W. B., & Kim, Y. Y. (1997). *Communicating with strangers: An approach to intercultural communication* (3rd ed.). Boston: McGraw-Hill.

Hall, E. T., & Hall, M. R. (1990). *Understanding cultural differences.* Yarmouth, ME: Intercultural Press.

Hanna, F. J., Bemak, F., & Chi-Ying Chung, R. (1999). Toward a new paradigm for multicultural counseling. *Journal of Counseling & Development, 77,* 125–134.

Ho, D. E. (1998). Indigenous psychologies: Asian perspectives. *Journal of Cross-Cultural Psychology, 29,* 88–103.

Hofstede, G. (1991). I, we, and they. In *Cultures and organizations: Software of the mind* (pp. 49–79). New York: McGraw-Hill.

Hvolbek, R. H. (1992). The role of meditative thinking within a curriculum of critical thinking. *Inquiry: Critical Thinking Across the Disciplines, 10*(2), 3–8.

Kim, U., & Park, Y-S. (2000). The challenge of cross-cultural psychology: The role of the indigenous psychologies. *Journal of Cross-Cultural Psychology, 31,* 63–75.

Lame Deer, Archie Fire, & Erdoes, R. (1992). *Gift of power: The life and teachings of a Lakota medicine man.* Sante Fe, NM: Bear & Co. Publishing.

Larson, C. U. (2001). *Persuasion: Reception and responsibility* (9th ed.). Belmont, CA: Wadsworth/Thomson Learning.

Meadows, K. (1996). *Earth medicine.* New York: Barnes & Noble Books.

Moemeka, A. A. (1998). Communalism as a fundamental dimension of culture. *Journal of Communication, 48,* 118–141.

Mpofu, E. (1994). Exploring the self-concept in an African culture. *Journal of Genetic Psychology, 55,* 341–354.

Neuliep, J. W. (2000). *Intercultural communication: A contextual approach.* Boston: Houghton Mifflin.

Ng, S. H., Loong, C. S. F., He, A. P., Liu, J. H., & Weatherall, A. (2000). Communication correlates of individualism and collectivism: Talk directed at one or more addressees in family conversations. *Journal of Language & Social Psychology, 19*(1), 26–45.

Norris, S. P. (1995). Sustaining and responding to charges of bias in critical thinking. *Educational Theory, 45,* 199–211.

Paul, R. (1993). *Critical thinking: What every person needs to survive in a rapidly changing world* (Rev. 3rd ed.). Rohnert Park, CA: Foundation for Critical Thinking, Sonoma State University.

Paul, R., Elder, L., & Bartell, T. (1997, March). *California teacher preparation for instruction in critical thinking: Research findings and policy recommendations.* Sacramento, CA: California Commission on Teacher Credentialing.

Perkins, D. N., Goodrich, H., Tishman, S., & Owen, J. M. (1993). *Thinking connections: Learning to think and thinking to learn.* Menlo Park, CA: Addison-Wesley.

Ramsey, S. (1979). Double vision: Nonverbal behavior East and West. In A. Wolfgang (Ed.), *Nonverbal behavior: Perspectives, applications, intercultural insights.* Lewiston, NY: C. J. Hogrefe.

Singelis, T. M., & Brown, W. J. (1995, March). Culture, self, and collectivist communication. *Human Communication Research, 21,* 354–389.

Swartz, R., & Parks, S. (1994). *Infusing the teaching of critical and creative thinking into content instruction.* Pacific Grove, CA: Critical Thinking Press and Software.

Triandis, H. C. (1995). *Individualism and collectivism.* Boulder, CO: Westview.

Triandis, H. C., Chen, X. P., & Chan, D. K.-S. (1998). Scenarios for the measurement of collectivism and individualism. *Journal of Cross-Cultural Psychology, 29,* 275–289.

Watkins, D., Mortazavi, S., & Trofimova, I. (2000). Independent and interdependent conceptions of self: An investigation of age, gender, and culture differences in importance and satisfaction ratings. *Cross-Cultural Research, 34,* 113–134.

Wheary, J., & Ennis, R. H. (1995). Gender bias in critical thinking: Continuing the dialogue. *Educational Theory, 45,* 213–224.

Witt-Miller, H. (1991, Fall). The soft, warm, wet technology of native oceania. *Whole Earth Review* (72), 64–69. Retrieved July 30, 2000, from INFOTRAC database. (Expanded Academic ASAP No. A11256652)

Wong, C. L., & Tjosvold, D. (1992, August). Managing conflict in a diverse work force: A Chinese perspective in North America. *Small Group Research, 23,* 302–321.

38

Reversing Underachievement in Urban Students: Pedagogy of Confidence

Yvette Jackson

My Stream of Consciousness

You think that I don't know that you think
I got an F because I'm lazy and indifferent.
But maybe I'm just underchallenged and underappreciated.
Deep down I am begging you to teach me
To learn and create—not just to memorize and regurgitate.
I'm asking you to help me find my own truth.
I'm asking you to help me find my own beauty.
I'm asking you to help me see my own unique truth.
We need a miracle
One for every kid who subconsciously wants
To be pushed to the edge/taken to the most extreme limits.
I want you to make my brain work in a hundred different
*   ways every day.*
I'm asking you to make my head ache with knowledge—
*   spin with ideas.*
I want you to make my mind my most powerful asset.

—Siem Tesfaslase, 10th grade, Arlington High School,
Indianapolis, Indiana

When we talk about people having undeveloped muscles or physiques, we say they're out of shape. We don't say they're deficient, like many say about underachieving urban students. The brain is like a muscle. It requires specific exercises that reflect and address the needs of the learner, guided personal training in skills to build strength and confidence, and a nutritional diet of relevant and meaningful instruction to build strength (competence in skills) and prevent deficiencies (underachievement).

So, given all the research we have about the brain and learning, why doesn't instruction reflect this understanding? Why don't more teachers feel competent and confident about reversing the underachievement of urban students?

THE LIMITING REALITY: FEAR

Ask Me

Ask me why a sour smell surrounds the sweet smell of
*   summer.*
Ask me why our bodies are made to live forever, but some
*   die at forty.*
Ask me why I get a lump in my throat when I talk to a
*   beautiful flower.*
Ask me why the brain is far more powerful than a
*   computer, but we are limited to what we use.*

—Priscilla Mitchell, 10th grade,
Arlington High School

Through the National Urban Alliance for Effective Education, I have worked with many school districts around the country where underachievement is the norm. These districts are predominantly in cities where urban is a euphemism for low-performing students of color, and where 73 percent of the teachers identify themselves as white or racially and culturally different from their students (Mahiri, 1998, p. 4). In these districts, teachers are under all kinds of pressure, but the one they articulate the most emotionally is fear: fear of the tests their students have to take; fear of their inability to address and translate standards and assessments into instruction; and, most poignantly, fear of not being able to reach their culturally different students to reverse underachievement.

This fear causes a type of paralysis that inhibits many well-meaning teachers from trying instructional strategies that motivate and support the learning of their culturally different students. Instead they continuously use methods that not only minimize learning but very often result in significant resistant behaviors from these students (Alpert, 1976). The classroom becomes one where "the rhythms of learning of these students are out of sync with the fearful cadence of their culturally different teachers" (Mahiri, 1998). Students feel the apprehension of their teachers and translate this as the teachers' not caring or not believing in their capacity to learn. Many of these students respond to these perceptions by shutting down or acting out. The teachers attribute this shutting down to a lack of connection between themselves and their students, and they often misinterpret the students' behavior as showing a lack of caring. Both sets of perceptions are often very far from reality. Most teachers and students care very much. What many of the teachers actually feel is that they don't know how to help their culturally different students learn (Archer, 1999).

The way the brain makes learning happen does not differ from one culture to another. The brain, unlike the mind, is a biological entity, not a social, cultural product (Eisner, 1994). When teachers understand intelligence, learning, and the powerful effects of culture, language, and cognition on these processes, they can better choose effective learning strategies that do not depend on race or ethnicity but rather build on each student's cultural frame of reference (Mahiri, 1998; Feuerstein, 1982). This understanding diminishes teachers' fears of being ineffective and enables them to appreciate the positive impact to be derived by recognizing the cultural experiences of their students.

UNDERSTANDING THE CONNECTION BETWEEN LEARNING AND INTELLIGENCE

Intelligence is the act of processing information in a way that enables an individual to solve problems and create products or strategies to successfully function in a particular situation (Feuerstein, 1982; Gardner, 2000; Caine & Caine, 1994). The processing involved in intelligence is the result of learning. Learning happens when the brain makes connections among experiences that engage students. They are engaged when they are actively involved and understand what they are studying. Dewey (1933) described this understanding as the ability to grasp meaning, to see something in relationship to something else familiar, and to make connections. The brain naturally constructs meaning when it perceives relationships (Caine & Caine, 1994), and those relevant or meaningful connections motivate the brain to be engaged and focused. Constructing meaning is the major requisite to learning and the core of intellectual processing.

RECOGNIZING THE IMPACT OF CULTURE, LANGUAGE, AND COGNITION ON LEARNING

The idea of constructing meaning is not an unfamiliar concept to teachers. When I ask teachers what affects how an individual constructs meaning from a piece of text or any other form of communication, they identify such factors as environment, culture, values, exposure, perception, language, background knowledge, and prior experiences.

These factors can be organized into three overarching categories: culture, language, and cognition. These categories are the key to accelerating learning, for they are the frame of reference from which all meaning is constructed and communicated, and therefore the frame of reference on which all achievement depends.

THE COGNITION APEX

Intelligence and learning are based on meaning that is constructed from information taken in through receptive functions such as reading, listening, and observing, and communicated through expressive functions such as talking, moving, and writing. The thinking processes involved in this behavior of human intelligence—going from receptive to expressive functions to construct meaning—is what we call cognition (Costa, 1985). It is what helps us understand and use the world around us by making relationships, seeing connections, and finding patterns. In reading, such behaviors are the basis for comprehending text, detecting language patterns, and focusing on generalizations.

COGNITION AND CULTURE

Reversing underachievement of urban students depends intricately on recognizing the impact of culture on cognition and the motivation necessary for learning. Prior experiences that students bring to school happen within their sociocultural environment. When teachers are unable to make links between these cultural references and build understanding, what Draschen described as an "affective filter" develops. When this occurs, students can't make connections, become unmotivated, and don't identify with the teacher. Often they are overanxious about their performance, which causes stress on a biological level (Draschen, 1982). This stress prevents input from reaching those parts of the brain responsible for language acquisition, thereby restricting how meaning is constructed (Delpit, 1995).

Culture also affects a learner's motivation at an even deeper level. Besides searching for relationships, the brain depends on cultural references when attaching relevance or meaning to an item or event (Feuerstein, 1982). Students need opportunities to share or express what is relevant and meaningful, and this sharing requires an environment where relationships between the teacher and student are built on mutual respect for cultural differences and recognition of cultural similarities.

CULTURE, LANGUAGE, AND COGNITION

Culture molds language, and language represents a way of thinking. Disconnections and misjudgments that teachers make about the potential of culturally different students are often affected by language differences. Many students in poor and low-performing urban districts are African-Americans with their own cultural linguistic form (language or dialect). Many culturally different teachers find this problematic. Teachers often don't know how to move the students from the linguistic form that has been practical and social for them to the standard form (Dewey, 1933). Many teachers often consider this language inferior and generalize this to signify inferior thinking. Often this perception is dealt with unconsciously. Cunningham's research shows that when teachers assess comprehension using miscue analysis, they are more likely to correct reading miscues that are dialect related than those that are not (Delpit, 1995). Moreover, this perception of inferiority is sometimes communicated directly to students, who naturally are sensitive to how their language is regarded. To demean the language is to demean their culture and identity.

Teachers' misjudgments about student language and potential can result from a lack of knowledge about how language develops. Language development and fluency are very much reliant on discussion for vocabulary building. "People acquire a new dialect most effectively through interaction with speakers of that dialect" (Delpit, 1995, p. 11). However, the way subjects are taught, very little discussion takes place using the vocabulary of the discipline or text in connection with the concepts, so language development is actually restricted (Dewey, 1933). Pogrow postulates that this lack of discussion can give rise to what he calls a "cognitive wall"— an inability to connect concepts to other experiences. It results from a lack of enriching conversation to build strategic understanding. Without such conversation, students cannot develop the cognitive structures to which ideas or concepts can be linked or expanded. This cognitive wall deflates motivation, inhibits learning, and can breed resistant behaviors (Pogrow, 2000).

PEDAGOGY OF CONFIDENCE

To you I might just be another child lost in society's
   universal negativity.
I suppose now is the time for heads to turn away and
   shoulders to shrug.

Know this . . .
Stereotypes can only go so far,
Last so long, and mean so much.
Why listen to rumors with no definition or destination?

Not only can I name all the states and capitals
Memorized since the third grade,
I can read Romeo and Juliet with no hesitation,
Because that one English teacher is not in it for the money
   and free summers.
Because she cares with the heart that goes past the extreme
For not only me,
But ALL 150 of her students, her children.
Miracles can happen,
Dreams can come true.

   — *Kaycee R. Grisby, 10th grade,*
      Arlington High School

Students' responses of either resistance or acceptance are at least in part predicated on the specific nature of the pedagogy and curriculum to which they are exposed (Mahiri, 1998, p. 3). Pedagogy is an art or method of teaching, developed and refined when teachers are confident in their ability to successfully affect their students. This sense of confidence results from knowing what to do and believing you have the skills and abilities to meet those expectations.

Confident teachers of urban students demonstrate their beliefs in the capacity of their students to learn by insisting on the expectation that they will be productive contributors to society and providing what Delpit calls "the codes of power" that will enable them to achieve these expectations. "Codes of power" are usable knowledge and skills that enable students to communicate effectively in standard literary forms. This relates to linguistic forms, critical and creative thinking, communicative strategies, and presentation of self—that is, ways of talking, writing, dressing, and interacting. Confident teachers use strategies that empower. Students become competent, learning increases, achievement improves, and both students and teachers are more confident (Delpit, 1995; Feuerstein, 1982; Jackson, Lewis, Feuerstein, & Samuda, 1998).

CULTURE, LANGUAGE, AND COGNITION AS THE INSTRUCTIONAL MODEL

The poetry in this chapter was written by the 10th grade urban students of a culturally different teacher whom I have the pleasure of mentoring through the Indianapolis Public Schools/National Urban Alliance Literacy Initiative. During her first two years of teaching at Arlington High School, Audra Jordan taught these students 9th and 10th grade English and reversed their trend of underachievement to performances of excellence. She has used writing—particularly poetry, similes, and metaphors—as a vehicle for her and her students to share cultural experiences, creating a deep, bonding relationship so crucial to the learning process of urban students. Her teaching practice exemplifies the *pedagogy of confidence*, which is based on the fearless expectation that all her students will learn. When teachers practice this pedagogy, they do not doubt the potential of their culturally different students, and they switch their instructional focus from what has to be taught to how to maximize learning. Through this practice, a teacher uses the interconnectedness of culture, language, and cognition as a frame for an "instructional model that guides the development of his or her teaching methods, the selection of learning strategies, and the design of assessments," which in turn accelerates and enriches the learning of urban students (Costa, 1985, p. 137). The model has three core concepts that act as instructional objectives within the context of culture, language, and cognition:

- Self-discovery
- Mediated learning
- Literacy enrichment

Each of these objectives is a symbiotic node in the model; that is, they depend on each other and require each other for support.

SELF-DISCOVERY

Two of the greatest motivators of learning are confidence in one's abilities and self-worth. Both strengthen the sense of identity that is critical to developing the motivation to achieve. Self-discovery is a process of reflection that is built into instruction as a learning ritual, connecting to students on both an affective level and a cognitive one. It is designed around a set of questions that the students must think through and react to with concrete responses.

The affective level addresses a student's sense of personal identity. The following questions can be used for personal reflection:

- How do I see myself?
- How do I think others see me?
- How do I see others?
- How do I want others to see me?

As a format for identity building, these questions allow students to measure how they see themselves as individuals as well as in relation to others. This exploration can set the groundwork for developing personal goals. They also provide a vehicle for teachers to learn about the cultural identity of their students, which includes the affiliations and references that individuals connect to and value.

The cognitive level of self-discovery is a cycle of reflection. It begins with the introduction of new material, moves through self-assessing for understanding, and then recycles to incorporate new material. It requires teachers to analyze what is being taught, identify what they want the students to understand, and decide which conceptual understandings to focus on. This helps to ensure that students make relevant personal connections, which can motivate them to form lasting memories.

Introduction questions for students include:

- What do I know about this (concept or theme)?
- What connections can I make to this?

Closure questions include:

- What did I learn about myself ?
- How does this connect to my world?
- What else does this remind me of and why?

Student journals provide an excellent vehicle for thinking through the questions, but they must be shared through individual conferences with the teacher. This sharing, in a safe and mutually respectful environment, opens communication and trust between students and teachers.

MEDIATED LEARNING

Feuerstein describes mediated learning as an interactive process that bonds the teacher and student in a nurturing relationship, which is so culturally important to urban students. The goal of mediated learning is to elicit from the students a personal motivation for learning. The teacher engages the student around purposely selected activities that build their confidence by guiding them in discussion to critically analyze tasks and identify relevant connections and applications to their personal experiences. Through this discussion, the teacher builds background in the understandings of the discipline or text to be studied (preventing the "cognitive wall" mentioned earlier) and facilitates acquisition of the relationships, verbal tools, and cognitive skills necessary to master the task (Feuerstein, 1982). This dynamic interaction between the teacher and student is the most important aspect of the mediation process for it allows assessment of understanding and learning to be part of the instructional process (Jackson et al., 1998). Mediated learning develops the cognitive functions that are the foundations of literacy and are necessary for achievement throughout life. These include:

- Focusing on problems or issues
- Inferring connections
- Organizing information
- Sorting relevant and irrelevant information
- Labeling

Mediated learning facilitates a balance between self-discovery, relationship building, and mastering content understanding.

LITERACY ENRICHMENT

Underachievement among urban students is most evident in literacy skills (Levine, Cooper, & Hilliard, 2000). Literacy is the key to empowering students. It is the primary focus of mediated learning and the context in which the "codes of power" described earlier are developed. Eisner (1994) described it as an individual's ability to construct, create, and communicate meaning in many forms—for example, written text, drawing, mathematical symbols, or dance. It is the engagement of both receptive and expressive capabilities in a student. Literacy for urban learners is best developed when the teacher mediates the learning process by providing lessons that foster social interaction for language development and guide the application of cognitive skills that help students construct and communicate.

Five critical experiences help accelerate literacy development:

- Responding to a variety of texts.
- Composing—oral and written.
- Studying and mastering language patterns.
- Sustained reading of a variety of self-selected books.
- Learning how to learn. (Nessel, 1999)

There are some very powerful strategies that provide mediated learning experiences in literacy. These strategies translate into skills and ensure development of critical thinking, fluency, and organization within the context of culture, language, and cognition (Levine, Cooper, & Hilliard, 2000).

Constructing Meaning Through Talking: Read-Talk-Write

This strategy helps students read carefully and put information into their own words. Students pair up and read part of a short text individually. Then they share what they've read.

After talking, they decide collaboratively on a sentence to summarize what they've read. They continue this process until the entire selection is read. This interactive strategy helps students paraphrase information, remember information, and monitor their own reading. It also helps students crystallize their thinking by comparing their thoughts to their partner's (Nessel & Baltas, 2000).

Thinking Maps for Constructing and Communicating Meaning

Thinking Maps are eight visual-verbal organizers developed by David Hyerle to support the brain's natural learning process by helping students identify patterns and relationships in their thinking as well as in textual material. They are based on the eight fundamental cognitive processes that form the core of cognition and learning: defining a concept, describing qualities or attributes, comparing and contrasting, sequencing, classifying, part-whole relationships, cause and effect, and seeing analogies. The Thinking Maps provide a common language for teachers to use with culturally different students in developing both critical thinking and language, or "codes of power," needed to strengthen their ability to construct meaning from text and to communicate their learning. They are tools that facilitate lessons around the five critical experiences necessary to develop literacy. When students use the Thinking Maps, teachers can quickly assess their thinking and identify specific comprehension issues (Hyerle, 1995).

TAXONOMIES AND LANGUAGE DEVELOPMENT

Fluency in standard English is one of the most important language goals for reversing underachievement in urban students. It is the basis for reading, writing, and speaking. The key to developing fluency is building vocabulary through strategies that provide a venue for 1) recognizing students' cultural experiences; 2) creating bridges from those experiences to relevant, theme-related vocabulary; and 3) making connections between their language and standard English.

One motivating strategy for building fluency is a taxonomy-based writing system developed by Evelyn Rothstein. Students brainstorm about a topic and place the resulting items alphabetically on a list. The list helps the writers recognize what they already know on a subject. A taxonomy also helps students connect their language with the standard English form. Figure 38.1 shows examples of three taxonomies from Jordan's Arlington High School class. The students created taxonomies around themes they were studying in literature. The taxonomies stimulated their creativity and strengthened their

—Figure 38.1—
Student-Created Taxonomies

Taxonomy of Slang	Images of Sorrow Taxonomy	Images of Love Taxonomy
A ain't, all 'dat	A addicts, anger, ashtrays	A African drums, Aphrodite
B bump, bousta (about to)	B bitter voices, broken glass	B bayou, babies
C crib, chillin'	C conflicts, crucifixion, captivity	C Caribbean Sea, couples
D dis, dang	D dead flowers, dreams	D doves, diaries, dreams
E e-z	E excuses, endangered species	E emotions, everlasting
F fixin', frontin'	F frowns, fantasies never realized	F flowers, France, flames
G gonna, gots/gat (got)	G greenhouse effect, ghetto	G God, ginger
H homie, hookup	H heartbreak, homeless people	H hot springs, hugs
I I's, ice	I infants (neglected), injustice	I infatuation, innocence
J ju (you)	J junkies, jail cells	J jasmine, Jesus
K kinda, killa	K killings	K kisses, kites
L lil, loot	L love lost, labyrinths	L labryinth, love letters
M mo', mutha	M mobs, melted wax, memories	M mothers, magnolias
N nuttin'	N 911, neglected people	N notes, northern lights
O off the hook	O orphans, obituaries	O optimism, only you
P phat	P poverty, painkillers	P proposals, poems
Q quad	Q quiet rooms	Q quiet, quality time
R rowdy	R Romeo and Juliet, racists	R reggae, rainstorms
S scratch, somethin'	S stillborns, slaves, sunsets	S songs, solitude
T tight, triflin'	T tension-filled rooms, tribulations	T temples, tickles, time
U us's	U unsatisfied love, unsaved people	U Uranus, Utopia, universe
V violation	V victims, violent homes	V victory, virtues, velvet
W wuz-up	W war, weapons, weeping	W waves, willow trees
	X X-rays	X x-citement
Y yo	Y yelling	Y yo-yos, you
		Z zoos

confidence in language. The students moved from personal taxonomies to sharing with the entire class, which allowed them to interact while developing their vocabulary (Rothstein & Lauber, 1999). The richness of the vocabulary shows the students' potential and creativity.

Immense potential exists in the classrooms of urban students. Finding the combination of interactions to unlock it requires an ardent belief in this potential, the desire to try all means to tap it, and the confidence to connect to the students through what we all value most: personal identity. When our perceptions and expectations expand to recognize the power of culture and language in the learning process, we can explore the endless opportunities for creating the bridges that confi-

dent teachers such as Jordan provide. These bridges allow students to see connections and relationships between their world and the world we are trying to open to them. We provide the motivation to pursue the dreams of success that all these students harbor.

Dreamkeeper
Listen to me tell you why they said I couldn't.
They said there was NO WAY
Me being Black, them being White —
Oh wait, other way around
    See what I mean
They said it wouldn't be possible

I'm too sensitive
Too nice
Too open
Too honest
They said I wouldn't last
Too many threats-dangers-risks
> *Oh really?*
They continued—I couldn't succeed
> *Too naïve*
> *Too young*
Too idealistic
There is NO WAY to save them all
> *By the way—for future reference—Do not refer to*
> *my children as "them"*
They said I couldn't because too much damage has already been done
No motivation
Nothing to work with
> *Please, I do not have time for your lies*
They said I wouldn't be happy
I would become bitter, sarcastic, disillusioned
> *Oh yeah? Let me know when that begins.*
They said I couldn't because I'm only motivated by Anglo guilt
Races stick together
There is no way I could relate
I must be a fake, a phony
> *Do you even know me?*
They said I could do "better"
> *But that's YOUR better—not MINE*
They said I couldn't because they are the other people's children
Now listen to me tell you why I must
I must because both lives and dreams depend on it
I must because nowhere in the quote does it say that the village is
> *exclusive*
I must because love is round
I must because in doubting my faith, I would betray my innermost
> *being*
I must because it is your problem not mine
I must because neither racism, reverse racism, fear, insecurity or
> *elitism rules my world*
I must because lyrical words and powerful rhythms are yet to be sung
I must because my passion propels me
I must because it is my daily benediction
I must because MY children, YOUR children, OUR children
They are MY laughter
> *MY tears*
MY screams

MY TRUTH
YES, MY TRUTH
I must because each of their individual faces float in and out of my
> *dreams*
I must because I am a natural born DREAMKEEPER
> —*Audra Jordan, Teacher, Arlington High School,*
> *Indianapolis, Indiana*

REFERENCES

Alpert, R. D. (1976). *Talking black*. Rowley, MA: Newbury.

Archer, J. (February 3, 1999). Teachers suggest the need for better training. *Education Week*, 8(21), 12.

Caine, R. N., & Caine, G. (1994). *Making connections: Teaching and the human brain*. Menlo Park, CA: Addison-Wesley.

Costa, A. (Ed.). (1985). *Developing Minds*. Alexandria, VA: Association for Supervision and Curriculum Development.

Delpit, L. (1995). *Other people's children: Cultural conflict in the classroom*. New York: New Press.

Dewey, J. (1933). *How we think*. New York: D.C. Heath and Co.

Draschen, S. (1982). Principles and practices in second language. New York: Pergamon.

Eisner, E. (1994). *Cognition and curriculum reconsidered*. New York: Teachers College Press.

Feuerstein, R. (1982). *Instrumental enrichment*. Baltimore: University Press.

Gardner, H. (2000, March 12). *Intelligence reframed: Multiple intelligences for the 21st century*. Opening address at Teaching for Intelligence Conference, Orlando, FL.

Hyerle, D. (1995). *Thinking Maps*. Cary, NC: Innovative Learning Group.

Jackson, Y., Lewis, J., Feuerstein, R., & Samuda, R. (1998). Linking assessment to intervention with instrumental enrichment. In R. Samuda (Ed.), *Advances in cross-cultural assessment*. Thousand Oaks, CA: Sage Publishing.

Levine, D., Cooper, E., & Hilliard, A., III. (2000). National Urban Alliance professional development for improving schools in the context of effective schools research. *Journal of Negro Education*.

Mahiri, J. (1998). *Shooting for excellence: African American and youth culture*. New York: National Council of Teachers of English and Teachers College Press.

Nessel, D. (1999). The Indianapolis/National Urban Alliance reading plan. In *The Indianapolis/National Urban Alliance Literacy Initiative Proposal*. Indianapolis: National Urban Alliance.

Nessel, D., & Baltas, J. (2000). *Thinking strategies for student achievement*. Arlington Heights, IL: National Urban Alliance and Skylight Publications.

Pogrow, S. (2000, April 19). Beyond the 'good smart' mentality: Overcoming the cognitive wall. *Education Week*, 19(32), 44, 46–47.

Rothstein, E., & Lauber, G. (1999). *Writing as learning: A content-based approach*. Arlington Heights, IL: SkyLight Publications.

39

Thinking in a Culture of Poverty

Ruby K. Payne

Economic realities create cause and effect patterns of thinking and behaving. People keep these mind-sets and behaviors, even when they no longer need them, unless one of two things happens: They get relationships or they get education. When an individual must work 12 to 15 hours a day just to survive, then little time and energy is left over for other endeavors. However, if in that same amount of time an individual can make enough money or food for two people to survive, the individual's partner or family member is freed up to devote time to learning.

Learning takes time. Time must be set aside for learning because it has become so abstract, so unrelated to daily life. As a rule of thumb, a civilization cannot progress until some of its people can get far enough away from survival mode to devote time to learning. When people are living in poverty, they devote a great deal of time to survival. In order to survive, they develop a mind-set. To better understand the thinking in poverty environments, the concept of hidden rules is important.

HIDDEN RULES

Hidden rules are those unspoken cues that people use to know whether or not an individual belongs to a group. We have hidden rules based on race, religion, or region of the country, but we also have them based on economic class. Hidden rules tend to originate from repeated, familiar situations and then become absorbed into daily life.

Figure 39.1 includes some of the hidden rules based on economic class (Payne, 1995).

Three factors drive the hidden rules in poverty: survival, relationships, and entertainment. When an individual's family has been living in poverty for two generations or more, life revolves around survival. Things (the possessions of the middle class) are not all that available. And in that person's reality of simply surviving, people become the possessions. When that happens, education is often feared—the familiar pattern is when people get educated, they tend to leave.

Because hidden rules in part determine inclusion and exclusion, they can affect school success. Furthermore, because some mind-sets are valued more than others, hidden rules can affect opinions about a student's intelligence. In school and work settings, the abilities and potential of a student are often linked to the ability to use the hidden rules of the middle class, because those are the ones followed at school.

COGNITIVE ISSUES

The school setting requires the ability to be verbal and abstract, in other words, to use an abstract representational system and models. However, to survive in poverty, it is necessary to be very nonverbal and concrete (sensory-based).

To be verbal and abstract, an individual must be able to use the formal register of the language. In his research on language, Dutch linguist Martin Joos (1972) found that no matter what language one speaks in the world, there are five registers (see Figure 39.2).

Maria Montano-Harmon (1991), a Hispanic linguist in California, found in her research with poor secondary students that very few of them knew much beyond casual register and that neither did their parents. One of the characteristics of individuals living in poverty around the world is that often they cannot speak the formal register of the country in which they live.

One of the hidden rules of middle class is that a person will speak formal register for at least the first three minutes of an interview. Yet a person from a poor neighborhood must speak casual register to survive. Therefore, students in poverty environments must be able to follow at least two sets of hidden rules in order to survive. They must be able to use casual register to survive in the neighborhood and formal register at school.

Copyright © 2001 by Ruby K. Payne

—Figure 39.1—

Hidden Rules Based on Economic Class

Generational Poverty	Middle Class	Wealth
The driving forces for decision making are survival, relationships, and entertainment.	The driving forces for decision making are work, achievement, and material security.	The driving forces for decision making are social, financial, and political connections.
People are possessions. A relationship is valued over achievement. Too much education is often feared—when people get educated, they often leave.	Things are possessions. If material security is threatened, the relationship is in danger.	Legacies, one-of-a-kind objects, and pedigrees are possessions.
The "world" is defined in local terms. Often the individual has not been out of the neighborhood.	The "world" is defined in national terms. The national news is watched; travel tends to be in the home country.	The "world" is defined in international terms. Often land holdings, bank accounts, and so on are in several countries.
Physical fighting is how conflict is resolved. If you only know the casual register of a language, you do not have the abstract words to negotiate a resolution. Respect is given to those who can physically defend themselves.	Fighting is done verbally. Physical fighting is viewed with distaste.	Fighting occurs through social inclusion or exclusion and through lawyers.
Food is valued for its quantity. The question after a meal is "Are you full? Did you have enough?"	Food is valued for its quality. The question after a meal is "Did you like it? Was it good?"	Food is valued for its presentation. The question after a meal is "Was it aesthetically pleasing? How was the presentation?"
The important information is conveyed nonverbally. The noise level is higher. Emotions are openly displayed.	The important information is conveyed verbally.	The important information is conveyed verbally and through social inclusion or exclusion. Emotional response is muted.
A person's future is viewed as being fated and lucky or unlucky. Discipline is about punishment and forgiveness because the behavior cannot be changed.	A person's future is viewed as the result of choices that are made. Discipline is about developing self-governing behavior and change.	A person's future is viewed in terms of the right to rule and the need to learn to rule responsibly. Discipline is related to learning those responsibilities.

The greater issue with casual register is that it has virtually no abstract words—words that represent concepts or ideas that have no sensory form. An individual cannot taste, touch, smell, see, or hear an idea or concept. Yet formal schooling is about understanding and using abstractions and abstract systems of representation.

ABSTRACT REPRESENTATIONAL SYSTEMS

For example, in the winter the body cannot tell the difference between minus 20 degrees Fahrenheit and minus 40 degrees.

A thermometer represents the difference, even though the sensory data do not. Measured heat and cold are the abstract representational systems that allow one to communicate the sensory information.

Formal schooling teaches abstract systems of representation such as language, numbers, the periodic table, algorithms, organizational patterns in writing, genetics, computer software, and so on. These systems are learned. Those of us who are successful in school settings have built representational structures inside of our heads that correspond to external reality. For example, when I am looking for my keys, I go inside my head and

—Figure 39.2—
Joos's Five Registers

Register	Explanation
Frozen	Words that are always the same. Pledge of Allegiance, Lord's Prayer, etc.
Formal	The word choice and sentence structure of the business and educational communities. About 1,200–1,600 word vocabulary.
Consultative	A mix of formal and casual registers.
Casual	Language between friends. Comes from the oral tradition of a culture. About 400–800 word vocabulary. Many broken sentences, frequent nonverbal assists, general word choice, and few abstract words.
Intimate	Language between twins and lovers. A highly private language about private activities.

Source: Adapted from Joos, M. (1972). The styles of the five clocks. In R. D. Abrahams & R. C. Troike (Eds.), *Language and cultural diversity in American education.* Englewood Cliffs, NJ: Prentice-Hall.

look. I say they are lost when I cannot see them in the mental picture I've created or when they are not located where I thought they would be.

The development of these structures inside our heads comes in part from the exposure to language *and* from significant relationships of mutual respect. Those relationships are the motivation for learning. In the work of Hart and Risley (1995, 1999), the authors researched the amount of language that children have an opportunity to learn from age 1 to 3 in different economic classes. Children who lived in welfare households heard 10 million words in the first three years of life. Children in working-class homes heard 20 million words, and children in professional households heard 30 million words. For example, in an educated household, when a child hits another child, the adult will often say, "We don't hit. We do not participate in violence." The abstract word "violence" is integrated into the conversation. In a poor household, it is not unusual that the child is slapped and told, "Quit hitting." The exposure to abstract language helps build cognitive structures or architectures inside the head. These architectures replicate external reality in an abstract fashion and allow us to negotiate new situations.

Because the important information in poverty environments is relayed nonverbally, language is not as valued. (The brain recognizes nonverbal information and the intent of the message more quickly, and therefore it is more important for survival). According to cognitive scientists, about 50 percent of who you are is inherited (i.e. built into your brain) and about 50 percent is developed by your environment (i.e. as the mind is developed). Feuerstein (1985) said that the mind could be developed through mediated learning (see Figure 39.3). He stated that when individuals did not have much opportunity to be mediated or learn abstract systems, then another pattern often surfaced: The individual could not plan. Taking that pattern even further:

- When people cannot plan . . . they cannot predict.
- When people cannot predict . . . they do not understand cause and effect.
- When people do not understand cause and effect . . . they cannot identify consequences.
- When people cannot identify consequences . . . they do not control impulsivity.
- When people do not control impulsivity . . . they have an inclination toward criminal behavior.

WHAT INTERVENTIONS HELP STUDENTS IN POVERTY ACHIEVE?

For students from poverty to survive in school and work, the first step is to teach that there are two sets of rules. The school needs to directly teach the hidden rules that are to be followed at school. The rules that students bring with them are not to be denigrated, but educators must explain that they do not work as well at school.

The second step is to develop relationships of mutual respect with students. Relationships of mutual respect are the key motivators for learning. Comer (1995) states that without relationships of mutual respect among students and teachers, no significant learning can occur.

The third step is to mediate or directly teach the processes and abstract representational systems. The concept of mediation is simply that one teaches what, why, and how.

What are these abstract processes? At the very basic level are processes Feuerstein identifies as input strategies. These include the following:

- Use planning behaviors.
- Focus perception on a specific stimulus.
- Control impulsivity.

—Figure 39.3—
Mediation of Processes

Identify the Stimulus	Give It Meaning	Provide a Strategy
What	Why	How

- Explore data systematically.
- Use appropriate and accurate labels.
- Organize space using stable systems of reference.
- Orient data in time.
- Identify constancies across variations.
- Gather precise and accurate data.
- Consider two sources of information at once.
- Organize data (for example, into parts of a whole).
- Visually transport data.

Intelligence is often assessed based on task and context. Therefore, it is imperative that the processes get taught directly along with the particular content and task being studied.

The fourth intervention that makes a significant difference for these students is to directly teach the mental model of the subject area or discipline. A mental model is how a person keeps abstract information in her head. The mental model reflects either the purpose or structure. A mental model is usually a two-dimensional drawing, a story, or an analogy. For example, when people are talking about building a house, the talk is very abstract. When the house finally is finished in three dimensions, a mental model is used to translate between the two. That mental model can be represented by a set of blueprints.

Schulman (1988) identified the difference between an excellent teacher and a good teacher. He found that an excellent teacher understood the structure of the discipline or subject area and used visual representations, stories, and analogies to teach those structures.

Even if a student holds all possible meanings inside his head, if he does not communicate them back in the discipline's accepted mental models, then we say the student does not understand. By directly teaching mental models, the teacher can provide an abstract framework for the student. Then the student will know what is important and what is not. Only when structure and purpose are understood can students successfully identify levels of importance. And that ability to classify information is a building block in the process of remembering it. Memory is linked to the ability to chunk information. That chunking process depends on the ability to sort information by importance and group it in some fashion based on that importance.

When teachers provide a framework for the information—or a mental model—they collapse the amount of time needed to teach something. And when students from poverty are directly taught the abstract processes, they tend to achieve as well as students from educated households.

EQUITY AND EXCELLENCE

In conclusion, the push for equity and excellence will only arrive when there are relationships of mutual respect between student and teacher. I am always amused when poor children who achieve are written off by the comment: "Well, all they did is drill and kill for the test." Having worked with those students, it can be simply said that they will not learn unless there is first and foremost a relationship of mutual respect. And secondly, when we directly teach the abstract processes and mental models that are needed to learn abstract systems, we provide them with the tools to be educated. It will always be their choice to use the education; but it is our sacred responsibility to teach the tools that will allow them to make the choice.

REFERENCES AND BIBLIOGRAPHY

Brandt, R. (1988, November). On assessment of teaching: A conversation with Lee Schulman. *Educational Leadership, 46*(3), 42–46.

Caine, R. N., & Caine, G. (1991). *Making connections: Teaching and the human brain.* Alexandria, VA: Association for Supervision and Curriculum Development.

Comer, J. (1995). Speech at Region IV Education Service Center, Houston, TX.

Feuerstein, R. (with Rand, Y., Hoffman, M. B., & Miller, R.) (1985). *Instrumental enrichment: An intervention program for cognitive modifiability.* Glenview, IL: Scott, Foresman & Co.

Hart, B., & Risley, T. (1995). *Meaningful differences in the everyday experience of young American children*. Baltimore: Brookes Publishing.

Hart, B., & Risley, T. (1999). *The social world of children learning to talk*. Baltimore: Brookes Publishing.

Idol, L., & Jones, B. F. (Eds.). (1991). *Educational values and cognitive instruction: Implications for reform*. Hillsdale, NJ: Lawrence Erlbaum.

Joos, M. (1972). The styles of the five clocks. In R. D. Abrahams & R. C. Troike (Eds.), *Language and cultural diversity in American education*. Englewood Cliffs, NJ: Prentice-Hall.

Marzano, R. J., & Arredondo, D. E. (1986). *Tactics for thinking*. Aurora, CO: Mid-continent Regional Educational Laboratory.

Montano-Harmon, M. R. (1991). Discourse features of written Mexican Spanish: Current research in contrastive rhetoric and its implications. *Hispania, 74*(2), 417–425.

Payne, R. K. (1995). *A framework for understanding poverty*. Baytown, TX: RFT Publishing.

Payne, R. K., & Slocumb, P. (1999). *Removing the mask: Giftedness in poverty*. Baytown, TX: RFT Publishing.

Palinscar, A. S., & Brown, A. L. (1984). The reciprocal teaching of comprehension-fostering and comprehension-monitoring activities. *Cognition and instruction, 1*(2), 117–175.

Schulman, L. S. (1988). A union of insufficiencies: Strategies for teacher assessment in a period of educational reform. *Educational Leadership, 46*(3), 36–41.

Sharron, H., & Coulter, M. (1994) *Changing children's minds: Feuerstein's revolution in the teaching of intelligence*. Exeter, Great Britain: BPC Wheatons.

40

The Biological Basis for Learning

LAWRENCE F. LOWERY

With a head that swivels and tilts and eyes that perceive color and depth, the human body is built to move about and explore unknown territory. The upright stance frees the forelimbs, and the hands, with their opposable thumbs, can manipulate the environment. These biological attributes enable us to explore our environment, note what happens, and then, on the basis of our observations, alter our understanding of it. There is no separating the intricate relationship of bipedalism, hand manipulation, sensory input, and brain development. Their interdependence is important to us throughout our lives.

In much the same way that young children observe objects in their environment by looking, touching, listening, tasting, and smelling, adults observe objects on the surface of Mars with remote probes. A TV eye "sees." A mechanical hand touches the surface and "feels" it. Antennae "listen." Sensors "smell" the atmosphere. With each of these actions—the youngster's firsthand, sensory experiences and the adult's inventive extensions of the senses—humans gather knowledge about the universe.

BIOLOGICAL STAGES AND THINKING

Compared with other living organisms, humans enter this world quite empty-headed in terms of content. Many species of birds, fish, and other animals are born with brains preprogrammed with information that enables them to survive, gather food, and reproduce their own kind. For example, some migrating birds can travel to locations where they have never been. Other animals also behave in instinctive ways

that are independent of learning. But the human baby is quite helpless. It must construct its knowledge of the world for itself.

From a biological perspective, not being born with prior knowledge is superb. It strengthens a species' ability to survive. Humans can reproduce their kind in virtually any environment, and the offspring will learn that environment through observations and interactions with it. Instead of coming into life prepared with prior knowledge, we have been endowed with a powerful genetic gift—a set of thinking capabilities that are programmed to appear at intervals and are spaced well enough apart so that the current capability has time to establish itself. The power of these capabilities is that they allow us to learn how to survive in practically any environment.

These capabilities are like a series of transparent maps superimposed one on another to depict an increasing complexity of surfaces, streets, cities, terrain, and continents. But they are maps without content: The names, terms, and qualities do not come with the maps. Each individual's interactions with the environment gradually fill in the content—first with one map and then with others.

Researchers in both biology and psychology have established the nature of thinking capabilities and the sequence in which they appear. The *biological* basis underlying their appearance is established by periodic increases in brain size and weight (Epstein, 1974), cellular growth within the brain (Winick & Ross, 1969), electrical functioning within the brain (Monnier, 1960), head circumference (Eichorn & Bayley, 1962), general brain development (Restak, 1980; *Scientific American*, September 1992), and evidence of brain reorganizations in roughly two-year cycles (Wright, 1997).

The *psychological* basis is established through evidence of the individual's capacity to deal with independent ideas and to relate them in increasing combinations in two- or three-year spurts from about age 3 through age 17 (Case, 1974; Pascual-

This chapter is adapted with permission from *The Biological Basis of Thinking and Learning*, University of California, Berkeley. Copyright © 2001 by Lawrence F. Lowery.

Leone, 1970). Psychologic research has also established the individual's tendency to exhibit the same kinds of behaviors as other people within two- to three-year ranges and, as a person grows older, to replace each view with a more sophisticated one (Piaget, 1969; Bloch, 2000).

PATTERN-SEEKING STAGES OF DEVELOPMENT

Pattern-seeking, or inquiry processes, lie at the very heart of human learning and set humans apart from most primates and other animals. Scientists use the processes whenever they define scientific concepts or develop taxonomies. We all use them frequently: Every word we speak, hear, read, write, or think denotes a group or class of objects or ideas. Humans have become proficient in these processes, making them the most powerful tools we have for producing and arranging information about our world.

In early stages of development, children tend to be perceptually oriented and can usually sort objects on the basis of certain characteristics, but not others (Gelman & Kremer, 1991). For example, in our culture, sorting objects by *color* is the earliest capability to appear. By age 7, sorting by *shape* is predominant. Sorting by *pattern* is next, followed by *size*. The sorting of objects by the materials of which they are made or by other abstract characteristics, such as molecular structures, develops much later.

Some researchers disagree about the placement of specific, identified abilities in the developmental sequence of our pattern-seeking abilities. Figure 40.1, which shows several perspectives on children's development, represents only the identified abilities for which there is broad agreement in independent researchers' findings on the order of development (Allen, 1967; Hooper & Sipple, 1974; Kofsky, 1966; Kroes, 1974; Lowery, 1981a; Piaget, 1969, 1997).

INABILITY TO IMPOSE PATTERNS

Stage 1: Accidental Representation

How are thoughts structured during the first stage of cognitive development? (See Preschool Level 1 in Figure 40.1.) We can see this structure best by observing what children do. When given objects to play with, the very young child will explore them *one at a time*, attracted by their perceptual features. When the child has finished exploring an object like the leaf in Figure 40.2, she will discard it.

The thinking capability at this stage is highly sensory, and actions are imposed on the object one at a time:

- Looking at it and perceiving aspects of color, size, and shape.
- Touching it and sensing texture and firmness.
- Pushing, pulling, or throwing it and noting how it behaves from such actions.
- Tasting it and noting its flavor, firmness, and texture.

These experiences provide the fundamental repertoire for future stages. Biologically, we are given about three years in which to establish the basic repertoire of the environment in which we live.

In addition, the brain is designed to encode words easily in our early years. Children will encode, on average, about 10 new words every day between ages 2 and 5 (Jackendoff, 1994). Very young children actively and vigorously construct concepts and associate those concepts with words. Even at this early stage, children can be seen deliberately carrying out inquiry processes that contribute to building the child's personal repertoire.

From birth until about age 3, the child explores objects randomly and indicates no system that suggests an organized, rational plan, although the final arrangement of objects might be a design or might accidentally represent something such as a face or train. For this reason, researchers have described this stage as the stage of "accidental representations." Children at this stage often create arrangements like those in Figure 40.3 and give similar accompanying statements.

PRE-PATTERNING ABILITIES

Stage 2: Resemblance Sorting

The second stage of cognitive development begins to unfold at about age 3. Now, when the child thinks about objects and acts on them, she produces pairings on the basis of size, shape, color, or other properties. Her rationale for each pairing is derived from the repertoire she has acquired through previous experiences. From this action, she establishes additional mental constructs about the world and how the objects and events in it are related. All her thinking is characterized by the ability to match *two objects* on the basis of one common attribute or to link two events on the basis of one relationship. Figure 40.4 illustrates how a child might use Stage 2 thinking to sort leaves. This continues to be the dominant way in which she thinks and solves problems until about age 6 (Allen, 1967; Kofsky, 1966; Lowery, 1981a), and the capacity will be available to her for the rest of her life.

This stage is characterized by the child's ability to compare one action with another, or to pair objects on the basis of one

—Figure 40.1—
Order of Development of Pattern-Seeking Abilities

General Description	Lowery's Descriptors	Research Descriptors	Piaget's Descriptors
Preschool Level 1: No ability to impose intent on objects	Repertoire building: learning characteristics (size, shape, color)	Accidental representation	Sensory-motor operations
Preschool Level 2: Ability to put two objects together on the basis of a single property	Learning by one-to-one correspondence	Resemblance sorting	Pre-operational stage
Primary Level: Ability to put all objects together on a consistent, single-property rationale	Putting things together; returning things to the way they were	Consistent or exhaustive sorting	Early concrete operations
Upper Elementary Level: Ability to coordinate two or more properties or concepts at a time	Simultaneity of ideas	Multiple membership classifying	Late concrete operations
Middle School Level: Ability to conceptualize ideas that are remote in time and space	Superordinate/ subordinate relationships	Inclusive classifying	Early formal operations
Junior High School Level: Ability to reason with permutations	Combinatorial reasoning	Horizontal reclassifying	Middle formal operations
High School Level: Ability to reason with relationships among progressively superordinate ideas	Flexible thinking	Hierarchical reclassifying	Late formal operations

Source: This figure and others in this chapter are adapted from *The Biological Basis of Thinking and Learning* by Lawrence F. Lowery, 1998, monograph, Lawrence Hall of Science, University of California, Berkeley, pp. 3–22. Adapted by permission of the author.

property, such as color, shape, or size. The thought is carried out in advance of doing the pairing.

Without prior instruction, children at this stage can be seen pairing objects in one-to-one correspondences because the objects resemble each other. The pairings appear as groups, piles, or chains of objects that allow the child to make basic comparisons of single attributes.

Children at this stage do not put together all the objects that belong together without going through a sequence of steps. And although children can recognize several different properties, they do not yet use them in combinations (that is, sort by multiple properties) at the same time.

Card games that children enjoy and have success with at this stage are Slap Jack, Concentration, and Old Maid (in both traditional and newer versions).

Stage 3: Consistent and Exhaustive Sorting

The next stage of cognitive development begins at about age 6 and is established for most children by age 8 (Lovell, Mitchell, & Everett, 1962; Lowery, 1981b; Taylor, 1996).

Arrangements made by a child will use up, or exhaust, all the pieces in a set. When grouping objects, the child will give a rule that is logical, or consistent, for all the objects within the set. For example, if the child puts all the blue objects together,

—*Figure 40.2*—

Stage 1 Thinking: Example of What Learners Do

Given a set of objects—in this case, leaves—of different shapes, sizes, colors, and textures, the child explores each object one at a time. By looking, touching, smelling, listening, and tasting, the child learns about the properties of each leaf. Through interactions with adults, the child develops a descriptive vocabulary. When the child has finished with the exploration, he or she seems to randomly discard the objects.

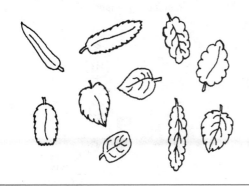

he will continue to sort the yellows, reds, and other colors into groups and say, "I've grouped all of these by their colors."

The sorting ability at this stage is characterized by the child's grouping of *all* objects in a set on the basis of *one* common attribute. For example, Figure 40.5 shows how a child at Stage 3 might sort leaves of different sizes and shapes.

If earlier experiences have been rich, children at this stage have acquired a broad repertoire of possible properties that

—*Figure 40.3*—

Examples of Thinking: Stage 1

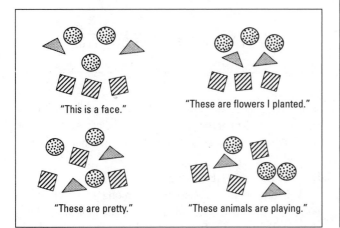

"This is a face."

"These are flowers I planted."

"These are pretty."

"These animals are playing."

—*Figure 40.4*—

Stage 2 Thinking: Example of What Learners Do

Given a set of objects, such as leaves, the student matches a familiar object with a new, unfamiliar object on a pairing or one-to-one basis. When finished with the action, the student displays pairs of objects, piles of objects, or chains linking pairs together.

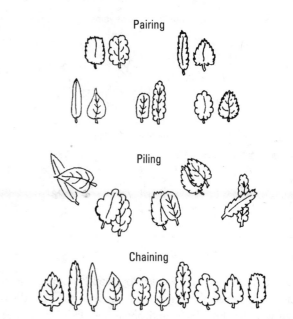

Pairing

Piling

Chaining

make up objects. They can sort objects to the extent of that repertoire. Each sorting, however, is always based on one property, because children cannot yet mentally combine more than one property at a time. Evidence of this stage appears in children's creative writing wherein each adjective used to describe something (a property) is placed in its own sentence ("It is an *old* house. It is a *brown* house. It is an *empty* house") or is chained together with connectors ("It is an old *and* brown *and* empty house").

A card game that children play successfully at this stage is Go Fish, in which sets are collected (all four aces, all four 7s, and so forth). A child at this stage is often frustrated when playing with a child at the previous level who saves only two cards in each set.

TRUE PATTERNING ABILITIES

Stage 4: Multiple Membership Classifying

When children exhibit thinking that indicates they can mentally combine more than one idea at a time, they have

—*Figure 40.5*—

Stage 3 Thinking: Example of What Learners Do

Given a set of objects, such as leaves, the student groups together or takes apart sets of objects based on a single, consistent rationale. When finished, the student displays sets of objects with a logic to their arrangement.

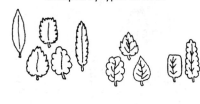

Grouped by types of veins

Grouped by types of edges

—*Figure 40.6*—

Stage 4 Thinking: Examples of What Learners Do

Given a set of objects, such as shapes or leaves, the student places certain objects between others so as to reveal multiple properties of those objects. The student explains that the objects belong to more than one class or set at the same time. When finished, the student's arrangement of objects indicates the intersection of multiple properties.

Intersecting properties

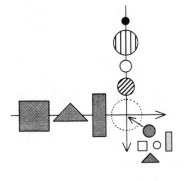

Multiple groupings

	Smooth Edge	Lobed Edge	Serrated Edge
Long Shape			
Heart Shape			
Rectangular Shape			

entered Stage 4 of cognitive development. For most children, this takes place at about age 8 and continues to be the dominant way the child thinks until about age 11 (Inhelder & Piaget, 1964; Vernon, 1965). This capacity will be available to learners for the rest of their lives.

At this stage the student can classify an object into more than one category at the same time, or into one category on the basis of two or more simultaneous properties. Figure 40.6 shows two examples of this stage of thinking: the first example is symbolized by abstract shapes; the second, by analysis of leaf characteristics.

The student realizes the simultaneity of properties inherent in objects—that is, that an object is *both* brown *and* square at the same time, rather than being brown *and then* being square. Arrangements of objects and ideas at this stage of thinking are complex.

Although younger children can produce results that *seem* to exemplify this stage, the way they attain them is quite different. For example, the younger child might first sort objects by their colors, then by a desired shape. The older child will mentally select the "correct" object by both properties before moving it into a grouping.

A card game that students begin to play well at this stage is gin rummy, in which sets (all the 3s, all the jacks, and so forth) or runs (three or more cards in sequence in a suit) can be

saved simultaneously. A student at this stage will consistently win over a student at the previous stage who can save only one possibility at a time—either the run or the set, but not both.

Stage 5: Inclusive Classifying

Thinking about the relationships among groups of objects and a superordinate conception of them are indicators of this stage of development. It appears at about age 11. Such think-

—Figure 40.7—
Stage 5 Thinking: Example of What Learners Do

Given a set of objects, such as leaves, the student abstracts multiple commonalities among them, thus achieving a superordinate concept that relates them all together. When finished, the student has arranged a collection of objects and has described the collection for its abstract qualities.

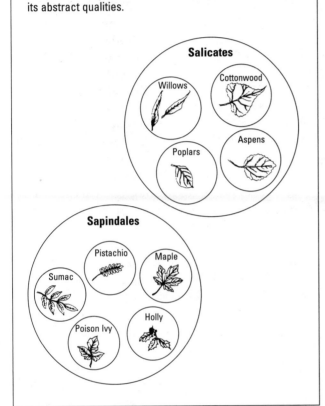

ing realizes that if one collection of objects is included in another, then all the objects in the smaller grouping are but a part of the larger. Conversely, a part of the larger class contains all of the smaller grouping. At this stage, a person recognizes that the whole is equal to the sum of its parts and that an example to represent the whole does not exist. For example, Figure 40.7 shows how a student might classify groups of leaves, as parts within a larger whole.

One characteristic of this stage of thinking is the emergence of deductive reasoning, which allows students to make inferences logically between the more general and the less general:

All women are mortal;
All queens are women;
Thus, all queens are mortal.

Given the opportunity, the student can learn to recognize logical relationships between larger and smaller classes. Experts understand the relationships between the whole of an idea and its parts; novices either understand the whole in a general way or some of the parts, but not both.

At this stage, students can fully understand that they live in a particular city and a particular state at the same time, and that one is superordinate to the other.

FLEXIBILITY IN PATTERNING ABILITIES

Stage 6: Horizontal Repatterning

As the next stage unfolds, at about age 14 (Brownlee, 1999; Lawson & Renner, 1975; Lowery, 1981c), the student becomes more flexible in his thinking. An individual at this stage can classify objects by one or more attributes, then reclassify them in numerous different ways, realizing that each way is possible at the same time and that the choice for an arrangement depends on one's purpose. For more complex analysis of the leaf example, see Figure 40.8.

For another example, if you give a young person at Stage 6 a set of books with the identifying characteristics of size (number of pages), shape, color, and content, she realizes that the books can be organized on the basis of

- size; shape; color; content
- size and shape; size and color; size and content; shape and color; shape and content; color and content
- size, shape, and color; size, shape, and content; shape, color, and content; size, color, and content
- size, shape, color, and content

Given the goal of locating information in the books, the person selects only the content as the organizing attribute because the other attributes are not useful to achieve the goal. Given a different goal, such as the determination of the ratio of books with fewer than 100 pages to those with more than 100, she would reclassify the books for a different attribute to achieve that goal.

Experts use this capacity when playing master's-level bridge or chess. It is also valuable in playing games not based solely on chance, such as blackjack (e.g., keeping track of cards consumed in earlier dealings).

Stage 7: Hierarchical Repatterning

When the seventh stage appears at about age 16 (Karplus & Karplus, 1972; Lowery, 1981c), the student is able to develop a framework based on a logical rationale about the relationships among the objects or ideas, while at the same time

—Figure 40.8—
Stage 6 Thinking: Example of What Learners Do

Given a set of objects, such as leaves, the student classifies, takes apart, reclassifies, and continues to do so throughout all the possible combinations of classes that can be created with the objects. When finished, the student describes the various classes and under which conditions each arrangement has value.

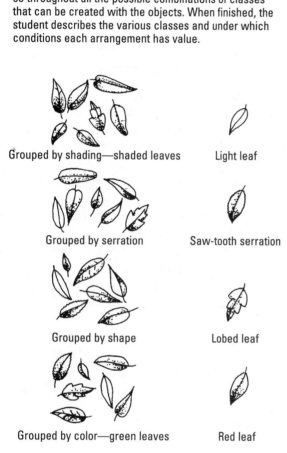

Grouped by shading—shaded leaves   Light leaf

Grouped by serration   Saw-tooth serration

Grouped by shape   Lobed leaf

Grouped by color—green leaves   Red leaf

realizing that the arrangement is one of many possible ones that eventually may be changed based on fresh insights. This stage is characterized by a person's ability to classify and reclassify objects or ideas into hierarchies of increasingly related or inclusive classes.

At this stage of ability, students need expertise in a content area. The patterning that the human mind is capable of at this stage is complex and is expressed in many different ways, such as the periodic table of the elements or the patterns of a strand of DNA. The patterns created exemplify the highest order of flexible thinking. For example, to follow our leaf analogy, Figure 40.9 shows a few of the branches in the classification of flowering plants. It is at this level that solutions to games or the best pathways (e.g. moves) to win a game can be worked out and generalized.

EDUCATIONAL IMPLICATIONS

The notion of stages is more than the sequential progression of thinking development. It includes the patterning of responses throughout the sequence and the time periods necessary for consolidating each capability. Researchers have found that all humans progress through the seven biologically based stages described here (Allen, 1967; Cowan, 1978; Hooper & Sipple, 1974; Inhelder & Piaget, 1964; Kofsky, 1966; Kroes, 1974). This developmental learning sequence is common to all cultures (Bransford, Brown, & Cocking, 1999; Cowan, 1978; Lovell et al., 1962; Lowery & Allen, 1978; Price-Williams, 1962; Schmidt & Nzimande, 1970; Wei, Lavatelli, & Jones, 1971). As learners move through the stages, they integrate all learning acquired during prior stages, including behaviors, concepts, and skills.

The result is a broad structural network of interrelated capabilities appearing not all at once but within a fairly narrowly defined period, followed by a plateau of several years. For thinking to develop properly, people need a long childhood—one in which children are free from having to carry out survival activities until all the stages are in place. This is why humans have a longer, biologically determined childhood than any other animal on earth.

Too often, educators overlook the importance of this biological basis for the development of thinking as a foundation for learning. The periodic, rapid increases in brain growth (perhaps the establishment of cellular networking), coupled with the appearance of new, content-free thinking capabilities that overlay earlier content-related capabilities, are followed by plateaus in time that allow the person to integrate new capabilities, use them, and make them functional. Unfortunately, the organization of curriculum and instruction in most U.S. schools and the design of commercial textbooks do not match the thinking capacities of learners. Teachers often introduce topics at a stage before students can comprehend them. Schools and districts do not arrange content so that students can learn it and build on it over a period of years.

VERTICAL CURRICULUM AND INSTRUCTION

Most teachers are familiar with the *vertical* sequencing of content in the curriculum. Unfortunately, it is business as usual in schools. Skills and concepts increase constantly in complexity as students move through the grades. Curriculum expectations for a student's performance are based on school

—Figure 40.9—
Stage 7 Thinking: Example of What Learners Do

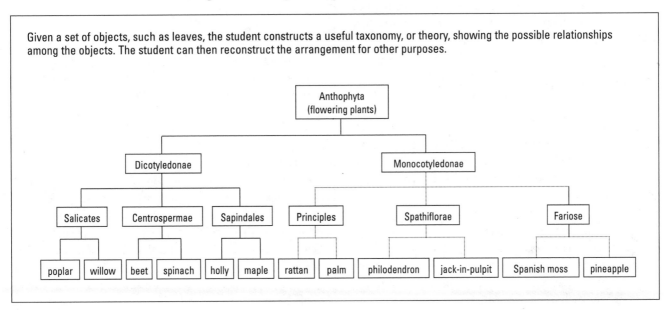

Given a set of objects, such as leaves, the student constructs a useful taxonomy, or theory, showing the possible relationships among the objects. The student can then reconstruct the arrangement for other purposes.

grade, chronological age, or achievement scores, rather than on cognitive development.

In the competitive social context of schools, educators try to accelerate the stages of development through school intervention by moving advanced topics and skills into earlier grades (Furth, 1977). For example, in science, plate tectonics and atomic structures are taught abstractly in the primary grades. In math, the distributive property and coordinate graphing are taught before aspects needed for prior knowledge. In language arts, homonyms are taught before students can grasp parallel and double meanings. Educators act as if the distance from childhood to intellectual adulthood is measured only in terms of quantity—that is, as students grow older, they acquire more experience, greater information, and broader knowledge. This is an incomplete view of intellectual growth. The most significant differences between youngsters and adults rest in the nature and quality of their understanding. As youngsters develop, they pass through ways of thinking, each stage representing a different organization of experience, information, and knowledge and each leading to a different view of the world.

HORIZONTAL CURRICULUM AND INSTRUCTION

Curriculum and instruction should reflect what we know about the biological basis for thinking and learning. Students perform best in a *horizontal* curriculum, which challenges them to use a particular stage of thinking with different materials

at various levels of abstraction. This model allows students at an identified stage of development to explore many experiences within that stage. Teachers do not compare a student's progress with that of other students. Rather, they select worthwhile experiences appropriate to each child's developmental stage, organize them for meaningful interpretation, and orchestrate them to provoke the student's thinking. Many researchers have helped to validate this model in the sciences (Askham, 1972; Loggins, 1972; Lowery & Allen, 1978) and in mathematics (Ginsburg, 1977; Langbort, 1982; Rupley, 1981).

This approach is derived from the biological basis for thinking and learning, which shows that thinking capabilities are independent of the objects involved in a given task. Students experience small, sequential steps of understanding through an inexhaustible set of possible experiences.

For example, a teacher might design sorting tasks to challenge a student who is at or beyond Thinking Stage 2 (resemblance sorting—see Figure 40.4). The teacher could ask the student to find two marbles that are alike in *color* from an array of marbles. The activity can be repeated using *size* as the feature for pairing the marbles. The activity can also be done with other objects, using color, size, or another physical property. In each variation, the thinking capability required remains the same—pairing two objects on the basis of a single property. Studies show that when instructed in this way, students become more proficient in their thinking capabilities and transfer these skills more easily to new tasks.

EXPANDING STUDENTS' THINKING

Teachers can also use the horizontal curriculum approach to extend students' thinking into higher levels of abstraction without requiring a higher stage of thinking.

CONCRETE REALITY

For example, if a student who is at or beyond Thinking Stage 3 (consistent and exhaustive sorting) can group all objects within a set so that they logically belong together, the action is considered to be firsthand, or *concrete* (see Figure 40.10a). The action involves manipulations of real objects, not abstractions of reality.

One cannot say enough about the value of firsthand experiences, which activate a multiplicity of our five senses, the only avenues into the brain. The brain receives and stores, in effect, a record of the neural activity in the sensory and motor systems from each sense when an individual interacts with the environment. Each record is a pattern of connections among

—*Figure 40.10*—
Formats for Learning

a
Concrete

b
Pictorial

c
Symbolic

neurons, patterns that can be reactivated to re-create the component parts of the experience later.

PICTORIAL REPRESENTATIONS

The same student is able to impose the same Stage 3 thinking on *representations* of reality without having to be at a more advanced stage. Representations, such as pictures, videos, and simulations, are considered to be one step removed from reality (see Figure 40.10b). Fewer of our five senses are used in studying them.

The use of representations in teaching has great value. A representation of planets in motion provides a way to look at the relationships among the objects within our solar system, a view that cannot be seen concretely. Running water through earth materials in a stream table exemplifies the cause-and-effect relationships that create landforms over centuries of time.

The power of representational instruction is that it can simplify complex ideas (as with illustrations) and truncate space and time (as with simulations). Sometimes representational instruction is important to *precede* firsthand experiences. Experience with a stream table enables students to better interpret certain landforms in the area where they live. Experiences with modeling circuitry provide prior knowledge for working with electrical circuits. Experiences with building a model of a human skeleton enable the learner to interpret the arrangement of bones found in an archaeological dig or even work with materials found in some popular science kits, such as the packages of small bones called "owl pellets," which owls regurgitate after eating an animal.

Sometimes firsthand experiences are important to precede representational experiences. Various direct studies of plants and animals, rocks and minerals, and balance and motion enhance understandings of videotapes, simulations, and other representations encountered after the studies. Some examples of such representations include the showing of plants and animals in distant natural habitats, simulations of how earth materials are transformed into various forms, and animations of how objects move and fall.

SYMBOLIC REPRESENTATION

Again, without having to be at a more advanced stage, this same student at Stage 3 thinking has the potential to successfully carry out the same thinking process on *symbols* or abstractions that are several steps away from reality (see Figure

40.10c). For symbols to carry meaning, the brain must be able to interpret the symbol in terms of prior knowledge. If there is no match between what the brain has stored and the symbol, then the student cannot interpret the symbol. The great value of reading books, whether narrative, technical, or expository, is that the words (symbols) are used to take a reader's prior knowledge and rearrange it in fresh ways. What we learn from books is essentially rearrangements of our stored knowledge. We can establish new insights and understanding through analogies and metaphors that we had not thought about previously.

Being Human

Our biological heritage provides us with a sequence of thinking capabilities—originally designed to enhance our chances for survival. As humans, however, we have enlarged on these capabilities: The interplay between thinking and actions has brought about understanding about the world that transcends the immediacy of survival. As humans we have the leisure to fantasize and contemplate. We create through art, music, and architecture; we imagine and communicate through books. We explore frontiers that are beyond the tangible and experiential.

An understanding of the biological basis for thinking can lead to a school curriculum—and creative instruction—that is far more responsive to the realities of how humans learn and to the intellectual differences among students at all grade levels, from early childhood through adolescence.

References

Allen, L. R. (1967). An examination of the classificatory ability of children who have been exposed to one of the "new" elementary science programs. Unpublished doctoral dissertation, University of California, Berkeley.

Askham, L. R. (1972). Classification of plants by children in an outdoor environment. Unpublished Doctoral dissertation, University of California, Berkeley.

Bloch, H. (2000, July). What is the target? Post-Piagetian psychology. Child Development, 857–862.

Bransford, J. D., Brown, A. L., & Cocking, R. R. (Eds.). (1999). How people learn. Washington, DC: National Academy Press.

Brownlee, S. (1999, August 9). Inside the teen brain. U.S. News and World Report, 45–54.

Case, R. (1974). Structures and strictures: Some functional limitations on the course of cognitive growth. Cognitive Psychology, 16, 544–573.

Cowan, P. A. (1978). Piaget with feeling. New York: Holt, Rinehart & Winston.

Eichorn, D., & Bayley, N. (1962). Growth in head circumference from birth through young adulthood. Child Development, 33, 257–271.

Epstein, H. T. (1974). Phrenoblysis: Special brain and growth periods. Developmental Psychobiology, 17, 207–216.

Furth, H. G. (1977). Piagetian theory and its implications for the helping professions. Paper presented at Sixth Annual Piagetian Conference, University of Southern California.

Gelman, S., & Kremer, K. (1991, April). Explanations of how objects and their properties originate. Child Development, 396–415.

Ginsburg, H. (1977). The psychology of arithmetic thinking. The Journal of Children's Mathematic Behavior, 14, 1–89.

Hooper, F., & Sipple, T. (1974). A cross-sectional investigation of children's classificatory abilities. [Technical report]. Madison: Research and Development Center for Cognitive Learning, University of Wisconsin.

Inhelder, B., & Piaget, J. (1964). The early growth of logic in the child (E. A. Lunzer & D. Papert, Trans.). New York: W. W. Norton.

Jackendoff, R. (1994). Patterns in the mind: Language and human nature. New York: Basic Books.

Karplus, R., & Karplus, E. (1972). Intellectual development beyond elementary school. Ratio: A longitudinal study. School Science and Mathematics, 8, 735.

Kofsky, E. (1966). A scalogram study of classificatory development. Child Development, 37, 190–204.

Kroes, W. (1974). Concept shift and the development of the concept of class in children. Journal of Genetic Psychology, 125, 119–126.

Langbort, C. R. (1982). An investigation of the ability of fourth grade children to solve problems using hand-held calculators. Unpublished doctoral dissertation, University of California, Berkeley.

Lawson, A. E., & Renner, J. W. (1975). Piagetian theory and biology teaching. American Biology Teacher, 37, 336–343.

Loggins, P. (1972). Visual multiple-class membership sorting abilities among second grade children: Tasks of increasing difficulty across categories of sex and socioeconomic status. Unpublished doctoral dissertation, University of California, Berkeley.

Lovell, K., Mitchell, B., & Everett, I. R. (1962). An experimental study of the growth of some logical structures. British Journal of Psychology, 53, 175–188.

Lowery, L. F. (1981a). Learning about learning: Classification abilities. Berkeley: Graduate School of Education, University of California.

Lowery, L. F. (1981b). Learning about learning: Conservational abilities. Berkeley: Graduate School of Education, University of California.

Lowery, L. F. (1981c). Learning about learning: Propositional abilities. Berkeley: Graduate School of Education, University of California.

Lowery, L. F., & Allen, L. R. (1978). Visual resemblance sorting abilities of U.S. and Malaysian first grade children. Journal of Research in Science Teaching, 15, 287–292.

Monnier, M. (1960). Definition of stages of development. In J. Tanner & B. Inhelder (Eds.), Discussions on child development (pp. 133–135). New York: International Universities Press.

Pascual-Leone, J. (1970). A mathematical model for the transition rule in Piaget's developmental stages. Acta Psychologica, 63, 301–345.

Piaget, J. (1969). Psychology of intelligence. Totowa, NJ: Littlefield Adams.

Piaget, J. (1997). The language and thought of the child. London: Routledge.

Price-Williams, D. R. (1962). Abstract and concrete modes of classification in a primitive society. British Journal of Educational Psychology, 32, 50–62.

Restak, R. M. (1980). The brain, the last frontier. New York: Warner Books.

Rupley, W. (1981). The effects of numerical characteristics on the difficulty of proportional reasoning tasks. Unpublished doctoral dissertation, University of California, Berkeley.

Schmidt, W. H. O., & Nzimande, A. (1970). Cultural differences in color/form preferences and in classificatory behavior. *Human Development, 13*(2), 140–148.

Scientific American (1992, September). The decade of the brain (special issue).

Taylor, J. B. (1996, Midsummer). Piagetian perspectives on understanding children's understanding. *Childhood Education,* 258–260.

Vernon, P. E. (1965). Environmental handicaps and intellectual development. *British Journal of Educational Psychology, 35,* 9–20.

Wei, T., Lavatelli, T., & Jones, C. (1971). Piaget's concept of classification: A comparative study of socially disadvantaged and middle class young children. *Child Development, 42,* 919–977.

Winick, M., & Ross, P. (1969). Head circumference and cellular growth of the brain in normal and marasmic children. *Journal of Pediatrics, 74,* 774–778.

Wright, K. (1997). Babies, bonds, and brains. *Discover, 18*(10), 75–78.

VI

Thinking
Across the
Curriculum

Introduction

ARTHUR L. COSTA

When you are face to face with a difficulty, you are up against a discovery.

—Lord Kelvin

Traditionally, school curriculum has been built upon content from the "scholarly disciplines": history, mathematics, biology, economics, and literacy. Yet, every significant statement of the goals and outcomes of education has been expressed in terms of desired characteristics of the student—effective problem solver, responsible citizen, complex thinker, competent learner, and effective communicator (Leibowitz, 2000). We are interested in focusing on student performance under challenging conditions that demand strategic reasoning, insightfulness, perseverance, creativity, and precision to resolve a complex problem.

It is implied, therefore, that if teachers taught academic subjects and if students were to learn and be evaluated on how well they learned the content, they would somehow become the kind of people we want them to become (Seiger-Ehrenberg, 1991).

An imperative mind-shift is essential, and therefore this section is based on a different premise. We must finally admit that process *is* the content. If we want students to develop certain behavioral characteristics—taking a critical stance with their work, inquiring, thinking flexibly, learning from another person's perspective—then we should start with those attributes and focus the entire curriculum on achieving them. View the scholarly disciplines as sources of needed information, ideas, and procedures. Select and use content to achieve the desired student characteristics. The core of our curriculum must focus on such processes as learning to learn, knowledge production, metacognition, transference, decision making, creativity, and group problem solving. These *are* the subject matters of instruction. Content, judiciously selected for its rich contributions to thinking and learning, be-

comes the vehicle to carry the learning processes. The focus is on learning *from* the objectives instead of learning *of* the objectives (Costa & Liebmann, 1997).

Barry Beyer opens this section by presenting a scope and sequence for a curriculum focused on thinking skills. Next, Bena Kallick and Marian Leibowitz invite teachers to think simultaneously about content objectives, process outcomes, and long-range habits of mind as they design units of study. A trio of authors, John Barell, Cheryl Hopper and Ann White, show how teaching based on real, relevant, and engaging problems serves as the core for integrating learning from not only a variety of subject areas but also from problem-solving processes.

Using the metaphor of a gourmet meal, Burton Cohen and Peter Hilts describe sample lessons built around the integration of thinking processes—much as a master chef thinks about the blend of flavors in a meal, so too does a curriculum planner design "delicious" lessons. Robert Swartz next describes a model of infusing critical and creative thinking into content instruction with many rich examples drawn from several classroom teachers' experiences.

Finally, Barry Beyer provides the research that supports not only the need to teach thinking but also the benefits to students when thinking becomes the focus of instruction and assessment.

Changing curriculum means changing your mind from valuing knowledge acquisition as an outcome to valuing knowledge production as an outcome. The critical attribute of intelligent human beings is not only having information but also knowing how to act on it. As our paradigm shifts, we will need to let go of our obsession with acquiring content knowledge as an end in itself and make room for viewing content as a vehicle for developing broader, more pervasive, and complex goals such as students' personal efficacy, flexibility, craftsmanship, consciousness, and interdependence (Costa & Garmston, 1994).

REFERENCES

Costa, A., & Garmston, R. (1994). *Cognitive coaching: A foundation for renaissance schools.* Norwood, MA: Christopher-Gordon.

Costa, A., & Liebmann, R. (1997). *Envisioning process as content.* Thousand Oaks, CA: Corwin Press.

Leibowitz, M. (2000). The work ethic and habits of mind. In A. Costa & B. Kallick (Eds.), *Discovering and exploring habits of mind* (pp. 62–78). Alexandria, VA: Association for Supervision and Curriculum Development.

Seiger-Ehrenberg, S. (1991). Educational outcomes for a K–12 curriculum. In A. L. Costa (Ed.), *Developing minds: A resource book for teaching thinking* (Rev. ed., Vol. 1, pp. 6–9). Alexandria, VA: Association for Supervision and Curriculum Development.

41

Developing a Scope and Sequence for Thinking Skills Instruction

BARRY K. BEYER

I n spite of the importance of a well-organized scope and sequence for the teaching of any subject, few, if any, thinking skills scope and sequences have been disseminated. Even scarcer are explications of principles that can guide the construction of such scope and sequences. Here I suggest such basic principles, with illustrations from a thinking skills scope and sequence I have developed.

SELECTING THE CONTENT OF A THINKING SKILLS CURRICULUM

A well-structured thinking skills scope and sequence identifies the skills and strategies to be learned throughout a curriculum; arranges them in the order in which they are to be introduced, practiced, generalized, and elaborated; and keys them to the various subjects in which they are to be taught. Such a scope and sequence provides a framework that is not overwhelmed by academic subject matter.

To build such a framework, first identify the thinking operations that will constitute your curriculum. Figure 41.1 presents some operations that could make up such a curriculum. I selected these skills because they are repeatedly used in most academic subjects, are commonly used outside school, and are often identified by experts as significant thinking operations. These three criteria should prove useful in selecting the cognitive operations for inclusion in any districtwide, building, or subject area thinking skills curriculum.

Figure 41.1 presents the thinking operations in three levels of complexity.

Level I. Thinking strategies are broad, inclusive, complex operations such as problem solving, decision making, and con-

ceptualizing. These skills are described in the figure in terms of their major subordinate operations.

Level II. Critical thinking is not a process in the same sense as the Level I strategies. Rather, critical thinking is a set of discrete mental operations used to determine the worth or accuracy of something as well as a set of dispositions that guide their use and execution. These operations combine both analysis and evaluation and are used repeatedly in various stages of the Level I thinking strategies.

Level III. Information processing skills are the most basic thinking operations. Each skill is relatively simple in terms of the procedures it involves or the rules it employs. Moreover, these skills are used repeatedly in various combinations to carry out the more complex Level I and II skills and strategies.

For further explication of this thinking skills hierarchy, see Beyer (1987).

ORDERING OPERATIONS BY GRADE LEVEL AND SUBJECT AREA

Next, the thinking skills and strategies selected for instruction need to be arranged by grade level and subject area (see Figure 41.2). After these skills have been introduced, they must be practiced in succeeding grades in the given subjects, elaborated where they appear a second or third time in Figure 41.2, and then transferred to other subject areas at later grade levels. They can also be introduced or reinforced in subject areas other than those shown here, of course.

The skills in Figure 41.2 have been placed for introduction at the grade levels and in the subjects designated based on (1) how they relate to each other, with instruction in the less complex or prerequisite skills preceding instruction in the more complex and inclusive skills; (2) the opportunities presented by various subjects for continuing instruction in these skills; and (3) the relative ease of learning these skills as determined by presumed levels of student experience and development.

Adapted with permission of author from *Educational Leadership* 45(7), April 1988, 26–30. Copyright © 1988 Barry K. Beyer

—Figure 41.1—
Major Thinking Skills and Strategies

I. Thinking Strategies

Problem Solving
1. Recognize a problem
2. Represent the problem
3. Devise/choose solution plan
4. Execute the plan
5. Evaluate the solution

Decision Making
1. Define the goal
2. Identify alternatives
3. Analyze alternatives
4. Rank alternatives
5. Judge highest-ranked alternatives
6. Choose "best" alternative

Conceptualizing
1. Identify examples
2. Identify common attributes
3. Classify attributes
4. Interrelate categories of attributes
5. Identify additional examples/nonexamples
6. Modify concept attributes/structure

II. Critical Thinking Skills

1. Distinguishing between verifiable facts and value claims
2. Distinguishing relevant from irrelevant information, claims, or reasons
3. Determining the factual accuracy of a statement
4. Determining the credibility of a source
5. Identifying ambiguous claims or arguments
6. Identifying unstated assumptions
7. Detecting bias
8. Identifying logical fallacies
9. Recognizing logical inconsistencies in a line of reasoning
10. Determining the strength of an argument or a claim

III. Information Processing Skills

1. Recall
2. Translation
3. Interpretation
4. Extrapolation
5. Application

6. Analysis (compare, contrast, classify, seriate, etc.)
7. Synthesis
8. Evaluation

9. Reasoning (inferencing):
   inductive
   deductive
   analogical

The specific rationale for why these skills and strategies have been arranged as shown in Figure 41.2 is as follows:

1. *Information processing skills.* The skills of classifying and seriating (sequencing), for example, can be introduced in grades K–1 and taught to a high degree of proficiency in simple form by the end of 1st grade. Piaget and other developmentalists assert that mastery of these operations is essential to cognition and that if students do not master them by the end of the primary grades, they will be less successful at later cognitive tasks (Inhelder & Piaget, 1958). To these skills can be added instruction in comparing/contrasting and observing in grades 1 or 2, and all four can be elaborated in terms of more sophisticated attributes and applications in a variety of subjects and increasingly abstract contexts in succeeding grades. Instruction in all these skills may be readily provided in reading and/or social studies or language arts throughout these grade levels.

2. *Problem-solving strategies and techniques.* Starting in 3rd grade, problem solving can be introduced in mathematics and science through a simple, four-step problem-solving strategy and several basic techniques or plans for producing solutions. The number of steps in the overall strategy and the complexity of operations that constitute each step can be elaborated periodically as students progress through the grades (see Figure 41.2). As teachers introduce and reinforce the overall strategy, they can then use it as a framework for introducing and reinforcing a wide variety of solution plans, formulas, and techniques, such as hypothesis making and testing, working backward from a tentative answer, and so on. As these skills are introduced, students may incorporate them into the overall problem-solving strategy. After they have been taught to some degree of proficiency in the initial subject areas, problem-solving strategies and various solution plans and techniques can then be transferred to other subject areas (such as vocational education) on a "need-to-use" basis. Math and science are

—Figure 41.2—

A Thinking Skills Scope and Sequence

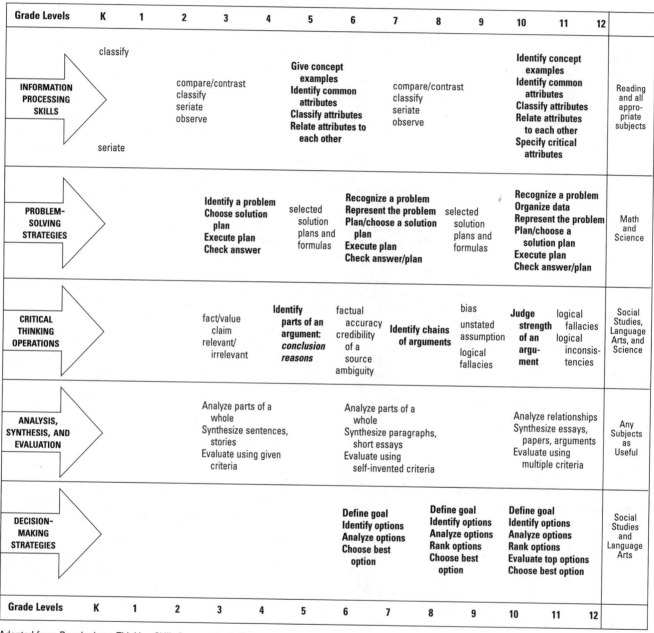

Adapted from *Developing a Thinking Skills Program*, by B. K. Beyer, 1988. Boston: Allyn and Bacon, Inc. Copyright © 1988 Barry K. Beyer.

convenient vehicles for introducing both this overall thinking strategy and a wide range of specific solution plans.

3. *Critical thinking operations.* Starting in 3rd or 4th grade, selected critical thinking skills can be introduced throughout science, language arts, and/or social studies. Several of these skills can be introduced in one or more of these subjects in

each succeeding year, with previously introduced critical thinking skills being practiced, elaborated, and transferred to other subjects over subsequent grades. Moreover, the skill of argument analysis may be taught as an "umbrella" operation to assist students in understanding these specific critical thinking skills. Argument analysis thus serves as a framework to which students can attach specific critical thinking skills, especially if argument analysis is gradually elaborated from identifying the components of an argument in early grades, to identifying chains of arguments in intermediate or middle school grades, to judging the strength of arguments and producing arguments in high school grades.

4. *Analysis, synthesis, and evaluation.* Beginning in 3rd, 4th, or 5th grade, simplified versions of the more complex information-processing skills of analysis, synthesis, and evaluation can be introduced in appropriate subjects. They can be refined, added to, and transferred to other subjects in succeeding grades. Language arts is a particularly good vehicle for introducing these skills at this level because of the customary study of parts of a paragraph or story or play (analysis); creation of sentences, paragraphs, and compositions or reports (synthesis); and assessing the quality of various written productions (evaluation).

5. *Decision-making strategies.* Social studies and language arts (and health education) provide useful contexts for introducing a simplified model of decision making in the first year of middle or junior high school and for elaborating this process in subsequent years. Students at these grade levels are increasingly pressed to make important personal, academic, and even career choices. Moreover, the content of language arts and social studies courses in these grades is replete with opportunities for and examples useful in teaching this strategy. Figure 41.2 outlines the attributes of an increasingly sophisticated decision-making strategy that might be included in any thinking skills program.

The thinking skills scope and sequence presented in Figure 41.2 might well serve as a model for the core of any school's thinking skills program. Of course, other skills might be added. The outline presented here is necessarily less detailed than it may need to be for successful implementation. For additional information on this scope and sequence, see Beyer (1988).

STRUCTURING THE SCOPE AND SEQUENCE

The scope and sequence model described here illustrates and clarifies important principles that can guide the development of a workable scope and sequence for teaching thinking in any curriculum.

First, limit the number of thinking operations included in the curriculum. Mastery of any complex thinking operation requires repeated attention and considerable time. A K–12 program with more than two dozen thinking skills and strategies can result in skill overload and superficial teaching and learning.

Second, avoid skill overload at each grade level. In grades K–5 or K–6, introduce only two or three *new* skills at a *single grade* level or even at every other grade level. Introduce only two or three new skills in each *cluster* of related subjects in grades 6 or 7 through 12. It takes considerable time to learn a new skill and to transfer it to other contexts. While new skills are being introduced, previously introduced skills need to be elaborated and reinforced through repeated application with instructive feedback, as necessary. Skill overload must be minimized for teachers as well as for students.

Third, stagger the introduction of specific skills across grade levels and subjects, reducing the number of new operations to be learned each year in each subject, thus making it possible for students to learn thoroughly—or overlearn—these skills at first.

Fourth, assign responsibility for introducing each new thinking skill or strategy to several subjects at the same grade level rather than to a single subject. Doing so will avoid skill learning overload; help ensure skill learning proficiency even if instruction in one subject area is less than successful; and create numerous opportunities for systematic teaching for transfer. For example, assign the same two critical thinking skills to social studies and science at a given grade level, or assign the introduction of problem solving to both math and science at another grade. In either case, allow one subject area to introduce the skill formally and teach it to some proficiency in the context or media in which it was originally introduced. Then transfer the skill into the second subject while skill instruction continues in the first subject.

Fifth, build complex skills on simpler ones. That is, initially introduce skills that are prerequisite to other skills. For example, instruction in comparing, contrasting, and classifying should precede instruction in more complex forms of analyzing.

Sixth, provide instruction in any single skill across several grade levels. Thinking skills develop in degree of complexity over time and are useful in a variety of subjects or contexts, both in school and beyond. Instruction and independent application should continue over several years until students can use on their own initiative and without guidance a variety of thinking skills to solve problems, make decisions, conceptualize and analyze, assess, or produce arguments.

Next, introduce and teach specific thinking skills in the context of major "umbrella" strategies or related skills that give these skills utility and function. When introducing a new skill, hook it to other operations with which it is often used. Thus, specific skills such as *distinguishing relevant from irrelevant*, when introduced as part of argument analysis or of identifying a problem in the context of a problem-solving strategy, take on more value than if introduced merely as one of a long list of isolated skills.

Finally, go slowly. Add new thinking skills and strategies to the sequence gradually. Allow teachers to gain confidence and proficiency in their teaching of those introduced earlier before adding new skills to their teaching responsibilities.

AN EFFECTIVE THINKING SKILLS CURRICULUM

There is, of course, more to an effective thinking skills curriculum than a list and a sequence of skills to be taught. Attention must also be given to teaching the habits and values of skillful thinking, what Robert Ennis (1985) calls "thinking dispositions" and Richard Paul (1987) calls "passions" of critical thinking. (See also Ennis's Chapter 8 and Shari Tishman's Chapter 13 in this book.) Furthermore, attention also must be given to the teaching of metacognitive strategies and techniques. For classroom instruction in thinking to be productive, scope and sequence guides need to be devised for these important dimensions of thinking also. At least one effort to develop such an integrated scope and sequence now exists (Beyer, 1988), and others will undoubtedly follow.

In addition, an effective program contains (1) sample lesson plans, (2) thorough training, (3) detailed descriptions of the skills, and (4) model skills tests to incorporate into teachers' regular subject area exams. All of these resources combine to provide the support necessary for teaching thinking.

The first order of business in any effort to develop a thinking skills curriculum, though, should be to design an appropriate scope and sequence. Use of the principles presented here promises development of a scope and sequence that can contribute dramatically to making skillful thinking a reality in our classrooms.

REFERENCES

Beyer, B. K. (1987). *Practical strategies for the teaching of thinking*. Boston: Allyn and Bacon.

Beyer, B. K. (1988). *Developing a thinking skills program*. Boston: Allyn and Bacon.

Ennis, R. (1985, October). A logical basis for measuring critical thinking skills. *Educational Leadership, 43*(2), 44–48.

Inhelder, B., & Piaget, J. (1958). *The growth of logical thinking in children from childhood to adolescence*. New York: Basic Books.

Paul, R. (1987). Dialogical thinking: Critical thought essential to the acquisition of rational knowledge and passions. In J. Baron & R. Sternberg (Eds.), *Teaching thinking skills: Theory and practice* (pp. 127–148). New York: W. H. Freeman and Company.

42

Teacher as "Thought-Full" Designer

BENA KALLICK AND MARIAN LEIBOWITZ

When teachers are designing new units of study, developing units, themes, projects, or lessons, they have an opportunity to make thinking a significant part of the design. As a teacher plans, there needs to be consideration as to where thinking skills are best integrated into the course of study. Instruction for higher-level thinking is best integrated when there is time for explicit and direct teaching, student-engaged guided practice, an opportunity for student-centered, self-directed application, and time for assessment feedback.

Designing for "thought-full" work requires differentiating between a lesson, which one hopes will be accomplished within a short amount of time, and a unit, which can be extended over a longer period. A series of lessons and activities often serves as a scaffold for a larger theme or unit of study. When choosing such themes, it is important to work with content that is generative—that lends itself to generating many questions, ideas, and interpretations. We usually find that the most generative topics or themes have the following characteristics:

- Are of interest to the student.
- Have some pathway for students to find a relationship between their own experience and the content to be studied.
- Present problems that have not yet been solved.
- Allow for more than one interpretation or point of view.
- Are universal rather than particular in meaning.
- Require primary as well as secondary source material.
- Have not been studied from the same perspective.

Examples of possible themes are:

- Power
- Connections
- Change
- Justice
- Discovery
- Patterns
- Relationships
- Honor
- Conflict
- Forces

These themes or topics are worthy of more time and attention than individual lessons might be. Themes also serve as a connector for student thinking in more than one discipline, for example, in math and science or in science and English. They help students think in larger ways about the material they are studying. In addition, because there is often as much known as not yet known, they provide a rich opportunity for students to practice their thinking skills.

When teachers plan, many factors need to be considered and identified as important. Teachers need to establish clearly the content knowledge on which the lesson will focus. Will certain process areas, such as thinking, communication, or collaboration, be required? Will certain habits of mind, work-related behaviors, or dispositions be required for students to demonstrate their learning? (See Arthur L. Costa's Chapter 15 in this book for more details on habits of mind.)

The following framework of critical elements is helpful as teachers plan their units. The process usually begins with brainstorming: Which topic or theme in the curriculum are you most interested in expanding into a unit? Which aspect do you feel you can devote more time and depth to studying?

Once you decide what you want the students to know, be able to do, and become intrigued with as a result of this unit, project, or problem, you can fill in this organizational form:

UNIT DESIGN

Context for Unit: What is going on in your classroom at the time you are planning this unit or lesson? How would you describe the students for whom it is being planned?

Essential Questions: This lays out an overarching question or set of questions to help frame the unit for the students and is usually related to the "big ideas" that the unit deals with. Two examples follow.

On the topic of immigration:

1. What evidence is there that immigration is a periodic phenomenon and a recurring event in history?

2. What factors have contributed to immigration events throughout the history of the United States?

3. What have been the effects of immigration on the development of American culture?

From Frelinghuysen Middle School in Morristown, New Jersey, on the theme of change:

1. What do we mean by change?

2. How has change impacted our lives personally and as a society?

3. What are the factors that contribute to or impede change?

Content: Think of the facts, concepts, and larger understanding that you want the students to have by the end of the unit. Then link the content to standards and benchmarks.

Skills: Name the specific skills for thinking and processing the content. For example, decision making and problem solving; generating ideas; and comparing and contrasting.

Habits of Mind: Identify specific dispositions for developing a work ethic—for example, persisting; listening with understanding and empathy; and checking for accuracy.

Assessment: What is the final assessment product whereby students will demonstrate their learning? Describe the task. Include the scoring rubric for the content, skills, and habits of mind you have identified. An example from Sir Francis Drake High School in California's Tamalpais School District, follows:

Individual Assessment

• An informative speech on a community issue with governmental or economic implications.

• Brief analysis of individual research on a group topic.

• A persuasive speech.

• Reflection of work on a project in a journal.

• A test of the student's mastery of government and economic terms and principles.

Group Assessment

• A summary of research.

• A product the group worked on, such as a video or play.

Assessment Indicators

The student should

• Be willing to change his mind when presented with evidence or rationale.

• Accept or offer multiple solutions to the problem.

• Seek alternative sources of data.

• Stay on task.

• Ask clarifying questions related to the task.

Product Indicators

The student's project should

• Apply content knowledge from the research paper.

• Follow the product plan as specified.

• Be completed in a timely manner.

• Reflect care and attention to detail and organization.

Presentation Indicators

The student should

• Use language that is appropriate for the audience.

• Enhance the presentation by using visuals or multimedia products.

• Present ideas in a logical, well-organized manner.

The teacher as designer needs to be clear about the emphasis in this unit. What are the most important facts, concepts, and ideas to be learned? Where along the way can the unit move along like an "express" train, skipping certain stops because none of the passengers needs to get off? Where does it need to move like a "local," with time spent at individual stations?

The design also requires the teacher to be reflective about the work, constantly seeking ways to refine and polish. When thoughtfully applied to work from assessment back out to instruction, the design process is a shift in the paradigm of developing units. It requires the designer to think first about how she will know if the student has learned the material and demonstrates good thinking skills, then make certain she has designed a "test" worth teaching to. Instructional planning follows. For example, Beth Checkovich, a science teacher at Harper Park Middle School in Loudoun County, Virginia, developed a process to reflect on her work as a designer (see Figure 42.1).

The level of thoughtful planning required to teach for thinking often also requires time to collaborate with colleagues. As new teachers enter our systems, design work will become an even more important and demanding task; experienced teachers will need time to both mentor and design with beginning teachers. In addition, teachers who are leaving the system may not leave a legacy of expertise for the system unless there is some established way for that to happen. For that reason, we suggest that a school system adopt a unit planning

—Figure 42.1—
Reflection for My Design Work

Design Component	What I Used to Do	How I Now Think About It
Specifying the objective for the lesson	I listed the objectives or copied them from the teacher's manual. I wrote in detail about every activity we do in class and how many minutes each activity would take.	**Overarching Understanding** Identify the relationship between the unit and independence in sustaining a team. **Essential Questions** • How do the functions of these teams represent the unit? Independence? Both? • What factors contribute to sustaining a team?
Effective use of assessment	Based assessment on all tests, quizzes, and some reports and projects.	**Evidence of Mastery** • Take vocabulary test. • Classify examples of team functions as either unity or independence. Choose two examples and explain or demonstrate how they sustain a team. **Projects** • Complete two labs on teams or parts of a team, and turn in lab reports on how parts of a team function. • Interview or report on a person in charge of a team (a coach, principal, corporate executive, or manager). • Record observations of ecosystems, specifically on examples of unity and independence. • Create a poster labeling a team and its parts. • Find similarities and differences between teams. • Simulate how such a team would work. **Portfolio**—Keep a reflective journal focusing on examples of teams, unity, independence, feelings about the topic, and questions about the topic or project.
Promoting higher-level thinking and life skills	I used cooperative groups some-times, but I never taught students how to cooperate or had them reflect on the process. I taught communication skills but did not use rubrics to explain what was expected. Used questioning skills and followed Bloom's Taxonomy, but did not plan these approaches.	**Life Skills** **Collaboration**—Assign and complete group tasks. Assign roles within group. Contribute ideas to group. Plan. Participate willingly. **Communication**—Keep accurate notes. Defend point of view with evidence. Write and present clear, well-organized thoughts. Question credibility of sources. Use technology. **Thinking**—Compare and contrast. Make decisions. Be persistent. Categorize and classify. Make analogies. Form and evaluate conclusions. **Quality**—Self-evaluate. Monitor progress. Meet deadlines. Vary presentation methods. Seek additional information as needed. **Citizenship**—Show respect for peers, adults, and oneself. Handle conflicts appropriately. Offer honest evaluations with constructive criticism.

form; the previous outline is only one example. Over time, staff development can give teachers opportunities to collaborate on design, and the system will build a bank of well-developed plans. Technology can help greatly in developing information on design resources so teachers can easily modify their designs.

We are often asked, as children do on a long car trip, "Are we there yet?" This kind of planning suggests that our trip has no end. It is a dynamic journey of teaching and learning that fosters innovative design, constantly informed and modified by information about student learning.

43

Big Rocks and Powerful Kingdoms: Problem-Based Learning in Science and Social Studies

JOHN BARELL, CHERYL HOPPER, AND ANN WHITE

How big is the biggest rock ever found?
Are there rocks in outer space?
How are rocks formed?
If continents didn't move, would we have volcanoes?

These questions poured forth from Ann White's 4th graders at Jackson Academy in East Orange, New Jersey, as they set upon their inquiry into the nature of rocks. "Rock Hounds" is what White calls her eager 4th graders. Such questions provide a focus for a unit on the mysteries and wonders of nature's building blocks. These questions also form the foundation of one approach to what some call "problem-based learning."

Problem-based learning seeks to challenge students to think through ill-structured, realistic problems found within the curriculum. A "problem" is anything that involves doubt, uncertainty, or difficulty. We encounter problems of all kinds, from personal to professional, from spiritual to economic. What these situations have in common is that they often cause us to question, to wonder how to solve them, to seek strategies for resolving the issue.

Now, why do we want to challenge students to identify and resolve problematic situations? The reasons are many. First, our minds are good at it. Research on brain function (Caine & Caine, 1997; Jensen, 1998; Diamond & Hopson, 1998) has indicated that engagement with such high levels of challenge fosters development of our brains and hence our ability to think productively. We as a species have confronted the challenges of walking upright on the savannas of east Africa, of how to honor our kings in Egypt, and of how to bring water to parched deserts. We did this without formal education in schools.

Second, these kinds of challenges engage our minds and bodies in thinking via complex, multifaceted situations where there are no easy, one-word answers. What to do about pollution in a local stream or how to get more citizens involved in local politics requires what some call higher-order thinking. If we want our students engaged in productive thought, problem-based learning is one approach.

Third, thinking through situations like these requires problem identification—one of the most important aspects of problem solving. Being able to identify the problem without referring to a textbook is a life skill (Barell, 1995).

Fourth, working through ill-structured problems requires teamwork and collaboration skills, which are required in most work environments. We have to be able to listen, compromise, analyze and synthesize ideas, and draw conclusions on our own and as a group to solve most difficult problems today.

Fifth, most state standards in the various disciplines call for inquiry in the disciplines—for example, thinking as scientists and historians do. These professionals do not spend hours reading and memorizing databases. They poke around in their fields for intriguing situations that spark their curiosity and call forth their best thinking.

Sixth, research from cross-cultural studies by Stigler and Hiebert (1999) indicates that this problem-based approach is used in countries such as Japan where teachers often start a math lesson with a challenging problem to struggle through, trying out various approaches and solutions. These teachers see working through problems as a way of learning the relationships among concepts, facts, and procedures. Some teachers in the United States, by contrast, seem more interested in helping students perform a procedure or practice a set of discrete skills. Thus a problem-based approach may be one of the best ways to come to a deeper understanding of the subject's fundamental concepts and problem-solving processes. Ralph Tyler noted this in his classic book *Basic Principles of Curriculum and Instruction* (1949): The best way to learn concepts and ideas is within the context of a problematic situation.

Finally, perhaps, the effort expended on posing and resolving such problems more than likely develops our capacity to do so in the future and helps us apply learning from one problem to another (Bransford, Franks, & Sherwood, 1986; Mayer, 1989).

Thus there are many reasons for challenging students with complex problems drawn from our curriculum or directly related to it.

What particularly interests the authors of this chapter is the inquiry aspect of problem-based learning. It seems that one of the challenges of such learning is for students to pose their own problems, and one way to do this is for us to give prominence to their questions. We know from classroom observations that students ask very few complex questions about content during a class session (Dillon, 1988).

The stories presented below, therefore, focus more on questions students generated than on teachers' deciding what problem students are to investigate. What we want to see is the kind of student self-direction McCombs writes about as a way of fostering students' metacognitive reflection and growth toward independent thinking—taking more control of and responsibility for their own learning (1991).

THE ROCK HOUNDS

Ann White's students had begun their studies by carefully observing various kinds of rocks, some from science kits and others they had brought from home. Then they identified what they already knew about rocks and minerals using the KWHLAQ strategy (Barell, 1998), which is outlined in Figure 43.1. The KWHLAQ strategy, developed at Montclair State University, involves a series of probing questions to explore current knowledge and learning goals. Starting any unit with what students know acknowledges and honors their knowledge, taps into their schemata about the subject, and may identify misconceptions. For example, one 6th grader doing a unit on the Age of Exploration thought Christopher Columbus was married to Queen Isabella.

Students then posed their own questions, identified ways to gather answers, and conducted research using the Internet, books, and local geologists. Having students identify what they're curious about gives the unit focus and pro-

—Figure 43.1—

Problem-Based Learning Strategy: An Inquiry Approach

KWHLAQ

This strategy is designed to encourage students to assume more responsibility for and control of their learning. The acronym KWHLAQ derives from the boldface words in the questions below.

We ask ourselves:

"What do we think we already **know** about the subject?"

"What do we **want** or **need** to find out?"

"**How** will we go about finding our answers?"

"What have we **learned**—about the subject, about ourselves as inquirers, about working with others?" [daily as we proceed through the unit and after its culmination]

"What concepts or skills can we **apply** to this and other subjects and to our lives?"

"What **questions** do we have now?"

vides them with personal reasons for engaging in the learning experiences.

Some of their other questions included the following:

- Can you eat other rocks besides halite?
- Do rocks have energy?
- What's the most popular rock?

As White conducted her lessons introducing students to various kinds of rocks, their origins, and Earth's history, they generated more questions each day.

HIGH SCHOOL SOCIAL STUDIES

Not too far away in Paramus, Cheryl Hopper has been guiding her 9th graders through a unit on Africa using the same KWHLAQ strategy.

Her students first webbed out what they thought they knew about Africa (see Figure 43.2).

Then she asked them what they wanted and needed to know about Africa. The "need" to know is important because we want our students to think like historians and scientists, and not all 4th or 9th graders are fascinated by rocks and Africa.

—Figure 43.2—
Using Problem-Based Learning with the Africa Unit

Cheryl Hopper
Paramus High School
Grade level: 9th grade
Model: KWHLAQ

Introduction:
I showed my students slides taken in Africa of a traditional village, a modern city, a marketplace, a mosque, a discotheque, dam construction, and other sights, without any comments about the content.

Then I asked: **What do we think we *know* about the continent of Africa and the people who live there?** I organized student responses on a concept map (see example below).

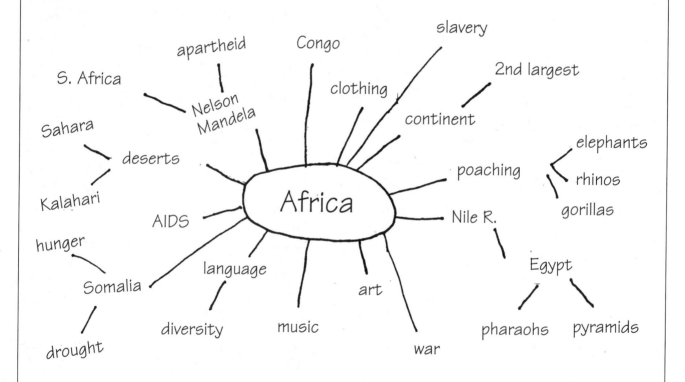

My students are very familiar with this type of activity. At the beginning of the year when I introduced concept maps, I put students in pairs so each duo could create a map of their own and then share it in a large-group discussion.

The concept map can be displayed throughout the unit and referred to regularly. The class can update it as new information is learned and thereby correct misconceptions or misinformation.

Here are some of their questions:

• How and why did powerful kingdoms emerge in Africa, especially West Africa?
• How do geographic features account for the continent's cultural diversity?
• What were the effects of European rule? of apartheid?

Hopper's students then combined these into core questions that reflected their personal interests and her curricular priorities. The core questions provided an organizing focus for the unit and for additional questions that students raised. As one of her students said, "How come every time I answer one question, another one pops up?" He thought this process would never end, and, of course, if he were lucky it never would!

As in White's class, students teamed up to research different questions, but Hopper's 9th graders assumed the roles of experts in different areas, such as geography, Atlantic slave trade, and art. They made assignments for the whole class. For example, the geography experts gave this homework assignment:

> Read about the geography of the continent of Africa in your textbook. Now, imagine you are taking a hot air balloon trip across the continent. In your journal describe what you see. Include geographic features, changes in climate, and so forth.

Students, in effect, mapped out the entire unit, not only giving assignments but also planning trips to a local African art museum where they became the knowledgeable experts who designed challenging learning experiences around the artifacts.

PERSONAL AND PROBLEM-BASED LEARNING

Both White and Hopper have engaged their students in a form of problem-based learning that focuses on the KWHLAQ inquiry strategy.

In 4th and 9th grades the students investigate topics found within the curriculum but do so in ways that challenge them to identify their own questions. Dewey said reflective thought begins with a perplexity (1933); their questions reflect these kinds of personal doubts and put them right at the center of constructing the unit.

Both teachers are also engaged in a personal learning approach that consists of sharing control with their students. Students become more personally involved in their own learning when it offers choices. McCombs points out that giving students opportunities to make choices taps into their inherent motivation to learn (1991). Furthermore, Jensen (1998) notes how brain research supports educators offering such opportunities:

> We've come to understand that the two critical ingredients in enrichment are challenge and feedback. Since what's challenging for one student may not be challenging for another, this principle makes a tremendous argument for choice in the learning process, including self-paced learning, and more variety in the strategies used to engage learners better. (p. 39)

Brain research also supports our tapping into students' inquisitiveness. "The brain is essentially curious, and it must be to survive. It constantly seeks connections between the new and the known" (Wolfe & Brandt, 1998, p. 11).

Students make choices not only in the kinds of questions they will research in a personalized, problem-based unit but also in the ways they gather information and how they process it and make it meaningful through their assessment projects.

Personally posing and resolving problems gives students opportunities to become more meaningfully involved, because educators trust their students, to varying degrees, both to organize their learning and fashion meaningful culminating experiences.

THE PROBLEMATIC SCENARIO

In both New Jersey classes, teachers used the principles of authentic assessment to create a scenario that would challenge students to use the information they learned in practical and real-world ways.

White's Rock Hounds took what they had discovered about sedimentary, igneous, and metamorphic rocks around their school building to create an exhibit on local geology for their school and a partner school several miles away. And a visit from geologist Jonathan Lincoln of Montclair State University helped them answer some of their questions and generated the intriguing discovery that those indentations in a purple rock were the fossilized footprints of dinosaurs running around New Jersey back when it was part of Africa, around 200 million years ago.

As for Hopper, she presented her 9th graders with her core concepts and skills in the form of a scenario:

> You are an African nation that desires a substantial loan from the World Bank. Your goal is to convince the World Bank that your country's needs are great and you deserve a loan. The World Bank has a limited amount to lend, and many other countries are asking for loans. Therefore, you must prepare a strong case for receiving a loan and be able to defend your need for the money.

Such a scenario meets Wiggins's (1998) criteria for authentic assessment:

- Students make judgments involving critical thinking and problem solving.
- They replicate contexts in which adults are "tested" in the workplace.
- They "do" the subject as historians or economists would.
- They present their findings in settings where they can rehearse and receive immediate, direct feedback, and can thereby modify their conclusions.

ASSESSING OUR UNDERSTANDING

These scenarios are designed to incorporate the major content that teachers want students to show they understand. As

Perkins (1992) has noted, three of our primary goals in education are ensuring that students can retain, understand, and use knowledge. We want our students to be able, through a variety of strategies, to demonstrate their understanding of concepts, ideas, principles, and information (Barell, 1995).

The Rock Hounds had to figure out what kinds of rocks were to be found around Jackson Academy, determine how they were formed, and then design an exhibit to communicate these findings to their classmates and to students in their partner school. In the process they engaged in collaborative problem solving.

In Paramus, the 9th grade appellants to the World Bank had to become very familiar with one African nation, assess its economic status, and engage in problem solving to determine priorities and how to fulfill them.

The final three steps in the process—L A Q—provide us with additional opportunities for students to demonstrate understanding. White asked students daily what they had learned, as she did at the end of the unit. So there was always new learning and, of course, new questions for students to add to their list posted on the bulletin board.

The A question—How can we apply what we have learned?—is designed to help students transfer new knowledge and skills into the same and other subjects as well as to their personal lives. "If I compared my country to a state in the U.S. or another developed country about the same size, it was easier for the World Bank to understand our problems," noted one of Hopper's students.

Pictures and video simulations of the moving continents, of plate tectonics, and how one plate subducted beneath another, causing volcanoes to spew forth molten magma, intrigued a student in White's class. During the geologist's visit, the student posed this question, "If the continents didn't move, would there still be volcanoes?"

"No," he said. "It's the moving of the plates that causes volcanoes to erupt."

Finally, we bring the strategy full circle by asking for new questions. Where do we go from here?

"I ended with the question of why people continue to reproduce if their lives are so hard," observed one 9th grader.

And White's class wondered, "Where will the continents be in a million years?"

WHAT STUDENTS SAY

McCombs (1991) has noted that students who set goals for their learning and reflect on their progress are well on their way to becoming self-directed. Students in White's 4th grade classes found this inquiry approach "fun, because you get to ask your own questions. . . . I never knew that you could eat some minerals. . . . I found out that the biggest rocks in the world are not as important as the oldest . . . the oldest rocks are millions of years old. . . ."

Hopper's students had these reflections:

- "The information was easy to get, but we had to focus on the problems and that was hard."
- "I enjoyed working with the Internet. We really understood what our country symbolized."

In general, we have found that when we tap into students' interest in sharing some control over their learning, we energize them, the learning process, and the whole class experience. Indeed, as so many have pointed out, having a choice among alternatives that you select is a very powerful way of transforming the classroom.

PROBLEM-BASED LEARNING IN OTHER SUBJECTS

In John Barell's university English literature classes, he challenged students with the problem of transforming a classic novel, for example Fyodor Dostoevsky's *Crime and Punishment* or *The Brothers Karamazov*, into film. This class project required multiple roles and opportunities for students with varying talents to participate in various fashions.

Jane Rowe provided her 6th graders with this mystery: "Who really discovered America?" This led to their doing research, using a variety of text and Internet resources to generate their own conclusions.

Jude Desotelle and Lynn Lierman had their middle school class of learning-disabled students design a community that could support a major widget factory with sufficient resources, facilities, and personnel.

Michelle Maguire presented her biology students with this problem: "Aliens have landed. They are in need of resources and have come to negotiate a deal. In exchange for one half of Earth's water, the aliens have agreed to share with us the information needed to produce enzymes that prevent cancer. Should we accept the deal?"

Sharlene Prinsen challenged her students in Spanish class to identify a problematic situation worth investigating in Mexico and to pose questions that could be answered while doing on-site research in that country using their newly acquired language skills.

Lynné Cassellius asked her high school students to play the roles of the Future Civic Planning Committee, charged with ensuring a smooth transition for immigrants moving into Wisconsin's local communities from various countries.

These are but a few examples of the kinds of long-term, inquiry-based learning experiences in which teachers in K–12 classrooms and beyond have engaged their students for years. These approaches may seem like nothing new. What is exciting is seeing students at the center of posing problems and questions, conducting their own research using the World Wide Web, and presenting their findings using Wiggins's criteria for authentic assessment.

TRANSFERABLE SKILLS

Problem-based inquiry provides us with excellent opportunities for personalizing students' learning. By offering them chances to pose their own meaningful questions, to research them in ways that are fun and involve transferable skills, and to wrap all their knowledge in an authentic task as a culminating experience, we offer students experiences that can help them learn content. Furthermore, we provide them with knowledge and skills that are potentially transferable to other life situations (Bransford et al., 1986; Mayer, 1989; Stepien, Gallagher, & Workman, 1992).

France (1890) once noted that "the whole art of teaching is only the art of awakening the natural curiosity of young minds for the purpose of satisfying it afterwards." Yes! And in problem-based learning, with a focus on personalized and group inquiry, we have a vehicle to do just that.

REFERENCES

Barell, J. (1995). *Teaching for thoughtfulness: Classroom strategies to enhance intellectual development* (2nd ed.). New York: Longman.

Barell, J. (1998). *Problem based learning: An inquiry approach.* Arlington Heights, IL: SkyLight.

Bransford, J., Franks, N., & Sherwood, R. (1986, June). *New approaches to instruction: Because wisdom can't be taught.* Paper presented at a conference on Similarity and Analogy. Urbana-Champaign, IL: University of Illinois.

Caine, R., & Caine, G. (1997). Education on the edge of possibility. Alexandria, VA: Association for Supervision and Curriculum Development.

Dewey, J. (1933). *How we think.* Lexington, MA: D. C. Heath.

Diamond, M., & Hopson, J. (1998). *Magic trees of the mind: How to nurture your child's intelligence, creativity, and healthy emotions from birth through adolescence.* New York: Dutton.

Dillon, J. T. (1988). *Questioning and teaching: A manual of practice.* New York: Teachers College Press.

France, A. (1890). *The crime of Sylvestre Bonnard.* New York: Harper and Brothers.

Jensen, E. (1998). *Teaching with the brain in mind.* Alexandria, VA: Association for Supervision and Curriculum Development.

Mayer, R. (1989). Models for understanding. *Review of Educational Research,* 59(1), 43–64.

McCombs, B. (1991). *Metacognition and motivation for higher-level thinking.* Paper presented at the annual meeting of the American Educational Research Association, Chicago.

Perkins, D. (1992). *Smart schools: From training memories to educating minds.* New York: Free Press.

Stepien, W., Gallagher, S., & Workman, D. (1992). *Problem-based learning for traditional and interdisciplinary classrooms.* Aurora, IL: Center for Problem-Based Learning, Illinois Mathematics and Science Academy.

Stigler, J., & Hiebert, J. (1999). The teaching gap: Best ideas from the world's teachers for improving education in the classroom. New York: Free Press.

Tyler, R. (1949). *Basic principles of curriculum and instruction.* Chicago: University of Chicago Press.

Wiggins, G. (1998). *Educative assessment: Designing assessments to inform and improve student performance.* San Francisco: Jossey-Bass.

Wolfe, P., & Brandt, R. (1998, November). What do we know from brain research? *Educational Leadership,* 56(3), 8–13.

44

Resetting the Table: A Balanced Diet of Thought-Filled Integration

Burton Cohen and Peter Hilts

The flavorful burst of apples, cinnamon, and sugar confirms to our tongue what the nose had only suspected: Apple pie has arrived! At that single, sumptuous moment a complex revelation blossoms. That first taste is both a simple pleasure and a complex measure of all we are capable of knowing. Each bite speaks volumes about careful preparation and promises forks full of pleasure to come.

Why can't learning be just as self-evident? Without rubrics, checklists, or even a curriculum, we would enjoy each flaky morsel and spontaneously assess the pie as not so hot, decent, good, or "May I have another slice, please?" Even though we do not normally equate eating with learning, both are fundamental human drives. Eating is so essential to survival that we are hard-wired with all sorts of systems to ensure that we keep finding, preparing, and enjoying food. The same is true for learning. Our natural craving is to gather new insights, combine them to make meaning, and share that meaning with others. Like a great meal that combines flavors creatively, integrated opportunities keep learners hungry for more.

The traditional disciplines, with their focus on specialization and discrete knowledge, are like cooking classes that focus on only one course. Imagine a restaurant where each part of the meal came from a different kitchen, with chefs that never talked to each other and serving times that were defiantly uncoordinated—hardly a recipe for gustatory greatness. Yet precisely the same chaos runs rampant in traditional education. Is it any wonder that many learners nibble around the edges of academic opportunity? Fortunately there is a cognitive cuisine that can excite even the most jaded and demanding critics. By folding thought-filled processes into integrated curriculum, we can present a banquet of opportunities to serve all learners.

Pie makes our mouths water because we are biologically prepared to appreciate sweet and spice. So what can make our minds respond with equal anticipation? The answer is as old as survival. Just as food must be gathered, prepared, and consumed, learners must gather, prepare, and present the fruits of their learning for evaluation. Each phase of the learning process requires a different set of thinking processes, and each phase is powerfully present in every traditional academic discipline. Experiences that weave appropriate thinking and processes across disciplines activate our best learning potential.

GATHERING

Consider first the learning phase of gathering, which is present across the curriculum. Because gathering is an inquiry process, it requires learners to develop skills in questioning and research. These skills transcend any single discipline and can serve as powerful links. The collection aspect of gathering can employ library skills, interviewing techniques, brainstorming methods, electronic research, and any other means by which learners accumulate information. Because this skill set is so universal, it is an excellent starting point to help teachers coordinate foundational skills.

Reading and literature teachers employ inquiry when they ask students to read and comprehend new material. History teachers may direct students to books, videos, or computers to help them gather new knowledge for a report. Science classrooms are full of labs and problems that require students to use inquiry when they generate hypotheses and design experiments. Art teachers use examples and models; language instruction includes books, materials, and posters. All these experiences expose students to new, raw information. When teachers talk and plan across disciplinary boundaries, they can introduce and reinforce skills with confidence that they are part of a coherent effort. Imagine a student who learns the skill of questioning in preparing to research a history question. By learning what constitutes a useful and precise question, that student will be better prepared when the science curriculum requires written questions to prove a hypothesis.

Taking the curriculum to the next level is even more engaging. By relating the scientific experiment to the historical period under study, both teachers magnify the importance of their subject's curriculum. Whether this connection takes place across a segmented school day, in a team-taught class, or during a project-based experience, it fulfills the craving for meaning and coherence that is fundamental to a learner's motivation.

LIGHTHOUSE LESSON 1

At a public high school in Minnesota, teachers collaborate with each other and with students to launch a complex, inquiry-based project. The project, called the Pond Profile, is conducted by students at the School of Environmental Studies in Apple Valley. Under the broad question "What is the relationship between humans and water?" students focus on the effects of suburban development on surface-water quality. Students begin by reading novels and stories that present water as a significant topic. They supplement those fictional insights with reports and textual materials about water quality testing and principles of effective fieldwork. Social studies teachers offer historical insights into human development and the importance of water in community life. Mathematics instruction includes units on statistics and measurement, which foreshadow the work to come. Students in art and photography choose local ponds as the subjects of their work.

The teaching and learning resonate with two common notes, the skill of inquiry and the topic of ponds. The school buzzes with the confidence of a skilled kitchen staff preparing a coordinated gourmet menu. In every classroom and at all times, the thinking process of inquiry energizes and unifies learning. Because their final presentation is made to city officials, students are motivated to accurately collect relevant information, prepare it completely, and present it effectively. Students and staff are not only highly motivated but also satisfied by the sense of real accomplishment that is a hallmark of thought-filled, authentic learning.

PREPARATION

Learner satisfaction is almost tangible, but learner frustration can be just as evident when thinking skills do not match up with the task at hand. That is why excellent teachers help students monitor and adjust their own thought processes to best meet the needs of the current learning phase. Inquiry is an excellent beginning. But a presentation filled with questions and hypotheses would leave the audience hungry for more. Just as we would never make a full meal out of appetizers, we must not imagine that inquiry alone is sufficient to complete the learning process. Between gathering and presenting lies a

critical phase—the time of preparation. When the ingredients of an excellent presentation have been collected, learners must decide which are most credible, which need additional treatment, and how they can best be assembled into a coherent whole.

Preparation involves the skills of evaluation, interpretation, and many forms of analysis. Learners who have collected a large body of information must now mine it to discover meaningful patterns. Inquiry questions such as what, who, when, and why give way to analytic questions such as "To what degree?"; "Based on what criteria?"; and "According to which comparison?" These questions require judgment and discrimination, thinking skills that build on inquiry but are distinct from it.

It is in the area of preparation that academic disciplines diverge most dramatically. Mathematics instruction relies heavily on the use of formulas and symbolic representations to move from data to conclusion. The specialized language and procedures of math set clear parameters on this middle phase, with a heavy emphasis on precision. If an equation is reversed, an operation left undone, or sequence not followed, the final product will suffer. This reality spawns a valuable form of disciplined precision. In science there is a different approach. Because the scientific tradition embraces a self-correcting method, it is more tolerant of mistakes along the way. Even a flawed hypothesis or experiment can generate useful learning, *if it is documented and leads to reflection on the process.*

The social sciences approach preparation from a third perspective. Their tradition is the marketplace of ideas. In this approach the credibility, consistency, and support of an argument determine its value. Learners must compare the clarity and accuracy of others' claims so that their own conclusions are consistent and defensible. By placing ideas in competition with each other, the learner practices powerful analytic and evaluative techniques. What is often lost, as specialists advocate their particular flavor of preparation, is that these techniques can be highly complementary. It is mathematical precision which gives us bridges and BMWs. It is science's tolerance for imperfection which led to penicillin, while the abstract approach of social studies helps put all our formulas and discoveries in a meaningful human context. All these processes are valuable. And each relies, at times, on a fourth preparation method—communication. Both writing and speaking are foundational processes of preparation that combine insights and evaluation for public consumption.

Rather than letting these skills simmer in isolation, integrated projects and opportunities bring them together, adding valuable new applications to each approach. When student scientists conduct fieldwork, it is completely reasonable that they collect their data with mathematical precision. This integration sparks application when students become adept at using the right thinking "tool" for the job. Soon they begin to see that scientific tolerance of ambiguity is similar to the writing process of drafting, revising, and finalizing. All of these processes make students better at defending their conclusions, which is both a mandate of the social sciences and a full-circle return to math teachers' expectation that students show their work.

LIGHTHOUSE LESSON 2

At a high school in Iowa, interdisciplinary teams of teachers created the European Odyssey as a way to engage students in a complex suite of activities focusing on content and cognition. The teachers at Valley Southwoods Freshman High School in West Des Moines begin by assigning groups of students to a country and a crisis. Students must create a travelogue of their imagined odyssey, including currency, language, travel distances, cultural customs, and many other factors.

At some point in their journey they are faced with the crisis. This may be an unexpected travel delay, loss of their travel documents, health problems, unanticipated trouble with the law, or any number of other realistic problems. As they prepare their final report, complete with maps, illustrations, and other supplements, the students employ a full set of thinking processes. Not only do they have to analyze a variety of primary and secondary sources, but they have to choose between routes, accommodations, and potential solutions to their problems. Once they collect as much information as possible, each group of students digs in to assemble their best possible project.

Although the final projects are all unique, their preparation draws consistently on the same set of transdisciplinary skills. Because the teachers have made a commitment to coherence, they also link other aspects of their curriculum to the central project. All of these elements are integrated, and each reinforces the importance of thoughtful processes.

PRESENTATION

The odyssey of integration can be as intriguing as a European adventure, especially when it engages teachers as the authors of their own professional development. This excitement is most obvious during the presentation phase of a learning experience. The presentation, like a gourmet meal, shows the expertise and execution of a team of specialists. Like the savory offerings from a creative kitchen, a polished presentation

reflects the contributions of many teachers and their associated disciplines. This collaboration is most potent when teachers embrace the dual synergy of *teaching* from their expertise and *learning* from expert colleagues. It is not unusual for teachers to rediscover their own joy for learning. In fact, it is unusual for teachers newly involved in interdisciplinary lessons not to get excited.

Part of the excitement happens naturally as projects and lessons culminate in all kinds of student presentations. Teachers themselves are constantly engaged in making presentations, whether they are presenting lectures, directing labs, leading discussions, creating art, or solving equations. Of course, gathering and preparing are critical to these presentations. But it is when teachers present their lessons to students that they come alive. It is no coincidence that teachers are confident and creative when they help students develop the thinking skills necessary for dynamic presentations. As role models, teachers can show students how to analyze their audiences, build rapport with them, and evaluate themselves as they present. These are the three critical thinking skills associated with every presentation, and they draw heavily from the practice and insights of effective communication.

The process of audience analysis and self-adjustment is driven by a set of related questions: Who will receive my presentation? What do they want or need from the presentation? What methods best match my audience? and How well am I executing my plan? These questions operate equally well for a variety of disciplines. In math, the audience is most concerned about precisely correct answers, so the effective presenter uses symbols with precise meaning. An effective math student also checks for accuracy along the way. This application is quite specific to math, but the underlying thought-filled principle transcends any one discipline. Consider that art and math are often considered poles apart, but creative artists also ask themselves about their audience, its needs, and their ability to meet those needs. A student constructs a sketch with a working sense of how it will be viewed. A photographer checks the contrast or composition of a picture and makes adjustments to enhance the final image. The storyteller chooses written or spoken words to evoke feeling and understanding. All of these students are engaged in the same complex set of learning behaviors. All pause and evaluate their own efforts. The sketch artist steps back to see the work progressing. The photographer emerges from the darkroom to see how the print looks in natural light. The writer or speaker checks to see if the chosen words flow smoothly to create the right kind of feeling and meaning. All are thinking hard in this phase of learning, which uses very different skills from either gathering or preparing.

Presenting builds on inquiry; it packages what has been prepared but requires special attention to the relationship between the product and the audience.

LIGHTHOUSE LESSON 3

A school in the hills above Guatemala City boasts a vibrant example of an excellent presentation. There at Colegio Decroly Americano, on a long retaining wall separating a playground from a soccer field, visitors find a colorful painting filled with cultural and personal images. Placed just down the hill from the main classrooms, the mural is a spirited addition to the place where students gather each day. Because Colegio Decroly Americano is an international school serving a diverse population, some of the images may be unfamiliar to students, teachers, or visitors new to Guatemala. To respond to this unfamiliarity, the students who created the mural also wrote a script explaining the various elements and telling something about the student artists who put paint to stone. The content of the mural draws from the entire student experience and so reflects all disciplines. The choice of images reflects the priorities and themes of each class. In addition, the teachers use mural presentations regularly to give students opportunities to practice speaking English. The pride and excitement on display are even more remarkable considering that the artists, authors, and speakers are only in 3rd grade, and many are making presentations to adult visitors using their second language. Decroly teachers, even those not involved with the project, are justifiably proud of their school and their students. They know that they are building basic skills that will last through a lifetime of learning.

Such shared projects help build a sense of school community. Sometime in the distant past, our ancestors gathered fruits, grains, and meats and brought them home to a village. With steam, fire, and spices they made a meal, and in the flickering light of a common fire, the whole village shared the result. The shared enjoyment of eating together was a natural outcome of successful gathering and skillful preparation. The shared success of that ancient village can be found in classrooms today. Learning and sharing are still as fundamental as gathering and eating. When gathering transcends disciplines, the preparation and presentation can be as satisfying and compelling as the best buffet. Learning *can* be that good. When thoughtful teachers use thought-filled processes to introduce and reinforce the phases of learning, students' hunger for learning is fully satisfied.

45

Infusing Critical and Creative Thinking into Content Instruction

Robert J. Swartz

The movement to bring the explicit teaching of thinking into the classroom stimulated the creation of a variety of special courses and programs for students during the 1980s. However, when a separate program is used as the sole vehicle for instruction in thinking, the application of what is learned to other academic work and to everyday thinking appears to be far less automatic than we would like, however effective the program may be otherwise (Perkins & Salomon, 1988; Salomon & Perkins, 1989). In this chapter I describe a contrasting approach to helping students improve their thinking: the infusion of the teaching of thinking into standard content instruction. What interests me especially about this approach is not so much the work of professional curriculum specialists in prescribing how thinking should be taught along with content; rather it is the work of creative classroom teachers who have redesigned the way they teach. Since 1987, when I first used the word "infusion" to describe what certain teachers were doing to blend instruction in specific thinking skills into their content instruction (Swartz, 1987), much activity has occurred in school classrooms to implement this approach. From the late 1980s to the present, K–12 teachers in a wide variety of schools throughout the United States—and indeed in other countries—have restructured the way they teach standard content to infuse instruction in a variety of thinking skills, using those early teachers' work as models. The results have been impressive.

Our challenge today is twofold. It is first to learn from these models by articulating, analyzing, and adapting what they represent so that local curricula can include significant and workable objectives, standards, and themes related to teaching

thinking. The goal is to transform these local curricula into thinking-oriented curricula while retaining the integrity of their content focus. The second challenge is to implement this shift in focus in *every* classroom in light of what we have learned over the past 25 years about staff development and educational change. To be successful, both of these enterprises must be motivated and carried forth from within the school and school district. They are formidable tasks that themselves require time and careful, critical, creative thinking. Their importance cannot be overstated. This chapter is designed to establish the groundwork for these tasks by discussing some of the key things we learn from the process of infusion, especially as it has been implemented in classrooms in the United States.

WHY SHOULD WE TEACH THINKING IN THE CONTENT AREAS?

Much of the effort to teach thinking has focused on "higher-order thinking." What is involved in this is neither esoteric nor technically difficult. In fact it typically involves processes that we use regularly. Comparing and contrasting, predicting, finding causes, locating reliable sources of information, and deciding on things to do, for example, are forms of thinking that we use almost every day of our lives. They are representative of many other activities no less familiar to us. Each of these processes complements and builds on the important acts of recollection and recognition that have been characterized, though misleadingly, as "lower-order thinking." Figure 45.1 identifies some of the key forms of thinking that have been categorized as "higher-order thinking."

Performing these "higher-order" activities, however, does not necessarily mean performing them *well*, nor does it necessarily entail either creative or critical thinking. That is a matter of *how* we perform them. For example, we all know of situations in which people have compared and contrasted things superficially just by listing a few similarities and differences;

This chapter is adapted, with permission of the publisher, from "What Is Infusion," in *Infusing the Teaching of Critical and Creative Thinking into Content Instruction: A Lesson Design Handbook for the Elementary Grades*, by R. Swartz, & S. Parks, 1994, pp. 3–27. Pacific Grove, CA: Critical Thinking Books and Software.

—Figure 45.1—
Important Types of Thinking That We Should Teach Students to Engage in Skillfully

I. Generating Ideas
    A. Alternate Possibilities
        1. Multiplicity of Ideas
        2. Varied Ideas
        3. New Ideas
        4. Detailed Ideas
    B. Composition
        1. Analogy/Metaphor

II. Clarifying Ideas
    A. Analyzing Ideas
        1. Compare/Contrast
        2. Classification/Definition
        3. Parts/Whole
        4. Sequencing
    B. Analyzing Arguments
        1. Finding Reasons/Conclusions
        2. Uncovering Assumptions

III. Assessing the Reasonableness of Ideas
    A. Assessing Basic Information
        1. Accuracy of Observation
        2. Reliability of Sources
    B. Inference
        1. Use of Evidence
            a. Causal Explanation
            b. Prediction
            c. Generalization
            d. Reasoning by Analogy
        2. Deduction
            a. Conditional Reasoning (If . . . then. . . .)
            b. Categorical Reasoning (Some . . . all. . . .)

IV. Complex Thinking Tasks
    A. Decision Making
    B. Problem Solving

Source: Adapted from *Infusing the Teaching of Critical and Creative Thinking into Content Instruction: A Lesson Design Handbook for the Elementary Grades,* by R. Swartz, & S. Parks, 1994, p. 6. Pacific Grove, CA: Critical Thinking Books and Software.

for example, we take the time to generate and consider a variety of options, going out of our way to think about new and interesting possibilities, we are exercising creativity in our decision making. And if we make well-founded and well-considered judgments about the reasonableness of these options, paying particular attention to their expected consequences, we are exercising careful thought. We do not always do either, of course.

It is not too hard to help our students shift from less skillful to more skillful ways of thinking in these important ways and to incorporate the more skillful practices into the conduct of their lives. The idea that it is important to spend time with *all* students to reorganize their thinking in this way and the notion that there are clear instructional strategies to do so with demonstrable results were two fundamental tenets of the thinking skills movement of the 1980s. Showing how this could be done on a large scale in classrooms has been one of the great successes of the 1990s. Disseminating these results around the globe is the great challenge of the next decade. Why, though, should content instruction in the subject areas be the primary framework of this approach, and how can the blending of thinking and content be accomplished in a system that for many years has focused solely on content?

What we teach students in the content areas is not inert pieces of information; it is the primary material that informed and literate people use in much of their thinking. We want information about nutrition taught in a science class to influence students' dietary choices and habits. We want an understanding of the political history of the country where students live to affect their choices of political candidates and their national and public policy positions. Reliable and relevant information, shaped by the conceptual frameworks we use to convey it, should fuel the natural thinking tasks that guide us through our lives. Yet too often what students learn in school is learned just to pass tests; it has little influence in their lives after they leave school. Infusion as a strategy for teaching thinking is based on the ideal we all have as educators of the natural fusion of what we normally teach students with the forms of thinking we all use every day.

WHAT KINDS OF LESSONS TEACH THINKING WITH CONTENT?

Kevin O'Reilly, a high school American history teacher in the Hamilton-Wenham Regional School District in Massachusetts, is interested in helping his students become skillful at determining the accuracy of information by judging the reliability of its sources. He begins his initial lesson on this skill by

more careful thought is needed to bring insight. The predictions people make about the future often involve no more than guessing; more careful thought is needed to ascertain how likely the predictions are. Likewise, people often make decisions without much forethought, deciding to do the first thing that occurs to them; more careful thought is needed to know what is the best thing to do, and it is often imperative to know this before making a choice, rather than afterward.

What does it mean to perform these mental activities *carefully* and *skillfully*? There are no surprises here, either. If, staging a scuffle in the corridor outside his classroom and asking student witnesses in his classroom what happened. He compares the conflicting accounts his students give to the conflicting accounts given about the Battle of Lexington in 1775, at the start of the Revolutionary War. As students attempt to determine which of 20th century historians, and then which of the eyewitnesses, gave the most accurate account of the battle, they reflect on why one historical account may be more accurate than another. This activity yields a checklist of factors to take into account in judging skillfully the accuracy and reliability of sources of information. The students use the checklist again and again in O'Reilly's classroom; it enables them to back up their assessments of accuracy with reasons. These skills focus on the accuracy and reliability of eyewitnesses, of observation, and of secondary sources of information in general and are very important in life outside the classroom. In the immediate context of the Revolutionary War, O'Reilly's students use these skills to make informed critical judgments about the accuracy of various textbook accounts of the Lexington incident that students who are simply directed to read the historical texts to "get the facts" cannot and do not make.

Besides developing vital critical thinking skills, O'Reilly's students learn a tremendous amount about the context for the battle and the biases that people might have had in describing what happened. (The battle occurred a few years after the Boston Massacre trials, and some colonists wanted to use it as a rallying cry to turn the uncommitted against the British.) They also gain a critical perspective on the role of such reports in the construction of a history and on the way that histories can be written from various points of view.

Infusion is not restricted to American history or to high school. Cathy Skowron, a 1st grade teacher at Provincetown Elementary School in Provincetown, Massachusetts, uses the same technique. She reads her students the tale of Henny Penny and follows it with a discussion, prompted by her questioning, of whether the other animals should have trusted Henny Penny and how they could have determined whether she was a reliable source of information. After all, it might have paid for them to consider this question; believing her without doing so is one of the primary reasons they were led into the fox's den.

Many primary grade teachers use such stories only to help students build listening skills or vocabulary. Skowron appreciates these goals but wants to do more, in both content and thinking. Integrating questions that help students consider the reliability of Henny Penny's information helps them understand the story at a different level: They begin to grasp the "moral" of the Henny Penny story, that uncritical thinking can

be dangerous. This new understanding in turn allows Skowron to begin teaching about what the moral of a story is.

Skowron's lesson differs from O'Reilly's 9th grade American History lesson in the sophistication of content, vocabulary, and the expectations of her students' background knowledge. Nonetheless, like O'Reilly she tries to help her students consider factors that are often overlooked in making judgments about the reliability of information. Students learn not only to raise questions of reliability in appropriate contexts but also to think more thoroughly about how to answer these questions.

The same critical thinking skill can be taught, reinforced, and elaborated in many other contexts, subjects, and grade levels. For example, one 5th grade teacher helps her students with library research by referring them to a variety of books on the same topic and then helping them draft questions they need to answer in deciding which source is likely to give them the most accurate information. In doing so they focus on factors such as the date of the books, the authors' expertise, whether the account is firsthand or secondhand, whether the book is fictional, the reputation of the publisher, and so on. She reports that students' interests in the topic are piqued, and better research skills result.

Other types of thinking have also been made the focus of infused lessons. I mentioned decision making, a relatively complex thinking process. Traci Whipple and Gina Blaisdell, 3rd and 4th grade teachers from the Meadow Glens and the Highlands Elementary Schools in Naperville, Illinois, ask their students to "become" Sarah in the book *Sarah, Plain and Tall* by Patricia MacLachlan (1985). Given the information in the book, the students think about the best thing for Sarah to do when she has to decide whether to stay with the family she has joined in Oklahoma from her home in Maine, close to 2,000 miles away, in the latter part of the 19th century. The students don't try to predict what Sarah will do; rather they consider what her options are, trying to come up with unusual and creative ones, then weigh the consequences of these options, rating the pros and cons and evaluating their importance to Sarah. At that point they can compare the options and choose the best one. These students are guided by a strategy for skillful decision making that they then reflect on, and—having tried it in the context of Sarah's decision—they assess its effectiveness. At the same time, of course, they get practice in reading comprehension, one of the lesson's primary content objectives.

Skillful decision making, like determining the reliability of sources of information, can be taught in the primary grades. The Dr. Seuss book *Horton Hatches the Egg* (1940) is the basis for another decision-making lesson for 1st grade students, developed by Sandra Parks for use in elementary schools in the Cypress-Fairbanks Independent School District in Texas, and now used in many 1st grade classrooms. The students become little Hortons, sitting on Mayzie's egg after she goes off on a vacation, just as he spots some hunters. What should he do? He's promised Mayzie to take care of her egg, but these hunters pose a real threat to him. The students develop a set of options—run away without the egg, fight the hunters, or tell them what he is doing and ask them not to harm him—and then consider the consequences, which they rate as pros and cons of specific options. Then they compare the options in light of these pros and cons and decide which is best. These students also learn how to explain why they think their chosen option is best.

As with this technique of "becoming" a fictional character who has to make a decision, students may be asked to "become" historical characters with important decisions to make. In a high-school history lesson, for example, students become President Harry S Truman in July 1945 after the atomic bomb has been tested. Truman must decide how to bring World War II to a close. The students develop and consider options such as invading the Japanese mainland, demonstrating the bomb, using the bomb on a populated city, negotiating peace, and so forth. Then they predict the consequences of each, being as thorough as they can. In determining the consequences of these options, the students have to explore in some depth the historical situation of the period. Would heavy casualties result from an invasion? Why? Would negotiations secure a lasting peace? Why? In each case answering "why" requires a deep understanding of the situation, which the students get through research orchestrated in cooperative learning groups, each working on a specific option.

Similarly, Rita Hagevik, a teacher at Ligon Middle School in Raleigh, North Carolina, helps her students learn the same decision-making strategy in 7th grade science (Swartz, 1997). She asks them to imagine that they have been asked to serve on a commission to report to the president about what the United States should rely on as its dominant source of energy over the next 25 years. The students develop options including standard sources such as nuclear, wind, solar, fossil fuel, and hydroelectric, but they also include such sources as geothermal and some innovative sources such as "human power": "Imagine that a law was passed requiring every person on earth to push a treadmill for an hour each day." They determine what factors need to be taken into account in making this decision—cost, safety, and environmental impact, for example—and then, once again through small-group collaboration, they divide the task and search for relevant and reliable information on the consequences of each option, considering the identified factors.

The students learn how to get information on the Internet, through library research, and so forth. The results are decisions that each student can support with hard scientific information about the energy sources they have studied.

As taught by these teachers, skillful decision making and its mate, problem solving, involve students in an integrated set of thinking activities that engage them in the creative generation of ideas, an analysis of those ideas, and the exercise of critical judgment in determining what the best idea is. In essence, skillful decision making is a complex task incorporating a number of different but complementary thinking skills, such as the quartet often referred to as "fluency, flexibility, originality, and elaboration" by specialists in creative thinking, predicting likely consequences, focused comparing and contrasting, ranking/prioritizing, and determining the accuracy and reliability of sources of information. If students have difficulty with any of these, a teacher can always teach lessons that focus on a specific type of skillful thinking. For example, Rebecca Reagan, a 5th grade teacher in the Lubbock Independent School District in Texas often supplements her lessons on skillful decision making by teaching students a lesson in which they first brainstorm ideas about how they might communicate with people in their community about educational issues in their school. Reagan teaches students a number of enhancement strategies that go beyond simple brainstorming and help to dramatically increase the number of ideas they generate while also explicitly fostering originality. Stephen Fischer, a science teacher at Millville Alternative High School in Millville, New Jersey, teaches a lesson on the population explosion in which students learn how to find, collect, and assess evidence about likely scenarios for mankind as our population continues to grow.

Lessons on these types of thinking can stand on their own, of course, as well as being used to enhance decision making. This is especially true of thinking that yields a deeper understanding of what is being taught. We can compare and contrast options, but to do so skillfully it is important to not just list some similarities and differences between them. We need to sort out the key similarities and differences and draw conclusions from them, perhaps after we have thought about any patterns they display. Classroom teachers from the primary grades through high school now use infusion as a technique to help students learn this enhanced strategy for comparing and contrasting. They teach initial lessons on comparing and contrasting in which they might focus, for example, on two characters in a story, such as in Rebecca Reagan's 5th grade lesson on Matt and Attean, two characters from the novel *The Sign of the Beaver*, by Elizabeth Speare (1983). Other examples of such lessons include comparing and contrasting fruits and cones (grade 2 science), triangles and pyramids (grade 2 mathematics), Abraham Lincoln and Frederick Douglass (grade 5 history), plant cells and animal cells (grade 8 science), RNA and DNA (grade 11 science), and the play *Romeo and Juliet* and the film *West Side Story* (grade 12 English).

Other types of skills that enhance deep understanding (and hence fall into the thinking category of "analysis") include the examination of parts of a whole, in which students don't just list the parts of something but also formulate statements about their function and put those ideas together in a concept of how the parts work together to make the whole object operate as it does. Good examples of such lessons range from the systems of the human body (Stephen Fischer, Millville, New Jersey, High School) to the parts of a short story (Rebecca Reagan, Lubbock, Texas, public schools) to a 1st grade lesson on simple machines in which students analyzed the parts of a screw and explained how it worked (Beebe Elementary School, Naperville, Illinois). This list could go on and on. In many of these cases, reports of enhanced content learning and increased test scores testify to the depth of understanding the lessons generate about concepts and ideas in the standard curriculum.

Good writing built on good thinking can also be a goal of infusion lessons. The students of Traci Whipple and Gina Blaisdell in Naperville don't just make decisions about what Sarah should do in their lesson on the children's novel *Sarah, Plain and Tall*. They also write a persuasive letter to Sarah explaining why she should do what they think is best. In doing this they make use of a "template" for persuasive writing that was developed by Rebecca Reagan, who, in teaching her own infusion lessons on decision making, extended them with a writing component that would enable the students to communicate the thinking behind their decisions. The template provides students with a paragraph-by-paragraph and sentence-by-sentence guide to writing persuasive prose based on their thinking. Similarly, as an extension of the lesson on the bombing of Hiroshima, the teachers often ask students to write a persuasive letter to President Truman about what they think his best choice is, using a version of Reagan's template. A similar technique is used by Rita Hagevik in extending her lesson on energy sources. All of these teachers report that the quality of students' writing in their classrooms improves as they show great improvements in their thinking.

These examples show what can be done to infuse the teaching of how to engage skillfully in key types of thinking into the curriculum by finding natural contexts in the curriculum in which students can use thinking strategies. Imagine the richness of the curriculum and the depth of learning possible when this happens schoolwide. There are now such schools.

HOW SHOULD WE TEACH STUDENTS THINKING IN THE CONTENT AREAS?

USE AN EXPLICIT STRUCTURE FOR SKILLFUL THINKING

Teachers are often told to stop asking only "what" questions and ask more "why" questions to prompt more than simple recall. This is one of the main insights gained from Benjamin Bloom's work on his famous thinking taxonomy (Bloom, Englehart, Furst, Hill, & Krathwohl, 1956). The infusion lessons I have described seem to exemplify this practice. Indeed, some who use the term "infusion" refer only to asking more challenging, "higher-order questions" in the context of content instruction. A comparison of textbooks of the 1990s with those of the early 1980s also reflects this tendency. Nonetheless, there are important subtleties in the lessons I have described that go beyond merely asking higher-order questions.

There is no doubt that a lot of thinking beyond simple recall occurs in classrooms where many "why" and "how" questions are asked. But is this enough to teach skillful thinking? If a teacher asks, "Why did Huck Finn's father abduct him?" this indeed gives students the opportunity to think beyond simple recall. But if they are in the habit of guessing or making hasty judgments about what causes things to happen, all the teacher usually provides is another opportunity for the same. That does not help them improve their thinking. To use an early and powerful conceptualization, this constitutes teaching *for* thinking (Brandt, 1984; Costa, 1985b). To be sure, some students do meet the challenge of careful thinking in this case, but many do not. Such questioning doesn't make an impression on students who are generally unaware of how they think and doesn't help them modify any bad habits they have in thinking.

What all of the teachers I have mentioned in this chapter do is what has come to be called the teaching *of* thinking (Brandt, 1984; Costa, 1985b; McTighe, 1987). This involves the use of some very specific instructional strategies designed to make the lessons they teach more effective in achieving their thinking objectives as well as their content goals. Specifically, these teachers make thinking strategies explicit and guide students to follow them reflectively. For example, Rita Hagevik in Raleigh, North Carolina, works with her students to develop a list of specific focus questions—such as "What options do I have?" and "What short- and long-term consequences could these options have?"—that can be built into an organized, though by no means rigid, way of thinking about decisions before they are made. Hagevik posts this set of questions—the "thinking strategy"—on the wall of her classroom to guide her students through the process. I have called this a map of skillful decision making (Swartz & Perkins, 1989). It is a flexible guide; students can reword some of the questions or add others. Hagevik also uses a set of graphic organizers to give students places to "download" their ideas for further reflection, structured in a way that is consonant with this thinking strategy map. This is what I mean by using an explicit structure for the kind of thinking being taught.

One important thing we have all learned in the thinking skills movement is that the more explicit the thinking that we are trying to help students with, the more likely it is that they will learn to change and improve their thinking habits. Infusion teachers also often supplement the use of thinking strategy maps and graphic organizers by explicitly guiding students through the thinking process orally while they are focused on content. The teachers may ask such prompting questions as, "What options does Horton have in protecting himself against the hunters?" or "What options does President Truman have to bring World War II to a close?" This combination of techniques is a key distinguishing characteristic of the teaching *of* thinking in contrast to teaching *for* thinking. During the early and middle 1980s, the primary use of this technique was in instructional efforts that were separate from the regular curriculum. From the mid-1980s on, this emphasis started to shift, until now a vast range of explicit thinking skills instruction takes place in infused lessons.

HELP STUDENTS REFLECT ON THEIR THINKING

Using focus questions that make explicit use of the language of thinking has a specific function in the lessons of teachers such as O'Reilly, Whipple, and Fischer. It helps focus students' attention on certain ingredients in their thinking—such as the consideration of evidence—that they often miss. From there, teachers move toward the use of another important and more general technique they employ: prompting students to be aware of how they are thinking so that they can reflect on it, monitor it, and direct it themselves, rather than relying on the teacher to do so. This is *metacognition*—thinking about thinking. Metacognition requires that we have a conceptual apparatus and language that enables us to articulate what is going on in our thinking (Costa, 1985a; Swartz & Parks, 1994; Beyer, 1997).

All the teachers whose work I have commented on have found it extremely important to build metacognitive prompts into their thinking skills lessons. The rationale for this practice is simple. Our goal in teaching thinking is for students to internalize strategies that make their thinking more effective. We want the teaching of thinking to prompt an internal

monologue in students: "Wait a minute, before I make this decision shouldn't I think about what my options are?" Metacognitive reflection prompted by the teacher in a thinking skills lesson is a necessary and powerful transition to this type of internalization.

The importance of metacognitive reflection as an effective tool in enhancing learning is supported by a considerable amount of research (Bransford, Sherwood, Vye, & Riser, 1986). When we think about our thinking, we can become aware of how we are doing it and modify it; we can set goals, develop a plan to meet them, and then act on this plan. This is a familiar technique for taking charge of our *actions*. The great insight about metacognition as a tool for good thinking is that *thinking is not just something that happens* to us; rather it is subject to our deliberate control just as our overt behavior is. By taking charge of our own thinking we can reorganize it to counter shortfalls we may detect in the way we ordinarily think.

This is reflected in the infusion lessons I have described. In Hamilton, Massachusetts, for instance, Kevin O'Reilly often asks his students to list the factors they considered in reflecting on the reliability of eyewitness accounts of the battle of Lexington. This helps students monitor their thinking. O'Reilly then asks his students to share these and to develop, as a class, a comprehensive list of factors that should be considered in assessing the reliability of any eyewitness report. When students use these guidelines they may see that they may not have considered all the relevant factors (evaluating their thinking), and they can decide to broaden the way that they think about reliability in the future (planning their thinking). Descriptive, evaluative, and projective episodes of metacognitive reflection are also prompted by teachers of infusion lessons that focus on other types of thinking such as comparing and contrasting, predicting, and decision making (Perkins & Swartz, 1992; Swartz, 1989; Swartz, Fischer, & Parks, 1998; Swartz & Parks, 1994).

There are, of course, myriad other instructional strategies to promote metacognition. They range from the very directive—such as giving students an explicit plan or a graphic organizer to guide their thinking in the lesson—to techniques such as "Think-Pair-Share," in which students "think out loud" so that other students can help them. Whatever techniques are used, keeping in mind the goals of metacognitive instruction is crucial to making them effective in infusion lessons.

GIVE STUDENTS MORE GUIDED PRACTICE FOR TRANSFER

Helping students reflect on and plan their thinking seems hollow unless they have a chance to actually follow the plan a number of times so that they get used to thinking that way. This is the motivation behind other practices used by the teachers whose works I have described. They explicitly *teach for transfer* of specific types of skillful thinking, following up and building on their initial infusion lessons. Research supports explicit transfer activities as an important ingredient in teaching thinking (Perkins & Salomon, 1988). Such activities usually build directly on the kinds of metacognitive activities described above.

Shortly after the decision-making lesson based on the book *Sarah, Plain and Tall*, Whipple and Blaisdell work with their 3rd and 4th grade students on the landing of the pilgrims in what was to become Plymouth, Massachusetts, in 1620. They highlight the fact that when the Pilgrims arrived they found natives living on the land. Whipple and Blaisdell ask the students to use their plan for decision making to guide them through a similar process focused on the pilgrims' situation. What should they do? Similarly, American history teacher Kevin O'Reilly, months after the lesson on the Battle of Lexington, and after a number of other activities on reliable sources, has his students read several eyewitness accounts of conditions under slavery in the United States before the Civil War—accounts from slaveholders, abolitionists, Northern newspaper articles, and so on. He then asks the students to certify which of these are likely to be the most reliable, using the checklist they developed in class when they worked on the Battle of Lexington.

These lessons by Whipple and Blaisdell and O'Reilly are examples, respectively, of *immediate transfer activities* following a specific thinking skill lesson and *reinforcement of skillful thinking* later in the school year. Teachers report that it usually takes only three or four such transfer activities for students to apply their plans for thinking without the need for teacher prompting.

Many teachers supplement this follow-up by asking questions like: "What are the sorts of situations that call for the kind of thinking we have practiced?" Students may make lists of sources of information, types of situations calling for serious decision making, and so forth. They can write these in student journals or on charts posted on the classroom wall. As they practice the types of skillful thinking they are being taught and assimilate these lists, they become more and more proficient in identifying situations in which the specific kind of skillful thinking they are being taught is called for and in using it on those occasions.

Most teachers, of course, hope that the habits of guided thinking stick with students outside of school. Some teachers, though, reinforce this habit more directly. Helping students

apply the specific critical and creative thinking skills taught in infused lessons to their own lives is an obvious way to carry this out. This is also practiced by the teachers mentioned in this chapter. Once again, making thinking an up-front question has brought the greatest success.

HELPING STUDENTS DEVELOP DISPOSITIONS TO ENGAGE IN SKILLFUL THINKING

John Dewey, in his landmark book *How We Think* (1933) remarks that we can teach students what constitutes good thinking, but that without their being motivated and disposed to engage in it when the occasion arises, such instruction comes to naught. Most teachers who infuse the teaching of critical and creative thinking into content instruction recognize this problem (Beyer, 1987; Beyer, 1997). To overcome it, they rely on a combination of three things: (1) students' reflection on how best to practice specific types of thinking—such as decision making and parts/whole analysis; (2) practice directed at building the habit of engaging in specific types of thinking skillfulness; and (3) familiarity with occasions on which such thinking is called for. I have described these techniques already in this chapter. It is important to note here that these kinds of infusion lessons already incorporate instructional techniques that speak to the issue of helping students develop the disposition to engage in specific forms of skillful thinking.

Some have suggested, however, that besides teaching specific forms of skillful thinking and helping students develop a disposition to engage in them when needed, other things that they call *thinking dispositions* must also be taught (Ennis, 1987; Perkins, Jay, & Tishman, 1993). The extreme case is the notion that teaching thinking is no more than teaching students these "dispositions." Proponents of this idea give as examples open-mindedness, deliberateness, and adventurousness in thinking. What is the role of these dispositions in infusion?

First, let me comment that in my experience such things as open-mindedness and deliberateness should *not* be described as thinking dispositions, in contrast with thinking skills, nor should they be thought to require different instructional strategies as a result. Practicing open-mindedness, for example, involves not just a *disposition* to do something but *actively* doing various things. An open-minded person seeks alternative points of view before making up his mind; takes alternative points of view seriously by listening to them or reading them carefully; and considers their force, value, and reliability. Similar behavioral descriptions can be provided for the other so-called dispositions. Thus they are not merely dispositions; they are forms of skillful thinking in the same sense as decision making, determining the reliability of sources, and comparing and contrasting, except that they are general in nature and apply to any of the more specific forms of thinking that I have reported on. These more general forms of thinking can be taught using the same techniques, and they should be taught so that students don't just learn how to engage in them skillfully but they also develop the disposition to do so when it is called for.

Some teachers of infusion lessons combine instruction in these broader and very important kinds of intelligent behaviors with the instruction they provide in specific types of skillful thinking. For example, a 5th grade teacher asks students whom she is teaching how to analyze and evaluate arguments skillfully in their study of the Revolutionary War to read Thomas Paine's *Common Sense*, promoting independence from Britain. Before students make up their minds on this issue, however, they are asked to imagine that they are "on the fence" about it and want to hear other points of view. In seeking other arguments, they find one that favors loyalty to Britain. They have to reserve judgment and practice open-mindedness until they have assessed both arguments. If they think that neither one supports its conclusions well—as many students do—they have to search for information and construct their own arguments, taking a stand only when they feel it is well supported. This assignment is not easy for students to do, because most are so committed to Thomas Paine's point of view. But most teachers feel it is well worth helping students respond to the challenge of being open-minded, especially in such contexts. As with any of the more specific thinking skills discussed earlier, asking students to reflect metacognitively on how to be open-minded and whether it is worthwhile to do so, and to develop a plan for being open-minded are coupled with repeated practice as a follow-up to this lesson for broader application. Logging occasions when open-mindedness is important—for example, when trying to decide who to vote for—can build it into a valuable habit of mind for the students.

HELPING OUR STUDENTS BECOME GOOD THINKERS

There are no pat formulas for constructing the more elaborate types of infused lessons, and their follow-ups, found in the work of the teachers I have commented upon. They use a variety of practices to accomplish their goals as teachers of thinking. What stands out, however, is that these practices include five basic components that make a great difference in the lessons' success:

- They help students develop and learn explicit strategies that inform and organize the way they do specific types of thinking (the teaching of thinking).
- They build into their instruction significant opportunities for students to reflect on, monitor, evaluate, and plan their thinking (metacognition).
- They prompt specific engagement by students in the types of skillful thinking being taught in the context of the content they are learning (active thinking).
- They follow up specific lessons with opportunities for students to get more practice in guiding themselves to apply the same sort of thinking in new situations (teaching for transfer).
- They are conducted in an open classroom environment where good thinking attitudes are modeled and where students are given opportunities to manifest those attitudes and reflect on their value (building the disposition to engage in skillful thinking).

Learning to think better enhances student learning in the content areas and will improve the quality of their lives and their professional work after they leave school. Indeed, it is through careful thinking that human beings can make the most of their minds, and it is through such behavior that great civilizations are built. The lessons I have analyzed here are examples of what can be done to teach the skillful practice of important types of thinking across the curriculum's content areas. The curricula of any country abound with opportunities for such lessons, and they are a must if we are to help our students realize their full potential as thinkers.

REFERENCES

Beyer, B. (1987). *Practical strategies for the teaching of thinking.* Needham Heights, MA: Allyn and Bacon.

Beyer, B. (1997). *Improving student thinking: A comprehensive approach.* Needham Heights, MA: Allyn and Bacon.

Bloom, B. S., Englehart, M. D., Furst, E. J., Hill, W. H, & Krathwohl, D. R. (Eds.). (1956). *Taxonomy of educational objectives: The classification of educational goals. Handbook I: Cognitive domain.* New York: David McKay.

Brandt, R. (1984). Teaching of thinking, for thinking, about thinking. *Educational Leadership, 42*(1), 3.

Bransford, J., Sherwood, R., Vye, N., & Riser, J. (1986, November). Teaching thinking and problem solving: Research foundations. *American Psychologist, 41*(10), 1078–1089.

Costa, A. (1985a). Mediating the metacognitive. In A. Costa (Ed.), *Developing Minds.* Alexandria, VA: Association for Supervision and Curriculum Development.

Costa, A. (1985b). Teaching for, of, and about thinking. In A. Costa (Ed.), *Developing Minds.* Alexandria, VA: Association for Supervision and Curriculum Development.

Dewey, J. (1933). *How we think* (2nd ed.). Boston: D. C. Heath.

Ennis, R. (1987). A taxonomy of critical thinking abilities and dispositions. In J. Baron & R. Sternberg (Eds.), *Teaching thinking skills: Theory and practice.* New York: W. H. Freeman.

MacLachlan, P. (1985). *Sarah, plain and tall.* New York: Harper & Row.

McTighe, J. (1987). Teaching for, of, and about thinking. In M. Heinman & J. Slomnienko (Eds.), *Thinking skills instruction: Concepts and techniques.* Washington, DC: National Education Association.

Perkins, D. N., & Salomon, G. (1988, September). Teaching for transfer. *Educational Leadership. 46*(1), 22–32.

Perkins, D. N., & Salomon, G. (1989, January–February). Are cognitive skills context-bound? *Educational Researcher, 18*(1), 16–25.

Perkins, D. N., & Swartz, R. (1992). The nine basics of teaching thinking. In A. Costa, J. Bellanca, & R. Fogarty (Eds.), *If minds matter: A foreword to the future.* (pp. 53–69). Palatine, IL: Skylight.

Perkins, D. N., Jay, E., & Tishman, S. (1993). Beyond abilities: A dispositional theory of thinking. *Merrill-Palmer Quarterly, 39*(1), 1–21.

Salomon, G., & Perkins, D. N. (1989). Rocky roads to transfer: Rethinking mechanisms of a neglected phenomenon. *Educational Psychologist, 24*(2), 113–142.

Seuss, D. (1940). *Horton hatches the egg.* New York: Random House.

Speare, E. G. (1983). *The sign of the beaver.* Houghton Mifflin.

Swartz, R. (1987). Teaching for thinking: A developmental model for the infusion of thinking skills into mainstream instruction. In J. Baron & R. Sternberg (Eds.), *Teaching thinking skills: theory and practice.* New York: W. H. Freeman.

Swartz, R. (1989). Making good thinking stick: The role of metacognition, extended practice, and teacher modeling in the teaching of thinking. In D. Topping, D. Crowell, & V. Kobayashi (Eds.), *Thinking across cultures: The third international conference.* Hillsdale, NJ: Erlbaum.

Swartz, R. (1997). Teaching science literacy. In A. L. Costa & R. M. Liebmann (Eds.), *Supporting the spirit of learning: When process is content* (pp. 117–141). Thousand Oaks, CA: Corwin Press.

Swartz, R., & Parks, S. (1994). *Infusing the teaching of critical and creative thinking into content instruction: A lesson design handbook for the elementary grades.* Pacific Grove, CA: Critical Thinking Books and Software.

Swartz, R., & Perkins, D. N. (1989). *Teaching thinking: Issues and approaches.* Pacific Grove, CA: Critical Thinking Books and Software.

WORKS CONTAINING PUBLISHED EXAMPLES OF INFUSION LESSONS

Barman, C., et al. (1989). *Addison-Wesley science.* Menlo Park, CA: Addison-Wesley.

Dorin, H. (1989). Critical and creative thinking. In *Chemistry: The study of matter (teacher's resource book).* Needham Heights, MA: Allyn and Bacon.

O'Reilly, K. (1983). *Critical thinking in American history.* Pacific Grove, CA: Critical Thinking Books and Software.

Schraer, R., & Stolze, J. (1988). Critical and creative thinking. In *Biology: The study of life (teacher's resource book).* Needham Heights, MA: Allyn and Bacon.

Sterns, P., Schwartz, D., & Beyer, B. (1989). *World history: Traditions and new directions.* Menlo Park, CA; Addison Wesley.

Swartz, R., Fischer, S. D., & Parks, S. (1998). *Infusing the teaching of critical and creative thinking into secondary science: A lesson design handbook.* Pacific Grove, CA: Critical Thinking Books and Software.

Swartz, R., Larisey, J., & Kiser, M. A. (2000). *Teaching critical and creative thinking in language arts: A lesson book, grades 1 & 2.* Pacific Grove, CA: Critical Thinking Books and Software.

Swartz, R., & Parks, S. (1994). *Infusing the teaching of critical and creative thinking into content instruction: A lesson design handbook for the elementary grades.* Pacific Grove, CA: Critical Thinking Books and Software.

Swartz, R., Reagan, R., & Kiser, M. A. (1999a). *Teaching critical and creative thinking in language arts: A lesson book, grades 5 & 6.* Pacific Grove, CA: Critical Thinking Books and Software.

Swartz, R., Whipple, T., Blaisdell, G., & Kiser, M. A. (1999b). *Teaching critical and creative thinking in language arts: A lesson book, grades 3 & 4.* Pacific Grove, CA: Critical Thinking Books and Software.

46

What Research Says About Teaching Thinking Skills

BARRY K. BEYER

Classroom research provides a powerful basis for making decisions about teaching. This is especially true of research related to the teaching of thinking skills. Unfortunately, however, much of this research is not readily accessible to the classroom teachers, supervisors, and instructional designers who can benefit most from it, because it is so diverse and widely scattered. My purpose here is to pull together the findings of this research and present it in a way that makes it immediately accessible and meaningful to those educators who seek guidance in teaching thinking skills more successfully than by the traditional exhortations "make 'em think," "drill and kill," and other equally dysfunctional methods still used in many classrooms.

A considerable body of research exists related to teaching thinking skills. This research covers many fields, including motivation, learning and cognition, skill teaching, skill acquisition, information processing, cognitive psychology, learning styles, creativity, memory, brain functioning, and the nature of thinking skills themselves. It consists also of a wide variety of quantitative and qualitative research, including experimental studies in natural and controlled settings, observational studies, and analyses of think-aloud protocols. This research can provide guidance on why we should teach thinking in our schools; what attributes of those skills might be most useful to teach; and when, how, and where teachers can effectively provide purposeful instruction in these skills.

WHY THINKING SKILLS ARE WORTH TEACHING

Research indicates that teaching thinking skills is worth doing. This research clearly demonstrates a major gap between the crucial role that skillful thinking plays in learning and in out-of-school life and the less-than-optimal ability of many of our

students and young people to engage effectively in such thinking, as demonstrated in these findings:

1. Learning requires thinking (Dewey, 1910; Glaser, 1984; McPeck, 1981; Perkins, 1993).
2. Most young students and novices at higher-order thinking do not customarily attend to the kinds of factors required to solve problems effectively (Chi, Glaser, & Rees, 1982; Gettys, 1983; Gettys & Engleman, 1983; Nickerson, 1989; Perkins, 1985; Siegler, 1998).
3. Significant proportions of secondary school and college students cannot effectively carry out higher-order thinking skills required for success in postsecondary education or in the world of work (Bloom & Broder, 1950; Browne & Keeley, 1988; Carnegie Foundation, 1989; Commission on Achieving Necessary Skills, 1991; Mullis, 1984; National Assessment of Educational Progress, 1990; National Science Board Commission, 1983; Research and Policy Committee, 1985; Task Force on Education for Economic Growth, 1983).
4. Improved thinking does not normally occur as an incidental outcome of subject-matter learning (Glaser, 1941; Newmann, 1990; Nickerson, 1989; Taba, 1965; Taba, Levine, & Elzey, 1964).

Clearly we need to teach our students the skills of good thinking. Research on the effectiveness of such teaching and the benefits derived from it also indicate an effective way of meeting this need, to wit:

1. Systematic classroom instruction in cognitive skills improves student proficiency in applying these skills and the quality of student thinking (Edwards, 1988; Glenn & Ellis, 1982; Herrnstein, Nickerson, Sanchez, & Swets, 1986; Lipman, 1985; Schoenfeld, 1979a, 1979b; Sternberg & Davidson, 1989; Whimbey, 1980).
2. In courses that provide continuing, systematic instruction in the thinking skills needed to understand the subject

Copyright © 2001 by Barry K. Beyer.

matter, students score higher on end-of-course assessments of subject-matter learning than do students who do not receive such instruction (Estes, 1972; Nickerson, 1989; Schoenfeld, 1979a).

Teaching thinking skills is worth doing, then, not only because it is necessary but also because it can be done effectively and it produces valued results.

WHAT TO TEACH ABOUT THINKING SKILLS

Although thinking is a complex phenomenon, researchers and specialists agree on some basic tools of effective thinking (Brown, J. S., Collins, & Duguid, 1989; Perkins, 1992; Resnick & Klopfer, 1989). These skills are of two kinds: those essential for learning in general and those most useful for learning specific subjects, such as history, science, or mathematics.

Researchers have found, for example, that mastery of at least four thinking skills—comparing, classifying, sequencing, and predicting—is essential for students to become effective readers, writers, and learners (Commission on Reading, 1985; Hayes & Flower, 1981; Jones, Amiran, & Katims, 1985; Paris, Wixon, & Palincsar, 1986; Siegler, 1998). Youngsters who do not master these basic cognitive skills in the primary grades rarely achieve grade-level performances in reading comprehension and independent learning (Siegler, 1998).

Moreover, subject-matter specialists, as well as specialists in various types of thinking, have identified additional thinking skills as especially useful in learning various subjects and in being effective citizens in our democratic society—skills such as decision making, problem solving, making conclusions, identifying cause-and-effect relationships, and various critical thinking skills, such as judging the strength of an argument, distinguishing factual claims from value judgments, detecting bias, identifying points of view, and determining the credibility of a source (Lipman, 1991; National Council for the Social Studies, 1989; Schoenfeld, 1985). Not surprisingly, proficiency in all of these thinking skills is precisely what is required to meet current national, state, and local standards for English, mathematics, writing, history, social studies, science, and other subjects—as stipulated, for example, in the *National Standards for United States History* (National Center for History in the Schools, 1995) and the *Principles and Standards for School Mathematics* (National Council of Teachers of Mathematics, 2000).

Many researchers emphasize that teaching students how to apply these and other thinking skills is an important goal of classroom instruction. As a result of their research and that of

their colleagues, many have specifically recommended teaching students explicit procedures (also called strategies or routines), heuristics, rules, and other related skill knowledge used by experts in carrying out these thinking operations (Anderson, 1983; Brown, Bransford, Ferrara, & Campione, 1983; Doyle, 1983; Glaser, 1976; Palincsar & Klenk, 1991; Nickerson, 1989; Nickerson, Perkins, & Smith, 1985; Perkins, 1992; Pressley & Harris, 1990; Resnick, 1976; Resnick & Klopfer, 1989; Simon, 1980; Snow, 1982). (See also Chapter 74 by Michael Pressley and Karen Harris in this volume.) Researchers have also affirmed the value of providing students with information about the usefulness of a skill and the conditions in which they can and should employ it (Baker & Brown, 1984; Borkowsky & Krause, 1985; Nickerson, 1989; Perkins, 1985; Simon, 1980).

Through the analysis of skilled performances, cognitive researchers and specialists have identified the thinking procedures of experts—or, more correctly, of those identified as skilled in carrying out specific thinking operations. These procedures can be found in the work of noted scholars, such as

- Nationally respected philosopher/educators Robert Ennis (1962) and Matthew Lipman (1988).
- Decision science specialists Charles Kepner and Benjamin Tregoe (1997).
- Educator Joe B. Hurst and his colleagues (1983).
- Reading researcher Anne Brown and her colleagues (1981).
- Writing researchers John R. Hayes and Linda S. Flower (1981).
- Cognitive psychologist Robert Siegler (1998).

HOW TO TEACH THINKING SKILLS EFFECTIVELY

Skillful thinking is the product of a cumulative, developmental process (Case, 1992; Dreyfus, 1984), but it does not occur as the result of maturation alone. Nor do all individuals become skillful thinkers if left to their own devices. Developing proficiency in any thinking skill takes time and experience. As noted earlier, researchers have found that such proficiency can be sharply enhanced through instruction (Doyle, 1983; Frederiksen, 1984; Resnick, 1976; Sigel, 1984).

A RESEARCH-BASED INSTRUCTIONAL FRAMEWORK

Researchers find that young learners, left on their own, develop proficiency in a thinking procedure by first taking it apart and practicing its components and then gradually integrating these components (Dreyfus, 1984; Siegler, 1998). Effective thinking skill instruction appears to parallel closely the natural development of such proficiency, and this progression suggests a useful framework for instruction. For instance, students master few if any thinking skills because of a single instructional experience. In fact, research demonstrates that people may require anywhere from 5 or 6 to 50 or more such experiences to develop proficiency in the independent application of a thinking skill (Joyce, 1985; Joyce & Showers, 1983; Pasnak, 1989; Pasnak et al., 1987). Research furthermore attests to the difficulty people have in applying a skill to a context other than that in which they initially "learned" it; therefore, teachers need to provide additional thinking skill instruction in a variety of contexts beyond an initial lesson (Perkins & Salomon, 1989).

Investigators have shown that continuing systematic instruction in explicit skill-using procedures, over an extended period, is especially effective in helping children of all abilities to develop increased proficiency in these skills (Bryson & Scardamalia, 1991; Doyle, 1983; Edwards, 1988; Gersten & Carnine, 1986; Glenn & Ellis, 1982; Nickerson, 1989; Perkins, 1987; Posner & Keele, 1973; Pressley & Harris, 1990; Resnick, 1976, 1987b). Such instruction in a single skill provides a highly focused introduction to a step-by-step procedure for applying it. After this introduction, students need continuing guided practice featuring gradually fading (reducing) of instruction and support until they demonstrate proficiency in effectively using the procedure on their own in a variety of contexts and subjects (Doyle, 1983; Frederiksen, 1984; Nickerson, 1989; Posner & Keele, 1973). Researchers sometimes describe this instructional framework as consisting of three phases: *modeling, coaching,* and *fading* (Nickerson, 1989). We discuss these phases here as *introduction; practice,* which consists of coaching followed by fading; and *transfer.*

INTRODUCING A THINKING SKILL

A student's initial instructional experience with a new or complex thinking operation, or skill, is clearly a key to effective skill instruction and learning. Research strongly suggests that an introductory thinking skill lesson should exhibit several important features. It should make explicit the key procedural steps and any skill-related knowledge (such as heuristics or criteria) to be applied in carrying out the skill (Doyle, 1983; Frederiksen, 1984; Posner & Keele, 1973). It must also keep the focus on the skill by eliminating or, at least, minimizing interference from the use of complex or unfamiliar subject mat-

ter, the emotions connected with the subject matter, and the attributes of other recently introduced skills (Dempster, 1993; Posner & Keele, 1973; Pressley & Harris, 1990). This lesson should also make explicit the benefits of applying the skill (Baker & Brown, 1984; Borkowsky & Krause, 1985). And it should help students identify conditions in which it is appropriate to use the skill so students can later learn to apply it in contexts other than that in which is was introduced (Baker & Brown, 1984; Perkins & Salomon, 1989; Posner & Keele, 1973; Feuerstein, 1980; Simon, 1980). This introduction and those that follow also benefit from helping students develop the mental set required to tap their prior knowledge related to the skill (Ausubel, 1960; Mayer, 1983; Posner & Keele, 1973).

Modeling and Metacognitive Reflection. Classroom research has demonstrated that two specific techniques prove especially useful in these introductory lessons: modeling and metacognitive reflection (Brown, Campione, & Day, 1981; Posner & Keele, 1973; Rosenshine & Meister, 1992; Sternberg, 1984; Taba, 1965). In fact, this research indicates that metacognitive reflection is an extremely powerful technique because it encourages students, by reflecting on and sharing with others how they just carried out a skilled operation, to become more aware of the cognitive procedures they employ and thus be better able to modify them if necessary. Doing this each time they apply the same skill helps them gradually construct, reconstruct, and internalize effective procedures (Brown, Campione, and Day, 1981; Brown et al., 1983; Cognition and Technology Group, 1993; Hudgins, 1977; Larkin, McDermott, Simon, & Simon, 1980; Nickerson, 1989; Nickerson et al., 1985; Papert, 1980; Paris & Winograd, 1990; Vygotsky, 1962; Whimbey, 1980).

The usefulness of modeling has also been demonstrated in skill learning (Doyle, 1983; Posner & Keele, 1973; Pressley & Harris, 1990; Resnick, 1987b; Rosenshine & Meister, 1992; Simon, 1980). Modeling is especially effective when it combines an explanation of the principles modeled with an actual demonstration of the skill procedure by which they are applied (Palincsar & Brown, 1984). This makes accessible to students an explicit, ready-made, effective procedure for carrying out that skill. The modeled procedure in turn provides a takeoff point from which students can gradually construct or develop more personalized but equally effective procedures (Resnick, 1976, 1987b; Pressley & Harris, 1990). Whether used separately or combined in introducing a thinking skill, these techniques of metacognitive reflection and modeling assist students of all ability levels to initiate and begin to refine their efforts to improve their execution of a thinking skill.

Constructivist and Didactic Teaching. Research indicates that teachers can effectively use either constructivist or didactic teaching strategies, or some combination of the two, to organize the application of these techniques. Allowing students to inductively construct a skill-using procedure from their own experiences in applying it, then to articulate what they did and hear their peers do the same proves helpful for average or above-average students, especially when they are dealing with routine thinking skills (Anderson, Marcham, & Dunn, 1944; Doyle, 1983; Frederiksen, 1984; Glenn & Ellis, 1982; Mulcahy & Associates, 1993; Sigel, 1984). A didactic, more directive approach emphasizing modeling, however, seems to benefit and appeal most to less able students (Doyle, 1983; Frederiksen, 1984; Mulcahy and Associates, 1993; Means, Chelemer, & Knapp, 1991; Peterson, 1979). The latter approach also appears helpful in introducing an especially complex or difficult skill to students of any ability level. Sternberg (1997), however, suggests that this difference in effectiveness may be related more to student preferences for certain types of instruction than to student ability or skill complexity. Taken together, this research suggests strongly that the combination of metacognitive reflection and modeling in the same lesson may well support skill learning in heterogeneous classrooms. Educators have designed many teaching strategies to do exactly this (Beyer, 1987, 1997; Beyer & Pasnak, 1993; Lochhead, 2001; Sternberg & Davidson, 1989; Whimbey & Lochhead, 1999).

PROVIDING THINKING SKILL PRACTICE

Frequent practice over an extended period has been shown to be essential for developing thinking skill proficiency (Anderson, 1982; Brown, et al., 1981; Frederiksen, 1984; Glaser, 1979; Mayer, 1983; Posner & Keele, 1973). This research indicates that two types of practice should be applied to a new thinking skill—immediate, frequent practice with considerable instructional guidance, support, and feedback. At this stage a student's performance is halting, often laborious, and fragmented (Dreyfus, 1984; Frederiksen, 1984). The second stage of practice requires intermittent application and gradual fading of instructional support until it disappears altogether. At this point, student performance becomes more rapid, smooth, and self-directed—in effect, autonomous (Anderson, 1982; Frederiksen, 1984; Posner & Keele, 1973).

Scaffolded Support. Researchers indicate that the most effective skill practice exhibits a number of important features, chief of which are scaffolded and cued instructional support

and corrective feedback (Doyle, 1983; Frederiksen, 1984; Glaser, 1979; Jones et al., 1985; Resnick & Klopfer, 1989; Rosenshine & Meister, 1992). A scaffold consists of a diagram or series of written prompts that "walk" students explicitly through each skill step and thereby allow them to concentrate on performing and perfecting each of the key steps without trying also to remember what the steps are or a useful sequence for performing them. According to Rosenshine and Meister's (1992) analysis of thinking skill instruction, procedural checklists, skill-specific graphic organizers, and process-structured questions serve as useful scaffolds for the initial practice of newly introduced thinking skills. For detailed descriptions of these and other scaffolding techniques, see Armbruster, Anderson, & Mall, 1991; Beyer, 1997; Dillon, 1982; Jones et al., 1985; McTighe & Lyman, 1988; Winne, 1979; also see Chapter 61 by Jay McTighe and Frank Lyman in this volume.

Cued Practice. Cued practice is useful in building proficiency in a new thinking skill, especially when it follows scaffolded practice. A cue is a reminder of what to do next, but it does not provide explicit guidance in exactly what to do. Research indicates that cues help students to recall an operation they have internalized through prior learning and to then scaffold the application of that skill (Doyle, 1983; McTighe & Lyman, 1988). Cues demonstrated by research to be effective include rehearsal of a skill procedure before applying it; emphasizing or highlighting the name (or related terms) of a thinking skill that is to be or has just been applied; and the use of mnemonic devices to help students recall appropriate skill procedures (McTighe & Lyman, 1988; Rosenshine & Meister, 1992). Research in the physiology and functioning of the brain and in information processing also suggests a number of techniques that may improve skill learning along with subject-matter retention and recall. Especially useful are techniques that strengthen and expand associations in the brain, such as cumulative rehearsal, multiple association, and information restructuring (Jensen, 1998; Lehman, 1990; Sprenger, 1999).

Feedback. Feedback, to be most effective in improving thinking skill proficiency, must be prompt (Frederiksen, 1984; Posner & Keele, 1973). Teachers can apply such feedback by engaging students in metacognitive reflection (Brown et al., 1981; Sternberg, 1984) and by various scaffolding and cueing devices (Jones et al., 1985; Rosenshine & Meister, 1992). Not only do the scaffolding techniques noted previously provide "feed-*back*" during or immediately after a student has learned about a thinking skill, but like the cueing techniques noted here, they even *feed forward* to the students information about steps in a skill procedure before students apply them. The research of Olson and Astington (1990) also suggests that consistent use of the language of thinking in everyday classroom discourse not only can provide such feedback—as well as feed information forward, or in advance, to students—but also supplies important cues for storing and retrieving skill procedures and related knowledge. This involves using the name of a skill to trigger its application, as in "Evaluate this essay" rather than "Tell me what you think about this essay," and using the technical terms of major thinking steps, such as alternatives or options in decision making (Astington & Olson, 1990; Olson & Astington, 1990; Perkins, 1992).

TEACHING THINKING SKILLS FOR TRANSFER

Because, as researchers have noted, people rarely transfer thinking skills without assistance beyond the context in which they are initially applied (Nickerson, 1989; Perkins & Salomon, 1989; Stonewater, 1977), students benefit from instruction in making such transfer (Brown et al., 1989; Perkins & Salomon, 1988, 1989). This can be accomplished by reintroducing in a new context a thinking skill applied earlier in a different context. Such transfer lessons usually include several additional follow-up practice opportunities in the new context until students demonstrate their ability to apply the skill with ease. In transferring the application of a skill to new contexts, students especially need to be able to identify the general similarities between the contexts so that later they can identify other new contexts in which the skill is applicable (Hudgins, 1977; Nickerson, 1989; Perkins & Salomon, 1988).

Researchers and specialists have also suggested that teachers can facilitate transfer even while they are introducing a new skill. Helping students to generalize about the circumstances when it is appropriate to apply a skill and about principles for applying it also facilitates their transfer of the skill to new contexts (Borkowsky & Krause, 1985). So, too, does helping students predict (or bridge) when or where use of a skill they have been applying might be appropriate (Feuerstein, 1980; Perkins & Salomon, 1988).

WHERE AND WHEN TO TEACH THINKING SKILLS

Many researchers recommend teaching thinking skills in academic subject-matter courses as the ideal approach to improving the quality of student thinking (Joyce, 1985; Pressley & Harris, 1990; Resnick, 1987b; Resnick & Klopfer, 1989). Research suggests three main reasons for this recommendation:

1. The subject matter and one's knowledge of it inform the selection and application of thinking skills, just as their selection and application shape the insights and knowledge derived from subject-matter study (Glaser, 1984; Resnick & Klopfer, 1989). Throughout every classroom, thinking skills serve as tools for achieving subject-matter learning goals, just as subject matter serves as a vehicle and context for applying these thinking skills. This symbiotic relationship between subject matter and thinking skills thus provides repeated opportunities for instruction in thinking. Subject-matter learning and thinking skill improvement can reinforce and contribute to each other's development in a highly integrated fashion (Prawat, 1991).

2. Students' motivation to learn a new or complex cognitive skill is sharply enhanced when teachers provide instruction in the skill at a point where students perceive a need to use it to accomplish a subject-matter objective. When learning subject matter is what counts, learning how to do the skill then required takes on a special urgency, and students attend better to instruction in that skill (Bereiter, 1973; Dempster, 1993; Posner & Keele, 1973; Pressley & Harris, 1990; Sigel, 1984).

3. Instruction in thinking skills in subject-matter courses improves both subject-matter learning and the quality of student thinking (Estes, 1972; Nickerson, 1989; Schoenfeld, 1979a). Thus, integrating the two kinds of instruction is not only feasible but also highly desirable.

IMPROVING THE QUALITY OF STUDENT THINKING AND LEARNING

The research cited here offers considerable evidence of the need to teach thinking skills. It also offers substantial guidance on how to meet this need, suggesting an effective framework for sequencing specific types of lessons most likely to advance skill proficiency, as well as instructional techniques and materials to use in conducting these lessons. The research also suggests ways to combine these techniques into classroom strategies to maximize their effectiveness for students of various abilities. Most important, this research provides tantalizing evidence of the beneficial results one might expect to achieve through systematic and appropriate use of these instructional techniques and strategies and of exactly when and where their application may be most productive.

Obviously, however, the research is not all in, relative to teaching thinking skills. Nor may it ever be. There are still gaps, even apparent contradictions. But the research and its interpretations by the researchers and specialists cited here suggest extremely useful techniques and strategies for teaching thinking skills—techniques and strategies considerably more likely to improve the quality of student thinking and learning than continued reliance on the still all-too-frequently used techniques of exhortation, rote drill and practice, and simply telling kids to think.

Many other chapters in this volume present practical suggestions and detailed examples for applying many of the teaching strategies and techniques suggested by this research to the everyday teaching of thinking skills in our classrooms. To the degree that we, as teachers, apply these consistently and continuously throughout our teaching, we ought to be able to help our students think much smarter—rather than harder—than many of them are wont to do when left on their own. That is a goal they—and we—should most assuredly appreciate.

References

Anderson, H. C., Marcham, F. G., & Dunn, S. B. (1944, December). An experiment in teaching certain skills of critical thinking. *Journal of Educational Research, 38*(4), 241–251.

Anderson, J. R. (1982). Acquisition of cognitive skill. *Psychological Review, 89,* 369–406.

Anderson, J. R. (1983). *The architecture of cognition.* Cambridge, MA: Harvard University Press.

Armbruster, B. B., Anderson, R. C., & Mall, V. C. (1991, November). Preparing teachers of literacy. *Educational Leadership, 49*(3), 21–24.

Astington, J. W., & Olson, D. R. (1990). Metacognitive and metalinguistic language: Learning to talk about thought. *Applied Psychology: An International Review, 39,* 77–87.

Ausubel, D. (1960). The use of advance organizers in the learning and retention of meaningful verbal material. *Journal of Educational Psychology, 51,* 267–272.

Baker, L., & Brown, A. L. (1984). Metacognitive skills and reading. In P. D. Pearson, M. Kamil, R. Barr, & P. Mosenthal (Eds.), *Handbook of reading research.* New York: Longman.

Bereiter, C. (1973, May). Elementary schools: Convenience or necessity? *Elementary School Journal, 73*(8), 435–446.

Beyer, B. K. (1987). *Practical strategies for the teaching of thinking.* Boston: Allyn and Bacon.

Beyer, B. K. (1997). *Improving student thinking.* Boston: Allyn and Bacon.

Beyer, B. K., & Pasnak, R. (1993). Helping children think better: The developmental lesson set approach. *Journal of Research and Development in Education, 26*(2), 97–105.

Bloom, B., & Broder, L. (1950). *Problem solving processes of college students.* Chicago: Chicago University Press.

Borkowsky, J. G., & Krause, A. J. (1985). Metacognition and attributional beliefs. In G. d'Yewalle (Ed.), *Cognition, information processing and motivation.* Amsterdam: North-Holland.

Brown, A., Campione, J., & Day, J. J. (1981, February). Learning to learn: On training students to learn from texts. *Educational Researcher, 10*(2), 14–21.

Brown, A. L., Bransford, J. D., Ferrara, R. A., & Campione, J. S. (1983). Learning, remembering, and understanding. In J. H. Flavell & E. M. Markham (Eds.), *Handbook of child psychology: Vol. 3. Cognitive development* (4th ed.) (pp. 77–166). New York: Wiley.

Brown, J. S., Collins, A., & Duguid, P. (1989, January–February). Situated cognition and the culture of learning. *Educational Researcher, 18*(1), 32–42.

Browne, M. N., & Keeley, S. (1988, Spring). Do college students know how to think critically when they graduate? *Research Serving Technology, 1*(9).

Bryson, M., & Scardamalia, M. (1991). Teaching writing to students at risk for academic failure. In B. Means, C. Chelemer, & M. S. Knapp (Eds.), *Teaching advanced skills to at-risk students* (pp. 141–167). San Francisco: Jossey-Bass.

Carnegie Foundation for the Advancement of Teaching. (1989). *The condition of the professorate.* Princeton, NJ: Princeton University Press.

Case, R. (1992). *The mind's staircase.* Hillsdale, NJ: Erlbaum.

Chi, M. T. H., Glaser, R., & Rees, E. (1982). Expertise in problem solving. In R. J. Sternberg (Ed.), *Advances in the psychology of human intelligence: Vol. 1.* Hillsdale, NJ: Erlbaum.

Cognition and Technology Group at Vanderbilt University. (1993). *Anchored instruction and situated cognition revisited* [unpublished paper]. Nashville, TN: Vanderbilt University.

Commission on Achieving Necessary Skills. (1991). *Work force 2000.* Washington, DC: U.S. Department of Labor.

Commission on Reading. (1985). *Becoming a nation of readers.* Washington, DC: National Institute of Education.

Dempster, F. N. (1993, February). Exposing our students to less should help them learn more. *Phi Delta Kappan, 74*(6), 433–437.

Dewey, J. (1910). *How we think.* Boston: D. C. Heath.

Dillon, J. T. (1982, April). The multidisciplinary study of questioning. *Journal of Educational Psychology, 74*(2), 147–165.

Doyle, W. (1983, Summer). Academic work. *Review of Educational Research, 53*(2), 159–199.

Dreyfus, H. L. (1984, May 29). *Expert systems versus intuitive enterprise.* Unpublished paper delivered at George Mason University Conference on Cognitive Development, Fairfax, Va.

Edwards, J. (1988, Fall), Measuring the effects of the direct teaching of thinking skills. *Human Intelligence Newsletter, 9*(3), 9–10.

Ennis, R. H. (1962, Winter). A concept of critical thinking. *Harvard Educational Review, 32*(1), 81–111.

Estes, T. H. (1972). Reading in the social studies: A review of research since 1950. In J. Laffery (Ed.), *Reading in the content areas* (pp. 178–183). Newark, DE: International Reading Association.

Feuerstein, R. (1980). *Instrumental enrichment.* Baltimore: University Park Press.

Frederiksen, N. (1984). Implications of cognitive theory for instruction in problem solving. *Review of Educational Research, 54,* 363–407.

Gersten, R., & Carnine, D. (1986, April). Direct instruction in reading comprehension. *Educational Leadership, 46*(7), 70–78.

Gettys, C. F. (1983). *Research and theory on predecision processes.* Norman, OK: Decision Processes Laboratory, University of Oklahoma.

Gettys, C. F., & Engleman, P. D. (1983). *Ability and expertise in act generation.* Norman, OK: Decision Processes Laboratory, University of Oklahoma.

Glaser, E. M. (1941). *An experiment in the development of critical thinking.* New York: Bureau of Publications, Teachers College, Columbia University.

Glaser, R. (1976). Components of a psychology of instruction. *Review of Educational Research, 46,* 1–24.

Glaser, R. (1979). Trends and research questions in psychological research on learning and schooling. *Educational Researcher, 8,* 6–13.

Glaser, R. (1984). Education and thinking: The role of knowledge. *American Psychologist, 39*(2), 93–104.

Glenn, A. D., & Ellis, A. K. (1982, February). Direct and indirect methods of teaching problem solving to elementary school children. *Social Education, 46*(2), 134–136.

Hayes, J. R., & Flower, L. S. (1981). Writing as problem solving. *Visible Language, 14,* 388–399.

Herrnstein, R. J., Nickerson, R. S., Sanchez, M., & Swets, J. A. (1986). Teaching thinking skills. *American Psychologist, 41*(11), 1279–1289.

Hudgins, B. B. (1977). *Learning and thinking.* Itasca, IL: F. E. Peacock Publishers.

Hurst, J. B., Kinney, M., & Weiss, S. J. (1983, Fall). The decision making process. *Theory and Research in Social Education, 11*(3), 17–43.

Jensen, E. (1998). *Teaching with the brain in mind.* Alexandria, VA: Association for Supervision and Curriculum Development.

Jones, B. F., Amiran, M. R., & Katims, M. (1985). Teaching cognitive strategies and text structures within language arts programs. In J. W. Segal, S. F. Chipman, & R. Glaser (Eds.), *Thinking and learning skills: Vol. 1. Relating instruction to research* (pp. 259–290). Hillsdale, NJ: Erlbaum.

Joyce, B. (1985, May). Models for teaching thinking. *Educational Leadership, 42*(8), 4–7.

Joyce, B., & Showers, B. (1983). *Power in staff development through research on training.* Alexandria, VA: Association for Supervision and Curriculum Development.

Kepner, C. H., & Tregoe, B. B. (1997). *The new rational manager.* Princeton, NJ: Princeton Research Press.

Larkin, J., McDermott, J., Simon, D. P., & Simon, H. A. (1980). Expert and novice performance in solving physics problems. *Science, 208,* 1335–1342.

Lehman, E. B. (1990, January–February). Some suggestions for the teaching of thinking from an information processing perspective. *Teaching Thinking and Problem Solving, 12*(1).

Lipman, M. (1985). Thinking skills fostered in philosophy for children. In J. W. Segal, S. F. Chipman, & R. Glaser (Eds.), *Thinking and learning skills: Vol. 1. Relating instruction to research* (pp. 83–108). Hillsdale, NJ: Erlbaum.

Lipman, M. (1988, September). Critical thinking: What can it be? *Educational Leadership, 45*(1), 38–43.

Lipman, M. (1991). *Thinking in education.* Cambridge, England: Cambridge University Press.

Lochhead, J. (2001). *Thinkback: A user's guide to minding the mind.* Mahwah, NJ: Erlbaum.

Mayer, R. E. (1983). Can you repeat that? Qualitative effects of repetition and advanced organizers on learning from science prose. *Journal of Educational Psychology, 75,* 40–49.

McPeck, J. E. (1981). *Critical thinking and education.* New York: St. Martin's Press.

McTighe, J., & Lyman Jr., F. T. (1988, April). Cueing thinking in the classroom: Theory-embedded tools. *Educational Leadership, 45*(7), 18–24.

Means, B., Chelemer, C., & Knapp, M. S. (Eds.). (1991). *Teaching advanced skills to at-risk students.* San Francisco: Jossey-Bass.

Mulcahy, R., & Associates. (1993). Cognitive education project. *Teaching Thinking and Problem Solving, 15*(6), 1, 3–9.

Mullis, V. S. (1984, May 17–19). *What do NAEP results tell us about students' higher order thinking abilities?* Unpublished paper delivered at ASCD Wingspread Conference on Teaching Thinking Skills, Racine, Wisc.

National Assessment of Educational Progress. (1990). *Learning to read in our nation's schools.* Princeton, NJ: Princeton University Press.

National Center for History in the Schools. (1995). *National standards for United States history.* Los Angeles: University of California-Los Angeles.

National Council for the Social Studies Task Force on Scope and Sequence. (1989, October). In search of a scope and sequence for social studies. *Social Education, 53*(6), 376–387.

National Council of Teachers of Mathematics. (2000). *Principles and standards for school mathematics.* Reston, VA: Author.

National Science Board Commission on Precollege Education in Mathematics, Science and Technology. (1983). *Educating Americans for the 21st century.* Washington, DC: National Science Foundation.

Newmann, F. M. (1990). Higher order thinking in teaching social studies. *Journal of Curriculum Studies, 22*(1), 41–56.

Nickerson, R. (1989). On improving thinking through instruction. In E. Z. Rothkopf (Ed.), *Review of Research in Education: Vol. 15* (pp. 3–57). Washington, DC: American Educational Research Association.

Nickerson, R. S., Perkins, D. N., & Smith, E. E. (1985). *The teaching of thinking.* Hillsdale, NJ: Erlbaum.

Olson, D. R., & Astington, J. W. (1990). Talking about text: How literacy contributes to thought. *Journal of Pragmatics, 14,* 705–721.

Palincsar, A. S., & Brown, A. L. (1984). Reciprocal teaching of comprehension-fostering and comprehension-monitoring activities. *Cognition and Instruction, 1,* 117–175.

Palincsar, A., & Klenk, L. (1991). Dialogues promoting reading comprehension. In B. Means, C. Chelemer, & M. S. Knapp (Eds.), *Teaching advanced skills to at-risk students* (pp. 112–130). San Francisco: Jossey-Bass.

Papert, S. (1980). *Mindstorms: Children, computers and powerful ideas.* New York: Basic Books.

Paris, S. G., & Winograd, P. (1990, November–December). Promoting metacognition and motivation of exceptional children. *Remedial and Special Education, 11*(6), 7–15.

Paris, S. G., Wixon, K. K., & Palincsar, A. S. (1986). Instructional approaches to reading comprehension. *Review of Educational Research, 13,* 91–128.

Pasnak, R. (1989, Spring–Summer). Teaching basic cognitive operations to at-risk students. *Human Intelligence Newsletter, 10*(2), 5.

Pasnak, R., Brown, K., Kurkjian, M., Mattran, K., Triana, E., & Yamamoto, N. (1987, August). Cognitive gains through training on classification, seriation, and conservation. *Genetic, Social and General Psychology Monographs, 113*(3), 295–321.

Perkins, D. (1985, October). Postprimary education has little impact on informal reasoning. *Journal of Educational Psychology, 77*(5), 562–571.

Perkins, D. (1987, March–April). Myth and method in teaching thinking. *Teaching Thinking and Problem Solving, 9*(2), 1–2, 8–9.

Perkins, D. (1992). *Smart schools.* New York: Free Press.

Perkins, D. (1993, November). Creating a culture of thinking. *Educational Leadership, 51*(3), 98–99.

Perkins, D. N., & Salomon, G. (1988, September). Teaching for transfer. *Educational Leadership, 46*(1), 22–32.

Perkins, D. N., & Salomon, G. (1989). Are thinking skills context-bound? *Educational Researcher, 18,* 16–25.

Peterson, P. (1979, October). Direct instruction: Effective for what and for whom? *Educational Leadership, 37*(2), 46–48.

Posner, M., & Keele, S. W. (1973). Skill learning. In R. M. W. Travers (Ed.), *Second handbook of research on teaching* (pp. 805–831). Chicago: Rand McNally College Publishing.

Prawat, R. S. (1991, March). The value of ideas: The immersion approach to the development of thinking. *Educational Researcher, 70*(2), 3–10.

Pressley, M., & Harris, K. B. (1990, September). What we really know about strategy instruction. *Educational Leadership, 48*(1), 31–34.

Research and Policy Committee. (1985). *Investing in our children.* New York: Committee on Economic Development.

Resnick, L. B. (1976). Task analysis in instructional design: Some cases from mathematics. In D. Klahr (Ed.), *Cognition and instruction.* Hillsdale, NJ: Erlbaum.

Resnick, L. B. (1987a). *Education and learning to think.* Washington, DC: National Academy Press.

Resnick, L. B. (1987b, December). Learning in school and out. *Educational Researcher, 16,* 13–29.

Resnick, L. B., & Klopfer, L. E. (Eds.). (1989). *Toward the thinking curriculum: Current cognitive research* (pp. 1–18). Alexandria, VA: Association for Supervision and Curriculum Development.

Rosenshine, B., & Meister, C. (1992, April). The use of scaffolds for teaching higher-level cognitive strategies. *Educational Leadership, 49*(7), 26–33.

Schoenfeld, A. (1979a). Can heuristics be taught? In J. Lochhead & J. Clement (Eds.), *Cognitive process instruction.* Philadelphia: Franklin Institute Press.

Schoenfeld, A. (1979b). Explicit heuristic training as a variable in problem-solving performance. *Journal for Research in Mathematics Education, 10*(2), 173–187.

Schoenfeld, A. (1985). *Mathematical problem solving.* New York: Academic Press.

Siegler, R. S. (1998). *Children's thinking* (3rd ed.). Upper Saddle River, NJ: Prentice-Hall.

Sigel, I. E. (1984, November). A constructivist perspective for teaching thinking. *Educational Leadership, 42*(3), 18–21.

Simon, H. (1980). Problem solving and education. In D. T. Tuma & R. Reif (Eds.), *Problem solving and education: Issues in teaching and research.* Hillsdale, NJ: Erlbaum.

Snow, R. E. (1982). The training of intellectual aptitude. In D. K. Detterman & R. J. Sternberg (Eds.), *How and how much can intelligence be increased?* Norwood, NJ: Ablex.

Sprenger, M. (1999). *Learning and memory: The brain in action.* Alexandria, VA: Association for Supervision and Curriculum Development.

Sternberg, R. (1984, September). How can we teach intelligence? *Educational Leadership 42*(1), 38–50.

Sternberg, R. J. (1997). *Thinking styles.* New York: Cambridge University Press.

Sternberg, R., & Davidson, J. (1989). A four-prong model for intellectual development. *Journal of Research and Development in Education, 22*(3), 22–28.

Stonewater, J. K. (1977). *Instruction in problem solving and Piaget's theory of cognitive development.* Unpublished doctoral dissertation, Michigan State University, East Lansing.

Taba, H. (1965, May). Teaching of thinking. *Elementary English, 42*(15), 534–542.

Taba, H., Levine, S., & Elzey, F. F. (1964). *Thinking in elementary school children.* San Francisco: U.S. Office of Education Cooperative Research Project, No. 1574, San Francisco State College.

Task Force on Education for Economic Growth. (1983). *Action for excellence.* Denver, CO: Education Commission of the States.

Vygotsky, L. S. (1962). *Thought and language.* Cambridge, MA: MIT Press.

Whimbey, A. (1980). Students can learn to be better problem solvers. *Educational Leadership, 38*(8), 560–565.

Whimbey, A., & Lochhead, J. (1999). *Problem solving and comprehension* (6th ed.). Mahwah, NJ: Erlbaum.

Winne, P. N. (1979). Experiments relating teachers' use of higher cognitive questions to student achievement. *Review of Educational Research, 49,* 13–50.

VII

Thinking in School Subjects

The real voyage of discovery consists not in seeking new landscapes but in having new eyes.

—MARCEL PROUST

Introduction

JOHN BARELL

The true voyage of discovery for educators today may be to see our classrooms not as repositories of knowledge handed down within textbooks, but as communities wherein students and teachers, together, are inquiring about the nature of life and the world. Within these learning communities, all participants share more or less equally in the pursuit of knowledge and understanding within the major subject areas of humankind.

I have been able to witness such learning communities, from kindergarten through 12th grade, in several, but not all, schools. In the best communities, like those of Ann White and Cheryl Hopper (see Chapter 43 in this volume), students and teachers are engaged in authentic learning and assessment; together they are exploring the mysteries of science and the wonders of history, geography, economics, and philosophy.

In White's 4th grade and Hopper's high school classrooms, we can see the fundamental elements that the authors in this section are speaking about:

- Establishing learning communities.
- Teaching for understanding and continual inquiry.
- Challenging students to use specific thinking processes.
- Bringing to consciousness the dispositions that nurture thoughtfulness, such as openness and curiosity.
- Believing in the notion that children construct meanings.
- Engaging in authentic learning, communicating, and problem solving in settings that reflect realities of life.

All these elements are potentially present in everybody's classroom if we are open to seeing with Proust's "new eyes."

Marcy Cook realizes that within such communities we can both think through problems and practice math skills and facts until we achieve what is especially important: deep understanding of concepts and skills. The person who influenced my thinking more than any other during the past decade, Barbara M'Gonigle, is a math teacher who told me several years ago, "My students can get the right answers, but they do not understand the concepts." That makes all the difference.

Cathy Block also stresses the need for learning in authentic settings, which may mean, for example, interpreting the "cultural and social contexts" of messages on the World Wide Web. *Information*, someone noted, is data in formation, and without the thoughtful reading and interpretation thereof, we are confronted by meaningless facts.

Art Whimbey, Jack Lochhead, Myra Linden, and Carol Welsh present us with the most specific thinking challenges, based on the interconnections between writing and thinking. Again, one of their emphases is upon attempting to achieve understanding of text and of our own thinking.

Science is an area in which people engage in what some call "the scientific method." What Robert Swartz and Stephen Fischer point out is that the intellectual processes of, for example, trying to figure out what caused a group of animals to die must be accompanied by dispositions such as inquisitiveness and openness to possibilities. Without the deep sense of inquiry—or the desire to plumb the depths of nature's mysteries—we wouldn't have the scientific advancements we enjoy. Their emphasis on problem-based learning in authentic settings reinforces an idea presented in several of our chapters—that learning can be enhanced when students are engaged in thinking through complex situations present in life in which they have to identify the real problem and work toward solutions.

One of the things we as educators may take for granted is how children construct meaning. They put ideas into words. But, as Elliot Eisner points out, this reflects only one kind of literacy. It is because the human mind attempts to create meaning in many different aesthetic, linguistic, physical, and mathematical forms that we have the rich culture we do, full of multiple representations of meanings. Unfortunately, schools focus narrowly upon the linguistic and the mathematical to the detriment of those forms present naturally in the arts and physical movement.

Barry Beyer discusses two of the major dispositions necessary for active intelligence: curiosity and skepticism. If all schools nurtured a strong sense of wonder and inquisitiveness and then a healthy skepticism toward all possibilities generated thereby, we would provide students with two attributes for success in the Internet century.

Again, Virginia Rojas reinforces the need for inquiry within authentic situations while, for example, teaching foreign languages and the concept of food. What questions can students ask about the customs and practices of food and nutrition in different countries? Language learning, in other words, is not mere memorization of tenses and cases.

Ruth Loring brings to the forefront the importance of brain research to undergird her support for music education. The value of exposure to music, she asserts, is the creation of environments in which curiosity, playfulness, and imagination can flourish.

Next, Rebecca Reagan describes what it means to be literate from a thoughtful point of view.

And finally, Bill Maxwell and his coauthors extend thinking into the gym, the playing field, and the stadium as athletes are shown to depend not only on their physical prowess but their intellectual stamina as well.

In all of our chapters, we see with "new eyes" the wonders of learning in communities of inquiry where thinking processes are taught explicitly in order to achieve deeper understanding and applications to the world of experience. Our voyages of discovery toward developing the minds and hearts of our children are guided by the thoughtfulness and sense of true north provided by this squadron of authors.

47

Mathematics: The Thinking Arena for Problem Solving

Marcy Cook

I believe in the power of mathematics to engage young minds and the power of young minds to engage in mathematics.

—*A. G. Andrews*

A historical overview of math education reveals its ever-changing philosophies. In the first half of the 20th century, the focus was primarily on arithmetic computation, with a strong emphasis on the memorization of facts and procedures. With the Soviet launching of *Sputnik I* in 1957 came a realization by individuals in the United States that something needed to be changed in our teaching of mathematics. New math was introduced, with abstractions and symbols that befuddled students, parents, and many teachers. By the early 1970s, the general perception was that students did not have basic skills, and thus a back-to-basics movement occurred. When the realization hit that students who had done much drill and practice were incapable of thinking mathematically and unable to solve complex mathematical problems, many decreed the United States a nation at risk. The National Council of Teachers of Mathematics (NCTM) declared problem solving to be the theme of the 1980s, and the Curriculum and Evaluation Standards of 1989 outlined expectations including mathematics as problem solving, reasoning, communication, and connections. The decade of the 1990s focused on reforms, with most states developing standards and frameworks. *Everybody Counts* (National Research Council, 1989) reported to the nation that mathematics should become a pump rather than a filter in the pipeline of American education and that math literacy was essential as a foundation for democracy in a technological age. Even the U.S. government became involved by establishing Goals 2000.

Near the end of the 20th century came a wave of discontent; once again advocates and adversaries of the reform movement took their stand. Practices such as students' using manipulatives and constructing knowledge rather than being fed information were questioned. Math instruction became politicized, eliciting questions on who should make decisions for what is taught and how that teaching should be measured. Testing revealed that children in the United States scored below those in many other countries in the Third International Mathematics and Science Study (TIMSS) (U.S. National Research Center Reports, 1996). In general, the performance of the U.S. students was considered disappointing, reinstating the need for focused vision and high standards. A push for accountability, with teachers being assessed in terms of gains in student achievement, put pressure on teachers to have their students test well. This led to a drive to consider a set curriculum with the need to teach to a set of standards in a prescriptive approach to produce high test scores.

THEORIES BEHIND MATHEMATICAL LEARNING

The instructional practices related to the pendulum swing in teaching mathematics seem founded in various theories of how children think and learn. Many opposing theories have been put into practice over the years, with a move to the other side occurring when people perceive a failure in mathematical performance.

Drill and practice, a common feature of many math programs, is based on the suggestion that learning results directly from establishing bonds between specific stimuli and responses. Continual drill will strengthen those bonds.

In contrast to the drill philosophy is the argument that students learn mathematics best if it is taught in a meaningful way. Because mathematics is such a large field, it is impossible to drill on all aspects, so it is best to understand and then see relations among the various mathematical ideas.

Jean Piaget's learning theory of stage development (sensorimotor, preoperational, concrete operational, and formal operational led to a movement to use manipulative materials to teach mathematics and an awareness of students moving from manipulative to representational to abstract levels. Piaget's theory is often viewed as the forerunner of constructivism, which asserts that formal mathematics must be constructed, not merely taught. Students construct knowledge by interpreting what they see and hear to coincide with what they already know or believe to be true about the world. Students constantly reconstruct knowledge rather than just accept, without question, information they are told.

Information processing theories rely on the idea that stored memory is vital. The belief that math concepts are best remembered if they are taught in relation to information that has been previously stored suggests that teachers should constantly strive to explain new information in terms of knowledge the students already possess.

Because no one theory completely describes how children acquire mathematical understandings, no theory emerges as the panacea for mathematical instruction. Educators differ in their beliefs on how children learn. Furthermore, they do not all agree on the goals for mathematics instruction. Some regard the learning of math as the acquisition of algorithmic skills; others see it as the understanding of concepts and relationships within mathematics; and many view it as the development of problem-solving skills.

MATH FOR THE 21ST CENTURY

We live in a mathematical world that relies on quantitative mathematical understanding. Thanks to computers and recent technological advances, a wealth of information is now easily accessible. We need to ensure that this use of technology is not accompanied by intellectual laziness. We do not want to lose tomorrow's creative thinkers! With the onrush of data acquisition, we need to avoid the feeling of "data, data, everywhere, but not a thought to think," as stated by John Allen Paulos at the annual NCTM meeting in Chicago in April 2000.

In our rapidly changing technological world, workers will need higher-order skills to face unknown, nonroutine encounters. The typical worker will change jobs numerous times in the coming years. Throughout their lives individuals will need to be adaptable to meet changing conditions and actively seek and create new knowledge. Thinking is the intellectual activity imperative for confronting those new and unusual situations. To be the thinkers of tomorrow, students need to be able to adapt, to innovate, and to invent; to use logic and reasoning; to make decisions; and to persevere. The classroom must become a forum for critical thinking where good questions and

problems provoke curiosity and are perceived as a challenge rather than an intimidating situation. The justification of thinking should be the measure of the effectiveness of our possession of mathematical competence.

Because the National Council of Teachers of Mathematics believes that mathematical competence will open doors to productive futures, their *Principles and Standards for School Mathematics* (2000) sets high standards for students and teachers alike. It makes the case that a stronger and bolder vision of the basics for tomorrow is needed today. Educators must help students succeed in understanding and doing mathematics—not just passing the test. We do not want the intellectual life of a classroom turned into a training ground for test preparation. Our goal should be to enhance learning so our students become mathematically competent and mathematically confident. We need to maintain a balance, in which students are expected to master basic skills of computation, attain conceptual understandings, and have the ability to solve new problems. They need to make meaningful connections between existing knowledge and the structured system of formal mathematics and be able to creatively apply past learning to new situations. If we believe that students are thinking individuals with the ability to interpret and remember what they see and hear in relation to what they already know, we can combine the best of past theories. It is possible to teach with meaning, use manipulatives and visual models, use drill and practice when appropriate, and expect students to make connections between the conceptual knowledge (the mathematical concepts) and the procedural knowledge (the formal language, algorithms, and symbol representations for completing math tasks). We need to value understanding the concept and making sense of the mathematical world, not merely computation proficiency and high test scores. Our goal should be to provide students with the opportunity to gain competence and confidence in mathematical solving of problems so they will be resourceful and flexible when dealing with future problems.

Our focus needs to be on helping each student learn to learn and learn to think, making education a lifetime endeavor. With the political rush embracing accountability, standards, and assessments, we need high expectations; but we need to be sure that we continue to value thinking. Teaching for what is tested threatens creativity, flexibility, and fluency of thought. To cope confidently with the demands of the future, number crunching is not enough; students need to experience challenges and justify their thinking. They need to be taught to learn—not merely to remember what has been taught; they need to learn how to think and to apply that thinking to those nonroutine situations they will encounter.

MATHEMATICAL MISUNDERSTANDINGS

Mathematics has engendered many misconceptions, which often inhibit mathematics from becoming a thinking endeavor.

Misunderstanding #1: Math is essentially computation, in which memorizing and following rules are the important mathematical procedures. Instead, conceptual understanding should precede the memorization, and students should be enabled to move to higher-level actions in mathematics, such as thinking combinatorially, holding variables constant, seeing probabilistically and proportionally, and searching for patterns. They need to go beyond manipulating, drawing, counting, matching, reading, writing, computing, and reciting, and proceed to thinking, which includes applying, categorizing, classifying, comparing, investigating, inferring, analyzing, relating, generating hypotheses and mathematical models, reasoning (inductively and deductively), making generalizations, synthesizing, evaluating, and verifying. Although students can be successful in learning to follow rules, such as the three-step process for word problems (in which they find the numbers in the problem, look for key words to determine the operation to use, and perform the appropriate computation), they probably will not be able to apply this procedure to more complex problems that do not fit the three outlined steps. The well-known expression "Yours is not to reason why. Just invert and multiply" expresses a philosophy that says students are expected to apply a rote rule when dividing common fractions. By the same token, it is possible for algebra students to learn procedures without understanding the meaning of what they are learning. If students are only to memorize facts and rules told to them by the teacher, they are being treated as empty receptacles to be filled with knowledge rather than as decision-making, thinking individuals who will succeed with new, different problematic situations.

Misunderstanding #2: The only important outcome in mathematics is to obtain the correct answer. Instead, we need a balance that values the process as well as the answer. If students are encouraged to answer the question "What are you thinking?" rather than merely to find the solution, their learning will be enhanced. We need to know whether students understand mathematics, not merely whether they can obtain the correct answer. To know whether students understand mathematics we need to ask them to use mathematics to solve real problems. The application and transfer of previously learned material to the new situation shows the extent of understanding. We need to remember that teaching and learning are multiple interactive processes; correct answers and high test scores are not enough to evaluate whether a student is mathematically powerful.

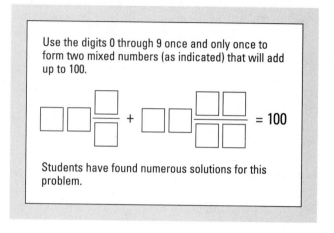

—Figure 47.1—
Finding the Right Answers

Use the digits 0 through 9 once and only once to form two mixed numbers (as indicated) that will add up to 100.

Students have found numerous solutions for this problem.

Misunderstanding #3: Mathematical problems have only one right answer. Instead, problems should be posed that have numerous solutions so that students can pursue various answers. Open-ended problems should be used often in classrooms to encourage divergent thinking. See Figure 47.1 for an example of a problem with numerous solutions.

Misunderstanding #4. There is only one way to solve a problem, and by following a rule or a formula, we can always find the right answer. Instead, students should be encouraged to use creative thinking and problem-solving strategies when attacking a problem. Teachers need to provide problems with multiple methods of solution and encourage students to attack a problem in a variety of ways and to talk about their approaches. Here is an example: If it costs 12 cents for 20 straws, how much would you spend for 35 straws? How many different ways can you prove the answer?

Misunderstanding #5: The teacher and the text are the authority and should not be questioned. Instead, students should be encouraged to have a questioning attitude and to challenge others with their thinking. Disagreement should be encouraged within the math classroom. The belief that learning to argue about mathematical ideas is fundamental to understanding mathematics is common in Asian classrooms and should become common in U.S. classrooms as well.

For mathematics to be a thinking event we must dispel these myths or misconceptions and allow math to have the breadth it deserves (rather than believing that math is the hardest of all subjects because it is so narrow-minded about the answers).

CREATING THE THINKING MATH ENVIRONMENT

Because a major goal in mathematics teaching should be to involve students in higher-level thinking, and a very small percentage of textbook pages involve higher-level thinking, it is up to educators to create an environment that encourages students to explore, experiment, take risks, share failures and successes, and question one another.

Many students seem to automatically move through math books looking at examples and following those examples; they often show evidence that they can push paper and crunch numbers, but not that they can logically think through a problem. Too many learning situations are dominated by telling, lecturing, questioning for a specific answer, and assigning seatwork. Instead, we need to present challenging thinking experiences in which students have an opportunity to inquire, to question, to probe, to experiment, to hypothesize, to find alternate solutions for a problem, or to discover alternate ways to obtain a solution. We need to provide numerous opportunities for attacking open-ended problems—alias *problem solving*. Critical thinking, which includes understanding the situation and dealing with the data and assumptions to arrive at a conclusion or solution that can be supported, needs to be at the heart of instruction; reasoning should pervade all mathematical activity. We need to think of mathematics as an arena with many events that can be entered into by students who have developed a critical spirit that makes them feel comfortable questioning, challenging, and justifying their thinking.

We should encourage students to think constantly during a daily mathematics period. By having a starter problem that focuses on thinking rather than rote regurgitation of previously learned material, the student has the opportunity to make decisions, hypothesize, and engage the brain in modifying solutions when appropriate. Here is an example: "In what month do you think most people, worldwide, eat less food?" After students have made an initial response, they should be encouraged to communicate with a partner what the mathematically logical answer would be. Usually that "ah-ha!" light flashes—revealing that thinking is taking place. Another example of a starter thinking problem is to ask students to determine which single-digit number is X by eliminating digits as constraints are imposed by the teacher. Here is an example:

$X - 7 =$ a negative number

$3X \neq$ an even number

$X^2 =$ a 2-digit number

As they deal with each direction, students figure out which digits to eliminate; communication with a partner to tell why those digits are being eliminated engages students in the process of thinking each step of the way.

All students have the right to think, and the classroom climate should promote, encourage, recognize, support, and reward mathematical thinking. Teachers need to make learning activities more challenging and engaging, and they should encourage students to cooperatively attack problems and discuss their reasoning. Students who are mathematically powerful exhibit curiosity as well as the willingness and ability to probe, explore, experiment, and persevere. A daily challenge, or stumper problem, can ensure continual problem-solving experience. See Figure 47.2 for an example.

We cannot teach students to do every problem in the world, because there is an infinite set of problems. But if we encourage them to read critically and to analyze the conditions of the problem, they will be successful when encountering new or unique problems. Many algebra students are capable of routine learning and yet cannot simplify the following expression, because they have not been pushed to think ahead and see the whole picture.

$$(X - A)(X - B)(X - C) \ldots (X - Z)$$

Classrooms must become mathematical communities that thrive on conjecturing, inventing, reasoning, and constructing proofs. The art of questioning becomes the key to the thinking classroom. Educators should be questioning not to guide student thinking in line with theirs but to provoke thinking and to discover what students know and understand. Open-ended questions with multiple responses or those that require reasons or conclusions should invite students to take intellectual risks and justify their answers.

Students should be actively thinking by making conjectures, developing mathematical arguments about those conjectures, and evaluating mathematical arguments and proofs. They should display a sense of mathematical competence by validating and supporting ideas with mathematical argument. Students should be encouraged to reflect on what they did and what they are thinking. Probing understanding with questions such as "What makes you think that it will always work?" "What other ways can you think of to prove your solution?" and "Why do you think it worked that way?" will result in higher-level mathematical thinking. Because correct answers do not necessarily show understanding, we should not settle for answers alone, but ask for reasoning. "Why?" should be a

—Figure 47.2—
Finding Number Values for Food Names

Ask students to find the name of a food we eat that has a value between 50 and 60 if we use the code below.

A	B	C	D	E	F	G	H	I	J	K	L	M
1	2	3	4	5	6	7	8	9	10	11	12	13

N	O	P	Q	R	S	T	U	V	W	X	Y	Z
14	15	16	17	18	19	20	21	22	23	24	25	26

(Note: An apple is worth 1 + 16 + 16 + 12 + 5 = 50, which is not between 50 and 60 and thus is not a solution to this problem.)

Students should be encouraged to select foods that seem reasonably possible for the limit (estimation) and then test their premise. We would hope that they would think through the reasonableness of a word and would not bother testing such foods as brussels sprouts or watermelon. Thinking—not merely adding numbers in a column—is inherent in this problem, which has at least 60 solutions.

standard question in a learning environment and should be asked whether the answers are correct or incorrect. Students need to understand why the computations work and what the answers represent. We need to listen to students. Because communication often leads to deeper understanding of a problem, they should have opportunities to communicate their thinking both orally and in written form to the teacher and to each other. We need to respect and value students' ideas, ways of thinking, and mathematical dispositions. Statements by students and teachers alike should be open to questions, reactions, and elaborations from others.

Students need to be taught to stop what they are doing periodically and assess if what they are doing makes sense; they should evaluate whether the current plan of action should be continued or whether they should try a new action plan. When working on a complex problem, they should be encouraged to consider alternative solution paths when the one they have chosen does not seem productive.

PRINCIPLES OF PROBLEM-SOLVING INSTRUCTION

The NCTM professional teaching standards (National Council of Teachers of Mathematics, 1991) stress providing tasks that engage students' intellect and call for problem formulation, problem solving, and mathematical reasoning. Because a primary goal of math teaching and learning is to develop the ability to solve a variety of complex mathematics problems and to be confident and persistent when solving problems, students need to experience many problems to gain problem-solving ability. Problem solving involves more than word problems; it involves dealing with such areas as patterning, interpreting information, developing geometric constructions, and proving theorems as well as reflecting on the methods used and the solution obtained. Quality rather than quantity should prevail with problems that provoke thought and allow for the application of strategies. Problems that challenge students' curiosity and allow them to solve them by their own means often lead to a triumphant feeling of discovery.

Students benefit from instruction in planned problem solving, including the use of various strategies or techniques for attacking mathematical problems. They should be aware of such strategies as trial and error (guess and check), drawing a diagram or making a model, elimination, looking for a pattern, simplifying the problem, working backwards, organizing information (often in table or graph form), and writing an equation. Students should be able to assess how they solved a problem rather than merely cite the answer to the problem. Students need experiences to know when the various strategies are appropriate, and they need the motivation to apply the strategies even though such strategies may involve more effort and risk than routine performances.

Students need to believe that the teacher values problem solving; thus educators need to be problem solvers themselves and share that enthusiasm with students; it is important for students to know that teachers are not always in the know but have to think through problem-solving situations just like they do. The teacher needs to create the right kind of atmosphere so that thinking prevails. As Polya (1973) says,

Thus a teacher of mathematics has a great opportunity. If he fills his allotted time with drilling his students in routine operations, he kills their interest, hampers their intellectual development, and misuses his opportunity. But if he challenges the curiosity of his students by setting them problems proportionate to their knowledge, and helps them to solve their problems with stimulating questions, he may give them a taste for, and some means of, independent thinking. (p. v)

Preparing for Mathematical Success

Contrary to many people's belief, mathematics is much more than the study of numbers and shapes with routine problems, memorization of facts and formulas, and rote procedures followed to arrive at a specific answer. It needs to be measured in ways beyond standardized testing formats. Our goals for mathematically powerful students include thinking and communicating, estimating, interpreting data, seeking alternative approaches, and dealing with technology and creative problem solving. The *Mathematics Framework for California Public Schools* (California Department of Education, 1992) states that mathematically powerful students effectively deal with mathematical ideas and mathematical thinking, individually and cooperatively, with confidence and enthusiasm.

The joy of teaching is seeing students authentically and enthusiastically involved in learning, reasoning, and solving problems. By asking good questions, providing good problems, challenging and perhaps even frustrating students by provoking thought, we can increase the probability for developing thinkers for tomorrow. Although exercising and improving in the ability to do math computation does not necessarily lead to the improvement of critical thinking, improving in the ability to think critically does contribute to mathematical success. We need to model problem solving and other thinking processes and make students conscious of their own thinking. We need to ensure that mathematical thinking, creativity, and communication remain important personal and national goals. Mathematics should be viewed neither as a set of facts and formulas nor as the memorization of theorems and postulates, but as a way of thinking—an arena for problem solving at its best.

References

California Department of Education. (1992). *Mathematics framework for California public schools*. Sacramento: Author.

National Council of Teachers of Mathematics. (1989). *Curriculum and evaluation standards for school mathematics*. Reston, VA: Author.

National Council of Teachers of Mathematics. (1991). *Professional standards for teaching mathematics*. Reston, VA: Author.

National Council of Teachers of Mathematics. (2000). *Principles and standards for school mathematics*. Reston, VA: Author.

National Research Council. (1989). *Everybody counts*. Washington, DC: National Academy Press.

Polya, G. (1973). *How to solve it*. Princeton, NJ: Princeton University Press.

U.S. National Research Center Reports. (1996). *Third international mathematics and science study*. East Lansing: Michigan State University.

48

Improving Thinking Abilities Through Reading Instruction

Cathy Collins Block

The principal goal of education is to create men who are capable of doing new things, not simply of repeating what other generations have done, and to form minds which can be critical, can verify, and not accept everything they are offered.

—*Jean Piaget*

Thinking and reading develop along parallel trajectories. Recent research suggests that the instructional methods and materials in literacy classes can become the perfect vehicle to teach higher-level thinking (Beck, 1989; Block, 2000; Block & Mangieri, 1995, 1996a, 1996b). Among the reasons cited are that literature—more than any other curriculum—provides the opportunity for students to come face-to-face with powerful thinkers. Through the magic of literary license, authors can transport students into people's minds. While there, students can listen to literary figures' reflections, judge their reasoning, and recognize thinking processes that lead to the characters' success in lifelike situations. Literary characters continuously model thinking-in-progress. They solve problems effectively and ineffectively. Through reading, students can also experience vicariously the consequences of acting on inadequate evidence.

Powerful teachers can develop thinking and reading abilities simultaneously. For example, when educators teach comprehension strategies, concomitantly they can raise students' abilities to think on high levels outside of class. Similarly, when literacy lessons focus on advancing the capabilities to deduce, summarize, and synthesize, students are more likely to engage such processes when they receive information throughout their lives from sources other than print. Today, many educators want their reading programs to realize these potentials. This chapter can help them achieve their goals.

The Need for Parallel Development in Thinking and Reading

Why is there a need for dual-focused literacy instruction—that is, instruction that focuses on both reading and thinking? Several reasons exist.

As recently as 1997, most students in K–12 schools were not developing the habits of thinking and problem solving needed to succeed in a rapidly changing world. Only 43 percent of high school graduates could interpret, summarize, and explain sophisticated expository and narrative text (National Center for Education Statistics, as reported in Delisle, 1997). In addition, society demands that children make responsible decisions earlier in their lives than in the past. Often by the age of 10, "youth will have already had their last best chance to choose a path which will lead toward a productive and fulfilled life" (Commission on Excellence in Education, 1983, p. 20). Many students live in unsafe neighborhoods, and many are tempted or pressured to experiment with drugs and alcohol at young ages. Without sound thinking strategies (and surrounded by equally confused peers), many children make choices that have enormously harmful consequences. As Hahn, Dansberger, and Lefkowitz (1987) found, there is a significant correlation between an inability to think effectively and the use of destructive means to fulfill a need for power and importance. Unfortunately, without instruction, many thinking patterns developed in youth will not alter or advance in adulthood (Eichhorn, 1989; Mangieri & Block, 2000).

It is also unacceptable that students in the United States do not perform well on measures of higher-level thinking and reading when compared with peers in other industrialized nations (International Assessment of Educational Progress, 2000; TEIMS, 1998). If our youth are to continue to become international leaders, we must teach them how to (1) use mature thinking strategies, (2) employ fair-minded consensus-building procedures in groups, (3) create ideas cooperatively, (4) honor diverse voices, (5) encourage multiple options, and (6) effectively select among equally attractive alternatives. To begin with, we must devote more time to practices of thinking critically about printed materials and "move the development of higher-level thinking into the mainstream of instruction" (Beck, 1989, p. 682).

Research demonstrates that language and thinking competencies shape each other. As students enlarge their reading powers, they must think more and at a higher level in order to understand the density of ideas in their readings. At the same time, as students learn more mature thinking strategies, they can transform the ephemeral thoughts that are ignited during reading into lasting, life-guiding principles. Through a dual-focused literacy program, learning experiences, discussions, and emotions that students experience during reading can expand the density of dendrites and cognitive structures in the brain. As more and more dendrites intertwine, students' reflection and thoughtfulness increase (Jensen, 1998; Rosenblatt, 1978; Smith, 1978). As a result, students will regularly and continuously ignite new concept schema and strengthen previously existing understandings.

Another reason to push for dual-focused literacy programs relates to the exponential increase in information. Information is increasing at such a rapid pace that the knowledge necessary to survive in 2050 has not been created. Similarly, the technological competencies that adults possess today have been projected to represent only 10 percent of what present kindergartners will need when they become adults (Applebee, Langer, & Mullis, 1987; Boyer, 1983; Bloom, Englehart, Furst, Hill, & Krathwohl, 1956). This suggests that learning how to think by means of reading may be more valuable than learning any particular content through reading.

Contemporary literacy requires that students validate statements and solve problems with incomplete data and discern patterns among disparate sources of information. When reading instruction builds these capabilities, the time spent in instruction is well spent. When reading instruction does not build these capabilities, much valuable time is wasted because the content and information in most expository text will become obsolete by the time students become adults. In contrast, the thinking competencies and literacy strategies they develop will remain valuable throughout their lives.

Today's youth need to develop new forms of literacy that will help them acquire the skills needed for interacting with television, surfing the Web, reading e-mail, and participating in chat rooms. These communication tools have begun to func-

tion as primary information-gathering sources for young people. Students today also receive more multiculturally influenced information from around the world than students of earlier generations. Most will have received permission to traverse the information superhighway unescorted before they are allowed to cross the streets in front of their houses. Their literacy and thinking strategies will come less from parents and teachers and more from peers and a wide array of technology-based tools and sources. Most will have used computers and other technology long before they begin their first structured reading lessons. Similarly, technology will enable children to view ongoing research, as it happens. Adults will less frequently serve as mediators, filters, or interpreters of new information.

In addition, high-level literacy and thinking abilities will increasingly become the core around which groups of students socialize. The ability to read technology instruction manuals and to solve technological problems already has enormous exchange value in today's social groups. Social settings that involve other new types of literacy and high-level thinking abilities, such as "edutainment" and "virtual reality," are already prized.

Equally important, dual-focused literacy lessons may promote students' creativity. Creativity is an important tool, but students do not develop it fully without instruction. In a longitudinal study, 84 percent of kindergartners ranked high in aptitude for creative thinking, but by the end of 2nd grade, without instruction to develop innovative thinking processes, only 10 percent sustained even a significant level of inventive capacity (Block, in press). Most had stopped their exploratory, problem-solving thinking as soon as they stated a quick answer. Finally, unless reading programs help more students to recognize the complexities and relationships between seemingly disparate ideas, they may become convinced that problems can be solved simply, without sustained and creative reflection. For many children, the typical television episode tends to reinforce the notion that instant solutions are likely (Stuart and Graves, 1987).

In summary, the needs for a dual-focused literacy program are multifaceted. How can we begin to develop them in our schools today?

FOUR WAYS TO ENHANCE LITERACY INSTRUCTION

Eight domains of thinking are amenable to instruction during literacy lessons. These domains are (1) basic thinking skills, such as identifying the main idea, determining cause and effect, and questioning; (2) essential thinking processes that require two or more skills, such as drawing conclusions, inferring, and summarizing; (3) making decisions and using tools of reasoned judgment, such as detecting propaganda and suspending judgment; (4) solving problems; (5) metacognition; (6) thinking more effectively in groups; (7) thinking more effectively when reflecting and studying alone; and (8) creativity/inventiveness. By using four kinds of literacy enhancement lessons, teachers can increase students' literacy and thinking development in each of these domains.

LITERACY ENHANCEMENT LESSON #1: EXPLORING ISSUES OF TIMELESS IMPORTANCE

When students are guided to read and think about issues that define humanity, both their reading and thinking skills will improve. With well-planned choices of fictional text, students concomitantly learn thinking concepts and processes that they can engage to ensure that justice prevails and truth reigns in areas of their lives that they can control, that they can change proactively and productively, that environments can be enhanced, and so forth. With well-planned selections of nonfiction, they can learn (1) how scientists, artists, mathematicians, and historians think; (2) how to employ the cognitive tools that professionals use to discover knowledge; and (3) how they recognize the differences in format and style of varied professional writings.

Research demonstrates that such dual-focused lessons can also significantly increase students' self-regulation (Block & Pressley, in press). That is, readers become more motivated to (1) ferret out exact meanings, (2) study subtleties of complex sentences, (3) increase reading and thinking strengths to avoid compromising with the demands of a difficult text, (4) refrain from skipping important words so they can predict upcoming events, and (5) fill gaps in understanding by rereading rather than relying on personal experiences.

Thus, exploring issues of timeless importance presents thinking and reading as interactive processes constructed by students, authors, and teachers working together to create new levels of understanding. Students can be taught how to sustain their own purposes while accurately interpreting authors' intentions. They can be shown how to engage a broad continuum of thoughts as they read. This continuum (and teachers' thinking aloud that demonstrates it) is bordered at one end by authors' intended meanings and on the other by students' application of texts to their lives. Through repeated teacher modeling, pupils come to value reading and thinking as important windows that can be used to look onto the world anew and learn more about what we, as people, at our highest

levels of ability can become (Galda, 1997; Gaskins, Gaskins, & Gaskins, 1991; Mangieri & Block, 2000).

Another benefit of reading about timeless issues is that students tend to employ more cognitive tools learned outside of school because of increases in the depth and time invested in exploring single issues. Through television commercials and computer software, today's students have learned to instantly intake, connect, and organize rapidly moving, multisensory input communicated in milliseconds. More than previous generations, they can shift their attention from one stimulus to another without confusion or distraction (Block, 1999). Teachers can use issue-driven instruction to help students realize how all forms of modern print, audio, and visual literacies are shaping how (and what) they think and dream. Such instruction can partner with media to captivate students so that learning occurs exponentially faster and students can assimilate infinitely greater bodies of information. Moreover, when literacy programs target thinking development through curriculum that addresses the complexities in humanity, students are almost forced to immediately engage higher-level thinking as soon as they start each new text (Block, 2001). As they experience the intertwined events, emotions, and intricacies of human life, students are forced to instantly ignite their analytical, generative, and interpretive skills to merely make sense of the content (Langer, 1997).

Before students can reach such high levels of crafting abilities, however, schools must overcome the limitations in present forms of reading instruction. First, new lessons must teach students how to process authorial clues and their own thoughts interactively. Second, teachers must model, and allow students to practice, periodically stopping during reading to craft a sustained and valid interpretation. Dual-focused instruction must be neither too prescriptive and depersonalized, nor too freeflowing and noninstructive. Also, multiple genres must be studied so that students learn how to think within the richness of varied syntax structures.

LITERACY ENHANCEMENT LESSON #2: DEVELOPING LONG-TERM THINKING AND READING SKILLS

Reading instruction must teach students how to reread, reflect, and develop insights in the process of reading and thinking so that they can experience pleasure and respite from the speed with which technology thrusts information into their lives. In a technology-driven age, reading instruction must highlight the unique pleasure that arises from long-term thinking. Because students will spend less time gathering information today than in the past, reading instruction must focus on developing the facility to (1) analyze multiple sources of information, (2) engage multiple, interactive plans in problematic situations, (3) seek out valid experts, and (4) operate effectively within the constraints of the shorter shelf life of knowledge.

To accomplish this, reading lessons must begin to sustain students in an engaged, sustained flow experience that has continuous focused absorption in reading and thinking simultaneously. Lessons must provide enough time for students to not merely read but to live within books—to walk in the shoes of literary figures. They must be taught how to (1) establish their own reading and thinking goals before reading and (2) engage expert thinking strategies as they read. The following easy-to-implement methods develop these abilities.

The first activity requires a large block of uninterrupted time for silent reading and thinking. At the outset, teachers demonstrate how students can initiate thinking processes that expert readers use (e.g., taking risks as they infer, rereading when their minds begin to wander, adding new purposes and commitments when their motivations wane, and setting a goal before reading). Then students are taught to establish a purpose for each new reading by writing down or thinking about what they want to find out from a particular reading experience. Next, they select and silently read two pages about topics that are important to them. As they read, the teacher moves about the room to answer questions that arise as soon as students encounter a comprehension or decoding challenge in a specific sentence. The teacher eliminates confusions at specific places in the text and notes the exact difficulty for that student on a hand-held chart. Later in the week, needs-based groups or individual conferences are held to provide intense instruction concerning this particular thinking or literacy difficulty. Through these lessons, students (1) discover that printed stories are only glimpses of the messages and lives that writers have to offer, (2) free their creativity, (3) think empathetically as they learn to care more about authors' messages, (4) value their own worth as thinkers and readers, and (5) interpret ideas in the broader contexts of their own lives.

The second method is used during oral reading. In these shared reading experiences, students—not teachers—say the first words after a reading. The rationale is that whoever sets the agenda and does most of the talking during a reading lesson engages the most thinking. Before each shared reading experience, students decide whether the reading is to be completed without interruptions from peers or if classmates can stop the reading at any time to comment. If the choice is for uninterrupted reading, students raise their hands when they have something to share, but no one speaks. A volunteer records names in order, as well as the page number that triggered students' thoughts. This list determines who begins the conversation when the reading is complete. Pursuant discussions include insights that students discovered about themselves, humanity, reading processes, and thinking.

LITERACY ENHANCEMENT LESSON #3: TEACHING THINKING STRATEGIES AS PROCESSES

To teach thinking strategies as processes, teachers tell stories about themselves as readers and thinkers and use graphic depictions of thinking-in-action. Teachers show how they craft meaning at a difficult point in a specific text before students read the same text. They share expanded explanations and present at least three examples of high-level thinking as they introduce the text. Through such lessons, students (1) build connections between two different selections that they have read related to the same topic; (2) think on literal, inferential, and applied levels interchangeably; (3) expand the depth and breadth of their thinking; (4) make connections between words, facts, and concepts and the historical, social, political, and cultural context in which they were written; and (5) fill gaps in narrative and expository trajectories (Golden & Rumelhart, 1993).

When we teach literacy and thinking strategies as a process, we can also assist students to analyze seductive details, think about meaning making, and maintain metacognition during reading. We can directly instruct students to judge credibility and discern the cultural-social context in which messages, particularly on the Internet, have been constructed (Reinking, Labbo, & McKenna, 1997). As Stahl, Hynd, Britton, McNish, and Bosquet (1998) demonstrated, merely having rapid access via a computer to masses of textual information was not enough to enable high school students to interpret historical events more analytically. They needed basic instruction on how to compare and contrast critical information from various sources.

Thinking guides that visually depict stages of thinking/reading processes can help students learn thinking processes more rapidly (Block, 2001; Block & Mangieri, 1996a, 1996b). After students have been exposed to or create their own depiction of cognitive processes-in-action, they can recognize the components in their own thinking as they read (Block, in press). In turn, the repetition of these lessons significantly increases students' abilities to initiate metacognition as they read a specific book. Other methods of teaching thinking as a process appear in Block (2001) and in *Reason to Read* (Block & Mangieri, 1995, 1996a, 1996b), a three-volume curriculum that contains depictions of 45 cognitive processes.

LITERACY ENHANCEMENT LESSON #4: ALLOWING STUDENTS TO SELECT THE LITERACY AND THINKING PROCESSES THAT THEY WANT TO LEARN

It is important to create time in the reading curriculum for students to discuss literacy and cognitive processes that they want to learn to improve their reading and thinking abilities. We must teach students to create and speculate rather than recite and regurgitate. Dual-focused lessons that enable students to do this are especially important because today's youth are the first generation to learn from reading nonlinear environments. Although research about how to increase thinking abilities in such environments is extremely limited (Lanham, 1993), learning how to do so does involve non-traditional reading and thinking processes.

Reading classes can become the venue where students recognize new thinking processes. For instance, with the mass use of HDTV, more authorial intents will be communicated through facial features, expressions, and glimpses. Background knowledge will become more important as audiences (readers) are placed into real-world simulations through virtual reality technologies. What strategies will students need to balance such vivid input sources with character dialogue? What should we teach students in order to keep media from framing the meaning of a message without their consent? We don't have the answers. Indeed, students likely will be the ones who tell us, and then help us teach, the thinking processes that are needed.

Already, more and more literacy and media experiences intertwine future, past, and present events out of chronological sequence. Some interactive TV users can select what commercials they want to view and at what speed they want to view programs. Other viewers (readers) can play games and win prizes as they watch TV interactively (Carey, 1997). E-mail can subvert established hierarchies of authority and encourage candidness, imperviousness, and confrontational rudeness (Reinking, Labbo, & McKenna, 1997). Soon national elections and registrations will occur from home TVs. Methods of teaching the thinking skills needed in these new literacy environments are at http://www.abacon.com/collins-block.

Hypertext has also increased the need for student discussion of literacy and cognitive strategies that they have created or need. When ideas become multilayered in complex ways, students become more aware of the power of making interconnections during thinking. When students are allowed to describe the connections they are making as they read, the resulting intentional placement of juxtaposed ideas will reveal new and unique synergistic thinking strategies. We must schedule more time during reading lessons for students to talk not only about what they read but about how they are thinking as they read. What processes do students use when they create multidimensional mental images? In addition, how can students learn when it is appropriate or inappropriate to act on the basis of sound bites? For all of these reasons, providing time for students to create, discuss, and graphically depict thinking processes-in-action will be a great step forward in literacy instruction.

When students demonstrate processes they have created, their levels of metacognition, effort, and drive expand. They also can decide what it is that they need to learn in order to think and read better, and what they learn about themselves can help them sustain the will and volition to eliminate their individual literacy deficiencies and thinking weaknesses.

LOOKING TOWARD THE FUTURE

Although no one can predict the challenges that our youth will face in the coming years, we can deduce that teaching them to read and think simultaneously will significantly increase their resiliency, reflectivity, and problem-solving capabilities throughout their lives. In the hands of exemplary reading teachers, students may no longer be tempted simply to submit to being informed or refrain from analyzing texts that register on their minds.

Moreover, it is important that we not assume that our students understand how we think and read simply because they see us doing it. We must communicate that no matter how limited their level of literacy, with dual-focused literacy instruction, they can rise to higher levels of capability and learn more about authors' thinking patterns.

An enduring truth is that it is teachers who enable students to reach their potential as thinkers and readers. Teachers must model how to think with, about, and through reading. We must demonstrate how to approach knowledge as relative, rather than absolute. We must instruct students to think on higher levels with greater ease and efficacy and never abandon the value of forging their own meanings. At present, less than half the school districts in the United States provide incentives for teachers to engage in professional development to enhance their abilities to achieve these goals. The lessons described in this chapter can begin our march toward simultaneously developing our as well as our students' reading and thinking capabilities.

REFERENCES

Applebee, A. N., Langer, J. A., & Mullis, L. (1987). *Literature and U.S. history: The instructional experiences and factual knowledge of high school juniors.* Princeton, NJ: Educational Testing Service.

Beck, I. (1989). Reading and reasoning. *The Reading Teacher, 42*(9), 676–684.

Block, C. C. (1999). Comprehension: Crafting understanding. In L. B. Gambrell, L. M. Morrow, S. B. Neuman, & M. Pressley (Eds.), *Best practices in literacy instruction* (pp. 98–118). New York: Guilford Press.

Block, C. C. (2000, May). New research developments in comprehension instruction. Paper presented at the annual meeting of the International Reading Association, Indianapolis, IN.

Block, C. C. (2001). *Teaching the language arts.* 3rd ed. Boston: Allyn and Bacon.

Block, C. C. (in press). *Teaching comprehension.* Boston: Allyn and Bacon.

Block, C. C., & Mangieri, J. N. (1995). *Reason to Read: Thinking Strategies for Life Through Literature* (Vol. 1). Palo Alto, CA: Addison-Wesley.

Block, C. C., & Mangieri, J. N. (1996a). *Reason to Read: Thinking Strategies for Life Through Literature* (Vol. 2). Palo Alto, CA: Addison-Wesley.

Block, C. C., & Mangieri, J. N. (1996b). *Reason to Read: Thinking Strategies for Life Through Literature* (Vol. 3). Palo Alto, CA: Addison-Wesley.

Block, C. C., & Pressley, M. (Eds.) (in press). *Comprehension instruction.* New York: Guilford Press.

Bloom, B. S., Englehart, M. D., Furst, E. J., Hill, W. H., & Krathwohl, D. R. (Eds.). (1956). *Taxonomy of educational objectives: The classification of educational goals. Handbook I: Cognitive domain.* New York: David McKay.

Boyer, E. (1983). *High school.* New York: Harper & Row.

Carey, J. (1997). Exploring future media. In J. Flood, S. B. Heath, & D. Lapp (Eds.), *Handbook of research on teaching literacy through communication and visual arts* (pp. 62–67). New York: IRA.

Commission on Excellence in Education. (1983). *A nation at risk.* Washington, DC: U.S. Government Printing Office.

Delisle, R. (1997). *How to use problem-based learning in the classroom.* Alexandria, VA: Association for Supervision and Curriculum Development.

Eichhorn, D. (1989). *The middle school.* New York: Center for Applied Research in Education.

Galda, L. (1997). Mirrors and windows: Reading as transformation. In T. E. Raphael & K. H. Au (Eds.), *Literature-based instruction: Reshaping the curriculum* (pp. 13–27). Norwood, MA: Christopher-Gordon.

Gaskins, R. W., Gaskins, J. C., & Gaskins, I. W. (1991). A decoding program for poor readers—and the rest of the class, too! *Language Arts, 68*(4), 213–225.

Golden, R., & Rumelhart, D. (1993). A parallel distributed processing model of story comprehension and recall. *Discourse Processes, 16*(3), 203–237.

Hahn, A., Dansberger, J., & Lefkowitz, B. (1987). *Dropouts in America: Enough is known for action.* Washington, DC: Institute for Educational Leadership.

International Assessment of Educational Progress (2000). Washington, DC: Department of Education.

Jensen, E. (1998). *Teaching with the brain in mind.* Alexandria, VA: Association for Supervision and Curriculum Development.

Langer, J. (1997). Reading comprehension. *Research in the Teaching of English, 2*(1), 55–84.

Lanham, R. (1993). *The electronic word: Democracy, technology, and the arts.* Chicago: University of Chicago Press.

Mangieri, J., & Block, C. C. (2000). *Power thinking for success.* Houston, TX: Telemetrics International.

Reinking, D., Labbo, L., & McKenna, M. (1997). Navigating the changing landscape of literacy: Current theory and research in computer-based reading and writing. In J. Flood, S. B. Heath, & D. Lapp (Eds.), *Handbook of research on teaching literacy through communication and visual arts* (pp. 77–89). New York: IRA.

Rosenblatt, L. M. (1978). *The reader, the text and the poem.* Carbondale, IL: Southern Illinois University Press.

Smith, N. (1978). *The history of reading instruction.* New York: McGraw-Hill.

Stahl, S., Hynd, C., Britton, B., McNish, M., & Bosquet, D. (1998). What happens when students read multiple source documents in history? *Reading Research Quarterly, 34*(5), 556–589.

Stuart, V., & Graves, D. (1987). *How to teach writing.* Urbana, IL: National Council of Teachers of English.

TEIMS (1998). International Study of Math, Science and Higher Level Thinking. Washington, DC: Author.

49

What Is Write for Thinking?

Arthur Whimbey, Jack Lochhead, Myra J. Linden, and Carol Welsh

Good writing demands clear thinking. Good thinking often results in concise, clear prose. But neither of these facts implies that practice in writing will automatically develop strong thinking skills. Deep water may demand great swimming but usually does not develop it.

Claims made about the beneficial effects of writing often exhibit a reverse logic. Students who are able to complete writing assignments demonstrate an ability to think. Thus it is concluded that writing develops thinking. Unfortunately there is no evidence that the students' ability to think emerged from the writing; in most cases the thinking was already in place. Yet most of us have direct experience with situations in which writing helped clarify our thoughts. But we are not novices; our experience may not be a suitable guide to what is best for our students. Writing that is the right write for thinking can generate "write thinking"—skillful thinking for writing.

To develop skills in writing or thinking, we must do more than demand them. To actively develop any skill, we must provide learners with a structure that will produce the right sequence of progressively more complex actions. The best structures are extremely simple yet function effectively over many different levels of experience. One such simple structure is used for developing hand-eye coordination for sports ranging from baseball to golf. It is "keep your eye on the ball." This structure works as well for the professional athlete as it does for the complete novice. Such structures are essential for developing all skills and especially for developing skills in thinking and writing.

Unfortunately, in many educational settings we plunge students into tasks they do not know how to handle, and then we blame them for their inability to find a structure that will help them master the assignment. The student of baseball who keeps his eyes fixed on the bat will not become a better batter even with hours and hours of practice. Yet keeping one's eyes on the bat may seem to the student every bit as logical as keeping one's eyes on the ball. It is not easy to explain why one

strategy works and the other fails. Because it can take years of experience to separate the effective strategies from the rest, it is inefficient and fundamentally unfair to expect students to discover the best strategies on their own.

In this chapter we consider a few proven strategies that will simultaneously develop skills in writing and in thinking: jumbled text reconstruction, split text reconstruction, sentence combining, controlled writing, and four-color analysis. These structures are simple, powerful, and effective for all students. None is entirely new. If there is novelty in this chapter, it is in our attempt to distinguish between structures that promote thought and apparently similar structures that do not.

All of the above strategies involve reconstructing text. Students are asked to manipulate sentence parts into whole sentences, sentences into paragraphs, and eventually paragraphs into full-length pieces of writing. The strategies guide students through the thought processes used by successful writers to produce standard written English.

The first two strategies we discuss are forms of Text Reconstruction Across the Curriculum (TRAC), and their use is not limited to English classes. They can be used in any kind of course to improve reading, writing, and reasoning skills, along with mastery of subject matter content.

JUMBLED TEXT RECONSTRUCTION

To understand our definition of jumbled text reconstruction, or jumbled TRAC, number the following sentences, putting them in the best logical order:

_____ Then they discuss their arrangements, an activity that builds reasoning, communication, and cooperative learning skills.

_____ Text reconstruction is a powerful form of writing across the curriculum.

—— Finally, they write the sentences in logical order, internalizing the spelling, grammar, and vocabulary of standard written English.

—— Students number the sentences in jumbled paragraphs of papers from various academic fields.

Jumbled text reconstruction exercises similar to this example can be created out of almost any kind of text (see Linden & Whimbey, 1987). The paragraphs in a full-length article, essay, or chapter may be jumbled, or chapter summaries may be jumbled and used as review material. Applications exist in every discipline across the curriculum. Chapter Five of *Why Johnny Can't Write* (Linden & Whimbey, 1990) provides detailed instructions for creating such exercises.

Many outstanding writers have used forms of text reconstruction to improve their own writing and language skills. Among them are Somerset Maugham, Malcolm X, Joan Didion, and Benjamin Franklin.

Franklin describes in his autobiography a method he used to improve his writing skills. As a youth, Franklin worked in his brother's print shop, where articles by many fine writers were published. When he admired an essay, he wrote several words from each sentence. These he calls "short hints of the sentiment in each sentence." Next he rearranged the hints into random order and set them aside. Several weeks later Franklin tried to arrange the hints into their original order to re-create the logical organization of the essay. He says, "This was to teach me method in the arrangement of thoughts." Then he attempted to write each sentence from just the hints, checking the original and noting any deviations, trying to master the vocabulary, sentence structure, and style of the writer.

The text reconstruction technique described by Franklin requires the self-discipline and intelligence for which he was so famous. But simpler versions are available. A computer-assisted approach is probably the simplest (see www.new-intel.com). Exercise workbooks are another useful approach (see Whimbey & Blanton, 1995; also www.tracinstitute.com and www.whimbey.com). In these the task of disassembling the text has already been done, and the students need only to reconstruct the paragraph (as was the case in our definition of Text Reconstruction given above). This has an important advantage over Franklin's method. It is not always easy to create disassembled text that can be unambiguously reassembled. Workbooks and computer programs focus student attention on the most useful elements of the learning task and avoid frustrating encounters with large amounts of ambiguous material.

SPLIT TEXT RECONSTRUCTION: THE WEDGE OF UNDERSTANDING

Another form of text reconstruction, split TRAC, removes part of the end of each sentence in a paragraph. These ends of sentences are then mixed up and put in a random order below the paragraph. Students must determine which ending goes with which beginning to form a complete logical sentence. After matching the sentence parts, students discuss their choices with a classmate and proceed as with jumbled TRAC. The following example of split TRAC is from a software program, *Highlights of United States History: The Story of Our Nation* (Linden & Whimbey, 2000):

James Buchanan: 1857–1861

Paragraph 1

1. President Buchanan, who came from Pennsylvania, was personally
2. However, he was considered to be pro-slavery because
3. Buchanan also believed that the federal government did not have the right
4. Because of his stand on slavery, he

• he attacked abolitionists as agitators.
• against slavery, calling it "a great political and moral evil."
• was supported by the South.
• to end slavery in areas where it was already established.

Split sentence exercises force students to become active readers. Weak readers often do not understand the need to actively take apart and reassemble complex sentences. As a result, they get lost in a sea of disconnected words and phrases. Sentences that have already been split teach students to assemble a more complete understanding of the paragraph, and at the same time they model the active reading strategies these readers need to master.

Split sentence exercises are fairly easy to design and can be created from any existing text. Thus teachers can create their own exercises by using whatever material they may happen to have available or desire to use. Split TRAC, like jumbled TRAC, can be used to review materials or to preview textbook chapters. The introductions to most textbook chapters lend themselves to being adapted for Split TRAC previewing of the entire chapter. Of course, it is important that students not have access to the textbook while they are completing the exercise.

SENTENCE COMBINING

William Strong (1981) describes a useful introductory version of text reconstruction called sentence combining. In his sentence combining exercise presented here, the students' task is to combine short choppy sentences into one complex sentence, deleting all redundant material.

- The farmer was out standing in her field.
- This was after four years of training.
- The training was arduous.
- The training was in college.

Students who engage in the task of assembling one complex sentence that contains all the information of the four sentences discover for themselves the rules and conventions of effective writing. Lochhead (2001) provides a detailed example of two students engaged in such a task.

Sentence combining can also be employed to teach specific skills such as the use and function of conjunctions. For example, a unit on the use of the words *however, therefore,* and *moreover* might begin by defining the terms (Whimbey, Williams, & Linden, 1994, p. 47):

HOWEVER, THEREFORE, and MOREOVER are similar in meaning to BUT, SO, and AND, though somewhat more formal. They are used with a semicolon (;) and a comma (,) to connect sentences as follows:

$$\text{Sentence 1;} \begin{bmatrix} \text{however} \\ \text{therefore} \\ \text{moreover} \end{bmatrix}, \text{sentence 2.}$$

Use one of the above formats to join the following two sentences:

- Joan felt she would say the wrong thing and offend people.
- She said nothing at all.

Exercises of this kind can be designed to teach the most basic elements of composition without resorting to the kind of drills that put a stop to thinking. Dozens of research studies have demonstrated the effectiveness of sentence combining for improving writing skills, reading skills, and several aspects of verbal reasoning (Hillocks, 1986).

CONTROLLED WRITING

One key to "write thinking" is to use exercises that provide students with the support they need to succeed. Another key is to also provide intellectually demanding challenges. The split sentence task may be simple, but nearly every person, from the 1st grader to the college professor, finds that the task demands some thought and understanding.

Controlled writing exercises provide a powerful structure but a more limited level of challenge. Here's an example based on a paraphrase from *Ananse Tales* (Dykstra, Port, & Port, 1966, p. 1):

Ananse, the spider, managed to collect all the world's knowledge in one spot. He placed it in a gourd and then decided to climb a tree and hang the gourd there so that he might keep all the wisdom on earth for himself.

- Copy the passage.
- Rewrite the entire passage, changing the word gourd to basket each time it appears.
- Rewrite the entire passage, changing Ananse, the spider, to Ananse's wife.
- Remember to change the pronouns wherever it is necessary.

Controlled writing exercises such as this have long been a basic structure in teaching English as a second language (ESL). These exercises give ESL students practice necessary for internalizing the fundamentals of standard written English. There are, in fact, many English-speaking students for whom standard written English is for all practical purposes a second language. These students benefit immensely from controlled writing. Donna Gorrell's controlled writing text *Copy/Write* (1982) has been used for years with college-level basic writers; it can also be used with high school students.

Yet for most students the task of changing *gourd* to *basket* lacks the intellectual challenge that might engage their attention. Can controlled writing really be considered a thoughtful approach to writing? The answer depends not on the exercise itself but on the relationship between the demands of the exercise and the needs of the student. For some students controlled writing demands thought and attention; for others it does not. For those students for whom controlled writing is appropriate, a more difficult open-ended exercise would likely generate paralysis and hence no thought at all.

FOUR-COLOR ANALYSIS

Whereas most text reconstruction activities ask students to re-assemble separated elements, four-color analysis stresses the reverse process. The analysis can be used for either reading or for writing. It asks students to think about text in terms of four color categories:

- RED is for emotions and feelings.
- BLUE is for facts.
- PURPLE is for personal stories and experience.
- GREEN is for the big picture and meaning.

Students can be told to write in a manner that employs all four colors and to identify each part of their writing either by writing in the appropriate color or by underlining phrases with that color.

Suppose that an uncooperative student has to write a book report. He might start with the following stunning analysis:

I did not like this story. It was all wet.

The first sentence would be colored red and the second blue. But now two more colors must be added. Even our uncooperative student can see that two parts are missing, and he therefore attempts to write more:

—*Figure 49.1*—

301

I feel there were far too many words and no pictures.

But in attempting to add some personal experience (purple), our student really just adds more facts (blue.) So he tries again:

I lost interest when I did not see a picture of the fish that ate Jonah.

This sentence does add a personal story (purple), and so all that is left is to add the big picture and meaning (green):

I guess the point is to stay away from water and big fish.

After writing this penetrating analysis, our student might be asked to discuss with other students his report and its color coding. It is easy to imagine how such a discussion might lead to improvements.

Even students who have just started to write benefit from the four-color system. Figure 49.1 is an actual classroom example from 2nd grade. Although the execution of the four colors may be slightly confused, the effort nonetheless drives the writing forward. By 3rd grade, students can better separate the four colors.

WHICH WRITE IS RIGHT?

But though they wrote it all by rote
They did not write it right. (Collingwood, 1961, p. 362)

Not all writing is right for thinking. As long as national scores on reading and writing tests remain low in the United States (Learning First Alliance, 1998), we must question whether the techniques we are using meet the needs of our students. Yet the differences between effective and ineffective techniques can be difficult to see. The four-color system divides writing into four categories. A commonly used process approach also uses four stages: generating ideas, composing ideas, sequencing ideas, and expressing ideas.[1] What is the difference? Without classroom testing, it is impossible to tell which will work best. Experience has shown that the process approach requires that students employ a higher level of analysis; it is therefore effective with a much smaller number of students. It fails to give weak students the support they need to develop their fledgling skills. The four-step process model is logical, and it correctly specifies stages that many successful writers use, but it does not engage all of the students we have to teach.

What makes writing so incredibly difficult to teach is that assignments often are either too demanding or too demeaning to engage thought; sometimes they are both. Assignments that work well for one group of students fail with another. Teachers, however, are rarely in a position to custom-design every as-

signment for each student in the class. Thus there is a pressing need to find assignments that span the needs of a diverse student population. In this chapter, we have provided some examples of the kinds of exercises that do work well with a large range of student talents. These exercises have structures that are deceptively simple. On the surface they lack depth and sophistication. It is only when one carefully examines the mental activities of students that one begins to appreciate that these structures are write for thinking.

NOTE

[1]See, for example, pp. 28–41 of Howard and Barton (1986). Murray (1987) suggests a similar five-step process: collecting, focusing, ordering, developing, and clarifying.

REFERENCES

Collingwood, S. D. (Ed.). (1961). *Diversions and digressions of Lewis Carroll.* New York: Dover.

Dykstra, G., Port, A., & Port, R. (1966). *Ananse Tales manual: A course in controlled composition.* New York: Teachers College Press.

Gorrell, D. (1982). *Copy/write: Basic writing through controlled composition.* Boston: Little, Brown.

Hillocks, G., Jr. (1986). *Research in written composition.* Urbana, IL: ERIC Clearinghouse on Reading and Communication Skills/National Conference on Research in English.

Howard, V. A., & Barton, J. H. (1986). *Thinking on paper.* New York: William Morrow.

Learning First Alliance. (1998). *Every child reading: An action plan.* Washington, DC: Author.

Linden, M., & Whimbey, A. (1987). *Analytical writing and thinking: Facing the tests.* Mahwah, NJ: Lawrence Erlbaum Associates.

Linden, M., & Whimbey, A. (1990). *Why Johnny can't write.* Mahwah, NJ: Lawrence Erlbaum Associates.

Linden, M., & Whimbey, A. (2000). *Highlights of United States history: The story of our nation.* Grand Prairie, TX: New Intelligence.

Lochhead, J. (2001). *Thinkback: A user's guide to minding the mind.* Mahwah, NJ: Lawrence Erlbaum Associates.

Murray, D. M. (1987). *Write to learn.* New York: Holt, Rinehart and Winston.

Strong, W. (1981). *Sentence combining and paragraph building.* New York: Random House.

Whimbey, A., Williams, E., Sr., & Linden, M. (1994). *Keys to quick writing skills: Sentence combining and text reconstruction* (Rev. ed.). Birmingham, AL: EBSCO Curriculum Materials.

Whimbey, A., & Blanton, E. L. (1995). *The Whimbey writing program.* Mahwah, NJ: Lawrence Erlbaum Associates.

WEB SITES

www.newintel.com
www.tracinstitute.com
www.whimbey.com

50

Teaching Thinking in Science

Robert J. Swartz and Stephen David Fischer

Science is more than a collection of information about the natural world. It is a living enterprise involving a range of human activities, all focused on finding out how the world works and on applying this knowledge to serve our purposes in this world. The information often referred to as "science" is the product of these activities. Thinking is involved in all of them, and to do them well, the thinking must be done skillfully.

Is there any sort of thinking that is distinctively "scientific thinking?" If so, what are its characteristics?

The Scientific Method

The most common answer to the question about "scientific thinking" is an account of what has been called the "scientific method." The scientific method, in its most general form, is a methodology for gathering data to test hypotheses, usually about the causes of things. It involves gathering observational data that are public and reproducible, and that provide relevant support or countersupport to possible explanations. These data are often gathered through experimentation in which other possibly explanatory factors are controlled so that the data provided can be used to genuinely rule in or rule out specific possible causes.

For example, in trying to determine the cause of the death of game hens whose diet included a certain kind of worm, experimenters fed two groups of similar game hens the same food with one exception—one group's diet included the worms and the other's did not. Here the variables were *controlled*—that is,

the only thing that varied between the groups, as far as the experimenters knew, was the inclusion of the worms. When the hens that ate the worms died and the others didn't, the experimenters had observational data that supported the hypothesis that the worms were poisonous to these hens.

We should, of course, be cautious about thinking that the data show more than that these worms are poisonous to these game hens. Concluding that the data showed that these worms were poisonous to *all* game hens would be a mistake according to the principles of scientific investigation. This is because it is possible that these worms and certain microorganisms present only in the digestive system of the type of hens tested are *together* causing the deaths. To rule this out, another, different experiment would have to be conducted. In fact, to be able to generalize from the data, we need to know certain things about the sample: that it is representative of the total population of game hens. Only then is this kind of generalization justified.

The thinking that goes into judging whether a causal explanation is reasonable based on available data is, of course, critical thinking; and using the standards in science that relate to the need to make sure that all other variables are controlled is what makes this kind of judgment skillful. Similarly, we exercise critical thinking when we judge whether or not the sample tested provides sufficient support to generalize about all hens. But another important critical thinking skill must be involved in both these types of inferences: we must make sure that the observational reports are accurate and reliable. Here, there are standards that should be used to determine the accuracy of an observation—for example whether the observer has some expertise with regard to what is being observed; whether the observer was attending carefully to what was being observed; whether the observer had prior expectations of what would be seen, and so forth. Judging an observer to be a reliable source of information based on these standards involves critical thinking.

This chapter is adapted from "Critical and Creative Thinking in Science," by R. Swartz, S. D. Fischer, & S. Parks, in *Infusing the Teaching of Critical and Creative Thinking into Secondary Science: A Lesson Design Handbook* (pp. 29–32). Copyright © 1998 by Critical Thinking Books and Software. Adapted with permission of the authors and Critical Thinking Books and Software.

Several other kinds of skillful thinking go into the gathering of data from such an experiment. Skillfully comparing and contrasting the experimental and control groups is essential; classifying the data that result, making sure of the sequence of events, and so forth, are all involved to some degree. These are fundamentally analytical skills that are as essential in science as critical thinking skills are.

Now let's consider what kind of thinking goes into the process of designing an experiment of this sort. To do this well, prior knowledge of what sorts of results would support or count against the hypothesis under consideration is essential. When we design such experiments we are, in fact, thinking about what evidence we expect to find that could rule in or rule out the particular hypothesis, and how we could gather that evidence. This involves more skillful thinking. For example, we have to predict how certain things will likely react in the experiment. This type of prediction needs to be well supported, and ascertaining that it is, is another skill of critical thinking. And we have to do this in the context of making decisions about the best way to run the experiment. In short, to design such experiments well, we must use—or gather—a wide range of scientific and practical information that we ascertain is reliable and use the strategies of skillful decision making to make carefully thought-out choices.

Do we always have to conduct experiments like the game hen experiment described here in order to make truly scientific judgments about what is causing the deaths of the game hens? Certainly if no one knows why, or has relevant data about why, the hens died, such an experiment may well be called for. But science is a social and public enterprise. To find out whether certain microorganisms cause a certain disease, we may not have to conduct any experiment ourselves. The experiments may already have been carried out to establish conclusively that a cause-effect relationship exists. Then all we have to find out is that someone else has already obtained these experimental results. Of course, because we are relying on information from another source, we should make skillful judgments about the credibility of the source. But we may, indeed, find that the source is impeccable, and that the experiments have been repeated and the results confirmed many times. Then it may be silly to do this all over again. So we may simply identify the worms in the feed and find out, by reading a relevant book or article, or asking someone who knows about such worms, that research has already established that these worms are poisonous to these game hens.

All of this is proper science just as much as laboratory work is. In fact, some of the greatest scientific discoveries of the 20th century involved creatively putting together data derived from the work of others to generate new ideas that furnish us with powerful and well-supported explanatory hypotheses that are real breakthroughs in science. Fundamentally, the Nobel Prize–winning work that Crick and Watson did in developing a double-helix model for the structure of DNA involved drawing upon the results of others and was not derived from new experimentation of their own. Such innovations in science involve acts of creative synthesis, the creative use of models and metaphors, and other generative forms of thinking that are no less parts of scientific thinking than the rigorous reliance on observational evidence to establish the viability of such new ideas.

APPLYING SCIENCE TO SOLVE PROBLEMS

Is this what science is all about, and does this portrayal of scientific thinking capture the essence of this great enterprise? To be sure, science does involve hypothesizing, collecting data, analyzing data, and summarizing results. But this is too narrow a view of science to capture its richness and to explain its achievements. If we think about many of the great scientific advances of recent history, such as the development of space flight, of vaccination against diseases, and of computers, we realize that science, and scientific thinking, is a broader enterprise than just developing an understanding of how the world works.

Let's set the game hen example in a broader context—one in which, obviously, the hen farmers want to keep their hens from dying. Their perception of this as a problem is the overall context in which the described experiment becomes relevant. Information about what is causing the hens to die, once confirmed by the experiment, can then be used to make judgments about how to solve the problem. In fact, most contexts in which such experiments in "pure" science are conducted are contexts that call for careful problem solving and decision making—so-called "applied" science. Here the various types of thinking that are involved in problem solving and decision making must be done well if the problem is to be solved effectively. Problems that require action must be diagnosed and defined, possible solutions generated and their consequences assessed, and the best solution chosen based on this careful assessment. The use of accurate scientific information is crucial in this enterprise as well.

One should not take too lightly the kind of thinking that is needed to effectively solve such problems even after we know what is causing them. For example, knowing that it is the worms that are killing the hens may seem to lead to a simple solution—get rid of the worms. But that may be neither easy nor the best solution. It may be costly to ferret out the worms, and they may keep coming back. Less routine and more creative solutions may be necessary. Maybe moving the hens, or the whole farm, to a noninfested area is a better solution, or maybe something can be put in their feed that will counteract and neutralize the effects of the worms. All of these possibilities have to be explored with the same high standards as those applied to experiments in the laboratory in order to determine the best solution, while fully respecting the need for credible observational data to support judgments of cause and effect when they have to be made.

Let's consider another, better-known example. When it was determined that the distortion in the images sent back to Earth by the Hubble telescope was due to the misgrinding of the reflecting lens in the telescope, one obvious solution to the problem was to replace the lens with one that was ground properly. But that was not the best solution. Rather, the team of scientists working on the project opted for a correcting mechanism that saved millions of dollars and worked just as well, rather like eyeglasses work for people with poor eyesight. The thinking that goes into this kind of problem solving is as much the enterprise of science as the work in the laboratory that yields some of the basic knowledge needed to solve such problems.

A SCIENTIFIC FRAME OF MIND

It is easy to focus attention just on thinking processes and how to do them well when discussing scientific thinking. But being a scientific thinker involves more. Good, persistent scientific practice often involves overall attitudes and mental dispositions toward gaining knowledge about the world as well. If someone investigating possible causes of a plane crash does not accept any of the hypotheses until reliable evidence shows that one of them—and that one only—could have caused the crash, that person is displaying a disposition not to embrace a theory until it has been scientifically proven. Such a commitment to respect the standards of good scientific procedure in gaining knowledge, and to persist until all leads have been exhausted, is crucial to good science.

This presupposes another general attitude that is essential in science: open-mindedness. In solving complex problems in science, it is easy to miss crucial bits of data. Or if not overlooked, new data may come along later that may not confirm what we had accepted earlier. So we may have to change our minds. Good scientific thinking requires that we acknowledge the sometimes humbling fact that we could be wrong even in our most basic scientific beliefs, and that evidence might come along that shows this. Great scientific revolutions are few and far between, but we never know whether one is just around the corner. Open-mindedness respects this possibility.

In the case of the game hens, economics is the obvious motivator for finding out both why the hens died and how best to resolve this problem. Less evident, but just as pertinent to understanding what inspires good science, may be another driving force: a circumspect and probing frame of mind. Something unusual, or even not so unusual but not well understood, happens, and we don't know why. Why, then, did it happen? This is not simply curiosity, but a deeper bent of mind motivated by the desire to understand how things work and why things are the way they are. It is manifested by a person raising seemingly simple questions like "Why did these hens die?" "Why and how does DNA replicate itself?" "Why is the universe expanding?" We know that the answers to such questions are often not simple or easily obtainable. A person who raises such questions and is motivated to seek answers using the best scientific techniques is a person who has the kind of scientific frame of mind that has guided, and at times inspired, the great discoveries in science. These attitudes and commitments have always been as much a part of scientific thinking as the actual procedures used by scientifically minded people. Both a scientific frame of mind and sound scientific practice are essential to expand the body of scientific knowledge.

SCIENCE LITERACY AND SCIENTIFIC THINKING

Do only professional scientists use scientific thinking? Suppose that when we inquire about how we might deal with the poisonous worms we find out there is a well-known and totally effective low-cost remedy that completely counteracts the effects of these worms. Then we may find that our problem can be solved quite simply. Is our thinking still respectable scientific thinking? We believe that even such apparently "lowest common denominator" thinking is still scientific if practiced with the same standards as any other type of thinking we do in science. The scientifically literate person—a person who has a basic understanding of the concepts and ideas of modern science and knows how to get scientific information, how to certify that it is accurate and reliable, and then how to use it to solve problems well—can be engaging in quite respectable scientific problem solving even though he or she may not have and practice the technical and experimental skills of the research scientist.

Likewise, it doesn't take a research chemist to recognize that the laundry detergent "experiments" featured in the well-known "ring around the collar" television commercial are suspect. Two dirty shirts with heavily soiled collars are placed in separate washing machines with the sponsor's product in one and some other brand in the other. After a time lapse, the dirt on the collar of the shirt washed in the sponsor's detergent was gone, while the collar of the shirt washed in the other brand looked unchanged. When people question such an advertisement because they realize that we don't know that variables like the water temperature, amount of detergent, and so forth, have been controlled, they are using good scientific thinking to avoid making an ill-founded inference, even though they may not be research scientists.

TEACHING BASIC SCIENTIFIC KNOWLEDGE AND SCIENTIFIC THINKING

Science education should aim to help students learn to do the kind of thinking needed to solve problems in science. Yet, much of what goes under the name of teaching scientific thinking is very limited. For example, students are often asked to solve problems in science, especially in secondary school. But these are usually very narrowly conceived problems such as calculating the quantities of a certain substance needed to produce a given volume of another substance.

To be sure, science teachers sometimes take students through excursions into "the scientific method." But this is usually restricted to a few occasions when an instructor has students develop some hypotheses to explain things that are presented as mysterious and then test those hypotheses. Often these hypotheses fail the test, and the teacher tells the students what the right explanation is.

Hands-on, "discovery," and inquiry learning in science are also practiced as ways to promote scientific thinking, especially in the elementary grades. These are important instructional techniques, but although they do prompt a sense of wonder, questioning, and exploration of the world around us, they often fall short, *in themselves*, in helping students develop the skills of scientific investigation and the more complex kind of problem solving described earlier.

Teachers who take seriously the model for thinking in science presented here do not restrict themselves to encouraging thinking only in these contexts. Rather, they infuse instruction in the various types of skillful thinking into the standard content instruction in science. The dominant curricular configuration that most teachers of science work within is a standard sequenced-learning approach. This contrasts with a problem-based approach discussed later.

INFUSING THINKING INTO STANDARD SEQUENCED-LEARNING APPROACHES

A sequenced-learning curriculum stresses the study of specific topics that fall within the traditional divisions in science (life sciences, earth sciences, and so forth). Within each of these there is a sequenced study of a standard set of topics (for example, respiration and digestion in life sciences). Usually such a curriculum uses a textbook arranged according to this sequence of topics. Within these studies, basic concepts like the extinction of a species, kinetic energy, heredity, and plate tectonics are introduced, and basic scientific principles governing the application of these concepts—Mendel's laws, for example—are explained.

Teachers who infuse instruction in skillful thinking usually find contexts in which it is natural and appropriate to do these specific kinds of thinking. Thus, for a deep understanding of important phenomena in the world, they may ask students to compare and contrast fruits and cones as reproductive methods in the plant world (in the primary grades), plant cells and animal cells, or RNA and DNA (in middle and high school biology). Teachers may ask students to do a parts/whole analysis of the components of a simple machine such as a screw (elementary grades), a bird of prey such as the American kestrel (middle or high school life sciences or biology), or the systems of the human body (high school biology).

In engaging students in these activities, teachers do not usually just ask questions like "What are the similarities and differences between fruits and cones?" or "What are the parts of an American kestrel?" Rather, they teach thinking strategies. Figures 50.1 and 50.2 present strategies in the form of "thinking strategy maps" for compare/contrast and for parts/whole analysis.

—Figure 50.1—

A Thinking Strategy Map for Compare/Contrast Analysis

1. How are they similar?
2. How are they different?
3. What similarities and differences seem significant?
4. What major categories, patterns, or themes do you see in the significant similarities and differences?
5. What interpretation or conclusion is suggested by the significant similarities and differences?

Adapted from *Infusing the Teaching of Critical and Creative Thinking into Secondary Science: A Lesson Design Handbook,* by R. Swartz, S. D. Fischer, & S. Parks, p. 93. Copyright 1998 by Critical Thinking Books and Software. Adapted with permission.

—Figure 50.2—
A Thinking Strategy Map for
Determining Parts/Whole Relationships

1. What smaller things make up the whole?
2. For each part, what would happen to the whole if it was missing?
3. What is the function of each part?
4. How do the parts work together to make the whole operate the way it does?

Adapted from *Infusing the Teaching of Critical and Creative Thinking into Secondary Science: A Lesson Design Handbook,* by R. Swartz, S. D. Fischer, & S. Parks, p. 168. Copyright 1998 by Critical Thinking Books and Software. Adapted with permission.

After students identify these strategies as ways of engaging in in-depth thinking, teachers then have them reflect metacognitively on their thinking and develop plans for using the same kinds of thinking in other contexts. These teachers introduce such additional activities to give students more practice in the thinking strategies and opportunities to guide themselves in using the strategies. In this sense, such lessons involve the *teaching of thinking,* and not just *teaching for thinking* (Brandt, 1984; Costa, 1985).

Using the same techniques, many teachers also infuse instruction in strategies for more effective creative and critical thinking. So, for example, high school students who study environmental science are asked to brainstorm different ways of reducing the harmful effects of acid rain after reviewing various things that have been done already and the chemistry of acid rain. They learn a strategy that goes beyond simple brainstorming and incorporates techniques for blending ideas to generate original ones. And, indeed, the results are some really original ideas that they never would have thought of had they not used this strategy.

To emphasize critical thinking, some teachers have developed and used lessons on the extinction of dinosaurs in which students attempt to figure out what happened to these creatures. Such lessons do not involve either reviewing the different theories or just guessing about the extinction, but instead teach students an organized strategy in which they develop a number of hypotheses (possible causes) and then have to ascertain what the evidence shows about these different hypotheses. Elementary, middle, and high school versions of this

lesson are available. In each case, students learn the same basic strategy: generate alternative possible causes, figure out what information is needed to support these, and then search for information, asking, when all the evidence is in, what the evidence shows—does it render the hypothesis likely, unlikely, or uncertain? This activity teaches an important lesson: the realization that although some evidence exists for some of the hypotheses, there isn't enough evidence yet to establish any of them as the likely cause (Swartz & Parks, 1994; Swartz, Fischer, & Parks, 1998).

Similar lessons that instruct students in strategies for skillful causal explanation have been taught on why a specific electrical failure occurred (elementary school science), or why there was a breakdown in the production of sulfuric acid at a sulfuric acid processing plant (high school chemistry). In these lessons, students follow the same strategy and are able to support their judgments about the causes of these events with supporting reasons and evidence that they have gathered (see Figure 50.3).

Teachers who infuse instruction in thinking skills into their science content teaching instruct students in another important critical thinking skill, which has to do with the reliability and accuracy of sources of information, including both secondary sources and observation itself. Students identify factors to take into account (such as expertise, possible bias, use of adequate investigative techniques, and corroboration) and develop these into a checklist that they use to judge the reliabil-

—Figure 50.3—
A Thinking Strategy Map
for Skillful Causal Explanation

1. What are possible causes of the event in question?
2. What could you find that would count for or against the likelihood of these possibilities?
3. What evidence do you already have, or have you gathered, that is relevant to determining what caused the event?
4. Which possibility is rendered most likely, based on the evidence?

Adapted from *Infusing the Teaching of Critical and Creative Thinking into Secondary Science: A Lesson Design Handbook,* by R. Swartz, S. D. Fischer, & S. Parks, p. 359. Copyright 1998 by Critical Thinking Books and Software. Adapted with permission.

ity of sources—including their textbooks. In the case of direct observation, they add such factors as attention and the use of observation-enhancing instruments. They use the checklists to judge whether the information they get from a source is likely or unlikely to be accurate, or its accuracy is uncertain. One such elementary school lesson involves judging the likely accuracy of information in a *National Geographic* article about strange creatures discovered at the bottom of the ocean. The students investigate the characteristics of the submersible vehicle (the *Alvin*) used to gather the information as well as the reputation of the magazine and the credentials of the researchers. They can then explain why they think this information is accurate. A similar middle/high school lesson focuses on the reports of Percival Lowell, an astronomer and the discoverer of the planet Pluto, that he saw canals on the surface of the planet Mars (Swartz, Fischer, & Parks, 1998).

Teachers often help students combine many of these thinking skills in making decisions and solving problems. For example, one lesson that has been adapted and taught at the elementary, middle, and high school levels puts students in the position of decision makers trying to make well-founded judgments about which source of energy ought to be dominant over the next 25 years. They learn and use a strategy for decision making like the one already discussed, in which they brainstorm to generate options, investigate the consequences of those options by gathering reliable and accurate data, and compare and contrast the options in terms of their consequences. They then have to defend their views with reference to the projected consequences they have come up with. And, of course, they have to make sure that it is likely that the information they are using is accurate and reliable.

PROBLEM-BASED LEARNING IN SCIENCE CLASSROOMS

In problem-based curricula, the standard sequenced-learning approach is abandoned, textbooks are used only as reference material along with other sources, and the curriculum is built around a series of authentic problems for which the students must develop solutions. Constructing a whole curriculum around problems is difficult, and we know of no examples of such exclusively problem-based instruction for K–12 schools. However, this approach has been used extensively in medical schools, where it was first developed. Figure 50.4 sketches out the basic contrast between the two approaches to curriculum (Swartz, 1999).

Some limited problem-based units have been developed in secondary science education. For example, in one high school a physics teacher and a math teacher together developed a problem-based unit on sound. The problem revolved around the fact that people were continually complaining about the noise in the school cafeteria, and the students were to imagine that they had been hired to solve this problem. Similarly, in a middle school unit on minerals, light, and sound, students were asked to simulate having to survive in a cave for a certain period of time. The students were given information about the cave and had to develop plans supported by good data (Swartz, 1999).

One idea behind problem-based learning is that rich problems can lead students into learning everything they would have learned using a sequenced-learning approach—and more—in the same amount of time. The teachers who developed the high school unit on sound reported some success in students matching if not exceeding content-understanding levels compared with students who learned these basic concepts and ideas in more traditional ways.

At the same time, such problem-based units contain opportunities to teach students strategies for thinking through and trying to solve a problem using infusion as a technique. Such instruction can, in fact, be articulated so that it emphasizes the important subskills of skillful problem solving as the unit progresses, like skillfully comparing and contrasting, predicting consequences, and determining the reliability of sources of information.

SUMMARY AND CONCLUSION

Science is not merely a body of information; it is a human enterprise that requires careful thought in the form of creative, critical, and analytical thinking, and that usually links these types of thinking in complex problem-solving situations. It incorporates standards of judgment that depend on publicly observable data that rule out competing hypotheses and provide adequate support for accepted ideas. The creative development of those ideas is as crucial in the advancement of science as the use of the standards is in critically judging their acceptability. And, of course, all of this operates on a body of knowledge that represents the accumulated results of previous work that should be drawn upon. But this body of "knowledge" should be approached with an open-mindedness that recognizes that future discoveries may lead to revisions.

All of this—not just the base of scientific knowledge—should be taught in the name of science. Yet there is an imbalance in science teaching that allots far more time to teaching the body of knowledge than to teaching the kinds of skillful thinking needed to accumulate it, certify it, accumulate more of it, and, finally, use it in solving problems.

—Figure 50.4—
Two Models for the Delivery of the Science Curriculum

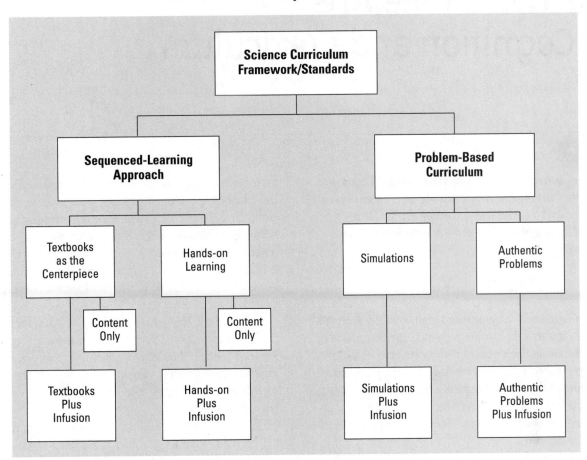

Just giving students narrow, well-defined, quantitative "problems" to solve in science classes is not enough; nor is adding on instruction in which students occasionally are asked to develop and test hypotheses in the name of the scientific method. Rather, educators must teach the full range of types of skillful thinking needed to engage in this enterprise. The best way to do this is by infusing such instruction into standard content teaching in science.

Infusion can be accomplished working within a standard sequenced-learning curriculum or within the more radical approach of problem-based learning projects. But in either case, it works best if it incorporates instructional techniques that make strategies for skillful thinking explicit, guide students through the use of these strategies, bring them to a metacognitive awareness and evaluation of the strategies' effectiveness, and engage them in more practices in which they guide themselves in using the strategies. Then, we believe, science education will be doing its students the greatest service it can—

aiming to make them scientific thinkers in the fullest and richest sense.

REFERENCES

Brandt, R. (1984). Teaching of thinking, for thinking, about thinking. *Educational Leadership, 42*(1), 3.

Costa, A. (1985). Teaching for, of, and about thinking. In A. Costa (Ed.), *Developing Minds.* Alexandria, VA: Association for Supervision and Curriculum Development.

Swartz, R. (1999). Teaching science literacy through problem-based learning and critical thinking. In A. Costa & R. Liebmann (Eds.), *Supporting the spirit of learning: When process is content* (pp. 117–141). Thousand Oaks, CA: Corwin Press.

Swartz, R., Fischer, S. D., & Parks, S. (1998). *Infusing the teaching of critical and creative thinking into secondary science: A lesson design handbook.* Pacific Grove, CA: Critical Thinking Books and Software.

Swartz, R., & Parks, S. (1994). *Infusing the teaching of critical and creative thinking into content instruction: A lesson design handbook for the elementary grades.* Pacific Grove, CA: Critical Thinking Press and Software.

51

The Role of the Arts in Cognition and Curriculum

ELLIOT W. EISNER

Must we always teach our children with books? Let them look at the stars and the mountains above. Let them look at the waters and the trees and flowers on Earth. Then they will begin to think, and to think is the beginning of a real education.

—David Polis

My thesis is straightforward but not widely accepted. It is that the arts are cognitive activities, guided by human intelligence, that make unique forms of meaning possible. I shall argue further that the meanings secured through the arts require what might best be described as forms of artistic literacy, without which artistic meaning is impeded and the ability to use more conventional forms of expression is hampered.

To talk about the cognitive character of the arts or about the kind of meaning that they convey is not particularly common. The models of mind that have typified U.S. educational psychology (particularly that aspect of psychology concerned with learning and knowing) have made tidy separations between thinking and feeling, feeling and acting, and acting and thinking![1] The view of thinking that has been most common is rooted in the Platonic belief that mind and body are distinct, and, of the two, body is base while mind, lofty.[2] Feeling is located in soma, idea in psyche. The literature distinguishes between cognition and affect, and we tend to regard as cognitive those activities of mind that mediate ideas through words and numbers. We consider words more abstract than images, icons less flexible than propositions. We regard words as high in that hierarchy of cognitive achievement we use to describe cognitive growth. Jean Piaget, for example, regarded

formal operations, those mental operations that deal with logical relationships, as the apotheosis of cognitive achievement (Inhelder & Piaget, 1958). For some cognitive psychologists, thinking is a kind of inner speech that allows one to reason.[3] Since reason is a condition of rationality, and since reasoning is believed to require the logical treatment of words, operations of the mind that do not employ logic are placed on the margins of rationality.

In this view, the arts, if not considered irrational, are thought of as a-rational. As for meaning, it is most commonly regarded as an attribute of propositions, the property of assertions for which scientific warrant can be secured. The arts are considered emotive forms that might provide satisfaction—but not understanding.

The consequences of this view of mind have, in my opinion, been disastrous for education. First, this view has created a dubious status hierarchy among subjects taught in schools. Mathematics is the queen of the hill; other subjects, especially those in which students "work with their hands," are assigned lower intellectual status. Simply recall the standard whipping boy at school activities, basket weaving. Basket weaving epitomizes low status and mindlessness. Let me state quickly that I reject mindless forms of basket weaving in school. But let me add just as quickly that I also reject mindless forms of algebra and that I find nothing inherently more intellectually complex in algebra than in basket weaving; it depends upon the nature of the algebra and the nature of baskets we choose to weave.

Besides making some subjects the targets of verbal abuse, the status hierarchy among subjects that emanates from such an indefensible conception of mind has practical day-to-day consequences in schools. Consider how time is allocated in school programs. Time is surely one of the most precious of school resources. As researchers of time on task have told us (Rosenshine, 1976), the relationship between the amount of time allocated and learning is a significant one. Partly because of our view of intellect, however, some subjects—the fine arts,

This chapter is adapted from *Developing Minds: A Resource Book for Teaching Thinking* (Rev. ed.), 1991.

for example—receive very little attention in school programs. On the average, elementary school teachers devote about four percent of school time each week to instruction in the fine arts.[4] And this time is not prime time, such as the so-called cognitive subjects command. For the fine arts, Friday afternoons are very popular.

Space does not permit a lengthy recital of sins that have been committed by schools in the name of cognitive development. Yet it is important to remember that the conception of giftedness used in many states excludes ability in the fine arts, that tax dollars support programs whose criteria discriminate against students whose gifts are in the fine arts, and that many colleges and universities do not consider high school grades in the fine arts when making admissions decisions.[5] We legitimate such practices by distinguishing between intelligence and talent, assigning the former to verbal and mathematical forms of reasoning and the latter to performance in activities we deem more concrete: playing a musical instrument, dancing, painting.

I could elaborate at length on each of these points. But I mention them simply to highlight the model of mind that has been so widely accepted and to provide a context for my remarks concerning the role of the arts in cognition and curriculum.

If you were to consult *The Dictionary of Psychology* (1934) regarding the meaning of cognition, you would find that cognition is "the process through which the organism becomes aware of the environment." Thus, cognition is a process that makes awareness possible. It is, in this sense, a matter of becoming conscious, of noticing, of recognizing, of perceiving. It is a matter of distinguishing one thing from another: a figure from its ground, the various subtleties and nuances that, when perceived, become a part of one's consciousness.

In this process, the functions of the senses are crucial. They bring to awareness the qualitative world we inhabit. To become aware of the world, two conditions must be satisfied. First, the qualities must be available for experiencing by a sentient human being. Second, the individual must be able to "read" their presence. When both of these conditions are met, the human being is capable of forming concepts of the world. These concepts take shape in the information that the senses have provided.

The process of forming concepts is one of construing general features from qualitative particulars. The perception of the qualitative world is always fragmented: We never see a particular immediately, in an instant. Time is always involved.[6] General configurations are formed—that is, differentiated from wholes to parts. Through time this process yields structured patterns that constitute a set. The patterns formed in

this way are concepts. They are root forms of experience that we are able to recall and to manipulate imaginatively.

The importance of the senses in concept formation is that (1) no concepts can be formed without sensory information,[7] (2) the degree to which the particular senses are differentiated has a large effect on the kind and subtlety of the concepts that are formed, and (3) without concepts formed as images (whether these images are visual, auditory, or in some other sensory form), image surrogates—words, for example—are meaningless.[8]

It is easy to see how such concrete concepts as dog or chair, red or blue, depend upon sensory information. But what about such abstract concepts as justice, category, nation, infinity? I would argue that these words are nothing more than meaningless noises or marks on paper unless their referents can be imagined. Unless we have a conception of justice, the word is empty. Unless we can imagine infinity, the term is nothing more than a few decibels of sound moving through space. I do not mean to imply that we conjure up an image every time we hear a word. Our automatic response mechanisms make this unnecessary. But when I say "the man was a feckless mountebank," the statement will have meaning only if you have referents for "feckless" and "mountebank." If you do not, then you turn to a friend or a dictionary for other words whose images allow you to create an analogy. It is through such analogies or through illustrative examples that so-called abstract concepts take on meaning. Concepts, in this view, are not linguistic at base; instead, they are sensory. The forms concepts take are as diverse as our sensory capacities and the abilities we have developed to use them.

The process of concept formation is of particular importance in the development of scientific theory. In the social sciences, for example, theoreticians form concepts by construing social situations in ways that others have not noticed. Terms such as class, social structure, adaptation, role, status, and reinforcement are meaningful because they bracket aspects of the social world for us to experience.[9] They call to our attention qualities of the world that otherwise would have gone unseen. But the reality is in the flesh and blood of experience, not simply in the words. Put another way, there is an icon—a stylized image of reality—underlying any term that is meaningful. The makers of such icons are people we regard as perceptive or insightful. Indeed, the Latin root of "intuition" is *intueri*, meaning to look upon, to see. In the beginning there was the image, not the word.

One important characteristic of concepts is that they can be not only recalled, but imaginatively manipulated. We can combine qualities we have encountered to form entities that never were, but that might become: hence unicorns, helixes, ideals of perfection toward which we strive, and new tunes to whistle. We can construct models of the world from which we can derive verbal or numerical propositions or from which we can create visual or auditory images. The point is that, while the sensory system provides us with information about the world in sensory form, our imaginative capacities—when coupled with an inclination toward play—allow us to examine and explore the possibilities of this information.[10] Although our imaginative lives might be played out in solitary fantasy or daydreaming, imagination often provides the springboard for expression. How is experience expressed? What vehicles are used? What skills are employed? And what do the arts have to do with it? It is to that side of the cognitive coin that I now turn.

Thus far I have emphasized the cognitive function of the sensory systems, and I have pointed out that concepts formed from sensory information can be recalled and manipulated through imagination. But thus far, this manipulation of concepts has been private, something occurring within the personal experience of individuals. The other side of the coin deals with the problem of externalization. In some way, an individual must acquire and employ a form that can represent to self and to others what has been conceptualized. This task requires what I call a form of representation.[11] The problem of representing conceptions is a problem of finding or inventing equivalents for those conceptions. In this task, the form or forms to be employed must themselves appeal to one or more of the senses. A visual concept, for example, might be externalized in a form that is visual, or the form might instead be auditory, verbal, or both. Thus, for example, we could represent an imaginary stream of rolling and flowing blue amoebic shapes either visually or through sound. The stream might be described through words, or it might be represented through movement—perhaps dance. Regardless of the form we select, it must be one that the sensory systems can pick up. Put another way, the form must be empirical.

The kind of information that we are able to convey about what we have conceptualized is both constrained and made possible by the forms of representation that we have access to and are able to use. Some of the things an individual knows are better represented by some forms than others. What one can convey about a river that slowly winds its way to the sea will be significantly influenced by the form of representation one chooses to use. The same holds true for portrayals of classrooms, teaching, love affairs, and memorable cities one has visited.

Consider suspense. Almost all of us are able to invent a way of conveying suspense through music. From old cowboy movies and mystery dramas on radio and television, we already have a repertoire of models to draw upon. But think about how suspense would be represented through painting or sculpture. Here the problem becomes much more difficult. Why? Because suspense is a temporal experience, and painting and sculpture are largely spatial. It is more difficult to use the latter to represent the former than to use music, which itself is temporal.

Some forms of representation can illuminate some aspects of the world that others cannot. What a person can learn about the world through visual form is not likely to be provided through auditory form. What an individual knows takes shape in the empirical world only through a vehicle or vehicles that make knowing public. The vehicles we use for this purpose are the forms of representation.

Although I have described the externalization of concepts as one-directional—that is, as moving from inside out—the process is actually reciprocal. For example, what a person knows how to do affects what he or she conceptualizes. If you walk around the world with black and white film in your camera, you look for contrasts of light and dark, for texture, for patterns of shadow against buildings and walls. As Ernst Gombrich (1969) put it, "Artists don't paint what they can see, they see what they can paint." The ability to use a form of representation skillfully guides our perception. The process flows, as it were, from representation to conception as well as from conception to representation.

Dialectical relationships between conception and representation occur in other ways as well. For example, the externalization of a conception through a form of representation allows the editing process to occur. By stabilizing what is evanescent, the conception can be modified, abbreviated, sharpened, revised, or discarded altogether. Further, in the process of representation new concepts are formed. Indeed, the act of discovery through expression is so important that R. G. Collingwood (1958) describes its presence as the difference between art and craft. The craftsman knows how to do a job well, but produces nothing essentially new. The artist not only has the skills of the craftsman, but discovers new possibilities as work progresses. The work of art is to make expressive form become a source of surprise, a discovery, a form that embodies a conception not held at the outset.

The selection of a form of representation does not adequately resolve the question of how that form, once selected, becomes "equivalent" to the conception. I suggest that we secure equivalence by treating forms of representation in one of three ways. The first of these modes of treatment is mimetic, the second is expressive, and the third is conventional.

Mimetic modes of treatment are efforts to imitate the surface features of perceived or conceptualized forms, within the constraints of some material. Early examples of mimesis are the running animals found on the walls of the Lascaux Caves. According to Gombrich (1969), the history of art is replete with efforts to create illusions that imitate the visual features of the environment as it was or as it was imagined. But mimesis as a way of treating a form of representation is not limited to what is visual. Mimesis occurs in auditory forms of representation, such as music and voice, and in movement through dance. Mimesis is possible in any of the forms used to provide information that the senses can pick up.

As I have already said, the creation of an equivalent for a conception is always both constrained and made possible by the medium a person employs. Different media appeal to different sensory systems. Thus, when a person transforms visual conceptions into sound or movement, he or she must find what Rudolf Arnheim (1954) calls the "structural equivalent" of the conception within the medium he or she elects to use. Such transformation requires the invention of analogies.

In language, analogic functions are performed by metaphor. When we move from the auditory to the visual, however, we must create a structural equivalent between the auditory and the visual. For example, the sounds "ooo loo loo" and "eee pee pee" are represented best by two very different kinds of graphic lines—one waving, the other pointed or jagged. Humans have the capacity to perceive and grasp these structural equivalences even when they take shape in different forms of representation—one visual, the other auditory. Thus, mimesis, the business of imitating the surface features of a conceptualization within the limits of some medium, is one way to secure equivalence between a conception and its forms of representation.

The second way to do this is by treating the forms expressively. By expressively, I mean that what is conveyed is what the object, event, or conception expresses—not what it looks like. Thus, "sorrow" can be represented mimetically, but it can also be represented expressively. In the arts, this expressive mode of treatment is of particular interest: the tense nervousness of Velasquez's Pope Innocent X, the celebration of color in a Sam Francis, the asceticism of a late Barnett Newman, the ethereal quality of Helen Frankenthaler's work, the symbolic undertones of an Edward Hopper, the crisp architecture of Bach's fugues, the romantic expansiveness of Beethoven's Seventh Symphony, the lighthearted whimsy of the poetry of e.e. cummings. What these artists have created are expressive images. In general, mimesis is a minor element in their works, used only to complement the dominant intent. Pablo Picasso succinctly stated the importance of the expressive mode of treatment in art when he said, "A painter takes the sun and makes it into a yellow spot, an artist takes a yellow spot and makes it into the sun."

By contrast, the conventional mode of treatment uses an arbitrary sign, on whose meaning society has agreed, to convey that meaning. Thus words and numbers are meaningful, not because they look like their referents, but because we have agreed that they shall stand for them. The use of convention is, of course, not limited to words and numbers. Swastikas, crosses, six-pointed stars, the iconography of cultures past and present are all examples of visual conventions. Conventions in music take such forms as anthems, wedding marches, and graduation processionals.

In much of art the three modes of treatment are combined. Erwin Panofsky (1955) made his major contribution to the history of art—to the study of iconography—by describing these relationships. The works of Jasper Johns, Marc Chagall, Joseph Cornell, Jack Levine, Robert Rauschenberg, and Andy Warhol demonstrate the ingenious ways in which visual artists have exploited all three modes of treatment in their effort to convey meaning.

I hope that I have made my point clear: Any form of representation one chooses to use—visual, auditory, or discursive—must also be treated in some way. Some forms tend to call forth one particular mode of treatment. The treatment of mathematics, for example, is essentially conventional, even though we may recognize its aesthetic qualities. The visual arts, by contrast, tend to emphasize the mimetic and the expressive. Language tends to be treated conventionally and expressively (save for occasional instances of onomatopoeia, which are obviously mimetic). The forms we choose provide potential options. The options we choose give us opportunities to convey what we know and what we are likely to experience.

Just as any form of representation we elect to use must be treated in a particular way, the elements within that form must also be related to each other. This relationship constitutes a syntax, an arrangement of parts used to construct a whole. Some forms of representation, such as mathematics and propositional discourse, are governed rather rigorously by publicly codified rules, through which the operations applied to such forms are to be performed. To be able to add, one must be able to apply correctly a set of prescribed operations to a set of numerical elements. To be able to punctuate, one must follow certain publicly articulated rules so that the marks placed within a sentence or paragraph are correct. Similarly, in spelling, rules govern the arrangements of elements (letters) that constitute words. There are only two ways to spell most words in English: correctly or incorrectly. Forms of representation that are treated through convention tend to emphasize the rule-governed end of the syntactical continuum. When forms are treated in this way, the scoring of performance can be handled by machines, because the need for judgment is small.

Forms of representation that are treated expressively have no comparable rules. There are, of course, rules of a sort to guide one in making a painting of a particular style or designing a building of a particular architectural period. But the quality of performance in such forms is not determined by measuring the extent to which the rules are followed (as is done for spelling and arithmetic). Instead, quality is judged by other criteria—in some cases, criteria that don't even exist prior to the creation of the work. Syntactical forms that are open rather than closed, that allow for the idiosyncratic creation of relationships without being regarded as incorrect, are figurative in character. Thus, it is possible to array forms of representation not only with respect to their modes of treatment, but in relation to the ends of the syntactical continuum toward which they lean. In general, the arts lean toward the figurative. That is why, given the same task, 30 students in music, poetry, or visual art will create 30 different solutions, all of which can be "right," while 30 students in arithmetic will—if the teacher has taught effectively—come up with identical solutions. That is also why the arts are regarded as subjective: One cannot apply a conventionally defined set of rules to determine whether the meanings that are conveyed are accurate. Idiosyncratic arrangements are encouraged when figurative syntaxes are employed.

The importance of this distinction between rule-governed and figurative syntactical emphases becomes apparent when we consider the kinds of cognitive processes that each type of syntax elicits. Learning of rules fosters acquiescence: One learns to obey a rule or to follow it. Figurative syntaxes, by contrast, encourage invention, personal choice, exploratory activity, and judgment. The use of forms whose syntax is figurative is an uncertain enterprise since there are no formally codified rules to guide judgments. The student, like the artist, is thrown on his or her own resources. How does one know when the painting is finished, the poem completed, the story ended? There is no predefined standard by which to check a solution. There is no correct answer given in the back of the book, no procedure for determining proof. The necessary cognitive op-

erations are what were known, in earlier psychological jargon, as "higher mental processes." At the least, tasks that emphasize the figurative give people opportunities to form new structures, to make speculative decisions, and to act upon them. Such tasks also enable people to learn to judge—not by applying clear-cut standards, but by appealing to a form of rationality that focuses on the rightness of a form to a function.

It would be well at this point to recall the theme of this article, the role of the arts in cognition and curriculum. I began by describing a commonly held view: Cognition requires that ideas be linguistically mediated, whereas the arts are expressive and affective activities depending more upon talent than intelligence or cognition. I next analyzed the role of the senses in concept formation, arguing that all concepts are basically sensory in character and that concept formation requires the ability to perceive qualitative nuances in the qualitative world and to abstract their structural features for purposes of recall or imaginative manipulation. From there I moved to a discussion of the task of representation. An individual who wishes to externalize a concept must find some way of constructing an equivalent for it in the empirical world. To do this, people invent new forms of representation or borrow from those already available in the culture. Because these forms can be treated in different ways and because they appeal to different sensory systems, the kind of meanings each yields is unique. What we can convey in one form of representation has no literal equivalent in another. I have labeled the modes of treating these forms as mimetic, expressive, and conventional. Because the elements within forms of representation can be ordered according to different rules, I have identified a syntactical continuum, highly rule-governed at one end and figurative at the other. The rule-governed end of the continuum prescribes the rules of operations that must, by convention, be followed in ordering these elements. The figurative end allows maximum degrees of latitude for idiosyncratic arrangement. The former is more of a code; the latter, more of a metaphor.

But what is the significance of such analysis for education? What bearing does it have on what we do in school? What might it mean for what we teach? There are four implications, I believe, for the conduct of education and for education theory.

First, the view that I have advanced makes it impossible to regard as cognitive any mental activity that is not itself rooted in sensory forms of life. This expands our conceptions of intelligence and literacy. Any conception of intelligence that omits the ordering of qualities through direct experience is neglecting a central feature of intellectual functioning. But no intelligence test that is published today includes such tasks. The models of mind that underlie current tests assign only marginal intellectual status to what is an intellectual activity. One no more plays the violin with one's fingers than one counts with his toes. In each case, mind must operate, and the kind and number of opportunities a person is given to learn will significantly affect the degree to which his or her ability develops. The concepts of talent and lack of talent have been used too long to cover up weak or nonexistent programs in the arts. To be sure, individual aptitudes in the arts vary, but such differences also exist in other content areas. So-called lack of talent is too often nothing more than an excuse for absent opportunity. It also serves as a self-fulfilling prophecy.

Second, the view that I have advanced recognizes that the realm of meaning has many mansions. Science, for example, despite its enormous usefulness, can never have a monopoly on meaning because the form of representation it employs is only one among the several that are available. It is not possible to represent or to know everything in one form. The way Willy Loman conveys his inability to cope with a sinking career can only be represented through the expressive treatment of form that Arthur Miller employed in Death of a Salesman. The quality of space in the paintings of Giorgio de Chirico or Hans Hofmann depends on the artists' arrangements of visual images; it cannot be rendered through number. When Dylan Thomas (1953) wrote, "Do not go gentle into that good night/ Old age should burn and rave at close of day;/Rage, rage against the dying of the light," he conveyed a message about being in the anteroom of death that cannot be translated fully, even in propositional prose.

What this means for education is that—insofar as we in schools, colleges, and universities are interested in providing the conditions that enable students to secure deep and diverse forms of meaning in their lives—we cannot in good conscience omit the fine arts. Insofar as we seek to develop the skills for securing such meanings, we must develop multiple forms of literacy. Such meanings do not accrue to the unprepared mind. The task of the schools is to provide the conditions that foster the development of such literacy. At present, for the vast majority of students, the schools fail in this task.

Third, educational equity is one consequence for students of the change in education policy that my arguments suggest. As I have already pointed out, the benefits derived from excellence in differing forms of representation are not equal. Students who perform at outstanding levels in the fine arts do not have these grades taken into account when they apply for admission to colleges and universities. The beneficiaries of the funds allocated to education for the gifted often do not include students whose gifts are in the fine arts.[12] The amount of school time devoted to cultivating abilities in the arts is extremely limited; hence, students with abilities and interests in the arts are denied the opportunities that students in science, mathematics, or English receive.

Such policies and practices amount to a form of educational inequity. This inequity would cease if the arguments I have presented were used as grounds for decisions about the allocation of school time, about the criteria used to identify gifted students, and about the aptitudes suitable for college and university study. It is an anomaly of the first order that a university should confer credit in the fine arts for courses taken on its own campus and deny credits to students who have taken such courses in high schools. At present, that's the way it is.

Finally, the view I have presented implies that the cultivation of literacy in, for example, visual and auditory forms of representation can significantly improve a student's ability to use propositional forms of representation. The ability to create or understand sociology, psychology, or economics depends on the ability to perceive qualitative nuances in the social world, the ability to conceptualize patterns from which to share what has been experienced, and the ability to write about them in a form that is compelling. Without such perceptivity, the content of writing will be shallow. Without the ability to manipulate conceptions of the world imaginatively, the work is likely to be uninspired. Without an ear for the melody, cadence, and tempo of language, the tale is likely to be unconvincing. Education in the arts cultivates sensitive perception, develops insight, fosters imagination, and places a premium on well-crafted form.

These skills and dispositions are of central importance in both writing and reading. Without them, children are unlikely to write—not because they cannot spell, but because they have nothing to say. The writer starts with vision and ends with words. The reader begins with these words, but ends with vision. The reader uses the writer's words in order to see.

The interaction of the senses enriches meaning. The arts are not mere diversions from the important business of education; they are essential resources.

NOTES

[1]These distinctions are reified most clearly in the customary separation between the cognitive and the affective domains, which are typically discussed as if they were independent entities or processes.

[2]See especially Plato. (1951). *The republic* (F. M. Cornford, Trans.). New York: Oxford University Press.

[3]See for example, Schaff, A. (1973). *Language and cognition.* New York: McGraw-Hill.

[4]If an elementary teacher provides one hour of instruction in art and one hour of instruction in music each week, the percentage of instructional time devoted to both is about 7 percent. Many teachers provide less time than this.

[5]The University of California, like many other state universities, provides no credit for grades received in the fine arts when computing grade-point averages for students seeking admission.

[6]The acquisition of visual information over time is a function of micromovements of the eye and brain called *saccades.*

[7]Insofar as something is conceivable, it must, by definition, be a part of human experience. Experience without sensory content is an impossibility.

[8]The view argues that the reception and organization of sensory material require the use of intelligence. Intelligence is not something that one applies after experiencing the empirical world. Rather, it is a central factor in the process of experience.

[9]See Weitz, M. (1956, September). The role of theory in aesthetics. *Journal of Aesthetics and Art Criticism.*

[10]In a sense, play is the ability to suspend rules in order to explore new arrangements. See Sutton-Smith, B. (Ed.). (1979). *Play and learning.* New York: Halsted Press.

[11]This concept is elaborated in greater detail in Eisner, E. W. (1985). *Cognition and curriculum: a basis for deciding what to teach.* New York: Longman.

[12]Until a few years ago, the Mentally Gifted Minor Program (MGM) in California—now Gifted and Talented Education (GTE)—did not include students who were gifted in the fine arts.

REFERENCES

Arnheim, R. (1954). *Art and visual perception.* Berkeley: University of California Press.

Collingwood, R. G. (1958). *Principles of art.* Oxford: Oxford University Press.

Gombrich, E. H. (1969). Visual discovery through art. In J. Hogg (Ed.), *Psychology and the visual arts.* Middlesex, England: Penguin Books.

Inhelder, B., & Piaget, J. (1958). *The growth of cognitive thinking from childhood to adolescence* (A. Parsons & S. Milgram, Trans.). New York: Basic Books.

Panofsky, E. (1955). *Meaning in the visual arts: Papers in and on art history.* Garden City, New York: Doubleday.

Rosenshine, B. (1976). Classroom instruction. In N. L. Gage (Ed.), *Psychology of teaching: 75th yearbook of the National Society for the Study of Education* (Part 1, pp. 335–371). Chicago: University of Chicago Press.

Thomas, D. (1953). Do not go gentle into that good night. *The collected poems of Dylan Thomas.* New York: New Directions.

Warren, H. C. (Ed.). (1934). *The dictionary of psychology.* Cambridge: Riverside Press.

52

Infusing Thinking in History and the Social Sciences

BARRY K. BEYER

At first glance, the title of this chapter may prompt the question—Infusing thinking in history and the social sciences? Isn't thinking already infused in these disciplines? Each of these disciplines is distinguished by a mode of thinking (Bruner, 1963; Bruner, Goodnow, & Austin, 1956; Phenix, 1964; Schwab, 1962). The bodies of knowledge that constitute each of these disciplines have been and continue to be produced by this way of thinking and the cognitive skills by which it is put into operation. One simply cannot understand or contribute anything to history, anthropology, economics, geography, political science, or sociology without applying continuously these cognitive skills—skills that range from simple recall to more complex and rigorous reasoning, critical evaluation, inference making, and other higher-order thinking operations (Gardner, 1999; Perkins, 1992; Resnick & Klopfer, 1989).

Infuse thinking into these disciplines? It's already there! That's the good news.

But there's bad news, too. The higher-order thinking that is so embedded in history and the social science disciplines seems to be missing from many of the elementary and secondary school courses derived from these disciplines (Cornbleth & Korth, 1981; Newmann, 1990). Yet, such thinking is required if students in these courses are to develop the understandings that many teachers seek and that current history, geography, and social studies standards and state learning standards call for. Infusing this thinking into these courses is what we really need to be concerned about. And, to accomplish this, we first must be clear about the kinds of thinking that are so much a part of their parent disciplines.

Two dimensions of thinking are embedded in history and the social sciences. One consists of the cognitive operations—commonly called skills and strategies—employed when learning about or doing any research in these disciplines. The second consists of dispositions that support and drive the application of these thinking processes.

CORE THINKING SKILLS AND STRATEGIES

Four types of thinking skills and strategies lie at the heart of history and the social sciences. Figure 52.1 lists the most significant of these core thinking skills and their major components. The cognitive skills and strategies presented in this figure are closely related to each other and deeply embedded in the knowledge claims generated by their application. The way problems are defined—and not defined; the ways in which information is collected, assessed, and analyzed—or left uncollected, poorly assessed, and sloppily analyzed; and the skilled—or unskilled—way that reasoning is applied affect considerably the substance of these disciplines.

PROBLEM SOLVING

Although each of the social science disciplines and history focus on a different aspect of the human condition, all share a common mode of thinking: problem solving. This cognitive strategy frames both learning and scholarly inquiry in these disciplines and provides a framework for the application of the other core thinking operations.

Figure 52.1 presents the four major steps in a general problem solving strategy as described by Gyorgy Polya (1945/1973), an internationally recognized expert in problem solving. In carrying out this strategy, historians and social scientists first become aware of a problem and narrow it down to make it as precise as possible (Step 1). Their problems commonly emerge from a wish or need to know more about an issue or topic, from discrepancies in information or in multiple accounts of the same thing, from questions of interest to their disciplines, from the analytical concepts that de-

Copyright © 2001 by Barry K. Beyer

—*Figure 52.1*—
History and Social Science Core Thinking Skills

Problem Solving

- Step 1: Defining the problem
- Step 2: Selecting or devising a solution strategy
- Step 3: Carrying out the strategy
- Step 4: Evaluating the solution and solution strategy

Solution Strategies*

- Analyzing sources
- Decision making
- Hypothesis making and testing
- Conducting a survey
- Conceptualizing
- Conducting an experiment
- Making a controlled observation
- Constructing an argument

Critical Thinking Skills**

- Distinguishing relevant from irrelevant
- Distinguishing verifiable facts from (reasoned) opinions and value claims

- Judging the factual accuracy of a claim
- Detecting bias
- Judging the credibility of a source
- Identifying unstated assumptions
- Identifying ambiguous claims or arguments
- Identifying logical fallacies
- Recognizing logical inconsistencies in a line of reasoning
- Determining the strength of an argument

Information Processing and Reasoning Skills

- Recall
- Translation
- Interpretation
- Extrapolation
- Application
- Analysis
- Synthesis
- Evaluation
- Reasoning: deductive and inductive

* Adapted from Beyer, 1997, and Marzano, 1991.
** Adapted from Ennis, 1962.

fine their disciplines, or from just plain curiosity. These problems may also be procedural in nature, such as whether or not a particular source is credible or accurate. This initial step also includes identifying the type of problem selected for investigation.

Historians and social scientists then adopt or adapt a plan or strategy for solving the type of problem identified or collecting the kind of information required to solve the problem (Step 2). In carrying out this solution strategy (Step 3), they monitor carefully what they are doing to ensure that they follow the strategy, identify and respond to unanticipated obstacles, and revise the strategy as necessary to solve the problem or answer the question on which they are working. Upon arriving at what they believe to be a defensible answer, conclusion, or solution, they then evaluate it for accuracy and thoroughness (Step 4). They also evaluate the efficacy of the solution strategy they used. Solution strategies that worked well are usually stored in memory for solving similar future problems; flawed solution strategies are revised or discarded. Solutions that pass this final evaluation are published—either formally or informally—and circulated. Solutions that fail require revision or a return to more problem solving, using perhaps a more precisely defined statement of the problem, a new

solution strategy, additional or more accurate information and analysis, and so on.

Like most complex cognitive strategies, this problem-solving strategy is not linear but recursive. Problems often get redefined, unanticipated information is uncovered, and new solution plans are adopted in the process of working out a solution. Moreover, there are variations on this process, most of which either elaborate one or more of the four steps, add additional steps, or incorporate solution strategies for only very specific types of problems (see, for example, Chapter 10 by Jack Lochhead and Aletta Zietsman and Chapter 71 by Robert Sternberg in this book, and the sources cited in Figure 52.4).

SOLUTION STRATEGIES

Solution strategies or plans are procedures for solving specific kinds of problems. Historians and social scientists employ a variety of such problem-specific strategies. Once the type of problem or the kind of information needed to answer a question has been identified, the solution strategy selected is plugged into the general problem-solving strategy (at Step 3) and carried out. These plans may be any of those previously used to resolve similar problems, adaptations of these, or new plans created especially for a specific question or problem. When no appropriate solution plan can be identified, these problem solvers often fall back on one of a number of all-purpose, or "emergency," solution strategies, such as breaking problems into smaller, less complex subproblems, each of which can be resolved in turn.

Figure 52.1 lists a number of solution strategies commonly used in history and the social sciences. Each helps resolve a specific type of problem. For instance, a question or problem involving what a group of people believe may require conducting a survey. When a problem requires making a choice from among several alternatives, a decision-making strategy can be employed. Conceptualizing enables scholars to invent or revise existing concepts that organize often unorganized information and make it meaningful. Hypothesis making and testing is a plan for working through a complex problem that at first suggests a number of possible answers or solutions.

Each solution strategy consists of a specific cognitive procedure or combination of procedures. For example, one especially important solution strategy for historians is that of analyzing historical sources. In spite of its label, however, this strategy consists of more than the skill of analysis. As deconstructed by cognitive psychologist Samuel Wineburg (1991), it includes (1) assessing a source to determine, among other things, its authenticity, credibility, and point of view; (2) corroborating the details presented by comparing them to details presented in other sources on the same topic; and (3) contextualizing—placing what is presented or described in the context of what preceded and followed—all as steps toward (4) inferring historical meaning. As is readily apparent, this strategy actually combines a number of thinking skills, including evaluation, inferencing, and recall, as well as analysis. Most social scientists also employ a similar strategy in the course of their research and inquiries.

CRITICAL THINKING

Critical thinking consists of applying criteria to judge the worth, authenticity, or some other quality of something. Historians and social scientists engage in critical thinking to—among other things—ensure the accuracy of the information they collect, the objectivity and thoroughness of their inquiries, the reasonableness and truthfulness of the concepts, conclusions, and other knowledge claims they produce, and the quality of the arguments they develop to support these claims. They also think critically about the assumptions and inferences they make and the thinking they and others employ throughout their problem solving.

Figure 52.1 identifies 10 of the critical thinking skills frequently applied in history and the social sciences (Ennis, 1962). Essentially each of these skills consists of two major components: (1) criteria, or standards, for judging some quality, such as credibility, and (2) a procedure for using these criteria to make this judgment. Proficiency in critical thinking requires knowledge of both.

Criteria are conditions, standards, or rules that must be met in order for something to be what it purports or is asserted to be. For example, scholars have identified the following as criteria that must be met for a written source to be judged as credible:

- Author's reputation for honesty and accuracy.
- Author's expertise in the topic or field being written about.
- Absence of any conflict of interest on the author's part.
- Known risk to the author's reputation.
- Author's use of accepted methods of inquiry.
- Corroboration by other sources.

The procedure for applying any criteria is essentially that of evaluation. To make any critical thinking judgment, we can follow these steps:

1. Identify the quality to be judged.
2. Recall or identify the criteria to be met for judging this quality.
3. Analyze whatever is being evaluated piece by piece to find evidence related to these criteria.
4. Identify any relationships and/or pattern among this evidence.
5. Match the evidence and patterns to the criteria being used.
6. Judge the extent or degree of fit between the evidence found and the criteria that must be met.

Critical thinking is employed throughout any effective application of problem solving, any solution strategy, and any other kind of thinking. As skilled thinkers engage in these kinds of thinking, they also monitor and evaluate *how* they are thinking as well as *what* they are thinking. The judgments they make about both en route to developing an understanding, theory, or other claim allow them to alter, correct, or otherwise modify what they are doing to make it as accurate and thorough as it can be. Critical thinking, in effect, is a sort of quality control for thinking as well as for the knowledge claims produced by thinking.

INFORMATION PROCESSING AND REASONING

The information processing and reasoning skills identified in Figure 52.1 are employed repeatedly and in varying combinations in carrying out the other core history and social science thinking skills and strategies described here. For example, recall and reasoning as well as analysis and evaluation are used in making any critical thinking judgment. Recall, translation, interpretation, analysis, reasoning, synthesis, and evaluation are used in defining a problem. Hypothesizing requires recall, analysis, extrapolation, synthesis, and reasoning. And so on. Although these skills are rarely used in isolation from each other, proficiency in each is essential to the successful execution of any thinking task no matter how simple it may appear to be.

Of all the information processing skills, analysis is one of the most used. It lies at the heart of most problem solving and learning tasks—tasks such as defining a problem, generating concepts, finding evidence to support or refute a claim, or judging the strength of an argument. Essentially this skill consists of taking things apart to identify their attributes or components, to identify how these features are related to each other, and to identify the structure or framework that holds them together (Beyer, 1988; Bloom, Englehart, Furst, Hill, & Krathwohl, 1956/1984; Marzano et al., 1988). Figure 52.2 presents a basic procedure commonly used by experts to apply this skill. It also outlines some of the knowledge that informs the application of this procedure.

As in most thinking strategies and skills, there is more to this skill than simply a procedure to be applied. Knowledge related to how the procedure is applied is also part of the skill. This consists of *conditional* knowledge—when and where it is appropriate to use the skill— and *declarative* knowledge, such as heuristics for applying the skill effectively and efficiently, as well as clues as to what to look for, what criteria are to be applied, and how to deal with obstacles that are likely to arise in its application. In terms of analysis, knowing prior to the application of the skill the possible parts or relationships or structural patterns to look for—although sometimes restrictive—facilitates the initial application of the skill in novel contexts, especially for novices. Individuals who lack this skill knowledge frequently find it extremely difficult, if not impossible, to analyze information in a meaningful or productive way.

—Figure 52.2—

Major Attributes of the Skill of Analysis

Definition	*Analyze:* To take apart; to separate a whole into its constituent parts; to dissect, disassemble, deconstruct
Procedure	1. State your goal. 2. Recall or otherwise identify the kinds of evidence or attributes you will look for. 3. Search or probe (document, data, etc.) line by line or piece by piece to find these parts, attributes, or features, being alert to finding other relevant items you had not thought of earlier. 4. Identify any connections (spatial, causal, functional, etc.) among these parts or attributes. 5. Identify any pattern(s) perceived or principle(s) structuring these interrelationships (such as persuasive techniques, inductive or deductive structures, etc.).
Supporting Knowledge	1. When to analyze? • To clarify a problem, test a hypothesis, produce a synthesis, or evaluate something. • To identify the particular features of something. • To establish relationships or patterns. • To judge the worth, accuracy, or relevance of something. 2. How to start? • State parts, attributes, or features to look for. • Scan to find "something" germane to the task. 3. What to do if . . . • You cannot identify parts or attributes to use? Consider what ought to "be there" if your purpose is to be achieved. • Contradictory clues are found? Consider the results ambiguous or insufficient. 4. What to look for: • Kinds of potential parts or attributes, such as facts, value judgments, assumptions, reasons, conclusions, arguments, etc. • Kinds of potential relationships, such as causal, spatial, functional, temporal, evidence-conclusion, etc. • Kinds of potential organizing principles, such as general to specific, specific to general, claim-example, persuasive technique, inductive or deductive, etc.

In practice, social science and history scholars combine the kinds of thinking described here into purposeful inquiry to produce knowledge. Problem solving provides the framework in which these skills are applied in different combinations at varying points in their inquiry and study. Skilled application of these cognitive operations is essential to developing knowledge and understanding in these disciplines.

THINKING DISPOSITIONS

Thinking in history and the social sciences involves more than the mental operations by which it is carried out. The dispositions that motivate and support the selection, application, and evaluation of these skills are equally important.

Dispositions are habitual ways of behaving. Skilled thinkers are disposed to—among other things—tolerate ambiguity, suspend judgment, and exhibit a healthy skepticism and curiosity. These habitual ways of behaving are derived from the value scholars and serious students of history and social science place on truth and proof in their quests for understanding and knowledge (Lipman, 1991). They reflect a willingness—indeed, almost a passionate desire—to manifest consistently these behaviors and employ the skills implied by these dispositions. Some of the more important dispositions that drive good thinking in history and the social sciences, as in all disciplines, are:

1. Seek clarity, accuracy, and precision.
2. Examine a variety of viewpoints.
3. Seek to be well informed.
4. Use credible sources.
5. Seek a number of alternatives.
6. Seek and give reasons.
7. Seek and provide evidence.
8. Be open-minded.
9. Persist in carrying out a thinking task.
10. Be slow to believe.
11. Be objective.
12. Be systematic rather than impulsive.
13. Judge in terms of situations, issues, purposes, and consequences rather than in terms of fixed, dogmatic precepts or emotional wishful thinking.
14. Suspend judgment when appropriate and sufficient evidence and reasoning are lacking.
15. Be willing to change a position or judgment when evidence and reasons are sufficient to do so.

Through the continuing application of these dispositions, individuals become what philosopher Matthew Lipman refers to as "self-regulating" and "self-correcting" autonomous thinkers (Lipman, 1991).

INFUSING DISCIPLINED THINKING INTO HISTORY AND SOCIAL STUDIES COURSES

As already noted, many of the kinds of thinking described here as integral to the disciplines of history and the social sciences are not embedded in many of our elementary and secondary school courses in history and the social studies derived from these disciplines (Newmann, 1990; Newmann, Secada, & Wehlage, 1995; Perkins, 1992). Consequently, students are not likely to be developing the levels of understanding sought in these courses. Nor are they likely to have the opportunities they need to practice—let alone improve—the kinds of thinking needed to continue learning beyond school and to become the kinds of citizens required for our democratic society (Taba, 1965). What can be done to ensure that this thinking is infused in courses where it is missing and what are some implications of doing so?

One productive way to infuse thinking into our history and social studies classrooms is to engage students in doing what historians and social scientists do in their disciplines: solve problems. Two ways to do this are problem-solving learning activities and problem-solving lessons and units.

PROBLEM-SOLVING LEARNING ACTIVITIES

We can interject into our teaching specific, short-range tasks that require students to engage in history and social science problem solving to produce knowledge new to them. Examples of such activities include the following:

• Search a text (or texts) for evidence to substantiate or refute a textbook or student claim or conclusion.

• Infer from a site map of or artifacts from a prehistoric (or other) settlement the kinds of technology or values of its inhabitants.

• Determine what can be said "for sure" about what happened at a specific event by comparing excerpts from several sources about that event.

• Evaluate the strength—the accuracy and soundness—of a given argument.

• Construct a convincing argument to support or refute a conclusion asserted by a student, the teacher, the class, or a textbook author.

• Apply a specific history, geography, or other social science concept to explain an example of it—or to distinguish an example from a nonexample of it.

• Evaluate several sources on a topic for accuracy, bias, point of view, and/or relevance to a given topic.

• Identify and judge the assumptions or inferences in a given argument.

Activities like these engage students in different aspects of problem solving, in using different solution strategies, in making critical thinking judgments, and in interpreting, analyzing, and reasoning. Students can usually complete the activities in less than a typical class period when they are provided with the necessary information. Additional activities like these and detailed examples of some of them are described elsewhere in this book (e.g., Robert Swartz's Chapter 45) and in Beyer, 1997.

PROBLEM-SOLVING LESSONS AND UNITS

We can also structure classroom teaching and learning to move students through complete problem-solving tasks, from problem identification to solution and "publication," just as historians and social scientists do, by employing a problem-solving strategy like that presented in Figure 52.3. This strategy elaborates Polya's general problem-solving model (as shown in Figure 52.1) by incorporating hypothesis making and testing as the overall solution plan. It is drawn from the work of John Dewey (1910) and from problem-solving strategies commonly used by history and social science scholars and educators (Beyer, 1971, 1979; Bruner, 1963; Fenton, 1967; Hunt & Metcalf, 1968).

The utility of this problem-solving strategy lies in the role played by hypotheses in both learning and research. Hypotheses help us to focus on specific aspects of a problem or topic. When converted into "if . . . then" statements, they direct us to the kinds of information required to develop a solution, as in "If (my hypothesis) is accurate, then I need or will be able to find (specific information) that indicates it is accurate." They also suggest the kinds of information collecting and processing methods and sources required. Hypotheses furthermore give rise to questions that can be used to probe and analyze the collected information in our efforts to make it meaningful. Making and testing hypotheses is a powerful tool for solving many types of problems in history and social studies classrooms.

Lessons structured around this strategy may be completed in a regular class period or extend over several class periods or longer. Students may, for example, launch their study of "What was life like (in a particular time in a specific place in history)?" by defining the meaning of the term *life* and then hypothesizing responses to this question by analyzing a list of words (in present-day English, of course) commonly spoken by the people of that time and place. After inferring the kinds of evidence they may expect to find if their hypotheses are accurate, they can then analyze artifacts left behind by these people, a list of laws that governed these people, excerpts from their written records, accounts by outside visitors, and drawings and paintings produced by these people, all the while revising, elaborating, and otherwise modifying their hypotheses after assessing and analyzing each source. After judging the accuracy of their revised hypotheses, they can draw conclusions about the lives of these people and present their conclusions as arguments, buttressed with evidence they have uncovered. Problem-solving lessons and units like these engage students in producing—or constructing—new ideas, understandings, and knowledge.

The role of the teacher in using this problem-solving strategy changes as students become increasingly skilled in using it and in applying the specific thinking operations required at each step of the way. Initially teachers may have to explain each step in some detail, model some specific operations as necessary, and distribute the data only as needed. After the strategy has been used several times and students become more familiar with it, however, teachers can increasingly stand back, intervening only to provide explicit instruction in skills that students need to improve or in the application of unfamiliar solution strategies or critical thinking skills. Eventually students can apply this problem-solving strategy autonomously to disorganized data and even vary its application depending on the problem being considered. At this point the teacher simply serves as a sounding board, troubleshooter, or "quality control" monitor. Throughout a problem-solving lesson or unit, students will be engaging in the kinds of higher-order, complex thinking that is an essential part of history and the social sciences.

IMPLICATIONS FOR TEACHING

Infusing into history and social studies courses the kinds of thinking that historians and social scientists customarily apply provides naturally recurring opportunities for students to engage in these kinds of thinking in a purposeful way. But such infusion has serious implications.

—*Figure 52.3*—

A Teaching and Learning Problem-Solving Strategy for History and Social Studies

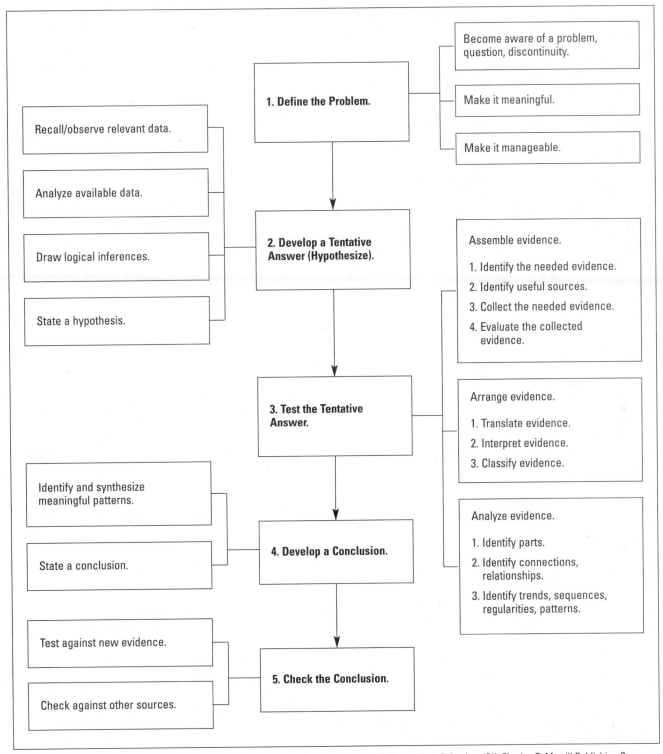

Adapted from *Inquiry in the Social Studies Classroom: A Strategy for Teaching* by Barry K. Beyer, 1971. Columbus, OH: Charles E. Merrill Publishing Co.

THE NEED TO TEACH THESE THINKING SKILLS

If we, as teachers, require students to engage in the kinds of thinking described here, they can't be made to do it unaided, because many can't—or won't (Newmann, 1990; Taba, 1965). We must be willing to help them become more proficient in applying these skills than they currently may be. And this means, in short, providing continuing instruction in the thinking skills, strategies, and dispositions of history and the social sciences in which students may be deficient while they attempt to use them to achieve prescribed substantive learning goals.

The required instruction consists essentially of making thinking procedures explicit, helping students become aware of how they and others carry out these procedures, and, frequently, showing—modeling—how these procedures can be better executed (Pressley & Harris, 1990). It also requires supporting and guiding students' continued application of these skills through the use of scaffolding, cueing, and other means (see Beyer's Chapters 62 and 66 in this book). We can use a variety of techniques and strategies to provide the instruction necessary for attaining proficiency (Beyer, 1997). In addition, we must help students internalize the dispositions that support these kinds of thinking by modeling the dispositions, by encouraging their application through discussion and questioning, by insisting that students exhibit them, and by rewarding those who do. Although such instruction initially takes time, it can be done as students use the information they are supposed to be learning about. The long-term result is better and deeper subject matter learning as well as improved thinking (Estes, 1972).

AUTHENTICITY OF SKILL PROCEDURES

In teaching students how better to carry out the thinking skills that they need to improve, care must be taken to ensure they master authentic procedures for carrying out these skills. Not just any skill-using procedure—or anyone's way of doing it—will suffice. It is crucial in any attempt to improve student thinking that we, as teachers, help our students become proficient in mental operations performed by skillful thinkers—rather than force on them hastily thought-up, inexpert, dysfunctional, or idiosyncratic versions of these operations.

Authentic thinking-skill procedures are those employed effectively by individuals with demonstrated expertise in carrying them out. Identifying or finding accurate, meaningful, complete descriptions of these authentic procedures for many thinking skills is sometimes difficult. A number of sources describe authentic skill-using procedures in a clear, detailed manner (see Figure 52.4).

ENHANCING THE ROLE OF THINKING

The disciplines of history and the social sciences are, indeed, infused with thinking. But the role and presence of this thinking is often obscured by a focus on subject matter and knowledge claims. Our task is not to infuse thinking in these disciplines but rather to expose the thinking that is already integral

—*Figure 52.4*—

Selected Sources of Authentic Thinking Skill Procedures

Problem Solving

Bransford, J. D., & Stein, B. S. (1997). *The ideal problem solver.* New York: W. H. Freeman & Co.

Hayes, J. R. (1989). *The complete problem solver.* (2nd ed.). Hillsdale, NJ: Erlbaum Associates.

Polya, G. (1945/1973). *How to solve it.* Princeton, NJ: Princeton University Press.

Solution Strategies

Beyer, B. K. (1997). *Improving student thinking.* Boston: Allyn and Bacon.

Hurst, J. B., et al. (1983, Fall). The decision making process. *Theory and Research in Social Education, 11*(3), 17–43.

Kepner, C. H., & Tregoe, B. B. (1997). *The new rational manager.* Princeton, NJ: Princeton Research Press.

Marzano, R. (1992). *A different kind of classroom: Teaching with dimensions of learning.* Alexandria, VA: Association for Supervision and Curriculum Development.

Critical Thinking

Beyer, B. K. (1988). *Developing a thinking skills program.* Boston: Allyn and Bacon.

Damer, T. E. (1995). *Attacking faulty reasoning.* (3rd ed.). Belmont, CA: Wadsworth Publishing Co.

Ennis, R. H. (1962, Winter). A concept of critical thinking. *Harvard Educational Review, 32*(1), 81–111.

Information Processing and Reasoning

Beyer, B. K. (1988). *Developing a thinking skills program.* Boston: Allyn and Bacon.

Fogarty, R., & Bellanca, J. (1986). *Teach them thinking.* Palatine, IL: IRI.

Swartz, R. J., & Parks, S. (1994). *Infusing the teaching of critical and creative thinking into content instruction.* Pacific Grove, CA: Critical Thinking Books and Software.

Toulmin, S., et al. (1984). (2nd ed.). *An introduction to reasoning.* New York: Macmillan.

to them and become more conscious of its nature and the role it plays. Then we must ensure that it is infused in the courses derived from these disciplines. Once we have accomplished these tasks, we can take advantage of the presence of this thinking and our students' need to employ it to improve, through instruction, their proficiency in applying it. Becoming aware of the nature and role of thinking in these disciplines is an important first step in accomplishing these crucial educational goals.

REFERENCES

Beyer, B. K. (1971). *Inquiry in the social studies classroom*. Columbus, OH: Charles E. Merrill Publishing Co.

Beyer, B. K. (1979). *Teaching thinking in social studies*. Columbus, OH: Charles E. Merrill Publishing Co.

Beyer, B. K. (1988). *Developing a thinking skills program*. Boston: Allyn and Bacon.

Beyer, B. K. (1997). *Improving student thinking: A comprehensive approach*. Boston: Allyn and Bacon.

Bloom, B. S., Englehart, M. D., Furst, E. J., Hill, W. H, & Krathwohl, D. R. (Eds.). (1956/1984). *Taxonomy of educational objectives: The classification of educational goals. Handbook I: Cognitive domain*. New York: David McKay.

Bruner, J. S. (1963). *The process of education*. Cambridge, MA: Harvard University Press.

Bruner, J. S., Goodnow, J. J., & Austin, G. A. (1956). *A study of thinking*. New York: John Wiley and Sons.

Cornbleth, C., & Korth, W. (1981, April). If remembering, understanding, and reasoning are important . . . . *Social Education*, 276–279.

Dewey, J. (1910). *How we think*. Boston: D. C. Heath.

Dreyfus, H. L. (1984, May 19). *Expert systems versus intuitive enterprise*. Unpublished paper delivered at the George Mason University Conference on Cognitive Development, Fairfax, Va.

Ennis, R. H. (1962). A concept of critical thinking. *Harvard Educational Review, 32*(1), 81–111.

Estes, T. H. (1972). Reading in the social studies: A review of research since 1950. In J. Laffery (Ed.), *Reading in the content areas* (pp. 178–183). Newark, NJ: International Reading Association.

Fenton, E. (1967). *The new social studies*. New York: Holt, Rinehart and Winston.

Gardner, H. (1999). *The disciplined mind*. New York: Simon and Schuster.

Hunt, M. P., & Metcalf, L. E. (1968). *Teaching high school social studies*. New York: Harper and Row.

Lipman, M. (1991). *Thinking in education*. Cambridge: Cambridge University Press.

Marzano, R. (1991, April). Fostering thinking across the curriculum through knowledge structuring. *Journal of Reading, 34*(7), 518–525.

Marzano, R. J., Brandt, R. S., Hughes, C. S., Jones, B. F., Presseisen, B. Z., Rankin, S. C., Suhor, C. (1988). *Dimensions of thinking: A framework for curriculum and instruction*. Alexandria, VA: Association for Supervision and Curriculum Development.

Newmann, F. M. (1990, January–February). Higher order thinking in teaching social studies. *Journal of Curriculum Studies, 22*(1), 41–56.

Newmann, F. M., Secada, W., & Wehlage, G. G. (1995). *A guide to authentic instruction and assessment*. Madison, WI: Wisconsin Center for Educational Research.

Perkins, D. (1992). *Smart schools*. New York: Free Press.

Phenix, P. H. (1964). *Realms of meaning*. New York: McGraw-Hill.

Polya, G. (1945/1973). *How to solve it*. Princeton: Princeton University Press.

Pressley, M., & Harris, K. R. (1990, September). What we really know about strategy instruction. *Educational Leadership, 48*(1), 31–34.

Resnick, L. B., & Klopfer, L. E. (1989). *Toward the thinking curriculum: Current cognitive research*. Alexandria, VA: Association for Supervision and Curriculum Development.

Schwab, J. J. (1962, July). The concept of the structure of a discipline. *The Educational Record, 43*, 197–205.

Taba, H. (1965, May). The teaching of thinking. *Elementary English, 42*(15), 534–542.

Wineburg, S. (1991). Historical problem solving: A study of cognitive processes used in the evaluation of documentation and written evidence. *Journal of Educational Psychology, 83*(1), 73–87.

53

A View from the Foxhole: Elevating Foreign Language Classrooms

Virginia Pauline Rojas

Foreign and second language teaching and learning approaches have been *reforming* for two decades. As in other academic disciplines, changes have focused on implementing a performance-based orientation to learning and assessment (Met, 1995). In language classrooms, this shift underscores learners' capacities to use what they know about language and, in so doing, to become better at it until they are competent or proficient enough to communicate in a linguistic and cultural context other than their own. Discussing the relationship of thinking to this process is ironic because the common expectation is that the study of another language naturally enhances "problem-solving skills, creativity, and general cognitive development" (Schultz, 1998, p. 6). Indeed, language plays a central role in all learning, and the use of discourse is basic to intellectual development (Barnes, 1995; Corson, 1999). The changes, however, must be calling for language teachers and learners to be able to do something they cannot yet do because little progress has been made in changing the daily practices of language classrooms (Rojas, 1996). Both teachers and learners must therefore gain clear insights into current reality and a willingness to work at closing the gap between the appearance of change and real reform.

Enhancing language instruction to make it more thoughtful might mean ordering new instructional materials, creating new tests, and pursuing new teaching practices. These forces may lead to changes in what teachers do in class but may also simply put a new label on what they have already been doing. It is easy as educators to use a catchphrase and mistakenly perceive the appearance of change as substantive reform, especially if we don't want the changes to be too disruptive (Widdowson, 1998). To examine critically, inquire into, or interrogate the presence or lack of congruence among our beliefs, knowledge, and practices—and never to assume that we have *the* answer—truly signals the process of reform (Short & Burke, 1996). It is in the ongoing search for and the asking of questions that new understandings come forth. Teaching for thinking should therefore itself be an inquiry; as such, this discussion asks four questions. Perhaps as we use inquiry as a tool for our own reflection, we can better understand how to construct our teaching contexts to do the same.

WHY DO WE DO WHAT WE DO?

Realizing that there is more to language learning than memorizing grammatical forms, the communicative and proficiency movements tried to shift our classrooms from language learning to language acquisition environments (Krashen, 1981). Theoretically, classrooms abandoned language drills in order to focus on meaning in social encounters and to position learners as active participants in the learning process (Curtain & Pesola, 1994; Markee, 1997; Ramirez, 1995; Richards & Rodgers, 1986). As a result, language teachers are now liberated to design interactive lessons, and students to experience authentic communication. Innovative principles of these curricula include linguistic functions or speech acts, topic-related vocabulary in communicative situations, and grammatical and sociocultural accuracy (Met, 1995; Ramirez, 1995). Remarkably and despite this heightened sense of the importance of meaningful context for language acquisition, language learners are no more able to authenticate these elements as discourse outside the classroom than they were when taught through the structuralist approach (Rojas, 1998). Widdowson (1998) attributes this plight to a lack of pragmatic engagement with semantically encoded meaning; that is, the language has little meaning for students. Missing is a pedagogic artifice to provoke a pragmatic reaction or to evoke "felt meaning"—the spark we feel when our brains make a connection (Caine & Caine, 1997; Widdowson, 1998).

That connection cannot occur without a vehicle for conceptual exploration in the target language. When asked to identify the content of what is being taught in their classrooms, many language teachers respond in terms of grammatical structures such as "present perfect tense," "articles," or "comparisons." If challenged to distinguish between content and skills, teachers might name a language function such as "requesting information in a restaurant" as content and grammatical items as skills. Sometimes the function and structure correlate but sometimes not. Some teachers choose to keep the grammatical structures as content and specify speaking or reading as the corresponding skills. Others propose a topic such as "food" as content and language functions or grammatical structures as skills. Although this last option appears most akin to curricular intent, teachers are frequently unable to answer the simplest question—"What are the concepts that students should know about food?"—making it seem that food is less a content element than a vocabulary list (Rojas, 1998). Some teachers eventually respond that they want their students to know something about culture; for example, that different foods are eaten across cultures and at varying times of the day. These are still facts, though, and facts are rarely engaging. Besides, these content-based attempts are most often reserved for the advanced levels of language study that few students reach (Met, 1995).

A skills-driven curriculum does not promote language or cognitive development (Freeman & Freeman, 1998). Our overreliance on instruction organized accordingly prevents us from finding our way to the language proficiency paradigm—a journey ultimately altering the instructional landscape of our classrooms and, more importantly, learners' linguistic and cognitive capacities. If we do not specify the concepts to be explored, skills remain nothing more than lists to be practiced in isolation, and lists do not inform us about learners' proficiencies. The best evidence of performance is the extended discourse that students speak, read, and write. What we hope for should be decided before we teach, and our daily activities should reflect our expectations. Helping our students collect and reflect on these daily products and performances will not only make our classrooms more pragmatically engaging but also help our students take increasing responsibility for the attainment of their own language proficiency (Rojas, 1998).

The inability to distinguish between content and skills binds classrooms in other ways as well. Discrete linguistic items—sequentially ordered and hierarchically placed—continue to dominate our discourse in canonized scripts and canned curriculum packages (Rojas, 1996). Students move from the simple to the complex as though the second language acquisition process is linear and cumulative—a proposition unsupported by the research (Collier, 1995). Student interaction is suppressed by the single-minded goal of sequencing prescriptive and contrived tasks around grammatical explanations, often not provided in the target language (Oxford, 1998b). Teachers statically dispense a litany of linguistic "dummy runs" disguised as communicative menus, allowing time-worn activities and assessment models to prevail (Barnes, 1995). Students regurgitate fixed formulas in ritualistic roles, and teachers lament an inherent lack of motivation for the study of another language. The emancipatory potential of the communicative and proficiency movements seems lost (Rojas, 1996).

What Would More Thoughtful Language Instruction Look and Sound Like?

Connecting second language acquisition principles to what we do in our classrooms is necessary if we are to find our way (Crookes, 1997; Gass, 1993; Ellis, 1990, 1997). Keeping up with the latest research is daunting, given the constantly changing perspectives on variables that are still unaccounted for (Titone, 1990). Nunan's (1995) review of the research on the effects of instruction on second language acquisition reveals the following: (1) formal instruction has an impact on language learning but not on language acquisition unless the learner is developmentally ready and the language rules are teachable, and (2) second language acquisition requires abundant amounts of comprehensible language input, the potential for input to become intake, and equally abundant opportunities for output. The lesson to be learned is straightforward: successful second language acquisition does not take place simply because teachers tell students how to "get it right" (Corson, 1999).

The internal processes of second language acquisition are consistent with constructivist models of learning (Met, 1995). Students are builders of knowledge—not recorders of information—and learning is a holistic, meaning-making process. What is needed is a model of teaching "that values risk-taking, welcomes conjecture, and sees error making as inevitable and necessary" (Corson, 1999, p. 89). Nunan (1995) offers advice on offering such an environment: gather information on students' readiness and cognitive styles, provide learning options and choices, design open-ended problems around key concepts, present information using diverse modalities, organize learners to work collaboratively in mixed groups, use assorted assessment options, and coach rather than teach. Most of us would concur with this "learner-centered and experience-based view of second language teaching" (Richards & Rodgers, 1986, p. 69). Our question is: What conditions must be met to create them?

As mentioned earlier, the language-immersion principle of teaching language *through* content rather than *as* content is necessary (Clyne, 1991; Genesee, 1994; Met, 1991; Snow, Met, & Genesee, 1989). Access to challenging content "provides for development of a wider range of discourse skills than does traditional second or foreign language instruction" (Met & Lorenz, 1998, p. 232). As students interact with content, they generate metaphors, clarify and assess the reasonableness of ideas, and use diverse vocabulary—the most important evidence available about the quality of their thought (Corson, 1999). If more advanced levels of proficiency are our goal, then full-blown immersion should play some part in students' learning experiences (Johnson & Swain, 1997). Several options are available, including any combination of early- or late-, partial- or total-immersion programs (Curtain & Pesola, 1994). Immersion—a method of foreign language instruction in which the regular school curriculum is taught in another language—"is the most effective form of language instruction ever implemented in a school setting" (Met & Lorenz, 1998, p. 211).

Inquiry learning is another essential condition because (1) inquiry is a process of both problem posing and solving, (2) inquiry casts learners as participants and not spectators, as does the transmission-of-knowledge model, and (3) inquiry generates dialogue as a tool for co-constructing meaning (Freire & Macedo, 1987; Wells, 1992). Inquiry is also immersion—into tasks and themes of mutual interest—to originate significant questions and responses. A guiding question directs the search for understanding, serving as a logical, coordinated instrument for attaining meaning (Jacobs, 1989). Criteria for guiding questions of quality establish that such questions should be open-ended, require high-level cognitive terminology for elaborated responses, contain emotive force or intellectual bite, and be succinct (Kaufman & Grennon Brooks, 1996; Traver, 1998). As apprentices of new cultures, for example, learners explore the concepts of how "food" is viewed between cultures, why eating customs differ, what it means to have a healthy diet, or even who is hungry in different parts of the world. Engaging in these pursuits—more so than rehearsing fictitious situations they may never encounter—may motivate learners to invest in learning (Widdowson, 1998).

Implementing an inquiry model involves more than asking conceptual questions or using new instructional strategies. It demands a theoretical shift in how we view curriculum, students, and language learning and teaching (Short & Burke, 1996). Open-ended, challenging, and interpretational tasks are the focus of inquiry and the medium of learning. Heterogeneously grouped students work together on differentiated tasks and materials, ensuring multiple paths to learning for diverse learners (Guntermann, 1992; Met & Lorenz, 1998; Schultz, 1998). A differentiated language classroom is "marked by a repeated rhythm of whole class preparation, review, and sharing, followed by opportunities for individual or small-group exploration, sense making, extension, and production" (Tomlinson, 1995, p. 9). Student-centered inquiry teaching enhances individual creativity, stimulates collaborative efforts, and emphasizes learning how to learn through hands-on experimentation with learner-generated questions, investigations, hypotheses, and models. This environment ultimately supports the variability of the second language acquisition process.

Because inquiry is theoretically grounded in collaborative relationships, classes must break away from their current format, in which teacher talk dominates; it is through interaction and negotiation of meaning that language is acquired and developed (Ramirez, 1995). Interaction must transcend the current "teacher-question/student-response" framework, for it is during "student-student interactions that most higher-order cognitive and linguistic discourse is observed" (Garcia, 1991, p. 4). Talk enables language acquisition as "meaning is continually created and recreated over stretches of discourse" (Corson, 1999, p. 89). Teachers therefore design cooperative learning activities to provide practice opportunities for learners to contribute their own ideas and experiences to the learning process (El-Khoumy, 1997; Jacob, Rottenberg, Patrick, & Wheeler, 1996; Kagan, 1994; Krahnke, 1987; Larsen-Freeman & Long, 1991; Lee & VanPatten, 1995; Nunan, 1995; Scarcella & Oxford, 1992).

Having pairs and groups of students work together on open-ended tasks means students will no longer sit quietly in rows but will move around the room engaging in conversations, reading materials, and executing experiential activities such as dialectical journals, public speaking, debates, reader's theater, writer's workshop, improvisations, found poetry, and instructional conversations (Olson, 1992; Tharp & Gallimore, 1991). Accompanying methods to prompt thoughtfulness and intellectual processes would include higher-order and Socratic questioning, analytical reading, strategic writing, cooperative learning, and the use of graphic organizers. Discussion groups are not places where students practice linguistic functions but rather where they construct mutual understanding through conversations and dialogue. The teaching of writing moves away from rhetorical templates, grammar lessons, and skill work to concentrate on an authoring process in which writing is thinking, clarifying, and communicating (Short & Burke, 1996).

Literacy of the "Net generation" demands attention as well, though our goal must not be to simply add computers to the old language learning environments but to have different environments that include computer assistance (Tapscott, 1999; Warschauer, 1998). Examples of such assistance include computer-mediated interactions for language development through instructional software activities and the use of the Internet for authentic input, synchronous output, or asynchronous research and distance-learning projects (British Council, 1998; Chapelle, 1998; Haas, Mink, Cristensen, & Yasui, 1998). Technology should be embraced as a means to further students' inquiries through instant access to information and interaction. Fresh content, plentiful raw data, and primary sources—ingredients for inquiry language learning—are readily available in our increasingly high-tech society (Kaufman & Grennon Brooks, 1996). Information technology does much more than expand information sources: it fundamentally alters classrooms.

The benefits for language acquisition are unmistakable: (1) increased collaboration, negotiation, and opportunities for quality thinking, (2) encouragement of risk taking and control of own learning, (3) active learning in a meaning-focused environment, (4) salience of input with potential for pragmatic engagement, (5) opportunities for production and output, (6) the advantage of extra time to elaborate and edit responses, (7) flexible differentiated instruction, and (8) our own professional growth (Al-Arishi, 1994; British Council, 1998; Cummins & Sayers, 1995; Feyten & Nutta, 1998; Haas et al., 1998; Owsten, 1997; Oxford, 1998a). The broader ecology of the language acquisition environment is affected as much by technology as by content and inquiry-based instruction.

A final prerequisite comes to mind: assessment. Language acquisition and development depend upon the quality of the feedback students receive and the opportunities they have to apply that data (Wiggins, 1998). The performing arts have long depended on feedback to inform students about what they can and can't do; it is a natural extension of performance-based achievement. The image of the language teacher going home at the end of the day with an armload of tests gives way to a spectrum of assessment scenarios: the teacher engaging in conferences with students about their projects and performances, students videotaping oral presentations for later viewing and self-assessment, students reflecting on what they and others have achieved in peer editing sessions, or students selecting from an extensive portfolio of completed tasks those best indicating their own growth and then being rewarded for the insight and justification of their choices.

Once again, the benefits of performance-based assessments are plentiful: (1) curriculum alignment, (2) added emphasis on learners' metacognitive development, (3) the element of real-world performance, (4) the focus on higher-order thinking and problem solving, (5) the natural extension of assessment from learning activities, (6) the open disclosure of rating criteria, (7) the potential for cultural sensitivity, and (8) the reciprocity of teachers as learners and learners as teachers (Brown & Hudson, 1998).

Assessment—if it is genuinely thoughtful—"encourages retention, higher-level cognitive skills, development of internal standards, creativity and variety in solving problems" (DeFazio, 1997, p. 102). The question "How can we make assessment unbounded events where students have occasion to revise, improve, and defend their performances?" resonates in a trustful climate of collegiality and respect (Wiggins, 1993).

HOW BEST CAN WE LEARN TO IMPLEMENT THESE CONDITIONS?

Reflective practice—or developing our expertise through a process of critical reflection in the context of collaboration—is flourishing as a means of professional development among language teachers (Glisan, 1996; Richards & Lockhart, 1994). Characterized by active inquiry through problem solving, "minds-on" manipulation of raw data, and opportunities for reflection, this model offers us a process to understand and to change as a result of our understanding (Kaufman & Grennon Brooks, 1996). Unlike other professional development efforts in which we might be told what to do, we embark on an ongoing inquiry and collaborative effort to improve our classrooms (Jaramillo, 1998). Principles of this process include the following: (1) change takes time, (2) responsiveness requires capacity, (3) teaching and learning are analogous to inquiry and reflection, (4) inquiry and reflection are needed to transcend cultural boundaries, (5) data analysis supports inquiry, and (6) responsive educators access research to investigate potential replication practices (Jaramillo, 1998). A guiding rationale prevails: we are learning in order to improve learning. The beauty of these efforts is that they recognize us as inquirers, decision makers, and creators of knowledge—giving us the opportunity to practice and model learning.

HOW WILL WE KNOW WHAT WE HAVE LEARNED?

The lesson to be learned from inquiry is the difficulty in our capacity to distinguish between the illusion of change and the reality of reform. Plato's parable of the cave ingeniously compares the two. Those who have always lived in the cave can only see what is directly in front of them and therefore assume reality to be nothing more than the shadows cast upon the wall by their fire. Once they look outward, their world of comfortable illusions is shattered, leaving them feeling frightened and confused. It is a natural aspect of the human condition to retreat rather than to pursue the anguish of gaining even the simplest of new understandings. As language educators, we sometimes long for a world filled with few questions, easy answers, and perfect practices. Yet such a situation is an illusion. The continual examination of, inquiry into, and interrogation of our beliefs, knowledge, and practices are difficult processes. The first step is the breaking away from the shadows of our conventional knowledge and believing that the questioning process is the beginning of knowing what we have learned.

REFERENCES

Al-Arishi, A. Y. (1994). An integrated approach to the use of technology in communicative language teaching. *Language Quarterly, 32*(1–2), 175–191.

Barnes, D. (1995). Talking and learning in classrooms: An introduction. *Primary Voices, 3*(1), 2–7.

British Council. (1998, June). The Internet and English language teaching. Available: www.britcoun.org/english/internet/engcont.htm

Brown, J. D., & Hudson, T. (1998). The alternatives in language assessment. *TESOL Quarterly, 32*(4), 653–677.

Caine, R. N., & Caine, G. (1997). *Education on the edge of possibility.* Alexandria, VA: Association for Supervision and Curriculum Development.

Chapelle, C. (1998). Research on the use of technology in TESOL: Analysis of interaction sequences in computer-assisted language learning. *TESOL Quarterly, 32*(4), 753–757.

Clyne, M. (1991). Immersion principles in second language programs: Research and policy in multicultural Australia. *Journal of Multilingual and Multicultural Development, 12*(1–2), 55–65.

Collier, V. P. (1995). *Promoting academic success for ESL students: Understanding second language for school.* Available from Bastos Book Co., P.O. Box 433, Woodside, NY 11377.

Corson, D. (1999). *Language policy in schools: A resource for teachers and administrators.* Mahwah, NJ: Lawrence Erlbaum Associates.

Crookes, G. (1997). SLA and language pedagogy: A socioeducational perspective, *Studies in Second Language Acquisition, 19*(1), 93–116.

Cummins, J., & Sayers, D. (1995). *Brave new schools: Challenging cultural illiteracy through global learning networks.* New York: St. Martin's Press.

Curtain, H., & Pesola, C. A. (1994). *Languages and children: Making the match.* (2nd ed.). New York: Longman.

DeFazio, A. (1997). Language awareness at the international high school. In L. van Lier & D. Corson (Eds.), *Knowledge about language* (pp. 99–107). Boston, MA: Kluwer.

El-Khoumy, A. S. A. (1997). *Review of recent studies dealing with techniques for classroom interaction.* (ERIC Document Reproduction Service No. ED 415 688).

Ellis, R. (1990). *Instructed second language acquisition.* Oxford: Blackwell.

Ellis, R. (1997). SLA and language pedagogy: An educational perspective. *Studies in Second Language Acquisition, 19*(1), 69–92.

Feyten, C., & Nutta, J. (1998). How can technology be used to promote language learning? In M. Met (Ed.), *Critical issues in second language learning* (pp. 125–130). Glenview, IL: Addison-Wesley.

Freeman, Y. S., & Freeman, D. E. (1998). *ESL/EFL teaching: Principles for success.* Portsmouth, NH: Heinemann.

Freire, P., & Macedo, D. (1987). *Literacy: Reading the word and the world.* South Hadley, MA: Bergin and Garvey.

García, E. (1991). *Education of linguistically and culturally diverse students: Effective instructional practices.* Santa Cruz, CA: National Center for Research on Cultural Diversity and Second Language Learning.

Gass, S. M. (1993). Second language acquisition: Past, present, and future. *Second Language Research, 9*(2), 99–117.

Genesee, F. (1994). Integrating language and content: Lessons from immersion. In *Educational Practice Report #11.* Santa Cruz, CA: National Center for Research on Cultural Diversity and Second Language Learning.

Glisan, E. (1996). A collaborative approach to professional development. In R. Lafayette (Ed.), *National standards: A catalyst for reform* (pp. 57–95). Lincolnwood, IL: National Textbook.

Guntermann, G. (1992). Developing tomorrow's teachers of world languages. Washington, DC: ERIC Clearinghouse on Languages and Linguistics (ERIC Document Reproduction Service No. ED 350 880).

Haas, M., Mink, S., Cristensen, P., & Yasui, A. (1998). Preparing students to fully participate in the future: Practical applications. In M. Met (Ed.), *Critical issues in second language learning* (pp. 130–137). Glenview, IL: Addison-Wesley.

Jacob, E., Rottenberg, L., Patrick, S. K., & Wheeler, E. (1996). Cooperative learning: Context and opportunities for acquiring academic English. *TESOL Quarterly, 30*(2), 253–280.

Jacobs, H. H. (1989). *Interdisciplinary curriculum: Design and implementation.* Alexandria, VA: Association for Supervision and Curriculum Development.

Jaramillo, A. (1998, Autumn). Professional development from the inside out. *TESOL Journal, 7*(5), 12–18.

Johnson, K. E., & Swain, M. (1997). *Immersion education: International perspectives.* New York: Cambridge University Press.

Kagan, S. (1994). *Cooperative learning.* San Clemente, CA: Kagan Cooperative Learning.

Kaufman, D., & Grennon Brooks, J. (1996). Interdisciplinary collaboration in teacher education: A constructivist approach. *TESOL Quarterly, 30*(2), 231–252.

Krahnke, K. (1987). *Approaches to syllabus design for foreign language teaching.* Englewood Cliffs, NJ: Prentice-Hall.

Krashen, S. D. (1981). *Second language acquisition and second language learning.* Oxford: Pergamon.

Larsen-Freeman, D., & Long, M. H. (1991). *An introduction to second language acquisition research.* New York: Longman.

Lee, J. F. & VanPatten, B. (1995). *Making communicative language teaching happen.* New York: McGraw-Hill.

Markee, N. (1997). *Managing curricula innovation.* Cambridge: Cambridge University Press.

Met, M. (1991). Learning language through content; learning content through language. *Foreign Language Annals, 24*(4), 281–295.

Met, M. (1995). Foreign language curriculum in an era of educational reform. In A. A. Glatthorn (Ed.), *Content of the curriculum* (pp. 69–99). Alexandria, VA: Association for Supervision and Curriculum Development.

Met, M., & Lorenz, E. (1998). Preparing global citizens: A foreign language program for all students. *ASCD curriculum handbook* (Case study, pp. 11.211–11.240). Alexandria, VA: Association for Supervision and Curriculum Development.

Nunan, D. (1995). Closing the gap between learning and instruction. *TESOL Quarterly, 29*(1), 133–158.

Olson, C. B. (1992). Interactive strategies for enhancing thinking and writing. In A. Costa, J. Bellanca, & R. Fogarty (Eds.), *If minds matter: A foreword to the future* (pp. 101–116). Arlington Heights, IL: SkyLight.

Owsten, R. D. (1997). The World Wide Web: A technology to enhance teaching and learning? *Educational Researcher, 26*(2), 27–33.

Oxford, R. L. (1998a). Uses of advanced technology for early language learning. In M. Met (Ed.), *Critical issues in second language learning* (pp. 137–147). Glenview, IL: Addison-Wesley.

Oxford, R. L. (1998b). Where is the United States headed with K–12 foreign language education? *ERIC/CLL News Bulletin, 22*(1), 1–4.

Ramirez, A. G. (1995). *Creating contexts for second language acquisition: Theory and methods.* New York: Longman.

Richards, J. C., & Lockhart, C. (1994). *Reflective teaching in second language classrooms.* Cambridge: Cambridge University Press.

Richards, J. C., & Rodgers, T. (1986). *Approaches and methods in language teaching: A description and analysis.* Cambridge: Cambridge University Press.

Rojas, V. P. (1996). Above the word: When content is process in foreign language teaching. In A. L. Costa & R. Liebman (Eds.), *Envisioning process and content: Toward a renaissance curriculum* (pp. 199–210). Thousand Oaks, CA: Corwin Press.

Rojas, V. P. (1998, April). Mapping the curriculum: Implications for EFL instruction. *English Teaching Professional,* (7), 34–35.

Scarcella, R., & Oxford, R. (1992). *The tapestry of language learning: The individual in the communicative classroom.* Boston: Heinle & Heinle.

Schultz, R. A. (1998). Foreign language education in the United States: Trends and challenges. *ERIC Review, 6*(1), 6–13.

Short, K. G., & Burke, C. (1996). Examining our beliefs and practices through inquiry. *Language Arts, 73*(2), 97–103.

Snow, M. A., Met, M., & Genesee, F. (1989). A conceptual framework for the integration of language and content in second/foreign language instruction. *TESOL Quarterly, 23*(2), 201–217.

Tapscott, D. (1999). Educating the net generation. *Educational Leadership, 56*(5), 6–11.

Tharp, R., & Gallimore, R. (1991). The instructional conversation: Teaching and learning in social activity. *Research Report #2.* Santa Cruz, CA: National Center for Research on Cultural Diversity and Second Language Learning.

Titone, R. (1990, April). *A psycho-sociolinguistic perspective in FL learning: The role of attitude as a dynamic factor.* Paper presented at the World Congress of Applied Linguistics in Halkidiki, Greece, sponsored by the International Association of Applied Linguistics. (ERIC Document Reproduction Service No. ED 326 073).

Tomlinson, C. A. (1995). *How to differentiate instruction in mixed-ability classrooms.* Alexandria, VA: Association for Supervision and Curriculum Development.

Traver, R. (1998). What is a good guiding question? *Educational Leadership, 55*(5), 70–73.

Warschauer, M. (1998). Researching technology in TESOL: Determinist, instrumental, and critical approaches. *TESOL Quarterly, 32*(4), 757–761.

Wells, G. (1992, November). *Language and the inquiry-oriented curriculum.* Paper presented at the annual meeting of the National Council of Teachers of English in Louisville, Kentucky. (ERIC Document Reproduction Service No. ED 355 539).

Widdowson, H. G. (1998). Context, community, and authentic language. *TESOL Quarterly, 32*(4), 705–716.

Wiggins, G. (1993). *Assessing student performance: Exploring the purpose and limits of testing.* San Francisco, CA: Jossey-Bass.

Wiggins, G. (1998). *Educative assessment: Designing assessments to inform and improve student performance.* San Francisco: Jossey-Bass.

54

Music and Skillful Thinking

Ruth M. Loring

Music and its connection to thinking has been the subject of a great deal of study and interest in recent years. From university research centers to the popular press, the possibility of enhancing intellectual capacity through music has captured the attention of the community at large. Does music instruction make a difference in the way human beings process information? Can music impact neural networking from the beginning of life and throughout adulthood? What can educators do to incorporate what is known about the positive effects of music into classroom instruction? In the quest for more skillful thinking, is music a fundamental?

MUSIC AND BRAIN DEVELOPMENT

After studying the impact of music instruction on the intellectual performance of preschoolers, researchers Frances Rauscher and Gordon Shaw think so. Reporting their findings in *Neurological Research* (Rauscher et al., 1997), they found that early music training dramatically boosts a child's brainpower. Specifically, the results indicate that piano instruction increases aptitudes for math and science, and the researchers speculate that this effect probably extends to all musical instruments. Shaw believes that music instruction may actually develop the hardware of the brain rather than merely building specific skills typically thought of as being musical—for example, reading musical notation, maintaining rhythm, and so on. The thinking skills apparently developed in these preschoolers are those needed to succeed in higher levels of math and science.

Preschoolers in the study demonstrated dramatic improvement in tests that measure spatial reasoning. The six-month experiment placed children in four groups, each receiving one of the following treatments: weekly piano instruction, computer training, singing, and no special training. Of these groups, the children given piano instruction performed at a 34 percent higher level on the spatial reasoning tests than the other three groups of preschoolers. Rauscher attributes the significant difference that piano instruction seems to make to the multiple modes of input. With feedback provided through various senses—for example, chords sound wide, feel wide, and look wide—patterns formed have greater opportunity to link, and stronger connections are made. The process of playing the piano mirrors the development of abstract reasoning, logic, and order—skills necessary in math and science.

Rauscher and colleagues' tentative conclusions are that instruction in music stimulates early brain development. Even though some proponents of music education advocate that music should be studied and appreciated on its own merits, students at all levels of "music ability" can benefit from musical instruction and a musical environment. The actual act of making music seems to be the vehicle through which intellectual capacity is shaped for higher-level thinking. Advocacy for incorporating music, as well as all the arts, across the curriculum comes from music educators who claim that "participation in music and arts builds literacy among children and helps them develop intuition, reasoning, imagination, and dexterity into unique forms of expression and communication" (Consortium of National Arts Education Associations, 1994). A study compiled by the College Board showed a direct correlation between improved SAT scores and the length of time spent studying music and other arts. Students studying the arts four or more years scored 59 points higher on verbal and 44 points higher on math portions of the SAT than did students with no coursework or experience in the arts, results only achieved through sequential arts education in public schools (Music Educators National Conference, 1995).

What is the significance of the development of spatial memory? Caine and Caine (1997) explain that spatial memory does not require rehearsal and allows for instant memory because it is always engaged, inexhaustible, and registers experiences in three-dimensional space. Spatial memory is unlike the set of memory systems that allow for rote memorization, in which unrelated information can be stored. If information and skills are separated from prior knowledge and actual experience, dependence on rote memory and repetition is increased. If music instruction enhances neural networking of the brain, then using music in experientially based, brain-compatible learning strategies could actually help reshape pedagogy.

There does appear to be a difference in the impact of listening to music and actually performing music. Studies of the impact of listening to music on learning have been conducted with college students (Rauscher, Shaw, & Ky, 1993). After 10 minutes of listening to a Mozart piano sonata, students demonstrated a 30 per cent improvement in intellectual processing as demonstrated on a test of spatial-temporal reasoning skills. This test measures ability to form mental images from physical objects or to see patterns in space and time. These are the skills used by architects and engineers, and they serve as the basis of understanding proportion, geometry, and other mathematical and scientific concepts. Although listening to Mozart appears to prompt and ready the brain to perform spatial reasoning tasks, the improved ability of the college students faded within an hour.

Nevertheless, listening to music as a means to enhance learning is becoming a widely accepted practice. For over 20 years, Campbell (1997) has researched the effects of sound and music on learning and health, promoting the idea that music can enhance intellectual performance. Sprenger (1999) points out that "when people hear music they like, the experience causes the release of endorphins, which makes them feel good" (p. 99). Perhaps it is the "feeling good" that is the behind the positive impact of music on learning. However, research findings do not support any claim that listening alone has a long-term impact on spatial reasoning ability. The "Mozart effect" seems to impact short-term memory only. In contrast, "music training, unlike listening, produces long-term modifications in underlying neural circuitry" (Rauscher et al, 1997, p. 7).

Even with cautionary words (Bruer, 1998) about the impact of music instruction, teachers are tapping into this "temporary IQ upsizing" with recordings such as those by Gary Lamb (1995), whose compositions are widely used by teachers seeking to create the environment that enhances brain activity. Mozart himself listened to music before he was born as his father played the piano and violin. By the time he was four, Mozart was composing and playing music for his father's friends. In only 36 years of life, he composed more than 600 major compositions, including symphonies, concertos, and choir pieces.

The value of music in the development of thinking is not that every child can be made into a Mozart or an Einstein but that the stimulus children receive early in life helps determine how well their brains will function throughout life. It appears that the best time to boost the synaptic density of the brain is between the ages of 2 and 10. Density of synapses increases sharply during the first months of life, reaches a maximum at ages 1 to 2, declines between the ages of 2 and 16, and then remains relatively constant until the age of 72 (Gardner, 1985). Extremely rapid learning of the young child may reflect an exploitation of the larger number of synapses available at that time (pp. 44–45). To a certain extent, then, the kind of brain that develops to maturity depends upon the types of experiences the brain has undergone (Sylwester, 1995).

However, we know from 40 years of research that the brain is modifiable, and it is never too late for the brain to learn. Throughout a lifetime, complex experiences stimulate neural connections. Diamond, Krech, and Rosenzweig (1964) found that rats in a complex, naturally enriched environment had larger brains compared with rats in an impoverished environment. Furthermore, even rats that had lived up to three-fourths of their lives in impoverished environments showed positive change in parts of their brains when put in enriched, complex environments. Recent studies on brain development of accomplished musicians (Schlaug, Jancke, Huang, & Steinmetz, 1995) have shown that early exposure to instruction does result in increased thickness of fibers connecting the two hemispheres of the brain. However, this does not cause exceptional music ability. Neither inherited characteristics nor the environment can ever be the sole determinant of development or behavior.

MUSIC IN THE LEARNING CONTEXT

As the research clearly indicates, children are not blank slates. Our experiences shape our brains, and then our brains shape our experiences. Diamond and Hopson (1998) offer guidelines for parents and other caregivers on how to use music to nurture a child's intelligence, creativity, and healthy emotions. Within the school setting they recommend arousing motivation to learn and building contexts for true understanding through apprenticeships, collaborative learning groups, and microcommunities.

They call for a "participatory school" (p. 284) where direct application of learning tools can be experienced in an apprenticeship-type environment. In schools that focus on authentic learning, such as the Met in Providence, Rhode Island, students are actively engaged in their own learning process. Music lets students be creators, producers, performers, and critics, behaving as skillful thinkers in authentic learning environments both in and out of school (Boardman, 1989). For example, as creator, students can write music. As producer, they can format the musical piece for distribution. As performer, students can play the piece themselves or conduct others. And as critics, students can make sensitive discriminations and evaluations. Furthermore, music can stimulate the 12 "qualities of genius" proposed by Armstrong (1998), who makes his claim on the basis of research in the neurosciences, anthropology, and developmental psychology. Both producing and consuming music creates an environment and expectation for these qualities to flourish: curiosity, playfulness, imagination, creativity, wonder, wisdom, inventiveness, vitality, sensitivity, flexibility, humor, and joy. Could it be that the absence of role models in a child's environment that display characteristics of some or all of the 12 qualities of genius may starve dendrites in those portions of the brain that support these behaviors?

> An environment that fails to recognize the importance of the 12 qualities of genius may starve those traits out of existence, while surroundings that are "genius friendly" may well create neurological connections that facilitate their growth. (Armstrong, 1998, p. 17)

In addition, developing creative and critical thinking is intricately connected to healthy emotions. The intelligent behaviors that Costa (1991) describes as the basis of thoughtful environments can be prompted through the discipline of musical performance. For example, persistence is needed to "analyze a problem, to develop a system, structure, or strategy of problem attack" (p. 101). This ability is also needed to learn to play an instrument with enough skill to play for pleasure or for entertainment. In the process, children can develop self-esteem and self-regulation, critical aspects of "emotional intelligence" (Goleman, 1995). Clearly, through music, students can experience "intelligence in the emotions and . . . intelligence can be

brought to emotions" (p. 40). As performing members of an ensemble, students exercise a whole range of emotive and cognitive abilities, giving meaningful context to experience. Students involved in the pursuit of musical accomplishment learn to trust the process of personal preparation and to regard the needs of the group even at the expense of personal recognition. This ability to be self-effacing while still practicing the kind of "complex thinking" Lipman (1991) describes as recursive, metacognitive, and self-corrective reflection on the process can be elegantly developed through musical expressions.

Strategic and reflective practices a skillful thinker uses to make decisions and solve problems are complex and can be expressed through music. For example, processing information includes a careful analysis of details, comparison of what is known to what else needs to be known, ability to predict possible consequences in light of a given set of circumstances, and, through it all, withholding judgment until all evidence to support a particular conclusion has been evaluated. Can music actually facilitate these "skillful thinking" processes? An environment that invites full participation among students to actively engage in meaningful learning experiences is enhanced through the use of music.

Using music in terms of both performing and listening helps to set a context for learning that permits connection making at complex levels of thinking. Perkins proposes that all learning is situated in a culture of needs and practices that gives the knowledge and skill being learned "context, texture, and motivation" (1992, p. 45). If students in "smart schools" are going to "practice their understandings" instead of "practicing remembering," how can music serve as an effective medium? Suggested connections between music learning and Perkins's theories of intellectual development are shown in Figure 54.1.

—*Figure 54.1*—
Connections Between Intellectual Development and Music Learning

Perkins suggests that intellect can be developed as you provide . . .	Music offers opportunities for students to actively engage this area of intellectual development by . . .
• Clear information.	• Performing in a relevant context that enables students to experience real connections.
• Thoughtful practice.	• Valuing daily practice that includes reflection and self-assessment.
• Informative feedback.	• Receiving feedback from coaching and critiquing from mentors, teachers, and peers.
• Strong intrinsic or extrinsic motivation.	• Performing for personal pleasure and for entertaining others.

—Figure 54.2—
Connections Between Goals of Teaching and Learning and Music Instruction

Goals of teaching and learning include . . .	Music instruction provides opportunities to meet these goals through . . .
• An appreciation of interconnectedness.	• Creation of musical pieces or production of compositions.
• A strong identity and sense of being.	• Enhancement of self-esteem through performance.
• A sufficiently large vision and imagination to see how specifics relate to each other.	• Opportunities to experience a blending of parts to create a whole musical presentation.
• The capacity to flow and deal with paradox and uncertainty.	• Collaboration as a member of an orchestra, ensemble, or other group.
• A capacity to build community and live in relationship with others.	• Meaningful context to develop personal discipline as an individual and as a team member.

Learning, then, is a consequence of thinking. Schools should be places where students can learn meaningful content through the process of thinking skillfully. Music offers the opportunity to be reflective and gather experiences (Perkins, 1995) that transfer to other areas of learning. For example, music and math are related in that both are about fractions, timing, and movement. Without math, there is no music.

Music offers similar opportunities to develop skillful thinkers who are metacognitive in the approach to deciding what to do and believe. Students learn to be aware, strategic, and reflective (Barell, 1991) as they solve problems and make decisions. As one who produces or processes music, a student is continuously becoming aware of what is being heard, reflecting on the quality, judging the quality against criteria, and drawing conclusions as to its appropriateness based on purpose.

Elliot (1995) refers to music as involving processes-and-products—that is, actions and outcomes intertwined. Revelation of the self and relationship to community is the outcome of action that is purposeful and situated. This process-and-product model may be familiar in other subject areas, such as sociology, which studies equity in human interactions; or science, with its focus on analyses of hypotheses in light of evidence. Music instruction also fits this process-and-product model with connections to teaching and learning goals (Caine & Caine, 1997), as shown in Figure 54.2.

Music, then, becomes a vehicle for prompting the questions: What is acceptable? What is excellent? (Mann, 1998). In classrooms where instruction addresses all types of intelligences (Gardner, 1999; Armstrong, 1993; Lazear, 1991), musi-

cal experience can serve as a foundation from which all other forms of intelligence can be expressed. For example, students can listen to a musical piece and then write a response (invoking the linguistic/verbal intelligence). After creating a musical piece, they may develop a hypothesis (mathematical/logical intelligence), create a display or picture (visual/spatial intelligence), act out an interpretation (bodily/kinesthetic intelligence), design a response with a friend (interpersonal intelligence), or meditate on their own response in a solitary fashion (intrapersonal intelligence). Watching animals in an environment that includes various types of music and recording field notes on their behavioral variations could incorporate the eighth intelligence, natural/environmental. Musical experiences then may "assume privileged roles in the organization of subsequent experiences" (Gardner, 1999, p. 82). The point is that musical experience is fundamental.

Why should students study music? In addition to improved academic achievement, transferable skills developed through the study of music seem self-evident: perseverance, confidence, responsibility, discipline, wise use of time, precision, motor control, overcoming fear of the public, following directions, creativity, self-expression, and intellectual and social development (Kavanaugh, 1995). If we as educators provide opportunities for students to create, produce, consume, and critique music throughout their educational experience, we foster both intellectual development and an attitude of confidence that encourages learning for a lifetime. The movement to recognize the significance of music could be the beginning of a revolution in understanding how we think and how we can think more skillfully.

References

Armstrong, T. (1993). *Seven kinds of smart: Identifying and developing your many intelligences*. New York: Plume.

Armstrong, T. (1998). *Awakening genius in the classroom*. Alexandria, VA: Association for Supervision and Curriculum Development.

Barell, J. (1991). *Teaching for thoughtfulness: Classroom strategies to enhance intellectual development*. New York: Addison-Wesley.

Boardman, E. (Ed.). (1989). *Dimensions of musical thinking*. Reston, VA: Music Educators National Conference.

Bruer, J. T. (1998, November). Brain science, brain fiction. *Educational Leadership, 56*(3), 14–19.

Caine, R. N., & Caine, G. (1991). *Making connections: Teaching and the human brain*. Menlo Park, CA: Addison-Wesley.

Caine, R. N., & Caine, G. (1997). *Education on the edge of possibility*. Alexandria, VA: Association for Supervision and Curriculum Development.

Campbell, D. (1997). *The Mozart effect: Tapping the power of music to heal the body, strengthen the mind and unlock the creative spirit*. New York: Avon Books.

Consortium of National Arts Education Associations. (1994). *National standards for art education: What every young American should know and be able to do in the arts*. Reston, VA: Music Educators National Conference.

Costa, A. (1991). The search for intelligent life. In A. Costa (Ed.), *Developing minds: A resource book for teaching thinking* (Rev. ed., Vol. 1, pp. 100–106). Alexandria, VA: Association for Supervision and Curriculum Development.

Diamond, M., & Hopson, J. (1998). *Magic trees of the mind*. New York: Plume.

Diamond, M. C., Krech, D., & Rosenzweig, M. R. (1964). The effects of an enriched environment on the histology of the rat cerebral cortex. *Journal of Comparative Neurology, 123*, 111–120.

Elliot, D. (1995). *Music matters: A new philosophy of music education*. New York: Oxford University Press.

Gardner, H. (1985). *Frames of mind*. New York: Basic Books.

Gardner, H. (1999). *The disciplined mind: What all students should understand*. New York: Simon and Schuster.

Goleman, D. (1995). *Emotional intelligence*. New York: Bantam Books.

Kavanaugh, P. (1995). *Raising musical kids: Great ideas to help your child develop a love for music*. Ann Arbor, MI: Servant Publications.

Lamb, G. (1995). Golden Gate Records, P.O. Box 4100, Santa Cruz, CA, 95063.

Lazear, D. (1991). *Eight ways of knowing: Teaching for multiple intelligences* (3rd ed.). Palatine, IL: SkyLight.

Lipman, M. (1991). *Thinking in education*. New York: Cambridge University Press.

Mann, L. (1998, Spring). Music education's forte. ASCD *Curriculum Update*, 8.

Music Educators National Conference. (1995). Profiles of SAT and achievement test takers. New York: College Board.

Perkins, D. (1992). *Smart schools: From training memories to educating minds*. New York: Free Press.

Perkins, D. (1995). *Outsmarting IQ: The emerging science of learnable intelligence*. New York: Free Press.

Rauscher, F., Shaw, G., & Ky, K. (1993, October 14). Music and spatial task performance. *Nature, 365*(6447), 611.

Rauscher, F., Shaw, G., Levine, L., Wright, E., Dennis, W., & Newcomb, R. (1997, February). Music training causes long-term enhancement of preschool children's spatial-temporal reasoning. *Neurological Research, 19*(1), 2–8.

Schlaug, G., Jancke, L., Huang, Y., & Steinmetz, H. (1995). In vivo evidence of structural brain asymmetry in musicians. *Science, 267*, 699–701.

Sprenger, M. (1999). *Learning and memory: The brain in action*. Alexandria, VA: Association for Supervision and Curriculum Development.

Sylwester, R. (1995). *A celebration of neurons: An educator's guide to the human brain*. Alexandria, VA: Association for Supervision and Curriculum Development.

Web Sites

http://www.mindinst.org
http://www.musica.uci.edu
http://www.amc-music.com
http://www.menc.org

55

Developing a Lifetime of Literacy

Rebecca Reagan

The importance of being truly literate came home to me recently. It was snowing as I drove my car on the slick highway, so I gripped the steering wheel as tightly as I could and focused on the road ahead. At the top of an incline, I realized the traffic in front of me had come to a standstill. Being cautious, I stopped well back of the 18-wheeler in front of me and placed my trust in the ability of those behind me to read the bumper sticker prominently displayed on the back of my car, which said, "If you can read this, YOU ARE TOO CLOSE!" My faith in my fellow drivers' literacy came into question rather quickly when the vehicle behind me crashed into my car. Calmly extricating myself from the automobile, I met the man who hit me and inquired a bit impatiently whether he was literate. To this he answered somewhat tersely, "I read the sticker, lady, but I didn't think about exactly what 'too close' implied!"

These words, uttered by a total stranger, reinforced my thinking about the nature of literacy and what we as educators should do to create truly literate lifetime learners.

Defining Literacy

Defined traditionally as "the ability to read and write," literacy as an educational term has come to mean the ability to decode and encode symbols. The driver of the other car decoded the words enough to understand what they meant literally when he used his knowledge to read the text. However, he didn't think about their implications or significance. He exhibited what some reading experts call "literal comprehension." Many of our students also meet this same standard of literacy when they are given material to read. Whether they are reading fiction or nonfiction, students use the text to obtain various pieces of knowledge but don't think about the significance and implication of what they have read. Many standardized tests only test for this kind of literacy. Decoding in this sense—that

is, literal comprehension—is not all that is needed for true literacy. True literacy is better described as understanding the deeper meaning of what is being read. Just as Bloom (1956) designates higher-level thinking skills, so, too, are there higher-level literacy skills. For example, the ability to make well-founded inferences and to draw well-supported conclusions from a text—as we do, for example, when we generalize, make judgments about motives and causes, or make predictions based on what is in a text—exceeds the standard level of literacy. The kind of thinking employed in higher-level literacy involves such "higher-level abilities" and not just simple decoding strategies. The high-level literate person combines textual clues with background knowledge to make accurate inferences that can be supported by evidence. The ability to make these inferences is a crucial part of higher-level literacy. The critical thinking skills that support higher-level literacy are crucial for its development.

Teaching for Higher-Level Literacy

Teaching for higher literacy can involve many different instructional techniques. In fiction and some nonfiction material, characters, both imagined and real, interact with each other and the events that take place around them. Well-founded inferences about characters do not simply manifest themselves. The most successful instruction that has been researched involves teaching students strategies—for example, questioning strategies—that guide them in approaching a text, and structural frameworks, or templates, that guide them in their writing. These strategies and templates are structures that help students to organize the thinking that lies behind higher-level literacy and to do it well. Therefore, teaching for higher-level literacy is a special case of teaching thinking skills applied to reading and writing texts. For example, when 5th grade students read *Shiloh* by Phyllis Reynolds

Naylor, if they just learn that Marty hides Shiloh from Judd, they are reading only for literal comprehension. However, if they use a reading strategy that focuses them on what consequences Marty's action will have both for himself and his family and then on finding evidence in the text to support their thinking, they are learning a higher level of literacy, one that has real-life implications. Engaging with the text and developing strategies to understand it in a deeper way takes much more than a few questions or a worksheet, no matter how well done each might be. Laying a foundation for deeper thinking is important not only to the students, but will make the teacher's job of developing more literate learners an easier one. The thinking skill/reading skill instruction that is involved here is, of course, instruction that is infused into language arts instruction, rather than in a separate course or thinking program.

Instruction that focuses on inferential abilities can be embedded in broader thinking tasks as well. Literal comprehension requires students to only read about what a character is doing. Readers do not make inferences about why a character is acting or reacting in a particular manner, what the consequences of a character's actions might be, or what the text tells the reader about the character's character. Again using *Shiloh* as an example, teachers typically might ask their students to describe Marty. However, deeper understanding of behavior both past, present, and future falls by the wayside. Decision making (Swartz & Parks, 1994) is a strategy that enables students to probe the motives and actions of people more intensely. Instead of merely describing Marty, students use Marty's character traits to determine what he should do about Shiloh. Key in this thinking task is making inferences about the consequences of Marty's actions. To do this, they not only must read the text carefully but also find evidence to support their inferences using previous behaviors, reactions to outside influences, and interaction with others.

In each of these instances, what is in the text becomes meaningful in a deep sense as readers combine their own background knowledge and experiences with textual clues in order to think like the character in a story or novel. We have a saying in Texas that goes somewhat like this: "Before you can fully understand another person, you need to walk a mile in his moccasins." For students to understand what another person would do in a particular situation, or to "walk a mile in their moccasins," they should first explore the various forces that influence not only their own perspectives, but also those of others. The following activity helps focus students on the many things that influence perspective. It uses the book *Two Bad Ants* by Chris Van Allsburg.

1. Have students fold a 12" × 18" sheet of white or manila paper into 16 rectangles. Students should write "Two Bad Ants" and their names in the upper left-hand box. Beginning with the box to the right of this one, number the rest of the boxes from 1 to 32 (using the back also).

2. Read each page *not* showing the pictures and allow students about a minute to sketch (using only a few lines to represent an object) what they hear. Proceed in this manner until the book is complete.

3. Reread the book showing the pictures and have the students compare what they drew to what is drawn by Van Allsburg.

4. Discuss with them the difference between their pictures and the illustrations and why they think these differences occurred.

Students will usually sketch from their perspectives and not take into consideration the size orientation of an ant. For example, the "mountain" is usually drawn as a mountain and not the side of a house. Emphasize that size creates attitude. The world is built for ordinary people. Here's an activity that will help them understand this:

1. Have students stand on their chairs and discuss the impact being "taller" has on them. Then have them briefly lie face down with their chins on the floor. Again discuss the impact of a much smaller size.

2. Using a large piece of paper or chart tablet, have students list influences on their lives. Lists usually include such things as home environment, parents, divorce, peers, siblings, religions, specific traumatic events, climate, teachers, economic status, handicapping conditions, and so forth. As students add items to the list, discuss how each one influences their lives regularly.

3. Have students think about what it would be like to be very different from who they are. Using either poetry or prose, have students write about what it would be like to be someone else. The following example uses a form of poetry called an acrostic:

M etal whizzing by my head
E ating mush with loads of dread

A lways drumming a fast retreat
T reating wounds and swollen feet

W alking hard through swamps and trees
A lways wondering what next I'll see
R aring to up front now, to feel the pain and honor somehow
—by David Boothe, age 10, Preston Smith Elementary School, Lubbock, Texas

These pieces of writing are usually amazing because students have put so much thought into them before writing. Students should also keep a copy of the class list of influences and add to it throughout the year. This may seem simplistic, but by looking at specific influences, students are much more aware of those things that determine the behavior not only of characters, but of real people as well. This activity is a stepping-stone to strategies that will require a departure from the traditional ways to teach literacy—and to assess it. The most effective method to demonstrate this is to show how a skill that is employed at every grade level can be taught differently in order to gain higher levels of literacy.

OTHER TYPES OF THINKING THAT ENHANCE LITERACY

Besides helping students develop critical thinking skills needed to make well-supported inferences from a text, working with them on strategies for more analytical thinking skills also enhances higher-level literacy. These skills include comparing and contrasting, classifying, sequencing and ranking, determining parts/whole relationships, uncovering assumptions, and analyzing reasons and conclusions in a text to support the points of view advanced. For example, a skill that is basic to any classroom is comparing and contrasting, which is a natural way we learn and think. When we meet someone new, we compare and contrast this new person with people we already know. When we learn a new skill, we use previous skills and think about how this new one is like and different from the old. Traditionally, when comparing and contrasting two items, teachers have students make lists of similarities and differences or use a Venn diagram, stopping there—much like reading the bumper sticker and not thinking about its implications. After making the lists, students may then be assigned a three-paragraph essay based on what they have "learned." The "crash" comes when the writing reflects that these activities required only superficial literacy and did not probe deeply into the implications of the similarities and differences.

Skillful comparing and contrasting (Swartz & Parks, 1994) redefines this traditional strategy by adding elements that on the surface may seem simple but that enhance the thinking of the students to such an extent as to create a much higher level of literacy. By infusing a content lesson with this analytical thinking strategy, skillful comparing and contrasting achieves at least three objectives: (1) it focuses the learner on reading and writing in a meaningful way, (2) the strategy itself becomes a reading strategy that can be used in other contexts, and (3) it requires the learner to draw conclusions about the items being compared and contrasted. Thinking strategy maps, graphic organizers, and probing questions precede the determination of patterns and the development of finely drawn conclusions. The language of thinking is as important as the language of content. It follows then that the thinking objective is also as important as the content objective. Richer content leads to more powerful thinking, generating a greater payoff. Whether the lesson is based on abolitionism using Lincoln and Douglass (Swartz & Parks, 1994), or the character traits of Matt and Attean in the novel *Sign of the Beaver* by Elizabeth George Speare (Swartz, Kiser, & Reagan, 1999), the process is uniformly consistent. Students are introduced to the thinking skill along with the content, developing a thinking strategy map (Swartz & Parks, 1994) that should be displayed in the classroom to be used as needed (see Robert Swartz's Chapter 50, Figure 50.1, in this book).

Notice that the thinking strategy map begins much like traditional comparing and contrasting with the questions: How are they similar? How are they different? Departure from the traditional comes with the third question: What similarities and differences seem significant? The fourth and fifth questions further extend students' thinking by asking them to find categories and patterns, and then to interpret what they have "listed" by drawing conclusions.

To aid them in writing down the information they find in the text of the novel or the social studies book, a blank graphic organizer like the one shown in Figure 55.1 is given to each student.

Using various classroom strategies such as independent reading, cooperative learning, and jigsaw, students are given the opportunity to think actively about the content. Because it is important that students be able to change and modify the information on the organizer, they should write in pencil. At first they should complete only the sections on the organizer that answer the first two questions and the "with regard to" section that links the differences. When students report their information, it is important that the teacher extend each response with probing questions about the implications of the fact presented. Otherwise the information has no greater meaning and is merely superficial literacy. Persistence pays off when students begin to realize a greater understanding of the content while internalizing the thinking skill. In the lesson on Lincoln and Douglass, a typical similarity is "They were both self-taught." By asking such questions as "What does this show about their character and goals?" "How easy would it have been to be self-educated in the early 1800s?" and, of course, "What were the influences in their lives that made them so determined?" teachers create a thoughtful classroom where there are no absolutes. "Right" answers take a backseat to answers

— Figure 55.1—

A Graphic Organizer for Open Compare and Contrast

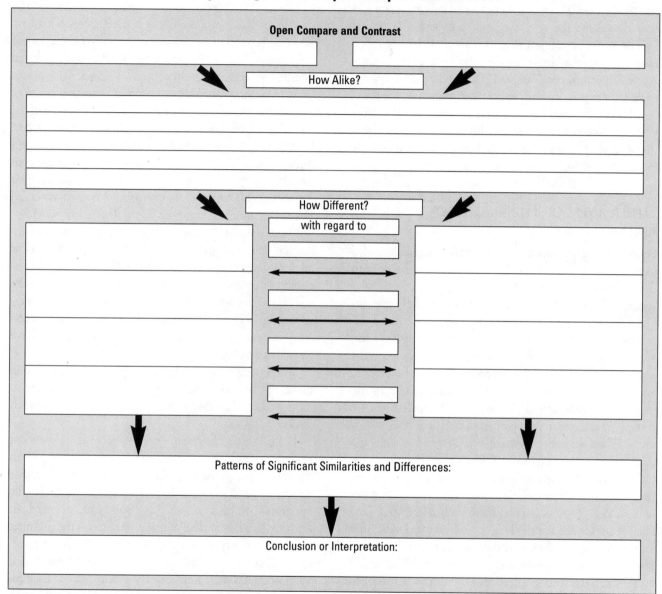

Adapted from *Teaching Critical and Creative Thinking in Language Arts: Infusion Lessons Grades 5 and 6,* by R. J. Swartz, M. Kiser, & R. Reagan (1999). Pacific Grove, CA: Critical Thinking Press and Software. Copyright 1999 by Critical Thinking Press and Software. Adapted with permission.

that have justification. Significant similarities and differences reveal themselves through discussion, and students often revert back to the content for more evidence to support their ideas. But the lesson is by no means over—otherwise it would just be extended literacy, not deep literacy.

Students are then asked to look for patterns found in the similarities and differences using the graphic organizer and the information from the discussion. The key to internalizing both

the content and the thinking process comes when the students are asked to make an inference and write a conclusion about the two things being compared. Figure 55.2 shows a completed graphic organizer for the lesson on Lincoln and Douglass. Notice the patterns that were found and the conclusion that was drawn about these two great men.

This higher level of literacy will manifest itself when students are asked to write an essay about what they have com-

—*Figure 55.2*—

Sample of a Completed Graphic Organizer for Open Compare and Contrast

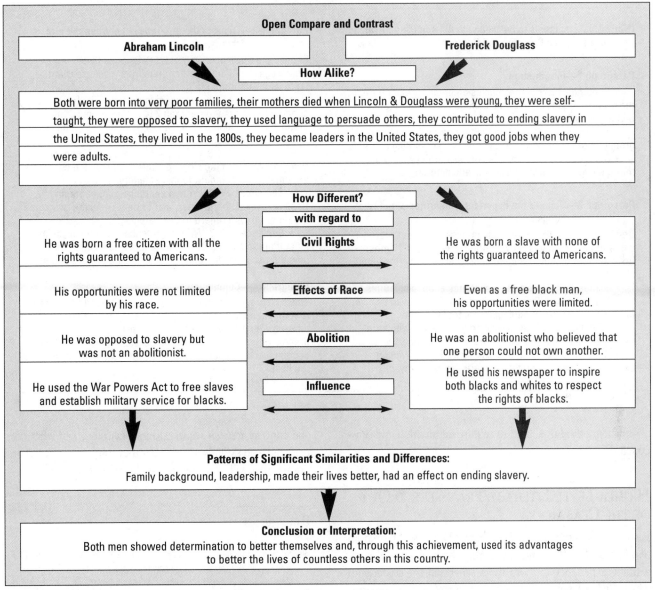

Open Compare and Contrast

| Abraham Lincoln | Frederick Douglass |

How Alike?

Both were born into very poor families, their mothers died when Lincoln & Douglass were young, they were self-taught, they were opposed to slavery, they used language to persuade others, they contributed to ending slavery in the United States, they lived in the 1800s, they became leaders in the United States, they got good jobs when they were adults.

How Different?

with regard to

| | **Civil Rights** | |
| He was born a free citizen with all the rights guaranteed to Americans. | | He was born a slave with none of the rights guaranteed to Americans. |

| | **Effects of Race** | |
| His opportunities were not limited by his race. | | Even as a free black man, his opportunities were limited. |

| | **Abolition** | |
| He was opposed to slavery but was not an abolitionist. | | He was an abolitionist who believed that one person could not own another. |

| | **Influence** | |
| He used the War Powers Act to free slaves and establish military service for blacks. | | He used his newspaper to inspire both blacks and whites to respect the rights of blacks. |

Patterns of Significant Similarities and Differences:
Family background, leadership, made their lives better, had an effect on ending slavery.

Conclusion or Interpretation:
Both men showed determination to better themselves and, through this achievement, used its advantages to better the lives of countless others in this country.

Adapted from *Teaching Critical and Creative Thinking in Language Arts: Infusion Lessons Grades 5 and 6,* by R. J. Swartz, M. Kiser, & R. Reagan (1999). Pacific Grove, CA: Critical Thinking Press and Software. Copyright 1999 by Critical Thinking Press and Software. Adapted with permission.

pared and contrasted. The inference that has been made in the form of a conclusion becomes the thesis sentence that will be supported by the information found on the graphic organizer. The richness of the writing reflects the depth of literacy in its language and structure. Once I asked a student what frightened him most about writing an essay. He replied, "The blank page." To assist those students who have difficulty with organization, teachers can provide a writing template such as the one shown in Figure 55.3. It does not tell the students what to say but gives them a way to structure their ideas. Higher-level literacy also includes the ability to use language to relate one's well-supported ideas to others in an organized and thoughtful manner.

In order for students to internalize these thinking and reading strategies, it is important that metacognition take place. By thinking about their thinking, they will also be thinking

—Figure 55.3—
Writing Template for Open Compare and Contrast

(Note: This template is to be used with the completed Graphic Organizer for Open Compare and Contrast.)

Paragraph 1—Introduction.
- Sentence 1: Write the conclusion or interpretation from the graphic organizer. It should include the names of the two things you are comparing.
- Sentence 2: Elaborate on Sentence 1 by giving background information on the two things you are writing about.
- Sentence 3: This sentence should inform your reader that the two items have similarities and differences.

Paragraph 2—Discuss the important similarities of the two things.
Before beginning this paragraph, choose the three most important similarities from your graphic organizer. Number them in order of importance from most important (1) to least important (3).
- Sentence 1: Write a topic sentence about similarities.
- Sentences 2 & 3: State similarity #2. Follow with an example of how the two things share that similarity.
- Sentences 4 & 5: State similarity #3. Follow with an example of how the two things share that similarity.
- Sentences 6 & 7: State similarity #1. Follow with an example of how the two things share that similarity.

Paragraph 3—Discuss the differences between the two things.
Choose the three most important categories (listed under "with regard to") and number them from most important (1) to least important (3).
- Sentence 1: Write a transition sentence. It should connect the topic of paragraph 2 to the new topic of paragraph 3. For example, "Although _____ and _____ have similarities, they also have differences."
- Sentences 2 & 3: Write a sentence about category #3. Using the boxes to the sides, elaborate on how the two items are different with regard to this category.
- Sentences 4 & 5: Write a sentence about category #2. Using the boxes to the sides, elaborate on how the two items are different with regard to this category.
- Sentences 6 & 7: Write a sentence about the most important difference. Using the boxes on the sides, elaborate on how the two items are different with regard to this category.

Paragraph 4—Conclusion.
This paragraph should contain at least two good sentences. It is your last opportunity to impress the reader with your thinking. You may rephrase your interpretation from the graphic organizer and further elaborate on this idea. The last sentence is the clincher. It is what your reader will remember the best.

---

about the method they used to acquire information and draw conclusions.

HIGHER-LEVEL LITERACY TRANSFERRED OUT OF THE CLASSROOM

Lessons such as the ones on Lincoln and Douglass, Marty from *Shiloh*, and *Two Bad Ants* are merely the beginning of a rewarding experience for both the teacher and the students in which higher-level literacy is an achievable goal. Often students extend their abilities by choosing to read other materials about the same topics or other related topics. To encourage internalization of the higher-level literacy and thinking skills, educators should take care to transfer them to other situations and content areas. If students think skillfully about what they read and read skillfully about what they think, it creates a continuum that will last a lifetime—a lifetime of literacy.

REFERENCES

Bloom, B. S., Englehart, M. D., Furst, E. J., Hill, W. H, & Krathwohl, D. R. (Eds.). (1956). *Taxonomy of educational objectives: The classification of educational goals. Handbook I: Cognitive domain.* New York: David McKay.

Swartz, B., Kiser, M., & Reagan, R. (1999). *Teaching critical and creative thinking in language arts: Infusion lessons Grades 5 and 6.* Pacific Grove, CA: Critical Thinking Press and Software.

Swartz, R., & Parks, S. (1994). *Infusing the teaching of critical and creative thinking into content instruction: A lesson design handbook for the elementary grades.* Pacific Grove, CA: Critical Thinking Press and Software.

56

Developing Thinking Skills in Physical Education

Daniel M. Landers, William Maxwell, Jessica Butler, and Lex Fagen

If the head is ready, the body will follow.

—*Alexander Popov,*
1996 Olympic Gold Medalist, Swimming

Physical education—defined here as the organized teaching of fitness, inventive movement patterns, games, physical skills, hygiene, and healthy lifestyles—is in decline in the United States, in part because of a mistaken belief that the body and mind are separate entities and physical education contributes little to an individual's mental functioning. In fact, the teaching of certain thinking and psychological skills is an integral part of effective physical education programs. Furthermore, research shows that exercise actually enhances thinking skills and a person's readiness to engage in mentally challenging activities. The curriculum for physical education takes in many disciplines, including anatomy, physiology, endocrinology, neuroscience, and body chemistry, that enable the student to understand all aspects or systems of the human body. It also includes inculcating life-long fitness patterns and habits.

THINKING IN PHYSICAL EDUCATION

Around the turn of the 20th century, it was common for children to play spontaneously many types of games without the intervention of adults. Compared with children a hundred years ago, children now engage in far fewer activities involving physical activity, and adults have taken more control over these activities (Sutton-Smith & Rosenberg, 1971). The neighborhood "pick-up game" of baseball or football has been transformed into highly organized and adult-run Little League and Pop Warner Football programs. As a result of these and other cultural developments—the dominance of television and time spent at the computer, for instance—children have fewer opportunities in games and sport to "think" on their own. Adults now do more of the "thinking" associated with

planning schedules, formulating rules, transporting children to practices and games, devising plays and strategies, choosing team members, adjudicating disputes, influencing decisions by referees and officials, and fund raising.

At the same time, and adding to the cause for concern, required daily physical education programs have been dramatically reduced nationwide. A recent survey published in *USA Today* (Weir, 2000) showed that only one state required daily physical education from 9th through 12th grade. Nineteen states required only one year; six states required one-half year. Three states had no requirement at all.

This is not to say children no longer have opportunities for developing thinking skills in sport and games. Children are naturally inventive—when adults stay out of their way. Children will spontaneously demonstrate the highest form of thinking—inventing—when the social organization and climate allow (see Brueghel, cited in Maxwell, 1983). Children will remember games and then modify them to their circumstances, thus demonstrating natural creativity. Children frequently formulate strategies, choose sides, and resolve disputes to keep the game going. They learn to cooperate and get along with teammates to optimize team performance, they learn agreed-upon rules, and sometimes they learn "set plays" of their own creation or out of a play book.

Physical educators need to be mindful of this inherent inclination in children when contemplating expanding the opportunities for children to think in the context of PE instruction. Many of the recent curricula in elementary school physical education emphasize more unstructured activities that allow children more flexibility in creating their own movement forms (Pangrazi, personal interview, 1999). The so-called new games movement is also an attempt to move away from the intentionally structured sports and games that are traditional in physical education classes.

Maxwell (1983) gives several examples of fundamental scientific principles being learned in traditional children's play and games. From playing with hoops, for instance, children learn the principles of centrifugal force, centripetal force, momentum, and inertia; and they learn that for a wheel to function well, all radii must be of equal length. No lecture or complicated theorem is needed, just the experience of play.

Every activity within physical education is an opportunity to teach one or more reasoning skills. For instance, children can learn the importance of accuracy by using a tape measure to assess broad-jump performance, their height, or the circumference of their flexed biceps. (Imagine the outcry if a child's leap is inaccurately measured.) Students can apply spatial skills by stepping off a basketball court and drawing it to scale, or musical skills by bouncing a ball in harmony with the instructor's changing rhythms. Students can learn analytic and interpersonal skills by carefully observing another child dribbling a basketball and then telling that child one thing that she is doing correctly or well and one thing she is doing incorrectly. Other activities can help students develop intrapersonal knowledge. They can develop self-awareness by examining their body shape and determining if it most closely resembles that of a gymnast, a basketball player, a wrestler, a swimmer, a football player, a long-distance runner, a sprinter, or a tennis player. One of the virtues that physical education has over other disciplines is that children can actually chart their progress on any physical attribute that they possess—height, weight, chest measurement, number of pushups achieved in three minutes, free-throw shooting percentages, and so forth. By charting such curves, students learn the power of graphical representation and that they can exercise enormous control over their bodies. Figure 56.1 lists additional examples of activities for all of Howard Gardner's original "seven intelligences" (Gardner, 1984).

PSYCHOLOGICAL SKILLS USED BY ELITE ATHLETES

Since the late 1970s, elite athletes have increasingly used cognitive-behavioral techniques (sometimes called psychological skills) to enhance their performance. Athletes have realized that the mental side of their sport is very important, and at the highest levels of competition, it is often the most important factor. This realization has led to the implementation of a host of cognitive-behavioral techniques that athletes use to help them control their arousal levels and focus their attention effectively. These techniques are not a substitute for practicing the physical skill, and, like physical skills, the mental skills work only if they are routinely practiced and perfected. Thus,

these mental skills are seen as an extension of training rather than a substitute for physical training.

Three of the most common psychological techniques are self-talk, goal setting, and imagery/visualization. Most athletes have goals and talk to themselves about their sport, but often the kind of goals they set and the kinds of things they say to themselves have not been shown by research to be effective. With self-talk, the emphasis is to teach athletes techniques that will prevent them from dwelling on negative self-statements (Zinsser, Bunker, & Williams, 1998). The goal is to prevent athletes from carrying the negative thinking into their next serve or next swing of the bat because it will prevent them from focusing on the task at hand and will not allow the kinesthetic sense to dominate the physical actions associated with the skill. To ward off, and thus control, negative thoughts, athletes are taught to use a cue, like saying the word *stop*. This makes them aware of the fact that negative thinking is taking place and this needs to be changed. They are taught how to reframe the negative thoughts into more positive thoughts. Once this is done, they are then required to reflect upon previous accomplishments and bring evidence to bear that would refute the previous negative statements. This final process is called "countering"; it is an important validating process that will help the athlete believe that the positive statement is realistic.

Research has shown that goals that are realistic and moderately difficult, are stated in absolute as opposed to relative terms, and combine short- and long-term objectives have the greatest effects in enhancing sport and motor performance (Kyllo & Landers, 1995). The goals must also be measurable, with an identified timeline for accomplishment (Gould, 1998). Athletes are taught how to set measurable goals that are based on their own levels of past performance (that is, a performance goal) rather than simply winning or beating a particular opponent (that is, an outcome goal). The advantage of a performance goal is that it allows for more personal control because the achievement is not dependent on things that may be out of the athlete's control (e.g., the skill and ability of the competitor). Athletes are also taught to set goals for practice and for competition, and how to set positive goals as opposed to negative goals.

Perhaps one of the most important cognitive aspects of a goal-setting program is that athletes—or any student for that matter—must carefully examine themselves and identify a goal-achievement strategy. This means that they need to find time to work out more, to lose weight, to gain more strength, to improve cardiovascular functioning, and so forth. This goal-setting process will provide all students with an opportunity to think about their daily activities and thus develop important

Sample PE Problems Related to Gardner's First Seven Intelligences[1]

—Figure 56.1—

Grade	Verbal[2]	Logical/Mathematical	Spatial	Kinesthetic	Musical	Interpersonal	Intrapersonal
K	Raise your left foot, right arm, etc.	Using a tape measure, measure the height of one student in your class.	Face north, south, east, west.	Stand on one foot, with arms outstretched, for 10 seconds.	Stomp your feet in rhythm with a runner seen here on video that I will show you.	Teach a smaller child how to dribble a basketball.	Analyze your height. Average? Above average? Below average?
1st	Turn 90 degrees to your right.	Measure the chest of three children in your class.	All class members form a circle. Who is at north, east, etc.?	Raise your left leg as high as possible.	Bounce a ball in rhythm with my bouncing.	Teach a smaller child how to hit a tennis ball.	Analyze your body weight. Average? Above average? Below average?
2nd	Answer orally five questions about soccer.	Measure the length of your hand.	All class members form a circle. Who is at 90 degrees, 180 degrees, etc.?	Close your eyes. Stretch your arms to horizontal. Bring your two index fingers together in front of your face.	Jump rope in rhythm with my counting.	You are captain of a basketball team. Who do you choose and why?	Compare your body shape to the ideal athlete in tennis, swimming, basketball, football, soccer, etc.
3rd	Describe orally three differences between two balls.	Measure the circumference of three balls.	Using your right arm as the hour hand and your left arm as the minute hand, show me 12 o'clock, 6 o'clock, etc.	Stand on one foot for 15 seconds.	Jump two ropes in rhythm with my counting.	You are a soccer team coach. Which daily drills will you insist upon?	For you to be a champion in _____, you need to _____.
4th	Paraphrase one of the major rules of tennis.	Guess the weight of each child in the class, then measure. Show the difference between the guess and the actual weight.	Using your right arm as the hour hand and your left arm as the minute hand, show me times such as 12:15, 6:30 and 10:45.	Stand on one foot for 45 seconds.	Stomp your feet in rhythm with a runner on video that I will show you.	Interview a top athlete in your nearby high school. Write the questions in advance.	Name one way for you to become more mentally tough. Chart over the semester your heart rate before, immediately after, and 120 seconds after rigorous exercise.
5th	Write a one-paragraph story of a sporting event that took place this week.	On a lab scale, measure the variations in weight of 10 baseballs.	Spin 720 degrees in four seconds.	Pat your stomach and rub your head simultaneously.	Stomp your feet in rhythm with a runner on video that I will show you.	Interview a top athlete in your nearby high school. Write the questions in advance.	My self-discipline regime consists of _____ _____ _____ _____.

(continued)

—Figure 56.1—

Sample PE Problems Related to Gardner's First Seven Intelligences[1] (continued)

Grade	Verbal[2]	Logical/Mathematical	Spatial	Kinesthetic	Musical	Interpersonal	Intrapersonal
6th	Watch a sporting event on TV and write a story for a sports newspaper.	Clock the maximum number of dribbles a classmate can do in 15 seconds.	Spin 1440 degrees in four seconds.	Stand on your right foot for 15 seconds while swinging your left arm.	Stomp your feet in rhythm with a runner I will show you on video.	Interview a top athlete in your nearby high school. Write the questions in advance.	To become a champion, I am prepared to sacrifice _____.
7th	Describe accurately the ritualistic motions of one major league baseball pitcher regularly seen in your city.	Obtain the heights of all the children in the class. Chart the average, mean, mode, and median heights.	Measure the areas of some common playing fields.	Lie on your back, raise your left leg toward zenith while holding your breath.	A PE Research Project (1) Problem: Does a particular type of music enhance athletic performance? (2) Method: Divide class into four equal groups. One group listens to waltzes, another to classical music, another to rock and roll, and the fourth to no music. (3) Observe and record performances in a variety of sports. (4) Refine hypothesis and retest. (5) Articulate "theory." [Note: This type of research may be repeated in the 8th, 9th, 10th, 11th, and 12th grades.]	Interview a top athlete in your nearby high school. Write the questions in advance.	The greatest fault I must correct to become a first-class _____ is _____.
8th	Describe accurately the motions of a diver in the first two seconds of a dive.	Measure the head circumference of another student. Record the measurements for the heads of every student in the class. List three reasons for variations.	Close your eyes and turn 270 degrees.	Stand on one foot for 120 seconds while counting backwards from 120.	(See 7th grade activity.)	If possible, interview a professional athlete.	I can visualize myself _____.

346

(continued)

—Figure 56.1—

Sample PE Problems Related to Gardner's First Seven Intelligences[1]   (continued)

Grade	Verbal[2]	Logical/Mathematical	Spatial	Kinesthetic	Musical	Interpersonal	Intrapersonal
9th	Write the script for a play-by-play description of a 30-second segment of a professional basketball game.	Measure reaction/response speeds for various stimuli chosen by the instructor.	In groups of three students, create the end points of a 140-degree angle with your bodies.	Bounce a ball with one hand and toss a smaller ball with the other hand.	(See 7th grade activity.)	If possible, interview a professional athlete.	I need ___ hours of sleep every night.
10th	Write a review of a classical film of a sporting event.	Chart the world record for one track and field event by age level.	Face north, south, east, and west and identify the building you are facing.	Stand on one foot for 15 seconds while bending 45 degrees.	(See 7th grade activity.) [Note: Although this research problem may be repeated, there can be sufficient variations to sustain interest.]	If possible, interview a professional athlete.	The ideal diet for me consists of ___ ___ ___
11th/12th	Describe your body accurately for a coach of your potential sport.	Compare the world records for one track and field event by gender.	Orienteering exercises: With a compass and four name cards in hand, each student runs northeast as fast as she can in order to locate a marker. Once she finds the marker, she places her name card there and then runs southeast from this marker to the second marker. The students continue in this fashion until they reach the finish line.	Stand on one foot for 45 seconds while catching baseballs.	(See 7th grade activity.)	The best athlete in your high school asks your advice on choosing a college. How do you respond?	My most likely area of athletic success is ___

[1]We define thinking as responding to recognized problems. Therefore, one of the tasks of the PE teacher is to "force" children to respond to problems appropriate to their physical and mental development. Obviously each problem in this figure represents a type within a larger class. The instructor should spend a great deal of time understanding students' perceived futures and then conceive problems for those students that reflect their individual futures and enlist the students' support in "inventing" problems suitable for their age levels.
[2]In the early years, "verbal skills" are demonstrated more by listening and responding physically than by speaking. At certain critical development stages, children love to "prove" that they have "listening" skills.

time management skills. Without this important process of self-awareness and commitment to the goal, it is unlikely that the goal can be achieved.

Relaxation and imagery/visualization skills are also important. Research has shown that imagery enhances motor and sports performance (Feltz & Landers, 1983). Athletes often use imagery to focus attention and prevent distracting or negative (worrisome) thoughts. Although the visual sense is often dominant (thus the term *visualization*), one important aspect is to teach athletes to use multiple senses in their imagery (auditory, visual, kinesthetic, gustatory, tactile). Visualization of the performance outcome as viewed from a first-person perspective (as seen through your own eyes) has been shown to be better for enhancing performance than the use of a third person perspective (as you would see yourself full-body on a movie screen) (Vealey & Greenleaf, 1998). In a first-person perspective, the diver, for example, "sees" through her own imagination the sky or water at exactly the right instant in the dive. It is also known that in developing imagery skills it is better if the athletes are relaxed. Thus, athletes need to learn techniques for achieving a relaxed state.

Laura Jansson (1983), a former Finnish diving champion, argues that mental rehearsal—a form of preperformance imaging—has other applications. "It could, for example, be effectively used in the rehabilitation of injured patients. With mental rehearsal, one can stimulate the nervous pathways associated with the use of those certain muscles while they are still weak or incapacitated. Secondly, I would suggest the use of mental rehearsal to overcome fear or anxiety" (p. 196).

Relaxation techniques consist of progressive muscle relaxation or meditation techniques (Williams & Harris, 1998). In the former, the muscles of the body are divided into six regions (arms, legs, back, chest and stomach, lower face, and upper face). Athletes then learn how to maximally tense the muscles in each of these regions while either in a sitting or a supine position. The muscles are tensed for 7 seconds and then relaxed for 30 to 40 seconds. During the relaxation phase, the group leader repeatedly reminds the athletes to focus on the process of relaxation occurring in the muscle group that was previously tensed. In this way, athletes become more self-aware of minor levels of muscular tension and can then begin mind and body techniques to reduce the unwanted tension before it increases to a level that handicaps their performance.

Meditation skills can also be taught (Williams & Harris, 1998). These include sitting in a comfortable position, having a quiet environment, developing a passive attitude, and repeating a mantra (that is, a cue word) over and over again. Sometimes meditation involves specific breathing techniques,

but this is not essential. By repeating the mantra and maintaining a passive attitude, one can learn to control arousal levels and ward off any distractions while maintaining a steady focus on the task at hand. These meditation skills can be practiced in combination, and the combinations can be individualized for each athlete. Often a preperformance routine is created (Zinsser et al., 1998). The psychological skills are put together in a set order and used routinely before every performance. For example, while on the diving platform, Olympic gold medalist Greg Louganis used a self-talk preperformance routine that served as an attentional cue or trigger right before performing his forward three-and-one-half somersault dive. He used the following cue words: "Relax, see the platform, spot the water, spot the water, spot the water, kick out, spot the water again." Note that he did this *before* and not during the dive.

The preperformance routine can also consist of a combination of imagery and positively framed cue words, or it might consist of relaxation combined with imagery and physical movements. For instance, a basketball player about to shoot a free throw may first look at the basket and imagine the ball going through it. The player may then approach the free throw line, place his feet in a predetermined position, close his eyes momentarily, and mentally scan his body looking for unwanted muscle tension. If the athlete identifies some tension, he may slightly tense that muscle and then let all of the tension out by fully relaxing that part of the body. If he finds no tension, he continues the preperformance routine by bouncing the ball two times while focusing all of his attention on the basket. At this time, all self-talk and imagery cease so that the kinesthetic sense can act to guide the actual execution of shooting the ball. Thinking that involves sequential analysis of the skill during the execution of the skill often results in "paralysis by overanalysis." After bouncing the ball twice, the athlete brings the ball to the shooting position, momentarily sets the ball, and then shoots the ball. Once the shot is completed, the athlete gains the necessary feedback from the outcome of the shot and then goes through the preperformance routine again in preparation for the next shot.

Once athletes learn to use imagery and relaxation skills, they can test their ability to effectively use these skills by providing themselves with challenging or stressful situations. The purpose is to help them maintain their composure (that is, arousal control) and attentional focus in the presence of distracting stimuli (Schmid & Peper, 1998). For instance, teammates can verbally taunt them while they are preparing to shoot a basketball free throw. The athletes use the preperformance routine they have learned to counter the taunts.

In addition to cognitive-behavioral skills, athletes also learn techniques to promote teamwork and group cohesion (Carron & Dennis, 1998). In high-tech industries, it is becoming readily apparent that the teamwork and group problem-solving skills so prevalent in athletics are also needed in industry. Athletes gain experience in interpreting subtle body cues or statements made by opponents or teammates. This ability to "read" opponents and teammates comes with extensive playing experience. By reading the signs in opponents, athletes can anticipate what their opponents are about to do and thereby gain a strategic advantage. By reading signs in their own teammates, athletes are better able to motivate or, if necessary, replace players who might be showing signs of fatigue or loss of motivation.

The psychological skills that elite athletes use can, of course, be taught to children in physical education classes, and in other classes as well. Teachers can implement a unit that gives examples of how these skills can be used in other areas of the school curriculum, in the workforce, or in everyday activities. For example, students can apply goal-setting techniques in math or English classes. Relaxation and imagery skills can be taught to pupils who are anxious about speaking in front of the class. Techniques for team building and group cohesiveness can be extended to group problem-solving activities in the classroom or in industries where it is important for people to work as a team to accomplish a project. The idea is to use sport and physical education as a means to motivate students to become more self-aware and to make them aware of how these psychological skills apply to other areas of their lives.

EXERCISE AND COGNITIVE FUNCTIONING

Research findings show that moderate levels of regular exercise or even a single bout of exercise can improve one's mood state (Landers & Arent, 2001). Findings across hundreds of studies with thousands of subjects have consistently shown that exercise can reduce anxiety and depression levels and increase positive affect and self-esteem. These effects are largest for people who are low in fitness to begin with or for people who have initially high levels of negative mood. The effects are small to moderate, and are equivalent to modern-day prescription drugs designed to reduce anxiety and depression. Like these drugs, a single bout of exercise produces increases in levels of the brain chemicals serotonin and norepinephrine (Chaouloff, 1997; Dishman, 1997). Clinically anxious or depressed individuals typically have lower than normal levels of serotonin and norepinephrine. Research studies comparing exercise to psychotherapy and cognitive-behavioral therapy

again show that exercise improves mood as much as these psychological techniques do (Landers & Arent, 2001).

In addition to psychological benefits, exercise also provides many physical benefits such as lower blood pressure, less cardiovascular disease, greater muscle tone, less body fat, and a longer life span (Corbin & Pangrazi, 1996). In addition, the cost of exercise is less than the cost of psychotherapy and cognitive-behavioral therapy, and the number and severity of side effects are less than those associated with drug therapy (Martinsen & Stanghelle, 1997).

A meta-analytic review of nearly 200 studies has shown that exercise has a small but positive effect on cognitive functioning (Etnier et al., 1997). This meta-analysis included cognitive tests of memory and perception, as well as verbal and math reasoning. In addition to increases in levels of brain neurotransmitters and improved mood state affecting thinking readiness, other mechanisms are believed to contribute to the small gains in cognitive functioning brought about by exercise. Researchers working with rats have found relationships between exercise and permanent structural changes in the brain (Black, Isaacs, Anderson, Alcantara, & Greenough, 1990). The initial results indicate that (1) exercise may result in changes either in the brain itself or in the brain environment, and (2) these changes may have a positive influence on the performance capabilities of the brain (Etnier & Landers, 1995).

SUMMARY

Research evidence supports the notion that exercise, sport, and games enhance thinking skills and the readiness to engage in mentally challenging activities. Unfortunately, many individuals seem to believe the opposite as the length and frequency of required physical education in grades K–12 continue to decline in the United States. We believe it is necessary for the public, school board members, and educational administrators to realize that physical education does play a role in educating students not only physically but also mentally. Physical education can also educate students in concepts that foster healthy lifestyles. Exercising in physical education classes can provide students with the necessary levels of brain neurotransmitters, and perhaps structural changes in the brain, that promote improved mood state, which in turn results in improved cognitive functioning. Psychological skills and other thinking activities can and should be taught in physical education programs. These skills can be generalized beyond physical education and sport examples so that students can realize their applicability in other academic subjects and in other areas of their lives.

REFERENCES

Black, J. E., Isaacs, K. R., Anderson, B. J., Alcantara, A. A., & Greenough, W. T. (1990). Learning causes synaptogenesis, whereas motor activity causes angiogenesis, in cerebellar cortex of adult rats. *Proceedings of the National Academy of Sciences, 87,* 5568–5572.

Carron, A. V., & Dennis, P. W. (1998). The sport team as an effective group. In J. M. Williams (Ed.), *Applied sport psychology* (pp. 128–141). Mountain View, CA: Mayfield.

Chaouloff, F. (1997). The serotonin hypothesis. In W. P. Morgan (Ed.), *Physical activity and mental health* (pp. 179–198). Washington, DC: Taylor & Francis.

Corbin, C. B., & Pangrazi, R. P. (1996, July). What you need to know about the Surgeon General's report on physical activity and health. *Physical Activity and Fitness Research Digest, 2*(6), 1–8.

Dishman, R. K. (1997). The norepinephrine hypothesis. In W. P. Morgan (Ed.), *Physical activity and mental health* (pp. 199–212). Washington, DC: Taylor & Francis.

Etnier, J. L., & Landers, D. M. (1995). Brain function and exercise. *Sports Medicine, 19*(3), 81–85.

Etnier, J. L., Salazar, W., Landers, D. M., Petruzzello, S. J., Han, M. W., & Nowell, P. (1997). The influence of physical fitness and exercise upon cognitive functioning: A meta-analysis. *Journal of Sport & Exercise Psychology, 19,* 249–277.

Feltz, D. L., & Landers, D. M. (1983). The effects of mental practice on motor skill learning and performance: A meta-analysis. *Journal of Sport & Exercise Psychology, 5*(1), 25–57.

Gardner, H. (1984). *Frames of mind: The theory of multiple intelligences.* New York: Basic Books.

Gould, D. (1998). Goal setting for peak performance. In J. M. Williams (Ed.), *Applied sport psychology* (pp. 182–196). Mountain View, CA: Mayfield.

Jansson, L. E., (1983). Mental training: Mental rehearsal and its use. In W. Maxwell (Ed.), *Thinking: The expanding frontier.* Philadelphia: Franklin Institute Press.

Kyllo B. L., & Landers, D. M. (1995). Goal setting in sport and exercise: A research synthesis to resolve the controversy. *Journal of Sport & Exercise Psychology, 17*(2), 117–137.

Landers D. M., & Arent, S. M. (2001). Physical activity and mental health. *Handbook of research on sport psychology.* New York: John Wiley.

Martinsen, E. W., & Stanghelle, J. K. (1997). Drug therapy and physical activity. In W. P. Morgan (Ed.), *Physical activity & mental health* (pp. 81–90). Washington, DC: Taylor & Francis.

Maxwell, W. (1983). Games children play: Powerful tools that teach some thinking skills. In W. Maxwell (Ed.), *Thinking: The expanding frontier.* Philadelphia: Franklin Institute Press.

Schmid, A., & Peper, E. (1998). Strategies for training concentration. In J. M. Williams (Ed.), *Applied sport psychology* (pp. 316–328). Mountain View, CA: Mayfield.

Sutton-Smith, B., & Rosenberg, B. G. (1971). Sixty years of historical change in the game preferences of American children. In R. E. Herron & B. Sutton-Smith (Eds.), *Child's play* (pp. 18–50). New York: John Wiley.

Vealey, R. S., & Greenleaf, C. A. (1998). Seeing is believing: Understanding and using imagery in sport. In J. M. Williams (Ed.), *Applied sport psychology* (pp. 237–260). Mountain View, CA: Mayfield.

Weir, T. (2000, May 2). The new PE: "Life" sports are emphasized instead of the team concept so that no child is left out. *USA Today* (Final ed.), p. C1.

Williams, J. M., & Harris, D. V. (1998). Relaxation and energizing techniques for regulation of arousal. In J. M. Williams (Ed.), *Applied sport psychology* (pp. 219–336). Mountain View, CA: Mayfield.

Zinsser, N., Bunker, L., & Williams, J. M. (1998). Cognitive techniques for building confidence and enhancing performance. In J. M. Williams (Ed.), *Applied sport psychology* (pp. 270–295). Mountain View, CA: Mayfield.

VIII

Techniques for Teaching Thinking

It's not the answers that enlighten us, but the questions.

—*Descouvertes de la Salle*

Introduction

ARTHUR L. COSTA

This section is constructed around a profoundly helpful "blueprint" for teaching thinking suggested by Ron Brandt in his editorial preface to the September 1984 issue of *Educational Leadership*. In it he proposes that a balanced program for teaching thinking should include three components: teaching *for* thinking, *of* thinking, and *about* thinking. The chapters in this section are arranged to illuminate each of these three components.

This is a "how to do it" section as it provides practitioners with specific instructional skills and techniques intended to enhance student thinking. The first chapter begins with an overview and an elaboration of these three components—teaching *for*, *of*, and *about* thinking.

The next chapter—the first one in the *for* section—invites teachers to consciously employ specific teacher behaviors that are critical to creating school and classroom conditions which enhance student thinking. I describe those behaviors—questioning, responding, structuring, and modeling—and then provide examples and references to substantiating research.

The purpose of all teaching is for students to transfer knowledge beyond the situation in which it was learned. David Perkins and Gavriel Salomon's chapter is a classic in the literature on transfer, illuminating the perennial problem of transfer of learning and providing suggestions for how to maximize a student's inclination to draw forth knowledge and transfer it to new and novel situations.

Much research has shown that most student learning and achievement can be attributed to certain teacher characteristics including verbal interactions, classroom organization and management, teacher clarity, and classroom reward systems—how you teach is what you get! The chapter I coauthored with Robert Marzano invites teachers to pay close attention to their own verbal interactions with students and to deliberately embed their classroom language with thought-full words and phrases.

The next chapters in this section focus on the teaching *of* thinking. Frank Lyman and Jay McTighe begin by providing a variety of concrete, practical tools with which teachers can engage and enhance students' thought processes. In an effort to help students master the tools of effective, skillful thinking, they must understand thinking and problem solving as procedural knowledge. Barry Beyer next provides specific, step-by-step instructional strategies for the explicit teaching of thinking skills.

"I see what you mean" is an expression often used in casual conversation. David Hyerle provides eight Thinking Maps as a way to help students really see how they are thinking—to aid in communicating about the workings of the human mind; to more creatively and effectively generate, hold, and organize their thoughts; and to provide mental models of such thinking skills.

One of the capacities unique to human beings, to the best of our belief and knowledge, is the ability to stand aside and examine our thought processes while we are engaging in thought. It is what is known as metacognition—thinking *about* thinking. Because we know that effective problem solvers monitor their own mental progress as they plan for, execute, and reflect on a learning task, students need opportunities to talk aloud overtly about what is going on inside their heads covertly. My chapter on metacognition illuminates what is meant by the term and provides several classroom strategies for enhancing students' consciousness of their own mental behaviors and their effects on others and the environment.

Jack Lochhead, an expert in "talk aloud problem solving" strategies, then enriches the classroom applications of metacognition by describing "sound thinking"—putting thoughts to words.

Finally, Barry Beyer concludes this section with a synthesis of all the techniques described in the preceding chapters. His summary brings together a helpful set of criteria with which teachers can monitor their own teaching. He provides a mental map for ensuring that the classroom is a place that invites thinking—teaching *for* thinking; that teachers provide instruction in what may seem obvious to us but obscure to children—teaching *of* thinking; and that there is classroom dialogue about what is going on in our heads when we think—teaching *about* thinking.

57

Teaching For, Of, and About Thinking

Arthur L. Costa

Treat people as if they were what they ought to be, and you help them to become what they are capable of being.
—*Johann Wolfgang von Goethe*

A most helpful guiding organizer for the teaching of thinking can be found in the September 1984 issue of ASCD's *Educational Leadership* magazine, and that approach stands the test of time. Ron Brandt's editorial preface in that issue suggests that a balanced program for the teaching of thinking should include three components, which I have interpreted here.

TEACHING FOR THINKING

Many authors and psychologists feel that children learn to think long before they come to school and that educators need to create conditions that give that natural, human inclination to think a chance to emerge and blossom. Leslie Hart (1983), in his book *Human Brain, Human Learning*, suggested that schools are "brain incompatible." Brewster Ghiselin (1952) and Howard Gardner (1982) in their studies of creativity found that what young children do prior to entering school and what practicing scientists and artists do is more similar than anything that goes on in between. Indeed, Senge (1990) states,

> Children come fully equipped with an insatiable drive to explore and experiment. Unfortunately the primary institutions of our society are oriented predominantly toward controlling rather than learning, rewarding individuals for performing for others rather than cultivating their natural curiosity and impulse to learn . (p. 7)

Teaching *for* thinking simply means that teachers and administrators examine, monitor, and strive to create school and classroom conditions that are conducive to children's thinking. This means that

1. Teachers pose problems, raise questions, and intervene with paradoxes, dilemmas, and discrepancies that challenge and engage students' minds.

2. Teachers organize the classroom for interaction by arranging the environment for large and small group collaborative problem solving.

3. Teachers and administrators structure the school environment for thinking—communicating it as a goal, valuing it, making time for it, securing a variety of materials—manipulatives, rich data sources, technology, and raw materials—to support it.

4. Teachers, administrators, and students make it a policy to gather evidence of, reflect on, evaluate, report, and celebrate growth in it.

5. Teachers and administrators respond to students' ideas in such a way as to maintain a school and classroom climate that creates trust, allows risk taking, and is experimental, creative, and positive. This requires nonjudgmental listening and the probing of students' and each other's ideas and assumptions.

6. Teachers, administrators, and all the significant adults in the school and home environments strive to improve and model the behaviors of thinking that are desired in students.

Accomplishing all of the above would be a major undertaking in and of itself. That alone would go far in encouraging students to use their native intelligence. However, there's more. Even using all those strategies, an educator is not yet teaching students to think.

TEACHING OF THINKING

Most authors and developers of major cognitive curriculum projects agree that direct instruction in thinking skills is imperative. Edward de Bono, Barry Beyer, Reuven Feuerstein, Arthur Whimbey, and Matthew Lipman would agree on at least this one point: That the teaching of thinking requires that teachers instruct students directly in the processes of thinking. Even David Perkins (1981) believes that creativity can be taught—by design.

Statewide standards are often focused on one or more performances of such thinking operations. Following are some examples taken from Virginia's Standards of Learning (1995), with italics added to denote the connection to thinking operations:

> Grade 6 Reading/Literature: The student will "*Compare* and *contrast* author's styles" (p. 68).
>
> Grade 7 Civics and Economics: "The student will *compare* the national, state, and local governments with emphasis on their structures, functions and powers" (p. 90).
>
> Grade 11 Research: "The student will *analyze, evaluate, synthesize,* and organize information from a variety of sources into a documented paper dealing with a question problem or issue" (p. 75).

This may require the analysis of the subject areas or skills being taught in the curriculum, identifying the cognitive abilities prerequisite to mastery of those subject areas or skills, and then teaching those thinking skills directly.

In a science class, for example, the teacher or a lab workbook might pose a question: What inferences might you draw from this experiment? This assumes that students know what an inference is and how to make inferences from data. In a social sciences class, the teacher or text might ask the question: What comparisons do you see in the lives of Abraham Lincoln and Frederick Douglass? This assumes that students know how to examine significant characteristics and to find similarities and differences between the two subjects. So that students might successfully complete such assignments, it is prerequisite that they know the procedural knowledge of how to compare, how to infer, how to draw logical conclusions, how to make a prediction, and so on.

Critical thinking skills might be taught directly during a social studies unit on the election process. Steps in the problem-solving process might be taught directly during math and science instruction. The qualities of fluency and metaphorical thinking might be taught directly during creative writing.

Nothing yet has been taught about the application of these thinking skills beyond the context in which they were learned in various thinking tasks such as information production, decision making, and problem solving. Such thinking tasks are also found in state standards. Another example from Virginia's Standards of Learning (1995) illustrates the focus on thinking

tasks that require the application of specific thinking operations and skills:

> Grade 5 Computation and Estimation: "The student will *create and solve problems* involving addition, subtraction, multiplication, and division of whole numbers using paper and pencil, estimation, mental computation, and calculators" (p. 11).

While students may be able to perform the steps in the problem-solving process and correctly distinguish between classification and categorization, the question still remains whether students have any inclination to use these skills in real life situations.

Teaching *of* thinking not only includes teaching the steps and strategies of problem solving, creative thinking, and decision making, it also includes habituating those attitudes, dispositions or habits of mind that characterize effective, skillful thinkers. Such habits are formed over time by encountering and applying them in a variety of settings and contexts.

Take, for instance, another excerpt from the Virginia Standards of Learning (p. 33):

> Students will be able to *develop* scientific dispositions and habits of mind including:
> - curiosity
> - demand for verification
> - respect for logic and rational thinking
> - consideration of premises and consequences
> - respect for historical contributions
> - attention to accuracy and precision
> - patience and persistence.

Teaching *of* thinking, therefore, means that these cognitive skills, operations, and dispositions are taught *directly*. Even with all of this—creating conditions for thinking and teaching it directly—there is still more.

TEACHING ABOUT THINKING

Teaching about thinking consists of at least four components: 1) brain functioning, 2) metacognition, 3) great thinkers, and 4) epistemic cognition. A brief explanation of these may be helpful.

BRAIN FUNCTIONING

All of us, particularly adolescents, are fascinated by the intricacies, complexities, and marvels of our own bodies. Recently, increasing neurobiological research has shed new light on how our brains work. Teaching *about* thinking would include investigating such curiosities as: How do we think? How does memory work? What causes emotions? Why do we dream? How do we learn? How and why do mental disorders occur? What happens when part of the brain is damaged? Such resources as Richard Restak's book *The Brain* (1984); Nancy Margulies's and Robert Sylwester's teaching kits, *Discover Your Brain* (1998), and Margulies's comic book series, *Inside Brian's Brain* (1997); Kapil Gupta's *Human Brain Coloring Workbook* (1997); and Rebecca Treays's *Understanding Your Brain* (1995) would be helpful.

METACOGNITION

Being conscious of our own thinking and problem solving during the acts of thinking and problem solving is known as metacognition. It is a uniquely human ability occurring in the neo-cortex of the brain. Interestingly, it has been found that good problem solvers employ metacognition—planning a course of action before beginning a task, monitoring themselves during execution of a plan, backing up or adjusting a plan consciously, and evaluating themselves upon completion.

Metacognition in the classroom might be characterized by having discussions with students about what is going on inside their heads while thinking is occurring; comparing different students' approaches to problem solving and decision making; identifying what is known, what needs to be known, and how to produce that knowledge; or having students think aloud while problem solving.

Metacognition instruction would include learning how to learn; how to study for a test; and how to use strategies of question asking before, during, and after reading. It might include helping students become acquainted with their own and other's learning styles; the intelligences in which they excel; their own learning preferences such as visual, auditory, or kinesthetic; and strategies that can help them in situations that do not match their best learning modalities.

GREAT THINKERS

Students should be exposed to others—scientists, artists, composers, anthropologists, philosophers—who solve problems well and whose products of creative and critical thought have left a significant and lasting impact on society: Confucius, Marie Curie, Charles Darwin, Emily Dickinson, Thomas Edison, Albert Einstein, Benjamin Franklin, Mahatma Gandhi, Vincent van Gogh, Langston Hughes, Wolfgang Mozart, Isaac Newton, Louis Pasteur, and Leonardo da Vinci. Their logic, creativity, perseverance, and risk-taking are models of the types of behavior we wish to instill in our youth.

It would be desirable if students would respect these traits in people with whom they interact—not only in such noteworthy scientists, artists, and historians. Ideally, students will learn to appreciate the productive, efficient thinking and problem solving shown by mechanics who use efficient and precise ways of repairing automobiles; parents who manage their impulsivity when emotionally overwrought; entrepreneurs who seek creative ways to offer innovative services and products; and, yes, even teachers who plan, monitor, evaluate, and strive to perfect their instructional skills.

EPISTEMIC COGNITION

Epistemology is the study of how knowledge is produced and the methods of inquiry of the various disciplines of science, anthropology, psychology, art, drama, poetry, economics, history, and so on. It might include discussions of questions such as:

- How do the work processes of scientists and artists differ?
- What are the processes by which scientific truths are discovered and proven?
- What are the processes of inquiry used by anthropologists as they live with and study a culture?
- What goes on inside a maestro's mind as she conducts an orchestra?
- What was it about Mozart's genius that allowed him to "hear" a total musical composition before writing it down?
- What is that process by which poets create?
- Why can't we use processes of scientific inquiry to solve social problems?

Epistemic cognition is the study and comparison of the methods of the great artists, scientists, and scholars, and the differential processes of investigation, inquiry, and creativity that underlie their productivity.

For an example of how the Michigan State Assessment of Educational Performance approaches epistemic cognition, see Figure 57.1.

Matthew Lipman's program, *Philosophy for Children* (1991), is especially well suited for this approach. Other resources include David Perkins's book *The Mind's Best Work* (Harvard University Press, 1981); Carol Madigan and Ann Elwood's book *Brainstorms and Thunderbolts: How Creative Genius Works* (Macmillan Publishers, 1983); and Howard Gardner's book *Art, Mind, and Brain* (Basic Books, 1982).

—Figure 57.1—

Recognizing Others' Thought Processes

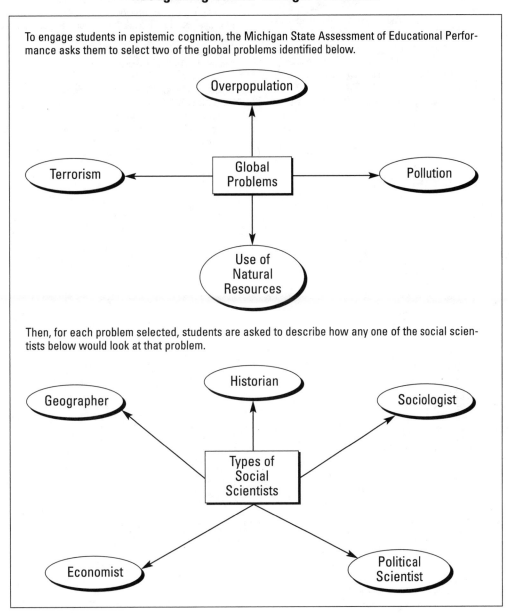

To engage students in epistemic cognition, the Michigan State Assessment of Educational Performance asks them to select two of the global problems identified below.

Then, for each problem selected, students are asked to describe how any one of the social scientists below would look at that problem.

STRIVING FOR BALANCE

By combining all three kinds of teaching thinking explained here, we can offer a well-balanced program. In summary, we should focus on

• Teaching *for* thinking—creating, monitoring and amplifying environmental conditions that maximize the possibility that innate thinking capacities will happen.

• Teaching *of* thinking—teaching thinking strategies directly, including specific cognitive operations, skillful performance of thinking tasks such as problem solving and decision making, and the dispositions or habits of mind that characterize skillful thinkers.

• Teaching *about* thinking—the attributes, conditions and processes of human thought.

REFERENCES

Brandt, R. (1984, September). Teaching of thinking, for thinking, about thinking. *Educational Leadership, 42*(1). Alexandria, VA: Association for Supervision and Curriculum Development.

Commonwealth of Virginia. (1995). *Standards of Learning for Virginia public schools.* Richmond: Board of Education, Commonwealth of Virginia.

Gardner, H. (1982). *Art, mind and brain: A cognitive approach to creativity.* New York: Basic Books. Basic Books Paperback, 1984.

Ghiselin, B. (Ed.) (1952). *The creative process.* Berkeley, CA: University of California Press.

Gupta, K. (1997). *Human brain coloring workbook.* Princeton, NJ: Princeton Review.

Hart, L. (1983). *Human brain, human learning.* New York: Longman.

Lipman, M. (1991). Philosophy for children. In A. L. Costa (Ed.) *Developing minds: Programs for teaching thinking* (Rev. ed., Vol. 2, pp. 35–38). Alexandria, VA: Association for Supervision and Curriculum Development.

Margulies, N. (1997). *Inside Brian's brain.* Tucson, AZ: Zephyr Press.

Margulies, N., & Sylwester, R. (1998). *Discover Your Brain* [Multimedia Kits]. Tucson, AZ: Zephyr Press.

Perkins, D. (1981). *The mind's best work.* Cambridge, MA: Harvard University Press.

Restak, R. (1984). *The brain.* New York: Bantam Books.

Senge, P. (1990, Fall). The leader's new work: Building learning organizations. *Sloan Management Review, 7.*

Treays, R. (1995). *Understanding your brain.* Tulsa, OK: Educational Development.

58

Teacher Behaviors That Enable Student Thinking

Arthur L. Costa

Act so as to elicit the best in others and thereby in thyself.
—*Felix Adler*

What the teacher says and does in the classroom greatly affects student learning. Certain teacher behaviors influence a student's achievement, self-concept, social relationships, and thinking abilities. Teacher behaviors that invite, maintain, and enhance students' thinking in the classroom fall into four major categories:

• *Questioning* to challenge students' intellect and to help students collect and recollect information, process that information into meaningful relationships, and apply those relationships in different or novel situations. Questions can focus students on their own emotions, motivations, and metacognitive processes.
• *Structuring* the classroom by arranging for individual, small-group, and total-group interaction; by managing the resources of time, energy, space, and materials to facilitate thinking; and by legitimizing thinking as a valid goal for students.
• *Responding* to students so as to create a trusting environment and to help maintain, extend, and become aware of their thinking.
• *Modeling* behaviors that reflect *desirable* intellectual capacities and dispositions teachers encounter in the day-to-day problems and strategies of the classroom and school.

Classroom interaction generally falls into two categories: *recitation and dialogue*. Recitation is characterized by recurring sequences of teacher questions and student answers, where students recite what they already know or are learning through the teacher's questioning. The interaction is teacher-centered because the teacher controls the classroom by asking questions and reinforcing responses. Dialogue, on the other hand, involves group interaction in which students discuss what they don't know, usually by considering a subject from more than one point of view. The teacher, as the facilitator, creates an atmosphere of freedom, clarity, and equality.

This latter form of classroom interaction—dialogue—must be kept in focus as we consider which teacher behaviors are facilitative. Analyses of those instructional strategies intended to enhance thinking, creativity, cooperation, and positive self-worth stress the need for this dialectic discussion strategy. (See Richard Paul's discussion of dialectical and dialogical discourse in Chapter 67.)

QUESTIONING TO CHALLENGE STUDENTS' INTELLECT

Learning is an engagement of the mind that changes the mind.
—Martin Heiddeger, *What Do We Mean*

Minds are generally engaged through some form of cognitive dissonance, a provocation or an inquiry. Effective teachers create that dissonance either by raising a point of uncertainty or discrepancy in the content, by pressing the students to raise such points as they try to understand what is being presented, and by challenging students' assumptions or conclusions. Ultimately, engagement occurs through student interest and teachers can set the conditions in which the student's interest is piqued.

Teacher's questions can provide rich invitations for developing such student engagement. Through their questioning strategies, teachers engage and transform the mind. To draw forth, become aware of, practice and apply skillful thinking, learners must be presented with problems and questions, the answers to which are not apparent. Both teachers and students are

This chapter is adapted from "Using Questions to Challenge Students' Intellect," by A. L. Costa and B. Kallick, 2000, in *Activating and Engaging Habits of Mind* (pp. 34–45), edited by A. L. Costa and B. Kallick. Alexandria, VA: Association for Supervision and Curriculum Development.

encouraged to raise their own dilemmas and paradoxes as they consider different points of view. Our purpose is to continuously reinforce the habit of questioning and problem posing as well as increase the possibility for a sense of wonderment and curiosity.

DESIGNING POWERFUL QUESTIONS

Careful, intentional, and productive questioning, therefore, is one of the most powerful tools of effective teachers. When a teacher begins a question with, "Who can tell me . . ." there is an immediate signal that only certain students can tell the teacher the answer to the question. If, on the other hand, a teacher begins the question with, "What do we know about . . ." the signal is that "we," all of us, probably have something to offer. If questions are posed with the implication that the answers are already known, there is a tendency for students to "guess what's in the teacher's head" and search for conformity or agreement. But if the implication is that neither the teacher nor the students know the answers, then there is a sincere and collaborative inquiry—searching together for approaches and solutions. The focus becomes one of developing strategies to resolve the problem and generate alternative answers to the question rather than to produce an answer that will be confirmed or negated by someone of higher authority.

The discussion on questioning strategies that follows is designed to help teachers gain linguistic skills and metacognitive maps that will help them

- Monitor their own questions.
- Formulate and pose questions that intentionally challenge students' intellect and imagination.
- Purposely draw forth student's awareness and employment of thinking skills, cognitive tasks, and dispositions.
- Model complex questions in their own interactions so students will increase their habit of posing complex questions and develop a questioning attitude.

Some questions may place limits on student's thinking. To heighten awareness of their own questions and to ensure that they are not miscuing, confusing, or limiting student thought, let us begin by examining some questioning don'ts before presenting some questioning do's.

SOME QUESTIONING PATTERNS TO AVOID

There are at least five types of questions that can miscue students' thinking by sending confusing and mixed messages. They do *not* belong in thoughtful lesson designs:

- *Verification questions*, the answers to which are already known by you or by the student.

  What is the name of . . . ?

  How many times did you . . . ?
- *Closed questions* that can be answered "yes," "no," or "I can."

  Can you recite the poem?

  Who can state the formula for . . . ?
- *Rhetorical questions* in which the answer is given within the question.

  In what year was the War of 1812?

  How long is the 100-yard dash?
- *Defensive questions*, which cause justification, resistance, and self-protection.

  Why didn't you complete your homework?

  Are you misbehaving again?
- *Agreement questions*, which are intended to invite others to agree with your opinion or answer.

  This is really the best solution, isn't it?

  We really should get started now, shouldn't we?

  Who can name the three basic parts of a plant? Root, stems, and leaves, right?

SOME QUESTIONING DO'S

Powerful questions evoke in students an awareness of and engagement in the mind. They have three characteristics (Costa & Garmston, 1999, pp. 48–49):

1. They are invitational.
- *An approachable voice is used.* There is a lilt and melody in the questioner's voice rather than a flat, even tenor.
- *Plurals are used to invite multiple rather than singular concepts.*

  What are some of your goals?

  What alternatives are you considering?
- *Words are selected to express tentativeness.*

  What conclusions might you draw?

  What hunches do you have to explain this situation?
- *Invitational stems are used to enable the behavior to be performed.*

  As you reflect on . . . .

  As you plan for . . . .
- *Positive presuppositions assume capability and empowerment.*

360

What are some of the benefits you will derive from engaging in this activity?

As you anticipate your project, what are some indicators that you are progressing and succeeding?

2. They engage specific cognitive operations at various levels of complexity.

3. They address external or internal content that is relevant to the learner.

- *External content* might be something appearing in the environment around the learner, such as a lesson content, a meeting, a playground experience, another student, a project, or a home experience.

- *Internal content* might be something occurring inside the person's mind, an emotion such as satisfaction or frustration, or metacognition.

LEVELS OF COMPLEXITY

Questions invite different levels of complexity of thinking. Early in children's lives they learn to be alert to certain syntactical cues to know how to behave or what to think. Teachers will want to deliberately use these linguistic tools to engage and challenge complex thinking in their students' minds. The following poem captures the increasingly complex levels of thinking:

The Three Story Intellect
There are one-story intellects, two-story intellects, and three-story intellects with skylights.
All fact collectors, who have no aim beyond their facts, are one-story men.
Two-story men compare, reason, generalize, using the labors of the fact collectors as well as their own.
Three-story men idealize, imagine, predict—their best illumination comes from above, through the skylight.
—Oliver Wendell Holmes

Oliver Wendell Holmes reminds us that all three levels of thinking are important. Teachers will want to design and pose questions that elicit all three levels of intellect. Figure 58.1 is a graphic representation of Holmes's poem. It might be used as a framework or mental map to assist teachers in posing questions. (For a similar guide to questioning, see also Robert Marzano's Chapter 32 in this book.) At the first story of this model are the data-gathering cognitive operations. The second story, or the processing level, involves the cognitive operations by which meaning is made of the data. The third story of the house invites students to go "beyond the skylights" to speculate, elaborate, and apply concepts in new and hypothetical situations.

Following are some examples of questions that incorporate the criteria for powerful questions and that are intended to invite specific cognitive operations at each level of the three-story intellect model.

COGNITIVE LEVELS OF QUESTIONS

Gathering and Recalling Information

Questions and statements can be designed to spark data **input,** in other words draw from students the concepts, information, feelings, or experiences they have acquired in the past and stored in long- or short-term memory. Questioning strategies can also be designed to activate the senses to gather data that the student can then process at the next higher level. There are several cognitive processes included at the input level of thinking. Some of the following verbs may be used in a behavioral objective statement if the teacher desires students to display cognitive behavior at the input level:

completing	listing	scanning
identifying	reciting	describing
observing	defining	naming
counting	matching	selecting

Examples of questions and statements designed to elicit these cognitive objectives are shown in Figure 58.2.

Making Sense Out of the Information Gathered

To cause students to **process** the data gathered through the senses and retrieve them from long- and short-term memory, questions and statements are designed to draw some relationships of cause and effect, to synthesize, analyze, summarize, compare, contrast, or classify the data that they have acquired or observed. Often, when students are doing research projects, they are inclined to copy or paraphrase the text that is in the resource book. When students understand that the research is, by definition, inquiry, then they can learn to raise questions that can be answered through their research rather than answer questions of completion. The list of words below can guide students to raise questions at a more complex level. The assignment might read, "In your research, you must be able to answer definitional questions as well as to answer any question you raise that uses one of the following verbs." The verbs that are listed below could be used in a behavioral objective statement if the teacher desires students to display cognitive behavior at the processing level. These verbs also can be useful when a teacher is trying to raise an "essential question" for a given unit of study:

—Figure 58.1—
The Three-Story Intellect Model

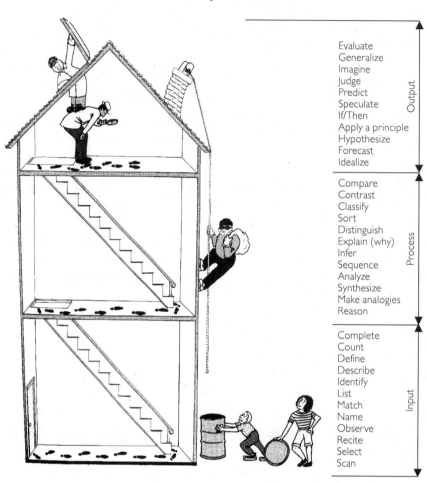

Output
- Evaluate
- Generalize
- Imagine
- Judge
- Predict
- Speculate
- If/Then
- Apply a principle
- Hypothesize
- Forecast
- Idealize

Process
- Compare
- Contrast
- Classify
- Sort
- Distinguish
- Explain (why)
- Infer
- Sequence
- Analyze
- Synthesize
- Make analogies
- Reason

Input
- Complete
- Count
- Define
- Describe
- Identify
- List
- Match
- Name
- Observe
- Recite
- Select
- Scan

Adapted by permission of the publisher from the "Three-Story Intellect Model" from *Brain Compatible Classrooms* by Robin Fogarty, © 1997 SkyLight Training and Publishing, Inc.

analyzing	organizing	grouping
distinguishing	classifying	synthesizing
making analogies	explaining	contrasting
categorizing	sequencing	inferring
experimenting	comparing	

Examples of questions designed to elicit these cognitive objectives are shown in Figure 58.3.

Applying and Evaluating Actions in Novel Situations

Questions and statements that cause **output** are designed to have students go beyond the concepts or principles they have developed and use this relationship in a novel or hypo-

thetical situation. Application invites students to think creatively and hypothetically, to use imagination, to expose their value systems, or make judgments. These questions most powerfully lend themselves to the research process, because the answers cannot be found in books or in databases. In addition, essential questions can be raised at this level and they can take on a more philosophical tone.

If the teacher desires student behaviors at the level of application, some of the following verbs could be used in a behavioral objective statement:

Applying a principle	Model building
Imagining	Predicting

—*Figure 58.2*—
Eliciting Input-Level Behaviors

Question or Statement	Desired Cognitive Behavior
Which states bound California?	Naming
How does the picture make you feel?	Describing
What word does this picture go with?	Matching
What does the word, "haggard" mean?	Defining
What were the names of the children in the story?	Naming
What did you see the man doing in the film?	Observing
Which ball is the blue one?	Identifying
How does the Gettysburg Address begin?	Reciting
How many coins are there in the stack?	Counting
Which words in this list are rhyming words?	Selecting
The Mexican houses were made of mud bricks called . . . what?	Completing
Watch what color it turns when I put the litmus paper in the liquid.	Observing
List the first four numbers in a set of positive integers.	Listing
How did you feel about the grade you received in science?	Recalling

Evaluating	Extrapolating
Judging	Speculating
Hypothesizing	Forecasting
Generalizing	Transferring

Examples of questions designed to elicit these cognitive objectives are shown in Figure 58.4.

STRUCTURING THE CLASSROOM FOR THINKING

Structuring may be described as the way teachers control such classroom environmental resources as time, space, human energy, and materials. Even the "unstructured" classroom imposes a structure to which students react and within which students interact. In a well-structured classroom where students know the objectives of the lesson, time is used efficiently, the teacher is clear about the directions, the classroom environment conveys a congenial sense of order, and student energies are engaged in meaningful learning tasks that, in turn, produce higher achievement.

Structuring the classroom for thinking should be conscious, deliberate, clear, and based on the desired outcomes for students. Knowing what learning tasks are to be accomplished and what type of interaction is desired, the teacher gives directions, states ground rules, describes objectives, places limits, and creates a classroom organizational pattern intended to best elicit the desired cognitive performance from students. Three central aspects of teacher structuring include

1. The clarity of verbal and written instructions.
2. The structuring of time and energy.
3. The different ways of organizing and arranging interaction patterns.

INSTRUCTIONAL CLARITY

Teacher: "Why do you think Robert Frost repeated the last line of this verse?"
Student: (No response)
Teacher: (After a long pause) "Well, what feelings did you have as you read the poem?"
Student: "Why don't you just tell us the answer?"
If you are specific in what you expect, then others will be specific in fulfilling your expectations.
—Rulon G. Craven

Students expend great amounts of energy trying to figure out teachers' intentions. If the messages and directions presented

—Figure 58.3—

Eliciting Processing-Level Behaviors

Question or Statement	Desired Cognitive Behavior
In what ways do you see the American Civil War like the Revolutionary War?	Comparing
What suggests to you that Columbus believed he could get to the East by sailing west?	Explaining
From our experiments with food coloring in different water temperatures, what might you infer about the movement of molecules?	Inferring
How might you arrange the rocks in the order of their size?	Sequencing
As you analyze the development of machines, what were some of their effects on the people living at that time?	Explaining, Causality
How might you arrange in groups the things that a magnet will and will not pick up?	Grouping
What other machines can you think of that work in the same way that this one does?	Making Analogies
What are some characteristics of Van Gogh's work that makes you think this painting is his?	Distinguishing
What might you do to test your idea?	Experimenting
In what ways are pine needles different from redwood needles?	Contrasting
In what ways might you arrange the blocks so that they have a crowded feeling?	Organizing
What data are we going to need in order to solve this problem?	Analyzing
Arrange the following elements of a set in ascending order: 13/4, 3/2, 5/6, 32/5.	Sequencing
How does the formula for finding the volume of a cone compare with the formula for the volume of a pyramid?	Comparing

by the teacher are confused, garbled, and unclear, then students will have a more difficult learning task. Because some students come from homes, previous teachers, or other schools where thoughtful behavior was not valued, they often are dismayed and resistant to the teacher's invitations to think. Such resistance and reluctance to respond would indicate that a program to develop creativity, flexibility, and risk-taking is sorely needed.

If students are to realize that thinking is a legitimate goal of education, then teachers must convey to students that the goal of instruction is thinking, that the responsibility for thinking is theirs, that it is often desirable to have more than one solution to a problem, that it is commendable when students take time to plan, that an answer can be changed with additional information.

STRUCTURING TIME AND ENERGY

Achievement correlates highly with the amount of time students are successfully engaged in learning. But an emphasis on thinking cannot be viewed by the student as an isolated event. Students must repeatedly receive cognitive skills instruction and encounter situations that require them to think throughout the school day, across academic content areas, and over extended periods of time. Only then can students transfer, generalize, and apply cognitive skills (Sternberg & Wagner, 1982, pp. 50, 53).

Structuring time alone, however, is inadequate. Schools must also consider the quality of the task during that time—the degree that students' energies are engaged. The extent to which teachers mediate the interaction of pupils with instructional materials and with the content of the lesson not only de-

—*Figure 58.4*—
Eliciting Application-Level Behaviors

Question or Statement	Desired Cognitive Behavior
What do you suppose will happen to our weather if a high pressure area moves in?	Forecasting
If our population continues to grow as it does, what do you suppose life will be like in the twenty-first century?	Speculating
Drawing on what you know about how heat affects the speed of movement of the molecules, what do you predict will happen when we put the liquid in the refrigerator?	Predicting
Imagine what life would be like if there were no laws to govern us.	Imagining
What might you say about all countries' economies that are dependent upon only one crop?	Generalizing
Design some ways to use this bimetal strip to make a fire alarm?	Applying
How could you use this clay to make a model of a plant cell?	Model Building
What would be a fair solution to this problem?	Evaluating
As you consider the periodic table and the invention of the microscope, which was more essential to organizing chemistry?	Judging
From what we have learned about its characteristics, what other examples of romantic music can you cite?	Applying a principle
What do you think might happen if we placed the saltwater fish in the tank of fresh water?	Hypothesizing

termines how well decision-making and problem-solving skills are learned, it also influences students' attitudes toward the school, the teachers, the content to be learned, and learning itself. In effective learning environments, students are encouraged to become active thinkers, not passive observers. This might include Socratic dialogue led by teachers and students, individual hands-on or heads-on manipulations, and cooperative small group or total group investigations.

STRUCTURING CLASSROOM ORGANIZATIONAL PATTERNS FOR THINKING

The lecture method has long been found wanting in terms of student learning. Early studies have shown that there are vast individual differences in the amount of learning assimilated by students through lecture (Jones, 1923). And Ebbinhous (1913) found that retention dropped from about 60 percent of immediate recall after the lecture to about 20 percent after eight weeks.

Different students need different classroom organizational patterns. Some students learn best individually; some learn best in groups. There are students who can only learn when an adult is present to constantly encourage and reinforce them; others can't learn when another person is nearby. Some students need noise, others need quiet. Some need bright light, some need subdued light. Some need formal settings, others need informal situations. Some need to move, others need to be stationary (Dunn & Dunn, 1978). Less able students seem to do better in highly structured situations where direct help is generous, while more able students seem to prefer less structured situations (Sternberg & Wagner, 1982).

What kind of classroom structure, then, produces the greatest achievement of cognitive skills and strategies? Thomas (1980) found that instructional strategies in which there was maximal teacher control through praise and structuring had little cognitive payoff for students. He suggested that students be given wide latitude for discovery of a range of appropriate cognitive strategies.

Roger and David Johnson (see Chapter 72 of this book) found that students working cooperatively in groups used more higher-level reasoning strategies and greater critical thinking competencies than students working in competitive and individualistic learning situations.

When higher-level thinking, creativity, and problem solving are the objectives, students must be in a classroom climate where they are in the decision-making role, where they construct strategies to solve problems, where they determine the correctness of an answer based on data they produced and validated, and where they play a key part in setting their own goals and devising ways to assess the accomplishment of those goals.

INTRINSIC RATHER THAN EXTRINSIC REWARDS

The reward system in such a classroom should be intrinsic. It must spring from an internal motivation to learn: an intellectual curiosity about phenomena; a proud striving for craftsmanship and accuracy; a sense of being a productive and interdependent member of a community of scholars; and a desire to emulate respected others (Lepper & Greene, 1978; Bruner, Goodnow, & Austin, 1956) (see Chapter 4 in this book, by Arthur L. Costa and Robert J. Garmston).

Teachers who value internal rather than external rewards, who engage students in structuring their own learning, who realize human variability in learning, and who can teach toward multiple goals use a repertoire of classroom organizational patterns. Classrooms organized for thinking are characterized by:

• Individual students working alone, engaged in a task requiring one or more cognitive skills, such as comparing, classifying, sorting, and evaluating. During individual work, teachers monitor students' progress and mediate their experiences.

• Groups working cooperatively, in pairs or small groups, on such collaborative problem solving as planning strategies for group projects, contributing data and ideas to the progress of the project, identifying information that needs to be gathered, devising strategies to generate that information, and evaluating individual and group social skills. During group work, teachers monitor students' progress, assess growth in social and cognitive abilities, and mediate both the intellectual skills required of the task and the cooperative group skills.

• Total group engagement in listening to presentations by, and interacting with, the teacher, resource people, media, and other students. Such total group interactive strategies as the Socratic and dialectic methods, and class meetings are also employed when the teacher or a student raises a dilemma, problem, or discrepancy for all to participate in debating and resolving.

TEACHER RESPONSE BEHAVIORS

"He who praises everybody praises nobody."
— Samuel Johnson

The manner in which teachers and administrators respond to students can create and maintain a thoughtful environment that creates trust, allows risk taking, is experimental, creative, and positive. This requires listening to students and each other's ideas, remaining nonjudgmental, and having rich data sources. The following five patterns of response behaviors—using silence, facilitating the acquisition of data, accepting without judgment, clarifying, and empathizing—are employed to create an atmosphere in which students may experience and practice complex and creative thought processes.

SILENCE (WAIT TIME)

In some classrooms, the teacher dominates the interaction using a rapid-fire pace and lower cognitive-level questions. The teacher may wait less than one second after posing a question before repeating the question, commenting on a student answer, redirecting the question to a new student, answering the question herself or starting a new questioning sequence. Students' answers are often terse, fragmentary, or show a lack of confidence with inflected tones. After a student replies, the teacher may wait less than one second before commenting or asking another question. There is little chance for students to have second thoughts or to extend their ideas. Many teachers appear to be programmed to accept one predetermined "right" answer. There is little room left for alternate answers or differing opinions.

Rowe first developed the concept of wait time in the late 1960s. In observing classrooms, she noticed that some teachers were using "purposeful pauses" as they conducted lessons and class discussions (Rowe, 1974). She noted students making speculations, holding sustained conversational sequences, posing alternative explanations, and arguing over the interpretation of data. She noted positive changes in the affective climate and the quality of classroom interactions. She also noticed an increase in the level of cognitive functioning and academic achievement; and a decrease in the number of behavior problems.

Wait Time 1 is the length of time a teacher pauses after asking a question. Wait Time 2 is the length of time a teacher waits after a student comments or asks a question. A minimum of three seconds of pausing is recommended. With higher-level cognitive tasks, five seconds or more of wait time may be required to achieve positive results. Wait Time 3 is pausing and modeling thoughtfulness after the student asks the teacher a question.

It takes time for students to be able to think flexibly or creatively. The use of longer pauses in group discussions provides students with the necessary think time that helps them manage their impulsivity and take responsible risks as they answer questions posed either by the teacher or by the work they are studying.

FACILITATING THE ACQUISITION OF DATA

If learners are to process data by comparing, classifying, making inferences, or drawing causal relationships for themselves, then data must be available for them to process. Facilitating the acquisition of data means that when the teacher perceives that a student needs information, or when a student requests additional information, the teacher provides it or makes it possible for the student to acquire the data, facts, or information needed or requested.

The teacher, therefore, creates a climate that is responsive to the student's quest for information. Teachers do this in a variety of ways:

- By *providing data (feedback) about a student's performance.*
  No, 3 times 6 is not 24; 3 times 8 is 24.
  Yes, you have spelled "rhythm" correctly.
- By *providing personal information or data (self-divulgence).* These are often in the form of "I" messages.
  I want you to know that chewing gum in this classroom really disturbs me.
  The way you painted the tree makes me feel like I'm on the inside looking out.
- By *making it possible for students to experiment with equipment and materials to find data or information for themselves.*
  Here's a larger test tube if you'd like to see how your experiment would turn out differently.
  We can see the video again if you want to check your observations.
- By *making primary and secondary sources of information accessible.*
  Catherine, this geography database gives information you will need for your report on the world's highest mountain ranges.
  Here's the dictionary. The best way to verify the spelling is to look it up.

- By *responding to a student's request for information.*
  You were wondering about this piece of equipment? It's called a DVD-ROM drive.
- By *surveying group members for their feelings or for input of information.*
  On this chart we have made a list of what you observed in the film. We can keep this chart in front of us so that we can refer to it as we classify our observations.
  Let's go around the circle and share some of the feelings we had when we found out the school board decided to close our school.
- By *labeling a thinking process or behavior.*
  That is a hypothesis you are posing, Gina.
  The question you are asking is an attempt to verify the data.

Data energizes learning and growth, and knowledge of results is the most important variable governing the acquisition of skillful thinking.

ACCEPTING WITHOUT JUDGMENT

Nonevaluative, nonjudgmental teachers accept what students say and do. When they accept, they give no clues through posture, gesture, or word as to whether a student's idea, behavior, or feeling, is good, bad, better or worse, right or wrong. In response to a student's idea or action, acceptance of it provides a psychologically safe climate where students can take risks, are entrusted with the responsibility of making decisions for themselves, and can explore the consequences of their own actions. Nonjudgmental acceptance provides conditions in which students are encouraged to examine and compare their own data, values, ideas, criteria, and feelings with those of others as well as those of the teacher. While teachers may respond nonjudgmentally in several ways, two types of nonjudgmental accepting responses are described here: acknowledgment and paraphrasing.

Acknowledging

Acknowledgment is responding by simply receiving without judging what the student says. It communicates that the student's ideas have been heard.

Examples of this type of response are passive, verbal accepting responses such as "Um-hmm," "That's one possibility," or "I understand." Other examples are passive, nonverbal accepting responses such as nodding the head during a student's statement or recording it without change on the chalkboard.

Another option is to acknowledge the student's gift of her thinking simply by saying "thank you."

Paraphrasing

Paraphrasing is responding to what the student says or does by rephrasing, recasting, translating, or summarizing. Teachers use this response when they want to extend, build on, compare, or give an example based on what the student has said. Using different words, the teacher strives to maintain the intent and accurate meaning of the student's idea. By paraphrasing, the teacher signals understanding and caring. Examples of this type of response are

• I understand. Your idea is that we should all write our legislators rather than send them one letter from the group.
• Shaun's idea is that the leaves could be classified according to their shapes while Sarah's way is to group them by size.

Praise Can Decrease Motivation and Creativity

Using rewards and praise as motivators of student learning can increase the student's dependency on others for learning rather than finding the learning inherently satisfying or involving the acquisition or exercise of skills that the students value themselves (Deci, 1978, 1995; Kohn, 1994; Lepper & Greene, 1978).

Surprisingly, while many teachers advocate the use of praise such as "good," "excellent," "great," in attempts to reinforce behaviors and to build self-worth, the research on praise indicates that the opposite is more often the case. Thus praise builds conformity and has been found to be a detriment to creativity (Kohn, 1994). Some examples of teacher responses that use praise

That was a very *good* answer, Linda.

Your painting is *excellent*.

If praise is given, it is important that the criteria for the praise be described—for example, what makes an act "good" or "excellent." If the student understands the criteria that make the act acceptable, then repeat performances are more likely.

Help Students Analyze Their Own Answers

Teacher: "Jane says San Francisco is the largest city in California. Bill says Los Angeles is the largest. Would each of you please tell us the population of the two cities? One way to find out is to compare our data."

Most teachers enjoy rewarding and praising their students. Brophy (1981), however, found that the one person in the classroom for whom praise has the most beneficial effect is, in-deed, the teacher. It is understandable, therefore, that educators respond with resistance to research studies showing the detrimental effects of rewards.

CLARIFYING WHEN YOU DON'T UNDERSTAND

Clarifying is similar to accepting in that both behaviors reflect the teacher's concern for fully understanding the student's idea. While active acceptance demonstrates that the teacher *does* understand, *clarifying* means that you *do not* understand what the student is saying and, therefore, more information is needed.

The teacher may seek further explanation of a student's idea, invite the student to provide a more specific elaboration or rephrasing, or seek descriptions of the thinking processes underlying the production of that idea.

The intent of clarifying is to better understand the students' ideas, feelings, and thought processes. Clarifying is *not* a devious way of changing or redirecting what the student is thinking or feeling. It is not a way of directing the class's attention to the "correct answer." Clarifying is often stated in the form of an interrogative but could also be a statement inviting further illumination. For example:

Could you explain to us what you mean by "charisma"?

Go over that one more time, Shelley, I'm not sure I understand you.

You say you are studying the situation. Tell us just exactly what you do when you study something.

Explain to us the steps you took to arrive at that answer.

By clarifying, teachers show the students that their ideas are worthy of exploration and consideration but that the full meaning is not yet understood. When a teacher responds to students' comments by encouraging them to elaborate further, students become more purposeful in their thinking and behaving.

EMPATHIZING

Sometimes students come to school from dysfunctional, abusive, drug-dependent, impoverished environments. The emotions and feelings they bring to school affect their learning and motivation.

Empathic acceptance is a response that accepts feelings in addition to cognition. Teachers respond empathically when they want to accept a student's feelings, emotions, or behaviors. Often teachers show empathy when they express similar feelings from their own experiences. Such responses communicate that the teacher not only "hears" the student's idea but also the emotions underlying the idea. Empathic acceptance does not mean that the teacher condones acts of aggression or destructive behavior. Some examples of this type of response are

I can see why you're confused. Those directions are unclear to me, too.

You're frustrated because you didn't get a chance to share your idea. We've all got to take turns, and that requires patience. It's hard to wait when you're anxious to share.

The student enters the room and slams a math workbook on the desk. The teacher responds empathetically to this behavior by saying: "Something must be upsetting you today. Did you have difficulty with that assignment?"

These teacher response behaviors fit the acronym SPACE. The use of Silence, Providing data, Accepting without judgment, Clarifying and Empathizing (SPACE) can be taught to students, parents, and groups of people meeting to consider school improvement. These strategies can serve as a mental map for building an environment in which thinking can flourish.

MODELING: BEHAVING CONGRUENTLY WITH COGNITIVE GOALS AND OBJECTIVES

Students are quick to pick up the inconsistencies between what a teacher says and what a teacher does. Effective teachers of thinking constantly strive to bring their words, actions, beliefs, values, and goals for students into harmony.

Children acquire much of their behavior, feelings, attitudes, and values not through direct instruction but through imitation of both adult and peer models. Students adopt new behavior patterns or modify their own behavior on the basis of observation alone. Thus, since there is such extended contact between teacher and student, the teacher is one of the most significant and influential models in a student's life.

Modeling tends to reinforce students' perceptions of the values and goals stated by the teacher or by the school. And by exhibiting the kinds of behavior desired in students, adults can strongly influence students' behavior patterns. For example:

• If listening to one another is a valued behavior, teachers who listen to students will greatly enhance the probability of achieving this objective.

• If solving problems in a rational, scientific manner is valued, students must observe teachers and administrators using rational, scientific ways to solve problems that arise in the school or classroom.

• If managing impulsivity is a characteristic of intelligent problem solving, students must witness teachers and administrators reacting calmly and patiently during stressful situations.

• If teachers want students to accept one another's points of view, values, and differences (overcoming egocentrism), they will accept students' differences.

• If teachers want students to become enthusiastic about thinking, they will show enthusiasm for challenges, puzzles, and complex tasks requiring thought.

Emulating others is a basic way of learning. Young people, especially, are very quick to imitate behavior. If we become "do as I say, not as I do" educators, we can make students feet hostile, frustrated, and confused. Our goal as educators should be to facilitate students' development of their own behavior, since in the end, each person is responsible for what he or she does.

REFERENCES

Bloom, B. S., Englehart, M. D., Furst, E. J., Hill, W. H, & Krathwohl, D. R. (Eds.). (1956). *Taxonomy of educational objectives: The classification of educational goals. Handbook I: Cognitive domain.* New York: David McKay.

Brophy, J. I. (1981, October). *Teacher praise: A functional analysis* [occasional paper no. 28]. East Lansing, MI: Michigan State University Institute for Research on Teaching.

Bruner, J., Goodnow, J., & Austin, G. A. (1956). *A study of thinking.* New York: Wiley.

Costa, A. L., & Garmston, R. (1999). Cognitive coaching: A foundation for Renaissance schools: Training syllabus. Norwood, MA: Christopher Gordon Publications.

Deci, E. (1978). Application of research on the effect rewards. In Lepper, M., & Greene, D. (Eds.), *The hidden cost of rewards: New perspectives on the psychology of human motivation.* New York: Lawrence Erlbaum.

Deci, E. (1995). *Why we do what we do.* New York: Grosset Putnam Inc.

Dunn, R., & Dunn, K. (1978). *Teaching students through their individual learning styles.* Reston, VA: Reston Publishing Company.

Ebbinhous, H. (1913). *Memory.* New York: Teachers College, Columbia University.

Jones, H. E. (1923, November). Experimental studies of college teaching. *Archives of Psychology, 68.*

Kohn, A. (1994). *Punished by rewards: The trouble with gold stars, incentive plans, A's, praise and other bribes.* New York: Houghton Mifflin.

Lepper, M., & Greene, D. (Eds.). (1978). *The hidden cost of rewards: New perspectives on the psychology of human motivation.* New York: Erlbaum.

Rowe, M. B. (1974, Spring). Wait time and rewards as instructional variables: Their influence on language, logic and fate control. *Journal of Research in Science Teaching, 11*(2), 81–84.

Sternberg, R. J., & Wagner, R. K. (1982). *Understanding intelligence: What's in it for educators?* Paper submitted to the National Commission on Excellence in Education, Washington, DC.

Thomas, J. (1980, Summer). Agency and achievement: Self-management and self-regard. *Review of Educational Research, 50*(2), 213–240.

59

Teaching for Transfer

DAVID PERKINS AND GAVRIEL SALOMON

Give me a fish and I will eat today. Teach me to fish and I will eat for a lifetime.

—*Chinese proverb*

Facing a move across town and concerned with economy, you rent a small truck to transport your worldly possessions. You have never driven a truck before and wonder whether you can manage it. However, when you pick the truck up from the rental agency, you find yourself pleased and surprised. Driving the truck is an experience unfamiliar, yet familiar. You guide the vehicle through the city traffic with caution, yet growing confidence, only hoping that you will not have to parallel park it.

This everyday episode is a story of transfer—something learned in one context has helped in another. The following line of poetry from Shakespeare also shows transfer: "Summer's lease hath all too short a date." Regretting the decline of summer in his Sonnet 18, Shakespeare compares it to, of all things, a lease. The world of landlords and lawyers falls into startling juxtaposition with the world of dazzling days, cumulus clouds, and warm breezes.

Your experience with the truck and Shakespeare's metaphor differ in many ways. From driving a car to driving a truck is a short step, while from leases to summer seems a long step. One might speak roughly of "near transfer" versus "far transfer." In the first case, you carry a physical skill over to another context, whereas in the second, Shakespeare carries knowledge associated with leases over to another context. One might speak of transfer of skill versus transfer of knowledge, and, although here we will focus on those two, other sorts of

things might be transferred as well—for instance, attitudes or cognitive styles. Finally, the first case is everyday, the second a high achievement of a literary genius. Nonetheless, despite these many contrasts, both episodes illustrate the phenomenon of transfer. In both, knowledge or skill associated with one context reaches out to enhance another. (It is also possible to speak of negative transfer, where knowledge or skill from one context interferes in another.)

Transfer goes beyond ordinary learning in that the skill or knowledge in question has to travel to a new context—from cars to trucks, from lawyers to summer, or across other gaps that might in principle block it. To be sure, that definition makes for a fuzzy border between transfer and ordinary learning. For example, if car to truck is a gap, so in some sense is automatic transmission to standard transmission, or Ford automatic to Chrysler automatic. But the last two, and especially the last, do not seem intuitively to be different enough to pose a significant gap. In practice, we have a rough sense of what gaps might be significant and, although that sense may not always be accurate, nothing in this article will depend upon drawing a perfectly sharp line between transfer and ordinary learning.

If transfer figures in activities as diverse as moving across town and writing sonnets, it is easy to believe that transfer has at least a potential role in virtually all walks of life. But transfer does not take care of itself, and conventional schooling pays little heed to the problem. With proper attention, we can do much more to teach for transfer than we are now doing.

WHY IS TRANSFER IMPORTANT TO EDUCATION?

Any survey of what education hopes to achieve discloses that transfer is integral to our expectations and aspirations for education. First of all, the transfer of basic skills is a routine target of schooling. For example, students learn to read *Dick and Jane* or *A Tale of Two Cities* not just for the sake of reading other texts but in preparation for a much wider range of reading—

This chapter is adapted from *Developing Minds: A Resource Book for Teaching Thinking* (Rev. ed.), 1991. The original chapter is adapted from D. N. Perkins and G. Salomon (1988, September). Teaching for transfer. *Educational Leadership, 46*(1), 22–32.

newspapers, job applications, income tax forms, political platforms, assembly instructions, wills, contracts, and so on. Students learn mathematical skills not just for the sake of figuring Sammy's age when it is two-thirds of Jane's, but for smart shopping in the supermarket, wise investment in the stock market, understanding of statistical trends, and so on.

Another expectation of education concerns the transfer of knowledge. The "database" students acquire in school ought to inform their thinking in other school subjects and in life outside of school. For example, European and American history should help students to think about current political events—the traditions that shape them, the economic and political factors that influence them, the reasons one votes or acts in certain ways in the political arena. Literary studies should help students think about fundamental problems of life—the cycle of birth and death, the struggle for dominance, the quest for love, and how one's own life incarnates those eternal dramas. Science instruction should help students to understand the world around them—the branch waving in the wind as an oscillator, a city as an artificial ecology, the threat and promise of nuclear power or genetic engineering.

Finally, transfer plays a key role in an aspiration of education that lately has attained great prominence: the teaching of thinking skills. As with basic skills and knowledge, here again the aim is not just to build students' performance on a narrow range of school tasks. One hopes that students will become better creative and critical thinkers in the many contexts that invite a thoughtful approach, such as making important life decisions, casting votes, interacting with others equitably, engaging in productive pursuits such as essay writing, and painting.

WHY IS TRANSFER WORRISOME IN EDUCATION?

The implicit assumption in educational practice has been that transfer takes care of itself. To be lighthearted about a heavy problem, one might call this the Bo Peep theory of transfer: "Let them alone and they'll come home, wagging their tails behind them." If students acquire information about the Revolutionary War and the westward emigration, if they learn some problem-solving skills in math and some critical thinking skills in social studies, all this will more or less automatically spill over to the many other contexts in and out of school where it might apply, we hope.

Unfortunately, considerable research and everyday experience testify that the Bo Peep theory is inordinately optimistic. While the basic skills of reading, writing, and arithmetic typically show transfer (for reasons to be discussed later), other sorts of knowledge and skill very often do not.

For example, a great deal of the knowledge students acquire is inert or passive. The knowledge shows up when students respond to direct probes, such as multiple choice or fill-in-the-blank quizzes. However, students do not transfer the knowledge to problem-solving contexts where they have to think about new situations. For example, Bransford and his colleagues have demonstrated that both everyday knowledge and the knowledge acquired in typical school study formats tend to be inert (Bransford, Franks, Vye, & Sherwood, 1986; Perfetto, Bransford, & Franks, 1983). Studies of programming instruction have shown that a considerable portion of beginning students' knowledge of commands in a programming language is inert even in the context of active programming, where there is hardly any gap to transfer across (Perkins & Martin, 1986; Perkins, Martin, & Farady, 1986). Studies of medical education argue that much of the technical knowledge student physicians acquire from texts and lectures is inert—not retrieved or applied in the diagnostic contexts for which it is intended (Barrows & Tamblyn, 1980).

It has often been suggested that literacy is one of the most powerful carriers of cognitive abilities. Olson (1976), for example, has argued that written language permits patterns of thinking much more complex than can be managed within the limited capacity of human short-term memory. Moreover, written texts, in their presentational and argumentative structures, illustrate patterns of thinking useful for handling complex tasks. Literacy, therefore, ought to bring with it a variety of expanded cognitive abilities. To put the matter in terms of transfer, literacy should yield cognitive gains on a number of fronts, not just the skills of reading and writing per se.

The difficulty with testing this hypothesis is that people usually learn to write in school at the same time they learn numerous other skills that could affect their cognitive abilities. This dilemma was resolved when Scribner and Cole (1981) undertook a detailed study of the Vai, an African tribe that had developed a written language that many members of the tribe learned and used, but that maintained no tradition of formal schooling. Remarkably, the investigators' studies disclosed hardly any impact of Vai literacy on the cognitive performance of Vai who had mastered the written language. The hypothesized transfer did not appear.

Another source of discouraging evidence about transfer comes from contemporary studies of the impact of computer programming instruction on cognitive skills. Many psychologists and educators have emphasized that the richness and rigor of computer programming may enhance students' cognitive skills generally (e.g., Feurzeig, Horwitz, & Nickerson, 1981; Linn, 1985; Papert 1980). The learning of programming demands systematicity—breaking problems into parts, diagnosing the causes of difficulties, and so on. Thinking of this sort appears applicable to nearly any domain. Moreover, as Papert (1980) has urged, programming languages afford the opportunity to learn about the nature of procedures, and procedures in turn provide a way of thinking about how the mind works. While all this may be true, the track record of efforts to enhance cognitive skills via programming is discouraging. Most findings have been negative (see reviews in Clements 1985b; Dalbey & Linn, 1985; Salomon & Perkins, 1987).

Another well-investigated aspect of learning has been the effort to teach mildly mentally disabled students the basic cognitive skills of memory. Learning some basic strategies of memory familiar to nondisabled students can substantially improve the performance of mentally disabled learners. However, in most cases, the learners do not carry over the strategies to new contexts. Instead, it is as though the memory strategies are "contextually welded" to the circumstances of their acquisition (Belmont, Butterfield, & Ferretti, 1982).

With this array of findings contrary to the Bo Peep theory, it is natural to ask why transfer should prove so hard to achieve. Several explanations are possible. Perhaps the skill or knowledge in question is not well learned in the first place. Perhaps the skill or knowledge in itself is adequately assimilated, but advice on when to use it is not provided in the instruction. Perhaps the hoped-for transfer involves genuine creative discovery that we simply cannot expect to occur routinely.

While all these explanations have a commonsense character, one other contributed by contemporary cognitive psychology is more surprising: there may not be as much to transfer as we think. The skills students acquire in learning to read and write, the knowledge they accumulate in studying the American Revolution, and the problem-solving abilities they develop in math and physics may be much more specific to those contexts than one would imagine. Skill and knowledge are perhaps more specialized than they appear. This is sometimes called the problem of "local knowledge"; that is, knowledge (including skill) tends to be local rather than general and cross-cutting in character.

The classic example of this problem of local knowledge is chess expertise, which has been extensively researched. Chess is an interesting case in point because it appears to be a game of pure logic. There is no concealed information, as in card games: all the information is available to both players. It seems that each player need only reason logically and make the best possible move within his or her mental capacity.

However, in contrast with this picture of chess as a general logical pursuit, investigations have disclosed that chess exper-

tise depends to a startling degree on experience specifically with the game. Chess masters have accumulated an enormous repertoire of schemata—patterns of a few chess pieces with significance for play (de Groot, 1965; Chase & Simon, 1973). One pattern may indicate a certain threat, another a certain opportunity, another an avenue of escape. Skilled play depends largely on the size of one's repertoire. A chess master may be no more adept at other intellectual pursuits, such as solving mysteries or proving mathematical theorems, than any layperson.

Findings of this sort are not limited to chess. They have emerged in virtually every performance area carefully studied with the question in mind, including problem solving in math (Schoenfeld & Herrmann, 1982), physics (Chi, Feltovich, & Glaser, 1981; Larkin, 1983; Larkin, McDermott, Simon, & Simon, 1980), and computer programming (Soloway & Ehrlich, 1984), for example.

In summary, diverse empirical research on transfer has shown that transfer often does not occur. When transfer fails, many things might have gone wrong. The most discouraging explanation is that knowledge and skill may be too local to allow for many of the expectations and aspirations that educators have held.

WHEN DOES TRANSFER HAPPEN?

The prospects of teaching for transfer might be easier to estimate with the help of some model that could explain the mechanisms of transfer and the conditions under which transfer could be expected. Salomon and Perkins (1984) have offered such an account, the "low-road/high-road" model of transfer. The model has been used to examine the role of transfer in the teaching of thinking (Perkins & Salomon, 1987), to forecast the impact of new technologies on cognition (Perkins, 1985), and to review the findings on transfer of cognitive skills from programming instruction (Salomon & Perkins, 1987).

At the heart of the model lies the distinction between two very different mechanisms of transfer—low-road transfer and high-road transfer. The way learning to drive a car prepares one for driving a truck illustrates low-road transfer. One develops well-practiced habits of car driving over a considerable period. Then one enters a new context, truck driving, with many obvious similarities to the old one. The new context almost automatically activates the patterns of behavior that suit the old one: the steering wheel begs one to steer it, the windshield invites one to look through it, and so on. Fortunately, the old behaviors fit the new context well enough so that they function quite adequately.

Must We Choose Between Cultural Literacy and Critical Thinking?

From certain quarters today comes a wave of pessimism about the prospects of transfer and the potentials of teaching for general cognitive skills. One recent and popular spokesperson for a negative position is E. D. Hirsch, Jr. (1987), who offers in his *Cultural Literacy* an eloquent plea for turning away from general skills and equipping youngsters with the varied basic knowledge that makes one culturally literate.

Such a response is quite understandable in the face of the naive approach to problems of learning and transfer typically found in schools. Often, educators have expected broad global nonspecific transfer from highly specialized activities such as the study of Latin or computer programming, as though these activities exercised up some generic mental muscle. Often, educators have not focused on exactly what about such activities might transfer nor made efforts to decontextualize the transferable aspects and bridge them to other contexts. Often, educators have sought to impart lengthy lists of "microskills" for reading or other performances, an approach that seems doomed to sink in the quicksand of its own complexity.

On the other hand, Hirsch and others who would turn their backs on general skills go a bit too far. Hirsch, for example, adopts a strong local knowledge position, asserting that the prospects for transfer are meager. However, we argue for the considerable potentials of transfer if attention is paid to fostering it. Throughout *Cultural Literacy*, Hirsch periodically snipes at the teaching of critical thinking, intimating that attention to such general skills pays no dividend. But we emphasize that some aspects of critical thinking plainly call for attention—thinking about the opposite side of an issue, for example.

Ironically, in framing his argument, Hirsch commits one of those lapses of critical thinking he sees no need for schools to address: he creates a false dichotomy, treating as contraries factors that are compatible and indeed complementary. This is one of the most common slips of critical thinking, one that well-designed education could help us all to become more mindful of. Specifically, although basic knowledge of our culture has a commonly neglected importance, as Hirsch argues, this does not imply that critical thinking and other kinds of general knowledge and skill are unimportant. Plainly, more than one thing can be important at the same time. Of course, an articulate monolithic view such as his makes better press. It may even work to correct the opposite excess better than would a balanced appraisal. But it rarely captures the real complexity of human skill and knowledge.

To generalize, low-road transfer reflects the automatic triggering of well-practiced routines in circumstances where there is considerable perceptual similarity to the original learning context. Opening a chemistry book for the first time triggers reading habits acquired elsewhere, trying out a new video game activates reflexes honed on another one, or interpreting a bar graph in economics automatically musters bar graph interpretation skills acquired in math. This low-road transfer trades on the extensive overlap *at the level of the superficial stimulus* among many situations where we might apply a skill or piece of knowledge.

High-road transfer has a very different character. By definition, high-road transfer depends on deliberate, mindful abstraction of skill or knowledge from one context for application in another. Although we know nothing directly of Shakespeare's mental processes, it seems likely that Shakespeare arrived at his remarkable "Summer's lease hath all too short a date" not by tripping over it, but by deliberate author-ial effort, reaching mentally for some kind of abstract metaphorical match with the decline of summer. After all, in contrast with the resemblance between car and truck cabs, no superficial perceptual similarity exists between the summer's end and leases to provoke a reflexive connection.

Whatever the case with Shakespeare, more everyday examples of high-road transfer are in order. It is useful to distinguish between at least two types of high-road transfer—forward reaching and backward reaching. In forward-reaching high-road transfer, one learns something and abstracts it in preparation for applications elsewhere. For instance, an enthusiastic economics major learning calculus might reflect on how calculus could apply to economic contexts, speculate on possible uses, and perhaps try some, even though the calculus class does not address economics at all and the economics classes the student is taking do not use advanced math. A chess player might contemplate basic principles of chess strategy, such as control of the center, and reflectively ask what such principles might mean in other contexts. What would control of the center signify in a business, political, or military context?

In backward-reaching high-road transfer, one finds oneself in a problem situation, abstracts key characteristics from the situation, and reaches backward into one's experience for matches. The same examples applied in reverse can illustrate this pattern. A different economics major, facing a particular problem, might define its general demands, search her repertoire, and discover that calculus can help. A young politician, developing strategies for the coming campaign, might reflect on the situation and make fertile analogies with prior chess experience: capture the center of public opinion and you've captured the election.

As these examples show, whether forward-reaching or backward-reaching, high-road transfer always involves reflective thought in abstracting from one context and seeking connections with others. This contrasts with the reflexive, automatic character of low-road transfer. Accordingly, high-road transfer is not as dependent on superficial stimulus similarities, since through reflective abstraction a person can often "see through" superficial differences to deeper analogies.

The low-road/high-road view of transfer helps in understanding when it is reasonable or not to expect transfer because it clarifies the conditions under which different sorts of transfer occur. To be sure, sometimes transfer happens quite automatically in accordance with the Bo Peep theory; but that is by the low road, with the requirements of well practiced skills or knowledge and superficial perceptual similarity to activate the skills or knowledge. Moreover, the transfer is likely to be "near" transfer, since the contexts have that surface perceptual similarity. High-road transfer can bridge between contexts remote from one another, but it requires the effort of deliberate abstraction and connection-making and the ingenuity to make the abstractions and discover the connections.

CAN FAILURES OF TRANSFER BE EXPLAINED?

We reviewed a number of worrisome failures of transfer earlier. It is by no means the case, though, that conventional education affords no transfer at all. As mentioned earlier, most students learn to read more or less adequately and do bring those reading skills to bear when introduced to new areas. They do apply their arithmetic skills to income tax forms and other out-of-school tasks. Can the low-road/high-road model help us to understand why education sometimes succeeds but all too often fails in achieving transfer?

Broadly speaking, the successes fit the description of low-road transfer. For example, students fairly readily carry over their basic reading skills to many new contexts. But the surface characteristics of those new contexts strongly stimulate reading skills—text appears in front of one's eyes, so what else would one do but read it? Arithmetic skills also transfer readily to such contexts as filling out income tax forms or checking bills in restaurants and stores. But again, the stimulus demand is direct and explicit: the tax forms provide places for sums, differences, and products; the bill displays addition.

Consider now one of the failures: the problem of inert knowledge. For instance, when students fail to interpret current events in light of their historical knowledge, what can be said about the problems of transfer? First, there is an issue of initial learning: the skill students have learned through their study of history is not the skill they need when they consider today's newspapers. We want them to make thoughtful interpretations of current events, but they have learned to remember and retrieve knowledge on cue. We can hardly expect transfer of a performance that has not been learned in the first place!

However, that aside, what about the conditions for low- and high-road transfer? As to the low road, there is little surface resemblance between the learned knowledge and the new contexts of application. For example, why should strife between Iraq and Iran automatically remind a student of certain of the causes of the Civil War, when the surface features are so different? As to the high road, this would require explicit, mindful abstraction of historical patterns and applications in other settings, to break those patterns free of their accidental associations in the Civil War or other settings. Conventional history instruction does little to decontextualize such patterns, instead highlighting the particular story of particular historical episodes.

Consider another failure: the impact of programming instruction on general cognitive skills. As for low-road transfer, in most of the studies seeking transfer from computer programming, the students have not learned the programming skills themselves very well, failing to meet the condition of practice to near automaticity. Moreover, there is a problem with the surface appearance condition for low-road transfer. In the context of programming, one might learn good problem-solving practices such as defining the problem clearly before one begins. However, the formal context of programming does not look or feel very much like the tense context of a labor dispute or the excited context of hunting for a new stereo system. Accordingly, other contexts where it is important to take time in defining the problem are not so likely to reawaken in students' minds their programming experiences.

As to high-road transfer from programming, this would demand emphasis on abstracting from the programming context general principles of, for instance, problem solving and transporting those principles to applications outside of programming. Most efforts to teach programming, however, include virtually no attention to building such bridges between domains; instead, they focus entirely on building programming skills. So the conditions for high-road transfer are not met.

Similar accounts can be given of the other cases of failure of transfer discussed earlier. In summary, conventional schooling lives up to its earlier characterization as following the Bo Peep theory of transfer—doing nothing special about it but expecting it to happen. When the conditions for low-road transfer are met by chance—as in many applications of reading, writing, and arithmetic, transfer occurs—the sheep come home by themselves. Otherwise, the sheep get lost.

To be sure, meeting the low-road and high-road conditions for transfer is not the whole story. There remains the deeper problem of "local knowledge." The most artful instructional design will not provoke transfer if the knowledge and skills in question are fundamentally local in character, not really transferable to other contexts in the first place. This problem will be revisited shortly.

CAN WE TEACH FOR TRANSFER?

Besides accounting for failure of transfer, the foregoing explanations hold forth hope of doing better: by designing instruction to meet the conditions needed to foster transfer, perhaps we can achieve it. In broad terms, one might speak of two techniques for promoting transfer: "hugging" and "bridging."

"Hugging" means teaching so as to better meet the resemblance conditions for low-road transfer. Teachers who would like students to use their knowledge of biology in thinking about current ecological problems might introduce that knowledge in the first place in the context of such problems. Teachers who want students to relate literature to everyday life might emphasize literature where the connection is particularly plain for many students—*Catcher in the Rye* or *Romeo and Juliet*, for example.

"Bridging" means teaching so as to better meet the conditions for high-road transfer. Rather than expecting students to achieve transfer spontaneously, one "mediates" the needed processes of abstraction and connection making (Delclos, Littlefield, and Bransford, 1985; Feuerstein, 1980). For example, teachers can point out explicitly the more general principles behind particular skills or knowledge or, better, provoke students to attempt such generalizations themselves: "What general factors provoked the American Revolution, and where are they operating in the world today?" Teachers can ask students

to make analogies that reach outside the immediate context: "How was treatment of blacks in the U.S. South before the Civil War like or unlike the treatment of blacks in South Africa in the 1980s?" Teachers can directly teach problem solving and other strategies and provoke broad-spectrum practice reaching beyond their own subject matters: "You learned this problem-defining strategy in math, but how might you apply it to planning an essay in English?"

Such tactics of hugging and bridging will sound familiar. Teachers already pose questions and organize activities of these sorts from time to time. However, rarely is this done persistently and systematically enough to saturate the context of education with attention to transfer. On the contrary, the occasional bridging question or assignment of a reading carefully chosen to hug a transfer target gets lost amid the overwhelming emphasis on subject-matter-specific, topic-specific, fact-based questions and activities.

There is ample reason to believe that bridging and hugging together could do much to foster transfer in instructional settings. Consider, once again, the impact of programming on cognitive skills. As emphasized earlier, findings in general have been negative. However, in a few cases, positive results have appeared (Carver & Klahr, 1987; Clements, 1985a, 1985b; Clements & Gullo, 1984; Clements & Merriman, 1988; Littlefield, Delclos, Lever, & Bransford, 1988). These cases all involved strong bridging activities in the instruction.

The same story can be told of efforts to teach people with mental disabilities some elementary memory skills. As noted earlier, transfer was lacking in most such experiments, but not in all. In a few experiments, the investigators taught learners not only the memory strategies themselves but habits of self-monitoring, by which the learners examined their own behavior and thought about how to approach a task. This abstract focus on task demands—in effect a form of bridging—led to positive transfer results in these studies (Belmont et al., 1982).

Even without explicit bridging, hugging can have a substantial impact on transfer. For example, inert knowledge has been a serious problem in medical education, where traditionally students memorize multitudinous details of anatomy and physiology outside the context of real diagnostic application. In an approach called "problem-based learning," medical students acquire their technical knowledge of the human body in the context of working through case studies demanding diagnosis (Barrows & Tamblyn, 1980). Experiments in science education conducted by John Bransford and his colleagues tell a similar story. When science facts and concepts were presented to students in the context of a story in which they could help resolve a problem or illuminate a question, the students proved much more able to transfer these facts and concepts to new problem-solving contexts (Bransford et al., 1986; Sherwood, Kinzer, Bransford, & Franks, 1987). In both the medical context and the science work, the instruction hugged much closer to the transfer performance than would instruction that simply and straightforwardly presented information.

Taken together, the notions of bridging and hugging write a relatively simple recipe for teaching for transfer. First, imagine the transfer you want—let's say, interpretation of contemporary and past conduct of societies and nations or perhaps problem solving where care is taken to define the problem before seeking solutions. Next, shape instruction to hug closer to the transfer desired. Teach history not just for memorizing its story but for interpretation of events through general principles. Teach programming or mathematical problem solving with emphasis on problem defining. Also, shape instruction to bridge to the transfer desired. Deliberately provoke students to think about how they approach tasks inside and outside history, programming, or math. Steal a little time from the source subject matter to confront students with analogous problems outside its boundary. Such teamwork between bridging and hugging practically guarantees making the most of whatever potential transfer the subject matter affords.

Moreover, there is an opportunity to go even further. Aside from how one teaches, one can help students develop skills of *learning for transfer*. Students can become acquainted with the problem of transfer in itself and the tactics of bridging and hugging. Students can develop habits of doing considerable bridging and hugging for themselves, beyond what the instruction itself directly provides. Accordingly, a major goal of teaching for transfer becomes not just teaching particular knowledge and skills for transfer but teaching students in general how to *learn for transfer*.

IS KNOWLEDGE TOO LOCAL FOR TRANSFER?

Encouraging as all this is, it nonetheless leaves untreated the nagging problem of "local knowledge." If by and large the knowledge (including skills) that empowers a person in a particular activity is highly local to that activity, there are few prospects for useful transfer to other activities. What, then, can be said about this contemporary trend in theorizing about expertise and its implications for the potentials of teaching for transfer?

The suggestion is that, while the findings supporting a "local knowledge" view of expertise are entirely sound, the implications drawn from those findings against the prospects of

transfer are too hasty. Despite the local knowledge results, there are numerous opportunities for transfer. At least three arguments support this viewpoint: (1) disciplinary boundaries are very fuzzy, not representing distinct breaks in the kinds of knowledge or skill that are useful; (2) while much knowledge is local, there are at least a few quite general and important thinking strategies; and (3) there are numerous elements of knowledge and skill of intermediate generality that afford some transfer across a limited range of disciplines.

The fuzziness of disciplinary boundaries. Even if knowledge and skill are local, are their boundaries of usefulness the same as the boundaries we use to organize disciplines and subject matters? For a case in point, history and current events might be treated in schools as different subjects, and, because they are partitioned off from each other, one might find scant transfer between them without special attention. Yet it seems plain that the kinds of causal reasoning and types of causes relevant to explaining historical events apply just as well to contemporary events. For another case in point, literature is a subject to study, life a "subject" to live. Yet plainly most literature treats fundamental themes of concern in life—love, birth, death, acquisition and defense of property, and so on. The relationships between literature and life offer an arena for reflection upon both and for transport of ideas from one to the other and back again.

To generalize, a close look at conventional disciplinary boundaries discloses not a well-defined geography with borders naturally marked by rivers and mountain ranges but, instead, enormous overlap and interrelation. If knowledge and skill are local, the boundaries surely are not the cleavages of the conventional curriculum. Yet because these cleavages are there as part of the organization of schooling, tactics of bridging and hugging are needed to take the numerous opportunities for fertile transfer across the conventional subject matters.

The existence of important cross-cutting thinking strategies. There are certainly some strategic patterns of thinking that are important, neglected, and cross-disciplinary in character (see Baron, 1985a, 1985b; Baron & Sternberg, 1986; Chipman, Segal, & Glaser, 1985; Nickerson, Perkins, & Smith, 1985; Perkins, 1986a, 1986b, 1986c). For example, in virtually all contexts people tend not to give full attention to the other side of an issue—the view opposite their own—in reasoning about a situation. People also tend to be "solution minded," orienting too quickly to a problem and beginning to develop candidate solutions at once. Often they could benefit by standing back from the problem, exploring its nature, defining exactly what the problem is, seeking alternative ways to represent it, and so on. Further, people tend not to monitor their own mental processes very much, when doing so would garner the perspective and leverage of greater metacognitive awareness.

To be sure, exactly how to consider alternative views, explore a problem, or self-monitor is somewhat a matter of local knowledge that will differ significantly from context to context. However, the strategy of allocating attention and effort to considering the other side of an issue, exploring a problem, or self-monitoring applies to many situations in general. Accordingly, when developing such strategies in any domain, one can then hope to transfer them to others.

Patterns of thinking of intermediate generality. Finally, if we do not demand universal generality, there are numerous kinds of knowledge and skill of intermediate generality that cut across certain domains and provide natural prospects for transfer. For example, many considerations of measurement, methodology, and the role of evidence apply fairly uniformly across the hard sciences. Any art yields interesting results when examined through the categories of style and form, though the particular styles and forms of importance will vary from art to art. Psychological concepts such as motive, intention, inner conflict, the unconscious, and so on have an obvious role to play in interpreting literature, history, current events, and everyday life, and they perhaps even have some part to play in examining scientific discovery.

Of course, conventional subject matter boundaries usually inhibit the emergence of these patterns of thinking of intermediate generality because the style of instruction is so very local that it does not decontextualize the patterns. Bridging and hugging are needed to develop out of the details of the subject matters the overarching principles.

MEMBERS OF THE SAME TEAM

Instead of worrying about which is more important—local knowledge or the more general transferable aspects of knowledge—we should recognize the synergy of local and more general knowledge. To be sure, students who do not know much about history are unlikely to enrich their thinking about the causes of the American Revolution by the general strategy of trying to reflect on both sides of an issue, American and British. And students who do not have the habit of reflecting on both sides of a case will not get much depth of understanding out of the history they do know. Similarly, students who lack an understanding of key mathematical concepts will not gain much from the general strategy of trying to define and represent a problem well before they start. But students who lack the habit of trying to define and represent a problem well

will often misuse the mathematical concepts they know when the problem is not routine.

So general and local knowledge are not rivals. Rather they are members of the same team that play different positions. Proper attention to transfer will make the best of both for the sake of deeper and broader knowledge, skill, and understanding.

REFERENCES

Baron J. (1985a). *Rationality and intelligence.* New York: Cambridge University Press.

Baron, J. (1985b). What kinds of intelligence components are fundamental? In S. S. Chipman, J. W. Segal, & R. Glaser (Eds.), *Thinking and learning skills. Vol. 2: Current research and open questions.* Hillsdale, NJ: Lawrence Erlbaum.

Baron, J. B., & Sternberg, R. S. (Eds.). (1986). *Teaching thinking skills: Theory and practice.* New York: W. H. Freeman.

Barrows, H. S., & Tamblyn, R. M. (1980). *Problem-based learning: An approach to medical education.* New York: Springer.

Belmont, J. M., Butterfield, E. C., & Ferretti, R. P. (1982). To secure transfer of training, instruct self-management skills. In D. K. Detterman & R. J. Sternberg, (Eds.), *How and how much can intelligence be increased?* Norwood, NJ: Ablex.

Bransford, J. D., Franks, J. J., Vye, N. J., & Sherwood, R. D. (1986, June). *New approaches to instruction: Because wisdom can't be told.* Paper presented at the Conference on Similarity and Analogy, University of Illinois.

Carver, S. M., & Klahr, D. (April 1987). *Analysis, instruction, and transfer of the components of debugging skill.* Paper presented at the biennial meeting of the Society for Research in Child Development. Baltimore, MD.

Chase, W. C., & Simon, H. A. (1973). Perception in chess. *Cognitive Psychology, 4,* 55–81.

Chi, M., Feltovich, P., & Glaser, R. (1981). Categorization and representation of physics problems by experts and novices. *Cognitive Science, 5*(2), 121–152.

Chipman, S. F., Segal, J. G., & Glaser, R. (Eds.). (1985). *Thinking and learning skills. Volume 2: Current research and open questions.* Hillsdale, NJ: Lawrence Erlbaum.

Clements, D. H. (1985a, April). *Effects of Logo programming on cognition, metacognitive skills, and achievement.* Presentation at the American Educational Research Association conference, Chicago.

Clements, D. H. (1985b). Research on Logo in education: Is the turtle slow but steady, or not even in the race? *Computers in the Schools, 2*(2/3), 55–71.

Clements, D. H., & Gullo, D. F. (1984). Effects of computer programming on young children's cognition. *Journal of Educational Psychology, 76*(6), 1051–1058.

Clements, D. H., & Merriman, S. (1988). Componential developments in Logo programming environments. In R. E. Mayer (Ed.), *Teaching and learning computer programming: Multiple research perspectives.* Hillsdale, NJ: Lawrence Erlbaum.

Dalbey, J., & Linn, M. C. (1985). The demands and requirements of computer programming: A literature review. *Journal of Educational Computing Research, 1*(3), 253–274.

de Groot, A. D. (1965). *Thought and choice in chess.* The Hague: Mouton.

Delclos, V. R., Littlefield, J., & Bransford, J. D. (1985). Teaching thinking through Logo: The importance of method. *Roeper Review, 7*(3), 153–156.

Feuerstein, R. (1980). *Instrumental enrichments: An intervention program for cognitive modifiability.* Baltimore: University Park Press.

Feurzeig, W., Horwitz, P., & Nickerson, R. (1981). *Microcomputers in education* [report no. 4798]. Cambridge, MA: Bolt, Beranek, and Newman.

Hirsch, E. D., Jr. (1987). *Cultural literacy: What every American needs to know.* Boston: Houghton Mifflin.

Larkin, J. H. (1983). The role of problem representation in physics. In D. Gentner & A. I. Stevens (Eds.), *Mental models.* Hillsdale, N.J: Lawrence Erlbaum.

Larkin, J. H., McDermott, J., Simon, D. P., & Simon, H. A. (1980). Modes of competence in solving physics problems. *Cognitive Science, 4,* 317–345.

Linn, M. C. (1985, May). The cognitive consequences of programming instruction in classrooms. *Educational Researcher, 14*(5), 14–29.

Littlefield, J., Delclos, V., Lever, S., & Bransford, J. (1988). Learning Logo: Method of teaching, transfer of general skills, attitudes toward computers. In R. E. Mayer (Ed.), *Teaching and learning computer programming: Multiple research perspectives.* Hillsdale, NJ: Lawrence Erlbaum.

Nickerson, R. D., Perkins, D. N., & Smith, E. (1985). *The teaching of thinking.* Hillsdale, NJ: Lawrence Erlbaum.

Olson, D. R. (1976). Culture, technology, and intellect. In L. B. Resnick (Ed.), *Nature of intelligence.* Hillsdale, NJ: Lawrence Erlbaum.

Papert, S. (1980). *Mindstorms: Children, computers, and powerful ideas.* New York: Basic Books.

Perfetto, G. A., Bransford, J. D., & Franks, J. (1983). Constraints on access in a problem solving context. *Memory & Cognition, 11*(1), 24–31.

Perkins, D. N. (1985). The fingertip effect: How information-processing technology changes thinking. *Educational Researcher 14*(7), 11–17.

Perkins, D. N. (1986a). *Knowledge as design.* Hillsdale, NJ: Lawrence Erlbaum.

Perkins, D. N. (1986b). Thinking frames. *Educational Leadership, 43*(8), 410.

Perkins, D. N. (1986c). Thinking frames: An integrative perspective on teaching cognitive skills. In J. B. Baron & R. S. Sternberg (Eds.), *Teaching thinking skills: Theory and practice.* New York: W. H. Freeman.

Perkins, D. N., & Martin, F. (1986). Fragile knowledge and neglected strategies in novice programmers. In E. Soloway & S. Iyengar (Eds.), *Empirical Studies of Programmers.* Norwood, NJ: Ablex.

Perkins, D. N., Martin, F., & Farady, M. (1986). *Loci of difficulty in learning to program* [Educational Technology Center technical report]. Cambridge, MA: Educational Technology Center, Harvard Graduate School of Education.

Perkins, D. N., & Salomon, G. (1987). Transfer and teaching thinking. In D. N. Perkins, J. Lochhead, & J. Bishop (Eds.), *The second international conference.* Hillsdale, NJ: Lawrence Erlbaum.

Salomon, G., & Perkins, D. N. (1984, August). *Rocky roads to transfer: Rethinking mechanisms of a neglected phenomenon.* Paper presented at the Conference on Thinking, Harvard Graduate School of Education, Cambridge, MA.

Salomon, G., & Perkins, D. N. (1987). Transfer of cognitive skills from programming: When and how? *Journal of Educational Computing Research, 3*(2), 149–169.

Schoenfeld, A. H., & Herrman, D. J. (1982). Problem perception and knowledge structure in expert and novice mathematical problem solvers. *Journal of Experimental Psychology: Learning, Memory, and Cognition, 8,* 484–494.

Scribner, S., & Cole, M. (1981). *The psychology of literacy.* Cambridge, MA: Harvard University Press.

Sherwood, R. D., Kinzer, C. K., Bransford, J. D., &. Franks, J. (1987, May). Some benefits of creating macro contexts for science instruction: Initial findings. *Journal of Research in Science Teaching , 24*(5), 417–435.

Soloway, E., & Ehrlich, K. (1984). Empirical studies of programming knowledge. *IEEE Transactions on Software Engineering, 10*(5), 595–609.

Authors' note: Some of the ideas discussed herein were developed at the Educational Technology Center of the Harvard Graduate School of Education, operating with support from the Office of Educational Research and Improvement (OERI), contract #OERI 400830041. Opinions expressed herein are not necessarily shared by OERI and do not represent office policy.

60

Teaching the Language of Thinking

ARTHUR L. COSTA AND ROBERT J. MARZANO

Schools should not be organized for teachers to teach, but for children to learn.

—McLean Briggs

Teaching and learning are predominantly linguistic phenomena; that is, we accomplish most of our learning through the vehicle of language, the daily exchange of words in classrooms. Therefore, language is a tool that teachers can use to enhance cognitive development. If we are to develop a successful program for teaching thinking, we must also develop a language of cognition.

THE LINGUISTIC NATURE OF INSTRUCTION

According to Feuerstein (1980), the teacher's interactive role is crucial in the mediated learning experience of children's cognitive development. In their major review of studies of linguistic interactions in classrooms, Green and Smith (1982) conclude that language is used by teachers to "frame" the presentation of content, the tasks students are to perform, and the norms of acceptable and unacceptable conduct. In other words, teachers tell students what to do, when to do it, and how to behave when they do it.

Language also creates classroom culture, which is defined as the set of important understandings that class members share. For example, Parelius (1980) and Purkey and Smith (1982) have identified such classroom culture variables as "tone of orderliness" and "atmosphere of acceptance" as keys to effective teaching. Burger (1977) asserts that culture actually "lives in language."

Labeling is another fundamental characteristic of language (Condon, 1968). When people create a name or a label for something, they also create a reality that previously did not exist for them. Condon uses the example of taking a course in astronomy. Before taking a course, a person will look at a night sky and see only stars. After a few weeks of instruction, he or she will begin to see *super novae, white dwarfs,* and *galaxies.* Thus, when we create labels, we structure our perceptions. New labels foster new perceptions. As Condon (1968) observed, "For better or for worse, when names are learned we see what we had not seen, for we know what to look for."

Given the nature and importance of language, creating a classroom language of cognition necessarily involves redefining terminology and perhaps inventing new terminology for specific situations. We have identified seven starting points.

USING PRECISE VOCABULARY

Teachers often admonish students to "think hard." They sometimes criticize students for not having the inclination to think: "These kids just go off without thinking."

The term *think* covers a range of thought processes. Students may fail to think because the vocabulary is foreign to them or because they may not know how to perform the specific skill implied. Thus, teachers should use specific cognitive terminology and show students how to perform particular skills. For example, instead of saying, "Let's *look at* these two pictures," say, "Let's *compare* these two pictures" (Figure 60.1), and then demonstrate how to find similarities and differences in them.

As children hear these terms daily and develop the cognitive processes that these labels signify, they will internalize the words and use them as part of their own vocabularies. Teachers can also provide specific instruction in cognitive processes

This chapter is adapted from *Developing Minds: A Resource Book for Teaching Thinking* (Rev. ed.), 1991. The original chapter is adapted from an October 1987 article in *Educational Leadership, 45*(2), 29–33.

—*Figure 60.1*—
Precise Terminology

Instead of Saying:
"Let's look at these two pictures."
"What do you think will happen when . . . ?"
"How can you put into groups . . . ?"
"Let's work this problem."
"What do you think would have happened if . . . ?"
"What did you think of this story?"
"How can you explain . . . ?"
"How do you know that's true?"
"How else could you use this . . . ?"

Say:
"Let's *compare* these two pictures."
"What do you *predict* will happen when . . . ?"
"How can you *classify* . . . ?"
"Let's *analyze* this problem."
"What do you *speculate* would have happened if . . . ?"
"What *conclusions* can you draw about this story?"
"What *hypotheses* do you have that might explain . . . ?"
"What *evidence* do you have to support . . . ?"
"How could you *apply* this . . . ?"

so that students will attach precise, shared meaning to the terms (Beyer, 1985). Teaching students what goes on in the head when comparisons are made, what are helpful steps in a decision-making process, and what techniques cause creative juices to flow when writing a story are examples of ways teachers can provide specific instruction in thinking skills.

POSING CRITICAL QUESTIONS

Teachers often make decisions about which classroom behaviors to discourage and which to reinforce. They do this by posing questions that cause children to examine their behavior, consider the consequences of that behavior, and choose more appropriate actions (Bailis & Hunter, 1985). For example, instead of saying, "Be quiet," the teacher can say, "The noise you're making is disturbing us. Is there a way you can work so that we don't hear you?" (Figure 60.2).

Discussions with children about appropriate behavior, classroom and school rules, and courtesy are necessary if students are to learn respect for other people. The language of thinking will help students determine which behaviors "work" within the culture of the classroom.

—*Figure 60.2*—
Questions That Encourage Appropriate Behavior

Instead of Saying:
"Be quiet."
"Sarah, get away from Shawn."
"Stop Interrupting."
"Stop running."

Say:
"The noise you're making is disturbing us. Is there a way you can work so that we don't hear you?"
"Sarah, can you find another place to do your best work?"
"Since it's Maria's turn to talk, what do you need to do?"
"Why do you think we have the rule about always walking in the halls?"

PROVIDING DATA, NOT SOLUTIONS

Sometimes teachers rob children of the opportunity to take responsibility for their behavior by providing solutions, consequences, and appropriate actions for them. Teachers can teach responsibility by giving data and sending "I" messages (Figure 60.3). By providing data as input for children to process, teachers will encourage them to act more autonomously, to be-

—*Figure 60.3*—
Data for Autonomous Decision Making

When Children:
Make noise by tapping their pencils.
Interrupt.
Whine.
Are courteous.
Chew gum.

Say:
"I want you to know that your pencil tapping is disturbing me."
"I like it when you take turns to speak."
"It hurts my ears."
"I liked it when you came in so quietly and went right to work."
"I want you to know that gum chewing in my class disturbs me."

—Figure 60.4—

Instructions That Teach Meaning

Instead of Saying:
"For our field trip, remember to bring spending money, comfortable shoes, and a warm jacket."
"The bell has rung; it's time to go home. Clear off your desks quietly and line up at the door."
"Get 52 cups, 26 scissors, and 78 sheets of paper to cover the desks."
"Remember to write your name in the upper right-hand corner of your paper."

Say:
"What must we remember to bring with us on the field trip?"
"The bell has rung. What must we do to get ready to go home?"
"Everyone will need two paper cups, a pair of scissors, and three sheets of paper. The desktops will need to be protected. Can you figure out what you'll need to do?"
"So that I can easily tell who the paper belongs to, what must you remember to do?"

—Figure 60.5—

Avoiding Generalizations

When You Hear:
"He *never* listens to me."
"*Everybody* has one."
"*Things* go better with . . ."
"Things *go* better with . . ."
"Things go *better* with . . ."
"You *shouldn't* do that . . ."
"The *parents* . . ."
"I want them to *understand* . . ."
"This cereal is *more nutritious.*"
"*They* won't let me . . ."
"*The administrators* . . ."

Say:
"Never? Never, ever?"
"Everybody? Who, exactly?"
"Which things, specifically?"
"Go? Go how, specifically?"
"Better than what?"
"What would happen if you did?"
"Which parents?"
"What exactly will they be doing if they understand?"
"More nutritious than what?"
"Who are they?"
"Which administrators?"

come aware of the effects of their behavior on others, and to become more empathetic by sensing verbal and nonverbal cues from others.

GIVING DIRECTIONS

When giving directions, teachers often spoonfeed students by providing so much information that they can comply without having to infer meaning (Figure 60.4). Instead, teachers can ask questions that require students to analyze a task, identify what is needed to complete the task, and then perform the task.

PROBING FOR SPECIFICITY

Oral language is rife with omissions, vagueness, and generalizations. It is conceptual rather than operational; value laden; and sometimes deceptive. To encourage careful thinking, teachers should try to get students to define terms, be specific about actions, make precise comparisons, and use accurate descriptors (Laborde, 1984). They should be alert to vague or unspecified terms, which fall into several categories:

- Universals, including *always, never, all, everybody.*
- Vague actions, such as *know about, understand, appreciate.*
- Comparisons, such as *better, newer, cheaper, more nutritious.*
- Unreferenced pronouns, such as *they, them, we.*
- Unspecified groups, such as *teachers, parents, things.*
- Assumed rules or traditions, including *ought, should, or must.*

Critical thinkers are characterized by their ability to use specific terminology, to refrain from overgeneralization, and to support their assumptions with valid data (Ennis, 1985) (Figure 60.5).

DEVELOPING METACOGNITION

Thinking about thinking begets more thinking (Costa, 1984). When teachers ask children to describe the thought processes they are using, the data they need, and the plans they are formulating, students learn to think about their own thinking—to metacogitate. Whimbey (1985) refers to this as "talk aloud problem solving" (Figure 60.6).

—Figure 60.6—
Thinking About Thinking

When Children Say:
"The answer is 43 pounds, seven ounces."
"I don't know how to solve this problem."
"I'm ready to begin."
"We're memorizing our poems."
"I like the large one best."
"I'm finished."

Say:
"Describe the steps you took to arrive at that answer."
"What can you do to get started?"
"Describe your plan of action."
"What do you do when you memorize?"
"What criteria are you using to make your choice?"
"How do you know you're correct?"

—Figure 60.7—
Linguistic Cues

Relationship
Addition
Comparison
Contrast
Sequence
Causality

Description
Two ideas go together in some way.
Common attributes are shared.
Two ideas don't go together.
One event happens before, during, or after another event.
One event occurs as a result of another.

Example of Linguistic Cue
"He is intelligent *and* he is kind."
"Shawn *and* Sarah *both* play the violin."
"He is healthy, *but* he doesn't exercise."
"He went home, *then* he went to the library, checked out some books, and returned to school."
"*Because* no one was home, he went to the gym."

As teachers require students to describe what's going on "inside their heads," students become aware of their thinking processes. Similarly, as they listen to their classmates describing their metacognitive processes, they develop flexibility of thought and an appreciation for the variety of ways to solve the same problem. Teachers, too, may share their thinking by making their inner dialogue external. Verbalizing questions they are asking themselves about ways to solve problems, and sharing their lesson plans and how they check their own accuracy, are ways teachers can model their metacognitive processes to students.

ANALYZING THE LOGIC OF LANGUAGE

Effective thinking can be fostered by having students analyze the logic implied by linguistic expressions. Certain words and phrases—linguistic cues—indicate logical relationships between ideas (Figure 60.7).

By examining these linguistic cues (*and, or, but, after, because*), students can learn to identify related ideas in a sentence between the ideas (*addition, comparison, contrast, sequence,* or *causality*).

HOW TO GROW INTELLIGENT BEHAVIOR

Teaching students to be alert to the cognitive processes embedded in written and spoken language can help them become aware of their own language and thought. It can help them decode the syntactic, semantic, and rhetorical signals found in all languages; and it can help them integrate the complex interaction of language, thought, and action (Marzano & Hutchins, 1985). By asking questions, selecting terms, clarifying ideas and processes, providing data, and withholding value judgments, teachers can stimulate and enhance the thinking of their students.

REFERENCES

Bailis, R., & Hunter, M. (1985, August). Do your words get them to think? *Learning 14,* 1.

Beyer, B. (1985). Practical strategies for the direct teaching of thinking skills. In A. L. Costa (Ed.), *Developing minds: A resource book for teaching thinking.* Alexandria, VA: Association for Supervision and Curriculum Development.

Burger, H. G. (1977). Panculture: A hominization-derived processed taxonomy from Murdock's universal basics. In B. Bernardi, *The concept and dynamics of culture.* The Hague, Netherlands: Mouton.

Condon, J. C. (1968). *Semantics and communication.* New York: MacMillan.

Costa, A. L. (1984, November). Mediating the metacognitive. *Educational Leadership, 42*(3), 57–62.

Ennis, R. (1985). Goals for a critical thinking curriculum. In A. L. Costa (Ed.), *Developing minds: A resource book for teaching thinking*. Alexandria, VA: Association for Supervision and Curriculum Development.

Feuerstein, R. (1980). *Instructional enrichment*. Baltimore: University Park Press.

Green, J. L., & Smith, D. C. (1982, February). Teaching and learning: A linguistic perspective. Paper presented at the Conference on Research on Teaching: Implications for Practice, Warrenton, VA.

Laborde, G. (1984). *Influencing with Integrity*. Palo Alto, Calif.: Syntony Press.

Marzano, R., & Hutchins, C. L. (1985). *Thinking skills: A conceptual framework*. Aurora, CO: Mid-continent Regional Educational Laboratory.

Parelius, R. J. (1980). *Faculty cultures and instructional practices*. New Brunswick, NJ: Rutgers University Press.

Purkey, S. C., & Smith, M. S. (1982). Effective schools: A review. Madison, WI: Wisconsin Center for Educational Research, University of Wisconsin.

Whimbey, A. (1985). Test results from teaching thinking. In A. L. Costa (Ed.), *Developing minds: A resource book for teaching thinking*. Alexandria, VA: Association for Supervision and Curriculum Development.

61

Cueing Thinking in the Classroom: The Promise of Theory-Embedded Tools

Jay McTighe and Frank T. Lyman Jr.

Throughout history, human progress has been propelled by the development and use of tools. The wheel, telegraph, microscope, computer—these and other tools greatly extend human capabilities. How can the concept of tools help to accelerate progress in education? Nathaniel Gage (1974) has proposed that teachers use "tools of the trade," tangible teaching/learning devices that are material embodiments of theoretically valid teaching/learning ideas. According to Gage, these tools should have

• *Psychological validity*—they reflect what is known about teaching and learning.
• *Concreteness*—they embody knowledge in materials and equipment.
• *Relevance to teachers*—they have practical value in the classroom.
• *Differentiation by type of learning*—a relationship exists between the type of tool and the way that a skill, concept, process, or attitude is best learned.

Successful classroom applications demonstrate that tool-assisted instruction is indeed a medium for blending theory and practice. Here we describe six tools for creating classroom conditions conducive to thinking.

THINK–PAIR–SHARE

After the teacher asks a question, 1st graders think for 10 seconds and then talk in pairs as the teacher moves an arrow on a cue chart from think *to* pair.

More than 20 years of research on "wait time" has confirmed numerous benefits from allowing three or more seconds of silent

thinking time after a question has been posed (wait time 1) as well as after a student's response (wait time 2). These benefits include longer and more elaborate answers, inferences supported by evidence and logical argument, greater incidence of speculative responses, increased student participation in discussion, and improved achievement (Rowe, 1986). Also, the use of cooperative learning structures promotes student involvement and increased verbal interaction, resulting in positive effects on attitude and achievement (Slavin, 1981; Johnson & Johnson, 1984). The Think–Pair–Share method (Lyman, 1981b; 1989) combines the benefits of wait time and cooperative learning.

Think–Pair–Share is a multi-mode discussion cycle in which students listen to a question or presentation, have time to *think* individually, talk with each other in *pairs*, and finally *share* responses with the larger group. The teacher signals students to switch from listening to the *think*, *pair*, and *share* modes by using cues (see Figure 61.1).

Cueing enables teachers to manage students' thinking by combating the competitiveness, impulsivity, and passivity present in the timeworn recitation model. Both wait time 1 and wait time 2 can be consistently achieved with Think–Pair–Share, as students raise their hands only on signal, not directly after the question or a response. Students, individually and in pairs, may write or diagram their thoughts. Other cues give options for how students are to think or work in pairs. For instance, teachers may cue them to reach consensus, engage in problem solving, or assume the role of devil's advocate (see Figure 61.2). The overall effect of these coordinated elements is a concrete, valid, and practical system, made manageable—and thereby acceptable to teachers—by cueing devices.

QUESTIONING/DISCUSSION STRATEGIES BOOKMARK

During classroom discussion of the limits of First Amendment rights, a high school social studies teacher glances at a laminated

This chapter is adapted from *Developing Minds: A Resource Book for Teaching Thinking* (Rev. ed.), 1991. The original chapter is adapted from an April 1988 article in *Educational Leadership, 45*(7), 18–24.

—*Figure 61.1*—
Cues for Think–Pair–Share

bookmark he's holding and assumes the role of devil's advocate in response to student comments.

More than 2,000 years ago, Socrates demonstrated the power of questioning to stimulate thinking. Educators today know that the way a teacher structures a question influences the nature of the thinking required to respond. We also know that follow-up discussion strategies, such as asking for elaboration, influence the degree and quality of classroom discussion. Despite this knowledge, however, Goodlad (1983) reports that most classroom questions require only factual responses and that, in general, students are not involved in thought-provoking discussions.

Teachers can integrate effective questioning and discussion strategies into their daily repertoires by referring to a "cueing" bookmark (McTighe, 1985), which features question starters on one side and discussion strategies on the other (see Figure 61.3). During classroom discussion, the bookmark reminds teachers to use these promising strategies.

THINKING MATRIX

After looking at a game board thinking matrix, a 5th grade boy asks his classmates: "what caused the hero's death—I mean, what was there about his life that made you think he had to die that way?"

—*Figure 61.2*—
Think–Pair–Share Structures

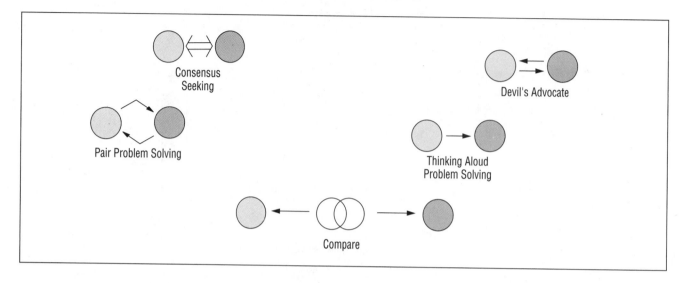

In addition to learning to ask questions that promote thinking (see Gall, 1970; Hare & Pulliam, 1980), teachers are recognizing a need to help students generate their own questions. Generating their own questions facilitates students' comprehension (Dave & McBride, 1986) and encourages them to focus attention, make predictions, identify relevant information, and think creatively about content.

The thinking matrix, or Thinktrix, is a device to aid teachers and students in generating questions and responses (Lyman, 1987). (See Figure 61.4.) The vertical axis of the matrix contains symbols of types of thought; the horizontal axis lists categories that give points of departure for inquiry, which vary according to the subject area. For example, using the matrix in language arts, teachers or students point to an intersection such as cause/effect and event or character and ask a question about the cause of the hero's death; in social studies, they could point to the intersection of idea to example and theme or concept and ask for historical examples of balance of power.

The Thinktrix has many uses in the classroom. Students can analyze classroom questioning or discourse; or they can create, analyze, and answer their own questions, using a desk-size matrix as a game board. Using a poster-size matrix, teachers can make up their own questions, teach question design to students, show students how to respond to information using different thinking types, and point out the possible visual representations, or cognitive mappings, of each thinking type. In essence, the thinking matrix allows for shared metacognition in which teacher and students have a common framework for generating and organizing thought as well as for reflecting upon it.

READY READING REFERENCE

While reading about sea lions in a recent issue of National Geographic World, *a 5th grader looks at his bookmark and creates a visual image of what he has just read.*

Analysis of the differences between good and poor readers points out the importance of the strategic behaviors that good readers spontaneously employ before, during, and after their reading. For example, they concentrate on their purpose for reading, monitor their comprehension, and adjust their approach when necessary. Poor readers, on the other hand, are less mindful of such effective strategies. In fact, they tend to perceive reading as "decoding" rather than as the construction of meaning (Garner, 1980; Garner & Reis, 1981).

The Ready Reading Reference bookmark in Figure 61.5 (Kapinus, 1986) was developed to summarize knowledge about "good reader" strategies (Paris & Jacobs, 1984). The bookmark serves as a tangible instructional tool and a concrete cue for students during independent reading.

PROBLEM-SOLVING STRATEGIES WHEEL

As students in an algebra II class struggle to solve a word problem, their teacher points to a poster of problem-solving strategies and suggests that they consider strategy no. 5, draw a picture or diagram.

—Figure 61.3—
Cueing Bookmark

Front	Back
Questioning for Quality Thinking	*Strategies to Extend Student Thinking*

Front

Questioning for Quality Thinking

Knowledge—Identification and recall of information.
   Who, what, when, where, how _____ ?
   Describe _____ .

Comprehension—Organization and selection of facts and ideas.
   Retell _____ in your own words.
   What is the main idea of _____ ?

Application—Use of facts, rules, principles.
   How is _____ an example of _____ ?
   How is _____ related to _____ ?
   Why is _____ significant?

Analysis—Separation of a whole into component parts.
   What are the parts or features of _____ ?
   Classify _____ according to _____ .
   Outline/diagram/web _____ .
   How does _____ compare/contrast with _____ ?
   What evidence can you list for _____ ?

Synthesis—Combination of ideas to form a new whole.
   What would you predict/infer from _____ ?
   What ideas can you add to _____ ?
   How would you create/design a new _____ ?
   What might happen if you combined _____
   with _____ ?
   What solutions would you suggest for _____ ?

Evaluation—Development of opinions, judgments, or decisions.
   Do you agree _____ ?
   What do you think about _____ ?
   What is most important _____ ?
   Prioritize _____ .
   How would you decide about _____ ?
   What criteria would you use to assess _____ ?

Back

Strategies to Extend Student Thinking

- **Remember wait time 1 and 2**
   Provide at least three seconds of thinking time after a question and after a response.
- **Use the Think-Pair-Share method**
   Allow individual thinking time, discussion with a partner, and then open up the class discussion.
- **Ask follow-ups**
   Why? Do you agree? Can you elaborate? Tell me more. Can you give me an example?
- **Withhold judgment**
   Respond to student answers in a nonevaluative fashion.
- **Ask for summary (to promote active listening)**
   "Could you please summarize John's point?"
- **Survey the class**
   "How many people agree with the author's point of view?" (thumbs up, thumbs down)
- **Allow for student calling**
   "Richard, will you please call on someone else to respond?"
- **Play devil's advocate**
   Require students to defend their reasoning against different points of view.
- **Ask students to "unpack their thinking"**
   "Describe how you arrived at your answer." (think aloud)
- **Call on students randomly**
   Not just those with raised hands.
- **Student questioning**
   Let the students develop their own questions.
- **Cue student responses**
   "There is not a single correct answer for this question. I want you to consider alternatives."

Source: Adapted from Language and Learning Improvement Branch, Division of Instruction, Maryland State Department of Education.

Math and science teachers often experience frustration when students who demonstrate an understanding of basic facts and concepts cannot apply this knowledge to word problems. Fortunately, inquiry into the problem-solving behaviors of experts and novices has revealed important strategic distinctions, with implications for problem-solving instruction. Effective problem solvers spend time understanding a problem before attacking it. To this end, they may create various representations or models. Expert problem solvers also report using problem-solving strategies, or heuristics, such as breaking the problem into subproblems. They also engage in metacognitive behaviors, including monitoring progress and checking the final solution (Schoenfeld, 1979, 1980; Mayer, 1983; Suydam, 1980).

Teachers who wish to improve student problem solving can spend classroom time examining the solution *process* along with the final answer, model their own strategic reasoning by "thinking aloud," and provide explicit instruction in problem-solving heuristics using a problem-solving strategies wheel (see Figure 61.6). Frequently found in the form of a large classroom poster, such an instructional tool is a visible cue that reminds teachers and students of the strategies of experts.

—Figure 61.4—
Thinktrix

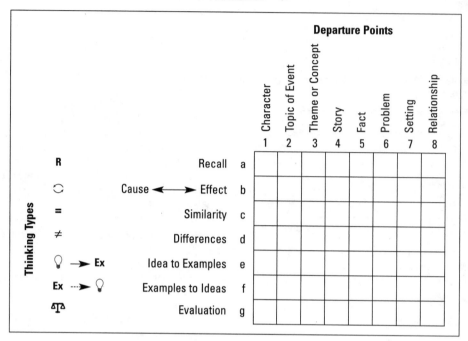

Cognitive Mapping

Upon completing a character analysis map as part of a "prewriting" activity, an 8th grader comments, "I like graphic organizers because they help me see what I'm thinking."

The ability to generate and organize information and ideas is fundamental to effective thinking. Cognitive maps and other visual organizers are effective tools for helping students to generate ideas and to organize their thoughts. Cognitive maps provide a visual, holistic representation of facts and concepts and their relationships within an organized framework. They help students to

- Represent abstract or implicit information in more concrete form.
- Depict the relationships among facts and concepts.
- Generate and elaborate ideas.
- Relate new information to prior knowledge.
- Store and retrieve information.

Cognitive mapping techniques show demonstrated success in improving retention of information (Armbuster & Anderson, 1980; Dansereau et al., 1979; Davidson, 1982; Vaughn, 1982). Teachers using the process approach to writing often use cognitive mapping during prewriting (Stahl-Gemake & Sinatra, 1986).

Cognitive map prototypes are now in use in classrooms from kindergarten through university levels. Perhaps the most widely used design is the web. Others include sequence steps or chains, vector charts for cause and effect, story maps, analogy links, and flowcharts for decision making and problem solving (see Figs. 61.7, 61.8, and 61.9, p. 391). Such cognitive maps become blueprints for oral discourse and written composition, particularly when used in conjunction with Think–Pair–Share and metacognitive cues, such as those on the Thinktrix and the bookmarks (Lyman, Lopez, & Mindus, 1986).

Through their regular use of cognitive mapping, students come to recognize that thought can be shaped, teachers discover a set of powerful tools for rendering the invisible process of thinking visible, and both experience the benefits of shared metacognition.

Why Instructional Tools Are Effective

The tools just described serve as catalysts for creating a responsive, "thinking" classroom. At least four factors may help explain the success of these and similar instructional tools: they provide an aid to memory, a common frame of reference, a practical incentive to act based on sound educational theory, and an inherent permanence.

—Figure 61.5—
Ready Reading Reference Bookmark

While you read—
Tell
yourself what the
author says.
Ask
yourself if what you are
reading makes sense.
Picture
what the author
describes.
Identify
the main ideas.
Predict
what will come next.

If you don't understand—
Identify
the problem.
Remind
yourself of what you want
to find out.
Look Back.
Look Ahead.
Slow Down.
Ask
for help.

After you read—
Retell
what you read in your own
words.
Summarize
the most important ideas.
Ask
yourself questions and
answer them.
Picture
in your mind what the
author described.
Decide
what was especially
interesting or enjoyable.

Maryland State Department of Education
Division of Instruction
Language and Learning Improvement Branch

52027/8/87

Source: Reprinted from *Ready Reading Reference* [bookmark], Maryland State Department of Education, Division of Instruction, Language and Learning Improvement Branch.

1. *An aid to memory.* Thinking tools serve as tangible cues for teachers and students. They provide immediate access to theoretical knowledge when it is needed most: at the point of decision making. In the complex and distracting dynamics of school, the concreteness and stability of these tools remind teachers and students to use what they know to enhance their thinking.

2. *A common frame of reference.* Thinking tools provide mutually understood frames of reference for teachers and students by offering common terminology (e.g., the thinking types on the Thinktrix) and specific cues for action (e.g., the signals associated with Think–Pair–Share). The tools provide congruence that can improve carryover from one classroom and subject area to others, resulting in consistency of approach within a school.

3. *Incentive to act.* Teachers are bombarded by advice and mandates, many of which appear to complicate their work. On the other hand, they welcome new ideas and materials that they think have practical value. The thinking tools described

—Figure 61.6—

Problem-Solving Strategies Wheel

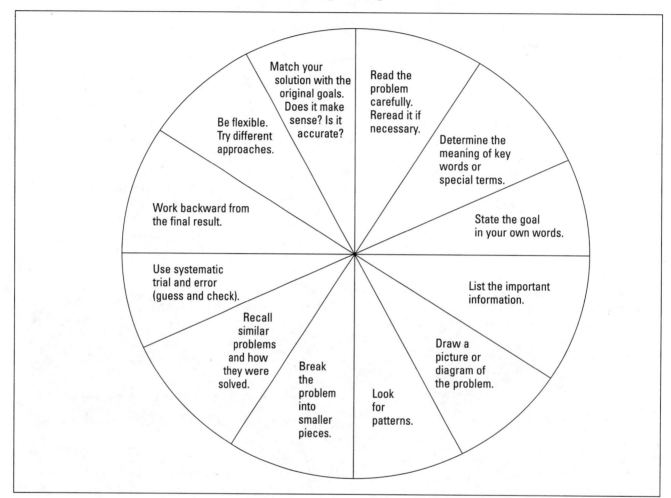

here have been enthusiastically received, in part because they are ready for immediate use.

4. *Permanence.* Even successful innovations are difficult to maintain in schools. These thinking tools, visible and concrete, may help to hold an innovation in place. Another dimension of permanence may be achieved through "mental templating": teachers and students frequently remember the message embedded in the tool even when the tool itself is not present. As a result, memories of ways to think and act may persist beyond the classroom.

THE PROMISE OF THEORY-EMBEDDED TOOLS

Instructional tools present a concrete, practical, and valid system for involving students from nursery school through graduate school in the active processing of ideas. Their use enables teacher educators to send novice teachers into the field with practical embodiments of theory. Staff developers who encourage the invention and use of instructional tools will see the elusive theory-into-practice connection made and maintained.

Furthermore, as Gage (1974) suggests, research on tools will test theory in practice and expand the knowledge base. These theory-embedded cueing devices promise to bring classroom teaching into closer harmony with known principles of effective instruction, thereby improving the quality of thinking and learning for all students.

REFERENCES

Armbuster, B. B., & Anderson, T. H. (1980). The effect of mapping on the free recall of expository test. (Technical Report 160). Urbana-Champaign, IL: Center for the Study of Reading, University of Illinois.

—*Figure 61.7*—
Flow Chart

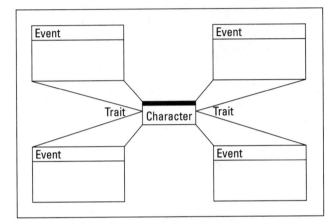

—*Figure 61.8*—
Decision-Making Model

—*Figure 61.9*—
Analogy Link

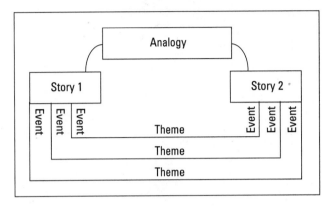

Dansereau, D., et al. (1979, February). Development and evaluation of a learning strategy training program. *Journal of Educational Psychology, 71*(1), 64–73.

Davey, B., & McBride, S. (1986). Effects of question-generation training on reading comprehension. *Journal of Educational Psychology, 78*(4), 256–262.

Davidson, J. L. (1982, October). The group mapping activity for instruction on reading and thinking. *Journal of Reading, 26*(1), 53–56.

Gage, N. L. (1974). *Teacher effectiveness and teacher education: The search for a scientific basis.* Palo Alto, CA: Pacific Books.

Gall, M. (1970). The use of questions in teaching. *Review of Educational Research, 40,* 707–721.

Garner, R. (1980). Monitoring of understanding: An investigation of good and poor readers. *Journal of Reading Behavior, 12,* 55–64.

Garner, R., & Reis, R. (1981). Monitoring and resolving comprehension obstacles: An investigation of spontaneous text lookbacks among upper-grade good and poor comprehenders. *Reading and Research Quarterly, 16*(4), 569–582.

Goodlad, J. I. (1983). *A place called school.* New York: McGraw-Hill.

Hare, V., & Pulliam, C. (1980). Teacher questioning: A verification and an extension. *Journal of Reading Behavior,* 69–72.

Johnson, D., & Johnson, R. (1984). Cooperative small-group learning. *Curriculum Report, 14*(1), 1–6.

Kapinus, B. (1986). *Ready reading readiness.* Baltimore: Maryland State Department of Education.

Lyman, F. T., Jr. (1981a, Spring). The development of tools. *Maryland A. T. E. Journal, 1,* 20–21.

Lyman, F. T., Jr. (1981b). The responsive classroom discussion: The inclusion of all students. In A. Anderson (Ed.), *Mainstreaming Digest.* College Park, MD: University of Maryland.

Lyman, F. T., Jr. (1987). The Thinktrix: A classroom tool for thinking in response to reading. In *Reading: Issues and Practices; Yearbook of the State of Maryland International Reading Association Council* (Vol. 4, 15–18). Wesminster, MD: State of Maryland International Reading Association Council.

Lyman, F. T., Jr. (1989, September–October). Rechoreographing: The middle level minuet. *The Early Adolescence Magazine (TEAM), 4*(1), 22–24.

Lyman, F. T., Jr., Lopez, C., & Mindus, A. (1986). Think-Links: The shaping of thought in response to reading. Unpublished manuscript. Columbia, MD: Authors.

Mayer, R. (1983, June). Implications of cognitive psychology for instruction in mathematic problem solving. Paper presented at the Conference on Teaching Mathematical Problem Solving, San Diego State University.

McTighe, J. (Speaker). (1985). *Questioning for quality thinking* (audiotape side 1) and *Strategies for extending student thinking* (side 2). Baltimore: Maryland State Department of Education.

Paris, S., & Jacobs. (1984, December). The benefits of informed instruction for children's reading awareness and comprehension skills. *Child Development, 55*(6), 2083–2093.

Rowe, M. B. (1986, January–February). Wait time: Slowing down may be a way of speeding up! *The Journal of Teacher Education, 31*(1), 43–50.

Schoenfeld, A. (1979). Can heuristics be taught? In J. Lochhead & J. Clement (Eds.), *Cognitive Press Instruction*. Philadelphia: Franklin Institute Press.

Schoenfeld, A. (1980). Heuristics in the classroom. In S. Krulik, & R. E. Reys (Eds.), *Problem solving in school mathematics*. Reston, VA: National Council of Teachers of Mathematics.

Slavin, R. E. (1981). Synthesis of research on cooperative learning. *Educational Leadership, 38*(8), 655–660.

Stahl-Gemake, J., & Sinatra, R. (1986, November–December). Using maps to improve writing. *Early Years*.

Suydam, M. (1980). Untangling clues from research on problem solving. In S. Krulik, & R. E. Reys (Eds.), *Problem solving in school mathematics*. Reston, VA: National Council of Teachers of Mathematics.

Vaughn, L., Jr. (1982, February). Use the construct procedure to foster active reading and learning. *Journal of Reading*.

62

Practical Strategies for Direct Instruction in Thinking Skills

Barry K. Beyer

There is an old saying that "Kids learn what they are taught." Stated more precisely, it goes: "Kids learn what they *perceive* is being taught." When students clearly understand or see—from the pattern of actions exhibited by the teacher—what it is they are supposed to do or know, and when instruction, including assessment, clearly focuses on this learning goal, they put effort into achieving this goal and usually *do* achieve it. Direct instruction is one way of applying the principles implicit in this adage to the teaching of thinking skills.

ESSENTIAL FEATURES OF
DIRECT INSTRUCTION IN THINKING SKILLS

Direct instruction, as applied to teaching thinking skills, is teaching that focuses continuously and explicitly on the procedures and heuristics—rules of thumb—for carrying out a specific cognitive operation, or thinking skill. It is distinguished by its (1) direct focus on step-by-step procedures and rules for carrying out a thinking skill, (2) efforts to eliminate or minimize any interference with this focus on the skill, and (3) continuous instruction in the thinking skill over an extended period of time and topics. Each of these features contributes directly to its effectiveness as a form of classroom instruction (Doyle, 1983).

Keeping the focus on the skill. Teachers who use direct instruction constantly focus student attention on how to carry out the skill. In every skill lesson they publicly affirm that learning the skill is the lesson's objective, and they display the name of the skill on the chalkboard. They continuously employ teaching techniques that make explicit the step-by-step procedures for applying the skill. They help their students learn important information about the skill, such as appropri-

ate circumstances for using it, some "expert" or authentic procedures for carrying it out, heuristics or rules that guide its application, criteria required to make any judgments essential in carrying it out, and contextual information that provides clues as to how to apply it.

Above all, when using direct instruction teachers engage students in applying the skill over and over again, initially with considerable support, guidance, and class discussions concentrating on what students did or can do mentally to carry out the thinking skill. They provide this practice before examining any subject matter claims or inferences generated by student application of the skill (Doyle, 1983). During the initial thinking skills lessons using direct instruction, students attend exclusively to the skill and how it can be executed.

Types of thinking skill lessons. Direct instruction in a single thinking skill consists of a series of lessons over an extended period of time, all focused on the same skill. The purpose of these lessons is to move students from halting, fragmented, incomplete, inexpert execution of a procedure for carrying out the skill to its increasingly skillful, integrated, self-directed, and effective application. Regardless of the specific skill being taught, direct instruction uses three basic types of lessons:

1. An *introduction* to an explicit procedure or procedures for carrying out the skill, usually a single 20–40 minute lesson focusing exclusively on the skill.

2. A series of 6 to 12 *guided practice* lessons in which students apply the skill and, as they do, receive scaffolded and then cued instruction in exercising the skill—with attention to the skill gradually decreasing from 15 minutes or so to finally fading out altogether, as they become increasingly proficient in carrying out the skill on their own.

3. An introduction and several practice lessons that *transfer* the skill from the context or media or subject in which it has been applied so far to a new context, medium, or subject.

Copyright © 2001 by Barry K. Beyer

—Figure 62.1—

A Sequence of Lessons for Direct Instruction in a Thinking Skill

Lesson # 1 2 3 4 5 6 7 8 9 10 11 12 13 14 15 16 17 18 19 20 21 22 23 24 25

Introduction →

Initial Scaffolded Practice

Guided Practice

Intermittent Cued Practice

Independent Practice to Autonomous Use

Initiating Transfer

26 27 28 29 30 31 32 33 34 35 36 37 38 39 40 41 42 43 44 45 46 47 48 49 50

Each ▢ represents a lesson in which a "target" skill is "taught."

Figure 62.1 illustrates a sequence of these types of lessons for a hypothetical thinking skill. Each number represents a subject matter lesson. Each box represents a lesson or portion of a lesson in which the thinking skill is the focus of instruction. Note the sequence of the three different types of lessons—from introduction through the various kinds of practice and the beginnings of transfer. Note, too, the spacing of the skill lessons within each type of thinking skill instruction for this single skill.

Although a number of strategies have been suggested for teaching these three kinds of lessons (Sternberg & Davidson, 1989; Whimbey & Lochhead, 1999), the strategies described here are especially practical because they can be employed to teach any thinking skill to students of any ability level in any subject. These strategies have been derived from research in skill learning, effective instruction, and cognition as well as from exemplary classroom practice (see Chapter 46 in this book, and also Doyle, 1983; Frederikson, 1984; Nickerson, 1989; Posner & Keele, 1973).

STRATEGIES FOR INTRODUCING A THINKING SKILL

Research indicates that in introducing a thinking skill students must focus exclusively on the skill. They should see the skill demonstrated by a teacher or peers skilled in executing it. They should apply the skill, reflect on how they did it, and receive feedback on how they did it (Posner & Keele, 1973).

While subject matter to which the skill is applied will be used to explain or illustrate how the skill can be carried out, it should not be elaborated, discussed, or probed at all during this lesson. What is crucial in this introductory lesson is that students see, hear, and actually engage in *how* the skill being introduced is carried out, especially by those more skillful in its application than they are (Brown et al., 1981; Hudgins, 1977; Posner & Keele, 1973; Sternberg, 1984; Taba, 1965). There are two basic strategies for conducting introductory direct instruction skill lessons: inductive and didactic.

An inductive strategy. Lessons using this strategy allow students to affirm the efficacy of the thinking procedure they presently use, or to construct from their own experience and from other sources a more effective and appropriate procedure. This inductive strategy for introducing a thinking skill consists of six major steps:

The teacher—
1. Previews the skill.

The students—
2. Apply it.
3. Reflect on what they did mentally to carry it out.
4. Apply the skill a second time.
5. Reflect again on what they did mentally to carry out the skill this time.
6. Review what they have verbalized about how, when, and where to apply this skill.

This strategy requires students—with teacher direction, prompting, and input as appropriate—to tease out of their verbalized experiences mental procedures for executing the skill on which they are focusing. What emerges is a tentative procedure (or several procedures that may differ from student to student) that can be gradually revised as they are applied and assessed in subsequent lessons.

Suppose, for example, your world history students have been studying England's industrial revolution and have just read about the early results of that event. You have found several interesting documents related to this topic. So you have decided to introduce your students to the skill of evaluating written sources for bias because, in your judgment, this is an important thinking skill and one in which they need to be more proficient. Here, in brief, is how you might use this inductive strategy to teach this introductory lesson:

Step 1. To *preview* the skill you write the words "evaluating for bias" on the board as you say them aloud, underline the word "bias," and announce that the goal of this lesson is for students to be able to apply an effective procedure for carrying out this skill. You then elicit some examples of bias, giving them yourself if none are forthcoming from the class. You do the same for some synonyms of bias, writing these on the board also. Then you ask for a tentative definition of bias and write on the board any reasonable definitions offered—or write your own if none is suggested. You also explain why this skill is useful and when applying it is appropriate. Doing these five things in this order provides a clear indication as to the purpose of the lesson. It also helps students search their memories to recall anything about this skill they might already know, allows volunteers to contribute immediately to the class, and helps them develop the (anticipatory) mental set required to maximize their subsequent learning.

Step 2. Without any further instruction, you now distribute copies of document A, introduce it briefly, and then direct your students to *apply* the skill individually to "evaluate this source for bias":

Document A
Some of these lords of the loom . . . employ thousands of miserable creatures . . . [who are] kept, fourteen hours in each day, locked up, summer and winter, in a heat of from *eighty to eighty-four degrees.* . . .

What then must be the situation of these poor creatures who are doomed to toil day after day . . .? Can any man, with a heart in his body . . . refrain from cursing a system that produces such slavery and cruelty?

. . . These poor creatures have no cool room to retreat to . . . [and] are not allowed to send for water to drink; . . . even the rain water is locked up by the mas-

ter's order. . . . Any spinner found with his window open . . . is to pay a fine.

. . . The notorious fact is, that well-constitutioned men are rendered old and past labour at forty . . . and that children are rendered decrepit and deformed . . . before they arrive at the age of sixteen. . . . (Cobbett, 1824, italics in original)

Step 3. After several minutes you ask for a show of hands on whether this excerpt shows any bias. Some students may assert that it *is* biased. Others hold back, waiting for you to give some signal as to the "right answer." But rather than following up and discussing the document's content, you now ask them to *reflect* silently for a moment on what they did mentally to carry out this task. Then you direct them each to explain to a student across the aisle what they recall doing. After a minute or two you have several volunteers report to the class—as best they can—what they believe they did, step by step, to execute this skill, prompting them to recall as much as they can while you list their steps (in their own words) on the board.

In reporting how they applied their "skill" of evaluating for bias, some students might cite emotionally charged words—"miserable creatures," "doomed," "slavery," for instance—or over generalizations, such as "any spinner," as evidence of or clues to an apparent one-sidedness here. You write the types of clues (not the specific clues) on the board in a box labeled "clues." Then you ask the class to evaluate the procedures and types of clues on the board, identify what to look for, and state useful steps for applying the skill.

Step 4. Leaving all the skill information on the board, you now distribute document B and direct the class to *apply* the skill again to "evaluate this excerpt for bias:"

Document B
I have just visited many factories . . . and I never saw . . . children in ill-humor. They seemed to be always cheerful and alert, taking pleasure in the light play of the muscles—enjoying the mobility natural to their age. The scene of industry . . . was exhilarating. It was delightful to observe the nimbleness with which they pieced the broken ends as the mule carriage began to recede from the fixed roller-beam and to see them at leisure after a few seconds exercise of their tiny fingers, to amuse themselves in any attitude they chose. . . . The work of these lively elves seemed to resemble a sport. . . . They evidenced no trace of exhaustion on emerging from the mill in the evening, for they . . . skip about any neighborhood playground. . . . (Ure, 1861, p. 301)

Again, you allow them only a few minutes to complete this task.

Step 5. At this point you have a choice. You could have your students *reflect* on how they applied the skill this time, guiding them through the sharing and reporting as in Step 3 above. But instead, you choose to have your students, after reflecting individually, report directly to the class any steps (and any clues, in this case) they used this time that they did not use before, telling why they switched to these. These you add to the lists of steps or clues already on the board. Then you guide a class appraisal of the additions to identify those that hold promise for executing this skill more easily and more effectively in the future.

Step 6. To conclude this lesson, you now have your students *review* what they have identified about the skill of evaluating for bias. They restate the apparent key steps in the procedures that look useful for applying this skill and note promising types of clues to look for. They suggest more accurate synonyms. They revise their initial definition of the skill to make it more precise. And they give additional examples of biases. The lesson ends with you and the students "bridging" the skill—suggesting where, in school and out, and under what conditions it might be useful—as, in this case, to evaluate any communication for evidence of bias (Feuerstein, 1980).

By moving students through this six-step strategy of introducing a skill—previewing, applying, reflecting, applying again, reflecting, and reviewing—you have helped them to articulate some major steps in one or more apparently useful procedures for carrying out a thinking skill, incomplete and somewhat ill-defined as these steps may be. And they have had two opportunities to apply it and reflect on how they did it. This inductive introduction strategy allows students to generate this skill knowledge—tentative as it is—from their own experience and to take an active role in constructing it. It also allows field-independent students—who tend to show interest in new concepts for their own sake and have more of an internal rather than an external motivation—to share their insights with their less venturesome classmates (Martorella, 1982). It is most useful in initiating instruction in all except the most complex thinking skills in heterogeneously grouped classes.

A didactic strategy. A didactic skill-introducing strategy may be useful when you are teaching at-risk or field dependent students (who tend to respond best to externally provided organizational structures and goals); when you suspect your students—due to their unfamiliarity with the skill—may confuse each other by volunteering completely irrelevant, misleading, or idiosyncratic procedures to use; or when time is precious (Means, Chelemer, & Knapp, 1991). In this strategy:

The teacher—
1. Previews the thinking skill.
2. Models and explains an authentic step-by-step procedure and rules for carrying out the skill.

The students—
3. Review the demonstrated procedure and rules.
4. Apply the skill procedure.
5. Reflect on what they did mentally to carry it out.

Teacher and students—
6. Review what they have articulated, heard, and seen about how, when, and where to carry out the skill.

This strategy presents the students with an authentic, or "expert," skill procedure to follow when they first apply it (not all students will follow it, however). But it also allows students the opportunity to adapt the procedure for applying the skill—or even generate their own—as they reflect on and consider alternative steps and procedures. Thus, while it appears to be "closed" or expository, it is not completely so. It provides a good take-off point for especially difficult skills or for students who need a push to get their cognitive gears meshing.

Here's how you might use this strategy—rather than the inductive strategy—to introduce the skill of evaluating for bias in your world history class:

Step 1. You *preview* the skill—with whatever aid you can get from your students—exactly as in using the inductive strategy above. Writing the name of the skill on the board and saying it aloud—perhaps having students repeat it—makes clear that this is the lesson's goal. Presenting examples, synonyms, and a precise definition are also crucial here, as noted in the explanation of the inductive lesson. So, too, is explaining briefly why it is useful and some conditions for employing it.

Step 2. Next, you (1) *explain* the key steps in an authentic procedure for carrying out this skill, displaying them on a poster or overhead as you do, then (2) *model* this procedure by explaining how and why you perform each step as you apply it to document A. You write on the board several clues to bias that you find. In essence, you walk students through the skill step-by-step, referring continuously to the posted steps and telling the class why you are taking each step.

Step 3. To help your students take ownership of this procedure, you now have them *review* it by paraphrasing the steps, any clues to look for and any rules you have suggested.

Step 4. Now it's the students' turn. Leaving the skill procedure clearly visible, you distribute document B and direct the students—individually or in pairs—to follow the procedure just modeled to *apply* the skill to evaluate this source for any bias.

Step 5. When they have completed this evaluation, you proceed exactly as in *Step 3* in the inductive strategy—having the students *reflect* silently on the steps each used and share this information with a partner. Then several volunteers can report their procedures to the entire class, especially if the steps differed from the procedure modeled. You can record on the board any steps or clues that differ from those you modeled, having students explain why they used these. Then you lead the class in evaluating the modeled procedure and clues and any alternative steps or clues to determine their potential value in carrying out this skill. Your students can perhaps even "recommend" procedures that seem to be especially promising.

Step 6. To conclude this lesson, students—with your prompting as necessary—now *review* the procedure demonstrated and any other skill attributes that have been noted in the preceding discussion. One especially effective review is to have volunteers imagine they are addressing an audience two grades lower than their own. In their own words, they should provide these students with step-by-step instructions for carrying out this skill and any hints or rules to follow. These procedures can be written on the board, if appropriate, or recorded to use as a checklist or on a poster in the next lesson on this skill.

This didactic strategy, as you can see, requires that the teacher know and be able to describe clearly the essential steps in an "expert" procedure for carrying out the skill to be introduced. It also requires the students to remain somewhat passive for the first part of the lesson. To alter this, you could, after Step 1, give them document A and ask them to evaluate it for bias, allowing them to fumble around a bit before interrupting to "let me show you how to do it," and proceed from there. This modification allows slower—more cautious?—students to simply copy or reproduce the modeled strategy while still enabling more thoughtful students to first try it on their own. This didactic strategy is not as restrictive as it may first appear.

The importance of introducing a new thinking skill by using an inductive or didactic strategy like these or very similar to them cannot be overstated. Appropriately conducted, these strategies raise student thinking to a level of consciousness that helps make students aware of gaps and dysfunctional steps in their own thinking procedures as well as of steps and procedures employed by others seemingly more skillful than they are. Thus, the stage is set for modifying in subsequent lessons the cognitive procedures they are using to improve the efficiency and effectiveness of their thinking. This introductory

lesson, in effect, thus creates a foundation for improving thinking. Subsequent practice in applying this skill must then build on this foundation to bring about the improvement sought.

STRATEGIES FOR GUIDING PRACTICE OF A THINKING SKILL

Once students have been introduced to a new thinking skill they need repeated opportunities to practice applying that skill. Each such opportunity provides a natural occasion for us as teachers to structure and guide their practice of the skill to help them learn from their efforts to apply it. Two kinds of such guided practice are essential: scaffolded practice and cued practice (Doyle, 1983; Posner & Keele, 1973). Each can be provided in a short mini-lesson that focuses directly on the skill. Each type of lesson can be organized around a different teaching strategy.

A PREP Strategy for Scaffolding Practice. Research indicates that for best results practice of a new thinking skill should immediately follow its introduction. It further indicates that this practice should be frequent, should be in the same context (use the same subject and media) as used in the introductory lesson, and provide considerable feedback (Doyle, 1983; Posner and Keele, 1973). As shown in Figure 62.1, these initial practice lessons may be a day or two apart or even daily, depending on the complexity of the skill and the ability levels of the students. A PREP strategy proves especially useful for conducting these initial practice lessons:

1. **P**review the skill.
2. **R**ehearse a procedure for applying it.
3. **E**xecute (apply) the skill, using a scaffolding technique.
4. **P**onder (reflect on) on how the skill was applied.

If, for instance, you were to use this strategy in a practice lesson the day after you had introduced the skill of evaluating to detect bias in your world history class, you might proceed as follows:

Step 1. When it's time for your students to apply the skill of evaluating a source for bias, you write the name of the skill on the board and announce this is a good time to learn more about how applying this skill works. You and your students then *preview* the skill of evaluating for bias exactly as you did to initiate your introductory lesson, naming the skill, giving synonyms and examples of it, and stating its definition. You also ask for or note some conditions under which applying the skill is appropriate.

Step 2. Your students then *rehearse* one or more procedures they generated in the previous skill lesson and any related rules and heuristics (and clues in the case of this particular skill) they "discovered" or learned in that lesson. They paraphrase these, rather than simply repeating them in rote fashion.

Step 3. Using a scaffold you provide—perhaps a checklist, a sequence of process-structured questions, or a graphic organizer for this skill—the students now *execute* the skill by analyzing a new document for evidence of bias.

Step 4. Upon completing this task your students now *ponder* what they did by reflecting on how they carried out the skill, step-by-step, exactly as they did in completing this step in their introduction to this skill. Next, they share how they did it with a partner and then with the whole class, while you prompt them and note on the board appropriate steps volunteered and clues used. Finally, they assess what they have reported. (If they have been using checklists they can now revise these to represent any changes in the preferred procedures for next time. If they had used process-structured questions or a graphic organizer and changes were necessary, you may have to alter these for use in the next practice lesson on this skill.) After bridging the skill to other contexts, your class can now turn to a discussion of the information in the document and the insights developed by its study.

The value of this PREP strategy lies in the feedback it provides and especially in the use of a scaffold that "walks" students through the steps of applying the skill. A scaffold enables students to concentrate on carrying out the steps in a procedure for executing a skill without simultaneously trying to recall which steps to use next. Their goal in these practice lessons is to develop an increasingly smooth, uninterrupted application of these steps while internalizing the sequential pattern of applying them. Scaffolding techniques like checklists (which students can make in Step 6 of either of the skill introducing lessons described above), a set of process-structured questions prepared by the teacher in the interval between lessons, or an appropriate graphic organizer are especially effective in these practice lessons. They not only provide feedback but they actually feed forward to the students what to do and when to do it—while they are applying the skill (see Chapter 66 in this book for detailed explanations of these types of scaffolds, and also see Beyer, 1997).

Each of the other steps in PREP also provides useful "feedforward" or feedback to students. Both the previewing of what they already know about the skill and the rehearsal of procedures to use can help students prepare mentally for carrying out what they are supposed to do. The final step in the strategy engages students in reflecting on, articulating, and sharing how they executed the skill, thus providing additional feedback. This strategy actually "preps" students for application of the thinking skill by providing the support and guidance so essential in the early stages of practice.

Lessons using this PREP strategy can be completed in 15 minutes or less. They are mini-lessons that can be plugged into any regular lesson at the point where students can practice the skill. Once this skill mini-lesson has been completed, the remaining class time can be devoted to discussing the subject matter insights generated by application of the skill.

A PEP Strategy for Cueing Practice. Once students demonstrate that they can carry out a recently introduced and practiced thinking skill without the extensive structure or feedback provided in the initial practice lessons, less guided practice is appropriate. Research indicates that this later practice may be less frequent and increasingly more intermittent than the initial practice. It can provide less structure and feedback, as well (Posner and Keele, 1973). Simply by dropping the rehearsal step from the preceding practice strategy and devoting less time to each of the remaining steps, we have a strategy appropriate for guiding this type of skill practice. In this PEP strategy teacher and students:

1. **P**review the skill
2. **E**xecute the skill, with cues as needed
3. **P**onder (reflect on) how they applied the skill

PEP provides just enough teacher guidance and student reflection to fine-tune the application of the skill, to embed in memory an appropriate procedure for applying it, and to energize the students to use it. Like the previous practice strategy, it also provides structure and guidance while the skill is being applied, but this structure is much more limited. In this PEP strategy cueing replaces scaffolding.

Other than the time devoted to applying the skill, only five to seven minutes may be required to provide the focus on the skill called for in Steps 1 and 3 of this strategy, so virtually the entire class period can be devoted to the pursuit of other learning objectives. After a few such PEP lessons, students should be able to apply this skill completely on their own and on their own initiative and direction, troubleshooting its application themselves and executing it rapidly and relatively flawlessly.

STRATEGIES FOR TRANSFER

Because thinking skills are tied closely (in learner's minds) to the context or content in which they are first encountered, their application is not readily transferred to other, especially remote, contexts or content. It is, therefore, necessary to provide instructional assistance to enable this transfer to occur (Brown, Collins, & Duguid, 1989; Perkins & Salomon, 1988, 1989). In direct instruction teaching for transfer occurs on two fronts.

Continuous bridging. Each of the four teaching strategies presented above generates or at least paves the way for transfer in two places—when the skill to be taught is previewed (Step 1) and in the final step where students pull together what they have learned about the skill. Identifying synonyms for the skill name alerts students to a variety of cues that can trigger its application. Noting general conditions under which it can be applied (as, in the case of evaluating for bias, whenever one wants to ascertain the truth or accuracy of information presented in any source, including news reports, textbooks, and speeches) informs students of appropriate uses. Identifying actual circumstances or examples of when the skill was last used or could be used in the future also helps to promote transfer. All these techniques, if used consistently in every lesson on the thinking skill, can bridge or extend student awareness of its applicability beyond the context in which it is presently being applied.

Direct transfer. But more than this is required to produce transfer. It is also usually necessary to teach students directly *how* to apply a skill learned in one context to a new context (Perkins & Salomon, 1988). This can be done by repeating the sequence of direct instruction lessons described previously, using the strategies presented here to conduct these lessons in the content or context in which the skill is to be transferred.

The *introductory transfer lesson* is especially important. It can be taught using either the inductive or didactic strategy, with one significant addition. This addition is a new step immediately following Step 1, previewing the skill. Here students *review* or *rehearse* what they recall about the skill before they try to apply it (in the inductive strategy) or see it modeled (in the didactic strategy) in the new context. The remainder of the lesson then proceeds exactly as it does in any skill introducing lesson.

For example, if you had initially taught your world history students how to evaluate written documents for bias, you might now wish to have them learn how to apply this skill to evaluating visuals such as films or video presentations for bias. To initiate this transfer, you might elect to introduce the skill using the didactic strategy outlined above. Because your students (presumably) already know a lot about this skill as a result of their earlier practice in applying it, *previewing* the skill

(Step 1) can be brief—merely naming it, eliciting a definition and citing where or when it was last applied. Students then *review* or *rehearse* (new step) the skill by briefly reporting one or more procedures they have been using to apply it. Then, in Step 2, you *model* (with their assistance, if you wish) the procedure for applying it to an excerpt from a video news broadcast perhaps and explain the visual clues to bias they might not be aware of at this point. Next, they *review* the revised skill procedure and new clues (Step 3). In Step 4 students *apply* it to an excerpt from a second video newscast, *reflect* on how they did it (Step 5), and *review* briefly what they have learned or confirmed about how the skill can be applied to this new medium (Step 6). Because of their previous experiences in applying the skill, this lesson might require only half the time required to teach the very first introductory lesson on this thinking skill some months earlier.

Thereafter, you should provide your students with several opportunities to apply the skill to videos using a PREP strategy and a graphic organizer to scaffold their practice. And several more cued practice lessons using a PEP strategy may also be needed until your students demonstrate the level of proficiency in using this skill with videos that you seek. At this point your guidance can be withdrawn altogether. In time and with such instruction, your students can generalize the skill to an increasingly wider range of contexts and eventually employ it independently.

DIRECT INSTRUCTION IN THINKING SKILLS

Researchers have long asserted that proficiency in thinking does not develop as a result of instruction that is directed—or appears to be directed—at subject matter learning only or to other ends (Anderson, 1942; Cornbleth & Korth, 1981; Russell, 1956; Taba, 1965). Instead, students need explicit, direct attention to improving their thinking even in subject matter courses. Such instruction does not, in each lesson, jump back and forth from thinking skill to subject matter to thinking skill to subject matter and so on, but rather provides a series of lessons and mini-lessons, each of which focuses in its entirety completely on explicit procedures for carrying out a skill, but while using the regular subject matter of the course to do so. The teaching strategies described here provide one practical way of conducting these lessons in any thinking skill for students of any ability levels in any subject or setting. Such direct instruction in thinking skills is one of the most powerful and efficient ways—for students and teachers alike—for helping our students to master the tools of good thinking.

REFERENCES

Anderson, H. (Ed.). (1942). *Teaching critical thinking in social studies.* Washington, DC: National Council for the Social Studies.

Beyer, B. K. (1987). *Practical strategies for the teaching of thinking.* Boston: Allyn and Bacon.

Beyer, B. K. (1997). *Improving student thinking.* Boston: Allyn and Bacon.

Brown, A., et al. (1981, February). Learning to learn: On training students to learn from texts. *Educational Researcher, 10,* 14–21.

Brown, J. S., Collins, A., & Duguid, P. (1989, January–February). Situated cognition and the culture of learning. *Educational Researcher, 18*(1), 32–42.

Cobbett, W. (1824, November 20). *Political Register, 52.*

Cornbleth, C., & Korth, W. (1981, April). If remembering, understanding and reasoning are important . . . . *Social Education, 45*(4), 276–279.

Doyle, W. (1983, Summer). Academic work. *Review of Educational Research, 53*(2), 159–199.

Feuerstein, R. (1980). *Instrumental Enrichment.* Baltimore: University Park Press.

Frederikson, N. (1984, Fall). Implications of cognitive theory for instruction in problem solving. *Review of Educational Research, 54*(3), 363–407.

Hudgins, R. (1977). *Learning and thinking.* Itasca, IL: F. E. Peacock.

Jones, B. F., Amiran, M. R., & Katins, M. (1985). Teaching cognitive strategies and text structures within language arts programs. In J. W. Segal, S. F. Chipman and R. Glaser (Eds.), *Thinking and learning skills. Volume 1: Relating instruction to research* (pp. 259–290). Mahwah, NJ: Lawrence Erlbaum Associates.

Martorella, P. (1982, Fall). Cognitive research: some implications for the design of social studies instructional materials. *Theory and Research in Social Education, 10*(3), 1–6.

McTighe, J., & Lyman Jr., F. T. (1988, April). Cueing thinking in the classroom: the promise of theory embedded tools. *Educational Leadership, 45*(7) 18–24.

Means, B., Chelemer, C. & Knapp, M. S. (Eds.). (1991). *Teaching advanced skills to at risk students.* San Francisco, Jossey-Bass.

Nickerson, R. (1989). On improving thinking through instruction. In E. Z. Rothkopf (Ed.), *Review of Research in Education, 15,* 3–57. Washington, DC: American Educational Research Association.

Perkins, D., & Salomon, G. (1988, September). Teaching for transfer. *Educational Leadership, 46*(1), 22–32.

Perkins, D. N., & Salomon, G. (1989, January). Are thinking skills context bound? *Educational Researcher, 18,* 16–25.

Posner, M., & Keele, S. W. (1973). Skill learning. In R. M. W. Travers (Ed.), *Second handbook of research on teaching* (pp. 805–831). Chicago: Rand McNally College Publishing Company.

Rosenshine, B., & Meister, C. (1992). The use of scaffolds for teaching higher-level cognitive strategies. *Educational Leadership, 49*(7), 26–33.

Russell, D. (1956). *Children's thinking.* Boston: Ginn.

Sternberg, R. (1984). *Teaching intellectual skills.* Unpublished paper. Yale University.

Sternberg, R., & Davidson, J. (1989, Spring). A four prong model for intellectual development. *Journal of Research and Development in Education, 22*(3), 22–28.

Taba, H. (1965). Teaching of thinking. *Elementary English, 42*(2), 534.

Ure, A. (1861). *The philosophy of manufacturers* (3rd ed.). London: H.G. Bohn.

Whimbey, A., & Lochhead, J. (1999). *Problem solving and comprehension.* Mahwah, NJ: Lawrence Erlbaum Associates.

63

Visual Tools for Mapping Minds

David Hyerle

From Parts to the Whole System

Over the past 50 years there has been a radical transformation in our understanding of the scientific underpinnings of life: we have moved from measuring isolated parts of structures to showing patterns within dynamic systems. As this shift has slowly taken place we have not yet changed the fundamental way we present or represent these new understandings in classrooms.

We know that the content—the organized systems of information that we want students to understand (for example, the human body, social-economic-political systems, ecosystems, solar systems)—are all nonlinear in form. Yet we still represent, talk, and write about systems in linear ways, expecting that learners will be able to put all the bits together and see the big picture. Simply, our students cannot "get their minds around" these systems, given the traditional thinking tools we have provided. This mismatch—or cognitive dissonance—between the nonlinear forms of knowledge we attempt to teach and the linear form in which students receive this knowledge is, I believe, the most important barrier to meaningful teaching, learning, and assessment that exists today in classrooms.

As summarized in this chapter, visual tools such as webs, organizers, and thinking process maps are the most compatible and effective tools for moving every student from the basic organization of information, to basic skills instruction and content specific learning, to thinking in patterns and systems (see Figure 63.1). First, let's look at these new sciences and understandings that rely on seeing patterns of organization, or systems.

This chapter is adapted with permission from *A Field Guide to Using Visual Tools*, by D. Hyerle, 2000. Alexandria, VA: Association for Supervision and Curriculum Development. Copyright © 2000 by David Hyerle.

The Web of Life

In *The Web of Life*, Fritjof Capra (1996) offers a unique integration of quantum physics, information theory, systems thinking, and theories linking the brain, mind, and cognition. Here is a summary view of Capra's definition of a living system:

> A living system has a pattern of organization that is physically structured and activated by a life process that embodies these patterns (1996, p. 79).

The key characteristic of this definition of a living system is the pattern of organization of an organism. Capra highlights the importance of how we represent and thus understand these patterns:

> In the study of structure we measure and weigh things. Patterns, however, cannot be measured or weighed; they must be mapped. To understand a pattern we must map a configuration of relationships (Capra, 1996, p. 81).

It is not only the attempted measurement of the parts of patterns that has hindered us from perceiving patterns: the problem is how we ultimately represent these patterns. Our dependency on linear strings of words and numerals for conveying nonlinear concepts prevents us from fully representing and understanding patterns, interdependencies, and systems. From Capra's view, we need to use mapping techniques with our traditional linear languages and mathematical expertise to expand the linear mind-set through which we regularly filter, think about, communicate, and assess ideas.

As a society and as educators, we are only now beginning to address the fundamental importance of interdependent relationships and patterns, the architecture of systems. This awareness is challenging teachers and educational leaders to utilize tools and techniques that support students in mapping the patterns of knowledge—the evolving blueprints—that ground every discipline we teach and that help connect every discipline together into interdisciplinary knowledge.

—Figure 63.1—
Overview of Visual Tools

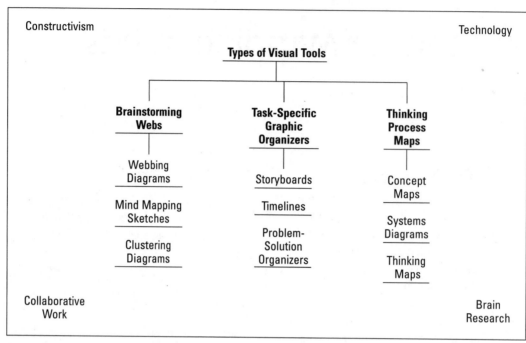

Source: Adapted with permission from *A Field Guide to Using Visual Tools* (p. viii), by D. Hyerle, 2000. Alexandria, VA: Association for Supervision and Curriculum Development. Copyright 2000 by David Hyerle.

THE BRAIN AS A PATTERN DETECTOR

Patterns exist in nature. One only has to look out the window, or to look at the human body's processes to see this. It is no wonder then that the experts in brain-based learning all agree on one thing: the brain as an organism is constantly self-organizing, re-creating organizational patterns. Certainly we get stuck in mental patterns, or behavioral ruts. But the brain is constantly making sense of the world by physically constructing patterns as neural networks. The focus on patterning is thus an entry point to understanding the connection between brain functioning, language, thinking, meaning making, and visual tools:

> The overwhelming need of learners is for meaningfulness. . . . We do not come to understand a subject or master a skill by sticking bits of information to each other. Understanding a subject results from perceiving relationships. The brain is designed as a pattern detector. Our function as educators is to provide students with the sorts of experiences that enable them to perceive "the patterns that connect." (Caine & Caine, 1991, p. 7)

"Visual tools" is an umbrella term for different mental mapping techniques (Hyerle, 1996); they include brainstorming webs, graphic organizers, and thinking process maps. Before turning to a review of the different types of visual tools, let's reflect on why the visual modality is so important. Certainly hands-on activities and manipulatives for kinesthetic patterning are essential, and auditory patterning is a staple of everyday classrooms.

One answer is found in the structure and processing of the brain. Practically, we retain snapshots of our past experiences, and we can visualize future possibilities. Why? The brain as a structure is capable of absorbing 36,000 visual images every hour. The sophisticated visual capacity of our brain system is beyond the conscious processing of our mind. Research approximates that between 80 percent and 90 percent of the information received by the brain is through visual means (Jensen, 1998). Though our auditory and kinesthetic modes of sensing are complex, the overwhelmingly dominant mode through which our brain filters information is through our eyes. From an evolutionary perspective, the human brain has evolved to become positively imbalanced toward being primarily a visual imager and processor.

Even if we each believe that we are dominantly "kinesthetic" or "auditory," consider that each of us is—by far—still taking in more patterns of information "visually" than through other modalities. We need to understand, and thus teach and learn with this imbalanced strength in mind: most of our students and most of us as we read this page, are strong if not dominantly visual processors of patterns. Consider that mostly what happens in classrooms is conveyed in spoken form or through linear text.

Current brain research has provided many insights into how the brain unconsciously takes in and consciously processes information. Wolfe and Sorgen (1991) have described three major stages of information processing within the dynamic system of the brain: paying attention, building meaning, and extending meaning. Most visual tools provide flexible cognitive patterns to students and teachers that are congruent with and facilitate each of these stages. A key to understanding and conceptual development is the capacity for accumulating and linking information in long-term memory. Wolfe and Sorgen (1998, personal communication) highlight the link between brain functioning, memory, and visual tools by pointing to a study by Standing reported in 1973 in *The Quarterly Journal of Experimental Psychology*:

> The impact of visualization on memory and recall has been demonstrated in numerous studies. In one, subjects were shown as many as 10,000 pictures, and then later shown some of these same pictures along with other pictures they had not seen. Under these conditions, they were able to recognize more than 90 percent of the pictures they had already seen. (Hyerle, 2000, p. 31)

As Wolfe and Sorgen noted, visual tools can help students initially process and make sense out of abstract information and also take advantage of the brain's almost unlimited capacity for images. Therefore, the use of visual tools needs to become more than an occasional strategy for isolated activities. These tools need to be fully integrated into classrooms as central to the communication of ideas—from preschool to college and into the workplace.

In summary, the brain and mind have a specialized, continuously evolving, multi-dimensional and dynamic spatial architecture. Architecture provides the basis for a good definition of high quality visual tools: they are dynamic blueprints of the mind's *conceptual* architecture. Visual tools provide one of the most direct routes for most learners—and maybe all but a few learners in our ever more inclusive classrooms—to show and communicate patterns of thinking. Much research and practical use in classrooms now shows that these tools shift learning to levels of understanding well beyond the common presentations of content information as blocks of static text—text that is but a linear wall, often a mere facade of the rich conceptual patterning of human thinking and understanding.

TYPES OF VISUAL TOOLS FOR THINKING

In *Visual Tools for Constructing Knowledge* (Hyerle, 1996) and *A Field Guide to Using Visual Tools* (Hyerle, 2000), three types of tools and related software are defined and reviewed: brainstorming webs, graphic "task-specific" organizers, and thinking process maps. These kinds of tools in different ways concretely support reading across disciplines, writing processes, and content specific learning. But there is an added benefit: they engage learners with lifelong tools for patterning and networking of information, organizing information into knowledge from various sources, seeking and sharing meanings, assessing, and the linking of isolated bits to holistic, interrelated systems. All of these visual tools are influenced by—or framed by—constructivism, brain research, visual technologies, and the requirement in the workplace and classrooms that learners interactively share their thinking in collaborative working groups (see Figure 63.1).

A phrase coined in the business world for thinking creatively is "thinking outside the box." Though this phrase has become a cliché, it provides a useful way to discriminate between types of visual tools. Below is a brief review of some of these types: brainstorming webs for thinking "outside the box," graphic organizers for thinking "inside the box," and thinking process maps for thinking "about the box."

BRAINSTORMING WEBS FOR THINKING OUTSIDE THE BOX

The associative power of the human brain is facilitated through and ignited by a high degree of open-ended brain networking. It is understandable and somewhat haunting that many webs look similar to the pictures we have of neural networks, as neurons are the brain's building blocks that communicate with each other. Axons send information to other neurons while dendrites (Greek for "tree") branch out with the cell body to receive information—networking neuron to neuron at a rate of 10 million billion transmissions per second. As shown in schematic views of a cortex, these connections are reflections of the complex webs we see children draw as they connect ideas on a page.

Brainstorming webs are open systems for thinking outside of the box. This means that there often is no formal or common representation system that is shared among those creating webs. Often private, idiosyncratic graphic languages develop in classrooms, each related to the personality of the thinker. But to believe that brainstorming webs should not or cannot evolve into more formal structures is to deny the great depth of these visual tools. Developers identify different forms of tools that can aid the process of moving from generation to organization to transformation of ideas and concepts. For example, some categories are called clustering and mindscaping tools, and Buzan Organisation, Ltd., has a set of visual techniques called Mind Maps. With advanced development of a brainstorming web—sometimes through software programs such as Inspiration (Portland, OR: Inspiration Software, Inc., 1998)—these visual representations may also be final products for presentation in a classroom or boardroom.

Unfortunately, many learners mistakenly believe that brainstorming webs are only a first step rather than an enduring process that continues and that even extends beyond a final product. I have even heard from teachers that students may brainstorm information and then not even refer to the document during the later processes of completing a project. Often, then, brainstorming webs are perceived as a static visual picture—the snapshot of a burst of creative energy—disconnected from further creative and analytical work, rather than a dynamic representation of evolving mental models.

GRAPHIC TASK-SPECIFIC
ORGANIZERS FOR THINKING INSIDE THE BOX

Unlike webs that facilitate thinking outside the box, graphic organizers are often structured so that students are supported in thinking inside the box. A teacher may create or may find in a teacher's guide a specific visual structure that students follow and sometimes fill in as they proceed through a complex series of steps. Often teachers match specific patterns of content or one content task to a graphic. These highly structured graphics may seem constraining at times. But often these templates are good starting points for students who have trouble systematically approaching a task, organizing their ideas, and staying focused (especially when the task is complex). For example, many organizers are sequential, showing the guiding steps for solving a word problem, organizing content information for a research report, learning a specific process for a certain kind of writing prompt, or for a story board highlighting essential skills and patterns for comprehending a story.

Because these types of visual tools are highly structured, they provide direct facilitation of several habits of mind (Costa, 1991): persistence, self-control (managing impulsivity), accuracy, and precision of language and thinking. Review most any graphic organizer—found in a textbook or teacher created—and you will find that the visual-spatial structure guides students through the steps, box by box, or oval by oval. Teachers report that task-specific graphic organizers provide a concrete system and model for proceeding through a problem

that otherwise students would give up on, because they have not developed their own organizational structures for persevering in a problem. An obvious reason is that the visual structure reveals a whole view of the process and, importantly, a vision of an end point.

This kind of structuring also provides some visual guidelines, much like a rope students can hang onto rather than impulsively jumping outside the problem to what Benjamin Bloom called "one-shot thinking." The visual modeling thereby shows students that they can decrease their impulsivity and stay "in the box" when they need to focus on following through to a solution. Oftentimes students don't have a record of their thinking, and the steps and missteps they took along the way. By visually capturing their ideas along a train of thought to a solution, students can review, refine, and share their ideas with others for feedback.

THINKING PROCESS MAPPING
FOR THINKING ABOUT THE BOX

Brainstorming webs are used for thinking creatively outside the box of the daily classroom and workplace mental routines. These open webs help us break mental and emotional barriers, reflecting the millions of rapid firing associations occurring in our brains. Typical graphic organizers help students think inside the box. These graphics provide a mental safety net for many students, leading them into success and future independent applications.

A third kind of visual tool—called thinking process maps—is in many ways an outgrowth and synthesis of brainstorming webs and graphic organizers. Thinking process maps are being used in classrooms and the workplace for explicitly focusing learners' attention on fundamental thinking patterns, conceptual development, and metacognition. Developers who have created these tools have a common interest in having learners think about the patterns of content, or about the box itself. These tools support students in asking: What are the thinking processes and structures embedded in this information? How am I thinking? What is the frame of reference or mental model that is influencing my organization of this concept?

These practical and conceptually elegant tools are designed to help students generate and efficiently share recurring patterns of thinking, from fundamental cognitive skills such as comparison, classification, and cause-effect reasoning, to integrated visual languages such as Novak's Concept Mapping (1998), inductive towers (Clarke, 1991), and systems diagraming. While thinking process maps scaffold some habits of mind to brainstorming webs and organizers, these tools also provide a foundation for deeper questioning, multisensory learning, metacognition, and empathic listening.

Thinking process maps provide a concrete way to work with complexity and abstractions, matching the capacities of our brains to see the big picture and the details in both linear and holistic forms. As we look at these different forms, we see that most of them have a common thread: consistent and expandable graphics. This matches, at the deepest levels, the structure and dynamism of the brain. We can see that the brain thrives on a consistent structure that expands dynamically toward novel and more complex configurations.

THINKING MAPS: A SYNTHESIS TOOL KIT

The wide array of visual tools are used for making sense of our own stored knowledge, to assimilate new information and concepts, and to improve our long-term thinking abilities. But one of the problems for students as they go up through the grade levels in elementary school and from classroom to classroom in secondary schools is that they are encountering a haphazard and discontinuous array of graphic tools. Each one of the graphics in isolation may be useful, but students can become overwhelmed when given dozens of graphics over the course of a year, or hundreds over the course of just a few years. These tools could be synthesized, coordinated, and organized in a meaningful way for teachers and students so that whole learning communities can unite around some common visual tools.

This is the idea behind a common visual language called Thinking Maps, which I developed in 1988 (see Figure 63.2). These are eight unique graphic "starter" patterns, each based, respectively, on a fundamental thinking skill (Hyerle, 1995; Hyerle & Grey Matter Software, 1999). This visual language is in many ways a synthesis of the three types of visual tools described here. As a language of visual tools, each of the eight Thinking Maps embodies the generative quality of brainstorming webs, the organizing and consistent visual structure of graphic organizers, and the deep processing capacity and dynamic configurations found in thinking process maps. Learners can use this thinking tool kit—on paper or through Thinking Maps Software—to construct and communicate networks of mental models of linear and nonlinear concepts.

Each map begins with a graphic primitive and may expand to an infinite number of configurations. And, while there are only eight maps, the maps are often used together in a variety of ways. This is analogous to a carpenter with a tool kit: There may be a set number of fundamental tools in the kit, yet an infinite number of combinations and uses helpful for constructing a building. By providing learners with common graphic starting points based on thinking skills definitions and processes, every learner is enabled to detect, construct, and communicate different patterns of thinking about content concepts.

The systematic use of Thinking Maps in whole schools is leading to successful improvements in test results and quality indicators (Hyerle, 2000). Previous research on graphic organizers has often focused on a single kind of graphic for isolated tasks. Thinking Maps results show how teachers and students are using these tools across disciplines and also for specific content tasks. The strongest documentation shows up in reading comprehension and writing scores. Test results across urban, rural, and suburban schools in different states—with wide disparities in needs—have found that reading comprehension and writing scores have changed dramatically, and in several cases over multiple years. A recent study from Mississippi showed statistically significant changes in junior college students who dramatically improved their reading test scores when using Thinking Maps (Ball, 1999).

The most dramatic effects are found as students quite naturally become the center of learning and thinking. After learning how to use each Thinking Map for independent and cooperative learning, students begin moving from novice to more expert applications. With very little modeling, they begin linking several maps together for identifying different patterns in reading comprehension (text structures: sequential, causal, or comparative). They use different maps for responding to writing prompts of different kinds (narrative, persuasive, informative, or personal expression). When accessing several resources for researching topics in the sciences and social studies, students build maps over time. These results are accumulated in schoolwide portfolios.

These kinds of results reveal a very different perspective on the use of visual tools from past success stories. Whereas most of us have perceived graphic organizers and webbing techniques as useful and relatively isolated strategies, when systematically used, these tools may become one of the linchpins for student-centered learning and whole school changes in performance.

VISUAL TOOLS FOR ASSESSING MENTAL MODELS

We want students to become self-assessing. We want students to go beyond looking at a final product and think about what they could have done better: we want them to become self-assessing during the processes of constructing knowledge and building final products. Visual tools provide a display of the

—*Figure 63.2*—
Eight Thinking Processes in Thinking Maps

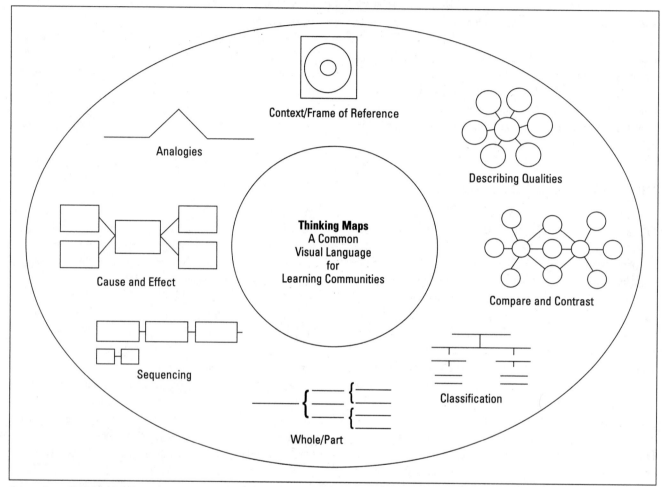

Source: From *Thinking Maps: Training of Trainers* manual, by D. Hyerle, 1999. Raleigh, NC: Innovative Sciences, Inc.

development of one's thinking, in differing patterns, for all to review. When a student is using visual tools and different software programs systematically and over time, teachers, peers, parents, and administrators may look down and begin a rich dialogue with the student about how the patterns of ideas have evolved. We also begin to see changes in how students pattern their thinking over multiple years.

Unlike any other period in the history of humankind, we also want learners of our time to know that as they are looking down on their maps, they are looking at only one perspective, one mental model. There are multiple models for reality. This is not relativism, but intellectual rigor. In a culturally diverse, information-rich, "networked" world, visual tools provide an additional way of sharing different points of view and cultural frames of reference.

Mental models are those rich schemas through which we filter our emotions (Goleman, 1985), drive our every thought, and hold onto our life experiences. Visual tools—in the most recently developed forms—are a new medium for helping us face our own mental models and begin an internal dialogue about what and how we know something, and how we value it.

Seeing is not believing. Our mental models are, by definition, models built on available resources, beliefs, values, and existing paradigms. These models are evolving and imperfect, much like

a pane of glass framing and subtly distorting our vision; mental models determine what we see . . . Human beings cannot navigate through the complex environments of our world without these cognitive mental maps, and all these maps, by definition, are flawed in some way. (Senge, 1990)

Without this critical perspective on mental models, visual tools such as static graphic organizers will merely become another set of worthy techniques for regurgitating the existing structures. Visual tools have great promise as authentic tools for all learners—teachers and students alike—for understanding the ways in which we are thinking and for building new insights.

BIBLIOGRAPHY

Ball, M. K. (1999). *The effects of Thinking Maps on reading scores of traditional and nontraditional college students.* Unpublished dissertation, University of Southern Mississippi, Hattiesburg.

Buzan, T. (1996). *The Mind Map book: How to use radiant thinking to maximize your brain's untapped potential.* New York: Plume/Penguin.

Caine, R. N., & Caine, G. (1991). *Making connections: Teaching and the human brain.* Alexandria, VA: Association for Supervision and Curriculum Development.

Capra, F. (1996). *The web of life.* New York: Anchor Books.

Clarke, J. H. (1991). *Patterns of thinking.* Needham Heights, MA: Allyn and Bacon.

Costa, A. (1991). *Developing minds.* Alexandria, VA: Association for Supervision and Curriculum Development.

Goleman, D. (1985). *Vital lies, simple truths.* New York: Touchstone.

Goleman, D. (1994). *Emotional intelligence.* New York: Bantam.

Hyerle, D. (1995). *Thinking Maps: Tools for learning training manual.* Cary, NC: Innovative Sciences, Inc.

Hyerle, D. (1996). *Visual tools for constructing knowledge.* Alexandria, VA: Association for Supervision and Curriculum Development.

Hyerle, D. (2000). *A field guide to using visual tools.* Alexandria, VA: Association for Supervision and Curriculum Development.

Hyerle, D., & Grey Matter Software. (1999). *Thinking Maps software.* Cary, NC: Innovative Sciences, Inc.

Inspiration Software. (1998). *Inspiration idea book.* Portland, OR: Inspiration Software, Inc.

Jensen, E. (1998). *Teaching with the brain in mind.* Alexandria, VA: Association for Supervision and Curriculum Development.

Novak, J. (1998). *Learning, creating, and using knowledge.* Mahwah, NJ: Lawrence Erlbaum Associates.

Senge, P. M. (1990). *The fifth discipline.* New York: Currency Doubleday.

Sylwester, R. (1995). *A celebration of neurons.* Alexandria, VA: Association for Supervision and Curriculum Development.

Wolfe, P., & Sorgen, M. (1991). *Teaching, learning, and memory.* Napa, CA: Authors.

64

Mediating the Metacognitive

Arthur L. Costa

I cannot always control what goes on outside. But I can always control what goes on inside.

—*Wayne Dyer*

Try to solve this problem in your head: How much is one half of two plus two? Did you hear yourself talking to yourself?

Did you find yourself having to decide whether you should take one half of the first two, then add it to two (which would make the answer three); or sum two plus two first, then take one half (which would make the answer two)?

If you caught yourself having an inner dialogue inside your brain, and if you had to stop to evaluate your own decision-making and problem-solving processes, you were experiencing *metacognition.*

Occurring in the neocortex, and therefore thought by some neurologists to be uniquely human, metacognition is our ability to know what we know and what we don't know. It is our ability to plan a strategy for producing what information is needed, to be conscious of our own steps and strategies during the act of problem solving, and to reflect on and evaluate the productiveness of our own thinking. While "inner language," which is thought to be a prerequisite, begins in most children around age 5, metacognition is a key attribute of formal thought, flowering about age 11. Interestingly, not all humans achieve the level of formal operations (Chiabetta, 1976). And as Alexander Luria, the Russian psychologist found, not all adults metacogitate (Whimbey & Whimbey, 1976).

We often find students following instructions or performing tasks without wondering why they are doing what they are doing. They seldom question themselves about their own learning strategies or evaluate the efficiency of their own performance. Some children virtually have no idea of what they should do when they confront a problem and are often unable to explain their strategies of decision making (Sternberg & Wagner, 1982). There is much evidence, however, to demonstrate that those who perform well on complex cognitive tasks, who are flexible and persevere in problem solving, and who consciously apply their intellectual skills, are those who possess well-developed metacognitive abilities (Bloom & Broder, 1950; Brown, 1978; Whimbey, 1980). They are those who "manage" their intellectual resources well: (1) their basic perceptual-motor skills; (2) their language, beliefs, knowledge of content, and memory processes; and (3) their purposeful and voluntary strategies intended to achieve a desired outcome (Aspen Systems, 1982).

If we wish to install intelligent behavior as a significant outcome of education, then instructional strategies, purposefully intended to develop children's metacognitive abilities, must be infused into our teaching methods, staff development, and supervisory processes (Costa, 1981). Interestingly, *direct* instruction in metacognition may *not* be beneficial. When strategies of problem solving are imposed by the teacher rather than generated by the students themselves, their performance may become impaired. Conversely, when students experience the need for problem-solving strategies, induce their own, and discuss and practice them to the degree that they become spontaneous and unconscious, their metacognition seems to improve (Sternberg & Wagner, 1982). The trick, therefore, is to teach metacognitive skills without creating an even greater burden on the students' ability to attend to the task.

Probably the major components of metacognition are developing a plan of action, maintaining that plan in mind over a period of time, then reflecting back on and evaluating the

This chapter is adapted from *Developing Minds: A Resource Book for Teaching Thinking* (Rev. ed.), 1991.

plan upon its completion. Planning a strategy before embarking on a course of action helps us keep track of the steps in the sequence of planned behavior at the conscious awareness level for the duration of the activity. It facilitates making temporal and comparative judgments, assessing the readiness for more or different activities, and monitoring our interpretations, perceptions, decisions, and behaviors. An example of this would be what superior teachers do daily: developing a teaching strategy for a lesson, keeping that strategy in mind throughout the instruction, then reflecting back upon the strategy to evaluate its effectiveness in producing the desired student outcomes.

Rigney (1980) identified the following self-monitoring skills as necessary for successful performance on intellectual tasks:

- Keeping one's place in a long sequence of operations.
- Knowing that a subgoal has been obtained.
- Detecting errors and recovering from those errors either by making a quick fix or by retreating to the last known correct operation.

Such monitoring involves both "looking ahead" and "looking back." Looking ahead includes the following:

- Learning the structure of a sequence of operations.
- Identifying areas where errors are likely.
- Choosing a strategy that will reduce the possibility of error and will provide easy recovery.
- Identifying the kinds of feedback that will be available at various points, and evaluating the usefulness of that feedback.

Looking back includes the following:

- Detecting errors previously made.
- Keeping a history of what has been done up to the present and thus what should come next.
- Assessing the reasonableness of the present immediate outcome of task performance.

A simple example of this might be drawn from a reading task. It is a common experience while reading a passage to have our mind "wander" from the pages. We "see" the words but no meaning is being produced. Suddenly we realize that we are not concentrating and that we've lost contact with the meaning of the text. We "recover" by returning to the passage to find our place, matching it with the last thought we can remember, and, once having found it, reading on with connect-

edness. This inner awareness and the strategy of recovery are components of metacognition.

STRATEGIES FOR ENHANCING METACOGNITION

Following are a dozen suggestions that teachers of any grade level can use to enhance metacognition.[1] Whether teaching vocational education, physical education, algebra, or reading skills, teachers can promote metacognition by using these and similar instructional techniques.

1. STRATEGY PLANNING

Prior to any learning activity, teachers will want to take time to develop and discuss strategies and steps for attacking problems, rules to remember, and directions to be followed. Time constraints, purposes, and ground rules under which students must operate should be developed and "interiorized." Thus, students can better keep these ideas in mind during the experience and evaluate their performance afterward.

During the activity, teachers can invite students to share their progress, thought processes, and perceptions of their own behavior. Asking students to indicate where they are in their strategy, describe the "trail" of thinking up to that point, and tell what alternative pathways they intend to pursue next in the solution of their problem helps them become aware of their own behavior. (It also provides the teacher with a diagnostic "cognitive map" of a student's thinking, which can be used to give more individualized assistance.)

Then, *after* the learning activity is completed, teachers can invite students to evaluate how well those rules were obeyed, how productive the strategies were, whether the instructions were followed correctly, and what would be some alternative, more efficient strategies to be used in the future.

I know a kindergarten teacher who begins and ends each day with a class meeting. During these times, children make plans for the day. They decide what learning tasks to accomplish and how to accomplish them. They allocate classroom space, assign roles, and develop criteria for appropriate conduct. Throughout the day the teacher calls attention to the plans and ground rules made that morning and invites students to compare what they are doing with what was agreed on. Then, before dismissal, another class meeting is held to reflect on, evaluate, and plan further strategies and criteria.

2. QUESTION GENERATING

Regardless of the subject area, it is useful for students to pose study questions for themselves prior to and during their reading of textual material. This self-generation of questions facilitates comprehension. It encourages the student to pause frequently and perform a "self-check" for understanding, to determine whether or not comprehension has occurred. They may check, for example, whether they know the main characters or events; they are grasping the concept; it "makes sense"; they can relate it to what they already know; they can give other examples or instances; they can use the main idea to explain other ideas; or they can use the information in the passage to predict what may come next. They then must decide what strategic action should be taken to remove obstacles and thereby increase comprehension. This helps students become more self-aware and take conscious control of their own studying (Sanacore, 1984).

3. CONSCIOUS CHOOSING

Teachers can promote metacognition by helping students explore the consequences of their choices and decisions prior to and during the act of deciding. Students will then be able to perceive causal relationships between their choices, their actions, and the results they achieved. Providing nonjudgmental feedback about the effects of their behaviors and decisions on others and on their environment helps students become aware of their own behaviors. For example, a teacher's statement, "I want you to know that the noise you're making with your pencil is disturbing me," will better contribute to metacognitive development than the command, "John, stop tapping your pencil!"

4. DIFFERENTIATED EVALUATING

Teachers can enhance metacognition by causing students to reflect on and categorize their actions according to two or more sets of evaluative criteria. Examples are: inviting students to distinguish between what was done that day that was was helpful and hindering; what they liked and didn't like; or what were pluses and minuses of the activity. Thus, students must keep the criteria in mind, apply them to multiple classification systems, and justify their reasons accordingly.

5. TAKING CREDIT

Teachers may cause students to identify what they have done well and invite them to seek feedback from their peers. The teacher might ask, "What have you done that you're proud of?" "How would you like to be recognized for doing that?" (name on the board, hug, pat on the back, handshake,

applause from the group, etc.). Thus students will become more conscious of their own behavior and apply a set of internal criteria for behavior they consider "good."

6. OUTLAWING "I CAN'T"

Teachers can inform students that their excuses of "I can't," "I don't know how to," or "I'm too slow to" are unacceptable behaviors in the classroom. Instead, having students identify what information is required, what materials are needed, or what skills are lacking in their ability to perform the desired behavior is an alternative and acceptable response. This helps students identify the boundaries between what they know and what they need to know. It develops a persevering attitude and enhances the student's ability to create strategies that will produce needed data.

7. PARAPHRASING OR REFLECTING IDEAS BACK TO THE STUDENT

Paraphrasing, building upon, extending, and using student ideas can make students conscious of their own thinking. For example, saying: "What you're telling me is . . . ," or "What I hear in your plan are the following steps . . . ," or "Let's work with Peter's strategy for a moment."

Inviting students to restate, translate, compare, and paraphrase each other's ideas causes them to become not only better listeners of other's thinking, but better listeners of their own thinking as well.

8. LABELING STUDENT BEHAVIORS

When the teacher places labels on students' cognitive processes, it can make them conscious of their own actions: "What I see you doing is making out a plan of action for . . ."; "What you are doing is called an experiment"; or "You're being very helpful to Mark by sharing your paints. That's an example of cooperation."

9. CLARIFYING STUDENT TERMINOLOGY

Students often use "hollow," vague, and nonspecific terminology. For example, in making value judgments students might be heard saying: "It's not fair . . ."; "He's too strict"; or "It's no good." Teachers need to get in the habit of clarifying these values: "What's *too* strict?" "What would be *more* fair?"

We sometimes hear students using nominalizations: "They're mean to me." (Who are they?) "We had to do that."

(Who is we?) "Everybody has one." (Who is everybody?) Thus, clarifying causes students to operationally define their terminology and to examine the premise on which their thinking is based. It is desirable that, as a result of such clarifying, students become more specific and qualifying in their terminology.

For older children, above age 11 or so, it appears helpful to invite them to clarify their problem-solving processes. Causing them to describe their thinking while they are thinking seems to beget more thinking. Some examples: inviting students to talk aloud as they are solving a problem; discussing what is going on in their heads when they confront an unfamiliar word while reading; or what steps they are going through in deciding whether to buy some item at the store. After solving a problem, the teacher can invite a clarification of the processes used: "Sarah, you figured out that the answer was 44; Shawn says the answer is 33. Let's hear how you came up with 44. Retrace your steps for us." Clarifying in this way helps students reexamine their own problem-solving processes, identify their own errors, and self-correct. The teacher might ask a question such as: "How much is three plus four?" The student may reply, "12." Rather than merely correcting the student, the teacher may choose to clarify: "Gina, how did you arrive at that answer?" "Well, I multiplied four and three and got . . . oh, I see, I multiplied instead of added."

10. Role Playing and Simulations

Having students assume the roles of other persons causes them to consciously maintain in their heads the attributes and characteristics of those persons. Dramatization serves as a hypothesis or prediction of how that person would react in a certain situation. This role-playing also contributes to the reduction of ego-centered perceptions.

11. Journal Keeping

Writing and illustrating a personal log or a diary throughout an experience over a period of time causes the student to synthesize thoughts and actions and to translate them into symbolic form. The record also provides an opportunity to revisit initial perceptions, to compare the changes in those perceptions with the addition of more data, to chart the processes of strategic thinking and decision making, to identify the blind alleys and pathways taken, and to recall the successes and the "tragedies" of experimentation. (A variation on writing journals would be making videotape or audiotape recordings of actions and performances over time.)

12. Modeling

Of all the instructional techniques suggested, the one with the probability of greatest influence on students is that of teacher modeling. Since students learn best by imitating the significant adults around them, the teacher who publicly demonstrates metacognition will probably produce students who metacogitate. Indicators of teachers' public metacognitive behavior might include:

- Sharing their planning by describing their goals and objectives and giving reasons for their actions.
- Making human errors but then being seen to recover from those errors by getting "back on track."
- Admitting they do not know an answer but designing ways to produce an answer.
- Seeking feedback and evaluation of their actions from others.
- Having a clearly stated value system and making decisions consistent with that value system.
- Being able to self-disclose by using adjectives that describe their own strengths and weaknesses.
- Demonstrating understanding and empathy by listening to and accurately describing the ideas and feelings of others.

Evaluating Growth in Metacognitive Abilities

We can determine if students are becoming more aware of their own thinking, as they are able to describe what goes on in their heads when they are thinking. When asked, they can list the steps and tell where they are in the sequence of a problem-solving strategy. They can trace the pathways and dead ends they took on the road to a problem solution. They can describe what data are lacking and their plans for producing those data.

We should see students persevering more when the solution to a problem is not immediately apparent. This means that they have systematic methods of analyzing a problem, knowing ways to begin, knowing what steps must be performed, and realizing when they are accurate or are in error. We should see students taking more pride in their efforts, becoming self-correcting, striving for craftsmanship and accuracy in their products, and becoming more autonomous in their problem-solving abilities.

These days, educators are putting greater emphasis on teaching for thinking. Metacognition is an attribute of the "educated intellect." It must be included if thinking is to become a durable reality for the future.

NOTES

[1]For several of these techniques I am deeply indebted to Fred Newton, Multnomah County (Oregon) Superintendent of Schools Office; Juanita Sagan, a therapist in Oakland, California; and Ron Brandt, formerly an executive editor at the Association for Supervision and Curriculum Development.

REFERENCES

Aspen Systems (1982, April). *Topics in learning and learning disabilities, 2*(1). Gaithersburg, MD: Aspen Systems Corp.

Bloom, B. S., & Broder, L. J. (1950). *Problem-solving processes of college students*. Chicago: University of Chicago Press.

Brown, A. L. (1978). Knowing when, where, and how to remember: A problem of metacognition. In R. Glaser (Ed.), *Advances in Instructional Psychology*. Hillsdale, NJ: Erlbaum.

Chiabetta, E. L. A. (1976). Review of Piagetian studies relevant to science instruction at the secondary and college level. *Science Education, 60,* 253–261.

Costa, A. L. (1981, October). Teaching for intelligent behavior. *Educational Leadership, 39*(1), 29–32.

Rigney, J. W. (1980). Cognitive learning strategies and qualities in information processing. In R. Snow, P. Federico, & W. Montague (Eds.), *Aptitudes, learning, and instruction* (Vol. 1). Hillsdale, NJ: Erlbaum.

Sanacore, J. (1984, May) Metacognition and the improvement of reading: Some important links. *Journal of Reading, 27*(8), 706–712.

Sternberg, R., & Wagner, R. (1982). Understanding intelligence: What's in it for education? Paper submitted to the National Commission on Excellence in Education, Washington, DC.

Whimbey, A. (1980, April). Students can learn to be better problem solvers. *Educational Leadership, 37*(7), 560–565.

Whimbey, A., & Whimbey, L. S. (1976). *Intelligence can be taught*. New York: Bantam Books.

65

Making Sense of Thinking

Jack Lochhead

I magine playing a game of tennis in the dark. You see nothing. Out there somewhere in front of you is the net. Suddenly you hear the sound of a racket hitting the ball, followed by the sound of the ball bouncing in your court. You take a step toward where you think the bounce may have been and swing your racket. In the very unlikely event that you hit the ball you get little sense of where it went or landed.

SENSELESS OBSERVATIONS

Not many people have attempted to learn tennis in the above manner. Yet we use a similar strategy to teach thinking. Thinking is invisible. It is also inaudible, intangible, and odorless. In short, thinking is not sensible. Yet we seem to forget this when we teach thinking. Most often the teacher goes to the board and solves a problem using a largely invisible, barely audible (even when loud), odorless, untouchable method, while students patiently observe the unobservable.

There are good reasons for this foolishness. We usually learn skills by observing experts as well as by observing our own efforts. We attempt to determine the differences between our efforts and those of skilled performers and then we try to modify our efforts to make them more like the experts' performance. Thus a student of tennis will watch superior players as they hit balls. He will then try to swing his racket in a similar manner and may have a coach watch and critique these attempts. The coach will tell the student to pay attention to particular parts of the swing, and she may even guide the swing by physically holding and pushing the learner's arms. Advanced athletes compare their actions, as recorded on digitized videotape, to computer models and may thereby improve skills beyond those of any previous human. It seems reasonable to apply a similar approach to thinking.[1] Unfortunately such an approach can work only if the learner can observe the thinking, both his own thinking and that of the teacher's. But thinking is not sensible! More accurately, thinking is not sensible

until we act to make it detectable by at least one of five senses. Sound is usually the simplest sense to employ.

Someday we may be able to place electrodes in the brain and produce computer displays that will allow us to improve thinking by comparing our brain activity with that of experts. For the time being we must make do with a simpler technology. Thinking Aloud Pair Problem Solving (TAPPS) is a technique that can help students learn to observe thinking—their own thinking and that of their fellow students. TAPPS makes thinking observable by having a problem solver talk aloud, describing what she is thinking. TAPPS makes thinking sensible by making it audible, and for that reason I will refer to it as Sound Thinking. Elsewhere (Lochhead, 2001) I have referred to a similar approach as Thinkback—emphasizing the relationship to video playback as used in coaching athletic performance.

INSECURE FEELINGS

Putting thoughts into words is not a natural act. When someone thinks aloud in public we usually consider that person to be crazy. Thus learning Sound Thinking requires some practice and a willingness to overcome certain inhibitions. When you have been in the dark, it takes time to adjust to lights.

Sound Thinking is a tool for teaching and learning thinking. It is not a quick fix. The process of making thinking audible is at first a barrier to optimal performance, and it dramatically slows down the thinking process. But while such slow, noisy thinking is not helpful to performance, it is essential for teaching and learning.

Although it takes time and effort to develop skills in Sound Thinking, getting started is quick and easy. Students are paired up and given some simple problems to solve. One student, the problem solver, is asked to talk aloud about everything he is thinking while working on the problem. The other student, the listener, listens carefully and asks questions that push the problem solver to describe each step in greater detail. First, the listener makes sure that the problem solver keeps talking: "What are you thinking?" "What is going on in there?" Next, the listener looks for gaps in the problem solver's descriptions: "How did you know to do that?" "What are you trying to do now?"

As soon as one problem is solved, the students switch roles and move on to the next problem. They continue to alternate roles while working through a list of problems. This alternation is important, because the eventual goal of Sound Thinking is to combine skill in thinking aloud with an equal level of skill in listening to thought. With both skills in place, students can listen to their own thoughts and understand their own thinking. But to do that, listening and thinking aloud need to be synchronized.[2] Learning two skills in parallel can be confusing. It may be difficult to remember to stay within one role. It is therefore important that students start with simple problems that do not demand a great deal of concentration. These problems leave some mental resources available to pay attention to how well one is functioning in the role of listener or problem solver. Some examples of suitable problems can be found in Chapter 4 of the book *Problem Solving and Comprehension* (Whimbey & Lochhead, 1999).

Before students begin the process of Thinking Aloud Pair Problem Solving, it is helpful to provide them with a model case such as the one in Figure 65.1.

SELF-CONSCIOUS THINKING

The culmination of Sound Thinking is reflective thinking, the ability to listen to and follow one's own thought processes. To reach this stage, students need to have internalized the two roles of listener and problem solver to such an extent that each is automatic. Students who have reached this stage are in a position to learn from their own mistakes. They know what route they took to get to a wrong answer, and they can go back and figure out where they went wrong. They are also able to learn from the performance of fellow students or from expert models. When they do not understand a process they are observing, they know how to ask questions to illuminate it. In short, they are no longer playing in the dark.

Reflective thinking is essential to metacognition, the process of thinking about thinking. We can understand another person's thinking only to the extent that we can model it with our own thinking. Thus, as long as our own thoughts remain opaque, the thoughts of others are even more obscure. Without reflective thinking we remain lost in a mental fog that we cannot see and have no reason to believe exists. Therefore

—*Figure 65.1*—
Example of Thinking Aloud Pair Problem Solving

If the second letter in the word WEST comes after the fourth letter in the alphabet, circle the letter A below. If it does not, circle the B.

A   B

Problem Solver: If the second letter in the word WEST comes after the fourth letter in alphabet, circle the letter A below. If it does not, circle the B.

Listener: You said "in alphabet" not "in *the* alphabet."

Problem Solver: Oh, yeah.

(pause).

Listener: What are you thinking?

Problem Solver: Nothing. I am just looking at it.

(pause).

Listener: What are you looking at?

Problem Solver: It's A. I circle the A.

Listener: Wait a minute. You just said you weren't thinking. Now you say it's A. How did you get that?

Problem Solver: Well, the fourth letter is D.

Listener: Yes.

Problem Solver: And so I circle the A.

Listener: How do you get the fourth letter is D?

Problem Solver: A, B, C, D. I count.

Listener: OK. So how come you circle the A?

Problem Solver: Because that's what it says to do.

Listener: I think you're wrong.

Reprinted from *Problem Solving and Comprehension* (6th ed.), by A. Whimbey & J. Lochhead, 1999, pp. 36–38, with permission from the publisher, Lawrence Erlbaum Associates, Mahwah, NJ.

until we can think reflectively, we have no idea what we have been missing.

SENSIBLE CHANGES

The process of Sound Thinking as implemented in *Problem Solving and Comprehension* tends to improve student performance on a wide variety of tests. About 40 hours of instruction has produced gains averaging 10 percent on tests such as the SAT (Whimbey, 1985; Whimbey, Johnson, Williams, & Linden, 1993). But these gains understate the potential. When Sound Thinking is used as part of a coherent thinking skills program, the outcomes can be astounding. There are many ways to implement such a program. Xavier University in New Orleans has one approach, and Morningside Academy in Seattle has quite a different one. When Sound Thinking is used in an educational environment that stresses many different approaches to developing thinking skills, it becomes a powerful tool for improving learning. Because Sound Thinking teaches students to think reflectively, it helps them get the most out of other methods for teaching thinking, including others described in this book. To produce the best results, a program needs to employ several different methods for teaching thinking and do this in a total educational environment that demands and rewards serious thinking.

At Xavier University, the TAPPS process has been used for more than 20 years as part of a comprehensive approach to improving thinking skills. During that period, medical school acceptances for Xavier students have increased more than 3000 percent. In just two decades, Xavier has lifted itself from a position of having no academic distinction to being recognized as one of the top 30 universities in the United States (Cose, 1997).[3]

Morningside Academy has been using TAPPS for more than 15 years in the middle school and high school years. It has repeatedly measured learning gains many times greater than normal. Student performance on the Iowa Test of Basic Skills consistently rises two to five grade levels after a single year of instruction in TAPPS. An adult version of the Morningside program used in Welfare to Work programs produces one grade level of change for each month of instruction, roughly 10 times the normal rate of learning (Johnson, 1997; see also http://www.morningsideinfo.com).

SENSING PROGRESS

Long-term use of Sound Thinking accomplishes much more than merely improving students' learning capabilities. Because Sound Thinking allows teachers to hear how their students think, it permits teachers, probably for the first time in their careers, to actually observe student thinking. Teachers generally assume they understand what their students are thinking, but this kind of strategy sheds new light on student thought processes and enlightens teachers. Normally teaching is conducted, like night tennis, without any clear sense of the impact of one's actions. With Sound Thinking, the rules are changed;

everything is different. For institutions such as Xavier and Morningside, this difference in faculty vision has created gains far beyond what is normally possible. And these gains have multiplied year after year.

But the greatest benefits require much more than just the long-term use of Sound Thinking. The gains at Xavier and Morningside are produced because all faculty were involved. While the practice of Sound Thinking may help one teacher to see students in a new light, such benefits are limited when other colleagues remain in the dark. Large educational gains demand a comprehensive, well-integrated approach that involves all faculty striving for common goals. Team performance will be erratic if most of the players cannot see the goal posts.

Even with Sound Thinking, much mental activity remains hidden or obscure. The image of thinking that emerges from thinking aloud (even highly practiced thinking aloud) is often blurry and open to extensive interpretation. Learning to interpret such blurry images is best accomplished in a community of colleagues who can challenge and defend various constructions. The task of making thinking sensible needs to be a schoolwide effort.

COMMON SENSE

Implementing a program of Sound Thinking raises many instructional challenges. The following issues have so far been ignored:

- How should students be paired up? A book could be written on the subject. Each teacher needs to discover the pairing strategies that work best in his classroom.
- What happens when both students in a pair are hopelessly stuck? Usually there are two sources for help, other students and the teacher. The problems that are assigned should be easy enough so that the teacher will not be overwhelmed by stuck students. Often the teacher can save time by enlisting the help of another group that has already solved the problem.
- What about the noise level? Sound Thinking is a noisy process. It will not work in schools that have either thin walls or thick principals.
- How does Sound Thinking work with a deaf student? It is extremely difficult to conduct Sound Thinking exercises with a single deaf student, but with two it is very easy.

WRITE ON

After students have internalized the listener role and are comfortable with detailed loud thinking, they are ready for the more challenging task of Write Thinking. In this exercise (usually assigned as homework), students write out everything they would have said to their partners. Write Thinking has many advantages, but it is quite difficult to learn. First, it requires a thorough mastery of Sound Thinking. Next, it requires the persistence to put thoughts into writing, a medium that is both slower and more taxing than speech. To date, few teachers have had the skill and determination to demand Write Thinking from all their students. But for those fortunate students who learn to use Write Thinking, the long-term advantages are considerable. An engineering student explained, "Whenever I see an exam question that I have absolutely no idea how to solve I start to use Write Thinking. At least I can get some partial credit. But, usually once I start writing, I discover I know how to solve the problem." Sensible thinking, whether in writing or speech, gives access to powers we never sensed before.

NOTES

[1] There is a long history of efforts to use thinking aloud episodes as a tool to study and improve thinking. William James often reflected on his own verbalized thoughts. Vygotsky and Piaget both studied the verbalized thinking of children. The most definitive recent theoretical work on Thinking Aloud is in Ericsson and Simon (1993, 1998).

[2] We have all encountered people, often professors, who are practiced in thinking aloud but not in listening to themselves or others. Their thinking may be untouchably brilliant, but it is not sensible.

[3] There are only 30 institutions in the United States that place more than 100 students per year into medical school. Most are very large university complexes containing a vastly greater faculty and student body than Xavier has. While Xavier is only in the top 30 based on medical school placements, there has also been remarkable growth in many other areas. For the latest statistics, see http://www.xupremed.com.

REFERENCES

Cose, E. (1997). *Color-blind: Seeing beyond race in a race-obsessed world.* New York: Harper Collins.

Ericsson, K. A., & Simon, H. A. (1993). *Protocol analysis verbal reports as data* (Rev. ed.). Cambridge, MA: MIT Press.

Ericsson, K. A.. & Simon, H. A. (1998). How to study thinking in everyday life: Contrasting think-aloud protocols with descriptions and explanations of thinking. *Mind Culture, and Activity, 5*(3), 178–186.

Johnson, K. (1997). *About Morningside.* Seattle: Morningside Academy.

Lochhead, J. (2001). *Thinkback: A user's guide to minding the mind.* Mahwah, NJ: Lawrence Erlbaum Associates.

Whimbey, A. (1985). Test results from teaching thinking. In A. L. Costa (Ed.), *Developing minds: A resource book for teaching thinking* (p. 269–271). Alexandria, VA: Association for Supervision and Curriculum Development.

Whimbey, A., Johnson, M. H., Williams, E., Sr., & Linden, M. J. (1993). *Blueprint for educational change: Improving reasoning, literacies, and science achievement with cooperative learning.* Birmingham, AL: EBSCO Curriculum Materials, Box 486; 800-633-8623.

Whimbey, A., & Lochhead, J. (1999). *Problem solving and comprehension* (6th ed.). Mahwah, NJ: Lawrence Erlbaum Associates.

66

Putting It All Together to Improve Student Thinking

BARRY K. BEYER

When you're through changing, you're through.

—*Bruce Barton*

As the chapters in this section indicate, specialists recommend a variety of teaching techniques for use in improving the quality of our student thinking. This variety, however, does not mean that we can simply choose which one of several to employ in our classrooms. Rather, if we wish to improve the thinking of our students we must use them all. Employing only one or two of these teaching techniques will fall short of what is required to reach this goal. For it is only by combining all of these into a comprehensive instructional effort that we can best help our students become as proficient in thinking as they could and should be. This chapter outlines how these techniques can be arranged in strategic combinations to carry out the teaching-learning functions essential to achieving this goal.

Before doing this, however, we should be clear about our purposes in using these techniques. Do we seek to *facilitate* student thinking or to *improve* it permanently? The two are not synonymous. Facilitating thinking is commonly a one-time intervention to help students overcome a temporary obstacle or to ease them through a difficult thinking task—a sort of quick-fix to a specific problem. *Improving* thinking, on the other hand, means making thinking work better—more rapidly, accurately, expertly—in the long run than it does now. This requires a continuing, systematic, purposeful effort to move students toward achieving and maintaining the highest levels possible of skilled, self-directed, self-correcting, autonomous thinking. Improving student thinking requires us to use many

techniques rather than one or two and to employ them frequently, not just once or twice.

Research, theory and exemplary practice indicate that there are at least five things we should do in our classrooms to improve the quality of our students' thinking (Doyle, 1983; Frederickson, 1984; Newmann, 1990; Nickerson, 1988–89; Perkins, 1992; Posner & Keele, 1973). And we can do these at the same time that we engage our students in achieving the various subject matter learning objectives called for by our curricula. Specifically, we should

- Provide a thoughtful classroom learning environment—one that makes thinking possible and students willing to engage in it.
- Make the invisible substance of thinking visible and explicit.
- Scaffold and cue student application of new thinking operations during the students' initial efforts to apply them.
- Provide continuing, direct instruction in procedures for applying difficult or complex thinking operations.
- Integrate instruction in thinking with instruction in subject matter.

Any instructional effort that seeks to bring about significant and lasting improvement in student thinking should include these five features. Each of the teaching techniques we employ in our teaching must contribute directly to one or more of them. The following paragraphs detail the importance of these five essential features of thinking skill instruction and how the techniques presented in this section can be used to carry them out.

PROVIDING THOUGHTFUL LEARNING ENVIRONMENTS

Unless the learning environments of our classrooms nurture and support student thinking, especially higher-order thinking,

Copyright © 2001 by Barry K. Beyer. Adapted from *The Clearing House*, 71(5), May/June 1998/99, pp. 262–267.

our students are unlikely to be very receptive to continued efforts on our part to help them improve their thinking. Among the features of such learning environments, two stand out as especially crucial: (1) repeated opportunities to engage in meaningful thinking beyond the level of recall and (2) encouragement to engage and remain engaged in such thinking. To ensure that our classrooms consistently exhibit these features we need to make them *thinker friendly* as well as *thinking friendly*. Specialists call such classrooms thoughtful classrooms (Wiggins, 1987).

Providing thinking opportunities. The secret to providing repeated classroom opportunities to engage in thinking is to engage students in *productive* learning tasks. These are tasks that require students to *produce* or construct knowledge new to them, rather than simply to reproduce information or knowledge claims that have already been presented to them by others. One powerful way to do this is to frame learning assignments or lessons around thoughtful questions (Wiggins, 1987).

A thoughtful question is a question that—to produce an acceptable response—requires students to go substantially beyond where they are and, like the crew of the Enterprise in "Star Trek," to go where they have never gone before. To answer these questions, students must locate and use information they may not yet possess as well as restructure familiar information to produce something they do not already know. "What did Columbus discover?" is not a very thoughtful question. "Who discovered Columbus—and why?" is much more thoughtful.

Thoughtful questions stimulate thinking and trigger additional related questions. To answer them students must engage in problem solving: they must define terms; pose hypotheses; identify, find, assess, and manipulate data; make and test inferences; generate and evaluate conclusions and arguments; and apply concepts, principles, and other kinds of knowledge. These questions are not yes-or-no questions. They cannot be answered simply by recall. They do *not* have a single preferred "right" answer (Newmann, 1990; Wiggins, 1987). By organizing lessons, units, or topics around such questions, we can provide students with continued opportunities to engage in all kinds of thinking to generate worthwhile and meaningful subject matter learning.

Productive learning activities also provide considerable opportunities for sustained thinking. Activities like judging the accuracy of a given claim or body of information or generating a strong argument in support of a conclusion may require as few as only one or two classroom periods (Beyer, 1997). Longer

tasks such as making and testing hypotheses in order to solve a problem, or projects like the following provide even more opportunities for continued higher-order student thinking:

> Create and justify good-citizenship merit-badge requirements for a specific kind of person in a given culture or place at a particular time in history, such as for a Nez Perce youth in the 1870s, an enslaved or free African American in the 1850s, or a king's vassal—or serf—in the Middle Ages.

Organizing lessons around thoughtful questions and productive learning tasks provides repeated built-in opportunities for and gives purpose to higher-order thinking in our classrooms.

Encouraging student thinking. Providing opportunities to think, however, is fruitless unless students take advantage of them. And, as we all know, too many students frequently do not. Providing encouragement that motivates students to seize and sustain engagement in the thinking opportunities we provide is thus also essential to creating and maintaining a thoughtful learning environment.

The kind of encouragement required to do this is not the "redouble your effort" kind derived from simple cheerleading or from exhortations like, "Think! Think again! Now think harder." On the contrary, it is the kind of encouragement that *emboldens* students to engage in thinking. This means providing them some tangible aid, prompt, or other support that gives them reason to feel that they will or can succeed at the task at hand.

We can provide such encouragement by arranging students in our classrooms so they face each other as well as by surrounding them with bulletin board displays of quotations, cartoons, puzzles, and copies of their own work that illustrate the importance and value of good thinking. Providing *wait time* for them to think *before we respond* to their assertions or answers *and before we demand that they respond to ours* also serves this purpose (Rowe, 1974). So, too, does our modeling the behaviors and dispositions of skillful thinking and helping our students exhibit these behaviors and dispositions. Rather than cutting thinking off with remarks such as "Good answer!" we can build on student responses to sustain continued thinking by, for instance, asking for evidence to support the accuracy of a response or for examples or more details or assumptions underlying it (see, for instance Chapter 58 in this book).

We can also encourage student thinking by minimizing or eliminating the negative risks of thinking (Lipman, 1991; Nickerson, 1988–89). For instance, we can consistently emphasize the positive value of rejected hypotheses and "wrong answers" in leading us to valid hypotheses and "correct answers." We can constantly employ the language of thinking by using precise thinking terms to denote the specific cognitive actions, skills, conditions, or products we wish students to engage in or produce (see Chapter 60 in this book). Instead of asking, "What do you think will happen next?" we should ask, "What do you *predict* will happen next?" (Beyer, 1997; Olson & Astington, 1990; Perkins, 1992). And we can keep classroom discourse focused on truth and proof rather than on who says what, welcome and explore divergent or unusual views, and reward the validated products of high-risk thinking (Newmann, 1990).

By having students engage in challenging higher-order thinking tasks as a normal and expected part of our classrooms, by providing emboldening boosts, and by helping them see how skilled thinkers carry out these tasks and then guiding student practice in doing so themselves, we give students reason to believe they can successfully carry out such thinking. It is this kind of support—combined with the topics we ask them to think about—that encourages them to take advantage of the thinking opportunities we provide.

MAKING THINKING VISIBLE

Before we can repair or strengthen something that is broken or is not working as well as it should be, we need to be aware of exactly how it presently functions. We also need to be aware of how it works or might work when functioning as it could or should function. This is as true of student thinking as it is of any other procedure or process. A crucial step in improving student thinking thus consists of making students conscious of how they currently carry out a given thinking operation and how others more skilled than they carry out the same thinking operation. This means we need to make visible and explicit the seemingly invisible processes of thinking, especially when introducing our students to new or complex thinking operations.

The invisible substance of thinking. What is there we can make visible and explicit about any act of thinking? Cognitive scientists assert that every thinking skill (operation, strategy, or act) consists of three elements: one or more *procedures* (series of steps or rules) by which it is or can be executed skillfully and efficiently; the *conditions* under which it is appropriately employed; and any *declarative knowledge*, like the criteria employed in making judgments or the rules of thumb that guide expert application of a procedure (Anderson, 1983: Nickerson, 1988–89). Students benefit immensely from becoming familiar with procedures for how they presently execute a given thinking operation as well as the procedures experts use, discussing where and when it is appropriate to employ the operation, and reviewing anything they know—or should know—that would make its application more efficient, effective, and expert (Papert, 1980; Vygotsky, 1962).

Making the invisible visible. We can help students make visible and explicit these normally unarticulated elements of any thinking skill in several ways. One is by engaging students in reflecting on what they did to carry out a thinking operation they have just completed. This is known as *metacognitive reflection* (see Chapter 64 by Arthur Costa in this book). Once students have completed a thinking task, we can have them think back on and share with their peers exactly what they did mentally, step-by-step, to complete this task and why they took these steps. In doing this, students verbalize what they recall doing, listen to how some of their peers believe they did the same thing, and then analyze these accounts to identify apparently useful and even additional unarticulated steps and rules. By continuously verbalizing and then comparing these procedural descriptions to each other and to explicit procedures employed by individuals more skilled than they in carrying out the same operation, students can spot weaknesses, dysfunctional steps or gaps in the way they do it, identify procedural steps or rules that appear to be more useful in carrying out the thinking operation, and adopt or incorporate these into how they execute it in the future (Beyer, 1997; Costa, 1984; Nickerson, Perkins, & Smith, 1985; Sternberg, 1984).

Another way to make the invisible of thinking visible and explicit is to *model* a thinking operation for students (Pressley & Harris, 1990; Rosenshine & Meister, 1992). Modeling consists of demonstrating step-by-step how a skill is executed with accompanying explanation, noting the key steps in the procedure and why these steps are important. If we are proficient at executing the thinking skill in question and can verbalize clearly how we do it, we ourselves can model it for our students. We may also use written protocols or videos or essays that model this procedure, if any are available. Occasionally, a few students who have demonstrated skill in carrying out a thinking operation can model the procedures they used. Then, if we provide an immediate opportunity to apply the modeled procedure while it is still visible to them, all students in our class can attempt to replicate it. With continued practice and reflection they can adopt or adapt it to develop a skilled routine of their own for executing the skill.

The key here is making students conscious of exactly how they presently carry out a thinking act or skill, of how their peers do it, and of how more skillful thinkers do it. Metacognitive reflection and modeling serve these ends well. Improving the quality of student thinking requires repeated use of both techniques in our classrooms.

GUIDING AND SUPPORTING STUDENT THINKING

Providing continuing guidance and support to students who are trying to apply newly encountered thinking skills proves indispensable to moving them toward skillful, autonomous use of these skills (Rosenshine & Meister, 1992). Two kinds of such guidance and support prove especially effective to this end: scaffolding and cueing. Once students have become consciously aware of a procedure for skillfully executing a new or complex thinking procedure, scaffolding and cueing can be used to guide their continuing follow-up practice and application of the procedure in a variety of contexts.

Scaffolding thinking. A scaffold is a skeletal framework of a thinking procedure—such as a checklist—that makes the steps in that thinking procedure explicit. Students use the scaffold to steer themselves through these steps as they try to carry them out. Such devices allow students to concentrate on applying the rules and steps of an unfamiliar or complex thinking procedure to a given body of information without having also to try to recall what the steps are. Use of thinking scaffolds minimizes procedural errors in trying to apply a newly encountered thinking skill and enables students to internalize a more effective skill-using routine sooner than they otherwise might if they had to carry out the skill, from memory, exclusively on their own (Beyer, 1997; McTighe & Lyman, 1988).

There are three kinds of devices that prove especially effective as scaffolds for thinking. *Procedural checklists,* such as the one for decision making shown in Figure 66.1, are the most explicit. They provide a list, in order, of the mental steps by which a specific thinking procedure can be effectively carried out. *Process-structured questions* are less explicit. Like the example in Figure 66.1, these devices walk students through the steps in a thinking procedure not by telling them the steps directly but by asking a series of questions that require students to execute in sequence each of the steps that constitutes the given thinking procedure. Thinking skill *graphic organizers* like the one in Figure 66.1 are charts or diagrams that present visually—and occasionally with written prompts as well—the steps in a thinking procedure (McTighe & Lyman, 1988). As students fill in the sections of this graphic organizer, they move through these steps (see Chapter 61 by Jay McTighe and Frank Lyman and Chapter 63 by David Hyerle in this book). Graphic

organizers provide less explicit support and guidance than either checklists or process structured questions, but can still effectively scaffold or structure student thinking.

Not all checklists, lists of questions, or graphic organizers scaffold thinking, however. Many checklists and questions trigger thinking but do not, by the way they are arranged or worded, effectively move students through the steps in a cognitive procedure. Furthermore, as commonly used, many webs, matrices, charts, and diagrams tend to represent the *products* of thinking, products such as concepts, arguments, and so on, rather than represent a *procedure* by which a thinking product is generated. To be most effective in scaffolding thinking, such checklists, questions, and thinking skill graphic organizers must present a cognitive procedure in step-by-step fashion. We also must explicitly introduce the procedure that we are trying to scaffold to students *prior* to using the scaffold.

Cueing thinking. A *cue* is a prompt that reminds us of what to do or say next, without telling us all that we are to do or say. Cueing thinking consists of prompting students to employ a specific thinking operation. A cue is usually much less explicit than a scaffold. It also depends much more than a scaffold for its effectiveness on the degree to which students have already internalized—stored in memory—under that cue or signal the procedures and rules that constitute the action or skill it seeks to call forth. Cueing thinking proves helpful to improving student thinking only after students have become consciously aware (through metacognitive reflection or modeling) of an effective skill-using procedure and have had enough scaffolded practice in applying it to have stored that specific knowledge in memory.

Thinking cues take many forms (Rosenshine & Meister, 1992). They range from the more explicit, like previewing and rehearsing a skill about to be applied, to simply naming that operation, to even less explicit devices such as mnemonics and symbols (see Chapter 61 in this book). We can *preview* a thinking operation that students are about to employ by having volunteers provide its various names, give examples of it, report any special rules or heuristics that they know might guide its use (including the criteria it applies, if it is a critical thinking operation), tell why it is appropriate to use at this point, and define it. Asking for the definition last allows students to use the preceding volunteered information as cues for searching their memories for this definition or as information from which to construct an appropriate working definition (Beyer, 1987).

We can help students *rehearse* a thinking skill they are about to practice by having volunteers report one or more routines by which it can be effectively employed or any rules, criteria, and heuristics that direct or inform its use. When stu-

—Figure 66.1—
Scaffolds for Student Thinking

A Procedural Checklist for Decision Making

___ Identify a choosing opportunity

___ State the problem or goal

___ State the criteria of the best choice or decision

___ List the possible alternative choices

___ List the possible consequences of selecting each alternative

___ Evaluate each consequence in terms of the criteria identified above

___ Select the alternative that best meets the identified criteria

Process-Structured Questions for Decision Making

1. What do you want to make a decision about?
2. What do you want to accomplish by making this decision?
3. How will you know when you have made the best choice?
4. What are all the alternatives you have to choose from?
5. What are the possible consequences of each alternative—long range as well as short range?
6. What are the pluses and minuses of each consequence?
7. Which alternative is best? Why?

A Graphic Organizer for Decision Making

Situation/Opportunity:					
Problem:		Goal/Criteria:			
Alternatives:	Consequences/Costs/Etc.:				Evaluation:
Decision:		Reasons:			

---

dents have been applying a skill for some time, however, merely *naming* the skill—or words associated with it—customarily serves as a sufficient cue. *Mnemonics*, if devised or learned earlier by the students when they were first articulating or devising more effective procedures for executing a skill, also can serve as useful thinking cues. Consider this acronym as a cue for the process of decision making, for example:

- Define goal.
- Enumerate alternatives.
- Consider consequences.
- Investigate (good and bad of each).
- Determine best choice.
- Execute.

Acronyms like this one not only aid students in recalling the skill to employ but can actually cue the appreciation of the steps in a procedure for executing it (Beyer, 1997).

Scaffolding and cueing thinking while it is being applied by the students provide exactly the kinds of guidance and support that help them become proficient in carrying such thinking skills with increasing degrees of autonomy. The selected techniques described here are especially effective for this purpose.

PROVIDING DIRECT INSTRUCTION IN THINKING SKILLS

Most thinking skills cannot be mastered in only one or two lessons. Research indicates that while it may take as few as six skill lessons to attain mastery, it may require fifty or more instructional lessons to achieve this goal (Pasnak et al., 1987). This is especially true for many at-risk students or for students of any ability when encountering a skill with which they are completely unfamiliar or which is an especially complex thinking operation such as identifying unstated assumptions, judging the strength of an argument, or solving highly technical problems (Pressley & Harris, 1990). For these skill learning situations, we need to employ teaching strategies that provide continuing explicit instruction in the strategies or procedures of the thinking skills in question.

Direct instruction in a thinking skill does exactly this. It consists of a series of lessons that focus explicitly on procedures for carrying out a specific skill and on knowledge related to those procedures. Three types of lessons are essential to this teaching—lessons that introduce the skill, that guide and support its practice, and that help students transfer its application to contexts other than the one in which it was initially introduced and practiced. Such instruction consists of anywhere from six to a dozen or more lessons over an extended period of time and in a variety of contents (Beyer, 1987, 1997).

Each of these types of lessons plays a significant role in moving students from unskilled to skillful application of a thinking operation (see Chapter 62 by Barry Beyer in this book). The major purpose of an introductory lesson on a skill is to make one or more procedures for applying it visible and explicit; these lessons focus almost exclusively on the skill procedure and may require anywhere from 20 to 40 minutes. Lessons in which students practice applying the skill require scaffolding by the teacher until students demonstrate their ability to execute the skill without this kind of structured support. They should be relatively close together and frequent and require only 10 to 15 minutes to complete the application of the skill and follow-up reflection on it. Opportunities to apply the skill may require only occasional cueing. While all of these lessons can include instruction that sets the skill up for transfer (Beyer, 1987), it is usually necessary to reintroduce the skill in some detail when it is to be applied in a new context with further scaffolded and cued practice (see Chapter 59 by David Perkins and Gavriel Salomon in this book).

At its best, direct instruction is a mix of didactic and constructivist teaching and learning. Various specific strategies have been designed to move students through the types of direct instruction described here (Beyer, 1997; Sternberg & Davidson, 1989; Whimbey & Lochhead, 1999). As noted here, some strategies incorporate many of the skill-teaching techniques described in the pages of this book as well as elsewhere (Beyer, 1997; Lochhead, 2000). Organizing continuing classroom instruction in how to carry out any thinking skill around these strategies provides a systematic structure for moving students from the status of novice to increasing proficiency in thinking.

INTEGRATING INSTRUCTION IN THINKING WITH SUBJECT MATTER

Thinking is affected and shaped as much by the subject matter to which it is applied as that subject matter is shaped by the kind of thinking that is employed to process it and the degree of expertise with which that thinking is applied. Instructional efforts to improve student thinking, therefore, need to be carefully integrated into instruction in subject matter (Resnick & Klopfer, 1989). *We can and should teach thinking and subject matter together.*

To accomplish this, we must ensure that our students have repeated opportunities throughout our courses to apply the thinking skills in which they need to improve. This can be done, in part, by focusing on topics and themes that raise puzzling or thoughtful questions. It can also be accomplished by building student study around problem solving and other productive thinking activities.

Prior to beginning a course, we can identify the specific thinking skills we believe our students will need to improve. Next, we can build in repeated opportunities for the students, once they have first encountered the need to use each of these skills, to apply each, at first frequently and then intermittently thereafter. Then we can design the appropriate skill instruction for each lesson in this skill-using sequence while using the subject matter our students are to be studying along the way.

While we are teaching, we can also be always alert to any thinking skills with which our students seem to be having difficulty. The first time we notice such difficulty we then can switch our instructional focus from subject matter to how to carry out the skill by *introducing* that skill using an appropriate direct instruction strategy for doing so. John Bransford (1993) calls this "just-in-time teaching." Appropriate scaffolded and cued practice and instruction can follow, over a sequence of subsequent skill-using lessons.

Teaching thinking skills in subject matter courses capitalizes on what research tells us about students' willingness to learn and focus on a new skill. Motivation increases when the skill's introduction and guidance in using it coincide with the student perceiving both a need for the skill and a lack of his or her ability to apply it effectively (Sigel, 1984). Such skill lessons do not ignore the topic being studied but rather help students learn content while improving proficiency in executing the skill.

COMBINING THESE TECHNIQUES AND FEATURES TO IMPROVE STUDENT THINKING

Some of the teaching techniques described here may not be new to many of us. However, we may not have realized the importance of using them all rather than only one or two in our teaching. The power of these techniques is derived as much from how they are employed strategically in combination with each other as it is from their own inherent value.

Each of the five essential features of thinking skill instruction described here addresses a different element of what is required to improve student thinking. Thoughtful classrooms provide the kind of nurturing thinking environment so essential for all the other approaches to take hold. Making the invisible substance of thinking visible and explicit requires such an environment and establishes the baseline from which improvement can proceed. Scaffolding and cueing student thinking can help students apply with increasing efficiency and ease—and eventually with what math instructors call "elegance"—the thinking procedures they are perfecting. Providing continued direct instruction in thinking skill procedures employs effective classroom strategies for teaching such complex skills to students of all ability levels, and especially to at-risk students (Beyer, 1997). And applying all of these techniques and teaching strategies in the subject matter being studied gives purpose to and motivates continued student thinking skill development (Bereiter, 1984). To improve the quality of student thinking and learning in our classrooms, we can and should combine all of the techniques presented here and employ them strategically to carry out the five features of thinking skill instruction so essential to accomplishing this important goal.

IS THIS WORTH DOING?

Is the effort to do this worth it? Of course it is. All our students think. But most of them can think better—more often—and with greater success than they now do. And many of them certainly can learn more in our courses than they do now. Interestingly, research demonstrates that in classes where teachers attend continuously and explicitly to the cognitive skills needed to understand subject matter, students not only improve their proficiency in these thinking skills but also attain higher achievement in subject matter (Estes, 1972). By using the essential features of effective thinking skill instruction described in this section of the book, we can accomplish these goals.

REFERENCES

Anderson, J. R. (1983). *The architecture of cognition*. Cambridge, MA: Harvard University Press.

Bereiter, C. (1984). How to keep thinking skills from going the way of all frills. *Educational Leadership, 42*(1), 76.

Beyer, B. (1987). *Practical strategies for the teaching of thinking*. Boston: Allyn and Bacon.

Beyer, B. K. (1997). *Improving student thinking: A comprehensive approach*. Boston: Allyn and Bacon.

Bransford, J. (1993, February 26). Presentation on teaching thinking presented at the Association for Supervision and Curriculum Development's National Conference on Thinking and Learning, San Antonio, TX.

Costa, A. (1984, November). Mediating the metacognitive. *Educational Leadership, 42*(3), 57–62.

Doyle, W. (1983, Summer). Academic work. *Review of Educational Research, 53*(2).

Estes, T. H. (1972). Reading in the social studies: A review of research since 1950. In J. Laffery (Ed.), *Reading in the content areas*. Newark, DE: International Reading Association.

Frederikson, N. (1984, Fall). Implications of cognitive theory for instruction in problem solving. *Review of Educational Research, 54*(3), pp. 363–407.

Lipman, M. (1991). *Thinking in education*. Cambridge: Cambridge University Press.

Lochhead, J. (2001). *Thinkback: A user's guide to minding the mind*. Mahwah, NJ: Lawrence Erlbaum Associates.

McTighe, J., & Lyman Jr., F. T. (1988, April). Cueing thinking in the classroom: The promise of theory embedded tools. *Educational Leadership, 45*(7), 18–24.

Newmann, F. (1990, January–February) Higher order thinking in teaching social studies. *Journal of Curriculum Studies, 22*(1), 41–56.

Nickerson, R. (1988–89). On improving thinking through instruction. In E. Z. Rothkopf (Ed.), *Review of research in education: Vol. 15*. Washington, DC: American Educational Research Association.

Nickerson, R. S., Perkins, D. N., & Smith, E. E. (1985). *The teaching of thinking*. Hillsdale, NJ: Lawrence Erlbaum Associates.

Olson, D., & Astington, J. W. (1990). Talking about text: How literacy contributes to thought. *Journal of Pragmatics, 14*, 705–721.

Papert, S. (1980). *Mindstorms: Children, computers and powerful ideas*. New York: Basic Books.

Pasnak, R., Brown, K., Kurkjian, M., Mattran, K., Triana, E., & Yamamoto, N. (1987). Cognitive gains through training on classification, seriation, and conservation. *Genetic, Social and General Psychology Monographs, 113*(3), 293–321.

Perkins, D. (1992). *Smart schools*. New York: The Free Press.

Posner, M. E., & Keele, S. W. (1973). Skill learning. In R. M. W. Travers (Ed.), *Second Handbook of Research on Teaching* (pp. 805–831). Chicago: Rand McNally College Publishing.

Pressley, M., & Harris, K. R. (1990). What we really know about strategy instruction. *Educational Leadership, 48*(1), 31–34.

Resnick, L., & Klopfer, L. E. (Eds.). (1989). *Toward the thinking curriculum*. Alexandria, VA: Association for Supervision and Curriculum Development.

Rosenshine, B. V., & Meister, C. (1992). The use of scaffolds for teaching higher level cognitive strategies. *Educational Leadership, 49*(7), 26–33.

Rowe, M. B. (1974). Wait time and rewards as instructional variables. *Journal of Research in Science Teaching, 11,* 81–94.

Sigel, I. E. (1984) A constructivist perspective for teaching thinking. *Educational Leadership, 42*(7), 18–22.

Sternberg, R. J. (1984). How can we teach intelligence? *Educational Leadership, 42*(1), 38–50.

Sternberg, R., & Davidson, J. (1989, April). A four-prong model for intellectual development. *Journal of Research and Development in Education, 22*(3), 22–28.

Vygotsky, L. S. (1962). *Thought and language.* Cambridge, MA: MIT Press.

Whimbey, A., & Lochhead, J. (1999). *Problem solving and comprehension* (6th ed.). Mahwah, NJ: Lawrence Erlbaum Associates.

Wiggins, G. (1987, Winter). Creating a thought-provoking curriculum. *American Educator, 11*(4), 12–13.

IX

Strategies for Teaching Thinking

Life is a succession of lessons which must be lived to be understood.

—RALPH WALDO EMERSON, IN "ILLUSIONS"

Introduction

Jack Lochhead

This section of *Developing Minds* concerns the search for teaching strategies suited to developing student thinking skills. Learning lots of "stuff" is not a good strategy for thinking. This is true despite the fact that people who think exceptionally well often also know a great deal. Indeed, the best strategies for learning thinking are often very different from those employed in the practice of thinking. It is therefore not surprising that curriculum designers have devised far too many ineffective strategies by asking students to do some of the things good thinkers can do, such as read Latin or solve Algebra problems, rather than by making a careful analysis of what students need to learn.

Some of the authors in this section discuss the benefits of having students develop their thinking skills through student-to-student dialog. Richard Paul leads off with a detailed analysis of dialogical thinking. He provides us with an image of how one should conduct dialog and what it should accomplish. Many educators place thinking and content at odds with one another. They view learning to think as an irrelevant luxury that steals time from the essential process of covering content. Sydelle Seiger-Ehrenberg shows how mistaken that view is by describing how students acquire concepts and by indicating the critical role thinking must play in the learning of content.

Turning to creative thinking, Donald Treffinger and Scott Isaksen review work on the teaching of creativity. They use the creative domain to highlight trends that have influenced all strategies for the teaching of thinking.

In his chapter, David Perkins describes the relation of thinking and understanding, showing why an education designed to develop a deep understanding of content must also be an education designed to teach thinking. Robert Sternberg suggests a framework for thinking skills and related learning strategies relevant to all aspects of daily life. He provides a comprehensive map of the territory ahead with a built-in guide to learning the terrain.

Cooperation is a critical feature of that terrain, according to Roger and David Johnson. They discuss why cooperative learning is key to most strategies for developing thinking and why intellectual conflict is crucial to such efforts. Thomas Jackson extends this discussion to show why Socratic instruction, as it is too often practiced, is a poor strategy for developing thinking. He also shows how to revise the Socratic method to place proper emphasis on the students' thinking and includes detailed instructional designs.

Michael Pressley and Karen R. Harris wrap up this section with their review of the cognitive research that has led to our current perspective on strategies for instruction.

Several authors in this section emphasize the need for conflict and clashing perspectives. After about 30 years of trial, error, and research, investigators from diverse origins have converged on a remarkably similar set of conclusions. Yet we need not fear any stifling of thinking; teachers should find ample room for conflict and mismatched perspectives as they strive to incorporate these conclusions into the mainstream of educational practice.

67

Dialogical and Dialectical Thinking

Richard W. Paul

> *It is far better to debate an issue without settling it than to settle an issue without debating it.*
>
> —*Joseph Joubert*

Part I: Theory

When as a result of a trial, a jury issues a verdict of guilty or innocent; when as a result of political debate, we decide to vote for a candidate; when as a result of reading about alternative political systems, we conclude that one is superior; when as a result of hearing various sides of a family argument, we are persuaded that one side is more justified and accurate; when as a result of reading many reports on the need for educational reform, we are prepared to argue for one of them; when as a result of entertaining various representations of national security, we reason to a position of our own; when after reading and thinking about approaches to raising children, we conclude that one is better than the others; when after interacting with someone and reflecting on conflicting interpretations of his or her character, we decide to marry that person—we are reasoning dialectically.

When students discuss their ideas, beliefs, or points of view with other students or the teacher; when they role-play the thinking of others; when they use their thinking to figure out the thinking of another (say, that of the author of a textbook or story); when they listen carefully to the thoughts of another and try to make sense of them; when they arrange their thoughts, orally or in writing, in such a fashion as to be understood by another; when they enter sympathetically into the thinking of others or reason hypothetically from the assumptions of others—they are reasoning dialogically.

An open society requires open minds. One-sided egocentric and sociocentric thought, joined with massive technical knowledge and power, are not the foundations of a genuine democracy. This basic insight, formed over a hundred years ago by John Stuart Mill (1947), is as true today, and as ignored, as it was when he first wrote it:

> In the case of any person whose judgment is really deserving in confidence, how has it become so? Because he has kept his mind open to criticism of his opinions and conduct. Because it has been his practice to listen to all that could be said against him; to profit by as much of it as was just, and expound to himself, and upon occasion to others, the fallacy of what was fallacious. Because he has felt that the only way in which a human being can make some approach to knowing the whole of a subject is by hearing what can be said about it by persons of every variety of opinion and study. (p. 3)

This is the dialogical ideal. Dialogical and dialectical thinking involve dialogue or extended exchange between different points of view or frames of reference. Both are multilogical (involving many logics) rather than monological (involving one logic) because in both cases there is more than one line of reasoning to consider, more than one "logic" being formulated. Dialogue becomes dialectical when ideas or reasonings conflict and we need to assess their various strengths and weaknesses.

In general, students learn best in dialogical situations, under circumstances in which they must continually express their views to others and try to fit others' views into their own. Even in dealing with monological problems (e.g., most math and science problems) students need to move dialogically between their own thinking and "correct" thinking on the subject before they come to appreciate the one "right" (monological) way to proceed. They cannot simply leap directly to "correct" thought; they need to think dialogically first. Unfortunately, the dominant mode of education at all levels is still didactic: teaching by telling, learning by memorizing. The problem it

Copyright © 2001 by Richard W. Paul. This chapter is adapted from *Developing Minds: A Resource Book for Teaching Thinking* (Rev. ed.), 1991.

creates is evident in this excerpt from a letter written by a teacher who has a master's degree in physics and mathematics:

> After I started teaching, I realized that I had learned physics by rote and that I really did not understand all I knew about physics. My thinking students asked me questions for which I always had the standard textbook answers, but for the first time made me start thinking for myself, and I realized that these canned answers were not justified by my own thinking and only confused my students who were showing some ability to think for themselves. To achieve my academic goals I had memorized the thoughts of others, but I had never learned or been encouraged to learn to think for myself.

Didactic teaching encourages monological thinking from beginning to end. There is little room for dialogical or dialectical thinking in the mind of the didactic teacher: The teacher, usually focused on content coverage, tells students directly what to believe and think about subject matter, while students, in turn, focus on remembering what the teacher said in order to reproduce it on demand. In its most common form, this mode of teaching falsely assumes that we can directly give students knowledge without their having to think their way to it, that knowledge can be implanted directly in students' minds through memorization. It confuses information with knowledge. And it falsely assumes that knowledge can be separated from understanding and justification. It also confuses the ability to state a principle with the understanding of it, the ability to supply a definition with the comprehension of it, and the act of saying something is important with the actual recognition of its importance. Didactic instruction flourishes when it appears that life's problems can be solved by one-dimensional answers and that knowledge is ready-made for passive absorption. Without recognizing it, most teachers teach as if this were so.

Students today have very little school experience in reasoning within opposing points of view. Indeed, students today have little experience with reasoning at all. Most students do not know what inferences are, what it is to make assumptions, what it is to reason from an assumption to one or more conclusions. In today's didactic classroom, the teacher is engaged in inculcating information. Classroom monologue (students passively listening) rather than active dialogue (students thoughtfully engaged) is the paradigm.

Unfortunately, students then come away with the impression that knowledge can be obtained without struggle, without having to hear from more than one point of view, without having to identify or assess evidence, without having to question assumptions, without having to trace implications, with-

out having to analyze concepts, without having to consider objections. The result is students with no real sense of what the process of acquiring knowledge involves, students with nothing more than a scattering of information and beliefs, students with little sense of what it is to reason their way to knowledge. The result is teachers oblivious of the fact that knowledge must be earned through thought, who teach as if knowledge is available to anyone willing to commit information to short-term memory. The result is school as a place where knowledge is didactically dispensed and passively acquired, something found principally in books, something that comes from authorities.

But if gaining knowledge really is a fundamental goal—and all curricula say it is—then most students should be spending most of their time actively reasoning. That is, most of the students most of time should be gathering, analyzing, and assessing information. They should be considering alternative competing interpretations and theories. They should be identifying and questioning assumptions, advancing reasons, devising hypotheses, thinking up ways to experiment and test their beliefs. They should be following up implications, analyzing concepts, considering objections. They should be testing their ideas against the ideas of others. They should be sympathetically entering opposing points of view. They should be role-playing reasoning different from their own. In short, they should be reasoning dialogically and dialectically.

Only when students have a rich diet of dialogical and dialectical thought do they become prepared for the messy, multidimensional real world, where opposition, conflict, critique, and contradiction are everywhere. Only through a rigorous exposure to dialogical and dialectical thinking do students develop intellectually fit minds.

ABSOLUTISTIC THINKING IN EARLY SCHOOL YEARS

Young children do not recognize that they have a point of view. Rather, they tend to make absolute judgments about themselves and others. They are not usually given an opportunity to rationally develop their own thoughts. Their capacity to judge reasons and evidence is usually not cultivated. Their intellectual growth is stunted.

As a result, young children uncritically internalize images and concepts of what they and others are like, of what, for example, Americans are like, of what atheists, Christians, communists, parents, children, business people, farmers, liberals, conservatives, left-wingers, right-wingers, salespeople, foreigners, patriots, Palestinians, Kiwanis Club members, cheerleaders, politicians, Nazis, ballet dancers, terrorists, union leaders, guerrillas, freedom fighters, doctors, Marines, scientists, mathematicians, contractors, and waitresses are like. They then "ego-identify" with their conceptions, which they assume to be accurate, spontaneously using them as guides in their day-to-day decision making.

Children need assignments in multilogical issues to break out of their uncritical absolutism. They need to discover opposing points of view in nonthreatening situations. They need to put their ideas into words, advance conclusions, and justify them. They need to discover their own assumptions as well as the assumptions of others. They need to discover their own inconsistencies as well as the inconsistencies of others. They do this best when they learn how to role-play the thinking of others, advance conclusions other than their own, and construct reasons to support them. Children need to do this for the multilogical issues—those involving conflicting points of view, interpretations, and conclusions—that they inevitably face in their everyday life. But they also need to do so for the disciplined monological questions that they must of necessity approach from within the context of their own undisciplined minds.

Because children are not exposed to dialogical and dialectical activities, children do not learn how to read, write, think, listen, or speak in such a way as to rationally organize and express what they believe. They do not learn how uncritically they are responding to the mass media nor to what extent the media reinforce their subconscious egocentric or sociocentric views. They feel deeply, principally about egocentric concerns, justifying getting what they want, and avoiding what they do not want. If school is to prepare students for life as it is, if it is to empower children to become rational persons, it must cultivate dialogical engagement and reasoned judgment from the outset.

Fact, Opinion, and Reasoned Judgment

When critical thinking is introduced into the classroom, though very often it is not, it is usually approached monologically—for example, by having students divide a set of statements into facts and opinions. Unfortunately, a taxonomy that divides all beliefs into either facts or opinions leaves out the most important category: reasoned judgment. Most important issues are not simply matters of fact, nor are they essentially matters of faith, taste, or preference. They are matters that call for reasoned reflection. They are matters that can be understood from different points of view through different frames of reference. We can, and many different people do, approach them with different assumptions, ideas and concepts, priori-

ties, and ends in view. The tools of critical thinking enable us to grasp genuine strengths and weaknesses in thought only when they are analytically applied to divergent perspectives in dialectical contexts. Dialogical and dialectical experience enables us to develop a sense of what is most reasonable. Monological rules do not. For example, it is exceedingly difficult to judge the case made by a prosecutor in a trial until we have heard the arguments for the defense. Only by stepping out of the perspective of the prosecutor and actually organizing the evidence in language designed to make the strongest case for the defense can we begin to grasp the true strength and weakness of the prosecutor's case.

This approach is the only proper way to deal with the important issues we face in our lives, and I am amazed that we and our textbooks refuse to recognize it. The most basic issues simply do not reduce to unadulterated fact or arbitrary opinion. True, they often have a factual dimension. Characteristically, however, some of what is apparently empirically true is also arguable. And we are often faced with the problem of deciding which facts are most important, which should be made central, and which should be deemed peripheral or even irrelevant. Finally, despite the common view, facts do not speak for themselves. They must be rendered meaningful by interpretation, by explanation, by construal. Make your own list of the 10 most important issues and see if is not true (but beware, of course, the tendency to see your own answers to these issues as self-evident facts).

Part II: Pedagogy

Everyday life, in contrast to school, is filled with multilogical problems for which there are competing answers. Furthermore, even when subject matter can be algorithmically and monologically expressed, students need to approach that subject matter through dialogical thought that brings their own thinking into play. Teachers do not, by and large, recognize these facts, nor when it is pointed out to them do they know how to take them into account in the classroom. Being habituated to didactic instruction, dialogical instruction that does not result in predictable "correct" answers is a puzzle to them. They do not know how to foster it. They do not know how to assess it. They do not know how to use it to aid students in mastering content. There are four interrelated skills teachers need to learn:

1. How to identify and distinguish multilogical from monological problems and issues.
2. How to teach Socratically.

3. How to use dialogical and dialectical thought to master content.

4. How to assess dialogical and dialectical thought.

I should add that one does not master these understandings overnight, but only by degrees over an extended period of time. They cannot be taught, for example, in a one-day workshop. Let us consider each of these four learnings in order.

LEARNING TO IDENTIFY AND DISTINGUISH MULTILOGICAL FROM MONOLOGICAL PROBLEMS AND ISSUES

This involves distinguishing problems for which there is an established step-by-step procedure for solving them (e.g., What is the square root of 653? What is the boiling point of water? In what year did the American Revolution begin?) from problems and issues that can be analyzed from multiple different points of view leading to multiple competing answers, resolutions, or solutions (e.g., Was the American Revolution justified? Should the colonists have used violence to achieve their ends? When should you conform to group pressure, and when should you resist that pressure? What is the meaning of this story? What would a true friend do in this situation? What caused World War II? Could it have been avoided? How important is it to get a good education? How important is it to make a lot of money? Is money the root of all evil? What kind of person are you? What are America's real values? How can you tell what to believe and what not to believe?). These kinds of questions, we should note, can be raised from the earliest school years (e.g., Who was right in your argument with your sister, she or you? When should you share your toys? Was it right for Jack, in "Jack and the Bean Stalk," to take the golden eggs and the harp as well? Should the big billy goat have killed the troll in "The Three Billy Goats Gruff"? Is this the best rule to have to avoid accidents in the playground or can you think of a better one? Do the advertisements on television for toys give you good information about toys, or do they mislead you about them?).

SOCRATIC QUESTIONING AND DIALOGICAL DISCUSSION

Dialogical discussion will naturally occur if teachers learn to stimulate student thinking through Socratic questioning. This consists of teachers wondering aloud about the meaning and truth of student responses to questions. The Socratic teacher models a reflective, analytic listener: One who actively pursues clarity of expression. One who actively looks for evidence and reasons. One who actively considers alternative points of view. One who actively tries to reconcile differences of viewpoint. One who actively tries to find out not just what people think but whether what they think is actually so.

Socratic discussion allows students to develop and evaluate their thinking, comparing it to that of other students. Since students inevitably respond to Socratic questions within their own points of view, the discussion inevitably becomes multidimensional.

By routinely raising root questions and root ideas in a classroom setting, multiple points of view get expressed, but in a context in which the seminal ideas, which must be mastered in order to master the content, are deeply considered and their interrelationships established. Over time, students learn from Socratic discussions a sense of intellectual discipline and thoroughness. They learn to appreciate the power of logic and logical thinking. They learn that all thoughts can be pursued in at least four directions:

- *Their origin.* "How did you come to think this?" "Can you remember the circumstances in which you formed this belief?"
- *Their support.* "Why do you believe this?" "Do you have any evidence for this?" "What are some of the reasons people believe this?" "In believing this aren't you assuming that such and so is true?" "Is that a sound assumption, do you think?"
- *Their conflicts with other thoughts.* "But some people might object to your position by saying _____ . How would you answer them?" "But what do you think of this contrasting view?" "But how would you answer the objection that _____ ?"
- *Their implications and consequences.* "But what are the practical consequences of believing this? What would we have to do to put it into action?" "But what follows from the view that _____ ? Wouldn't we also have to believe that _____ in order to be consistent?" "Are you implying that _____ ?"

Figure 67.1 shows an example of how one can pursue the thought "Most people are lazy" using Socratic discussion.

Before a Socratic discussion, teachers should think over the issues and connections that underlie the area or subject to be discussed. Whenever possible, they should figure out in advance what the fundamental ideas are and how they relate to fundamental problems. For example, before leading a Socratic discussion on the question "What is history?" teachers should "prethink" the issue so that they are clear about the essential insights that the Socratic discussion is to foster. For example, the discussion could yield the ideas that history is selective (it

—*Figure 67.1*—
Socratic Discussion

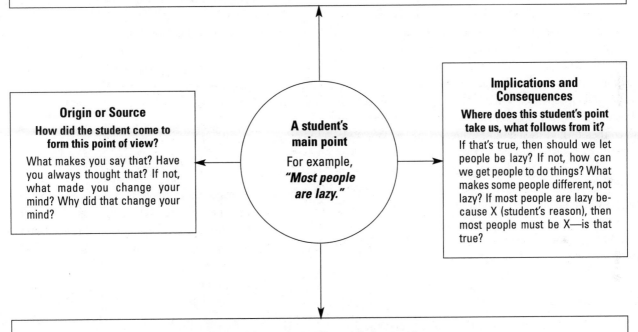

There are *four directions* in which thought can be pursued.

Conflicting Views
How does this student's thinking conflict with other points of view?

What would you say to someone who said that people basically *want* to accomplish things and learn about things, that people *need* to work and keep busy and feel that they contribute? Could there be other reasons why people seem lazy, like maybe people are afraid of messing up, and that's why they don't go out there and do stuff? Your history book is full of people who did things, worked hard, fought, and so on—how do you explain that?

Origin or Source
How did the student come to form this point of view?

What makes you say that? Have you always thought that? If not, what made you change your mind? Why did that change your mind?

A student's main point
For example, *"Most people are lazy."*

Implications and Consequences
Where does this student's point take us, what follows from it?

If that's true, then should we let people be lazy? If not, how can we get people to do things? What makes some people different, not lazy? If most people are lazy because X (student's reason), then most people must be X—is that true?

Support, Reasons, Evidence, & Assumptions
Can the student support his or her view with reasons or evidence?

Why do you think so? Are there certain kinds or groups of people that *aren't* lazy? Why are most people lazy? How do you know? How could we find out if that might be so? Do people choose to be lazy, or decide that it doesn't matter if they are lazy, or are they just that way naturally? Do you think most people think of themselves as lazy? Why?

is not possible to include all of the past in a book); that historians make value judgments about what to include and exclude; that history is written from a point of view; and that historians with different viewpoints often come to different historical judgments. Teachers should also recognize various related insights. Those could be, for example, that all human thinking has a historical dimension (in that all our thinking is shaped by our life and times), that memory is a kind of internal historian, that the news is like the history of yesterday, that

gossip is a form of historical thought, and so on. The pre-thinking enables teachers to look for opportunities in discussion to help students make connections and see the implications of their own thinking about history and things historical.

Of course, teachers must also follow up on the insights that are fostered through Socratic discussion. Hence, once a Socratic discussion has been held on the nature of history, students should be encouraged to raise questions about their history text (e.g., What sorts of things would you guess were left out of this account of the battle? What point of view does the writer seem to have? Which of the sentences in this paragraph state facts? Which of the sentences interpret the facts or draw a conclusion from them? If you were a Native American, do you think you would agree with this conclusion in your history text?). They should also have follow-up assignments that require them to further develop the insights being fostered (e.g., I'd like each of you to imagine that you are one of the colonists loyal to the king and to write one paragraph in which you list your reasons why you think that armed revolution is not justified).

No matter how much advance thinking the teacher has done, however, actual Socratic discussion will proceed, not in a predictable or straightforward direction, but in a crisscrossing, back-and-forth movement. Because Socratic instructors continually encourage students to explore how what they think about x relates to what they think about y and z, students' thinking moves back and forth between their own basic ideas and those being presented by the other students, between their own ideas and those expressed in a book or story, between their own thinking and their own experience, between ideas within one domain and those in another—in short, between any of a variety of perspectives. This dialogical process will sometimes become dialectical when ideas clash or are inconsistent.

Let us now look at a couple of excerpts from Socratic discussion carried out at different grade levels.

A 4TH GRADE SOCRATIC DISCUSSION

Teacher: How does your mind work? Where's your mind?

Student: In your head. (Numerous students point to their heads.)

Teacher: Does your mind do anything?

Student: It helps you remember and think.

Student: It helps, like, if you want to move your legs. It sends a message down to them.

Student: This side of your mind controls this side of your body, and that side controls this other side.

Student: When you touch a hot oven, it tells you whether to cry or say ouch!

Teacher: Does it tell you when to be sad and when to be happy? How does your mind know when to be happy and when to be sad?

Student: When you're hurt, it tells you to be sad.

Student: If something is happening around you is sad.

Student: If there is lightning and you are scared.

Student: If you get something you want.

Student: It makes your body operate. It's like a machine that operates your body.

Teacher: Does it ever happen that two people are in the same circumstance but one is happy and the other is sad? Even though they are in exactly the same circumstance?

Student: You get the same toy. One person might like it. The other gets the same toy, and he doesn't like the toy.

Teacher: Why do you think that some people come to like some things and some people seem to like different things?

Student: Because everybody is not the same. Everybody has different minds and is built different, made different.

Student: They have different personalities?

Teacher: Where does personality come from?

Student: When you start doing stuff and you find that you like some stuff best.

Teacher: Are you born with a personality, or do you develop it as you grow up?

Student: You develop it as you grow up.

Teacher: What makes you develop one rather than another?

Student: Like, your parents or something.

Teacher: How can your parents' personality get into you?

Student: Because you're always around them, and then the way they act as if they think they are good, and they want you to act the same way, then they'll sort of teach you, and you'll do it.

Student: Like, if you are in a tradition. They want you to carry on something that their parents started.

Teacher: Does your mind come to think at all the way children around you think? Can you think of any examples where the way you think is like the way children around you think? Do you think you behave like other American kids?

Student: Yes.

Teacher: What would make you behave more like American kids in your neighborhood than like Eskimo kids?

Student: Because you're around them.

Student: Like, Eskimo kids probably don't even know what the word "jump rope" is. American kids here know what it is.

Teacher: And are there things that the Eskimo kids know that you don't know about?

Student: Yes.

Student: And also we don't have to dress like them or act like them, and they have to know when a storm is coming so they won't get trapped outside.

Teacher: OK, so if I understand you then, parents have some influence on how you behave, and the kids around you have some influence on how you behave. Do you have some influence on how you behave? Do you choose the kind of person you're going to be at all?

Student: Yes.

Teacher: How do you do that, do you think?

Student: Well, if someone says to jump off a five-story building, you won't say okay. You wouldn't want to do that. . . .

(Discussion continues.)

A HIGH SCHOOL SOCRATIC DISCUSSION

Teacher: This is a course in biology. What kind of a subject is that? What do you know about biology already? Kathleen, what do you know about it?

Kathleen: It's a science.

Teacher: And what's a science?

Kathleen: Me? A science is very exact. They do experiments and measure things and test things.

Teacher: Right, and what other sciences are there besides biology? Marisa, could you name some?

Marisa: Sure, there's chemistry and physics.

Teacher: What else?

Blake: There's botany and math?

Teacher: Math . . . math is a little different from the others, isn't it? How is math different from biology, chemistry, physics, and botany? Blake, what would you say?

Blake: You don't do experiments in math.

Teacher: And why not?

Blake: I guess 'cause numbers are different?

Teacher: Yes, studying numbers and other mathematical things is different from studying chemicals or laws in the physical world or living things, and so forth. You might ask your math teacher about why numbers are different or do some reading about that. But let's focus our attention here on what are called the life sciences. Why are biology and botany called life sciences?

Peter: Because they both study living things.

Teacher: How are they different? How is biology different from botany? Jennifer, what do you think?

Jennifer: I don't know.

Teacher: Well, let's all of us look up the words in our dictionaries and see what is said about them.

(Students look up the words.)

Teacher: Jennifer, what did you find for biology?

Jennifer: It says, "The science that deals with the origin, history, physical characteristics, life processes, habits, et cetera, of plants and animals: It includes botany and zoology."

Teacher: So what do we know about the relationship of botany to biology? Rick?

Rick: Botany is just a part of biology.

Teacher: Right, and what can we tell about biology from just looking at its etymology. What does it literally mean? If you break the word into two parts, "bio" and "logy." Blake, what does it tell us?

Blake: The science of life or the study of life.

Teacher: So, do you see how etymology can help us get an insight into the meaning of the word? Do you see how the longer definition spells out the etymological meaning in greater detail? Well, why do you think experiments are so important to biologists and other scientists? Have humans always done experiments, do you think? Marisa.

Marisa: I guess not, not before there was any science.

Teacher: Right, that's an excellent point; science didn't always exist. What did people do before science existed? How did they get their information? How did they form their beliefs? Peter.

Peter: From religion.

Teacher: Yes, religion often shaped a lot of what people thought. Why don't we use religion today to decide, for example, what is true of the origin, history, and physical characteristics of life?

Peter: Some people still do. Some people believe that the Bible explains the origin of life and that the theory of evolution is wrong.

Teacher: What is the theory of evolution, José?

José: I don't know.

Teacher: Well, why don't you we all look up the name Darwin in our dictionaries and see if there is anything about Darwinian theory.

(Students look up the word.)

Teacher: José, read aloud what you have found.

José: It says, "Darwin's theory of evolution holds that all species of plants and animals developed from earlier forms by hereditary transmission of slight variations in successive generations and that the forms which survive are those that are best adapted to the environment."

Teacher: What does that mean to you, in ordinary language? How would you explain that? José.

José: It means the stronger survive and the weaker die?

Teacher: Well, if that's true, why do you think the dinosaurs died out? I thought dinosaurs were very strong.

Shannon: They died because of the ice age, I think.

Teacher: So I guess it's not enough to be strong; you must also fit in with the changes in the environment. Perhaps fitness or adaptability is more important than strength. Well, in any case, why do you think that most people today look to science to provide answers to questions about the origin and nature of life rather than to the Bible or other religious teachings?

Shannon: Nowadays most people believe that science and religion deal with different things and that scientific questions cannot be answered by religion.

Teacher: And by the same token, I suppose, we recognize that religious questions cannot be answered by science. In any case, how were scientists able to convince people to consider their way of finding answers to questions about the nature of life and life processes. Kathleen, you've been quiet for a while, what do you think?

Kathleen: To me, science can be proved. When scientists say something, we can ask for proof and they can show us, and if we want, we can try it out for ourselves.

Teacher: Could you explain that further?

Kathleen: Sure. In my chemistry class we did experiments in which we tested out some of the things that were said in our chemistry books. We could see for ourselves.

Teacher: That's right. Science is based on the notion that when we claim things to be true about the world we should be able to test them to see if, objectively, they are true. Marisa, you have a question?

Marisa: Yes, but don't we all test things? We test our parents and friends. We try out ideas to see if they work.

Teacher: That's true. But is there any difference between the way you and I test our friends and the way a chemist might test a solution to see if it is acidic?

Marisa: Sure. But I'm not sure how to explain it.

Teacher: Blake, what do you think?

Blake: Scientists have laboratories; we don't.

Teacher: They also do precise measurements and use precise instruments, don't they? Why don't we do that with our friends, parents, and children? Adrian, do you have any idea why not?

Adrian: We don't need to measure our friends. We need to find out whether they really care about us.

Teacher: Yes, finding out about caring is a different matter than finding out about acids and bases, or even than finding out about animal behavior. You might say that there are two different kinds of realities in the world, the qualitative and the quantitative, and that science is mostly concerned with the quantitative, while we are often concerned with the qualitative. Could you name some qualitative ideas that all of us are concerned with? Rick, what do you think?

Rick: I don't know what you mean.

Teacher: Well, the word qualitative is connected to the word quality. If I were to ask you to describe your own qualities in comparison to your brother or sister, would you know the sort of thing I was asking you?

Rick: I guess so.

Teacher: Could you, for example, take your father and describe to us some of his best and some of his worst qualities, as you see them?

Rick: I guess so.

(Discussion continues.)

In both cases a variety of follow-up activities and assignments would be necessary to build on the insights fostered in these discussions.

USING COOPERATIVE LEARNING TO FOSTER DIALOGICAL AND DIALECTICAL THINKING

Cooperative learning fosters dialogical and dialectical thinking because individual students will inevitably have different points of view and will need to argue out those differences. The key is students learning to assess their own thinking so that they can make logical choices among the various proposals and suggestions they meet in cooperative learning. For example, we want students in cooperative groups to Socratically question each other in a supportive way. We want them to develop confidence in their capacity to reason together to find insightful answers to important questions. To do this, they must probe each other's ideas for their support and implications. Along the way, they must develop a sensitivity to what they and others are assuming. Most important, if cooperative learning is not to be cooperative mislearning, it is essential that students learn how to bring intellectual standards into their work.

ASSESSING DIALOGICAL AND DIALECTICAL THINKING

Since dialogical and dialectical activities focus on the process rather than the product of thinking, it is essential that both students and teachers learn how to assess thought processes. To do this it is essential that definite standards for thinking be estab-

—Figure 67.2—
The Perfections and Imperfections of Thought

clear	vs. unclear
precise	vs. imprecise
specific	vs. vague
accurate	vs. inaccurate
relevant	vs. irrelevant
consistent	vs. inconsistent
logical	vs. illogical
deep	vs. superficial
complete	vs. incomplete
significant	vs. trivial
adequate	vs. inadequate
fair	vs. biased

lished (for example, see Figure 67.2). Unfortunately, few teachers have had an education that emphasized the universal standards for thought. This deficiency is linked with the fact that the logic of thinking is currently not emphasized in schooling. Teachers must learn—while already in the classroom—how to distinguish and explain the difference between clear and unclear, precise and imprecise, specific and vague, relevant and irrelevant, consistent and inconsistent, logical and illogical, deep and superficial, complete and incomplete, significant and trivial, open-minded and biased, and adequate and inadequate reasoning and expression. Students, in turn, need to recognize their responsibility to express themselves in reasoning that is as clear, precise, specific, accurate, relevant, consistent, logical, deep, complete, and open-minded as possible, irrespective of the subject matter. These are deep and substantial, even revolutionary, understandings. They provide an entirely new perspective on what knowledge and learning are all about.

HOW TO USE DIALOGICAL AND DIALECTICAL THINKING TO MASTER CONTENT

Because students do not come to the classroom with a blank slate for a mind; because their thinking is already developing in some direction; because they have already formed ideas, assumptions, beliefs, and patterns of inference; and because they learn new ideas, assumptions, and beliefs only through the scaffolding of their previously formed thinking, it is essential that dialogical and dialectical thinking form the core of their learning. There is no way around the need of minds to think their way to knowledge. Knowledge is discovered by thinking, analyzed by thinking, interpreted by thinking, organized by thinking, extended by thinking, and assessed by thinking. There is no way to take the thinking out of knowledge, nor is there a way to create a direct step-by-step path to knowledge that all minds can follow. In science classes students should be learning how to think scientifically, in math classes how to think mathematically, in history classes how to think historically, and so forth. It is scientific thinking that produces scientific knowledge, mathematical thinking that produces mathematical knowledge, historical thinking that produces historical knowledge. Dialogical exchange and dialectical clash are integral to acquiring all these forms of knowledge. To this day we have refused to face this reality.

TAKING UP THE CHALLENGE

Dialogical thinking refers to thinking that involves a dialogue or extended exchange between different points of view, cognitive domains, or frames of reference. Whenever we consider concepts or issues deeply, we naturally explore their connections to other ideas and issues within different domains or points of view. Critical thinkers need to be able to engage in fruitful, exploratory dialogue, proposing ideas, probing their roots, considering subject matter insights and evidence, testing ideas, and moving between various points of view. Socratic questioning is one form of dialogical thinking.

Dialectical thinking refers to dialogical thinking conducted in order to test the strengths and weaknesses of opposing points of view. Court trials and debates are dialectical in form and intention. They pit idea against idea, reasoning against counter-reasoning, in order to get at the truth of a matter. As soon as we begin to explore ideas, we find that some clash or are inconsistent with others. If we are to integrate our thinking, we need to assess which of the conflicting ideas we will accept and which reject, or which parts of the views are strong and which weak, or, if neither, how the views can be reconciled. Students need to develop dialectical reasoning skills so that their thinking moves comfortably between divergent points of view or lines of thought, assessing the relative strengths and weaknesses of the evidence or reasoning presented. Dialectical thinking can be practiced whenever two conflicting points of view, arguments, or conclusions are under discussion.

Because at present both teachers and students are largely unpracticed in either dialogical or dialectical thinking, it is important to move instruction in this direction slowly and carefully as part of a reflectively designed, long-term staff development plan, one with a sufficiently rich theoretical base and pedagogical translation to allow for individual teachers to proceed at their own rate. I recommend an approach that focuses on lesson remodeling and redesign, and the Recommended

Readings section of this chapter supplies some resources for this kind of work.

Most teachers need to work with other teachers to carry through needed reforms. They need to work together with much encouragement and many incentives. Very few districts have taken up the challenge. Most have created the mere appearance of change. In most districts, didacticism remains, unchallenged in its arrogance, in its self-deception, in its fruitlessness.

REFERENCE

Mill, J. S. (1947). *On liberty*. Arlington Heights, IL: AHM Publishing.

RECOMMENDED READINGS

Paul, R. W. (1984, September). Critical thinking: Fundamental to education for a free society. *Educational Leadership, 42*(1), 4–14.

Paul, R. W. (1987). Dialogical thinking: Critical thought essential to the acquisition of rational knowledge and passions. In J. Baron & R. Sternberg (Eds.), *Teaching thinking skills: Theory and practice*. New York: W. H. Freeman and Company.

Paul, R. (1990). *Critical thinking: What every person needs to survive in a rapidly changing world*. Rohnert Park, CA: Center for Critical Thinking and Moral Critique, Sonoma State University.

Paul, R. W., Binker, A. J. A., Jensen, K., & Kreklau, H. (1990). *Critical thinking handbook: 4th–6th grades. A guide for remodeling lesson plans in language arts, social studies, and science*. Rohnert Park, CA: Foundation for Critical Thinking, Sonoma State University.

Paul, R. W., Binker, A. J. A., Martin, D., Vetrano, C., & Kreklau, H. (1989). *Critical thinking handbook: 6th–9th grades. A guide for remodeling lesson plans in language arts, social studies, and science*. Rohnert Park, CA: Foundation for Critical Thinking, Sonoma State University.

Paul, R. W., Binker, A. J. A., Martin, D., Vetrano, C., & Kreklau, H. (1989). *Critical thinking handbook: High school. A guide for redesigning instruction*. Rohnert Park, CA: Center for Critical Thinking and Moral Critique, Sonoma State University.

Paul, R. W., Binker, A. J. A., & Weil, D. (1990). *Critical thinking handbook: K–3. A guide for remodeling lesson plans in language arts, social studies, and science*. Rohnert Park, CA: Foundation for Critical Thinking, Sonoma State University.

Scriven, M. (1985, Winter). Critical for survival. *National Forum, 65*(1), 9–12.

Siegel, H. (1980, November). Critical thinking as an educational ideal. *The Educational Forum 45*(1), 7–23.

68

Concept Development

Sydelle Seiger-Ehrenberg

The art of teaching is the art of assisting discovery.
—*Mark Van Doren*

Despite much talk about concept-centered curriculum, too many students still just learn facts. Teachers report, and tests show, that even those students who seem to have learned concepts often fail to apply them to new but similar situations. Let's explore some of the possible reasons.

Different Concepts of "Concept"

One reason may be that educators haven't been sufficiently clear and consistent about what they think a concept is. They haven't distinguished between concepts and other things they want students to learn, such as facts, principles, attitudes, and skills. Fuzziness or lack of common understanding among curriculum developers, teachers, and testers about what a concept is could account for disparity among what is taught, learned, and tested.

Lack of Understanding of Concept Learning/Teaching Processes

Another reason may be the assumption that concepts are learned (and therefore should be taught) in the same way facts are learned. While much attention has been given to differences in individual student learning "styles" (preferences related to *gathering* information), very little has been focused on

the differences in various learning "strategies" (procedures for *processing* information). The processes for learning and teaching concepts differ significantly from those appropriate for fact, principle, attitude, and skill learning. Lack of understanding of those differences on the part of the curriculum developer or the teacher could certainly contribute to students' failure to learn concepts.

Inadequate or Inappropriate Curriculum Materials

Curriculum guides, teachers' manuals, and student materials may not contain enough of the right kind of information. Neither commercial nor locally developed curriculum may be thorough enough in identifying, defining, and relating the concepts students are expected to learn; in outlining appropriate concept-learning processes; or in presenting the kind of information students need in order to form concepts. Too often, the concept is just "presented" (as though it were a fact). Teachers who have to work with an inadequate or inappropriate curriculum may well be misled as to how to help students learn concepts, or, if they know better, be burdened with the task of revising or even developing the curriculum from scratch.

These may not be the only reasons students are not learning concepts as well as we think they should, but since these factors are under our control, they should be addressed and, to the extent possible, eliminated.

Following are some ideas about concept learning and teaching, which, over the past 12 years, many educators have learned and successfully applied. Their success came not from merely reading about or listening to these ideas, but as a result of hard work during and after intensive training in a staff development program called BASICS (Ehrenberg & Ehrenberg, 1978; Project BASICS, 1975). This program and its predecessor, The Hilda Taba Teaching Strategies Program, focus on the thinking strategies students need to learn to achieve each of

This chapter is adapted from *Developing Minds: A Resource Book for Teaching Thinking* (Rev. ed.), 1991. The original chapter was adapted from "Concept Learning: How to Make It Happen in the Classroom," by S. D. Ehrenberg, October 1981, in *Educational Leadership* 38(1), 36–43.

the basic types of learning objectives of any curriculum: concepts, principles, attitudes, and skills (Durkin & Hardy, 1972).

WHAT IS A CONCEPT?

Following are three *examples* of concepts:

1. Any plane, closed figure having just three sides.
2. Any body of land bordered on all sides by water.
3. Any invertebrate having just three body parts and exactly six legs.

First, observe what each statement says. Note the *differences* among them. Then decide what is *true of all three statements*. What is true of all three is what makes all of them examples of "concept."

Now focus on the following three items. None of the three is a concept.

a. ABC is a plane, closed figure having three sides.
b. island.
c. ant.

Consider items "a," "b," and "c" one at a time. Compare and contrast each with the concept examples (#1, #2, and #3) and decide why "a," "b," and "c" are not examples of "a concept." Item "a" states certain facts about figure ABC—its characteristics—but it does not state the characteristics common to any and all examples of that type of figure. Item "b" gives the English label for a type of thing but does not state the set of characteristics common to any and all examples. Item "c"

gives the name of one example of concept #3, insect, but it does not state the characteristics common to any and all examples of insects, distinguishing all insects from any noninsect.

Based on the above, consider the following definitions and examples:

- **Concept**—The set of attributes or characteristics common to any and all instances (people, objects, events, ideas) of a given class (type, kind, category), *or* the characteristics that make certain items examples of a type of thing and that distinguish any and all examples from nonexamples.
- **Concept Label**—One or more *terms* used to refer to any and all examples of a given concept.
- **Examples**—Any and all *individual items* that have the characteristics of a given concept or class.
- **Nonexamples**—Any and all *individual items* that may have some but not all the characteristics that make items examples of a given concept or class.

The concept is the set of characteristics, not the label (see Figure 68.1). A person can know the label for a concept without knowing the characteristics of any and all examples, and vice versa. A concept is not the same as a fact. A fact is verifiable information about an individual item, while a concept is a generalization in a person's mind about what is true of any and all items (even those the person has never seen) that are examples of the same class. A few additional points about concepts:

All concepts are abstract. This is because a concept constitutes a generalized mental image of the characteristics that make items examples. However, the characteristics of individual items may be either concrete (*all* of the characteristics are

—*Figure 68.1*—
Concept Examples

Concept Label	Concept Characteristics	Examples	Nonexamples
Compound Word	Any word whose meaning is a combination of the meaning of the root words of which it is composed.	Nightgown Oversee Doorknob	Carpet Begun Understood
Fruit	The part of any plant that contains the seeds.	Apple Tomato Squash	Potato Celery Carrot
Improper Fraction	Any fraction whose numerator is equal to or greater than its denominator.	$\frac{8}{7}$ $\frac{16}{16}$ $\frac{4}{1}$	$\frac{7}{8}$ $\frac{4}{16}$ $\frac{1}{4}$

perceivable, as in an apple) or represented in some way. A representation may be quite "concrete" (many of the characteristics are perceivable, as in a model, film, or photo) or quite "abstract" (few or none of the characteristics are perceivable, as in a diagram, symbol, or spoken or written description).

A common misconception is that young children cannot conceptualize because they cannot yet form abstract ideas. Actually, young children can and do conceptualize but only when the characteristics of examples of the concepts are perceivable directly through the senses and they have the opportunity to perceive those characteristics firsthand in several individual items. They need these sense perceptions to form the generalized mental picture of the characteristics. (Is it any wonder that young children have so much trouble forming such concepts as "sharing" and "tidiness"?)

Concepts cannot be verified, like facts, as being "right" or "wrong." Although it is difficult for us to realize, our concepts are not what *is* but what we have learned to *think* is. As a cultural group, over time, we decide what things are and what to call them. We store our current sets of characteristics and the concept labels that go with them in the dictionary, and this becomes our authority to arbitrate any dispute. However, we all know how dictionaries differ and that dictionaries need to be updated periodically to keep up with our changing concepts that are newly developed and commonly agreed on.

If you want to test this idea about concepts, see how many different explanations you get when you ask several people whether each of the following is a family and why they think it is or is not:

- A husband and wife with no children.
- Several friends sharing the same home.
- Roommates at college.
- A separated husband and wife each having one of their children.
- A mother and grown daughter living together.

Concepts are hierarchical; that is, some classes include other classes. Living things include plants and animals; animals include vertebrates and invertebrates; vertebrates include mammals, fish, birds, amphibians, and reptiles; and so on. "My dog Spot" is a specific example of every one of the classes in the hierarchy until he separates out into the canine class because some of his characteristics distinguish him from examples of feline, equine, and so forth. Not only that but, by virtue of the unique characteristics that distinguish him from other mongrels in the world, Spot is himself a concept (in a class by himself).

We've already made the distinction between concept and fact. Let's now consider the relationship between concepts and other types of learning: principles, attitudes, and skills.

1. *Fact:* Verifiable information obtained through observing, experiencing, reading, or listening. Evidence of acquisition, comprehension, retention, and retrieval of information is the learner's expression of the specific, accurate, complete, relevant information called for.

2. *Concept:* Mental image of the set of characteristics common to any and all examples of a class. Evidence of conceptualization is the learner's demonstrated ability to consistently distinguish examples from nonexamples by citing the presence or absence of the concept characteristics in individual items.

3. *Principle:* Mental image of the cause-effect process which, under certain conditions, occurs between examples of two or more concepts. Evidence of understanding of the principle is the learner's demonstrated ability to make well-supported and qualified inferences of either cause or effect in new or changed situations.

4. *Attitude:* Mental set toward taking some action based on the desirability of anticipated consequences. Evidence of attitude learning is newly acquired willingness to take (or refrain from) an action based on the learner's concept of what the action is and predictions as to the desirable or undesirable effects of taking (or not taking) the action.

5. *Skill:* Proficiency and speed in performing a mental or physical action or set of procedures. Evidence of skill learning is the learner's performance of the action/procedure at the desired level of proficiency or speed and, where applicable, a product that meets desired standards for quality and/or quantity. This performance is based on the learner's concept of the action, predictions as to the effects of performing one way or another, and internalization of the procedures through repeated practice.

It is important to note (see Figure 68.2) that concept learning is distinctly different from any of the other levels of learning; therefore, the evidence of achievement is different. You can't, for example, appropriately test understanding of a concept by having the learners state facts or perform a skill. Note also that each level is prerequisite to, and an important component of, the next level of learning. This being the case, fact learning is necessary but not sufficient to concept learning, and concept learning is necessary but not sufficient to the learning of principles, attitudes, and skills. (Paradoxically, the learner needs to develop a certain degree of thinking, listening, and reading skill before achieving even the fact-learning level.)

—*Figure 68.2*—
Levels of Learning

1. Fact
2. Concept
3. Principle
4. Attitude
5. Skill

WHAT LEARNING/TEACHING STRATEGIES DEVELOP CONCEPTS?

Fundamental to helping students learn concepts is understanding that conceptualizing has to take place in the mind of the learner. That is, the learner needs to establish a mental image of the set of characteristics that makes something an example of the concept and that distinguishes examples from nonexamples. If the learner has access only to the concept label and a definition (only words), the learner's mental image of the characteristics of examples of the concept may be vague, inaccurate, or nonexistent. Being able to accurately state a definition one has read or heard amounts only to fact-level learning, not conceptualization; the learner is only recalling words.

One who has conceptualized, on the other hand, is able to consistently identify new examples, create new examples, distinguish examples from nonexamples, change nonexamples into examples, and, in every case, is able to explain what they have done by citing the presence or absence of the concept characteristics. The learner can do this because he or she is guided by a clear mental image of the characteristics that should be there.

There are a number of strategies through which the learner can be guided so as to gather the appropriate information, process the information appropriately, and end up with a clear mental image of the concept characteristics.

For example, using an inductive strategy, a teacher might have students record on worksheets information on the physical characteristics and life cycles of ants, grasshoppers, moths, and mantises. When the information has been reported, verified, and recorded on a large wall chart, the teacher might ask questions intended to direct students' attention to differences among the examples and then to characteristics common to all examples. Students would be asked to formulate a statement specifying "what is true of all invertebrates like these."

After giving or asking students for the concept label "insect," the teacher might have students complete another worksheet calling for information about the characteristics of spiders, centipedes, scorpions, and earthworms. The learning sequence would be completed by having students respond to the following questions:

- According to this information, what are some of the characteristics of these invertebrates that make them like insects?
- What is true of the insects that is not true of any of these other insectlike invertebrates?
- Based on what you've said here, finish the statement, "What makes insects different from other insect-like animals is _____ ."
- Identify the animals shown here that you think are insects and the ones you think are not. For each, be ready to tell what about the animal made you decide it was or was not an insect.

Using a deductive (classifying) strategy, a teacher would first present information about characteristics of all examples of the concept (a definition) along with the concept label. For the concept "contraction," for instance, the teacher might ask students to state in their own words what they had read that was true of all contractions. Next, students would be asked to identify and verify the characteristics in each of several examples of the concept. For instance, the teacher might say, "In the sentence, 'The girl's here,' the word 'girl's' is an example of a contraction. Referring to the definition we just discussed, what about 'girl's' in this sentence makes it an example of a contraction?"

Next, students would be asked to note the absence of one or more of the concept characteristics in each of several nonexamples. For example, the teacher might say, "In the sentence, 'The girl's coat is here,' the word 'girl's' is not a contraction. Referring to our definition, what about 'girl's' in this sentence makes it not a contraction?"

Then students would develop generalized personal statements giving characteristics of all examples of the concept and characteristics that distinguish examples from nonexamples. Finally, the teacher might have students identify which underlined words in a group of sentences were contractions and which were not. Students would be expected to explain what made each an example or a nonexample of contractions.

From these examples, you can see there are certain common elements to concept-learning strategies:

1. Students must focus on several examples of the concept.

2. Students must gather and verify information as to the *concept-relevant characteristics* of each individual example and nonexample.

3. Students must note how the examples vary and yet are still examples of the concept.

4. Students must note what is *alike* about all the examples of the concept.

5. Students must generalize that what is alike about all the examples they've examined is also true of all other examples of the concept.

6. Students must note how nonexamples resemble examples, but particularly, how they *differ* from them.

7. Students must generalize about the characteristics that *distinguish* all examples of the concept from any item that might resemble them in some way.

WHAT SHOULD CURRICULUM MATERIALS PROVIDE?

You might find it useful and enlightening to check a number of curriculum guides and text materials to see how they introduce concepts. How often is there nothing more than words, that is, the concept label and a definition? If examples are presented, are the concept characteristics clearly identified in each example, or is it assumed that the reader can and will identify the right ones? Here are five guidelines for developing curriculum materials to promote concept development:

1. Concepts should be clearly identified as concepts (not facts, principles, attitudes, and skills).

2. Concepts should be clearly stated in terms of the set of characteristics by which examples are identified and by which examples can be distinguished from nonexamples.

3. Several good examples and nonexamples should be suggested or provided for use with students.

4. One or more appropriate concept development learning sequences should be outlined for each concept. These should clearly state what the learner needs to do at each step of the sequence and what the teacher might provide, do, or say to guide students through the conceptualizing process.

5. Appropriate concept testing and reinforcing activities should be included, as in our example of having students distinguish contractions from possessives. Each should require students not only to identify new examples but also to cite the presence or absence of the concept characteristics.

None of the foregoing ideas is new. Nor is reading and understanding them all that we need in order to make concept learning a consistent reality in the classroom. To conceptualize these ideas, the reader needs to encounter and deal with a number of examples and nonexamples of their use in the classroom. To develop skill in the use of concept learning/teaching strategies requires not only conceptualization, but also firsthand experience with their results with students; willingness to take the required action to achieve the desired results; and enough practice and application to make the learning and teaching strategies an integral part of both curriculum and instruction.

REFERENCES

Durkin, M., & Hardy, P. (1972). *The Hilda Taba teaching strategies program.* Miami, FL: Institute for Staff Development.

Ehrenberg, S. D., & Ehrenberg, L. M. (1978). *BASICS: Building and applying strategies for intellectual competencies in students. Participant manual A.* Coral Gables, FL: Institute for Curriculum and Instruction.

Project BASICS. (1975). *Final report.* Ann Arbor, MI: Washtenaw Intermediate School District.

69

Teaching for Creative Learning and Problem Solving

Donald J. Treffinger and Scott G. Isaksen

The broad topic of teaching creativity has interested researchers for more than five decades, and interest among educators and business people continues to grow. "Teaching creativity" and "strategies" both lack consensus definitions among researchers and practitioners. Does teaching creativity mean making or enhancing potential where previously little or none existed? Does it mean to free potential to whatever extent it was previously present but unrealized or unexpressed? Is it a kind of thinking or problem solving open to anyone, or something reserved for a few exceptional geniuses? Or might it be none, or all, or any of these?

For us, teaching for creative learning means providing instruction in methods and tools; establishing an environment in which students can learn, practice, and apply those methods and tools; building metacognitive competence; and differentiating instruction to respond appropriately to learner characteristics and styles. In our discussion of strategies for teaching creativity, we mean deliberately planning, choosing, and applying alternative approaches for helping individuals and groups deal successfully with tasks, opportunities, and challenges that call for, or will benefit from, novel and useful responses.

Creativity Research over Five Decades

Treffinger, Sortore, and Cross (1993) identified three general periods in the 20th century relating to teaching creativity. These were *creativity as diverging* (1950s and 1960s), *packages and programs* (1970s and 1980s), and a contemporary *ecological* era. During the first era, creativity came to be synonymous for many people with divergent thinking. Guilford's (1967) concept of divergent production; Torrance's (1962, 1966) fluency, flexibility, originality, and elaboration; and Osborn's (1953) emphasis on deferred judgment and brainstorming influenced the era. Divergent thinking dominated our efforts, leading to many open-ended creativity exercises or creativity training activities for classroom use. Research established that students at many ages could significantly improve their ability to produce many, varied, and original ideas. Despite a great deal of confusion and critique, researchers and educators have found that scores on divergent thinking are relatively good predictors of creative accomplishment.

The activities of the 1960s paved the way for more complex models and programs in the 1970s and 1980s. For example, the Creative Problem Solving (CPS) framework evolved as a five-step model applying both creative and critical thinking (Noller, Parnes, & Biondi, 1976). The Productive Thinking Program (Covington, Crutchfield, Olton, & Davies, 1972) applied programmed instruction principles to creative thinking and problem solving. Torrance's work progressed beyond the four basic creative thinking variables, with new emphasis on the environment or conditions for creative teaching and learning. Numerous other programs appeared for developing creative or productive thinking. The major focus shifted from divergent thinking alone to nurturing more complex skills and processes such as creative and critical thinking, problem solving, and decision making.

Deliberate efforts for teaching creativity have continued to expand and evolve throughout the past decade. Torrance's studies of the complex and nonrational dimensions of creativity and sociodrama, led to the development of the Incubation Model of Teaching (Torrance & Safter, 1990). We no longer view creativity and Creative Problem Solving as processes that we can reduce to a simple set of prescriptive techniques or stages, follow dutifully from beginning to end, and use the same way for every kind of problem in all settings. Today we emphasize a natural, dynamic, and flexible approach to CPS

(Isaksen, Dorval, & Treffinger, 2000; Treffinger, Isaksen, & Dorval, 2000), linking CPS methods and tools to people's needs and tasks, rather than always deploying a single, fixed set of steps or stages. Instructional approaches such as problem-based learning, and contemporary programs such as Destination ImagiNation (see http://www.destinationimagination.org) or Community Problem Solving (a component of the Future Problem Solving Program, http://www.fpsp.org) highlight flexibility in process and engagement in real-life problems and challenges.

Researchers and practitioners generally agree that

- Creativity is complex and multi-faceted.
- Creativity is not a matter of characteristics or traits residing solely within the individual. Rather, creativity arises from the complex and interdependent interactions among each person's characteristics, the operations each is able to perform, the context in which each works, and elements of the tasks or outcomes themselves.
- Creativity and problem solving skills can be taught.

We need no more theses or dissertations on the simple question, "Can we, through some deliberate instructional or training program, enhance performance on some specified measure of creativity?" The answer, unequivocally, is, "If you devise and carry out a reasonable treatment, and choose variables carefully to represent a realistic operational definition of creativity, then, yes, you can enhance subjects' performance significantly." This is hardly mysterious, and certainly no longer controversial. We can enhance students' ability to be productive thinkers and creative problem solvers. Extensive research supporting this assertion has been summarized by Isaksen and DeSchryver (2000) and others.

CURRENT AND EMERGING ISSUES AND STRATEGIES

Teaching creativity also involves a number of current issues and strategic possibilities. Although there is no universally accepted, guaranteed-successful strategic plan for all people or groups, it is possible to identify several important questions and choices that one should consider in developing one's own strategy for teaching creativity. We describe here three major current and emerging issues and strategic choices:

Deciding how best to nurture creativity. What works best, for whom, for what purposes, and under what conditions? The most intriguing challenges regarding teaching creativity deal with how best to nurture creativity, rather than with

whether or not it is possible to do so. Our challenge is to explore new conceptions of thinking skills, new process variables, and, most importantly, to investigate the complex and varied interactions among learner characteristics, process variables, and situational or contextual variables (Isaksen, Puccio, & Treffinger, 1993). We need to understand better how to make creativity instruction more responsive to the learning styles or other unique characteristics of learners and to variables involving the situational context for creativity. The most promising directions in this area must extend considerably beyond the search for prescriptive, "one-size-fits-all" scope-and-sequence lists for specific tools or methods. Research might profitably investigate the extent to which certain tools function as prerequisites for others; that is, how well instruction in basic tools transfers to applications in more complex problem-solving applications. We might also investigate the most significant variables that distinguish "real" problems from contrived or practice problems. Many questions and possibilities concerning the power and impact of computer technology in promoting instruction in creativity will also be important to address in the coming decade.

Distinguishing among simple and complex tools. Is there a generalizable set of tools or strategies to nurture creativity? Too often, discussions about teaching creativity make little or no distinction between the development and application of a specific tool, such as brainstorming, and a more complex and extensive framework for solving problems creatively, such as Creative Problem Solving, in which brainstorming certainly plays an important role, but which includes many other tools as well. We need to make deliberate efforts to describe and distinguish among several possible levels of complexity, from simple tools for generating or focusing options or ideas, to more extensive and sophisticated frameworks for productive thinking.

Exploring a range of strategic choices. If people believed that creativity is a rare, natural genius or gift, the question of teaching creativity might not have been raised in any serious way at all. The challenge might only have been to discover those who "had it," create opportunities for them to use it, and then get out of the way. Building on the assumptions and supporting evidence that we can and should engage in deliberate instruction or training to help people deal with tasks that call for new and useful responses, the strategic choices are more numerous—and more complex. In the first two eras discussed above, the strategic options were often "What creativity tool or activity do you prefer to use?" or "What training package or program appeals to you?"

Today, other more powerful strategies are available. Direct instruction—teaching creativity as a stand-alone set of tools—

—Figure 69.1—
Instructional Model for Teaching Creativity

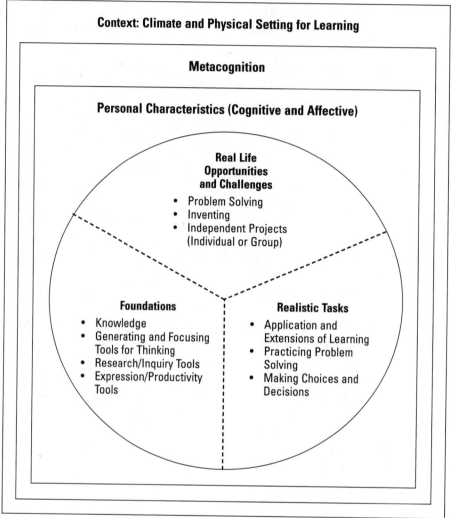

Source: Adapted with permission from *Planning for Productive Thinking and Learning* (p. 27), by D. J. Treffinger & J. F. Feldhausen, 1998, Sarasota, FL: Center for Creative Learning.

is an option that a number of experts support (e.g. deBono, 1983). Those who aim to integrate direct teaching of thinking into content instruction (Beyer, 1988), or use "infusion" approaches (Swartz & Parks, 1994), seek to blend both process and content.

Our strategic approach goes beyond the content curriculum as the context for teaching and learning productive thinking. Isaksen & Parnes (1985) have emphasized the importance of direct instruction, integration, and real-life application. Treffinger and Feldhusen (1998) proposed a systematic model (see Figure 69.1) for instruction. This model's three components are teaching the foundation tools for generating or focusing options (Isaksen, Dorval, & Treffinger, 1998; Treffinger & Nassab, 2000), guiding students in working on realistic tasks, and dealing with real-life problems and challenges. These instructional components are also influenced by the context or environment that supports (or inhibits) productive thinking, the development of metacognitive skills, and responsiveness to student characteristics and style preferences.

Teaching creativity has received considerable effort and attention in research and practice for more than 50 years.

Nonetheless, many unanswered questions remain. Educators have several promising strategic options for teaching creativity. Through continuing research and development, we must enhance and expand our ability to design and deliver effective, appropriate, and challenging opportunities for individuals and groups of all ages and in many content areas or organizational settings. To be powerful in our contemporary world, instruction that seeks to nurture creativity, critical thinking, or problem-solving must extend beyond simple activities, exercises, or packaged programs. We must learn, apply, and teach sophisticated approaches in which we tailor our methods and tools to the tasks we are addressing, including real life challenges; to the people with whom we are working; and to the situations in which our work takes place.

REFERENCES

Beyer, B. K. (1988). *Developing a thinking skills program.* Boston: Allyn and Bacon.

Covington, M. V., Crutchfield, R. S., Olton, R., & Davies, L. (1972). *The productive thinking program.* Columbus, OH: Charles E. Merrill.

deBono, E. (1983). The direct teaching of thinking as a skill. *Phi Delta Kappan, 64*(10), 703–708.

Guilford, J. P. (1967). *The nature of human intelligence.* New York: McGraw-Hill.

Isaksen, S. G., & DeSchryver, L. (2000). Making a difference with CPS: A summary of the evidence. In S. G. Isaksen (Ed.), *Facilitative leadership:*

Making a difference with creative problem solving (pp. 187–249). Dubuque, IA: Kendall/Hunt.

Isaksen, S. G., Dorval, K. B., & Treffinger, D. J. (1998). *Toolbox for creative problem solving.* Williamsville, NY: Creative Problem Solving Group—Buffalo.

Isaksen, S. G., Dorval, K. B., & Treffinger, D. J. (2000). *Creative approaches to problem solving* (2nd ed.). Dubuque, IA: Kendall/Hunt.

Isaksen, S. G., & Parnes, S. J. (1985). Curriculum planning for creative thinking and problem solving. *Journal of Creative Behavior, 19,* 1–29.

Isaksen, S. G., Puccio, G. J., & Treffinger, D. J. (1993). An ecological approach to creativity research: Profiling for creative problem solving. *Journal of Creative Behavior, 27*(3), 149–170.

Noller, R. B., Parnes, S. J., & Biondi, A. M. (1976). *Creative action book.* New York: Scribners.

Osborn, A. F. (1953). *Applied imagination.* New York: Scribners.

Swartz, R. J. & Parks, S. (1994). *Infusing critical and creative thinking into content instruction: A lesson design handbook for the elementary grades.* Pacific Grove, CA: Critical Thinking Press and Software.

Torrance, E. P. (1962). *Guiding creative talent.* Englewood Cliffs, NJ: Prentice-Hall.

Torrance, E. P. (1966). *Torrance tests of creative thinking.* Princeton, NJ: Personnel Press.

Torrance, E. P., & Safter, H. T. (1990). *The incubation model of teaching.* Buffalo, NY: Bearly Limited.

Treffinger, D. J., & Feldhusen, J. F. (1998). *Planning for productive thinking and learning.* Sarasota, FL: Center for Creative Learning.

Treffinger, D. J., Isaksen, S. G., & Dorval, K. B. (2000). *Creative problem solving: An introduction* (3rd ed.). Waco, TX: Prufrock Press.

Treffinger, D. J., & Nassab, C. A. (2000). *Thinking tool lessons.* Waco, TX: Prufrock Press.

Treffinger, D. J., Sortore, M. R., & Cross Jr., J. A. (1993). Programs and strategies for nurturing creativity. In K. A. Heller, F. J. Mönks, & A. H. Passow (Eds.), *International handbook of research and development of giftedness and talent* (pp. 555–567). New York: Pergamon.

70

Thinking for Understanding

David Perkins

How lasers work, the meaning of *Hamlet*, the prospects for peace and war, the worth of a close friendship, or even the properties of fractions, pesky confusing things that they are—these are among the many things worth understanding well. And it's worth adding understanding itself to the list. After all, if we do not understand understanding, at least in a practical operational sense, how can we expect to cultivate this trait so essential to a thoughtful and effective life?

What then is understanding? A good start on this puzzle comes from exploring a remarkably simple set of questions. These questions have been used with elementary school children, practicing teachers, college professors, and other groups, but the answers they inspire prove remarkably consistent. Readers may want to pause and jot down their own responses before reading on.

- What is something that you feel you understand really well? (It could be an academic topic, or a nonacademic topic such as gardening or child rearing.)
- How did you come to understand it?
- How do you know you understand it?

When people respond to these questions, their answers reveal a provocative pattern. As to what people feel they understand, sometimes people mention academic topics but more often they do not. They name areas like playing basketball, sustaining a friendship, coping with a difficult child or parent, dieting, managing an office, or planning a really good picnic. Lamentably, one reason for this nonacademic trend may be that academic experiences do not so often give us the depth of experience that leads us to say, "Here's something I understand really well."

As to how people come to understand something, they usually mention active experiences over time—practicing it, struggling with it, making mistakes and correcting them, watching others and trying to pick up tricks and insights. As to how people know they understand it, a similarly active spirit pervades their responses: "Because I can explain it." "Because I can do it." "Because I can solve problems around it." "Because I can teach it."

WHY UNDERSTANDING FRACTIONS IS LIKE KNOWING HOW TO SKATE

People's responses make an interesting contrast with a view of understanding embedded in our everyday language. We often speak of understanding as a matter of grasping something, apprehending it, "catching on," or "getting it." In other words, an understanding is something possessed, and achieving understanding is a process of quick incorporation, rather like a frog darting out its tongue to swallow a fly.

To be sure, there are moments when understanding something comes quickly and fluently. But this fly-catcher sense of understanding hardly appears at all when people speak of something that they understand really well. Instead, people's answers to the three basic questions can be generalized into a view of understanding that makes a great deal of psychological and philosophical sense. To put it in a single sentence: *Understanding something is a matter of being able to think and act flexibly with what you know and are coming to know.*

Does this formulation really work? Is thinking really so central to understanding? Let's test the idea. Imagine you under-

Copyright © 2001 by David Perkins

stand something like one of Newton's laws or cooking a good pasta. But suppose you could not explain it, nor generalize about it, nor critique it, nor solve problems with it, nor undertake practical activities with it. This would be a strange sort of understanding—in fact, not an understanding at all. Understanding and being able to think and act flexibly go hand in hand, just as people imply through their responses to the three questions. We need to consider understanding not as a possession but as a performance capability, something we are able to do.

All this has a punch line that concerns learning. If understanding is a performance capability, learning for understanding should be more like learning a flexible performance than acquiring bits of knowledge. It's more like learning to skate than learning facts and routines by rote. When you learn to skate, what do you spend most of your time doing? Skating, of course. And, if you learn to skate well, you engage in not just mindless repetition but thoughtful practice, perhaps with the help of a coach, focusing your attention on different challenges at different times, identifying and correcting problems, extending your reach.

Analogously, if you're learning to understand fractions, what should you be spending most of your time doing? Certainly not just doing fractions exercises. You should be thinking about fractions—analyzing them, generalizing about them, putting them to work, making up games using them, trying out alternative fractions notations. You should be thinking with what you know so far, even as you extend your knowledge. That's why understanding fractions is like knowing how to skate.

TfU is not a Sneeze

TfU may sound like a sneeze, but it's not. Instead, if you ran across TfU, it might be in a classroom where the topic of the day is Irish poet William Butler Yeats's poem, "Sailing to Byzantium." As the lesson unfolds, you find it framed in an interesting way. The larger topic is not, say, "Yeats's poetry." Instead it's "the poetry of immortality." Yeats's poem expresses a yearning for immortality through a journey to a mythical Byzantium, where the speaker would take on the form of a gold statue: "such a form as Grecian goldsmiths make / Of hammered gold and gold enameling / To keep a drowsy emperor awake." One might also read and ponder John Keats's "Ode on a Grecian Urn," where art achieves a timeless stasis, and William Shakespeare's sonnet "Shall I compare thee to a Summer's day?" which at the end promises immortality through the poet's immortal words.

Besides this theme, the class has some particular goals, which you might have helped shape through an earlier discus-

sion. These goals ask you and other participants to understand the allure of the immortal and the different ways poets have evoked that allure. The classroom process includes activities for individuals and small groups, followed by discussion. One activity challenges you to find a 20th century poem with much the same theme and compare and contrast it with these more classical treatments. Another asks you to respond personally, saying what kinds of meaning the poems evoke in you. As you proceed, you find yourself receiving a lot of feedback on your work, sometimes from the teacher, sometimes from other students, sometimes simply from yourself.

This is a TfU learning experience. TfU is an acronym for Teaching for Understanding, a pedagogical framework developed over several years at Project Zero of the Harvard Graduate School of Education with support from the Spencer Foundation. As one of the principal investigators on the project, I worked with Howard Gardner, Vito Perrone, and others. The research and practical results appear in a book of linked articles edited by Wiske (1998), a teachers' guide by Blythe (1998), and various articles (Perkins, 1993; Perkins & Blythe, 1994; Perkins & Unger, 1999). Besides developing a framework for TfU, the researchers conducted investigations suggesting that students learning English literature, history, science, and mathematics through TfU attained higher levels of understanding (Unger, Wilson, Jaramillo, & Dempsey, 1998; Hammerness, Jaramillo, Unger, & Wilson, 1998).

The idea of understanding as a performance capability lies at the center of TfU. Around it, we constructed a framework for planning instruction that emphasized four key categories. The framework encourages teachers who aim to teach for understanding to do the following:

- Identify a *generative topic*, something that puts a rich evocative spin on the content that will be the focus of learning; for instance, not so much Yeats's specific poem as the poetry of immortality.
- Articulate *understanding goals*—just what is it about the topic that the teacher wants students to understand, such as the allure of the immortal and how poets have used it.
- Organize the learning around *understanding performances*. This is the "skating part"— what the learners do to think with what they know and are coming to know, demonstrating their understanding and stretching it further. For the Yeats example, this might mean locating contemporary poetry with similar themes and examining the similarities and differences as well as pondering your own responses.
- Provide for *ongoing assessment*, with plenty of feedback early and often around those understanding performances.

By now, teachers at all levels, elementary to university, in various parts of the world have used this framework for extended periods. The flexibility of TfU stems from multiple factors. TfU adapts easily to different subject matters, ages, and levels of difficulty. TfU melds well with other pedagogical ideas, such as problem-based learning, project-based learning, and performance assessment. Finally, TfU allows for a range of individual styles and commitments. For example, it can be used in more-conservative ways in more-conservative settings, and in more break-the-mold ways in less-conservative settings.

GETTING THE THINKING INTO THE LEARNING

TfU hinges on "understanding performances"—activities that ask learners to think with what they know so far and thereby advance their understanding. It's there that the thinking gets into the learning and makes understanding happen. Getting the thinking into the learning may look easy, but it is a surprisingly tricky aspect of TfU.

Suppose, for example, that the theme of the month is ecology, certainly a generative topic. Learners are to come to a broad understanding of a number of aspects of ecology. Pitfalls such as the following commonly appear when teachers fresh to TfU attempt to put the thinking into the learning.

The not-much-thinking pitfall. One student activity might involve groups of students assembling a giant wall chart showing the complex ecology of a pond. This certainly can be an engaging collaborative project. It can produce a useful representation for later lessons. However, it doesn't involve much thinking in itself. The students simply need to follow the instructions to assemble the pieces. Whatever other utility it may have, putting together the wall chart is not an understanding performance.

The off-target-thinking pitfall. Another activity might present students with a crossword puzzle that involves vocabulary from ecology. There is plenty of thinking to be done here if it's a well-designed puzzle: Crossword puzzles can be quite intellectually challenging. The trouble is that the kind of thinking involved has less to do with understanding ecologies and more to do with close reasoning about how the words might intersect. Again, this does not mean that the crossword puzzle is a bad thing to do. It may serve certain purposes. But it is not an understanding performance about ecology. It does not get the right kind of thinking into the learning.

The easy-to-avoid-the-thinking pitfall. How about this then: The teacher asks the students to visit a local pond, identify as many organisms of various sizes as they can, and map the ecology of the pond. This sounds more promising than the

crossword puzzle. It's rather like the wall chart, only now the students have to make up their own chart.

Unfortunately, there is still a problem. In such a task, it's relatively easy for students to avoid the thinking. A group might identify a number of organisms and produce a large diagram showing where they were found, but with nothing about how they relate to one another. The students could well call this a "map of the ecology," only it does not show food webs and similar dependency relationships.

The problem with the mapping activity applies to many other activities that teachers often think of as good understanding performances—write an essay, write a story, produce a diagram, develop a discussion, create a dramatization, and so on. The trouble with all of these can be put in a sentence: They offer ample *opportunity* for understanding performances, but they do not typically *require* extensive thinking. Students can cruise through them, filling the essay, story, diagram, discussion, or dramatization with information about the topic without much real thinking.

What then would a reasonable understanding performance look like for the study of ecology? It's not difficult to extend the mapping activity into a true understanding performance. One might add to the basic charting activity, "Show with arrows the dependency relationships: X eats Y, X lives on Y, and so on; label what they are; and on the chart write down your evidence, either from observations or from the text, for the reality of that dependency relationship." It's very hard to accomplish this more defined activity without some real thinking about ecological relationships. You *have to* think with what you know, including what you can find out from the pond and the books at hand.

MAKING THINKING PORTABLE

TfU well done might seem to teach thinking automatically. There is a limited truth in this. Certainly by thinking about fractions in various ways, students will learn to think about fractions better. By thinking about poetry and the theme of immortality, students will learn to think about that better. By thinking about ecological relationships in the pond, students will learn to think about such relationships better in the lake or river or forest.

The problem is that this more able and insightful thinking probably will not reach beyond fractions, the immorality theme, or ecology for most students. A considerable body of research argues that transfer of learning from one domain to another is quite limited in the absence of specific efforts to promote transfer (e.g. see Perkins, 1995, chapter 9; Salomon & Perkins, 1989; Perkins & Salomon, 1988). Just because students are dealing deeply with dependencies in their analysis of the pond, this does not mean that they will start discerning webs of dependencies in family or political or economic life. A few may, but most of them probably will not. TfU by itself teaches what might be called local thinking but not portable thinking.

Yet it is not difficult to extend TfU to make the thinking more portable. There are two quite different ways to approach this challenge. The most straightforward way is to make an aspect of thinking the generative topic rather than taking a particular area of content as the generative topic. For instance, suppose a teacher chose the generative topic "webs of dependency." Particular understanding goals might include understanding how commonplace and important webs of dependency are, how loops and hierarchies occur within webs of dependency, and related themes. The same pond activity mentioned before might make up part of students' learning experiences, but so would activities that addressed different settings where webs of dependency have importance—family, political, and economic life; systems of the body such as respiratory, circulatory systems; manufacturing and transportation networks; and more. What a teacher can do to teach kinds of thinking such as analyzing webs of dependency she can also do for more general kinds of thinking, such as decision making, and for more specific kinds, such as developing formal proofs in Euclidean geometry.

However, making an aspect of thinking the generative topic is not the only approach. Another is to keep the topic focused on subject matter but get explicit about the thinking moves that are in play. Continuing with the example of ecology, a teacher might not only ask the students to construct their dependency webs but involve them in discussing the idea of dependency webs. The teacher might encourage them to bring in other examples—again, family, politics, economics, transport—not to shift the topic but as brief forays to foster a higher level of reflective abstraction. As the unit on ecology continues, the teacher might take care to return to the idea of dependency webs, deploying it in various contexts. This approach to the teaching of thinking often is called "infusion," meaning that explicit attention to thinking gets infused into the treatment of the subject matter, rather than itself becoming the subject matter (Swartz & Perkins, 1989).

DECLASSIFYING UNDERSTANDING

The scenes of learning for understanding so far have unfolded between the four walls of classrooms. Indeed, we often classify understanding as an academic sort of thing, a matter for classrooms. Yet none of the principles discussed applies exclusively to formal settings of learning. Indeed, they figure virtually everywhere. A few years ago, some colleagues and I were invited to take TfU out of the classroom, to "declassify it," so to speak. We were asked whether we could adapt TfU to organizational learning, working with middle and high-level managers during the day-to-day activities of the organization. We accepted the challenge, and the project that followed revealed much about understanding in the practical context of organizational life (Perkins & Wilson, 1999).

Early in that project, we applied TfU directly to help individuals and small groups understand and improve their circumstances. People undertook inquiry projects. Generative topics were often things like how to enhance communication and camaraderie within an office, how to streamline meetings, or how to advance personal leadership skills. Understanding goals were often things like understanding why communication broke down or meetings sprawled. Performances of understanding were the inquiry processes used to investigate these issues, including experiments that people tried to make things better. Ongoing assessments involved various sources of feedback, from personal observations, to counsel from others, to numbers tallying what a work group had done.

All this worked fairly well. But we discovered along the way that the vocabulary of generative topics, understanding goals, understanding performances, and ongoing assessment, which worked nicely in classrooms, seemed unnatural in the organizational setting and required a great deal of explanation. Responding to this problem, we produced an approximate translation of these four categories into a different language:

- Instead of generative topics, participants spoke of their dreams—for better communications, more efficient meetings, and so on.
- Instead of understanding goals, they spoke of mysteries—what needed to be figured out.
- Instead of understanding performances, they spoke of actions to pursue the dreams and investigate the mysteries.
- Instead of ongoing assessment, they spoke of evidence—the signs formal and informal that would gauge their progress.

Thus, the nomenclature of dreams, mysteries, actions, and evidence came to do the job in the organizational context that generative topics, understanding goals, understanding performances, and ongoing assessment had done in the academic context. The organizational approach used the same principles—thinking, with what you know still at the center—but different packaging.

Besides involving participating managers in inquiry projects, we also found that TfU provided a useful way to introduce particular understandings important to their roles. These included ways to understand and accomplish effective feedback, conflict resolution, and related matters. One useful understanding concerned what we called the Bermuda Triangle of leadership. People in leadership positions commonly find themselves in the midst of a three-way dilemma between person, process, and product. They could attend to and support the motivation and development of the person, debug the process underway, or move to ensure that a sound product emerged as quickly as possible, perhaps by assigning the task to another person altogether. All too often, leader figures fail to notice the Bermuda Triangle and take a precipitous and unwise action. Understanding the natural tensions and tradeoffs among person, process, and product is part of the art and craft of management. TfU provided a way to introduce this and other important understandings in a context of action.

What can be said of organizational learning can be said of any context—developing athletic abilities, running a small business, writing a book, planning a vacation, purchasing a used car. The world presents us with challenges of understanding and action. We need to understand to act well, and through those actions, if they are thoughtfully considered, we advance our understanding. Life lived as it should be is one big understanding performance. Understanding and basic principles of learning for understanding through thinking are not just for blackboards and desks. We need to declassify them and put them to work anywhere people do anything worth doing.

REFERENCES

Blythe, T. (1998). *The teaching for understanding guide.* San Francisco: Jossey-Bass.

Hammerness, K., Jaramillo, R., Unger, C., & Wilson, D. (1998). What do students in teaching for understanding classrooms understand? In Wiske, M. S. (Ed.), *Teaching for understanding: Linking research with practice* (pp. 233–265). San Francisco, CA: Jossey-Bass.

Perkins, D. N. (1993). An apple for education: Teaching and learning for understanding. *American Educator, 17*(3), 8, 28–35.

Perkins, D. N. (1995). *Outsmarting IQ: The emerging science of learnable intelligence.* NY: The Free Press.

Perkins, D. N., & Blythe, T. (1994). Putting understanding up front. *Educational Leadership, 51*(5), 4–7.

Perkins, D. N., & Salomon, G. (1988). Teaching for transfer. *Educational Leadership, 46*(1), 22–32.

Perkins, D. N., & Unger, C. (1999). Teaching and learning for understanding. In C. Reigeluth (Ed.), *Instructional design theories and models: Vol. 2* (pp. 91–114). Hillsdale, NJ: Erlbaum.

Perkins, D. N., & Wilson, D. (1999). Bridging the idea action gap. *Knowledge Directions,* the Journal of the Institute for Knowledge Management, *1,* 65–77.

Salomon, G., & Perkins, D. N. (1989). Rocky roads to transfer: Rethinking mechanisms of a neglected phenomenon. *Educational Psychologist, 24*(2), 113–142.

Swartz, R. J., & Perkins, D. N. (1989). *Teaching thinking: Issues and approaches.* Pacific Grove, CA: Midwest Publications.

Unger, C., Wilson, D., Jaramillo, R., & Dempsey, R. (1998). What do students think about understanding? In Wiske, M. S. (Ed.), *Teaching for understanding: Linking research with practice* (pp. 266–292). San Francisco, CA: Jossey-Bass.

Wiske, M. S. (Ed.). (1998). *Teaching for understanding: Linking research with practice.* San Francisco, CA: Jossey-Bass.

71

Teaching Problem Solving as a Way of Life

Robert J. Sternberg

Problem-solving skills are among the most valuable kinds of skills students can acquire. In teaching students how to problem-solve, teachers should prepare them to integrate problem-solving skills into their lives, rather than leaving students with the notion that these are special skills they should apply only in special instances. Teaching of problem solving should encompass all three of the types of problems individuals encounter in their lives: analytical, creative, and practical (Sternberg, 1997a, 1997b).

Analytical problem solving requires students to analyze, evaluate, compare and contrast, judge, and critique. In this type of problem, one might evaluate the validity of a theory, compare and contrast the personalities of two literary characters, critique a work of art, or analyze a mathematical proof. This is the kind of problem solving most frequently encountered in school settings.

Creative problem solving requires students to create, invent, discover, imagine, and suppose. Students might design an experiment to test a theory, invent something, create a work of art, imagine that a novel ended in a different way, or suppose that temperatures continue their steady rise and then consider the consequences. Students need to face this kind of problem solving more often in school because it is so important to success in a rapidly changing and often unpredictable world.

Practical problem solving requires students to use, apply, put into practice, and implement. Students might think about the implications of a scientific phenomenon such as gravity for their daily lives, use a lesson learned from a novel to solve a problem they have, or show how to apply a lesson of past international conflicts to a current international conflict. Unless we give students practical problems to solve, they may never learn how to take what they learn in school and apply it to their lives.

PROBLEM-SOLVING PROCESSES

I have found it useful to distinguish among three kinds of problem-solving processes (Sternberg, 1985; Sternberg & Spear-Swerling, 1996; Sternberg & Grigorenko, 2000) for solving the three types of problems. Other theorists make similar distinctions, although they may use other names for the same or similar processes. One may use these processes in solving all three types of problems; what differs in the three cases is the context to which they are applied. I apply the processes described here to a typical task in school: studying for an examination.

METACOMPONENTS: THE PROBLEM-SOLVING CYCLE

Metacomponents are higher order or executive processes used to plan, monitor, and evaluate one's problem solving. Taken together, the processes form a problem-solving cycle. In other words, the solution to or end of one problem typically represents the origin or beginning of the next problem. For example, solving the problem of loneliness by finding a companion may end the loneliness but may begin a set of problems associated with getting along with the new companion.

The processes listed here follow the sequence in which one might typically use them, but applying these steps in a flexible order maximizes their effectiveness in problem solving.

Recognizing the existence of a problem is a prerequisite for problem solving, because one cannot solve a problem one does not know one has. The student needs to recognize that an examination will take place, that studying for it is best done systematically, and that finding the optimal system is not a trivial matter, but rather represents a problem he or she must solve.

Defining the nature of a problem is also a prerequisite for problem solving, because it determines exactly what problem needs solving. The student may define the problem in different ways, such as "studying for an exam," "studying for a multiple-choice exam," or "studying for a multiple-choice exam that is a major part of the final grade." A more focused definition of the problem, such as the last example, helps in the more precise formulation of how to solve the problem. An incorrect definition of the problem (e.g., studying the big ideas that might help one on an essay exam but that prove to be irrelevant on a fact-based multiple-choice exam) can result in wasted time in problem solving and a suboptimal solution to the actual problem.

Allocating resources to problem solving is the step in the process in which one decides what resources are needed to solve a problem, and how much of each. One of the most important resources, of course, is time—for example, the amount of time that the student should devote to studying. Other resources include amount of concentration, type and extent of materials needed for studying, and funds. For a really important examination, the student may wish to buy special books or pay for a special cram course.

Representing information about the problem is particularly important because of the principle of encoding specificity (Tulving & Thomson, 1973). How the student encodes information at the time of study will determine how he or she will be able to retrieve it at test time. If a student encodes the information in a suboptimal way, he or she may not be able to access the information for the test, even though it is stored in long-term memory. Various tools students might use include a mind map (schematic representation of information), outline, detailed notes, or flash cards.

Formulating a strategy for problem solution involves deciding on an ordered series of steps for solving the problem. For example, the student might first want to study class notes and then a textbook, or vice versa, or study the class notes and the textbook in alternation. Another strategic decision is spacing: Should the student space studying over intervals or cram it into a small number of intensive sessions?

Monitoring problem solving involves taking care to make sure that the chosen strategy is actually leading toward a solution to the problem at hand. For example, the student may wish to self-test at regular intervals to see whether he or she is learning the material adequately. If not, the student then can devise an alternative strategy for learning the information.

Evaluating the problem solution is the final step in the process, the place to assess whether the solution was adequate. In the case of studying for an exam, the evaluation may well be the exam. Smart problem solvers build in their own prior evaluation in order to ensure that they have successfully achieved their goals. Thus, they will proofread their own term papers, or

test themselves after they have studied or otherwise completed their tasks.

In sum, people use a problem-solving cycle to solve problems. The order of processes is flexible. Problem solving is defective to the extent that one or more of these processes is omitted. Usually, the solution to one problem becomes the basis for the next problem, hence creating the cyclical nature of the problem-solving processes.

KNOWLEDGE-ACQUISITION COMPONENTS

Knowledge-acquisition components are processes used in learning. They make explicit the fact that learning is itself a form of problem solving. In a typical course, for example, no student could possibly learn or choose to study with the greatest of care everything the course covers. Students need to be selective in deciding what material is worth learning and how they will go about learning it.

Selective encoding is a process problem solvers use to determine what material is relevant for problem solving in the first place. In studying for an examination, for example, the student needs to decide which information is important (e.g., she might opt to focus on what the teacher emphasized, thinking it is likely to appear on the exam).

Selective comparison is a process used to determine what information one already knows from the past that is likely to be useful in the present. The student almost always has at least some relevant prior information. In this process, he determines what that prior information is. For example, he may know some of the material from a prior course and hence need to study it less intensively than material that is wholly new.

Selective combination involves combining and synthesizing all the relevant old and new information in a way that makes sense in terms of the problem the student wants to solve. In this step, the student forms a new integrated knowledge base that takes into account learning from prior courses with learning from the present course. Without this step, knowledge remains encapsulated and is usually largely inaccessible.

Performance components are lower-order processes of problem solving used in the actual execution of the strategy for solving a problem. The number of such components is extremely large (Sternberg, 1985). Listed here are a few of the components used frequently in solving problems:

• Inference—What is the relation between two pieces of information?

• Mapping—What is the relation between two relations?

• Application—How can one piece of information be applied in a new situation such that its use is parallel to the way it has been used before?

• Justification—When multiple responses to a problem exist and none appear to be quite "right," which one is nevertheless the best or the closest to the ideal?

How can the instructor ideally teach these processes involved in the various types of problem solving?

APPROACHES TO THE TEACHING OF PROBLEM SOLVING

We can characterize the approaches to teaching problem solving along three different dimensions: infused versus separate teaching of problem solving, domain-specific versus domain-general strategies, and implicit versus explicit teaching and learning.

INFUSED VERSUS SEPARATE TEACHING OF PROBLEM SOLVING

The instructor may infuse the teaching of thinking into a pre-existing curriculum or teach it as a separate course. In the first case, teaching of problem solving is an active part of an existing curriculum and may actually be incorporated into a textbook, teacher's manual, or student guide (Sternberg, 1998; Williams et al., 1996). The advantages of this approach are that (a) students learn that problem solving is an integral part of, rather than distinct from, their regular course work; (b) students see how to apply what they learn about problem solving directly to the course content they are learning; and (c) the school does not have to schedule a separate course into a curriculum that usually is already well-packed with material.

The disadvantages of this method are that (a) the students may not be able to see what the skills are, in order to separate them from other course content being taught; (b) sometimes the teaching of the problem-solving skills gets crowded out by other aspects of the course, such as the need to learn content material; and (c) the students may learn how to apply the problem-solving skills in particular content areas or subareas, but may not see how to generalize these skills beyond the contexts in which they learned the skills. The advantages and disadvantages of a separate course (Bransford & Stein, 1993; Feuerstein, 1980; Sternberg & Grigorenko, 2000) are complementary to those of an infused course.

DOMAIN-SPECIFIC VERSUS DOMAIN-GENERAL STRATEGIES

A second dimension is whether to teach problem solving in a way that is domain-specific or domain-general. Some methods of problem solving apply only within a given domain. For example, strategies of reading problematical X-rays, playing chess, or solving knowledge-rich physics problems apply primarily or exclusively to these domains. These methods are sometimes called "strong" because they are powerful, if limited. Other techniques are domain-general and can be taught in any subject-matter area. For example, the method of means-ends analysis applies in any domain. In this method, the student considers where she is in solving a problem, considers where she needs to get to, and takes the path that minimizes the distance she must traverse to get there. This method only works, of course, if the student knows what the final solution is but does not know quite how to get there. The advantage of using techniques based on knowledge-rich problems in specific domains is that the techniques are stronger and more likely to lead to an optimal solution. The disadvantage is that the techniques apply to only a limited range of problems.

IMPLICIT VERSUS EXPLICIT TEACHING AND LEARNING

Most problem-solving skills are taught and learned implicitly. A teacher may make no mention that he is teaching problem-solving skills, so that students are not aware they are learning how to solve problems. Rather, they pick up the skills by using them. Or the teacher may teach some skills explicitly. In this case, he deliberately teaches problem-solving skills, making students aware of this fact and expecting them to learn these skills. The advantage to implicit learning is that students are learning the strategies as part of their content learning rather than as something separate that they may or may not call upon when needed. The disadvantage is that students may not actually extract the strategy or be able later to use it. The advantages and disadvantages of explicit learning are complementary to these.

Fortunately, the contrasts presented here do not represent mutually exclusive options. By combining methods of instruction and learning (e.g., teaching problem-solving skills both in an infused and in a separate manner), it is possible to maximize the advantages and minimize the disadvantages of both approaches in the teaching of problem-solving processes.

A FOUR-PRONG MODEL FOR TEACHING PROBLEM SOLVING

Regardless of how one decides to teach problem solving, it helps to have a model for teaching it. We have found the following four-prong model particularly effective. This model derives from the Vygotskian notion (Vygotsky, 1978) that learning occurs best when it first occurs in a social setting and later is internalized (Sternberg & Davidson, 1989):

1. *Familiarization.* In this step, students become familiar with the problem-solving processes that the teacher is presenting. This step occurs through five sequential substeps:

a. Presentation and interactive solution in real-world problems. The teacher presents one or two real-world problems for discussion that require students to use the particular step or steps they are learning.

b. Labeling of processes and strategies. Once students have solved the problems, the teacher points out how they used the particular process, identifies the process, and labels it.

c. Application of labeled processes to initial problems. The teacher asks students to show explicitly how they used the new process or processes in solving the initial problems.

d. Application of labeled processes to new problems. The teacher gives students a few new problems and asks them to explicitly apply the processes they have learned to the new problem.

e. Student generation of new problems. Students generate their own problems using the process or processes they are learning.

2. *Intragroup problem solving.* Students work together in small groups to solve given problems and to generate their own problems for solving, using the new processes they have learned.

3. *Intergroup problem solving.* The small groups evaluate and constructively critique the other groups' work.

4. *Individual problem solving.* Students work individually on using the new processes in the solution of given and new problems.

In sum, the four-prong model provides an effective way of teaching for thinking. It combines individual with group learning, and enables students to capitalize on strengths and, at the same time, to correct or compensate for weaknesses.

Teaching problem solving raises a number of challenging issues for exploration by teachers and students. The benefit is that long after the students apply the skills to content that has ceased to be relevant to their lives, the problem-solving skills they have learned will continue to be relevant. If problem solving is taught well, students will not view these as special skills to take out of a dusty closet for special purposes, but rather as skills to hone and use on a daily basis.[1]

NOTES

[1]Preparation of this chapter was supported under the Javits Act Program (Grant No. R206R000001) as administered by the Office of Educational Research and Improvement, U. S. Department of Education. Grantees undertaking such projects are encouraged to express freely their professional judgment. This chapter, therefore, does not necessarily represent the position or policies of the Office of Educational Research and Improvement or the U. S. Department of Education, and no official endorsement should be inferred.

REFERENCES

Bransford, J. D., & Stein, B. S. (1993). *The ideal problem solver: A guide for improving thinking, learning, and creativity* (2nd ed). New York: W. H. Freeman and Co.

Feuerstein, R. (1980). *Instrumental enrichment: An intervention program for cognitive modifiability.* Baltimore, MD: University Park Press.

Sternberg, R. J. (1985). *Beyond IQ: A triarchic theory of human intelligence.* New York: Cambridge University Press.

Sternberg, R. J. (1997a). *Successful intelligence.* New York: Plume.

Sternberg, R. J. (1997b). *Thinking styles.* New York: Oxford University Press.

Sternberg, R. J. (1998). Applying the triarchic theory of human intelligence in the classroom. In R. J. Sternberg & W. M. Williams (Eds.), *Intelligence, instruction, and assessment* (pp. 1–15). Mahwah, NJ: Lawrence Erlbaum Associates.

Sternberg, R. J., & Davidson, J. E. (1989). A four-prong model for intellectual skills development. *Journal of Research and Development in Education, 22,* 22–28.

Sternberg, R. J., & Grigorenko, E. L. (2000). *Teaching for successful intelligence.* Arlington Heights, IL: Skylight.

Sternberg, R. J., & Spear-Swerling, L. (1996). *Teaching for thinking.* Washington, DC: American Psychological Association.

Tulving, E., & Thomson, D. M. (1973). Encoding specificity and retrieval processes in episodic memory. *Psychological Review, 80,* 352–373.

Vygotsky, L. S. (1978). *Mind in society: The development of higher psychological processes.* Cambridge, MA: Harvard University Press.

Williams, W. M., Blythe, T., White, N., Li, J., Sternberg, R. J., & Gardner, H. I. (1996). *Practical intelligence for school: A handbook for teachers of grades 5–8.* New York: HarperCollins.

72

Cooperation and Conflict: Effects on Cognition and Metacognition

David W. Johnson and Roger T. Johnson

Individuals who engage in higher-level cognitive reasoning and critical thinking, and in metacognitive reasoning (knowing what reasoning strategies they are using and how to modify them in order to improve performance and effectiveness), often outperform those who do not. While the value of higher-level cognitive and metacognitive reasoning in most situations is undisputed, there is less agreement about the conditions under which one might best develop them. We believe that two of the conditions necessary for higher-level cognitive and metacognitive reasoning are a cooperative context and intellectual conflict.

Cooperation, constructive controversy, cognition, and metacognition are all intimately related. Cooperative learning provides the context within which cognition and metacognition best take place. Once a teacher establishes the cooperative context, primarily through the use of cooperative learning, the intellectual challenge resulting from conflict among ideas and conclusions (i.e., controversy) creates perhaps the most effective instructional situation for promoting critical thinking, higher-level reasoning, and metacognitive thought.

Definitions

What Is Cooperative Learning?

Cooperative learning is the instructional use of small groups so that students work together to maximize their own and each other's learning (Johnson, Johnson, & Holubec, 1998). In order to be productive, cooperative efforts must be structured to include the essential elements of positive interdependence (each member can succeed only if all members succeed), individual accountability (all members must do their fair share of the work), promotive interaction (members encourage and assist each other's efforts to achieve), appropriate use of interpersonal and small group skills (such as leadership, communication, decision making, trust building, and conflict resolution skills), and group processing (groups must reflect on how well they are working together and how they might improve their effectiveness as a group). Cooperative learning contrasts with competitive learning, where students work against each other to achieve a goal that only one or a few students can attain, and with individualistic learning, where students work by themselves to accomplish learning goals unrelated to those of the other students. In both competitive and individualistic learning situations, the interpersonal exchange so necessary to cognition and metacognition tends not to take place.

What Is Constructive Controversy?

Constructive controversy exists when one person's ideas, knowledge, conclusions, theories, and opinions are incompatible with those of another and the two seek to reach an agreement (Johnson & Johnson, 1995). They can resolve controversies by engaging in what Aristotle called deliberate discourse (the discussion of the advantages and disadvantages of proposed actions) aimed at synthesizing novel solutions; that is, creative problem solving. Structured academic controversies differ from individualistic learning (students can work independently with their own set of materials at their own pace), debate (students present different positions, and a judge determines who presented best), and concurrence seeking (students can inhibit discussion to avoid any disagreement and compromise quickly to reach a consensus). In a constructive controversy, the teacher guides students through the steps of (a) researching and preparing a position, (b) presenting and advocating their position, (c) engaging in an open discussion in which they refute the opposing position and rebut attacks on their own position, (d) reversing perspectives to be able to see the issue from all points of view, and (d) synthesizing and integrating the best evidence and reasoning into a joint position that everyone can commit themselves to implementing.

COOPERATION'S IMPACT ON COGNITION AND METACOGNITION

Working cooperatively can have profound effects on students (Johnson & Johnson, 1989). During the past century, researchers have conducted over 900 studies that indicate that cooperative learning experiences promote higher achievement than do competitive and individualistic learning. In addition to aiding students' mastery and retention of material, cooperative efforts can improve achievement in the use of reasoning strategies used to complete the assignment, the generation of new ideas and solutions (process gain), and the transfer of what they learn in one situation to another situation (group-to-individual transfer). Cooperative learning is superior to competitive and individualistic learning in situations where the task is more conceptual, more problem solving is required, higher-lever reasoning and critical thinking are desirable, more creative answers are needed, more long-term retention is desired, and the application of what is learned is greater.

Many of the studies relating cooperative learning experiences and achievement have focused on quality of reasoning strategy, level of cognitive reasoning, and metacognitive strategies (Johnson & Johnson, 1989). In studies where students could solve tasks using either higher- or lower-level reasoning strategies, a more frequent discovery and use of higher-level reasoning strategies occurred within the cooperative than within competitive or individualistic learning situations. In a categorization and retrieval task, for example, 1st grade students were instructed to memorize 12 nouns during the instructional session and then to complete several retrieval tasks during the testing session the following day. The nouns were given in random order and students were told to (1) order the nouns in a way that makes sense and aids memorization and (2) memorize the words. Three of the words were fruits, three were animals, three were clothing, and three were toys. Eight of the nine cooperative groups discovered and used all four categories, and only one student in the competitive and individualistic conditions did so. Even the highest-achieving students failed to use the category search strategy in the competitive and individualistic conditions. Studies on both Piaget's cognitive development and Kohlberg's moral development theories have indicated that cooperative learning promotes the transition to higher-level cognitive and moral reasoning more frequently than competitive or individualistic experiences. The research confirms their theories (Johnson & Johnson, 1989).

WHY COOPERATION AFFECTS COGNITION AND METACOGNITION

Cooperative learning promotes higher-level cognitive and metacognitive reasoning for a number of reasons. First, the expectation that one will have to summarize, explain, and teach what one is learning impacts the strategies used. The way students conceptualize material and organize it cognitively is different when they are learning material to teach to others than when they are learning material for their own benefit (Murray, 1983). When learning material that they will teach to collaborators, students use higher-level strategies more frequently than when they learn the material for their own use.

Second, the discussion within cooperative learning situations promotes more frequent oral summarizing, explaining, and elaborating of what one knows (Johnson & Johnson, 1989). These processes are necessary for the storage of information into the memory (through further encoding and networking) and the long-term retention of the information. Such oral rehearsal provides a review that seems to consolidate and strengthen what students know and to provide relevant feedback about the degree to which they have achieved mastery and understanding. In one of the earliest studies on this subject, Johnson (1971b) found that a person's understanding of and level of reasoning about an issue were enhanced by the combination of explaining one's knowledge, and summarizing and paraphrasing the other person's knowledge and perspective. Subsequently, vocalizing what they learned was more strongly related to achievement than was listening to other group members vocalize (Johnson, Johnson, Roy, & Zaidman, 1985). Summarizing the main concepts and principles students were learning increased achievement and retention (Yager, Johnson, and Johnson, 1985). Both explaining relevant information and disagreeing with another group member were positively related to individual achievement (Vasquez, Johnson, & Johnson, 1993). These and other studies support the conclusion that one formulates meaning through the process of conveying it. It is while students are orally summarizing, explaining, and elaborating that they cognitively organize and systematize the concepts and information they are discussing.

Third, heterogeneity among group members nourishes cooperative learning groups. As students accommodate themselves to each other's different perspectives, strategies, and approaches to completing assignments, divergent thinking and creative thinking is stimulated. The exchange of ideas and perspectives among students from various achievement levels, physical abilities, genders, and cultural and ethnic backgrounds enriches learning experiences.

Fourth, in most cooperative learning situations students with incomplete information interact with others who have different perspectives and facts. Cooperative experiences have been found to promote greater perspective-taking ability than did competitive or individualistic experiences, and perspective taking resulted in better understanding and retention of others' information, reasoning, and perspectives (Johnson, 1971a; Johnson & Johnson, 1989). This evidence indicates that having information available does not ensure that someone will use it. Utilization depends on students' ability to understand others' perspectives.

Fifth, the members of cooperative learning groups externalize their ideas and reasoning for critical examination. As a result, considerable peer monitoring and regulation of one's thinking and reasoning tend to occur. Group-mates stimulate and focus the exploration of ideas. In comparison, individuals working by themselves more frequently get lost in lengthy and aimless wild goose chases. Individuals generally have difficulty monitoring their own cognitive activity. Within a cooperative group, however, each member can monitor the reasoning of other members and help enhance their understanding of the issue or material. In essence, the cooperative experience serves as a training ground for metacognitive skills to develop that are transferable to individual learning.

Sixth, group members may give each other feedback concerning the quality and relevance of contributions and how to improve one's reasoning or performance. Typically, group members give personalized process feedback (as opposed to terminal feedback) as part of the ongoing interaction. In cooperative learning groups, fellow group members give feedback, which they discuss face-to-face in ways that make clear its personal implications.

Finally, involved participation in cooperative learning groups inevitably produces controversy—conflicts among the ideas, opinions, conclusions, theories, and information of members (Johnson & Johnson, 1995). This intellectual conflict promotes higher-level reasoning and metacognitive activity.

CONTROVERSY'S IMPACT ON COGNITION AND METACOGNITION

Engaging in constructive controversy profoundly affects students' cognitive and metacognitive reasoning (Johnson & Johnson, 1989, 1995). During the past 30 years, researchers have conducted more than 40 studies that indicate constructive controversy produced higher achievement and retention than did concurrence seeking, debate, and individualistic learning. Controversy tends to result in higher-quality decisions and solutions to complex problems for which students can plausibly develop different viewpoints, even when one or both sides presents erroneous information.

Participants in academic controversies use more complex and higher-level reasoning strategies, recall more correct information, are better able to transfer learning to new situations, and are better able to generalize the principles they learned to a wider variety of situations. Controversy increases the exchange of expertise; the number, quality, and range of ideas; the use of more varied strategies; the ability to develop syntheses combining diverse perspectives; the quality and quantity of creative insights; and the number of imaginative and novel solutions. Controversy results in greater task involvement (the quality and quantity of the physical and psychological energy that individuals invest in their efforts to achieve), greater emotional involvement in and commitment to solving the problem, more feelings of stimulation and enjoyment, and more positive attitudes toward the task and the experience. Cognitive development theorists have posited that repeated interpersonal controversies, where individuals are forced again and again to recognize the perspectives of others, promote (a) cognitive and moral development, (b) the ability to think logically, and (c) the reduction of egocentric reasoning.

Finally, controversy promotes greater liking and social support among participants than does debate, concurrence-seeking, no controversy, or individualistic efforts. Controversy tends to result in higher academic self-esteem and greater perspective-taking accuracy. Controversy relies on "argumentative clash" to develop, clarify, expand, and elaborate one's thinking about the issues being considered.

WHY CONTROVERSY AFFECTS COGNITION AND METACOGNITION

Constructive controversy results in higher-level cognitive and metacognitive reasoning when participants use a four-step process (Johnson & Johnson, 1995). This process involves reaching a conclusion about the issue, becoming uncertain about the correctness of one's views (called epistemic curiosity) when challenged by a person representing an opposing position, actively searching for more information and reconceptualizing one's knowledge in an attempt to resolve the uncertainty, and reaching a new and refined conclusion. This process can be used as many times as needed.

Higher-level and metacognitive reasoning are required at each stage of the controversy procedure. They are used in researching, conceptualizing, organizing, and planning how to advocate persuasively a position. In presenting a persuasive case for their positions to opponents, participants orally summarize, explain, and elaborate their information, ideas, and conclusions (this facilitates encoding, networking, and long-term retention of the information) and reorganize the concepts and information they are discussing. Participants externalize their reasoning for critical examination and monitoring by peers. On a metacognitive level, they also critically evaluate how persuasive their presentations will seem from the opposing frames of reference. They present their arguments (e.g., thesis statement, rationale, conclusion) and conceptualize the information in various ways such as charts, graphs, maps, cartoons, songs, chants, dances, physical movement, or role playing. Furthermore, being exposed to a counter position reduces the need to conform to the majority opinion and stimulates divergent thinking.

In critically analyzing and refuting an opposing position, at the same time rebutting the opponent's attacks on their information and reasoning, participants monitor others' reasoning and help enhance others' understanding of the issue or material. The process of refutation and rebuttal stimulates divergent and creative thinking. Group members give personalized process feedback throughout.

The constructive controversy procedures require participants to reverse perspectives and see the issue from all sides. In order to understand all the relevant information and the variety of perspectives, students must (a) actively attempt to understand both the content of the information being presented and the cognitive and affective perspectives of the person presenting the information, and (b) be able to hold both their own and other people's perspectives in mind at the same time. Doing so is an essential ingredient for cognitive and moral growth.

The final step of the constructive controversy procedure is to seek a synthesis that incorporates the best reasoning from all sides. Synthesizing involves seeing new patterns within a body of evidence and arriving at the best possible solution in order to find a position to which all participants can commit themselves. Synthesizing requires creativity. To create is to cause something new to exist (Johnson & Johnson, 1995). Students arrive at a synthesis by using higher-level thinking and reasoning processes, critically analyzing information, and using both deductive and inductive reasoning. Synthesis requires that students keep conclusions tentative, accurately understand opposing perspectives, incorporate new information into their conceptual frameworks, and change their attitudes and positions.

Finally, participants discuss how well they followed the controversy procedure and give each other feedback concerning the quality of their reasoning or performance.

Cooperative learning groups promote the use of higher-level thinking strategies, higher-level reasoning, and metacognitive strategies. In such an environment, intellectual conflict often emerges, especially if teachers deliberately structure the controversies. To promote higher-level reasoning, critical thinking, and metacognitive skills, teachers are well-advised to first establish cooperative learning and then structure academic controversies.

REFERENCES

Johnson, D. W. (1971a). Role reversal: A summary and review of the research. *International Journal of Group Tensions, 1*, 318–334.

Johnson, D. W. (1971b). Effectiveness of role reversal: Actor or listener. *Psychological Reports, 28*, 275–282.

Johnson, D. W., & Johnson, F. (2000). *Joining together: Group theory and group skills* (7th ed.). Boston: Allyn & Bacon.

Johnson, D. W., & Johnson, R. (1989). *Cooperation and competition: Theory and research*. Edina, MN: Interaction Book Company.

Johnson, D. W., & Johnson, R. (1995). *Creative controversy: Intellectual challenge in the classroom* (3rd ed.). Edina, MN: Interaction Book Company.

Johnson, D. W., Johnson, R., & Holubec, E. (1998). *Cooperation in the classroom* (6th ed.). Edina, MN: Interaction Book Company.

Johnson, D. W., Johnson, R., & GATE Coordinators. (1999). *GATEway to learning: A teachers resource to learning cooperatively*. Boca Raton, FL: Florida Atlantic University's Genesis Academy for Teaching Excellence.

Johnson, D. W., Johnson, R., Roy, P., & Zaidman, B. (1985). Oral interaction in cooperative learning groups: Speaking, listening, and the nature of statements made by high-, medium-, and low-achieving students. *Journal of Psychology, 119*(4), 303–321.

Murray, F. (1983). *Cognitive benefits of teaching on the teacher*. Paper presented at American Educational Research Association Annual Meeting, Montreal, Quebec.

Vasquez, B., Johnson, D. W., & Johnson, R. (1993). Impact of cooperative learning on the performance and retention of U.S. Navy Air Traffic Controller Trainees. *Journal of Social Psychology, 133*, 769–783.

Yager, S., Johnson, D. W., & Johnson, R. (1985). Oral discussion, group-to-individual transfer, and achievement in cooperative learning groups. *Journal of Educational Psychology, 77*, 60–66.

73

The Art and Craft of "Gently Socratic" Inquiry

Thomas E. Jackson

"Gently Socratic" inquiry recognizes that a paramount objective of education is to help children develop their ability to think for themselves and to learn to use this ability in responsible ways. It also acknowledges that much of current schooling still falls short of helping children achieve this ability to think. Frequently, by the time children reach 3rd grade, the sense of wonder with which they entered kindergarten—wonder out of which authentic thinking and thus thinking for oneself develops—has begun to diminish. By 6th grade it has practically disappeared. Children's thinking focuses instead on what the teacher expects. A major contributing factor to this loss of wonder is the failure to properly nurture the true voices of children. Due to a variety of pressures, both internal and external, the typical classroom teacher does not appear to have time for children's genuine wondering and questioning, from which structured inquiries can grow. This apparent lack of time is exacerbated by the fact that most teachers simply have never been exposed to this type of inquiry. If teachers are ever to do this successfully in their own classrooms, they need time and guidance in learning how to conduct such inquiries.

WHAT IS GENTLY SOCRATIC INQUIRY?

The "gentle" in gently Socratic inquiry involves highlighting both a connection and distinction from what Socrates and Socratic method too often have come to represent. Socrates is often portrayed as the consummate lawyer, cleverly questioning and manipulating his adversary into an "Aha! Got you!" position of contradiction. Socratic method is construed as methodical questioning and cross-examining, peeling away layers of half-truths, exposing hidden assumptions. The Socratic method becomes an almost algorithmic, step-by-step procedure.

The term "gently Socratic" is meant to distance the nature of inquiry presented here from Socratic method or the Socrates described above. Hannah Arendt (1978) eloquently portrays the Socrates whom she contends would be worthy of the admiration that history has bestowed upon him as a model thinker and inquirer. Gently Socratic inquiry draws its inspiration from this portrayal of Socrates.

The first connection with Socrates in gently Socratic inquiry is dialogue. A salient feature of dialogue is not questioning (let alone, cross-examination) but listening. Dialogue's first interest is not to counter, debate, disagree, lead, or expose, but to genuinely and simply listen. This quality of listening requires setting aside one's own thoughts in order to be truly open to what the other is saying. This is especially important because the "other" in this case will most often be a child, and gentleness must be foremost in one's mind if one hopes to be privileged with an authentic response from a child.

Many factors in contemporary teaching and teacher preparation work against the kind of listening essential for genuine Socratic inquiry. As Peter Senge suggests, we all internalize a mental model of what it means to be a teacher. Central to this tendency is the idea that the teacher is the one who is "in the know" and the student is the "learner." Too often, the teacher focuses her listening on hearing an expected answer, or on probing the student's understanding of a particular idea or concept. "Has the student understood what I am trying to teach?" is a stance that precludes the kind of listening that is essential for the success of gently Socratic inquiry.

The focus on dialogue means that a particular relationship must develop among the members of the classroom community that is quite different from standard classroom practice. This new relationship places much more emphasis on listening, thoughtfulness, silence, and care and respect for the thoughts of others. The teacher provides ample time for students to express and clarify what they mean, to understand, to respond to what others have said, and to delve further into what other students intended. Above all, the classroom is an intellectually safe place that is not in a rush to get somewhere.

Whenever possible, students and teacher sit in a circle during inquiry time. Students call on each other, no longer relying on the teacher to carry this responsibility. Each has the opportunity to speak or to pass and remain silent. In this environment, inquiry will grow.

Gently Socratic inquiry is essentially about creating a particular place, time, and context in the classroom within which to establish a different relationship between teacher and students. The teacher becomes a co-inquirer in dialogue *with* the children, rather than their guide or sage. Over time, tools and criteria come into play that enhance the quality and rigor of the discourse and inquiry, but always within the context of an intellectually safe place.

To develop the classroom community and the needed skills, the teacher needs to deliberately set aside time for both. A minimum of two sessions per week is highly recommended. As the children internalize the skills and procedures, the strategies and skills that emerge from the inquiry sessions ultimately appear at other times of the school day and in other content areas. The children begin to ask qualitatively different sorts of questions; they persist in seeking to scratch beneath the surface of a text, or lesson, or personal situation.

WHAT GENTLY SOCRATIC INQUIRY IS NOT

Gently Socratic inquiry is not about having a particular answer in mind beforehand. Nor is it a method in any algorithmic sense. In particular, it is not a Socratic method. It involves certain skills, but no method.

Gently Socratic inquiry is also not a program specifically for a targeted group such as the gifted. It works with virtually any ability group, or mix thereof.

DEVELOPING A COMMUNITY OF INQUIRY

Gently Socratic inquiry begins by developing a context within which dialogue and inquiry unfold. Certainly, classrooms must be physically safe places. For dialogue and inquiry to occur they must be emotionally and intellectually safe as well. In an intellectually safe place there are no put-downs and no comments intended to belittle, undermine, negate, devalue, or ridicule. Within this place, the group accepts virtually any question or comment, so long as it is respectful of the other members of the circle. What develops is a growing trust among the participants and with it the courage to present one's own thoughts, however tentative initially, on complex and difficult issues.

Anyone who knows how to pretend they understand something even though they don't, or who has been in a context where they had a question but were afraid to ask it, has felt the influence of a place that was not intellectually safe. Intellectual safety is the bedrock upon which inquiry grows.

An important detail relevant to intellectual safety is proper acknowledgment of the diversity of views that emerge in the course of various inquiries. Intellectual safety arises, in part, out of acknowledging and celebrating this diversity. This is not the same as saying there are "no right or wrong answers" or "any answer is okay." Sometimes a student will fail to present reasons, or well-thought-out reasons, to support their answer. The group may not fully understand the implications of a particular answer, nor the assumptions that underlie them. Over time, the group begins to understand that it needs to take these criteria into account in considering a proposed answer. Mere opinion—unsupported opinion—does not suffice.

Equally important is this: The goal is not to persuade anyone to any particular answer, but rather for everyone to reach a deeper understanding of the complexity of the issues involved and a greater ability to navigate among these complexities.

CREATING THE COMMUNITY

The most favorable configuration for developing a community is for the class, including the teacher, to sit in a circle, on the floor if possible. Unlike the more traditional configuration with students in rows, the circle allows all members of the community to make eye contact, to *see* each other. In the ensuing dialogue, participants are better able to hear what others are saying and also to see how they are saying it; in other words, the facial expressions and mannerisms of those who are speaking. The circle also facilitates seeing the impact on each other of the interaction. What is the impact of acceptance or rejection? Of careful listening as opposed to indifference?

An early objective is to establish a protocol whereby students feel empowered to call on each other. One effective activity for accomplishing this is to create a "community ball" together as a way to give shape to what will become an inquiry community. This activity is effective with groups from kindergarten through university (see Figure 73.1). Once the group has made the ball, the agreement is that the person with the ball is the speaker of the moment. That person, when finished, passes to whomever he or she wishes. One caveat is that if the ball comes to a person who has not asked to speak or does not wish to speak, she has the absolute right to pass.

Another strategy is to introduce certain "magic words" (see Figure 73.2) that members of the community will use to facilitate procedures. The use of magic words has been effective in developing a safe place where inquiry can unfold in a non-

—Figure 73.1—
Making a Community Ball

Materials needed:
- 12" x 4" stiff cardboard
- Skein of multi-colored yarn
- One long piece of heavy-duty string for tying

Procedure:
1. Fold the cardboard in half lengthwise, so that it is 12" x 2".
2. Place the tie-string inside the center fold.
3. Wrap yarn from the skein around the width of cardboard.
4. Hold on to the tie-string while pulling the yarn off the cardboard. The tie-string will be running through the center of the yarn coil. Grasp both ends of the tie-string and tie them together securely, forming a bagel shape.
5. Cut through the yarn at the outer edge, creating a pom-pom ball.

The group sits in a circle. The teacher begins wrapping the yarn around the cardboard, while the student next to her feeds the yarn from the skein. The teacher responds to a question that each person in the circle will answer in turn. This question can be anything the teacher thinks will draw out the children, such as, "What is your favorite food or music?" or "What do you like best about school?" When the teacher finishes speaking, she passes the cardboard to the student beside her, who begins to wrap and rap(!) as the teacher takes over feeding the yarn. This process—one person wrapping and speaking, and his neighbor feeding the yarn—continues until all have had the opportunity to speak.

Source: From *Getting Started in Philosophy: A Start-Up Kit for K–1,* by T. Jackson & L. Oho, 1993. Unpublished manuscript.

—Figure 73.2—
Magic Words

- SPLAT = Speak a little louder, please. SPLAT means that what a person said just barely got out of their mouth and then went "splat" onto the floor. In other words, we need you to speak louder so we can hear you.
- IDUS = I don't understand. IDUS can empower students to be able to say when they don't understand. It has proven much easier for students to say IDUS than "I don't understand." Teachers find it encouraging when IDUS begins to show up in other content areas.
- POPAAT = Please, one person at a time. Once students learn that during inquiry time the group is *very* interested in what they have to say, they often all want to speak at the same time. POPAAT is effective in this context. When people start speaking out of turn, someone says POPAAT, which means that all must stop talking. The person holding the ball then continues.
- OMT = One more time. OMT is a request for the speaker to repeat what he has said.
- NQP = Next question, please.
- LMO = Let's move on.
- PBQ = Please be quiet.
- GOS = Going off subject. A group member can say GOS when the discussion is losing focus.

Source: From *Philosophy for Children: A Guide for Teachers,* by T. Jackson, 1989. Unpublished manuscript.

Once the teacher introduces the magic words, anyone may hold up a card. If the community seems bogged down in a topic and is not getting anywhere, someone may offer "LMO" to the community. At that moment, the community votes to see if the majority would indeed like to move on. If a minority still has interest in the topic, they can pursue it at a later time.

DEVELOPING AN UNDERSTANDING OF INQUIRY

Perhaps most basic to successful inquiry is the clear and shared understanding that "we aren't in a rush to get anywhere." In other content areas there is pressure to cover the material, to get on with it. The dialogue and inquiry sessions have a different feel.

Co-inquiry: In gently Socratic inquiry, no one, especially not the teacher, knows either "the" answer to the question (if the inquiry begins with a question) or where the inquiry will

threatening way. Children who are soft-spoken readily speak up when someone in the group says "SPLAT" (speak louder please). It's okay to say "IDUS" (I don't understand). And when several people are speaking at once, "POPAAT" (please, one person at a time) works. The teacher and students can write these "words" on cards and display them for all to see as needed. Each group can, of course, develop its own set of words. Whatever words you use, they can be powerfully instrumental in developing a community where all members, rather than just the teacher, share in the responsibility for moving an inquiry forward, and where the members share a common vocabulary with which to engage in this task.

lead. Any effort to guide an inquiry to a predetermined answer or outcome corrupts the process from the start. The dialogue develops its own integrity, its own movement, going where "it" wants or needs to go. At various points it may bog down and need an occasional nudge ("LMO") but in the main, the inquiry emerges from the context. It frequently pushes what Vygotsky (Vygotsky, 1986; Lipman, 1996) refers to as the "zone of proximal development" of all participants, including the teacher.

Gently Socratic inquiry is co-inquiry in the best sense. The teacher is not a privileged knower. In such inquiries, the children are not infrequently ahead of the thinking of the teacher, leading the inquiry down unexpected paths. Indeed, what the teacher knows can interfere with participation in the unfolding inquiry. Matthew Lipman, of New Jersey's Montclair University, has developed a curriculum called Philosophy for Children that is designed to nurture this form of inquiry (1980).

The source of the inquiry: Whenever possible, the inquiry arises out of the questions and interests of the children and moves in directions that the children indicate. There are a wide variety of possible triggers, occasions, and topics for inquiry. Plain Vanilla is one strategy for finding a trigger and then giving shape to an inquiry (see Figure 73.3). A salient feature of gently Socratic inquiry is its sensitivity to the interests and questions of the children, their thoughts, and where they take the topic. Even very young children generate sophisticated lines of inquiry from deceptively simple beginnings. One kindergartner, in response to the question, "What do you wonder about?" answered: "The other night, while I was gazing at the stars, I wondered whether anything came before space." In the discussion that ensued, the children's exploration ranged from dinosaurs to God. Other inquiries have explored such topics as "Could there be a greatest number?" (3rd grade); "What constitutes a right?" and "What is the purpose of rights?" (5th grade); and "What is more important—friends, fame, or fortune?" (6th grade). Once children realize that the topics can indeed come from them and be pursued along lines they are interested in, the quality of their thinking is truly astounding.

The self-corrective nature of inquiry: Matthew Lipman (1991), following in the pragmatist tradition of the American philosopher Charles Sanders Peirce, emphasizes the centrality of self-corrective inquiry. In classrooms where inquiry has become an essential and ongoing activity, community members

—Figure 73.3—

Plain Vanilla

Step 1. Read—A paragraph or two, an episode, a chapter, or a whole story. In the primary grades, the teacher may do the reading, or she may write the story on chart paper for everyone to read together. Alternatively, students could look at paintings, especially those by the students themselves; watch a video; read a poem; listen to a piece of music; or select a topic from a "wonder box" into which children have placed things they wonder about.

Step 2. Question—Ask the children for questions or comments they have about the story. Write them down on chart paper with the child's name next to their comment.

Step 3. Vote—As a class, the children vote for the question or comment they would like to inquire into first. Note this beside the question. Write NQP beside the question with the next highest number of votes.

Step 4. Dialogue/Inquiry—Inquire into the question selected, using WRAITEC (letters from the tool kit) and magic words as appropriate. If the children lose energy for the question selected, the group focuses on the question marked NQP.

Step 5. Evaluate—Use the criteria suggested in this chapter, some subset thereof, or other criteria you select.

Source: From *Philosophy for Children: A Guide for Teachers,* by T. Jackson, 1989. Unpublished manuscript.

will change and develop their thoughts about a particular topic. "Before I thought . . . , but now I realize that . . . ." becomes an increasingly common comment in a maturing inquiry community in the course of a school year.

INQUIRY TOOLS FOR SCRATCHING BENEATH THE SURFACE

Gently Socratic inquiry is more than a conversation or sharing of ideas within a group. It is characterized by an intellectual rigor that certain cognitive tools can facilitate. These tools comprise the "good thinker's tool kit." They are the means for giving shape and direction to the notion that, although we aren't in a rush to get anywhere, we *do* have an expectation that we will get *somewhere.*

One of the goals in developing inquiry skills is learning to scratch beneath the surface of any topic or question. The active use of the good thinker's tools is one indication that "scratching" is occurring. In addition, at least three types of progress can result from effective scratching.

One form of progress occurs when an inquiry reveals how complicated the question or topic really is. At the end of the session, things might well appear in a muddle, more mixed up than in the beginning. This muddle can be a form of progress when participants realize that the topic was much more complex than they thought at first.

Another form of progress is when connections begin to emerge among the various ideas that present themselves in the course of the inquiry. For example, an inquiry that began with the question, "What does it mean to say, 'That wasn't fair'?" led a group of 3rd graders to questions of whether it wasn't fair because someone was treated differently, and whether treating someone differently is ever consistent with being fair. The children thereby made a connection between "fair" and "how someone is treated."

A third type of progress is when the shape of an answer begins to emerge. In the fairness inquiry above, "how one is treated" might emerge as a criterion of fairness such that it might be proposed that "*If* a person is treated differently in a particular sort of way, *then* that wouldn't be fair."

Moreover, various participants in the same inquiry may individually experience different types of progress. For some, it may just be a muddle. For others, connections may begin to emerge, while still others may begin to have an answer in mind. Each form of progress has value and merit. A valuable exercise is to have students keep journals of inquiry sessions to promote an ongoing internal dialogue for each individual.

Certainly there will be days and times when it appears that students are not making progress in any of these ways. Yet there may be progress of a different, equally important kind. For example, in a given session, a particularly quiet student may feel moved to participate verbally for the first time.

THE GOOD THINKER'S TOOL KIT

Helping students and teachers internalize good thinkers' tools of inquiry equips them with the ability to think for themselves in a responsible way. With sustained experience in dialogue, students become more adept at giving and asking for reasons, detecting assumptions, anticipating consequences, reflecting on inferences they draw, asking for clarification, and seeking evidence and examples as well as counterexamples. They also learn to seek out alternatives and to form criteria for the judgments they make. The letters *W, R, A, I, T, E,* and *C* represent the good thinker's tools (Jackson, 1989):

W = What do you/we mean by . . . ? *W* highlights the importance of being sensitive to possible multiplicity of meanings and ambiguity; hence, a readiness to seek clarification when needed.

R = Reasons. *R* reflects that in inquiry one should expect that it is not enough to simply offer an opinion. Whenever possible, group members should support their opinions with reasons.

A = Assumptions. *A* represents the importance of making explicit, whenever appropriate, the assumptions that underlie the discussion during inquiry.

I = Inferences; If . . . then's; Implications. *I* highlights the central role of inferences we might make, of possible implications of what someone has said, and of hypothetical statements such as, "*If* what Jody said is true, *then* 'real' can't just be things we can see or touch."

T = True? *T* indicates that a major concern in our inquiry is the question of whether or not what someone has stated is in fact true, and how we might go about finding out.

E = Examples; Evidence. *E* points out the importance of giving examples to illustrate or clarify what someone is saying and of providing evidence to support a claim.

C = Counterexamples. *C* represents an important check on assertions or claims that possibly cast too wide a net. For example, "always" or "never" frequently occur in conversations, such as "The boys always get to go first" or "We never get to stay up late." The search for counterexamples is a way of checking the truth of such a claim. For example, "You get to stay up late if it's a holiday" is a counterexample.

An important class activity is to make tool kits together, so that each student has her own kit. Students design 3 x 5 cards, one for each letter, writing on the back of each card whatever clarifying notes will help them remember the significance of each letter. When desiring a reason from someone who is speaking, a student displays the *R* card. If an important assumption is going unnoticed, a student can show the *A* card, and so on.

The class should also devote time, separate from the inquiry sessions, to becoming more familiar with each tool. In the course of an inquiry, anyone can place a card representing a given tool in the circle when they want to use that particular tool. This can facilitate the evaluation of the session at the end, as it makes apparent which tools made their appearance in the course of the day's inquiry.

REFLECTING ON THE INQUIRY

Finally, it is important that the inquiry community reflect on how well it has done on any given day (Jackson, 1989). We suggest the following criteria, which the teacher can present to the group prior to beginning the inquiry cycle and again at the end of each session. The criteria fall into two categories, those dealing with how we did as a community and those dealing with the inquiry itself.

How did we do as a community?
• Listening—Was I listening to others? Were others listening to me?
• Participation—Did most people participate rather than just a few who dominated?
• Safety—Was it a safe environment?

How was our inquiry?
• Focus—Did we maintain a focus?
• Depth—Did our discussion scratch beneath the surface, open up the topic, or otherwise make some progress?
• Understanding—Did I increase my understanding of the topic?
• Thinking—Did I challenge my own thinking or work hard at it?
• Interest—Was it interesting?

At some point it is important for the group to discuss more fully what each criterion means. What, for example, counts as participation? Does one need to speak in order to participate? What does it mean to scratch beneath the surface? At an appropriate time, the teacher can introduce the notion of three types of progress and the use of the various tools as indicators of scratching or its absence.

The evaluation can occur in a variety of ways. The teacher can list each criterion on a separate card. He displays each card one at a time, and the members indicate how they thought the community did on that criterion with "thumbs up" or "thumbs down." A thumb midway between up and down indicates neutral. At first the teacher can handle the cards, but as soon as possible it is useful to ask individual students to take a particular card and ask the group for their response to that criterion. As the community gains experience, it can establish a standard for what "thumbs up" means within the context of the experiences of that community.

Related to evaluation of an inquiry session is a feature that will inevitably emerge wherever inquiry has become a regular part of the classroom: Once intellectual safety is firmly in place, diversity of viewpoints will make their appearance. One way of preparing for this is to make clear that with complex topics, one can expect a number of legitimate, different points of view. Indeed, as individuals, we may have differing points of view at different points in time.

At the end of a discussion into whether a particular action was fair, or indeed any other topic of similar complexity, it's important to acknowledge at least four possible places someone might be in their thinking at any given time. They might be prepared to answer, "Yes, I think it was fair," or "No, I don't think it was fair," but also, importantly, they might be at an "I don't know" or "Maybe so" place.

Asking students and teacher to raise their hands in response to where their thinking is on the particular topic is a way of displaying to the group the diversity of their thinking on a particular issue. Asking for such a display of hands is also a way of bringing closure to an inquiry that is still ongoing but must pause because it is time for lunch, recess, or another class.

THE ROLE OF THE TEACHER

The teacher is absolutely pivotal to the success of gently Socratic inquiry. In the beginning it will be the teacher who introduces the ideas behind such inquiry. She will be responsible for establishing, monitoring, and maintaining the safety within the group. This will include monitoring the proper use of the community ball and calling on each other, and seeing that members have ample opportunity to speak as well as permission to remain silent. With younger grades, for example, one problem that often appears initially is that boys only call on boys, girls call on girls, and close friends call on each other.

The teacher is responsible for introducing the magic words and seeing to their proper use. In some cases, students may initially abuse the freedom offered by these words and repeatedly utter "SPLAT" (speak louder please) to someone who is shy, or "LMO" (let's move on) the moment there is any pause in the dialogue.

The teacher conducts the lessons that involve making the tool kit and follow-up lessons that focus on a particular tool. For most students and many teachers, "inference" and "assumption" are little more than vocabulary words. The group needs to spend time on developing deeper understanding of what these terms mean. Similarly, what makes a reason a good reason, how counterexamples function, and how one might go about finding out whether a given claim or statement is true may be areas where understanding is currently quite shallow. In early sessions the teacher should call attention to uses of the various tools and encourage their use.

Most importantly, it is the teacher, especially in the beginning, who sets the tone for the group. "Not being in a rush" depends on a teacher sufficiently comfortable with silence and "wait time" beyond what is typical in most classrooms. It requires a teacher whose own sense of wonder is still very much alive and who is keenly interested in what the authentic thoughts of the children are on a given topic; one who is comfortable with uncertainty, not eager to push for closure, but willing to allow an inquiry to move where "it" and the children seem to want to take it. She must be willing to risk not knowing the answer, to indeed be a co-inquirer in the quest for an answer.

Initially the teacher needs to make the crucial judgments about using both magic words and good thinker's tools. The teacher is the one who asks for reasons, examples, and clarification, at the same time displaying letters that represent the particular tool requested, at once modeling and highlighting their use.

The teacher begins to weave threads of conversation into dialogue, asking who agrees or disagrees or has other thoughts about the topic at hand, offering a counterexample, asking "If what Tanya said is true, would it follow that . . . ?" or making some other comment to nudge the dialogue along. This is especially delicate and challenging because a major objective is

for the children to internalize and thus take over these skills and behaviors. They need as much opportunity as possible to try them out, and providing these opportunities is the teacher's responsibility.

It is the teacher who brings a given session to a close and sees to it that the group conducts an evaluation. How long are inquiry sessions? With kindergarten children they last from 10 minutes to more than an hour. Sessions with older children tend to be more predictable in terms of length, but also more subject to the time demands of the school day and curriculum.

In this kind of inquiry, the teacher's role is to be pedagogically strong but philosophically self-effacing. The teacher should be firmly in control of the procedures but allow the content of the inquiry to unfold as it needs to, rather than following the desires of the teacher.

REFERENCES

Arendt, H. (1978). *The life of the mind.* New York: Harcourt Brace Jovanovich.

Jackson, T. (1989). *Philosophy for children: A guide for teachers.* Unpublished manuscript.

Lipman, M. (1980). *Philosophy in the classroom* (2nd ed.). Philadelphia: Temple University Press.

Lipman, M. (1991). *Thinking in education.* New York: Cambridge University Press.

Lipman, M. (1996). *Natasha: Vygotskian dialogues.* New York: Teachers College, Columbia University.

Vygotsky, L. (1986). *Thought and language.* Cambridge, MA: MIT Press.

74

Teaching Cognitive Strategies for Reading, Writing, and Problem Solving

Michael Pressley and Karen R. Harris

It's easier to act your way into a new way of thinking than to think your way into a new way of acting.
　　　　　　　—Millard Fuller, founder of Habitat for Humanity

Cognitive psychologists made great progress in the latter half of the 20th century in identifying how competent readers read, good writers write, and effective problem solvers problem solve. One of the analytical tools most helpful in illuminating such cognitive processes was verbal protocol analysis, which involves asking readers, writers, and problem solvers to think aloud as they read, write, or solve problems. Such analyses revealed dramatic processing differences between those who perform these tasks effectively and those who do not.

For example, skilled readers are more active than unskilled readers before, during, and after reading passages (Pressley & Afflerbach, 1995). Before reading, they are likely to preview a text, sizing up what's in it and making decisions about how they are going to read it (e.g., deciding which sections are most relevant to their purposes and opting to read those more carefully). During reading, they adjust reading speed depending on a number of factors, including text relevance, density, and level of interest. Good readers sometimes choose to reread especially difficult or relevant sections of a text. After reading, good readers may reflect on the reading, deciding which parts of text are worth remembering and thinking about how they might use ideas from this text in the future.

Other researchers have conducted similar analyses of writing (Flower & Hayes, 1980) and problem solving (Burkell, Schneider, & Pressley, 1990). Good writers draw upon a rich store of strategies for planning, text production, and revising. They also draw upon knowledge of the patterns or schemas evident in different writing genres or models, developing novel or modified frameworks as the writing task becomes more complex. Further, skilled writers consider their audience's needs and perspective as well as the functions they intend their writing to serve. They are knowledgeable about their topic, doing research as necessary. Finally, they use effective self-regulation procedures throughout the recursive writing process until they achieve their goals (Harris & Graham, 1992).

Similarly, good problem solvers make certain they understand a problem before they attempt a solution. Once they comprehend the problem, they develop an initial plan, carry it out, and reflect on whether they successfully solved the problem. If they were unsuccessful, they plan some more, attempt to implement new plans, and continue to monitor the effectiveness of their effort. Problem solving continues until they have solved the problem (Polya, 1957).

Cognitive Strategy Instruction

The logic of cognitive strategy instruction is straightforward. Because learners who face significant challenges with reading, writing, and problem solving are not as strategic as good readers, writers, and problem solvers, a critical factor may be that they are not using the strategic processes that more effective learners use. If so, then supporting the development of such procedures should improve their reading, writing, and problem solving. In a classical analysis, Flavell, Friedrichs, and Hoyt (1970) referred to the failure to use strategies that one could carry out profitably as a production deficiency. Flavell and his colleagues also recognized that teachers could often help students overcome their production deficiencies by teaching them to use such strategies.

This general hypothesis stimulated many experiments in the past 30 years (see Pressley & Harris, 1994) in which struggling readers, writers, or problem solvers were the participants in the study. Researchers randomly assigned some of the par-

Copyright © 2001 by Michael Pressley and Karen R. Harris

ticipants to a condition in which they were taught appropriate and powerful strategies (i.e., reading, writing, problem-solving, and/or self-regulation strategies, depending largely on the specific interest of the researcher). They assigned other struggling learners to a control condition. Before cognitive strategies instruction, both groups of participants faced equivalent problems in reading, writing, or problem solving. Participants who received instruction in the strategies performed significantly and meaningfully better than control participants.

Such experiments were an enormous success. It proved possible to teach children who could not decode words to decode by applying sounding-out strategies (Pressley & Allington, 1999). Those with poor comprehension became better after they learned reading comprehension strategies (Pearson & Dole, 1987). Struggling writers showed important changes in both how and what they wrote, as well as changes in self-efficacy and attitudes about themselves as writers (Harris & Graham, 1999). Students were able to solve more problems when teachers taught them to understand a problem before attempting it, devise a plan rather than rush into the problem, monitor whether the plan worked, and revise the plan if necessary (Hembree, 1992).

MAINTAINING AND GENERALIZING THE STRATEGIES

That students could learn to carry out effective strategies did not mean that they would continue to use these strategies. In general, particularly in earlier research, maintenance failures following strategies instruction were frequent. Students failed to apply strategies to tasks and situations very similar to the training tasks and situations they had experienced. Transfer failures were even more frequent. Students failed to apply strategies to tasks and situations somewhat different from training tasks and situations, even though the trained strategies would improve performance if carried out (Gick & Holyoak, 1980, 1983).

Fortunately, instructional solutions exist that can increase the likelihood of maintenance and transfer of trained strategies. One is to provide information during instruction about when and where to use the instructed strategies, as well as opportunities for learners to discover and come to understand where and when they can profitably use these strategies (Pressley, Borkowski, & O'Sullivan, 1984, 1985). There is nothing like the opportunity for successful performance on a previously difficult task to convince a student to continue using that strategy with similar tasks in the future (Pressley, Levin, & Ghatala, 1984).

Researchers have attempted to identify how teachers can teach strategies so that students understand and are likely to continue using what they are learning. Roehler and Duffy (1984) dubbed one approach that produces good results as "direct explanation." In this approach, the components of which are now common among most strategy instruction models, the teacher initially models use of the strategies, thinking aloud and doing whatever is necessary to make explicit the strategic processes involved in the task. To support her modeling, the teacher might list the strategies on a wall chart or prepare prompts or mnemonics that students can keep in front of them as they work. This modeling of mental processes, known as "mental modeling" (Duffy, Roehler, & Herrmann, 1988), contains extensive explanations of the processes, including when and where the student might apply the strategies being modeled.

The teacher encourages students to attempt the strategies themselves by providing and pointing out opportunities to help students understand where they can use the instructed processes, and when doing so would improve performance. As students attempt to use strategies, the teacher monitors their attempts, providing assistance as necessary. Such assistance is in the form of scaffolding (Wood, Bruner, & Ross, 1976), with enough support to permit the student to carry out the procedure but not so much that the teacher is carrying out the strategy for the student. For example, if the student is having difficulty thinking of a comprehension strategy to apply to a text he is reading, the teacher might remind the student of the chart in the room listing possible comprehension strategies.

As students become facile in using strategies, the teacher provides more and more challenging situations to apply the processes—modeling, explaining, and scaffolding ever more savvy uses of strategies. Such instruction is decidedly long-term, consistent with the most impressive demonstrations of successful strategies teaching to promote reading (Brown, Pressley, Van Meter, & Schuder, 1996), writing (Danoff, Harris, & Graham, 1993; Englert, Raphael, Anderson, Anthony, & Stevens, 1991; Sawyer, Graham, & Harris, 1992), and problem solving (Charles & Lester, 1984).

In short, many strategies and processes have helped to address issues of maintenance and generalization. These include informed learning; modeling of effort and strategy attributions; recognition of gains following strategy execution; knowledge about when and where one can and cannot use the strategy; sufficient practice to allow automatization, fluency, and personalization of the strategy; diverse practice; encouraging, prompting, and supporting generalization and maintenance;

and collaboration and scaffolding (Harris & Graham, 1992). In addition, particularly with students whose challenges are most significant, booster sessions appear to be necessary for long-term maintenance (Meichenbaum, 1977; Graham, Harris, & Troia, 1998). Finally, some research indicates that explicit, scaffolded development of self-regulation strategies in tandem with targeted task strategies can enhance maintenance and generalization (Harris & Graham, 1996; Sawyer, et al., 1992).

Issues in obtaining and improving maintenance and generalization remain, however. Researchers are currently exploring ideas that include the use of "homework" assignments, long-term goal setting and self-monitoring, and peer support for maintenance and generalization (Graham et al., 1998; Harris & Graham, 1992). Further research on the breadth, depth, and course of development of maintenance and generalization abilities in students would enhance our understanding (Alexander, Graham, & Harris, 1998). Perhaps one of the most intriguing questions to us, however, is that of the long-term effects of strategy instruction and the development of self-regulation across the grades and among disciplines. The skillful reader, writer, or problem solver employs strategies the way a jazz musician uses a melody, profiting from the variations, the riffs, the twists, and ultimately the meaning. We believe teachers and parents can support the development and mature use of strategies by planning together to introduce and enhance task and self-regulation strategies developmentally across the grades. A great deal of additional research is needed to determine what the effects of such efforts would be.

USING COGNITIVE STRATEGIES WITH YOUNG CHILDREN

Educational researchers and theorists interested in cognitive strategies instruction have explored such instruction as a function of the age and abilities of students. Although the findings contain many subtleties, some generalizations are possible. Very young children are able to learn many of the strategies that are well-matched to important, age-appropriate tasks. Hence, 5- and 6-year-old children can learn the strategy of sounding out words in order to recognize them (Adams, Treiman, & Pressley, 1998), although such teaching involves a number of components including the teaching of letter-sound associations for single letters and blends. In general, however, the younger and less able the child, the more complete and explicit the instruction must be in order to make progress, a principle of strategy instruction that the earliest researchers on the teaching of cognitive strategies to children recognized (Rohwer, 1970).

That strategy instruction often can be successful with young children, even ones who are struggling in one or more areas, does not mean that young children are able to learn every type of strategy. Some strategies are probably too cognitively demanding for young children. Although by the end of the grade school years children have little trouble constructing mental images representing the ideas in text, imagery construction is quite difficult for kindergarten and Grade 1 children, seeming to overwhelm their short-term memory capacity (Cariglia-Bull & Pressley, 1990).

DISSEMINATING WHAT WE KNOW ABOUT COGNITIVE STRATEGIES

Cognitive psychologists have been able to make a strong case that good thinkers use cognitive strategies when they read, write, and solve problems. In addition, researchers interested in cognition and instruction have established that often those who do not use cognitive strategies spontaneously can learn to use such strategies, with improved comprehension, writing, and problem solving.

Some research on cognitive strategies instruction has produced revolutionary changes in approaches to teaching; other research on such instruction has had less impact. Thus, many elementary classrooms in the United States now include a great deal of writing instruction, including explicit teaching to plan, draft, and revise as part of writing. So, too, the reform of mathematics instruction as defined by the standards of the National Council of Teachers of Mathematics (2000) includes substantial instruction in problem-solving strategies. In contrast to these successes, some decided failures also exist. Despite almost a quarter of a century of research establishing that teaching comprehension strategies enhances the reading comprehension of students in the later elementary grades, little such comprehension instruction in contemporary 4th and 5th grade classrooms seems to be taking place (Pressley, Wharton-McDonald, Mistretta-Hampston, & Echevarria, 1998). Rather, many teachers seem to believe that students will become skilled at comprehension if they simply read a great deal. By the upper elementary grades, many teachers do not see it as their job to teach reading.

A bright spot with respect to cognitive strategies instruction is the area of special education. A number of special educators include teaching of cognitive strategies as a prominent part of their curriculum, especially for learning disabled children (Deshler, Schumaker, Harris, & Graham, 1999). The literature includes numerous examples in which such children have learned strategies, with substantial improvements in performance (Deshler & Schumaker, 1988; Englert et al., 1991; Danoff et al., 1993; Harris & Graham, 1996; Sawyer et al., 1992). In general, such instruction is consistent with the direct explanation model, including mental modeling, verbal explanations, and scaffolding. Strategies instruction provided to students with learning disabilities is very explicit and long-term, consistent with the conclusion that students who have significant learning problems often require more explicit instruction than normally achieving students in order to learn cognitive strategies (Deshler & Schumaker, 1988; Harris & Graham, 1996, 1999). Finally, research with elementary students with learning disabilities has tended to include explicit development of self-regulation strategies in tandem with task strategies, to address the difficulties with self-regulation that many of these students experience (Harris & Graham, 1996, 1999; Sawyer, et al., 1992).

More positively, recent analyses have shown that teachers in excellent classrooms incorporate many research-supported interventions (Pressley et al., in press). A further challenge will be to study how teachers can fit cognitive strategies instruction into classrooms that are already attractively complex. This work should be carried out in parallel with research intended to stimulate teachers who have not incorporated much in the way of innovation in their classroom environments, for there are many classrooms in this category (Pressley et al., 1998). Much work on the dissemination of cognitive strategies instruction remains to be done, with classrooms as the logical focus.

REFERENCES

Adams, M. J., Treiman, R., & Pressley, M. (1998). Reading, writing, and literacy. To appear in I. Sigel & A. Renninger (Eds.), *Handbook of child psychology. Vol. 4: Child psychology in practice* (pp. 275–355). New York: John Wiley & Sons.

Alexander, P. A., Graham, S., & Harris, K. R. (1998). A perspective on strategy research: Progress and prospects. *Educational Psychology Review, 10*(2), 115–127.

Brown, R., Pressley, M., Van Meter, P., & Schuder, T. (1996). A quasi-experimental validation of transactional strategies instruction with low-achieving second grade readers. *Journal of Educational Psychology, 88*, 18–37.

Burkell, J., Schneider, B., & Pressley, M. (1990). Mathematics. In M. Pressley & Associates, *Cognitive strategy instruction that really improves children's academic performance* (pp. 147–177). Cambridge MA: Brookline Books.

Cariglia-Bull, T., & Pressley, M. (1990). Short-term memory differences between children predict imagery effects when sentences are read. *Journal of Experimental Child Psychology, 49*, 384–398.

Charles, R. I., & Lester, F. K., Jr. (1984). An evaluation of a process-oriented instructional program in mathematical problem-solving in grades 5 and 7. *Journal of Research in Mathematics Education, 15*, 15–34.

Danoff, B., Harris, K. R., & Graham, S. (1993). Incorporating strategy instruction within the writing process in the regular classroom: Effects on the writing of students with and without learning disabilities. *Journal of Reading Behavior, 25*, 295–322.

Deshler, D. D., & Schumaker, J. B. (1988). An instructional model for teaching students how to learn. In J. L. Graden, J. E. Zins, & M. J. Curtis (Eds.), *Alternative educational delivery systems: Enhancing instructional options for all students* (pp. 391–411). Washington DC: National Association of School Psychologists.

Deshler, D. D., Schumaker, J. B., Harris, K. R., & Graham, S. (Eds.) (1999). *Advances in teaching and learning. Vol. 3: Teaching every adolescent every day: Learning in diverse schools and classrooms.* Cambridge, MA: Brookline Books.

Duffy, G. G., Roehler, L. R., & Herrmann, B. A. (1988). Modeling mental processes helps poor readers become strategic readers. *Reading Teacher, 41*, 762–767.

Englert, C. S., Raphael, T. E., Anderson, L. M., Anthony, H. M., & Stevens, D. D. (1991). Making writing strategies and self-talk visible: Cognitive strategy instruction in writing in regular and special education classrooms. *American Educational Research Journal, 28*, 337–372.

Flavell, J. H., Friedrichs, A. G., & Hoyt, J. D. (1970). Developmental changes in memorization. *Cognitive Psychology, 1*, 324–340.

Flower, L., & Hayes, J. (1980). The dynamics of composing: Making plans and juggling constraints. In L. Gregg & E. Steinberg (Eds.), *Cognitive processes in writing* (pp. 31–50). Hillsdale NJ: Erlbaum.

Gick, M. L., & Holyoak, K. J. (1980). Analogical problem solving. *Cognitive Psychology, 12*, 306–355.

Gick, M. L., & Holyoak, K. J. (1983). Schema induction and analogical transfer. *Cognitive Psychology, 15*, 1–38.

Graham, S., & Harris, K. R., & Troia, G. (1998). Writing and self-regulation: Cases from the self-regulated strategy development model. In D. Schunk & B. Zimmerman (Eds.), *Developing self-regulated learners: From teaching to self-reflective practices.* New York: Guilford.

Harris, K. R., & Graham, S. (1992). Self-regulated strategy development: A part of the writing process. In M. Pressley, K.R. Harris, & J.T. Guthrie (Eds.), *Promoting academic competence and literacy in school* (pp. 277–309).

Harris, K., & Graham, S. (1996). *Making the writing process work: Strategies for composition and self-regulation.* Cambridge, MA: Brookline Books.

Harris, K. R., & Graham, S. (1999). Programmatic intervention research: Illustrations from the evolution of self-regulated strategy development. *Learning Disability Quarterly, 22*, 251–262.

Hembree, R. (1992). Experiments and relational studies in problem solving: A meta-analysis. *Journal for Research in Mathematics Education, 23*, 242–273.

Meichenbaum, D. (1977). *Cognitive behavior modification: An integrative approach.* New York: Plenum Press.

National Council of Teachers of Mathematics (2000). *Curriculum and evaluation standards for school mathematics.* Reston VA: National Council of Teachers of Mathematics.

Pearson, P. D., & Dole, J. A. (1987). Explicit comprehension instruction: A review of research and a new conceptualization of instruction. *Elementary School Journal, 88*, 151–165.

Polya, G. (1957). *How to solve it.* New York: Doubleday.

Pressley, M., & Afflerbach, P. (1995). *Verbal protocols of reading: The nature of constructively responsive reading.* Hillsdale NJ: Erlbaum.

Pressley, M., & Allington, R. (1999). What should reading instructional research be the research of? *Issues in Education, 5*(1), 1–35.

Pressley, M., Borkowski, J. G., & O'Sullivan, J. T. (1984). Memory strategy instruction is made of this: Metamemory and durable strategy use. *Educational Psychologist, 19*, 94–107.

Pressley, M., Borkowski, J. G., & O'Sullivan, J. T. (1985). Children's metamemory and the teaching of strategies. In D. L. Forrest-Pressley,

G. E. MacKinnon, & T. G. Waller (Eds.), *Metacognition, cognition, and human performance* (pp. 111–153). Orlando, FL: Academic Press.

Pressley, M., & Harris, K. R. (1994). Increasing the quality of educational intervention research. *Educational Psychology Review, 6,* 191–214.

Pressley, M., Levin, J. R., & Ghatala, E. S. (1984). Memory strategy monitoring in adults and children. *Journal of Verbal Learning and Verbal Behavior, 23,* 270–288.

Pressley, M., Wharton-McDonald, R., Allington, R., Block, C. C., Morrow, L., Tracey, D., Baker, K., Brooks, G., Crinion, J., Nelson, E., & Woo, D. (in press). A study of effective grade-1 literacy instruction. *Scientific Studies of Reading.*

Pressley, M., Wharton-McDonald, R., Mistretta-Hampston, J., & Echevarria, M. (1998). The nature of literacy instruction in ten grade-4/5 classrooms in upstate New York. *Scientific Studies of Reading, 2,* 159–191.

Roehler, L. R., & Duffy, G. G. (1984). Direct explanation of comprehension processes. In G. G. Duffy, L. R. Roehler, & J. Mason (Eds.), *Comprehension instruction: Perspectives and suggestions* (pp. 265–280). New York: Longan.

Rohwer, W. D., Jr. (1970). Implications of cognitive development for education. In P. H. Mussed (Ed.), *Carmichael's manual of child psychology, Vol. 1* (pp. 1379–1454). New York: John Wiley & Sons.

Sawyer, R., Graham, S., & Harris, K. (1992). Direct teaching, strategy instruction, and strategy instruction with explicit self-regulation: Effects on the composition skills and self-efficacy of students with learning disabilities. *Journal of Educational Psychology, 84,* 340–352.

Wood, S. S., Bruner, J. S., & Ross, G. (1976, April). The role of tutoring in problem solving. *Journal of Child Psychology and Psychiatry, 17*(2), 89–100.

X

Teaching Thinking Through Technology

We live in a time of such rapid change and growth of knowledge that only he who is in a fundamental sense a scholar—that is, a person who continues to learn and inquire—can hope to keep pace, let alone play the role of guide.

—NATHAN M. PUSEY,
THE AGE OF THE SCHOLAR

Introduction

Bena Kallick

New tools often transform the way we think. Take the printing press, for example. Prior to the printing press, oral communication was essential. People had well-developed skills as story tellers, used verbal descriptive narrative as a form of reporting, and sharpened their memories for the details of events. Different thinking skills and capabilities were required, particularly the skills associated with short- and long-term memory. Likewise, the computer has changed the way we think. When used to its full potential, the computer is more than a tool for efficiency and automation: it transforms thinking and creates new knowledge.

The computer does some of the work; the "knowledge worker" does the rest. The computer provides the data in a form that we can continuously reconfigure in order to analyze information, seek patterns, and solve problems as they arise out of the material at hand. The knowledge worker is constantly dealing with new situations, learning from them, and attempting to respond in new and better ways. The chief implication of a shift to "knowledge work" is that knowledge workers adapt their responses to a given situation instead of carrying out standard operating procedures. They attempt to understand what would be an appropriate response to a situation, then marshal the necessary resources and capabilities to get it done. They are good problem solvers.

In order to make the best use of these capabilities, we have to develop them in ourselves as well as in our students. James Wilson focuses his chapter on an analysis of problem solving as seen through the window of software. He sorts problems into two categories, well-defined and ill-defined, and examines the issues for learning. Gary Morrison and Deborah Lowther focus on the knowledge worker and identify the skills students will need to become effective knowledge workers in the classroom and beyond. They provide a template for building curriculum units that integrate the uses of technology to enhance higher-level problem solving and learning. John Richards explores the

power and potential of the Internet and its influence on thinking. The work of Joanne Marien, Elaine Vislocky, and Linda Chapman offers a rich practical example of how a school district has focused on research as a key to building the skills needed to access and make sense out of the often undifferentiated and excessive information available to us over the Internet.

Each chapter reinforces the research findings from *How People Learn* by Bransford, Brown, and Cocking (1999). The authors summarize their findings regarding new technologies as follows:

> Because many new technologies are interactive, it is now easier to create environments in which students can learn by doing, receive feedback, and continually refine their understanding and build new knowledge.
>
> Technologies can help people visualize difficult-to-understand concepts, such as differentiating heat from temperature. Students are able to work with visualization and modeling software similar to the tools used in nonschool environments to increase their conceptual understanding and the likelihood of transfer from school to nonschool settings.
>
> New technologies provide access to a vast array of information, including digital libraries, real-world data for analysis, and connections to other people who provide information, feedback, and inspiration, all of which can enhance the learning of teachers and administrators as well as students. (p. xix)

The promise of the uses for new technologies in our schools must be accompanied by a change in the culture's dispositions for thinking. The habits of mind become central to building these dispositions. What Wilson refers to as "tenacity" is detailed in the habit of persisting. When confronted with data, the habits of questioning and problem posing become essential. The ultimate form of "adaptive expertise," in which one can take what is well-known and transfer it adaptively to a new situation, calls for two habits: applying past knowledge to new situations and thinking flexibly (Bransford, Brown, & Cocking, 1999).

Integrating technology as a meaningful tool that will transform the culture of schools requires attention to the habits of mind; newly defined thinking tasks such as problem solving; and the necessary cognitive operations such as analyzing, inferring, and evaluating.

REFERENCES

Bransford, J., Brown, A., & Cocking, R. (Eds.). (1999). *How people learn*. Washington, DC: Committee on Developments in the Science of Learning, Commission on Behavioral and Social Sciences and Education, National Research Council, National Academy Press.

75

Technology and Thinking: The Evolving Relationship

James M. Wilson III

Recent history has witnessed a rapid infusion of information technology into schools and classrooms. This change has created excitement about the prospects of enhancing learning, as well as skepticism and confusion about the role of technology in education. Such new media, as McLuhan (1964) presciently noted, will alter both the cognition and relationships of individuals and organizations by shaping and controlling the "scale and form of human association and action" (p. 24). Technology alters the workflow in organizations. In that students do engage in work through the process of learning and are managed by the work of teachers, the transformation of the school by such technology is inevitable. New methods of learning and new relationships to facilitate learning are in the pioneering or emergent stage. We are all discovering the implications of this new media for learning, creativity, and thinking.

This chapter will focus on two features of this new technology with regard to the cognitive task of problem solving. The first is the capacity of information technology to emulate and enhance many cognitive functions: memory, categorization, search for information, speed of processing information, range of methods for presenting information, and simulating authentic circumstances (the proverbial "virtual realities") for engaging in learning. These capabilities present many opportunities for learning and augmenting the process of thinking. The salient question here is "How can we best use these cybernetic enhancements to cognition and learning?"

The second factor is the variety of information born of the connectivity among technology users. The increased connectivity facilitated by sundry networks (Internet, television, telephones, fax machines, etc.) has created a flood of varied and unorganized information. Such interaction among diverse information and ideas has spawned a historical moment where space and time are compressed, and formerly insular cultures confront each other. It is a challenge for children to make sense of such a world—a world quite unbounded and anarchic. The new capabilities present many opportunities, as well as threats, for learning and enhancing the process of thinking. The salient question here is "What thinking skills do we need to cultivate in students so that they can assimilate and benefit from such unbounded variety and anarchy?"

There are no stock answers for these two concerns; the measurable influence of technology in the classroom is still in its emergent stages at the turn of the 20th century. However, we can beneficially consider certain matters before we have the empirical results in hand.

TRIAL AND ERROR, TYPES OF PROBLEMS, AND THE EVOLUTION OF THOUGHT

The work of Karl Popper (1979) and Donald Campbell (1969) in evolutionary epistemology provides a relevant, practical, and descriptive model of human creativity, thinking, and learning under such dynamic conditions. At the heart of evolutionary epistemology is the simple belief that trial and error is the basic mechanism by which knowledge evolves. Trial-and-error learning requires both the capability to generate a variety of trials and the capability to select among trials, in terms of correct and incorrect.

To learn, then, requires that we generate a number of trials with sufficient variety in order to find the appropriate fit to the conditions of the presented problem. However, the various trials alone are meaningless without criteria to select appropriately among them. Selection criteria must make explicit the conditions under which we identify incorrect trials. Otherwise, how would we determine if a trial is false?

WELL-DEFINED AND ILL-DEFINED PROBLEMS

This model of learning, with its focus on the generation of trials, helps in considering two types of problems: well-defined and ill-defined (Newell, 1969; Reitman, 1964; Simon, 1973).

In a well-defined problem the components are completely specified. For example, in certain well-defined problems a student must answer correctly from memory or by internally generating a variety of answers and then selecting among them. An example of this would be a drill problem such as "1 + 1 = ?" A variety of possible answers is not presented; the student must generate the variety and then select the appropriate answer. In this case the selection criterion relies largely on memory of the rules for numbers, operators, and counting.

The second kind of well-defined problem involves making the problem explicit and presenting a variety of possible responses. The student is then challenged to select the correct response from the presented variations. An example is the multiple-choice problem, where students have the variety generated for them:

Let $4x - 16 = 12$; solve for x.

a) 7   b) 8   c) 6   d) 4   e) none of these answers

Another variant of the well-defined problem challenges the student to imagine and explore a variety of possible solutions:

You are given a 4-gallon jug and a 3-gallon jug. Neither has any measuring markers on it. A pump can be used to fill the jugs with water. How can you get exactly 2 gallons of water in the 4-gallon jug? (Rich, 1983)

Here the user must imagine the variety of ways to fill and empty the jugs to arrive at the answer. A relatively small number of clear possibilities exists, thus making the problem manageable. However, one can imagine a well-defined problem that is more complicated (such as the traveling salesman problem below), where the number of possible combinations is so great that one cannot solve the problem by listing all the methods, as in the water jug problem.

The Traveling Salesman Problem

A salesman has a list of cities, each of which he must visit exactly once. There are direct roads between each pair of cities on the list. Find the route the salesman should follow so that he travels the shortest possible distance on a round trip, starting at any one of the cities and then returning there. (Rich, 1983)

With such problems, the sheer scope of possible solutions makes enumerating all possible answers unmanageable. In these cases one must engage in methods of estimation (heuristics) to attempt to approach a reasonable (albeit potentially suboptimal) answer. The method of solving is known, but the volume of possible answers is too great to consider.

Here the problem challenges our imagination to construct a method of estimation.

With ill-defined problems, considerable uncertainty exists about definitions, materials, and operations for solving the problem; much is not explicit. The student must ponder what the problem asks, considering a range of possible interpretations and selecting the best fit; generate a variety of possible solutions; and then engage in selecting among possible solutions. "What is the best way to invest $1,000?" is an example of this type of problem. The answer depends on considering variables such as risk-preference, duration of investment, age of investor, and so forth.

Each of these types of problems presents differing degrees of variation and selection as suggested by the evolutionary paradigm. In each case, rapid learning is facilitated by a) generating variety and/or b) rapid selection and accurate selection among that variety. These kinds of problems present both opportunities and threats when considered in conjunction with technology.

TENACITY, AND THE PROVISIONAL STATUS OF KNOWLEDGE

The creation of variation among trials is considered "blind" in the evolutionary paradigm. Much like brainstorming, it is random. Such trials are considered uncorrelated and independent of each other—a subsequent trial in no way suggests a moving in the "direction" of the solution (Campbell, 1987). Campbell identifies Bain (1874) as the first author to invoke the notion of trial and error in learning.

From the start, the importance of tenacity in trial-and-error learning is essential. One must engage with the problem in order to generate adequate trials to solve the problem. In the next step, evolutionary epistemology indicates that selection be uncompromising. One retains ideas that remain valid; ideas that fall become extinct. Retained ideas then spread to others as received knowledge. And, to follow Popper, these retained ideas remain only until new evidence (variation) invalidates the selection. Thus all knowledge is provisional, potentially subject to falsification. Discovery breaks with former knowledge when such knowledge can no longer accommodate anomalous variations and the imagination (blind variation) forges a new interpretation.

EDUCATION AND EVOLUTIONARY EPISTEMOLOGY

In focusing on the provisional nature of our knowledge and the role of teachers in creating an environment to promote trial and error, Perkinson (1993) states the implications for education eloquently:

> Let me first briefly summarize the critical approach [to education]. It is based on evolutionary epistemology, which claims that we never receive knowledge, but rather create it . . . by modifying knowledge we already have; and we modify our existing knowledge only when we uncover inadequacies in it that we have not recognized heretofore. Accepting this as an explanation of how knowledge grows, I have suggested that teachers construe their roles as facilitators of the growth of their students' knowledge. (p. 34)

I invoke this particular theory of learning because of the enormous variety of information presented to students through electronic media, and because electronic media allows for the creation of an ample variety of products, virtual environments, and information. Given this depth and breadth of information, the method of selection becomes essential. The process requires a means of thinking about information that includes having a set of selection criteria for deciding what information is analytically, aesthetically, or ethically appropriate. Further, given the numerous unbounded problems that the real world presents, the capacity and tenacity to generate variation in the trial-and-error process is essential—particularly in an age where continuous learning is emphasized.

TRIAL AND ERROR AND TECHNOLOGY

What is the relationship of technology to this process of trial and error? It depends on the kind of problem.

We have identified well-defined and ill-defined types of problems—or in terms of computer science, types of problem spaces. Tic-tac-toe is an example of a well-defined problem space. One can specify the optimal move, given any move by an opponent, because the response to any variation is known and all variation is known. Such problem spaces are tractable domains for computer programming: a computer can play an unbeatable game of tic-tac-toe. The game of checkers, likewise, is such a space (albeit far more complicated), and so is the game of chess (even more complicated). Such problem spaces offer an environment where a student can encounter an "expert." In other words, the computer can respond with the same level of complexity and accuracy as an expert. The chance to engage in much trial-and-error learning in relation to expert responses presents the opportunity for rapid learning.

Software developed for well-defined problem spaces can play an important role as students learn skills in such areas as addition, subtraction, letter sounds, or letter names, particu-

larly if the software is able to recognize and appropriately respond to common errors in a student's approach to solving the tasks. Expert systems like these can allow the student's errors (variation) to inform the software as to what set of problems are most appropriate for the student to focus on. This helps the student recognize the error that is preventing him or her from converging on the appropriate response. The student receives immediate and appropriate feedback on trials, offering the potential to accelerate learning.

The capability of software to provide this kind of expert diagnosis and an appropriate remedy presents an opportunity to restructure the classroom. A curriculum that presents well-defined problem spaces can potentially create resources in the classroom. Problems like these present the choice of offering practice with computer-based gaming via such expert systems, or through contact with a teacher. I am not suggesting a wholesale replacement of teachers for this type of problem. Rather, such problems present the opportunity for teachers to provide an environment for ample trial and error to build on instruction.

Over time it may seem more efficient and effective for teachers to spend the bulk of their time in teaching students those knowledge domains and problem spaces that are ill-ordered. For example, areas such as analyzing a student drawing or a hand-written story, or viewing a ballet performance or debate, are currently clearly beyond the diagnostic and prescriptive power of the computer. Those areas require teacher observation, diagnosis, and prescription.

Identifying the realm of problems presented to students as either well- or ill-ordered provides the basis for understanding what kinds of problems require direct teacher interaction with the student to guide the process of trial and error, versus teacher interaction augmented by interaction with computer software. This opens up the possibility of reconfiguring the classroom to use limited resources more efficiently and effectively.

WELL-DEFINED COMPLEXITY:
SIMULATION AND VIRTUAL WORLDS

In addition to expert systems that guide the trial-and-error process of learning, students and teachers also confront the prospect of simulated or virtual environments. These environments offer students contact with knowledge domains that were formerly too complex or required materials too expensive to allow broad access. Students can now engage in simulated chemistry and physics experiments, build cities, manage companies, and engage in strategic reasoning, all without leaving their keyboard. When well-constructed, such software removes the deadening presentation of abstract concepts and places the student in an environment that demands knowing particular information and concepts in order to proceed or even survive in the simulated environment. The software becomes a simulation of the "authentic," and exposes students to broader kinds of environments and processes, albeit simulated. Students can encounter very complex domains that are well-defined but have an enormous combination of possibilities.

Simulated environments allow for easy repetition of events that would take longer to repeat in real time. For example, a student can repeat a chemical experiment numerous times in simulation software. He can easily restart the experiment, thus encouraging ample trials to enhance learning. Real-world experiments differ in that the student learns how to handle lab equipment and actual chemicals. Indeed, this is invaluable. But in many cases, one can simulate the conceptual dimension of combining chemicals in particular proportions. These capabilities also exist in physical experiments, flight simulation, building construction, historical battles, and so on.

That such environments can be couched as a game further enhances the motivation to learn, to research, to be persistent—to have the tenacity to create variation. The test for educators is to make certain that these virtual environments are, in fact, valid. Are the relationships correct and the facts solid?

UNBOUNDED VARIATION: THE ILL-DEFINED INTERNET

A more complex issue is the problem of cultivating a student to manage the substantial and varied range of information with which they will come in contact. With the advent of the book, radio, television, and now the Internet, the tight boundaries of culture—which shape the personality and notions of self—have become increasingly permeable. Personal cognitive systems face much greater challenges today, as the variety of interpretations is vast. Under such conditions, establishing selection criteria becomes both problematic and increasingly important. The potential threat of such variety is echoed in the concerns about how such a range of information can influence student behavior. For example, the content of motion pictures is linked, rightly or wrongly, to incidents of student violence.

The responsibility for developing selection criteria among this broad range of information is also a topic of debate. Is the development of such criteria the responsibility of the parents, religious organizations, or the state? It seems a moot point, when the classroom and the home are now permeable, via the television and the Internet, to such a full range of information.

Throughout the nation, schools are in the process of selecting censoring tools to reduce full access to Internet sites. Educators expect that some students will potentially have inadequate criteria to make sense of an uncensored range of information. Schools therefore are supplying, rightly or wrongly, the criteria for students.

Recall that Plato expressed his concern about exposing children to the disturbing influence of minor scales in music, and society as a whole to the potentially deceitful influence of poets. For thousands of years, societies have seen children, who have not yet cultivated a solid set of selection criteria, as being at risk to the malevolent influence of uncensored and abundant information.

Educators have the formidable challenge of developing thinking skills to understand and select among such varied information. Evolutionary epistemology suggests that such variation is only tolerable if there is some means to determine which information is false and which is true. Without selection criteria, we cannot sort this insufferable amount of variation into true and false, and a state of confusion ensues. Indeed, as Maturana (1970/1980) has indicated, "A cognitive system is a system whose organization defines a domain of interactions in which it can act with relevance to the maintenance of itself" (p. 13).

This substantial variety confounds the definition of the domain of interactions, as well as the acts of relevance. Children today encounter a variety of cognitive domains while naturally seeking what Maturana calls "mutually orienting behavior." Such orienting behaviors, deriving from tradition, are now challenged by the trajectory of technological advance, democracy, and international trade. Now more than ever, secular and scientific thinking skills matter as change continues to challenge and dissolve existing social traditions and structures.

TECHNOLOGY AND THE ENHANCEMENT OF EDUCATOR THINKING

Information technology—in particular, well-constructed databases that contain a variety of student assessments—can also provide teachers with information about a student that will help them design appropriate work to enhance student thinking.

In many districts, a student profile is often difficult to access, as records of student performance and assessment are still in hard copy and dispersed across schools. A complete profile can provide a fully faceted view of the student, perhaps indicating a particular learning style or intelligence, which allows the teacher to more easily identify the student's particular strengths. Such a perspective could help teachers across subject areas to fashion instruction that plays on the student's strengths and thereby potentially enhance learning in the student's weaker areas.

Evaluating students in this way faces considerable, but not insurmountable, barriers in the current workflow and cultures of schools. The student as the central object of inquiry among a group of teaching practitioners provides a means for a collective evaluation of a student's capabilities. Teachers can discuss what approaches would best enhance the student's thinking skills, given their performance among a number of diverse knowledge domains. Or from the evolutionary view—presenting *variety* in terms of what the student can demonstrate helps educators converge on a more apropos solution for enhancing the student's performance—that is, *selecting* the appropriate course of study.

CONCLUSION

Technology presents educators with both threats and opportunities. The threats are that students may not be able to adequately integrate into their world view the enormous diversity of information to which they are exposed. Students then potentially could become confused, disoriented, or begin "tuning out" new information. This a case where too much variety drowns the capability of the student's existing set of selection criteria.

Alternately, the capacity for expert systems, simulation, and artificial intelligence within a gaming presentation offers the student the opportunity to directly engage with an expert and to be motivated to generate many trials (variation) in order to win and learn within such environments.

Current technology cannot displace the role of the educator in facilitating and assessing student performance in partic-

ular activities where the problem to be solved is not well-defined. The great bulk of problems in the world fall under this category, so educators need not fear their displacement by technology. However, there is the potential to restructure the classroom environment as students use software to work on well-defined problems, and teachers spend more time with their students cultivating approaches to ill-defined problems.

Finally, diverse information about a student's performance, facilitated by database technology, enhances the process by which teachers think about students—and about how to better craft instruction to improve students' processes of thinking and learning.

REFERENCES

Bain, A. (1874). *The senses and the intellect* (3rd ed.). New York: Appleton.

Campbell, D. (1969). Variation and selective retention in socio-cultural evolution. *General systems, 16,* 69–85.

Campbell, D. (1987). Blind variation and selective retention in creative thought as in other knowledge processes. In G. Radnitizky and W. W. Bartley, III (Eds.), *Evolutionary epistemology, rationality, and the sociology of knowledge* (pp. 91–114). La Salle, IL: Open Court.

Maturana, H. (1970/1980). Biology and cognition. In *Autopoieses and cognition: The realization of the living* (pp. 2–62). Dordrecht: Reidel.

McLuhan, M. (1964). *Understanding media: The extensions of man.* New York: Signet, McGraw-Hill.

Newell, A. (1969). Heuristic programming: Ill-structured problems. In J. S. Aronofsky (Ed.), *Progress in operations research,* Vol. 3. New York: Wiley.

Perkinson, H. J. (1993). *Since Socrates: Studies in the history of Western educational thought.* New York: Longman.

Popper, K. (1979). *Objective knowledge: An evolutionary approach.* Oxford: Clarendon Press.

Reitman, W. (1964). Heuristic decision procedures, open constraints, and the structure of ill-defined problems. In M. W. Shelley & G. L. Bryans (Eds.), *Human judgement and optimality.* New York: Wiley.

Rich, E. (1983). *Artificial intelligence.* New York: McGraw-Hill.

Simon, H. (1973). The structure of ill-structured problems. *Artificial intelligence, 4,* 181.

76

Thinking in the Information Age

Gary R. Morrison and Deborah L. Lowther

In education we have typically viewed our students as absorbers of knowledge. We give them a textbook, handouts, exercises, and lectures to help them learn the content. This view is consistent with Ausubel's (1968) approach to receptive learning, in which the student must master a body of knowledge in a meaningful manner. Today we might question the viability of such a model, in view of the massive growth of knowledge. Ten years ago a teacher could be comfortable teaching from a single, district-selected textbook. The world, as defined by the classroom, revolved around this textbook; in a sense, the textbook defined the world.

In 1999 there was one Internet-capable computer for every 13.8 students in the United States (Jerald & Orlofsky, 1999). Students with Internet access have a massive body of information ranging from facts to raw data that they can analyze to generate new knowledge. Schools can no longer focus on a body of knowledge a student must master. Rather, we must transition to helping our students locate, manipulate, analyze, interpret, and generate knowledge. Our emphasis must change from a focus on the content (for example, mastery of a subject) to a focus on the processes of learning and thinking.

INFORMATION TECHNOLOGY AND THE CLASSROOM

One approach to making this transition is to examine the processes and changes that have occurred in businesses as they have switched from an industrialized-based to a knowledge-based enterprise. Businesses have realized that they must change their method of doing business and come to grips with a knowledge society (Nonaka, 1994). To be successful, enterprises must move beyond simply processing information and begin to create new knowledge to solve today's challenges. One means of creating new knowledge is through the use of information technology.

Businesses, governments, health care, libraries, and other organizations use information technology to process information and to create new knowledge and solutions. O'Brien defines an information system as a "combination of people, hardware, software, communication networks, and data resources that collects, transforms, and disseminates information in an organization" (1998, p. 4). Notice the difference between this view of information and Ausubel's (1968) view of content. O'Brien describes a process where the worker is actively engaged in collecting, transforming, and disseminating information. Ausubel's receptive learning theory describes a passive student who is absorbing content from a textbook.

Within an information technology system, users transform information with hardware and software. For example, analysts, sales personnel, managers, and others use spreadsheets, databases, and statistical programs to transform information. Using these programs, they can manipulate the data to find trends or specific cases, or to summarize data into a manageable number such as a mean. They then use Web pages, multimedia presentations, and e-mail to disseminate this new knowledge to others. Others use this new information to solve problems, make decisions, and generate new knowledge.

For learners to go beyond simply "knowing" to actually understanding information, they must become engaged with reshaping and transforming information (Gardner, 1991). As the students manipulate, analyze, and interpret information, they identify discrepancies between what they know about their world and what the data indicate. This type of puzzlement (Savery & Duffy, 1995) or cognitive dissonance can lead students to search for solutions. This process of how the learner develops understanding is consistent with a constructivist approach to instruction. Compared to a receptive learning approach, the constructivist approach encourages students to explore, inquire, analyze, and solve problems as a means of learning and developing understanding.

A constructivist approach requires different teaching strategies than the more traditional "master a body of knowledge" approach that often results in an emphasis on memorization. One constructivist approach is to embed an information technology process within a problem-based learning environment. In this setting, the instructor guides the learners as they identify and define a problem, then gather information and data needed to solve the problem. As they gather the data, they manipulate it by sorting, analyzing, calculating, or transforming it in some other way, which yields new knowledge or, at least, new knowledge for the learner. This problem-based learning approach is very similar to the information technology process adults use in the workplace.

Since workplace requirements now focus on the ability to use technology to process information, it is imperative that our schools adopt a technology integration approach that prepares students to succeed in a digitized world. Both the American Association of University Women (2000) and Lowther, Bassoppo-Moyo, and Morrison (1998) have suggested that we need to redefine computer literacy. Students and teachers must go beyond traditional computer literacy goals to attain a level of technological competence: they must know how to use a computer to solve problems. To do this, schools must move away from primarily using computers to deliver a body of knowledge and start using them as problem-solving tools.

A MODEL FOR TECHNOLOGY INTEGRATION

We have developed a model for designing problem-based lesson plans that integrates computers with the information technology process (Morrison & Lowther, in press). This model creates a student-centered learning environment in which students collect and manipulate information to generate new knowledge. For example, students might create a database of earthquakes and volcanoes that occurred during the past 100 years to "discover" the set of plates that comprise the Earth's crust. Another example would involve students creating a rich database of information about U.S. presidents to use as a basis for predicting which presidential candidate has the characteristics most likely to result in election.

A search of the World Wide Web and textbooks produces a host of resources with the term "computer integration" in their title—resources that define the term in a multitude of ways. We propose a three-level definition of technology integration, with levels based on the student's control over processing of information and information flow. We define "control over processing" as degree of manipulation possible, and "information flow" as amount of information that the user can input.

Level 1 involves low student control of processing and information flow. The teacher selects software that matches the objectives for a specific unit of instruction (for example, drill-and-practice, tutorials, and simulations). If appropriate, all the students in the classroom can use the software, or a select group of students can use it as a remedial activity or enrichment exercise.

Level 2 is where student control of processing and information flow is moderate. Students use productivity software such as Internet search engines or word processing as part of a lesson. A student might search the Internet for information to use in a report or use a word processor to write a short story.

Level 3 involves high student control of processing and information flow. Students use productivity software such as spreadsheets, databases, Internet search engines, and presentation (e.g., PowerPoint) applications to find, collect, and manipulate data, and to present their new knowledge.

The evolution from Level 1 to Level 3 represents a shift in philosophy and methods from using the computer as a device to deliver instruction, to one where computer technology is embedded in the lesson as a tool. A Level 3 integration lesson also represents an information technology approach to learning where students are learning real-world skills as they also acquire knowledge that supports district, state, and national standards.

NTeQ, iNtegrating Technology for inQuiry, is a 10-step model for developing Level 3 integrated lesson plans. More detailed information about this model and sample lesson plans are available at http://www.nteq.com. The focus of the NTeQ model is on the teacher's development of the lesson plan (see Figure 76.1), hence some of the steps in the model are out of sequence for classroom use.

The first step to planning an integrated lesson is to specify *all* the objectives related to the specific lesson, not just those objectives directly related to computer activities. There are two reasons for specifying all objectives. First, not everything is best taught with the aid of a computer. Students typically need to read (books, magazines, encyclopedias, etc.) to gain an understanding and background for the problem. Second, if you have a limited number of computers in your classroom, students will need other meaningful activities to help them achieve the objectives.

Computer technology is most effective when there is a match between the functions of the computer software and the instructional objectives. Computer functions include analyzing data, sorting data, visualizing information, drawing, writing, editing, and so forth. These functions are the tasks or capabilities inherent in such applications as spreadsheets, word

—*Figure 76.1*—
NTeQ Model

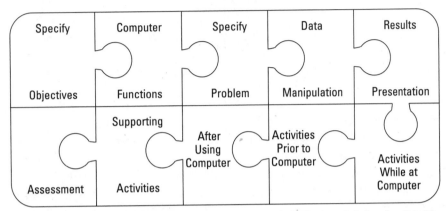

From *Integrating Computer Technology into the Classroom,* by G. R. Morrison, D. L. Lowther, & L. De-Meulle, 1999. Columbus, OH: Merrill. Used with permission.

processing, databases, and graphic programs. If a match exists between the verb in an objective and a computer function, then it follows that there is an appropriate use of the computer in the lesson. For example, if an objective requires the learner to *interpret* the effect on temperature of adding ice to tap water, then there is a match with the spreadsheet functions of calculating and graphing. Similarly, if an objective requires a learner to *categorize* or *select* information, then there is a match with the functions of a database. As a final example, if an objective requires the learner to *create a diagram or map,* then there is a match with the functions of a drawing program. Morrison and Lowther (in press) include a more detailed listing of computer functions in their appendix.

THE NTeQ PROBLEM-SOLVING PROCESS

Integrated lessons are problem-based; that is, students investigate a problem and learn required content and basic skills in a meaningful context. The next step of the model is to define the problem that students will solve. It is best when the problem uses real-world data and is meaningful to the students. Students can even participate in the final definition of the problem or suggest specific problems to solve as part of a unit.

Data manipulation. One aspect of the problem-solving process involves analyzing data to solve the problem. In this step, the teacher and students must determine the most appropriate ways to manipulate the data, such as creating graphs, sorting data, finding the means, creating a map, or using other computer functions. It is important that the teacher have a clear idea of the various ways that students can manipulate the

data. Keep in mind that the students may identify other questions for analysis as they work on the problem.

Results presentation. As the students reach solutions to the problems, they are simultaneously producing new knowledge. This step focuses on how the students will present their new knowledge. Forms of presentation include written and oral reports, multimedia presentations, newsletters, articles in a school magazine, Web pages, television, and radio shows, and books or pamphlets. These items might also be part of one or more portfolios a student creates during the semester or year.

Activities while at the computer. Once you have defined how the students will manipulate the data and the type of presentation the students will make, you can plan what they will do while using the computer. This is important, as computer time is limited. Are they using a computer to search for data, graph their results, write a paper, or create a multimedia presentation? In most lessons, students will use a computer more than once, so you need to consider all their computer activities.

Activities prior to using the computer. Now you can define what the students must do to get ready to use the computer. If they are doing an Internet search, then they should prepare a list of search terms. A group that is entering data into a spreadsheet or database should organize the data for easy entry. If they are creating a database, they should identify the database fields. Preparing for their computer time can make their time more efficient and allow each team member and group adequate access.

Activities after using the computer. Almost anyone can create a colorful, three-dimensional graph with a spreadsheet;

find hundreds of URLs related to a topic; or create a visually pleasing report from information in a database. But what does this information mean? You need to determine what the students will do with the results of their data manipulation. For example, what questions could we ask about a graph? One method to help the students interpret their results is to use a Think Sheet (Morrison and Lowther, in press), which provides students with a series of questions to guide their thinking and interpretation of the results.

Supporting activities. We consider learning activities that are not directly dependent on computer use as supporting or multidimensional activities. These activities support the achievement of both computer and noncomputer objectives through reading, exercises, discussions, small group activities, or a host of other instructional activities.

Assessment. The final step in planning the integrated lesson is to determine how you will assess student learning, which might include not only objective tests but also other forms of assessment. For example, you might develop rubrics to evaluate the students' products and presentations. Similarly, the students might assemble different parts of the project into portfolios that you will evaluate with a rubric. Or you might have the students write self-assessments that can provide insight into their approaches and thinking processes.

Introducing the lesson. Once you have completed planning the lesson, you can implement it in your classroom. If this is the first time your students have experienced a problem-based lesson, you may need to introduce them to the problem-solving steps. You might also establish ground rules for classroom work by allowing the students to suggest rules and strategies for enforcement, at the same time explaining each individual's responsibility. For example, if one of your objectives is that students demonstrate how to create a PowerPoint presentation, then you need to explain what you expect the presentation to include. Although students can work in groups, each student is responsible for demonstrating all aspects of the process. Providing clear guidelines will resolve some of the potential problems.

CHANGING ROLES FOR TEACHER AND STUDENTS

The iNtegrating Technology for inQuiry Model is based on a Level 3 integration approach in that the NTeQ lessons are problem-based, use real-world data, and create a student-centered learning environment. Since NTeQ is quite different from a traditional approach, both teacher and students need to adopt new roles.

Teachers assume three roles in the integrated classroom (Morrison & Lowther, in press). First, the teacher is a *designer*, creating integrated lesson plans by adapting existing plans or developing new ideas. The problems that students will investigate as part of the lesson plan need to be based in the real world and meaningful to the student. Computers are not the focus of the lesson, but rather they serve as a tool to achieve designated lesson objectives. A teacher must carefully design the lesson to incorporate the multiple learning resources needed to achieve the stated objectives.

Second, the teacher is a *facilitator*, no longer functioning as the main source of information, but rather helping students solve problems and find answers. When asked a question, the facilitator is more likely to prompt the learner to find an answer than to simply provide an answer herself. To help the students develop the necessary search and problem-solving skills, the teacher must model the appropriate processes.

Third, the teacher is a *manager* of the classroom. Most of today's classrooms that are fortunate enough to have computers have only a limited number for student use. As a result, the teacher must develop a viable rotation schedule that provides equitable student access to computers. The NTeQ model works well in a classroom with a ratio of one computer for four to six students. Teachers have also effectively implemented the model in classrooms where each student has a laptop computer. The teacher may assign individual roles on the team so that one student does not dominate the keyboard. Roles can include data entry, data checker, and reader. The teacher must also find solutions to technical problems. Given the complexity of today's computers and the skills of the students, a teacher needs to be *wise* rather than trying to be a technical wizard. Calling on students and support staff to solve technical problems is often more efficient for both teacher and students. Teachers must also manage the classroom environment. During a problem-based lesson, students will work on a variety of tasks, and that scenario often results in a higher noise level. The teacher must manage the environment to keep the students on task and noise at an acceptable level without dampening enthusiasm and creativity.

With this approach, the student's role changes from a passive absorber of knowledge to that of an active researcher who is discovering and producing knowledge. In the NTeQ model, students not only gain new knowledge, but also increase their problem-solving, research, and computer skills. They learn to think and behave like researchers. They must also learn to work as members of a collaborative team, where they grow to value team collaboration, develop teamwork skills, and solve problems within the group.

REFERENCES

American Association of University Women. (2000, April). *Tech-savvy: Educating girls in the new computer age* [On-line]. Available: http://www.aauw.org/2000/techsexecsum.html

Ausubel, D. P. (1968). *Educational psychology: A cognitive view*. New York: Holt, Rinehart, and Winston.

Gardner, H. (1991). *The unschooled mind: How children think and how schools should teach*. New York: McGraw-Hill.

Jerald, C. D. & Orlofsky, G. F. (1999). Raising the bar on school technology. *Education Week, 14*, 58–69.

Lowther, D. L., Bassoppo-Moyo, T., & Morrison, G. R. (1998). Moving from computer literate to technological competent: The next educational reform. *Computers and Human Behavior, 14*, 93–109.

Morrison, G. R. & Lowther, D. L. (in press). *Integrating computer technology into the classroom* (2nd ed.). Columbus, OH: Merrill.

Morrison, G. R., Lowther, D. L., & DeMeulle, L. (1999). *Integrating computer technology into the classroom*. Columbus, OH: Merrill.

Nonaka, I. (1994). A dynamic theory of organizational knowledge creation. *Organizational Science, 5*, 14–37.

O'Brien, J. A. (1998). *Introduction to information systems: An inter-networked enterprise perspective*. Boston: Irwin McGraw-Hill.

Savery, J. R. & Duffy, T. M. (1995). Problem-based learning: An instructional model and its constructivist framework. *Educational Technology, 45*, 31–38.

77

Learning in a Digital World

JOHN RICHARDS

The inevitable convergence of a wide range of communication and information systems, including video delivery, telephony, computer networks, and online services, is opening up new possibilities for thinking. For the most part, these are known technologies, and technological integration is a matter of time and money. In contrast, we have not yet begun to think about the integration of diverse media from a human perspective.

This convergence is about to have unique and somewhat unpredictable effects on learning, thinking, and our understanding of the educational enterprise. This goes well beyond the telecommunications industry's belief that a ubiquitous voice, video, and data infrastructure provides the opportunity for just-in-time learning throughout life.

People relate to the introduction or modification of even a single medium in different ways depending on the context of use, the individual's understanding of the situation, and the new ways in which this transforms people's imagination. The development of functional multiple-media learning environments is not simply the result of combining different media types (an additive process), but consists of creating a brand new kind of media (a transforming process). The development of educational uses of these new media types depends on understanding the ways people will see the world differently and come to use the media for learning. As real video and truly interactive networking are integrated, television "audiences" do not simply become network "users," and network "users" do not become audiences. Instead, qualitatively different experiences are in store.

Educators and researchers are concerned with integrating the Internet and the Web into classrooms, and how these media change the way children think. Today's teenagers watch television while they surf the Web, talk on the telephone, or visit several chat rooms with a CD playing in the background. This is a multi-tasking environment that goes way beyond the Internet (Richards, 2000).

ANALOG VERSUS DIGITAL

The transformation from analog to digital will have deep implications for human knowledge and even deeper implications for human communication and relationships, according to Kaufman and Smarr:

> Our analog modes of communication by voice, print, and video are gradually being replaced by digital modes. Ultimately most of human knowledge will be stored in a common digital library. (1993, p. ix)

Kaufman and Smarr argue that the fundamental idea of replacing the continuous world of nature with a model or simulation of that world formed of discrete units has transformed the pursuit of science. The digital perspective provides a controllable, visualizable representation that is becoming the key to a more comprehensible world.

How does our understanding of the content of media differ as we move from analog to digital? This is not an arcane question pertaining to the relevance of supercomputer simulations. Rather, it affects all of our interactions with voice, video, and data technologies. For example, in the most developed of these digitizations, consider how writing e-mail messages differs from writing letters. It seems that only yesterday we were seeing paeans to letter writing as a dying medium. The commonly accepted explanation was that culture was deteriorating and the literacy required for letters was a lost art. In retrospect, given the plethora of e-mail, the delays in letter delivery were not tolerable, especially when contrasted with the immediacy of telephones. But e-mail did not simply change the nature of letter writing; it replaced letter writing with a panoply of alternatives. Not only did a new, more informal genre evolve, but so did entirely new forms of written communication with entirely new rules for participation. E-mail, chats, bulletin boards, and electronic mailing lists do not have straightforward analogs in the letter-writing or, more generally, precomputer culture. Even more distinct forms of communication are only now appearing. As argued by Sherry Turkle (1995), chats and multi-user domains—also called MUDs and MUSEs—are developing unique and unprecedented participation structures. How will these conversations change with the easy availability of voice on the Internet? How will putting telephone (or video-telephone) on the Internet change the nature of a phone call? What new forms will evolve?

In my judgment, the most profound differences will occur with video. The control added to video through the digitization process changes the nature of video. More importantly, the digitization inherent in convergence brings together television and computers, two culturally distinct technologies that have also been distinct in development and production. As we talk about an infrastructure that integrates voice, video, and data, we must consider the power of the cultural differences of these technologies and their complex contexts of use.

McLuhan: Ceteris Paribus

> There is no *ceteris paribus* in the world of media and technology. Every extension or acceleration effects new configurations in the overall situation at once.
> —Marshall McLuhan, *Understanding Media* (1964)

McLuhan argues that the effects of a new technological extension cannot be measured in a test that assumes *ceteris paribus*, that is, all other things being equal. In this realm, once the innovation is introduced we can no longer imagine the world without it. This has nothing to do with the act of measuring, as with the Heisenberg Uncertainty Principle, which holds that measuring changes the object being measured. Rather, one aspect cannot be isolated for measurement because technological innovations change everything all at once. The extension is not just changing the media or the technology; it is changing how we imagine. The act of imagining has expanded to new dimensions.

This was true with the introduction of the technology of literacy as well. Literacy changed how humans perceive their reality. It created a sequential storytelling motif and almost eliminated the demands on memory. Logan (1986) argues that it actually changed the structure of our brain by exercising the logical dimension of thought.

> A medium of communication is not merely a passive conduit for the transmission of information but rather an active force in creating new social patterns and new perceptual realities. A person who is literate has a different world view than one who receives information exclusively through oral communication. The alphabet, independent of the spoken languages it transcribes or

the information it makes available, has its own intrinsic impacts. (Logan, 1986, p. 24)

The current rate of change in the introduction of new media is unprecedented in human history. Children are imagining and learning in new ways. Their ability to process information, media, and various sources of data is truly a modern phenomenon. ("Why can't we 'pause' the world?" "The problem with live sporting events is that you miss the replays.") They are experiencing a world that differs in deep ways from the world of their parents and teachers. This presents unique challenges to educators, who must accept that the Internet is only one part of what students are facing. The integration of voice, video, and data presents even more changes in the way we think and approach information. If every media extension changes everything all at once, in very unpredictable ways, then the multiple extensions that define convergence will undoubtedly shift the educational paradigm.

The Internet Is Not a Library

People tend to talk of the Internet as a library. But a library has structure, whether the Dewey Decimal System or the Library of Congress. In addition, there is at least a double selection process for what goes into a library. In order to be published, books, magazines, music, and video have undergone the scrutiny of at least a publisher and editor, and most often a copy editor and several outside readers. In order to be in a library, they must also be selected by a librarian. Admittedly, vanity publishers and publishers with extreme agendas exist, as do lazy librarians, and even librarians with hidden agendas. Books that many of us feel are not worthwhile do get into libraries. However, compared to the Internet, the library is an incredibly selective environment. When people speak about "publishing" on the Web, they often mean throwing stuff up on a site. There is no selection process. The Internet is the largest compendium of unfiltered and unsorted information ever assembled. The Internet is a yard sale. As with all yard sales, if you know what you are doing, sometimes you can find a masterpiece.

The inevitable result has been the emergence of the significance of brands. People trust CNN.com because they know there are editors and fact checkers. In the absence of brands, the challenge for students is to "know what they are doing." Search and selection capabilities are entirely different than they were 20 years ago. When I was in graduate school, the challenge was to find 10 or 20 references on a particular topic. The challenge now is to select 10 or 20 references from among the thousand that may appear on a list.

PARTICIPATION VERSUS DELIVERY

A philosophy of participation and user constructibility has dominated networking. From the beginning of the Arpanet—the U.S. Defense Department precursor to the Internet—networking has been distributed with no central locus of control. For national security reasons, the network was designed so that the removal of any node would have no effect on the rest of the system. Moreover, the World Wide Web has had such wild success because it so adeptly fits the underlying participatory philosophy of networking.

By contrast, centralized delivery models have dominated television and cinema. Beginning with Hollywood domination of movie making and continuing with the big three U.S. broadcast companies, television and cinema content have been tightly controlled, produced, and distributed. Researchers are only now recognizing that television audiences actively produce meaning from the programs they watch (Ang, 1995). As the plethora of programs provides choice, the audience is freer to construct meaning through participating in these choices. Furthermore, television itself is evolving as the surrounding technologies change. As Ang notes, "The VCR disrupted the modern entanglement between centralized transmission and privatized reception because it displaced the locus of control over the circulation of cultural texts to more local contexts" (p. 12).

The audience experience is different when the same movie is shown in a cinema, on TV, or as a tape played on a home VCR. The audience is different, with many different expectations. For example, consider continuity and control. In a cinema, movie viewing is continuous and initiated by the theater. Alternatively, television presentations are "geared" toward interruptions, and started and stopped by the design of the programmer. With a rented videotape, the audience can take a bathroom break without losing viewing time. In short, the nature of the medium is changing because of the role of the audience.

AUDIENCE VERSUS USERS

Each of the media carry with them different relationships with their users and audiences, and these relationships are not dependent solely on the medium in isolation. Consider the distinctions Ellis (1992) draws between cinema and television audiences. The cinema spectator is a voyeur. By contrast, television viewers are "uninvolved in the events portrayed" and "... are able to see 'life's parade at their fingertips,' but at the cost of exempting themselves from that parade for the du-

ration of their TV viewing" (pp. 169–170). The spectator pays for the cinema and resents any commercial intrusion. The television viewer accepts commercials as a part of the basic structure of watching. This too is evolving with the pay-tier channels on cable such as HBO.

How does this compare with the audience for video software? Or video on the Web? As software developers we have naively assumed that new media types fit in with the nature of the software. Videos, pictures, and sounds are included for motivational purposes, or as illustrations of some concept, and have little or no fundamental effect on the user. Moreover, the deep distinctions between viewers and spectators suggest that the computer-user relationship probably changes with the introduction of the Web. Typically, the computer-user relationship is one-to-one, essentially an individual participation structure. The Web is somewhat different without many precursors, as it is essentially a social structure. The underlying metaphor is that we are connecting with other individuals in a dynamic, changing, unstructured, cluttered world.

Different educational philosophies have grown up around the technologies. Distinct cultures exist in technology and education. These two cultures—the digital, consisting of computers and networking; and the analog, consisting of TV and the cable video world—know little of each other and in the past have rarely interacted.

CONVERGING MEDIA

At CNN we are trying to navigate between these cultures. Traditionally operating from a cable television perspective, we have produced a commercial-free news and features program for schools for more than a decade. Each evening we create a Teacher's Guide that provides a run-down of the program, suggestions for classroom use, and links to other materials. This was first distributed by fax and e-mail, and is now available at http://cnnfyi.com/newsroom or through an electronic mailing list.

The challenge for CNN NEWSROOM is to connect the news to the curriculum and to help students see the relevance of the curriculum in the context of their world. A news story on Bosnia allows a history teacher to ask what Muslims are doing in the middle of Europe, and what this has to do with the Ottoman Empire or with World War I. A story on the need to speed up the space station to prevent it from falling to Earth allows a science teacher to ask what the relationship is between altitude and velocity, or to introduce a discussion of vectors and combinations of forces (i.e., escape velocity). A triple heart bypass of a world leader or movie star allows the science teacher to talk about the heart, or a nutrition and health teacher to talk about cholesterol and exercise. The currency of the news responds to the perpetual student question, "Why do I need to know this?"

CNN NEWSROOM services middle and high school students, and we consistently conduct research to determine its effectiveness. Recently, we conducted focus groups in Atlanta, Boston, and Columbus, Ohio, with males and females ages 14 to 24. We were particularly interested in differentiating the teens' perceptions and usage of news and information. What we found has changed our thinking and contributed to the introduction of two new programs. News, almost all agreed, is predictable, passive, and boring, and delivered peripherally—perhaps received while walking through their parents' living room. News is not for them but for their parents. Most told us they do not follow a news story unless they experience it as relating to their lives. Very often they had no context for understanding a story. Many claimed they often lost interest within a matter of days, even during "relevant" stories such as the shootings at Columbine High School. Some said oversaturation in the media and prolongation of a story were factors.

Information, on the other hand, is something they seek—facts they think they need to know. Their primary sources of information are magazines, the Internet, and radio. Television provides information almost inadvertently, whether they happen to be watching a program containing important information (many said while watching programs their parents had selected) or by tuning in when they were aware of something special. The most widely mentioned news program was "20/20" for its "whole story" personal approach and Barbara Walters's candid questions, the kind "I'd want to ask."

It was clear that we needed to provide a voice for students. They wanted more control over information and were more interested in their peers than in adults as news sources. As a result we created CNN Student Bureau (CNNSB), a virtual, distributed, worldwide student news source. News from CNNSB can be regional, national, or global in scope. The constructive process of producing news and reflecting on the production process makes students much more effective and critical consumers of news.

CNNSB operates in high schools as an in-school program integrated into journalism, English, or history departments; as an interdisciplinary program; or as a club. At the university level, CNNSB works with mass communication and journalism departments. Almost 650 schools are involved in the program from 48 states and 42 countries. To date, we have aired more than 60 student-edited, student-produced stories on the CNN networks.

In addition, we have recently partnered with Harcourt Publishing, Riverdeep Interactive Learning, and HighWired. com to create CNNfyi.com, a news and information site for middle and high school students and teachers. The student edition provides context and stories designed to catch student interest, and a parallel teacher edition helps teachers make the curriculum connections that bring interest and relevance to their lessons. We are planning for as much as 30 percent of the student edition to be CNNSB stories. As we try to integrate CNN NEWSROOM programming with CNNfyi.com, we are learning the relative strengths and weaknesses of communicating in each medium. We can get so much more information on the Web, yet the television image is much more powerful. We are experimenting with these new formats and paradigms in order to understand how to reach a generation that is demanding multiple media and seeking control over their digital environments.

The rise of image in communication is more than a matter of educating ourselves to analyze and interpret visual experiences. Rather, as argued by Taylor and Saarinen (1994), the incorporation of images in presentations has changed the very nature of communication. Text by its very nature is linear and sequential; a picture or video allows for an infinite series of branches.

This may not be a new stage of meaning but a return to an old one. McLuhan (1964) argues that prior to Gutenberg, storytelling relied on images and metaphors that were much more generative, taking into account the multiple audiences and the individual construction of meaning. The integration of video media with computer technology is not a quantitative difference but a qualitative difference that requires us to rethink learning in this digital world.

Today's students are growing up in a different world than their parents did. They have a very different experience with media and therefore perceive a very different reality. They are products of a different upbringing. We have to adhere to all of our constructivist warnings that limit our access and understanding of another's reality as we try to anticipate how students think and how they will evolve in this media-rich information world.

REFERENCES

Ang, I. (1995). *Living room wars: Rethinking media audiences for a post-modern world.* London: Routledge.

Ellis, J. (1992). *Visible fictions: Cinema, television, video* (Rev. ed.). London: Routledge.

Kaufman, W. J., & Smarr, L. L. (1993). *Supercomputing and the transformation of science.* New York: Scientific American Library.

Logan, R. (1986). *The alphabet effect.* New York: William Morrow.

McLuhan, M. (1964). *Understanding media: The extensions of man.* New York: McGraw-Hill.

Richards, J. (2000, June 24). Testimony for the Congressional Web-Based Education Commission, Atlanta, Georgia. Available: http://www.webcommission.org

Taylor, M. C., & Saarinen, E. (1994). *Imagologies: Media philosophy.* London: Routledge.

Turkle, S. (1995). *Life on the screen.* New York: Simon and Schuster.

78

Integrating Research, Thinking, and Technology

Joanne Marien, Elaine Vislocky, and Linda Chapman

With the arrival of the 21st century, the challenge of preparing our students to be proficient at the sort of sophisticated thinking and problem solving required for life in the new millennium is no longer our distant goal; it is our reality. In suburban Somers School District, 50 miles north of New York City, we are using a research-based curriculum to develop in our students the thinking skills needed to survive in an ever-changing, information-driven society. We rely strongly on the use of technology to help us meet this challenge.

Given the digital information explosion, we can't possibly teach students all they will need to know—nor can we even predict what that will be. We can and must, therefore, equip them with the ability to access, evaluate, and use information to create new understandings. Like similar efforts throughout the country, New York State's Learning Standards in seven curriculum areas demand this. Despite differences in content, each of the 29 standards emphasizes the need for students to be good thinkers and effective users of information. Across all disciplines, students must be able to pose questions, analyze relevant information, and then construct and communicate new understandings and ideas. We have found that the process of conducting research provides rich opportunities for students to develop these essential life skills. Technology has become an indispensable aid to our student researchers not only as a means of accessing information but as a valuable tool for organizing, manipulating, and communicating information and ideas.

THE RESEARCH PROTOCOL

To bring direction to this work, we developed a districtwide road map—a research protocol—that clearly outlines the process of conducting research. Our protocol is based on the premise that we must teach research and its underlying skills, not assign them. Using a developmental approach that builds consistency throughout the grades, the research protocol guides the learner through the various thinking and information-processing strategies that the research process requires.

We have developed four increasingly complex versions for students in grades K–3, 4–6, 7–9, and 10–12 (see http://www.somers.k12.ny.us/intranet/research/protocols.html). For primary students, the research protocol includes only three steps, each with its own set of scaffolding questions. As students progress through the grades, their research protocol becomes more comprehensive, requiring more sophisticated thinking and more proficiency in using technology. For example, at the K–3 level, a student would consider "Where can I find answers to my questions?" (see Figure 78.1). In response, a student might determine the best two of four resources provided by the teacher or decide whether an atlas or an encyclopedia would be a more appropriate resource for the question being asked. The related step at the 10–12 level, "Identify appropriate resources and their location," requires students to find and then evaluate resources from a much broader array of possible choices (see Figure 78.2). Because of technology's impact, these resources have multiplied tremendously, now come in many formats, and are located in places beyond the school library.

As students work through the steps of the research protocol, they are actually progressing through a kind of problem-solving process: they identify and clarify a problem, devise and carry out a plan, distinguish between relevant and irrelevant information, and then evaluate their solution or conclusion and the plan used to produce it (see Figure 78.3). It is not realistic to expect students to independently carry out this level of thinking without a carefully designed support structure. We have embedded scaffolding questions within the protocol as one initial source of guidance (see Figure 78.2). Teachers use these to carefully lead students through each step of the process, often modeling steps and sharing other students' work

—*Figure 78.1*—
Research Protocol, K–3

1. I think about my subject:
What do I know?
What can I tell or show you?
What do I want to know?
What are my research questions?

2. I do my research:
Where can I find answers to my questions?
Are these sources I can understand?
Have I organized what I've learned?
How can I share my answers with others?

3. My research is done:
Does the information I've found answer my
   questions?
What have I learned?
Can I list the resources I used to answer my
   questions?

—*Figure 78.2*—
Research Protocol, 10–12

1. Define my task.
Have I completed preliminary assignments in order
   to begin the research?
What is my research problem?
How will I present the results of my research and to
   whom?

2. Determine the research questions.
Do I have sufficient background knowledge about
   my research problem to be able to define my
   research question?
What questions am I trying to answer?

3. Identify appropriate resources and their location.
Which collections should I investigate?
What types of resources may have the information I
   need?
Where am I likely to find the resources I need?
Am I keeping a list of potential resources including
   all of the information I will need for my list of
   Works Cited?

4. Plan my agenda.
To conduct my research, how should I plan my time,
   both in and outside of school, to meet my
   deadlines?
Do I need to coordinate my plans with others?

5. Gather information.
What is the best way to search for information
   within each recommended resource?
What is the best way for me to collect and organize
   my information?
Can I find enough relevant information to answer all
   of my research questions?
Did I save all pertinent information?
For each resource, did I collect all the information
   required for my notes and Works Cited?

6. Evaluate information.
For each resource, have I determined its reliability,
   currency, and relevancy to my research questions?
Given my findings so far, do I need to re-evaluate
   my research questions?
Do I need to repeat any of the steps listed above?

7. Organize my information.
Does the information make sense?
Do I have the information I need? What information
   am I missing, and what do I need to do to find it?
Is the information significant to my research
   question?
How will I answer my questions in my own words?
Did I create a logical structure to organize my
   information?
Do I need to repeat any of the steps listed above?

(continued)

as exemplars. Ultimately, our goal is for high school seniors to grapple with challenging research questions independently, without teacher support.

Our research-based curriculum has created thoughtful classrooms in which students are, as Beyer describes, engaged in "purposeful thinking in the pursuit of meaningful learning" (1997, pp. 55–56). By beginning with students' own questions, we ensure that they have a clear purpose for their research and that the work that follows will be meaningful to them. For example, after studying electricity, a 2nd grade teacher tapped into a student's interest in electric eels by helping her to pose the question, "How do electric eels get their electricity?" In an 8th grade course focusing on the 20th century, students asked, "What was so great about The Great Society?" And, as a culminating project in Advanced Placement U.S. History, juniors debated, "Whose America is it?" Compelling questions such as these engage students' interest, energize the research process, and foster lively thinking and discussions.

Once students have refined their research question, they are ready to progress through a series of three overlapping steps in the protocol:

- Identify appropriate resources and their location.
- Gather your information.
- Evaluate your information.

—Figure 78.2—
Research Protocol, 10–12 *(continued)*

8. Think and apply.
What are the implications of my findings? What conclusions have I reached?
Have I explained my conclusions?
Have I integrated all of the relevant pieces of my research into a coherent whole?
Have I answered my research questions?
Have I pushed beyond what I found in the text and given my research personal meaning?
After examining the information, does the research illuminate additional research questions?

9. Present my work.
What format will best reflect the connections among the various pieces of information that need to be communicated?
What ingredients will convey the message most clearly?

10. Reflect on my work.
How well did I answer my research questions?
Do I need to repeat any of the steps listed above?
Do I have more questions as a result of having done this research?
In thinking about the process of research, what was hard? What was easy?
What have I learned?

Information, traditionally confined by a library's four walls, now seems to defy boundaries. Technology's impact has been so profound that the challenge has shifted from simply finding *enough* information to answer a research question, to sorting through excessive amounts of information to determine the reliability and validity of potential sources that could easily number in the hundreds, even thousands. Recently, a high school junior spent 30 minutes online in his school library researching the controversy surrounding the Vietnam conflict. He found the following: 1,701 citations from magazines and newspapers; 3 encyclopedia articles; 55 historical documents; 2 timelines; 49 biographical essays; and 7,238 documents on the Internet, more than half of which were located either on commercial or personal home pages.

Today, sifting through typical search results to determine the reliability and usefulness of sources demands far more critical analysis and evaluation than ever before. As a student begins this process, he must first recognize that different types of resources require different levels of scrutiny. In the past, student researchers, knowing that a library had purchased a book,

or that a reputable publisher had published a particular essay, for example, were often reassured of quality. This is no longer the case. Especially when using "free" Internet resources, the evaluation task is monumental. Most sources, at first glance, look reputable even if they are not. Students need new ways to determine the reliability of sources. To help with this, we provide students with a Web Evaluation Checklist that leads them through the key questions in this decision-making process. Regarding the source, for example, we ask our students to consider: *Is the author of the site identifiable? Is the purpose of the Web site clear? Does the author have appropriate expertise? What kind of site is this? Is the sponsor or location of the site appropriate for the content?* Our school libraries' home pages publish the complete checklist, along with other research aids (see http://www.somers.k12.ny.us/intranet/skills/evaluating/wwwevalcheck.html).

THE NEED TO ORGANIZE INFORMATION

To make sense of disjointed collections of information and transform them into a focused, meaningful response to a research question is often the most difficult part of the process for our students. The protocol carefully guides the student through the next two interrelated steps:

- Organize your information.
- Think and apply.

We have drawn upon Hyerle's (1996) work to teach students to organize their information and findings using a common set of visual organizers that we distribute through our wide area network (see http://www.somers.k12.ny.us/intranet/skills/questioning/resquestiontypes.html). Throughout the district we have begun to use standard drawing tools as well as specialized programs such as Inspiration to create, modify, and share organizers to help students think about the information they gather. By representing their information in a sensible visual arrangement, students more readily detect patterns and relationships that may not have been apparent to them at first. Students use these tools not only to stay afloat in a sea of information, but also to recognize its currents and chart a path to swim to shore. Since each organizer relates to a different cognitive procedure (compare/contrast, cause/effect, etc.), students must first decide which one they should use to map out and then analyze their information. The organizers help students handle their information: to bring order and focus to it, to separate out what is useful from what is not, and to recognize what is missing. By using software, students can cut, paste,

—Figure 78.3—
Research and the Problem-Solving Process

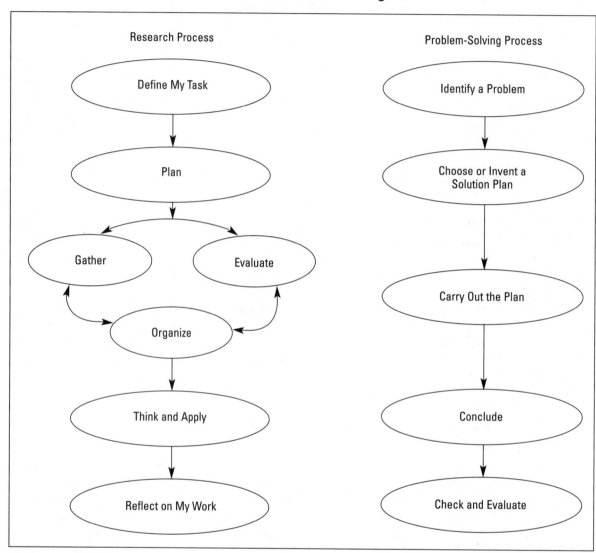

Source: Adapted with permission from *Improving Student Thinking* (p. 294), by B. K. Beyer. Copyright © 1997 by Allyn and Bacon.

add, and move information until they arrive at an organizational scheme that makes sense.

Technology has changed how students are able to wrestle with information in other ways as well. Unwieldy data is no longer an obstacle to insightful thinking. Many new software applications provide robust features that, when used effectively, help our students to examine different perspectives, explore possibilities, and gain new insights. Clearly, software such as spreadsheets and databases can sort, search through, and reorganize enormous amounts of information. However, in order to reach a worthwhile conclusion about the results, students

still need to know how to ask the right questions and think logically about the data as they manipulate it.

To teach is to learn. As the research process concludes, the very process of preparing to share results with others often moves students to yet another level of understanding. In a final series of scaffolding questions, we encourage our researchers to present their findings in any one of a variety of formats, beyond printed papers. We ask students to consider the following:

• *What format will best reflect the connections among the various pieces of information that need to be communicated?* Presentation and publishing software relies upon webbing, making it easier for students to think outside of the box, to break out of the usual linear mind-set.

• *What ingredients will convey the message most clearly?* Even word processing programs allow users to easily incorporate music, narration, photographs, maps, and videos.

Metacognitive reflection, thinking about one's own thinking, is a helpful means of clarifying and improving the thought process, especially when it is complex (Beyer, 1997). Students are reminded of this in one of the protocol's most important steps: Reflect on your work.

REFLECT ON YOUR WORK

Although the last step of the protocol guides students through a *final* reflection, ongoing self-reflection is embedded within many of the questions that guide students through each step of the protocol. Teachers constantly encourage students to review and revise their questions and their work, to integrate emerging new thoughts and understandings throughout the process, and to repeat steps of the protocol when necessary. Especially after they have postulated answers to their research questions, students reflect back and evaluate their solutions or conclusions, an important last step in any good problem-solving process. This reflective thinking often occurs during writing, and technology has had a tremendous influence here. Built-in editing features of word-processing programs make the

revision process much less tedious and thereby encourage reflective thinking. Writers no longer need to weigh the importance of a small change against the need to recopy the text. They can easily compare, side by side, different versions of an essay's introduction. The ability to clearly see revisions (potentially, from several different peer editors) and review them at any time enables the kind of thoughtful revision and reflection that is essential throughout the research process.

Unquestionably, technology is an important, often exciting tool for teaching complex thinking skills. Yet we are ever mindful of technology's dichotomous nature. On the one hand, it has created the problem of information overload. On the other hand, it has provided the tools that help to make sense of it all. Nonetheless, we have found that we must constantly guard against students' tendencies to confuse quantity with quality or to equate good information with good thinking. Our research protocol, with its multiple layers of scaffolding questions, helps guide students through these issues to critical understandings. Looking ahead, we know that this initiative will be a work in progress for as long as technology continues to change both the challenges and opportunities for conducting meaningful research—indeed, for a very long time!

REFERENCES

Beyer, B. K. (1997). *Improving student thinking.* Boston: Allyn and Bacon.

Hyerle, D. (1996). *Visual tools for constructing knowledge.* Alexandria, VA: Association for Supervision and Curriculum Development.

XI

Assessing Growth in Thinking Abilities

Accuracy of observation is the equivalent of accuracy of thinking.

—WALLACE STEVENS

Introduction

BENA KALLICK

The call for thinking is evident in many of the state and national standards. Witness the verbs that are pervasive in standards and, often, in state tests:

• Explore	• Compare	• Connect
• Contrast	• Describe	• Discuss
• Elaborate	• Respond	• Support
• Represent	• Visualize	• Reason
• Verify	• Solve	• Summarize
• Simplify	• Diagram	• Identify
• Interpret	• Judge	• Observe
• Organize	• Paraphrase	• Predict
• Analyze	• Apply	• Classify

Since the attention to thinking was made explicit in the late 1970s, with extensive accompanying research, educators have recognized that thinking can be taught and assessed, and students' thinking can be improved. By the 1990s, the call for higher-level thinking, particularly in the areas of communication, problem solving, and decision making, resounded from the workplace. The issue of *all* students working toward higher levels of thinking was at the center of the political and educational call for greater accountability to a higher set of standards.

Elliott Asp provides a thoughtful discussion about the issues that surround making thinking a focus for state and national tests. His chapter provides an analysis of the promise and limitations of any test that tries to measure what goes on in students' minds as they respond to testing tasks. He presents the continuing challenge inherent in measuring the mental activities highlighted in the verbs above. We have yet to devise a cost-effective system that is not overwhelmingly labor intensive (particularly for teachers).

Monty Neill examines the movement from state standards to state tests, making a strong case for the misalignment between calling for higher levels of thinking and actually testing for higher levels of thinking. He shows how state after state has not held to the task of designing assessments that truly measure a more thoughtful and deeper level of understanding of important concepts and ideas.

One might wonder, then, if it is indeed possible to design assessments that can measure how well students are thinking. Art Costa and Bena Kallick present an overview of alternative assessments that might do just that. Their chapter provides not only a variety of possible assessment forms but also a planning matrix so that individuals and systems might thoughtfully plan for alternatives that measure thinking. Robert Stone elucidates multiple measures from the perspective of the day-to-day classroom.

Performance assessments, although difficult to design, provide a rich window into the ways that students can demonstrate meeting standards. In her chapter on performance assessment, Kay Burke provides us with a set of criteria for high-quality design work and gives some examples from practice.

Barry Beyer suggests that thinking skills can be assessed directly. He offers a format for assessing thinking skills that provides a lens for knowing where a student is in relation to three levels of performance. We can then determine whether the student requires more instruction or more challenge. And finally, Alec Fisher extends the possibility for assessing for specific thinking skills in the context of performances and well-constructed tests.

79

To Think or Not to Think: Thinking as Measured on State and National Assessments

Elliott Asp

W
e have entered an era in public education in which accountability is not an option (Popham, 1998). People are generally dissatisfied with public schools and the level of student achievement (Herman, 1997), and the public and policymakers alike view assessment as the primary vehicle for reform (Linn, 1998).

Following the GOALS 2000 legislation passed by the U.S. Congress in 1994 and with the endorsement of the National Governors Association Conference in 1996, every state has established standards for student achievement or has mandated that local districts do so (Herman, 1997; Editorial Projects in Education, 1999). Forty-eight states have developed a state testing program based on those standards, and those that have not still require some public reporting of progress toward local standards. Along with these criterion-referenced measures, many districts and some states also employ national norm-referenced tests as part of their assessment programs.

Although the stakes associated with these tests vary from state to state, political consequences are attached to all of them, because the results are publicly reported. As a result, educators at every level feel the pressure to increase scores on these measures. This is particularly true for building administrators and classroom teachers. Such pressure has a powerful influence on classroom instruction. Teachers allocate a great deal of time to preparing students for these tests, and their instructional activities tend to mimic the format of the tests.

What does this mean for the teaching and learning of thinking? If these tests measure thinking (as defined in this volume), they could support the effort. However, if they do not, then thinking may go by the wayside in many classrooms.

Can state and national tests measure thinking in a meaningful way? Do they? This chapter explores those questions.

THOUGHTS ABOUT MEASURING THINKING

It is important to provide some context for "thinking" about assessing thinking. Thinking, as a cognitive process, cannot be directly observed. One has to make an inference about student thinking based on behavior in a particular situation—for example, a student's response to a test question or the manner in which she addresses an open-ended performance task. Thinking could also be assessed by having students engage in some form of metacognition in which they describe their thought processes.

It should also be noted that a student cannot think about nothing. That is, thinking is content bound. The more a student knows about the nature of a particular discipline, the more sophisticated the thinking will be. Experts in a field think much differently about the content of that field than do novices (Glaser, 1991). The manner in which thinking is assessed will vary across subject areas, although some researchers are looking for common frameworks for assessing cognitive activity in various domains (Baker, Freeman, & Clayton, 1991).

Regardless of the content area, if one is to encourage a thoughtful response, students need to be given test items that are, to some degree, purposefully ambiguous and lend themselves to a variety of correct approaches based on how one "thinks" about them. The best assessments of thinking will require students to apply knowledge and skills in novel situations. Clearly a performance assessment is the best way to construct such a situation for students.

An example will illustrate this point. Let's assume one wanted to assess a 5th grader's ability to categorize objects according to specific criteria. This could be done through a multiple-choice item such as that shown in Figure 79.1. The student must identify the properties of two groups of objects,

—Figure 79.1—

A Multiple-Choice Test Item to Assess a Student's Ability to Categorize Objects

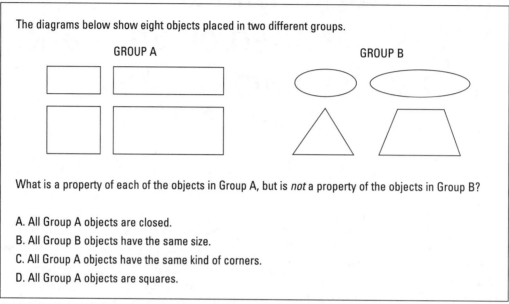

The diagrams below show eight objects placed in two different groups.

GROUP A   GROUP B

What is a property of each of the objects in Group A, but is *not* a property of the objects in Group B?

A. All Group A objects are closed.

B. All Group B objects have the same size.

C. All Group A objects have the same kind of corners.

D. All Group A objects are squares.

Source: Adapted from S. Rakow (2000). Personal communication.

with the assessment item including a set of properties to consider in the possible responses.

In Figure 79.2, the student is asked the same question but without the "hints" provided in the possible responses. The student must construct the properties of each group in order to answer the question.

Figure 79.3 is even more open-ended. The student must analyze the characteristics of all the objects and decide how to group them. However, the objects have a limited number of characteristics, and there is only one correct answer.

Figure 79.4 is the most open-ended and authentic. Here the student must examine real-life objects (seeds) and determine how to categorize them. The problem has a variety of correct answers depending on the characteristics the student uses to categorize the seeds. It provides the most insight into the student's ability to categorize objects. However, it is also the most time consuming to administer and score.

Another issue to consider when measuring thinking is coverage. One cannot observe all the behavior a student might engage in that would indicate achievement in a certain subject area. Any measurement effort is based on generating a representative sample of behavior that exemplifies students' mastery of knowledge and skills from a particular domain. To obtain a "good" sample one must specify the domain in advance and carefully construct assessment items to represent those

specifications so that the assessment covers the domain and provides an accurate representation of student performance within the domain. It is no different when measuring thinking.

How well have the designers of state and national tests done in specifying the "domain of thinking" and developing items that assess that domain? In some cases relatively well and in others not well at all. However, in fairness to the designers, state and national tests have some inherent characteristics that limit their utility in measuring thinking simply because they are large-scale tests.

CHARACTERISTICS OF LARGE-SCALE ASSESSMENTS AND WHY THEY MAKE MEASURING THINKING DIFFICULT

The state and national assessments examined in this chapter are designed primarily as accountability measures and are intended to measure the achievement of large groups of students across classrooms, schools, districts, states, and, in some cases, the nation. To generate meaningful data, they must meet some specific criteria or have certain characteristics that restrict (or at least influence) the kinds of assessment methodology used. A useful way to think about this is to consider two general characteristics or dimensions of assessment: standardization and item type.

—*Figure 79.2*—

An Alternative Test Item to Assess a Student's Ability to Categorize Objects

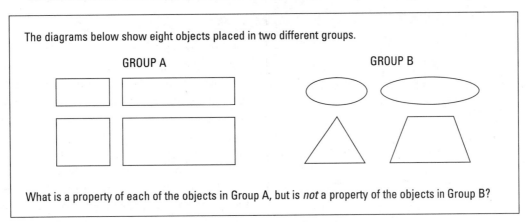

The diagrams below show eight objects placed in two different groups.

GROUP A   GROUP B

What is a property of each of the objects in Group A, but is *not* a property of the objects in Group B?

Source: Adapted from S. Rakow (2000). Personal communication.

STANDARDIZATION

Assessments can range from highly standardized to unstandardized. A highly standardized assessment is given in the same manner to all students taking the test according to a specified procedure and is scored the same way for all students. According to this definition, state and national tests are certainly standardized, but many classroom assessments are as well. Conversely, an unstandardized assessment is one in which the administration and scoring procedures are adjusted according to the needs of individual students. Teachers use such measures all the time. For example, they individualize assessments for special needs students such as special education or gifted and talented youngsters; or they differentiate assessment for different groups of students. Teachers can do this because they collect a large amount of data on the achievement of their students through a variety of assessment methodologies (some formal and some informal) and a number of assessment episodes. Therefore, they can consider the results from a single unstandardized assessment in the context of other information.

—*Figure 79.3*—

An Open-Ended Test Item to Assess a Student's Ability to Categorize Objects

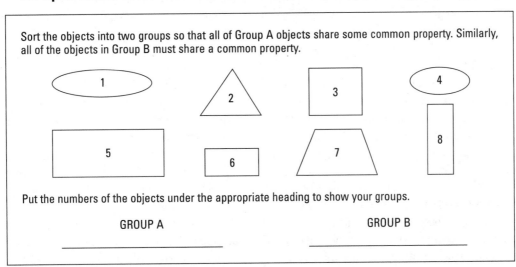

Sort the objects into two groups so that all of Group A objects share some common property. Similarly, all of the objects in Group B must share a common property.

1 2 3 4

5 6 7 8

Put the numbers of the objects under the appropriate heading to show your groups.

GROUP A   GROUP B

_____   _____

Source: Adapted from S. Rakow (2000). Personal communication.

—*Figure 79.4*—

A Performance Task to Assess a Student's Ability to Categorize Objects

In front of you is a plastic bag with seeds. Put the seeds into two groups so that there is something the same about all the seeds in each group. Be sure to use all the seeds.

A. What is the same about all of the seeds in your first group?

B. What is the same about all of the seeds in your second group?

Source: Adapted from S. Rakow (2000). Personal communication.

Large-scale assessors do not have that luxury. Their goal is to aggregate data across large groups of students, as they can usually assess students only one time. They have to use highly standardized procedures to minimize the impact of extraneous variables—things that are not being assessed (e.g., access to resources, the time allowed to complete the test) but that could influence scores.

ITEM TYPE

Assessments can range from items that ask students to select or choose the answer (e.g., multiple-choice, true-false) to those in which the student constructs the answer (e.g., performance assessments, portfolios).

Assessments on the "select" end of the continuum are more efficient—that is, they are relatively inexpensive in terms of both time and money to administer and score. A multiple-choice test, for example, can be scored in seconds by electronic means, allowing for "mass scoring" in a short time. The best use of this kind of assessment is in measuring recall of knowledge and low-level application of that information. Although these kinds of items can assess students' use of higher-level thinking to some degree, they provide no insight into student thinking or the rationale for choosing a particular answer. They can assess whether students can find the correct answer to a "higher-order" problem, but not how they did it.

Assessments on the "construct" or "performance" end of the continuum require much more time to administer and score. A single performance task could take several test ses-

sions or an extended single session to administer. And because they must be read or evaluated by human beings, not machines, they are much more time consuming and costly to score reliably. Also, they are narrow in scope. That is, to get a consistent or reliable picture of student performance requires multiple assessment episodes using a variety of tasks (Shavelson, Baxter, & Pine, 1991; Lane et al., 1993). However, these kinds of assessments provide much more insight into student thinking than those on the "select" end because there is a much larger and more in-depth (albeit narrower) sample of behavior that can be "observed." Assessments in which students "do" the answer rather than choose it can be constructed so that students have to apply knowledge and skills in context, solve problems using what they have learned, or engage in a number of other kinds of higher-order cognitive activity. Further, because these items are open-ended, a variety of correct answers are possible. This allows students' thinking to be the deciding factor in whether they get the question "right." Therefore, inferences about student thinking are better grounded.

SUMMARY

Figure 79.5 illustrates how these two dimensions fit together. In quadrant 1 are standardized measures in which students have to select the answer from a set of alternatives. In quadrant 2 are standardized measures that are more performance oriented. In quadrant 3 are those assessments that call for the student to construct the answer in a less standardized manner. The assessment in quadrant 4 is unstandardized (to a lesser or greater degree), and the student chooses the answer from several options on a scale.

Some state and national assessments incorporate assessments from quadrants 2 and 3, but problems with standardization and consistent scoring and their high cost in time and money limit their large-scale use. For example, some states have included literacy portfolios in their assessment programs. These kinds of assessments are highly valued by teachers, students, and parents because they can be tailored to the individual student. If the purpose is to document student growth in writing, then the teacher would work with the student to include particular pieces to illustrate that. If the purpose is to highlight the student's best work, then different work samples would be identified. In any case, individual students would probably choose different pieces depending on their own goals. One student might use a short story and research paper to document her growth as a writer, while another might select a poem and an expository piece.

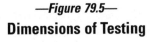

Dimensions of Testing

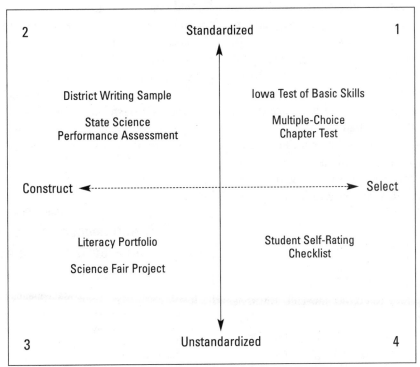

Source: Adapted from "The Relationship of Large-Scale and Classroom Assessment," by E. Asp, 1998, in R. Brandt (Ed.), *Assessing Student Learning: New Rules, New Realities.* Arlington, VA: Educational Research Service.

This works well in the classroom where the teacher can meet with students and parents to interpret the results. However, making sense on a large scale of hundreds or thousands of portfolios containing different pieces of writing is very difficult. States that have tried to use these more classroom-oriented measures have had to narrow the parameters of what can be included in the portfolios. This kind of restriction makes the assessment less useful for teachers. In addition, even with some restrictions, it may be impossible to score these assessments (when used on a large scale) with a level of consistency that would allow them to be used for reporting at the individual student level.

A related difficulty in using measures in quadrants 2 and 3 as part of large-scale testing has to do with the narrow scope of performance measures and the technical problems associated with generalizing students' scores on one task to other tasks in the same domain. It takes at least several performance episodes to get a stable score for students in regard to their use, for example, of the scientific method. This only compounds the high cost of using performance measures.

The point is that there are limitations in measuring thinking on state and national tests that have nothing to do with design or intent. They have more to do with feasibility. Because less standardized, more performance-oriented measures are the most useful in measuring higher-order thinking, the degree to which state and national tests assess thinking as it is defined in this volume is inherently limited.

Given those limitations, how effective have state and national assessment efforts been in measuring thinking?

THINKING AS IT APPEARS ON STATE AND NATIONAL TESTS

National tests used during the 1960s, '70s, and '80s (most of which were norm-referenced tests, or NRTs) and minimum competency tests (MCTs) developed as state assessments in the 1970s and '80s did not address thinking in a comprehensive manner and certainly did not promote the teaching of thinking in the classroom. Both NRTs and MCTs relied largely on a multiple-choice format. However, since the mid-1990s, both national and state tests have improved the manner and degree to which they address thinking. This is due in part to the reaction of test publishers to criticisms from performance assessment proponents and assessment experts, and to changes in our views of what students should know and be able to do. That is, national content area groups such as the National Council of Teachers of Mathematics and the American Association for the Advancement of Science have developed standards for student learning in their disciplines that emphasize the application of subject area knowledge and skills using higher-order thinking. Following suit, states and districts have adopted rigorous content standards for students that incorporate high-level application of subject area knowledge and skills. (In many cases these standards are based on the work of the national groups.)

CHANGES IN NATIONAL TESTS

To respond to the changing needs of their customers, all the major publishing companies (CTB/McGraw-Hill, Riverside Publishing, and Harcourt Brace), as well as many of the "minor" players in the market, have revised their instruments and reporting procedures to incorporate higher-order thinking. The most significant change has been the incorporation of performance (constructed-response) items with multiple-choice questions on NRTs.

A prominent example is the "multiple assessment" version of the Terra Nova. *Terra Nova* is the marketing name for the latest version of the Comprehensive Test of Basic Skills (CTB/McGraw-Hill, 1997). The Terra Nova incorporates both selected-response and constructed-response items on the same scale. For example, on the reading battery students answer multiple-choice items tapping their basic understanding of a story. In addition, there are constructed response items that require them to compare and contrast characters, predict how a particular character might act in another setting, or provide a different ending to a story on the test in their own words. On the math battery students might construct a bar graph or describe how they arrived at the solution to a problem as well as solve traditional computation and "story" problems. In some instances they are asked to apply math knowledge and skills in real-life settings. For example, students might read ratings of the characteristics of various products and then use that information (presented in charts and graphs) to make a decision about which is the best product. They have to justify their answer based on the data supplied in the problem.

The Terra Nova was designed with "thinking" in mind (Cizek, 1998). The test is organized around six cognitive

processes: gathering information, organizing information, analyzing information, generating ideas, synthesizing elements, and evaluating outcomes; it is based on the work of Hughes and Rankin (1987) and Marzano et al. (1988). Each of these processes is defined by a series of subskills. For instance, in "evaluating outcomes," students establish criteria for evaluating an outcome and verify that the criteria have been met. Both constructed-response and multiple-choice items are used to assess these thinking skills. Figure 79.6 shows an example of a performance item used to measure students' ability to evaluate outcomes in mathematics. Figure 79.7 is an example of a

—*Figure 79.6*—

A Performance Item in Mathematics from the *Terra Nova* Assessment

---

Mathematics

Verify   This constructed response requires the student to evaluate and verify the conclusions stated in the article for numerical accuracy and for the accuracy of the interpretation of the facts.

Examine the conclusions made in the following newsletter article. Explain how the data do or do not support the author's statements.

HOMES WITH COMPUTERS INCREASE

In 1985, computers were in 15% of American homes. By 1990, this figure had risen to 22%. During the following five years, an additional 15% of all homes were equipped with computers. This means that in 1995 more than half of all households owned at least one computer. At this rate, all American homes will have computers by the year 2000.

Source: From *Teacher's Guide to Terra Nova,* by CTB/McGraw-Hill, 1997, p. 133.

—*Figure 79.7*—

A Multiple-Choice Item in Reading/Language Arts from the *Terra Nova* Assessment

Reading/Language Arts

Verify The item requires the student to evaluate how well each sentence supports the central topic of the paragraph and contributes to the paragraph's coherence and cohesion. Then the student must identify the sentence that is least relevant to the central idea and provides the least support for the development of meaning.

Choose the sentence that does *not* belong in the paragraph.

1. Henri Matisse was an important French artist. 2. Though he is best known as a painter, Matisse enjoyed working with other art forms, too. 3. When he was eighteen, he studied to be a lawyer. 4. His works include sculptures, book illustrations, and a chapel.

  A Sentence 1

  B Sentence 2

✔ **C** Sentence 3

  D Sentence 4

Source: From *Teacher's Guide to Terra Nova,* by CTB/McGraw-Hill, 1997, p. 133.

multiple-choice item intended to tap students' ability to evaluate outcomes in reading.

The thinking skills assessed on the Terra Nova follow a "developmental" pattern of sorts. That is, the levels of the Terra Nova used with elementary students focus more on gathering and organizing information and give little attention to synthesis of elements and evaluation of outcomes. The latter two skills are more heavily emphasized in versions of the test designed for middle school and high school students. The cognitive skill most heavily emphasized across all levels of the test is analyzing information.

There are three versions of the Terra Nova: the complete battery, the survey battery, and multiple assessments. The complete battery is a "traditional NRT" made up of a relatively large number of items (all multiple-choice). The survey battery is a scaled-down version of the complete battery with a limited number of items. It is intended to provide a "quick and dirty" overview of student achievement. Because they use multiple-choice items exclusively, the complete and survey batteries do not address higher-order thinking skills to the same degree as the multiple assessments version (see Figure

79.8). In all versions, the reading/language arts subtests have far more items that address such thinking skills as synthesis and evaluation than do those for mathematics, science, and social studies. Even though items from the Terra Nova can be classified according to the type of thinking they reflect, no data regarding students' thinking are reported.

There are some national tests that do report specific information about students' "ability to think." The performance assessments developed by Riverside Publishing as companions to the Iowa Tests of Basic Skills are an example. These measures provide student scores for several types of cognitive processes (for instance, organizing, analyzing, and evaluating, as classified by the Association for Supervision and Curriculum Development) based on a four-point rubric that designates a student's performance as showing "proficient," "basic," "emerging," or "little or no evidence of" understanding of the processes. Another example is the Integrated Assessment System published by Harcourt Brace Educational Measurement (2000), which provides scores in various categories of thinking (that is, problem solving and communication in math; making inferences and supporting conclusions in science).

Several publishers provide normative data (that is, percentile ranks, grade equivalent scores, normal curve equivalent scores, and so forth) based on student performance on an open-ended task. The performance tasks from Riverside, for example, generate normative as well as criterion data. Other examples are the Stanford 9 Open-Ended Reading Assessment and GOALS, produced by Harcourt Educational Assessment.

The New Standards Reference Exams, published by Harcourt Brace and Company in 1997, are another "national" effort to assess student thinking. These instruments are primarily performance-based and require students to apply knowledge and skills in reading, writing, and math. For instance, in math, middle-level students deal with a series of short tasks in which they interpret graphs to understand the relationship between two variables—such as birth rate and life expectancy—and communicate their understanding. These assessments are based on the New Standards Performance Standards (National Center on Education & the Economy and the University of Pittsburgh, 1997), which reflect the work of many national groups such as National Council of Teachers of Mathematics and the National Research Council. These assessments are designed to serve as an "anchor" or "benchmark" of student performance in an on-demand setting that can be used in conjunction with other performance exams and a portfolio to make an overall judgment about student learning. They provide a criterion score for the knowledge and skills

—Figure 79.8—

Number of Items on the Terra Nova Related to Various Thinking Skills

Test Type	Thinking Skill					
	Gather Information	Organize Information	Analyze Information	Generate Ideas	Synthesize Elements	Evaluate Outcomes
Complete Battery						
Reading/Language Arts	9	3	44	2	14	8
Mathematics	5	10	24	6	1	0
Science	6	7	13	10	3	1
Social Studies	5	7	23	2	1	2
Survey						
Reading/Language Arts	5	2	29	2	11	6
Mathematics	4	5	11	5	0	0
Science	6	4	9	5	1	0
Social Studies	5	2	15	1	1	1
Multiple Assessments						
Reading/Language Arts	6	2	37	6	7	8
Mathematics	5	3	21	6	2	4
Science	3	7	17	4	2	2
Social Studies	3	4	18	8	1	1

Source: "Thinking Skills Classification for Terra Nova, Level 19, Form A," in *Teacher's Guide to Terra Nova*, CTB/McGraw-Hill, 1997, p. 261.

being assessed (for example, math problem solving) but do not address levels of thinking in the specific way that the Riverside performance tasks do.

CHANGES IN STATE TESTS

State tests have also changed dramatically over the past decade. This new generation of state tests was designed to assess state content standards that incorporate higher-level thinking as part of the targets for student learning. Figure 79.9 shows an example from the Colorado State Model Content Standards in science. The standards adopted in many states are similar. Because of the "content" of their content standards, a number of state assessment programs include some form of performance assessment in an effort to assess thinking.

A report conducted for the Council of Chief State School Officers (CCSSO) by the North Central Regional Educational Laboratory provides evidence for this (Bond, Roeber, & Braskamp, 1997). As shown in Figure 79.10, many states are incorporating various types of performance items into their assessment systems, ranging from performance tasks to projects and portfolios. (The most common performance assessment is a writing sample.) This survey also documents that only a rel-

atively small number of states rely on multiple-choice items exclusively. Twenty-three states indicated that they had at least one component of their assessment program that had no multiple-choice items. Most states report using a blend of selected-response and performance items.

What do these combinations of multiple-choice and performance items look like? The Colorado Student Assessment Program (CSAP) is an example. Using a mixture of multiple-choice, short-answer, and performance tasks, it is typical of many of the new generation of state tests. In a 4th grade reading assessment, for example, students read a poem and a story and respond to multiple-choice and short-answer items that tap several levels of meaning (from literal to more inferential). In addition, they have to compare and contrast in writing the manner in which a common theme is treated in each type of text.

A similar blend of multiple-choice, short-answer and performance tasks appears in the math portion of the CSAP. There are basic computation items, items that call for students to apply math knowledge and skills to solve problems, and still others that require students to show how they solved a problem and/or to communicate their reasoning. On this assessment students engage in application and problem solving and

—Figure 79.9—
Colorado Model Content Standards in Science

1. Students understand the processes of scientific investigation and design, conduct, communicate about, and evaluate such investigations.

2. Physical Science: Students know and understand common properties, forms, and changes in matter and energy.

3. Life Science: Students know and understand the characteristics and structure of living things, the processes of life, and how living things interact with each other and their environment.

4. Earth and Space Science: Students know and understand the processes and interactions of Earth's systems and the structure and dynamics of Earth and other objects in space.

5. Students know and understand interrelationships among science, technology, and human activity and how they can affect the world.

6. Students understand that science involves a particular way of knowing and understand common connections among scientific disciplines.

Source: Colorado Content Standards, 1995.

—Figure 79.10—
Types of Test Items on
State Assessments in 1996

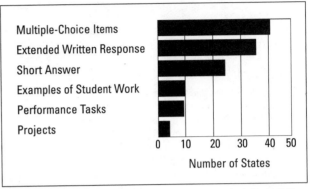

Source: Trends in State Student Assessment Programs, by L. Bond, E. Roeber, & D. Braskamp, 1997. Washington, DC: Council of Chief State School Officers.

metacognition about their own understanding of the problem-solving process.

The writing portion of the CSAP, as is typical of many state tests, combines an extended writing task with several shorter tasks, a "hands-on" editing section, and traditional multiple-choice items. Students use the writing process to draft and revise a piece over several days. The shorter pieces are completed in one testing session. Although some would argue that the writing required on these kinds of assessments is not authentic, there is no doubt that to be successful students need to engage in higher-order cognitive activity such as planning and organizing their work and synthesizing and evaluating ideas.

The Maryland State Performance Assessment (MSPAP) goes beyond the hybrid models like Colorado's to focus more heavily on performance assessment and higher-level thinking. MSPAP consists mainly of extended performance items. Figure 79.11 shows an example from the science assessment. This item requires students to use a variety of cognitive processes such as analysis, synthesis, and evaluation.

These new state assessments look much like the new national tests described earlier. This is because most of the contractors who developed them are the major test publishers, and some of the items from their norm-referenced products

appear on their state tests. For example, items from the Terra Nova are also used in the Colorado Student Assessment Program. This occurs because of the tight timelines for developing these products imposed by policymakers. To be able to develop a "customized state test" in a relatively short time frame, test publishers must use existing items from their NRT item banks. This makes for some tricky going in terms of the use of their NRT products. For instance, one form of the multiple assessment version of the Terra Nova cannot be used in Colorado because it contains items that appear on the state test.

Although state tests may never invoke the level of thinking that can be addressed in high-quality classroom assessment, there has been much improvement. However, this is not a universal phenomenon. In fact, some states have regressed in how they address thinking.

What is behind this "regression" in some state assessment programs? Certainly, the "learning theories" of psychometricians and others who are charged with overseeing the development of state tests influence whether and how thinking is assessed on state assessments. Sheppard (1990) argues that some state assessment directors conceive of learning as a linear, step-by-step process in which large concepts or ideas can be broken down into smaller pieces and then combined to generate the overall concept or skill being learned. She believes that this view of the nature of learning is reflected in the construction of some state assessments.

The views on learning held by state testing directors and test developers certainly contribute to differences among state assessment programs. But I believe the greatest influence is the

—Figure 79.11—
Maryland State Performance Assessment in Science

MSPAP Through the Eyes of an 8th Grade Student

How might a Maryland School Performance assessment item—or task—be described by a student taking the MSPAP? Here is how a task on "Planetary Patterns" might be viewed by an 8th grader.

1. Exploring a new solar system.

Today, my teacher asked us to imagine that we were scientists working at the Goddard Space Flight Center in Greenbelt, Maryland. The Voyager spacecraft has been sending back data on a newly discovered solar system. There are four planets in this new system, and they have nearly circular orbits that do not overlap. A chart tells us the surface temperature, number of moons, tilt of axis and chemical composition of each planet. Based on this data and an orbit diagram, we have to identify similarities between patterns present in this new solar system and our own solar system. Looking at the model provided, I see that the planets in the new solar system orbit around a sun which is at the center of the system, just like ours. I also notice that the surface temperature of any planet in the system decreases as its distance from the sun increases.

2. More questions, more patterns.

Next we are asked to come up with at least three questions about the new solar system which are not answered by the chart. I have quite a few questions about the system, including the size of each planet, each planet's distance from the sun, the atmospheric pressure of each planet, and the age of the planet. Next, I am asked to identify and write about three repeating patterns of astronomical change that occur in the sky. I remember that the moon goes through phases regularly, the sun rises and sets each day, and there is a difference in the position of the of the stars in the sky as the seasons change.

3. Completing the orbit data logs and predicting planet positions.

My classmates and I are given a chart listing the position of the four planets in the new solar system for the months of January, February, March and April. Working with three other students, we must complete the orbit data logs, also provided in our packet, to show in a picture form where each planet is at each of these times. Working carefully, we pinpoint the position of each planet in each of the four months using the data given. Then, on our own, we use what we have learned about the rate of the orbit of each planet to predict the position of all four planets in the month of May. We are allowed to use pennies on our chart to represent planets and move them around the diagram to help make our predictions. Once our predictions are made, we write about our methods. I figured out how far each planet moved around its orbit in a month and moved the penny representing each planet the right distance, and there it was, at the right spot.

4. Reserving time on the orbiting space telescope.

The next instructions I read ask me to imagine that *Space and Telescope Magazine* wants to record the next planetary alignment of this new solar system. To do this, I need to figure out when the planets will be aligned so I can reserve time on the orbiting space telescope. This takes a little more doing than the last task, and I find that using the pennies on my diagram helps me keep track of the motion of the planets. Carefully keeping track of which month I am in, I move each planet around its orbit the right number of spaces. Finally, after moving all the planets around their orbits several times, I come to a month when they are all in a row, or aligned. This is the month I predict should be reserved for the use of the orbiting space telescope.

5. Conclusions and explanations for younger students.

Next, I write about how predicting the alignment of the planets was different from predicting their position in the month of May, one month after our data ended. It was a little more difficult to predict the alignment, but I found that by moving the pennies around the diagram one at a time and keeping track of the month, I was able to find the answer. In the space on our worksheet I write a paragraph for a younger student describing how the model of the solar system using orbit diagrams and pennies helped with my predictions. Finally, I write about how working with others in a group influenced or changed our beginning ideas about the position of the planets. My group basically agreed on how to go about predicting the positions of the planets, and our idea worked.

6. When we put it to the test, it was confirmed.

Planetary Patterns was challenging, I had to think carefully and logically. I also got a chance to use information I learned in my science class.

Source: Adapted from Fact Sheet 13, *MSPAP Through the Eyes of an 8th Grade Student,* Maryland State Department of Education, March 1995.

opinions of state policymakers with regard to what are appropriate learning targets for students. Cognitive psychologists and other researchers have abandoned the behavioral view of learning for a more constructivist approach in which learning is defined as more than the reception of information. From this point of view, learning involves the integration of new knowledge with what one has already learned and the application of that new learning, in cognitively complex ways, to construct additional knowledge (Glaser & Silver, 1994; Wittrock, 1991). Some form of performance assessment in which students are required to organize information and use it to solve complex problems within a real-life context is required to address this kind of learning (Herman, 1997).

Although many cognitive scientists, along with professional educators and their professional organizations, have endorsed this new understanding of the nature of learning and how it takes place, the public at large has not (McDonnell, 1997). The opposition to the new view of learning has led to the revision or complete dismantling of some state assessment systems—those in California and Kentucky, for example. Those states were among the leaders in developing state assessment systems that addressed higher-level cognitive processes. But over the past several years, policymakers in both states (particularly within the state legislature) have demanded that state standards, assessments, and curriculum frameworks focus more on basic knowledge and skills rather than on application and problem solving. This has occurred in other states as well.

This trend toward a more "basic" view of what students should be learning (and what the appropriate content of assessments should be) has been countered in some states by the business community, which also has strong views about the kinds of things students should be learning. Business leaders have been outspoken in their desire for students to bring more than a knowledge of basic skills to the workplace (e.g., Secretary's Commission on Achieving Necessary Skills, 1991)— although they do want kids to know the "basics." Not only do they want their future employees to be able to apply knowledge in meaningful ways, they also stress the need for schools to train students to work effectively in groups, to solve problems and make decisions, and to meet deadlines, among other things. The type of assessments needed to measure these kinds of skills and knowledge are performance oriented, and several national publishers (mostly notably ACT) have developed testing programs that tap this kind of learning. The leadership of the business community has played a major role in improving student achievement in several states (Grissmer & Flanagan, 1998), and its influence may balance the impact of citizens groups and policymakers who are calling for a more "traditional" view of school learning.

It is hard to say who will win the "learning wars," but it is clear that the views of learning of those who hold political power have a great influence on the nature of state testing and national testing and, in turn, the degree to which thinking is assessed. So far, thinking is winning, as evidenced by the improvements in the manner and extent that higher-order thinking has been incorporated into state and national testing programs over the past 10 years. But what does the future hold? Or at least, what can we hope for?

Best Hopes for the Future

There will always be a limit to how well state and national tests address thinking, especially compared with classroom assessment. However, as we have seen, it is possible to incorporate the higher-order application of knowledge and skills in these instruments to a greater degree than we have seen in the past. Although predicting the future of assessment with any degree of "validity" is not a very "reliable" process, there are some reasons to be optimistic.

The Continued Use of Performance Assessment

I believe that performance assessment will continue to be incorporated into large-scale assessment for several reasons. First, test publishers and states have invested a large amount of resources into the development and implementation of these instruments. More importantly, national curriculum groups and professional organizations support including performance measures on state and national tests, and most state standards require some form of performance assessment in order to be adequately assessed. Further, business leaders are demanding that students be able to apply what they have learned in school on the job (Grissman & Flanagan, 1998). However, because of the issues associated with the large-scale use of performance items, "hybrid" models such as the Terra Nova and the Colorado assessment program may be the best we can hope for on a widespread basis.

In regard to promoting the teaching and learning of thinking in the classroom, it is especially important that state and national assessments include some open-ended performance items as an "instructional symbol."

New Assessment Technology

Another development that will encourage the use of performance items in large-scale testing and, in turn, promote an emphasis on thinking is the emergence of new types of assessment technology (Asp, 2000). For example, emerging technology will allow the use of a variety of test and response formats that are not widely available today. With new forms of technology, test items could be contextualized in very authentic ways using the video and audio capabilities of computers. Questions could be posed orally, and students could respond in the same manner or by constructing answers on the screen, enabling them to describe their thinking processes in solving a math problem, for instance, without confounding the description with their writing ability.

Through the use of such tools as HyperCard stacks, digital cameras, and video production software, students can display the results of research and other complex tasks without having to compose a "research paper." Researchers at the Center for Research on Evaluation, Standards, and Student Testing (CRESST) at the University of California, Los Angeles, are experimenting with using networked computers to assess students' ability to synthesize new information about a topic; for example, they have students create cognitive maps on particular concepts (Herman, 1999). They are using the same technology to assess how well students can locate information, collaborate with others, and communicate their findings.

These advances will no doubt continue, making it possible to assess aspects of student learning that are not readily assessed by more print-bound methods. Whereas today's state and national assessments include the content knowledge students need to "think about," tomorrow's assessment technology may make it possible for students to authentically search for information within the testing situation as part of the assessment process.

A side benefit of the new assessment technology may be its impact on the "learning wars." When students are not bound by what they can remember or have close at hand, then their ability to locate and evaluate information and apply it for a particular purpose becomes critically important. New forms of assessment technology may serve as a catalyst for bringing the content and process factions together and ending the conflict over what is most important, making it "OK" to think on large-scale tests. In addition, the business community in many states is becoming more vocal about the need for employees to be able to find appropriate information and process it at a high level. This combination of the emergence of new information processing tools (which will also serve as assessment instruments) and the demand by employers that students be able to use them may change the public's (and some educators') ideas about learning and what schools should be emphasizing and, in turn, what should be measured on large-scale tests.

"DESIGNING-IN" THINKING

Although the new generation of state and national tests emphasize thinking to a greater degree than in the past, few are actually designed to report on thinking specifically. Currently, test developers typically identify the "kind" or level of thinking included on the test after the fact. That is, they review the items and label them according to some schema or theoretical perspective on thinking after the instrument is completed. Usually the developers begin by specifying the content domain and developing items that reflect the specification. They may have identified (a priori) some thinking skills or levels they want to include, but they don't develop a set of items that would reflect student performance in a particular domain of thinking. They do not specify particular domains of thinking (for example, evaluation, synthesis, analysis, and so forth) and then develop items to specifically provide a score on that domain. The table of thinking skills measured on the Terra Nova (Figure 79.8) provides an example. Recall that a variety of levels of thinking are covered on the Terra Nova, but students do not receive a score on their ability to, for example, evaluate or synthesize. Also remember that there is an imbalance in the number of items associated with each level of thinking, and some "kinds" of thinking receive more emphasis than others.

The performance assessments designed for use with the ITBS are somewhat different. Recall that students receive a score in some aspect of thinking (for example, organizing, generating, integrating). Content specifications were developed in advance for each of the kinds of thinking included in the assessments. Items were designed to tap one or more of those types of thinking, and a scoring system was developed to evaluate student responses in terms of the predetermined definitions or content specifications.

Even more of this kind of upfront work is needed if state and national assessments are to address thinking in a meaningful manner that provides specific data about student use of higher-order cognitive processes. Test developers need to specifically identify what it "looks like" to engage in various kinds of higher-order cognitive activity and develop items that adequately measure the full scope of that domain. This would lead to more focused, in-depth assessments that would provide a much more accurate measure of thinking. The good news is that many assessment experts and cognitive psychologists have been experimenting with this kind of assessment development. The bad news is that test publishers and other developers of large-scale assessment are not highly represented in that group.

A NEW ROLE OR CRITERION FOR QUALITY ASSESSMENT

A new role for assessment has been emerging over the past decade, in which assessment is viewed as a tool that can inform instruction, improve student achievement, and ultimately provide more and better education for the learner. This is exemplified in the assessment design process. For example, in many states the assessment development procedure includes an instructional impact review. This process considers an assessment item's predicted effect on teaching and curriculum along with content appropriateness as a criterion for inclusion into the item pool from which the state assessment will be constructed. Items that would tend to encourage teachers, schools, and districts to emphasize low-level knowledge and skills are typically excluded from the pool.

All of this is really about defining the purpose of assessment. The focus of almost all state and national testing has been accountability. This new criterion for quality assessment actually defines a new purpose for large-scale assessment—promoting improved educational opportunities for students. After the negative impact on instruction of the first generation of state and national tests, our best hope for large-scale tests in the 1990s was to (at the very least) "do no harm" (when it comes to teaching and learning). Now we expect more. A quality large-scale assessment program should promote best practice and lead to improved instruction for students. In the context of our discussion, this means promoting an emphasis on higher-order thinking in classrooms.

SUMMARY

If we want state and national tests to address higher-order cognition, then promoting the teaching and learning of higher-order thinking needs to be spelled out as a goal and included in the "test specs." Then we must design the test to measure specific aspects of thinking (Newmann & Archbald, 1992). That means defining the particular domains of thinking beforehand and purposefully developing items to tap that domain (Herman, 1991). This will force us to continue to incorporate performance assessment items into large-scale efforts (Berlak et al., 1992). One would hope that the use of new technology will make that effort easier and the items more authentic and "thought provoking." If all that comes to pass, as I think it will, then the future of assessing thinking on a large scale is a rosy one.

REFERENCES

Asp, E. (2000). Assessment in education: Where have we been? Where are we headed? In R. Brandt (Ed.), *Education in a new era*. Alexandria, VA: Association for Supervision and Curriculum Development.

Baker, E., Freeman, M., & Clayton, S. (1991). Cognitive assessment of history for large-scale testing. In M. Wittrock and E. Baker (Eds.), *Testing and Cognition*. Englewood Cliffs, NJ: Prentice-Hall, Inc.

Berlak, H., Newmann, F., Adams, E., Archbald, D., Burgess, T., Raven, J., & Romberg, T. (1992). *Toward a new science of educational testing and assessment*. Albany, NY: State University of New York Press.

Bond, L., Roeber, E., & Braskamp, D. (1997). *Trends in state student assessment programs*. Washington, DC: Council of Chief State School Officers.

Cizek, G. (1998). *Filling in the blanks, putting standardized tests to the tests*. Washington, DC: The Thomas B. Fordham Foundation.

CTB/McGraw-Hill. (1997). *Teacher's guide to Terra Nova*. Monterey, CA: CTB/McGraw-Hill.

Editorial Projects in Education. (1999, January 11). Quality counts: Rewarding results, punishing failure. *Education Week, 28*(17).

Glaser, R. (1991). Expertise and assessment. In M. Wittrock and E. Baker (Eds.), *Testing and cognition*. Englewood Cliffs, NJ: Prentice-Hall, Inc.

Glaser, R., & Silver, E. (1994). Assessment, testing and instruction. *Annual Review of Psychology, 40*, 631–666.

Grissmer, D., & Flanagan, A. (1998). *Exploring rapid achievement gains in North Carolina and Texas*. Washington, DC: National Goals Panel.

Harcourt Brace Educational Measurement. (2000). *Integrated Assessment System*. San Antonio, TX: Author.

Herman, J. (1991). Research in cognition and learning: Implications for Achievement testing practice. In M. Wittrock and E. Baker (Eds.), *Testing and cognition*. Englewood Cliffs, NJ: Prentice-Hall, Inc.

Herman, J. (1997). *Large-scale assessment in support of school reform: Lessons in the search for alternative measures* (CSE Technical Report 446). Los Angeles: University of California, National Center for Research on Evaluation, Standards, and Student Testing.

Herman, J. (1999). *Why standards-based assessment systems ought to improve classroom practice*. Presentation at the annual meeting of the American Association of School Administrators, New Orleans, LA.

Hughes, C., & Rankin, S. (1987). The Rankin-Hughes framework. In *Developing thinking skills across the curriculum*. Westland, MI: Michigan Association for Computer Users in Learning.

Johnson, J., & Immerwahr, J. (1994). *First things first: What Americans expect from the public schools*. New York: Public Agenda.

Lane, S., Silver, E., Cai, J., Magone, M., Wang, N., Stone, C., Ankenmann, R., & Liu, M. (1993). *Assessing performance assessments: Do they withstand empirical scrutiny?* Symposium at the Annual Meeting of the American Educational Research Association, Atlanta, GA.

Linn, R. (1998). *Assessments and accountability.* (CSE Technical Report 490). Los Angeles: University of California, National Center for Research on Evaluation, Standards, and Student Testing (CRESST).

Marzano, R., Brandt, R., Hughes, C., Jones, B., Presseisen, B., Rankin, S., & Suhor, C. (1988). *Dimensions of thinking: A framework for curriculum and instruction*. Alexandria, VA: Association for Supervision and Curriculum Development.

McDonnell, L. (1997). *The politics of state testing: Implementing new student assessments.* (CSE Technical Report 424). Los Angeles: University of California, National Center for Research on Evaluation, Standards, and Student Testing.

National Center on Education & Economy and the University of Pittsburgh. (1997). *New Standards performance standards: Vol. 2. Middle school*. Orlando, FL: Harcourt Brace and Company.

National Center on Education and Economy and the University of Pittsburgh. (1997). *New standards reference exams*. Orlando, FL: Harcourt, Brace and Company.

Newmann, F., & Archbald, D. (1992). The nature of authentic academic achievement. In Berlak, H., Newmann, F., Adams, E., Archbald, D., Burgess, T., Raven, J., and Romberg, T. (eds.), *Toward a new science of educational testing and assessment*. Albany, NY: State University of New York Press.

Popham, J. (1998). *Standardized tests should not be used to evaluate educational quality: A debate.* Paper presented at the Annual Meeting of the American Educational Research Association, San Diego, CA.

Secretary's Commission on Achieving Necessary Skills. (1991). *What work requires of schools.* Washington, DC: United States Department of Labor.

Shavelson, R., Baxter, G., & Pine, J. (1991). Performance assessment in science. *Applied Measurement in Education, 4,* 347–362.

Sheppard, L. (1990). *Psychometricians' beliefs about learning.* (CSE Technical Report 318). Los Angeles: University of California, National Center for Research on Evaluation, Standards, and Student Testing (CRESST).

Wittrock, M. (1991). Testing and recent research in cognition. In M. Wittrock and E. Baker (Eds.), *Testing and cognition.* Englewood Cliffs, NJ: Prentice-Hall.

80

State Exams Flunk Test of Quality Thinking

Monty Neill

It is better to know some of the questions than all of the answers.

—*James Thurber*

Today, "standards and assessments" is the ubiquitous—we would say "iniquitous"—theme of school reform. Following political winds and federal law, every state but Iowa has adopted at least some standards and has mandated standardized tests.[1] In 1997, nineteen required students to pass a test to graduate (only a few allowed alternative routes to earn a diploma), and about six more soon would.[2] A small but increasing number of states require students to pass tests for grade promotion. Half the states in 1997 used test scores as the basis for action toward schools, teachers, or administrators, from cash bonuses to accreditation or to school takeovers.[3] Quite explicitly, most states now want schools to teach to the tests, thereby defining curriculum and instruction as what is on the tests.

School board members need to think about the consequences of this approach for student learning, for attracting and retaining a high-quality teaching staff, for school improvement, and for the ability to meaningfully participate in shaping the education provided their community's children. Most immediately, they need to weigh in on the dangers of allowing test scores to become the sole factor in making educational decisions, ignoring or overriding other information.

The testing profession's recently revised official principles, the Standards for Educational and Psychological Testing,[4] state clearly, "In educational settings, a decision or characterization that will have a major impact on a student should not be made on the basis of a single test score." The National Academy of Sciences publication *High Stakes*[5] makes the same case, calling for the use of multiple sources of information for determining student placement, grade retention, or graduation.

The high-stakes testing on which many states are beginning to rely is a clear instance of test misuse. Further, high-stakes applications intensify all the other problems associated with too great a reliance on testing. For many students and schools, the consequences are very harmful.

Consequences for Student Learning

Test-based teaching, rewards, threats, and controls will, we are told, lead to improved learning. Thus far, the evidence does not support such a claim. For example, states which have not implemented graduation tests are more likely to show improvement on the National Assessment of Educational Progress (NAEP) than are states which have such exams. Moreover, states with the heaviest test burden tend to be states with the lowest scores on NAEP.[6]

Often, when scores on state tests go up, scores on NAEP, a relatively independent measure, do not. Tests are only samples of the knowledge and skills found in a subject area. Teaching to the test almost always means focusing on the tested sample rather than on the whole subject. Thus, test scores may increase while real learning in the whole subject does not. Further, as test-score gains based on teaching to the state exam cease to be valid measures of broader learning, the results mislead the public about educational achievement.

Nor does test-based teaching seem to lead to closing test-score gaps among racial groups. Texas, for example, claims that test-driven reform works because scores on the Texas Assessment of Academic Skills (TAAS) for African Americans and

This chapter is adapted by permission of the publisher from "State Exams Flunk Test of Quality" by M. Neill, in *The State Education Standard*, Spring 2000, pp. 31–35. Copyright © 2000, the National Association of State Boards of Education.

Latinos have gone up while racial gaps narrowed. However, while the state's mean NAEP 4th grade reading score for whites rose six points from 1992 to 1998, average black scores dropped three points and Hispanic average scores rose only three points.[7]

There are many reasons why test-based "reform" will not produce improved learning. Fundamentally, school improvement driven by tests is not likely to be better than the tests themselves. For that reason, a careful look at the tests is essential. Unfortunately, the tests remain secret in most states, hidden from public scrutiny behind copyright law and bureaucratic restrictions.

However, a few states do make substantial portions of their tests available. If these tests represent what our children should know and control schooling in those states, they, and we, are in trouble.

Today, all state testing programs include some of the following components: criterion- and/or norm-referenced (CRT/NRT) tests with multiple-choice items; some open-ended short-answer questions; and a writing sample. A few states add a couple of questions requiring a more extended response. Vermont includes portfolios.[8]

None of the commercial NRTs match even the most impoverished of state standards. That does not prevent some states from using them as part of what they claim to be standards-based reform. California, for example, relies on Harcourt's Stanford 9, and Wisconsin's state test is simply CTB's Terra Nova under another name. Since most state standards are voluminous,[9] it would be hard to prove that any test item would not fit somewhere in the standards. Nonetheless, the tests in no way constitute a balanced reflection of the standards.

Most states attempt to assess to the standards using customized CRTs or "standards-based tests." Even with these, much of what is in the standards is not tested and cannot be assessed using the methods employed.[10]

For example, Massachusetts's science standards call for students to do science, but the tests involve no aspect of "doing" science. The 1999 grade 8 exam contains a mix of multiple-choice and constructed-response items. Virtually all the multiple-choice items can be answered if the test taker knows the name of a concept or process—but that is not evidence that they understand it or that they are able to apply the knowledge. Some of the five open-ended questions do require some thought to answer, others are fairly trivial.[11]

Multiple-choice questions have long been criticized as nonauthentic. After all, how many real-world problems present four or five brief answer choices? While these types of items can have some use in assessing factual, declarative knowledge,

and can extend to lower-level inferencing, they cannot assess more complex thought in any area.[12] Even in states with mixed-method exams, low-level multiple-choice items typically account for more of the score than any other parts, and those items remain low-level.[13]

If the goal is regurgitation of facts, these tests may be adequate. But that is not the purpose of model national standards such as those in science, math, or history. Few states claim factual recall and basic procedures as their goal.

Even when efforts at memorization "succeed" in raising test scores, the learning is neither substantial nor long lasting. Students still cannot think in the subject area, nor use knowledge. What has been memorized to pass a test is soon forgotten.[14]

When states include short open-ended items, the actual questions rarely require critical, divergent, complex, and creative thinking, synthesis and evaluation, or the application of knowledge. Many short-answer items on the "new" state tests are not much more than multiple-choice questions with the answer options removed. For example, the Wisconsin state test for grade 4 students asked students to list "two reasons why geese migrate each year"—a question which simply asked for recall of memorized information.[15]

Mathematics appears to be a partial exception in some states, in part because short-answer items can be of real use in math. In Massachusetts, for example, independent reviewers of the grade 4 exam thought that the questions reasonably reflected the standards of the National Council of Teachers of Mathematics. However: 1) the language in the items was often way beyond typical grade 4 reading ability[16]; 2) too few teachers are prepared well to teach to the NCTM standards; and 3) the state is now changing the standards to move away from NCTM, a reflection of the intense politicization of the standards, which further undermines the legitimacy of the standards-and-test approach.[17]

State tests rarely require extended responses. To be reasonably sure that the scores reflect how well the student really knows the subject, a large number of extended-response items would be required.[18] Since these items are harder and more expensive to score, states might include one or two, but few even do that. The Maryland State Performance Assessment Program is an exception. However, it uses a sampling procedure which produces school scores, not individual-level data. No other state uses this sensible approach.

Most state tests now include writing samples. However, the typical state writing exam is a completely formulaic exercise in the irrelevant. Such "essays" typically reduce writing to a "five-paragraph paper," penned in response to a generic prompt. What is evaluated is not writing, but compliance with the state scoring guide.[19] This often controls how writing is taught, leaving many students unable to communicate well for a variety of purposes, never mind actually wanting to write.

Many argue that the problems with the tests can be fixed. The chimera of better tests has been chased for decades. No matter what proponents claim, multiple-choice items cannot assess most higher-level skills, short-answer items provide no space for real thought, and "extended response" items consistently embody narrow cultural experiences, triviality, or are even nonsensical.[20] Even if the questions could be improved, no state will ever spend the money to create tests composed of extended-response items to obtain individual scores—and if they did, they would devour even more of the school year than tests now do. In short, test-driven school reform cannot be expected to produce high-quality schooling because the technology and economics of testing do not allow this desirable outcome.

High-stakes tests—for promotion, graduation, school rewards, or punishments—intensify the problem because they intensify the imperative to teach to these flawed instruments.[21] Whenever the tests are intentionally made very difficult, as with Massachusetts's MCAS or Virginia's Standards of Learning (SOL) exams, the failure rate is enormous, and more than enormous for African American and Latino students, as well as those with special needs, in vocational education programs, or for whom English is a second language.[22]

Even with a seemingly less-difficult test, such as Texas's TAAS, the failure rate is high: only 68 percent of those who first took the test as sophomores in 1994 passed it by the end of their senior year.[23] Further, such tests increase the dropout rate. When the TAAS was introduced as a graduation exam, the graduation rate for black and Hispanic students plunged 10 percentage points. Many students who were retained in grade 9 dropped out before taking the grade 10 TAAS. No more than half the 8th-grade students from these groups now graduate from Texas high schools.[24]

It might appear contradictory to argue that the tests are simultaneously too difficult and intellectually impoverished. Not so. The tests are difficult because they demand memorization of masses of information, not thinking. Items are made difficult by their obscurity, not their cognitive rigor.

Unfortunately, too few U.S. students are prepared to use their minds well. But memorization-dependent exams will exacerbate, not solve, this problem. Another approach to assessment, accountability, and school reform is needed if the nation is to have schools where students learn to think.

BETTER TEACHING?

According to proponents, the tests will focus teachers' attention on what is most essential, leading to better teaching.[25] However, since most state tests focus primarily on memorization, teachers are forced to make this their instructional focus. One consequence is profoundly tedious instruction which turns most students off to learning. It rarely even leads to significant and lasting changes in test scores.[26] Many teachers have made clear the damage this approach causes for high-quality instruction,[27] largely because the memorization demands of the tests occupy all available time, leaving none for thinking, exploring, debating, evaluating, or doing.

Defenders of tests maintain that students must memorize, they must have facts and information to use in thinking.[28] There is some truth to this, but this approach has a fundamentally flawed understanding of learning.

For example: Johnny comes to school from a home in which the parents provide school-type knowledge, which can be a basis for thinking in a subject. Teachers can build on this, as many good suburban and private schools do now. But Sally comes from a home where school-type knowledge is in short supply; she is not immersed in a culture in which she will almost effortlessly absorb much of the kinds of knowledge schools expect. One response is to drill Sally in the facts, to defer asking her to think about these facts until Sally has "mastered" enough of them. For most Sallys, that day never comes.[29] That is largely because having facts poured into one's head doesn't even lead to success at memorization for most students, often, in turn, because students are simply turned off to such forms of "instruction."[30]

Since children, like adults, mostly learn through active engagement,[31] what is necessary is to create classrooms in which students learn facts by being engaged in interesting work, creating a virtual spiral of declarative knowledge and thinking skills. But test-driven reform precludes that possibility because there is not enough time in the day, week, or year to engage in this sort of learning activity. Thus, the best sorts of teaching practices are driven out of schools where they do exist and prevented from developing where they do not. Rather than improve teaching, test-driven "reform" undermines it.

There is one further, very nasty consequence: test-driven reform also drives out the best teachers.[32] How absurd to believe that the "best and brightest" will want to enter teaching when test-driven reform treats them as clerks in a Dickens novel—other than that many care deeply for children. Once again, high stakes renders the situation worse. In Florida, where schools are ranked almost entirely on test scores, teachers are abandoning low-scoring schools, leaving them even more understaffed and less able to improve learning.[33] This works wonderfully well as a scheme to destroy public education, but not very well as a plan to improve educational outcomes in low-scoring schools.

SCHOOL REFORM

Attempting to improve schools through tests ignores what it really takes to improve schools. The best models for low-income children can be found in the network of small schools created in the wake of the Central Park East schools initiated by Deborah Meier. In these schools, a percentage of students far beyond demographic expectations not only enroll in college but also succeed. However, while the students succeed in real life, their test scores go up only modestly.[34]

Why and how these schools work requires a book,[35] but there are some essentials. There are high expectations and standards, but they are not the insane overload of most state standards imposed in a one-size-fits-all manner of the sort Susan Ohanian so eloquently lambastes.[36] There is continuous professional development, organized by the staff using time within a reorganized school day; but it is professional development rooted in the needs of the school, not in response to items on a bad test. Real power and accountability rest with the school staff. The schools are communities, small enough for people to actually know each other, creating a human institution rather than the kind of school of which a student could say, "This place hurts my spirit."[37]

Test-driven reform maintains the factory model of schooling, created following the Taylorist "cult of efficiency"[38] and behaviorist psychology.[39] High-stakes tests speed up the assembly line for both students and teachers. The content knowledge covered by tests has expanded, but there remains no serious effort to engage students as thoughtful humans. This approach to schooling is antithetical to learning to think as well as to being an active participant in a democracy.

DEMOCRACY NOW?

Local control has its pitfalls. It can maintain racism or refuse to educate the poor. It can honor the worst forms of narrow parochialism. It can isolate educators from engagement with valuable change. It even can perpetuate the very kinds of schooling being reinforced by testing. But without local engagement in public schooling, democracy is impoverished. If all significant decisions about content—and, as a consequence, about instruction—are made by a far-away bureau-

cracy, not only teachers but also community residents are reduced to powerless functionaries. Deborah Meier argues that such people are poor role models for children, that children need powerful and engaged adults around them.[40]

Arguably, some local school boards have not served well the interests of all the children in their districts. But test-driven reform compounds this problem, imposing bad education at the level of the state and mandating it for every district. It is one thing for a state to develop mechanisms through which schools must demonstrate what they are doing and how they are going to do it better,[41] and quite another to reduce accountability and improvement to test scores.

Local school committees ought to take the lead in opposing these destructive mandates. If parents or teachers have already begun to resist, school boards should support them. In doing so, they should work to construct a new paradigm of governance and participatory democracy in shaping schools. That is, they should ally with genuine reform at the local level against bureaucratic deformations imposed from above. Doing so has not been a common practice among school boards,[42] but is now essential.

Left unchecked, test-driven reform will re-create for another generation the factory model of schooling developed early in the 20th century that never has and never will work for most students. Ironically, schools for the rich don't use that model, but schools for everyone else are now expected to—in the name of reform.

It need not be this way. Change requires two things: organizing and a feasible alternative. In Massachusetts, the Coalition for Authentic Reform in Education (CARE) has proposed a community-based accountability system to replace the state's reliance on tests.[43] Key elements of this plan are:

1. Local authentic assessments approved by regional boards. Schools, rather than the state, would determine graduation. The state would define an essential, but limited, body of knowledge, skills, and habits of mind that all students should acquire, while allowing local schools and districts the freedom to create assessment systems that meet the needs of their unique student populations.

2. A school quality review process to assess the effectiveness of school practices, based on existing successful models.

3. Standardized testing solely in literacy and numeracy, to provide one method for tracking progress of schools from year to year.

4. Annual local reporting by schools to their communities, using a defined set of indicators, including evidence of achievement of the state's "common core" of learning, which

also focus on equal opportunity and access to knowledge for all students.

CONCLUSION

Testing has taken over school reform efforts in many states. It is an approach to school improvement that lacks evidence of success and has many well-documented damaging consequences, from damaging the lives of individuals to misdirecting resources to inhibiting real reform. School boards should step forward and help lead our schools toward genuine reform by embracing approaches to accountability that enhance student learning, improve teaching, strengthen schools, and promote democracy.

NOTES

[1]*Education Week.* (2000, January 13). *Quality Counts 2000*, p. 72. Though it is not noted there, Nebraska does have a statewide test: S. Bauer, "State told it cannot order schools to test," *Lincoln Journal-Star*, received via e-mail, February 15, 2000.

[2]Neill, M. (1997). *Testing our children: A report card on state assessment systems.* Cambridge: FairTest. FairTest keeps track of state policy changes on high-stakes testing and regularly updates its table on graduation tests. Available: http://www.fairtest.org/states/intro.htm.

[3]Roeber, E., Bond, L., & Connealy, S. (1997, Fall). *Annual survey of state student assessment programs.* Washington, DC: Council of Chief State School Officers.

[4]American Educational Research Association (AERA), American Psychological Association, & National Council on Measurement in Education. (1999). *Standards for educational and psychological testing.* Washington, DC: AERA.

[5]Heubert, J. P., & Hauser, R. M. (1998). *High stakes: Testing for tracking, promotion, and graduation.* Washington, DC: National Academy Press.

[6]Neill, M., with Gayler, K. (1998, December 4). *Do high stakes graduation tests improve learning outcomes? Using state-level NAEP data to evaluate the effects of mandatory graduation tests.* Paper presented at the conference "High-Stakes Testing in K-12: Reconciling Standards-Based Reforms with Civil Rights and Equity," sponsored by the Civil Rights Project at Harvard University with Teachers College and Columbia Law School, New York. Draft available: http://www.law.harvard.edu/civilrights/conferences/testing98/drafts.html.

[7]Kauffman, A. H. (1999). Plaintiffs' post-trial brief, *GI Forum, et al., v. Texas Education Agency, et al.* (Civil Action No. SA-97-CA-1278EP, U.S. District Court for the Western District of Texas, San Antonio Division).

[8]Neill, M. (1997). *Testing our children: A report card on state assessment systems.* Cambridge: FairTest; Roeber, E., Bond, L., & Connealy, S. (1997, Fall). *Annual survey of state student assessment programs.* Washington, DC: Council of Chief State School Officers.

[9]Ohanian, S. (1999). *One size fits few: The folly of educational standards.* Portsmouth, NH: Heineman; Kendall, J. S., & Marzano, R. J. *Content knowledge: The McREL standards database.* Aurora, CO: Mid-continent Research for Education and Learning. Available at http://www.mcrel.org/standards-benchmarks/.

[10]Cf., Are state-level standards and assessments aligned? (1999, Fall). *WCER Highlights.* Wisconsin Center for Education Research, University of Wisconsin–Madison, pp. 1–3; Nichols, P., & Sugrue, B. (1999, Summer).

The lack of fidelity between cognitively complex constructs and conventional test development practice. *Educational Measurement: Issues and Practice 18*(2), 18–29; Shafer, M. C., and Foster, S. (1997, Fall). The changing face of assessment. *Principled Practice in Mathematics & Science Education.* Wisconsin Center for Education Research, University of Wisconsin–Madison, pp. 1–7; Neill, M. (1997). *Testing our children: A report card on state assessment systems.* Cambridge: FairTest.

[11]http://www.doe.mass.edu/mcas/. The Massachusetts CARE group has for a second time reviewed the MCAS exams, and its report will be forthcoming and available from FairTest.

[12]Frederiksen, N. (1984). The real test bias: Influences of testing on teaching and learning. *American Psychologist 39*(3), 193–202; Nichols, P., & Sugrue, B. (1999, Summer). The lack of fidelity between cognitively complex constructs and conventional test development practice. *Educational Measurement: Issues and Practice 18*(2), 18–29; Shafer, M. C., and Foster, S. (1997, Fall). The changing face of assessment. *Principled Practice in Mathematics & Science Education.* Wisconsin Center for Education Research, University of Wisconsin–Madison, pp. 1–7.

[13]Neill, M. (1997). *Testing our children: A report card on state assessment systems.* Cambridge: FairTest.

[14]Kohn, A. (1999). *The schools our children deserve.* Boston: Houghton Mifflin; Ryan, R. M., & La Guardia, J. G. (1999). Achievement motivation within a pressured society: Intrinsic and extrinsic motivations to learn and the politics of school reform. In T. Urdan (Ed.), *Advances in motivation and achievement, Vol. 11* (pp. 45–85). Greenwich, CT: JAI Press.

[15]Wisconsin Student Assessment System. (1996–97). *Knowledge and concepts examinations, science.* San Antonio: CTB/McGraw Hill, 12.

[16]Ad hoc MCAS Group (1998, November). *MCAS Review.* Cambridge, MA. Photocopies available from FairTest.

[17]Hayward, E. (2000, February 11). Math curriculum panel quits to protest meddling. *Boston Herald*, p. 14.

[18]Shavelson, R. J., Baxter, G. P., and Pine, J. (1992). Performance assessments: Political rhetoric and measurement reality. *Educational Researcher 21*(4), 22–27.

[19]Mabry, L. (1999, May). Writing to the rubric. *Phi Delta Kappan, 80*(9), 673–679.

[20]Cf., Heifetz, J. (2000, February 10). Regents exam is "unpossible." *New York Daily News*, Opinion.

[21]Madaus, G. F. (1988). The influence of testing on the curriculum. In L. N. Tanner (Ed.), *Critical issues in the curriculum; 87th yearbook of the National Society for the Study of Education, Part I* (pp. 83–121). Chicago: University of Chicago Press.

[22]Uriarte, M., & Chavez, L. (1999, November). *Latino students in Massachusetts public schools.* Boston: Gaston Institute, University of Massachusetts–Boston.

[23]Mexican American Legal Defense and Educational Fund. (1997, October 14). The effect of the TAAS on Texas 1996 Public School Seniors. San Antonio: Author.

[24]Haney, W. (1999). *Supplementary report on Texas Assessment of Academic Skills Exit Test (TAAS-X),* (prepared for plaintiffs and submitted to the court in *GI Forum, et al., v. Texas Education Agency, et al.,* Civil Action No SA-97-CA-1278EP, U.S. District Court for the Western District of Texas, San Antonio Division).

[25]Education Trust. (1999, Fall). *Ticket to nowhere: Thinking K–16.* Washington, DC: Author.

[26]Hoff, D. (2000, January 26). Testing's ups and downs predictable. *Education Week*, pp. 1, 12–13.

[27]Cf., Stoskopf, A. (2000, February 2). Clio's lament: Teaching and learning history in the age of accountability. *Education Week*, pp. 38, 41; McNeil, L. M. (1988, March). Contradictions of control, part 3: Contradictions of reform. *Phi Delta Kappan, 69*(7), 478–485; and a more recent study in this vein will be McNeil, L. M. (2000, April). *Contradictions of school reform: The educational costs of standardized testing.* New York: Routledge.

[28]Cf., Hirsch, E. D. (2000, February 2). The tests we need, and why we don't have them. *Education Week*, pp. 64, 40–41; Hirsch, E. D. (1996). *The schools we need and why we don't have them.* New York: Doubleday.

[29]Newmann, F. M., Lopez, G., & Bryk, A. S. (1998, October). *The quality of intellectual work in Chicago schools: A baseline report.* Chicago: Chicago Consortium on School Research.

[30]Kohn, A. (1999). *The schools our children deserve.* Boston: Houghton Mifflin; Ryan, R. M., & La Guardia, J. G. (1999). Achievement motivation within a pressured society: Intrinsic and extrinsic motivations to learn and the politics of school reform. In T. Urdan (Ed.), *Advances in motivation and achievement, Vol. 11* (pp. 45–85). Greenwich, CT: JAI Press.

[31]There is now an enormous body of literature on this, though with much debate on particulars. For a recent summary, see A. Kohn, *The schools our children deserve.* Boston: Houghton Mifflin, 1999.

[32]McNeil, L. M. (1988, March). Contradictions of control, part 3: Contradictions of reform. *Phi Delta Kappan,* 69(7), 478–485; McNeil, L. M. (2000, April). *Contradictions of school reform: The educational costs of standardized testing.* New York: Routledge.

[33]Dougher, C. (2000, February). Big weight, little shoulders. *City Link,* Palm Beach, FL (posted to the Assessment Reform Network listserv).

[34]Meier, D. (1995). *The power of their ideas.* Boston: Beacon Press; Bensman, D. (1994). *Lives of the graduates of Central Park East Elementary School.* New York: Center for Collaborative Education (CCE) and National Center for Restructuring Education, Schools, and Teaching Education; Bensman, D. (1987). *Quality education in the inner city: The story of Central Park East Elementary School.* New York: CCE; Meier, D. (2000, January). Personal communication.

[35]Meier, D. (1995). *The power of their ideas.* Boston: Beacon Press.

[36]Ohanian, S. (1999). *One size fits few: The folly of educational standards.* Portsmouth, NH: Heinemann.

[37]Poplin, M., & Weeres, J. (1992). *Voices from the inside: A report on schooling from inside the classroom, part 1.* Claremont, CA: Claremont Graduate School, Institute for Education in Transformation.

[38]Callahan, R. (1962). *Education and the cult of efficiency.* Chicago: University of Chicago Press.

[39]Resnick, L. B., and Resnick, D. P. (1992). Assessing the thinking curriculum: New tools for educational reform. In B. R. Gifford & M. C. O'Connor (Eds.), *Changing assessments: Alternative views of aptitude, achievement, and instruction* (pp. 37–75). Boston: Kluwer.

[40]Meier. D. Educating a democracy. *Boston Review.* Available: http://bostonreview.mit.edu/BR24.6/meier.html.

[41]Coalition for Authentic Reform in Education. (1999). *A call for an authentic statewide assessment system.* Cambridge, MA: FairTest. Available: http:www.fairtest.org/arn/masspage.html.

[42]Gelberg, D. (1997). *The "business" of reforming America's schools.* Albany, NY: SUNY Press.

[43]Coalition for Authentic Reform in Education. (1999). *A call for an authentic statewide assessment system.* Cambridge, MA: FairTest. Available: http:www.fairtest.org/arn/masspage.html. See also Neill, D. M. (1997, September). Transforming student assessment. *Phi Delta Kappan* 79(1), 34–40, 58.

81

Building a System for Assessing Thinking

Arthur L. Costa and Bena Kallick

How much do students really love to learn, to persist, to passionately attack a problem or a task?
... to watch some of their prized ideas explode and to start anew?
... to go beyond being merely dutiful or long-winded?
Let us assess such things.

—*Grant Wiggins*

Although many would agree that thinking is required both in the workplace and to sustain our democracy, we are caught in an age of accountability in which achievement is measured in discrete and often reductive terms. When we hear such terms as *measurement, evaluation,* and *accountability*, what often comes to mind is *testing*. Although testing is one form of gathering data to inform our evaluation, to assess growth in thinking abilities requires other forms as well. We cannot evaluate process-oriented outcomes exclusively through product-oriented assessment strategies.

INTERDEPENDENT ASSESSMENTS

In this chapter, we deal with evaluation as a balanced set of interdependent assessments, each contributing to the whole picture of students who are becoming more thoughtful. Some of the measures can be reduced to numbers, others are narratives revealing qualitative differences, and others are less tangible but nonetheless significant. How we manage these measures will help create a picture of how well students are

This chapter is adapted from "Assessing the Habits of Mind," by A. L. Costa and B. Kallick, 2000, in *Assessing and Reporting on Habits of Mind* (pp. 29–53), edited by A. L. Costa and B. Kallick. Alexandria, VA: Association for Supervision and Curriculum Development.

improving in their thinking and how we can help them to become even better at it.

Section II of this book, "Thinking: Building Common Understandings," defines thinking as a composite of various skills, abilities, strategies, capacities, and inclinations. Here we describe the relationship of cognitive operations, thinking tasks, and habits of mind as interdependent (see Figure 81.1). To function successfully, thoughtful people continue to gain skills in each of these arenas. Although we may have assessments that isolate each of these capabilities, the assessment that weaves them together makes the most sense.

Cognitive operations. Being successful in school, at work, and in life depends on acquiring and performing certain basic, discrete thinking skills such as recalling, comparing, classifying, inferring, generalizing, evaluating, experimenting, and analyzing. According to Barry Beyer in Chapters 41 and 62 of this book, as well as deBono (1980), and Feuerstein and colleagues (1980), these skills may need to be taught directly. In Chapter 84 in this volume, Beyer suggests a way of assessing students' knowledge of specific thinking skills.

Thinking tasks. Such specific skills are seldom performed in isolation. Rather, they are embedded within a larger context in response to some stimulus. They are strategically organized into and employed in combinations and sequences that we refer to as thinking tasks, such as creative problem solving, information processing, and decision making (see Chapter 8 by Robert Ennis and Chapter 71 by Robert Sternberg in this volume.) Thinking tasks are larger strategies employed over time and require the application of clusters of discrete cognitive operations. For example, decision making may require observing accurately, inferring causal relationships, comparing and contrasting alternative choices, predicting consequences, and deducing (see Chapter 45 by Robert Swartz in this volume). Although some cognitive operations such as reasoning and problem solving may be assessed using tests (such as those sug-

—Figure 81.1—
A Composite View of Thinking

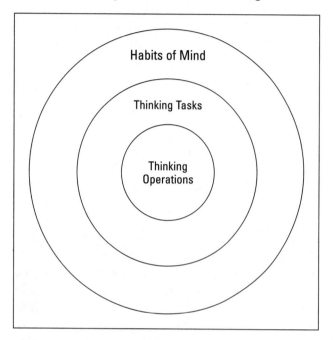

Habits of Mind

Thinking Tasks

Thinking Operations

gested by Ennis and described by Alec Fisher in Chapter 85), cognitive operations generally require demonstration and performance in real-life problem-solving and decision-making tasks. Kay Burke provides many examples in Chapter 83.

Habits of mind. Even though individuals may know the labels and procedures of these thinking skills and be able to perform tasks requiring skillful thinking, they must also recognize opportunities in which such skills may be employed and, furthermore, be inclined to employ them. To achieve a habit of mind, therefore, requires more than simply possessing these basic skills and having the capacities to carry through with the behaviors (see Chapter 13 by Shari Tishman and Chapter 15 by Art Costa.) To make a pattern of intellectual behaviors habitual requires time—time beyond that required for one problem-solving task, one lesson, one unit, one class, or even one school year. Students must encounter, practice, and reflect on these behaviors in numerous settings using a variety of contents and with adequate time for self-evaluation. Therefore, assessment strategies must be designed to gather data about increasing and spontaneously applying habits of mind over time and in a rich variety of contexts.

Distinguishing these three ways of thinking helps us realize the necessity of finding multiple ways of acquiring data about student growth in thinking. There is merit in assessing think-

ing as a set of isolated skills. We can learn more specifically what a student can or cannot do. Distinguishing this information can help us make better teaching interventions (Feuerstein, Rand, Hoffman, & Miller, 1980). However, the skill does not remain in isolation. When we put it into a context, we can assess how a student applies the skill when a situation or task requires its use. The assessment of habits of mind requires yet different modes of assessment. To assess only cognitive operations discloses nothing about their application to thinking tasks. To assess performance of only cognitive operations and thinking tasks discloses nothing about a student's inclination toward or sensitivity to the need and opportunity to employ those cognitive operations. Thus, we need a balance of assessment strategies.

TRIANGULATION

If we were to assess the competencies of an airline pilot, a physician, or a bus driver, we would want them not only to indicate their knowledge of laws, regulations, and procedures, but also to demonstrate their competencies under supervised performance of their tasks. Even with these two measures, our confidence in them would still need to be satisfied by observing them during periods of internship over time and in crisis situations. This systematic gathering of balanced assessment data about growth from three different vantage points may be referred to as "triangulation" (see Figure 81.2).

Chapters 79, 80, 82, and 83 in this volume provide rich suggestions about how to assess cognitive operations and thinking tasks. This chapter focuses on several tools that may be used to assess habits of mind, discussed in more detail by Costa and Kallick (2000). Each of these tools, when used regularly, can provide a longitudinal record of student growth, of students' "getting into the habit." This process of assessment and feedback should ultimately lead to learners' becoming self-assessing.

CHECKLISTS

Checklists are a useful way to help students assess themselves and the groups they work in. Checklists are developed through classroom conversations. For example, a teacher asks the students, "What would it look like if a person were a good listener?" "What would it sound like if a person were a good listener?" Students then generate a list of positively constructed, observable behaviors. In the "looks like" category, responses might include "maintains eye contact" or "nods head when agreeing." The "sounds like" category might include such re-

—Figure 81.2—

Triangulation: Assessing Three Components of Thinking

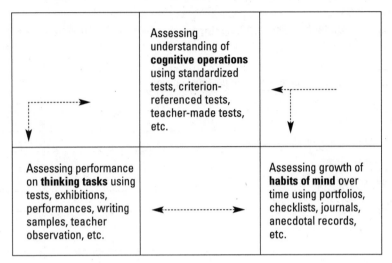

sponses as "builds on the other person's ideas" or "clarifies when does not understand." Finally, the students and teacher agree to observe for these behaviors. Figure 81.3 shows a checklist developed for the habit of mind of listening with understanding and empathy.

Once students feel comfortable assessing themselves, the teacher asks them to rate themselves as well as the others in their group. Students then compare ratings and see whether their self-perceptions are accurate. Finally, the teacher rates the students and gives specific examples of how students are showing evidence of the positive behaviors of good listening. Parents may also collect data at home with a "How Is My Child Doing?" checklist.

As the students begin to collect data about their behavior over time, they may create a graph of their progress (or lack of it). They will find it helpful to receive feedback from their peers, their teacher, and their self-assessment.

RUBRICS

Once students are familiar with checklists, teachers often want to help them discern qualitative differences in their behaviors. Rubrics can be designed to provide a differentiated scoring system that describes performance at increasing levels of mastery. Each category should be sufficiently clear so that students can learn from the feedback about their behavior and thus learn how to improve. The example in Figure 81.4 was developed in an elementary school classroom and is intended for students' self-assessment of their own interdependent thinking while

working cooperatively in groups. (See also Marzano, Pickering, & McTighe, 1993.)

PORTFOLIOS

Many teachers use the habits of mind as an organizer for student portfolios. The portfolio is sectioned with folders, each labeled with an attribute. Students choose work based on their best example of the various habits of mind. The work is entered in the portfolio, and the student reflects on why the work has been chosen and what it should say to the reader of the portfolio. In peer conferences, students coach one another as they build these portfolios; they read their work and, with the help of the peer, reflect on why they have chosen particular pieces.

> Keeping track is a matter of reflective review and summarizing in which there is both discrimination and record of the significant features of a developing experience . . . It is the heart of intellectual organization and of the disciplined mind. (Dewey, 1938)

When portfolios are developed around the habits of mind, they are transdisciplinary. This answers the question many teachers face about how to have one portfolio that can work across all subjects. This is especially useful for high school students.

As an example of the habits of mind approach to portfolios at the elementary level, consider Lucy, a 6th grade student who was asked to choose a piece for her portfolio that demonstrated her development as a problem solver. The teacher was

—Figure 81.3—

A "How Am I Doing?" Checklist for a Habit of Mind

Habit of Mind: Listening with Understanding and Empathy	Often	Sometimes	Not Yet
Verbal Behaviors			
Restates or paraphrases a person's idea before offering personal opinion.			
Clarifies a person's ideas, concepts, or terminology.			
Expresses empathy for other's feelings and emotions.			
Poses questions intended to engage thinking and reflection.			
Expresses personal regard and interest.			
Takes an allocentric point of view (e.g., "If I were in your position . . .").			
Changes mind with addition of new information.			
Nonverbal Behaviors			
Faces the person who is speaking.			
Establishes eye contact if appropriate.			
Nods head.			
Uses facial expression congruent with speaker's emotional message.			

surprised by the choice but understood when she heard Lucy's reflection:

> This piece was written after my grandfather died. I was so sad that he died and I did not know how to rid myself of the sadness. We went on a class trip and I took photos of where we were. I placed those photos around my bed and laid on my bed for hours looking at the photos and thinking about my grandfather. Finally, I got up and wrote this piece. It shows how I was able to solve my problem of sadness through writing.

Lucy was showing evidence of her disposition for problem solving and drawing from previous experiences to reflect on her learning.

In a 10th grade English class, student portfolios are framed with the habits of mind. Each student has a list of the habits of mind permanently fixed on the inside of the portfolio cover, with checklists that help them look at the habits of mind in their work. Students are asked to choose habits of mind that they sense will help them to write better essays, for example, *persistence, precision,* and *accuracy.* Later in the school year, students are pushed further in their reflections about essays, asking peers to assume the role of "coach," and respond to peer judgment. Tenth grader Parin tells Brian, for example, that his essay illustrates his flexibility in thinking because he ". . . uses many metaphors for the journey: development, emotional progression, humility. . . ." Parin also notes that Brian shows precision of language in his ". . . good use of synonyms . . . decreases redundancy."

By the end of the year, students can show where their strengths have been made conscious, and they can articulate the reasons for their improvement. This is the most meaningful assessment because it holds the promise that students will continue to progress after they leave the classroom.

PERFORMANCES

The habits of mind become increasingly significant as students prepare for presentations of their work. These performances require orchestration and a great deal of social thinking. Students can receive feedback about the development of their habits of mind at three points during the performance process:

- When they are starting to plan for a performance.
- When they are in the process of working on the performance.
- When they are presenting their work to an audience.

DURING THE PLANNING

Exemplifying thinking about the habits of mind during the planning stage, a science teacher asks his students to set goals

—Figure 81.4—
A Scoring Rubric for Group Cooperation

4	Demonstrates interdependence. All members contribute. Shows indicators of cooperation and working together, compromising, and staying on task. Disagreements are welcomed as learning opportunities. Completes task with accuracy and within time limits. Members listen to others' points of view. Paraphrasing, clarifying, and empathizing are in evidence.
3	Members disagree but reach agreements through arguing and debate. Some paraphrasing and clarifying is in evidence. Group sometimes strays from task. Some members remain silent or refrain from participating.
2	Some members are off task. Group rushes to complete task in the most expedient way because of the pressure of time. Evidence of arguing or encouraging others to get it over with.
1	Few on task. Evidence of arguing and disinterest. Some members occupied with other work.
0	Chaos. Task not completed. Many put-downs. Some members leave before task is complete. Complaints about having to participate in task.

Source: Tamalpias Elementary School, Marin County, California.

for their work. He asks the students to choose one habit they feel especially strong in and one that they need to work on. They make a plan for how they will work to develop the habits through the actions they take. Then, as a group, they develop a list of indicators that answer the question "What will a particular habit of mind look and sound like when we see and hear it happening?" They agree to keep a record of incidences in which they observe the use of a disposition. What is important about this process is that they plan to pay attention to the habits of mind before they begin their work.

DURING THE PROCESS

Record-keeping forms are provided for students as they work on their performance, and they document their observations. In one high school class, the students keep a collective log of their process during project development. Group members rotate responsibility for log entries for each day they work together. They reflect on the following points:

- What did we learn today?
- What did we notice about the way the group is working?
- What did the group and group member do to contribute to the group's success?
- What might we do to be more effective as a group?
- Which habits of mind would help us to be more productive?

DURING THE PRESENTATION

This is when students are required to focus on checking for accuracy and precision, using precise language, creativity, problem posing, and metacognition. During the presentation, the audience is asked to pay attention to the accuracy of the information. They also take note of the use of proper terminology.

ANECDOTAL RECORDS

Being constantly alert to students' demonstration of particular habits of mind, teachers can document student work. The most significant part of this strategy is to be systematic about record keeping. One teacher at John Lyman Elementary School in Middlefield, Connecticut, found that she was able to observe all of the children in her class when she designed a notebook, tabbed each section with a student's name, and used Post-it notes to record information about the student's habits of mind. At the end of the first marking period, she had a good database to draw from when she wanted to write narrative comments about students, as this example shows:

> Jean picks up mathematical concepts quickly and is able to apply the new knowledge immediately to solve problems. She has been working on activities involving sorting, graphing, and estimating and place value. She has also been doing a lot of group problem solving. She is able to generate multiple solutions to a problem and can usually explain in words how she arrived at her solution. She is developing efficient strategies for doing

mental computations. She enjoys a mathematical challenge and is willing to struggle with a problem when the answer is not immediately apparent.

Parents as well as teachers can provide anecdotal records. Many teachers send a copy of the habits of mind home and ask parents to notice when the child is using the behaviors. During conference time, the parents share their observations with the teacher.

Besides documenting performances, teachers should also be alert to students' comments before, during, and after learning activities, projects, and assignments. Students often reveal their awareness, understanding, and application of the habits of mind as they plan for and reflect on their work. Following are some student comments, collected by Michele Swanson at Sir Francis Drake High School in San Anselmo, California:

Persisting: In the last project when I couldn't have been more stressed, I wanted to quit and walk away, but no matter how much I wanted to give up because I had no idea what I was doing or how it was going to be done, no matter how much I wanted to throw the Makita because it wasn't working, no matter how much responsibility I was forced to take on I stuck with it until the end always knowing (hoping) it would turn out great.

Listening with understanding and empathy: Listening before prejudging someone's contribution makes sense. Being patient helps. I was surprised at the great ideas and how much everyone added.

Finding humor: Getting to know these people can really impact your life and your work very positively, so you always have to keep a light and open heart and humor can aid in this.

Humor keeps people relaxed and much more comfortable even while working on serious subject matter.

INTERVIEWS

Interviews can be an effective way for students to share their reflections on and attainment of the habits of mind. By creating an atmosphere of trust and by constructing well-designed questions, teachers can help students reveal their insights, understandings, and applications of the habits of mind. Here are some examples of effective questions:

• As you reflect on this semester's work, which of the habits of mind were you most aware of in your own learning?

• Which habit of mind will you focus your energies on as you begin our next project?

• What insights have you gained as a result of employing these habits of mind?

• As you think about your future, how might these habits of mind be used as a guide in your life?

Interviews provide teachers with opportunities to model their own use of precise language, their own listening with understanding and empathy, and their own use of questioning strategies. Teaching students to conduct interviews provides situations in which they must practice these habits of mind themselves. When they are practicing the art of questioning, they are reinforcing their habits of mind. In addition, the experience makes them more conscious about their own thinking about the same questions. The ultimate purpose is to lead students to the use of a powerful strategy: self-interview.

JOURNALS AND LOGS

Consciousness about habits of mind often begins with journal entries designed to help students focus on how they are developing. Learning logs and journals are a way to integrate content, process, personal feelings, and habits of mind. These tools are especially powerful in engaging metacognition and helping students to draw forth previous knowledge because they invite students to learn from writing as thinking. Before or directly following the end of a unit, a project, or an area of study, teachers can ask students to make entries in their logs or journals. Teachers, too, can join in by reflecting on their teaching, analyzing students' learning, preserving anecdotes about the class interactions, and projecting ideas for how they might approach a unit of study differently in the future.

Sometimes students complain, "I don't know what to write." To stimulate thinking, teachers can post "questioning stems" on a chart or ask students to keep a copy of them in the front of the log or journal. Here are some examples of possible questioning stems, or starters, that can stimulate reflection on use of the habits of mind:

• One thing that surprised me today was . . .
• I felt particularly flexible when I . . .
• I used my senses to . . .
• As I think about how I went about solving the problem I . . .
• A question I want to pursue is . . .
• When I checked my work I found . . .
• Because I listened carefully I learned . . .

Such thought starters can help students use the lens of the habits as a way of documenting their learning.

Teachers can collect specific log entries from time to time, read them, and share written comments with students. This helps build stronger teacher-learner relationships and provides a useful way to informally assess how well students are doing and how their conscious use of the habits of mind is developing. Students can choose journal or log entries from the beginning, middle, and end of the learning period to include in their portfolios along with their reflections and synthesis connecting the entries or generalizing about their learning over time (Lipton, 1997).

A PLANNING MATRIX

Obviously, collecting evidence of growth in all three of these areas—cognitive operations, thinking tasks, and habits of mind—cannot be done using the same techniques or strategy. Each requires a different data collection tool. The matrix in Figure 81.5 can help organize planning for how to collect evidence of thinking using a variety of assessment strategies.

Following is a classroom scenario that illustrates how a teacher might collect evidence of the use of cognitive operations, thinking strategies, and habits of mind. The students are presented with a complex, multistep math problem. To solve the problem, the student must do the following:

• *Use a strategy for problem solving.* It is assumed that the teacher has instructed the students in strategies for math problem solving. The assessment question is whether the student will independently use a helpful strategy to solve the problem. To know whether a strategy is being used, the teacher states in the problem task: "Show your reasoning."

• *Use cognitive operations such as reasoning by analogy.* Once again, the teacher is assumed to have taught such skills, and the students should be demonstrating their reasoning process with an explanation of how they came to their conclusion.

• *Use the habits of mind such as questioning and problem posing, striving for accuracy, and thinking about thinking.* In a classroom in which thinking is being taught, students will have ex-

—*Figure 81.5*—
A Planning Matrix for Assessment Strategies

Assessment Tools	Cognitive Operations	Thinking Tasks	Habits of Mind
Standardized Tests			
Criterion-Referenced Tests			
Writing Samples			
Journals and Logs			
Exhibitions			
Performances			
Anecdotes: School/Classroom			
Anecdotes: Home			
Teacher Observation			
Portfolios			
Interviews			
Rubrics			
Checklists			
Other			

perience with being able to call upon these habits and will be able to explain how the habits played a role in their problem solving.

The indicators for many of these strategies, skills, and habits of mind either directly state or imply evidence of thinking. For example, here are the indicators for problem solving and decision making:

- Identifies whether a situation, task, or problem needs an individual or a collaborative plan of action.
- Identifies needed resources.
- Accesses research of past practices for relevance, accuracy, and value.
- Uses multiple resources and generates new ways of viewing situations, tasks, or problems.
- Outlines possible solutions and ramifications of each solution.
- Draws logical conclusions/solutions.
- Implements action plan.
- Evaluates plan to make continual modifications.

Looking at the indicators, we begin to see which methods from the planning matrix would work best to gather evidence. In addition, use of the matrix paves the way for a rich portfolio of carefully selected work that can be transdisciplinary. The portfolio can be kept over time to show clear evidence that a student is improving in thinking.

TECHNOLOGY: A BURGEONING RESOURCE

The tools of technology enable an electronic record of student progress over time, using multiple measures, with actual student work to provide concrete examples of the quality of work produced. Among the most powerful aspects of using technology to provide an information management system are the following:

- Access to actual student work rather than numbers that attempt to describe it.
- Portfolios that include multimedia examples of performance that demonstrate a student's multiple intelligences.
- The ability to see a student's performance in multiple domains simultaneously (for example, simultaneous evidence of problem solving in the arts, science, and writing).

The technology is available, and an increasing number of educators are using it. Incorporating rich examples of student work, however, will require not only the infrastructure and memory of computers, but also a shift in thinking about demonstrations of learning.

SELF-EVALUATION: THE ULTIMATE GOAL

Employed over time, the assessment strategies described in this chapter can provide rich information for teachers as they cultivate their students' habits of mind. More importantly, however, this process of self-assessment provides students with data that promote their learning and growth.

Success depends on gathering information from a variety of feedback sources. In some cases, individuals change after consciously observing their own feelings, attitudes, and skills. Some depend on the observations of outsiders (so-called critical friends). And in other cases, those directly involved in a change collect specific kinds of evidence about what is happening in the organization's environment. Once these data are analyzed, interpreted, and internalized, actions are modified to more closely achieve the goals. Thus, individuals—and the organization—are continually self-learning, self-renewing, and self-modifying.

Building a system for measuring thinking will require considerable work in schools. They will have to define specifically which cognitive operations, thinking tasks, and habits of mind they want students to develop; they will have to decide on the best methods for collecting evidence; and they will have to persist in collecting evidence over time. They will have to have many conversations to find agreement among teachers about what is valued and how to interpret the evidence presented. All of this work is in progress in many schools. It is the task we face if we are to really invest in a more thoughtful future.

REFERENCES

Costa, A., & Kallick, B. (2000). *Assessing and reporting on habits of mind.* Alexandria, VA: Association for Supervision and Curriculum Development.

deBono, E. (1980). *Teaching thinking.* New York: Penguin.

Dewey, J. (1938). *Experience and education.* New York: Collier.

Feuerstein, R., Rand, Y., Hoffman, M., & Miller, R. (1980). *Instrumental enrichment: An intervention program for cognitive modifiability.* Baltimore: University Park Press.

Lipton, L. (1997). *50 ways to literacy.* Arlington Heights, IL: SkyLight Publishers.

Marzano. R. J., Pickering, D., & McTighe, J. (1993). *Assessing student outcomes: Performance assessment using the dimensions of learning model.* Alexandria, VA: Association for Supervision and Curriculum Development.

82

How Teachers Can Assess the Thinking Skills They Are Teaching

Robert Stone

A generation ago, teachers taught a myriad of facts, concepts, and skills to students, and the assumption was that students would then, at some future time and place, use those bits of knowledge to solve problems and to communicate effectively. Today's effective teachers continue to immerse students in the factual knowledge of the various disciplines but take students to the next level by challenging them to use that information to think critically, to create products, or to demonstrate performance in the students' real world of today.

It is relatively simple to assess most facts and skills through the time-honored strategies of drill and practice, short answer, fill in the blank, and so forth. However, if we stop there, we are only helping to create what Madeline Hunter described as "Champions of Trivial Pursuit." Students must be able to apply that knowledge in new and different situations, not just learning situations.

That is where authentic and performance assessments come into play. An industrial technology teacher would never have students pound nails simply for the sake of pounding nails or measure and cut boards into various lengths to demonstrate the ability to use a saw. Once students are familiar with the tools and their functions and can use them effectively, the real assessment begins. The tools, although introduced and practiced singularly, are meant to be used in conjunction with each other to produce a more complex project.

Students who are taught the tools of math, science, history, or language but are never asked to "build" anything are short-changed by our educational system. As teachers, how do we go about assessing beyond the knowledge and comprehension levels of Bloom's taxonomy; beyond the fill-in-the-blank, true-false, or short-answer response? How do we discover that students truly understand and can use what we have taught them?

Although each subject area offers its own unique opportunities for assessing thinking, most good assessments will allow students to pull together learning from multiple subjects. Very few important tasks that we do as adults are limited to single subject content. Planning the family vacation, organizing a community fund-raiser, or preparing for a dinner party all require complex thinking and problem solving based on knowledge from multiple subject areas.

One of the advantages of teaching elementary school is the opportunity to mesh several subject areas into one assessment. Here is an example. Following a math unit on perimeter and area, the teacher creates a multidisciplinary task to assess student understanding. Each student lays out the design for a schoolyard ornamental garden on grid paper, calculating the area devoted to each type of planting and the amount of border (fencing, rock wall, etc.) required. Once the design work has been done, students calculate the total cost of the project, adding the cost of border materials and plantings. In the final step of the project, students develop a presentation to be made to the parent-teacher organization, which they hope will fund their proposal. A final score is determined by the accuracy of the calculations and a student-developed rubric for scoring the presentation—an assessment that logically links math with language arts.

Imposing our own ways of thinking on students can be easy, but when students are allowed to demonstrate their understanding in their own ways, great thinking emerges. Open-ended assessments can capture creative thinking. When asked to create a poster that an educational publisher might market to teachers showing the three branches of the U.S. government, students are "turned loose" to show their understanding of the people involved in each branch, their responsibilities, and the concept of checks and balances. What the teacher may have pictured as a simple three-column chart with a few arrows becomes, on the student canvas, a three-ring circus (no editorial comment intended on their part) with the president portrayed as the ringmaster and the Congress portrayed as lions ready to bite back. Others' analogies might see the federal government as a spreading oak tree with each branch armed with chainsaws to keep the others trimmed back, or as a schoolhouse with the principal, teachers, and students playing the roles. Students make the learning authentic for themselves by finding examples in their "real" world that relate to the topic. Sometimes the best assessments of thinking emerge when we let the students know what we are looking for—"Show me your understanding of the three branches of the federal government"—and then get out of the way.

This doesn't mean that the traditional type of assessment might not precede a project like this one. In order to build, students need materials and tools. Being able to state the three branches of the government, the people who work in each branch, the responsibilities of each branch, and the way they all keep each other in check is critical to the success of creating a well thought out finished product. Recall is good, but the possession of that knowledge should lead to something.

There are many days when it just feels easier to pass out the worksheet or to assign the matching questions at the end of the chapter. Teachers don't always have the energy to develop creative ways to assess thinking. Luckily, other sources are available that teachers can rely on for quality assessment.

AIMS (Activities Integrating Math, Science, and Technology), of Fresno, California, publishes a monthly magazine full of clever, creative, "hands-on" ways for students to learn and for teachers to assess that learning. Most have a math/science connection. One such activity called "Pack and Post" requires students to serve as postmaster by wrapping packages for mailing, weighing the packages, calculating the cost of shipping, and affixing the correct postage to the packages.

Math teachers at all levels can take advantage of the wide variety of assessments available in the Math Exemplars program, available from Exemplars, A Teacher's Solution, RR 1, Box 7390, Underhill, VT 05489. This wealth of authentic math tasks, stored in large notebooks and also available on computer disks, is a great reference for teachers looking to tap students' thinking beyond mere computation. Tasks are categorized by grade level, strands (geometry, fractions, decimals, etc.), and skills, so that a teacher can find, for example, a task for 4th graders that assesses addition of fractions with unlike denominators. A rubric is included that ranks students from the novice level through the apprentice, practitioner, and expert levels. The real understanding and thinking of students is revealed in the writing component of each task. Students not only use math skills to determine the answer but also must explain how they chose a strategy and carried it out.

We can assess student thinking informally every day in several ways. One effective way to have students demonstrate

their thinking is through journaling. Practical at any level (once students have learned to express themselves in written form) and for all subjects, the journal allows students to reflect on the material covered and to make their own connections to it. For example, a journal entry in a 7th grade U.S. history class might be prompted by this question: "How was the relationship between the American colonies and 'Mother England' like your relationship with your own parents?" A journal entry in a math class might be based on a statement such as this: "Now that you know how to calculate the area of a triangle, explain how you would teach the process to a friend who was absent during the past few days." This gives students the chance to really reflect on what they know and gives the teacher a clearer picture of what students are thinking.

We see student thinking when we ask students to web or map based on material read. After reading a short story, students might be asked to create a web showing the main characters, the unique characteristics of each, and the relationships among them. We see much more of their ability to organize, reason, and compare/contrast than if we had them respond to a series of short-answer questions.

Actually, we informally assess student thinking all the time when we ask questions about the content being covered. We push students toward the higher levels of Bloom's taxonomy when we ask, "How would you have reacted in that situation?" "How might your life be different today if the Civil War had not been fought?" or "Which problem-solving strategy did you use and why?"

Checklists can be used to have students evaluate their own progress (or their group's progress) toward the habits of good thinking. If the demonstration of "Reducing Impulsivity" is the target for the day, students can brainstorm a list of indicators for that habit and develop a checklist they will use to self-assess. The checklist can be as simple as "never," "sometimes," and "always." Indicators may include "We got input from all members before making a decision," "We considered all options before deciding," "We were not interested in being the first group done," and so forth.

Formal assessments answer the question "What is it I want my students to know and be able to do?" There are three tiers of assessment: drill/practice, rehearsal, and authentic performance. It is through the last tier that we get a clear picture of student thinking. One reason we don't do enough assessment of student thinking is that it takes a great deal of time—something we never have enough of in education. In our effort to "get through the book," we look for the shortcuts that drill/practice and rehearsal give us. By covering less content, we can have the time to go deeper.

When we ask students to show their best thinking, we need to provide them with adequate time to do so. Think about the last time you were asked to produce a finished product that required a great deal of thought and then imagine how you would have reacted if your administrator or supervisor had told you on Friday that it was due in the office on Monday afternoon. Students who are overly concerned about time are going to spend more time worrying about time than they spend thinking.

We can slow students down in several ways. First, we can set realistic deadlines and be willing to adjust those for individual needs. Treating every student the same is not necessarily fairness. We can require that students show at least two or three possible approaches to the task before they choose one. This forces students to think of the pluses and minuses of each rather than barreling ahead with the first idea that strikes them (again reducing impulsivity).

Students can demonstrate thinking in a wide variety of ways. Howard Gardner's eight intelligences tell us that not only do all students learn in different ways, but also they may all have different ways in which they can show their thinking. Giving students a choice of assessments can produce a wide variety of authentic performances. The culminating projects on a unit on colonial America might produce a report on Benjamin Franklin, a handmade quilt, a demonstration on candle dipping, a model of a slave-trading ship, or the teaching of a colonial game to the rest of the class. Even though the projects may be very different, they can all still be held to the same standard by a rubric that focuses more on the thinking and research involved than on the specific content learned.

In order for students to be good thinkers, they must have those building blocks that come from the teaching and assessment of the lower levels of Bloom's taxonomy. There is a place for drill and practice and assessments that ask students to match terms with their meanings, fill in the short answer, and identify statements as true or false. But, because we are preparing our students for a diverse and complicated world that will require competent problem solving, we must prepare them to be good thinkers as well. We need to not only assess their thinking but also teach them to assess their own thinking. We can do this by asking questions such as "How did this unit of study change your thinking about Native Americans?" "Which of the HOTS (Higher Order Thinking Skills) did you use to complete this task, and explain the process you went through?" "What problem-solving strategy did you use, and why did you choose it over the others?" "In completing this project, how did your planning sheet help you to make good decisions?"

With essential learnings pointing education toward such broader goals as communication, citizenship, and thinking skills, it is our obligation as teachers to make thinking something that students do every day in our classrooms and not just on assessment day.

83

Performances to Assess Standards and Intellectual Growth

Kay Burke

Performance assessment typically requires students to respond to a small number of more significant tasks rather than respond to a large number of less significant tasks.
— *W. James Popham,* Classroom Assessment: What Teachers Need to Know

How many times have educators been told to "Teach basic skills!" "Help students meet the standards!" "Raise test scores!" Teachers bombarded by such directives from the public and from policymakers often find it overwhelming to balance teaching with these mandates. In addition to teaching the curriculum and meeting the diverse needs of their students, they are also accountable for monitoring students' progress toward meeting the standards. Teachers can achieve these goals by creating integrated performance tasks that address the curriculum and standards as well as engage students in meaningful learning experiences that promote deep understanding.

PERFORMANCE TASKS AND ASSESSMENTS

Performance tasks allow educators to teach curriculum and performance standards in a way that is relevant and meaningful to students. A performance task presents a realistic problem scenario that requires students to apply their content knowledge and their thinking skills. The task clusters several standards from one or more content areas so students see the connections among the subject areas and the importance of integrating skills to achieve success. The task requires students to work individually and collaboratively to create high-quality projects and performances, often based on prespecified criteria embedded in the standards. Lewin and Shoemaker (1998) believe that a performance task should allow students some choice in selecting or shaping the task, and the task should be designed for "an audience larger than the teacher, that is, oth-

ers outside the classroom would find value in the work" (p. 5). Gronlund (1998) believes that performance tasks and the assessments that are built into them usually take more time "due to the difficulty of designing tasks, the comprehensive nature of the tasks, and the increased time needed to evaluate the results" (p. 136). There are, however, several criteria educators use to make developing and assessing performance tasks a more focused process. Popham (1999) discusses seven evaluative criteria that measurement specialists regard as the most important factors for educators to consider when judging potential tasks for performance assessments (see Figure 83.1).

The performance task in Figure 83.2 correlates to the standards, addresses an audience outside of the teacher, and allows students some choice in demonstrating their mastery of the content and the standards. The task challenges middle school students to use persuasive strategies to convince members of the Chamber of Commerce to ban smoking from all local businesses. Teachers provide the direct instruction and background information the students need before they engage in individual or group work. For example, the whole class reads and discusses the chapters in the textbook and researches information in magazines and newspapers and on the Internet. The school nurse lectures on the effects of smoking. The teacher shows a video on the effects of secondhand smoke and the costs of health care related to smoking. Once the students have a basic understanding of the content, they are ready to apply what they have learned in their campaign to ban smoking. The projects and performances require students to use their cooperative learning skills, their multiple intelligences, and their thinking skills. Groups are asked to *predict* health care costs, *classify* responses, *compare and contrast* businesses, *draw conclusions* from data, and *prioritize* action steps. Although the projects may be correlated specifically to the unit on smoking, the thinking skills embedded in each task are generalizable to all content areas and transferable to life.

—Figure 83.1—

Factors to Consider When Evaluating Performance-Test Tasks

• **Generalizability.** Is there a high likelihood that the students' performance on the task will generalize to comparable tasks?

• **Authenticity.** Is the task similar to what students might encounter in the real world as opposed to encountering only in school?

• **Multiple foci.** Does the task measure multiple instructional outcomes instead of only one?

• **Teachability.** Is the task one that students can become more proficient in as a consequence of a teacher's instructional efforts?

• **Fairness.** Is the task fair to all students—that is, does the task avoid bias based on such personal characteristics as students' gender, ethnicity, or socioeconomic status?

• **Feasibility.** Is the task realistically implementable in relation to its cost, space, time, and equipment requirements?

• **Scorability.** Is the task likely to elicit student responses that can be reliably and accurately evaluated?

Source: Classroom Assessment: What Teachers Need to Know (2nd ed.) (p. 165), by W. J. Popham, 1999. Boston: Allyn and Bacon. Used with permission.

—Figure 83.2—

Performance Task for a Health Unit on Smoking

Standards

Health: Explain the effects of smoking on the body system.

Mathematics: Organize, describe, and make predictions from existing data (construct, read, and interpret tables, graphs, and charts to organize and represent data).

Language Arts: (1) Analyze and evaluate information acquired from various sources. (2) Communicate ideas in writing to accomplish a variety of purposes.

Technology: Use available technology to produce multimedia work for a specified audience.

Life Skills: Apply basic troubleshooting or problem-solving techniques.

Task Description

As part of our school's Health Fair week, your class has been selected by the local Board of Health to conduct a campaign to convince the members of the Chamber of Commerce to ban smoking from all local businesses. You have two weeks to conduct your campaign that will end on May 15 when you present a multimedia presentation at the monthly meeting of the Chamber of Commerce.

Individual Work

Each student will complete the following assignments and assessments:

1. Read the chapters on smoking in the text and take a multiple-choice and essay test.

2. Write a letter to the editor of the local newspaper stating your view on banning smoking in local businesses. You will be assessed on the following criteria: accuracy of your information, persuasiveness, organization, style, and mechanics. See the Letter to the Editor Rubric for expectations of quality work (Figure 83.3).

3. Develop a portfolio that contains key individual and group assignments from this unit. You will be assessed on the quality of your format, visual appeal, organization, knowledge of key concepts, and reflections.

Group Work

Each student will also select a group project and create the rubric to assess it. Each group will be assessed on its ability to work cooperatively to troubleshoot problems and apply appropriate problem-solving techniques to meet or exceed expectations. See the Problem-Solving Rubric for expectations of quality work (Figure 83.4).

Group One: Create tables, graphs, and charts to *predict* the long-term effects of smoking on the health-care costs of the business people and the community.

Group Two: Conduct a telephone poll of local residents and *classify* their responses by age, gender, race, occupation, and smoking habits. Prepare a PowerPoint presentation to share the results of your poll.

Group Three: Create a pamphlet to distribute to business leaders, citizens, and Chamber of Commerce members *comparing and contrasting* business establishments that allow smoking and those that have banned smoking.

Group Four: Present to the Chamber of Commerce a multimedia presentation that *draws conclusions* from all the data collected and *prioritizes* the steps that must be taken to ban smoking in all businesses.

Source: Adapted from *The Mindful School: How to Assess Authentic Learning* (3rd ed.), by K. Burke, 1999 (p. 80). Arlington Heights, IL: SkyLight Training & Publishing. Adapted by permission of SkyLight Professional Development.

—Figure 83.3—

Letter to the Editor Rubric

Standard: Students will communicate ideas in writing to accomplish a purpose.

Criteria	1 Rejected by Church Bulletin Committee	2 Published in High School Newspaper	3 Published in Local Newspaper	4 Published in *The New York Times*	Score
Accuracy of Information	• 3 or more factual errors	• 2 factual errors	• 1 factual error	• All information is accurate	___ × 5 ___ (20)
Persuasiveness • Logic • Arguments	• No logic • No examples	• Faulty logic • 1 example	• Logical arguments • 2 appropriate examples	• Logical and convincing arguments • 3 examples	___ × 5 ___ (20)
Organization • Topic sentence • Support sentences • Concluding sentence	• Includes 1 element • Incoherent	• Includes 2 elements • Coherent	• Includes 3 organizational elements • Coherent	• Includes 3 elements • Coherent • Clear transitions	___ × 5 ___ (20)
Style • Grammar • Sentence structure • Transitions	• 4 or more errors • Distracts from arguments	• 2–3 errors • Choppy	• 1 error • Reinforces arguments	• No errors • Fluid style that informs and convinces readers	___ × 5 ___ (20)
Mechanics • Capitalization • Punctuation • Spelling	• 4 or more errors	• 2–3 errors	• 1 error	• 100% accuracy	___ × 5 ___ (20)

Source: Adapted from *The Mindful School: How to Assess Authentic Learning Training Manual,* by K. Burke, 2000. Arlington Heights, IL: SkyLight Training & Publishing. Adapted by permission of SkyLight Professional Development.

EXPECTATIONS FOR QUALITY WORK

Since performance tasks require students to produce products and performances, assessments such as quizzes and teacher-made tests, are not always appropriate measurements. Gronlund (1998) states that with performance assessment, teachers base evaluation on subjective judgment. He believes that teachers "are more likely to have to depend on identification of the *criteria* of a quality performance and then apply the criteria by means of a rating scale or set of scoring rubrics" (p. 17). Rubrics are scoring guides that can be used to measure such criteria. They include the specific criteria that should be components of the performance and describe the level of proficiency necessary to score at each level. The score that meets the standard is usually the third score, and the fourth score exceeds the standards. The descriptions of what is necessary to

achieve each rating help make the judgment of performance more objective, thereby making the grading process more consistent and fair. The first step in creating the rubric is to establish multiple criteria before judging the quality of the student's performance. Students who are involved in the process of developing the rubric internalize the criteria for high-quality work and feel more confident about what they are supposed to do. Rubrics help teachers become more accountable for assessing whether students are meeting the standards. They also allow teachers to evaluate work more consistently and provide documentation to students, parents, and administrators concerning the student's progress in meeting or exceeding the standards.

The rubric in Figure 83.3 for a letter to the editor assesses a language arts standard that states students should be able to "communicate ideas in writing to accomplish a purpose." In the

—*Figure 83.4*—
Problem-Solving Rubric

Standard: Applies basic troubleshooting or problem-solving techniques.

Criteria	1 Novice	2 In Progress	3 Meets Expectations	4 Exceeds Expectations
Identifies problem	Does not recognize there is a problem.	Recognizes there could be a problem but can't identify cause.	Recognizes there is a problem and understands underlying cause.	Recognizes the real problem, the underlying cause, and the extent of the problem.
Collects information	Does not collect information to solve problem.	Collects inaccurate or incomplete information.	Collects accurate and complete information.	Collects accurate, complete, and relevant information.
Applies techniques to solve problem	Does not apply any techniques to solve problem.	Applies one plausible technique to solve problem.	Applies two or three appropriate techniques to solve problem.	Applies four or more creative techniques to solve problem.
Evaluates effectiveness of solutions to problems	Shows little evidence of reasoning skills to evaluate effectiveness of solutions.	Analyzes the effectiveness of one or two of the solutions; demonstrates knowledge of the problem-solving process.	Analyzes and evaluates the effectiveness of all of the solutions; demonstrates understanding of the problem-solving process.	Evaluates the effectiveness of all the solutions and reflects on their implications; demonstrates in-depth understanding of problem-solving process.

Source: Adapted from *The Mindful School: How to Assess Authentic Learning* (3rd ed.), by K. Burke, 1999 (p. 51). Arlington Heights, IL: SkyLight Training & Publishing. Adapted by permission of SkyLight Professional Development.

assignment, students synthesize the data and present a persuasive written argument that includes statistics and quotes to convince readers to support a ban on smoking in all businesses. Students are better able to self-evaluate their own strengths and weaknesses because rubrics provide concrete guidelines. In addition, students who can self-assess their work have what Sternberg and Grigorenko (2000) call the "successful intelligence." They state, "People are successfully intelligent by virtue of recognizing their strengths and making the most of them at the same time that they recognize their weaknesses and find ways to correct or compensate for them" (p. 6). A student may not get a 4 on every criteria for the assignment in his first attempt, but at least he is aware of what he needs to do to meet or exceed the standard the next time. Students who are able to reflect honestly and accurately on their learning develop the critical thinking skills necessary for intellectual growth.

Popham (1999) says the most important factor when judging potential tasks for performance assessments is "generalizability," or the ability to generalize accurately what skills and knowledge the students possess. Since students engage in fewer performance tasks than conventional paper-and-pencil tests, the selected tasks should optimize the likelihood of accurately generalizing the students' capabilities. One way to ensure students are developing thinking skills is to embed the skills in each performance. Students brainstorm ideas, classify information, draw conclusions, make decisions, and solve problems on different tasks in all content areas. Teachers assess students' thinking abilities through observations, checklists, rubrics, portfolios, and reflections. The assessments provide feedback that helps students improve their cognitive skills each time they encounter a new task. The Problem-Solving Rubric in Figure 83.4 provides guidance to assess students' abilities to identify a problem, collect information, solve the problem, and evaluate the effectiveness of the solutions. The life skill of problem solving can be taught, monitored, reinforced, and transferred to all curriculum areas so that teachers have evidence that students have mastered the thinking skill of solving problems in a variety of contexts.

ASSESSMENT OF THINKING SKILLS

By clustering the standards to create performance tasks, teachers can embed thinking skills in the context of real-life experiences. Creating authentic assessments that evaluate students' mastery of the content, the standards, and the thinking processes helps students become independent learners and critical self-evaluators. Students who can solve problems independently and self-assess their ability to think critically and creatively can refocus and redirect their own learning. As stated by Costa and Kallick

> We must constantly remind ourselves that the ultimate purpose of evaluation is to have students become self-evaluating. If students graduate from our schools still dependent upon others to tell them when they are adequate, good, or excellent, then we've missed the whole point of what education is about. (1992, p. 280)

REFERENCES

Burke, K. (1999). *The mindful school: How to assess authentic learning* (3rd ed.) Arlington Heights, IL: SkyLight Training & Publishing.

Burke, K. (2000). *The mindful school: How to assess authentic learning training manual.* Arlington Heights, IL: SkyLight Training & Publishing.

Costa, A. L., & Kallick, B. (1992). Reassessing assessment. In A. L. Costa, J. A. Bellanca, & R. Fogarty (Eds.), *If minds matter: A foreword to the future: Vol. 2* (pp. 275–280). Arlington Heights, IL: SkyLight Training & Publishing.

Gronlund, N. E. (1998). *Assessment of student achievement* (6th ed.). Boston, MA: Allyn and Bacon.

Lewin, L., & Shoemaker, B. J. (1998). *Great performances: Creating classroom-based assessment tasks.* Alexandria, VA: Association for Supervision and Curriculum Development.

Popham, W. J. (1999). *Classroom assessment: What teachers need to know* (2nd ed.). Boston, MA: Allyn and Bacon.

Sternberg, R. J., & Grigorenko, E. L. (2000). *Teaching for successful intelligence: To increase student learning and achievement.* Arlington Heights, IL: SkyLight Training & Publishing.

84

A Format for Assessing Thinking Skills

Barry K. Beyer

If we are going to teach thinking skills with much hope of success, we should regularly assess student proficiency in applying these skills. Such assessments can provide information useful in improving instruction as well as student learning. Moreover, they can also, as research suggests, enhance student motivation to master—or try to master—the skills being taught (Doyle, 1983). This chapter describes a proposed format for a performance assessment that can serve these important functions by directly assessing knowledge and proficiency in thinking skills.

Direct Assessment of Proficiency in a Thinking Skill

The thinking skill assessment described here is based on the premise that if we want to find out how well students can apply a specific thinking skill, we ask them to perform it and to explain or show how and why they carry it out as they do. That's what this assessment format does. It asks students to perform a given thinking skill several times as well as to report what they know about this skill and how they carry it out. This assessment thus provides specific, direct evidence of what students know and do to execute the assessed skill. And this, in turn, allows us to judge not only the degree of proficiency exhibited by their performance but also to identify—and then to remedy through subsequent instruction—dysfunctional, erroneous, or irrelevant moves made in attempting to execute the thinking skill. When administered repeatedly over the duration of a course or courses, use of this assessment format can also identify changes in student proficiency in applying a thinking skill.

Basic Format

The assessment format consists of six basic tasks, all dealing with the *same* thinking skill. These six tasks assess knowledge and performance of the skill at three distinct levels. The first two tasks assess basic knowledge of the skill—its meaning and what it looks like when someone is doing it. The next three tasks assess student "expertise" in executing (performing) the skill. The final task assesses students' metacognitive understanding of *how* they execute the skill.

These tasks make up a self-contained oral or paper-and-pencil instrument that can be administered as a stand-alone assessment or be attached to any subject matter test. The tasks can also use subject matter the students have been studying as a vehicle for student application of the skill being assessed. Presenting all six skill tasks together, especially as a section in a regular subject matter unit test, reinforces the fact that mastering the skill is as important a learning goal as is mastering subject matter. Providing a separate evaluation of student performance on this skill assessment reinforces this fact even more.

Sample Instruments

The examples of the format presented in Figures 84.1 and 84.2—representing its use at the extremes of the K–12 spectrum—show its key components. What is important in these examples is not the specific skill being assessed, but the tasks and their structures, the task questions and directions, and the sequence in which these tasks are arranged on the assessments at these levels.

Figure 84.1 presents a primary grade assessment for the skill of sorting, using the six-task format. Although this could be a paper-and-pencil instrument, it is presented here as an oral assessment to be administered to students individually. Figure 84.2 presents an example of the same format for assessing the same skill (commonly called "classifying" at these grade levels)

Copyright © 2001 by Barry K. Beyer

—*Figure 84.1*—

A Format for a Thinking Skill Performance Assessment for Primary Grades

Thinking Skill: Sorting

To the teacher: Administer this assessment orally to individual students. Record student responses and groupings.

1. Tell me which of the following things I say tells what *sorting* is:
    a. Finding an answer to a problem
    b. Putting things together that are alike
    c. Saying what will happen next

2. Tell me if each of these people is sorting:
    a. My friend figuring which tree is taller   yes/no
    b. My brother putting dishes away in the
       cupboard   yes/no
    c. My sister choosing which TV show to
       watch   yes/no

3. Here are some objects. Sort these into groups.
    *(Materials: 1 banana, 1 red apple, 1 red ribbon,
    1 yellow ribbon)*

4. Here are other objects. Sort these for me.
    *(Materials: 1 small blue toy car, 1 large red toy car,
    1 small blue toy truck, 1 large red toy truck,
    1 small blue toy airplane, 1 large red toy airplane)*

5. Here are some other objects. Group these.
    *(Materials: 3 bronze keys—1 small, 1 medium, 1
    large; 3 silver keys—1 small, 1 medium, 1 large)*

6. Here are some other objects. Show me how to sort
   these into groups. (Ask the student why he or she has
   you make the moves shown. Record what the student
   says and does.)
    *(Materials: 1 small green star, 1 large green square,
    1 small orange square, 1 large orange star, 1 small
    orange triangle, 1 large green triangle)*

in the secondary grades. It is designed as a paper-and-pencil instrument to be administered simultaneously to all students in a class. These samples typify the first formal assessment of a skill at the given grade levels following its introduction and continued practice over several weeks of class. Again, it is important to remember that what's noteworthy here are the components of the assessment format rather than the skill being assessed. The format may be used to assess student proficiency in *any* thinking skill.

TASK STRUCTURE AND SEQUENCE

The tasks that make up this assessment may be presented to the students as directions or questions.

Task 1 on both grade level examples requires students to define the skill being assessed. Because students usually have had only limited instruction in the skill by the first time it is assessed at any grade level, this task is presented as a multiple-choice item so students merely have to recognize the correct definition rather than recall it, unaided, from memory. The sample assessments in Figures 84.1 and 84.2 illustrate this task. In subsequent assessments of this same skill at each grade level, students state or write the definition from memory, without any prompts whatsoever.

Task 2 asks students to select from several possible scenarios an example of the skill being used—or having just been used—by someone else. The sample assessments in Figures 84.1 and 84.2 do this in different ways. The task in Figure 84.2 is most useful only on the initial assessment of the skill being assessed, for sometimes its very form may actually serve as a prompt for completing subsequent tasks on the assessment. However, in this initial assessment it proves especially useful for diagnostic purposes. On later assessments it can be replaced by a task similar to that shown in Figure 84.1, but at the appropriate level of complexity.

Tasks 3, 4, and 5 require the students to apply the skill three times, each time to a different set of given information. Three applications serve to eliminate or reduce the effects of guessing, of any confusion caused by a misunderstanding of the given information, and of cheating (Dick & Carey, 1985). Giving students three tries at carrying out the skill also sets up their response to the final task by helping them to become increasingly conscious of how they do the skill so they can tap this information more readily to perform the final task.

Note that the skill names or referents in the directions to each of these three tasks are not identical. Where possible, each task direction or question employs a different synonym or cue word associated with the thinking skill being assessed. In Figure 84.1, for instance, items 3 and 6 use the combination of *sort* and *groups*—two cues; the directions for item 4 use only the word *sort*; and item 5 uses only the word *group*. Figure 84.2 illustrates different cues for these same tasks. Part of skill proficiency is knowing different words that cue, trigger, or call for use of the same thinking operation. These cues should be taught from the very beginning of instruction in any thinking skill. The extent to which students respond to these cues correctly gives us a measure of their understanding of the skill being assessed.

—*Figure 84.2*—

A Format for a Thinking Skill Performance Assessment for Secondary Grades

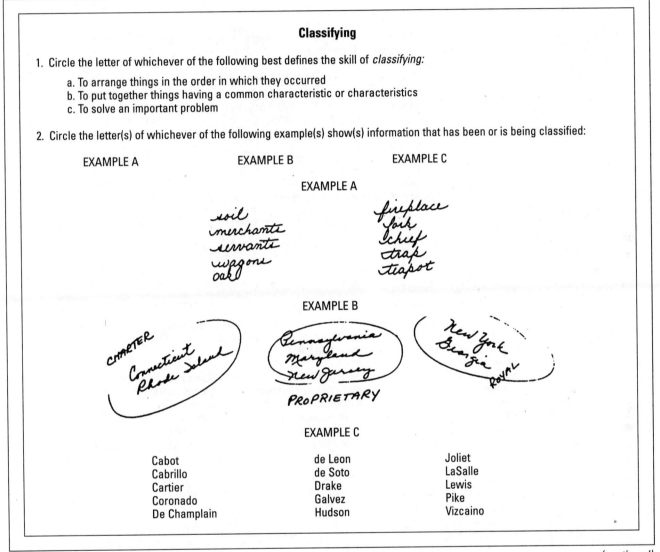

Classifying

1. Circle the letter of whichever of the following best defines the skill of *classifying:*

   a. To arrange things in the order in which they occurred
   b. To put together things having a common characteristic or characteristics
   c. To solve an important problem

2. Circle the letter(s) of whichever of the following example(s) show(s) information that has been or is being classified:

   EXAMPLE A   EXAMPLE B   EXAMPLE C

   EXAMPLE A

   EXAMPLE B

   EXAMPLE C

Cabot	de Leon	Joliet
Cabrillo	de Soto	LaSalle
Cartier	Drake	Lewis
Coronado	Galvez	Pike
De Champlain	Hudson	Vizcaino

(continued)

Source: Adapted from *Practical Strategies for the Teaching of Thinking,* by Barry K. Beyer, 1987. Boston: Allyn & Bacon. Used with permission of author.

The kind of information used in these three tasks is crucial to a valid assessment. Regardless of grade level, this information must be of a nature and in a form already familiar to the students. Ideally, it should be on the same subject in which the skill was introduced and practiced in the lessons preceding this assessment. However, the students should not have processed this particular information using this thinking skill before. Primary grade assessment tasks often involve the use of objects or drawings of objects in shapes and colors familiar to the students (as identified in Figure 84.1). Secondary grade assessment tasks (like those in Figure 84.2) should use content related to the topic students have been studying in class when they were learning about the thinking skill being assessed.

Assessment tasks that present information—or present it in a form—that students are unfamiliar with actually meas-

—*Figure 84.2*—

A Format for a Thinking Skill Performance Assessment for Secondary Grades *(continued)*

3. The following words were commonly spoken by people living in London, England, around the year 1750. Classify these words to identify what life was like for these Londoners at that time.

customs house	journeyman	stock exchange	squire
lottery ticket	workhouse	ale house	chimney sweep
apprentice	milkmaid	mugger	debtors prison
watchman	cesspool	pauper	gin
dock worker	poor house	typhus	coffee house
typhoid	butcher	cow	night soil
weaver	small pox	judge	wool comber

[Leave additional blank space for student notes.]

4a. The items listed below were found near a place where people lived in colonial America around 1750. The place where each item was made is indicated where known. Group these items in a way that will tell you about the people who used these items. *Be sure to show your work.* Then answer question 4b below.

1 iron candle chandelier (France)	1 porcelain teapot (China)	1 iron hoe (America)
2 pewter mugs (Germany)	1 glass wine decanter (France)	3 hand-painted pearl ware plates (China)
7 pewter spoons (America)	3 bone-handled toothbrushes	
9 medicine bottles (England)	8 perfume bottles (France)	1 silk glove
3 hand-painted porcelain plates (England)	2 printed silk cloths (China)	3 bone-handled forks (England)
	1 leather shoe (England)	2 stoneware pots (Germany)

[Leave additional blank space for student notes.]

4b. Circle the letter preceding the phrase that best completes this statement:

The people who once used the items on the above list
    a. lived on the western frontier.
    b. made a living as craftsmen.
    c. were upper-class, wealthy.

(continued)

ure student abilities to transfer a skill rather than their abilities to execute a skill as they have begun to "learn" it. Such transfer is not automatic (Hudgins, 1977; Perkins & Salomon, 1989; Posner & Keele, 1973; Sternberg, 1984). Only after considerable instruction has been provided in transfer-

ring (generalizing) a thinking skill to a variety of contexts should students be assessed on their abilities to execute it in novel contexts.

As tasks 3, 4, and 5 in Figure 84.1 indicate, primary grade students are required to simply apply the skill three times. As

—*Figure 84.2*—

A Format for a Thinking Skill Performance Assessment for Secondary Grades *(continued)*

5a. Classify the information below so you can answer this question: What was the economy of the thirteen British colonies in North America like around 1763? *Be sure to show all your work.* Then answer question 5b below.

Major Colonial Exports 1763

Export	*Colony*	*Export*	*Colony*
lumber	Massachusetts	fish	Rhode Island
iron tools	Pennsylvania	flour	Delaware
tobacco	Virginia	wool cloth	New York
lumber	Connecticut	rum	Rhode Island
indigo	South Carolina	rum	Massachusetts
fur hats	New Jersey	rice	North Carolina
farm products	Georgia	iron goods	Delaware
flour	Pennsylvania	pitch, tar	New Hampshire
tobacco	Maryland	rice	South Carolina

[Leave additional blank space for student notes.]

5b. Complete the following: Based on how you classified the above items, write a sentence that accurately describes the colonial economy in 1763.

_____

_____

_____

6. In the space beneath the following information, give *specific, detailed directions* that a 5th grader could follow to classify the information to answer this question: What was colonial culture in America like?

Phyllis Wheatley	poet	Cotton Mather	minister/scientist
Ben Franklin	printer/inventor	John Copley	painter
Benjamin West	painter	Jonathan Edwards	minister/writer
Sarah Kimble Knight	writer	Roger Williams	minister
David Rittenhouse	astronomer	Anne Bradstreet	poet

[Leave additional blank space for student notes.]

they do so, it is important to remember that the assessment administrator must not provide any assistance to or prompt students in any way as they proceed through each task.

The directions for these three tasks on the assessment for secondary grades are more complex than those for these same tasks at the primary level. For example, tasks 4 and 5 in the secondary form direct the students not only to perform the skill but also, in effect, to *show their work*, because we want to know as explicitly as possible *how* they carry out the skill. It is inappropriate, however, to ask elementary school students to "show their work," because doing so interferes with their execution of the skill, often actually blocking their efforts to carry it out. Such a task may also prove frustrating or impossible for them because most primary grade students seem to lack the language to report in the abstract to others how they carried out a specific thinking operation.

Task 3 in the secondary grade assessment could ask students to explain how they did the skill or to show their work, but it does not because experience suggests that the initial try on an assessment of a newly learned thinking skill ought to have students concentrate just on applying it. Once they have done the skill in task 3, it appears easier for them to articulate it when they apply it the next several times, in tasks 4 and 5. Note the directions used in these two tasks in the sample assessment in Figure 84.2. Other similar directions may be just as appropriate as long as they produce explanations, symbols (circled words, lines connecting words, etc.), or some other notations that reveal what the students do or did to carry out the skill. This is a crucial part of the task because it provides insights into the procedure, rules, and criteria used by a student to execute the skill being assessed. And this information, presumably, is precisely what we are trying to teach.

It is also necessary to leave enough blank space below the given information in each of these secondary grade assessment tasks (including task 3, even though it does not ask students to show their work) so students can use it for any explanation, notations, or other markings they may have become accustomed to making as they apply a skill, or to "show their work," or to explain how they carried out the skill.

Tasks 3, 4, and 5 on the secondary-level assessment also tie the application of the skill to a substantive learning task. That is, students are directed to find out or learn something by applying the skill to the given data or information. This provides them a substantive purpose for applying the skill and appears to motivate them to expend more effort in completing the task than they might if they sense this is simply an "exercise." To make this task even more legitimate, a subquestion can be added, as in tasks 4 and 5, asking students to actually indicate what they did learn by applying the skill. Figure 84.2 shows two forms this subquestion can take; question 4b asks only for recognition of a correct response, whereas question 5b asks students to generate the correct response from their application of the skill without any prompts at all. No matter how this additional substantive learning question is framed, it is important to note that it should not be evaluated for any skill grade, because the execution of the skill is what we are assessing.

Task 6, like tasks 3, 4, and 5, provides data or information familiar to the students for use as a vehicle for applying the skill. However, here the students do not simply perform the skill and then tell what they learned by so doing. Instead, they show, explain, or actually give directions to someone else on how to carry out this skill in step-by-step fashion. This ques-

tion allows students to verbalize or demonstrate their metacognitive knowledge of the skill procedure they have been using. The task is made easier by their preceding three applications of the skill and, for middle and high school students, their efforts to "show their work" at least twice before completing this final task.

Because many primary grade students lack the words to describe in detail how to carry out a cognitive operation or cannot write out how to do so, task 6 on their assessment simply requires them to *show* the assessment administrator how, step-by-step, to carry out the skill. It is useful in this task for the listener to prompt students to verbalize, as well as they can, *why* they are making these steps (moves) and to record for later analysis both the steps (moves) and explanations given.

Secondary students, however, can be asked to explain in writing to another student who is in a grade or two lower than theirs exactly how, step-by-step, to carry out the skill to complete the given substantive task. They can produce their responses in a paragraph, as a list of steps, as a flow chart, or in any other form appropriate to describing a procedure. Because secondary school students have been "showing their work" in at least two previous applications of the skill (tasks 4 and 5), they are more prepared to do this now than if this task were the first time they were required to articulate or show how they "do" the skill. The key to this task is the audience to whom the students are to address their explanation. As research on writing tells us, when students explain things to younger students or anyone else they can assume knows *less* about their topic than they do, they provide more detail, are more specific, and give relevant examples as part of their explanations (Britton, Burgess, Martin, McLeod, & Rosen, 1975). What we seek here is the clearest and most explicit step-by-step procedural description and explanation that the student can generate without direct prompting or intervention.

This six-task assessment format is useful for at least three reasons. First, it makes clear the importance of the thinking skill being assessed. Second, it provides information about the level of student proficiency in the skill. Those who complete tasks 1 and 2 satisfactorily and who successfully carry out the skill in at least two of tasks 3 through 5 (it is important to allow one slip-up somewhere in executing these three tasks because of possibly confusing content information) can be considered as demonstrating an acceptable proficiency in the skill. Students who provide acceptable responses to tasks 1 and 2 but not to tasks 3 through 6 reveal only a low-level knowledge of the skill. Those who satisfactorily complete task 6 as well as the other tasks demonstrate a high level of proficiency in the skill.

Finally, this type of skill test format provides information useful for planning instruction. By identifying those tasks that students have trouble with, we can determine exactly the kind and level of skill instruction required for follow-up, whether it be of a remedial or an enrichment nature.

MODIFYING THE BASIC FORMAT

The basic assessment format described so far covers only the first formal assessment of student proficiency in a thinking skill. However, this format can be expanded in a number of ways to elicit additional skill information. It also must be modified when it is used a second, third, or more times to assess continuous development of proficiency in the same skill.

ADAPTATIONS FOR OTHER GRADES AND STUDENTS

This format can be used for students of any ability or grade level. However, the wording of the task directions or questions as well as the nature and complexity of the information or data in the performance tasks may need to be revised to accommodate different ability levels and grade levels. Students at any grade level who do not read English well may need an oral version of the assessment (adapted to their grade level and language, of course), as may some students with learning disabilities. Indeed, the sample primary grade format (Figure 84.1) may be especially suited for assessing the proficiency of at-risk or ESL students in any grade in the cognitive skills of seriation, comparing, and predicting that lie at the heart of reading comprehension (Siegler, 1998).

Average to above-average students in upper-elementary or intermediate grades can use a simplified version of the Figure 84.2 assessment with much shorter sets of given information in tasks 3 through 6. Tasks 1 and 2 (and any additional skill-knowledge questions) may be multiple choice in the first several assessments on the same skill before being changed to open-ended items. Experience with this format may necessitate other adaptations as well. But whatever changes are made, the essential six-task, three-level structure should remain—two tasks assessing knowledge about or of the skill, three tasks requiring students to apply the skill (with several of these for middle or high school students, requiring them to also "show their work"), and a final metacognitive task that calls for a description or demonstration of *how*, step by step, to execute the skill.

ALTERING OR ADDING QUESTIONS

Tasks can be added in the first part of the instrument to assess student knowledge of various other skill attributes in ad-

dition to those already described. For example, a question asking students to identify synonyms for the skill label could follow item 1, which asks for a definition of the skill. A question asking students to state or identify a basic rule relating to the skill might be added to this sequence as well. So, too, could a question asking students to identify circumstances or conditions in which use of the skill is appropriate or essential. If the skill is a critical thinking skill, requiring students to judge the quality or worth of something, a question calling for students to identify or explain criteria appropriate to this judgment can be added.

It seems advisable, however, to limit the number of such questions in the initial assessment of a new skill to the two tasks in the basic format exemplified here, in order to avoid overloading the students when they have just begun to "get into" the skill. The additional skill questions described here might best be added to this assessment the second or third time it is administered on the same skill. Whenever additional questions are added, however, care must be taken that they do not "telegraph" answers to subsequent questions or provide any assistance whatsoever to student performance of the skill.

MODIFYING SUBSEQUENT INSTRUMENTS

We can use the assessment format described here to assess the extent to which student proficiency in executing a thinking skill is improving, as it should be with continued instruction and guided practice, by administering the assessment repeatedly over an extended period of time. The format must be somewhat modified, however, when it is used to assess the same skill a second, third, or more times.

For instance, the second assessment might incorporate several of the kinds of additional tasks or questions noted above (in a multiple-choice or open-ended format) but include only two performance tasks (of the type used in tasks 3 through 5) and conclude with the metacognitive task (item 6 in the Figure 84.1 or 84.2 examples). To bring variety to this final task, we could present an incomplete or erroneous or dysfunctional step-by-partial-step description of how a novice executed the skill and ask students to correct it or write an alternative, more "expert," procedure.

Subsequent assessments of this same skill might be limited to four tasks—one task asking for a definition or condition under which the skill should be applied, two tasks calling for application of the skill "showing all your work," and a fourth task asking for a step-by-step description of its application to a given set of information or material. Continued assessment of a single thinking skill reinforces skill learning as a legitimate classroom goal and provides information useful in altering teaching and remediating student weaknesses in applying it. It also gives teachers and students a permanent record of actual performances and of changes in the proficiency—or lack of it—with which they are carrying out the skill.

ASSESSING MULTIPLE SKILLS

A variation of this basic format can also be used to assess several skills on the same instrument. For example, the basic six-task format can be used for the most recently introduced skill; for a thinking skill introduced earlier we can then add four more items, such as a task asking students to identify or explain something about the second skill, two tasks like numbers 4 and 5, and a task like number 6. Thus, a thinking skills assessment of two thinking skills in which students have been receiving instruction would consist, at a minimum, of 10 tasks. An assessment of three newly taught skills using this format would then consist of six tasks for the most recently introduced thinking skill, four tasks for the skill introduced before that, and three tasks for the skill introduced before that.

MEETING ASSESSMENT NEEDS

Clearly, we should assess the thinking skills we teach if we are to have students value their mastery and if we are to improve student thinking and our teaching of thinking skills in our classrooms. The assessment format presented here offers one promising way to accomplish these goals. Moreover, this performance assessment format allows us to appraise the quality of students' thinking skill proficiency directly, rather than by the more questionable and unreliable method of inferring skill expertise from an answer to a subject matter question, a paragraph the students have written, or some other product of presumed thinking. With some practice, most of us can create thinking skill assessments using this format to assess student performance in any thinking skill using any subject matter at any grade level.

REFERENCES

Britton, J. N., Burgess, T., Martin, N., McLeod, A., & Rosen, H. (1975). *The development of writing abilities (11–18)*. London: Macmillan Education.

Dick, W., & Carey, L. (1985). *The systematic design of instruction* (2nd ed.). Glenview, IL: Scott, Foresman and Company.

Doyle, W. (1983, Summer). Academic work. *Review of Educational Research, 53*(2), 159–199.

Hudgins, B. B. (1977). *Learning and thinking*. Itasca, IL: F. E. Peacock.

Perkins, D. N., & Salomon, G. (1989). Are thinking skills context-bound? *Educational Researcher, 18*(1), 16–25.

Posner, M., & Keele, S. W. (1973). Skill learning. In R. M. W. Travers (Ed.), *Second handbook of research on teaching* (pp. 805–831). Chicago: Rand McNally College Publishing Co.

Siegler, R. (1998). *Children's thinking.* (2nd ed.). Englewood Cliffs, NJ: Prentice-Hall.

Sternberg, R. J. (1984, September). How can we teach intelligence? *Educational Leadership, 42*(1), 52.

85

Assessing Thinking Skills

Alec Fisher

Teachers who want to teach thinking skills will at some point want to assess the effectiveness of what they have tried to do. This can be done in a number of different ways, and this chapter explains some approaches that are relatively easy to use.

All teachers are used to evaluating their students' work—it is a central part of a teacher's job. If they think about it explicitly, teachers can probably specify what they are looking for when they grade the different kinds of work they ask students to do. They may be looking for students to exhibit some skill (such as reading well, solving problems, or being inventive) or to show what they know about the subject being taught. Imagine a teacher who has been teaching about evolution; such a teacher might want to test whether students have grasped the ideas taught and might ask questions that simply require the students to recall what was said—or apply it in some simple and obvious cases. Alternatively, the teacher might want to see how good the students are at thinking about the subject—for example, by asking them to figure out something that goes beyond what they have been told. Most of us are familiar with the distinction between saying "He knows a lot about X/doesn't know much about X" and "He is thinking about X very well/poorly." In this chapter we are interested in assessing the process of thinking rather than the facts known.

Elements of Effective Thinking Skill Assessments

The key to assessing the quality of students' thinking is the teacher's own expertise in the area of thinking skills; that is, teachers must know, reasonably clearly, what they are looking for in terms of the thinking involved. If, for example, they wish to assess critical thinking skills, they need a reasonably clear view of what these skills are and how they would be demonstrated in a particular discipline at a particular grade level. Let's take an example that I saw demonstrated in a Singapore Col-

lege classroom. In this case the students would soon be graduating, and the teacher decided to give them a "job simulation exercise." She explained that they would soon be working in laboratories and their employer might want them to conduct an experiment in cloning plants. She gave them some background data about two different ways of cloning a plant and then asked them to compare and contrast the alternatives, choose their preferred method, and present their decision as a recommendation to an employer. In this case the students had been taught how to compare and contrast things using Swartz's approach (see Swartz, Fischer, & Parks, 1998); the teacher knew she wanted the students to find the important similarities and differences between the two methods of cloning, to identify any important patterns, and to produce a well-reasoned case. Because she knew what the students should know about cloning and how they ought to think to come to a good decision in this case, she had no difficulty in grading their responses. (Incidentally, because the biology and the thinking skill had been well taught, most of the students were able to do a superb job.)

If teachers are going to assess student thinking in their own discipline, their expertise both in the discipline and in what would count as "good thinking" is the guarantee of their good judgment. Most teachers feel reasonably confident of their expertise in their discipline. They feel less sure, however, about assessing their students' thinking, because most teachers have received very little explicit training in the teaching of thinking skills.

The following discussion concentrates mostly on what are usually called critical thinking skills (though most of the ideas also apply, with some adjustments, to other kinds of thinking skills, such as creative thinking). Obviously the teacher who wishes to assess critical thinking skills needs to know what these are (for good surveys, see Norris & Ennis, 1989; Fisher & Scriven, 1997). Critical thinking skills include identifying and evaluating arguments, decision making, problem solving, creating analogies and metaphors, judging credibility, clarifying ideas, extracting and evaluating assumptions, constructing and evaluating explanations, comparing and contrasting, classifying, and so forth.

There is clearly a great difference between asking students to name the first three presidents of the United States (they either know them or they don't) and asking students to respond to the argument in the following passage. (The passage is an example from the United Kingdom, where there is a problem with young people stealing cars and driving them too fast, especially around cities; these young people are commonly called "joyriders.")

> The police force should ban their officers from driving at high speed in pursuit of young joyriders who steal cars. Many deaths, both of joyriders and of innocent bystanders, have occurred as a result of such chases. The police say that they have policies that are aimed at preventing danger to the public during car chases, by requiring police drivers to abandon the chase when speeds become too high for safety. But the excitement of the chase inevitably makes the police drivers forget the policy and disregard public safety. No stolen car is worth a human life.

It is clear that a question such as "How would you evaluate the argument presented in this passage?" is not a question to which one either does or does not know the answer; it requires some thought; in particular it requires some reasoning to figure out how to respond. This illustrates the first point about assessing thinking: it is important to ask the right kind of question. It is no use asking a question that simply requires the student to recall something he or she has learned (like names of presidents). It has to be a question that requires students to engage in the kind of thinking being assessed; thus, if the teacher is interested in assessing how good students are at arguing a case (a core skill in critical thinking), the students must be given a task that requires them to do precisely that, and they may need to be provided with suitable background material (e.g., the stimulus passage). Of course, merely asking students to present an argument does not necessarily require them to do much thinking. Suppose a teacher has already presented them with a detailed case in favor of the "separation of powers" in the U.S. Constitution; asking them to present a case for this may require little more than recalling what they have been taught.

To assess students' critical thinking skills or higher-order thinking skills, teachers must (1) be clear about what they are looking for and (2) ask the right kind of question. Assessing critical thinking skills requires asking questions that genuinely require students to do the following:

- Evaluate something—for example, an argument, a decision, an experiment, an advertisement, or a film.
- Explain something—for example, a phenomenon, an event, or an action.
- Justify something—for example, a decision, a judgment, an action, or a belief.
- Clarify something—for example, an idea, a claim, or a proposal.
- Analyze something—for example, a problem or an argument.
- Compare and contrast things—for example, points of view, ideas, or objects.

It is important to remember that such questions do not require students to think critically if the teacher has already told them an answer that they are simply required to reproduce.

A corollary of the requirement to ask the right kind of question is the need to provide the right kind of stimulus material or experiences; the stimulus material must be carefully chosen so that it provides adequate scope for the critical thinking being assessed. For example, the passage about joyriders is rich in assumptions, implications, and argumentative possibilities; if students were asked to evaluate its argument in 50 words or in 1,000 words, they probably would have plenty to say. By contrast, a simple newspaper report of an event might provide little scope for an evaluative response to an argument. It is a characteristic of higher-order thinking skills that the judgments involved are not routine, but are complex and require thought. Thus if we want students to exhibit such skills, we have to provide them with material that requires them to engage in that kind of thinking.

To take a completely different example, at the K–3 level, suppose the teacher has read Beatrix Potter's story of Peter Rabbit to her pupils. She could ask them questions about what happened at various points in the story (requiring simple recall), or she could ask a quite different kind of question—for example, one requiring them to exercise their decision-making skills. Thus she might ask, "What should Peter Rabbit think about to decide what to do when he arrives at the gate of Mr. McGregor's garden?" This would require the students to think about the consequences, risks, and other factors involved. If they had also been taught the thinking skill of decision making (for a good approach and good examples see Swartz & Parks, 1994), a student might produce the following answer:

> Peter Rabbit is greedy and likes excitement. If he wasn't he wouldn't want to go into Mr. McGregor's garden. Maybe he should think about that. He could instead go and pick berries with his sisters; maybe he

should do that, though it wouldn't be so exciting. He knows he will not get into trouble if he goes with his sisters, and he knows he may get into trouble if he goes into Mr. McGregor's garden. Maybe he should look to see where Mr. McGregor is—and the cat. Maybe he should go home and change his clothes if it is risky to go in Mr. McGregor's garden. Maybe he should look for other ways out besides the gate before he goes in, and maybe he should mark his trail so he can get out quickly if necessary. He knows his mother will be very cross if she finds out that he went in Mr. McGregor's garden. Probably he shouldn't go in the garden.

How should the teacher grade such a response? This depends upon such factors as the age of the children and how much practice they have had at similar tasks. But it is surely not difficult to see that such a response shows that the pupil has asked questions like these: What other things could Peter do? What might happen if he does this rather than that? How likely is trouble/excitement? How enjoyable/painful would it be if X happened? These are just the sort of questions a child should ask in a decision-making situation. From that point of view, this is a very good answer.

In some classroom situations, it doesn't matter much if the teacher's grade is rather quickly given, perhaps a bit too generous or too harsh, or perhaps subjective and hard to defend objectively. However, sometimes it does matter—as with end-of-semester tests. In those situations, the best way to be reasonably confident of one's judgment about the quality of the thinking involved in student responses is to sketch out "model answers" or to prepare schemes that show what is expected and to discuss these with a colleague who knows what the students have been taught, in terms of both subject matter and thinking skills. If further checks are needed, the teacher can ask the same colleague to independently grade some of the students' answers; to the extent that the colleague agrees, the teacher can have confidence in the objectivity of his or her grades (though this is still dependent, of course, on the expertise both teachers have in the area of thinking skills).

KINDS OF QUESTIONS THAT TEACHERS CAN USE TO ASSESS THINKING SKILLS

Teachers have various options for constructing questions that assess thinking skills. Two possibilities are the *essay/constructed-response* option and the *multiple-choice* option. Using the passage about joyriders, we might ask students to construct a written argumentative response of a given length. Such an assessment would look like this:

The police force should ban their officers from driving at high speed in pursuit of young joyriders who steal cars. Many deaths, both of joyriders and of innocent bystanders, have occurred as a result of such chases. The police say that they have policies that are aimed at preventing danger to the public during car chases, by requiring police drivers to abandon the chase when speeds become too high for safety. But the excitement of the chase inevitably makes the police drivers forget the policy and disregard public safety. No stolen car is worth a human life.

Write a critical evaluation of the above argument in not more than X words (here the teacher inserts a number for X).

A typical multiple-choice question based on the same passage might look like the following example, which comes from the Test of Reasoning Skills (UEA) (Fisher & Thomson, 1993):

Which one of the following, if true, would most strengthen the above argument?

A. A ban on car chases might lead to an increase in car crime.

B. Most joyriders drive very unsafely at high speed because they lack driving experience.

C. Many high-speed car chases result in the arrest of car thieves.

D. Some car thieves are arrested without the occurrence of a high-speed car chase.

E. Officers who undertake high-speed car chases have special training in such driving. (p. 40)

Multiple-choice questions have a place in assessing higher-order/critical thinking skills (in national tests, for example), but they do have some problems: they are difficult to design well; they may (as the above example does) involve quite a lot of reading for the information the examiner gets about the respondent's critical thinking skill; guessing has a one-in-five chance of being correct; and it can be difficult to be sure such questions are assessing the skill the examiner is really interested in because the examiner has no direct evidence of the respondents' thinking—only their choice.

One of the best options for assessing thinking skills is the *multiple-rating item*. (For a full account of multiple-rating items, which are essentially an invention of Michael Scriven's, see Chapter 6 in Fisher and Scriven, 1997. The multiple-rating item is a kind of hybrid of the multiple-choice and constructed-response options and combines the merits of both.

This kind of question is easy to construct. The teacher first chooses a question that is designed to elicit higher-order/critical thinking and that meets the criteria discussed earlier. Again using the joyride passage, possible questions might be "Write a critical response to the passage in not more than 50 words" or "Say in no more than 20 words what additional information (if true) would most strengthen or most weaken the argument in the passage." Let us suppose that students are asked to respond to the second question. The teacher collects their answers and grades them. Possible replies might include the following (where "S" means "strengthen" and "W" means "weaken"):

A. Police forces that have banned car chases have not seen an increase in car crime. (S)

B. Joyriding is most serious where police forces do not pursue such drivers. (W)

C. Joyriders cause many serious accidents and some deaths even when not being pursued. (W)

D. Many high-speed car chases result in the arrest of car thieves. (W)

E. Some highly trained police officers overestimate their skill when driving at high speed. (S)

F. If not pursued, joyriders cause very few accidents; police pursuit causes most accidents. (S)

G. The police say that there are no realistic alternatives to their present policy. (S)

Suppose that in grading these responses (bearing in mind the students' background knowledge and expertise), the teacher judges that A and E strengthen the argument but that F strengthens it most. Suppose also that the teacher judges that B and D weaken the argument but that C weakens it most. And finally suppose the teacher judges that G doesn't really strengthen or weaken the argument to any significant degree. Now the teacher has all the material needed to construct a multiple-rating item for another class or for next year's students. Here it is:

Assume each of the following statements is true and assess the extent to which it strengthens or weakens the above argument. Write "GS" if it greatly strengthens the argument, "S" if it strengthens it but not greatly, "N" if it neither strengthens nor weakens the argument, "W" if it weakens the argument to some extent, and "GW" if it weakens the argument a great deal.

A. Police forces that have banned car chases have not seen an increase in car crime.

B. Joyriding is most serious where police forces do not pursue such drivers.

C. Joyriders cause many serious accidents and some deaths even when not being pursued.

D. Many high-speed car chases result in the arrest of car thieves.

E. Some highly trained police officers overestimate their skill when driving at high speed.

Of course, the teacher could have chosen any other subset of the original responses—smaller or larger, depending on the purpose.

Multiple-rating items offer several advantages over other options. In responding to multiple-rating questions the students are being asked to do the very task the teacher just did in grading their work: they are being asked to recognize good answers and poor ones—an evaluative task that is quite characteristic of critical thinking. The teacher gets far more information from their answers than from the multiple-choice question because the student has to evaluate each statement. (Depending on the level of confidence in grading, the teacher can give two points for a correct answer and one point for a near miss, and can penalize badly wrong answers—thus penalizing guessing.) Multiple-rating items are easy to construct (the teacher needs only to put good representative examples from the earlier assessment—which asked for students to respond with a statement—on one side while grading them), and they are easy to grade. The assessment also has a certain authenticity for other similar students because the sentences being evaluated are the very things that their peers are inclined to say about the argument. Finally, multiple-rating items are excellent vehicles for teaching thinking skills. Students get very engaged in arguing about the worth of "authentic" responses to the question (in the sense that these have been written by their peers—though presented anonymously, of course).

Needless to say, the teacher's own expertise in the area of critical thinking or higher-order thinking is the only guarantee that the initial grading is correct, that the question really is assessing the targeted skill (has "validity," to use the technical jargon), and that the grade given is one that others would agree with (has "inter-rater reliability," again to use the technical jargon). However, as mentioned earlier, if it matters enough, the teacher can seek the advice of a colleague who also has expertise in the relevant area.

In addition to the basic format, many variations of the multiple-rating item are possible. One variation of the earlier example would require respondents to give brief reasons for their judgments. Clearly this would be more difficult to grade, but it would give even more direct evidence of the quality of students' thinking/reasoning and might suit the teacher's purpose—if, for example, the teacher had identified a weakness that needed to be remedied.

CONCLUSION

Clearly there are many thinking skills teachers may wish to assess, and many reasons for wishing to assess them. Teachers may wish to assess how well students have mastered some thinking skill that has been taught—for example, problem solving or decision making; alternatively they may wish to diagnose areas in which students are having difficulties with particular kinds of thinking—for example, understanding complex texts or designing experiments; yet again, teachers may simply wish to know how good students are at a given kind of thinking, whether it has been taught or not—for example, brainstorming or doing a compare and contrast exercise.

Whatever the reason for wishing to assess the quality of students' thinking, the following points should be kept in mind:

• It's important to be reasonably clear about what would count as good thinking or poor thinking in the domain in question for the students being assessed (allowing for their background, what teaching they have had, and so forth). If teachers are not confident they have the relevant professional expertise (and most of us have not been given explicit training in teaching thinking), they should consult colleagues who have that expertise.

• Students should be provided with the right kind of stimulus material for doing the kind of thinking being assessed. If decision making, for example, is the target thinking skill, the teacher should devise a task for which it is reasonable to assume that the students have the necessary information about such things as the likely consequences of various options, the risks, and so forth; or the teacher should give them the information they need in order to do the task.

• It's important to ask students the right kind of question. It should not be one that just requires them to recall something they have learned; it should require them to do the kind of thinking the teacher wishes to assess. For example, if students' ability to understand a complex text is the target skill, the teacher could present them with an example containing a thousand words and ask them to summarize it in a hundred words.

• When grading student responses, the only guarantee of the correctness of the grade is the teacher's own expertise in the subject area and in the thinking skills concerned; if it matters and if there is any doubt about grading, teachers should consult colleagues with the relevant expertise and ask them to do some "double-marking."

• Answers that have been given by one group of students can be used to construct multiple-rating items for other students. Multiple-rating items are easy to construct, can be easy to grade, and will have an air of authenticity about them. They also make excellent teaching material.

REFERENCES

Fisher, A., & Scriven, M. (1997). *Critical thinking: Its definition and assessment.* Norwich, United Kingdom: Center for Research in Critical Thinking, University of East Anglia.

Fisher, A., & Thomson, A. (1993). *Testing Reasoning Ability.* United Kingdom: The Centre for Research in Critical Thinking, University of East Anglia.

Norris, S., & Ennis, R. (1989). *Evaluating critical thinking.* Pacific Grove, CA: Critical Thinking Press and Software.

Swartz, R. J., Fischer, S. D., & Parks, S. (1998). *Infusing the teaching of critical and creative thinking into secondary science: A lesson design handbook.* Pacific Grove, CA: Critical Thinking Press and Software.

Swartz, R. J., & Parks, S. (1994). *Infusing the teaching of critical and creative thinking into content instruction: A lesson design handbook for the elementary grades.* Pacific Grove, CA: Critical Thinking Press and Software.

Appendixes and Resources: Introduction

Arthur L. Costa

While no list of resources is ever complete, we have drawn upon numerous sources to compile this one. You should continue to note in the Bibliography and Resources sections the books, articles, audio, video, and electronic materials you find helpful that enrich your understanding of the nature of teaching for thinking.

This list of human and material resources is supplemented with the Developing Minds Web site, CD-ROMs, and other publications from ASCD listing programs, assessment strategies, organizations, and newsletters. They are contained in a more flexible format so they may be updated periodically. You will want to browse the Web site periodically.

Contained here are checklists to help assess classroom, school, and community readiness and such groups' efforts to teach thinking, and a glossary of terms so that meanings can become more precise and coherent. Rather than have a huge bibliography, several key leaders in the field of cognitive education were invited to recommend a few classics for those who may wish to become students in the field. Also included are biographical sketches of the numerous contributors to this publication, so you may become better acquainted with their credentials, points of view, and experiences.

Glossary of Thinking Terms

Barry K. Beyer, Arthur L. Costa, and Barbara Z. Presseisen

"Aha" experience: instantaneous apprehension of an idea or understanding

Abstract: general; symbolic; not applied or specific

Accuracy: free from error; correctness

Algorithm: a procedure that, if followed exactly, will always yield the solution to a particular problem or type of problem

Alternative: option; another potential choice; one of a number of mutually exclusive possibilities

Ambiguity: having more than one meaning or interpretation; the state of being uncertain

Analogy: correspondence in some way between dissimilar things

Analyze: to take apart, disassemble, or deconstruct in order to identify the parts of something, the connections between these parts, or the pattern or structure that holds them together

Argument: a claim (conclusion) with supporting reasons and evidence tied together by logical reasoning

Assertion: a claim, conclusion, or declaration affirmed as if it were true but without proof or support

Assumption: a fact or condition taken for granted; a supposition that something is true without proof or evidence

Bias: a slanted or one-sided view or opinion; a preference that interferes with impartial judgment

Brainstorm: rapid generation of a number of ideas without elaboration or critical examination of each

Categorical reasoning: syllogistic reasoning using quantifiers such as "some," "all," "no," or "none" to indicate category membership

Categorize: to group together things having identical attributes; to put into a specifically defined class in a classification system

Causation: the process of bringing about some result or effect

Cause/effect: a condition, action, or event (cause) that makes something happen, and the result (effect) or outcome brought about by the cause or event

Claim: assertion affirmed as true but without proof or support

Classify: to sort things having similar attributes into groups, each group identified by a label specifying the distinguishing commonalities of all items in that group

Cognition: the mental process of acquiring knowledge

Cognitive operation: a specific thinking skill, such as comparing, classifying, synthesizing, analyzing, etc.

Compare and contrast: to note the similarities and differences between two or more things

Comprehension: the act or state of knowing or understanding

Conceive: to generate or invent in the mind

Conclusion: an inferential belief that is derived from premises; a belief drawn from systematic analysis of evidence

Concrete: specific, actual, real, or particular, as opposed to general, abstract, or theoretical

Conditional logic: reasoning from premises that may or may not be true; *if . . . then* reasoning

Contingency relationship: relationships expressed in *if . . . then* statements in which the consequent is dependent on the truth or accuracy of the antecedent

Contrast: to set in opposition; to show differences

Convergent thinking: thinking that requires or leads to a single correct response or answer

Creative thinking: the act of producing original or new thoughts (see *aha, elaborate, flexibility, fluency, originality*)

Critical thinking: judging the worth or other quality of something against criteria or standards

Data: information, especially numerical information, organized for analysis

Decision making: choosing from alternatives evaluated in light of their consequences

Deduce: to infer from a general principle

Develop criteria: to create standards, rules, or tests for making judgments

Discriminate: to differentiate between or among things

Disposition: inclination to perform one or more patterns of intellectual behaviors, such as being accurate, precise, etc.

Divergent thinking: thinking that generates many different correct responses or answers

Elaborate: to expand on or provide greater detail about something

Epistemic thinking: related to the collective knowledge produced by various forms of thinking, such as scientific, aesthetic, or political, and the ways these bodies of knowledge are developed and extended

Error: incorrectness; not right; untruth

Estimate: to judge or infer based on rough calculations or cursory consideration of limited information

Evaluate: to judge something against criteria or standards

Evidence: information that offers proof of some claim or conclusion

Factual claim: a statement that can be verified or proven; information presented as having objective certainty

Fallacy: an error or mistake in reasoning; a false idea, belief, or claim

Flexibility: the ability to take alternative points of view, to try several different approaches, or to apply concepts to a variety of situations

Fluency: the ability to produce a variety of responses

Generalization: a statement that expresses a relationship between two or more concepts, usually without limit in time or space; a principle that explains any number of related situations

Group: to place together things or ideas having common attributes

Habit of mind: An intellectual pattern of behaviors that has become habituated, for example, curiosity

Hierarchy: objects, events, or ideas arranged by rank, grade, or class according to some criterion

Heuristic: a general strategy or "rule of thumb" used in carrying out a particular skill or task; while such a guideline may not always produce a correct response or product, it is usually helpful in completing the task; for example, "Look before you leap" is an effective decision-making heuristic

Hypothesis: a tentative statement, claim, or answer, based on limited information and subject to further proof

Hypothesize: to generate, construct, or form a hypothesis

Ideational fluency: the ability to generate many ideas

Identical: sharing all attributes exactly

Identify: to point out or ascertain

Illogical: not in accord with the principles of logic

Induce: to infer a principle, conclusion, or hypothesis from specific instances

Infer: to arrive at a conclusion that evidence, facts, or assertions point toward but do not absolutely establish; to draw tentative conclusions from incomplete data

Information: facts, claims, statistical data, and other forms of knowledge

Inquiry: seeking information

Insight: sudden knowledge of something, such as finding a new relationship between seemingly unrelated events, conditions, or objects

Interpretation: explanation of the perceived meaning of something

Intuition: the power or faculty of attaining knowledge without apparent rational thought and inference

Irrelevant: not pertaining to

Judge: to determine whether something meets certain criteria or standards

Knowledge: understanding, developed through study, experience, or instruction

Label: to assign a name to something or a category of items that is indicative or descriptive of what it is

Lateral thinking: thinking around a problem to generate new ideas (compare to *vertical thinking*)

Logic: principles of reasoning

Logical reasoning: thinking in a systematic fashion to determine or establish the truth or validity of a claim

Meaning: the sense, significance, or import of something

Memory: that portion of the brain where information and knowledge are stored

Metacognition: consciousness of one's own thinking process; directing, monitoring, and evaluating one's thinking while engaged in doing that thinking

Metacognitive reflection: reviewing through reflection how one carried out a just-completed thinking operation

Metaphor: linguistic comparisons formed by transferring a term commonly associated with one object to another dissimilar object

Mnemonics: techniques, such as rhymes or acronyms, used to aid memory

Observe: using the senses, especially sight, to gather information

Opinion: a personal belief, judgment, appraisal, or claim not objectively verified or substantiated by proof

Order: to arrange or sequence things according to an established scheme or criterion

Originality: the ability to generate novel, nontraditional, or unexpected responses

Part-to-whole relationship: the links or connections between the individual components of something and the complete unit they constitute when combined

Pattern: an arrangement of constant traits or repetitive features or combinations of features

Perceive: to become aware of through the senses

Point of view: the position—such as cultural, intellectual, or political—from which events, objects, or principles are perceived, compared, judged, or given meaning

Predict: to formulate what is most likely to follow based on a perceived pattern; to foretell

Premise: a proposition upon which a conclusion is based

Prioritize: to order according to precedence or urgency

Principle: a fundamental law, doctrine, or rule; a basic truth or assumption

Problem: a situation that is uncertain, perplexing, or unresolved

Problem solve: to resolve an uncertainty or perplexity by the systematic application of an appropriate solution strategy

Procedure: a series of steps for performing a task or carrying out an action

Process: a series of actions that brings about intended results

Qualification: finding unique characteristics of a particular identity or description

Question: to formulate relevant inquiries in order to evaluate something, locate, or verify information, clarify an idea, etc.

Reasoned conclusion: a conclusion derived from and supported by logical reasoning and evidence

Reasoning: the mental process of drawing conclusions or inferences from observations, facts, experiences; *deductive:* inferring a valid conclusion from two or more premises; *inductive:* inferring a tentative conclusion or hypothesis from limited specifics

Recall: to retrieve from memory

Relationship: a connection or link between two or more things, such as temporal, spatial, functional, syllogistic, transitive, mathematical, cause/effect, part-whole, evidence-conclusion, etc.

Relevant: pertaining to; having a significant bearing on or relationship to

Rule: an underlying or governing principle

Sequence, Seriate: to arrange events, objects, or ideas in ascending or descending order according to some value or criterion

Skill: a learned ability to do something with proficiency; expertness

Slanted argument: a one-sided line of reasoning that seeks to demonstrate the purported truth of a claim

Sort: to classify or group information

Steps: individual movements in a series of actions designed to achieve some end

Strategy: a plan of action for accomplishing some end

Structure: an organization or arrangement that gives form to something

Summary: a condensed, concise statement of the essence of some communication

Syllogistic reasoning: drawing a logical conclusion from two statements or premises; reasoning from the general to the specific

Synthesize: to unite parts into a whole; to pull together into a whole; for example, to conclude, hypothesize, conceptualize, or compose

Test: to determine whether an assertion, conclusion, hypothesis, theory, or other kind of knowledge claim is accurate, true, or justified by evidence

Thinking: the mental processing of sensory input and recalled perceptions to achieve a specific end through reasoning, formulating thoughts, and judging

Thinking task: a discrepancy, problem, dichotomy, dilemma, or paradox, the answer to which is not immediately apparent, thus requiring some form of strategic reasoning; for example, decision making, problem solving, data generation, or creative thinking

Transformation: relating known to unknown characteristics; creating meaning

Value: worth assigned to something as a guide to behavior or as a measure of quality

Value conflict: the opposition of several values to each other

Value judgment: a judgment based on one's personal standards of worth

Vertical thinking: logical and straightforward thinking, used in refining and elaborating ideas and solutions (compare to *lateral thinking*)

These definitions are taken from a variety of sources. Readers interested in more detailed explanations of these terms should refer to the following sources:

Beyer, B. K. (1984). What's in a skill: Defining the skills we teach. *Social Studies Record, 21*(2), 19–23.

Commission on Science Education. (1963). *Science: A process approach.* Washington, DC: American Association for the Advancement of Science.

Halpern, D. F. (1984). *Thought and knowledge: An introduction to critical thinking* (pp. 357–372). Hillsdale, NJ: Lawrence Erlbaum Associates.

Kurfman, D. G. (Ed.). (1977). *Developing decision-making skills.* Arlington, VA: National Council for the Social Studies.

Miller, G. A., et al. (1960). *Plans and the structure of behavior.* New York: Holt, Rinehart & Winston.

Appendix A: Self-Reflection on Our Own Models of Teaching

By John Barell

Please rate your beliefs and practices using the scale of 1 to 5 on the following items.

5 = Very Often   4 = Often   3 = Sometimes   2 = Seldom   1 = Hardly Ever

CLASSROOM PRACTICES

1. When teaching I usually work at or near my desk.

2. We display examples of students' work around the room.

3. I group students in different configurations during class for instructional purposes.

4. I ask most of the questions during class.

5. Students pose thought-provoking questions related to content.

6. Students reflect on their work, progress, and thought processes orally or in writing.

7. I emphasize the thought processes used to arrive at answers, responses, and questions by asking, "How did you arrive at that answer, solution or idea?"

8. Students spend time working collaboratively in our class.

9. Students support their conclusions with evidence, giving reasons for their thinking.

10. Most answers to questions can be found in textbooks.

11. I encourage students to seek alternative ways of approaching problems, interpretations, and solutions.

12. Students spontaneously comment on each others' responses and ideas.

13. We ask questions in class that require complex thought processes.

14. Students respond to my questions with short, one- or two-word answers.

15. Students spend time on projects or problems to solve.

16. Covering content is one of my major goals.

17. My students use or create Internet resources.

18. I use a wide variety of assessment experiences.

19. One of my considerations is ensuring that students understand and can apply concepts to other subjects, to life experiences.

20. We work to build a community of inquiry in our class.

SCHOOL PRACTICES

1. We discuss teaching strategies in department and faculty meetings.

2. Assessment of my teaching focuses on the kinds of intellectual or physical challenges I present to students.

3. There are professional development opportunities geared toward challenging students to think productively.

4. There are professional development opportunities that help teachers and students use Internet resources.

5. We work to build a community of inquiry in our school.

Author's note: This checklist was revised by John Barell, Jason Allen, Giovanni Aliano, Sean Adams, Maria Gencarelli, Jessica Kazimir, Shannon Muller, Mark Lopes, Tracy Mitchell, Shannon Renaut, Suzanne Snyder, Monique Sarfity, Art Settembrino, Karen Vicari, Deborah VanderGroef, and Andreanna Xanthos by using these questions with teachers in the Paramus, New Jersey, school system in a research attempt to identify their mental models. (The concept of mental models was developed from Caine & Caine's ASCD book, *Education on the Edge of Possibility*.)

Appendix B:
Classroom Observation Checklist

LEE WINOCUR FIELD

Teacher _____ School _____ District _____

Observer _____ Subject _____ Date _____

Directions:
Mark an "x" in the appropriate column for each classroom behavior. If the statement is generally true of this classroom, mark *yes*. If the statement is generally not true of this classroom, mark *no*. If you are unsure, mark the third column.

	<u>Yes</u>	<u>No</u>	<u>Unsure</u>

Affective Indicators

1. Fosters a Climate of Openness
- Eye contact is frequent between teacher and students, and students and students.
- Teacher moves around the room.
- Students listen attentively to others.
- Teacher calls on students by name.

2. Encourages Student Interaction/Cooperation
- Students work in pairs or small groups.
- Students respond to other students.
- Students help others analyze and solve problems.

3. Demonstrates Attitude of Acceptance
- Teacher accepts all valid student responses.
- Incorrect student responses elicit encouraging, supportive comments.
- Teacher acknowledges student comments with a nod or other signal.

Cognitive Indicators

4. Encourages Students to Gather Information
- Reference materials are readily available.
- Students use reference materials.
- Student mobility is allowed to obtain information.
- Teacher acts as facilitator.
- Students record data in notebooks or journals.

This appendix is reprinted from "Classroom Observation Checklist," by S. L. Winocur, 1991, *Developing Minds: A Resource Book for Teaching Thinking* (Rev. Ed., Vol. 1, pp. 386–388), edited by A. L. Costa. Alexandria, VA: ASCD. Copyright 1983 by S. Lee Winocur, Costa Mesa, California.

5. **Encourages Students to Organize Information**
   - Teacher works from organized lesson plans.
   - Students classify and categorize data.
   - Students take notes systematically.
   - Teacher's presentation is logical, organized.
   - Ideas are graphically symbolized during instruction.

6. **Encourages Students to Justify Ideas**
   - Teacher probes for correct responses.
   - Teacher seeks evidence for stated claims.
   - Students analyze sources of information for reliability, relevance.
   - Teacher frequently asks, "Why do you think so?"
   - Students relate learning to past experience or similar situations.

7. **Encourages Students to Explore Alternatives and Others' Points of View**
   - Teacher establishes expectations for divergent solutions.
   - Teacher allows time to consider alternatives/points of view.
   - More than one student is queried for point of view/solution.
   - Teacher asks students to justify and explain their thoughts.

8. **Asks Open-Ended Questions**
   - Teacher asks open-ended questions with multiple answers as *frequently* as single-answer questions.

9. **Provides Visual Cues for Developing Cognitive Strategies**
   - Teacher appropriately uses a variety of visual media (charts, chalkboard, maps, pictures, gestures).
   - Teacher uses symbolic language to illustrate a point (simile, metaphor).
   - Teacher uses outlining.

10. **Models Reasoning Strategies**
    - Teacher uses "if/then" language.
    - Teacher poses "what if " or "suppose that" questions.
    - Teacher uses clear examples to facilitate logical thought.

11. **Encourages Transfer of Cognitive Skills to Everyday Life**
    - Teacher encourages transfer at end of lesson with comments like, "This will help you in your everyday life in this way . . . ."

12. **Elicits Verbalization of Student Reasoning**
    - Teacher poses questions at different levels of Bloom's Taxonomy.
    - Teacher allows at least 10 seconds wait time for student answer before restating or redirecting the question.
    - Teacher asks students to clarify and justify their responses.
    - Teacher probes "I don't know" responses.
    - Teacher reinforces students for responding to open-ended questions.

<u>Yes</u>   <u>No</u>   <u>Unsure</u>

13. Probes Student Reasoning for Clarification
- Teacher asks questions to elicit reasoning by students.
- Teacher requires students to expand on answers.
- Teacher cues students for most logical answers.

14. Encourages Students to Ask Questions
- Teacher poses problematic situations.
- Teacher withholds "correct" responses; encourages students to explore possibilities.
- Teacher encourages students to answer other students' questions.

15. Promotes Silent Reflection of Ideas
- Teacher allows time for reflection.

Appendix C:
How Thoughtful Is Your School?

ARTHUR L. COSTA

Use the following 15 questions as criteria to rate your school's effectiveness in developing thoughtful education.

Degree of Effectiveness: 5 = high; 1 = low

	To what degree:	5	4	3	2	1
1.	Do your community and staff value thinking as a primary goal of education?	5	4	3	2	1
2.	Does the staff believe that with appropriate intervention, human intelligence can continue to develop throughout a lifetime?	5	4	3	2	1
3.	Have you reached consensus on what it means to be an effective thinker?	5	4	3	2	1
4.	Are students aware that learning to think is a goal of their education?	5	4	3	2	1
5.	Do teachers use language (questioning and structuring) that invites students to think?	5	4	3	2	1
6.	Do teachers' response behaviors extend and maintain higher levels of thinking?	5	4	3	2	1
7.	Are learning activities arranged in order of increasing complexity and abstraction?	5	4	3	2	1
8.	Do instructional materials support higher cognitive functioning?	5	4	3	2	1
9.	Is adequate time devoted to thinking and reflecting?	5	4	3	2	1
10.	Does curriculum, instruction, and assessment provide for differences in modality strengths, cognitive styles, and learning styles?	5	4	3	2	1
11.	Are students' thoughtful behaviors celebrated in daily classroom life?	5	4	3	2	1
12.	Are tasks requiring thoughtful strategies of problem solving and decision making encountered repeatedly over time and throughout, across, and outside the curriculum?	5	4	3	2	1
13.	Do students and teachers discuss their thinking (metacognition)?	5	4	3	2	1
14.	Is growth in thinking skills, cognitive strategies, and habits of mind monitored, assessed, and reported?	5	4	3	2	1
15.	Do significant adults model thoughtful behavior?	5	4	3	2	1

Appendix D:
Checklist for Thinking Skills Programs

BARRY K. BEYER

	Yes	In Progress	No
1. Does your building or district have			
a. A list of major thinking skills to be taught throughout the school or district?	_____	_____	_____
b. Provisions for teaching these skills in subject-matter courses?	_____	_____	_____
c. Agreement among all subject areas that these skills should be taught?	_____	_____	_____
d. Detailed descriptions of authentic procedures, rules, and skill knowledge for each thinking skill to be taught?	_____	_____	_____
e. A scope-and-sequence document that clearly delimits which thinking skills are to be introduced and taught at each grade level in each subject area?	_____	_____	_____
f. Appropriate thinking skill descriptions in the immediate possession of every teacher and administrator?	_____	_____	_____
g. Provisions for continuing instruction in these thinking skills across multiple grade levels and subjects?	_____	_____	_____
h. Provisions for instruction in each skill with a variety of media in a variety of settings on a variety of subjects?	_____	_____	_____
2. Do your teachers			
a. Use common terminology and instructional language to describe the thinking skills they are required to teach?	_____	_____	_____
b. Provide instruction in thinking skills when these skills are needed to accomplish subject-matter learning goals?	_____	_____	_____
c. Understand the major components of the thinking skills they are teaching?	_____	_____	_____
d. Provide continuing instruction in each thinking skill through the stages of introduction, scaffolded practice, cued application, and transfer?	_____	_____	_____

	Yes	In Progress	No

e. Introduce thinking skills as explicitly as possible by explaining and modeling each skill and having students reflect on how they apply the skill? _____ _____ _____

f. Provide frequent scaffolded practice in each skill, with appropriate instructive feedback, once it has been introduced? _____ _____ _____

g. Provide intermittent cued practice to autonomous use? _____ _____ _____

h. Require students to reflect on and discuss how they apply each skill? _____ _____ _____

i. Use instructional materials appropriate to learning each thinking skill? _____ _____ _____

j. Assess student proficiency in the skills taught on their unit tests? _____ _____ _____

3. Do your provisions for assessing student thinking skills include

a. Regular classroom assessment of student proficiency in thinking skills being taught? _____ _____ _____

b. Use and knowledge of instruments that reveal student performance on skills being taught? _____ _____ _____

c. Use of instruments that are valid measures of thinking skill proficiency? _____ _____ _____

d. Use of instruments that provide the maximum data for diagnostic and monitoring purposes? _____ _____ _____

4. Do your supervisors and instructional leaders

a. Understand the nature of the thinking skills being taught and how to teach and assess them? _____ _____ _____

b. Provide inservice instruction in the nature of the thinking skills to be taught and in different ways to teach these skills? _____ _____ _____

c. Help teachers in different subject areas and grade levels share methods for teaching thinking skills? _____ _____ _____

d. Ensure that teachers follow the thinking skills curriculum? _____ _____ _____

e. Ensure the revision of the thinking skills curriculum, instructional strategies, assessment instruments, and instructional materials as appropriate? _____ _____ _____

Recommended Resources

World Wide Web

ASCD Resources

ASCD provides many educational resources on the Web (http://www.ascd.org). Here, find online excerpts of this book and many other ASCD books, articles, and multimedia. Search for "thinking skills" to find many related resources.

Bibliography

Rather than have a vast list of books on thinking, as was included in the revised edition of *Developing Minds*, many of the contributors to this book were invited to suggest books they thought every "student of thinking" should be acquainted with. Readers will also want to take advantage of the reference lists and bibliographies included in most chapters of the book. In our desire to serve educators who are intent on building programs of thoughtful education, therefore, what follows is a highly selected list of the most significant and prominent books in cognitive education suggested by the leaders in this field. Many are "classics" and provide the foundation for our modern thinking about cognition and instruction. In some instances, annotations by the contributors are included.

Appreciation is expressed to the contributors to this list:

Jonathon Baron, Larry Lowery, Barry Beyer, David Martin, John Edwards, Jay McTighe, Robert Ennis, Robert Sternberg, Scott Isaksen, Donald Treffinger, Sherry King, Robin Fogarty, Cathy Block, Art Costa, and Yvette Jackson.

Anderson, H. H. (Ed.). (1956). *Creativity and its cultivation.* New York: Harper.

A seminal collection of essays on the nature and nurture of creativity that was influential in stimulating research and development on creativity in both business and education.

Argyris, C. (1999). *On organizational learning* (2nd ed.) Malden, MA: Blackwell.

This book draws together the seminal work on organizational learning done by Chris Argyris over many years. It provides powerful insights into how organizations work, evolve, and learn.

Baron, J. (2000). *Thinking and deciding* (3rd ed). New York: Cambridge University Press.

Baron, J., & Sternberg, R. (Eds.). (1987). *Teaching thinking skills: Theory and practice.* New York: W. H. Freeman.

A classic and comprehensive compendium of articles dealing with the teaching of critical thinking.

Benner, P. (1984). *From novice to expert.* Menlo Park, CA: Addison-Wesley.

For anyone interested in skill acquisition, this is essential reading. It looks at the growth of nurses from novice to expert status.

Beyer, B. K. (1997). *Improving student thinking: A comprehensive approach.* Boston: Allyn and Bacon.

Block, C. C., & Mangieri, J. N. (1996). *Reason to read: Thinking strategies for life through literature.* Palo Alto, CA: Scott Foresman/Addison-Wesley.

This is a three-volume curriculum for grades 2–9. It contains 45 lessons with complete instructional, assessment, and home connections, and research reports. Each volume is designed as a complete instructional package.

Boden, M. A. (1991). *The creative mind: Myths and mechanisms.* New York: Basic Books.

Boden breaks down the mystery of creativity by mapping various views of the mind, including both artistic and scientific perspectives. Emphasizes the universality of creative potential.

Boshyk, Y. (2000). *Business driven action learning: Global best practices.* Basingstoke, UK: Macmillan Business.

Reviews the lessons learned by major international corporations about organizational thinking and learning.

Bransford, J., Brown, A., & Cocking, R. (Eds.). (1999). *How people learn: Brain, mind, experience, and school.* Washington, DC: National Academy Press.

Bransford, J. D., & Stein, B. S. (1993). *The ideal problem solver* (2nd ed.). New York: W. H. Freeman.

Browne, M. N., & Keeley, S. M. (1990). *Asking the right questions.* Englewood Cliffs, NJ: Prentice-Hall.

Bruner, J. S. (1960). *The process of education.* Cambridge, MA: Harvard University Press.

Bruner, J. S. (1968). *Toward a theory of instruction.* New York: W. W. Norton.

For more than three decades, Bruner's efforts to link cognitive development with the opportunities and challenges of curriculum and instruction served as a springboard for many researchers and developers who were concerned with "process education."

Burke, J., & Ornstein, R. (1997). *The axemaker's gift.* New York: Putnam.

A fascinating account of how scientific thinking and technology have gained control over how we perceive and value the world.

Caine, G., & Caine, R. N. (1991). *Making connections: Teaching and the human brain.* Alexandria, VA: Association for Supervision and Curriculum Development.

Seminal piece; meta-analysis of the research findings on the brain and learning translated into 12 guiding principles.

Collins, C. D., & Mangieri, J. (1994). *Teaching thinking: An agenda for the 21st century.* Mahwah, NJ: Lawrence Erlbaum.

This is an edited volume of renowned cognitive researchers who propose suggestions for enhancing curriculum to become more reflective and thoughtful.

Costa, A., & Kallick, B. (Eds.). (2000). *Habits of mind: A developmental series. Discovering and exploring habits of mind; Activating and engaging habits of mind; Assessing and reporting on habits of mind; Integrating and sustaining habits of mind.* Alexandria, VA: Association for Supervision and Curriculum Development.

This series of books identifies and describes 16 dispositions related to thinking, how to teach and assess growth in them, and how to infuse them into the culture of the school.

Costa, A., & Lowery, L. (1989). *Techniques for teaching thinking.* Pacific Grove, CA: Midwest Publications.

de Bono, E. (1976). *Teaching thinking.* New York: Penguin.

Advocating creative thinking, this book introduces the term "lateral thinking" to the business and educational communities.

de Bono, E. (1993). *Teach your child how to think.* New York: Penguin.

Probably the best of de Bono's books for those interested in how to go about actually teaching thinking directly.

Delpit, L. (1998). *Other people's children.* New York: The New Press.

Dewey, J. (1933). *How we think.* Boston MA: D. C. Heath.

Dewey, J. (1938). *Experience and education.* New York: Collier.

A thesis advocating experiential, hands-on learning that takes learning beyond the classroom walls and into the realm of real-world experiences.

Diamond, M., & Hobson, J. (1998). *Magic trees of the mind: How to nurture your child's intelligence, creativity and healthy emotions from birth through adolescence.* New York: Dutton.

Wonderfully readable book that describes Diamond's research at Berkeley on enriched environments and the growth of dendrites in the cerebral cortex; full of listings of resources to stimulate brain activity.

Edwards, J. (Ed.). (1994). *Thinking: International interdisciplinary perspectives.* Melbourne, Australia: Hawker Brownlow.

These are the top 30 papers, as selected by an international panel, from the Fifth International Conference on Thinking, held in Australia. They give a powerful international overview of the field.

Edwards, J., Butler, J., Hill, B., & Russell, S. (1997). *People rules for rocket scientists.* Brisbane, Australia: Samford Research Associates.

An excellent introduction to thinking in the workplace for those without workplace experience. Great for novices, and an interesting refresher for the experienced.

Elder, L., & Paul, R. (1995). *Critical thinking development: A stage theory.* Rohnert Park, CA: Foundation for Critical Thinking.

A theory involving stages of critical thinking development is presented and elaborated on.

Ennis, R. H. (1996). *Critical thinking.* Upper Saddle River, NJ: Prentice-Hall.

A comprehensive up-to-date critical thinking textbook containing many examples, appropriate for gifted high school students, undergraduates, and adults. More advanced material is so indicated.

Ennis, R. H. (1998). Is critical thinking culturally biased? *Teaching Philosophy, 21*(1), 15–33.

Argues that critical thinking is essentially not culturally biased, though ways of teaching it and the form of presenting its results might be on some occasions.

Ennis, R. H., & Millman, J. (1985). *Cornell critical thinking test, level 10.* Pacific Grove, CA: Critical Thinking Books and Software.

A fairly comprehensive multiple-choice critical thinking test aimed at middle and high school students.

Feuerstein, R., Rand, Y., Hoffman, M. B., & Miller, R. (1980). *Instrumental enrichment: An intervention program for cognitive modifiability.* Baltimore: University Park Press.

Fisher, A., & Scriven, M. (1997). *Critical thinking: Its definition and assessment.* Point Reyes, CA: Edgepress.

A stimulating treatment of critical thinking assessment and conceptual issues.

Gardner, H. (1983). *Frames of mind: The theory of multiple intelligences.* New York: Basic Books.

The book that started it all! Introduces Howard Gardner's theory of multiple intelligences.

Hare, R. M. (1981). *Moral thinking: Its levels, method and point.* Oxford, UK: Oxford University Press (Clarendon Press).

An excellent introduction to thinking about moral questions. This book introduces the normative/prescriptive distinction. For more on moral questions, see *The expanding circle: Ethics and sociobiology,* and *Practical ethics* (2nd ed.), by P. Singer, below.

Hart, L. (1983). *Human brain and human learning.* New York: Longman.

Seminal, early work that predicted that the future of teaching and learning would hinge on the study of the brain.

Hayes, J. R. (1989). *The complete problem solver.* Mahwah, NJ: Lawrence Erlbaum.

Heiman, M., & Slomianko, J. (Eds.). (1987). *Thinking skills instruction: Concepts and techniques.* Washington, DC: National Education Association.

Isaacs, W. (1999). *Dialogue and the art of thinking together.* New York: Currency.

Distinguishes dialogue and dialectical discourse. Through true and respectful listening we can achieve greater group intelligence.

Isaksen, S. G., Dorval, K. B., & Treffinger, D. J. (2000). *Creative approaches to problem solving* (2nd ed.). Dubuque, IA: Kendall/Hunt.

This book provides the most comprehensive presentation currently available on the Creative Problem Solving (CPS) framework. Builds on more than five decades of prior work. By drawing on the authors' current research and the contributions of many cognitive and organizational scholars, the framework is now flexible, natural, descriptive, and dynamic. CPS is no longer a fixed or "prescriptive" set of steps and stages.

Jensen, E. (1998). *Teaching with the brain in mind.* Alexandria, VA: Association for Supervision and Curriculum Development.

Keeney, R. L. (1992). *Value-focused thinking: A path to creative decision making.* Cambridge, MA: Harvard University Press.

A good example of modern decision theory and its practical applications, written by one of the field's leaders. This book is highly readable despite the threatening mathematical formalisms scattered throughout, which can be (but should not be) skipped.

Lipman, M. (1991). *Thinking in education*. Cambridge, MA: Cambridge University Press.

MacKinnon, D. W. (1968). *In search of human effectiveness*. Buffalo, NY: Bearly Limited/Creative Education Foundation.

Donald MacKinnon's research pointed the way to many promising directions for linking personality, cognitive characteristics, and organizational settings, and gave us a richer foundation for understanding the dynamics, development, and expression of creativity. This book includes a cross-section of many of MacKinnon's most significant essays and journal articles.

Mahiri, J. (1998). *Shooting for excellence*. New York: Teachers College Press.

Mangieri, J. N., & Block, C. C. (Eds.). (1994). *Creating powerful thinking in teachers and students: Diverse perspectives*. Orlando, FL: Harcourt Brace.

This is an edited volume written by 15 leading educators—including Howard Gardner, David Berliner, Anne Palinscar, Robert Sternberg, and Shirly Brice Heath—who project what is needed to enlarge the circle of educators contributing to a more thought-filled and thoughtful world.

Marzano, R., Pickering, D., & McTighe, J. (1993). *Assessing student outcomes: Performance assessment using the Dimensions of Learning model*. Alexandria, VA: Association for Supervision and Curriculum Development.

A practical guide to developing performance assessment tasks that emphasize complex reasoning skills; includes sample tasks and scoring rubrics.

Maclure, S., & Davies, P. (Eds.). (1991). *Learning to think: Thinking to learn: The proceedings of the 1989 OECD conference organised by the Centre for Educational Research and Innovation*. Oxford, UK: Pergamon.

An impressive collection of papers from the Organisation for Economic Co-operation and Development (OECD) conference in Paris. They provide an excellent basis for understanding European views on teaching thinking.

McTighe, J., & Wiggins, G. (1999). *Understanding by Design handbook*. Alexandria, VA: Association for Supervision and Curriculum Development.

A practical guide containing design tools, templates, exercises, and design standards based on the book *Understanding by Design*.

National Research Council. (1999). *How people learn: Brain, mind, experience and school*. Washington, DC: National Academy Press.

A current, readable summary of research in cognitive psychology and the educational implications.

National Science Foundation. (2000). *Inquiry: Thoughts, views and strategies for K–5 classrooms*. In *Foundations* (Vol. 2). Arlington, VA: National Academy Press.

Nickerson, R., Perkins, D., & Smith, E. (1985). *The teaching of thinking*. Hillsdale, NJ: Erlbaum.

Nonaka, I., & Takeuchi, H. (1995). *The knowledge-creating company*. New York: Oxford University Press.

For those interested in the innovative edges of thinking in Japanese business. Looks at the specific organizational structures and processes involved in organizational creativity and innovation.

Norris, S. P. (Ed.). (1992). *The generalizability of critical thinking: Multiple perspectives on an educational ideal*. New York: Teachers College Press.

Incorporates a variety of viewpoints about the basic issue that sometimes takes the form, "Should critical thinking be taught separately, incorporated in subject matter instruction, or both?"

Norris, S. P., & Ennis, R. H. (1989). *Evaluating critical thinking*. Pacific Grove, CA: Critical Thinking Books and Software.

A useful discussion of existing critical thinking tests and the process of making your own critical thinking test.

Osborn, A. F. (1953). *Applied imagination*. New York: Scribners.

Alex Osborn was one of the pioneers in bringing the concept of creativity into the realm of the practical and the everyday life of people and organizations. That his work is still widely cited after nearly 50 years is a testimony to the power of his ideas and the clarity and scope of his vision.

O'Tuel, F. S., & Bullard, R. K. (1993). *Developing higher order thinking in the content areas K–12*. Pacific Grove, CA: Critical Thinking Press and Software.

Paul, R., & Elder, L. (2001). *Critical thinking: Tools for taking charge of your learning and your life*. New York: Prentice-Hall.

Provides a holistic theme, approaching critical thinking as a process of taking responsibility for one's thinking.

Paul, R., et al. Critical thinking handbook series. Rohnert Park, CA: Foundation for Critical Thinking, Sonoma State University.

Paul, R., Binker, A. J. A., & Weil, D. (1995). *Critical thinking handbook: K–3rd grades. A guide for remodeling lesson plans in language arts, social studies, and science.*

Paul, R., Binker, A. J. A., Jensen, K., & Kreklau, H. (1990). *Critical thinking handbook: 4–6th grades. A guide for remodeling lesson plans in language arts, social studies, and science.*

Paul, R., Binker, A. J. A., Martin, D., Vetrano, C., & Kreklau, H. (1995). *Critical thinking handbook: 6–9th grades. A guide for remodeling lesson plans in language arts, social studies, and science.*

Paul, R., Martin, D., & Adamson, K. (1989). *Critical thinking handbook: High school. A guide for redesigning instruction.*

The four grade-level handbooks in this series can be used either as the basis for critical thinking staff development, or as an independent resource for teachers. Starting from standard lessons and standard practice, the teacher sees, in case after case, what the weaknesses are in standard lessons and how they can be remedied. A book from this series is an essential resource for any teacher serious about fostering the critical thinking of students.

Paul, R., & Elder, L. (2000). *Critical thinking handbook: Basic theory and instructional structure.* Rohnert Park, CA: Foundation for Critical Thinking.

This book, used in professional development workshops, provides an outline of the most fundamental theory of critical thinking and suggests ideas for incorporating the theory into the structure of the curriculum.

Paul, R., Elder, L., Bartell, T. (1997). *California teacher preparation for instruction in critical thinking.* Rohnert Park, CA: Foundation for Critical Thinking.

Research report on the extent to which college faculty teach for critical thinking and the extent to which prospective teachers are prepared to teach critical thinking.

Perkins, D. N. (1981). *The mind's best work.* Cambridge, MA: Harvard University Press.

Still a great book, although we've learned a little more in the last 20 years.

Perkins, D. N. (1986). *Knowledge as design: Critical and creative thinking for teachers and learners.* Hillsdale, NJ: Erlbaum.

Perkins, D. N. (1995). *Outsmarting IQ: The emerging science of learnable intelligence.* New York: The Free Press.

Perkins postulates a theory of a "learnable intelligence" influenced by the experiences of the learner.

Perry, T., & Delpit, L. (1998). *The real ebonics debate: Power, language, and the education of African-American children.* New York: The Beacon Press.

Piaget, J. (1970). Piaget's theory. In P. Mussen (Ed.), *Carmichael's manual of child psychology.* New York: Wiley.

The "Father of Constructivism," Piaget develops his theory of developmental learning, explaining how the "mind makes meaning" of an experience.

Polya, G. (1957). *How to solve it* (2nd ed.). Princeton, NJ: Princeton University Press.

Raiffa, H. (1982). *The art and science of negotiation.* Cambridge, MA: Harvard University Press.

Resnick, L. B., & Klopfer, L. E. (Eds.). (1989). *Toward the thinking curriculum: Current cognitive research (1989 Yearbook).* Alexandria, VA: Association for Supervision and Curriculum Development.

Rothenberg, A., & Hausman, C. R. (Eds.). (1976). *The creativity question.* Durham, NC: Duke University Press.

This collection addresses philosophical, historical, and psychological perspectives on the nature and nurture of creativity.

Senge, P., Kleiner, A., Roberts, C., Ross, R. B., & Smith, B. J. (1994). *The fifth discipline fieldbook: Strategies and tools for building the learning organization.* New York: Currency Doubleday.

A practical handbook for those interested in broad coverage of thinking about organizational learning.

Siegler, R. S. (1998). *Children's thinking.* Englewood Cliffs, NJ: Prentice-Hall.

Singer, P. (1982). *The expanding circle: Ethics and sociobiology.* New York: Farrar, Strauss, & Giroux.

An excellent introduction to thinking about moral questions, and the role of thinking in shaping morality. For more on moral questions, see next entry and also *Moral Thinking: Its levels, method and point* by R. M. Hare, above.

Singer, P. (1993). *Practical ethics* (2nd ed.). Cambridge: Cambridge University Press.

A highly readable introduction to moral argument, from a utilitarian perspective.

Sternberg, R. J., & Grigorenko, E. L. (2000). *Teaching for successful intelligence*. Arlington Heights, IL: SkyLight.

Sternberg, R. J., & Spear-Swerling, L. (1996). *Teaching for thinking*. Washington, DC: American Psychological Association.

Swartz, R., & Parks, S. (1994). *Infusing the teaching of critical and creative thinking into content instruction: A lesson design handbook for the elementary grades*. Pacific Grove, CA: Critical Thinking Press & Software.

Swartz, R., & Perkins, D. (1989). *Teaching thinking: Issues and approaches*. Pacific Grove, CA: Midwest Publications.

Sylwester, R. (1995). *Celebration of neurons: An educator's guide to the human brain*. Alexandria VA: Association for Supervision and Curriculum Development.

Comprehensive, user-friendly book for educators by a biology teacher/education professor who brings it all together in metaphorical language that is easy to understand.

Taylor, C. W., & Barron, F. (Eds.). (1963). *Scientific creativity: Its recognition and development*. New York: Wiley.

For more than two decades, Calvin Taylor was instrumental in bringing together scholars from many disciplines to explore and analyze the construct of creativity and its implications for research on creativity in individuals and in organizations. Through a series of invitational working meetings on creativity, known generally as "the Utah conferences," Taylor created an international forum for research and development. This book is representative of the proceedings from those conferences.

Taylor, I. A., & Getzels, J. W. (1975). *Perspectives in creativity*. Chicago: Aldine.

An edited collection of essays and summaries of major views on research and development in creativity. Covers many historical models, programs, and projects. Emphasizes synthesis of approaches and points of view.

Torrance, E. P., & Myers, R. (1970). *Creative learning and teaching*. New York: Harper & Row.

This book extended Torrance's initial ideas and described a variety of practical ways to incorporate creative thinking into teaching and learning experiences. Torrance's ideas continue to influence both research and practice on creativity in education.

Vygotsky, L. S. (1978). *Mind in society: The development of higher psychological process*. Cambridge, MA: Harvard University Press.

An explanation of the critical role of social interaction and its impact on cognitive learning. This thesis states that one learns first in the social setting and then that learning is internalized in a personal understanding.

Wasley, P. A., Hampel, R. L., & Clark, R. W. (1997). *Kids and school reform*. San Francisco: Jossey-Bass.

This book spotlights students in transforming high schools across the country. It asks what differences there are for students when adults undertake changes from new instructional methods to block schedules to new assessments. The book is unique in using the actual voices and experiences of six students (of the 150 students studied) of varied backgrounds as well as offering a set of connections that seem critical to making genuine differences in kids' performance.

Wertheimer, M. (1945/1959). *Productive thinking* (rev. ed.). New York: Harper & Row.

Although Wertheimer's theory is obscure, his examples are wonderful.

Whimbey, A., & Lochhead, J. (1999). *Problem solving and comprehension* (6th ed.). Mahwah, NJ: Lawrence Erlbaum.

Whimbey, A., & Whimbey, L. S. (1975). *Intelligence can be taught*. New York: Lawrence Erlbaum.

Debunking the theory of a genetically inherited intelligence, Whimbey makes the case that intelligence is a learned skill and can be improved through instruction.

Wiggins, G., & McTighe, J. (1998). *Understanding by Design*. Alexandria, VA: Association for Supervision and Curriculum Development.

A framework for curriculum and assessment design that focuses on developing and deepening student understanding of the key ideas in content standards.

Williamson, J. L. (1991). *The Greensboro Plan: Infusing reasoning and writing into the K–12 curriculum*. Rohnert Park, CA: Foundation for Critical Thinking.

A national model for school staff development in critical thinking.

About the Authors

Elliott Asp has been a classroom teacher in both traditional and alternative settings, curriculum developer, university professor, and an administrator at the building and district level. He has contributed to books, edited volumes, and research and professional journals on a wide variety of subjects. He has consulted with school districts and educational agencies in a number of states on standards-based education and assessment design and has made numerous presentations to state and national audiences. Asp has served on the national advisory board for the Biological Sciences Curriculum Study's Middle Level Science Project. He has served as an advisor with the New Standards Project and was one of the original members of the ASCD National Assessment Consortium. In addition, he contributed to the ASCD video series on performance assessment and standards-based education and assisted in the development of legislation establishing standards-based education in Colorado. He has served on a variety of state advisory boards and is currently on the Advisory Council for Colorado Reads and the Commissioner of Education's Assessment Management Team, appointed by the Governor and the Commissioner of Education.

Asp was formerly Curriculum and Assessment Specialist with Littleton Public Schools in Littleton, Colorado. He has also served as the Director of the Colorado Assessment Consortium, a group of districts from across the state working together to improve instruction and student achievement through better assessment. He is currently Assistant Superintendent for Research and Assessment for Douglas County Schools, Colorado. He continues to consult with schools, districts and states on assessment and instructional issues. His professional interests include the relationship between curriculum, assessment, and instruction in promoting student achievement and data-based decision making at the classroom, school, and district levels.

John Barell is former Director of the Teaching Thinking Network of the Association for Supervision and Curriculum Development. He also served as Professor of Curriculum and Teaching and Adjunct Professor of Literature at Montclair State University. Currently he is a consultant to the American Museum of Natural History in New York City. His primary interest is in fostering inquiry within learning communities and within problem-based learning experiences. He may be reached at 444 E. 82 St., Apt. 10A, New York, NY 10028; e-mail: jbarell@nyc.rr.com.

Jonathan Baron is Professor of Psychology at the University of Pennsylvania, where he has been since 1974. He is the author of *Rationality and Intelligence, Judgment Misguided*, and the textbook *Thinking and Deciding*, as well as other books and articles. His research concerns the heuristics and biases that impair judgments and decisions, particularly those about matters of public policy, where impaired judgments often lead to undesired outcomes. His e-mail address is baron@psych.upenn.edu, and his Web page is http://www.sas.upenn.edu/~jbaron.

Sheldon Berman is the Superintendent of the Hudson Public Schools in Massachusetts. Prior to coming to Hudson he was a founder and President of Educators for Social Responsibility. He is the author of *Children's Social Consciousness* and coeditor of *Promising Practices in Teaching Social Responsibility*, as well as the author of numerous articles on systemic change, thinking skills, community service learning, and the development of social responsibility. He can be reached at Hudson Public Schools, 155 Apsley St., Hudson, MA 01749. E-mail: shelley@concord.org.

Barry K. Beyer is Professor Emeritus in the Graduate School of Education of George Mason University in Fairfax, Virginia. He received his master's degree in history and education from Syracuse University in 1954 and his doctorate in history from the University of Rochester in 1962. His professional career included 37 years of public school and university teaching, research, and administration.

During his career, Beyer has served as a consultant and staff developer in more than 120 school systems, colleges and universities, and state education agencies throughout the United States and Canada and conducted numerous national clinics and institutes for ASCD, National Council for the Social Studies, the National Association of Secondary School Principals, and other major professional and governmental organizations. As a specialist in the teaching of thinking and writing and in history and social studies teaching, Beyer has authored more than 100 articles and monographs in professional journals such as *Educational Leadership*, *Phi Delta Kappan*, and *Social Education*. His eight major books include *Inquiry in the Social Studies Classroom*, *Teaching Thinking in Social Studies*, *Practical Strategies for the Teaching of Thinking*, and, most recently, *Improving Student Thinking*. He is also a coauthor of the nation's leading elementary school social studies programs, *The World Around Us*, and its successor, *Adventures in Time and Place*.

Beyer and his wife, Judy, reside in Fairfax, Virginia, where he continues his writing, research, consulting, and staff development activities. He may be reached by phone at 703-239-0178, or via e-mail at bkbeyer@erols.com.

Cathy Collins Block, an author of the *Stanford Early School Achievement Test* and Professor of Education at Texas Christian University, received her doctorate in Curriculum and Instruction from the University of Wisconsin–Madison. She was a Research Assistant at the Wisconsin Research and Development Center for Cognitive Development, served as Chairperson of the National Commission to Infuse Thinking Development into the Curriculum from 1991 to 1992, and was a Visiting Professor at The University of Notre Dame.

Block has written more than 50 articles and several books. She is the author of *Teaching the Language Arts* (3rd ed.), and *Literacy Difficulties: Diagnosis and Instruction*, which are widely read by preservice and practicing teachers. In addition to being a frequent consultant to school districts in the United States and Canada, Block also served on the EduQuest Board of Directors for IBM and along with John Mangieri coauthored the *Educational Planning Document* for the Walt Disney Corp. In 1998, she was the recipient of the prestigious Paul A. Witty Award for Meritorious Service from the International Reading Association. Block can be reached at Texas Christian University School of Education, 2800 S. University Dr., Fort Worth, TX 76129; phone: 817-257-6789; e-mail: c.block@tcu.edu.

Ron Brandt is currently Senior Research Associate to the National Study of School Evaluation, Schaumburg, Illinois. He is also a member of the board of directors of Mid-conti-

nent Research for Education and Learning. Brandt is the former Executive Editor of *Educational Leadership* and other publications at ASCD. He is the author of *Powerful Learning*, and editor of *Assessing Student Learning* and *Education in a New Era*. His articles have appeared recently in *Phi Delta Kappan*, *Education Week*, *Educational Leadership*, *Principal* magazine, and *Leadership News* of the American Association of School Administrators.

In 1996, he was named to the EdPress Hall of Fame for his contributions to education publishing. In 1997, he was honored by the National Staff Development Council for lifetime contributions to staff development for educators. Brandt taught at a teacher training college in Nigeria, West Africa, in the 1960s as part of a University of Wisconsin project. He has been a junior high school principal, staff member of the Upper Midwest Regional Educational Laboratory, director of staff development for the Minneapolis public schools, and associate superintendent in Lincoln, Nebraska. He has a master's degree from Northwestern University and a doctorate in educational administration from the University of Minnesota. He may be contacted at 1104 Woodcliff Drive, Alexandria, VA 22308-1058. Phone: 703-765-4779. Fax: 703-765-8038. E-mail: ronbrandt@erols.com.

Douglas F. Brenner is Associate Professor of Speech Communication, Department of Speech Communication, University of South Dakota. His interests include critical thinking, rhetorical criticism, technology in instruction, building learning communities, multicultural education, and the wisdom of indigenous peoples, especially Native Americans. Brenner has a doctorate in speech communication. He is working toward a master's degree in educational media and computers at Arizona State University. He may be reached at 414 E. Clark St. Vermillion, SD 57069; phone: 605-677-6208; fax: 605-677-8876; e-mail: dbrenner@usd.edu.

Jacqueline Grennon Brooks is Director of the Science Education Program at the State University of New York at Stony Brook, a program that prepares secondary science teachers and conducts research into constructivist pedagogy. She holds a doctor of education degree from the Department of Curriculum and Teaching at Teachers College, Columbia University. Formerly a middle school teacher and coordinator of gifted and talented programs, she is a past president of the Association of Constructivist Teaching.

Martin G. Brooks is Superintendent of the Plainview-Old Bethpage School District on Long Island, New York.

Previously, Brooks has been a superintendent of other districts, deputy superintendent, school principal, guidance counselor, and teacher. He holds a doctor of education degree from the Department of Educational Administration at Teachers College, Columbia University. He is the founder of ASCD's Network on Understanding Educational Change, an executive board member of Long Island ASCD and the Metropolitan School Study Council, and past president of the Nassau County Council of School Superintendents. His primary interests are constructivism, curriculum development, and social change.

Kay Burke is the Senior Vice President of Academics of Sky-Light Professional Development, part of Pearson Education. She has presented training and keynote speeches on positive discipline, professional portfolios, students portfolios, and performance assessment throughout the United States, Canada, and Australia. Burke is the author of *What to Do with the Kid Who: Developing Cooperation, Self-Discipline, and Responsibility in the Classroom* (2nd ed.); *How to Assess Authentic Learning* (3rd ed.); *Designing Professional Portfolios for Change*, and co-author of *The Portfolio Connection*.

Jessica Butler recently graduated from Ottawa University with a bachelor's degree in psychology. She aspires to move on to Arizona State University to attend its doctoral program in clinical psychology. Butler's future goal is to become a child psychologist. Before attending Ottawa, she obtained an associate of arts degree in Interpreter Training for the Deaf at Phoenix College. She can communicate in sign language and plans to incorporate this knowledge into her future practice.

Geoffrey Caine is a learning and education consultant with a background in law and management. **Renate Nummela Caine** is a Professor Emeritus of education at California State University, San Bernardino, and was an award winning teacher. The Caines are coauthors of *Making Connections: Teaching and the Human Brain*; *Education on the Edge of Possibility*; *Unleashing the Power of Perceptual Change: The Promise of Brain Based Learning*; and, with Sam Crowell, of *Mindshifts*, and *The ReEnchantment of Learning*. The Caines work nationally and internationally with schools, districts, other educational organizations, and businesses. They are co-directors of Caine Learning LLC and may be reached at 909-659-0152 or at www.cainelearning.com (e-mail: info@cainelearning.com).

Linda Chapman is Director of Technology & Libraries, Somers Central School District, Somers, New York. She may be reached via e-mail at Linda_Chapman@somers.k12.ny.us.

Burton Cohen has been an educator, consultant, and organizational analyst for 32 years. He has served as classroom teacher, building administrator, and district office administrator. His major areas of focus have included curriculum and instruction, professional development, and effective planning and implementation systems. Working internationally in Europe and Latin America, he has provided leadership in helping teachers and administrators effect changes in professional practice and implement interdisciplinary and thematically based learning experiences. He is currently the Director of Secondary Education in the Palo Alto Unified School District in Palo Alto, California.

Marcy Cook, master educator, author, and staff development specialist for mathematics, has presented workshops for teachers throughout North America. Having taught in the International School in Thessaloniki, Greece, she also has provided math in-service training for International Schools in Africa, Asia, Europe, and South America. With a bachelor of arts from the University of California, Santa Barbara, and a master's degree from Stanford University, she has taught all grades from elementary through university level. Her experiences with classroom teaching, gifted and talented education, and student teaching supervision have provided her with ideas galore to share with others. Author of more than 110 mini–math centers and 75 books, Marcy continually motivates teachers to make math a meaningful and exciting experience. She may be reached at P.O. Box 5840, Balboa Island, CA 92662-5840; phone: 949-673-5912; Web site: http:\\www.marcycookmath.com.

Arthur L. Costa is an Emeritus Professor of Education at California State University, Sacramento, and Co-Founder of the Institute for Intelligent Behavior in El Dorado Hills, California. He has served as a classroom teacher, a curriculum consultant, and an assistant superintendent for instruction, and as the director of educational programs for the National Aeronautics and Space Administration. He received his bachelor's and master's degrees from the University of Southern California and his doctorate of education from the University of California, Berkeley. He has made presentations and conducted workshops in all 50 states and throughout Canada, as well as

Africa, Asia, Australia, Central America, Europe, the Islands of the South Pacific, and South America.

Costa has written numerous books, including *Techniques for Teaching Thinking* (with Larry Lowery), *The School as a Home for the Mind*, and *Cognitive Coaching: A Foundation for Renaissance Schools* (with Robert Garmston). He is editor of *Developing Minds: a Resource Book for Teaching Thinking*, co-editor (with Rosemarie Liebmann) of the Process as Content Trilogy: *Envisioning Process as Content, Supporting the Spirit of Learning*, and *The Process Centered School*; and as coeditor (with Bena Kallick) of the four books in the Habits of Mind Series: *Exploring and Discovering Habits of Mind, Activating and Engaging Habits of Mind, Assessing and Reporting on Habits of Mind*, and *Integrating and Sustaining Habits of Mind*.

Active in many professional organizations, Costa has served as president of the California Association for Supervision and Curriculum Development and was the national President of the Association for Supervision and Curriculum Development from 1988 to 1989.

Dee Dickinson is Chief Executive Officer and founder of New Horizons for Learning, an international education network based in Seattle, Washington (the Web address is http://www.newhorizons.org). She has taught on all levels from elementary through university, has produced several series for educational television, and has created nine international conferences on education. She is an internationally recognized speaker, consultant, and author. Her publications include *Positive Trends in Learning* (commissioned by IBM), *Creating the Future*, and she is co-author, with Linda Campbell and Bruce Campbell, of *Teaching and Learning Through Multiple Intelligences*. She can be reached at 2128 38th Ave. E., Seattle, WA 98112, and by phone at 206-726-6169.

John Edwards is the Managing Director of Edwards Explorations, an Australian-based company concerned with exploring and developing human potential. He is also Adjunct Professor of Education at the University of Queensland in Brisbane, Australia. Edwards is internationally recognized for his research and consultancy work on organizational learning, knowledge generation, the direct teaching of thinking, and innovative management of change. This research has been translated into award-winning industrial practice. He has worked as a research metallurgist; a full-time author; a university professor; and a consultant and researcher in education, business, and industry. He has worked successfully for schools, governments, companies, and international agencies in more

than 20 countries. He may be reached by mail: Dr. John Edwards, P.O. Box 1934, Brisbane 4001, Queensland, Australia.

Elliot W. Eisner is Lee Jacks Professor of Education and Professor of Art at Stanford University. His major interests focus on arts education, curriculum studies, and qualitative research methodology. He has written 15 books in these areas, among them *The Educational Imagination, The Enlightened Eye*, and *The Kind of Schools We Need*, and has lectured throughout the world. He served as president of the American Educational Research Association, the International Society for Education Through Art, the National Art Education Association, and the John Dewey Society. Eisner can be reached at Stanford University, Stanford, CA 94305-3096.

Robert H. Ennis is a former high school science teacher who tried to incorporate critical thinking in his instruction. Ennis then became involved in the nature and assessment of critical thinking while working on a critical thinking research project during his doctoral study at the University of Illinois, leading to his doctoral dissertation, *The Development of a Critical Thinking Test*. After a 12-year period on the faculty of Cornell University as a philosopher of education, he joined the faculty of the University of Illinois in 1970 with a similar post. Although he retired in 1994, he continues to pursue his interests in the nature and assessment of critical thinking, philosophy of science, and the analysis of educational concepts.

Having published some 50 articles, most of which deal with critical thinking, and having been author, coauthor, or co-editor of six books (including a textbook, *Critical Thinking*) and three critical thinking tests, Ennis appreciates support from Cornell University, the U.S. Department of Education, the University of Illinois, and the Center for Advanced Study in the Behavioral Sciences. He is currently working on two critical thinking tests and two articles and a book in the area of critical thinking, and he continues to consult in the field.

His academic Web site at http://faculty.ed.uiuc.edu/rhennis/, provides further detail about his work. His e-mail address is rhennis@uiuc.edu.

Lex Fagen is a recent Ottawa University graduate. Originally from Des Moines, Iowa, Fagen attended high shool there and then went on to play college basketball with a full athletic scholarship in Iowa and Missouri, majoring in physical education and English. He was recruited by an agent from the European Basketball League to play professionally, and spent sixteen seasons playing in France, (Montpellier, Avignon, Reims,

Lourdes, Strasbourg, Marseille) from 1979 to 1995. He has been a dual national (French-American) since 1987. After retiring from basketball, he returned to the United States with his French wife in 1996 and is now a physical education and fitness instructor at Horizon Community Learning Center in Phoenix, Arizona. He may be reached at 1168 W. Elgin Street, Chandler, AZ 85224; phone/fax: 480-722-0104; e-mail: lexlyn@ aol.com.

Lee Winocur Field is a consultant and was President and Executive Director of the former Center for the Teaching of Thinking in Huntington, California. She has been an administrator in the Huntington Beach Union High School District, a principal, and a teacher, as well as a coordinator of innovative educational programs for the Orange County Department of Education. She received her doctorate from the U.S. International University, San Diego; her master's degree in education administration from California State University, Fullerton; and her bachelor's degree from University of California, Berkeley.

Stephen David Fischer received his bachelor's degree in biology from the University of California at San Diego and his master's in teaching science from Rowan University in Glassboro, New Jersey. Currently he is completing doctoral studies in computer technology in education. Fischer is presently District Supervisor, Science and Technology, for the Pinelands Regional School District, Tuckerton, New Jersey. He is a staff-development consultant in the United States and abroad on the topic of infusing the teaching of critical and creative thinking into science through the National Center for Teaching Thinking at 815 Washington Street, Suite 8, Newtonville, MA 02460. He is coauthor of the lesson design handbook, *Infusing the Teaching of Critical and Creative Thinking into Secondary Science*. He may be reached via e-mail at stephendf@msn.com.

Alec Fisher is Director of the Centre for Research in Critical Thinking at the University of East Anglia, Norwich. He has also worked for many years for the University of Cambridge Examinations Board, for whom he recently designed a new national critical thinking exam for 17-year-olds. He conducts workshops for schools and other educational institutions on teaching critical thinking and on assessing critical thinking—especially for teachers in higher education. He has provided this kind of training in Britain, Canada, Germany, Holland, Russia, Singapore, South Africa, and the United States. During 1992–93 he was Assistant Director of the Center for Critical Thinking at Sonoma State University, California. His books include *The Logic of Real Arguments*; and, coauthored with Michael Scriven, *Critical Thinking: Its Definition and Assessment*. He has organized three British conferences on critical thinking and education and is currently organizing—with Philip Adey of King's College London—the 10th International Conference on Thinking, to take place in the United Kingdom in June 2002. He may be reached at the Old Rectory, Church Rd., Booton, Norwich, NR10 4N2, and via e-mail at alec.fisher@uea.ac.uk.

Robin Fogarty is President of Fogarty and Associates, Ltd., an educational consulting company. Her doctorate is in curriculum and human resource development from Loyola University of Chicago. A leading proponent of the thoughtful classroom, Fogarty has trained educators throughout the world in cognitive strategies and cooperative interaction. She has taught at all levels, from kindergarten to college, served as an administrator, and consulted with state departments and ministries of education in Australia, Canada, the Netherlands, New Zealand, Puerto Rico, Russia, and the United States. Fogarty is the author, coauthor and editor of numerous publications, including *Brain-Compatible Classrooms*, *Problem-Based Learning and Other Curriculum Models for the Multiple Intelligences Classroom*, *How to Integrate the Curricula*, *The Portfolio Connection*, *Think About Multiage Classrooms*, and *Integrating Curricula with Multiple Intelligences: Teams, Themes, and Threads*.

Robert J. Garmston conducts presentations and workshops for educators, managers, and professionals in Africa, Asia, Canada, Europe, the Middle East, and throughout the United States. Professor Emeritus of Educational Administration at California State University, he is an educational consultant specializing in leadership, learning, and personal and organizational development. Formerly a classroom teacher, principal, director of instruction, and superintendent, Garmston is codeveloper of the Cognitive Coaching model and cofounder of the Institute for Intelligent Behavior with Arthur Costa. He is developer of the Adaptive School model with Bruce Wellman.

Garmston is the author of several books, including *Cognitive Coaching: A Foundation for Renaissance Schools* (with Arthur Costa), *The Adaptive School: A Sourcebook for Developing Collaborative Groups* (with Bruce Wellman) and *The Presenter's Fieldbook: A Practical Guide*. He served as president of the California Association for Supervision and Curriculum Development from 1989 to 1991 and as a member of ASCD's Executive Council at the international level from 1991 to 1994. He received the 1996 Learned Article of the Year award from the National Education Press Association and the 1999 Book of the Year award by the National Staff Development

Council. With his wife Sue, he was corecipient of the Helen Heffernan Memorial Award for distinguished service to California education. He currently is a reviewer for the *International Journal of Leadership in Education*.

Karen R. Harris is Professor of Special Education and Distinguished Scholar-Teacher, University of Maryland. Her research focuses on theoretical and intervention issues in the development of academic and self-regulation strategies among students who are at risk and those with severe learning challenges such as learning disabilities and attention deficit hyperactivity disorder. Author of more than 70 articles and 20 chapters, she contributes to the leading journals in special education, general education, and educational psychology. She is codirector of the federally funded Center for Accelerating Student Learning, in collaboration with Vanderbilt and Columbia Universities. She currently serves as Associate Editor of the *Journal of Educational Psychology*. She is coauthor or coeditor of five books and coeditor of the series Advances in Teaching and Learning. She can be reached at the Department of Special Education, University of Maryland, College Park, MD 20742.

LeRoy Hay is an educational futurist who concentrates his studies on reshaping U.S. schools for the information age. Currently he is the Assistant Superintendent for Instruction for the Wallingford Schools in Connecticut. He has also been an adjunct instructor at the University of Connecticut and Boston College and is a founding faculty member of an accredited online graduate program for Walden University. He was President of the Association for Supervision and Curriculum Development for 2000–01. In 1983 he was honored as the U.S. National Teacher of the Year. He may be contacted at 33 Risley Road, Vernon, CT 06066; e-mail:leehay@aol.com.

Peter Hilts is an educator and consultant from Wilmington, North Carolina. He holds a master of arts degree in teacher education and eagerly pursues practical applications for new learning theories. As a specialist in interdisciplinary design, instruction, and assessment, Hilts consults widely with schools who are redefining their structures and practices to support the learning brain. By specializing in creative integrations of brain theory, interdisciplinary methods, and educational technology, Hilts brings unique insight and enthusiasm to his work with clients and colleagues. In his role as Upper School Director at Cape Fear Academy, Hilts supports the teachers and students engaged in a rigorous college preparatory curriculum. Because he is active in the field and works with many schools, Hilts is able to draw on a wealth of examples, models, and techniques to help schools design optimal learning environments and experiences.

Cheryl Hopper is a former teacher of social studies at Paramus High School, Paramus, New Jersey. She is currently Assistant Director, Center of Pedagogy, Montclair State University, Upper Montclair, NJ 07043. Her priorities include creating authentic learning and assessment experiences for students. She may be reached via e-mail: hopperc@mail.montclair.edu.

David Hyerle is an independent author, consultant, and researcher focused on integrating content learning and thinking process instruction. Hyerle completed doctoral work at the University of California, Berkeley, and Harvard School of Education, where he refined a language of visual tools he created calling Thinking Maps, now being used in more than 2000 schools. He has written and produced a dozen resource guides, videos, and software based on Thinking Maps as tools for student-centered learning and whole-school and districtwide change. His second book on the general topic of visual tools, *A Field Guide to Using Visual Tools*, offers the reader both a theoretical and practical view of these essential tools for developing minds. He may be reached at 144 Goose Pond Road, Lyme, NH 03768, 603-795-2757; or through his Web site at http://www.mapthemind.com.

Scott G. Isaksen is President of the Creative Problem Solving Group–Buffalo, and Senior Fellow of its Creativity Research Unit. He has previously served as Professor and Director of the Center for Studies in Creativity at Buffalo State College, and has published more than 120 books, chapters, and articles in a variety of professional journals. He has been a consultant or trainer for more than 200 organizations in 18 countries. Isaksen serves on the advisory boards of the National Invention Center and the American Creativity Association. Since 1983, he has been a consulting editor for the *Journal of Creative Behavior*. He can be reached at the Creative Problem Solving Group–Buffalo, 1325 N. Forest Road, Suite 340, Williamsville, NY 14221-21423; phone: 716-689-2176; fax: 716-689-6441; e-mail: cpsb@cpsb.com; Web site: www.cpsb.com.

Thomas E. Jackson is a member of the University of Hawaii Philosophy Department and Director of the Philosophy in the Schools Project. He received his doctorate in Comparative Philosophy from the University of Hawaii at Manoa. He regularly works in public school classrooms with teachers and their students. In addition to work in Hawaii, he has conducted workshops in Australia, Brazil, Singapore, and most recently

Nanjing, Beijing, and Jiaozuo, China, with teachers eager to learn how to facilitate gently Socratic inquiries with children. He may be reached at the University of Hawaii, Dept. of Philosophy, 2530 Dole St., Honolulu, HI 96822; e-mail: tjackson@hawaii.edu; phone: 808-956-7287.

Yvette Jackson is internationally recognized for her work in assessing the learning potential of disenfranchised urban students. She has applied her research in literacy, gifted education, and the cognitive meditation theory of Reuven Feuerstein to develop instructional processes that translate assessment information into practices that enable students to reach and extend their potential.

While serving as the New York City Board of Education's Executive Director of Instruction and Professional Development, she created New York City's Gifted Programs Framework as well as its Comprehensive Educational Plan, which optimizes the coordinated delivery of all core curriculum and support services.

Jackson currently serves as the Co-Executive Director of the National Urban Alliance, founded at the College Board and Teachers College, Columbia University. She works with school district administrators and teachers across the United States to customize and deliver systemic approaches to literacy development through instructional practices that integrate culture, language, and cognition.

Jackson received a bachelor of arts degree from Queens College of the City University of New York with a double major in education and French. At Columbia University's Teachers College she was awarded a master's degree in curriculum, a master of education degree in educational administration, and a doctorate in educational administration. She has been called upon to testify before the U.S. Congress and is on the board of Dr. Feuerstein's International Center for the Enhancement of Learning Potential in Jerusalem.

David W. Johnson is a Professor of Educational Psychology at the University of Minnesota and Co-Director of the Cooperative Learning Center. He held the Emma M. Birkmaier Professorship in Educational Leadership at the University of Minnesota from 1994 to 1997. He received his doctoral degree from Columbia University. He has published more than 400 research articles and book chapters, and is the author of more than 40 books. He is a former Editor of the *American Educational Research Journal*. Johnson is the recipient of awards for outstanding research and teaching from numerous professional organizations. He has served as an organizational consultant to schools and businesses throughout the world, and is

a practicing psychotherapist. He may be reached at 60 Peik Hall, University of Minnesota, Minneapolis, MN 55435; phone: 612-624-7031; fax: 612-626-1395.

Roger T. Johnson is a Professor of Education at the University of Minnesota and is Co-Director of the Cooperative Learning Center. He holds his doctoral degree from the University of California at Berkeley. In 1965, Johnson received an award for outstanding teaching from the Jefferson County Schools, and has since been honored with several national awards. He taught in the Harvard-Newton Intern Program as a Master Teacher. He was a curriculum developer with the Elementary Science Study in the Educational Department at Harvard University. For three summers he taught classes in the British Primary Schools at the University of Sussex near Brighton, England. He has consulted with schools throughout the world. Johnson is the author of numerous research articles, book chapters, and books.

Bena Kallick is a private consultant providing services to school districts, state departments of education, professional organizations and public sector agencies throughout the United States. Her areas of focus include group dynamics, creative and critical thinking, and alternative assessment strategies in the classroom. Her written work includes "Literature to Think About" (a whole language curriculum); *Changing Schools into Communities for Thinking; Assessment in the Learning Organization*, coauthored with Arthur Costa; coeditor with Arthur Costa of the Habits of Mind Series: *Exploring and Discovering Habits of Mind, Activating and Engaging Habits of Mind, Assessing and Reporting on Habits of Mind*, and *Integrating and Sustaining Habits of Mind*. She is cofounder of TECHPATHS, a software company designed to facilitate teachers' networks and communications about performance assessment. Kallick received her doctorate in educational evaluation with Union Graduate School. Her teaching appointments have included Yale University School of Organization and Management, University of Massachusetts Center for Creative and Critical Thinking, and Union Graduate School. She was on the boards of JOBS for the Future and the Apple Foundation. She may be reached via e-mail: bkallick@aol.com.

Sherry P. King has been the Superintendent of the Mamaroneck Union Free School District since February 1996. Prior to that she was the superintendent of the Croton-Harmon Schools, a high school principal, assistant principal, and teacher of English.

King received her doctorate in educational administration from Columbia University in 1984. She was a senior researcher for *Small Schools: Great Strides, A Study of New Small Schools in Chicago*, which was funded by the Joyce Foundation and published by Bank Street College of Education. She is also a trustee on the board of directors for Jobs for the Future. Among her publications are "Leadership in the 21st Century: Using Feedback to Maintain Focus and Direction" in *Preparing Our Schools for the 21st Century* (1999 ASCD Yearbook), and "Portfolios, Students' Work, and Teachers' Practice: An Elementary School Redefines Assessment" in *Assessing Student Learning: From Grading to Understanding*, edited by David Allen and just published in Spanish. She can be reached via e-mail at sking@mamkschools.org.

Daniel M. Landers is a Regents' Professor in the Department of Exercise Science and Physical Education at Arizona State University. He has served as President of three national-level U.S. sport and exercise psychology societies, and in 1995 he received the Distinguised Scholar Award for one of these societies. He has also served on committees of the National Academy of Science, the U.S. Olympic Committee, and more recently the International Olympic Committee. In the role of exercise and sport psychology, he has presented more than 300 papers, written over 115 journal articles, and contributed to or written 29 books. He may be reached at Box 870404 PEBE 112, Arizona State University, Tempe, AZ 85287-0404; phone: 480-965-7664; fax: 480-965-8108; e-mail: Landers@asu.edu.

David G. Lazear has had many years of international experience in the development of human capacities in both the public and private sectors. He and his family lived for extended periods of time in Africa, India, Italy, and Korea, providing training and leadership in implementing human development projects in rural village situations. He has also conducted professional development institutes and training programs for educators in some 15 other countries.

Lazear's expertise is in translating current brain research, research from the cognitive sciences, and cutting-edge educational research into practical classroom and school applications. He is the founder of his own company, called New Dimensions of Learning. New Dimensions specializes in staff development programs that demonstrate the how-to's of applying contemporary brain research and the theory of multiple intelligences. The programs of New Dimensions share numerous teaching and learning techniques, strategies, methods, exercises, and model lessons for developing a multiple intelligence approach to the task of today's education.

Lazear has authored seven books dealing with the practical application and implementation of the theory of multiple intelligences in the local school and classroom. He has appeared on a number of TV programs and has been a featured presenter on several videotapes that promote a wider understanding of the importance of multiple intelligences in the renewal and restructuring of our current educational systems.

Lazear can be reached at New Dimensions of Learning, 729 W. Waveland, Suite G, Chicago, IL 60613; phone: 800-726-8605; fax: 810-461-6364; e-mail: laserbeem@worldnet.att.net.

Marian Leibowitz is currently an educational consultant providing a variety of services to school districts, state departments of education, professional organizations, and agencies throughout the United States and abroad. She has traveled around the United States giving seminars for groups such as the Association for Supervision and Curriculum Development (ASCD) and I/D/E/A, and has built a wide diversity of professional experiences. Leibowitz's major areas of focus are in school renewal—leadership, change, instructional design, curriculum, and assessment. Much of her work is currently focusing on secondary school reform.

Leibowitz brings a variety of both teaching and administrative experience to her role, having been an Assistant Superintendent in Teaneck, New Jersey. She was a site visitor for the U.S. Office of Education Secondary School Recognition Program and works extensively in staff development and program evaluation at the secondary level. She is currently working with a number of school districts in aspects of change with major long-term projects in Albuquerque, New Mexico; Loudoun County, Virginia; New Rochelle, New York; San Antonio, Texas; and Stamford, Connecticut. Her writings include "Instruction for Process Learning" as well as numerous audio and video professional development programs produced for ASCD, Video Journal, and Canter and Associates. She may be reached at 283 Glenn Avenue, Lawrenceville, NJ 08648; phone: 609-882-5051.

Myra J. Linden is Professor Emeritus of English at Joliet Junior College. She is a member of the National Council of Teachers of English and a lifetime member of the College English Association. Having spent more than 35 years teaching English and speech at the high school and college levels, she is the co-author of *Why Johnny Can't Write: How to Improve Writing Skills; Analytical Writing and Thinking: Facing the Tests;* and *Keys to Quick Writing Skills.* Her e-mail address is mlinden@uswest.net.

Laura Lipton is codirector, along with Bruce Wellman, of MiraVia, LLC, a training and development firm dedicated to creating and sustaining learning-focused educational environments. Their publications, workshops, and seminars aim to provide effective strategies, practical resources, and innovative ideas for thoughtful educators grappling with critical professional issues.

Lipton brings a rich background of experience as a teacher, staff developer, and curriculum and instructional specialist to her work as a systems change agent. She has authored or co-authored numerous publications related to organizational and professional development, learning-focused schools, and classrooms and group development. In addition to collaborating with Wellman on *Pathways to Understanding: Patterns and Practices for the Learning-Focused Classroom* and *Shifting Rules, Shifting Roles: Transforming the Work Environment to Support Learning* (with Arthur Costa), she and Wellman have recently completed, *Mentoring Matters: A Practical Guide to Learning-Focused Relationships*. She can be contacted at 3 Lost Acre Trail, Sherman, CT 06784; phone: 860-354-4543; fax: 860-354-6740; e-mail: pthwytound@aol.com.

Jack Lochhead has been an active innovator, developer, and researcher in the field of Cognitive Process Instruction for more than 20 years. While at the University of Massachusetts, 1975 to 1990, he established new programs in both research and teaching including the Basic Math Program and the Scientific Reasoning Research Institute. He is the Founding Director of DeLiberate Thinking, a company dedicated to helping schools, public agencies, and private business develop instructional programs in the basic cognitive skills required for success in mathematics, science, and technology. His most recent book is *Thinkback: A User's Guide to Minding the Mind*. He can be reached at DeLiberate Thinking, P. O. Box 539, Conway, MA 01341; e-mail: deliberate@mindspring.com.

Ruth M. Loring is a freelance education consultant who specializes in designing professional development in teaching and learning for teachers in all content areas. With 30 years of experience as an educator and a doctorate in reading, she focuses on how people learn both in school and throughout life. Loring conducts workshops and coaches teachers in the process of incorporating principles of reflective teaching, skillful thinking, and authentic assessment within instructional practice. She undertakes schoolwide reform initiatives by presenting at national and regional conferences, consulting at the district level, and leading a national standards-based project that connects school to the workplace while integrating academic and technical education. She may be

contacted at Loring & Associates: Professional Development in Teaching and Learning, 2925 North 15-A Street, Waco, TX 76708; phone: 254-752-7244; fax: 254-752-8208; e-mail: ruth@learningbyloring.com or ruthloring@mindspring.com.

Lawrence F. Lowery is a Professor Emeritus at the University of California at Berkeley. He is affiliated with the Graduate School of Education and the Lawrence Hall of Science there. He remains active as the Principle Investigator for the Full Option Science System (FOSS), a research-based, field-tested science curriculum for grades K–8 that was developed at the Lawrence Hall of Science. He continues to publish and edit articles and books, the most recent being *The Kingfisher Science Encyclopaedia, Pathways—Guidelines to Implementing the Science Standards*, and "How Science Curriculums Reflect Brain Research" in the November 1998 issue of *Phi Delta Kappan*. He may be reached at Lawrence Hall of Science, University of California, Berkeley, CA 94720; e-mail: llarry@sirius.com.

Deborah L. Lowther is currently Associate Professor of Instructional Design and Technology at the University of Memphis. Her research is centered on school restructuring and factors influencing the integration of technology into various learning environments. She received her doctorate in educational technology from Arizona State University in 1994.

Lowther has coauthored *Integrating Computer Technology into the Classroom*, a textbook with Gary Morrison, and several book chapters and refereed journal articles. Her involvement also includes numerous presentations at international and national educational conventions, co-guest editing a national journal's special edition on technology in K–12 schools, working with multiple grants focused toward technology integration, and providing professional development to K–12 schools across the country. She may be reached at Instructional Design and Technology, University of Memphis, COE: 419 Ball Hall, Memphis, TN 38152; e-mail: dlowther@memphis.edu.

Armando Lozano is a master in education and doctoral student at Virtual University of the Monterrey Institute of Technology (ITESM) in México. He has designed several workshops in microteaching, learning strategies, and learning styles in the continuing education program at ITESM. Currently he is in charge of the area of cognition and instruction, one of the majors in the master of education program at ITESM that is offered in a distance education modality. He may be reached via mail: Avenida Eugenio Garza Sada 2501 Sur, Edificio CEDES Sotano 1, Col. Tecnologico, Monterrey, N.L., C.P. 64849 México; or e-mail: alozano@campus.ruv.itesm.mx.

Frank T. Lyman Jr., formerly an elementary teacher and field-based teacher educator, is an educational consultant, college instructor, and writer. He has invented, coinvented, and co-developed teaching and learning strategies to benefit children, teachers, and teacher educators. Some of these are Think-Pair-Share, Thinktrix, and Thinklinks for cognitive mapping. His focus in teacher education has been on accelerating the development of teachers from novice to expert through their use of reflective tools, such as the B Wheel and the Principle-based Teaching/Coaching Wheels. Lyman is a graduate of Haverford College, and received a master's in education from Harvard University and a doctorate from the University of Maryland. He may be reached at 5418 Killingworth Way, Columbia, MD 21044; e-mail: Lymanlink@aol.com.

Joanne Marien is Assistant Superintendent for Curriculum, Instruction, and Staff Development, Somers Central School District, Somers, New York. She may be reached via e-mail at Joanne_Marien@somers.k12.ny.

David S. Martin is on the faculty of the Education Department at Gallaudet University in Washington, D.C. Martin has done extensive work in the area of cognitive education as a trainer of experienced teachers, as a teacher of teachers in the university, and in writing professionally about research. He has previously been a teacher, a principal, a curriculum developer, a director of curriculum and instruction, and Dean of Education at Gallaudet. He has also contributed to the literature in the field of social studies education and teacher education. He serves as Co-Chair (with Nicholas Michelli of Montclair State University) of the Special Study Group on the Infusion of Critical Thinking into Teacher Education, within the American Association of Colleges for Teacher Education.

William C. Martin has used teaching for, of, and about thinking to become a public school change agent in Texas and Michigan. As a school principal, he has used the learning from personal mentors Art Costa, Robert Swartz, and John Edwards to create positive learning environments for adults and children. Martin has earned national recognition as a National Blue Ribbon School principal, a National Principal of the Year finalist, and Principal of Leadership. He has designed and presented workshops as a consultant for individual schools and a presenter at local, state, and national conferences for organizations that include the Association for Supervision and Curriculum Development and National Association of Secondary School Principals. He has been a presenter at the Annual Conference on Critical Thinking and Educational Reform, as well

as at both the Eighth and Ninth International Conferences on Thinking. Martin is the founder of the Continual Learning Coalition. He can be reached at P. O. Box 1070, Monroe, MI 48161-6070; e-mail: martinb@monroe.k12.mi.us.

Robert J. Marzano is a former Senior Fellow at Mid-continent Research for Education and Learning, responsible for translating research and theory into classroom practice. He has published a number of books, articles, and chapters in books on such topics as reading and writing instruction, thinking skills, school effectiveness, classroom assessment, and standards implementation. He can be reached via e-mail at robertjmarzano@aol.com.

William Maxwell is a Professor of Education and Educational Psychology at Ottawa University–Phoenix. He earned his bachelor's degree in science education at Oregon State University, and his master's and doctorate degrees at Harvard University. He has taught in Fiji, Korea, and Nigeria. He also has served as a dean of schools of education at The Advanced Teacher Training College, Port Harcourt, Nigeria; California State University, Fresno; North Carolina State University; and The University of The South Pacific, Suva, Fiji. He edited the book *Thinking: The Expanding Frontier.* Maxwell also serves on the Board of the Arizona Sports Council and is helping to establish an international sports academy near Phoenix to train future Olympians from around the world, especially from the 111 nations that have never won an Olympic medal. He may be reached at 12212 Paradise Village Parkway, #12-335-C, Phoenix, AZ 85032; phone: 602-996-9927; e-mail: willgaia@ aol.com.

Jay McTighe served as Director of the Maryland Assessment Consortium, a state collaboration of school districts working together to develop and share performance assessments. He has published articles in a number of leading journals and books, including ASCD's *Educational Leadership* magazine, the revised edition of *Developing Minds, Thinking Skills: Concepts and Techniques,* and *The Developer.* He coauthored three recent books on assessment, and is coauthor, with Grant Wiggins, of the Understanding by Design series. McTighe has an extensive background in staff development and is a regular speaker at national, state, and district conferences and workshops. He may be reached at 6581 River Run, Columbia, MD 21044-6066; phone: 410-531-1610, fax: 410-531-1971, e-mail: jmctigh@aol.com.

Nicholas M. Michelli is University Dean for Teacher Education for the City University of New York and Professor of Urban

Education in the CUNY Graduate Center Ph.D. program in urban education. He is responsible for enhancing teacher education across the senior colleges of the CUNY system and collaborating with the New York City Public Schools. He previously served as Dean of the College of Education and Human Services at Montclair State University (NJ) and has advocated preparing future teachers for critical thinking throughout his career. He serves as Chair of the Governmental Relations Committee of the American Association of Colleges for Teacher Education, Chair of the Governing Council of the National Network for Educational Renewal, and, with David Martin, Co-Chair of the Special Study Group on the Infusion of Critical Thinking into Teacher Education within AACTE.

Gary R. Morrison is a Professor in the Instructional Technology program at the Wayne State University, Detroit. He received his doctorate in Instructional Systems Technology from Indiana University in 1977. Since then, he has worked as an instructional designer at the University of Mid-America and three Fortune 500 companies. Prior to his work at Wayne State University, he was a Professor at the University of Memphis.

Morrison has written more than 100 papers on topics related to instructional design and computer-based instruction. He is senior author of *Designing Effective Instruction* (3rd ed.) and *Integrating Computer Technology into the Classroom*. He may be reached at Wayne State University, 399 Education, Detroit, MI 48202; e-mail: gary_morrison@wayne.edu.

Mary C. Murdock is an Associate Professor and member of the graduate faculty at the Center for Studies in Creativity at Buffalo State College. She teaches creativity, leadership, and Creative Problem Solving in both the center's master of science program and its undergraduate minor program. A former teacher of English and gifted education, Murdock has extensive public school experience including specialized experience in areas such as staff counselor in residential gifted and talented summer programs. Murdock is a member of various professional organizations and currently serves as Editor of the National Association for Gifted Children's Creativity Division newsletter. She has also been an evaluator for the Future Problem Solving National Scenario Writing Competition and is a Colleague of the Creative Education Foundation. Her publications include articles on qualitative and quantitative research and two texts: *Role Playing and Creative Problem Solving*, coauthored with E. Paul Torrance; and *Creativity Assessment: Readings and Resources*, with Gerard Puccio. She is also the co-editor, along with center colleagues, of *Understanding and Recognizing Creativity: The Emergence of a Discipline*, and *Nurturing*

and Developing Creativity: The Emergence of a Discipline. Murdock has a bachelor's degree in English from the University of North Carolina at Greensboro; a master's in gifted education; and a doctorate in educational psychology from the University of Georgia. She can be reached via e-mail at murdocmc@buffalostate.edu.

Monty Neill is the Executive Director of the National Center for Fair & Open Testing (FairTest). He has directed FairTest's work on testing in the public schools since 1987 and has taught and administered in pre-school, high school, and college.

His many publications include *Implementing Performance Assessments: A Guide to Classroom School and System Reform* and *Testing Our Children: A Report Card on State Assessment Systems*, the first comprehensive evaluation of all 50 state testing programs. He also led the National Forum on Assessment in writing *Principles and Indicators for Student Assessment Systems*, which has been signed by more than 80 education and civil rights organizations. The FairTest Web site is at http://www.fairtest.org. Neill can be reached at 342 Broadway, Cambridge, MA 02139; phone: 617-864-4810; e-mail: monty@fairtest.org.

Sandra Parks has served as a curriculum and staff development consultant for school systems for more than 20 years and has presented Professional Development Institutes for the Association for Supervision and Curriculum Development. She conducted research on teaching critical thinking at the Indiana State University Laboratory School and was founding president of the Indiana Association for the Gifted. She taught gifted education courses at the University of North Florida and the University of Miami and served as codirector for the National Center for Teaching Thinking. With Howard Black, she coauthored *Building Thinking Skills* and *Organizing Thinking*, two series of lesson books for K–12 students. She and Robert Swartz coauthored *Infusing the Teaching of Critical and Creative Thinking into Elementary Instruction*. With Bernard Juarez and Howard Black, she coauthored *Learning On Purpose*. She serves as cofacilitator of the ASCD Teaching Thinking Network. She may be reached via e-mail at thnkgwks@aug.com, or by mail at P. O. Box 468, St. Augustine, FL 32084.

Richard W. Paul is Director of Research and Professional Development at the Center for Critical Thinking and Chair of the National Council for Excellence in Critical Thinking. He is an internationally recognized authority on critical thinking, with seven books and more than 200 articles on the subject. He has written books for every grade level and has done extensive experimentation with teaching tactics and strategies. His latest book, coauthored by Linda Elder, is *Critical Thinking: Tools for Taking Charge of Your Learning and Your Life*, which details for students steps they can take to develop lifelong thinking skills. Paul can be reached at Foundation for Critical Thinking, P. O. Box 220, Dillon Beach, CA 94929; or via e-mail at cct@ criticalthinking.org. The Center for Critical Thinking's Web site is www.criticalthinking.org.

Ruby K. Payne is a national and international consultant who speaks on improving the achievement of students from poverty. Her book, *A Framework for Understanding Poverty*, is in its sixth printing. Payne's career experience includes nine years as a high school teacher and chairperson; six years as a consultant for regional service centers in Illinois and Texas; six years working in a school district central office in instruction, curriculum, and staff development; and two years as an elementary principal. She has a bachelor's degree in English education from Goshen College in Goshen, Indiana; a master's in English literature from Western Michigan University in Kalamazoo, Michigan; and a doctorate in educational leadership and policy studies from Loyola University, Chicago, Illinois.

Her writing about poverty began in 1994, when she began conducting training that included poverty-related issues affecting school discipline. In 1996, she resigned from her public school position to do full-time consulting on the poverty topic. Payne lives near Houston, Texas, with her husband, Frank, and their son, Tom. She can be contacted through aha! Process, Inc. via phone at 800-424-9484 or online at http://www.ahaprocess.com.

David Perkins is a Senior Professor of Education at Harvard Graduate School of Education and a founding member of Harvard Project Zero. He is author of *Archimedes' Bathtub*; *Smart Schools*; *From Training Memories to Education Minds*; *Outsmarting IQ: The Emerging Science of Learnable Intelligence*; *Knowledge as Design* and several other books and articles. Perkins has helped develop instructional programs and approaches for teaching understanding and thinking, including initiatives in Israel, Latin America and South Africa. He is a former Guggenheim Fellow.

Jane E. Pollock is a researcher and international trainer in the areas of standards, curriculum and instruction, thinking skills, assessment and grading, and supervision; and is a Principal Consultant for Mid-continent Research for Education and Learning. Pollock consults regularly with school districts and states to improve student learning. She is the coauthor of var-

ious books including *Dimensions of Learning Teacher's Manual* (2nd ed.), *Dimensions of Learning Trainer's Manual* (2nd ed.), and *Classroom Instruction That Works: Research-Based Strategies for Increasing Student Achievement*.

Michael Pressley is the Notre Dame Professor of Catholic Education and Professor of Psychology. He has studied student cognition, especially students' use of strategies, for about 20 years, including programs of research on children's imagery, mnemonics, cognitive monitoring, reading comprehension, and the nature of excellent beginning reading instruction. He is the author or coauthor of more than 200 scientific publications. In recent years, he has been honored by the American Educational Research Association for outstanding contributions to research on learning and by the International Reading Association for outstanding contributions to research on children at risk for reading and writing failure. Pressley currently directs Notre Dame's innovative teacher education program, which is sponsored by the Alliance for Catholic Education. This program places teachers in schools across the southern United States, especially ones serving children living in poverty.

Barbara Z. Presseisen is an experienced educator and consultant in cognitive development and professional staff preparation. Recently retired as Chief Education Officer and Vice President at Nobel Learning Communities, a network of private schools across the United States, she continues as educational advisor with that company. Presseisen has authored a number of books and articles on teaching thinking and problem solving, most recently *Teaching for Intelligence*. She has taught at Swarthmore College and Temple University and has been active in the educational laboratory network. Currently, Presseisen is working on integrating critical thinking instruction in history and archaeology with museum experience and Internet research. Her e-mail address is LEARN1943@aol.com.

Gerard J. Puccio is the Director and an Associate Professor at the Center for Studies in Creativity, Buffalo State College, an internationally known program that offers courses and academic credentials in creativity. He has written more than 30 articles, chapters, and books. His articles have appeared in such journals as the *British Journal of Educational Psychology*, the *Journal of Creative Behavior*, and the *Creativity Research Journal*. Puccio has provided consultative services to schools, corporations, and institutions of higher education. He has delivered courses and workshops in Canada, the Dominican Republic, England, Singapore, Spain, and Tanzania. He holds a master's degree in creativity from Buffalo State College and a doctorate in Organizational Psychology from the University of Manchester, England. His e-mail address is pucciogj@buffalostate.edu.

Rebecca Reagan is currently a 5th grade teacher in Lubbock, Texas, specializing in reading and writing. She received her bachelor's degree and Master of Science in education from Texas Tech University. Reagan has done extensive staff-development work in the United States and other countries in the areas of critical and creative thinking and of gifted education through the National Center for Teaching Thinking in Newtonville, Massachusetts. She is coauthor of *Teaching Critical and Creative Thinking in Language Arts: A Lesson Book for Grades 5 & 6* with Robert Swartz and Mary Anne Kiser. Her personal e-mail address is rebreagan@aol.com. She may also be reached at the National Center for Teaching Thinking, 815 Washington St., Ste. 8, Newtonville, MA 02460; and at 5320 85th St., Lubbock, TX 79424.

Lauren B. Resnick is an internationally known scholar in the cognitive science of learning and instruction. Her recent research has focused on socializing intelligence, the nature and development of thinking abilities, and the relation between school learning and everyday competence, with special attention on mathematics and literacy. Resnick's current work lies at the intersection of cognitive science and policy for education. She founded and directs the Institute for Learning, which focuses on professional development based on cognitive learning principles and effort-oriented education. She is also cofounder and codirector of the New Standards Project, which has developed standards and assessments that have widely influenced state and school district practice. Her mailing address is Lauren B. Resnick, Director, Learning Research and Development Center, University of Pittsburgh, 3939 O'Hara Street, Pittsburgh, PA 15260.

John Richards is Senior Vice President and General Manager of Turner Learning, Inc., the educational division of Turner Broadcasting System, Inc. Turner Learning uses the assets of Turner Broadcasting (CNN, TNT, TCM, TBS, Cartoon Network) to create high quality, innovative, educational products and services to educate and inspire youth and develop global citizens. An education pioneer, Richards has spent more than 25 years as an educator, researcher, software developer and published book author. Principal interests include student media production, the effects of convergence of media on the classroom, media literacy, and school restructuring and reform. Richards has managed the Educational Technologies Division at Bolt Beranek and Newman, was cofounder and Chief Exec-

utive Officer of Window, Inc. (a magazine-on-a-disk), and has taught at the University of Georgia, Lesley College, and M.I.T. Richards earned his doctorate in philosophy from the State University of New York at Buffalo. He may be reached at Turner Learning, Inc., One CNN Center Atlanta, GA 30303; e-mail: john.richards@turner.com.

Virginia Pauline Rojas develops language programs and conducts professional training for schools in the United States, international schools, and Ministries of Education. She advocates having first, second, and foreign language teachers critically and collaboratively converge their pedagogical distinctions in order to construct an inquiry-based model of literacy. Rojas holds her academic credentials in language education, applied linguistics, and educational philosophy from Ohio State and Rutgers Universities and was formerly the Director of the Office of Language and International Education for the New Jersey Department of Higher Education and an Associate Professor at the College of New Jersey. She can be reached at vprojas@aol.com or at 732-940-1860.

Gavriel Salomon, past Dean of the Faculty of Education at the University of Haifa, Israel, is a professor of educational psychology there. He is currently Co-Director of the Center for Research on Peace Education and Director of the University's Center for Advanced Studies. Salomon received his bachelor's and master's degrees in geography, education, and psychology from the Hebrew University of Jerusalem, Israel, and his doctorate in educational psychology and communication from Stanford University. He has taught at the Hebrew University and Tel-Aviv University in Israel; Universidad Ibero Americana in Mexico; and at Harvard, Indiana University, Stanford, University of Southern California, University of Michigan, and University of Arizona in the United States. He spent a year at the Center for the Advanced Study in the Behavioral Sciences at Stanford. Salomon is the author of *Interaction of Media, Cognition and Learning; Communication and Education;* and *Technology and Education in the Information Age;* and he edited *Distributed Cognitions.* He may be reached at University of Haifa, Faculty of Education; phone: 972-4-824-9373; fax: 971-4-824-9354; e-mail: gsalomon@research.haifa. ac.il.

Sydelle Seiger-Ehrenberg (deceased), was Director, Institute for Curriculum and Instruction, P.O. Box 747, Coshocton, OH 43812.

Robert J. Sternberg is IBM Professor of Psychology and Education in the Department of Psychology at Yale University.

Sternberg is best known for his triarchic theory of successful intelligence, investment theory of love, mental self-government theory of thinking styles, and balance theory of wisdom. He is the author of more than 800 publications and winner of numerous awards, including the Research Review, Outstanding Book, Sylvia Scribner, and Palmer O. Johnson Awards of the American Educational Research Association. He has been president of four divisions of the American Psychological Association and is editor of *Contemporary Psychology*. He may be reached via e-mail at robert.sternberg@yale.edu.

Robert Stone, a graduate of the University of Northern Iowa with a master's degree in Curriculum and Instructional Media from Iowa State University, has taught for 25 years in the Ankeny (Iowa) Community Schools. During that time he has taught in grades 3–7, spent four years as a staff development trainer, and looped with one group of students for three years. He also teaches several courses for Drake University in its master's program in Effective Teaching Learning and Leadership and serves as a team leader in Drake's distance learning program. He may be reached via e-mail at rstone@ aol.com.

Robert J. Swartz is a faculty member at the University of Massachusetts at Boston. He is Director of the National Center for Teaching Thinking in Newtonville, Massachusetts. Through the center he provides staff-development to educators across the country and abroad on restructuring curriculum by infusing critical and creative thinking into content instruction. Swartz received his bachelor's and doctorate degrees in philosophy from Harvard University and studied under a Fulbright Scholarship at Oxford and Cambridge Universities in England. He is lead author of a lesson design handbook series, Infusing the Teaching of Critical and Creative Thinking into Content Instruction, a series of follow-up infusion lesson books on the same topic, and an overview of teaching thinking, *Teaching Thinking: Issues and Approaches*, coauthored with David Perkins. He may be reached at the National Center for Teaching Thinking, 815 Washington Street, Suite 8, Newtonville, MA 02460; phone: 617-965-4604; Web site: http://www. javanet.com/~natlctt; personal e-mail: rjscct@prodigy.net.

Shari Tishman, Ed.D., is a Research Associate at Harvard Project Zero, Harvard Graduate School of Education. Her interests include the development of high-level cognition in the arts and in other areas. She has written extensively about the teaching of thinking and has developed a variety of thinking-centered educational materials. Much of her work focuses on the dispositional side of high-level thinking. Among other projects, she is currently working with art museums in Massachusetts and New York to develop and assess programs that teach thinking through looking at art.

Donald J. Treffinger, President of the Center for Creative Learning, has taught at the elementary school, middle school, and university levels. He is Professor Emeritus of Creative Studies at Buffalo State College. He has also worked with groups from schools, churches, museums, and science centers throughout the world. Treffinger is the author or coauthor of more than 300 books, chapters, and articles on creativity, creative problem solving, and talent development. He has served as the editor or as an editorial board member for several professional journals. Treffinger received the National Association for Gifted Children's Torrance Creativity Award in 1995. He can be reached at the Center for Creative Learning, P. O. Box 14100, NE Plaza, Sarasota, FL 34278-4100; phone: 941-351-8862; fax: 941-351-9061; e-mail: cclofc@gte.net; Web site: www.creativelearning.com.

Elaine Vislocky is Staff Development Specialist, Somers Central School District, Somers, NY. She may be reached via e-mail at Elaine_Vislocky@somers.k12.ny.us.

Bruce Wellman is Co-Director, along with Laura Lipton, of MiraVia, LLC, a training and development firm dedicated to creating and sustaining learning-focused educational environments. Their publications, workshops, and seminars aim to provide effective strategies, practical resources, and innovative ideas for thoughtful educators grappling with critical professional issues.

Wellman brings a rich background of experience as a teacher, staff developer, and curriculum and instructional specialist to his work as a systems change agent. He has authored or co-authored numerous publications related to organizational and professional development, learning-focused schools, and classrooms and group development. In addition to collaborating with Lipton on *Pathways to Understanding: Patterns and Practices for the Learning-Focused Classroom* and *Shifting Rules, Shifting Roles: Transforming the Work Environment to Support Learning* (with Arthur Costa), he and Lipton are currently working on their next publication, *Mentoring Matters: Templates and Tools for the Learning-Focused Mentor*. Wellman may be reached at 229 Colyer Rd., Guilford, VT 05301; phone: 802-257-4892; fax 802-257-2403; e-mail: bwellman@aol.com.

Carol Welsh is the designer of Four-Color Analysis of Text, developed to bridge the gap between whole language literary journal writing and teacher-directed questions for response to text. She is a doctoral candidate at the California Institute of Integral Studies in San Francisco, California, and works online with an international cohort group. Research studies applying four-color analysis as a constructivist methodology in classrooms, elementary through graduate level, are being conducted as part of her dissertation research. Since 1987 she has been an Instructional Support Teacher and Enrichment Facilitator for the School District of Lancaster, Pennsylvania. She may be reached via e-mail at cwelsh@redrose.net.

Arthur Whimbey holds a doctorate in experimental psychology from Purdue University and is Director of the TRAC Institute (TRAC stands for Text Reconstruction Across the Curriculum). His publications include *Intelligence Can Be Taught*; *Mastering Reading Through Reasoning*; *Analyze, Organize, Write*; and *Thinking Through Math Word Problems*. He may be reached via the Web at http://www.tracinstitute.com.

Ann White is a 4th and 5th grade science teacher at Jackson Academy in East Orange, New Jersey. One of her major interests is creating an urban-suburban partnership focused on environmental science activities that include the surrounding communities. She may be reached via e-mail: rwhite8073@aol.com.

James M. Wilson III, Co-Founder and Co-Director of Technology Pathways, focuses on knowledge engineering in schools to help teachers develop useful information on student performance. He is also founder and director of Data and Decision Analysis, a management-consulting firm that develops decision support systems. Over the past 15 years, he has worked with 16 state educational agencies, as well as numerous school districts, to improve their data collection practices, management of information, and knowledge creation.

Wilson has a Master of Business Administration degree, a master's in applied economics, and a doctorate in strategic management. He has written numerous articles on the use of information to guide strategic decision making in organizations, and specializes in the use of computer simulation to model and test theories of complex systems in organizations and markets. He has designed, produced, and launched more than 20 pieces of software. His most recent publication (coauthored with Bena Kallick) is *Information Technology in Schools: Creating Practical Knowledge to Improve Student Performance*.

Aletta Zietsman is a faculty member in the Department of Science Studies, Western Michigan University. She earned her doctorate at the University of Massachusetts, Amherst, and earlier degrees at the University of Witwatersrand, Rand Afrikaans University and Stellenbosch University. While a member of the Witwatersrand Physics Department she developed an innovative two-year program that enabled hundreds of underprepared high school students to succeed in university programs and to continue their education in graduate degree programs.

Index to Authors

Asp, Elliott, 497
Barell, John, *106, 256, 284, 551*
Baron, Jonathan, 76
Berman, Sheldon, *11*
Beyer, Barry K., *35, 87, 248, 275, 317, 393, 417, 533, 548, 556*
Block, Cathy Collins, *292*
Brandt, Ron, *169*
Brenner, Douglas F., *216*
Brooks, Jacqueline Grennon, *150*
Brooks, Martin G., *150*
Burke, Kay, *528*
Butler, Jessica, *343*
Caine, Geoffrey, *96*
Caine, Renate Nummela, *96*
Chapman, Linda, *489*
Cohen, Burton, *262*
Cook, Marcy, *286*
Costa, Arthur L., *2, 18, 42, 80, 94, 135, 246, 352, 354, 359, 379, 408, 517, 547, 548, 555*
Dickinson, Dee, *101*
Edwards, John, *23*
Eisner, Elliot W., *310*
Ennis, Robert H., *44*
Fagen, Lex, *343*
Field, Lee Winocur, *552*
Fischer, Stephen David, *303*
Fisher, Alec, *541*
Fogarty, Robin, *142, 144*
Garmston, Robert J., *18*

Harris, Karen R., *466*
Hay, LeRoy, *7*
Hilts, Peter, *262*
Hopper, Cheryl, *256*
Hyerle, David, *401*
Isaksen, Scott G., *442*
Jackson, Thomas E., *459*
Jackson, Yvette, *222*
Johnson, David W., *455*
Johnson, Roger T., *455*
Kallick, Bena, *253, 472, 496, 517*
King, Sherry P., *131*
Landers, Daniel M., *343*
Lazear, David G., *202*
Leibowitz, Marian, *253*
Linden, Myra J., *298*
Lipton, Laura, *118*
Lochhead, Jack, *54, 298, 413, 426*
Loring, Ruth M., *332*
Lowery, Lawrence F., *174, 234*
Lowther, Deborah L., *479*
Lozano, Armando, *192*
Lyman, Frank T. Jr., *384*
Marien, Joanne, *489*
Martin, David S., *111, 123, 211*
Martin, William C., *126*
Marzano, Robert, J., *29, 180, 379*
Maxwell, William, *343*
McTighe, Jay, *384*
Michelli, Nicholas M., *111*

Morrison, Gary R. *479*
Murdock, Mary C., *67*
Neill, Monty, *511*
Parks, Sandra, *190, 216*
Paul, Richard W., *427*
Payne, Ruby K., *229*
Perkins, David, *158, 370, 446*
Pollock, Jane E., *29*
Presseisen, Barbara Z., *47, 548*
Pressley, Michael, *466*
Puccio, Gerard J., *67*
Reagan, Rebecca, *337*
Resnick, Lauren B., *3*
Richards, John, *484*
Rojas, Virginia Pauline, *326*
Salomon, Gavriel, *370*
Seiger-Ehrenberg, Sydelle, *437*
Sternberg, Robert J., *197, 451*
Stone, Robert, *525*
Swartz, Robert J., *58, 164, 266, 303*
Tishman, Shari, *72*
Treffinger, Donald J., *442*
Vislocky, Elaine, *489*
Wellman, Bruce, *118*
Welsh, Carol, *298*
Whimbey, Arthur, *298*
White, Ann, *256*
Wilson, James M. III, *474*
Zietsman, Aletta, *54*

Index

Note: Page numbers followed by an *f* indicate figures.

AACTE. *See* American Association of Colleges for Teacher Education
ability, 158–161
absolutism, uncritical, 428–429
absolutistic thinking, 428–429
abstract concepts, 311, 438–439
abstract representational systems, 230–231
acceptance
 in collectivist culture, 218
 empathic, 368–369
accidental representation, 235, 237*f*
accomplishment, recognition of, 5. *See also* motivation
accountable talk, 5
accuracy
 in critical thinking, 218
 monitoring, 184, 185*f*, 187*f*
 striving for, 82
acknowledging, as teacher response behavior, 367–368
acronyms, 421
action(s), in systems thinking, 127
action learning, *vs.* linear management, 24–25
action plan, creating, 127–130
action research, 121
active reasoning
 importance of, 428
 for learning-disabled students, 211
Activities Integrating Math, Science, and Technology (AIMS), 526
activity-centered approach of learning styles, 193
activity posters, 209
ACTT. *See* Association Collaborative for Teaching Thinking
adaptive intelligence. *See* successful intelligence
administrators, 123–125
adolescent(s)
 behavior disorders in, 212
 cognitive capacities of, 50
 parenting, 104
adult(s)
 becoming successful, 104–105
 complex, 101
 teaching as cognitive activity for, 113
advanced beginner, 25
advocacy, and inquiry, 139
"affective filter," 223
affective skills, developed though CPS training, 70*f*
Agenda for Education in a Democracy, 114

agreement questions, 360
AIMS. *See* Activities Integrating Math, Science, and Technology
algorithms, 54–55
allocentrism, 19
alternative test, 499*f*
American Association of Colleges for Teacher Education (AACTE), 112
American Association of University Women, 480
American Federation of Teachers, 29
analog modes of communication, 484
analogy link, 391*f*
analysis, 184
 of answers, 368
 argument, 44–45, 88, 250–251
 audience, 264
 compare/contrast, 306*f*
 cues and questions for, 187*f*
 error, 184, 185*f*, 187*f*
 factor, 200
 four-color, 301–302, 301*f*
 goals of, 48, 185*f*
 of logic of language, 382, 382*f*
 meta-analysis, 349
 in preparation stage of learning, 263
 self-analysis, 209
 skills of, 270, 320*f*
 teaching, grade level and, 250*f*, 251
 use of term, 152
"analysis paralysis," 24
analytical intelligence, 147, 194
analytical problem solving, 451
Ananse Tales (Dykstra, Port and Port), 300
anarchic form of self-regulation, 194, 198
anecdotal records, 521–522
Ang, I., 486
anger, 166–167
animals
 knowledge born in, 234
 nonspecialized, 176
 specialized, 175
answers
 analysis of, 368
 vs. questions, 13–14
application, goals of, 48
apprenticeship, 6
approximated spelling, 153
aptitude, 3
Aquinas, Saint Thomas, 165
argument(s)
 analysis of, 44–45, 88, 250–251

argument(s) *(continued)*
 in collectivist culture, 218
 deductively valid, 45
 evaluation of, 88
 inductively valid, 45
 making, 88
 recognition of, 88
Aristotle, 76, 213, 455
Art, Mind, and Brain (Gardner), 356
artificial intelligence, 148
arts
 cognition and, 310–315
 inquiry in, 262
 presentation in, 264
ASCD. *See* Association for Supervision and Curriculum Development
Asian culture, 217–218
assessment. *See also* test(s)
 authentic, 259
 of cognition, 49
 of decision making, 65–66, 65*f*
 of dialogical and dialectical thinking, 434–435
 fair and credible, 5
 of foreign language acquisition, 329
 inappropriate, 39–40
 of intelligence, 207, 232
 interdependent, 517–518
 in problem solving, 482
 self-assessment, 209, 405–407, 524, 531
 taxonomy of, 49*f*
 technology and, 507–508, 524
 of thinking skills
  format for, 533–540, 534*f*–537*f*
  national tests in, 501–504
  performance tasks in, 528–532
  state tests in, 498–501, 504–507, 511–515
  system for, 517–524
  teachers in, 525–527, 541–545
  tests *vs.* staff-collected data, 137
 visual tools for, 405–407
Association Collaborative for Teaching Thinking (ACTT), 112
Association for Supervision and Curriculum Development (ASCD), 112
assumption(s), 45, 463
The Astonishing Hypothesis (Crick), 170
athletes, psychological skills used by, 344–349
attention, 20
attitude, 439
audience
 analysis of, 264
 vs. users, 486

auditory intelligence, 203, 208f
authentic assessment, 259
authentic professional development, 119–120
authoritarianism, 160–161
autism, 212
autonomy, student, accepting, 151–152
awe, responding with, 83–84
axons, 403

backward-reaching high-road transfer, 374
balanced literacy curriculum, 134
Basic Principles of Curriculum and Instruction (Tyler), 257
BASICS, 437
beginner, advanced, 25
behavior
    disorders, 212
    model of, 182f
    patterns of, 127
belief, methodological, 14
belonging, sense of, 105
Benchmarks for Science Literacy, 30
Berlak, Harold, 39, 509
biology
    and learning, 234–243
    and thinking, 175–180, 234–235
bird's-eye view, 19
black hat, 194, 194f
Blaisdell, Gina, 268, 270, 272
blind variation, 475
block scheduling, 131
Bloom, Benjamin, xiii, 7, 36, 37, 47–48, 55, 61, 70, 115, 143, 181, 270, 275, 293, 320, 337, 404, 408
Bloom's taxonomy, 143, 181, 183–184, 525, 526, 527
blue hat, 194, 194f
board of education study sessions, 131–133
bodily intelligence, 146, 202, 205f, 208f
"body intelligence," 102
"booktalks," 153–154
Bo Peep theory, 371, 372
brain
    associative power of, 403
    at birth, 176
    connections in, 178–179
    development of
        in infants, 103, 177
        music and, 332–333
    emotional side of, 164
    encoding words in, 235
    filing system of, 177–178
    functioning of, 355–356
    imaging techniques, 177
    injuries, 213
    learning in, xvi, 223
    as pattern detector, 401–403
    plasticity of, 102
    research on, 113
    and thinking, 176–179
The Brain (Restak), 356
brainstorming, 127, 226, 307
brainstorming webs, 402f, 403–404
Brainstorms and Thunderbolts: How Creative Genius Works (Madigan and Elwood), 356
bridge (card game), 239
bridging, 375, 399
Butler's Model of Human Action and Change, 129, 129f

capability, 80
Capra, Fritjof, 401
card games, 237, 238, 239
CARE. *See* Coalition for Authentic Reform in Education
case studies, 121
casual register of language, 231f
categorizing, 498f, 499f
causal explanation, 307f
CCSSO. *See* Council of Chief State School Officers
A Celebration of Neurons (Sylwester), 170
Center for Research on Evaluation, Standards, and Student Testing (CRESST), 508
challenge, daily, 289, 290f
challenge-and-support structures, 27, 27f
change
    key to real, 96
    reflection as trigger mechanism of, 129
checkers, 476
checklists
    in assessment, 518–519, 520f
    procedural, 420
chess, 239, 372, 476
child(ren). *See also* adolescent(s); student(s)
    brain development in, 103, 177, 332–333
    cognitive development in, 48, 102
    cognitive strategies for, 468
    conceptualizing in, 439
    encoding words, 235
    intelligence shutdown in, 204
    language development in, 231
    pattern seeking in, 235–240
    physical activity of, adults controlling, 343
    privileged *vs.* underprivileged, 160
    uncritical absolutism in, 428–429
childhood
    first, 172
    need for long, 240
    second, 172
Chinese culture, 217, 219
clarifying, 139, 368, 410–411
clarity
    instructional, 363–364
    monitoring, 184, 185f, 187f
    thinking and communicating with, 83
class constitution, 12
classifying, 173, 184
    cues and questions for, 187f
    inclusive, 238–239, 239f
    introducing, 249
    multiple membership, 237–238, 238f
    objectives for, 185f
    taxonomy of, 49f
    use of term, 152
classifying strategy, and concept development, 440
classroom, safe, creating, 12–13
classroom activity, 33
classroom observation checklist, 552–554
A Climate for Thinking (Costa), 126
closed questions, 360
closure questions, 225
CNN NEWSROOM, 486–487
CNN Student Bureau (CNNSB), 487
coaching
    intelligence, 209
    for learning-disabled students, 211
    peer, 121, 138
    thinking, 161–162

Coalition for Authentic Reform in Education (CARE), 514
"codes of power," 226
cognition
    arts and, 310–315
    assessment of, 49
    constructive controversy and, 457–458
    cooperative learning and, 456
    and culture, 223–224
    definition of, 52, 311
    development of, 48
    distributed, 102, 159
    enhancing, 138–139
    epistemic, 52, 52f, 356, 357f
    exercise and, 349
    skills of, CPS training and, 70f
    stress and, 135–136
cognition-centered approach of learning styles, 192
cognitive-behavioral techniques, used by athletes, 344–349
cognitive deficits, 212
cognitive mapping, 388, 391f
cognitive modifiability, 146
cognitive science, 3–4
cognitive strategies, 466–469
    maintaining and generalizing, 467–468
    for young children, 468
cognitive-strategy instructional techniques, 212
cognitive system, 182, 183f
"cognitive wall," 225
co-inquiry, 461–462
Colegio Decroly Americano, 265
collaboration, 120, 136–138
collaborative thinking, 13
collective learning, 99–100
collectivist culture, 217–218, 218–219
College Board, 29
collegiality, 139
color, sorting by, 235
Colorado State Model Content Standards, 504, 505f
Colorado Student Assessment Program (CSAP), 504–505
The Color Purple (Walker), 109
combination, selective, 452
Commission on the Humanities, 29
commitment, 80
Common Sense (Paine), 273
communication. *See also* dialogue
    analog *vs.* digital modes of, 484–485
    in collectivist culture, 217
    in individualist culture, 217
    lines of, in learning organization, 98
community
    building, 97–98, 99
    in collectivist culture, 217
    diversity in, 137–138
    sense of, 20–21
"community ball," 460, 461f
Community Problem Solving, 443
comparison, 173
    analysis, 306f
    in experiments, 304
    graphic organizer for, 340f, 341f
    selective, 452
    skillful, 339
    writing template for, 342f
competency, 25

The Complete Book of Parenting (Meyerhoff), 104
complexity, well-defined, 476–477
componential intelligence, 194
comprehension, 184
    cues and questions for, 188f
    goals of, 48, 186f
    monitoring, 212
Comprehensive Test of Basic Skills (CTB), 502
computation
    "natural," 148
    "organs of," 148
computational theory of mind, 148
computer(s). *See* information age; technology
computer-assisted language learning, 329
computer-assisted problem solving, 8–9, 55, 56, 476
computer literacy, 480
computer programming, and transfer, 371, 374–375
conation, 51–52, 52, 52f
concept(s)
    abstract, 311, 438–439
    characteristics of, 438–439
    definition of, 438, 439
    developing, 311, 440–441
    examples of, 438, 438f
    externalization of, 312
    learning
        lack of understanding of, 437
        missing from curriculum, 437
    and representation, 312–314
    revising existing, 319
    "structural equivalent" of, 313
"concept application," 156
"concept introduction," 156
concept map, 258f
conclusions, 49f
concrete reality, 242, 242f
conditional knowledge, 320
The Conditions of Learning (Gagne), 183
confidence
    encouraging, 12–15
    pedagogy of, 224, 225
    value of, 18
conflict, 21
confusion, as precursor to learning, 26
conjunctions, 300
conscientious students, 151–152
consciousness, 18–20
consequences, in decision making, 59, 60
conservative leaning of self-regulation, 195, 198
consistent sorting, 236–237, 238f
constitution, class, 12
constraints, 98
constructed learning, 145
constructive controversy
    and cognition and metacognition, 457–458
    definition of, 455
constructivism, xvi, 150–157, 278
    definition of, 150
    description of, 151–157
    vs. receptive learning, 479–480
    teachers resisting, 151
"consultant groups," 154
consultative register of language, 231f
Content Knowledge (Kendall and Marzano), 31
contextual intelligence, 194
contextualization corollary, 68f
continuous learning, 18, 85, 99

contrasting
    analysis, 306f
    in experiments, 304
    graphic organizer for, 340f, 341f
    skillful, 339
    writing template for, 342f
control groups, 304
controlled writing, 300
controversy, constructive
    and cognition and metacognition, 457–458
    definition of, 455
conventional modes of treatment, 313
convergent thinking, 193
cooperative groups, 209
cooperative learning
    and cognition and metacognition, 456
    definition of, 455
    and dialogical and dialectical thinking, 434
    student-to-student dialogue and, 154
Copy/Write (Gorrell), 300
Council of Chief State School Officers (CCSSO), 504
counterexample, 463
CPS. *See* Creative Problem Solving
craftsmanship, 18, 19–20, 82
creating, use of term, 152
creative intelligence, 147, 194
Creative Problem Solving (CPS), 69–70, 70f, 442–443
creative tension, 136, 136f
creative thinking, 50f, 67–71
    vs. creativity, 67
    definition of, 50, 68, 70–71
    developing, 69–70, 70f
    motivation in, 83
    music and, 334
    necessity of, 68–69
    in problem solving, 451
creativity, 442–445
    basic nature of, 67–68, 68f
    characteristics of, 68f
    vs. creative thinking, 67
    literacy and, 293
    praise and, 368
    research on, 442–443
    stress and, 135–136
    teaching, 68f, 443–445, 444f
credibility, judging, 45
CRESST. *See* Center for Research on Evaluation, Standards, and Student Testing
criteria, 88–89
criterion-referenced tests (CRT), 512
critical judgment, 88
critical questions, 380, 380f
critical thinking, 49–50, 50f, 88, 248, 249f
    abilities in, 44–46
    approaching monologically, 429
    culture and, 216, 218–219
    definition of, 44, 216
    dialogue in, 89–90
    dispositions in, 44
    in history, 267–268, 318f, 319
    in literacy, 339
    in mathematics, 289
    music and, 334
    in science, 250, 303–304, 307
    in social studies, 250, 318f, 319
    subject matter emphases on, 31–32, 31f
    teaching, 115, 373

critical thinking *(continued)*
    with content, 267–268
    grade level and, 250–251, 250f
    for learning-disabled students, 212
    strategies, 12–15
Critical Thinking (Ennis), 44
criticism, openness to, 83
CRT. *See* criterion-referenced tests
CSAP. *See* Colorado Student Assessment Program
Csikszentmihalyi, M., xvii, 21, 101, 103
CTB. *See* Comprehensive Test of Basic Skills
cueing
    in thinking skill practice, 278, 398, 420–421
    in Think-Pair-Share, 384, 385f
Cueing Bookmark, 387f
Cultural Literacy (Hirsch), 373
culture
    collectivist, 217–218
    and critical thinking, 216, 218–219
    definition of, 216
    individualist, 217
    of poverty, 229–232
    and problem solving, 216–220
    rules of, 129
    and thinking, 161
    urban, 222–228
cummings, e. e., 313
Cuomo, Mario, 82
curiosity, 109, 156
curriculum
    academic rigor in, 5
    arts in, 310–315
    balanced literacy, 134
    concept learning missing from, 437–438
    connecting news to, 486–487
    creative thinking, 266–273
    critical thinking, 44–46, 266–273
    horizontal, 241
    in multicultural education, 219
    multiple intelligence in, 204–206
    problem-based, 308, 309f
    research-based, 490
    sequenced-learning, 306–308, 309f
    teachers as designers of, 253–255, 255f
    thinking skills. *See* thinking skills curriculum
    vertical, 240–241
Curriculum and Evaluation Standards for School Mathematics, 30
Cypress-Fairbanks Independent School District, 269

daily challenge, 289, 290f
Darwin, Charles, 164
data
    acquisition of, facilitating, 367
    for decision making, 133, 380–381, 380f
    manipulation of, 481
    providing, in communication, 139
    raw, teachers using, 152
deaf students, 213
de Bono, Edward, xii, 24, 25, 29, 82, 193–194, 194f, 444, 517
decision making, 49, 50f, 184
    assessing, 65–66, 65f
    autonomous, data for, 380f
    collectivist, 219
    in critical thinking, 218
    cues and questions for, 187f

decision making (*continued*)
    data-based, 133, 380–381, 380*f*
    emotions in, 165
    good, 60–61
    in history, 269, 319
    incorporating strategies of, 64–65
    model of, 391*f*
    monitoring, 62
    "myside bias" in, 59
    objectives for, 185*f*
    poor, 58–60
    reflective, 133–134
    in social studies, 251, 319
    teaching, 62–64, 64*f*
        with content, 268–269
        grade level and, 250*f*, 251
    thinking skills involved in, 61*f*
declarative knowledge, 320, 419
deductive reasoning, emergence of, 239
deductive strategy, and concept development, 440
deep understanding, 270
defensive questions, 360
deliberate discourse, 455
delivery, *vs.* participation, 486
dendrites, 147, 179, 403
dependency webs, 449
deprivatization, 136, 138
descriptive models, of thinking, 77
Designing a New Taxonomy of Educational Objectives (Marzano), 181
Desotelle, Jude, 260
Destination ImagiNation, 443
Developing Cognitive Abilities Test, 49
"development trajectory" of intelligence, 210
Dewey, John, xii, 47, 55, 144–145, 223, 224, 259, 272, 275, 322, 519
"diagnostic evaluations," 210
dialectical thinking, 427–436
dialogical thinking, 427–436
dialogue. *See also* question(s)
    in critical thinking, 89–90
    dialectical, 427
    encouraging students to engage in, 153–154
    in gently Socratic inquiry, 459
    in professional development, 122
    vs. recitation, 359
    reflective, 136, 138–139
    in systems thinking, 129
Diamond, Marian, 102, 103, 144, 147, 333
The Dictionary of Psychology, 311
didactic strategy, for introducing thinking skills, 278, 396–397
diffusion corollary, 68*f*
digital modes of communication, 484–485
Dimensions of Thinking (Marzano et al.), xiii
directions, 381, 381*f*
direct transfer, 399
discipline, 105
disciplined thinking, 321–322
Disciplines of a Learning Organization (Senge), 126
"discovery," in learning cycle, 156
discovery learning, 145
Discover Your Brain (Margulies and Sylwester), 356
discussion strategies bookmark, 384–385, 387*f*
dispositions, thinking. *See* thinking dispositions
distress, 136

distributed cognition, 102, 159
distributed intelligence, 159
divergent thinking, 193, 442
"diversification," 214
diversity, 137–138
Dr. Seuss, 63–64, 268–269
doctrine, 160–161
domain-general teaching of problem solving, 453
domain-specific teaching of problem solving, 453
"do no harm" rule, 76, 77
"double-loop" learning, 26
"downshifting," 171
Dreyfus model of skill acquisition, 25
duration, 19

each one teach one (activity), 209
"ecology of thought," xvii
economic class, hidden rules based on, 229, 230*f*
education
    effort-based, 4
    industrial-age model of, 7, 9
    inservice, 124–125, 210
    multicultural, 219
    passions in, 21–22
    politics of, change in, 150
    propagandistic, 15
    public, purposes of, 2, 115
educational disadvantage, 212–213
educational innovation, learning, 119
Educational Leadership (magazine), xii, xiii, 352
Education and Learning to Think (Resnick), xiii–xiv, 29
educator(s). *See* teacher(s)
Educators for Social Responsibility (ESR), 11–17
Edwards, John, 23–28, 129, 275, 277, 568
EEG. *See* electroencephalography
effective thinking, origins of, 18–22
efficacy
    examining, 184, 185*f*, 187*f*
    passion for, 18
effort-based education, 4
egocentrism, 19
eight-in-one activities, 209
Elbow, Peter, 14
electroencephalography (EEG), 177
elementary school years
    parenting during, 104
    physical education in, and intelligence, 345*f*
The Emotional Brain (LeDoux), 164
emotional intelligence, 148, 168
Emotional Intelligence (Goleman), 164
emotional response, examining, 184, 185*f*, 187*f*
emotions
    vs. feelings, 172
    and learning, 102, 164–169
    respecting, 164–165
    students coping with, 165–166
    and thinking, 166–167
    thinking about, 167–169
empathy
    in emotional intelligence, 148
    listening with, 522
    in teacher behavior, 368–369
employee(s), desired characteristics of, 117
empowerment, 12–15
encoding, selective, 452
enculturation, 161
endorphins, 84
energy, structuring, 364–365

English as second language (ESL), 300
"enlightened self-interest," 59
environment
    enriched, 147–148
    learning, 417–419
"episodic grasp of reality," 83
epistemic cognition, 52, 52*f*, 356, 357*f*
epistemology, evolutionary, 474–477
error analysis, 184, 185*f*, 187*f*
ESL. *See* English as second language
ESR. *See* Educators for Social Responsibility
essays, persuasive decision-making, 65*f*, 66
Estes, T. H., 276, 279, 324, 422
estimation, 475
European Odyssey, 264
eustress, 136
evaluation. *See also* assessment
    goals of, 48
    in preparation stage of learning, 263
    teaching, grade level and, 250*f*, 251
events, in systems thinking, 127
Everybody Counts (National Research Council), 286
evidence
    as thinking tool, 463
    in Western culture, 219
evolution, 172
evolutionary epistemology, 474–476, 475–476, 477
execution, 186*f*, 188*f*
executive function of self-regulation, 194, 197, 199
exercise (physical), 343–349
exercises, *vs.* problem solving, 54
exhaustive sorting, 236–237, 238*f*
expectations, 5, 109
experiential intelligence, 147
experiential learning, 144–145
experimental inquiry, 184, 185*f*, 187*f*
experimental intelligence, 194
experiments
    and data acquisition, 367
    "scientific method" and, 153, 303–304
    simulated, 477
expert, 25
explanation, causal, 307*f*
explicitness corollary, 68*f*
explicit teaching of problem solving, 453
The Expression of the Emotions in Man and Animals (Darwin), 164
expressive modes of treatment, 313
externalization, of concepts, 312
external scope of self-regulation, 195, 198
extreme relativism, 161
extrinsic motivation, 74, 83, 366

facilitative questioning, 26
fact, 439
factor analysis, 200
faculty development, 113
familiarization, 454
"far transfer," 370
fear, 222–223
feedback
    data acquisition and, 367
    honest, 26
    personalized process, 457
    as teacher behavior, 108–109, 359, 366–369
    and thinking skill proficiency, 278–279

feelings, 172
Feuerstein, R., 48, 102, 146, 211, 231, 379
A Field Guide to Using Visual Tools (Hyerle), 403
flexibility
    consciousness and, 19
    interdependence and, 20–21
    passion for, 18–19
    in thinking, 81–82
flow chart, 391*f*
fMRI. *See* functional magnetic resonance imaging
focus questions, 271
follow-up questions, 272
foreign language acquisition
    assessment of, 329
    benefits of, 329
    computer-assisted, 329
    internal processes of, 327
    research on, 327
formal register of language, 231*f*
forward-reaching high-road transfer, 373–374
four-color analysis, 301–302, 301*f*
Frames of Mind (Gardner), 102
Franklin, Benjamin, 299
freedom, 105
frozen register of language, 231*f*
frustration, as precursor to learning, 26
functional magnetic resonance imaging (fMRI), 177
fuzzy language, 83
fuzzy thinking, 59, 83

Gage, Nathaniel, 384, 390
Gardner, Howard, xii, 102, 144, 146–147, 202, 203, 204, 209, 210, 223, 317, 333, 335, 344, 345*f*–347*f*, 354, 447, 453, 479
"gateway" standard, 218
gathering, in learning, 262–263
Gazzaniga, Michael, 172
generalizing, 184, 185*f*, 187*f*, 381*f*
general-purpose problem solving, 55
generation, 129
gently Socratic questioning, 459–465
Ghiselin, Brewster, 354
gifted students, 213–214
gin rummy (card game), 238
global level of self-regulation, 195, 198
GOALS 2000, 497, 503
goal setting, 344
Go Fish (card game), 237
Going off subject (GOS), 461*f*
Goleman, D., 48, 80, 144, 148, 164, 334, 406
Goodlad, John, 9, 111, 115, 135, 385
Gorrell, Donna, 300
GOS, *see* going off subject
graphic organizer
    for decision making, 63, 64*f*, 421*f*
    for open compare and contrast, 340*f*, 341*f*
    task-specific, 402*f*, 404
green hat, 194, 194*f*
Greenspan, Stanley, 171
Grigorenko, E., 192, 197, 199, 200, 451, 453, 531
groups, 121–122. *See also* cooperative learning
Guilford, J. P., 47–48, 193, 442

habits of mind, 80–85, 146, 404, 518
Hagevik, Rita, 269, 270

Hamilton-Wenham Regional School District, 267
"hands-on learning," 52, 179–180
Harcourt Brace Educational Measurement, 503
Harcourt Educational Assessment, 503
hard-of-hearing students, 213
harmony, 219
Hart, Leslie, 172, 354
Harvard Graduate School of Education, 447
hastiness, in decision making, 59
Heisenberg Uncertainty Principle, 485
Hercules (movie), 193
Herman, J., 497, 507, 508, 509
heuristics, 475
hidden rules, 229, 230*f*
hierarchical repatterning, 239–240, 241*f*
hierarchic form of self-regulation, 194, 198
hierarchy of human needs, 104–105
"high-context" communication, 217
"higher-order thinking," 61, 266
Highlands Elementary Schools, 268
Highlights of United States History: The Story of Our Nation (Linden and Whimbey), 299
high-road transfer, 372, 373–374, 375
    backward-reaching, 374
    forward-reaching, 373–374
high school
    physical education in, and intelligence, 347*f*
    research protocol in, 490*f*–491*f*
    social studies in, 257–259
    Socratic questioning in, 433–434
High Stakes (publication), 511
high-stakes testing, 511, 513
history
    critical thinking in, 267–268, 318*f*, 319
    decision making in, 269, 319
    disciplined thinking in, 321–322
    information processing skills in, 318*f*, 320–321
    inquiry in, 262
    problem solving in, 317–318, 318*f*, 321–322, 323*f*
    reasoning skills in, 318*f*, 320–321
    solution strategies in, 318–319, 318*f*
    thinking dispositions in, 321
Hobbes' Internet Timeline, 8
Hoffman, M. B., 80, 83, 517, 518
Holmes, Oliver Wendell, 361
horizontal curriculum, 241
horizontal repatterning, 239, 240*f*
Horton Hatches the Egg (Seuss), 63–64, 268–269
How People Learn (Bransford, Brown and Cocking), 472
How We Think (Dewey), xii, 272
"hugging," 375–376
Human Brain, Human Learning (Hart), 354
Human Brain Coloring Workbook (Gupta), 356
human needs, hierarchy of, 104–105
humor, 84, 522
Hurst, Joe B., 276
Hynd, C., 295
HyperCard, 508
hypertext, 296
hypothesis, 31*f*, 319, 320, 322

identity building, 225
I don't understand (IDUS), 461, 461*f*
ill-defined problem, 474–475, 476
imagery, 344, 348

imagining, 83
"immediate self-interest," 59
immersion, 328
implication, 463
implicit teaching of problem solving, 453
importance, examining, 184, 185*f*, 187*f*
impulsivity, managing, 81
inclination, 74, 80, 158–161
inclusive classifying, 238–239, 239*f*
inconsistencies, 429
Incubation Model of Teaching, 442
individualist culture, 217, 218–219
individual problem solving, 454
inductive strategy
    and concept development, 440
    for introducing thinking skills, 394–396
industrial age, thinking in, 7
inert knowledge, 371, 374, 375
infant(s), brain development in, 103, 177
inference, 76, 77, 452, 463
information, organization, 491–493
information age, thinking in, 7–8, 479–482
information flow, control of, 480
information literacy, 9–10
information processing skills, 248, 249*f*
    in history and social studies, 318*f*, 320–321
    teaching, grade level and, 249, 250*f*
information processing theory, 287
infused teaching of problem solving, 453
infusion lessons, 266–273
Inhelder, B., 238, 240, 249, 310
initiative, student, accepting, 151–152
innovating, 83
input, 361, 363*f*
inquiry. *See also* question(s); questioning
    and advocacy, 139
    experimental, 184, 185*f*, 187*f*
    in foreign language acquisition, 328
    gently Socratic, 459–465
    as learning phase, 262–263
    reflecting on, 464
    self-corrective nature of, 462
    source of, 462
"inquiry probes," 127
In Search of Understanding: The Case for Constructivist Classrooms (Brooks and Brooks), 150
inservice education, 124–125, 210
Inside Brian's Brain (Margulies), 356
Institute for the Advancement of Philosophy for Children, 114
instructional clarity, 363–364
Integrated Assessment System, 503
iNtegrating Technology for inQuiry, 480–482, 481*f*
intellect, levels of, 361, 362*f*
intellectual interdependence, 21
intellectual safety, 460
intelligence(s)
    analytical, 147, 194
    artificial, 148
    assessment of, 207, 232
    auditory, 203, 208*f*
    bodily, 146, 202, 205*f*, 208*f*
    "body," 102
    changing perspective of, 144–149
    coaching, 209
    in cognitive science, 4
    componential, 194

intelligence(s) *(continued)*
  contextual, 194
  creative, 147, 194
  of critical thinkers, 16
  development of, 20, 102, 142, 144
  "development trajectory" of, 210
  distributed, 159
  emotional, 148, 168
  experiential, 147
  experimental, 194
  interpersonal, 146, 203, 205*f*, 208*f*,
    345*f*–347*f*
  intrapersonal, 146, 203, 205*f*, 208*f*,
    345*f*–347*f*
  kinesthetic, 202, 205*f*, 208*f*, 345*f*–347*f*
  learnable, 4–6, 147
  learning and, 223
  linguistic, 203, 205*f*, 208*f*
  logical, 146, 202, 205*f*, 208*f*, 345*f*–347*f*
  mathematical, 202, 205*f*, 208*f*, 345*f*–347*f*
  "meta-intelligence," 207
  moral, 148
  multiple. *See* multiple intelligences
  music and, 333–335
  musical, 146, 203, 205*f*, 208*f*, 345*f*–347*f*
  naturalist, 146, 202, 205*f*, 208*f*
  neural, 147
  object-free, 202–203
  object-related, 202
  personal, 203
  physical education and, 345*f*–347*f*
  practical, 147
  qualifying criteria for, 204
  reflective, 147
  rhythmic, 203, 205*f*, 208*f*
  socializing, 5–6
  in social psychology, 4
  spatial, 202, 205*f*, 208*f*, 345*f*–347*f*
  successful, 147, 194
  technology and, 102–103
  triarchic theory of, 147, 194–195
  unalterable, xii, 4, 144
  verbal, 146, 203, 205*f*, 208*f*, 345*f*–347*f*
  vibrational, 203, 208*f*
  visual, 146, 202, 205*f*, 208*f*
intelligence diary, 209
"intelligence-fair," 210
intelligence scavenger hunt, 209
The Intelligent Curriculum (Lazear), 204
intelligent quotient (IQ). *See* intelligence
intentionality, 20, 139
interconnectedness, 14, 21
interdependence, 84–85
  intellectual, 21
  in learning communities, 138
  passion for, 18, 20–21
  vs. systems thinking, 14
interdependent assessment, 517–518
intergroup problem solving, 454
internalization, cycle of, xvi, 20
internal scope of self-regulation, 195, 198
Internet, 8, 9, 124, 477, 479, 485
interpersonal intelligence, 146, 203, 205*f*, 208*f*,
    345*f*–347*f*
interpretation, 263
intervention, 165, 168
interviews, 522
intimate register of language, 231*f*
intragroup problem solving, 454

intrapersonal intelligence, 146, 203, 205*f*, 208*f*,
    345*f*–347*f*
intrinsic motivation, 74, 83, 366
introduction questions, 225
intuition, 15
invented spelling, 153
investigation, 184, 185*f*, 187*f*
invitational environment, 106–110
Iowa Tests of Basic Skills, 503
IQ tests, 3

job-embedded learning, 119
"job simulation exercise," 541
John Lyman Elementary School, 521
Johns Hopkins University, 212
John-Steiner, Vera, 13
Jones, B. F., 47, 49, 170, 276, 278, 320, 502
Joos, Martin, 229
Jordan, Audra, 227–228
journals, thinking, 13, 109, 225, 411, 522–523
Joyce, B., 120, 138, 277, 279
judgment(s)
  accepting without, 367–368
  critical, 88
  making and evaluating, 45
  reasoned, 429
judicial function of self-regulation, 194, 197, 199
jumbled text reconstruction, 298–299
Jung, Carl, 192

Kendall, John, 29, 31
Kepner, Charles, 276
kinesthetic intelligence, 202, 205*f*, 208*f*,
    345*f*–347*f*
King, Martin Luther King, Jr., 136
kinship, in collectivist culture, 217–218, 219
knowledge, xvi
  active use of, 5
  applying past, to new situations, 83
  conditional, 320
  constructing, 146, 179–180
  declarative, 320, 419
  doubling of, 123
  goals of, 48
  inert, 371, 374, 375
  personal, practical, 23, 129, 129*f*
  provisional status of, 475
  public, 129, 129*f*
  scientific, 306–308
  and thinking, 5
  three systems and, 182–183, 183*f*
knowledge-acquisition components, 452–453
Kohlberg, Lawrence, 12
Kraus, Leah, 109
KWHLAQ strategy, 109, 257–258, 257*f*, 258*f*

labeling, 379, 410
"ladder of inference," 26
Lakota culture, 218, 219
Lamb, Gary, 333
language
  analogic functions in, 313
  and classroom culture, 379
  clear, 83
  development of, taxonomies and, 226–228
  foreign. *See* foreign language acquisition
  labeling in, 379
  and learning, 224
  logic of, analyzing, 382, 382*f*

language *(continued)*
  poverty and, 229–231
  precision of, 19–20
  registers of, 229, 231*f*
  sign, 213
  storage of, in brain, 178
  of thinking, 162, 379–382
language arts
  critical thinking in, 250
  decision making in, 251
language-delayed students, 211
language-immersion principle, 327–328
lateral thinking, 193
leadership, 98
Leadership and the New Science (Wheatley),
  131
learnable intelligence, 4–6, 147
learning
  active engagement and, 513
  as apprenticeship, 6
  biological basis for, 234–243
  brain and, xvi, 223
  collective, 99–100
  constructed, 145
  constructivist, xvi, 479–480
  continuous, 18, 85, 99
  cooperative, 154, 434, 455
  creative, 442–445
  culture and, 223–224
  discovery, 145
  "double-loop," 26
  emotions and, 102, 164–169
  experiential, 144–145
  foster responsibility for, 162
  gathering in, 262–263
  "hands-on," 52, 179–180
  inquiry, 328
  and intelligence, 223
  job-embedded, 119
  language and, 224
  levels of, 439, 440*f*
  mathematical, theories on, 286–287
  mediated, 146, 225–226, 231, 232*f*, 379
  motivators of, 225, 231
  music and, 333
  norms of, 136–139
  organizational, 96–100
  personal, 259
  precursors of, 26
  preparation in, 263–264
  presentation in, 264–265
  problem-based, 107, 109, 256–261, 308,
    309*f*, 375, 480
  receptive, 479
  self-management of, 6
  "single-loop," 26
  social interaction and, 102, 145–146
  student-centered, 480
  taking responsibility for one's own, 151
  for transfer, 376
  transformational, 26
  trial-and-error, 474–476
  in workplace, 23–28
"learning courage," 26
learning curve, 26
learning cycle model, 156
learning disability, 206, 211–212
learning environment, 417–419
learning-focused professional development, 119

learning organization
creative tension in, 136, 136f
definition of, 96–97
lessons for, 97–99
learning partnerships, professional, 120–121
learning styles
activity-centered approach of, 193
cognition-centered approach of, 192
vs. multiple intelligences, 203
personality-centered approach of, 192–193
"learning wars," 507, 508
LeDoux, Joseph, 164
legislative function of self-regulation, 194, 197, 199
Lehman, E. B., 278
Lehman College, 114
Let's move on (LMO), 461f
Letter to the Editor Rubric, 530f
liberal leaning of self-regulation, 195, 198
Lierman, Lynn, 260
Ligon Middle School, 269
Lincoln, Jonathan, 259
linear management, *vs.* action learning, 24–25
linear thinking, 193
linguistic intelligence, 203, 205f, 208f
Lipman, Matthew, xii, 88, 89, 90, 114, 115, 275, 276, 334, 356, 418, 462
listening
to adolescents, 104
to alternative perspectives, 14
in collectivist culture, 217
in gently Socratic inquiry, 459
to music, 333
in productive ways, 26
with understanding and empathy, 81, 522
waiting and, 108
literacy, 337–342. *See also* reading; writing
and cognitive abilities, 371
computer, 480
critical thinking in, 339
definition of, 337
enrichment of, 226
information, 9–10
science, 305–306
teaching for higher-level, 337–339
and transfer, 371
literacy instruction, dual-focused
enhancing, 293–296
need for, 292–293
living system, 401
LMO, *see* let's move on
"local knowledge," and transfer, 376–377
local level of self-regulation, 195, 198
logic, 89. *See also* multilogical thinking
temporal, 19
vs. thinking, 76
logical intelligence, 146, 202, 205f, 208f, 345f–347f
logs, 522–523
Louganis, Greg, 348
love, images of, taxonomy of, 227f
"low-context" communication, 217
"lower-order" thinking, 266
low-road transfer, 372–375
Lubbock Independent School District, 269
Luria, Alexander, 408

MacLachlan, Patricia, 268
macrocentrism, 19

"magic words," 460–461, 461f
magnetic resonance imaging (MRI), 177
magnetoencephalography (MEG), 177
Maguire, Michelle, 260
Making Connections (Caine and Caine), 97
Mall, V. C., 278
Mamaroneck Board of Education, 132
mapping, cognitive, 388, 391f
Marshall University, 114
Maryland State Performance Assessment
Program (MSPAP), 124, 505, 506f, 512
Marymount University, 114
Maslow, Abraham, 101, 104–105
matching, 184, 185f, 187f, 235–236, 237f
mathematical intelligence, 202, 205f, 208f, 345f–347f
mathematics
critical thinking in, 289
learning, theories on, 286–287
misconceptions about, 288
performance item in, 502f
preparation in, 263
presentation in, 264
problem solving in, 54, 55, 249, 286–291
teaching thinking in, 12, 289–290
technology and, 287
MBTI. *See* Myers-Briggs Type Indicator
McREL. *See* Mid-continent Research for
Education and Learning
MCTs. *See* minimum competency tests
meaning
communicating, 226
constructing, xvi, 223, 226
multiplicity of, 463
media, introduction of new, 485
mediated learning, 225–226, 231, 232f, 379
mediated learning experiences (MLE), 146
meditation techniques, 348
MEG. *See* magnetoencephalography
Meier, Deborah, 514
Meister, C., 277, 278, 419, 420
membership classifying, multiple, 237–238, 238f
memorization, 9, 512
memory(ies)
aids to, 389
learning, 372
spatial, 332–333
storage of, 178
mental models, 128, 232, 405–407
mental rehearsal, 348
mental retardation, 212
mental self-realization, 194–196
meta-analysis, 349
metacognition, xvii, 50–52, 82, 159, 171, 356
constructive controversy and, 457–458
cooperative learning and, 456
cues and questions for, 187f
in decision making, 62
developing, 381–382, 382f
enhancing, 409–411
importance of, 271
objectives for, 185f
skills of, 6, 51f
and CPS training, 70f
in students, 271–272
metacognitive reflection, 271, 277, 419
"meta-intelligence," 207
metaphors, 156, 313, 373
methodological belief, 14

MI. *See* multiple intelligences
Michigan State Assessment of Educational
Performance, 356
microcentrism, 19
microperceptions, 178
microphysical actions, 178
Mid-continent Research for Education and
Learning (McREL), 29, 124
middle class, hidden rules of, 229, 230f
middle school, physical education in, and
intelligence, 346f
Mill, John Stuart, 427
Millville Alternative High School, 269
mimetic modes of treatment, 313
mind
computational theory of, 148
habits of, 80–85, 146, 404, 518
scientific frame of, 305
The Mind's Best Work (Perkins), 356
"mindshifts" process, 99
minimum competency tests (MCTs), 501
Mitchell State College, 114
MLE. *See* mediated learning experiences
mnemonics, 421
modeling
mental, 128, 232, 405–407, 467
as teacher behavior, 359, 369, 411
in thinking skill practice, 277, 419
Model of Human Action and Change (Butler), 126
modifiability, cognitive, 146
monarchic form of self-regulation, 194, 197–198
monological thinking, 427, 428, 430
moral intelligence, 148
Morningside Academy, 415
motivation
in emotional intelligence, 148
examining, 184, 185f, 187f
extrinsic, 74, 83, 366
intrinsic, 74, 83, 366
for learning, 231
praise and, 368
recognition of accomplishment, 5
self-actualization and, 101
motor mechanisms, 177–178
"Mozart effect," 333
MRI. *See* magnetic resonance imaging
MSPAP. *See* Maryland State Performance
Assessment Program
MUDs. *See* multiuser domains
multicultural education, 219
multilogical thinking, 427, 429, 430
multiple-choice test, 498f, 500, 503, 503f, 504, 512
multiple intelligences (MI), 202–210
implications of, 202–203
integrating into curriculum, 204–206
vs. learning styles, 203
lesson ideas, 208f
teaching about, 207–210, 209f
teaching for, 203–204
teaching with, 206–207, 208f
multiple membership classifying, 237–238, 238f
"multisensory" learning experiences, 206
multiuser domains (MUDs), 485
muscle relaxation, 348
music, and thinking, 332–335
musical intelligence, 146, 203, 205f, 208f, 345f–347f
Myers, Isabel Briggs, 192

Myers-Briggs Type Indicator (MBTI), 200
"myside bias," 59, 77

NAEP. *See* National Assessment of Educational Progress
National Academy of Sciences, 511
National Assessment of Educational Progress (NAEP), 511
National Association for the Education of Young Children, 104
National Commission on Excellence in Education, 8
National Council for Accreditation of Teacher Education (NCATE), 112
National Council of Teachers of English (NCTE), 30–31
National Council of Teachers of Mathematics (NCTM), 30, 286, 287, 290, 468, 503, 512
National Council on Education Standards and Testing (NCEST), 30
National Education Association, 29
National Education Goals Panel (NEGP), 29
The National Education Goals Report: Building a Nation of Learners (NEGP), 29
National Education Standards and Assessment Council (NESAC), 30
National Governors Association Conference, 497
National Network for Educational Renewal, 114
National Research Council, 503
National Science Board Commission on Precollege Education in Mathematics, Science, and Technology, 29
National Science Education Standards, 30, 33
National Standards for History: Basic Edition, 33
national testing, 498–501, 501–504
National Urban Alliance for Effective Education, 222
A Nation at Risk (report), 8
Native American culture, 217–218, 219
"natural computation," 148
naturalist intelligence, 146, 202, 205*f*, 208*f*
Naylor, Phyllis Reynolds, 337–338
NCATE. *See* National Council for Accreditation of Teacher Education
NCEST. *See* National Council on Education Standards and Testing
NCTE. *See* National Council of Teachers of English
NCTM. *See* National Council of Teachers of Mathematics
"near transfer," 370
needs, hierarchy of, 104–105
neocortex, 408
NESAC. *See* National Education Standards and Assessment Council
networks, 120, 486
neural intelligence, 147
neural processes, 178
neurons, 173, 179
New Jersey Network for Educational Renewal, 115
New Standards Project, xiv
New Standards Reference Exams, 503
Next question, please (NQP), 461*f*
normative models, of thinking, 77
norm-referenced tests (NRTs), 501, 512
norms, shared, 136–137

North Central Regional Educational Laboratory, 504
novice, 25
NQP, *see* next question, please
NRTs. *See* norm-referenced tests
NTeQ, 480–482, 481*f*

object-free intelligences, 202–203
object-related intelligences, 202
observation(s), 45
observation checklist, 209
observation reports, 45
"Ode on a Grecian Urn" (Keats), 447
Odyssey, xii
OERI. *See* U.S. Office of Educational Research and Improvement
Of Mice and Men (Steinbeck), 154
Ohanian, Susan, 514
oligarchic form of self-regulation, 194, 198
One more time (OMT), 461*f*
"one-shot thinking," 404
open-ended questions, 289, 512
open-ended test, 499*f*
open-mindedness
    active, 76–78, 272–273
    in decision making, 61
    developing, 11–17
    encouraging, 77–78
    in science, 305
oral reporting, 65
orderliness
    establishing, 99
    importance of, 98
O'Reilly, Kevin, 267, 271, 272
organizational learning, 96–100
"organs of computation," 148
Othello (Shakespeare), 168
output, 362–363, 365*f*
overconfidence, 77

Paine, Thomas, 273
pair problem solving, 162
pairs, 384
Panel on the General Professional Education of the Physician and College Preparation for Medicine, 29
paraphrasing, 139, 368, 410
parent(s)
    of adolescents, 104
    dependency on, weaning from, 172
    of elementary school children, 104
    helping children developing intelligence, 102
    of infants, 103
    of preschool children, 103–104
    teaching thinking, 101–105
parenting, learning, 103
participation, *vs.* delivery, 486
partnerships, professional learning, 120–121
parts/whole relationships, 307*f*
passions, 18–22, 90
passive knowledge. *See* inert knowledge
pattern seeking, 175–176
    flexibility in patterning abilities, 239–240
    inability of, 235
    pre-patterning abilities, 235–237, 237*f*
    true patterning abilities, 237–239, 238*f*
Paulos, John Allen, 287
pausing, 139

PBQ, *see* please be quiet
pedagogy, 429–436
pedagogy of confidence, 224, 225
peer coaching relationships, 121, 138
peer support, 162
Peirce, Charles Sanders, 462
Peper, E., 348
PEP Strategy for Cueing Practice, 398
perfectionism, 19
performance components, 452–453
performance task(s), 507, 520–521, 528–532
    for assessing categorization, 500*f*
    evaluating, 529*f*
    for health unit on smoking, 529*f*
    in mathematics, 502*f*
    in national tests, 502
    and quality of work, 530–531
    in state tests, 504
    thinking skills used in, 33
perplexity, 259
Perrone, Vito, 447
Perry, William, 14
persistence, 81, 522
personal, practical knowledge (PPK), 23, 129, 129*f*
personal action, model of, 23–24, 24*f*
personal intelligences, 203
personality-centered approach of learning styles, 192–193
personalized process feedback, 457
personal learning, 259
perspectives, alternative, 14–15
persuasion, in collectivist culture, 218
PET. *See* positron emission tomography
Philosophy for Children (Lipman), 356
physical education (PE), thinking in, 343–349
physical needs, 105
Piaget, Jean, 19, 48, 144, 145, 235, 238, 240, 249, 286, 310
Picasso, Pablo, 313
pictorial representations, 242, 242*f*
Plain Vanilla, 462, 462*f*
planning matrix, 523–524, 523*f*
Plato, 477
Please, one person at a time (POPAAT), 461, 461*f*
Please be quiet (PBQ), 461*f*
Plotkin, Henry, 172
point of view, 89, 429
Pond Profile, 263
Poole, R. L., 181
POPAAT, 461, 461*f*
portfolios, 519–520
The Portrait of a Teacher (Jacobowitz and Michelli), 115
positron emission tomography (PET), 177
poverty, 229–232
    and educational disadvantage, 212
    hidden rules of, 229, 230*f*
    and language, 229–231
PPK. *See* personal, practical knowledge
practical intelligence, 147
practical problem solving, 451
precision
    striving for, 82
    thinking and communicating with, 83
prediction, 152
pregnancy
    development during, 103, 177

pregnancy *(continued)*
    risk factors in, 177
prejudice, 161
preparation, in learning, 263–264
preperformance routine, 348
PREP Strategy for Scaffolding Practice, 397–398
prescriptive models, of thinking, 77
presentation
    assessment of, 520–521
    in learning, 264–265
    in problem solving, 481
presuppositions, positive, 139
principals, learning focus of, 121
principle, 439
Principles and Standards for School Mathematics
    (NCTM), 287
Prinsen, Sharlene, 260
privileged children, 160
probing, 139
problem(s)
    defining nature of, 451–452
    ill-defined, 474–475, 476
    posing, 82. *See also* question(s)
    recognizing existence of, 451
    representation of, 56, 452
    well-defined, 474–475, 476
problem-based learning, 107, 109, 256–261, 308,
    309f, 375, 443, 480
problem solving, 49, 50f, 184
    allocating resources to, 452
    analytical, 451
    attitude about, 55
    and brain development, 107
    cognitive strategies for, 466–467
    as complex challenge, 56
    computer-assisted, 8–9, 55, 56, 476
    creative, 451
    cues and questions for, 187f
    culture and, 216–220
    evaluating, 452
    vs. exercises, 54
    familiarization with, 454
    formulating strategy for, 452
    general-purpose, 55
    in history, 317–318, 318f, 321–322, 323f
    importance of, 54–55
    individual, 454
    intergroup, 454
    intragroup, 454
    in learning-disabled students, 211–212
    mathematical, 54, 55, 249, 286–291
    monitoring, 452
    NTeQ, 481–482
    objectives for, 185f
    in pairs, 162
    and perception of context of problem,
        55–56
    practical, 451
    processes, 451–453
    research and, 492f
    in science, 249, 257, 304–305, 308
    in social studies, 257–259, 317–318, 318f,
        321–322, 323f
    spatial metaphor for, 56
    in students with behavior disorders, 212
    subject-specific, 55
    teaching
        domain-specific *vs.* domain-general, 453
        four-prong model for, 454

problem solving *(continued)*
    grade level and, 249–250, 250f
    implicit *vs.* explicit, 453
    infused *vs.* separate, 453
Problem Solving and Comprehension (Whimbey
    and Lochhead), 414
problem-solving cycle, 451–452
Problem Solving Rubric, 531, 531f
problem-solving strategies wheel, 386–387, 390f
"problem space," 56
"Problem Story Teams," 128
procedural checklists, 420
process, 361–362, 364f
process group, 99
process monitoring, 184, 185f, 187f
process-structured questions, 420
productive learning tasks, 418
Productive Thinking Program, 442
professional, definition of, 118
Professional and Pedagogical Studies for Initial
    Teacher Preparation, 112
professional development. *See* teacher-
    preparation programs
professional learning partnerships, 120–121
proficiency, 25
programming, computer, and transfer, 371,
    374–375
progressive leaning of self-regulation, 195, 198
Project Intelligence, xii
Project Zero, 202, 447
propagandistic education, 15
protocol
    for board of education study sessions,
        131–132
    research, 489–491
    tuning, 122
Provincetown Elementary School, 268
provisional knowledge, 475
psychological basis for thinking, 234–235
psychological skills, used by athletes, 344–349
psychology, 87
public education, purposes of, 2, 115
public knowledge, 129, 129f

qualifying, 49f
The Quarterly Journal of Experimental Psychology,
    403
Quellmalz, E. S., 29
question(s). *See also* dialogue; inquiry
    agreement, 360
    vs. answers, 13–14
    for assessment, 543–544
    of clarification and challenge, 45
    closed, 360
    closure, 225
    cognitive levels of, 361–363
    complex, and brain development, 108
    critical, 380, 380f
    defensive, 360
    designing powerful, 360–361
    for enhancing metacognition, 409–410
    facilitative, 26
    focus, 271
    focusing on, 44
    follow-up, 272
    introduction, 225
    in KWHLAQ strategy, 257, 257f
    levels of complexity of, 361
    open-ended, 289, 512

question(s) *(continued)*
    for personal reflection, 225
    process-structured, 420
    rhetorical, 360
    self-probing, xvii–xviii
    stimulus, for reasoning and thinking skills,
        33f
    students developing, 109, 270–271
    textbook, 37–38
    thoughtful, 418
    as tools for thinking, 384–385, 387f
    verification, 360
    wait time and, 155–156
questioning. *See also* inquiry
    as cultural attribute, 127
    as habit of mind, 82
    Socratic, 90, 430–434, 431f
    as teacher behavior, 154, 359–363

race, of teachers and of students, 222–223, 224
Raths, Louis, 37
Rathunde, Kevin, 101, 103
Rauscher, Frances, 332, 333
reading. *See also* literacy; literacy instruction
    cognitive strategies for, 466–467
    inquiry in, 262
    silent, 295
    skills of, developing long-term, 294–295
    thinking and, 292–296
Ready Reading Reference, 386–387, 389f
reality, concrete, 242, 242f
reasoned judgment, 429
reasoning, 87–88
    active, 428
    deductive, 239
    spatial, music and, 332–333
reasoning skills, 29–32
    in history and social studies, 318f, 320–321
    stimulus questions for, 33f
    subject matter emphases on, 31–32, 31f
    use of, 33–34
Reason to Read (Block and Mangieri), 295
recall, 186f, 188f, 320
receptive learning, 479
reciprocal relationships, 139
recitation, 359
recognition, 5
reflection
    of behavior, 165–166
    and change, 129
    cycle of, 225
    metacognitive, 271, 277, 419
reflection stage, 128
reflective decision making, 133–134
reflective dialogue, 136, 138–139
reflective intelligence, 147
reflective study sessions, 131–133
reflective thinking, 414
reflexive system, 171
rehearsal, mental, 348
relationships
    building, 97–98
    finding, 49f
    of mutual respect, 231, 232
    parts/whole, 307f
    peer coaching, 121, 138
    reciprocal, 139
    substantial negative, 200
    substantial positive, 200

relativism, extreme, 161
relaxation, 348
repatterning
    hierarchical, 239–240, 241f
    horizontal, 239, 240f
representation, 184
    accidental, 235, 237f
    concepts and, 312–314
    cues and questions for, 188f
    objectives for, 186f
    pictorial, 242, 242f
    symbolic, 242–243, 242f
representational systems, abstract, 230–231
research, and problem solving, 492f
research protocols, 489–491
resemblance sorting, 235–236, 237f
respect, mutual, 231, 232
responding, as teacher behavior, 108–109, 359, 366–369
"restraining impulsivity," 171
retrieval, 184, 186f, 188f
"reverse-engineering," 148
rewards, detrimental effects of, 368
rhetorical questions, 360
rhythm, 19, 98
rhythmic intelligence, 203, 205f, 208f
risk(s), taking, 84
Riverside Publishing, 503
role playing, 63, 411, 429
Rothstein, Evelyn, 226, 227
Rowe, Jane, 260
Rowe, M. B., 108, 366, 384, 418
rubrics, 519, 530–531
    Letter to the Editor, 530f
    Problem Solving, 531, 531f
    Scoring, 521f
rules, hidden, 229, 230f

safety
    intellectual, 460
    need for, 105
"Sailing to Byzantium" (Yeats), 447
Santos Haliscak, M. E., 192
Sarah, Plain and Tall (MacLachlan), 268, 270, 272
SAT scores, music and, 332
saving face, 217, 218
scaffolding, 104, 278, 397–398, 420, 421f
SCANS. See Secretary's Commission on Achieving Necessary Skills
Scarcella, R., 328
Scardamalia, M., 212, 277
scattered thinking, 59
scheduling, block, 131
Schoenfeld, A., 54, 55, 275, 276, 279, 372, 387
school administrators, 123–125
School of Environmental Studies, 263
school reform
    goal of, 3–6
    test-driven, 513–514
science
    critical thinking in, 250, 303–304, 307
    decision making in, 269
    inquiry in, 262
    open-mindedness in, 305
    problem solving in, 249, 257, 304–305, 308
science literacy, 305–306
scientific inquiry, benchmarks for, 31f
scientific method, 153, 303–304

scientific thinking, 305–308
Scoring Rubric, 521f
Scriven, Michael, 88
search, 76, 77
second language. See foreign language acquisition
Secretary's Commission on Achieving Necessary Skills (SCANS), 101
security, need for, 105
selective combination, 452
selective comparison, 452
selective encoding, 452
self-actualization, 101, 103
self-adjustment, 264
self-analysis, 209
self-assessment, 209, 405–407, 524, 531
self-awareness, 148
self confidence. See confidence
self-conscious thinking, 414
self-determination, 217
self-discovery, 225
self-divulgence, 367
self-esteem
    boosting, 209
    in collectivist culture, 217
    development of, 104, 105
    in individualist culture, 217
self-government. See self-regulation
self-gratification, 59
"self-instructional tracking plans," 207
self-interest
    "enlightened," 59
    "immediate," 59
self-monitoring, 211, 409
self-organization, 97
self-probing questions, xvii–xviii
self-reference, 97, 98
self-reflection checklist, 551
self-regulation, 148, 194–195
    forms of, 194–195, 197–198
    functions of, 194, 197
    leanings of, 195, 198
    levels of, 195, 198
    literacy and, 294
    scopes of, 195, 198
self-reliance, 217
self-system, 182, 183f, 185f, 187f
self-talk, 109, 344, 348
self-understanding, 209
senses, 83, 206, 311
sensitivity, 80
    and ability, 73
    cultivating, 74
    in dialogue, 139
    and thinking, 73–74
    as thinking disposition, 158–161
sentence combining, 300
separate teaching of problem solving, 453
sequence, 19
sequenced-learning curriculum, 306–308, 309f
sequencing, 249
Serious Creativity (de Bono), 25
Seven Pathways of Learning (Lazear), 210
Shakespeare, William, 168, 370, 373, 447
shape, sorting by, 235
shared norms, 136–137
shared values, 136–137
shared visioning, 126–127
Sherwood, R., 257, 271, 371, 376

Shiloh (Naylor), 337–338
short-answer test, 504
Sigel, Irving, 108
sign language, 213
The Sign of the Beaver (Speare), 269
silence, 218, 366–367
silent reading, 295
simulations, 411, 476–477, 541
simultaneity, 19
"single-loop" learning, 26
Sioux culture, 217–218
Six Thinking Hats (de Bono), 193
size, sorting by, 235
skepticism, 16
skill(s)
    acquisition of, 25
    affective, 70f
    of analysis, 270, 320f
    definition of, 439
    information processing. See information processing skills
    of metacognition, 6, 51f, 70f
    psychological, used by athletes, 344–349
    reasoning. See reasoning skills
    vs. substantive generalizations, 36
    teaching vs. testing, 37
    thinking. See thinking skills
skills overload, 38–39
Skowron, Cathy, 268
"skunkworks," 138
slang, taxonomy of, 227f
social cultivation of thinking, 159–160
social distribution of thinking, 159
social inhibition of thinking, 160–161
social interaction
    in emotional intelligence, 148
    and learning, 102, 145–146
    and teaching thinking, 161–162
socializing intelligence, 5–6
social psychology, 4
social responsibility, developing sense of, 11–12
social studies
    critical thinking in, 250, 318f, 319
    decision making in, 251, 319
    disciplined thinking in, 321–322
    in high school, 257–259
    information processing skills in, 318f, 320–321
    preparation in, 263
    problem solving in, 257–259, 317–318, 318f, 321–322, 323f
    reasoning skills in, 318f, 320–321
    solution strategies in, 318–319, 318f
    thinking dispositions in, 321
Socrates, 385, 459
Socratic inquiry, gently, 459–465
Socratic questioning, 90, 430–434, 431f
SOL. See Standards of Learning
"solution paths," 56
solution strategies, in history and social studies, 318–319, 318f
sorrow, images of, taxonomy of, 227f
sorting. See also pattern seeking
    consistent, 236–237, 238f
    exhaustive, 236–237, 238f
    resemblance, 235–236, 237f
Sound Thinking, 413–415
source, judging credibility of, 45
SPACE, 369

spatial intelligence, 202, 205f, 208f, 345f–347f
spatial memory, 332–333
spatial reasoning, music and, 332–333
Speak a little louder, please (SPLAT), 461, 461f
Speare, Elizabeth, 269
Spear-Swerling, L., 451
special-needs learners, 211–214
specifying, 184, 185f, 187f
spelling, approximated, 153
SPELT. *see* Strategies Program for Effective Learning and Thinking
Spencer Foundation, 447
SPLAT, *see* speak a little louder, please
split text reconstruction, 299
sprawling thinking, 59
staff, definition of, 118
staff development. *See* teacher-preparation programs
standardization, of tests, 499–500
Standards for Educational and Psychological Testing, 511
Standards for the English Language Arts, 31
Standards of Learning (SOL), 513
Stanford 9 Open-Ended Reading Assessment, 503
state testing, 498–501, 504–507, 511–515
Steinbeck, John, 154
stereotypes, 161
Steven Foster State University, 114
stimulus questions, for reasoning and thinking skills, 33f
stories, 106–110, 127–128
strategies
    creating, 127–130
    selecting appropriate, 51, 51f
Strategies Program for Effective Learning and Thinking (SPELT), 212
"streamlining," 214
stress
    culture and, 223
    effects of, 135–136
    in teaching, 135–136
Strong, William, 300
"structural equivalent," 313
structuring, as teacher behavior, 359, 363–366
student(s). *See also* adolescent(s); child(ren)
    asking questions, 154
    autonomy and initiative of, accepting, 151–152
    behavior and performance of, teachers' intellectual development of and, 136
    challenging
        problem-based learning and, 256–261
        questioning and, 359–363
    changing roles for, 482
    conscientious, 151–152
    constructing relationships and metaphors, 156
    coping with emotions, 165–166
    cultural identity of, teachers learning about, 225
    developing thinking dispositions, 272–273
    driving lessons, 152–153
    engaging in dialogue, 153–154
    and fear in teachers, 222–223
    intelligence shutdown in, 204
    listening to, 108
    metacognition in, 271–272
    and music, 332–333

student(s) *(continued)*
    natural curiosity of, 156
    in poverty, 229–232
    questioning their initial hypotheses, 154–155
    special-needs, 211–214
    thinking styles of, 199, 200
    urban, 222–228
student-centered learning, 480
student-created taxonomy, 227f
student profile, 477–478
Students' Thinking Styles Evaluated by Teachers, 199–200
student-to-student interaction, 145, 154
study groups, 121–122
study sessions, reflective, 131–133
stumper problem, 289, 290f
subject-specific problem solving, 55
substantial negative relationships, 200
substantial positive relationships, 200
successful intelligence, 147, 194
superintendents, role of, 131
support structures. *See* challenge-and-support structures
"suppositional thinking," 45–46
survival, 97, 229, 234
Swaney, Madeline, 108
Swanson, Michele, 522
The Sword in the Stone (movie), 193
Sylwester, R., 144, 164, 170–174, 202, 206, 207, 333, 356
symbolic representation, 242–243, 242f
synchronization, 19
synthesis, 184
    cues and questions for, 188f
    goals of, 48, 186f
    teaching, grade level and, 250f, 251
synthesis thinking, 16
systematic cognitive intervention approach, 212, 213
systemic structures, 127
systems thinking, 14, 21, 127–130

TAAS. *See* Texas Assessment of Academic Skills
Taba, Hilda, 35, 37, 275, 321, 324, 394, 399
talented students, 213–214
TAPPS. *See* Thinking Aloud Pair Problem Solving
task performance, monitoring, 51, 51f
task-specific graphic organizers, 402f, 404
taxonomy
    Bloom's, 143, 181, 183–184, 525, 526, 527
    and language development, 226–228
    new model of, 184–186, 185f–188f
    student-created, 227f
The Taxonomy of Educational Objectives, The Classification of Educational Goals (Bloom, Engelhart, Furst, Hill and Krathwohl). *See* Bloom's Taxonomy
"teachable moments," 152
teacher(s)
    allowing wait time after questions, 155–156
    asking questions, 154
    behaviors of, 359–369
    changing roles for, 482
    classroom observation checklist for, 552–554
    constructivist, 150–157
    and cultural identity of students, 225
    as curriculum designers, 253–255, 255f, 482

teacher(s) *(continued)*
    effective behaviors for, 112–113
    encouraging students to engage in dialogue, 153–154
    excellent *vs.* good, 232
    as facilitators, 482
    fear in, 222–223
    inquiring about students' understandings, 153
    intellectual development of, and student behavior and performance, 136
    leading students to question initial hypotheses, 154–155
    as manager, 482
    nurturing students' curiosity, 156
    overlooking importance of biological basis for development of thinking, 240
    preparing, of thinking, 111–117
    resisting constructivist pedagogy, 151
    role in, in gently Socratic inquiry, 464–465
    seeking elaboration of students' initial responses, 154
    self-reflection checklist for, 551
    sources of stress for, 135–136
    and student autonomy and initiative, 151–152
    and students in poverty, 231–232
    technology and, 477–478
    thinking skills checklist for, 556–557
    thinking styles inventory of, 199
    thinking styles of, 200
    using raw data, 152
teacher-preparation programs
    attributes for, 119–120
    form and function in, 122
    models of, 113–115, 120–122
    research on, 116–117
    steps in, 116
teaching
    as cognitive activity, 113
    constructivist, 278
    coping with emotions, 165–166
    creativity, 68f, 443–445, 444f
    critical thinking, 115
    decision making, 62–64, 64f
    didactic, 278
    about multiple intelligences, 207–210, 209f
    for multiple intelligences, 203–204
    with multiple intelligences, 206–207, 208f
    special-needs students, 211–214
    about thinking, xiii, 112, 270, 352, 355–356, 357
    for thinking, xiii, 112, 270, 307, 352, 354, 357
    of thinking, xii–xiii, 112, 270, 307, 352, 354–355, 357
    thinking skills
        importance of, 275–276
        research on, 275–280
    for transfer, 272, 375–376
Teaching for Critical Thinking, 115
Teaching for Understanding (TfU), 446–450
teams, 128
teamwork, 349
technology, 471–493
    and assessment, 507–508, 524
    and intelligence, 102–103
    literacy and, 293
    and mathematical thinking, 287

technology *(continued)*
    research and, 491
    and teachers, 477–478
    trial-and-error learning and, 476
teenagers. *See* adolescent(s)
television, 486
temporal logic, 19
tenacity, 475
tension, creative, 136, 136*f*
term(s), defining, 45
Terra Nova tests, 124, 502–503, 502*f*, 504*f*, 508
test(s)
    alternative, 499*f*
    defenders of, 513
    dimensions of, 500–501, 501*f*
    high-stakes, 511, 513
    multiple-choice, 498*f*, 500, 503, 503*f*, 504, 512
    national, 498–501, 501–504
    open-ended, 499*f*
    short-answer, 504
    standardization of, 499–500
    state, 498–501, 504–507, 511–515
    Terra Nova, 124, 502–503, 502*f*, 504*f*, 508
test-driven school reform, 513–514
Texas Assessment of Academic Skills (TAAS), 511, 513
textbook questions, 37–38
Text Reconstruction Across the Curriculum (TRAC), 298–299
TfU. *See* Teaching for Understanding
Thinkback, 413
thinking
    absolutistic, 428–429
    acting on, 15
    aloud, 387, 413–415
    big, xviii
    biological basis for, 175–180, 234
    brain and, 176–179
    coaching, 161–162
    coherent, importance of, 42
    collaborative, 13
    composite view of, 518
    convergent, 193
    creating climate for, 126
    creative. *See* creative thinking
    critical. *See* critical thinking
    about decisions. *See* decision making
    definitions of, 47, 76–77, 310
    descriptive models of, 77
    dialectical, 427–436
    dialogical, 427–436
    dimensions of, 170–171
    disciplined, 321–322
    divergent, 193, 442
    effective, origins of, 18–22
    about emotions, 167–169
    emotions and, 166–167
    exploring different meanings of, 115–116
    flexibly, 81–82
    foreign language and, 326–330
    fuzzy, 59, 83
    "higher-order," 61, 266
    industrial-age, 7
    information-age, 7–8, 479–482
    invisible substance of, 419
    knowledge and, 5
    language of, 162, 379–382
    lateral, 193

thinking *(continued)*
    linear, 193
    "lower-order," 266
    meaningful problems and, 11–12
    meditative type of, 219
    monological, 427, 428, 430
    multilogical, 427, 429, 430
    music and, 332–335
    normative models of, 77
    "one-shot," 404
    organizational patterns for, 365–366
    parents teaching, 101–105
    pattern seeking in, 175
    philosophy and, 87–91
    in physical education, 343–349
    poverty and, 229–232
    preparing teachers of, 111–117
    prescriptive models of, 77
    about problems. *See* problem solving
    psychological basis for, 234–235
    and reading, 292–296
    reflective, 414
    responsibility for, 162
    safe environment and, 12–13
    scaffolding, 104, 278, 397–398, 420, 421*f*
    scattered, 59
    scientific, 305–308
    self-conscious, 414
    sensitivity and, 73–74
    silent, 295
    social cultivation of, 159–160
    social distribution of, 159
    social inhibition of, 160–161, 162
    socialization and, 161–162
    and special-needs learners, 211–214
    sprawling, 59
    structuring classroom for, 363–366
    student
        encouraging, 418–419
        expanding, 242–243
        improving, 417–423
        skillful, 266–267, 267*f*
    "suppositional," 45–46
    synthesis, 16
    systems, 14, 21, 127–130
    teaching about, xiii, 112, 270, 352, 355–356, 357
    teaching for, xiii, 112, 270, 307, 352, 354, 357
    teaching of, xii–xiii, 112, 270, 307, 352, 354–355, 357
    about thinking. *See* metacognition
    together, xvii
    tools for, 384–391
    for understanding, 446–450
    vertical, 193
    visual tools for, 403–405
    in workplace, 23–28
    writing and, 298–302
Thinking: International Interdisciplinary Perspectives (Edwards), 25
Thinking Aloud Pair Problem Solving (TAPPS), 413–415
thinking dispositions, 72–75, 90, 158
    definition of, 72
    elements of, 73
    helping students develop, 272–273
    in history and social studies, 321
    recognizing, 73

thinking guides, 295
thinking hats, 193–194, 194*f*
"thinking in context," 12
thinking journals, 13, 109, 225, 411, 522–523
Thinking Maps, 226, 405, 406*f*
thinking matrix, 385–386, 388*f*
thinking process maps, 402*f*, 404–405
thinking skills
    assessment of
        format for, 533–540, 534*f*–537*f*
        national tests in, 501–504
        performance tasks in, 528–532
        state tests in, 498–501, 504–507, 511–515
        system for, 517–524
        teachers in, 525–527, 541–545
    checklist for, 556–557
    complex, 49–50, 50*f*
    CPS training and, 70*f*
    in decision making, 61*f*
    direct instruction in, 422
    essential, 47–49
    guided practice of, 393, 397–398
    incorporating into curriculum, 123–125
    introducing, 277–278, 393, 394–397
    levels of, 248, 249*f*
    long-term, 294–295
    metacognitive, model of, 51*f*
    previewing, 420
    providing practice, 278–279
    questions and, 37–38
    rehearsing, 420–421
    stimulus questions for, 33*f*
    taxonomy of basic, 49*f*
    teaching
        effectively, 276–279
        importance of, 275–276
        research on, 275–280
    transfer of. *See* transfer
    use of, 33–34
thinking skills curriculum, 12
    grade level and subject area and, 248–251, 250*f*
    scope and sequence for, 248–252, 250*f*
    selecting content for, 248
thinking strategy map, 167, 167*f*, 306, 306*f*, 307*f*, 339
thinking styles, 193–201
    in classroom, 199
    collectivist, 220
    elements of, 195*f*
    measurement of, 199–200
    properties of, 198–199
Thinking Styles Inventory, 199
Thinking Styles Questionnaire for Teachers, 199
Think-Pair-Share, 271, 384, 385*f*, 386*f*
Thinktrix, 385–386, 388*f*
Third International Mathematics and Science Study (TIMSS), 286
Thomas, Dylan, 315
tic-tac-toe, 476
time, structuring, 364–365
time perspectives, 19
TIMSS. *See* Third International Mathematics and Science Study
Tishman, Shari, 72–75, 73, 158, 159, 160, 161, 216, 272, 578
Torrance, E. P., 67, 68, 69, 442

TRAC. *See* Text Reconstruction Across the Curriculum
Tracey, D., 469
transfer, 393
    definition of, 370
    direct, 399
    failure of, 371–372, 374–375
    "far," 370
    high-road, 372, 373–374, 375
        backward-reaching, 374
        forward-reaching, 373–374
    importance of, 370–371
    learning for, 376
    "local knowledge" and, 376–377
    low-road, 372–373, 374, 375
    "near," 370
    strategies for, 398–399
    teaching for, 272, 375–376
    thinking skills for, 279
transformational learning, 26
transforming, 49f
Traveling Salesman Problem, 475
Treays, Rebecca, 356
Tregoe, Benjamin, 276
trial-and-error learning, 474–476
triangulation, 518, 519f
triarchic theory of intelligence, 147, 194–195
Truman, Harry S., 269
trust, 138–139
tuning protocols, 122
Tuskegee University, 114
Two Bad Ants (Van Allsburg), 338

uncritical absolutism, 428–429
underachievement, in urban students, 222–228
underprivileged children, 160
understanding
    declassifying, 449–450
    deep, 270
    definition of, 446
    listening with, 81, 522

understanding *(continued)*
    teaching for, 446–450
    thinking for, 446–450
Understanding Your Brain (Treays), 356
unit design, 253–255
University of California, 508
University of Georgia, 114
University of Massachusetts, 114
University of Northern Iowa, 114
University of Virginia, 114
upper class, hidden rules of, 230f
urban students, 222–228
U.S. Department of Education, 7
U.S. Department of Labor, 101
U.S. Office of Educational Research and Improvement (OERI), 30
usefulness corollary, 68f
utilization, 184, 185f, 187f

Valley Southwoods Freshman High School, 264
value, 80
values, shared, 136–137
Van Allsburg, Chris, 338
variation, blind, 475
verbal intelligence, 146, 203, 205f, 208f, 345f–347f
verification questions, 360
vertical curriculum, 240–241
vertical thinking, 193
vibrational intelligence, 203, 208f
Virginia Standards of Learning, 355
vision, shared, 126–127
visual intelligence, 146, 202, 205f, 208f
visualization, 344, 348
visual tools, 401–407, 402f
Visual Tools for Constructing Knowledge (Hyerle), 403
vocabulary
    building, in urban students, 226–227
    precise, 379–380, 380f
voting format, 127

Vygotsky, Lev, xvi, 20, 104, 138, 144, 145–146, 159–160, 419, 454, 462

waiting, 108
wait time, 155–156, 366–367, 384, 418
Wake Forest University, 114
Walker, Alice, 109
Warschauer, M., 329
Watkins, D., 217
Watson-Glaser Critical Thinking Appraisal, 114
The Web of Life (Capra), 401
well-defined complexity, 476–477
well-defined problem, 474–475, 476
Western culture, 218–219
white hat, 194, 194f
whole/parts relationships, 307f
Why Johnny Can't Write (Linden and Whimbey), 299
Wineburg, Samuel, 319
wonderment, responding with, 83–84
"word walls," 134
workplace
    importance of creativity in, 69
    learning and thinking in, 23–28
workshop, 127–128
world view, 129, 129f
worm's-eye view, 19
Write Thinking, 416
writing. *See also* literacy; literacy instruction
    cognitive strategies for, 466–467
    controlled, 300
    good thinking and, 270
    thinking and, 298–302

Xavier University, 415

Yeats, William Butler, 447
yellow hat, 194, 194f
yin and yang, 219

"zone of proximal development," 160, 462

RELATED ASCD RESOURCES: THINKING SKILLS

ASCD stock numbers are in parentheses.

AUDIOTAPES

Taking the Ho-Hum Out of Teaching: Strategies for Embedding Thinking Skills into the Curriculum by Robert Hanson and T. Robert Hanson (#200179)

Teaching Thinking to Multiple Intelligences and Diverse Student Populations (#294022)

Thinking Maps: Highlights from A Field Guide to Using Visual Tools by David Hyerle (#201111)

Designing Integrated Curriculum that Promotes Higher-Level Thinking by Lynn Erickson (#296202)

ONLINE RESOURCES

Visit ASCD's Web site (www.ascd.org) for the following professional development opportunities:

Online Tutorial: *The Brain and Learning* (http://www.ascd.org/frametutorials.html) (free)

Professional Development Online Course: *Memory and Learning Strategies* (http://www.ascd.org/framepdonline.html) (for a small fee; password protected)

PRINT PRODUCTS

Dimensions of Learning multimedia program (complete program, #614239), by educational consultants: Robert J. Marzano and Debra J. Pickering. This complete program includes:

Dimensions of Learning Trainer's Manual (2nd ed.) (#197134)

Dimensions of Learning Teacher's Manual (2nd ed.) (#197133)

A Different Kind of Classroom: Teaching with Dimensions of Learning (#61192107)

Dimensions of Learning Video Series (6 videotapes) (#614236)

Learning About Learning (free videotape with complete program)

Dimensions of Thinking: A Framework for Curriculum and Instruction, by Robert J. Marzano, Ronald S. Brandt, C. S. Hughes, B. F. Jones, B. Z. Presseisen, S. C. Rankin, & C. Suhor (#61187040S25)

A Field Guide to Using Visual Tools by David Hyerle (#100023)

Habits of Mind: A Developmental Series, edited by Arthur L. Costa and Bena Kallick (complete series, #100036)

Discovering and Exploring Habits of Mind (#100032)

Activating and Engaging Habits of Mind (#100033)

Assessing and Reporting on Habits of Mind (#100034)

Integrating and Sustaining Habits of Mind (#100035)

VIDEOTAPES

Dimensions of Learning Video Series (6 videotapes) (#614236)

How to Conduct Successful Socratic Seminars ("How To" Series, Tape 4) (#499046)

How to Engage Students in Critical Thinking ("How To" Series, Tape 8) (#400050)

For additional resources, visit us on the World Wide Web (http://www.ascd.org), send an e-mail message to member@ascd.org, call the ASCD Service Center (1-800-933-ASCD or 703-578-9600, then press 2), send a fax to 703-575-5400, or write to Information Services, ASCD, 1703 N. Beauregard St., Alexandria, VA 22311-1714 USA.